New International Fifth Edition

ABBREVIATIONS DICTIONARY

RALPH DE SOLA

New International Fifth Edition

ABBREVIATIONS DICTIONARY

Abbreviations · Acronyms · Anonyms and Eponyms · Appellations · Contractions · Geographical Equivalents · Historical and Mythological Characters · Initials and Nicknames · Short Forms and Slang Shortcuts · Signs and Symbols

ELSEVIER · NEW YORK
NEW YORK · AMSTERDAM · OXFORD

Elsevier North-Holland, Inc.
52 Vanderbilt Avenue, New York, New York 10017

Elsevier Scientific Publishing Company
335 Jan Van Galenstraat, Box 211
Amsterdam, The Netherlands

Library of Congress Cataloging in Publication Data

De Sola, Ralph, 1908–
Abbreviations dictionary.

1. Abbreviations, English. 2. Acronyms. 3. Signs and symbols. I. Title.
PE1693.D4 1977 423′.1 77-22195
ISBN 0-444-00213-8

Manufactured in the United States of America

Contents

Preface

Contemporary conversation, as well as modern printed communication, is filled with undefined bits of jargon. Abbreviations, acronyms, appellations, conversational shortcuts, eponyms, geographical equivalents, and specialized terms occupy more than twenty-five percent of the mass of words heard and overheard. Anyone from another industry, profession, or walk of life will be almost completely baffled if subjected to such talk and writing.

Readers will discover this expanded fifth edition contains many items not usually found in other reference works. Such things as place-name nicknames, pseudonyms, fishing vessel registration symbols, musical nicknames, and many other short-form categories would not seem to be germane to such a dictionary were it not that such terms serve as cultural abbreviations in contemporary conversation. Symbolic entries have been expanded into the alphabetically arranged entries to reflect the impact of centuries of Athenian and Roman culture on our own where we still hear about Bacchus or Dionysus, Aphrodite or Venus, et cetera. Many such entries appear under God, Goddess, Muse, Personification, as well as Father of, Mother of, and so forth. Reference librarians and school teachers, as well as many users of this dictionary, assure me such items are necessary and add much to this expanded international fifth edition.

Numerous entries appearing for the first time in this edition of the *Abbreviations Dictionary* are the result of suggestions made by many friends and associates. To all of them, my sincere thanks and appreciation. Critics of previous editions graciously lent their support by providing fresh material or more correct material and by suggesting new sources of information.

World traveller and good friend George F. Drake of Santa Barbara continued to supply many new items and even a few corrections; his many contributions to this expanded fifth edition reflect his travels through the British Isles, the Commonwealth countries, and the Continent, as well as his wide reading of American, British, and Canadian publications.

Reference libraries continued to provide encouragement and to help in compiling short forms. At Mesa College, aid was received from Warren Heyer, Jeanne Newhouse, Keith Anderson, and their many student assistants. At San Diego City College gratitude is owing its chief librarian James Newbold, his assistants Gabriella Jacks, Jane Romita, and their aides.

At the San Diego Public Library many helpful eyes continued to assist in this compilation. Librarians include Patricia Allely, Michael J. Archuleta, Barbara Barth, Dalton Degitz, David Gault, Mary Grauzinis, Jean Hughes, Matt Katka, Anna Martinez, Angela Patterson, Margaret Queen, Evelyn Roy, Vere Wolf, and other professionals.

Mr Patrick D. Wright, reference librarian of the University of Manitoba, gave of his time in providing Canadian terms appearing for the first time in any comparable lexicon. Other cooperating Canadians include Ben and Lorraine Sherkin, Marc Sherkin, Kari Sherkin, Judy Jordan, Harry and Mildred Lewis, Sam and Nancy Roth, the good doctors Joe Greenberg, Gordan Kerbel, Morris Shusterman, and Joanne Ritter, R.N.

British friends who assisted include George Alfred (Pete) and Gwen Ballin of Surrey and the Brownes (Patrick, Patricia, and Vanessa) also of Surrey. James B. T. Norris of Clacton-on-Sea, Essex, also provided many new entries. San Diegan consultants include Daniel Russell, Dr Kenneth C. Forror, Dr Ira Levine, and Dr Elizabeth Weldon Keating, Teacher-Coordinator of the Language Art and Humanities Department of San Diego Evening College. They all gave splendid encouragement and much help in the preparation of this compilation.

Bonnie Blair of Bala Cynwyd, Pennsylvania also contributed entries as did the late George F. Drake of Santa Barbara who kept sending them in up to the last week of his life.

Dorothy, my wife and companion for more than thirty years, continued to help in every way and to contend with the author on a day-and-night basis. She assisted by reading a vast number of periodicals in search of new short forms.

The entire staff of Elsevier North-Holland, including Ellen Blissman, Michael Connolly, Caroline Correll, William Drischler, Liza Gyllenhaal, Linda Hering, Ethel Langlois, Linda Leopold, and Ann Streimer, in New York, and their printer's staff manifested enthusiastic cooperation in the production of this expanded international fifth edition of the *Abbreviations Dictionary*. To them my heartfelt thanks.

Introduction

Definitions of Terms

abbreviations abridged contractions such as acdt: accident; AEC: Atomic Energy Commission; NASA: National Aeronautics and Space Administration.

acronyms words formed from letters in a series of related words such as ABLE: Activity Balance Line Evaluation; AGREE: Advisory Group on Reliability of Electronic Equipment; DYNAMO: Dynamic Action Management Operations.

anonyms attempts of authors to enjoy anonymity while maintaining their identity by such devices as the capitalized diphthong AE standing for Aeon, pen name of George William Russell.

contractions words shortened by dropping non-pronounced letters; omitted letter(s) which are indicated by apostrophes as in can't: can not; li'l: little; doesn't: does not; and let's: let us.

eponyms designations derived from family names, nicknames, or names of places or persons; e.g., Hapsburg dynasty, *Eroica* symphony, Paris of America (Montreal), Raynaud's disease, etc.

geographical equivalents entries such as Far East: countries and islands of East Asia or in the Pacific—eastern Siberia, China, Japan, Taiwan, Korea, Indochina, the Philippines, the Malay Peninsula.

initials FDR: Franklin Delano Roosevelt; HST: Harry S. Truman; JFK: John Fitzgerald Kennedy; LBJ: Lyndon Baines Johnson; initials of all American Presidents are included as well as initials of other noted personalities.

nicknames Al: Alfred; Bea: Beatrice; Hal: Harold; Ike: Dwight David Eisenhower; Isaac.

short forms amps: amperes; Olds: Oldsmobile; pots.: potentiometers.

sign $ & ¢—dollars and cents.

slang shortcuts B-girl: bar girl; C-note: $100 bill; 1-G: $1000.

symbols Al: aluminum; Pt: platinum; Rx: prescription; recipe.

Editors—Teachers—Writers

Editors, teachers, and writers will perform a splendid service for readers if they insist that abbreviations and acronyms be defined the first time they are used. The old argument, "everyone knows what that stands for," no longer is true. Many abbreviations stand for at least ten different things. Many acronyms, also, stand for several different things.

The style of writing abbreviations and acronyms requires the attention of editors, teachers, and writers. They should be unwilling to let things get out of hand to the point that a paragraph comes cluttered with unexplained capital-letter combinations. Technical literature will become almost impossible to read if the permissive trend continues wherein all abbreviations and acronyms appear in solid capital letters and without benefit of preliminary definition.

Throughout this *Abbreviations Dictionary* an attempt is made to follow the rules of English grammar. Capital letters are reserved for proper nouns. Lowercase letters are used for common nouns. However, when custom has become so strong that correctly written short forms are not recognized quickly, their more common equivalents are added parenthetically: icbm (ICBM): intercontinental ballistic missile.

Explanations

If readers and researchers did not continue to find themselves engulfed and ensnared in the modern abracadabra of abbreviations and acronyms, in the bewildering bafflegab and gobbledygook of corporationese, initialese, officialese, pentagonese, politicalese, and technicalese, there would be no need to provide this new international fifth edition of the *Abbreviations Dictionary*.

Because so many creators of abbreviations and coiners of acronyms fail to define their shortcuts the first time they use them, and because so many who use them also fail to define these things, it becomes increasingly difficult to understand what people are saying or writing when their sayings and writings are filled with abbreviations, acronyms, anonyms, contractions, initials, nicknames, pseudonyms, short forms, signs, slang shortcuts, and symbols created for their own convenience, without regard for their ability to create communicative and easily understood statements.

Daily speech, newspapers, magazines, books, and signs along the airways, highways, railways, and waterways reveal the universality of these shortcuts to communication and the growing tendency to use and devise more and more of them. This appears to be done in response to the rapid development of technological civilization. But witness the confusion compounded when someone without a knowledge of Spanish turns on the C tap in a shower bath in Acapulco, Buenos Aires, or Madrid. Hot water steams out instead of cold. North is N in most languages of western civilization, but west can be W or O or even V.

Abbreviations of every sort cover contemporary civilization like a deep and ever-deepening snowdrift, concealing the main features of the landscape: leaving the beholder mystified and perplexed by the overwhelming obscurity imposed by these letter and number combinations. Usually these shortcuts to communication are created without reference to the niceties of typography, the requirements of official and logical regulations, or even the rules of grammar. Most appear without definitions. More and more appear each year. And more and more duplicate already existing abbreviations standing for other things. The letter *a*, for example, stands for more than twenty-five different things. Capital *A* stands for more than thirty different things. And so it goes throughout the alphabet, with many varied combinations of letters and numbers, signs and symbols.

Arrangement

Everything in this book is arranged in alphabetical and numerical order. particles, prepositions, and the ampersand (&) are ignored in the arrangement. For example, U of P is alphabetized as UP; A & M and IT & T are placed as if they were AM and ITT. The singular and plural and tense of words do not alter the general sense of the abbreviation defined.

Golden Rule

"When in doubt, spell it out," insisted Ralph Bayless when he was chief engineer of all General Dynamics engineering organizations of Convair. He urged all to define abbreviations the first time they were used.

If, for example, a Gulf Missile Range is being described, and the term *GMR* will be used again and again, the text should begin something like this:

> The Gulf Missile Range (GMR) affords facilities for national defense and space exploration. GMR personnel are active in all phases of aerospace research, development, and engineering. GMR headquarters are in Mobile.

Common sense rules about abbreviations are most often ignored.

Therefore it is necessary to repeat that short words like Maine, Ohio, Samoa, etc., should not be abbreviated, although their unofficial abbreviations exist and are shown in this book. Similarly it is best to avoid the truncation of words spelling other words when abbreviated: cat.: catalog; king.: kingdom; man.: management.

Because this is a reference dictionary there are many duplications. Airlines have two and three-letter designations. The same is true of many place names. Many items are included so it will not be necessary for readers to try to guess what the abbreviations are intended to mean. Many unauthorized abbreviations are included for the same reason—to help readers find their way through the alphabet soup.

Capitalization

Capitalization of abbreviations, according to Department of Defense Military Standard 12-B (Mil-Std 12-B), must follow the rules of English grammar. All proper nouns are capitalized. All common nouns are written in lowercase letters. Units of weight, measure, and velocity, such as lb, kg, in., cc, mm, rpm, and the like, appear in lowercase to avoid confusion with other letter combinations they resemble.

Many military establishments and offices use full capitals for everything because message machines are provided only with capital letters. That is why many engineering drawings supplied the armed forces contain all abbreviations in capital letters. It is also true many draftsmen are afraid small letters will fill up, especially *a's, b's, d's, e's, g's, o's,* and the like. Therefore they also like to use capital letters. In text, however, 1500 RPM presents a typographical blob, as compared to the more sophisticated 1500 rpm.

At first loran was LORAN. As people became more used to it, it became Loran. Today it is loran. The same is true of other combinations. The trend is to capitalize only those letters standing for proper nouns, running all common nouns in lowercase. Nevertheless, for the sake of readers and researchers, some incorrectly rendered abbreviations appear in this book. Many people have a marked tendency to capitalize everything they think is important. If this tendency is unchecked, confusion follows. All abbreviations and acronyms look alike. So follow the commonsense rules of good grammar and correct usage.

Chemical element symbols, however, have the first letter capitalized: Au (gold), Zn (zinc), etc. The second letter of a chemical symbol always appears in lowercase.

Exceptions

The singular, plural, and tense of the words abbreviated do not alter abbreviations except in a few instances, such as fig.: figure; figs.: figures; lb:

pound; lbs: pounds; no.: number; nos: numbers; p: page; pp: pages; S: Saint; *SS: Saints.*

However, readers should be aware the International (*SI*) System of Measurements calls for the abolition of all pluralized abbreviations. Hence in. stands for inch or inches, lb for pound or pounds, oz for ounce or ounces. This system will probably gain widespread approval.

Documentary abbreviations are rendered as follows: FARs (Failure Analysis Reports), or IRs (Inspector's Reports) or RARs (Reliability Action Reports). In the singular they appear as FAR, IR, RAR.

Italics

Items from Latin and other non-English languages, as well as titles of books and periodicals, are usually set in italic type. Many physical symbols are also set in italics to differentiate them from other letter combinations they resemble.

Punctuation

Short forms are devised to save time and space and to overcome the necessity of repeating long words and phrases. All punctuation is avoided in modern practice unless the form is taken from Latin or there is some conventional use demanding punctuation, as in the case of academic degrees and a few governmental designations. U.S.A. is the country; USA is the army. D.C. is the District of Columbia; DC is direct current when used as a noun. Cash on delivery is not cod but c.o.d. Similarly, fig., figs. and no. require periods to keep readers from thinking they may be words instead of abbreviations for figure, figures, and number. Again, when in doubt, spell it out.

Capitalization and Punctuation Trends

American as well as British and Canadian publishers appear to be following the sensible trend to capitalize only those letters normally capitalized: proper nouns and important words in titles. They reserve lowercase letters for abbreviations consisting of adjectives and common nouns. This obviates the chaos brought about by those who capitalized all the letters in every abbreviation and then compounded their error by placing unnecessary full stops or periods after every letter as was the custom in bygone times.

Most periods are dropped because it is generally realized the purpose of all abbreviations is the thoroughgoing promotion of brevity. More than a decade ago, when Rudolf Flesch compiled one of his many useful books, *How To Be Brief—An Index to Simple Writing,* he stated: "To save even more space, leave out abbreviation periods whenever you can. The British omit them regularly . . . *Mr, Mrs, Dr, St* (Saint), *Thos, Chas, jr.* Periods are often left out after standard abbreviations like *US, UN, FCC, PTA* . . . following the pattern of most telephone books (e.g., *plmbg & heatg supls, atty, first, acctnts, svce, rl est*)."

Chemists, dentists, doctors, medical reference librarians, nurses, and psychiatrists used to write as if they were completely unaware of the rules of correct and effective English communication, confounding many chemical symbols with abbreviations and then capitalizing everything. They seemed to be in a world of their own and quite unaware that what they capitalized also stood for one or more other things in other and even everyday fields. Hence it sometimes becomes necessary to show abbreviations in both styles, correct and incorrect, so people may find out what they mean one way or another.

Hence **gmp (GMP)**: guanosine monophosphate. It precedes **GMP**: Green Mansion Properties. The reason for following the rules becomes apparent if we examine another entry: **hpl**: high(est) point level; human parotid lysozyme (HPL); human placental lactogen (HPL). It is followed by **HPL**: Halifax Public Library; Hamilton Public Library; Hartford Public Library; Houston Pipe Line; Houston Public Library.

Signs and Symbols

Frequently used signs and symbols are in the back of this dictionary. Many are found on typewriters (&: ampersand—the *and* sign; *: asterisk; ¢: cent; $: dollar; %: percent).

Symbols include the chemical elements (Al: aluminum; Au: gold—from the Latin *aurum*; C: carbon; Sn: tin—from the Latin *stannum*). All are listed in the alphabetical section without special definition to indicate they are not abbreviations but symbols. The chemical elements are also grouped together in the back of this dictionary.

Airlines use two-letters symbols for convenience in baggage handling, ticketing, and scheduling operations. Thus American Airlines is AA, Delta Air Lines is DL, National Airlines is NA, Pan American World Airways is PA, United Air Lines is UA. All airlines are shown in these two-letter code symbols as well as in other multiletter combinations. Railroads and steamship lines are included in the alphabetical sections.

Naval craft are designated by many arbitrary symbols. All available are shown.

This is the short and the long of it.
— SHAKESPEARE

A

a: abbreviation; absent; acceleration in feet per second; account; acre; adjective; adult; aerial; afternoon; altitude intercept; amateur; ampere; annealing; anthracite; arc; are (unit of metric land measure); area; argent; at; atmosphere; audit; auditor; automatic; available; aviation; aviator; axis; azure; distance from leading edge to aerodynamic center (symbol)

a′: all (contraction); minute (angle); prime

a″: second (angle); doubleprime

a: *am, an, an der* (German—on the, at the); angle of attack; *annus* (Latin—year); *arteria* (Latin—artery); attenuation constant (symbol)

A: absolute; absolute temperature; academy; acid; acoustic source; actual weight of an aircraft; adulterer; adulteress (capital letter A branded on the foreheads of all who were convicted of this crime in the early days of New England)—also known as the scarlet letter because branding caused bleeding; aircraft; airman; Alaska Steamship Company; Alcoa Steamship Company; Alfacode for A; ambassador; America; American; Americanization; Americanize; Amos, The Book of; amphibian; Anchor Line; anode; anterior; April; argon; Army; artillery; aspect ratio; astragal; Atlantic; atomic weight; attack; August; Austria (auto plaque); chemical activity; first van der Waals constant; Fraunhofer line due to oxygen; linear acceleration; mean sound absorption coefficient; total acidity

A-1: air personnel officer; excellent; first class; first rate; *Lloyd's Register* symbol indicating a vessel's equipment is first rate; personnel section of an air force staff; skyraider single-engine general-purpose attack aircraft flown from aircraft carriers; top quality; tops; very best

A-I: (motion pictures) for general patronage

A1c: Airman, first class

A_2: aortic second sound; Asian influenza virus

A-2: air intelligence officer; almost A-1 in quality; intelligence section of an air force staff; just short of being the best

A-II: (motion pictures) for adults and adolescents only

A-3: air operations and training officer; operations and training section of an air force staff; Skywarrior twin-engine turbojet tactical all-weather attack aircraft operating from aircraft carriers; training and operations

A-III: (motion pictures) for adults only

A-4: air material and supply officer; material and supply section of an air force staff; Skyhawk single-engine turbojet attack aircraft operating from aircraft carriers; supply and materiel

A-IV: (motion pictures) for adults with reservations

A-5: planning; supersonic twin-engine turbojet all-weather attack aircraft operating from aircraft carriers

A-6: communications

A-6A: Intruder twin-engine turbojet long-range carrier-based low-altitude attack aircraft

A: *abajo* (Spanish—down); *abasso* (Italian—down); *alas* (Finnish—down); *albus* (Latin—white); *Alteza* (Spanish—Highness); *aprobado* (Spanish—approved)—passed in an examination; arrival; *arrivare* (Italian—arrival); arrive; *arrive* (French—arrival); *auf* (German—up); *Aulus* (Latin—Aulus Gellius)—2nd-century author noted for his *Noctes Atticae* about languages and literature as well as natural history; *aus* (German—out); *avbeta* (Swedish—departure)

Å: angstrom unit

Å: *aas* (Dano-Norwegian—hills)

$\bar{a}\bar{a}$: acting appointment; adjectives; always afloat; approximate absolute; armature accelerator; author's alteration

aa (AA): achievement age; antiaircraft

$\bar{a}\bar{a}$: equal parts

a-a: air-to-air

a/a: antiaircraft

aa: *arterias* (Latin—arteries); (Hawaiian—block lava)—pronounced *ah-ah*

a & a: abbreviations and acronyms; additions and amendments

AA: absolute alcohol; absolute altitude; achievement age; Addicts Anonymous; Administrative Assistant; Aerolineas Argentinas (Argentine Airlines); Airman Apprentice; Alcoholics Anonymous; Aluminum (Company of) America; American Airlines; American Association; Ann Arbor (railroad); Ansett Airways; antiaircraft; Appropriate Authority; arithmetic average; Arlington Annex; Asian-African; Athletic Association; author's alteration(s); Automobile Association; Aviation Annex; *Aviatsionnaya Armiya* (Russian—Air Army)

AA: *Air Almanac; Astronautica Acta* (Journal of the International Astronautical Federation)

A.A.: Associate in Accounting; Associate in Arts

aaa: acute anxiety attack; amalgam

aa & a: armor, armament, and ammunition

Aaa: Alaska (government style is to spell it out); unofficial abbreviation—

AAA: Agricultural Adjustment Administration; Agricultural Aircraft Association; Alaska (unofficial abbreviation—government style is to spell it out); All American Aviation; Allegheny Airlines (3-letter coding); Allied Artists of America; American Academy of Advertising; American Academy of Allergy; American Accordionists Association; American Accounting

Association; American Airship Association; American Antartic Association; American Anthropological Association; American Arbitration Association; American Association of Anatomists; American Astronomers Association; American Australian Association; American Automobile Association; antiaircraft artillery; Antique Airplane Association; Appraisers Association of America; Archives of American Art; Army Audit Agency; Associated Agents of America; Association of Attenders and Alumni (Hague Academy of International Law); Association of Average Adjusters

A.A.A.: Amateur Athletic Association (British)

AAAA: American Association for the Advancement of Atheism; American Association of Advertising Agencies; Army Aviation Association of America; Associated Actors and Artists of America

AAAB: American Association of Architectural Bibliographers

AAAC: American Association for the Advancement of Criminology; Antiaircraft Artillery Command

AAACE: American Association of Agricultural College Editors

AAAD: American Athletic Association for the Deaf

AAAE: American Association of Airport Executives

AAA (AFL-CIO): Actors and Artistes of America

AAAEE: American Afro-Asian Educational Exchange

A.A. Ag.: Associate of Arts in Agriculture

AAAI: Affiliated Advertising Agencies International

AAAIMH: American Association for the Abolition of Involuntary Mental Hospitalization

AAAIP: Advanced Army Aircraft Instrumentation Program

AAAIS: Antiaircraft Artillery Information Service; Antiaircraft Artillery Intelligence Service

aaal: abolish all abortion laws

AAAL: American Academy of Arts and Letters

AAALAC: American Association for Accreditation of Laboratory Animal Care

AAAM: American Association of Aircraft Manufacturers; American Association for Automotive Medicine

AAAN: American Academy of Applied Nutrition

AAAOC: Antiaircraft Artillery Operation Center

AAAR: Association for the Advancement of Aging Research

AAARC: Antiaircraft Artillery Reception Center

AAAS: American Academy of Arts and Sciences; American Academy of Asian Studies; American Association for the Advancement of Science

A.A.A.S.: Associate in Arts and Science

AAASS: American Association for the Advancement of Slavic Studies

AAASUSS: Association of Administrative Assistants and Secretaries to United States Senators

AAAUS: Association of Average Adjusters of the United States

AAB: Aircraft Accident Board; American Association of Bioanalysts; Army Air Base; Army Artillery Board; Association of Applied Biologists

AABB: American Association of Blood Banks

AABC: American Amateur Baseball Congress; Association for the Advancement of Blind Children

AABD: Aid to the Aged, Blind, or Disabled

AABEVM: Association of American Boards of Examiners in Veterinary Medicine

AABGA: American Association of Botanical Gardens and Arboretums

AABI: Antilles Air Boats Incorporated

AABL: Associated Australian Banks of London

AABM: Association of American Battery Manufacturers

AABPDF: Allied Association of Bleachers, Printers, Dyers, and Finishers

AABT: Association for the Advancement of Behavior Therapy

AABTM: American Association of Baggage Traffic Managers

aaBm: analytical anatomy by the Braille method

aaby: as amended by

aac: automatic aperture control; average annual cost

AAC: Aeronautical Advisory Council; Aeronautical Approach Chart; Aircraft Armament Change; Alaskan Air Command; All-American Canal (serving California and Baja California); Alumnae Advisory Center; American Academy of Criminalistics; American Alpine Club; American Alumni Council; American Association of Criminology; American Cement Corporation (stock exchange symbol); Antiaircraft Command; Army Air Corps; Association of American Choruses; Association of American Colleges; Automotive Advertisers Council

AAC: Associação Academica de Coimbra (Portuguese—Coimbra Academic Association)

A.A.C: anno ante Christum (Latin—year before Christ)—same as before Christ

AACA: Antique Automobile Club of America; Automotive Air Conditioning Association

AACAP: Association of American Colleges Arts Program

AACB: Aeronautics and Astronautics Coordination Board

AACBC: American Association of College Baseball Coaches

AACBP: American Academy of Crown and Bridge Prosthodontics

aacc: all-attitude control capability; automatic approach control complex

AACC: American Association of Cereal Chemists; American Association of Clinical Chemists; American Association for Contamination Control; American Association of Credit Counselors; American Automatic Control Council; Association for the Aid of Crippled Children

A.A.C.C.A.: Associate of the Association of Certified and Corporate Accountants

AACCLA: Association of American Chambers of Commerce in Latin America

AACCP: American Association of Colleges for Chiropody-Podiatry

AACE: American Association of

Cost Engineers
AACFT: Army Aircraft
AACHS: Afro-American Cultural and Historical Society
AACI: American Association for Conservation Information; Association of Americans and Canadians in Israel
AACJC: American Association of Community and Junior Colleges
AACM: American Academy of Compensation Medicine
AACO: American Association of Certified Orthoptists; Assault Airlift Control Office(r)
AACOBS: Australian Advisory Council on Bibliographical Services
AACOMS: Army Area Communications System
AACP: American Academy for Cerebral Palsy; American Academy for Child Psychiatry; American Association of Colleges of Podiatry; American Association of Commercial Publications; American Association of Convention Planners; American Association of Correctional Psychologists
AACPR: American Association for Cleft Palate Rehabilitation
AACR: American Association for Cancer Research
***AACR:** Anglo-American Cataloguing Rules*
AACRAO: American Association of Collegiate Registrars and Admissions Officers
AACS: Airborne Astrographic Camera System; Airways and Air Communications Service; Army Airways Communications System
AACSA: Anglo-American Corporation of South Africa
AACSB: American Association of Collegiate Schools of Business
AACSL: American Association for the Comparative Study of Law
AACSM: Airways and Air Communications Service Manual
AACT: American Association of Commodity Traders
AACTE: American Association of Colleges for Teacher Education
AACUBO: American Association of College and University Business Officers
aad (AAD): alloxazine adenine dinucleotide
AAD: Aircraft Assignment Directive; American Academy of Dentists; American Academy of Dermatology; Army Air Defense
AADA: Advanced Air Depot Area; American Academy of Dramatic Arts; Army Air Defense Area
AADC: Army Air Defense Command(er)
AADCP: Army Air Defense Command Post
AADE: American Association of Dental Editors; American Association of Dental Examiners
AADIS: Army Air Defense Information Service
AADLA: Art and Antique Dealers League of America
AADM: American Academy of Dental Medicine
AADN: American Association of Doctors' Nurses
AADOO: Army Air Defense Operations Office(r)
AADPA: American Academy of Dental Practice Administration
AADS: Advanced Army Defense System; American Association of Dental Schools; American Association of Dermatology and Syphilology; Army Air Defense System
AAE: American Association of Endodontists; American Association of Engineers; Army Aviation Engineers
aae: acute allergic encephalitis (AAE)
AAEA: American Agricultural Editors Association
AAEC: Association of American Editorial Cartoonists; Australian Atomic Energy Commission
A.Ae.E.: Associate in Aeronautical Engineering
AAEE: American Academy of Environmental Engineers; American Association of Economic Entomologists
AAEH: Association to Advance Ethical Hypnosis
AAEKNE: American Association of Elementary-Kindergarten-Nursery Educators
AAEP: American Association of Equine Practitioners
AAES: Australian Army Education Service
AAEW: Atlantic Airborne Early Warning
aaf: acetylaminofluorine (AAF); ascorbic acid factor (AAF)
a-a-f: acetic-alcohol-formalin (fixing fluid)
AAF: American Advertising Federation; American Air Filter (company); American Architectural Foundation; American Architectural Foundation; American Astronautical Federation; Army Air Field; Army and Air Force; Army Air Forces
A.A. Fair: Erle Stanley Gardner
AAFB: Auxiliary Air Force Base
aafc (AAFC): antiaircraft fire control
AAFC: Air Accounting and Finance Center; Army Air Forces Center; Army Air Force Classification Center; Association of Advertising Film Companies
AAFCE: Allied Air Force, Central Europe
AAFCO: Association of American Feed Control Officials; Association of American Fertilizer Control Officials
AAFCWF: Army and Air Force Central Welfare Fund; Army and Air Force Civilian Welfare Fund
AAFE: American Association of Feed Exporters
AAFEC: Army Air Forces Engineering Command
AAFEMPS: Army and Air Force Exchange and Motion Picture Service
AAFES: Army and Air Force Exchange Service
AAFIS: Army Air Forces Intelligence School
AAFM: American Association of Feed Microscopists
AAFMC: Army Air Forces Materiel Center
AAFMPS: Army and Air Force Motion Picture Service
AAFNE: Allied Air Force, Northern Europe
AAFNS: Army Air Forces Navigation School
AAFOIC: Army Air Forces Officer in Charge
AAFP: American Academy of Family Physicians
AAFPS: Army and Air Force Pilot School; Army and Air Force Postal Service
AAFRS: American Academy of Facial Plastic and Reconstructive Surgery
AAFS: American Association of Foot Specialists; American Academy of Forensic

Sciences
AAFSE: Allied Air Force, Southern Europe
AAFSS: Advanced Aerial Fire Support System
AAFSW: Association of American Foreign Service Women
AAFTS: Army Air Forces Technical School
AAFWB: Army and Air Force Wage Board
AAG: Air Adjutant General; Association of American Geographers
AAGC: American Association of Gifted Children
AAGFO: American Academy of Gold Foil Operators
AAGp: Aeromedical Airlift Group (USAF)
AAGP: American Academy of General Practice
A. Agr.: Associate in Agriculture
A.Agri.: Associate in Agriculture
AAGR: Air-to-Air Gunnery Range
AAGS: All-American Gladiolus Selections
AAGUS: American Association of Genito-Urinary Surgeons
AAH: American Academy of Homiletics
aaha: awaiting action of higher authority
AAHA: American Animal Hospital Association; American Association of Homes for the Aging; American Association of Hospital Accountants
AAHC: American Association of Hospital Consultants
AAHD: American Academy of the History of Dentistry
AAHDC: American Association of Hospital Dental Chiefs
AAHE: American Association for Higher Education; American Association of Housing Educators
A.A.H.E.: Associate in Arts in Home Economics
AAHM: American Association for the History of Medicine; Association of Architectural Hardware Manufacturers
AAHP: American Association for Hospital Planning; American Association of Hospital Podiatrists; American Association for Humanistic Psychology
AAHPA: American Association of Hospital Purchasing Agents
AAHPER: American Association for Health, Physical Education, and Recreation
AAHPhA: American Animal Health Pharmaceutical Association
AAHQ: Allied Air Headquarters
AAHS: American Aviation Historical Society
aai: air-to-air identification; angle-of-approach indicator
AAI: African-American Institute; Afro-American Institute; Agricultural Ammonia Institute; Akron Art Institute; Alfred Adler Institute; Allied Armies in Italy (World War II); American Association of Immunologists
A.A.I.: Associate of the Chartered Auctioneers' and Estate Agents' Institute
AAIA: Association of American Indian Affairs
AAIAN: Association for the Advancement of Instruction about Alcohol and Narcotics
AAIB: American Association of Instructors of the Blind
AAIC: Allied Air Intelligence Center
AAICD: American Association of Imported Car Dealers
AAID: American Academy of Implant Dentures; American Association of Industrial Dentists
AAIE: American Association of Industrial Editors; American Association of Industrial Engineers
AAII: Association for the Advancement of Invention and Innovation
AAIM: American Association of Industrial Management
AAIN: American Association of Industrial Nurses
AAIPS: American Association of Industrial Physicians and Surgeons
AAIT: American Association of Inhalation Therapists
AAJ: Arab Airways, Jerusalem; Axel Axelson Johnson (Johnson Line)
AAJC: American Association of Junior Colleges
AAJE: American Association for Jewish Education
AAJR: American Academy for Jewish Research
AAJS: American Association for Jesuit Scientists
AAJSA: American Association of Journalism School Administrators
AAK: Alfred A. Knopf
aal: anterior axillary line
AAL: American Airlines; Ames Aeronautical Laboratory; Arctic Aeromedical Laboratory; Association of Assistant Librarians; Australian Air League
AA de L: *Academia Argentina de Letras* (Spanish—Argentine Academy of Letters)
AALA: American Auto Laundry Association; American Automotive Leasing Association
AALAPSO: Afro-Asian-Latin-American People's Solidarity Organization (Cuban overseas subversives)
AALC: African-American Labor Center (AFL-CIO)
AALD: Australian Army Legal Department
AALL: American Association of Law Libraries
aalmg (AALMG): antiaircraft light machine gun
AALPA: Association of Auctioneers and Landed Property Agents
AALPP: American Association for Legal and Political Philosophy
AALS: American Association of Language Specialists; Association of American Law Schools; Association of American Library Schools
AALT: American Association of Library Trustees
AALU: Association for Advanced Life Underwriting
aam (AAM): air-to-air missile
AAM: American Association of Microbiology; American Association of Museums; Australian Air Mission
AAMA: American Academy of Medical Administrators; American Apparel Manufacturers Association; American Association of Medical Assistants; Architectural Aluminum Manufacturers Association
AAMBP: Association of American Medical Book Publishers
AAMC: American Association of Marriage Counselors; American Association of Medical Clinics; Army Air Materiel Command; Association of American Medical Colleges; Australian Army Medical Corps
AAMCH: American Association for Maternal and Child Health
AAMD: American Association

on Mental Deficiency; Association of Art Museum Directors
AAMES: American Association for Middle East Studies
AAMF: American Association of Music Festivals
aamg (AAMG): antiaircraft machine gun
AAMGA: American Association of Managing General Agents
AAMI: American Association of Machinery Importers; Association for the Advancement of Medical Instrumentation; Association of Allergists for Mycological Investigation
AAMIH: American Association for Maternal and Infant Health
AAML: Arctic Aeromedical Laboratory
AAMMC: American Association of Medical Milk Commissioners
AAMOA: Afro-American Music Opportunities Association
AAMP: American Academy of Maxillofacial Prosthetics
AAMR: American Academy on Mental Retardation
AAMRL: American Association of Medical Record Librarians
AAMS: American Air Mail Society
AAMSW: American Association of Medical Social Workers
AAMU: Army Advanced Marksmanship Unit
AAMVA: American Association of Motor Vehicle Administrators
AAMW: Association of Advertising Men and Women
AAMWS: Australian Army Medical Women's Service
AAN: American Academy of Neurology; American Academy of Nutrition; American Association of Neuropathologists; American Association of Nurserymen
AANA: American Association of Nurse Anesthetists; Australian Association of National Advertisers
AANR: American Association of Newspaper Representatives
AANS: American Association of Neurological Surgery; Australian Army Nursing Service
AANSW: Archives Authority of New South Wales
aao: amino-acid oxidase
aaO: *am angeführten Ort* (German—in the place cited); *an anderen Orten* (German—elsewhere; in the place cited)
AAO: Academy of Applied Osteopathy; American Academy of Optometry; American Association of Orthodontists
AAO: *Abastumanskaya Astrofizicheskaya Observatoriya* (Russian—Abastumani Astrophysical Observatory)
AAOA: Ambulance Association of America
AAOC: American Association of Osteopathic Colleges; Antiaircraft Operations Center; Australian Army Ordnance Corps
AAOD: Army Aviation Operating Detachment
AAODC: American Association of Oilwell Drilling Contractors
AAOG: American Association of Obstetricians and Gynecologists
AAOGAS: American Association of Obstetricians, Gynecologists, and Abdominal Surgeons
AAOM: American Academy of Occupational Medicine; American Academy of Oral Medicine
AAOME: American Association of Osteopathic Medical Examiners
AAONMS: Ancient Arabic Order of Nobles of the Mystic Shrine
AAO & O: American Academy of Ophthalmology and Otolaryngology
AAOP: American Academy of Oral Pathology; Antiaircraft Observation Post
AAOPB: American Association of Pathologists and Bacteriologists
AAOPS: American Association of Oral and Plastic Surgeons
AAOR: American Academy of Oral Roentgenology
AAOS: American Academy of Orthopaedic Surgery
AAP: Academy of American Poets; Affirmative Action Program; Allied Administrative Publication; American Academy of Pediatrics; American Academy of Periodontology; Association for the Advancement of Psychoanalysis; Association for the Advancement of Psychotherapy; Association of American Physicians; Association of American Publishers; Association of Applied Psychoanalysis; Australian Associated Press
AAPA: American Amateur Press Association; American Association of Physical Anthropologists; American Association of Port Authorities
A-A PA: Anglo-American Press Association
AAPB: American Association of Pathologists and Bacteriologists
AAPC: All-African Peoples' Conference
AAPCC: American Association of Poison Control Centers; American Association of Psychiatric Clinics for Children
AAPCM: Association of American Playing Card Manufacturers
AAPCO: Association of American Pesticide Control Officials
AAPD: American Academy of Physiologic Dentistry
AAPE: American Academy of Physical Education
AAPG: American Association of Petroleum Geologists
AAPH: American Association of Professional Hypnologists
AAPHD: American Association of Public Health Dentists
AAPHI: Associate of the Association of Public Health Inspectors
AAPHP: American Association of Public Health Physicians
AAPICU: American Association of Presidents of Independent Colleges and Universities
AAPIU: Allied Aerial Photographic Interpretation Unit
AAPL: Afro-American Policemen's League; American Artists Professional League; American Association of Petroleum Landmen
aapm: amphiapomict
AAPMR: American Academy of Physical Medicine and Rehabilitation
AAPO: All-African Peoples' Organization
AAPOR: American Association for Public Opinion Research
AAPP: Association of Amusement Park Proprietors
AAPRM: American Association of Passenger Rate Men
AAPS: American Association of Plastic Surgeons; American Association for the Promotion of Science; Association for Ambulatory Pediatric Ser-

vices; Association of American Physicians and Surgeons
AAPSE: American Association of Professors in Sanitary Engineering
AAPSS: American Academy of Political and Social Sciences
AAPSW: Associate of the Association of Psychiatric Social Workers
AAPT: American Association of Physics Teachers; Association of Asphalt Paving Technologists
AAPTO: American Association of Passenger Traffic Officers
AAPTSR: Australian Association for Predetermined Time Standards and Research
aar: after action report; against all risks; average annual rainfall
Aar: Aarhus
AAR: Aircraft Accident Record; Aircraft Accident Report; American Academy in Rome; Army Area Representative; Association of American Railroads; Automotive Affiliated Representatives
aa rating: average-audience rating (percentage of tv-equipped homes viewing the average minute of a national telecast)
AARC: Ann Arbor Railroad Company
AARD: American Academy of Restorative Dentistry
AARDCO: Association of American Railroad Dining Car Officers
aarg: *aargang* (Dano-Norwegian or Swedish—yearbook)
Aarh: Aarhus
Aarhusium: (Latin—Aarhus)
AARL: Advanced Applications and Research Laboratory
aarp: annual advance retainer pay
AARP: American Association of Retired Persons
AARPS: Air-Augmented Rocket-Propulsion System
AARR: Ann Arbor Railroad
AARRC: Army Aircraft Requirements Review Committee
AARS: American Association of Railroad Superintendents; American Association of Railway Surgeons; Army Aircraft Repair Ship; Army Amateur Radio System
AART: American Association for Rehabilitation Therapy
AARTA: American Association of Railroad Ticket Agents
aarv: aerial armored reconnaissance vehicle
AARWBA: American Auto Racing Writers and Broadcasters Association
aas: advanced antenna system; aortic arch syndrome
AAs: author's alterations
AAS: Aircraft Airworthiness Section; All-America Selections; American Amaryllis Society; American Antiquarian Society; American Astronautical Society; American Astronomical Society; Army Air Service; Army Attache System; Arnold Air Society; Association for Asian Studies; Australian Academy of Science
A.A.S.: Academiae Americanae Socius (Latin—Fellow of the American Academy of Arts and Sciences)
AASA: American Association of School Administrators; Associate of the Australian Society of Accountants
AASB: American Association of Small Business
AASC: Allied Air Support Command; Australian Army Service Corps
aascm: awaiting action summary court martial
AASCO: Association of American Seed Control Officials
aasd: antiaircraft self-destroying
AASDJ: American Association of Schools and Departments of Journalism
AASE: American Academy of Sanitary Engineers; Association for Applied Solar Energy
AASEC: American Association of Sex Educators and Counselors
AASF: Advanced Air Striking Force
AASFE: American Association of Sunday and Feature Editors
AASG: Association of American State Geologists
AAS & GP: American Association of Soap and Glycerin Producers
AASH: American Association for the Study of the Headache
AASHO: American Association of State Highway Officials
AASI: Advertising Agency Service Interchange; American Academy for Scientific Interrogation
aasl: antiaircraft searchlight
AASL: American Association of School Librarians; American Association of State Librarians
A & ASL: American & Australian Steamship Line
AASLH: American Association for State and Local History
AASM: Association of American Steel Manufacturers
AASND: American Association for the Study of Neoplastic Diseases
AASO: Association of American Ship Owners
AASP: American Association for Social Psychiatry
AASPA: American Association of School Personnel Administrators
AASPRC: American Association of Sheriff's Posses and Riding Clubs
aasr: airport and airways surveillance radar
AASR: Abhazian Autonomous Soviet Socialist Republic; Adjarian Autonomous Soviet Socialist Republic
AASRI: Arctic and Antarctic Scientific Research Institute
AASRM: Ancient and Accepted Scottish Rite Masons
AASS: Afro-American Students Society; American Association for Social Security
AAST: American Association for the Surgery of Trauma
AASTC: Associate in Architecture—Sydney Technical College
AASTD: Association for the Advancement of the Science and Technology of Documentation
AASU: Afro-American Student Union
AASWA: American Association for the Study of World Affairs
AASWI: American Aid Society for the West Indies
aat: after acid treatment
aat (AAT): alpha-1 antitrypsin
AAT: Achievement Anxiety Test; Australian Antarctic Territory
A-AT: Anglo-Australian Telescope
AATA: Anglo-American Tourist Association
AATB: Advanced Amphibious Training Base
AATC: Anti-Aircraft Training Center; Army Aviation Test Command

AATCC: American Association of Textile Chemists and Colorists
AATCLC: American Association of Teachers of Chinese Language and Culture
AATEA: American Association of Teacher Educators in Agriculture
AATF: American Association of Teachers of French
AATG: American Association of Teachers of German
AATI: American Association of Teachers of Italian
AATM: American Academy of Tropical Medicine
AATOE: American Association of Theatre Organ Enthusiasts
AATP: American Academy of Tuberculosis Physicians
AATPA: American Association of Traveling Passenger Agents
AATRACEN: Anti-Aircraft Training Center
AATRIS: Army Air Traffic Regulation and Identification System
AATS: American Academy of Teachers of Singing; American Association of Theological Schools; American Association for Thoracic Surgery
AATSEEL: American Association of Teachers of Spanish and Portuguese
AATT: American Association for Textile Technology
AATTA: Arab Association of Tourism and Travel Agents
AAT & TC: Anti-Aircraft Training and Test Center
AATU: Association of Air Transport Unions
AATUF: All-African Trade Union Federation
AAU: Administrative Area Unit; Al-Azhar University; Amateur Athletic Union; Association of American Universities
AAUN: American Association for the United Nations
AAUP: American Association of University Presses; American Association of University Professors
AAUQ: Associate in Accountancy—University of Queensland
AAUTI: American Association of University Teachers of Insurance
AAUUS: Amateur Athletic Union of the U.S.
AAUW: American Association of University Women
aav: airborne assault vehicle
AAV: Antiaircraft Volunteer
AAVA: American Association of Veterinary Anatomists
AAVB: American Association of Veterinary Bacteriologists
AAVC: Australian Army Veterinary Corps
AAVCS: Automatic Aircraft Vectoring Control System
aavd: automatic alternate voice/data
AAVMC: Association of American Veterinary Medical Colleges
Aavn: Army aviation
AAVN: American Association of Veterinary Nutritionists
AAVP: American Association of Veterinary Pathologists
AAVRO: American Association of Vital Records and Public Health Statistics
AAVS: American Anti-Vivisection Society
AAVSO: American Association of Variable Star Observers
AAW: Advertising Association of the West; Anti-Air Warfare
AAWA: American Automatic Weapons Association
AAWB: American Association of Workers for the Blind
AAWC: Australian Advisory War Council
AAWD: Association of American Women Dentists
AAWg: Aeromedical Airlift Wing USAF)
AAWPI: Association of American Wood Pulp Importers
AAWS: American Association of Wardens and Superintendents
AAWU: Amateur Athletic Western Union
AAXICO: American Air Export and Import Company
AAYM: American Association of Youth Museums
AAZK: American Association of Zoo Keepers
AAZPA: American Association of Zoological Parks and Aquariums
ab: abscess; abortion; about; adapter booster; afterburner; airbrake; anchor bolt; antibody; asthmatic bronchitis; axiobuccal
ab: *abril* (Spanish—April)
a/b (A/B): airborne
a & b: applejack and benedictine; assault and battery
aB: *auf Bestellung* (German—on order)
Ab: abnormal; alabamine
Ab: *Abade* (Portuguese—Abbot)—also means fat man
AB: able-bodied seaman; Aid to the Blind; Air Base; Arnold Bernstein (steamship line); Assembly Bill
A-B: Allen-Bradley; Ambrose Bierce; Anton Bruckner
A.B.: *artium baccalureus* (Latin—Bachelor of Arts)
A/B: Aid to the Blind; Airman Basic
A/B: *Aktiebolag* (Swedish—limited company)
aba: antibacterial activity
ab-a: abampere
ABA: American Badminton Association; American Bakers Association; American Bandmasters Association; American Bankers Association; American Bar Association; American Bell Association; American Berkshire Association; American Booksellers Association; American Bowhunters Association; American Brazilian Association; American Buddhist Association; Annual Budget Authorization
ABAA: Antiquarian Booksellers Association of America
ab ab.: *ab absurdo* (Latin—to the absurd)
abac: a basic coursewriter
ABAC: Abraham Baldwin Agricultural College
ABACUS: Air Battle Analysis Center Utility System; Autonetics Business and Control United Systems
ABAD: Air Battle Analysis Division
ab aet.: *ab aeterno* (Latin—until eternity)
ABAG: Association of Bay Area Governments (San Francisco)
A-bahn: *Autobahn* (German—superhighway)
ABAI: American Boiler and Affiliated Industries
ABAK: *Asociation di Biblioteka i Archivo di Korsow* (Papiamento—Association of Libraries and Archives of Curaçao)
abamp: absolute ampere (10 amperes)
aband: abandoned
abandt: abandonment
ABAO: *Asociación Bilbaina de Amigos de la Opera* (Spanish—Bilbaoan Association of

Friends of the Opera)
ABAS: American Board of Abdominal Surgeons
abat: abattoir
ABATU: Advance Base Air Task Unit; Advance Base Aviation Training Unit
abb: *abbonamento* (Italian—subscription); *abbuono* (Italian—allowance; bonus; discount)
Abb: Abbess; Abbey; Abbot
Abb: *Abbildung* (German—illustration)
Abb.: *abbas* (Latin—abbot)
Ab of B: Archbishop(ric) of Bremen
ABB: Akron & Barberton Belt (railroad)
ABBA: American Blind Bowling Association; American Board of Bio-Analysis; American Brahman Breeders Association
ABBB: Association of Better Business Bureaus
ABBF: Association of Bronze and Brass Founders
Abbild: *Abbildungen* (German—illustrations)
ABBMM: Association of British Brush Machinery Manufacturers
abbr: abbreviate; abbreviated; abbreviation
ABBRA: American Boat Builders and Repairers Association
abbrev: *abbreviatura* (Italian—abbreviation)
abbreviaz: *abbreviazione* (Italian— abbreviation)
abbrev(s): abbreviation(s)
Abby: Abigail
abc: abecedarium (alphabet primer); advanced biomedical capsule (ABC); acid-balance control; aconite, belladonna, chloroform; alphabet; atomic, biological, chemical (ABC); alum, blood, charcoal; automatic bass compensation; automatic brightness control; axiobuccocervical
Ab of C: Archbishop(ric) of Cologne
ABC: Aerated Bread Company; Alcohol Beverage Control; American Bowling Congress; American Brass Company; American, British, Canadian; American Broadcasting Company; Argentina, Brazil, Chile; atomic, biological, chemical (warfare); Audit Bureau of Circulation; Australian Broadcasting Commission; Australian Broadcasting Corporation; Automotive Boosters Clubs
ABC: Spain's most prestigious daily newspaper
AB & C: Atlanta, Birmingham and Coast (railroad)
ABC^3: Airborne Battlefield Command and Control Center
ABCA: American-British- Canadian-Australian; Antique Bottle Collectors Association; Army Bureau of Current Affairs
ABC-ASP: American-British-Canadian—Army Standardization Program
abcb: air-blast circuit breaker
ABCB: American Bottlers of Carbonated Beverages; Australian Broadcasting Control Board
ABCC: Association of British Chambers of Commerce; Atomic Bomb Casualty Commission
ABCCC: Airborne Battlefield Command and Control Center
ABC—Clio: American Bibliographical Center—Clio Press (Santa Barbara, California)
ABCCTC: Advanced Base Combat Communication Training Center
abcd: airway (opened), breathing (restored), circulation (restored), definitive (therapy); atomic, biological, chemical, and damage (control); awaiting bad conduct discharge
ABCD: Accelerated Business Collection and Delivery (of mail); Action for Boston Community Development; Advanced Base Construction Depot; America, Britain, China, Dutch East Indies (ABCD Powers during World War II); American Society of Bookplate Collectors and Designers
ABCDCAL: Alcoholic Beverage Control Department—California
A-B-C-Dieren: German musical exercises wherein names of notes replace words
ABCFM: American Board of Commissioners for Foreign Missions
ABCH: American Board of Clinical Hypnosis
ABC Islands: Aruba, Bonaire, Curaçao (Netherlands Antilles)
ABC Latin American Powers: Argentina, Brazil, Chile
ABCM: Association of British Chemical Manufacturers; Aviation Chief Boatswain's Mate
ABCMR: Army Board for Correction of Military Records
abcoulomb: absolute coulomb (10 coulombs)
ABCP: Association of Blind Chartered Physiotherapists
ABC Powers: Argentina, Brazil, Chile
ABCR: Association for Beautiful Colorado Roads
ABCRS: American Board of Colon and Rectal Surgery
ABCS: American Board on Counseling Services
ABCSP: American-British-Canadian Standardization Program
ABC Std: American-British-Canadian Standard(s)
abcw (ABC or ABCW): atomic chemical, biological warfare
ABCW: American Bakery and Confectionery Workers
abd: abdicated; abdomen; abdominal; abduction; abductor; average body dose (radiation)
Abd: *Abdias* (Spanish—The Book of Obadiah); *Abdul* (Arabic—servant)
ABD: Abadan, Iran (airport); Advanced Base Depot; Advanced Base Dock; American Board of Dermatology
ABD: *Association Belge de Docomuntation* (Belgian Documentation Association)
A.B.D.: All But Dissertation (doctoral lacking)
ABDA: American-British-Dutch-Australian (forces in World War II)
ABDACOM: Advanced Base Depot Area Command; American-British-Dutch-Australian Command (World War II)
abdc: after bottom dead center
abde: airport bird-detection equipment
abd hyst: abdominal hysterectomy
ABDI: Administrative Board of the Dress Industry
abdl: automatic binary data link
abdom: abdomen; abdominal
ABDPH: American Board of Dental Public Health
Abdr: *Abdruck* (German—copy, printing)
abd's: all but their dissertations (Ph.D. candidates)
ABDSP: Anza-Borrego Desert

State Park (California)
abe: airborne bombing evaluation; augmented ballast expulsion
Abe: Abel; Abelarde; Abelardo; Abraham; Abrahán; Abram; Abrán
ABE: Adult Basic Education; Airborne Bombing Evaluation; Allentown-Bethlehem-Easton (Pennsylvania airport)
ABEA: American Broncho-Esophagological Association
Abeceds: Abecedarians
ABEC: Annular Bearing Engineers Committee
Abelard: Abelard-Schuman, Ltd
Abel Shufflebottom: Robert Southey's pseudonym
ABEM: *Association Belge pour l'Etude, l'Essais, et l'Emploi des Matériaux* (Belgian Association for the Study, Testing, and Use of Materials)
ABEP: Adult Basic Education Program
ABEPP: American Board of Examiners in Professional Psychology
aber: aberration
Aber: Aberdeen; Aberdonian
Aberc: Abercrombie; Abercrombian
Abercrombie: Abercrombie and Fitch
abes: aerospace business environment simulator
abets: airborne beacon electronic test set
ab ex: *ab extra* (Latin—from outside)
ABEX: American Brake Shoe Company
Abf: *Abfahrt* (German—departure)
ABF: Aircraft Battle Force; American Bar Foundation; American Beekeeping Federation; Associated British Foods
abfarad: absolute farad ($10^2/_3$ farads)
ABFLO: Association of Bedding and Furniture Law Officials
ABFM: American Board of Foreign Missions
ab'ft: abaft (toward the stern)
abg: axiobuccogingival
Abg: *Abgeordnete* (German—Member of Parliament)
ABG: Air Base Group; American Ship Building Company (stock exchange symbol)
abgk: *abgekürzt* (German—abbreviated)
ABGP: Air Base Group
abh: alpha-benzene-hexachloride
Abh: *Abhandlungen* (German—transactions, treatises)
abhenry: absolute henry (10^{-9} henries)
ABHP: American Board of Health Physics
abi: assignment of beneficial interest
Abi: Abigail
ABI: American Butter Institute; Associated Bank International; Authorized Break of Inspection
ABI: *Advance Book Information; Associação Brasileira de Imprensa* (Portuguese—Brazilian Press Association); *Associazione Bancaria Italiana* (Italian Bankers' Association); *Associazione Bibliotecari Italiani* (Italian Librarians Association)
ABIA: Associate of the Bankers' Institute of Australasia
Abie: Abraham
Abies: five-dollar bills bearing the portrait of President Abraham Lincoln
ABIM: American Board of Internal Medicine; American Board of International Missions; Association of British Insecticide Manufacturers
ab in.: *ab intra* (Latin—from within)
ab init.: *ab initio* (Latin—from the beginning)
ABJS: Association of Bone and Joint Surgeons
Abk: *Abkürzung* (German—abbreviation)
ABK: American Brake Shoe (stock exchange symbol)
Abkurz: *Abkürzungen* (German—abbreviations)
abl: ablative; axiobuccolingual
Abl: Atlas basic language (data processing)
Abl: *Abril* (Spanish—April)
ABL: Academia Brasileira de Letras (Brazilian Academy of Letters); Alameda Belt Line (railroad); Allegheny Ballistic Laboratory; Animated Biological Laboratories (NASA); Aquatic Biological Laboratory; Automated Biological Laboratory
ABLA: Amateur Bicycle League of America; American Business Law Association
ablat: ablative
ablb: alternate binaural loudness balance
ABLC: Association of British Launderers and Cleaners
ABLE: Action for Better Law Enforcement; Activity Balance Line Evaluation; Agricultural-Biological Literature Evaluation
ABLISS: Association of British Library and Information Studies Schools
ABLM: American Board of Legal Medicine
ABLS: Association of British Library Schools; Atlas Biomedical Literature System
A.B.L.S.: Bachelor of Arts in Library Science
abm: automated batch mixing
abm (ABM): antiballistic missile
Abm: Abraham
ABM: Advance Bill of Material; Aviation Boatswain's Mate
A.B.M.: Associate in Business Management
AB de M: *Acadêmia Brasileira de Música* (Portuguese—Brazilian Academy of Music)
ABMA: American Boiler Manufacturers Association; American Brush Manufacturers Association; Army Ballistic Missile Agency
ABMAC: Association of British Manufacturers of Agricultural Chemicals
ABMC: American Battle Monuments Commission
ABMD: Air Ballistics Missile Division
ABMEWS: Antiballistic Missile Early Warning System
ABMIS: Airborne Anti-Ballistic Missile Intercept System
ABMPM: Association of British Manufacturers of Printing Machinery
ABMRF: American Business Men's Research Foundation
ABMS: American Bureau of Metal Statistics
ABM System: Antiballistic Missile System
ABMU: American Baptist Missionary Union
abn: abnormal; airborne
Abn: Aberdeen
ABN: American Bank Note (stock exchange symbol)
ABN: *Algemene Bank Nederland* (Dutch—Netherlands General Bank)
A-BN: Anti-Bolshevik Nations
ABNCO: American Bank Note Company
ABNE: Association for the Benefit of Non-contract Em-

ployees
Abner: Norris Goff
abni: available but not installed
ABNI: *Atlas of Britain and Northern Ireland*
ABNINF: Airborne Infantry
ABNM: American Board of National Missions
abnor: abnormal
abnorm: abnormal(ity)
ABNPHSBM: Advisory Board on National Parks, Historic Sites, Buildings, and Monuments
ABNS: American Board of Neurological Surgery
abo: aboriginal; aborigine; absent bed occupancy
ABO: American Board of Opthalmology; American Board of Opticianry; American Board of Orthodontics; American Board of Otolaryngology; Association of Buying Offices
Abode of the Blest: the Isle of Avalon described in the Arthurian tales
Abode of Cold Darkness: Niffleheim (Norse underworld)
Abode of the Giants: Jotunheim (Norse mythology)
Abode of the Gods: Asgard, according to the Norse; Mount Olympus, according to the Greeks
Abode of Man: Midgard (the mid earth of the Norse mythology)
ABOF: Association of British Organic Fertilisers
ABOG: American Board of Obstetrics and Gynecology
abohm: absolute ohm (10^{-9} ohms)
Abolitionist African Nations: Liberia and Sierra Leone, created respectively by American and British abolitionists
Abolitionist Quaker: Lucretia Mott and John Greenleaf Whittier have equal title to this eponym
Abol(s): Abolitionist(s)
A-bomb: atomic bomb; (underground slang—cigarette containing hashish or marijuana plus heroin or opium)
abon: *abonné* (French—subscriber)
abonn: *abonnement* (French—subscription)
ABOPS: Association of Business Officers of Preparatory Schools
abos: aborigines
ABOS: American Board of Oral Surgery; American Board of Orthopedic Surgery
ab ov.: *ab ovo* (Latin—from the egg; from the start)
abp: arterial blood pressure
Abp: Archbishop
ABP: American Board of Pathology; American Board of Pediatrics; American Board of Pedodontics; American Board of Peridontology; American Board of Prosthodontics; American Business Press
ABPA: Advanced Base Personnel Administration; Australian Book Publishers' Association
ABPC: American Book Publishers Council
ABPD: American Board of Pediatric Dermatology
ABPG: Advanced Base Proving Ground
ABPI: Association of the British Pharmaceutical Industry
ABPM: American Board of Preventive Medicine
ABPMR: American Board of Physical Medicine and Rehabilitation
ABPN: American Board of Psychiatry and Neurology
ABPO: Advanced Base Personnel Officer
ABPsS: Associate of the British Psychological Society
ABPS: American Board of Plastic Surgery
ABPU: Advanced Base Personnel Unit
ABPVM: Association of British Plywood and Veneer Manufacturers
ABQ: Albuquerque, New Mexico (airport)
abr: abridge; abridgment
abr: *abril* (Portuguese or Spanish—April)
Abr: Abraham
ABR: American Board of Radiology; American Commercial Barge Line (stock exchange symbol); Real Aerovias Brasil (Brazilian airline symbol)
ABR: *American Bankruptcy Reports*
Abra: Abraham
abracadabra: abbreviations and related acronyms associated with defense, astronautics business and radio-electronics (acronym devised by the Office of Public Relations of Raytheon in an effort to abolish acronyms)
Abram: Abraham
Abrams: Fredrica Abrams; Harry N. Abrams; etc.
abras: abrasions
ABRB: Advanced Base Receiving Barracks
A & B R C: Antofagasta and Bolivia Railway Company
ABRD: Advanced Base Repair Depot; Advanced Base Reshipment Depot; American Bill of Rights Day (association)
ABRES: Advanced Ballistic Reentry System
abrev: *abréviation* (French—abbreviation); *abreviatura(s)* (Spanish—abbreviation(s))
abrew: *abrewiacja* (Polish—abbreviation)
abrid: abridged; abridgement
ABRO: Animal Breeding Research Organization
ABRRM: Association of British Reclaimed Rubber Manufacturers
ABRS: Association of British Riding Schools
ABRSM: Associated Board of the Royal Schools of Music
abrsv: abrasive
abr sw: airbrake switch
abs: abalones; abcesses; abortions; absent; absolute; abson; abstrene; acrylonitrilebutadiene-styrene (ABS) resin(s); air-break switch; alkyl benzene sulfonate
abs (Abs): antibodies
abs: *aux bons soins de* (French—in care of)
Abs: *Absatz* (German—paragraph); *Absender* (German—sender)
Ab of S: Archbishop(ric) of Salzburg
ABS: Air Base Squadron; American Begonia Society; American Berlioz Society; American Bible Society; American Board of Surgery; American Boxwood Society; American Brake Shoe; American Bureau of Shipping
ABSA: African Boy Scouts Association; Association of British Secretaries in America
abs alt: absolute altitude
absap: airborne search and attack plotter
abs art: abstract art
ABSC: American Brake and Screw Company
Abschn: *Abschnitt* (German—chapter, paragraph)
absd: advanced base sectional

dock
ABSD: Advanced Base Supply Depot
abse. rec: *absente rec* (Latin—in the absence of the accused)
abs. feb.: *absente febre* (Latin—in the absence of fever)
ABSI: Associate of the Boot and Shoe Institution
ABSIE: American Broadcasting Station in Europe (World War II)
ABSM: Associate of the Birmingham School of Music
ABSMA: American Bleached Shellac Manufacturers Association
absol: absolute
ABSP: Aid to the Potentially Self-supporting Blind
abs.re.: *absente reo* (Latin—the defendant being absent)
abst: abstract
abst jdg: abstract of judgment
abstr dict: abstract diction (indefiniteness)
abs vis: absolute viscosity
ABSW: Association of British Science Writers
abs z: absolute zero (—273 degrees centigrade)
abt: about; abundant
Abt: *Abteilung* (German—part)
Ab of T: Archbishop(ric) of Trier
ABT: Abbott Laboratories (stock exchange symbol); American Ballet Theater
ABTA: Association of British Travel Agents
ABTAC: Australian Book Trade Advisory Committee
ABTAPL: Association of British Theological and Philosophical Libraries
ABTF: Airborne Task Force
ABTICS: Abstract and Book Title Index Card Service (Iron and Steel Institute)
ABTTA: American Bridge, Tunnel, and Turnpike Association
ABTU: Advanced Base Torpedo Unit; Advanced Base Training Unit; Air Bombers Training Unit
ABTUC: All-Burma Trade Union Congress
ABU: Alliance Biblique Universelle (Universal Biblical Alliance)
A.Bus.: Associate in Business
abu: (Arabic—father)
abut: abutment
abv: above
abvolt: absolute volt (10^{-8} volts)
abw: anterior bite wing
abw: *Abwehr* (German—defense)
ABWA: American Bottled Water Association; American Business Writing Association; Associated Business Writers of America
ABWG: Air Base Wing
abwik: assault and battery with intent to kill
A-BU: Anglo-Belgian Union
ABWRC: Army Biological Warfare Research Center
aby: acid bismuth yeast
Aby: Abraham
ABY: Albany, Georgia (airport)
ABYA: Association of British Yacht Agents
ABYC: American Boat and Yacht Council
ac: absolute ceiling; accelerator; acetyl; acetyl-choline; adrenal cortex; aerodynamic center; air conduction; air cool; air-cooled; anodal closure; anticorrosive; antiphlogistic corticoid; arithmetic computation; asbestos cement; atriocarotid; auriculocarotid; auxiliary console; axiocervical
a-c: alternating-current
a/c: account; account current; aircraft
a/c: *ao cuidado de* (Portuguese—in care of)
a & c: addenda and corrigenda
a.c.: *ante cibos* (Latin—before meals)
a C: *avanti Cristo* (Italian—before Christ)
Ac: actinium; altocumulus
AC: Adelbert College; Adelphi College; Aden Colony; Adrian College; aerodynamic center (symbol); Air Canada; Alabama College; Albion College; Albright College; Allegheny College; Alliance College; Alma College; alternating current; Alverno College; Amarillo College; Ambulance Corps; Amherst College; Anderson College; Andrew College; Annhurst College; anodal contraction or closure; Antioch College; Aquinas College; Arcadia College; Arithmetic Computation (test); Arkansas College; Armstrong College; Asbury College; Ashland College; Assumption College; Athens College; Athletic Club; Augusta College; Augustana College; Aurora College; Austin College; Averett College; Azusa College
AC: *Atlanta Constitution*
AC: *Ação Catolica* (Portuguese), *Acción Católica* (Spanish), *Action Catholique* (French), *Azione Cattolica* (Italian)—Catholic Action
A.C.: *année courante* (French—current year); *Año Cristo* (Spanish—Year of Our Lord)—A.D.
A-C: Allis-Chalmers
A/C: Air Commodore; aircraft; Aviation Cadet
A & C: *Antony and Cleopatra*
A/1C: Airman First Class
A/2C: Airman Second Class
A^2C^2: *see* AACC
A/3C: Airman Third Class
aca: adenocarcinoma
ac a: acetic acid
Aca: Acapulco (inhabitants—Acapulqueños)
ACA: Acapulco, Mexico (airport); Aircraft Castings Association; Alberta College of Art; American Camping Association; American Canoe Association; American Carnivals Association; American Casting Association; American Cat Association; American Cemetery Association; American Chiropractic Association; American Civic Association; American College of Allergists; American College of Anesthesiologists; American College of Apothecaries; American Communications Association; American Composers Alliance; American Congregational Association; Americans for Constitutional Action; American Correctional Association; American Cryptogram Association; American Crystallographic Association; Arts Council of America; Arts Council of Australia; Assembly Constitutional Amendment; Associated Chiropodists of America; Association of Correctional Administrators
A.C.A.: Associate of the Institute of Chartered Accountants (of England and Wales)
ACAA: Agricultural Conservation and Adjustment Administration
ACAB: Army Contract Adjustment Board
ACAC: Allied Container Advisory Committee; Association of College Admission Counsel-

lors
acad: academic; academician; academy
Acad: Acadia; Academy
ACAD: American Conference of Academic Deans
Acad aper: Academy of Motion Picture Arts and Sciences aperture (of sound films)
Acad B-A: *Académie des Beaux Arts* (French—Academy of Fine Arts)
Academic: Academic Press
Acad Fran: *Académie Française* (French Academy)
Acadia(n): Novia Scotia(n); native Louisians of French origin are also called Acadians or Cajuns
Acadian(s): native Louisianian(s) of French origin; also called Cajun(s)
Acad Ins B-L: *Académie des Inscriptions et Belles-Lettres* (French—Academy of Inscriptions and Literature)
Acad mask: Academy of Motion Picture Arts and Sciences mask (enclosing the aperture area of sound films)
Acad Med: Academy of Medicine
Acad Mus: Academy of Music
Acad Sci: *Académie des Sciences* (French—Academy of Science); Academy of Science
Acad Sin: Academia Sinica (Chinese Academy of Science)
Acad St Cec: Academia di Santa Cecilia, Rome
Acad U: Acadia University
AC & AE: Association of Chemical and Allied Employees
ACAF: Amphibious Corps, Atlantic Fleet
ACAN: Army Command and Administrative Network
ACAnes: American College of Anesthetists
a. cant.: after cant frames
Acanth: Acanthocephala
acanthite: silver sulfide
Acap: Acapulco
ACAP: American Council on Alcohol Problems; Army Contract Appeals Panel
ACAPA: American Concrete Agricultural Pipe Association
a capp: *a cappella* (Italian—in chapel style, without musical accompaniment)
ACAS: Association of Casualty Accounts and Statisticians
AC/AS: Assistant Chief of Air Staff
ACAST: Advisory Committee on Applications of Science and Technology (UNESCO)
acata: acatalectic(al)
acb: air circuit breaker; asbestos cement board
ACB: Advertising Checking Bureau; Airman Classification Battery; Army Classification Battery; Association Canadienne des Biblioth*èques (Canadian Library Association); Association of Customers' Brokers; Association of the Customs Bar*
ACB: *Association Canadienne des Bibliothèques* (French—Canadian Library Association)
ACBA: Academy of Comic Book Artists
ACB of A: Associated Credit Bureaus of America
ACBB: American Council for Better Broadcasts
ACBL: American Commercial Barge Line; American Contract Bridge League
acbm: atomic cesium beam maser
ACBM: Associated Corset and Brassiere Manufacturers; Aviation Chief Boatswain's Mate
ACBs: Associated Credit Bureaus
ACBS: Accrediting Commission for Business Schools
ACBWS: Automatic Chemical Biological Warning System
acc: account; altocumulus castellatus (clouds); anodal closing contraction; astronomical great circle course (ACC); automatic chroma circuit (tv)
Acc: Lucius Accius (Roman poet)
ACC: Accra, Ghana (airport); Adirondack Community College; Administrative Committee on Coordination; Air Center Commander; Air Control Center; Air Coordinating Committee; Allied Control Commission; Allied Control Council; American College of Cardiology; American Concert Choir; American Conference of Cantors; American Craftsmen's Council; Army Chemical Center; Army Cooperation Command; Association of Choral Conductors; Auburn Community College
A-C-C: Appleton-Century-Crofts
ACCA: Aeronautical Chamber of Commerce of America; American Clinical and Climatological Association; American College of Clinic Administrators; American Cotton Cooperative Association; Art Collectors Club of America
acc & aud: accountant and auditor
ACCC: Alternate Command and Control Center
ACCCE: Association of Consulting Chemists and Chemical Engineers
ACCCF: American Concert Choir and Choral Foundation
AC & CCI: American Coke and Coal Chemicals Institute
acce: acceptance
ACCE: American Chamber of Commerce Executives
accel: accelerate
accel: *accelerando* (Italian—accelerating)
ACCELS: Automated-Circuit Card-Etching Layout System
accepon: *acceptation* (French—acceptance)
access: accessory
ACCESS: Automatic Computer-Controlled Electronic Scanning System
ACCF: American Committee for Cultural Freedom; Association of Community College Facilities
ACCFA: Agricultural Credit Cooperative Finance Administration
ACCHAN: Allied Command Channel (NATO)
acci: accidental injury
ACCI: American Cottage Cheese Institute
accid: accident(al)
ACCION: Americans for Community Cooperation in Other Nations
accis: accismus
accl: anodal closure clonus
ACCL: American Council of Commercial Laboratories
ACCM: American College of Clinic Managers
ACCN: Associated Court and Commercial Newspapers
acco: *accompagnamento* (Italian—accompaniment)
ACCO: Associate of the Canadian College of Organists; Association of Child Care Officers
accom: accommodation
accomp: accomplish
ACCORD: Action Coalition to

Create Opportunities for Retirement with Dignity
ACCP: American College of Chest Physicians
ACCR: American Council on Chiropractic Roentgenography
ACCRA: Abortion and Contraception Counselling and Research Association; American Chamber of Commerce Researchers Association
accrd int: accrued interest
accred: accredited
ACCS: Automated Calibration Control System
A.C.C.S.: Associate of the Chartered Corporation of Secretaries
acct: account; accountant; accounting
acctd: accented
ACCTU: All-Union Central Council of Trade Unions (USSR)
accum: accumulate
accur: *accuratissime* (Latin—most accurately)
accus: accusative
accw: alternating current continuous wave
accy: accessory
acd: absolute cardiac dullness; accord; accordion; acid-citrate-dextrose; active duty commitment; adopted child; advance delivery of correspondence; advice of duration and charges; anodal duration contraction; average daily census; axiodistocervical
ACD: Administrative Commitment Document; Allied Chemical Corporation (stock exchange symbol); American Choral Directors; American College of Dentists
ACD: *American College Dictionary*
ACDA: American Choral Directors Association; Arms Control and Disarmament Agency; Aviation Combat Development Agency
a-c/d-c: alternating current/direct current; underground slang—bisexual
ACDCM: Archbishop of Canterbury's Diploma in Church Music
a-c/d-c's: bisexuals
ACDM: Association of Chairmen of Departments of Mechanics
acdt: accident
acdu: active duty
A Cdre: Air Commodore
acdutra: active duty for training
ACDUTRA: Active Duty Reserve Army
ace.: acetic; adrenal cortical extract; aerospace control environment; air crash equipment; alcohol-chloroform-ether (anesthetic mixture); attitude control electronics; automatic checkout equipment; automatic circuit exchange
ACE: Allied Command, Europe; American Cinema Editors; American Council on Education; American Hard Rubber Company (trademark); Army Corps of Engineers; Aviation Construction Engineers
ACEA: Air Line Communication Employees Association
ACEAA: Advisory Committee on Electrical Appliances and Accessories
ACEC: Army Communications and Electronic Command; Ateliers de Constructions Electriques de Charleroi (Electrical Construction Workshops of Charleroi—Belgium)
A.C.Ed.: Associate in Commercial Education
ACEF: Asian Cultural Exchange Foundation; Association of Commodity Exchange Firms
a-c-e-g: (musical mnemonic—all cows eat grass)—bass clef note names of the four spaces (a-c-e-g)
ACEI: Association for Childhood Education International
ACEJ: American Council on Education for Journalism
ACEL: Air Crew Equipment Laboratory
ACELF: *Association Canadienne des Educateurs de Langue Française* (Canadian Association of French Language Teachers)
ACEM: Aviation Chief Electrician's Mate
ACEN: Assembly of Captive European Nations
ACEORP: Automotive and Construction Equipment Overhaul and Repair Plant
ACEP: American Council for Emigrés in the Professions
ACEPD: Automotive and Construction Equipment Parts Depot
ACER: Australian Council for Educational Research
ACERP: Advanced Communications-Electronics Requirements Plan
aces: automatic control evaluation simulator
ACES: Alternative Consumer Energy Society; Americans for the Competitive Enterprise System; Association for Counselor Education and Supervision
ACESA: Australian Commonwealth Engineering Standards Association
ace-s/c: acceptance checkout equipment—spacecraft
acet: acetome
ACET: Advisory Committee on Electronics and Telecommunications
ACE Test: American Council on Education Test
acetl: acetylene
acetyl-co A: acetyl-coenzyme A
ACEUR: Allied Command, Europe
ACEWR: American Committee for European Worker's Relief
acf: accessory clinical findings
ACF: Alternate Communications Facility; American Car & Foundry; American Checker Federation; American Chess Foundation; American Choral Foundation; American Culinary Federation; Association of Consulting Foresters
ACF: *Académie Canadienne Française* (French-Canadian Academy); *Automobile-Club de France* (Automobile Club of France)
ACFA: American Cat Fanciers Association; Association of Commercial Finance Attorneys
ACFAS: *Association Canadienne-Française pour l'Avancement des Sciences* (French—Canadian Association for the Advancement of Science)
ACFC: Aviation Chief Fire Controlman
ACFEA: Air Carrier Flight Engineers Association
ACFEL: Arctic Construction and Frost Effects Laboratory (Greenland)
ACFL: Atlantic Coast Football League
ACFM: Association of Canadian Fire Marshals
ACFN: American Committee for Flags of Necessity
ACFO: American College of Foot Orthopedics

ACFR: Advisory Committee of the Federal Register; Advisory Council on Federal Reports; American College of Foot Roentgenologists
ACFS: American College of Foot Surgeons
ACFSA: American Correctional Food Service Association
acft: aircraft
ac ft: acre feet; acre foot
ACFT: Aircraft Flying Training
acftc: aircraft carrier
acg: automatic caution guard; automatic control gear
ACG: Airborne Coordinating Group; Air Cargo Express (symbol); Airline Carriers of Goods; American College of Gastroenterology; American Council on Germany; Association for Corporate Growth
ac-g: accelerator globulin
acg (ACG): apex cardiogram
ACG: *An Comunn Gaidhealach* (The Gaelic Society)—also called the Highland Society
ACGA: American Cranberry Growers' Association
ACGB: Arts Council of Great Britain
ACGBI: Automobile Club of Great Britain and Ireland
ACGD: Association for Corporate Growth and Diversification
ACGF: American Child Guidance Foundation
ACGFC: Associate of the City and Guilds Finsbury College
ACGI: Associate of the City and Guilds Institute
ACGIH: American Conference of Governmental Industrial Hygienists
ACGM: Aircraft Carriers General Memorandum
ACGP: Army Career Group
ACGPOMS: American College of General Practitioners in Osteopathic Medicine and Surgery
ACGS: Aerial Cartographic and Geodetic Squadron; American Council on German Studies
ACGSq: Aerial Cartographic and Geodetic Squadron (USAF)
ach: acetylcholine (Ach); arm, chest, height
ach (Ach) (ACH): acetylcholine; adrenal cortical hormone
ACHA: American Catholic Historical Association; American College Health Association; American College of Hospital Administrators
AC & HBR: Algoma Central and Hudson Bay Railway
ache.: acetylcholinesterase
ACHE: Alabama Commission on Higher Education
achiev: achievement
ach index: arm (girth), chest (depth), hip (width) index (of nutrition)
ACHNHP: Appomattox Court House National Historical Park
ACHR: American Council of Human Rights
achrom: achromatism
A Ch S: Associate of the Society of Chiropodists
ACHS: Association of College Honor Societies
aci: airborne-controlled interception; automatic car identification
aci (ACI): anticlonus index
aci: *assure contre l'incendie* (French—insured against fire)
ACI: Air Cargo Incorporated; Air Combat Information; Air Combat Intelligence; Alliance Coopérative Internationale (International Cooperative Alliance); Alloy Casting Institute; American Carpet Institute; American Concrete Institute; American Cryogenics Incorporated
ACIA: Associated Cooperage Industries of America
ACIAA: Australian Commercial and Industrial Artists' Association
ACIAS: American Council of Industrial Arts Supervisors
ACIASAO: American Council of Industrial Arts State Association Officers
ACIATE: American Council of Industrial Arts Teacher Education
ACIB: Associate of the Corporation of Insurance Brokers
acic: acicular
ACIC: Aeronautical Chart and Information Center; Allied Captured Intelligence Center; Auxiliary Combat Information Center
acid: acidosis; acidulated drop; hallucinogenic drug such as LSD-25
acid phos: acid phosphatase
acid p'tase: acid phosphatase
ACIGS: Assistant Chief of the Imperial General Staff
ACII: Associate of the Chartered Insurance Institute
ACIID: A Critical Insight Into Israel's Dilemmas
ACIL: American Council of Independent Laboratories
acim: axis-crossing interval meter
ACIM: American Committee on Italian Migration
ACIO: Air Combat Intelligence Office(r)
ACIPCO: American Cast Iron Pipe Company
ACIR: Advisory Committee on Intergovernmental Relations; Automotive Crash Injury Research
AC/IREF: American Chapter—International Real Estate Federation
ACIS: American Committee for Irish Studies
A.C.I.S.: Associate of the Chartered Institute of Secretaries
acit: air-cannon impact tester
ACIV: Associate of the Commonwealth Institute of Valuers
ACIWLP: American Committee for International Wild Life Protection
ACJ: American Council for Judaism
ACJP: Airways Corporations Joint Pensions
ack: acknowledge; acknowledgment
ACK: accidentally killed; Armstrong Cork (stock exchange symbol)
ack-ack: antiaircraft
Ack-Ack: Aluminum Company of America (stock exchange nickname)
ackt: acknowledgment
acl: air-cushion landing; allowable cabin load
aCl: aspiryl chloride
ACL: American Classical League; Association of Cinema Laboratories; Atlantic Coast Line (railroad); Aviation Circular Letter
ACL: *Automobile Club de Luxembourg* (Automobile Club of the Grand Duchy of Luxembourg)
ACLA: American Comparative Literature Association; American Cotton Linter Association; Anti-Communist League of America
ACLAM: American College of Laboratory Animal Medicine
AClant: Allied Command, Atlantic

ACLC: Air Cadet League of Canada
acld: aircooled
ACLD: Association for Children with Learning Disabilities
aclg: air-cushion landing gear
ACLM: American College of Legal Medicine
ACLP: Association of Contact Lens Practitioners
acls: automatic carrier landing system
ACLS: American Council of Learned Societies; Automatic Carrier Landing System
ACLU: American Civil Liberties Union; American College of Life Underwriters
aclv: accrued leave
acm: anatomy-covering material; anatomy-covering memo; asbestos-covered metal
ACM: Air Chief Marshal; Air Commerce Manual; Air Court-Martial; American Campaign Medal; Association for Computing Machinery; auxiliary mine layer (3-letter symbol); Aviation Chief Metalsmith
a-c-m: albumin-calcium-magnesium
ACM: Automobile Club de Monaco (French—Automobile Club of Monaco)
ACMA: Acidproof Cement Manufacturers Association; Air Carrier Mechanics Association; Alumina Ceramic Manufacturers Association; American Certified Morticians Associations; American Circus Memorial Association; American Comedy Museum Association; American Cutlery Manufacturers Association
acme.: attitude control and maneuvering electronics
ACME: Advisory Council on Medical Education; Association of Consulting Management Engineers
ACMET: Advisory Council on Middle East Trade
ACMF: Air Corps Medical Forces; Allied Central Mediterranean Forces; American Corn Millers' Federation; Australian Commonwealth Military Forces
ACMI: American Cotton Manufacturers Institute; American Cystoscope Makers, Incorporated
ACML: Association of Canadian Map Libraries
ACMM: Aviation Chief Machinist's Mate
A.C.M.M.: Associate of the Conservatorium of Music—Melbourne
acmp: accompany
ACMP: Amateur Chamber Music Players; Assistant Commissioner of the Metropolitan Police
ACMRR: Advisory Committee on Marine Resources Research (FAO)
acmru: audio commercial-message repeating unit
ACMS: Advanced Configuration Management System; Army Command Management System
ACMT: American College of Medical Technologists
ACMWA: Amon Carter Museum of Western Art (Fort Worth)
acn: acute conditioned necrosis (ACN); all concerned notified; assignment control number (ACN); automatic celestial navigation (ACN)
ACN: American Chain & Cable (stock exchange symbol); American College of Neuropsychiatrists; American Council on NATO; Authorized Code Number
A.C.N.: Ante Christum Natum (Latin—before the birth of Christ)
ACNA: Advisory Council on Naval Affairs; Arctic Institute of North America
ACNB: Australian Commonwealth Naval Board
ACNE: Alaskans Concerned for Neglected Environments
ACNHA: American College of Nursing Home Administrators
ACNIL: Azienda Comunale Navigazione Interna (Italian—City and Lagoon Rapid Transit Shipping Company)
ACNM: American College of Nurse Midwifery
ACNO: Assistant Chief of Naval Operations
ACNOT: Assistant Chief of Naval Operations—Transportation
ACNS: American Council for Nationalities Service; Associated Correspondents News Service
ACNY: Advertising Club of New York
ACNYC: Art Commission of New York City
aco: anodal closing odor
a co: a cargo (Spanish—against)
ACO: Administrative Contracting Officer; Air Cargo (Leopoldville—Republic of the Congo); American Academy of Optometry
ACOFO: American College of Foot Orthopedists
acog: (ACOG): aircraft on ground
ACOG: American College of Obstetricians and Gynecologists
ACOHA: American College of Osteopathic Hospital Administrators
ACOI: American College of Osteopathic Internists
ACOM: Aviation Chief Ordnanceman
A.Comm.: Associate in Commerce
A.Comm.A.: Associate of the Society of Commercial Accountants
ACOOG: American College of Osteopathic Obstetricians and Gynecologists
ACOP: American College of Osteopathic Pediatricians; Association of Chief Officers of Police (England and Wales)
ACORD: Advisory Council on Research and Development
ACORDE: A Consortium on Restorative Dentistry Education
ACORN: Associative Content Retrieval Network
ACOS: American College of Osteopathic Surgeons
acous: acoustics
acp: acetyl-carrier protein (ACP); acid phosphatase; anodal closing picture; aspirin, caffeine, phenacetin; auxiliary control panel
ACP: Automóvel Clube de Portugal (Automobile Club of Portugal)
a & cp: anchors and chains proved
ACP: Agricultural Conservation Program; Air Control Point; Airline Carriers of Passengers; Allied Communications Publications; American College of Pharmacists; American College of Physicians; Anti-Comintern Pact; Associated Collegiate Press; Association of Clinical Pathologists; Association of Correctional Psychologists
ACPA: Affiliated Chiropodists-Podiatrists of America; American Capon Producers As-

sociation; American Cleft Palate Association; American College Personnel Association; American Concrete Paving Association; American Concrete Pipe Association

A-CPA: Asbestos-Cement Products Association

ACPAE: Association of Certified Public Accounts Examiners

a/c pay: accounts payable

ACPC: American College of Probate Counsel; American Council of Parent Cooperatives

ACPD: Anti-trust and Consumer Protection Division; Army Control Program Directive

ACPE: American Council on Pharmaceutical Education

ACPF: Amphibious Corps, Pacific Fleet

ACPFB: American Committee for Protection of Foreign Born

ACPIC: American Council for Private International Communications

acpm: attitude-control propulsion motor(s)

ACPM: American Congress for Preventive Medicine

ACPMR: American Congress of Physical Medicine and Rehabilitation

acpp (ACPP): adrenocorticopolypeptide

ACPRA: American College Public Relations Association

ACPS: American Coalition of Patriotic Societies

ACPSAHMWA: American Commission for the Protection and Salvage of Artistic and Historical Monuments in War Areas

acpt: accept

acpu: auxiliary computer power unit

acq: acquire; acquittal

ACQT: Aviation Cadet Qualifying Test

acquis: acquisition(s)

acr: acrylic; advanced capabilities radar; aerial combat reconnaissance; airfield-controlled radar; anti-constipation regimen

ACR: Advisory Commission on the Realm; Aircraft Control Room; Allied Commission on Reparations; American Academy in Rome; American College of Radiology

AC & R: American Cable and Radio (Corp)

ACRA: American Collegiate Retailing Association

ACRB: Aero-Club Royal de Belgique (Royal Belgian Aero Club); Army Council of Review Boards

ACRC: Air Compressor Research Council

acrd: accrued

ACRE: Automatic Checkout and Readiness Equipment

a/c rec: accounts receivable

acre ft: acre foot

ACRES: Airborne Communication Relay Station

acrg: acreage

ACRI: Air Conditioning and Refrigeration Institute; American Cocoa Research Institute

ACRL: Association of College and Research Libraries

ACRM: Aviation Chief Radioman

acro: acrobat(ic); acrophobe; acrophobia

acron: acronym

ACRONYMS: Acceptable Contractions of Randomly-Organized Names Yielding Meritorious Spontaniety

Acropolis of America: New York City's Morningside Heights—site of Columbia University

across: acrostic

ACRR: American Council on Race Relations

ACRS: Advisory Committee on Reactor Safeguards

ACRT: Aviation Chief Radio Technician

ACRW: American Council of Railroad Women

acs: alternating current synchronous; anodal closing sound; autograph card signed

acs (ACS): antireticular cytotoxic serum

Ac of S: Academy of Sciences (USSR)

Ac of S: Assistant Chief of Staff

ACS: Airline Charter Service; Alaskan Communications System; American Camellia Society; American Cancer Society; American Carnation Society; American Ceramic Society; American Chemical Society; American College of Surgeons; American Colonization Society; American Crystal Sugar (company); Armament Control System; Assistant Chief of Staff; Association of Clinical Scientists

ACS: Automobile Club de Suisse (French—Swiss Automobile Club)

A.C.S.: Associate in Commercial Science

AC/S: Assistant Chief of Staff

ACSA: Allied Communications Security Agency (NATO); American Cotton Shippers Association; Association of Collegiate Schools of Architecture

ACSC: Air Carrier Service Corporation; Air Command and Staff College; American Council on Schools and Colleges; Association of Casualty and Surety Companies; Australian Coastal Shipping Commission

ACSCP: Association of California State College Professors

ACSDO: Air Carrier Safety District Office(r)

ACSE: Association of Consulting Structural Engineers

ACSEA: Air Command—Southeast Asia; Allied Command South-East Asia

ACSF: Attack Carrier Striking Force

ACSI: Assistant Chief of Staff for Intelligence

ACSIL: Admiralty Centre for Scientific Information and Liaison (United Kingdom)

ACSI-MATIC: Assistant Chief of Staff—Intelligence (automatic processing system for large scale intelligence information)

ACSL: Assistant Cub Scout Leader

ACSM: American Congress of Surveying and Mapping

ACSMA: American Cloak and Suit Manufacturers Association

ACSN: Association of Collegiate Schools of Nursing

ACSOC: Acoustical Society of America

ACSP: Advisory Council on Scientific Policy (United Kingdom)

ACSPA: Australian Council of Salaried and Professional Associations

A/cs Pay: Accounts Payable

acsr: aluminum cable, steel reinforced

A/cs Rec: Accounts Receivable

acss: automated color-separation system (ACSS)

ACSS: Air Command and Staff School; American Cheviot Sheep Society; Army Chief of Support Services

ACSSAVO: Association of Chief State School Audio-Visual Officers
ACSSN: Association of Colleges and Secondary Schools for Negroes
ACSSRB: Administrative Center of Social Security for Rhine Boatmen
acst: acoustic; acoustical; acoustics
ACST: Army Clerical Speed Test
acst plas: acoustical plaster
acst t: acoustical tile
act.: acting; action; activated coagulation time; active; actor; actress; actuate; actuating; anticoagulant therapy; atropine coma therapy
act. (ACT): advanced coronary treatment
ACT: Action for Childrens Television; Air Control Team; American College Testing (program); American Conservatory Theatre; Associated Community Theaters; Association of Classroom Teachers; Australian Capital Territory; Aviation Classification Test
a cta: *a cuenta* (Spanish—on account)
ACTA: Aircoach Transport Association; American Community Theatre Association
ACTB: Aircrew Classification Test Battery
ACTC: Air Commerce Type Certificate
A.C.T.C.: Art Class Teacher's Certificate
act. ct: actual count
acte: anodal closure tetanus
ACTFL: American Council on the Teaching of Foreign Languages
actg: acting
ACTG: Advance Carrier Training Group
acth (ACTH): adrenocorticotrophic hormone
act/ic: active—in commission
actinolite: (*see* asbestos)
ACTION: American Council To Improve Our Neighborhoods
ACTION: (not an acronym but the current fusion of U.S. government youth agencies such as the Peace Corps and VISTA)
act/is: active—in service
ACTIV: Army Concept Team in Vietnam
ACTL: American College of Trial Lawyers
ACTM: Association of Cotton Textile Merchants of New York
ACTMC: Army Clothing, Textile and Material Center
actn (ACTN): adrenocorticotrophin
actnt: accountant
acto: automatic computing transfer oscillator
ACTO: Advisory Council on the Treatment of Offenders
act/oc: active—out of commission
actol: air-cushion takeoff and landing
Acton Bell: pseudonym of Anne Brontë
ACTOR: Askania cine-theodolite optical-tracking range
act/os: active—out of service
actp (ACTP): adrenocorticotrophic polypeptide
ACTR: Air Corps Technical Report
Acts: The Acts of the Apostles
ACTS: Acoustic Control and Telemetry System; Air Corps Tactical School; Airline Computer Tracing System (for identifying and returning lost luggage or other objects); Automatic Computer Telex System
ACTT: Association of Cinematograph and Television Technicians; America's Christmas Train and Trucks
ACTU: Association of Catholic Trade Unionists; Australian Council of Trade Unions
actv: activate
act. val: actual value
act. wt: actual weight
acu: address control unit
ACU: American Church Union; American Congregational Union; American Conservation Union; American Cycling Union; Association of College Unions; Association of Commonwealth Universities; Autocycle Union
ACUA: Association of Cambridge University Assistants
ACUCM: Association of College and University Concert Managers
ACUE: American Committee of United Europe
ACUHO: Association of College and University Housing Officers
ACUNY: Associated Colleges of Upper New York
ACUP: Association of College and University Printers
ACUS: Administrative Conference of the United States; Atlantic Council of the United States
acv: actual cash value; air-cushion vehicle
ACV: air-cushion vehicle; auxiliary aircraft carrier or tender (3-letter symbol)
ACVAFS: American Council of Voluntary Agencies for Foreign Service
ACVC: American Council of Venture Clubs
acvd: acute cardiovascular disease
ACVP: American College of Veterinary Pathologists
acw: aircraft control and warning; alternating continuous waves; automatic car wash
ACW: Air Control and Warning (system); Aircraftwoman; American Chain of Warehouses
AC & W: Air Communications and Weather (naval group)
ACWA: Amalgamated Clothing Workers of America
A.C.W.A.: Associate of the Institute of Cost and Work Accountants
ACWAI: Automatic Car Wash Association International
ACWC: Advisory Committee on Weather Control
ACWF: Army Central Welfare Fund
ACWL: Army Chemical Warfare Laboratory
ACWO: Aircraft Control and Warning Officer
ACWRON: Aircraft Control and Warning Squadron
ACWRRE: American Cargo War Risk Reinsurance Exchange
ACWS: Aircraft Control and Warning System
AC & WS: Aircraft Control and Warning Station(s)
ACWW: Associated Country Women of the World
acy: average crop yield
ACY: Akron, Canton & Youngstown (railroad); American Cyanamid Company (stock exchange symbol); Atlantic City, New Jersey (airport)
AC & Y: Akron, Canton & Youngstown (railroad)
acyl-co A: coenzyme A ester (general symbol for an organic compound)
acyro: acyrologia; acyrologic(al); acyrology

ad: active duty; a drink; a drug (addict); advertisement; advertising; aerodynamic decelerator; after drain; air dried; airdrome; area drain; average deviation

a/d: altitude/depth; analog-to-digital

'ad: had

a & d: ascending and descending

a & d (A & D): accounting and disbursing

a d: *a droit* (French—to the right)

a.d.: *auris dexter* (Latin—right ear)

ad 2 vic.: *ad duas vices* (Latin—for two doses; for two times)

a D: *ausser Dienst* (German—retired)

Ad: Ada; Adah; Adalbert; Adam; Adams; Adán; Addington; Addis; Addison; Adela; Adelaide; Adelard; Adelardo; Adelbert; Adele; Adelina; Adeline; Adelle; Adelsteen; Adeodato; Adlai; Adna; Adolf; Adolfine; Adolfo; Adolph; Adolphe; Adolpho; Adolphus; Adriaan; Adriaen; Adrian; Adriano; Adrianus; Adrien; Adrienne; Aedh

AD: Aden Airways; Air Defense; Air Depot; Air Division; Airdrome; Airframe Design (division); Airworthiness Directive; Appellate Division; Assembly District; Astia Document; Atlantic & Danville (railroad); *Aviatsionnaya Diviziya* (Russian—Aviation Division); destroyer tender (naval symbol)

A-D: Albrecht Dürer; Antonin Dvořák

A/D: Air Depot

A & D: Atlantic & Danville (railroad)

AD: *Acción Democratica* (Spanish—Democratic Action Party)—Venezuela's democratic movement begun by Romulo Betancourt

A.D.: *Anno Domini* (Latin—in the Year of our Lord)

ada: action data automation; actuarial data assembly; average daily attendance; average deviation adjustment

ada (ADA): adenosine deaminase

ada: *adalah* (Arabic—equity; justice)

Ada: Adelaida; Adelaide

Ad of A: Archduchy of Austria; Archduke of Austria

ADA: Air Defense Area; American Dairy Association; American Dehydrators Association; American Dental Association; American Dermatological Association; American Diabetes Association; American Dietetic Association; Americans for Democratic Action; Atomic Development Authority; Automobile Dealers Association

ADA: American Diabetes Association diet number

ADAA: American Dental Assistants Association; Art Dealers Association of America

adac: automatic direct analog computer

ADAC: *Allgemeiner Deutscher Automobilclub* (The German Automobile Club)

adacx: automatic data acquisition and computer complex

adad: air defense artillery director

Adag: *adagio* (Italian—slowly and expressively)

adaline: adaptive linear neuron

adam: adamantine; advanced data management; air deflection and modulation; automatic distance and angle measurement

A'dam: Amsterdam

ADAM: Agriculture Department Automated Manpower

adamite: basic zinc arsenate

adaml: advise by airmail

adamm (ADAMM): area defense anti-missile missile

adandac: administrative and accounting purposes

ADAOD: Air Defense Artillery Operations Detachment

ADAOO: Air Defense Artillery Operations Office(r)

adap: adapted

ADAP: Airport Development Aid Program (FAA)

ADAPS: Automatic Display and Plotting System

ADAPSO: Association of Data Processing Service Organizations

ADARF: Alcoholism and Drug Addiction Research Foundation (Ontario, Canada)

adapt.: adaption of automatically-programmed tools

adapticom: adaptive communication

ADAPTS: Air-Deliverable Anti-Pollution Transfer System (USCG)

adar: advanced development array radar; analog-to-digital-to-analog recording

ADAR: Air Defense Area

ADAS: Action Data Automation System; Agricultural Development Advisory Service

ADASC: Auto Dismantlers Association of Southern California (often called ADA)

ada(si): (Turkish—island)

ad ast.: *ad astra* (Latin—to the stars)

adat: automatic data accumulation and transfer

adaval: advise availability

ADAWS: Action Data Automation and Weapons System

A-day: assault day

ADB: Apollo Data Bank (NASA); Asian Development Bank; Atlantic Development Board (Canada)

ADB: *Australian Dictionary of Biography*

A.D.B.: Bachelor of Domestic Arts

ADBC: American Defenders of Bataan and Corregidor

ADBM: Association of Dry Battery Manufacturers

ADBPA: *Association pour le Développement des Bibliothèques Publiques en Afrique* (French—Association for the Development of Public Libraries in Africa)

adc: active-duty commitment; adopted child; advance delivery of correspondence; albumin, dextrose, catalase; anodal duration contraction; axiodistocervical

ADC: Aerophysics Development Corporation; Aerospace Defense Command; Agricultural Development Council; Aide-de-Camp; Aid to Dependent Children; Air Defense Command; Air Development Center; Air Diffusion Council; Alaska Defense Command; American Distilling Company; American Dock Company; Aviation Development Council

adcad: airways data collection and distribution

ad cap.: *ad captandum* (Latin—for pleasing; made attractive)

ADCC: Air Defense Control Center

ADCI: American Die Casting Institute

ADCO: American Dredging Company

ADCOC: Area Damage Control Center

Development of Research)
ADRA: Animal Diseases Research Association
adrac: automatic digital recording and control
ADRB: Army Disability Review Board; Army Discharge Review Board
ADRDE: Air Defense Research and Development Establishment
adren: adrenal; adrenalin
adrenals: adrenal glands
ADRI: Angkatan Darat Republik Indonesia (Indonesian Army)
Adrian: Hadrian
ADRIS: Automatic Dead Reckoning Instrument Systems
adrm: airdrome
ADROBN: Airdrome Battalion
ADRS: Analog-to-Digital Data Recording System
adrt: analog data recording transcriber
adr tel: *adresse telegraphique* (French—telegraphic address)
ads: advertisements; antibody deficiency syndrome; antidiuretic substance; area, date, subject; autograph document signed; automatic door seal
ADS: *Academie des Sciences* (French Academy of Science); Aerial Delivery System; Air Defense Sector; American Daffodil Society; American Dahlia Society; American Denture Society; American Dialect Society; American Dental Service; Association of Diesel Specialists
ADSA: American Dairy Science Association; American Dental Society of Anesthesiology; Atomic Defense Support Agency
ad. saec.: *ad saeculum* (Latin—to the century)
ADSAS: Air-Derived Separation Assurance System
adsc: average daily service charge (in hospitals)
ADSC: Advanced Section Communication Zone; Automatic Data Service Center
ADSCAT: Association of Distributors to the Self-service and Coin-operated Laundries and Allied Trades
adscom: advanced shipboard communications
ad sec.: *ad sectam* (Latin—at suit of (legal))
AdSec: Advanced Section
adshpdat: advise shipping data
ADSID: Air Defense Systems Integration Division
ADSL: Assembly Department Shortage List
ADSM: American Defense Service Medal
ADSMO: Air Defense Systems Management Office
ADSN: Accounting and Disbursing Station Number
ADSOC: Administrative Support Operations Center
adss: analysis of digitized seismic signals
ADSS: Aircraft Damage Sensing System; Australian Defense Scientific Service
ADST: Atlantic Daylight Saving Time
adstadis: advise status and/or disposition
adst.feb.: *adstante febre* (Latin—when fever is present)
adstkoh: advise stock on hand
ADSUP: Automatic Data Systems Uniform Practice(s)
adt: any damn thing (abbreviation for a placebo); automatic damage template; average daily dose
adT: *an demselben Tage* (German—the same day)
ADT: American District Telegraph; Applied Drilling Technology; Atlantic Daylight Time
ADTA: American Dental Trade Association
ADTC: Armament Development Test Center (USAF)
adtech: advanced decoy technology
ADTIC: Arctic, Desert, Tropic Information Center
ADTS: Automatic Data and Telecommunications Service
ADTSEA: American Driver Traffic Safety Education Association
adtu: automatic digital test unit; auxiliary data translator unit
ad 2 vic.: *ad duas vices* (Latin—for two doses)
adu: acceleration-deceleration unit; accumulation-distributionunit
ADU: Aircraft Delivery Unit
adult.: adulterant; adulterate; adulteration
ad us.: *ad usum* (Latin—according to custom)
ad us. ext.: *ad usum externum* (Latin—for external use)
adv: advance; adverb
adv.: *adversum* (Latin—adversely; against)
a/dv: arterio/deep venous (injection)
Adv.: Adventist; Adviser
ad val.: *ad valorem* (Latin—according to value)
Advance Agent of Emancipation: Lucretia Mott
advb: adverb; adverbial
Adv Bse: Advanced Base
adv chgs: advance charges
advdisc: advance discontinuance of allotment
advec: advection
adven: adventure; adventurer
adversat: adversative
advert: advertising
advertique: advertising antique (old coffee can, old tobacco tin, old decanter bottle, old trade-marked tray, etc.)
advert(s): advertisement(s)
adv frt: advance freight
Adv Intel Cen: Advanced Intelligence Center
ad virus: adenovirus
ADVISE: Area Denial Visual Identification Security Equipment
advl: adverbial
advon: advanced echelon; advanced operations unit
adv pmt: advance payment
adv poss: adverse possession
ADVS: Assistant Director of Veterinary Services
advst: advance stoppage
advt: advertise; advertisement; advertiser; advertising
adw: assault (with) deadly weapon
ADW: Air Defense Warning
ADWA: Atlantic Deeper Waterways Association
ADWC: Air Defense Weapons Center (USAF)
ADWKP: Air Defense Warning Key Point
adx: automatic data exchange
ADX: Adams Express Company (stock exchange symbol)
Adyg: Adygey
Adzh: Adzhar
ae: above the elbow; account executive; aircraft equipment; air escape; almost everywhere
ae: *aetatis* (Latin—aged; at the age of)
a & e: aerospace and electronic; armaments and electronics
AE: Agricultural Engineering (Department of Agriculture research division); Airborne Equipment (naval division); Air Explorer; ammunition ship (naval symbol); Auto-

matic Electric

A-E: Adam and Eve; Astro-Eugenics

AE: *Aeon* (pen name of George William Russell); *Aktiebolaget Atomenergi* (Swedish—Atomic Energy Corporation)

AE: *Atomnaya Energiya* (Russian—Atomic Energy)

AE: *American Ephemeris*

A.E.: Aeronautical Engineer; Agricultural Engineer; Architectural Engineer; Associate in Education; Associate in Engineering

A & E: Agricultural and Engineering; Architectural and Engineering

A & E: *Adolphus and Ellis*

AEA: Actors' Equity Association; Adult Education Association; American Economic Association; American Education Association; American Enterprise Association; American Export Airlines; Artists Equity Association; Atomic Energy Authority; Automotive Electric Association

AEAA: *Asociación de Escritores y Artistas Americanos* (Spanish—Association of American Writers and Artists)

AEAF: Allied Expeditionary Air Force

AEAO: Airborne Emergency Actions Officer

AEAs: American Entertainers Abroad

aea sol: alcohol-ether-acetone solution

AEAUSA: Adult Education Association of the United States of America

AEB: Area Electricity Board

aec: altitude engine control

AEC: Aeronautical Research Council; Agricultural Economics (division of Department of Agriculture); Aircraft Radio Corporation; Airworthiness Examination Committee; Alaska Engineering Commission (Alaska Railroad); Aluminum Extruders Council; American Engineering Council; Army Education Center; Army Educational Center; Army Educational Corps; Army Electronics Command (formerly Signal Corps); Atlantic & East Carolina (railroad); Atlas Educational Center; Atomic Energy Commission

A & EC: Atlantic & East Carolina (railroad)

AEC-A: Atomic Energy Commission—Albuquerque Operations Office

AEC-AI: Atomic Energy Commission—Argonne, Illinois

AEC-ANM: Atomic Energy Commission—Albuquerque, New Mexico

AEC-ASC: Atomic Energy Commission—Aiken, South Carolina

AECB: Atomic Energy Control Board (Canada)

AEC-BC: Atomic Energy Commission—Berkeley, California

AECC: Aeromedical Evacuation Control Center

AEC-CC: Atomic Energy Commission—Canoga Park, California

AECE: *Asociación Española de Cooperación Europea* (Spanish—Association for European Cooperation)

AEC-FOA: Atomic Energy Commission—Fernal Office Area, Cincinnati, Ohio

AEC-HW: Atomic Energy Commission—Hanford, Washington

AECI: African Explosives and Chemical Industries

AEC-II: Atomic Energy Commission—Idaho Falls, Idaho

AECL: Atomic Energy of Canada, Limited

AEC-LN: Atomic Energy Commission—Las Vegas, Nevada

AEC-LOC: Atomic Energy Commission—Lockland Aircraft Reactors Operations, Cincinnati, Ohio

AECM: Albert Einstein College of Medicine

AECP: Airman Education and Commissioning Program

AEC-NY: Atomic Energy Commission—New York Operations Office

AECOM: Army Electronic Command

AEC-OR: Atomic Energy Commission—Oak Ridge Operations Office

AEC-OT: Atomic Energy Commission—Oak Ridge, Tennessee

aecp: altitude engine control panel

AECP: Airman Education and Commissioning Program

AEC-PP: Atomic Energy Commission—Pittsburgh, Pennsylvania

AEC-PR: Atomic Energy Commission—Pittsburgh Naval Reactors Operations Office

AEC-RW: Atomic Energy Commission—Richland, Washington

AECT: Association for Educational Communications and Technology

AEC-UN: Atomic Energy Commission—Upton, L.I., N.Y.

aed (AED): automatic engineering design

AED: Associated Equipment Distributors; Association of Electronic Distributors

A.Ed.: Associate in Education

A.E.D.: *artium elegantium doctor* (Latin—Doctor of Fine Arts)

AEDB: Apollo Engineering Development Board

AEDC: Arnold Engineering Development Center

AEDD: Air Engineering Development Division

AEDE: *Association Européenne des Enseignants* (French—European Teachers' Association)

AEDO: Aircraft Engineering District Office

AED-RCA: Astro-Electronics Division-RCA

AEDS: Association of Educational Data Systems; Atomic Energy Detection System

AEDU: Admiralty Experimental Diving Unit

aee: absolute essential equipment; absolutely essential equipment

Ae.E.: Aeronautical Engineer

AEE: Atomic Energy Establishment

AE.E.: Associate in Engineering

AEEB: *Association Europeenne de l'Equipement de Bureau* (French—European Office Equipment Association)

AEEC: Airlines Electronic Engineering Committee

AEEL: Aeronautical Electronic and Electrical Laboratory

AEEN: Agence Européenne pour l'Energie Nucléaire (European Agency for Atomic Energy)

AEET: Atomic Energy Establishment, Trombay (India)

AEEW: Atomic Energy Establishment—Winfrith

AEF: Advertising Educational Foundation; Aerospace Education Foundation; Aircraft

Engineering Foundation; Allied Expeditionary Force; American Economic Foundation; American European Foundation; American European Foundation; American Expeditionary Force; Americans for Economic Freedom; Artists Equity Fund; Aviation Engineer(ing) Force

A-effect: alienation effect

AEFM: *Association Européenne des Festivals de Musique* (French—European Association of Music Festivals)

AEFORT: American-European Friends of ORT (Organization for Rehabilitation through Training)

AEFR: Aurora, Elgin & Fox River (railroad)

aeg: active element group(ing); air encephalogram(s)

aeg.: *aeger* (Latin—sick)

Aeg: Aegean

AEG: Association of Engineering Geologists

AEG: *Allgemeine Elektrizitäts Gesellschaft* (German—General Electric Company)

Aegian Ethicist: Aristotle

AEGIMRDA: Army Engineer Geodesy, Intelligence and Mapping Research and Development Agency

AEGIS: Aid for the Elderly in Government Institutions

AEGp: Aeromedical Evacuation Group (USAF)

AEH: A(lfred) E(dward) Housman

AEHA: Army Environmental Health Agency

AEHL: Army Environmental Health Laboratory

AEI: Air Express International; American Express Institute; American Express International; Annual Efficiency Index; Associated Electrical Industries

AEI: *Association des Écoles Internationales* (French—Association of International Schools)

AEIB: Association for Education in International Business

AEIC: Association of Edison Illuminating Companies

AEIDC: American Express International Development Company

AEIL: American Export Isbrandtsen Lines

A.E.I.O.U.: *Austria Erit In Orbe Ultima* (Latin—Austria will be the world's last survivor)—ancient acrostic of House of Hapsburg

AEIPPR: American Enterprise Institute for Public Policy Research

AEJ: Association for Education in Journalism

AEJI: Association of European Jute Industries

aek: all-electric kitchen

ael: audit error list

AEL: Aeronautical Engine Laboratory; Aircraft Engine Laboratory; American Electronic Laboratories; American Emigrants League; Americanism Education League; Animal Education League; Automation Engineering Laboratory

AELE: Americans for Effective Law Enforcement

AELE: *Association Européenne de Libre-Echange* (French—European Free Trade Association)

AELTC: All England Lawn Tennis Club

AEM: Advance Engineering Memorandum; Aircraft and Engine Mechanic; American Meter Company (stock exchange symbol); Association of Electronic Manufacturers; Aviation Electrician's Mate

AE & MP: Ambassador Extraordinary and Minister Plenipotentiary

AEMS: American Engineering Model Society

AEMSA: Army Electronics Material Support Agency

aen: advance evaluation note

aen.: *aeneus* (Latin—made of bronze or copper)

Aen.: *Aeneid* (Virgil's epic poem)

A.En.: Associate in English

AENA: All-England Netball Association

A.Eng.: Associate in Engineering

AEO: Air Engineer(ing) Office(r); Appeal Examining Office(r)

AEOB: Advanced Engine Overhaul Base

Aeol: Aeolian; Aeolic

Aeolians: Aeolian Islands off Sicily's north coast where they are called Isole Eolie and include Lipari, Stromboli, and Vulcano

AEOO: Aeromedical Evacuation Operations Officer

aeop: amend existing orders pertaining to

AEOS: Ancient Egyptian Order of Sciots

aep: accrued expenditure paid; average evoked potential

AEP: Addo Elephant Park (South Africa); Adult Education Program; American Electric Power

AEP: *Agencé Européenne de Productivité* (French—European Production Agency)

AE & P: Ambassador Extraordinary and Plenipotentiary

AEPC: Appalachian Electric Power Company

AEPCO: American Elsevier Publishing Company

AEPEM: Association of Electronic Parts and Equipment Manufacturers

AEPG: Army Electronic Proving Ground

AEPI: American Educational Publishers Institute

AEPS: American Electroplaters Society

aeq: age equivalent

aeq.: *aequales* (Latin—equal(s)]

aer: auditory-evoked response

AER: Abbreviated Effectiveness Report; Aeronautical Engineering Report; Airman Effectiveness Report; Army Emergency Relief; Association for Education by Radio; Association Européenne pour l'Etude du Probleme des Réfugies (European Association for the Study of the Refugee Problem)

aera: aeration

AERA: American Educational Research Association; American Engine Rebuilders Association

AERB: Army Education Requirements Board

AERC: Association of Executive Recruiting Consultants

aercab: advanced escape/rescue capability; advanced aircrew escape/rescue capability

AERDL: Army Electronics Research and Development Laboratory

AERE: Atomic Energy Research Establishment

Aer.E.: Aeronautical Engineer

AERI: Automotive Exhaust Research Institute

AERNO: Aeronautical Equipment Reference Number

aero: aerographer; aeronautical; aeronautics

AERO: Association of Electronic Reserve Officers

aerobatics: aeronautical acrobatics
aerobee: aerojet/bumblebee (naval missile)
aerob(s): aerobic exercise(s)
aerodyn: aerodynamics
Aero E: Aeronautical Engineer
Aer Of: Aerological Officer
AEROFLOT: Aero Flotilla (Soviet Air Lines)
aerol: aerological
aeromed: aeromedical
aeron: aeronautical
AERONAVES: Aeronaves de México
AERONORTE: Empresa de Transportes Aereos Norte do Brasil (North Brazil Airways)
Aero O/Y: Finnair (Finnish Airlines)
aerosp: aerospace
aerospace: aeronautics + space
aerospacecom: aerospace communication(s)
aerotel: airplane hotel (hangar)
Aerovias "Q": Aerovias Cubana (Cuban Airlines)
AERS: Atlantic Estuarine Research Society
AERT: Association for Education by Radio-Television
Aes: *Aesop* (Greek fabulist)
Aes: (Latin—bronze or copper)—used by numismatists to denote bronze or copper coins or coins of such colors
AES: Aerospace Electrical Society; Agricultural Estimates (division of Department of Agriculture); Agricultural Experiment Station; Aircraft Electrical Society; Airways Engineering Society; American Electrochemical Society; American Electroencephalographic Society; American Electroplaters Society; American Entomological Society; American Epidemiological Society; American Epilepsy Society; American Equilibration Society; American Ethnological Society; American Eugenics Society; Apollo Extension System; Army Exchange Service; Atlantic Estuarine Society; Audio Engineering Society
AESBOW: Association of Engineers and Scientists of the Bureau of Weapons (USN)
AESC: American Engineering Standards Committee
Aescul: Aesculapius (Greek god of medicine killed by Jupiter who cast a bolt of lightning at him because he had restored life to several persons)
AESE: Association of Earth Science Editors
AESHS: Alfred E. Smith High School
AESOP: Artificial Earth Satellite Observation Program; Automated Engineering and Scientific Optimization Program (NASA)
AESq: Aeromedical Evacuation Squadron (USAF)
AESQ: Air Explorer Squadron
aesth: aesthete; aesthetic; aesthetician; aesthetics
Aesthetic Post-Impressionist: Vasili Kandinski
AESU: Aerospace Environmental Support Unit
aet: absorption-equivalent thickness
aet.: *aetatis* (Latin—at or of the age of)
AET: *Aerlinte Eireann Teoranta (Irish Airlines)*
A.E.T.: Associate in Electrical Technology; Associate in Electronic Technology
AETA: American Educational Theatre Association
AETE: Aerospace Engineering Test Establishment (Canada)
AETFAT: Association pour l'Etude Taxonomique de la Flore d'Afrique Tropicale (Association for the Taxonomic Study of African Tropical Flora)
AETM: Aviation Electronic Technician's Mate
AETR: Advanced Engineering Test Reactor
AETS: Association for the Education of Teachers in Science
aeu: accrued expenditure unpaid
AEU: Amalgamated Engineering Union; American Ethical Union
aev (AEV): Aerothermodynamic elastic vehicle
aevac: air evacuation
AEW: Airborne Early Warning
AEW & C: Airborne Early Warning and Control
AEWES: Army Engineers Waterways Experiment Station
AEWHA: All-England Women's Hockey Association
AEWLA: All-England Women's Lacrosse Association
AEWRON: Airborne Early Warning Squadron
AEWS: Advanced Earth Satellite Weapon System (USAF); Aircraft Early Warning System (DoD)
aex: automatic electronic exchange (facilitating telephony)
AExO: Assistant Experimental Officer
af: ale firkin; audio fidelity (AF)
af: *afgang* (Danish—departure); *anno futuro* (Italian—next year)
a-f: anti-foam; audio-frequency
a/f: *a favor* (Spanish—a favor)
a & f (A & F): accounting and finance
Af: Africa; Afrikaans; African(s); Académie française (French Academy)
AF: Africa(n); Air Force; air freight; Anglo-French; Armored Force; Aviation Photographer's Mate; provision stores ship (2-letter symbol)
A-F: Anglo-French
A & F: Agriculture and Forestry (Senate Committee)
A of F: Admiral of the Fleet
AFA: Aerophilatelic Federation of the Americas; Air Force Association; Alien Firearms Act; American Finance Association; American Forestry Association; American Foundrymens Association; American Freedom Association; Association of Federal Appraisers
A.F.A.: Associate in Fine Arts
AF of A.: Advertising Federation of America
AFAA: Adult Film Association of America; Automatic Fire Alarm Association
AFAAEC: Air Force Academy and Aircrew Examining Center
AFAC: Air Force Armament Center; American Fisheries Advisory Committee
AFADO: Association of Food and Drug Officials
AFAFC: Air Force Accounting and Finance Center
AFAG: Airforce Advisory Group
AFAIM: Associate Fellow of the Australian Institute of Management
AFAITC: Armed Forces Air Intelligence Training Center
AFAL: Air Force Avionics Laboratory
AF & AM: Ancient Free and Accepted Masons
Af-Am(s): Afro-American(s)
AFAPL: Air Force Aero-Propulsion Laboratory
AFAR: Azores Fixed Acoustic Range (NATO)

Afars and Issas: Djibouti or French Somaliland (Côte française des Somalis)
AFAS: Air Force Aid Society
AFASE: Association for Applied Solar Energy
AFA-SEF: Air Force Association—Space Education Foundation
AFASIC: Association For All Speech-Impaired Children
AFAUD: Air Force Auditor General
afb: acid-fast bacillus; antifriction bearing
afb: *afbeelding* (Dutch—illustration)
AFB: Air Force Base; American Farm Bureau; American Foundation for the Blind
AFBF: American Farm Bureau Federation
AFBMA: Antifriction Bearing Manufacturers Association
AFBMD: Air Force Ballistic Missile Division
AFBNM: Agate Fossil Beds National Monument (Nebraska)
AFBS: American and Foreign Bible Society
AFBSD: Air Force Ballistic Systems Division
afc: automatic frequency control
AFC: Air Force Cross; American Football Conference; Apollo Flight Control (NASA); Area Forecast Center; Australian Flying Corps
AFCAI: Associate Fellow of the Canadian Aeronautical Institute
AFCAL: Association Française de Calcul
AFCC: Air Force Communications Center
AFCCB: Air Force Configuration Control Board
AFCCDD: Air Force Command and Control Development Division
AFCCP: Air Force Component Command Post
AFCD: Air Force Cryptologic Depot
afce: automatic flight-control equipment
AFCE: Associate in Fuel Technology and Chemical Engineering
AFCEA: Armed Forces Communications and Electronics Association
AFCent: Allied Forces, Central Europe
AFCI: American Foot Care Institute
AFCM: Air Force Commendation Medal
AFCMA: Aluminum Foil Container Manufacturers Association
AFCMD: Air Force Contract Management Division
AFCMO: Air Force Contract Management Office
AFCN: American Friends of the Captive Nations
afco: automatic fuel cutoff
AFCO: Admiralty Fleet Confidential Order; Air Force Contracting Office(r)
AF Compt: Air Force Comptroller
AFCON: Air Force Controlled (units)
AFCOS: Armed Forces Courier Service
AFCR: American Federation for Clinical Research
AFCRC: Air Force Cambridge Research Center
AFCRL: Air Force Cambridge Research Laboratories
AFCS: Active Federal Commissioned Service; Adaptive Flight Control System; Air Force Communications Service; Automatic Flight Control System
AFCSL: Air Force Communications Security Letter
AFCSM: Air Force Communications Security Manual
AFCSP: Air Force Communications Security Pamphlet
AFCW: Association of Family Case Workers
AFCWF: Air Force Civilian Welfare Fund
afd: accelerated freeze drying
afd: *afdeling* (Dano-Norwegian or Dutch—part)
AFD: Air Force Depot; Association of Food Distributors; Association of Footwear Distributors; mobile floating drydock (naval symbol)
AFDA: American Flag Day Association
AFDAP: Air Force Directorate of Advanced Technology
AFDATACOM: Air Force Data Communications System
AFDB: African Development Bank; Air Force Decorations Board; large auxiliary floating drydock (naval symbol)
AFDC: Aid for Dependent Children; Aid for Families with Dependent Children
AFDCB: Armed Forces Disciplinary Control Board
AFDCMI: Air Force Policy on Disclosure of Classified Military Information
AFDCUF: Aid to Families with Dependent Children of Unemployed Fathers
AFDE: American Fund for Dental Education
AFDEA: American Funeral Directors and Embalmers Association
AFDL: small auxiliary floating drydock (naval symbol)
AFDM: medium auxiliary floating drydock (naval symbol)
AFDO: Air Force Duty Officer; Association of Food and Drug Officials
AFDOA: Armed Forces Dental Officers Association
AFDOUS: Association of Food and Drug Officials of the United States
AFDP: Air Force Development Plan
AFDRB: Air Force Disability Review Board; Air Force Discharge Review Board
AFDRD: Air Force Director of Research and Development
AFDRQ: Air Force Director of Requirements
AFDS: Air Fighting Development Squadron
AFE: Administración de Ferrocarriles del Estado (State Railway Administration of Uruguay)
AFEA: American Farm Economic Association; American Film Export Association
AFEB: Armed Forces Epidemiological Board
AFEE: Airborne Forces Experimental Establishment
AFELIS: Air Force Engineering and Logistics Information System
AFEM: Armed Forces Expeditionary Medal
AFEMS: Air Force Equipment Management System
AFERB: Air Force Educational Requirements Board
AFERO: Asia and the Far East Regional Office (FAO)
AFES: Air Force Exchange Service; American Far Eastern Society; Armed Forces Examining Stations
AFETR: Air Force Eastern Test Range (see ETR)
AFEX: Air Forces Europe Exchange
aff: affairs
AFF: Army Field Forces

AFFA: Air Freight Forwarders Association
AFFC: Air Force Finance Center
AFFDL: Air Force Flight Dynamics Laboratory
AFFE: Air Force Far East; Allied Forces Far East; Army Forces Far East
affec: affectation; affection; affective
affet: *affettuoso* (Italian—tenderly; with pathos)
AFFFA: American Forged Fitting and Flange Association
AFFI: American Frozen Food Institute
Affie: Alfred
affil: affiliated
AFFJ: American Fund for Free Jurists
AFFL: Agricultural Finance Federation, Limited
afflat: afflatus
AFFLC: Air Force Film Library Center
affores: afforestation
affret: *affrettando* (Italian—speeding the tempo)
AFFS: American Federation of Film Societies
afft: affidavit
AFFTC: Air Force Flight Test Center; Air Force Flying Training Command
afg: analog function generator
afg: *afgang* (Danish—departure)
Afg: Afghan; afghani (currency); Afghanistan; Afghans
AFGC: American Forage and Grassland Council
AFGCM: Air Force Good Conduct Medal
AFGE: American Federation of Government Employees
Afghan: Afghanistan
AFGIS: Aerial Free Gunnery Instruction School
AFGM: American Federation of Grain Millers
AFGU: Aerial Free Gunnery Unit
AFGW: American Flint Glass Workers
AFGWC: Air Force Global Weather Central
AFH: Air Force Hospital; American Foundation for Homeopathy; Associated Federated Hotels
AFHC: Air Force Headquarters Command
AFHF: Air Force Historical Foundation; American Foot Health Foundation
AFHQ: Air Force Headquarters; Allied Forces Headquarters; Armed Forces Headquarters
AFHW: American Federation of Hosiery Workers
afi: amaurotic familial idiocy
AFI: Air Filter Institute; American Film Institute; American Filter Institute; American Friends of Israel; Armed Forces Institute; Atlantic Refining Company (stock exchange symbol)
AFIA: American Foreign Insurance Association
AFIAS: Associate Fellow of the Institute of the Aerospace Sciences
afib: atrial fibrillation
afic: *aficionado* (Spanish—admirer; devotee; fan)
AFIC: Air Force Intelligence Center
AFICCS: Air Force Interim Command and Control System
AFICE: Air Forces—Iceland
AFIED: Armed Forces Information and Education Division
AFII: American Federation of International Institutes
AFIIM: Associate Fellow of the Institute of Industrial Managers
AFINE: *Association Française pour l'Industrie Nucleaire d'Equipement* (French Association for the Nuclear Equipment Industry)
AFINS: Airways Flight Inspector
AFIP: Air Force Intelligence Publication; Armed Forces Information Program; Armed Forces Institute of Pathology
AFIPS: American Federation of Information Processing Societies
AFIR: Air Force Installation Representative
AFIRAN: Africa-Indian Ocean Region Air Navigation
affirm: affirmative
AFIRO: Air Force Installations Representative Officer
AFIS: Armed Forces Information School
afism: aluminum-free inorganic suspended material
AFISR: Air Force Industrial Security Regulations
AFIT: Air Force Institute of Technology
AFITAE: *Association Française d'Ingénieurs et Techniciens de l'Aéronautique et de l'Espace* (French Association of Aeronautical and Aerospace Engineers and Technicians)
AFJKT: Air Force Job-Knowledge Test
afk: *afkorting* (Dutch—abbreviation)
afl: abstract family of languages; anti-fatty liver; atrial flutter
afl: *aflevering* (Dutch—part)
AFL: Aeroflot (Soviet Air Lines); Air Force Letter; American Federation of Labor; American Football League; Applied Fisheries Laboratory (University of Washington); Association for Family Living
AFLA: Amateur Fencers League of America; American Foreign Law Association; Asian Federation of Library Associations
AFLAT: Air Force Language Aptitude Test
AFLC: Air Force Logistics Command
AFL-CIO: American Federation of Labor and Congress of Industrial Organizations
afld: airfield
AFLP: American Farmer Labor Party; Armed Forces Language Program
AFLS: Air Force Library Service
AFLSA: Air Force Longevity Service Award
aflt: afloat
afm: antifriction metal
AFM: Air Force Manual; Air Force Medal; Air Force Museum; American Federation of Musicians; Associated Fur Manufacturers
AFMA: American Footwear Manufacturers Association; Armed Forces Management Association
AFMA: *Air Force Manual of Abbreviations*
AFMBT: Artificial Flower Manufacturers Board of Trade
AFMDC: Air Force Missile Development Center
AFME: American Friends of the Middle East
AFMEC: African Methodist Episcopal Church
AFMed: Allied Forces, Mediterranean
AFMF: Air Fleet Marine Force
AFMH: American Foundation for Mental Hygiene
AFML: Air Force Materials Laboratory; Armed Forces Medical Library
AFMMFO: Air Force Medical Materiel Field Office
afmo: *afectísimo* (Spanish—most

affectionate)
AFMPA: Armed Forces Medical Publication Agency
afmr: antiferromagnetic resonance
AFMR: American Foundation for Management Research; Armed Forces Master Records
AFMS: Air Force Medical Service; American Federation of Minerological Societies
AFMSC: Air Force Medical Specialist Corps
AFMTC: Air Force Missile Test Center
AFMVOP: Air Force Motor Vehicle Operator Test
AFN: Afrique du Nord (French North Africa); Air Force Finance Center; American Forces Network; Armed Forces Network
AF of N: Alaska Federation of Natives
AFNA: Air Force with Navy
AFNB: Armed Forces News Bureau
AFNC: Air Force Nurse Corps
AFNE: Allied Forces, Northern Europe
AFNIL: *Agence Francophone pour la Numérotation Internationale du Livre* (French Agency for the International Numbering of Books)
AFNOR: Association Française de Normalisation (French Standards Association)
AFNorth: Allied Forces, Northern Europe
AFO: Accounting and Finance Office(r); Airports Field Office; Atlantic Fleet Organization
AFOAR: Air Force Office for Aerospace Research
AFOAS: Air Force Office of Aerospace Sciences
AFOAT: Air Force Office for Atomic Energy
AFOB: American Foundation for Overseas Blind
AFOC: Air Force Operations Center
AFOECP: Air Force Officer Education and Commissioning Program
AFOIC: Air Force Officer in Charge
AFOQT: Air Force Officer Qualifying Test
AFORG: Air Force Overseas Replacement Group
a fort: *a fortiori* (Italian—with greater force)
AFOSI: Air Force Office of Special Investigations
AFOSR: Air Force Office of Scientific Research
AFOUA: Air Force Outstanding Unit Award
afp: anterior faucial pillar
afp (AFP): alphafetroprotein
AFP: Agence France-Presse (successor to Havas); Air Force Pamphlet; Alternate Flight Plan; Annual Funding Program; Armed Forces Police; Authority for Purchase
AF of P: American Federation of Police
afpa: automatic flow process analysis
AFPA: Aquarama and Fairmount Park Aquarium; Australian Fire Protection Association
AFPAO: Air Force Property Accountable Office(r)
AFPB: Air Force Personnel Board
AFPC: Air Force Personnel Council; Air Force Procurement Circular; American Food for Peace Council; Armed Forces Policy Council
AFPCB: Armed Forces Pest Control Board
AFPD: Armed Forces Police Detachment
AFPE: American Foundation for Pharmaceutical Education; American Foundation for Political Education
AFPH: American Federation of the Physically Handicapped
AFPI: Air Force Procurement Instructions; American Forest Products Industries
AFPP: Air Force Procurement Procedures
AFPPA: American Federation of Poultry Producers Associations
AFPR: Air Force Plant Representative
AFPRO: Action for Food Production; Air Force Plant Representative's Office
AFPs: American Freeway Patrol cars (American Oil Company's free service to motorists in trouble on freeways)
AFPS: Armed Forces Press Service
AFPT: Air Force Personnel Test
AFPTRC: Air Force Personnel and Training Research Center
AFPU: Air Force Postal Unit
AFQ: Association Forestière Québeçoise (Quebec Forestry Service)
AFQA: Air Force Quality Assurance
AFQC: Air Force Quality Control
AFQT: Armed Forces Qualification Test
afr: airframe; air-fuel ratio
Afr: Africa; African; Africans; Afrikaans (South African Dutch)
A Fr: Algerian franc
A-Fr: Anglo-French
AFR: Air Force Regulation(s); Air Force Reserve
afra: average freight rate assessment
AFRA: American Farm research Association; American Federation of Television and Radio Artists
AFRAeS: Associate Fellow of the Royal Aeronautical Society
A-frame: capital-A-shaped support frame
Aframerican: African + American
AFRASEC: Afro-Asian Organization for Economic Cooperation
Afrasia: Africa + Asia
AFRB: Air Force Retiring Board
AFRBA: Armed Forces Relief and Benefit Association
AFRBSG: Air Force Reserve Base Support Group
AFRC: Air Force Regional Civil Engineer
AFRCSTC: Air Force Reserve Combat Support Training Center
afrd: acute febrile respiratory disease (AFRD)
AFRD: Air Force Research Division; Air Force Reserve Division; Association of Fund-Raising Directors
AFRes: Air Force Reserve
AFRESM: Armed Forces Reserve Medal
AFRESNAVSQ: Air Force Reserve Navigation Squadron
AFRFI: American Friends of Religious Freedom in Israel
afri: acute febrile respiratory illness (AFRI)
AFRI: Applied Forest Research Institute
Afric: Africa; African
Africa in Miniature: Cameroon
African Queen: Mrs Ian Smith of Salisbury, Rhodesia
Africa's big five: Cape buffalo, elephant, leopard, lion, rhinoceros
Afrik: Afrikaans

Afr Nat Cnl: African National Council
Afro: prefix meaning African or Black
AFRO: African Regional Office (FAO)
Afro-Am: Afro-American(ese)
Afro-American: African-American
Afro-America's First Great Poet: Paul Laurence Dunbar
Afro(s): Afro-American(s)—Black(s), Negro(es)
AFROTC: Air Force Reserve Officers Training Corps
AFRPL: Air Force Rocket Propulsion Laboratory
AFRR: Air Force Reserve Region
AFRRG: Air Force Reserve Recovery Group
AFRRI: Armed Forces Radiobiology Research Institute
AFRS: Air Force Reserve Sector; Armed Forces Radio Service
AFRTS: Armed Forces Radio-Television Service
AFRVN: Air Force of the Republic of Viet Nam
afs: aforesaid; atomic fluorescence spectroscopy
afs: *afsender* (Danish—sender)
AFS: Air Force Specialty; Air Force Station; Air Force Supply; Airline Feed System; Airways Facilities Shop; Alaska Ferry Service; American Feline Society; American Fern Society; American Field Service; American Fisheries Society; American Folklore Society; American Foundrymen's Society; American Fuchsia Society; Aviation Facilities Service
AFSA: Air Force Sergeants Association; American Flight Strips Association; American Foreign Service Association; Armed Forces Security Agency
AFSAB: Air Force Science Advisory Board
AFSAW: Air Force Special Activities Wing
Af-Sax: Afro-Saxon (black person of part Anglo-Saxon parentage; white-oriented person of African origin)
AFSB: American Federation of Small Business
AFSBO: American Federation of Small Business Organizations
AFSC: Air Force Service Command; Air Force Specialty Code; Air Force Supply Catalog; Air Force Systems Command; American Federation of Soroptimist Clubs; American Friends Service Committee; Armed Forces Staff College
AFSCC: Air Force Special Communications Center; Armed Forces Supply Control Center
AFSCF: Air Force Satellite Control Facility
AFSCM: Air Force Systems Command Manual
AFSCME: American Federation of State, County, and Municipal Employees
afsd: aforesaid
AFSec: Air Force Section
AFSF: Air Force Stock Fund
AFSIL: Accommodations for Students in London
AFSMAAG: Air Force Section—Military Advisory Group
AFSN: Air Force Serial Number; Air Force Service Number; Air Force Stock Number
AFSouth: Allied Forces, Southern Europe
AFSS: Air Force Security Service; Air Force Service Statement
AFSSD: Air Force Space Systems Division
AFSSO: Air Force Special Security Office
AFSTC: Air Force Space Test Center
AFSUB: Army Air Forces Anti-Submarine Command
AFSWA: Armed Forces Special Weapons Agency
AFSWC: Air Force Special Weapons Center
AFSWP: Armed Forces Special Weapons Project
aft: after; afternoon; at, near, or toward the rear; automatic fine tuning
Aft: *Aftenposten* (Evening Post—Oslo)
AFT: Air Freight Terminal; American Federation of Teachers; Annual Field Training (USA)
AFTA: Atlantic Free Trade Area
AFTAC: Air Force Technical Applications Center
AFT (AFL-CIO): American Federation of Teachers
AFTAU: American Friends of Tel Aviv University
AFTB: Air Force Test Base
AFTC: Airborne Flight Training Command; American Fair Trade Council; American Fox Terrier Club; American Free Trade Clubs
AFTE: American Federation of Technical Engineers
AFTF: Air Force Task Force
AFTLI: Association of Feeling Truth and Living It
AFTM: American Foundation for Tropical Medicine
aftn: afternoon
AFTN: Aeronautical Fixed Telecommunications Network
afto: *afecto* (Spanish—affectionate; fond)
AFTO: Air Force Technical Order
AFTOSB: Air Force Technical Order Standardization Board
AFTR: *American Federal Tax Reports*
AFTRA: American Federation of Television and Radio Artists
AFTRC: Air Force Technical Training Command
AFTTH: Air Force Technical Training Headquarters
AFU: Advanced Flying Units; American Fraternal Union; Assault Fire Unit (U.S. Army)
AFU: *Association Fonciere Urbaine* (French—Urban Land Association)
AFULE: Australian Federated Union of Locomotive Enginemen
AFUS: Air Force of the United States; Armed Forces of the United States
afv: armored fighting vehicle; armored force vehicle
AFVA: Air Force Visual Aid
AFvg: Anglo-French variable geometry
AFVN: Armed Forces Vietnam Network
AFW: Association for Family Welfare
AFWA: Air Force with Army
AFWETS: Air Force Weapons Effectiveness Testing System
AFWL: Air Force Weapons Laboratory; Armed Forces Writers League
AFWN: Air Force with Navy
AFWOFS: Air Force Weather Observing and Forecasting System
AFWR: Atlantic Fleet Weapons Range
AFWST: Armed Forces Women's Selection Test
AFWTR: Air Force Western Test Range (see WTR)
Afyon: *Afyonkarahisar* (Turkish—Black Castle of Opi-

um)—town in western central Turkey where much of the world's opium is grown
ag: armor grating; atrial gallop; axiogingival
a g: *à gauche* (French—to the left)
a-g: air-to-ground; anti-gas
a/g: air-to-ground; albumin-globulin ratio
Ag: Agostino
Ag: *argentum* (Latin—silver)
AG: Adjutant General; Aeronautical Standards Group; Air Group; Aktiengesellschaft (German—Joint stock company); Allegheny Ludlum Steel (stock exchange symbol); Artists Guild; Attorney General; Auditor General; escort research vessel (naval symbol); miscellaneous auxiliary vessels (naval symbol); sonar research ship (naval symbol); technical research ship (naval symbol)
AG: *Arkansas Gazette; Astronomische Gesellschaft; Alberghi per la Gioventu* (Italian—Youth Hostels)
a/g/a: air-to-ground-to-air
aga: accelerated growth area; appropriate for gestational age
AGA: Abrasive Grain Association; Adjutants General Association; Alabama Gas (symbol); American Gas Association; American Gastroenterological Association; American Gastroscopic Association; American Genetic Association; American Glassware Association; American Goiter Association; American Gold Association
AGAA: Art Galleries Association of Australia
AGAAC: *Acuerdo General sobre Aranceles Aduaneros y Comercio* (Spanish—General Accord concerning Custom's Duties and Commerce)
AGAC: American Guild of Authors and Composers
Aga cooker: Aktiebolaget gas-accumulative cooker
agacs: automatic ground-air-communication system
AGAFBO: Atlantic and Gulf American Flag Berth Operators
agalmatolite: talc
AGARD: Advisory Group for Aeronautical Research and Development (NATO)
agate: chalcedony
Agate Capital: Prineville, Oregon's place-name nickname
Agatha Christie: Agatha Christie Mallowan
agave.: automatic gimballed antenna vectoring equipment
agb: any good brand
AGB: Audits of Great Britain (television survey); icebreaker (3-letter symbol)
AGBAD: Alexander Graham Bell Association for the Deaf
AGBI: Artists' General Benevolent Institution
AGBUC: Association of Governing Boards of Universities and Colleges
agc: automatic gain control
AGC: Adjutant General's Corps; Aerojet-General Corporation; American Grassland Council; amphibious force flagship (naval symbol); Armed Guard Center; Associated General Contractors; astronomical great circle (course)
agca: automatic ground control approach
AGCA: Associated General Contractors of America
AGCan: Auditor General of Canada
agcl: automatic ground-controlled landing
AGCM: Army Good Conduct Medal
AGCMWA: Amon G. Carter Museum of Western Art
AGCRSP: Army Gas-Cooled Reactor Systems Program
AGCSD: Attorney General's Consumer Services Department
AGCT: Army General Classification Test
AGCTS: Armed Guard Center Training School
Ag-Cu al: silver-copper alloy (new U.S. coin facing)
agcy: agency
agd: agreed; axial gear differential
AGD: Academy of General Dentistry; Adjutant General's Department; American Gage Design; Auditor General's Department
AGDA: American Gasoline Dealers Association; American Gun Dealers Association
AGDC: Assistant Grand Director of Ceremonies
AGDE: escort research ship (naval symbol)
Ag. *Dei:* *Agnus Dei* (Latin—Lamb of God)
Ag Dept: Agriculture Department
AGDS: American Gage Design Standard
age. (AGE): aerospace ground equipment; automatic guidance electronics
Age: *The Age* (Melbourne)
Age of Anxiety: Bernstein's Symphony No. 2
Ag.E.: Agricultural Engineer
AGE: Amarillo Grain Exchange
A.G.E.: Associate in General Education
AGEC: Army General Equipment Command
AGED: Advisory Group on Electronic Devices
AGEH: hydrofoil research ship (naval symbol)
AGEHR: American Guild of English Handbell Ringers
Age of Voltaire: the Enlightenment
ageocp: aerospace ground equipment out of commission for parts
AGEP: Advisory Group on Electronic Parts
AGER: environmental research ship (naval symbol)
agerd: aerospace ground-equipment requirements data
AGERS: Auxiliary General Electronics Research Ship(s)
AG & ES: American Gas & Electric System
AGET: Advisory Group on Electronic Tubes
AGF: Army Ground Forces; miscellaneous command ship (naval symbol)
AGFA: Aktiengesellschaft für Anilinfabrikation (Corporation for Aniline Manufacture)
ag.feb.: *aggrediente febre* (Latin—when fever increases)
Ag and Fish: Ministry of Agriculture and Fisheries
AGFRTS: Air and Ground Forces Resources and Technical Staff (U.S. Army)
AGFSRS: Aircraft Ground Fire Suppression and Rescue System (DoD)
agg: agammaglobulinaemia(c); agglutination(ed); aggravated (ed); aggregated(ed); aggregation
aggie: agriculture
Aggie: Agatha; Agnes
aggies: agate playing marbles; students of agricultural colleges or schools
agglut: agglutination (ed)
aggr: aggregate

AGGR: Air-to-Ground Gunnery Range
aggred. feb.: *aggrediente febre* (Latin—while fever is developing)
aggro: aggression; aggressiveness
aggs: anti-gas gangrene serum
AGGS: American Good Government Society
Aggy: Agatha; Agnes
AGH: Australian General Hospital
agi: adjusted gross income
AGI: American Geographical Institute; American Geological Institute; Annual General Inspection
AGI: *Agenzia Giornalistica Italiana* (Italian News Agency); *Associazione Guide Italiane* (Italian Girl Guides' Association)
AGIC: Air-Ground Information Center
AGIFORS: Airlines Group of International Federation of Operations Research Societies
agil: airborne general illumination light
AGILE: Autonetics General Information Learning Equipment
AGIP: *Azienda Generale Italiana Petroli* (National Italian Oil Company)
agit.: *agitatum* (Latin—shaken)
agit. ante sum: *agita ante sumendum* (Latin—shake before using)
agit-prop: agitation and propaganda
agit. vas.: *agitato vase* (Latin—shaking the vessel)
agl: above ground level; acute granulocytic leukemia; airborne gun laying; aminoglutethimide
AGL: lighthouse tender (3-letter symbol)
AGLC: Air-to-Ground Liaison Code
aglm: agglomerate
AGLS: Association of General and Liberal Studies
A-glue: airplane glue
agm (AGM): air-to-ground missile
AGM: American Guild of Music; missile range instrumentation ship (naval symbol); Annual General Meeting (of shareholders)
AGMA: American Gear Manufacturers Association; Athletic Goods Manufacturers Association
AGMA (AFL-CIO): American Guild of Musical Artists
AGMR: major communications relay ship (naval symbol)
agn: acute glomerulonephritis; again; agnomen
Agn: Augustín
AGN: Aerojet-General Nucleonics
Agncy: Agency (postal placename abbreviation)
agnos: agnostic; agnosticism
AGO: Adjutant General's Office; Air Gunnery Officer; American Guild of Organists; Attorney General's Office; Attorney General's Opinion
AGOR: Auxiliary General Oceanographic Research (vessel)
AGP: Academy of General Practice; Adjutant General's Pool; Army Ground Pool; motor torpedo boat tender (naval symbol)
AGPA: American Group Psychotherapy Association
agpe: angle plate
agpi: automatic ground position indicator
ag prov: agent provocateur
AGPL: *Administração-Geral do Pôrto de Lisboa* (Portuguese—Port of Lisbon Authority)
agr: agree(ment); agricultural; agriculture
AGRA: Australian Garrison Royal Artillery
agrar: agrarian; agrarianism; agrarians
a/g ratio: albumin-globulin ratio
Agra U: Agra University
AGREE: Advisory Group on Reliability of Electronic Equipment
AGRF: American Geriatric Research Foundation
agri: agricultural; agriculturalist; agriculture; agriculturist
agribusiness: agricultural business (large-scale farming)
agric: agriculture
Agric E: Agricultural Engineer
Agricola: George Bauer
agripower: agricultural power
AGRM: Adjutant General—Royal Marines
agro: aggravation; agrobiological; agrobiologist; agrobiology; agrologic; agrological; agronomical; agronomics; agronomist; agronomy; etc.
agrogeol: agrogeology
agron: agronomy
agros: agrostology
ags: adrenogenital syndrome; agencies
ags (Ags): antigens
Ags: Aguascalientes (inhabitants—Hidrocalidos)
AGS: Aircraft General Standards; Alabama Great Southern (railroad); Allied Geographic Section; American Gem Society; American Geographical Society; American Geriatrics Society; American Goat Society; American Gynecological Society; Army General Staff; Army Guard School; surveying ship (naval symbol)
A.G.S.: Associate in General Studies
AGSM: American Gold Star Mothers; Associate of the Guildhall School of Music
AGSRO: Association of Government Supervisors and Radio Officers
AGSS: American Geographical and Statistical Society
agst: against
agt: agent; agreement
agt (AGT): antiglobulin test
AGT: Art Gallery of Toronto, Association of Geology Teachers
AGTE: Association of Group Travel Executives
agto: *agosto* (Portuguese and Spanish—August)
agtt (AGTT): abnormal glucose tolerance test
AGU: American Geophysical Union
Aguacates: Aguacate Mountains (avocado-colored hills and mountains of Costa Rica)
Agu Cur: Agulhas Current
agv: aniline gentian violet
AGVA: American Guild of Variety Artists
AGvga: Anglo-German variable-geometry aircraft
agw: allowable gross takeoff weight
AGWAC: Australian Guided Weapons and Analog Computer
AGWI: American Gulf and West Indies (steamship line)
agy: agency
agz: actual ground zero
ah: abdominal hysterectomy; acetohexamide; after hatch; alter heading; amenorrhea and hirsutism; aminohippurate; antihalation; antihyaluronidase; arterial hypertension; astigmatism hyper-

metropic
a-h: ampere-hour
a & h: accident and health; alive and healthy
Ah: ampere-hour; hyperopic astigmatism
AH: Airfield Heliport; Alfred Holt's Blue Funnel Line (house flag and funnel mark); Allis Chalmers (stock exchange symbol); Animal Husbandry (division of Department of Agriculture); Army Hospital; hospital ship (naval symbol)
AH: *Akademiya Nauk* (Russian—Academy of Sciences)
A-H: American-Hawaiian Line; Arrow-Hart & Hegeman Electric Company
A.H.: *Anno Hebraico* (Latin—in the Hebrew Year)
A & H: Arm and Hammer (trade mark)
aha: acquired hemolytic anemia; all have automobiles; autoimmune hemolytic anemia
AHA: Adirondack Historical Association; American Hardboard Association; American Heart Association; American Hereford Association; American Historical Association; American Hospital Association; American Hotel Association; American Humane Association; American Humanist Association; American Hypnotherapy Association; Association of Handicapped Artists; Association for Humane Abortion
AHAM: Association of Home Appliance Manufacturers
AHAUS: Amateur Hockey Association of the U.S.
AHC: Academy of Hospital Counselors; American Hardware Corporation; American Hockey Coaches; American Horticultural Council; American Hospital Corps; Army Hospital Corps
AHCEI: American Histadrut Cultural Exchange Institute
ahd: ahead; airhead; aired head; arteriosclerotic heart disease; atherosclerotic heart disease; auto-immune haemolytic disease
AHD: *American Heritage Dictionary*
A-H DT: Alaska-Hawaii Daylight Time
ahe: acute hemorrhagic encephalomyelitis
AHE: Association for Higher Education
A.H.E.: Associate in Home Economics
AHEA: American Home Economics Association
A-head: acid head (underground slang—LSD addict); amphetamine addict
AHEL: Army Human Engineering Laboratory (USA)
AHEM: Association of Hydraulic Equipment Manufacturers
AHEPA: American Hellenic Educational Progressive Association
AHES: American Humane Education Society
ahf: anti-hemophilic factor
AHF: American Health Foundation; American Heritage Foundation; American Hobby Federation; American Hungarian Foundation; Associated Health Foundation
AHF: American Hospital Formulary
AHFCR: Anderson Hospital for Cancer Research
ahg: antihemolytic globulin; antihuman globulin
ahg (AHG): antihemophilic globulin
AHG: American Housing Guild
ahh: alpha-hydrazine analog of histidine; arylhydrocarbon hydroxylase
AHHS: Alexander Hamilton High School
AHI: American Health Institute; American Honey Institute; American Hospital Institute
AHIL: Association of Hospital and Institution Libraries
AHIS: American Hull Insurance Syndicate
a.h.l.: *ad hunc locum* (Latin—at this place)
AHL: Alaska Historical Library; American Hockey League; Associated Humber Lines
ahle: acute hemorrhagic leukoencephalitis
AHLMA: American Home Laundry Manufacturers Association
ahls: antihuman-lymphocyte serum
ahm: ampere-hour meter
Ahm: Ahmadabad; Arnhem
ahma: advanced hypersonic manned aircraft
AHMA: American Hardware Manufacturers Association; American Hemisphere Marine Agencies; American Hotel and Motel Association
AHMC: Association of Hospital Management Committees
AHMI: Appalachian Hardwood Manufacturers Incorporated
AHMPS: Association of Headmistresses of Preparatory Schools
AHMS: American Home Missionary Society
AHN: Assistant Head Nurse
AHNA: Accredited Home Newspapers of America
ahp: acute hemorrhagic pancreatitis; air at high pressure; air horsepower; aviation horsepower
AHP: Assistant House Physician; Association for Humanistic Psychology
AHPA: American Horse Protection Association
AHPC: American Heritage Publishing Company
AHPR: Academy of Hospital Public Relations
ahps: auxiliary hydraulic power supply
AHQ: Air Headquarters; Allied Headquarters; Army Headquarters
ahr: acceptable hazard rate
AHR: Association for Health Records
AHRC: Australian Humanities Research Council
AHRGB: Association of Hotels and Restaurants of Great Britain
AHS: Aerospace High School; American Harp Society; American Hearing Society; American Helicopter Society; American Hibiscus Society; American Horticultural Society; American Hospital Supply (stock exchange symbol); American Humane Society; American Hypnodontic Society; Assistant House Surgeon; Aviation High School; Aviation Historical Society
AHSA: American Hampshire Sheep Association; American Horse Shows Association; Art, Historical, and Scientific Association
AHSB: Authority Health and Safety Branch
AHSC: American Hospital Supply Company
ahse: assembly, handling, and shipping equipment
ahsr: air height-surveillance radar
AHSS: Association of Home

Study Schools
A-H ST: Alaska-Hawaii Standard Time
aht: antihyaluronidase titer
AHT: Animal Health Trust; Augmented Histamine Test
a.h.v.: *ad hunc vocem* (Latin—at this word)
AHV: Altos Hornos de Vizcaya
AHWA: Association of Hospital and Welfare Administrators
AHWG: Ad Hoc Working Group (USA)
ai: accidentally incurred; airborne intercept; anti-icing; aortic incompetence; aortic insufficiency; apical impulse; articulation index; artificial insemination; axioincisal
a. i.: *ad interim* (Latin—in the interim)
a & i: abstracting and indexing
A & I: Afars and Issas (formerly French Somaliland); agricultural and industrial (college or school or subjects); Arts and Industries
A o I: Aimsw of Industry
AI: Aaland Islands; Admiralty Islands; Air India; Air Inspector; Air Installation(s); Airways Inspector; Alianza Interamericana (Inter-American Alliance); American Institute; Arctic Institute; Army Intelligence; Astrologers International
A/I: Aptitude Index
A & I: Arts and Industries
AIA: Aerospace Industries Association; Allergy Information Association; American Institute of Accountants; American Institute of Aeronautics; American Institute of Architects; Archeological Institute of America; Arctic Institute of America; Association Internationale d'Allergologie
A.I.A.: Associate of the Institute of Actuaries
AIAA: Aerospace Industries Association of America; American Institute of Aeronautics and Astronautics
AIAC: Air Industries Association of Canada
AIAE: Association of Institutes of Automobile Engineers
AIAESD: American International Association for Economic and Social Development (AIA)
AIAL: Associate of the Institute of Arts and Letters
AIAOS: Academic Instructor and Allied Officer School
AIAP: Ardmore Industrial Air Park
AIArb: Associate of the Institute of Arbitrators
AIAS: Australian Institute of Agriculture and Science
aib: aminoisobutyric acid
AIB: American Institute of Baking; American Institute of Banking; Assassination Information Bureau
AIB: *Association des Industries de Belgique* (Association of Belgian Industries)
AIB: *Associazione Italiana Biblioteche* (Italian Library Association)
A.I.B.: Associate of the Institute of Bankers
aiba: amino-isobutyric acid
AIBA: American Industrial Bankers Association
AIBC: Architectural Institute of British Columbia
AIBD: Associate of the Institute of British Decorators and Interior Designers
aibm (AIBM): anti-intercontinental ballistic missile
AIBM: *Association Internationale des Bibliothèques Musicales* (French—International Association of Music Libraries)
AIBP: Associate of the Institute of British Photographers
AIBS: American Institute of Biological Sciences
aic: aminoimidazole carboxamide
aic (AIC): aircraft in commission
AIC: Advanced Intelligence Center: Allied Intelligence Center; Allied Intelligence Committee; American Institute of Chemists; American Institution of Cooperation; Ammunition Identification Code; Arab Information Center; Arab Investment Company; Army Industrial College; Army Intelligence Center; Art Information Center; Art Institute of Chicago
AICA: Association Internationale des Critiques d'Art (International Association of Art Critics)
aicar: amino-imidazolecarboxamide ribonucleotide
AICB: *Association Internationale Contre le Bruit* (French—International Association Against Noise)
aicbm (AICBM): anti-intercontinental ballistic missile
AICC: All-India Congress Committee
AICCC: American Institute of Child Care Centers
AICE: American Institute of Chemical Engineers; American Institute of Consulting Engineers
AI-CE: Atomic International—Combustion Engineering
aicf: auto-immune complement fixation
AICF: America-Israel Cultural Foundation
AIChE (preferred abbreviation): American Institute of Chemical Engineers
AICMA: Association Internationale des Constructeurs de Matériel Aéronautique
AICO: American Insulator Corporation
AICPA: American Institute of Certified Public Accountants
AICQ: *Associazione Italiana per il Controllo della Qualità* (Italian Association for Quality Control)
AICS: Air Induction Control System; American Institute of Ceylonese Studies
AICS: *Association Internationale du Cinéma Scientifique* (French—International Scientific Film Association)
A.I.C.S.: Associate of the Institute of Chartered Shipbrokers
AICTA: Associate of the Imperial College of Tropical Agriculture
aicv: armored infantry combat vehicle (AICV)
aid: acute infectious disease; artifical insemination donor; avalanche injection diode
AID: Agency for International Development; Airline Interline Development; American Institute of Decorators; American Instructors of the Deaf; Army Information Digest; Army Intelligence Department; Artificial Insemination Donor; Association for International Development
AID: *Acronyms and Initialisms Dictionary*
A & ID: Acquisition and Improvement District
aida: attention-interest-desire-action (marketing formula); automatic instrumented diving assembly; automobile information data advertising

AIDA: Associated Independent Dairies of America
AIDD: American Institute of Design and Drafting
aide.: airborne insertion display equipment; aircraft installation diagnostic equipment
AIDE: American Institute of Driver Education
AIDE: *Association Internationale des Distributions d'Eau* (French—International Water Supply Association)
AIDI: *Associazione Italiana per la Documentazione e l'Informazione* (Italian Association for Documentation and Information)
AIDIA: Associate of the Industrial Design Institute of Australia
AIDIS: Asociación Interamericana de Ingenaria Senitaria (Inter-American Association of Sanitary Engineering)
AIDL: Auckland Industrial Development Laboratory
AIDP: Associate of the Institute of Data Processing
AIDP: *Association Internationale de Droit Pénal* (French—International Association of Penal Law)
AIDS: Abstracts Information Dissemination System; Automatic Inventory Dispatching System
AI & DSC: Army Information and Data System Command
AIEA: *Agence Internationale de l'Energie Atomique* (International Atomic Energy Agency)
AIECF: American Indian and Eskimo Cultural Foundation
A.I.Ed.: Associate in Industrial Education
AIEE: American Institute of Electrical Engineers
AIEF: Association Internationale des Etudes Françaises (International Association for French Studies)
aiep: amount of insulin extracted from the pancreas
AIERI: *Association Internationale des Etudes et Recherches sur l'Information* (French—International Association for Mass Communication Research)
AIEST: Association Internationale d'Experts Scientifiques du Tourisme (International Association of Scientific Experts in Tourism)
AIF: Air Intelligence Force; American Institute of France; Amphibian Imperial Forces; Army Industrial Fund; Atomic International Forum; Australian Imperial Forces
AIF: *Agencia Internacional de Fomento* (Spanish—International Development Agency); *Agenzia Internazionale Fides* (Italian—International Faith Agency—Vatican State news service); *Alliance Internationale des Femmes* (French—Women's International Alliance); *Asociación Internacional de Fomento* (Spanish—International Development Association)—IDA
AIFA: Associate of the International Faculty of Arts
AIFCS: Airborne Interception Fire-Control System
AIFD: Alaska Institute for Fisheries Development
AIFE: Associate of the Institution of Fire Engineers
AIFLD: American Institute for Free Labor Development
AIFM: Association Internationale des Femmes Médecins (International Association of Women Doctors)
AIFS: American Institute for Foreign Study
AIFT: American Institute for Foreign Trade
AIFTA: Anglo-Irish Free Trade Area
aig: all inertial guidance
AIG: Adjutant Inspector General; Association Internationale de Géodesia (International Geodesy Association)
AIGA: American Institute of Graphic Arts
AIGCM: Associate of the Incorporated Guild of Church Musicians
AIGS: Agricultural Investment Grant Scheme
AIGT: Association for the Improvement of Geometrical Teaching
aih: artificial insemination by husband
AIH: American Institute of Homeopathy; Aspen Institute of the Humanities
AIH: *Association Internationale de l'Hôtellerie* (French—International Hotel Association)
aihia: autoimmune hemolytic anemias
AIHA: American Industrial Hygiene Association
AIHC: American Industrial Health Conference
AIHED: American Institute for Human Engineering and Development
AIHS: American Irish Historical Society; Association Internationale d'Hydrologie Scientifique (International Association of Scientific Hydrology)
AIHSC: Auto Industry Highway Safety Committee
AII: Air India International
AIIA: Association of International Insurance Agents
AIIC: Army Imagery Intelligence Corps
AIID: American Institute of Interior Designers
AIIE: American Institute of Industrial Engineers
AIIMS: All-India Institute of Medical Sciences
AIInfSc: Associate of the Institute of Information Scientists
AIKD: American Institute of Kitchen Dealers
ail: aileron
AIL: Aeronautical Instruments Laboratory; Airborne Instruments Laboratory; Air Intelligence Liaison; American Institute of Laundering; American Israeli Lighthouse; Art Institute of Light; Association of International Libraries; Aviation Instrument Laboratory
A.I.L.: Associate of the Institute of Linguistics
AILA: American Institute of Landscape Architects
A.I.L.A.: Associate of the Institute of Landscape Architects
AILAS: Automatic Instrument Landing Approach System
Aileen: (Anglo-Irish—Helen)
Ailie: Aileen; Alice; Alicia; Alison; Helen; Helena
AILO: Air Intelligence Liaison Office(r)
AILS: Advanced Integrated Landing System
aim: aerotriangulation (by observation of) independent models; air intercept missile; air-isolated monolithic (circuit)
AIM: Academy Introduction Mission (USCG); Accuracy In Media; American Indian Movement; American Institute of Management; American Institute of Musicology; Army Installation Management; Association for the Integration of Management;

Australian Institute of Management
AIM: *Abstracts of Instructional Material; Airman's Information Manual*
aima: as interest may appear
AIMA: All-India Management Association
AIMBW: American Institute of Men's and Boy's Wear
AIMES: Association of Interns and Medical Students
AIMF: American International Music Fund
AIMH: Academy of International Military History
AIMILO: Army/Industrial Material Information Liaison Office(s)
AIMIT: Associate of the Institute of Musical Instrument Technicians
AIML: All-India Muslim League
AIMM: Australasian Institute of Mining and Metallurgy
AIMME: American Institute of Mining and Metallurgical Engineers
AIMMPE: American Institute of Mining, Metallurgical, and Petroleum Engineers
aimo: air mold; audibly-instructed manufacturing operations
aimp: air intercept missile package
AIMPE: Australian Institute of Marine and Power Engineers
AIMS: Advanced Intercontinental Missile System; Air Traffic Control Radar Beacon/Identification Friend or Foe/Mark XII/System; American Institute for Marxist Studies; American Institute for Mathematical Statistics; American Institute for Mental Studies; Association for International Medical Study; Automatic Industrial Management System
A.I.M.T.A.: Associate of the Institute of Municipal Treasurers and Accountants
AIMU: American Institute of Marine Underwriters
AIN: American Institute of Nutrition; Association of Interpretive Naturalists
AINA: Arctic Institute of North America
A-Ind: Anglo-Indian
AINEC: All-India Newspaper Editors' Conference
AINS: Assateague Island National Seashore (Maryland and Virginia)
ainsuf: aortic insufficiency
ain't: ungrammatical contraction—am not, are not, has not, have not, is not
AINWR: Aleutian Islands National Wildlife Refuge (Alaska)
aio: activity-interest-option (marketing factor scores)
Aio: Aioi
AIO: Air Installation Office; Americans for Indian Opportunity; Arecibo Ionospheric Observatory
aip: accident insurance policy; acute intermittent porphyria; average intravascular pressure
AIP: Aeronautical Information Publication; Aerovias Panama (Panamanian airline); American Independent Party; American Institute of Planners; American Institute of Physics; American Institute for Psychoanalysis
AIPA: American Indian Press Association
AIPC: Association Internationale des Ponts et Charpentes (International Association of Bridges and Scaffolds); *Association Internationale de Prophylaxie de la Cécité* (French—International Association for the Prevention of Blindness)
AIPCEE: *Association des Industries du Poisson de la Communauté Economique Européenne* (Association of Fishing Industries of the European Economic Community)
AIPCN: *Association Internationale Permanente des Congrés Navigation* (French—International Association of the Permanent Congress of Navigation)
AIPCR: *Association Internationale Permanente des Congrés de la Route* (French—International Association of the Permanent Congress of Routes)
AIPE: American Institute of Park Executives; American Institute of Plant Engineers
AIPG: American Institute of Professional Geologists
AIPHE: Associate of the Institution of Public Health Engineers
AIPLU: American Institute for Property and Liability Underwriters
AIPO: American Institute of Public Opinion
AIPR: American Institute of Pacific Relations
AIPs: Association of Irish Priests
AIPS: Automatic Indexing and Proofreading System
AIQ: Associate of the Institute of Quarrying
A.I.Q.S.: Associate of the Institute of Quantity Surveyors
AI & Q: Animal Inspection and Quarantine
air.: average injection rate
AIR: Action for Industrial Recycling; Air Control Products; All-India Radio; American Institute of Refrigeration; American Institute of Research; Army Intelligence Reserve; Arkansas Intermediate Reformatory
AIRA: Air Attaché
AIRB: Alabama Inspection and Rating Bureau; Arkansas Inspection and Rating Bureau
Air Capital of America: Wichita, Kansas
Air Capital of the World: Montreal, Quebéc—headquarters of the International Civil Aviation Organization and the International Air Transport Association
airbm (AIRBM): anti-intermediate-range ballistic missile
AIRCAL: Air California
Air Can: Air Canada (formerly Trans-Canada Air Lines)
Air Cav: Airmobile Cavalry
Air Cdr: Air Commander
AIRCENT: Allied Air Forces, Central Europe
AIRCEY: Air Ceylon
Air Cmdre: Air Commodore
AIRCO: Air Reduction Chemical Company
AIRCOM: Air Force Communication Complex
AIRCOMNET: Air Communications Network
AIRCOMS: Airways Communications System
AIREA: American Institute of Real Estate Appraisers
AiRepDn: Aircraft Repair Division
airew: airborne infrared early warning
AIRH: Association Internationale des Recherches Hydrauliques (International Association of Hydraulic Research)
air hp: air horsepower
AIRI: Atomic Industry Research Institute

AIRIMP: ATC/IATA (*q.q.v.*) reservations interline message procedures
Air Jam: Air Jamaica
AIRL: Aeronautical Icing Research Laboratory
Air LO: Air Liaison Officer
AIRLORDS: Airlines Load Optimization Recording and Display System
Air Mad: Air Madagascar
airmada: airplane aramada
airmiss: aircraft-in-flight collision barely missed
AirNorth: Allied Air Forces, Northern Europe
Air NZ: Air New Zealand
AIROPNET: Air Operational Network
AIRPASS: Aircraft Interception Radar and Pilots Attack Sight System
Air Res Squad: Air Reserve Squadron
AIRS: Airline Interline Reservations System
AIRSouth: Allied Air Forces, Southern Europe
airsurance: air insurance
airvan: airmobile van
AIRWORK: Airwork Atlantic Limited
AIRX: American Industrial Radium and X-Ray Society
ais: agreed industry standard
ais (AIS or Lunik III): automatic interplanetary station
AIS: Aeronautical Information Service; Air Intelligence Service; Alexander I. Solzhenitsyn; American Israeli Shipping (Zim Lines); Army Intelligence School; *Association Internationale de la Savonnerie et de la Detergence* (French—International Association of Soaps and Detergents); *Association Internationale de Sociologie* (French—International Sociology Association); Association of Iron and Steel
AI & S: Army Intelligence and Security
aisa: analytical isoelectrofocusing scanning apparatus
AISA: Associate of the Incorporated Secretaries Association
AISC: American Institute of Steel Construction
AISE: Association of Iron and Steel Engineers
AISI: American Iron and Steel Institute
AISM: *Association Internationale des Sociêtês de Microbiologie* (French—International Association of Microbiology Societies)
AISS: *Association Internationale de la Science du Sol* (French—International Solar Science Association)
ait: auto-ignition temperature
AiT: Anjuman-i-Tarikh (Historical Society of Afghanistan)
AIT: *Académie Internationale du Tourisme* (French—International Academy of Tourism); American Technology Institute; Army Intelligence Translator; Automatic Information Test
AITA: Air Industries and Transport Association
AITC: American Institute of Timber Construction
AITI: Aero Industries Technical Institute
aiu: abort interface unit; absolute iodine uptake; advanced instrumentation unit
AIU: American International Underwriters
AIU: *Alliance Israelite Universelle* (French—Universal Israelite Alliance)
aiv: accelerated inverse voltage
AIV: *Association Internationale de Volcanologie* (French—International Association of Vulcanology)
AIVAF: American-Israeli Vocal Arts Foundation
aiw: auroral intrasonic wave
AIW: Atlantic Intracoastal Waterway (Cape Cod to Florida Bay)
AIWM: American Institute of Weights and Measures
Aix: Aix-en-Provence
aj: ankle jerk; antijamming
aj: *a jini* (Czech—and others)
AJ: Air Jordan; Alma & Jonquieres (railroad); Andrew Jackson (7th U.S. President); Andrew Johnson (17th U.S. President); Associate Justice
AJ: *American Jurisprudence; Architects Journal; l'Armée Juife* (French—Jewish Army) —anti-Nazi resistance group
A.J.: Associate in Journalism
AJA: American Jewish Archives
A-JA: Anglo-Jewish Association
AJAG: Assistant Judge Advocate General
ajai: antijamming anti-interference
AJAs: Americans of Japanese Ancestry
AJASS: African Jazz Art Society Studios
AJAZ: American Jewish Alternatives to Zionism
AJB: *Association des Juifs de Belgique* (French—Association of the Jews of Belgium)
AJC: Altus Junior College; American Jewish Committee; American Jewish Congress; Anderson Junior College
A de JC: *Antes de Jesucristo* (Spanish—before Jesus Christ)
AJCC: Alternate Joint Communications Center
AJC-RC: American Jewish Committee—Records Center
AJCSA: All Japan Cotton Spinners Association
AJCW: Association of Jewish Center Workers
AJDC: American Joint Distribution Committee
AJHS: American Jewish Historical Society; Andrew Jackson High School
AJJUST: Automated Juvenile Justice System Technique
AJL: Association of Jewish Libraries; Association of Junior Leagues
AJLAC: American Jewish League Against Communism
AJNHS: Andrew Johnson National Historic Site (Greeneville, Tennessee)
AJPA: American Jewish Press Association
AJR: Association of Jewish Refugees
AJRC: American Junior Red Cross
AJRJ: Association of Japanese Residing in Japan
AJS: American Judicature Society
AJS: *American Journal of Sociology*
AJSJ: American Justinian Society of Jurists
AJY: Association for Jewish Youth
AJYB: *American Jewish Year Book*
ak: above the knee (amputation); ass kisser (underground slang)
a k: *alter kocker* (Yiddish colloquialism—old man)
AK: Alaska Coastal—Ellis Airlines; cargo ship (2-letter naval designation)
AK: *Avtomat Kalasnikov* (Russian—submachine gun)
AK 47: automatic rifle developed by the communists for use in Vietnam

aka: above-the-knee amputation
AKA: Associated Klans of America; cargo vessel, attack (3-letter coding)
Akad: Akademie (German—Academy)
Akad Nauk: Akademiya Nauk (USSR Academy of Sciences)
AKAG: Albright-Knox Art Gallery
ak amp: above-the-knee amputation
AKBS: Advanced Kinematic Bombing System
AKC: American Kennel Club; Associate King's College
AKI: American Kynol Incorporated
AKL: Algemene Kunstzijde Unie (Artist's Union); Auckland, New Zealand (airport)
AKN: King Salmon, Alaska (airport)
Akr: Akron
AKR: vehicle cargo ship (naval symbol)
AKS: general stores issue ship (3-letter symbol)
Akt: *Aktiebolag* (Swedish—limited company)
Akt Ges: *Aktiengesellschaft* (German—corporation or joint stock company)
Aktieb: *Aktiebolag* (Swedish—limited company)
Akties: *Aktieselskab* (Swedish—joint stock company)
AKV: cargo ships and aircraft ferries (3-letter symbol)
al: albumin; alcohol; axiolingual
Al: accommodation ladder; air lock; alcohol; alias; all lengths; annual leave; autograph letter
a l: *apres livraison* (French—after delivery)
aL: assumed latitude
Al: Alan; Albert; Albin; Alden; Alex(ander); Alf; Alfred; Allan; Allen; Alley; Allied; Alton; aluminum; Alva; Alvah; Alvin; Alvina; Alyn
Alo: Alonso
AL: Abraham Lincoln (16th President U.S.); Accession List(s); Acoustics Laboratory; Aeronautical Laboratory; Air Liaison; Aircraft Laboratory; Aircraft Logistics; Allegheny Airlines; Aluminum Limited; aluminum (machine shop symbol); América Latina (Portuguese or Spanish—Latin America); American League; American League (of Professional Baseball Clubs); American Legion; Angkatan Laut (Indonesian—Naval Forces); Anglo-Latin; Annual Lease; Annual Leave; Architectural League; Assumed Latitude; Astronomical League; Aviation Electronicsman
A-L: Allegheny-Ludlum; Anglo-Latin
A.L.: *Anno Lucis* (Latin—in the Year of Light)
A/L: airlift
ala: alanine; axiolabial
Ala: Alabama; Alabamian
ALA: Amalgamated Lithographers of America; American Landscape Architects; American Laryngological Association; American Latvian Association; American Legion Auxiliary; American Liberal Association; American Library Association; Assembly of the Librarians of the Americas; Authors League of America
A.L.A.: Associate in Liberal Arts; Associate of the (British) Library Association
ALAA: Associate of the Library Association of Australia
alaar: air-launched air-recoverable rocket
Alabama's Only Port: Mobile's place-name nickname
alabaster: calcite (onyx marble); variety of gypsum
ALABEL: American Library Association Board of Education for Librarianship
alabol: algorithmic and business-oriented language
ALACP: American League to Abolish Capital Punishment
alad: abnormal left axis deviation; aminolevulinic acid dehydrase
aladdin: atmospheric layer and density distribution of ions and neutrons
alag: axiolabiogingival
Al Ahr: *Al Ahram* (Arabic—The Pyramids)—Cairo's daily paper
ALA (I): Amalgamated Lithographers of America (Independent)
ALA—ISAD: American Library Association—Information Science and Automation Division
alal: axiolabiolingual
ALALC: Asociación Latinoamericana de Libre Comercio (Latin American Free Trade Association)
ALAM: Associate of the London Academy of Music
Alamo City: San Antonio, Texas
Alan: Alain; Allan; Allen
Alanders: Aland islanders
Alands: Aland Islands
alanon: alcoholics' anonymous (rehabilitation program)
Alaric Cottin: Voltaire's nickname for Frederick the Great, inferring his majesty was a poor poet but a splendid soldier
alarm.: automatic light aircraft readiness monitor
Alas.: Alaska; Alaskan; (unauthorized abbreviation)
Alas Cur: Alaska Current
Alas DST: Alaskan Daylight Saving Time
Alaska's Scenic Capital: Juneau
Alasia: Australasia
Alas ST: Alaskan Standard Time (150th meridian west of Greenwich; however, Alaskans use four time zones: 120, 135, 150, and 165 degrees west of Greenwich)
Alastair: Alexander
a la v: *a la vista* (Spanish—at sight; payable upon presentation)
alb: albumin
Alb: Albania; Albanian; Albany; Albert; Alberta; Albertan; Albion; Albalasserdam
ALBA: American Lawn Bowling Association; American Leather Belting Association
Albac: Albacete
Alban: Albania; Albanian
Alban: *Albanensis* (Latin—of St. Albans)
Albany beef: Hudson River sturgeon
ALBE: Air League of the British Empire
Albers-Schönberg disease: abnormal bone calcification resulting in spontaneous fracturing
Albert: Halbert
Albert's disease: inflammation of the bursae over the Achilles tendon
Alberto Moravia: (pseudonym—Alberto Pincherle)
Alberto Savinio: (pseudonym—Andrea de Chirico)
Albion: Britain's ancient name
albm (ALBM): air-launched ballistic missile
Alb Mus: Albany Museum (Grahamstown, South Africa)
Albn: Albanian
Albq: Albuquerque

Albr: Albrecht
Albt: Albert
Albturist: Albanian Tourism
albus: all bureaus (naval coding)
alc: alcohol; approximate lethal concentration; avian leukosis complex; axiolinguocervical
a l c: *a la carte* (French—on the menu)
ALC: Alabama Central (railroad); Associated Lutheran Charities
ALCA: American Leather Chemists Association; Associated Landscape Contractors of America
ALCAC: Airlines Communications Administrative Council
AlCan: Alaska-Canada (as in Al-Can Highway)
ALCAN: Aluminium Company of Canada
ALCC: Airborne Launch-Control Center
ALCC: *Asociación de Libre Comercio del Caribe* (Spanish—Caribbean Free Trade Association)
Alc^{de}: *Alcalde* (Spanish—justice of the peace; mayor)
alch: approach-light contact height
alchem: alchemy
alcism: alcoholism (addiction to alcohol)
ALCL: Association of London Chief Librarians
alcm (ALCM): air-launched cruise missile
ALCM: Associate of the London College of Music
ALCO: American Lava Corporation
ALCOA: Aluminum Company of America
alcoh: alcohol
alcohol: ethyl alcohol (C_2H_5OH)
alcon: all concerned
ALCOP: Alternate Command Post
alcr: aluminum crown (dental)
ald: aldolase; a later date
Ald: Aldabra; Alderman; Aldermanic
ALDA: Air Line Dispatchers Association; American Land Development Association; Australian Land Development Association
aldehyde: al(cohol) dehy(-drogenated)—dehydrogenated (oxidized) alcohol
aldep: automated layout design program
ALDEV: African Land Development
Aldm: Alderman
aldo: aldosterone
aldp: automatic language-data processing
ALDS: Apollo Launch-Data System
ALE: Association for Liberal Education
ALEA: Airline Employees Association
alec: algebraic components and coefficients
Alec(k): Alexander
Ale^{jo}: Alejandro
ALERT: Automatic Linguistic Extraction and Retrieval Technique
ALERT II: Automatic Law Enforcement Response Time (Kansas City, Missouri police file)
Ales: Alessandro
ALESCO: American Library and Educational Service Company
Aleut: Aleutian; Aleutian Islands
Aleut Cur: Aleutian Current
Aleutians: Aleutian Mountains; Aleutian islanders; Aleutian Islands
Aleut Is: Aleutian Islands
A-levels: advanced levels (of educational tests)
alex: alexandrine (verse)
Alex: Alexander; Alexandra; Alexandria
Alexa: Alexandra
Alexander of the North: Charles XII of Sweden
Alexander Serafimovich: Alexander Serafimovich Popov
Alexandrian Century: the 4th century before the Christian era when Alexander of Macedonia conquered Egypt, Persia, and India as well as encouraging Greek philosophers and poets—the 300s
Alexanders: Alexander Archipelago; Alexander cocktails
Alex City: Alexander City, Alabama
Alexes: ten-dollar bills bearing the portrait of America's first Secretary of the Treasury—Alexander Hamilton
Aleksei Maksimovich Peshkov: Maxim Gorki
alf: automatic letter facer
alf: (Swedish—river)
Alf: Alfonso; Alfred
ALF: American Life Federation; Arab Liberation Front
Alfa: code for letter A
ALFA: Anonima Lombarda Fabbrica Automobili
Alfalfa Bill: Governor William Henry Murray of Oklahoma
Alfie: Alfred
Alfo: Alfonso
ALFORD: Appalachian Laboratory for Occupational Respiratory Diseases
ALFSEA: Allied Land Forces—South-East Asia
alft: airlift
alg: algae; algal; algebra; algebraic; allergic; allergical; allergy; along; alongside; antilymphocyte globulin (ALG)
Alg: Algeria
ALG: Air Algérie; Algiers, Algeria (airport)
Alge: Algeciras
Algerian onyx: stalagmitic calcite
Algie: Algernon
alglyn: aluminum glycinate
algol: algebraically oriented language (algorithmic international language)
ALGU: Association of Land Grant Colleges and Universities
Algy: Algernon
alh: anterior lobe hormone; anterior lobe of the hypophysis
Alh: Alhambra
ALH: Australian Light Horse
ALHS: Abraham Lincoln High School
ali.: *alibi* (Latin—elsewhere)
'ali: (Arabic—high)
Ali: Alicante
ALI: American Law Institute; American Library Institute
ALIA: Royal Jordanian Airlines
Alianza: *La Alianza Federal de las Mercedes* (Spanish—Federal Alliance of Mercedes)—New Mexican organization founded by Reies Lopez Tijerina to reclaim Mexican land acquired by the United States
Alic: Alicante
alice (ALICE): automatic laundering instrument control equipment
Alice: The Alice—Alice Springs, Northern Territory, Australia; Allis-Chalmers Manufacturing Company (stock exchange slang)
Alice Markova: Alice Marks
Alick: Alexander
ALICS: Advanced Logistics Information and Control System (USAF)
alien:' alienist
'Alifax: (Cockney contraction—Halifax)
align.: alignment

alim (ALIM): air-launched interceptor missile
ALIMDA: Association of Life Insurance Medical Directors of America
Aline: Adeline
ALIS: Advanced Life Information System
alit: automatic line insulation tester
ALITALIA: Italian International Airline
A.Litt.: Associate in Letters
aljak: aluminum-jacketed coaxial cable
ALJC: Alice Lloyd Junior College
ALJH: Association of Libraries of Judaica and Hebraica (in Europe)
ALJR: *Australian Law Journal Reports*
alk: alkali
alki: alcohol; homeless alcoholic
alk phos: alkaline phosphatase
all.: above lower limit; acute lymphocytic leukemia; allergy
al.l.: *alia lectio* (Latin—a different reading)
All: Alloa
Al-L: Alsace-Lorraine
ALL: Admiralty Lines Limited
ALLA: Allied Long Lines Agency (NATO)
All-American Mirror: Upton Sinclair
allcat: all critical atmospheric turbulence (programs)
All 8va: *all'ottava* (Italian—in the octave)
Alld: Allahabad
alleg: allegation; allegoric; allegorical; allegory
Alleghenies: Allegheny Mountains
Allem: *Allemagne* (French—Germany)
allergol: allergologic(al)
allg: *allgemein* (German—general)
All H: All Hallows (Halloween)
Allie: Alice; Alison
Alligator Alley: Florida's Everglades Parkway or Tamiami Trail linking Tampa with Miami
Alligator State: sobriquet shared by Alabama, Florida, Louisiana, Mississippi, and Texas
all'ingr: *all'ingrosso* (Italian—wholesale)
Allison: Allison Division, General Motors
allit: alliteration; alliterative
ALLNAVSTAS: All Naval Stations
allo: allonym
Allo: *allegro* (Italian—lively, quickly)
alloc: allocate; allocation
allop: allophone
all'ott: *all'ottava* (Italian—an octave higher)
allp: audiolingual language programming
ALLS: Apollo Lunar Logistic Support
Alltto: *allegretto* (Italian—lively but less so than *allegro*)
allu: allude; allusion; allusively
allus: allusion
Ally Pally: Alexandra Palace in North London
alm.: alarm
Alm: Almería
ALM: American Leprosy Missions
ALM: *Antilliaanse Luchtvaart Maatschappij* (Dutch—Antillean Airline Company)
A.L.M.: *Artium Liberalium Magister* (Latin—Master of Liberal Arts)
A & LM: Arkansas & Louisiana-Missouri (railroad)
ALMA: Aircraft Locknut Manufacturers Association; Association of Literary Magazines of America
Alma Gluck: Reba Fierson
ALMAJCOM: All Major Commands
ALMC: Army Logistic Management Center
alme: acetyl-lysine methyl ester
almi: anterior lateral myocardial infarct
ALMS: Analytic Language Manipulation System
ALMT: Association of London Tailors
aln: anterior lymph node
alnico: aluminum, nickel, copper (magnet alloy also containing iron and cobalt)
alnmt: alignment
ALNP: Abraham Lincoln National Park
ALNZ: Air League of New Zealand
alo: axiolinguoclusal
Alo: Alonso
ALO: Air Liaison Office(r); Allied Liaison Office(r); Aloha Airlines; Amalgamated Lace Operatives; American Liaison Office(r); Army Liaison Office)r)
ALOA: Amalgamated Lace Operatives of America; Amalgamated Lithographers of America; Assembly of Librarians of the Americas; Associated Locksmiths of America
aloc: air lines of communication; allocation
ALOC: Air Line of Communication
ALOHA: Aloha Airlines
Aloha State: Hawaii's official nickname
ALOE: A Lady Of England—pseudonym of Charlotte Maria Tucker
alor: advanced lunar orbital rendezvous
alot: allotment
aloteen: alcoholic teenagers (rehabilitation program)
alotm: allotment
ALOTS: Airborne Lightweight Optical Tracking System
Aloys: Aloysius
Aloysha: (Russian nickname—Aleksei)—Alex; Alexander
alp.: anterior lobe (of) pituitary; assembly language program (data processing); autocode list processing
Alp: Alphen; Alpine
ALP: Air Liaison Party; Allied Liaison and Protocol; Ambulance Loading Post; American Labor Party; Australian Labour Party; Automated Learning Process; Automated Library Program
ALP: *Agence Lao Press* (French—Lao Press Agency)
ALPA: Air Line Pilot's Association
ALPAC: Automatic Language Processing Advisory Committee (National Research Council)
alpak: algebra package
ALPB: American Lutheran Publicity Bureau
ALPCA: Auto License Plate Collectors Association
Alph: Alphonse
alpha: alphabetical
ALPHA: Action League for Physically Handicapped Advancement
alphameric: alphanumeric and alphabetic-numeric
alphametic: alphabet arithmetic
alphanumeric: alphabetical-numerical
ALPHAS: Automatic Literature Processing, Handling, and Analysis System
Alpine Principality: Liechtenstein
Alpine Republic: Switzerland
ALPO: Allen Products; Amalga-

mation of Left Political Organizations; Association of Lunar and Planetary Observers

Alps: Alpine Mountains

ALPS: Advanced Linear Programming System

ALPSP: Association of Learned and Professional Society Publishers

ALPURCOMS: All-Purpose Communications System

alr.: *aliter* (Latin—otherwise)

ALR: *American Law Reports*

ALRA: Abortion Law Reform Association

ALRC: Anti-Locust Research Center

alri: airborne long-range input

ALRI: Angkatan Laut Republik Indonesia (Indonesian Navy)

ALROS: American Laryngological; Rhinological, and Otological Society

a l r p de V M: *a los reales pies de Vuestra Majestad* (Spanish—at the royal feet of Your Majesty)

ALRTF: Army Long-Range Technological Forecast

als: amyotrophic lateral sclerosis; antilymphocytic serum; autograph letter signed

ALS: Alton & Southern (railroad); American Littoral Society; Approach Light System

A.L.S.: Associate of the Linnean Society

ALSA: American Law Student Association

ALSAA: Americans of Lebanese-Syrian Ancestry for America

alsam (ALSAM): air-launched surface-attack missile

Alsat: Alsatian

ALSC: American Lumber Standards Committee

ALSCP: Appalachian Land Stabilization and Conservation Program

Al seg: *al segno* (Italian—return to the sign *:S:* and play to end or finale)

alsep (ALSEP): apollo lunar surface experiments package

Also: *Also Sprach Zarathustra* (German—Thus Spake Zarathustra)—symphonic poem by Richard Strauss

ALSO: Alex Lindsay String Orchestra (New Zealand)

alsor: air-launch sounding rocket

alss: airline system simulator

ALSS: Apollo Logistics Support System

ALST: Alaska Standard Time

alt: alternator; altimeter; altitude

Alt: alternating (light)

Alt: *Altesse* (French—Highness)

ALT: Aer Lingus (Irish Air Lines)

Alta: Alberta

ALTA: American Land Title Association; American Library Trustee Association; Association of Local Transport Airlines

altac: algebraic translator and compiler

altair (ALTAIR): ARPA (*q.v.*) long-range tracking and instrumentation radar

Altais: Altai Mountains

altan: alternate alerting network

alt. dieb.: *alternis diebus* (Latin—alternate days)

Alte Fritz: (German—Old Fritz) —Frederick the Great of Prussia

alter.: alteration

Alt Fl: alternating flashing (light)

Alt F Fl: alternating fixed and flashing (light)

Alt F Gp Fl: alternating fixed and group flashing (light)

Alt Got: Alternate Gothic

Alt Gp Occ: alternating group occulting (light)

Alt Gr Fl: alternating group flashing (light)

alt. hor.: *alternis horis* (Latin—at alternate hours)

altm: altimeter

alt. noc.: *alternis noctibus* (Latin—on alternate nights)

Alt Occ: alternating occulting (light)

Alto Perú: (Spanish—High Peru)—Bolivia

ALTPR: Association of London Theatre Press Representatives

altran: algebraic translator

altru: altruism; altruist; altruistic

ALTS: Advanced Lunar Transportation System

alt set.: altimeter setting

ALTUC: All-India Trade Union Congress

alt udk: *alt udkomne* (Dano-Norwegian—all published)

alu (ALU): arithmetic and logic unit

alue: admissible linear unbiased estimator

alum.: alumna; alumnae; alumni; alumnus; hydrated potassium aluminum sulfate

alv: alveolar

älv: (Swedish—river)

alv. adstrict.: *alvo adstricto* (Latin—bowels being constipated)

alv (ALV): avian leukemia virus(es)

alv. deject.: *alvi dejectiones* (Latin—intestinal discharges)

Alv^{o}: Alvaro

alvx: alveolectomy

alw: allowance; arch-loop whorl

Alweg: Axel Lennert Wenner-Gren (Swedish industrialist's name applied to monorailroad systems)

ALWL: Army Limited War Laboratory

Alx: Alexandria

aly: alloy

Aly: Alley

Alzheimer's disease: degenerative pre-senile brain disease

am.: aircooled motor; ammeter; amplitude modulation

a.m.: *ante meridiem* (Latin—before noon)

a & m: agricultural and mechanical; ancient and modern; architectural and mechanical; archy and mehitabel

a M (a/M): *am Main* (German—on the Main River)

Am: Amazonas; America; American; americium; myopic astigmatism (symbol)

Am.: *Amós* (Spanish—The Book of Amos)

AM: Academy of Management; Aeronaves de México (Mexican Airlines); Air Marshal; Air Medal; Air Ministry; Alexander Mackenzie (Canada's Prime Minister); Almacenes Maritimos; Alpes Maritimes (Maritime Alps); amplitude modulation; angular momentum; Arthur Meighen (Canada's tenth and twelfth Prime Minister); Aviation Medicine; Aviation Structural Mechanic; large minesweeper (naval symbol); metric angle (symbol)

A.M.: Air Mail

A.M.: *artium magister* (Latin—Master of Arts); *Ave Maria* (Latin—Hail Mary)

A-M: Addressograph-Multigraph; Alpes-Maritimes

A & M: Agricultural and Mechanical; Agricultural and Mechanical College of Texas; Ancient and Modern (hymns)

A of M: Academy of Music

a/m^2: amperes per square meter

ama: against medical advice

am^{a}: *amiga* (Spanish—female friend)

AMA: Academy of Model Aeronautics; Acoustical Materials Association; Aerospace Medical Association; Agricultural Marketing Administration; Aircraft Manufacturers Association; Air Matériel Area; Amarillo, Texas (airport); Amateur Trapshooting Association; Ambulance Manufacturers Association; American Machinery Association; American Management Association; American Maritime Association; American Marketing Association; American Medical Association; American Ministerial Association; American Monument Association; American Motel Association; American Motorcycle Association; American Municipal Association; Arena Managers Association; Automobile Manufacturers Association

A & MA: Advertising and Marketing Association

AMAA: Adhesives Manufacturers Association of America; Army Mutual Aid Association; Association of Medical Advertising Agencies

AMAB: Army Medical Advisory Board

AMACUS: Automated Microfilm Aperture Card Updating System

Amad: Amadeus

AMAE: American Museum of Atomic Energy; Association of Mexican-American Educators

AMAERF: American Medical Association Education and Research Foundation

amal: amalgam; amalgamate; amalgamation

AMAL: Aero-Medical Acceleration Laboratory; American Medical Acceleration Laboratory

amalg: amalgamated

amalgam: mercury and silver mixture

AMARC: Army Materiel Acquisition Review Committee

AMARS: Air Mobile Aircraft Refueling System; Automatic Message Address Routing System

AMAS: American Military Assistance Staff

amat: amateur

AMATC: Air Materiel Armament Test Center

amatol: ammonia & toluene (explosive)

A-matter: advance matter (written in advance of a newspaper story)

AMAUS: Aero Medical Association of the United States

AMAWA: American Medical Association Women's Auxiliary

AMAX: American Metal Climax

Amazon of the Keyboard: Teresa Carreño

amb: amber; ambient; ambulance

Amb: Ambassador

AMB: Airways Modernization Board; Associação Médica Brasileira (Brazilian Medical Association)

AMBAC: American Bosch Arma Corporation

Am Baptist: American Baptist Historical Society

Ambassador of the Air: Charles A. Lindbergh

Ambassador of Good Will: Will Rogers

AMBBA: Associated Master Barbers and Beauticians of America

Amb Brdg: Ambassador Bridge (Detroit—Windsor)

Amb Col: Ambassador College

ambel: ambiguity eliminator

Amber: *Amberes* (Spanish—Antwerp)

A.M. Bernard: Louisa M. Alcott's pseudonym she used for popular novels

Amb Ex: Ambassador Extraordinary

Amb Ex/Plen: Ambassador Extraordinary and Plenipotentiary

Am Bibl: American Bibliographic Center—Clio Press

ambig: ambiguity; ambiguous

ambish: ambition

ambit: algebraic manipulation by identity translation

ambiv: ambivalence; ambivalent

Am Bk: American Book Company

ambl: ambulatory

Amb Lib: Ambrosian Library (Milan)

Am Booksellers: American Booksellers Association

Ambridge: American Bridge (company)

AMBRL: Army Medical Biomechanical Research Laboratory

ambros: ambrosia

Ambrosian: Ambrosian Library (Milan)

ambt: ambulant

ambul: ambulation; ambulatory

amc: arthrogryposis multiplex congentia (AMC); automatic mixture control; axiomesiodistal

AMc: coastal minesweeper (3-letter naval symbol)

AMC: Aerospace Manufacturers Council; Air Mail Center; Air Materiel Command; Aircraft Manufacturers Council; Albany Medical Center; Albany Medical College; American Maritime Cases; American Mining Congress; American Mission to the Chinese; American Motors Corporation; Animal Medical Center; Appalachian Mountain Club; Army Materiel Command; Army Medical Center; Army Medical Corps; Army Missile Command; Army Mobility Command; Army Munitions Command; Association of Management Consultants

AMCA: Air Moving and Conditioning Association; American Mosquito Control Association

Am Camping: American Camping Association

AMC-ASC: Air Materiel Command—Aeronautical Systems Center

amcbh: auxiliary machine casing bulkhead

AMC & BW: Amalgamated Meat Cutters and Butcher Workmen

AMCEA: Advertising Media Credit Executives Association

Am Chem: American Chemical Society

AMCL: African Metals Corporation Limited; Association of Metropolitan Chief Librarians

AMCM: Air Materiel Command Manual

AMCMFO: Air Materiel Command Missile Field Office

AMCO: American Manufacturing Company

AMCOA: AiResearch Manufacturing Company of Arizona

AMCOM: American Stock Exchange Communications

Am Con: American Consul(ate)

AMCOS: Aldermaston Mechanized Cataloguing and Ordering System

AMCR: Air Materiel Command Regulation

AMCS: Airborne Missile Control System; Association of Military Colleges and Schools

AMCSA: Army Materiel Command Support Activity
AMCSOF: Amry Combat Surveillance Office
AMCST: Associate of the Manchester College of Science and Technology
am. cur.: *amicus curiae* (Latin—a friend at court)
amd: air movement designator; alpha-methyldopa; axiomesiodistal
AMD: Aerospace Medical Division; Air Movement Data; Army Medical Department
AMD: *Aerospace Material Document*
AMDA: Airlines Medical Directors Association
AMDB: Agricultural Machinery Development Board
a.m. D.g.: *ad majorem Dei gloriam* (Latin—to the greater glory of God)—also A.M.D.G.
AMDEA: Associated Manufacturers of Domestic Electrical Appliances
AMDEC: Associated Manufacturers of Domestic Electric Cookers
Am Dent: American Dental Association
AMDI: Associazione Medici Dentisti Italiani (Association of Italian Medical Dentists)
AmdlEvac: aeromedical evacuation
Amdoc: American Doctors (organization)
Am Doc Inst: American Documentation Institute
AMDS: Association of Military Dental Surgeons
amdt: amendment
ame: angle-measuring equipment
AME: African Methodist Episcopal
A.M.E.: Advanced Master of Education
AMEC: Airframe Manufacturing Equipment Committee
amecd: antimechanized
AMedD: Army Medical Department
AMedS: Army Medical Service
AMEE: Admiralty Marine Engineering Establishment
Ameer Baraka: Lee Roy Jones
AMEG: Association for Measurement and Evaluation in Guidance
AMEIC: Associate Member of the Engineering Institute of Canada
AMEL: Aero Medical Equipment Laboratory
amelior: amelioration
Am Elsevier: American Elsevier Publishing Company
AMEM: African Methodist Episcopal Mission
Am Emb: American Ambassador; American Embassy
AMEME: Association of Mining, Electrical, and Mechanical Engineers
AMEMIC: Association of Mill and Elevator Mutual Insurance Companies
amend.: amendment(s)
Am Engr: *American Engineer*
Amer: America; American
AMERADC: Army Mobility Equipment Research and Development Center
AMERICAL: Americans in New Caledonia (Army division)
Amerind: American & Indian (American Indian or Eskimo)
Amer Ind: American Indian
Amerindians: American Indians
Ameringlish: American English
Amer Men Sci: *American Men of Science*
AmerSp: American Spanish
Amer Std: American Standard
Amer Trauma Soc: American Trauma Society
AMeS: American Meteorological Society
AMES: Association of Marine Engineering Schools
AMETA: Army Management Engineering Training Agency
AMETS: Artillery Meteorological System
AMEWA: Associated Manufacturers of Electric Wiring Accessories
Amex: American Stock Exchange
AMEX: *Agencia Mexicana de Noticias* (Mexican News Agency)
Amexco: American Express Company
AMEZ: African Methodist Episcopal Zion
AMEZC: African Methodist Episcopal Zionist Church
amf (AMF): airmail facility
AMF: Air Material Force; American Machine and Foundry; Arctic Marine Freighters; Australian Marine Force
AMF(A): Allied Mobile Force (Air)—NATO
Am Feed: American Feed Manufacturers Association
AMFGC: Association of Midwest Fish and Game Commissioners
AMFIE: Association of Mutual Fire Insurance Engineers
AMFIS: Automatic Microfilm Information System
AMF(L): Allied Mobile Force (Land)—NATO
am/fm: amplitude modulation/frequency modulation
Am Friends: American Friends Service Committee
amg: automatic magnetic guidance; axiomesiogingival
AMG: Aircraft Machine Gunner; Albertus Magnus Guild; Allied Military Government
Am Geophysical: American Geophysical Union
AMGNY: Associated Musicians of Greater New York
AMGOT: Allied Military Government
amh: astigmatism with myopia predominating; automated medical history
Amh: Amharic
AMHA: American Motor Hotel Association
AMHCI: Associate Member of the Hotel and Catering Institute
Am Heart: American Heart Association
AMHIS: American Marine Hull Insurance Syndicate
AMHS: Alaska Marine Highway Authority; American Material Handling Society
AMHT: Automated Multiphasic Health Testing
ami: acute myocardial infarction; advanced manned interceptor; air mileage indicator; amitriptyline; axiomesioincisal
AMI: Advanced Manned Interceptor; American Meat Institute; American Military Institute; American Museum of Immigration; American Mushroom Institute; Association of Medical Illustrators
AMI: *Aeronautica Militare Italiana* (Italian Air Force)
AMIA: American Metal Importers Association; American Mutual Insurance Alliance
AMIADB: Army Member—Inter-American Defense Board
AMIAE: Associate Member of the Institute of Automobile Engineers
AMIAMA: Associate Member of the Incorporated Advertising Managers Association

AMIC: Aerospace Materials Information Center
AMICA: Automobile Mutual Insurance Company of America
AMICE: Associate Member of the Institution of Civil Engineers
AMICI: Association Mondiale des Interprètes de Conférences International
AMICO: American Measuring Instrument Company
AMICOM: Army Missile Command
Ami des Hommes: (French—Friend of Mankind)—Marquis de Mirabeau's nickname
Ami du Peuple: (French—Friend of the People)—nickname of Jean Paul Marat; title of the revolutionary journal he edited
AMIGOS: Americans Interested In Giving Others a Start
AMII: Association of Musical Instrument Industries
AMILO: Army-Industry Materiel Information Liaison Office
AMIN: Advertising and Marketing International Network
Am Ind: American Indian
AMINOIL: American Independent Oil (company)
Am Inst: American Institute
AMIOP: Associate Member of the Institute of Printing
AMIPA: Associate Member of the Institute of Practitioners in Advertising
Amirantes: Amirante Islands
AMIS: Aircraft Movement Information Section
AMJ: *Assemblée Mondiale de la Jeunesse* (French—World Assembly of Youth)
Am Jour Sci: *American Journal of Science*
aml: acute monocytic leukemia; acute myelocytic leukemia; acute myoblastic leukemia
aml (AML): amplitude-modulated link
AML: Admiralty Materials Laboratory; Aeromedical Laboratory; American Mail Line; Applied Mathematics Laboratory
AMLC: Aerospace Medical Laboratory (USAF)
Am Lib Dir: American Library Directory
Am-Lib(s): Americo-Liberian(s)
amls: antimouse lymphocyte serum
AMLS: Master of Arts in Library Science
amm: agnogenic myeloid metaplasia; ammonia; ammunition; anti-missile missile (AMM)
AMM: Air Mining Mission; Amman, Jordan (airport); Anti-Missile Missile; Associated Millinery Men; Association Medicale Mondiale (World Medical Association); Aviation Machinist's Mate
AM & M: Applied Mathematics and Mechanics
AMMA: American Museum of Marine Archeology
Am Mach: *American Machinist*
Am Management: American Management Association
Am Math Soc: American Mathematical Society
ammeter: amperemeter (current-measuring instrument)
AMMI: American Merchant Marine Institute
AMMIS: Aircraft Maintenance Manpower Information System (USAF)
amml: acute myelomonocytic leukemia
AMMLA: American Merchant Marine Library Association
ammo: ammunition
Ammo: American Motors (stock exchange slang)
ammon: ammonia
Ammon: Ammonite
Ammonia King: Edward Mallinckrodt
ammonia water: ammonium hydroxide (NH_4OH)
AMMPE: American Mining, Metallurgical, and Petroleum Engineers
amn: airman
AMNH: American Museum of Natural History
amnip: adaptive man-machine nonarithmetic information processing
AmnM: Airman's Medal
AMNZIE: Associate Member of the New Zealand Institution of Engineers
amo: axiomesio-occlusal
amo: *amigo* (Spanish—male friend)
amo (AMO): air mail only; alternant molecular orbit
AMO: Advance Material Order; Aircraft Material Officer; Air Ministry Order; American Motors (stock exchange symbol)
amob: automatic meterological oceanographic buoy
AMOCO: American Oil Company
amol: acute monocytic leukemia
amor: amorphous
AMORC: Ancient Mystic Order Rosae Crusis (Rosicrucian Order)
amorph: amorphous
AMOS: Automatic Meterological Observation Station
Amos and Andy: Freeman F. Gosden and Charles J. Correll
amp: ampere; amplitude; ampule
amp: acid mucopolysaccharide; adenosine monophosphate (hormonal chemical); amperage; ampere; amphetamine; ampicillin; amplification; amplifier; amplitude; ampule; amputation; average mean pressure
AMP: Air Mail Pioneers; American Museum of Photography; Army Mine Planter; Aurora Memorial Park (Philippines); Aviation Modernization Program
AMPA: Associate of the Master Photographers Association
AMPAC: American Medical Political Action Committee
AMPAS: Academy of Motion Picture Arts and Sciences
AMPC: Automatic Message Processing Center
AMPCO: Associated Missile Products Corporation; Association of Major Power Consumers of Ontario
Am Peace: American Peace Society
ampersand: and per se and
Ampersand: Ampersand Press (Princeton)
Ampersand NYC: Ampersand Press (New York City)
AMPFTA: American Military Precision Flying Teams Association
amph: amphibian; amphibious; amphimict; amphoric
Amph: Amphibia
AMPH: Association of Management in Public Health
amphet: amphetamine (stimulant)
amphetamine: alphamethylpenethylamine
amphets: amphetamines
amphib: amphibia(n); amphibious
amphibex: amphibious exercise
amphig: amphigoric; amphigorical; amphigorist; amphigory
Am Philos Soc: American Philosophical Society
amp hr: ampere hour

AMPI: Associated Milk Producers, Incorporated; Associated Music Publishers, Incorporated
Ampico: American Piano Company
ampl: amplifier
ampl: *ampliata* (Italian—enlarged); *amplus* (Latin—large)
ampr: advanced multipurpose radar; automatic manifold pressure regulator
AMPR: Aeronautical Manufactures Planning Report; Airframe Manufacturers Planning Report
amps: amperes; ampules
AMPS: Accrued Military Pay System; American Metered Postage Society; Army Mine Planter Service; Army Motion Picture Service; Associated Music Publishers; Automatic Message Processing System
AMPSS: Advanced Manned Precision Strike System
AMPTP: Association of Motion Picture and Television Producers
amp-turns: ampere-turns
Am Public Health: American Public Health Association
ampul.: *ampulla* (Latin—ampule)
AMQ: American Medical Qualification
AMR: Advanced Material Request; Airman Military Record; American Airlines (stock exchange symbol); Atlantic Missile Range
A.M.R.: Master of Arts in Research
AMRA: American Medical Records Association; Army Materials Research Agency
AMRAC: Anti-Missile Research Advisory Council
Am Radio: American Radio Relay League
AMRC: Advanced Metals Research Corporation; Army Mathematics Research Center; Automotive Market Research Council
AMRCA: American Miniature Racing Car Association
AMR & DL: Air Mobility Research and Development Laboratory (USA)
Am Res: American Research Council
AM & RF: African Medical and Research Foundation
AMRINA: Associate Member of the Royal Institution of Naval Architects
Amrit: Amritsar
AMRL: Aerospace Medical Research Laboratories; Army Medical Research Laboratory
AMRNL: Army Medical Research and Nutrition Laboratory
AMRO: Association of Medical Record Officers
amrpd: applied manufacturing research and process development
AMRS: Air Ministry Radio Station; American Moral Reform Society
ams: aggravated in military service; auditory memory span; automated multiphasic screening
AMs: auxiliary motor minesweeper
AMS: Administration Management Society; Aeronautical Material Specification; Agricultural Marketing Service; American Mathematical Society; American Meteor Society; American Meteorological Society; American Microscopical Society; American Mineral Spirits; American Museum of Safety; American Musicological Society; Army Map Service; Army Medical Service; Association of Messenger Services; Association of Museum Stores
amsa (AMSA): advanced manned strategic aircraft
AMSA: American Metal Stamping Association
amsam: anti-missile surface-to-air-missile
Am Sam: American Samoa
AMSC: Army Medical Specialist Corps
Am School: American Scholar
AMSCO: American Mineral Spirits Company; American Sterilizer Company
AMSE: Associate Member of the Society of Engineers
amsef: anti-mine-sweeping explosive float
AMSGA: Association of Manufacturers And Suppliers for the Graphic Arts
AMSH: Association for Moral and Social Hygiene
amsl: above mean sea level
AMSMH: Association of Medical Superintendents of Mental Hospitals
AMSO: Air Member for Supply and Organisation (RAF)
AMSOC: American Miscellaneous Society
Am Soc Afr Cult: American Society of African Culture
Am Soc HRAC Eng: American Society of Heating, Refrigerating, and Air-Conditioning Engineers
Am Soc Metals: American Society for Metals
Am Soc Not: American Society of Notaries
Am Soc Tool and Mfg Eng: American Society of Tool and Manufacturing Engineers
AMSP: Army Master Study Program
AMSq: Avionics Maintenance Squadron (USAF)
a *ms* s: autographed manuscript signed
AMSS: Advanced Meterological Sounding System
AMSSFG: Association of Manufacturers of Small Switch and Fuse Gear
a *mss* s: autographed manuscripts signed
Amst: Amsterdam
Amstelodamun: (Latin— Amsterdam)
Amstelredamun: (Latin—Amsterdam)
AMSUS: Association of Military Surgeons of the United States
amt: alpha-methyltryrosine; amethopterin; amount; amphetamine
AMT: Academy of Medicine, Toronto, Canada; Aerial Mail Terminal; American Medical Technologists; Astrograph Mean Time
A.M.T.: Associate in Mechanical Technology; Associate in Medical Technology; Master of Arts—Teaching
amta: airborne moving target attack
amtank: amphibious tank
AMTC: Airframe Manufacturing Tooling Committee
A.M.T.C.: Art Master's Teaching Certificate
AMTCL: Association for Machine Translation and Computational Linguistics
AMTDA: Agricultural Machinery and Tractor Dealers Association
Am Tech Soc: American Technical Society
Am Tel & Tel: American Telephone and Telegraph
amti: airborne moving target in-

dicator
Amtorg: Amerikanskaya Torgovlya (Russian-American Trading Company)
amtrac: amphibious tractor
AMTPI: Associate Member of the Town Planning Institute (UK)
Amtrak: (American railroad tracks)—the National Railway Passenger Corporation
amtran: automatic mathematical translator
amt(s): amphetamine(s)
AMTS: Associate Member of the Television Society
amu: air mileage unit; air mission unit; astronaut maneuvering unit; atomic mass unit
AMU: Alaska Methodist University; American Malacological Union; American Marksmanship Unit; Army Marksmanship Unit; Associated Midwestern Universities; Association of Marine Underwriters
AMUA: Associate in Music—University of Adelaide
AMURT: Anada Marga Universal Relief Team (India)
A.Mus.: Associate in Music
A.Mus.A.: Associate in Music—Australia
A.Mus.C.: Associate in Music—Canada
A.Mus.L.C.M.: Associate in Music—London College of Music
A.Mus.N.Z.: Associate in Music—New Zealand
A.Mus.S.A.: Associate in Music—South Africa
A.Mus.T.C.L.: Associate in Music—Trinity College of Music—London
amv: alfalca-mosaic virus; avian myeloblastitis virus
AMV: *Association Mondiale Vétérinaire* (Franch—World Veterinary Association)
AMVAP: Associate Manufacturers of Veterinary and Agricultural Products
AMVERS: Automated Merchant Vessel Reporting System
AMVETS: American Veterans (World War II, Korea, Vietnam)
AMW: Association of Married Women
AMWA: American Medical Women's Association
Am West: American West Publishing Company
AMWM: Association of Manufacturers of Woodworking Machinery
amy: amytal (barbituate depressant and sedative)
Amy: Amelia; Amoy, China
an.: airman; anode; annual
an.: *anno* (Latin—year); *ante* (Latin—before)
an': and
a/n: acidic and neutral
An: Annam; Annamese
A_n: normal atmosphere
AN: Acid Number; Aerodynamic Note; Air Force-Navy; Airmail Notice; Air Navigation; Air Navigator; Air Reduction (stock exchange symbol); Anglo-Norman; Apalachicola Northern (railroad); Army-Navy; net laying vessel (naval symbol)
A.N.: Associate in Nursing
A & N: Army and Navy
AN-22: Antonov 22 (Soviet super transport plane)
ana: anesthesia; anesthesiac
ana (ANA): antinuclear antibodies
Ana: Anita
ANA: Air Force-Navy Aeronautical; All Nippon Airways; American Nature Association; American Neurological Association; American Newspaper Association; American Numismatic Association; American Nurses' Association; Army-Navy Aeronautical; Asociación Nacional Automovilista (National Automobile Association); Association of National Advertisers; Australian National Airways
ANA: *Automotive News Almanac*
ANAAS: Australian and New Zealand Association for the Advancement of Science
anab: anabasis
anac: anachronism; anachronistic
anacol: anacoluthon
anacom: analog computer
anacreon: anacreontic(s); anacreontist
anacru: anacrusis
anaesth: anaesthesia; anaesthetic(s); anaesthesiologist; anaesthesiology
ANAF: Army, Navy, Air Force
anag: anagram; anagrammatic(al) (ly); anagramist; anagrams
anal: analogy; analysis; analytical
analg: analgesic
anal psychol: analytical psychology
analyt: analytical
anap: agglutination negative, absorption positive
ANAP: *Asociación Nacional de los Agricultores Pequeños* (Spanish—National Association of Small Farmers)
ANAPO: *Alianza Nacional Popular* (Spanish—Popular National Alliance)—fusion of Columbia's conservative and liberal political forces
ANARC: Association of North American Radio Clubs
anarch: anarchist; anarchism; anarchy
Anarchist Protagonist: Michael Bakunin
ANARE: Australian National Antarctic Research Expeditions
anat: anatomical; anatomist; anatomy
anath: anathema; anathematize
Anatole France: Jacques Anatole François Thibault
Anatolia: Asia Minor
anatran: analog translator
anav: area navigation
ANB: Army-Navy-British Standard
anbs (ANBS): armed nuclear bombardment satellite
ANB & TC: American National Bank and Trust Company
anc: all numbers calling; ancient
Anc: Ancona
ANC: African National Council; Air Force-Navy-Civil; American News Company; Arlington National Cemetery; Army and Navy Civil Committee on Aircraft; Army Nurse Corps
ANCA: Allied Naval Communications Agency; American National Cattlemen's Association
ANCAP: Administratión Nacional de Combustibles Alcohol y Portland
ANCAR: Australian National Committee for Antarctic Research
ancc: anodal closure contraction
anch: anchorage
Anco: Ancohuma
ANCO: Andersen-Collingwood (tanker service)
ancr: aircraft not combat ready
ANCs: African National Congress members
ANCS: American Numerical Control Society
ANCUN: Australian National

Committee for the United Nations
ANCXF: Allied Naval Commander Expeditionary Force
And: Andalucía; Andaman Islands
and: *andante* (Italian—of moderate speed)
AND: Army-Navy Design
andalusite: aluminum silicate
Andamans: Andaman islanders; Andaman Islands
ANDB: Air Navigation Development Board
Andes: Andes Mountains
And I: Andaman Islands
Andie: Andrew
Andno: *andantino* (Italian—slower than andante)
Ando: Andorra; Andorran
Andrea del Sarto: Andrea Domenico d'Agnolo di Francesco
Andreaofs: Andreaof Islands
Andre Maurois: Emile Salomon Wilhelm Herzog
Andrew Furuseth: Anders Andreassen
Andrews: twenty-dollar bills bearing the portrait of President Andrew Jackson
andro: androsterone
Andryusha: (Russian nickname—Andrei)—Andrew; Andy
Ands: Andreas
andte: anodal duration tetanus
Andte: *andante* (Italian—of moderate speed)
Andy: Andrew
anec: anecdotal; anecdote(s)
Aneda: (Latin—Edinburgh)
ANEDA: *Association Nationale d'Etudes pour la Documentation Automatique* (National Association for Automatic Documentation Studies)
anes: anesthesia; anesthesiologist; anesthesiology; anesthetician; anesthetic(s)
anesth: anesthetic
anesthesiol: anesthesiology
an. ex: anode excitation
anf: anchored filament; antinuclear factor(s)
ANF: American Nurses; Foundation; Atlantic Nuclear Force (NATO)
anfe (ANFE): aircraft not fully equipped
ANFIA: *Associazione Nazionale fra le Industrie Automobilistiche* (Italian—National Association of Automobile Industries)
anfo: ammonium nitrate fuel oil (explosive)
ang: angiogram; angle; angular
ang: *angaende* (Danish, Norwegian, Swedish—concerning)
Ang: Angel (phonograph records); Anglo-; Angola
ANG: Air Force-Navy-Army Guided Missiles; Air National Guard; American Newspaper Guild; Australian New Guinea
ANGAU: Australian New Guinea Administrative Unit
Angela: Angelica
Angel of the Battlefield: Clara Barton
Angelenos: natives of Los Angeles, California
Angelic Doctor: Thomas Aquinas
Ångfart: *Ångfartygas* (Swedish—steamship company)
Angie: Angela; Angelina; Angeline
angiol: angiology
angkor: (Khmer—city)
Angkor Thom: (Khmer—Great City)
Angkor Vat: (Khmer—Temple City)
Angl: Anglican
Angl: *Angleterre* (French—England)
Anglic: Anglican; Anglicism
ANGLICO: Air and Naval Gunfire Liaison Company
Anglo-Afg: Anglo-Afghan
Anglo-Afr: Anglo-African
Anglo-Amer: Anglo-American
Anglo-Ant: Anglo-Antarctic(an); Anglo-Antillean
Anglo-Arab: Anglo-Arabian
Anglo-Arg: Anglo-Argentine
Anglo-Art: Anglo-Arctic
Anglo-Aus: Anglo-Australian; Anglo-Austrian
Anglo-Bah: Anglo-Bahaman
Anglo-Barb: Anglo-Barbadian
Anglo-Bas: Anglo-Basque
Anglo-Bel: Anglo-Belizian
Anglo-Belg: Anglo-Belgian
Anglo-Bhu: Anglo-Bhutanese
Anglo-Bol: Anglo-Bolivian
Anglo-Bots: Anglo-Botswana
Anglo-Braz: Anglo-Brazilian
Anglo-Bul: Anglo-Bulgarian
Anglo-Bur: Anglo-Burman; Anglo-Burundian
Anglo-CA: Anglo-Central American
Anglo-Cam: Anglo-Cameroonian
Anglo-Can(ad): Anglo-Canadian
Anglo-Cat: Anglo-Catalan
Anglo-Cath: Anglo-Catholic
Anglo-Cey: Anglo-Ceylonese
Anglo-Chi: Anglo-Chinese
Anglo-Chil: Anglo-Chilean
Anglo-Col: Anglo-Colombian
Anglo-Cub: Anglo-Cuban
Anglo-Cyp: Anglo-Cypriot
Anglo-Czech: Anglo-Czechoslovak(ian)
Anglo-Dah: Anglo-Dahomean
Anglo-Dan: Anglo-Danish
Anglo-Du: Anglo-Dutch
Anglo-Ecu: Anglo-Ecuadorean
Anglo-Egypt: Anglo-Egyptian
Anglo-Epis: Anglo-Episcopal(ian)
Anglo-Ethio: Anglo-Ethiopian
Anglo-Fin: Anglo-Finnish
Anglo-Fr: Anglo-French
Anglo-Gam: Anglo-Gambian
Anglo-Ger: Anglo-German
Anglo-Gr: Anglo-Greek
Anglo-Guy: Anglo-Guyanese
Anglo-Hond: Anglo-Honduran
Anglo-Hung: Anglo-Hungarian
Anglo-Ice: Anglo-Icelandic
Anglo-Ind: Anglo-Indian
Anglo-Indo: Anglo-Indonesian
Anglo-Ir: Anglo-Iranian; Anglo-Iraqi; Anglo-Irish
Anglo-Isr: Anglo-Israeli
Anglo-Ital: Anglo-Italian
Anglo-Jam: Anglo-Jamacian
Anglo-Jap: Anglo-Japanese
Anglo-Jew: Anglo-Jewish
Anglo-Jor: Anglo-Jordanian
Anglo-Ken: Anglo-Kenyan
Anglo-Kuw: Anglo-Kuwaiti
Anglo-Lat: Anglo-Latin
Anglo-Mal: Anglo-Malawian; Anglo-Malaysian; Anglo-Maltese
Anglo-Mald: Anglo-Maldivian
Anglo-Mex: Anglo-Mexican
Anglo-Nep: Anglo-Nepalese
Anglo-Nig: Anglo-Nigerian
Anglo-Nor: Anglo-Norwegian
Anglo-Norm: Anglo-Norman
Anglo-NZ: Anglo-New Zealand
Anglo-Pak: Anglo-Pakistani
Anglo-Para: Anglo-Paraguayan
Anglo-Per: Anglo-Persian; Anglo-Peruvian
Anglo-Pol: Anglo-Polish
Anglo-Port: Anglo-Portuguese
Anglo-Rho: Anglo-Rhodesian
Anglo-Rom: Anglo-Romanian
Anglo-Rus(s): Anglo-Russian
Anglo(s): Anglo-Saxon(s)
Anglo-SA: Anglo-South African; Anglo-South American
Anglo-Sam: Anglo-Samoan
Anglo-Scot: Anglo-Scottish
Anglo-SL: Anglo-Sierra Leonean
Anglo-Som: Anglo-Somali
Anglo-Sov: Anglo-Soviet
Anglo-Span: Anglo-Spanish
Anglo-Sud: Anglo-Sudanese
Angl-Swe: Anglo-Swedish
Anglo-Swi: Anglo-Swiss
Anglo-Tanz: Anglo-Tanzanian

Anglo-Tob: Anglo-Tobagan
Anglo-Togo: Anglo-Togolese
Anglo-Ton: Anglo-Tongan
Anglo-Trin: Anglo-Trinidadian
Anglo-Turk: Anglo-Turkish
Anglo-Ugan: Anglo-Ugandan
Anglo-Uru: Anglo-Uruguayan
Anglo-Ven: Anglo-Venezuelan
Anglo-W: Anglo-Welsh
Anglo-Yem: Anglo-Yemini
Anglo-Yugo: Anglo-Yugoslav(ian)
Anglo-Zamb: Anglo-Zambian
Angola: Portuguese West Africa
Angry Eagle of Aviation: General William (Billy) Mitchell
Ang-Sax: Anglo-Saxon
Angus: Aeneas
ANGUS: Air National Guard of the United States
anh: anhydrite; anhydrous
Anh: *Anhang* (German—appendix)
ANHA: American Nursing Home Association
anhed: anhedral
anhic: anhydritic
ANHS: Adams National Historic Site
anhyd: anhydrous
ani: automatic number identification
ani: *atmosphère normale internationale* (French—international normal atmosphere)
ANI: Agencia Nacional de Informaciones (Uruguayan press service); Army-Navy-Industry
ANI: *Agéncia Nacional de Informaçao* (Portuguese—National Information Agency); *Agencia Nacional de Informationes* (Spanish—National Information Agency)
A & NI: Andaman and Nicobar Islands
ANIB: Australian News and Information Bureau
ANICA: *Associazione Nazionale Industrie Cinematografiche e Affini* (Italian—National Association of Cinematographic and Related Industries)
ANICO: American National Insurance Company
anil: aniline
aniline: phenyl amine
anim: animal; animate; animism
anim: *animato* (Italian—animated)
ANIM: Association of Nuclear Instrument Manufacturers
animad: animadversion
ANIP: Army-Navy Instrumentation Program
ank: ankle
ank: *ankomen* (Dutch—arrival); *ankomst* (Danish—arrival); *ankunft* (German—arrival)
Ank: Ankara
ANK: Ankara, Turkey (airport)
Ankerplatz: *Ankerplatz der Freude* (German—Anchorage of Joy)—St Pauli's Reeperbahn section of Hamburg featuring naughty nightlife
anl: annoyance level (aircraft noise); automatic noise limiter
ANL: Argonne National Laboratory; Australian National Library; Australian National Line; net-laying ship (naval symbol)
ANLCA: Alaska Native Land Claims Act
anld: annealed
an. lt: anchor light
anlys: analysis
anm: *anmaerkning* (Danish, Norwegian, Swedish—footnote, note, remark, observation)
Anm: *Anmerkung* (German—footnote; note)
ANM: *Admiralty Notices to Mariners*
ANMCC: Alternate National Military Command Center
ann: announce(ment); announcer; annual(ly); annuity; annuciator
ann.: *anni* (Latin—years); *anno* (Latin—year)
Ann: Anastasia; Angela; Angelina; Angeline; Anita; Anna; Annabelle; Anne; Annelida; Annetta; Annette; Annie; Antoinette
Ann: *Annalen* (German—annals); *Annales* (French—annals); *Annali* (Italian—annals)
Anna: Annabella; Annapolis, Maryland; Annette
ANNA: Army, Navy, NASA, Air Force
Anna Akhmatova: Anna Andreyevna Gorenko
Anna O: Bertha Pappenheim—feminist crusader against white slavery and first person to be psychoanalyzed
Annapolis of the Air: Pensacola, Florida
Ann Arbor Pub: Ann Arbor Publishers
Anna Seghers: (pseudonym—Netty Radvanyi)
Annng: Annapolis graduate
Annie's Town: Anniston, Alabama
anniv.: *anniversarium* (Latin—anniversary)
annot.: annotated; annotation
Ann Rept: Annual Report
annu: annual; annuale; annuario
annuit: annuitant
annul.: annulment
Annunc: Annunciation
ANO: Air Navigation Office; Anti-Narcotics Office
anoc: anodal opening contraction
anod.: anodize
anom: anomia; anomiac; anomiacal
Anon.: *anonymous* (Latin—nameless)
anorex: anorexia nervosa
anorm: aircraft not operationally ready—maintenance
anors: aircraft not operationally ready—supplies
anot: annotate
anov: analysis of variance
anova: analysis of variance
anp: aircraft nuclear propulsion
A-np: A-norprogesterone
ANP: Aberdare National Park (Kenya); Acadia National Park (Maine); Aircraft Nuclear-propulsion Program; Akan National Park (Japan); Albert National Park (Zaire); Angkor National Park (Cambodia); Arusha National Park (Tanzania); Associated Negro Press; Awash National Park (Ethiopia)
ANP: *Administración Nacional de Puertos* (Colombia's National Administration of Ports); *Algemeen Nederlandsch Persbureau* (Netherlands Press Bureau)
ANPA: American Newspaper Publishers Association
ANPI: *Associazione Nazionale Partigiani d'Italia* (National Association of Italian Partisans)
ANPO: Aircraft Nuclear Propulsion Office
anpod: antenna-positioning device
ANPP: Aircraft Nuclear Propulsion Program
ANPPF: Aircraft Nuclear Power Plant Facility
ANPPIA: *Associazione Nazionale Perseguitati Politici Italiani Antifascisti* (National Association of Italian Antifascist Political Victims)
ANPS: American Nail Producers Society
anpt: aeronautical national taper pipe threads

anr: another
ANR: American Natural Resources (formerly American Natural Gas); American Newspaper Representatives; Antwerp, Belgium (airport)
ANR: *Asociación Nacional Republicana* (Spanish—National Republican Association)—Paraguay's Colorado Party
ANRA: Amistad National Recreation Area (Texas); Arbuckle National Recreation Area (Oklahoma)
anrac: aids navigation radio control
ANRC: American National Red Cross; Animal Nutrition Research Council; Australian National Research Council
ANRT: *Association Nationale de la Recherche Technique* (National Association of Technical Research)
ans: answer; answered; answering; autograph note signed; autonomic nervous system
Ans: Anselm; Anselmo
ANS: Agencia Noticiosa Saporiti (Argentine press service); American Name Society; American Nuclear Society; American Numismatic Society; American Nutrition Society; Army Newspaper Serivce; Army News Service; Army Nursing Service; Astronomical Netherlands Satellite (first joint United States-Netherlands satellite)
ansa: aminonapthosulfonic acid; automatic new structure alert
ANSA: *Agenzia Nazionale Stampa Associata* (Italian—National Press Association Agency)
A(N)SA: American (National) Standards Association
ansam (ANSAM): antimissile surface-to-air missile
ANSCO: Anthony and Scovill (New York camera and film manufacturer who merged with AGFA to become Agfa-Ansco and more recently GAF—General Aniline and Film Corporation)
ANSETT: Ansett Airways
ANSETT-ANA: Ansett Australian National Airways
ANSI: American National Standards Institute
ANSIC: Aerospace Nuclear Safety Information Center
ANSL: Australian National Standards Laboratory
ANSP: Academy of Natural Sciences of Philadelphia
ANSS: American Nature Study Society
answ (ANSW): antinuclear submarine warfare
ant.: antenna(s); anterior; anticipated; antilog; antilogarithm; antiquarian; antique; antiquities; antiquity; antonym
ant.: *antico* (Italian—antique); *antiporta* (Italian—half-title)
Ant: Antigua; Antillea—West Indian Federation; Antillean; Antilles; Antwerp
ANT: Australian Northern Territory
ANTA: American National Theater and Academy; Australian National Travel Association
antag: antagonistic
Antarc: Antarctic; Antarctica
Antarc O: Antarctic Ocean
ant. ax line: anterior axillary line
Ant & Cl: *Antony and Cleopatra*
Ant Cur: Antilles Current
ant. d: anterior diameter
ante: (Latin—before)
antec: annual technical conference
ANTELCO: Administración Nacional de Telecomunicaciones (Paraguayan National Telecommunication Administration)
Antelope State: Nebraska
antennafier: antenna + radiofrequency amplifier
antennamitter: antenna + transmitter
antennaverter: antenna + converter
Antf: Antofagasta
Ant f: Antillean florin (guilder)
anthol: anthological(ly); anthologist, anthologize, anthology
Anthony Hope: nom de plume of Sir Anthony Hope Hawkins
Anthracite City: Scranton, Pennsylvania
anthro: anthropogeography; anthropological; anthropologist; anthropology; anthropometry; anthropomorphism; anthropophagy
anthrop: anthropology
anthropom: anthropometry
Anthroposophic: Anthroposophic Press
anticli: anticlimactic(al)(ly); anticlimax; anticlinal; anticline; anticlinorium
Anthy: Anthony
antifreeze: grain or methyl alcohol (CH_3OH) mixture
Antig: Antigua
Antilles: Greater and Lesser Antilles comprising most of the West Indies
antilog: antilogarithm
antichlor: anti + chlorine; antichloristic
antidis: antidisestablishmentarianism
antimag: antimagnetic
Antioch: Antioch Press
antiphon: antiphonal(ly)
antipol: antipollutant; antipollution
antiporn: antipornographic; antipornography
antiq: antiquarian, antique; antiquities; antiquity
antiquar: antiquarian
Antiques: Antiques Publications
antisex: antisexual
ant. jentac.: *ante jentaculum* (Latin—before breakfast)
Ant Lat: Antique Latin
ant. ld: antique laid
Anto: Antofagasta
Ant^o: Antonio
anton: antonym
ant. pit.: anterior pituitary
antr: apparent net transfer rate
Antr: Antrim
ant. sup. spine: anterior superior spine
antu: alpha-naphthyl-thiourea (rat poison)
Antuér: *Antuérpia* (Portuguese—Antwerp)
Antverpia: (Latin—Antwerp)
Antw: *Antwerpen* (Dutch, Flemish, German—Antwerp)
ant. wo: antique wove
ANU: St. John's, Antigua; Australia National University
Anver: *Anversa* (Italian—Antwerp)
ANWG: Apollo Navigation Working Group (NASA)
ANWR: Agassiz National Wildlife Refuge (Minnesota); Aransas NWR (Texas); Arrowhead NWR (North Dakota); Audubon NWR (North Dakota)
anx.: annex
Anx: Annex (postal place-name abbreviation)
Anz: Anzania (African name for South Africa)
ANZ: Air New Zealand
ANZAAS: Australian and New Zealand Association for the Advancement of Science
ANZAC: Australia and New Zealand Army Corps
ANZAM: Australia, New Zealand, and Malaysia (defense

pact)
Anzania: (black African—South Africa)
ANZ Bank: Australia and New Zealand Bank
ANZIA: Associate of the New Zealand Institute of Architects
ANZIC: Associate of the New Zealand Institute of Chemists
ANZLA: Associate of the New Zealand Library Association
ANZUK: Australia, New Zealand, United Kingdom
ANZUS: Australia, New Zealand, United States (mutual security pact)
ao: access opening; anodal opening; anterior oblique; anti-oxidant; aorta; aortic opening; area of operation(s); axio-occlusal
a/o (A/O): account of
***a O* (a/O):** *an der Oder* (German—on the Oder River)
AO: Administration Office; Airdrome Office(r); American Optical (company); Arkansas & Ozarks (railroad); Autonomous Oblast; Aviation Ordnanceman; fleet tanker (2-letter naval designation)
AO: *Ahonim Ortaklik* (Turkish—joint stock company)
aoa: at or above
AoA: Administration on Aging (HEW)
AOA: American Oceanology Association; American Optometric Association; American Ordnance Association; American Orthopedic Association; American Orthopsychiatric Association; American Osteopathic Association; American Overseas Airlines; American Overseas Association
AOAC: Association of Official Agricultural Chemists; Association of Official Analytical Chemists
AOAD: Army Ordnance Arsenal District
aob: alcohol on breath; any other business; at or below
AOB: Advanced Operational Base
AO-BIRMDis: Army Ordnance—Birmingham District
AOBMO: Army Ordnance Ballistic Missile Office (USA)
AO-BOSTDis: Army Ordnance—Boston District
AOBs: Antediluvian Order of Buffaloes
AOBSR: Air Observer
aoc: anodal opening contraction
AoC: Architect of the Capitol (D.C.)
AOC: Air Officer Commanding; Air Operations Center; Airport Operators Council; American Optical Company (stock exchange symbol); American Orthoptic Council; Arabian Oil Company; Army Ordnance Corps; Aviation Officer Candidate
AOCA: American Osteopathic College of Anesthesiologists
AO-CHIDis: Army Ordnance—Chicago District
AOCI: Airport Operators Council International
aocl: anodal opening clonus
AO-CLEVDis: Army Ordnance—Cleveland District
aocm (AOCM): aircraft out of commission for maintenance
AOCO: Atomic Ordnance Cataloging Office
aocp (AOCP): aircraft out of commission for parts
AOCs: American Olympic Committee members
AOCS: American Oil Chemists' Society
aod: arterial occlusive disease; as of date
AOD: Air Officer of the Day
ao diag: acridine-orange diagnosis (cancer)
AODs: Ancient Order of Druids
AODS: All Ordnance Destruct System
aoe: airborne operational equipment; auditing order error
AoE: Aerodrome of Entry
AOEHI: American Organization for the Education of the Hearing Impaired
AOEM: Automotive Original Equipment Manufacturers
AOER: Amry Officers' Emergency Reserve
AOF: Afrique Occidentale Française (French West Africa); Ancient Order of Foresters
aog (AOG); aircraft on ground
AOG: Atlantic Oceanographic Group; gasoline tanker (3-letter symbol)
AOGM: Army of Occupation of Germany Medal
AOH: Ancient Order of Hibernians
aoi: angle of incidence
aoiv: automatically-operated inlet valve
aok: all okay; everything in good order
aol: absent over leave
AOL: American-Oriental Lines; Atlantic Oceanography Laboratories
AO-LADis: Army Ordnance—Los Angeles District
aolo: advanced orbit laboratory operations
AOLP: Action Organization for the Liberation of Palestine
AOM: Army of Occupation Medal
A.O.M.: Master of Obstetric Art
AOMAA: Apartment Owners and Managers Association of America
AOMC: Army Ordnance Missile Command
AOMSA: Army Ordnance Missile Support Agency
aonb: area of outstanding natural beauty
AO-NYDis: Army Ordnance—New York District
aoo: anodal opening odor
AOO: American Oceanic Organization
aop: anodal opening picture; aortic-pressure pulse
AOP: Association of Optical Practitioners; Association of Osteopathic Publications
AOPA: Aircraft Owners and Pilots Association
AO-PHILDis: Army Ordnance—Philadelphia District
aoProf: *auserordentlicher Professor* (German—associate professor or special lecturer)
AOPU: Asian Oceanic Postal Union (China, Korea, Philippines, Thailand)
aoq: average outgoing quality
aoql: average outgoing quality limit
aor: angle of reflection; aorist
a/or: and/or
AOR: Army Operational Research; auxiliary oil replenishment (USN)
AORB: Aviation Operational Research Branch
AORG: Army Operational Research Group (United Kingdom)
AORL: Apollo Orbital Research Laboratory
AORN: Association of Operating Room Nurses
AOrPA: American Orthopsychiatric Association
AORT: Association of Operating Room Techniques
AORTF: American Organization for Rehabilitation through Training Federation

aort regurg: aortic regurgitation
aort sten: aortic stenosis
aos: acquisition of signal; add or subtract; angle of sight; anodal opening sound
AOS: American Opera Society; American Ophthalmological Society; American Orchid Society; American Oriental Society; American Otological Society
AOSC: Association of Oilwell Servicing Contractors
AOSE: American Order of Stationary Engineers
AOSO: Advanced Orbiting Solar Observatory
aosp: automatic operating and scheduling program
AOSPS: American Otorhinologic Society for Plastic Surgery
AOSs: Ancient Order of Shepherds
AO-STLDis: Army Ordnance—St. Louis District
AOSW: Association of Official Shorthand Writers
aot: anodal opening tetanus
Aot: Askania optical tracker
AOT: Alameda-Oakland Tunnel; Association of Occupational Therapists
AOTA: American Occupational Therapy Association
ao technique: acridine-orange technique (two-color fluorescent test for cancer)
AotOS: Admiral of the Ocean Sea (U.S. Merchant Marine award recalling title of Christopher Columbus)
AOtS: American Otological Society
aou: apparent oxygen utilization
AOU: American Ornithologists' Union
AOUW: Ancient Order of United Workmen
AOW: Articles of War
ap: access panel; acid phosphatase; action potential; acute proliferation; aerial port; aiming point; airplane; alkaline phosphatase; alum precipitated; aminopeptidase; angina pectoris; antepartum; anterior pituitary; anteroposterior; aortic pressure; appendectomy; appendices; appendix; arithmetic progression; armor piercing; arterial pressure; artificial pneumothorax; as prescribed; association period; author's proof; axiopulpal; (Welsh prefix—son of)
ap: *anno passato* (Italian—last year)
ap.: *apud* (Latin—according to)
a.p.: *ante prandium* (Latin—before a meal)
a/p: after perpendicular; air port (porthole); angle point; authority to pay; authority to purchase; autopilot
a&p: agricultural and pastoral; anterior and posterior; apogee and perigee (apex and antapex); auscultation and percussion
a_p: geomagnetic index
Ap: Apothecary
Ap.: *Apostolus* (Latin—Apostle)
AP: Air Police; Airport, Air Publication: American President Lines; Associated Press; Aviation Pilot; personnel transport (naval symbol)
AP: *Acción Popular* (Spanish—Popular Action); *Arbeiderpartiet (Norwegian—Labor Party—Det Norske Arbeiderpartiet* (The Norwegian Labor Party); *Atlanska Plovidba* (Russian—Atlantic Press); ment)
A.P.: *a protester* (French—to be protested later)
A-P: American Plan (includes meals)
A/P: allied papers; authority to pay
A & P: Great Atlantic & Pacific Tea Company
apa: aldosterone-producing adenoma; aminopenicillanic acid; antipernicious anemia factor; axial pressure angle
APA: Aerovias Panama Airways; Agricultural Publishers Association; Airline Passenger Association; American Patients Association; American Pharmaceutical Association; American Philological Association; American Philosophical Association; American Photoengravers Association; American Physiotherapy Association; American Pilots Association; American Podiatry Association; American Poultry Association; American Press Association; American Protective Association; American Psychiatric Association; American Psychoanalytical Association; American Psychological Association; American Psychosomatic Association; American Psychotherapy Association; American Pulpwood Association; Animation Producers Association; Anti-Papal Association; Association of Paroling Authorities; transport attack vessel (naval symbol)
APA: *Austria Presse Agentur* (German—Austrian Press Agency)
apache: analog programming and checking
APACHE: Application Package for Chemical Engineers
Apache State: Arizona—land of the Apache Indians
APACL: Asian People's Anti-Communist League
apacs: adaptive planning and control sequence (marketing)
APADS: Automatic Programmer and Data System
APAE: Association of Public Address Engineers
apaf: antipernicious anemia factor
APAG: Atlantic Political Advisory Group (NATO)
APAL: American Puerto-Rican Action League
AP & AM: Adler Planetarium and Astronomical Museum
APANZ: Associate of the Public Accountants of New Zealand
apar: apparatus
APAR: Automatic Programming and Recording
apart.: apartment
a-part: alpha particle(s)
APAS: Automatic Performance Analysis System
APATS: Antenna Pattern Test System (USA)
apb: atrial premature beat; auricular premature beat
APB: barracks ship, self-propelled (3-letter symbol)
APB: *All-Points Bulletin*
APBA: American Power Boat Association; Association Press Broadcasters Association
APBPA: Association of Professional Ball Players of America
APBS: Accredited Poultry Breeding Scheme
apc: acoustical plaster ceiling; all-purpose capsule (aspirin, phenacetin, caffeine); antiphlogistic corticoid; aperture current; armor-piercing capped (ammunition); aspirin-phenacetin-caffeine (mixture); atrial premature contractions; automatic phase control
a/p c: autopilot capsule
APc: coastal transport (3-letter

symbol)

APC: Aeronautical Planning Chart; Aerospace Primus Club; American Parents Committee; American Philatelic Congress; Area Positive Control; Arkansas Polytechnic College; Armored Personnel Carrier; Army Petroleum Center; Army Policy Council; Association of Private Camps; Association of Pulp Consumers

APCA: Air Pollution Control Association; American Petroleum Credit Association; American Planning and Civic Association; Anglo-Polish Catholic Association

APCB: Air Pollution Control Board

apc-c: aspirin, phenacetin, caffeine—with codeine

APCD: Air Pollution Control District

APCG: Association of Pacific Coast Geographers

apche: automatic programmed checkout equipment

apci: armor-piercing capped with incendiary

apcit: armor-piercing capped incendiary with tracer

APCK: Association for Promoting Christian Knowledge

APCM: Asiatic-Pacific Campaign Medal

APCO: Air Pollution Control Office; Alabama Power Company

APCS: Air Photographic and Charting Service

apct: armor-piercing capped with tracer

a/p ctl: autopilot control

apc virus: adenoidal, pharyngeal, conjuctival virus

apd: action potential duration; aiming point determination; anteroposterior diameter

APD: Air Pollution Division (U.S. Dept Agriculture); Air Procurement District; high-speed troop transport (3-letter naval symbol)

APDC: Albany Port District Commission

Ap Del: Apostolic Delegate

APDF: Asian-Pacific Dental Federation

APdS: American Pediatric Society

APDSMS: Advanced Point Defense Surface Missile System

APDUSA: African People's Democratic Union of Southern Africa

ape.: adapted physical educator; aerial port of embarkation (APE): aminophylline, phenobarbital, ephedrine; anterior pituitary extract; apparent effect; automatic photomapping equipment

APE: aerial port of embarkation; Amalgamated Power Engineering

A.P.E.: Air Pollution Engineer

Apeco: American Photocopy Equipment Company

apers: antipersonnel

apex.: advance-purchase excursion (airline fare); assembler and process executive

APEX: Advance-Purchase Excursion (Plan)—pay 90 days ahead of excursion flight

apf: acidproof floor; animal protein factor

APF: American Progress Foundation; Association of Pacific Fisheries; Association of Protestant Faiths

APFA: American Pipe Fittings Association

APFC: Asia-Pacific Forestry Commission

APFRI: American Physical Fitness Research Institute

Apg: Appingedam

APG: Aberdeen Proving Ground; Air Proving Ground; American Pewter Guild; Army Planning Group; Army Proving Ground; Australian Proving Ground

APGA: American Personnel and Guidance Association

APGC: Air Proving Ground Center

apgcu: autopilot ground control unit

APG/HEL: Aberdeen Proving Ground—Human Engineering Laboratory

APG/OBDC: Aberdeen Proving Ground—Ordnance Bomb Disposal Center

APGOEF: Air Proving Ground—Eglin, Florida

aph: antepartum hemorrhage; anterior pituitary hormone (APH)

APH: transport fitted for evacuation of wounded (3-letter symbol)

A.P.H.: A(lan) P(atrick) Herbert

APhA: American Pharmaceutical Association

APHA: American Public Health Association

APHB: American Printing House for the Blind

aphet: aphetic

APHI: Association of Public Health Inspectors

APHIS: Animal and Plant Health Inspection Service

aphor: aphorism; aphorist(ic)(al-ly); aphorize

aphp: antipseudomonas human plasma

Aphrodite: (Greek—Venus)—goddess of beauty and love

aphro(s): aphrodisiac(s)

APHS: Arizona Pioneer Historical Society

api: air position indicator; armor-piercing incendiary tracer

API: Alabama Polytechnic Institute; American Paper Institute; American Petroleum Institute; American Potash Institute; American Press Institute; armor-piercing incendiary

API: *Association Phonetique Internationale* (French—International Phonetic Association); *Associazione Pionieri Italiani* (Italian Boy Scouts Association)

APIC: Apollo Parts Information Center; Army Photo Interpretation Center

APICP: Association for the Promotion of the International Circulation of the Press

APICS: American Production and Inventory Control Society

APICSC: Atlantic-Pacific Interoceanic Canal Study Commission

apicult: apiculture

APID: Army Photo Interpretation Detachment

A-pill: abortion pill

APIM: Association Professionelle Internationale des Médecins (International Professional Association of Physicians)

APIN: Atlas Propulsion Information Notice

apipocc: appropriating property in possession of (a) common carrier

APIS: Army Photographic Intelligence Service

apivr: artificial pacemaker ventricular rhythm

APJ: American Power Jet (company)

apl (APL): anterior pituitary-like hormone

a/pl: armorplate

Apl: Appledore

APL: Air Provost Marshal; Akron Public Library; Albany Public Library; Albuquerque Public Library; American Pioneer Line; American President Lines; Applied Physics Laboratory; Assembly Parts List; Augusta Public Library; barracks ship (naval symbol)
A-PL: All-Purpose Linotype
APLA: American Patent Law Association; Armenian Progressive League of America; Atlantic Provinces Library Association
ap/lat: anteroposterior and lateral
APLC: Automated Parking Lot Control
APLE: Association of Public Lighting Engineers
APLS: American Plant Life Society
APLU: American President Line (container) Unit
apm: apomict; associative principle for multiplication
apm (APM): antipersonnel missile
APM: Academy of Physical Medicine; Association for Psychoanalytic Medicine
apma: advance payment of mileage authorized
APMA: Absorbent Paper Manufacturers Association; Automatic Phonograph Manufacturers Association
APMAC: A.P. Moller Associated Concerns
APMC: Academy of Physchologists in Marital Counseling
a/p mcu: autopilot monitor and control unit
APME: Associated Press Managing Editors (Association)
APMG: Assistant Postmaster General
apmi: area precipitation measurement indicator
APMR: Association for Physical and Mental Rehabilitation
APMT: Antenna Pattern Measuring Test (USA)
apn: average peak noise
APN: *American Practical Navigator*
APNP: Arthur's Pass National Park (South Island, New Zealand)
apo: apogee
APO: Accountable Property Office(r); Advanced Post Office; Air Force (Army) Post Office; American Potash & Chemical (stock exchange symbol); Animal Procurement Office(r); Area Patrol Office(r); Area Petroleum Office(r); Association of Physical Oceanographers
apob: airplane observation
Apoc: Apocalypse; Apocrypha; Apocryphal
APOC: Army Point of Contact
APOD: Aerial Port of Debarkation
APOE: Aerial Port of Embarkation
apol: apologete; apologetic(al); apologetics; apologia; apologise; apologist(s); apologize; apology
Apollo: (Latin—Apollon)—the Sun
Apollon: (Greek—Apollo)—the Sun
Apollyon: The Devil
apos: apostrophe
APOS: Advanced Polar Orbiting Satellite
apota: automatic positioning of telemetering antenna
apotek: *apoteket* (Danish—apothecary)—drugstore
apoth: apothecaries' (weight); apothecary
A-powered: atomic-powered
app: apparatus; apparel; apparent; appeal; appelate; appendage; appended; appendix; apperception; appetite; appetizer; applause; applied; appointed; apprehended; apprentice; approach; appropriate; appropriation; approval; approve; approximate
App: Appellate; Lucius Appuleius
App: *Apparat* (German—apparatus); Lucius Appuleius (Roman philosopher)
App.: *Apostoli* (Latin—Apostles)
APP: Air Parcel Post; Algonquin Provincial Park (Ontario); *Alianza Para Progreso* (Spanish—Alliance for Progress); Army Procurement Procedure; Association of Professional Photogrammetrists
APPA: American Pulp and Paper Association
appar: apparatus
Appalachians: Appalachian Mountains
Appassionata: Beethoven's Piano Sonata No. 23 in F minor (opus 57); nicknamed for its impassioned mood
APPC: Advance Procurement Planning Council
appd: approved
appellat: appellative
Appennines: Appennine Mountains
appi: advanced planning procurement information
APPITA: Australian Pulp and Paper Industries Technical Association
appl: applicable; application; applied
APPL: Advance Procurement Planning List(s)
applan.: *applanatus* (Latin—flattened)
Apple Blossom: state flower of Arkansas and Michigan
Apple Capital of the World: Wenatchee, Washington
Apple Island: Tasmania's nickname
Apple Islanders: Tasmanians
Apple Isle: Tasmania
Appleton: Appleton-Century-Crofts
applican.: *applicandus* (Latin—applied; to be applied)
APPM: Association of Publication Production Managers
appmt: appointment
appn: appropriation
a/p poi: autopilot positioning indicator
appr: approval; approve; approved
APPR: Army power package reactor
appren: apprentice
approx: approximate(ly)
apps: appendices; appendixes
appt: appoint; appointment
apptd: appointed
appx: appendix
appy: appendectomy
apr: amoebic prevalence rate; annual percentage rate; anterior pituitary reaction; apprentice
apr: *aprile* (Italian—April)
Apr: April
Apr: *Aprel* (Russian—April)
APR: Airman Performance Report; Air Pictorial Service; Air Priority Raging; Annual Progress Reports; Association of Petroleum Re-Refiners; Association of Publishers' Representatives
APRA: Aircraft Resources Production Agency
APRA: *Alianza Popular Revolucionaria Americana* (Spanish—Popular American Revolutionary Alliance)—Peru's Aprista Party of Haya de la Torre

aprax: apraxia(1)
APRC: Army Physical Review Council
APRDC: Army Polar Research and Development Center
APRE: Air Procurement Region—Europe
après JC: *après Jesus Christ* (French—after the birth of Jesus Christ; A.D.)
APRF: Army Pulse Radiation Facility
APRFE: Air Procurement Region—Far East
APri: air priority
A/Prin: Assistant Principal
APRL: American Prosthetic Research Laboratory
Aprmay: April and May
APRO: Aerial Phenomena Research Organization; Army Personnel Research Office
AprS: American Proctologic Society
APRS: Association of Professional Recording Studios
aprt: airport
APRTA: Associated Press Radio and Television Association
aprthd: *Apartheid* (Afrikaans—apartness)
aprx: approximately
aps: accessory power supply; adenosine phosphosulfate; autograph postcard signed; auxiliary power supply; auxiliary propulsion system
APS: Academy of Political Science; Adenosine Phosphosulfate; American Metal Products (stock exchange symbol); American Pediatric Society; American Pheasant Society; American Philatelic Society; American Philosophical Society; American Physical Society; American Physiological Society; American Phytopathological Society; American Plant Selections; American Poinsettia Society; American Polar Society; American Proctologic Society; American Proctologic Society; American Prosthodontic Society; American Psychosomatic Society; Army Pilot School; Army Postal Service; Association of Photo Sensitizers; submarine transport (naval symbol)
APS: *Algerie Presse Service* (French—Algerian Press Service)
APSA: Aerolíneas Peruanas, South America; American Political Science Association; Associate of the Photographic Society of America
A & PSA: Aden and Protectorate of South Arabia
APsaA: American Psychoanalytic Association
APSB: Aid to the Potentially Self-supporting Blind
APSF: Alfred P. Sloan Foundation
APSq: Aerial Port Squadron
APSS: Association for the Psychophysiological Study of Sleep
APsychoA: American Psychoanalytic Association
APsychosomS: American Psychosomatic Society
APsychpthA: American Psychopathological Association
apt.: alum-precipitated toxoid; apartment; armor-piercing with tracer; automatically-programmed tool(s); automatic picture transmission
apt: *apartadero* (Spanish—platform)
APT: Advanced Passenger Train; Automotive Professional Training; Airman Proficiency Test; Automatic Picture Transmission
APTA: American Physical Therapy Association; American Pioneer Trails Association; American Platform Tennis Association; American Public Transit Association
APTC: Allied Printing Trades Council
Aptdo: *apartado* (Spanish—post office box)
apte: advance passenger train express (149 mph British turbine-powered train)—APTE
apth: apthong (a silent letter like the *p* in pneumatic)
APTI: Association of Principals of Technical Institutions
apto: aluminum plastic tearoff (container cover)
apt(s): apartment(s)
APTs: Advanced Passenger Trains
APTS: Automatic Picture Transmission System
APTU: African Postal and Telecommunications Union
apu: auxiliary power unit
APU: Army Postal Unit
APV: Avenida Presidente Vargas, Rio de Janeiro, Brazil
apw: architectural projected window
APW: Accelerated Public Works; American Prisoner of War
APWA: American Public Welfare Association; American Public Works Association
APWU: American Postal Workers Union
apx: appendix
APZ: Assiniboine Park Zoo
aq: accomplishment quotient; achievement quotient; any quantity; aqueous
aq.: *aqua* (Latin—water)
a-q: aircraft quality
AQ: achievement quotient; aviation fire-control technician (USAF symbol); Schreiner Aerocontractors (Hague)
AQ: *Australian Quarterly*
AQAB: Air Quality Advisory Board
aq.astr.: *aqua adstricta* (Latin—ice)
aq. bull.: *aqua bulliens* (Latin—boiling water)
aq. cal.: *aqua calida* (Latin—warm water)
aq. com.: *aqua communis* (Latin—ordinary water)
AQCR: Air Quality Control Region (EPA)
aq. dest.: *aqua destillata* (Latin—distilled water)
aqdm: air quality display model
AQE: Airman Qualifying Examination
aq. ferv.: *aqua fervens* (Latin—hot water)
aq. fluv.: *aqua fluvii* (Latin—river water)
aq. font.: *aqua fontana* (Latin—spring water)
aql: acceptable qualifying levels; acceptable quality level; approved quality level
aq. mar.: *aqua marina* (Latin—sea water)
aq. ment. pip.: *aqua menthae piperitae* (Latin—peppermint water)
AQMG: Assistant Quartermaster General
aq. niv.: *aqua nivalis* (Latin—snow water)
aq. pluv.: *aqua pluvialis* (Latin—rain water)
aq. pur.: *aqua pura* (Latin—pure water)
AQREC: Army Quartermaster Research and Engineering Command
aq. reg.: (Latin—royal water) hydrochloric and nitric acid
aqs: additional qualifying symptoms
AQT: Applicant Qualification

Test

aq. tep.: *aqua tepida* (Latin—tepid water)

aqu: aqueous

aqua.: aquaria; aquarium; aquatic

aquacult: aquaculture

aqua fortis: (Latin—strong water) nitric acid

aquamarine: gemstone beryl

aquar: aquarium

Aquar: Aquarius

aqua regia: (Latin—royal water) hydrochloric and nitric acid

aque: aqueduct

Aqueduct: Aqueduct Books

Aquisgranum: (Latin—Aachen or Aix-la-Chapelle)

ar: achievement ratio; acid resisting; active resistance; alarm reaction; all rail; all risks; allocated reserve; analytical reagent; aromatic; arrival; artificial respiration; aspect ratio

ar: *avis de reception* (French—return receipt)

a/r: all risks; armed robbery; at the rate of

a & r: approved and removed; assault and robbery

a/R: *am Rhein* (German—on the Rhine River)

Ar: Arab; Arabia; Arabian; Arabic; Aragon; argon; Aries; aryl

AR: Aberdeen & Rockfish (railroad); Administrative Ruling; Aerodynamic Report; Aerolineas Argentinas (Argentine Airlines); Aeronautical Radionavigation; Airman Recruit; Airship Rigger; Amendment Request; American Smelting & Refining (stock exchange symbol); Annual Report; Army Regulation(s); Army Reserve; repair ship (naval symbol)

AR: *Aller et Retour* (French—roundtrip); *Andata-Ritorno* (Italian—roundtrip)

A.R.: *Anno Regni* (Latin—In the Year of the Reign of)

A/R: *Aksjerederi* (Norwegian—shipping company)

A & R: assembly and repair

ara: assigned responsible agency (DoD)

ara (ARA): aerial rocket artillery

Ara: Argentina

ARA: Aerospace Research Association; American Radio Association; American Railway Association; American Rationalist Association; American Relief Association; American Rental Association; American Republics Area; American Rheumatism Association; Arcade & Attica (railroad); Area Redevelopment Administration; Armada República Argentina (Argentine Navy); Artists' Representatives Association; Automatic Retailers of America

ARA: *Acção Revolucionaria Armada* (Portuguese—Armed Revolutionary Action)

A.R.A.: Associate of the Royal Academy

ARA (AFL-CIO): American Radio Association

Arab.: Arabia; Arabian; Arabic

Arabiya as-Sa'udiya: (Arabic—Saudi Arabia)

Arab League: League of Arab States (Algeria, Bahrain, Egypt, Iraq, Jordan, Kuwait, Lebanon, Libya, Morocco, Oman, Qatar, Somalia, Southern Yemen, Sudan, Syria, Tunisia, United Arab Emirates, Yemen)

ARAC: Aerospace Research Applications Center; Associate of the Royal Agricultural College

arach: arachnology

Arach: Arachnida

ARACI: Associate of the Royal Australian Chemical Institute

arad: airborne radar and doppler

ARAD: Associate of the Royal Academy of Dancing

ARADCOM: Army Defense Command

ARAeS: Associate of the Royal Aeronautical Society

ARAgS: Associate of the Royal Agricultural Society

ARAIA: Associate of the Royal Australian Institute of Architects

aral: automatic record analysis language

Aram: Aramaic

ARAM: Association of Railroad Advertising Managers

A.R.A.M.: Associate of the Royal Academy of Music

Aramco: Arabian-American Oil Company

aras: ascending reticular activating system

ARAS: Associate of the Royal Astronomical Society

araucanos: (Latin American nickname—Chileans or *chilenos*)—sobriquet recalls the liberty-loving Araucanian Indians who were never conquered by the Spaniards

arb: arbitrary; arbitration

arb: *arbeid(er)* [Dano-Norwegian—work(s)]

Arb: Arbroath

ARB: Accident Records Bureau (NYC Police Dept.); Air Registration Board; Air Research Bureau; Armored Rifle Battalion; Army Rearming Base; Army Retiring Board; ASTIA Report Bibliography; battle damage repair ship (naval symbol)

ARBA: American Railway Bridge and Building Association; American Road Builders Association; Associated Retail Bakers of America

ARBA: *American Reference Books Annual*

arb & aw: arbitration and award

ARBED: Aciéries Réunies de Burbach-Eich-Dudelange

ARBM: Association of Radio Battery Manufacturers

arbo: arthropod-borne (viral diseases)

arbor.: arboriculture

arbor. virus: arthropod-borne virus

ARBs: Air Resources Boards (pollution-control agencies)

ARBS: Associate of the Royal Society of British Sculptors

arbtrn: arbitration

arbtror: arbitrator

arc.: arcade; auto-refrigerated cascade

arc: *arco* (Italian—bow, indicating end of *pizzicato* passages)

Arc: Arachon; Arcade; Archaic; Arctic

ARC: Agricultural Relations Council; Agricultural Research Council; Aircraft Radio Corporation; Air Reserve Center; Air Rescue Center; Airworthiness Requirements Committee; American Red Cross; Ames Research Center (NASA); Appalachian Regional Commission; Armada República de Colombia (Colombian Navy); Asian Research Center (Harvard); Association of Retail Confectioners; Association of Rehabilitation Centers; Atlantic Research Corporation; Atomedic Research Center; cable laying or repair ship (naval symbol)

ARCA: Associate of the Royal College of Art

ARCAA: Associate of the Royal Canadian Academy of Arts
Arc Arch: Arctic Archipelago (Canadian Arctic)
ARCAS: Automatic Radar Chain Acquisition System
Arc Cur: Arctic Current
arce: amphibious river-crossing equipment
ARCen: Air Reserve Center
arch.: archaic; archipelago; architect(s); architectural; architecture
Arch-Bish: Archbishop
Arch City: St Louis dominated by the monumental Jefferson National Expansion Memorial arch commemorating the Louisiana Purchase making St Louis the Gateway to the West
Archd: Archdeacon; Archduke
Arch de Cln: Archipelago de Colón
Archduke: Beethoven's Trio in B minor (opus 97) for violin, cello, and piano; dedicated to his patron the Archduke Rudolph
Arch E: Architectural Engineer
archeo: archeological; archeologist; archeology
Archeoz: Archeozoic
Arches: Arches National Monument near Moab, Utah
archi: archival; archive; archivist
ARCHI: Asociación de Radiodifusoras de Chile (Association of Chilean Broadcasters)
Archie: Archibald
Archie: Archie Bunker (archetype of the average white American bigot; role created by actor Carroll O'Connor in the television serial entitled *All In The Family*)
archip: archipelago
Architect in Chief of St Peters: Raphael (Raffaello Santi)
Archive: Archive Press
archv: archive
Archy: Archibald
ARCI: American Railway Car Institute
Arclos: Army Close support
ARCM: Associate of the Royal College of Music
ARCNS: American Red Cross Nursing Services
Arc O: Arctic Ocean Command
Arco: Arco Publishing Company
ARCO: Associate of the Royal College of Organists; Atlantic Richfield Company
ARCom: Army Research
ARCON: Advanced Research Consultants
ARCOS: Anglo-Russian Cooperative Society
ARCOV: Army Combat Operations Vietnam
arcp: air refueling control point
ARCR: Arthritis and Rheumatism Council for Research
ARCRL: Agricultural Research Council Radiobiological Laboratory
ARCS: Air Resupply and Communication Service
A.R.C.S.: Associate of the Royal College of Science; Associate of the Royal College of Surgeons
ARCSA: Aviation Requirements for the Combat Structure of the Army
ARCST: Associate of the Royal College of Science and Technology
arct: air refueling control time
Arctic: Vassilenko's Fourth Symphony
Arctic big three: muskox, polar bear, walrus
Arctic Canada: Northwest Territories
Arctic Territories: Canadian Northwest Territories
ARCUK: Architects' Registration Council of the United Kingdom
ARCVS: Associate of the Royal College of Veterinary Surgeons
arc/w: arcweld
ard: acute respiratory disease
ar&d: aeronautical research and development; air research and development
Ard: Ardrossan
ARD: *Arbeitsgemeinschaft Rundfunkanstalten Deutschland* (German National Broadcasting)
ARD: Accelerated Rural Development; Air Reserve District; American Research and Development (corporation); Army Renegotiation Division; Association of Research Directors; auxiliary floating dock (naval)
AR & D: air research and development
ARDA: Advanced Reactor Development Associates; American Railway Development Association
ARDC: Aberdeen Research and Development Center; Air Research and Development Command; American Racing Drivers Club
ARDCM: Air Research and Development Command Manual
ARDCO: Applied Research and Development Company
ARDE: Armament Research and Development Establishment (Ministry of Supply)
ARDG: Army Research and Development Group (USA)
ARDG(E): Army Research and Development Group (Europe)
ARDG(FE): Army Research and Development Group (Far East)
ARDIS: Army Research and Development Information System
ARDM: medium auxiliary repair drydock (naval symbol)
ard's: analog recording dynamic analyzers
are. (ARE): air reactor experiment
ARE: Arab Republic of Egypt; Association for Research and Enlightenment
A.R.E.: Associate in Religious Education
AREA: Aerovias Ecuatorianas (Ecuadorian Airways); American Railway Engineering Association; American Recreational Equipment Association; Army Reactor Experimental Area; Association of Records Executives & Administrators
AREC: Amateur Radio Emergency Corps
AREFS: Air Refueling Squadron
AREI: Associate of the Real Estate and Stock Institute (Australia)
Arelate: (Latin—Arles)
ARENA: *Aliança Renovadora Nacional* (Portuguese—National Renovating Alliance)—political party in Brazil
aren't: are not
ARENTS: ARPA Environmental Test Satellite
Ares: (Greek—Mars)—god of war
AREUEA: American Real Estate and Urban Economics Association
arf: acute respiratory failure; (cartoonist's symbol—dog's bark)—*arf-arf*
ARF: Advertising Research Foundation; African Research Foundation; Air Reserve Force(s); American Radio Forum; American Rationalist Federation; American Rehabilitation Foundation; American Retail Foun-

dation; American Rose Foundation; Armour Research Foundation; Arthritis and Rheumatism Foundation

ARFA: Allied Radio Frequency Agency

ARFCOS: Armed Forces Courier Service

ARFDC: Atomic Reactor and Fuel Development Corporation

arfor: area forecast

ARFPC: Air Reserve Forces Policy Committee

arg: argent; argot; argument; argumentation; argumentative; argumentator (a controversialist); argus; arresting; arresting gear

arg: *argang* (Dano-Norwegian—yearbook); *argol* (Mongolian—dried camel or cattle dung fuel)

arg (Arg): arginine

arga: appliance, range, adjust (data processing)

Arg: Argentina; Argentinian

ARG: Aerolineas Argentinas; repair ship, internal combustion engine

ARGCA: American Rice Growers Cooperative Association

Argel: *Argelia* (Spanish—Alberia); *Argelía* (Portuguese—Algeria); (Portuguese or Spanish—Algiers)

Argen: Argentine; Argentinian

Argosy: Argosy-Antiquarian Limited

argus: advanced research on groups under stress

ARGUS: Automatic Routine Generating and Updating System

Argyll: Argyllshire

Argyrol King: Dr Albert C. Barnes

a Rh: *am Rhein* (German—on the Rhine)

ARH: heavy-hull repair ship (3-letter symbol)

ARHA: Associate of the Royal Hibernian Academy

ARHS: Associate of the Royal Horticultural Society

Ari: Aristotle

ARI: Air-Conditioning and Refrigeration Institute; Aluminum Research Institute; American Reciprocal Insurers; American Refractories Institute; American Russian Institute

ARIANA: Ariana Afghan Airlines

ARIB: Asphalt Roofing Industry Bureau

ARIBA: Associate of the Royal Institute of British Architects

ARIC: Associate of the Royal Institute of Chemistry

ARICRSU: American Russian Institute for Cultural Relations with the Soviet Union

ARICS: Associate of the Royal Institution of Chartered Surveyors

ARIEL: Automated Real-Time Investments Exchange Limited

ARIEM: Army Research Institute of Environmental Medicine

ARIES: Advanced Radar Information Evaluation System

ARINA: Associate of the Royal Institution of Naval Architects

ARINC: Aeronautical Radio Incorporated

arip: automatic rocket impact predictor

aris (ARIS): advanced range instrumentation ships

ARIS: Advanced Research Instrument System; Aircraft Research Instrumentation System

Arist: Aristotle

ARIST: *Annual Review of Information Science and Technology*

Arista: high-school honor society

aristocat(s): aristocratic cat(s)

Aristoph: Aristophanes

aristo(s): aristocrat(s)

ARISTOTLE: Annual Review and Information Symposium on the Technology of Training, Learning, and Education (DoD)

arit: *aritmética* (Portuguese or Spanish—arithmetic)

A.R.I.T.: American Registered Inhalation Therapist

arith: arithmetic

Ariz: Arizona; Arizonian

Ariz Hist Found: Arizona Historical Foundation

Ark: Arkansas; Arkansan

Arkansawyer: Arkansan nickname for a native of Arkansas also called Arkie

Ark City: Arkansas City, Arkansas

ARKIA: Israel Inland Airlines

Arkie: migratory farm worker or sharecropper from Arkansas

Arkopolis: Little Rock, Arkansas

arl: acceptable reliability level; air run landing; average remaining lifetime

ARL: Aeromedical Research Laboratory; Aeronautical Research Laboratory; Aerospace Research Laboratory; American Reefer Line; American Republics Line; American Roque League; Anesthesia Research Laboratories; Applied Research Laboratory (Johns Hopkins University); Association of Research Libraries; landing craft repair ship (3-letter naval symbol)

ARLD: Army Logistics Research and Development

Arletty: French actress Léonie Bathiat

Arlington: Arlington Books (Louisville, Ky); Arlington House (New Rochelle, NY)

Arlington House: Robert E. Lee's home in Arlington, Virginia overlooking the Potomac and Washington, D.C.

ARLIS: Arctic Research Laboratory Island (USN)

ARLIS/NA: Art Libraries Society/North America

ArLO: Army Liaison Officer

ARLO: Art Reference Libraries of Ohio

arm.: anti-radar missile (ARM); anti-radiation missile; armature; arming

Arm: Armagh; Armenia(n)

Ar.M.: Architecturae Magister (Master of Architecture)

ARM: Auditory Rehabilitation Mobile

ARMA: American Bosch Arma Corporation; American Records Management Association; Association of Records Managers and Administrators

a&r man: artist and repertory man (supervising phonograph record production)

ARMCM: Associate of the Royal Manchester College of Music

armd: armored

Armen: Armenia(n)

armet: area forecast (given in metric system)

armgrd: armed guard

ARMI: American Rack Merchandisers Institute; American Research Merchandising Institute; Army Resources Management Institute

ARMIT: Associate of the Royal Melbourne Institute of Technology

ARMM: Association of Reproduction Materials Manufacturers

ARMMA: American Railway

Master Mechanics' Association
ARMMS: Automated Reliability and Maintainability Measurement System
AR/MONP: Ayers Rock/Mount Olga National Park (Northern Territory, Australia)
armpl: armorplate
armr: armorer
ARMS: Advanced Receiver Model System; Aerial Radiological Measuring Survey; Amateur Radio Mobile Society
arm-saf: arm-safe (switch)
armt: armament
ARMU: Associated Rocky Mountain Universities
a Rn: *am Rhein* (German—on the Rhine)
Arn: Arnold
ARN: Stockholm, Sweden (Arlanda Airport)
ArNa: Army with Navy
arng: arrange
ARNG: Army National Guard
Arnhem Land: northern end of Australia's Northern Territory
A Rn I: Association of Rhodesian Industries
ARNM: Aztec Ruins National Monument
ARNMD: Association for Research in Nervous and Mental Disease
Arnold Bennett: Enoch Arnold Bennett
aro: after receipt of order; airborne range only
ARO: Air Radio Office(r); Applied Research Objective; Army Research Office; Army Routine Order; Asian Regional Organization; Association for Research in Ophthalmology; Association of Roentgenological Organizations
arod: airborne range and orbit determination
ARO-FE: Army Research Office—Far East
arom: aromatic
AR-ONP: Ayers Rock-Olgas National Park (Australia)
arp: airborne radar platform; airport reference point; alternator research package; (cartoonist's symbol — dog's bark)
ARP: Advanced Research Project(s); Aeronautical Recommended Practice(s); Air Raid Precautions; American Registry of Pathologists; Ammunition Refilling Point; Area Redevelopment Program; Association for Realistic Philosophy; Australian Reptile Park (New South Wales)
ARP: *Anti-Revolutionaire Partij* (Dutch—Anti-Revolutionary Party)
ARPA: Advanced Research Projects Agency
ARPAS: Air Reserve Pay and Allowance System
ARPAT: Advanced Research Projects Agency Terminal (defense system)
ARPC: Air Reserve Personnel Center
arpd (ARPD): applied research planning document
ARPEL: *Asistencia Recíproca Petrolera Estatal Latinoamericana* (Spanish—Latin American State Petroleum Reciprocal Assistance)—international agency
Arpo: *arpeggio* (Italian—producing the tones in a chord successively rather than simultaneously)
ARPO: Association of Resort Publicity Officers
Arprt: Airport (postal place-name abbreviation)
ARPS: Associate of the Royal Photographic Society
Arpt: Airport
ARPT: American Registry of Physical Therapists
a-r pulse: apical-radial pulse
arq: *arquitecto* (Spanish—architect); *arquitectura* (Spanish—architecture); *arquiteto* (Portuguese—architect) *arquitetura* (Portuguese—architecture)
Arq ^{to}***:*** *Arquitecto* (Portuguese or Spanish—Architect)
arr: airborne radio receiver; arrestor; arrival; arrive; arriving
Arr: *arrondissement* (French—district)
ARR: Air Regional Representative; Air Reserve Record(s); Army Retail Requirements
ARRC: Air Reserve Records Center; Associate of the Royal Red Cross
ARRF: Automatic Recording and Reduction Facility
ARRGp: Aerospace Rescue and Recovery Group (USAF)
Arri: Arnold and Richter (reflex motion-picture camera)
ARRL: American Radio Relay League
arr n: arrival notice
arrowhead: symbol used to indicate direction
Arroyo del Ajo: (Spanish—Garlic Gulch)—John Steinbeck's name for his home near Los Gatos, California
ARRS: Aerospace Rescue and Recovery Service; American Roentgen Ray Society
ARRSq: Aerospace Rescue and Recovery Squadron (USAF)
ARRT: American Registry of Radiologic Technologists
ARRTC: Aerospace Rescue and Recovery Training Center (USAF)
ARRWg: Aerospace Rescue and Recovery Wing (USAF)
ars: aerospace research satellite; arsenal; asbestos roof shingles
ARs: Action Requests
ARS: Aerospace Research Satellite; Agricultural Research Service; Airail Service (monorail); Air Rescue Service; American Records Society; American Recreation Society; American Repair Society; American Rescue Service; American Rhododendron Society; American Rocket Society; American Rose Society; Army Relief Society; salvage ships (naval symbol)
ARSA: Associate of the Royal School of Art
ARSC: Association of Recorded Sound Collections
arsen: arsenal
ARSH: Associate of the Royal Society for the Promotion of Health
Arsl: Arsenal (postal place-name abbreviation)
ARSL: Associate of the Royal Society of Literature
ARSM: Associate of the Royal School of Mines
ARSP: Aerospace Research Support Program
ARSPH: Associate of the Royal Society for the Promotion of Health
arsr: air route surveillance radar
ARST: salvage craft tender (naval symbol)
ARSTRAC: Army Strike Command
ARSV: armored reconnaissance scout vehicle (USA)
art.: airborne radiation thermometer; arterial; artery; article; articulate; articulation; artifact; artificial; artillery; ar-

tisan; artist; artistic; artistry
art^o: *artículo* (Spanish—article)
Art: Arthur; Arturo
Art: *Artikel* (German—article)
ART: Accredited Record Technician; Air Reserve Technician; Arithmetic Reading Test; Arithmetic Reasoning Test; Aviation Radio Technician
ARTA: American River Touring Association; Association of Retail Travel Agents
artac: advanced reconnaissance and target acquisition capabilities
ARTC: Air Route Traffic Control
ARTCC: Air Route Traffic Control Center
Art Center of Rhode Island: Wickford
Art Center of the Southwest: Taos, New Mexico
Art C-Part: articles of co-partner ship
ARTE: Admiralty Reactor Test Establishment
Artemis: (Greek—Diana)—goddess of the hunt and the Moon; protectress of women
Artemus Ward: (pseudonym—Charles Farrar Browne)
Arth: Arthropoda; Arthur; Arthurian
artic: articulate(d); articulation
Artichoke Capital: Castroville, California
Artie: Artemas; Artemisia; Artemus; Arthur; Artur; Arturo; Artus
Artie Shaw: Arthur Arshawsky
artif: artificer(s); artificial(ly)
Artigas: José Gervasio Artigas—defender of Uruguayan independence after leading Gaucho revolt against Spanish misrule
art. insem: artificial insemination
arto: air run takeoff
art^o: *artículo* (Italian—article); *artículo* (Spanish—article); *artigo* (Portuguese—article)
ARTOC: Army Tactical Operational Control; Army Tactical Operations Central
ARTP: Army Rocket Transportation System
art. pf: artist's proof
artrac: advanced range testing, reporting, and control
artron(s): artificial neuron(s)
arts.: articles
ARTS: Advanced Radar Traffic Control System; Automatic Radar Traffic Control System
ArtSci: Arts and Sciences (students or studies)
ARTSM: Association of Road Sign Makers
artu: automatic range tracking unit
arty: artillery
aru: analog remote unit; audio response unit
Aru: Aruba
ARU: Air Reserve Unit; American Railway Union
arv (ARV): aeroballistic reentry vehicle
Arv: *Arvoisa* (Finnish—esteemed)
ARV: aircraft engine overhaul and structural repair ship; American Revised Version
ARVA: aircraft repair ship for aircraft (4-letter designation)
ARVE: aircraft repair ship for engines (4-letter designation)
ARVH: aircraft repair ship—helicopter (naval symbol)
ARVIA: Associate of the Royal Victorian Institute of Architects
ARVN: Army of the Republic of Vietnam
ARVSG: Air Reserve Volunteer Support Group
arw: attitude reaction wheel
ARW: Air Raid Warden; Air Raid Warning; Air Reserve Wing (Canada)
ARWC: Army War College
ARWH: Air Reserve Wing Headquarters
ARWS: Associate of the Royal Society of Painters in Water Colours
Aryabhata: Indian spacecraft named for the fifth-century astronomer
Arz: *Arzobispo* (Spanish—Archbishop)
Arzbpo: *Arzobispo* (Spanish—Archbishop)
as.: airscoop; air-to-surface missile; alloy steel; antiseptic; aortic stenosis; asymmetric
a-s: ascendance-submission
a/s: airspeed; antisubmarine
a.s.: *auris sinistra* (Latin—left ear)
a/s.: *aux soins de* (French—in care of)
As: altostratus; arsenic; Asia; Asian; Asiatic; astigmatism; aunicles; Australia(n)
AS: Abilene & Southern (railroad); Academy of Science(s); Aeronautical Standard(s); air-to-surface missile; Air Service; Air Speed; Air Staff; Air Station; Airports Service; Air Surveillance; Alaska Airlines; Anglo-Saxon; antisubmarine; Apprentice Seaman; Army Security; Army Staff; submarine tender (naval symbol)
A.S.: Antonius Stradivarius (initials usually accompanied by a Maltese cross, both enclosed in a double circle)
A/S: alongside (barge, cargo carrier, lighter)
AS: *Anonim Sirket* (Turkish—joint stock company); *Aviaeskadra* (Russian—air squadron)
A/S: *Aksjeselskap* (Norwegian—limited company); *Aktieselkab* (Danish—joint stock company)
A & S: Alton & Southern (railroad)
A de S: *Académie des Sciences*
A of S: Academy of Science
asa: acetylsalicylic acid (aspirin); antistatic additive
asa: (Norwegian or Swedish—hill)
A-S a: Adams-Stokes attack
ASA: Acoustical Society of America; Actuarial Society of America; Aerovias Sud Americana (South American Airways); African Studies Association; Alaska Airlines; Aluminum Siding Association; Amateur Softball Association; Amateur Swimming Association; American Scientific Affiliation; American Shorthorn Association; American Sightseeing Association; American Society for Abrasives; American Society for Aesthetics; American Society of Agronomy; American Society of Anesthesiologists; American Society of Appraisers; American Society of Auctioneers; American Sociological Association; American Sociometric Association; American South African Line; American Soybean Association; American Standards Association; American Statistical Association; American Stockyards Association; American Studies Association; American Sunbathing Association; American Surgical Association; Anthroposophical Society of America; Army Seal of Approval; Army Security Agency; Assistant Secretary

of the Army; Associated Stenotypists of America; Association of Southeast Asia; Atomic Security Agency; Aviation Supply Annex
A of SA (ASA): Association of Southeast Asia
ASAA: Amateur Softball Association of America; Armenian Students Association of America
ASAALH: Association for the Study of Afro-American Life and History
ASAB: Association for the Study of Animal Behavior
ASAC: American Society for African Culture; American Society of Agricultural Consultants; Army Study Advisory Committee; Assistant Special Agent in Charge
ASAE: American Society of Agricultural Engineers
AS of AF: Assistant Secretary of the Air Force
ASAH: American Society of Association Historians
Asahi: *Asahi Shimbun* (Japanese—Rising Sun Newspaper)
ASALA: Associate of the South African Library Association
ASAM: American Society for Abrasive Methods
ASAN: Adriatica Società per Azioni di Navigazione
ASAnes: American Society of Anesthesiologists
ASAO: Association for Social Anthropology in Oceania
asap: as soon as possible
ASAP: Airlines of South Australia; antisubmarine attack plotter
ASAPS: Anti-Slavery and Aborigines Protection Society
ASARCO: American Smelting and Refining Company
ASAS: American Society of Abdominal Surgery; American Society of Animal Science; Army Security Agency School
asb: aircraft safety beacon; asbestos
as & b: aloin, strychnine, and belladona (pills)
ASB: Administration and Storage Building; Aircraft Safety Beacon; Air Safety Beacon; Air Safety Board; Air Staff Board; American Society of Bacteriologists
ASBAH: Association for Spina Bifida and Hydrocephalus
asb c: asbestos covered
ASBC: American Society of Biological Chemists
ASBC: *American Standard Building Code*
ASBCA: Armed Services Board of Contract Appeals
ASBCO: American Ship Building Company
ASBD: Advanced Sea-Based Deterrent Program
ASBDA: American School Band Directors Association
ASBE: American Society of Bakery Engineers
asbestos: actinolite (calcium magnesium silicate varying to calcium magnesium iron silicate)
asb & i: aloin, strychnine, belladona, and ipecac
asbl: assemble
ASBPA: American Shore and Beach Preservation Association
ASBPE: American Society of Business Press Editors
asc: altered state of consciousness; arteriosclerosis; arteriosclerosistic; ascarid; ascaridian; ascend; ascender; ascending; ascension; ascent; ascertain; ascertainable; automatic switching center; auxiliary switch closed
as & c: aerospace surveillance and control
Asc: Ascidian
A.Sc.: Associate in Science
ASC: Adelaide Steamship Company; Aeronautical Systems Center; Air Service Command; Air Support Command; Air Support Control; Air Systems Command; Alabama State College; Alaska Steamship Company; Albany State College; American Security Council; American Silk Council; American Society of Cinematographers; American Society of Criminology; American Society of Cytology; Arizona State College; Arkansas State College; Army Service Corps; Army Subsistence Center; Asian Socialist Conference; Associated Sandblasting Contractors
A & SC: Adhesive and Sealant Council
asca: automatic science citation alerting
ASCA: American School Counselor Association; American Senior Citizens Association; American Speech Correction Association; Association of State Correctional Administrators
ASCAA: Automobile Seat Cover Association of America
ASCAC: Antisubmarine Contact Analysis Center
ASCAP: American Society of Composers, Authors, and Publishers
ASCAT: Antisubmarine Contact Analysis Team
ASCATS: Apollo Simulation Checkout and Training System
ASCC: Adams State College of Colorado; Air Standardization Coordinating Committee; American Society for the Control of Cancer; Army Strategic Communications Command; Association of Senior Citizens Clubs
ASCD: Association for Supervision and Curriculum Development
ASCE: American Society of Civil Engineers
ASCEA: American Society of Civil Engineers and Architects
ASCET: American Society of Certified Engineering Technicians
ASCHAL: American Society of Corporate Historians, Archivists, and Librarians
ASCHE: American Society of Chemical Engineers
ASCI: Ameican Society for Clinical Investigation
ASCII: American Standard Code for Information Interchange
ASCLU: American Society of Chartered Life Underwriters
ASCM: Association of Steel Conduit Manufacturers
ASCMA: American Sprocket Chain Manufacturers Association
ASCN: American Society of Clinical Nutrition
asco: automatic sustainer cutoff
Asco: Automatic Switch Company
ASCom: Army Service Command
ascore: automatic shipboard checkout and readiness equipment
A Scot: type-A Scottish influenza virus
ASCP: American Society of Clinical Pathologists; American Society of Consulting Pharmacists; American Socie-

ty of Consulting Planners
ASCPT: American Society for Clinical Pharmacology and Therapeutics
ascr.: *ascriptum* (Latin—ascribed to)
ASCRO: Active Service Career for Reserve Officers
asc's (ASCs): altered states of consciousness
ASCS: Agricultural Stabilization and Conservation Service; Automatic Stabilization and Control System
ASCU: Association of State Colleges and Universities
ascvd: arteriosclerotic cardiovascular disease; atherosclerotic cardiovascular disease
A Sc W: Association of Scientific Workers
asd: aldosterone secretion defect; atrial septal defect
ASD: Aeronautical Systems Division; Army Shipping Document; Artillery Spotting Division; Assistant Secretary of Defense; Association of Steel Distributors; Aviation Supply Depot
ASD: *Association Suisse de Documentation* (Swiss Association of Documentation)
ASDA: American Safe Deposit Association; American Seafood Distributors Association; American Stamp Dealers Association; Asbestos and Danville (railroad); Association of Structural Draftsmen of America; Atomic and Space Development Authority
ASDAE: Association of Seventh-Day Adventists Educators
ASD–ALA: Adult Services Division—American Library Association
AsDB: Asian Development Bank
ASDC: Aeronomy and Space Data Center (NOAA)
asde: Aircraft surface detection equipment
a/s de: *aux soins de* (French—in care of)
ASDF: Air Self-Defense Force (Japanese Air Force)
ASDG: Aircraft Storage and Disposition Group
asdi: automatic selective dissemination of information
ASDIC: Anti-Submarine Detection Investigation Committee (British sonar, named for this wartime committee)
ASDIRS: Army Study Documentation and Information Retrieval System
asdr: airport surface-detection radar
ASDR: American Society of Dental Radiographers
A/S D/S: *Akties Dampskibsselskab* (Danish—steamship company, limited)
ase: airborne search equipment
ASE: Amalgamated Society of Engineers; American Society of Enologists; American Steel Equipment; American Stock Exchange; Association of Science Education
ASEA: Allmänna Svenska Elektriska Aktiebolaget; American Society of Engineers and Architects
ASEAN: Association of Southeast Asian Nations
ASEB: Aeronautics and Space Engineering Board
ASEC: All Saints' Episcopal College; American Standard Elevator Code
ASECA: Association for Education and Cultural Advancement (South Africa)
ASECS: American Society for Eighteenth-Century Studies
ASEE: American Society of Electrical Engineers; American Society for Engineering Education
ASEP: American Society for Experimental Pathology
ASESA: Armed Services Electro-Standards Agency
ASESB: Armed Services Explosive Safety Board
ASESS: Aerospace Environment Simulation System
ASETC: Armed Services Electron Tube Committee
asf: additional selection factor; amperes per square foot
a-s-f: aniline-formaldehyde-sulfur
ASF: Advisory Support Force; Aircraft Services Facility; Alaskan Sea Frontier; American Scandinavian Foundation; American Schizophrenia Foundation; Ammunition Storage Facility; Army Service Forces; Army Stock Fund; Association of State Foresters; Automative Safety Foundation
ASFA: American Steel Foundrymen's Association
ASFC: Atlantic Salt Fish Commission (Canada)
ASFCO: American Soda Fountain Company
ASFE: American Society For Aesthetics
ASFEC: Arab States Fundamental Education Center
ASFH: Albert Schweitzer Friendship House
asfir: active swept-frequency interferometer radar
ASFMRA: American Society of Farm Managers and Rural Appraisers
ASFP: Association of Specialized Film Producers
asfts: airborne systems functional test stand
asfx: assembly fixture
asg: assignment
ASG: Aeronautical Standards Group (Air Force and Navy); American Saint Gobain (glass); American Society of Genetics
ASGB: Aeronautical Society of Great Britain
ASGBI: Association of Surgeons of Great Britain and Ireland
asgd: assigned
asgmt: assignment
asgn: assign; assignment
ASGp: Aeronautical Standards Group (USAF)
ASGS: American Scientific Glassblowers Society
ash.: airship; armature shunt
Ash: Ashbel; Ashburton; Ashbury; Ashdown; Asher; Asheto; Ashley; Ashman; Ashton; Ashur; Ashville; Ashvillian
Ash: *Asahi Shimbun* (leading Japanese newspaper)
AsH: hyperopic astigmatism
ASH: Action on Smoking and Health; American Society of Hematology; Ashland Oil and Refining (stock exchange symbol)
A–S–H: Allen-Sherman-Hoff
A & SH: Argyll and Southerland Highlanders
ASHA: American School Health Association; American Social Health Association; American Social Hygiene Association; American Speech and Hearing Association
ASHACE: American Society of Heating and Air-Conditioning Engineers
ASHBM: Associate Scottish Hospital Bureau of Management
ASHC: All-States Hobby Club
ashd: arteriosclerotic heart disease
ASHE: American Society of

Hospital Engineers
Ashenden: W. Somerset Maugham
ASHG: American Society of Human Genetics
ASHH: American Society for the Hard of Hearing
ASHI: Association for the Study of Human Infertility
Ashken: *Ashkenazim* (Hebrew—Jews of central and northern Europe)
Ashland: Henry Clay's home in Lexington, Kentucky
Ash Mus: Ashmolean Museum
ashp: airship
ASHP: American Society of Hospital Pharmacists
ASHRAE: American Society of Heating, Refrigerating, and Air-Conditioning Engineers
ASHS: American Society for Horticultural Science
asi: airspeed indicator
ASI: Advanced Scientific Instruments; Aero-Space Institute; Aerospace Studies Institute; Africa Service Institute; Air Society International Amended Shipping Instruction(s); American Specifications Institute; American Swedish Institute; Audience Studies, Incorporated
ASIA: Army Signal Intelligence Agency
Asia's big five: elephant, leopard, rhinoceros, tiger, water buffalo
ASIC: Air Service Information Circular
ASID: American Society of Interior Designers
ASIDIC: Association of Scientific Information Dissemination Centers
ASIF: Airlift Service Industrial Fund
ASI & H: American Society of Ichthyologists and Herpetologists
ASII: American Science Information Institute
ASIL: American Society of International Law
a sin: *a sinistra* (Italian—at (to) the left)
ASIRC: Aquatic Sciences Information Retrieval Center (U of RI)
asis: anterior superior iliac spine
ASIS: Abort-Sensing Implementation System; American Society for Information Science; ammunition stores issue ship (naval designator)
ASIWPCA: Association of State and Interstate Water Pollution Control Administrators
ASJSA: American Society of Journalism School Administrators
ask.: amplitude shift keying
ASK: Association for Social Knowledge
ASKA: Automatic System for Kinematic Analysis
ASKS: Automatic Station-Keeping System
ASKT: American Society of Knitting Technologists
asl: abandon ship ladder; above sea level
Asl: American sign language
ASL: American Association of State Libraries; American Scantic Line; American Shuffleboard Leagues
A-SL: Abelard-Schuman Limited
ASLA: American Society of Landscape Architects
ASLB: Atomic Safety and Licensing Board (AEC)
ASLE: American Society of Lubrication Engineers
ASLEC: Association of Street Lighting Erection Contractors
ASLEF: Associated Society of Locomotive Engineers and Firemen
ASLEP: Apollo Surface Lunar Experiments Package
ASLH: American Society for Legal History
ASLIB: Association of Special Libraries and Information Bureaus
ASLNY: Art Students League of New York
aslo: assembly layout
ASLO: American Society of Limnology and Oceanography
ASLP: Association of Special Libraries in the Philippines
ASLRA: American Short Line Railroad Association
aslt: assault
aslv: *assurance sur la vie* (French—life insurance)
ASLW: Amalgamated Society of Leather Workers
asm: air-to-surface missile; assembly
AsM: myopic astigmatism
ASM: Air-to-Surface Missile; American Society of Mammalogists; American Society for Metals; American Society for Microbiology; Antarctic Service Medal
ASMA: Aerospace Medical Association; American Society of Music Arrangers
asmblr: assembler
ASMC: Army Supply and Maintenance Command (formerly Quartermaster Corps)
ASME: American Society of Magazine Editors; American Society of Mechanical Engineers; Association for the Study of Medical Education
As Mem: Associate Member
ASMFC: Atlantic States Marine Fisheries Commission
ASMFS: American Society of Maxillo-Facial Surgeons
ASMH: Association for Social and Moral Hygiene
asmi: airfield surface movement indication
ASMM: American Supply and Machinery Manufacturers
ASMP: American Society of Magazine Photographers
ASMPA: Armed Services Medical Procurement Agency
ASMPE: American Society of Motion Picture Engineers
asmr (ASMR): advanced short-to-median-range (twin-engine aircraft)
ASMRO: Armed Services Medical Regulating Office
ASMS: Advanced Surface Missile System
asmt: assortment
ASMT: American Society of Medical Technologists
Asmus Rasmus: nickname of the Rasmus Meyer Museum in Bergen, Norway and of J.T. Miller
asn: average sample number
asn (ASN): asparagine (amino acid)
Asn: Association
As of N: Assistant Secretary of the Navy
ASN: Allotment Serial Number; American Society of Naturalists; Army Serial Number; Army Service Number; Asiatic Steam Navigation; Assistant Secretary of the Navy
ASNC: Atlantic Steam Navigation Company (ferries)
ASNDE: Associate of the Society of Non-Destructive Examination
ASNE: American Society of Naval Engineers; American Society of Newspaper Editors
ASNLH: Association for the Study of Negro Life and History
A's & N's: Andamans and Nico-

bars (Andaman and Nicobar Islands)
aso: arteriosclerosis obliterans; auxiliary switch open
ASO: Aeronautica Supply Office(r); Air Signal Officer; Air Staff Officer; Air Staff Orientation; Air Surveillance Officer; Akron Symphony Orchestra; Albany Symphony Orchestra; Albuquerque Symphony Orchestra; American School of Orthodontists; American Sokol Organization; American Symphony Orchestra; Area Supply Office(r); Assistant Secretary's Office; Athens Symphony Orchestra; Atlanta Symphony Orchestra; Aviation Supply Office(r)
ASOC: Air Support Operations Center
ASOK: Ångfartygas Svenska Ostasiatiska Kompaniet (Swedish East Asiatic Steamship Line)
ASOL: American Symphony Orchestra League
ASOR: American Schools of Oriental Research
ASOS: American Society of Oral Surgeons
aso titer: antistreptolysin titer
asp.: affirmative self protection; ammunition supply point; aspartic acid; aspen
a s p: *accepté sous protêt* (French—accepted under protest)
asp (ASP): aspartic acid
Asp: American selling price
ASP: American Society of Parasitologists; American Society of Pharmacognosy; American Society of Photogrammetry; Ammunition Supply Point; Antisubmarine Patrol; Arizona State Prison; Astronomical Society of the Pacific; atmosphere-sounding projectile; Atomic Strike Plan; Automatic Schedule Procedure
A.S.P.: *accepté sans protêt* (French—accepted without protest)
A-S P: Anglo-Saxon Protestant
A/S/P: Aleksander Sergeevich Pushkin—apostle of freedom and father of Russian literature
ASPA: American Society for Personnel Administration; Australian Sugar Producers' Association
ASPAC: Asia and South Pacific Area Council
A-span: anticipation span (eye-voice span); capital-A-shaped span
Asparagus Capital: Isleton, California
ASPB: Armed Services Petroleum Board
aspc: *accepté sous protêt pour acompte* (French—accepted under protest for account)
ASPC: American Sheep Producers Council
ASPCA: American Society for the Prevention of Cruelty to Animals
ASPD: American Society of Professional Draftsmen
ASPERS: Armed Services Procurement Regulations
ASPET: American Society for Pharmacology and Experimental Therapeutics
ASPF: Association of Specialized Film Producers; Association of Superannuation and Pension Funds
asph: asphalt; asphaltic
asphalt: solid bitumen pitch
Asphaltic Lake: the Dead Sea's sobriquet
asphaltum: mineral pitch
asphic: asphaltic
asph mac: asphalt macadam
asphy: asphyxia
ASPI: American Society for Performance Improvement
ASPIRE: Associated Students Promoting Individual Rights for Everyone
aspirin: acetylsalicylic acid
ASPIRIN: Automatic System for Passenger Reservation by Notation
ASPM: *Armed Services Procurement Manual*
aspn: asparagine
ASPO: American Society of Planning Officials
aspp: alloy-steel protective plating
ASPP: American Society of Plant Physiologists; American Society of Polar Philatelists; American Society for the Perfection of Punctuation
ASPPA: Armed Service Petroleum Purchasing Agency
ASPPO: Armed Services Procurement Planning Office
ASPQ: *Association Suisse pour la Promotion de la Qualité* (Swiss Association for Quality Improvement)
ASPR: American Society of Psychical Research; Armed Services Procurement Regulations; Association of South Polar Research
ASPRL: Armament Systems Personnel Research Laboratory (USAF)
ASPRS: American Society of Plastic and Reconstructive Surgery
ASPs: Anglo-Saxon Protestants
ASPSPOM: American Society for the Preservation of Sacred, Patriotic, and Operatic Music
ASPT: American Society of Plant Taxonomists
ASQC: American Society for Quality Control
ASQDE: American Society of Questioned Document Examiners
asr: airport surveillance radar; air-sea rescue; automatic send-receive; available supply rate
ASR: American Society of Rocketry; American Sugar Company (stock exchange symbol); Association of Southeastern Railroads; Aviation Safety Regulation(s); submarine rescue vessel (naval symbol)
ASRC: Air-Sea Rescue Craft; Alabama Space and Rocket Center
asrd: aircraft shipment readiness date
ASRE: American Society of Refrigeration Engineers
ASRI: Aluminum Smelters Research Institute
ASRM: American Society of Range Movement
asroc (ASROC): antisubmarine rocket
ASRP: American Society for the Republic of Panama
ASRPP: American Society for Research in Psychosomatic Problems
a-s rs: air-sea rescue service
ASRT: Air Support Radar Team; American Society of Radiologic Technologists
asrv: angle-stop radiator valve
ass.: anterior superior spine; assurance
ASS: Accordion Sumphony Society; Anglo-Swedish Society; Army Special Staff; Associated Scholastic Society; Associated Sociologists Society; Australian Security Service
A.S.S.: Associate in Secretarial

Science; Associate in Secretarial Studies
A-SS: Anti-Slavery Society
ASSA: American Society for the Study of Allergy; Army Signal Supply Agency; Astronomical Society of South Australia
ASSArthr: American Society for the Study of Arthritis
assce: assurance
ASSCO: American Steam Ship Company
Ass Com Gen: Assistant Commissary General
assd: assigned
ASSE: American Society of Safety Engineers; American Society of Sanitary Engineers
assem: assemble
Assemblyman from the Bowery: Al Smith (Alfred E. Smith)
Assem God: Assemblies of God
assess.: analytical studies of surface effects of submerged submarines
ASSET: Aerothermodynamic Elastic Structural System Environmental Tests
ASSGB: Association of Ski Schools in Great Britain
ASSH: American Society for Surgery of the Hand
assigt: assignment
assim: assimilated
assist.: assistant
assmt: assessment
Assn: Association
Assn Brit Zool: Association of British Zoologists
Assn Clin Biochem: Association of Clinical Biochemists
assnd: assigned
Assn Study Anim Behav: Association for the Study of Animal Behaviour
ASSOBANCA: *Associazione Bancaria Italiana* (Italian Bankers' Association)
assoc: associate; associated; association
Assoc: Associate
Assoc Eng: Associate in Engineering
Associated States: Caribbean island states (Antigua-St Kitts-Nevis, Dominica, Grenada, St Lucia, St. Vincent)
Assoc IEE: Associate of the Institution of Electrical (Electronic) Engineers
Assoc I Min E: Associate of the Institute of Mining Engineers
Assoc INA: Associate of the Institute of Naval Architects
Assoc ISI: Associate of the Iron and Steel Institute
Assoc Met: Associate of Metallurgy
Assoc Sci: Associate in Science
assoc w: associated with
asson: assonance
ASSPHR: Anti-Slavery Society for the Protection of Human Rights
ASSR: Armenian Soviet Socialist Republic; Autonomous Soviet Socialist Republic; Azerbaijan Soviet Socialist Republic
ASSS: American Society for the Study of Sterility
asst: assist; assistance; assistant
ASST: American Society for Steel Treating
Asst Chf Engr: Assistant Chief Engineer
asstd: assented; assorted
ASSU: American Sunday School Union
assy: assembly
Assyr: Assyria(n)
Assyr-Babyl: Assyro-Babylonian
Assyrian Century: the 7th century before the Christian era when Assyria ruled the Middle East and conquered Egypt—the 600s
Ast: astigmatism; Asturias
AST: Surveillance Technician; Alaskan Standard Time; American Radiator and Standard Sanitary (stock exchange symbol); Army Specialized Training; Association for Student Training; Astronomical Society of Tasmania; Atlantic Standard Time
ASTA: American Society of Travel Agents; American String Teachers Association; Army Strategy and Tactics Analysis
ASTA: *Allgemeiner Studentenausschuss* (German—General Students Committee)
ASTANO: *Astilleros y Talleres del Noroeste* (Spanish—Dockyards and Workshops of the Northwest)
ASTAS: Antiradar Surveillance and Target Acquisition System
ASTC: Appalachian State Teachers College; Arkansas State Teachers College; Aroostook State Teachers College
A.S.T.C.: Associate of the Sydney Technical College
ASTD: American Society of Teachers of Dancing; American Society for Training and Development; American Society of Training Directors
ASTE: American Society of Tool Engineers
astec: advanced solar turboelectric concept; advanced solar turboelectric conversion
ASTEC: Antisubmarine Technical Evaluation Center
a sten: aortic stenosis
ASTEO: *Association Scientifique et Technique pour l'Exploration des Océans* (French Scientific and Technical Association for the Exploration of the Oceans)
asth: asthenopia
asti: antispasticity index
ASTI: American School of Technical Intelligence
ASTI: Applied Science and Technology Index
ASTIA: Armed Services Technical Information Agency
astig: astigmatic; astigmatism; astigmatizer; astigmatoscope; astigmatoscopy; astigmia; astigmometer; astigmoscope; etc.
'astinator: procrastinator
ASTM: American Society for Testing and Materials; American Society of Tropical Medicine
ASTME: American Society of Tool and Manufacturing Engineers
ASTMH: American Society of Tropical Medicine and Hygiene
ASTMS: Association of Scientific, Technical, and Managerial Staffs
asto: antistreptolysin
as tol: as tolerated (by the patient)
astor (ASTOR): antisubmarine torpedo
ASTP: Apollo-Soyuz Test Project; Army Specialized Training Program
astr: astronomy
astra: automatic scheduling with time-integrated resource allocation
ASTREA: Air Support to Regional Enforcement Agencies (helicopter surveillance)
astro: astrograph(ic); astrolabe; astrology; astrometry; astronautics; astronomer; astronomical; astronomy; astrophysics
Astro: Astronautics
ASTRO: Air-Space Travel Research Organization

astrochronies: astrochronological relatives
ast t: astronomical time
astrog: astrogeological; astrogeologist; astrogeology
astrol: astrology
astromonk: astronautical monkey (specimen used in biological tests)
astron: astronomy
Astro Obsv: Astrophysical Observatory
astrophys: astrophysics
ASTSECNAV: Assistant Secretary of the Navy
ASTECNAVAIR: Assistant Secretary of the Navy for Air
ASTT: American Society of Traffic and Transportation
A.S.T.T.: Associate in Science Teacher Training
ASU: American Secular Society; American Student Union; Arab Socialist Union; Arizona State University; Asunción, Paraguay (airport)
ASUA: Amateur Swimming Union of the Americas
ASUC: American Society of University Composers; Associated Students of the University of California
ASUSSR: Acadamy of Sciences of the USSR
ASUUS: Amateur Skating Union of the U.S.
asv: airborne radar for detecting surface vessels; aircraft-to-surface vessel; angle stop valve
a-s v: anti-snake venom; arterio-superficial venous
a/sv: arterio/superficial venous
ASV: American Standard Version
ASVA: Associate of the Society of Valuers and Auctioneers
asveo: advance space vehicle engineering operation
ASVU: Army Security Vetting Unit
asw: antisubmarine warfare
ASW: Anti-Submarine Warfare; Association of Scientific Writers
A/S WA: Aviation/Space Writers Association
asw/aaw: antisubmarine warfare/ anti-air warfare
ASWE: Admiralty Surface Weapons Establishment
ASWEPS: Anti-Submarine Warfare Environmental Prediction System
ASWG: American Steel and Wire Gage
ASWS: Audubon Shrine and Wildlife Sanctuary
asy: asylum
asym: asymmetrical
async: asynchronous
ASZ: American Society of Zoologists
ASZD: American Society for Zero Defects
at.: accounting tabulating (card); airtight; asphalt; asphaltic; asphalt tile; atmosphere (technical); atomic
a/t: antitank; antitorpedo
a & t: assemble and test
At: ampere-turn; astatine
AT: Adirondack Trail; Advanced Trainer; Air Travel; antitank; Appalachian Trail; Atherton Tablelands (Queensland parks)
A/T: American terms
***AT:** Antico Testamento* (Italian—Old Testament)
***A-T:** 'Alef-Tav:* (Hebrew—from the first to the last letter of the alphabet)—similar to the English expression from A to Z
ata: actual time of arrival; air-to-air
ATA: Advertising Typographers Association; Air Transport Association; Amateur Trapshooting Association; American Taxicab Association; American Taxpayers Association; American Teachers Association; American Thyroid Association; American Title Association; American Topical Association; American Transit Association; American Translators Association; American Tree Association; American Trucking Association; American Tunaboat Association; Army Transportation Association; Atlantic Treaty Association; auxiliary ocean tug (naval symbol)
A.T.A.: Associate Technical Aide
***ATA:** Agence Telegraphique Albanaise* (French—Albanian News Service)
ATAA: Advertising Typographers Association of America; Air Transport Association of America; Amateur Trapshooting Association of America
ATAC: Air Transport Association of Canada; Allied Tactical Air Force; Army Tank Automotive Center; Army Tank and Automotive Command
atacamite: basic copper chloride
ATAD: Air Transport and Delivery (service)
ATAE: Association of Tutors in Adult Education
ATAF: Allied Tactical Air Force
ATAG: Air Training Advisory Group
ATAI: Air Transport Association International
***ATALA:** Association pour l'Etude et de la Linguistique Appliquée* (Association for the Study of Applied Linguistics)
ATAM: Association for Teaching Aids in Mathematics
atar (ATAR): antitank aircraft rocket
ATAR: Automated Travel Agents Reservation
ATARS: Anti-Terrain-Avoidance Radar System
ATAS: Air Transport Auxiliary Service
Ataturk: (Turkish—Chief Turk) —sobriquet of General-President Mustafa Kemal—first president of Turkey
atav: atavism; atavist; atavistic-(al) (ly)
atb: asphalt tile base; at the time of bombing
ATB: Air Transportation Board
ATBI: Allied Trades of the Banking Industry
atbm: average time between maintenance
atbm (ATBM): antitactical ballistic missile
atc: acoustical tile ceiling; aerial tuning condenser; allergic to combat; approved type certificate; automatic temperature control; automatic tint control(tv)
atc (ATC): automatic train control
ATC: Air Traffic Conference; Air Traffic Control; Air Training Command; Air Transport Command; Air Transportation Corps; Aircraft Technical Committee; Airport Traffic Control; Airway Traffic Control; Alpine Tourist Commission; Appalachian Trail Conference; Armament Test Center; Army Training Center; Army Transportation Corps; Associated Traffic Clubs; Associated Travel Clubs
ATCA: Air Traffic Conference of America; Air Traffic Control Association
ATCC: Air Traffic Control Cen-

ter; Automatic Train Control Center

ATCDE: Association of Teachers in Colleges and Departments of Education

atce: ablative thrust chamber engine

atceu: air traffic control evaluation unit

ATCF: Automobile and Touring Club of Finland

atch: attach; attaching; attachment

atchd: attached

ATCL: Associate of Trinity College of Music—London

ATCMD: Atlanta Contract Management District

ATCO: Air Traffic Coordinating Office(r)

ATCOM: Atoll Commander

ATCOS: Atmospheric Composition Satellite

ATCRBS: Air Traffic Control Radar Beacon System

atd: actual time of departure; anthropomorphic test dummy

atd: *a tak dale* (Czech—et cetera)

ATD: Actual Time of Departure; Aid to the Totally Disabled; Armament Test Division; Art Teachers Diploma

atda: augmented target docking adapter

ATDA: American Train Dispatchers Association

atdc: after top dead center (valve setting)

ATDS: Airborne Tactical Data System; Association of Teachers of Domestic Science

ate: altitude transmitting equipment; automatic test equipment

Ate: *Almirante* (Spanish—admiral)

ATE: Associated Telephone Exchanges

ATEA: American Toy Export Association

ATEC: Air Transport Electronics Council

A.Tech.: Associate in Technology

ATEM: Aircraft Test Equipment Modification

Aten: *Atenas* (Portuguese or Spanish—Athens); *Atene* (Italian—Athens); *Athenes* (French—Athens)

A temp: *a tempo* (Italian—in the speed written)

ATEN: *Association Technique pour la production et l'utilisation de l'Energie Nucleaire* Technical Association for the Production and Use of Nuclear Energy)

ATerm: Air Terminal

ATESL: Association of Teachers of English as a Second Language

Atex: Atlantic tradewind experiment

atf: accounting tabulating form; actual time of fall

ATF: Air Task Force; American Type Founders; ocean tug (3-letter symbol)

ATFAC: American Turpentine Farmers Association Cooperative

atfr: automatic terrain-following radar

ATFS: Association of Track and Field Statisticians

atg: air-to-ground

ATG: Accordion Teachers Guild; Army Technical Group

atgar (ATGAR): anti-tank guided air rocket

ath: atheism; atheist(ic); athletic

Ath: Athens

ATH: Athens, Greece (airport)

AT-H: August Thyssen-Hütte

Athab: Athabasca(n)

athc: allotetrahydrocortisol

Atheist's Bible: Thomas Paine's *The Age of Reason*

Athel: Athel Line

Athen: Athenian

Athene: (Greek—Minerva)—goddess of wisdom

Athenian Century: the 5th century before the Christian era when the Athenians destroyed the Persian fleet at Salamis and completed the Parthenon in Athens—the 400s

atheol: atheological; atheologist; atheology

athodyd: aerothermodynamic duct (ramjet engine)

athsc: atherosclerosis

athw: athwartship

ati: actual time of interception; aerial tuning inductance; average total inspection

ATI: Air Technical Intelligence; American Television Institute; Asbestos Technical Institute; Asbestos Textile Institute

ATI: *Aero Transporti Italiani* (Italian Air Freight Line); Air Technical Index; *Azienda Tabacchi Italiani* (Italian State Tobacco Board)

A & TI: Agricultural and Technical Institute

ATIC: Aerospace Technical Intelligence Center; Air Technical Intelligence Center; Antigua Tourist Information Center

ATII: Associate of the Taxation Institute Incorporated

ATIL: Air Target Intelligence Liaison Program (USAF)

atis: automatic terminal information service

ATIS: Air Technical Intelligence Study

ATISC: Air Technical Intelligence Services Command (USAF)

ATJ: Association of Teachers of Japanese

ATJS: Advanced Tactical Jamming System

atk: attack

a-tk: anti-tank

atl: analog threshold logic

Atl: Atlanta; Atlantic

Atl: *Atlantico* (Italian or Spanish—Atlantic); *Atlantico* (Portuguese—Atlantic); *Atlantique* (French—Atlantic)

ATL: Associated Truck Lines; Atlanta, Georgia (airport); Atlantic Tankers Limited

ATLA: American Theological Library Association; American Trial Lawyers Association

ATLANTIC: Atlantic Refining Company

Atlantic Community: NATO nations

Atlantic Provinces: New Brunswick, Newfoundland, Nova Scotia, Prince Edward Island

Atlantic Scandinavia: Denmark, Iceland, Norway

ATLAS: Abbreviated Test Language for Avionic Systems; Automated Tape Label Assignment System

Atlas-Agena: two-stage launch vehicle

Atlas-Centaur: first American high-energy launch vehicle for space exploration—D-Series Atlas boosts Centaur space vehicle

Atlas-E: intercontinental ballistic missile designed to place a thermonuclear warhead on a 9000-mile-distant target

atlas fol: atlas folio—a book about 25 inches high

Atlas icbm: first American intercontinental ballistic missile

ATLB: Air Transport Licensing Board (UK)

ATLIS: Army Technical Library

Improvement Studies
Atl C: Atlantic City
Atl O: Atlantic Ocean
Atl Pil Aut: Atlantic Pilotage Authority
atm: atmosphere (normal)
at. m: atomic mass
at/m: ampere turns per meter
AT_7: hexachlorophene (disinfectant)
AT_{19}: dihydrotachysterol
ATM: Apollo Telescope Mount; Association of Teaching Aids in Mathematics; Associated Tobacco Manufacturers
ATM: *Azienda Tranviaria Municipale* (Italian—Municipal Rapid Transit Board)
ATMA: Adhesive Tape Manufacturers' Association
ATMC: Army Transportation Materiel Command
ATMI: American Textile Manufacturers Institute
atmos: atmosphere; atmospheric(al)(ly)
atm press: atmospheric pressure
ATMS: Automatic Transmission Measuring System
atn: acute tubular necrosis
ATN: Alabama, Tennessee and Northern (railroad)
ATNA: Australian Trained Nurses' Association
atndt: attendant
at. no.: atomic number
ATNP: Atherton Lablelands National Parks (Queensland)
ato: according to others; assisted takeoff; automatic train operation
ATO: ocean tug, old (3-letter symbol)
atoll.: acceptance, test, or launch language
atomdef: atomic defense
atomdev: atomic device
Atomic Cities: Los Alamos, New Mexico; Oak Ridge, Tennessee; Richland, Washington—created during World War II for generation of atomic bombs as well as nuclear energy sources
Atomic City: place-name nickname shared by Los Alamos, New Mexico and Oak Ridge, Tennessee
Atomic Energy City: Oak Ridge, Tennessee
atoms.: automated technical order maintenance sequence(s)
atorp: antitorpedo; atomic torpedo
ATOS: American Theatre Organ Society; Association of Temporary Office Services
atp (ATP): adenosine triphosphate, material found in almost all terrestrial life
atp: *a tout prix* (French—at any price)
ATP: Allied Technical Publication; Army Training Program
atpa: auxiliary turbopump assembly
ATPAS: Association of Teachers of Printing and Allied Subjects
ATPase: adenosine triphosphate
atpd: ambient temperature and pressure—dry
ATPE: Association of Teachers in Penal Establishments
ATPI: American Textbook Publishers Institute
ATPM: Association of Toilet Paper Manufacturers
at pres: at present
atps: ambient temperature and pressure—saturated with water vapor
atpu: air transport pressurizing unit
atr: advanced test reactor; anti-transmit-receive; transmitter-receiver
Atr: Achilles tendon reflex
ATR: Advanced Test Reactor; Association of Teachers of Russian; ocean tug, rescue (3-letter naval symbol)
atran: automatic terrain recognition and navigation
atrax: air-transportable communications complex
atrc: anti-tracking control
ATRC: Air Traffic Regulation Center
atr fib: atrial fibrillation
atrid: automatic target recognition, identification, and detection
atrima: as their respective interests may appear
ATRIS: Air Traffic Regulation Identification System (USA)
atro: actual time of return to operation
atrop: atrophy
atrt: anti-transmit-receive tube
ats: advanced technological satellite; air-to-ship; anxiety-tension state; astronomical time switch
ATs: Achievement Tests
ATS: Advanced Technological Satellite; Aeronautical Training Society; Air Tactical School; Air Traffic Services; American Therapeutic Society; American Trudeau Society; Application Technology Satellite; Army Transport Service; salvage tug (naval symbol)
ATSA: Aero Transportes
ATSC: American Traffic Safety Council
ATSE: Alliance of Theatrical Stage Employees
AT & SF: Atchison, Topeka and Santa Fe (railway)
ATSFSD: Air Traffic Service Flight Services Division (FAA)
atsit: automatic techniques for the selection and identification of targets
ATSOCC: Applications Technology Satellite Operations Control Center (NASA)
ATS's: Advanced Technological Satellites
AtST: Atlantic Standard Time
att: attach; attorney
a t & t: all tacos and tamales (American Southwestern roadside-stand short form); always talking and talking
Att: Attic(a)
ATT: Army Training Test
A & TT: Alcohol and Tobacco Tax
AT & T: American Telephone & Telegraph
atta: *atenta* (Spanish—attentively)
ATTC: American Towing Tank Conference
atten: attenuation, attenuator
Atterdag: (Danish—Another Day)—nickname of King Valdemar IV
ATT & F: Alcohol, Tobacco Tax, and Firearms (Division of U.S. Treasury Dept)
Att Gen: Attorney General
ATTI: Association of Teachers in Technical Institutions
Attic Muse: the Athenian historian Xenophon
attn: attention
atto: attorney
atto: *atento* (Spanish—attentively); 10^{-18}
attr: attractive
attrib: attributive
attrit: attrition
ATTS: Automatic Telemetry Tracking System
Attunusia: (Arabic—Tunisia)
atty: attorney
atty & c: attorney and client
Atty Gen: Attorney General
AT type: adenine and thymine type
Atu: *Atmosphärenüberdruck*

(German—atmospheric excess pressure)

ATU: Alliance of Telephone Unions; Amalgamated Transit Union

atum: antitank nonmetallic

atv (ATV): all-terrain vehicle

ATV: Associated Tele Vision

ATV: *Akademiet for de Tekniske Videnskaber* (Danish—Academy of Technical Sciences)

atvm: attenuator thermo-element voltmeter

at. vol: atomic volume

at/w: atomic hydrogen weld

ATW: American Theater Wing

at/wb: ampere turns per weber

ATWE: Association of Technical Writers and Editors

ATWg: Air Transport Wing (USAF)

atws: automatic track while scanning

at. wt: atomic weight

A Typ I: *Association Typographique Internationale* (French—International Typographic Association)

at. xpl: atomic explosion

au: angstrom unit; antitotxin unit; arbitrary unit(s); author; azauridine

au: *aurum* (Latin—gold)

a.u.: *aures unitas* (Latin—both ears); *au usum* (Latin—according to custom)

Au: angstrom unit; astronomical unit; gold (symbol)

Au^{198}: radioactive gold (symbol)

AU: Aarhus Universitet (University of Aarhus); Air University; Alfred University; Allen University; American University; Andrews University; Army Unit; Assumption University; astronomical unit; Atlanta University; Auburn University

AÜ: Ankara Üniversitesi (University of Ankara)

A/U: advanced undersea weapons

A & U: Allen & Unwin

AUA: American Unitarian Association; American Urological Association; Aruba, Netherlands West Indies (airport); Associated Unions of America; Austrian Airlines

A.U.A.: Associate of the University of Adelaide

AUB: American University of Beirut

AUBC: Association of Universities of the British Commonwealth

AUBTW: Amalgamated Union of Building Trade Workers

auc: average unit cost

a.u.c.: *ab urbe condita* (Latin—from the founding of the city; usually refers to Rome)

AUC: Aberystwyth University College

AU of C: American University of Cairo

AUCA: American Unitarian Christian Association

AUCAS: Association of University Clinical Academic Staff

AUCC: Association of Universities and Colleges of Canada

Auck: Auckland

Aucklands: Auckland Islands

AUCOA: Association of United Contractors of America

AUCSRLFRVWAM: All-Union Central Scientific Research Laboratory for the Restoration of Valuable Works of Art in Museums

auct: auction(eer)

auct: *auctorum* (Latin—of authors)

AUCTU: All-Union Council of Trade Unions

aud: audible; audit; audition; auditor; auditorium

audar: autodyne detection and ranging

Aud[a]: *audiencia* (Spanish—court of justice; hearing)

aud disb: auditor disbursements

Aud Gen: Auditor General

Aud Gen Nav: Auditor General of the Navy

Audie: Audry

auding: auditory hearing, listening, and understanding

audio: audiofrequency; audiogenic; audiogram; audiology; audiometer; audiometry; audiophile; audiovisual; audiovisual aids; etc.

audiol: audiology

audiovis: audiovisual; audiovisual aids

audre: audio response; automatic digit recognizer

AUEC: association of University Evening Colleges

AUEW: Amalgamated Union of Engineering Workers

Aufdr: *Aufdrucke* (German—imprint)

Aufl: *Auflage* (German—edition)

AUFS: American Universities Field Staff

AUFUSAF: Army Unit for United States Air Force

aug: augment; augmentation; augmentative

Aug: August; Augusta; Augustan

Augember: August and September

Augie: August; Augustine; Augustus

augm: *augmente* (French—augmented)

Augustan Age: Latin literature's golden era when Horace, Livy, Ovid, and Virgil flourished during the reign of the Emperor Augustus (27 B.C. to A.D. 14)

Augustina de Aragón: Augustina Domenech Zaragoza

Au_2H_2O: political campaign nickname of Arizona's Senator Barry Goldwater

AUI: Associated Universities Incorporated

auj: *aujourd'hui* (French—today)

Auk: Auckland

aul: above upper limit

AUL: Aberdeen University Library; Air University Library

AULC: American University Language Center

Auld Ane: (Scottish Gaelic—Old One)—the devil

Auld Clootie: (Scottish Gaelic—Old Cloven)—cloven-footed devil

Auld Reekie: (Scottish Gaelic—Old Smelly)—smogbound Edinburgh's nickname

Auld Sod: (Scottish Gaelic—Old Land)—Scotland

AULLA: Australasian Universities Language and Literature Association

aum (AUM): air-to-underwater missile

aum: *aumentado* (Spanish—augmented)

AUMLA: Australian Universities Modern Language Association

a. u. n.: *abesque ulla nota* (Latin—without annotation)

AUNT: Alliance for Undesirable but Necessary Tasks

auntie.: automatic unit for national taxation and insurance (UK)

AUO: African Unity Organization

AUP: Australian United Press

AUPG: American University Publishers Group

aur: auricle; auricular; auricularis; aurum

AUR: Association of University Radiologists

AURA: Association of Universi-

ties for Research in Astronomy
Aurelian Century: the 100s—reign of Roman emperor-philosopher Marcus Aurelius—the 2nd century
aur fib: auricular fibrillation
AURI: Angkatan Udara Republik Indonesia (Indonesian Air Force)
auric: auricular
aurora australis: (Latin—southern lights)
aurora borealis: (Latin—northern lights)
Aus: Austin; Austria; Austrian
AUS: Army of the United States; Austin, Texas (airport)
AUSA: Association of the United States Army
ausc: auscultation
AUSCS: Americans United for Separation of Church and State
Ausg: *Ausgabe* (German—edition)
Au sh: Australian serum hepatitis
AUSLFL: All-Union State Library of Foreign Literature (Moscow)
AUSS: Association of University Summer Sessions
Aussieland: Australia
Aussie(s): Australian(s)
Aust: Australia; Australian
Aust Cur: Australian Current
austen: austenitic
Austin: Augustina; Augustine
austral: (Spanish—southern)
Austral: Australian
Australas: Australasian
Australian States: New South Wales, Queensland, South Australia, Tasmania, Victoria, Western Australia
Australian Territories: Australian Antarctic; Australian Capital Territory (Canberra), Northern Territory, Papua New Guinea (Admiralty Islands, Heard and McDonald Islands, New Britain, New Guinea, New Ireland, the Solomons)
Australia's Little England: Tasmania
aut: *autore* (Italian—author)
Aut: *Autriche* (French—Austria)
AUT: American Union Transport; Association of University Teachers
AUTEC: Atlantic Underwater Test Evaluation Center
auth: authentic; authenticate; authenticity; author; authority; authorization; authorize(d)
Auth: Authority
authab: authorized abbreviation (USAF)
Author of the Declaration of Independence: Thomas Jefferson
Auth Ver: Authorized Version
AUT(I): Association of University Teachers (Ireland)
auto.: automobile; automatic; automotive
autiobio: autobiograph; autobiographer; autobiographic(al); autobiography
autocade: automobile parade
autodin: automatic digital network
autodoc: automatic documentation
autog: autograph
auto. lean: automatic lean
autom: automobile; automotive
autom: *automobile* (Italian—automobile); *automóvel* (Portuguese—automobile); *automóvil* (Spanish—automobile)
automap: automatic machining program
automast: automatic mathematical analysis and symbolic translation
automatic: automatic revolver
automation: automation action; automatic operation
Automobile City: Detroit, Michigan
Automobile Wizard: Henry Ford
automtn: automation
auton: autonomous; autonomy
autonet: automatic network
autop: automatic pistol; autopsy
AUTOPIC: Automatic Personal Identification Code
autopilot: automatic pilot
autopistol: automatic pistol
autogrom: autoprompter (tape)
autoprompt: automatic programming of machine tools
AUTOPSY: Automatic Operating System (IBM)
auto. recl: automatic reclosing
auto. rich: automatic rich
autorotic(s): automobile neurotic(s)
autos: automobiles; automatics
autosate: automatic data systems analysis technique
autoscript: automated system for composing, revising, illustrating, and typesetting
auto s & sv: automatic stop and check valve
AUTOSERVCEN: Automated Service Center
autosevcom: automatic secure voice communications
autospot: automatic system for positioning tolls
Auto State: Michigan
autostatis: automatic statewide auto theft inquiry
autostrad: automated system for transportation data
autosyn: automatically synchronous
autotran: automatic translation
autovon: automatic voice network
au tr: aural training
autran: automatic target-recognition analysis
AUT(S): Association of University Teachers (Scotland)
AUT(W): Association of University Teachers (Wales)
AUU: Association of Urban Universities
auv: armored utility vehicle
Au virus: Australian antigen
auw: airframe unit weight
AUWE: Admiralty Underwater Weapons Establishment
aux: auxiliary
aux m: auxiliary machinery
AUXOPS: Auxiliary Operational Members (USCG)
auxrc: auxiliary recording control
av: anteversion; aortic valve; arteriovenous; assessed valuation; atrioventricular; auriculoventricular; average; aviator; avoirdupois
a-v: atriventricular; audio-visual
av: *avril* (French—April)
a v: *a vista* (Italian—at sight)
a/v (A/V): *ad valorem* (Latin—as valued)
Av: Aves; Avian; Avila(n)
Av: *avenida* (Portuguese or Spanish—avenue)
AV: *alta voltagem* (Portuguese—high voltage); *alto voltaggio* (Italian—high voltage); *alto voltaje* (Spanish—high voltage); American viewpoint; Antonio Vivaldi; arteriovenous; audiovisual; Authorized Version; large seaplane tender (naval symbol)
A.V.: *Anno Vixit* (Latin—he (she) lived (a given number of) years)
ava: arteriovenous anastomosis
AVA: Aerodynamische Versuchsanstalt; American Vocational Association; Audio-Visual Aids
av/af: anteverted/anteflexed
aval: availability; available
avb: *avbeta* (Swedish—departure)

AVB: advanced aviation base ship (naval symbol)
avbl: armored vehicle bridge launcher
avc: allantoid vaginal cream; automatic volume control
av *C:* *avanti Cristo* (Italian—Before Christ)
AVC: American Veterans Committee; Antelope Valley College; Association of Vitamin Chemists; Audio-Visual Center
AvCad: Aviation Cadet
Av Cert: Aviation Certificate
avcs: atrioventricular conduction system
AVCS: Advanced Videcon Camera Systems; Assistant Vice Chief of Staff
avd: automatic voice data; automatic voltage digitizer
avd: *avdeling* (Dano-Norwegian—part; section)
AvD: Automobil Club von Deutschland (German Automobile Club)
AVD: Army Veterinary Department; high-speed seaplane tender (3-letter naval symbol)
Avda: *Avenida* (Spanish—Avenue)
AVDA: American Venereal Disease Association
a-v difference: arteriovenous concentration difference
AVDO: Aerospace Vehicle Distribution Office(r)
avdp: avoirdupois
ave: automatic volume expansion
'ave: have
Ave: Avenue
avec: amplitude vibration exciter control
AVEM: Association of Vacuum Equipment Manufacturers
Avennio: (Latin—Avignon)
AVENSA: Aerovias Venezolanas (Venezuelan Airlines)
avf: arteriovenous fistula; azimuthally varying field
avfr: available for reassignment
avg: average
Avg: *Avgust* (Russian—August)
Av Gar: Avant Garde
avgas: aviation gasoline
avge: average
avh: acute viral hepatitis
Avh: *Avhandlinger* (Swedish—transactions)
avi: airborne vehicle identification; air velocity index; aviation
AVI: American Virgin Islands; Association Universelle d'Aviculture Scientifique (Universal Association of Scientific Aviculture)
Aviaco: Aviación y Comercio (Spanish airline)
AVIANCA: Aerovias Nacionales de Colombia (National Airlines of Colombia)
AVIATECA: Empresa Guatemalteca de Aviacion (Guatemalan Aviation Enterprise)
Avicenna: Arabian astronomer-mathematician-physician Abu ibn Sina (980-1037)
AVID: Audio-Visual Instruction Department
avigation: aircraft navigation
avionics: aviation and astronautics electronics
AVISCO: American Viscose Corporation
AVISPA: Aerovias Interamericanas de Panamá (Interamerican Airways of Panama)
av JC: *avant Jesus Christ* (French—before Jesus Christ; B.C.)
avl: average versus length
av l: average length
AVL: Asheville, North Carolina (airport)
AVLA: Audio-Visual Language Association
Av Labs: Aviation Laboratories (USA)
AVLINE: Audiovisuals On-Line (computer retrieval system)
avlm: anti-vehicle land mine
avlub: aviation lubricant
avm: automatic voting machine
AVM: guided-missile ship (naval symbol)
AVMA: American Veterinary Medical Association
AVMF: *Aviatsiya Voenno Morskikh Flota* (Russian—Soviet Naval Aviation)
avn: atrioventricular node; aviation
Avn: Avonmouth
AVN: Air Vietnam
AVNMED: Aviation Medicine (DoD)
av node: arterioventricular node
avo: ampere-volt-ohm
AVO: Állam Védelmi-Osztály (Hungarian—Hungarian-Secret Soviet Police); avoid verbal orders
Avog: Avogadro
avoid.: airfield vehicle obstacle indication device
avoil: aviation oil
avoir: avoirdupois
avolo: automatic voice link observation
Avon: Avonmouth (Port of Bristol)
AVP: seaplane tender, small (3-letter symbol); Wilkes-Barre, Pennsylvania (airport)
avr: aortic valve replacement
AVR: Army Volunteer Reserve
AVRA: Audio-Visual Rsearch Association
AVRI: Animal Virus Research Institute
AVRO: A.V. Roe (Ltd)
AVRO: *Algemeene Vereeninging Radio Omroep* (Dutch—General Broadcasting Association)
avrp: atrioventricular refractory period; audiovisual recording and presentation
avs: aerospace vehicle simulation
AVS: American Vacuum Society; Association for Voluntary Sterilization; aviation supply ship (naval symbol)
A-V S: Anti-Vivisection Society
AVSA: African Violet Society of America
AVSC: Audio-Visual Support Center (USA)
AVSL: Assistant Venture Scout Leader
avst: automated visual-sensitivity test(er)
AVSYCOM: Aviation Systems Command (USA)
avt: audiovisual tutorial
Avt: Allen vision test
AVT: Adult Vocational Training; auxiliary aircraft transport (naval symbol); Aviation Medicine Technician
avta: automatic vocal transaction analyzer
AVTRW: Association of Veterinary Teachers and Research Workers
AVUS: *Automobile Versuchs and Untersuchungs Strecke* (German—Automobile Test Track)
avv: *avvocato* (Italian—advocate)—lawyer
av vales: atrioventricular (heart) valves
av w: average width
AVWV: *Antilliaans Verbond van Werknemers Verenigingen* (Dutch—Antillean Confederation of Workers' Unions)
AVX: Avalon Bay, Catalina Island, California (airport)
aw: air-to-water; anterior wall; antiwear; atomic warfare
a/w: actual weight; all-water; all-weather

a & w: alive and well
AW: air warning; Air Work, Ltd; American Welding; Articles of War; atomic warfare; atomic weight; automatic weapons(s); distilling ship (naval symbol)
A-W: Addison-Wesley
A & W: Atlantic & Western (railroad)
AWA: Air Warfare Analysis; All-Weather Attack; Aluminum Wares Association; American Warehousemen's Association; American Watch Association; American Waterfowl Association; American Wine Association; American Woman's Association; Association of Women in Architecture; Aviation/Space Writers Association
***AWA:** All the World's Aircraft*
awac: airborne warning and control
AWACS: Airborne Warning and Control System
AWADS: All-Weather Aerial Delivery System
Awakener of Bulgaria: George Venelin
AWAL: American-West African Line
AWAM: Association of West African Merchants
awar: area-weighted average resolution
AWARE: Addiction Workers Alerted to Rehabilitation and Education (NYC); Association for Women's Active Return to Education
AWARS: Airborne Weather and Reconnaissance System
AWAS: Australian Women's Army Service
AWASM: Associate of the Western Australia School of Mines
awb: air waybill
AWB: Agricultural Wages Board (UK)
AWBA: American World Boxing Association
AWB/CN: Air Waybill or Consignment Note
AWC: Air War College; American Watershed Council; American Wool Council; Anaconda Wire & Cable (stock exchange symbol); Area Wage & Classification (office); Arizona Western College; Army War College; Army Weapons Command
AWCO: Area Wage and Classification Office
awcs: agency-wide coding structure
AWCS: Air Weapons Control System
awd: awards
AWD: Air Worthiness Division
AWDA: Automotive Warehouse Distributors Association
awdr: advanced weapon-delivery radar
AWEASVC: Air Weather Service
A Weld I: Associate of the Welding Institute
AWES: Army Waterways Experiment Station
a wf: acceptable work-load factor; adrenal weight factor
AWF: American Wildlife Foundation
AWFS: All-Weather Fighter Squadron
AWG: American Wire Gage
AWH: Association of Western Hospitals
AWHA: Australian Women's Home Army
awi: anterior wall infarction
AWI: Animal Welfare Institute
AWIS: Association of Women in Science
AWIU: Allied Workers International Union
AWK: Wake Island (airport)
awl.: absent with leave; artesian well lease
AWLC: Association of Women Launderers and Cleaners
AWLF: African Wildlife Leadership Foundation
AWLS: All-Weather Landing System
awm: automatic washing machine
AWM: American War Mothers; Association of Women Mathematicians
AMWC: Association of Workers for Maladjusted Children
awmi: anterior wall myocardial infarction
awn: awning
AWN: Automated Weather Network
AWngSvc: Air Warning Service
AWNL: Australian Women's National League
AWO: Accounting Work Order; American Waterways Operators
awol: absent without leave
AWOP: All-Weather Operations Panel
awp: amusements with prizes
A & WP: Atlanta and West Point (railroad)
AWPA: American Wood Preservers Association
AWPB: American Wood Preservers Bureau
AWPL: Australia-West Pacific Line
awr: adaptive waveform recognition
AWR: Association of Western Railways
AWRA: American Water Resources Association
AWRE: Atomic Weapons Research Establishment
AWRIS: Army War Room Information System
AWRNCO: Aircraft Warning Company (Marines)
AWRT: American Women in Radio and Television
AWS: Aircraft Warning Service; Aircraft Warning System; Air Warning Service; Air Warning Squadron; Air Warning System(s); Air Weather Service; Air Weapon Systems; American War Standards; American Watercolor Society; American Weather Service; American Welding Society; Atlas Weapon System; Attack Warning System; Aviation Weather Service
AWSA: American Water Ski Association
AWSG: Army Work Study Group
***AW & ST:** Aviation Week & Space Technology*
awt: advanced waste treatment
AWTE: Association for World Travel Exchange
awu: atomic weight unit
AWU: Aluminim Workers Union
AWWA: American Water Works Association
AWWU: American Watch Workers Union
awy: airway
ax.: axiom(atic); axes; axis
AX: American Air Export & Import Company (stock exchange symbol)
axbt: aircraft-expendable bathythermograph
axgrad: axial gradient
axio: axiological(ly); axiologist; axiology; axiom; axiomatic (al)(ly)
AXO: Assistant Experimental Officer
***Axon:** Axelson* (Swedish—son of Axel)
Ay: Ayala
AY: Allied Youth
AYA: American Yachtsmen's

Association

AYC: Albany Yacht Club; American Yacht Club; American Youth Congress; Atlantic Yacht Club; Audubon Yacht Club

AYD: American Youth for Democracy

ayer: (Malay—water); (Spanish—yesterday)

Ayer: N.W. Ayer and Son

ayf: anti-yeast factor

AYH: American Youth Hostels

AYI: Academic Year Institute (NSF)

AYLC: Association of Young Launderers and Cleaners

Aym: Aymara

AYM: Ancient York Mason; Ancient York Masonry

AYM–YWHAs: Association of Young Men-Young Women's Hebrew Associations of Greater New York

AYP: Alaska-Yukon Pioneers

Ayr: Ayrshire

Ayrshire Poet: Robert Burns born in Alloway, Ayrshire, Scotland

az: azure

a Z: *aan Zee* (Dutch—on sea); *auf Zeit* (German—on account; on credit)

Az: azimuth; Azores; Aztec; Aztecan; azure

Az: *Azote* (Greek—nitrogen)

AZ: Active Zone; Alitalia (Linee Aeree Italiane)

AZ: *Akademisch Ziekenhuis* (Dutch—Academic Hospital)

A–Z: Ascheim-Zondek (pregnancy test)

A to Z: from A to Z; from the beginning to the end; thoroughly covered

AZA: American Zionist Association

Azalea Trail City: Lafayette, Louisiana

azas: adjustable-zero adjustable-span

Azb: Azerbaijan; Axerbaijani; Azerbaijanian

AZC: American Zionist Counicl

azel: azimuth elevation

AZF: American Zionist Federation

azg: azaguanine

AZGS: Azusa Ground Station

azi: azimuth

Az I: Azores Islands

AZI: American Zinc Institute

az ld: azure laid (paper)

Azorin: (pseudonym—Jose Martinez Ruis)

Azr: Azores

azran: azimuth and range

AZRI: Arid Zone Research Institute

azrock: asbestos rock

azs: automatic zero set

azt: azusa transponder

Azt: Aztec; Aztecan

Azores: Azores Islands

AZT: Ascheim-Zondek Test

aztc: azusa transponder coherent

Aztecan and Incan Century: the 1000s—great stone structures still standing in the highlands of Mexico and Peru are mute witnesses to these indigenous American cultures—the 11th century

Aztec type: microcephalic idiocy

A–Z Test: Ascheim-Zondek Test (for pregnancy)

azur: azauridine

azusa: azimuth, speed, altitude

az wo: azure wove (paper)

azy: azyme (matzos; unleavened bread)

B

b: baby; base; bicuspid; bituminous; black; blue; book; born; brass; breadth; bridge; wing span (symbol)

b: span

b.: *bis* (Latin—twice)

b 1: booster 1

b 1 p: booster 1 pitch

b 1 y: booster 1 yaw

b 2: booster 2

b 2 p: booster 2 pitch

b 2 y: booster 2 yaw

B: Bacillus; bad; *bajar* (Spanish—to descend); balboa (Panamanian currency); Baltic; band-width; Barber Lines; *bas* (French—down); bastard; Baume; Baume scale; bay; *Bay* (Turkish—Mister); Beatrice (Beatrice Foods) Beech; Belgium (auto plaque); belted; Bendix; Benoist scale; unit of marijuana measurement consisting of just enough to fill a small matchbox; benzene; body; Boeing; boils at; bolivar (Venezuelan currency); boliviano (Bolivian currency); bomber; bonded; borderline; boron; Boston; bowels; Bravo—code for letter B; British; brightness (symbol); Brother; Bruning; Buddhist; Bull Lines; buoyancy; Burroughs; flux density (symbol); Fraunhofer line caused by terrestrial oxygen

B-1: long range supersonic bomber

B2F: Boeing 720 fan jet airplane

B2F: Boeing 320 fan jet airplane

b4: before

B7F: Boeing 707 fan jet airplane

B-47: Stratojet all weather strategic medium bomber

B-52: Stratofortress all-weather intercontinental strategic heavy bomber

B-57: Canberra two-place twin-engine turbojet all-weather tactical bomber

B-58: Hustler strategic all-weather supersonic bomber

B-66: Destroyer twin-engine turbo-jet tactical all-weather light-bombardment aircraft

B 77: Bratislava 77 (viral) strain

B-707: one of a Boeing aircraft series containing other popular transport planes such as the 727, 737, 747, etc.

B/: balboa (Panamanian currency unit = $1.00 U.S.)

B: *bueno* (Spanish—good)—examination grade

B': *Ben* (Hebrew—son; son of)

ba: base line; blind approach

b/a: backache; billed at; boric acid

b.a.: *balneum arenae* (Latin—sand bath)

Ba: Baia (Portuguese—Bahia); barium (symbol)

BA: Basic Airman; Bellas Artes (Fine Arts); Berkshire Atheni-

um; Boeing (stock exchange symbol); Boston & Albany (railroad); British Academy; British Admiralty; British Army; British Association (for the Advancement of Science); Buenos Aires; Bureau of Accounts; Bureau of Apprenticeship; Busted Aristocrat (an officer reduced to the ranks)
BA: *Bowker Annual*
B-A: Basses-Alpes
B.A.: *Baccalaureus Artium* (Latin—Bachelor of Arts)
B/A: Bank of America; British American (oil company)
B & A: Bangor & Aroostook (railroad); Boston & Albany (railroad)
BA: *Biological Abstracts; Bonne Action* (French—Good Deed)
B es A: *Bachelier des Arts* (French—Bachelor of Arts)
baa: benzoyl arginine amide; bleat of a sheep
Baa: Baal; Baalam
BAA: Brewers Association of America; British Acetylene Assotiation; British Airports Authority; British Archeological Association; British Astronomical Association; Bureau of African Affairs
B.A.A.: Bachelor of Applied Arts
BAAA: British Association of Accountants and Auditors
BAAB: British Amateur Athletic Board
BAADS: Bangor Air Defense Sector
BAAF: Brigade Airborne Alert Force
baai: (Dutch—bay)
Baal: Baalbek
BAAL: Black Academy of Arts and Letters
BAAR: Board of Aviation Accident Research
BAAS: British Association for the Advancement of Science
bab: (Arabic—gate; strait)
Bab: Barbara; Babylon; Babylonia; Babylonian; W.S. Gilbert's nickname
Babette: Elizabeth
Bab(s): Barbara
BAB: British Airways Board; B.T.Babbitt (Babo cleanser)
Babar: Jean de Brunhoff's little elephant of storybook fame; Zahir ud-Din Muhammad (founder of India's Mogul dynasty)
Babars: Babar Islands of Indonesia
babb: babbit metal
Babbie: Barbara
Bab-el-Mandeb: (Arabic—Gate of Tears)—strait linking the Indian Ocean's Gulf of Aden with the Red Sea; scene of many shipwrecks and hence its name
Babe Ruth: George Herman Ruth the Sultan of Swat
Babs: blind approach beacon system
BABS: Babbage Society
BABT: Brotherhood of Associated Book Travelers
Babushka: (Russian—grandmother)—nickname of Ekaterina Breshkovskaya the turn-of-the-century revolutionary leader
Baby: Babylon(ia); Babylonian
Baby Langdon: Harry Langdon
bac: bacilli; bacillus; bacteria; bacterial; bacterial antigen complex; bacteriologist; bacteriology; blood-alcohol concentration; buccoaxiocervical
Bac.: *Baccalaureus* (Latin—Bachelor)
BAC: Bendix Aviation Corporation; Boeing Airplane Company; British Aircraft Corporation; British Association of Chemists; Bureau of Air Commerce; Business Advisory Council (U.S. Department of Commerce)
BAC: *Baile Atha Cliath* (Gaelic—Dublin)
BACAH: British Association of Consultants in Agriculture and Horticulture
BACAIC: Boeing Airplane Company Algebraic Interpretive Computing
BACAL: Butter and Cheese Association Limited
BACAN: British Association for the Control of Aircraft Noise
bac bag: bactine bag (underground slang—plastic bag containing bactine antiseptic sniffed by some school children in imitation of drug-addicted elders)—results often fatal due to suffocation
B.Acc.: Bachelor of Accountancy
BA & CC: Billiards Association and Control Council
Bacchus: (Latin—Dionysos)—god of revelry and wine
BACD: Boeing Airplane Company Design
BACE: Bureau of Agricultural Chemistry and Engineering
bach: bachelor
Bach: (German—brook; stream)
Bachelor Painter: Sir Joshua Reynolds
Bachelor President: James Buchanan—fifteenth President of the United States
B.A. Chem.: Bachelor of Arts in Chemistry
Bach Soc: Bach Society
BACIE: British Association for Commercial and Industrial Education
back.: backwardation
Back Bay: Boston's old residential section built on mud flats reclaimed from Boston Bay more than a century ago
Back-of-Beyond: Australia's sparsely-inhabited interior
Backbone of Asia: the Himalayas
Backbone of the Confederacy: the Mississippi River
Backbone of England: Pennine Ridge extending from the Cheviots to the south Midlands
Backbone of Europe: the Alps
Backbone of North America: the Rockies
Backbone of South America: the Andes
'backs: wetbacks (illegal immigrants from Mexico)
BACM: British Association of Colliery Management
BACMA: British Aromatic and Compound Manufacturers Association
BACO: British Aluminium Company
bact: bacteria; bacteriological; bacteriologist; bacteriology; bacterium
bacter: bacteriologist
Bactrian Sage: Zoroaster (founder of the Magian religion and native of Bactria)
BACU: Battle Area Control Unit
Bad: Badajoz
BAD: Bantu Administration and Development; Base Air Depot; Berlin Airlift Device; Black, Active, and Determined; British Association of Dermatology
BADA: Base Air Depot Area; British Antique Dealers' Association
BADAS: Binary Automatic Data Annotation System
Baden: Baden-Baden
BADGE: Basic Air Defense Ground Environment
Badger(s): Wisconsinite(s)

Badger State: Wisconsin's official nickname
BADGES: Base Air Defense Ground Environment System
Badlands: arid and eroded areas of Nebraska and South Dakota as well as other places
B.Admin.: Bachelor of Administration
BADS: British Association of Dermatology and Syphilology
bae: Beacon antenna equipment
BAE: Bureau of Agricultural Economics; Bureau of American Ethnology
B.A.E.: Bachelor of Aeronautical Engineering; Bachelor of Agricultural Engineering; Bachelor of Architectural Engineering; Bachelor of Art Education; Bachelor of Arts in Education
BAE: *Buque Armada Ecuatoriana* (Ecuadorian Naval Ship)
BA of E: Badminton Association of England
BAEA: British Actors' Equity Association
BAEC: British Agricultural Export Council
B.A.Econ.: Bachelor of Arts in Economics
B.A.Ed.: Bachelor of Arts in Education
B.Ae.E.: Bachelor of Aeronautical Engineering
Ba enem: barium enema
BAEng.: Bureau of Agricultural Engineering
baf: baffle
ba & f: budget, accounting, and finance
BAF: British Air Force; Burma Air Force; Burundi Air Force
BAFCom: Basic Armed Forces Communication Plan
bafgab: bafflegab—synonym for gobbledygook, jet-age jargon or officialese sometimes called pentagonese
BAFM: British Association of Forensic Medicine
BAFMA: British and Foreign Maritime Agencies
BAFO: British Air Forces of Occupation; British Army Forces Overseas
BAFS: British Academy of Forensic Science
BAFSC: British Association of Field and Sports Contractors
BAFSV: British Armed Forces Special Vouchers
BAFTM: British Association of Fishing Tackle Makers
bag.: bagasse; baggage; ballistic attack game; buccoaxiogingival
Bag: Baghdad
B.Ag.: Bachelor of Agriculture
BAG: Beaverbrook Art Gallery
BAGA: British Amateur Gymnastics Association
BAGBI: Booksellers Association of Great Britain and Ireland
BAGDA: British Advertising Gift Distributors Association
Bagdad by the Bay: San Francisco
Bagdad-on-Hudson: New York
Bagdad on the Subway: one of O Henry's nicknames for New York City. He also called it the City of Razzle Dazzle
B.Ag.E.: Bachelor of Agricultural Engineering
bagg: buffered azide glucose glycerol
B. Agr.: Bachelor of Agriculture
B.Agr.Eco.: Bachelor of Agricultural Economics
B.Agric.: Bachelor of Agriculture
BAGR: Bureau of Aeronautics General Representative
B.Ag.Sc.: Bachelor of Agricultural Science
Bag Town: San Diego, California, where so many sailors tote their seabags as they go afloat or ashore
Bah: Bahamas; Bahrain
Bahamas: Bahama Islands
BAH: Bahrain Island, Persian Gulf (airport)
Baha'i: (Abdul) Baha Bahai
Bahia: Sao Salvador de Bahia
Bah Ind: Bahasa Indonesian (national language)
BAHOH: British Association of the Hard of Hearing
BAHS: British Agricultural History Association
Ba I: Bahama Islands
BAI: Barrier Industrial Council; Bureau of Animal Industry
B.A.I.: *Baccalaureus in Arte Ingeniaria* (Latin—Bachelor of Engineering)
baib: beta-amino-isobutyric (acid)
BAIC: Bureau of Agricultural and Industrial Chemistry
baid: boolean array identifier
BAIE: British Association of Industrial Editors
BAINS: Basic Advanced Integrated Navigation System
bait.: bacterial automated identification technique
B.A.J.: Bachelor of Arts in Journalism
Baja: *Baja California* (Spanish—Lower California)
Bajan: Barbadan (inhabitant of Barbados)
B.A.Jour.: Bachelor of Arts in Journalism
Bajuns: Barbadans
bak: bakery
bakelite: bormaldehyde formaldehyde plus phenol resin
baking soda: sodium bicarbonate ($NaHCO_3$)
bakke: (Danish—hill)
bal: balance; balcony; baloney
Bal: Baleares; Ballarat; Balthasar; British anti-lewisite
BAL: Baltimore, Maryland (Friendship Airport); Belgian African Line; Bonanza Airlines (3-letter coding); Borneo Airways Ltd.
balance.: basic and logically applied norms—civil engineering
Balanchine: Georgi Balanchivadze
bal. arenae: *balneum arenae* (Latin—sandbath)
balast: balloon astronomy
Balb: Balboa
balc: balconette; balconied; balcony
Bald: Baldwin
Baldie: Archibald; Baldassare; Baldomero; Balduin; Baldur; Baldwin; Baldwina
baldie(s): bald person(s)
Baldy: Baldwin
Balearics: Balearic Islands
Baleful Prophet: Cassandra
balid: ballistics identification
balkan: (Turkish—mountain range)
Balkans: Balkan mountains, peoples, and states in southeastern Europe (Albania, Bulgaria, Greece, Romania, Turkey, Yugoslavia)
ball.: ballast
Ball: Ballerup
Ball Coll: Balliol College—Oxford
Ballenys: Balleny Islands
ballute: balloon parachute
bally: ballyhoo
bal. mar.: *balneum maris* (Latin—salt-water bath; seawater bath)
balop: balopticon (projector)
B Alp: Basses-Alpes
balpa: balance of payments; ballpark
BALPA: British Airline Pilot's Association
B-alpes: Basses-Alpes
bals: balsam

bals.: *balsamum* (Latin—balsam)
B.A.L.S.: Bachelor of Arts in Library Science
Balt: Balthasar; Baltic; Baltimore
balth: balthazar (16 bottle capacity)
Balti: Baltimore (slang)
Baltic: Baltic and Mercantile Shipping Exchange (in London); Baltic Sea
Baltic Scandinavia: Finland and Sweden (Denmark sometimes included although much of its coast is on the Atlantic)
Baltic States: Estonia, Latvia, Lithuania (secret protocol of the Hitler-Stalin Pact of 1939 assigned all three to the Soviet sphere)
Balto: Baltimore
Balts: Baltic peoples; Balto-Slavs (East Prussians, Estonians, Latvians, Lithuanians); Balto-Slavic-speaking peoples
Baluch: Baluchistan
balun: balance-to-balance (network)
balute: balloon parachute
bal. vap.: *balneum vapour* (Latin—steambath; vapor bath)
Balzac: Honore de Balzac
bam: broadcasting am
Bam: Bamberger
BAM: broadcasting AM; Brooklyn Academy of Music
'Bama: Alabama
BAMA: British Amsterdam Maritime Agencies
bambi (BAMBI): ballistic missile bombardment interceptor
Bambino: George Herman (Babe) Ruth
Bamboo Curtain: old nickname for the barrier between anticommunist and communist countries of Southeast Asia
bame: benzoylarginine methyl ester
BAMIRAC: Ballistic Missile Radiation Analysis Center
BAMO: BuAer Material Officer
BAMR: BuAer Maintenance Representative
B.A.M.S.: Bachelor of Ayurvedic Medicine and Surgery
BAMTM: British Association of Machine Tool Merchants
B.A.Mus.: Bachelor of Arts in Music
BAMW: British Association of Meat Wholesalers
Ban: Bantu; Byron Bancroft Johnson
BAN: Base Activation Notice; British Association of Neurologists
Banamex: Banco de Mexico
Banana City: Brisbane—a big banana export port
Bananagate: Honduran-style Watergate-type scandal involving some of the banana republic's highest officials bribed to lower export taxes on bananas
Bananaland: Queensland, Australia
Bananalanders: people of banana-growing Queensland, Australia
Banana Republics: countries of Central and northern South America where bananas are the principal export; Jamaica often included
BANC: British Association of National Coaches
Banco: *El Banco* (Spanish—The Bank)—World Bank for Reconstruction and Development
Banc.Sup.: *Bancus Superior* (Latin—Upper Bench)—King's or Queen's Bench
band: (Persian—mountain range)
Band: Bandung
Banda Oriental: (Spanish—Eastern Ribbon)—former name and present-day nickname of Uruguay
Bandas: Banda Islands of Indonesia
Band City: Elkhart, Indiana, where so many band instruments are made
banded agate: chalcedony
Banffs: Banffshire
Bang: Bangalore
Bangla: Bangladesh (formerly East Pakistan)
banir: bombing and navigation inertial reference
bank.: banking
Bank: Bangkok
BANK: International Bank for Reconstruction and Development
banks clgs: bank clearings
Bankers: Bankers Publishing (Boston); Bankers Trust (New York)
BANKPAC: Bankers Political Action Committee
banks.: bank holidays (West Indian English)
BANS: British Association of Numismatic Societies
Batham: Bantam Books
BANTSA: Bank of American National Trust and Savings Association
B.A. Nurs.: Bachelor of Arts in Nursing
BANWR: Bosque Apache National Wildlife Refuge (New Mexico)
BANZARE: British, Australian, New Zealand Antarctic Research Expedition
bao: basal acid output
BAO: British-American Oil; British Association of Otolaryngologists
B.A.O.: Bachelor of the Art of Obstetrics; Bachelor of Arts in Oratory
BAOP: British Atlantic Ocean Possessions (Ascension, St Helena, and Tristan da Cunha islands)
BAOR: British Army on Rhine
bap: baptism; baptized; beginning at a point; blood-agar plate; brachial artery pressure
b a p: beginning at a point
bap: *billets a payer* (French—bills payable)
Bap: Baptist; Baptista; Baptiste
BAP: Booksellers Association of Philadelphia
B A & P: Butte, Anaconda & & Pacific (railroad)
BAPA: British Airline Pilots' Association
BAPCO: Bahrain Petroleum Company
bape: baseplate
B.A.P.E.: Bachelor of Arts in Physical Education
BA Phys Med: British Association of Physical Medicine
BAPL: Bettis Atomic Power Laboratory (AEC)
BAPM: British Association of Physical Medicine
B.App.Arts: Bachelor of Applied Arts
B.App.Sci.: Bachelor of Applied Science
BAPS: British Association of Pediatric Surgeons; British Association of Plastic Surgeons; Bureau of Air Pollution Sciences
BAPSA: Broadcast Advertising Producers Society of America
Bapt: Baptist
BAPT: British Association of Physical Training
Bapu: (Gujerati—father)—Gandi's title affectionately bestowed by his many followers in India and elsewhere
baq: basic allowance for quarters
BAQ: Barranquilla, Colombia

(airport)
bar.: barometer; barometric
bar: *billets à recevoir* (French—bills receivable)
Bar: *Barone* (Italian—Baron)
Bar: Baroque; Baruch, Book of
B.Ar.: Bachelor of Architecture
BAR: Broadcast Advertisers' Reports; Browning automatic rifle; Bureau of Aeronautics Representative
BARA: *Bureau d'Analyse et de Recherche Appliquées* (French—Bureau of Analysis and Applied Research)
barb.: barbarian; barbecue; barber; barbiturate
Barb: Barbados Islands; Barbara; Barbary
Barbarossa: (Italian—Red Beard)—nickname of Frederick II of Germany
Barbary Coast: North African coast once infested by pirates; San Francisco's gambling, redlight, and waterfront district a century ago
Barbary States: Algeria, Libya (Tripolitania), Morocco, Tunisia
Barber Poet: Provençal poet Jacques Jasmin—a barber by profession and also called the Last of the Troubadors as he died in 1864
Barbie: Barbara
bar-b-q: barbecue
Barbra: Barbara
barbs.: barbiturates
barbus: *barbudos* (Spanish—bearded ones)
Barc: Barcelona
BARC: British Aeronautical Research Committee
Barca: Barcelona
Barca the Carthaginian: Maharbal
B.Arch.: Bachelor of Architecture
B.Arch.E.: Bachelor of Architectural Engineering
B.Arch. & T.P.: Bachelor of Architecture and Town Planning
Barcino: (Latin—Barcelona)
Bard of Avon: William Shakespeare
Bard of Ayrshire: Robert Burns
Bard of Prose: Boccaccio
barg(s): bargain(s)
bari: baritone; baritone saxophone
Bari: Bari delle Puglie, Italy
Barisans: Barisan Mountains of Sumatra
barite: barium sulfate
Barme: Bartolome
barn.: bombing and reconnaissance navigation
Barn: Barnard
Barna: Barcelona
Barney: Barnabas; Barnett; Bernard; Bernardino
BARNS: Bombing and Reconnaissance Navigation System
Baroness Orczy: Mrs Montagu Bartstow—author of *The Scarlet Pimpernel*
Baron Munchausen: Rudolf Erich Raspe who told many tall tales under his own name as well as under the pseudonym of Baron Munchausen—an aristocrat of Gottingen
Baron Stiegel: ironmaster Henry William Stiegel
b & arp: bare and acid resisting paint
barq: barquentine
Barq: Barranquilla
barr: barrister
barra: (Spanish—reef)
BARS: Backup Attitude-Reference System; Ballistic Analysis Research System
BARSTUR: Barding Sands Underwater Test Range
Bart: Baronet; Bartholomew; Bartolomeo
BART: Bay Area Rapid Transit (San Francisco); Brooklyn Army Terminal (New York)
BARTD: Bay Area Rapid Transit District
Barts: Saint-Barthelemy in the French West Indies; Saint Bartholomew's Hospital in London
barv: beach armored recovery vehicle
bas: basenji; basic airspeed; basic allowance for subsistence; basilica; basophil(s); basset; benzyl analog of serotonin
Bas: Basel; Basil; Basilica; Basilicata; Bass Strait; Bastogne; Bastrop; Basuto; Basutoland
BAs: Business Agents (of unions)
BAS: Basic Allowance for Subsistence; Behavioral Approach Scale; Brazilian-American Society; British Acoustical Society; British Antarctic Survey
B.A.S.: Bachelor of Agricultural Science; Bachelor of Applied Science
Basa: *Baronessa* (Italian—Baroness)
BASA: British Architectural Students' Association
BASAF: British and South Africa Forum
basalt: gabbro-type igneous rock
B. A. Sc.: Bachelor of Applied Science
BASC: Booth American Shipping Corporation
basc b: bascule bridge
basd: basic active service date
BASEEFA: British Approvals Service for Electrical Equipment in Flammable Atmospheres
BASF: Badische Anilin und Soda Fabrik
bash.: body acceleration given synchronously with the heartbeat
BASI: British Association of Ski Instructors
basic. (BASIC): battle-area surveillance and integrated communications; beginner's all-purpose symbolic instruction code (computer language)
BASIC: British-American Scientific International Commercial (English)
BASIC: *Biological Abstracts Subjects in Context*
BASICO: Behavior Science Corporation
BASIE: British Association for Commercial and Industrial Education
Basilia: (Latin—Basle)
Bask: Baskir(ia)
Bask(er): Baskerville
Basket of Eggs: egg-shaped hills of Downs in Northern Ireland
BASMA: Boot and Shoe Manufacturers' Association
BASO: Base Accountable Supply Officer; Bureau of Aeronautics Shipping Order
basops: base operations
baso(s): basophile(s)
Basque Provinces: Alava, Guipuzcoa, and Viscaya in northeastern Spain where Basque is spoken
BASR: Bureau of Applied Social Research (Columbia University)
BASRA: British Amateur Scientific Research Association
bass.: bassoon
BASS: Bass Anglers Sportsman Society
B.A.S.S.: Bachelor of Arts in Social Science
bass con: *basso continuo* (Italian—continuous bass)—figured bass background
BASSR: Bashkirian Autonomous Soviet Socialist Republic; Buriat Autonomous Soviet So-

cialist Republic
bas tit.: bastard title (half title)
ba sw: bell-alarm switch
bat.: battery; battle
Bat: Bartholomew; Battista
BAT: Blind Approach Training; Boeing Air Transport; Bureau of Apprenticeship and Training
B-AT: British-American Tobacco
BA & T: Bureau of Apprenticeship and Training
Batavian Republic: name for the Netherlands during the French Revolutionary wars (1795 to 1806)
BATC: British Amateur Television Club
bat. chg: battery charger; battery charging
BATDIV: battleship division
bate: base activation test equipment
b-a test: blood-alcohol test (used to determine if an automobile driver is under the influence of an intoxicating beverage)
BATFOR: battle force
bath.: bathroom; best available true heading
batho: bathometer
bathy: bathymeter; bathysphere; bathyscaphe
BATM: British Admiralty Technical Mission
bato: baloon-assisted takeoff
B.A.T.P.: Bachelor of Arts in Town Planning
BATRON: battleship squadron
batrop: baratropic
Bat Rou: Baton Rouge
Bats: British-American Tobacco (stock-exchange sobriquet)
BATS: Business Air Transport Service
batt: batter; batteries; battery
Battle-Born State: Nevada—admitted as territory in 1848 following the Mexican War
Battlefield City: Gettysburg, Pennsylvania
Battling Bob: Robert M. La Follette, Sr
bau: basic assembly unit; British absolute unit (BTU, Btu)
Bau: Bauer; Bauhaus
BAU: British Association Unit
BAUA: Business Aircraft Users' Association
Baubie: (Scottish—Barbara)
BAUS: British Association of Urological Surgeons
bauxite: hydrated aluminum-oxide mixture (source of aluminum)
bav: *bon à vue* (French—good at sight)
bav: *bon à vue* (French—good at sight)—sight draft
Bav: Bavaria; Bavarian
BAVA: Bureau of Audio-Visual Aids (NY)
BAVE: Bureau of Audio-Visual Education (Calif)
BAVTE: Bureau of Adult, Vocational, and Technical Education (HEW)
baw: bare aluminum wire
BAWA: British Amateur Wrestling Association
BAWHA: Bide-A-Wee Home Association
BAWRA: British Australian Wool Realization Association
Bay: The Bay—Algoa Bay or Port Elizabeth Bay in South Africa
Bay of Biscuits: (naval nickname—Bay of Biscay)
bay cand dc: bayonet candelabra double contact
Bay City: San Francisco
Bayer: *Bayerisch* (German—bavarian)
Bayou City: Houston, Texas
Bayou State: Louisiana and Mississippi vie for this nickname
BAYS: British Association of Young Scientists
Bay State: official nickname of Massachusetts known in colonial times as the Colony of Massachusetts Bay
Bay Stater(s): Massachusettan(s)
Bay Street: financial center of the Bahamas in Nassau on New Providence Island
bb: ball bearing; bank burglar(y); bayonet base (lamp or socket); below bridges; bill book; blood bank; blood buffer (base); blue bloaters; both bones (fractured); both to blame; breakthrough bleeding; breast biopsy; buffer base; bungling bureaucrat; double black; pellet fired from or made for a bb gun
b-b: black bordered
b/b: bail bond; bottled in bond
b & b: bed and board; bed and breakfast; benedictine and brandy
b or b: brass or bronze (cargo)
bb: *babord* (Swedish—port side)
b de b: *brut de brut* (French—naturally tart champagne or wine)
BB: Banco do Brasil (Bank of Brazil); battleship; B'nai B'rith; Brigitte Bardot; Bureau of the Budget
B.B.: Bernard Berensen; Bjornstjerne Bjornson; Boys' Brigade
B-B: Bora-Bora
B & B: Brown and Bigelow
B of B: Bureau of the Budget
bba: born before arrival
BBA: Big Brothers of America; British Bankers' Association
B.B.A.: Bachelor of Business Administration
bbb: basic boxed base; bed, breakfast, and bath; blood brain barrier; triple black
BBB: Best Berlin Broadcast; Best British Briar (pipes); Better Business Bureau
BBBC: British Boxing Board of Control
BB & BU: Bagel Boilers and Bakers Union
bbc: barrels, boxes, and crates (cargo); bromobenzylcyanide (gas)
BBC: Bank of British Columbia; Beautiful British Columbia; British Broadcasting Corporation
BBCC: Big Bend Community College
BBC dissociation: Braid-Berheim-Charcot dissociation
BBC English: cultured way of speaking English
BBCF: British Bacon Curers' Federation
BBCL: Bermuda Broadcasting Company Limited
BBCM: Bandmaster—Bandsmen's College of Music
BBCMA: British Baby Carriage Manufacturers' Association
BBCS: Browne Book-Charging System
bbcw: bare beryllium copper wire
bbdc: before bottom dead center
BB (DCO): Barclays Bank (Dominion, Colonial and Overseas)
BBEA: Brewery and Bottling Engineers Association
bb & em: bed, breakfast, and evening meal
bbf: boron-based fuel
BBF: Biblioteca Benjamin Franklin (Mexico City); Boilermakers, Blacksmiths, Forgers (union)
BBFC: British Board of Film Censors
BBG: Bermuda Botanical Gardens; Brooklyn Botanic Garden
BBGA: British Broiler Growers'

Association
bb-gun: airgun shooting bb's (ball bearings)
BBHC: Buffalo Bill Historical Center
BBHF: B'nai B'rith Hillel Foundations
BBI: Barbecue Briquet Institute
B Bibl: *Bachelier en Bibliothéconomie* (French—Bachelor in Library Science)
BBiP: *British Books in Print*
BBIRA: British Baking Industries Research Association
B Bisc: Bay of Biscay
bbj: ball-bearing joint
bbk: breadboard kit
bbl: barrel
BBL: bahia Blanca
BBL: Bangkok Bank Ltd; Big Brothers League
bbl roll: barrel roller
bbls/day: barrels per day
bbm: break-before-make
BBMRA: British Brush Manufacturers Research Association
BBNNR: Braunton Burrows National Nature Reserve (England)
BBNP: Big Bend National Park (Texas)
BBNR: Back Bay National Refuge (Virginia)
Bbo: Bilbao
B-Bomb: benzedrine bomb (underground slang—benzedrine inhaler)
B-boy: busboy; mess sergeant
bbp: boxes, barrels, packages, (cargo); building block principle
BBP: Beech Bottom Power Company
b&b pericarditis: bread-and-butter pericarditis
bbq: barbecue
BBQ: Brooklyn, Bronx, Queens
bbr: balloon-borne radio
BBRR: Brookhaven Beam Research Reactor (AEC)
BBRS: Balloon-Borne Radio System
bbs: ball bearings; barrels of basic sediment; box bark strips
Bbs: British biscuits
BBS: Bermuda Biological Station; Brunei Broadcasting Service
B.B.S.: Bachelor of Business Science
BBSATRA: British Boot, Shoe and Allied Trades Research Association
BBSI: British Boot and Shoe Institution
bbsj: ball-bearing swivel joint
B & B SNC: British and Burmese Steam Navigation Company
BBSR: Bermuda Biological Station for Research
bbs & w: barrels of basic sediment and water
bbt: basal body temperature; bombardment
BBT: Basal Body Temperature
BBTA: British Bureau of Television Advertising
BB & TC: Bahamas Broadcasting and Television Commission
BBU: Bagel Boilers Union
bbw: bare brass wire
BBWAA: Baseball Writers' Association of America
BBYO: B'nai B'rith Youth Organization
bbz: bearing bronze
bc: bad check; base (shield) connection; between centers; binary code; binary counter; birth control; bogus check; bolt circle; bone connection; bottom (dead) center; broadcast control
b/c: bales of cotton; bills for collection; birth control
BC: Before Christ
BC: Bacone College; Baja California; Bakersfield College; Bard College; Barnard College; Barrington College; Barry College; Bates College; Beaver College; Beckley College; Belgian Congo; Belhaven College; Bellarmine College; Belmont College; Beloit College; Benedict College; Bennett College; Bennington College; Berea College; Berry College; Bethany College; Bethel College; Bishop College; Blackburn College; Blinn College; Bliss College; Bloomfield College; Bluefield College; Bluffton College; Bomber Command; Boston College; Bourget College; Bowdoin College; Brandon College; Brenau College; Brentwood College; Brescia College; Brevard College; Briarcliff College; Bridgewater College; British Columbia; Brooklyn College; Bruyere College; Bryant College; Burdett College; Butler College
BC: *Biological Conservation*
B.C.: Bachelor of Chemistry; Bachelor of Commerce; Baja California; Before Christ; British Columbia
B-C: Barber-Colman
B & C: Banking and Currency (Senate Committee)
B of C: Bank of Canada; Bureau of the Census
B C: *basso continuo* (Italian—continuous bass background)
bca: best cruise altitude; blood color analyzer
bca: *barrica* (Spanish—cask; keg); *biblioteca* (Portuguese or Spanish—library)
BCA: Battery Control Area; Billiard Congress of America; Blue Cross Association; Boys' Clubs of America; British Caledonian Airways; British Colonial Airlines
B/C of A: British College of Aeronautics
BCAB: Birth Control Advisory Bureau
BCAC: British Conference on Automation and Computation
BCAir: British Commonwealth Air Force
BCAR: British Civil Airworthiness Requirements; British Council for Aid to Refugees
BCAS: British Compressed Air Society
BCAT: Birmingham College of Advanced Technology
bcb: binary code box; broadcast band; button-cell battery
BCBC: British Cattle Breeders' Club
bcbh: boiler casing bulkhead
bcc: beam-coupling coefficient; body-centered cubic
BCC: Battery Control Central; Berkshire Community College; British Communications Corporation; British Crown Colony; Bronx Community College; Bureau Central de Compensation; Burlington Community College
BCCA: Beer Can Collectors of America; British Cyclo-Cross Association
BCCCUS: British Commonwealth Chamber of Commerce in the United States
BCCF: British Cast Concrete Federation
BCCG: British Cooperative Clinical Group
BCCO: Base Consolidation Control Office(r)
BCCR: Banco Central de Costa Rica
BCCs: Birth-Control Clinics
bccw: bare copper-clad wire
bcd: bad conduct discharge; binary-coded decimal

BCD: Bad Conduct Discharge
BCD: *Business Cycle Developments*
bcdc: binary-coded decimal cunter
BCDC: Bay Conservation and Development Commission (San Francisco)
bcdp: battery control data processor
BCDTA: British Chemical and Dyestuffs Traders' Association
bce: base checkout equipment; bubble chamber equipment; bundle-controlled expansion.
bce (BCE): basal cell epithelioma
BCE: Base Civil Engineer; Before the Christian Era; Before the Common Era; British Columbia Electric (railroad)
B.C.E.: Bachelor of Civil Engineering; Before the Christian Era
BCECC: British and Central European Chamber of Commerce
BCEM: Bureau of Community Environmental Management (HEW)
BCER: British Columbia Electric Railway
bcf: bandpass crystal filter; basic control frequency; bulked continuous fiber
BCF: British Columbia Ferries; British Cycling Federation; Bureau of Commercial Fisheries
BCfa: Baja California
BCFA: British-China Friendship Association; British Columbia Ferry Authority
BCFGA: British Columbia Fruit Growers Association
BCFK: British Commonwealth Forces in Korea
BCFP: Bureau of Consumer Frauds and Protection
BCFS: British Columbia Forestry Society
bcg: ballistocardiogram; bidirectional categorical grammar; bucking current generator
BCG: Bacillus Calmette-Guerin (anti-tubercular vaccine)
BCGA: British Commercial Gas Association; British Cotton Growing Association
BCGLO: British Commonwealth Geographical Liaison Office
BCGNM: Black Canyon of the Gunnison National Monument (Colorado)
bcg test: bicolor guaiac test
bch: bunch
Bch: Beach
B. Ch.: *Baccalaureus Chirurgiae* (Latin—Bachelor of Surgery)
B.Ch.D.: *Baccalaureus Chirurgiae Dentium* (Latin—Bachelor of Dental Surgery)
B. Ch. E.: Bachelor of Chemical Engineering
B.Chem.: Bachelor of Chemistry
Bches-du-R: Bouches-du-Rhone
B. Chir.: Bachelor of Surgery
B.Chrom.: Bachelor of Chromatics
bci: battery-conditioned indicator; binary-coded information; broadcast interference
BCI: Bureau of Criminal Investigation
BCI: *Banca Commerciale Italiana* (Italian Commercial Bank)
BCIA: British Columbia Institute of Agrologists
BCIC: Birth-Control Investigation Committee
BCIE: Banco Centroamericano de Integracion Economica (Central American Bank of Economic Integration)
BCII: Bureau of Criminal Identification and Investigation
BCINA: British Commonwealth International Newsfilm Agency
BCIPPA: British Cast Iron Pressure Pipe Association
BCIRA: British Cotton Industry Research Association
BCIS: Binary Constitution Information Service
BCIS: *Bureau Central International de Séismologie* (French—International Central Bureau of Seismology)
BCISC: British Chemical Industrial Safety Council
BCIT: British Columbia Institute of Technology
B Cities: six leading cities of the Central African Republic—Bangui, Berberati, Bossangoa, Bambari, Bouar, Bangasu
BCJC: Bay City Junior College
Bck: Buckie
b-c kit: battle-casualty kit; bouillon-cigarette kit (containing bouillon cubes, cigarettes, matches)
bcl: broadcast listener; broom closet
Bcl: Barcelona
BCL: Belfast City Libraries; British Council Library
BCL: *Books for College Libraries*
B.C.L.: Bachelor of Civil Law
BCLA: British Columbia Library Association
BCLS: Bristol City Line of Steamships
bcm: beyond capability of maintenance; binary choice model; business center map
BCM: Baylor College of Medicine; Boston Conservatory of Music; British Commercial Monomark; British Consular Mail
BCM: *British Catalogue of Music*
BCMA: Biscuit and Cracker Manufacturers' Association; British Colour Makers; Association; British Columbia Medical Association
BCMD: Boston Contract Management Division
BCMFA: Bowdoin College Museum of Fine Arts
BCMR: Board for Correction of Military Records
bcn: beacon
BCN: Banque Canadienne Nationale (Canadian National Bank); Barcelona, Spain (airport); British Commonwealth of Nations
BCNP: Bryce Canyon National Park (Utah)
BCNRA: Bighorn Canyon National Recreation Area (Montana and Wyoming)
BCO: Baltimore Civic Opera
bcoe: bench checkout equipment
b coef: block coefficient
BCOF: British Commonwealth Occupation Force
B. Comm.: Bachelor of Commerce
B.Com.Ed.: Bachelor of Commerce in Education
B.Com.Sc.: Bachelor of Commercial Science
bcp: bromcresyl purple
BCP: Bootstrap Commissioning Program (USAF); Budget Change Proposal; Bulgarian Communist Party; Bureau of Consumer Protection
BCP: *Book of Common Prayer*
B.C.P.: Bachelor of City Planning
BCPA: British Commonwealth Pacific Airlines
BCPC: British Crop Protection Council
BC Pen: British Columbia Penitentiary
BCPIT: British Council for Promotion of International Trade
BCPMA: British Chemical Plant Manufacturers Association

BCPO: British Commonwealth Producers' Organization
bcps: beam candlepower seconds
bcp's: birth-control pills
bcr: battery control radar
BCR: Bituminous Coal Research; British Columbia Railway; Business Community Roads
BCRA: British Ceramic Research Institution; British Coke Research Association
BCRC: British Columbia Research Council
BCRD: British Council for the Rehabilitation of the Disabled
BCRUM: British Committee on Radiation Units and Measurements
BCS: British Cardiac Society; British Computer Society; Bureau of Criminal Statistics
B.C.S.: Bachelor of Chemical Science
B & CS: British and Commonwealth shipping
BCSA: British Constructional Steelwork Association
BCSC: Blue Cross of Southern California
BCSO: British Commonwealth Scientific Office
BCSO (NA): British Commonwealth Scientific Office (North America)
bcss: back spotfacer
bcst: broadcast
BCSTA: British Columbia School Trustees' Association
BCT: Battersea College of Technology; Bristol College of Technology; Brunel College of Technology
BCTA: British Canadian Trade Association; British Children's Theatre Association
BCTC: British Cycle Tourist Competition; Buffalo County Teachers College
BCTF: British Columbia Teachers' Federation
BCTN: Baja California—Territorio Norte (Northern Territory)
BCTS: Baja California—Territorio Sur (Southern Territory)
bcu (BCU): big closeup
BCURA: British Coal Utilization Research Association
bcu's: big closeups
BCVA: British Columbia Veterinary Association
bcw: bare copper wire; biological and chemical warfare; buffer control word
BCW: Bakery and Confectionery Workers (union); Bureau of Child Welfare
BCWA: British Cotton Waste Association
BCWMA: British Clock and Watch Manufacturers Association
bd: band; base (of prism) down; board; bomb disposal; brought down; buccodistal; bundle
b.d.: *bis die* (Latin—twice daily)
b/d: bank draft; barrels per day; bills discounted; brought down
bd: *band* (Swedish—volume); *bind* (Dano-Norwegian—volume)
Bd: Bahrain dinar; Bernhard; Board
Bd: *Band* (German—volume)
BD: Birlesik Devletler (Turkish—United States); Bomb Disposal; Bundesrepublik Deutschland (German—Republic of Germany)
B-D: Becton-Dickenson
B.D.: Bachelor of Divinity
B & D: Black & Decker
bda: bomb damage assessment; breakdown acid
Bda: Baroda
BDA: British Deaf Association; British Dental Association; British Dermatological Association; Bermuda (airport and tracking station—3-letter code symbol)
B.D.A.: Bachelor of Domestic Arts; Bachelor of Dramatic Art
BDAC: Bureau of Drug Abuse Control (Food and Drug Administration)
b & daf: bounded and described as follows
BDART: Battle Damage Assessment and Reporting Team
B-day: Barbarossa Day (German attack on Russia—June 22, 1941)—Barbarossa was code word for this offensive
bdb: bis-diazotized benzidine
bdc: bonded double center; bottom dead center
BDC: Boeing Development Center; Bomb Data Center; Book Development Council; Bureau of Domestic Commerce
BD & C: British Dominions and Colonies
bdd: binary-to-decimal decoder
BDDA: British Deaf and Dumb Association
bddi: beading die
bde: bile duct exploration; brigade
Bde: *Bände* (German—volumes)
bded: bounded
Bd of Ed: Board of Education
B.Den.Sci.: Bachelor in Dental Science
B.Des.: Bachelor of Design
bdf: base detonating fuse
BDFA: British Dairy Farmers Association
bd ft: board feet
bdg: binding, buffered desoxycholate glucose
Bdg: Bridgewater
B de G: Bahia de Guantanamo (Guantanamo Bay)
BDH: British Drug Houses
bdhi: bearing distance heading indicator
bdhsa: bomb director high-speed aircraft
bdi: bearing deviation indicator
Bdi: Beck depression inventory
BDI: Bureau of Dairy Industry
BDI: *Bundesverband der Deutschen Industrie* (Federation of German Industries)
BDIAC: Batelle Defender Information Analysis Center
BDIC: Batelle Defense Information Center
B.Did.: Bachelor of Didactics
BDJ: *Bund Deutscher Jugend* (League of German Youth)
b dk: bridge deck
bdl: bundle
BDL: beach landing lighter (Army); Hartford, Connecticut (Bradley Field)
bdl(s): bundle(s)
bd lt: bow designation light
bdm: births, deaths, marriages
bdm (BDM): bomber defense missile
BdM: *Bund Deutscher Mädchen* (League of German Girls)
BDMA: British Disinfectant Manufacturers Association
BDMAA: British Direct Mail Advertising Association
Bdmr: Bandmaster
bdn: bend down
Bdo: Bernardo; Bodo
BDO: Boom Defense Officer
bdp: breakdown pressure
Bdp: Budapest
BDP: Botswana Democratic Party
BDPA: Bureau of Data Processing and Accounts (Social Security Administration)
BDPEC: Bureau of Disease Prevention and Environmental Control
B en Dr: *Bachelier en Droit* (French—Bachelor of Law)

B.Dr.Art: Bachelor of Dramatic Art
bdrm(s): bedroom(s)
bd rts: bond rights
bdry: boundary
bds: boards; bonded double silk; bound in boards; brass divider strip
b.d.s.: *bis in die sumendus* (Latin—take twice daily)
bd & s: blowing dust and sand
Bds: Barbados
BDS: Bomb Damage Survey
B.D.S.: Bachelor of Dental Surgery
BDSA: Business and Defense Services Administration
B.D.Sc.: Bachelor of Dental Science
BDSC: Black Diamond Steamship Corporation
bdsd: base detonating, self-destroying
BDST: British Double Summer Time
Bd of Sup: Board of Supervisors
bdt: bidet
bdu: basic display unit
BdU: *Befehlshaber der Unterseeboote* (German—U-boat Command)
BDU: Bomb Disposal Unit
bdw: buffered distilled water
Bdx: Bordeaux
bdy: boundary
Bdy Mon: boundary monument
BDZ: *Borsen-Data Zentrale* (German—Stock-exchange Data Center)—computerized stock exchange
bdzr: bulldozer
be.: below the elbow; beveled edge; booster engine
b/e: bill of entry; bill of exchange
b & e: beginning and ending; breaking and entering
Be: Baume; Belgian; Belgium; beryllium
BE: Board of Education; Bucyrus-Erie
B.E.: Bachelor of Economics; Bachelor of Education; Bachelor of Elocution; Bachelor of Engineering
B-E: Bucyrus-Erie
B & E: Baltimore & Eastern (railroad)
B of E: Bank of England; Board of Education
BE: *Berkshire Eagle; Brockhaus Enzyklopadie* (German—Brockhaus' Encyclopedia)
Bea: Beatrice; Beatrix
BEA: British East Africa; British Electricity Authority; British European Airways; Bureau of Economic Analysis
BEAB: British Electrical Approvals Board (for household appliances)
BEAC: Boeing Engineering Analog Computer; British Export Advisory Committee
Beacon: Beacon Press
BEACON: British European Airways Computer Network
BEAIRA: British Electrical and Allied Industries Research Association
BEAM: Building Equipment Accessories and Materials (Canadian program)
BEAMA: British Electrical and Allied Manufacturers Association
Bean Town: Boston, Massachusetts
BEAPA: Bureau of East Asian and Pacific Affairs (Dept of State)
bear.: bearing
bearb: *bearbeitet* (German—revised)
bear market: stock market short form indicating a downward trend in securities as if a bear were clawing downward and biting into the back of its victim; *see* bull market
Bear State: old nickname for Arkansas where many bears resided
BEAS: British Executive Air Services
Beast of Belsen: Joseph Kramer, Nazi commandant of the concentration camp at Belsen
Beast of Berlin: Kaiser Wilhelm II during World War I; Führer Adolf Hitler during World War II
Beast of Budapest: Soviet Marshal Georgi Konstantinovich Zhukov also known as the Butcher of Poland and as the Butcher of South Korea
BEAT: Breaking, Entering, and Auto Theft (computerized criminal file in Lowell, Mass)
Beatie: Beatrice
Beatles: Beat + Beetles
beat(s): beatnik(s)
Beatty: Beatrice
Beau Brummel: nickname of George Bryan Brummel
Beau & Fl: Francis Beaumont and John Fletcher
Beau Nash: nickname of Richard Nash
Beau Sabreur: (French—Handsome Swordsman)—sobriquet of Napoleon's cavalry leader—Joachim Murat
beaut: beautiful; beauty
Beautiful Bob: Robert Taylor (Spangler A. Brugh)
beauts: beauties
Beauty Queen of the Balkans: Yugoslavia
Beaux-Arts: École de Beaux-Arts (fine arts academy established in Paris in 1648)
Beaverbrook: Lord Beaverbrook (William Maxwell Aitken)
Beaver(s): Oregonian(s)
Beaver State: Oregon's official nickname
beb: best ever bottled
BEB: Beach Erosion Board
bec: because
BEC: Base Engineering Course; Base Extension Course; Brevard Engineering College; Bureau of Employee's Compensation
BECA: Bureau of Educational and Cultural Affairs (US Department of State)
BECC: British Empire Cancer Campaign
Becca: Rebecca
BECGC: British Empire and Commonwealth Games Council
Bech: Bechstein; Bechuanaland
Bechu: Bechuana (formerly Bechuanaland)
Beck: Rebecca
Becky: Rebecca
BECM: British Electric Conduit Manufacturers
BECMA: British Electro-Ceramic Manufacturers Association
beco: booster engine cutoff
B.Eco.: Bachelor of Economics
BECO: Boston Edison Company
BECTO: British Electric Cable Testing Organisation
bed.: bridge-element delay
B.Ed.: Bachelor of Education
BEDA: British Electrical Development Association
Bedaks: Bureau of Drug Abuse Control officers
Bedford-Stuyvesant: section of Brooklyn, New York
Bedlam: nickname of St Mary of Bethlehem's lunatic asylum in old London
Bedroom of New York: Brooklyn
Bedroom of Washington, D.C.: Arlington, Virginia
bed(s): bedroom(s)
Beds: Bedfordshire
Bed-Stuy: Bedford-Stuyvesant
BEDT: Brooklyn Eastern District Terminal (railroad)
Bee: Beatrice

BEE: Basic Economic Education
B.E.E.: Bachelor of Electrical Engineering
Beeb: BBC (British Broadcasting Corporation)
beec: binary error-erasure channel
Beecham: Beauchamp
Beedle: General Walter Bedell Smith
beef.: business-and-engineering-enriched fortran
beefalo: beef cattle + buffalo (hybrid)
Beef Barons: Armour, Cudahy, Morris, Swift, and their ilk
Beefeaters: Her (His) Majesty's Honourable Corps of Gentlemen at Arms
Beef State: Nebraska's nickname
Bee Gee: British Guiana (now called Guyana)
Beehive of Industry: Providence, Rhode Island
Beehive State: Utah whose great seal displays a beehive symbolic of the energy of its settlers
Beethoven Town: Bonn, Germany—birthplace of Ludwig van Beethoven
beet sugar: sucrose
Bee Wee: nickname for a British West Indian
bef: before; blunt end first; buffered emitter follower
Bef: *Befehl* (German—command; order)
BEF: Bonus Expeditionary Force; British Expeditionary Force
BEFA: British Emigrant Families Association
befm: bending form
beg.: begin; beginning
BEG: Belgrade, Yugoslavia (airport)
Beggars of the Sea: Dutch pirates and privateers
begr: *begrundet* (German—established)
BEH: Bureau of Education for the Handicapped
BEHA: British Export Houses Association
behav: behavior; behavioral; behaviorist(ic)
Behavioral Res: Behavioral Research Laboratories
BEHC: Bio-Environmental Health Center
bei: butanol-extractable iodine
BEI: Bridgeport Engineering Institute
BEI: *British Education Index*
BEIA: Board of Education Inspectors' Association
Beibl: *Beiblatt* (German—supplement)
beif: *beifolgend* (German—sent herewith)
Beih: *beihft* (German—supplement)
beil: *beiliegend* (German—enclosed)
Beil: *Beilage* (German—appendix, supplement)
BEIS: British Egg Information Service
Beitr: *Beitrag* (German—contribution)
bel: below; 10 decibels
bel: (Turkish—pass)
Bel: Belem; Belfast; Belize; Belorussia
Bel: *Bacharel* (Portuguese—Bachelor)—academic degree
BEL: Belem do Para, Brazil (airport)
Bel Anglais: (French—Handsome Englishman)—nickname of John Churchill—Duke of Marlborough
Belchers: Belcher Islands
belcrk: bellcrank
Bel & Dr: *Bel and the Dragon*
B.Elec. & Tel. Eng.: Bachelor of Electronics and Telecommunication Engineering
Belém: (Brazil) Amazon River port also known as Belém do Para; (Portugal) Lisbon suburb
bel ex: *bel example* (French—fine example)—fine copy of a book, engraving, map, etc.
Belf: Belfast; Belfastian(s)
Belg: Belgian; Belgium
Belg: *Belgio* (Italian—Belgium)
Belg: *Belgica* (Portuguese or Spanish—Belgium)
Belgium Film Pioneer: Jacques Feyder
Belgolux: Belgian and Luxembourg
Belial: The Devil
Bell: Bell System (American Telephone and Telegraph and associated companies)
bella: belladonna (drug stimulant whose overdose results in delirium and death)
Bella: Arabella; Isabella
Bellas Artes: *Instituto Nacional de Bellas Artes* (Spanish—National Institute of Fine Arts)—in Mexico City
Belle: Bella; Arabella; Isabella
Belle Riviere: (see *La Belle Riviere)*
bells.: bell-bottom pants
Bell Town: East Hampton, Connecticut
Belmo: Belmopan
Below Sea-Level Cities: Brawley and El Centro in the Imperial Valley of southern California
Belvac: *Societe Belge de Vacuologie et de Vacuotechnique* (Belgian Society for Vacuum Science and Technology)
Bem: *Bemerkung* (German—comment; note; observation)
BEM: British Empire Medal
B.E.M.: Bachelor of Engineering of Mines
BEMA: Business Equipment Manufacturers Association
BEMB: British Egg Marketing Board
BEMO: Base Equipment Management Office
bems: bug-eyed monsters (science-fiction jargon)
BEMS: Bakery Equipment Manufacturers Society
BEMSA: British Eastern Merchant Shippers Association
ben: (Gaelic—mountain; summit); (Hebrew—son)
ben.: *bene* (Latin—good; well); *benedictio* (Latin—blessing)
Ben: Benedict; Benjamin
BEN: *Bureau d'Études nucleaires* (Belgian Bureau of Nuclear Studies)
Ben Block: nickname for a British sailor
Ben Cur: Benguela Current
Bend: Bendigo
BENDEX: Beneficial Data Exchange (linking Social Security Administration with state welfare agencies)
bene: benzine
Bened: Benedict; Benedictine
Benedictines: monastic order founded by St Benedict
benef: beneficiary
Benef: Benefice
Ben Eil: Benedenwindse Eilanden (Dutch—Leeward Islands)
Benelux: economic union of Belgium, Netherlands, and Luxembourg
Bene't: Benedict
benev: benevolent
Beng: Bengal; Bengali
B.Eng.: Bachelor of Engineering
bengals: bengal tigers; thick cigars
B.Eng. Sci.: Bachelor of Engineering Science
B.Eng.Tech.: Bachelor of Engineering Technology
Ben-Gurion: (Hebrew—Son of a Lion)—name adopted by Da-

vid Green
Benj: Benjamin
Benjies: hundred-dollar bills bearing the portrait of America's libertarian-patriot philosopher-scientist Benjamin Franklin
Benjn: Benjamin
Benjy: Benjamin
Bennie: Benjamin
bennies: benzedrine stimulants
benny: (underground slang—benzedrine)
Benny: Benjamin
ben sug: beneficial suggestion
bent-nail syndrome: medical nickname for Peyronie's disease (malady wherein the penis is bent out of shape)
b & ent & pl: breaking and entering and petty larceny
benz: benzedrine; benzine
BEO: Borough Education Office(r)
beoc: battery echelon operating control
B.E.P.: Bachelor of Engineering Physics
BE & P: Bureau of Engraving and Printing
B EpA: British Epilepsy Association
BEPI: Budget Estimates Presentation Instructions
BEPO: British Experimental Pile Operation
bepoc: Burrough's electrographic printer-plotter for ordnance computing
BEPQ: Bureau of Entomology and Plant Quarantine
beq: bequeath
beqd: bequeathed
beqt: bequest
ber: *berechnet* (German—computed)
Ber: Berlin; Berwickshire
Ber: *Bericht* (German—report)
BER: Berlin, West Germany (Tempelhof airport); Bureau of Economic Regulation
Berb: Berber
BERC: Biomedical Engineering Research Corporation; Black Economic Research Center
BERCO: British Electric Resistance Company
Berdoo: San Bernardino, California
berg: iceberg (sometimes written 'berg)
BERH: Board of Engineers for Rivers and Harbors
Berk: Berkeley
Berks: Berkshire
Berkshires: Berkshire Mountains
Berl: Berlin
Berlin Bach: Karl Philipp Emanuel Bach—also nicknamed Hamburg Bach
Berl Tid: *Berlingske Tidende* (Danish—Berling's Times)—a leading daily newspaper
Berm: Bermuda Islands
Bermudas: Bermuda Islands
bermudite: gabbro-type ignenous rock plus biotite crystals and iron ores
Bern: Bernhard
Bernh: Bernhard
Bernhardt: Sarah Bernhardt—stage name of Rosine Bernard
Bernie: Bernard
Berno: Bernardo
Bert: Albert; Alberta; Albertina; Bertha; Bertillon (system); Bertram; Bertrand; Cuthbert; Delbert; Elbert; Elberta; Filbert; Gilbert; Herbert; Hilbert; Ibert; Lambert; Norbert; Philbert; Roberta; Wilbert; Zilbert
Bertie: (affectionate nickname—Bertrand Russel—colossus of twentieth-century philosophy)
Ber Tri: Bermuda Triangle (North Atlantic Ocean shipwreck area within a triangle extending from Bermuda to Cape Hatteras to Key West and back to Bermuda)
Berts: Bertillon Measurements
Berw: Berwick
beryl: beryllium aluminum silicate
bes: balanced electrolyte solution
bes: *besonders* (German—especially)
Bes: Bessel's functions
BES: Biological Engineering Society; Bureau of Employment Security
B.E.S.: Bachelor of Engineering Science
BESA: British Engineering Standards Association
BESE: Bureau of Elementary and Secondary Education
BeShT: Baal Shem-Tov (Israel Ben Eliezer)
besi: bus electronic-scanning indicator
BESL: British Empire Service League
BESN: British Empire Steam Navigation (company)
BESRL: Behavioral Science Research Laboratory (USA)
Bess: Bessemer; Mrs Harry S. Truman
BESS: Bank of England Statistical Summary
Bessie: Bethlehem Steel (Wall Street slang); Elizabeth
Bessie Love: Juanita Horton's stage name
Bessy: Elizabeth
best: *Bestellung* (German—order)
BEST: Basic Essential Skills Training; Black Efforts for Soul in Television
bet.: best estimate of trajectory; between
Bet: Betsy; Elizabeth
BET: British Electric Traction
BETA: Business Equipment Trade Association
Beth: Bethlehem; Elizabeth
Beth Israel: (Hebrew—House of Israel)—many synagogues bear this name
Bethlehem: (Hebrew—House of Bread)
Bethlehem: Bethlehem Steel Corporation
betr: *betrefend* (German—concerning)
Betsy: Elizabeth
Betsytown: Elizabeth, New Jersey
Betty: Elizabeth
BEU: British Empire Union
BEUC: *Bureau Européen des Unions Consommateurs* (Bureau of European Consumer Unions)
bev: bevel; beverage; billion electron volts
Bev: Beverly
BEV: Blake E. Vance
Beverly Sills: Belle Silverman
BEW: Board of Economic Warfare
bexec: budget execution
BEY: Beirut, Lebanon (airport)
bez: *bezahlt* (German—paid); *bezuglich* (German—referring to)
Bez: *Bezirk* (German—district)
bezw: *bezichungsweise, beziehungsweise* (German—respectively)
bf: back feed; beer firkin; before; bold face; both faces; boy friend; buffered; butter fat
bf: *bassa frequenza* (Italian—bass frequency); *bouillon filtrate* (French—filtered bouillon)
b.f.: *bona fide* (Latin—genuine; sincere)—in good faith; without deception; without fraud
b-f: beat-frequency
b/f: black female; brought forward; brown female

b & f: bell and flange
b4: before
BF: Banque de France (Bank of France); Battle Fleet; Battle Force
B.F.: Bachelor of Forestry
B de F: Banque de France (Bank of France); Banco de Fomento (Development Bank of Puerto Rico)
***BF:** Beogradska Filharmonica* (Serbo-Croat—Belgrade Philharmonic)
BFA: British Fellmongers' Association; British Film Academy; Broadcasting Foundation of America
B.F.A.: Bachelor of Fine Arts
BFAP: British Forces—Arabian Peninsula
BFB: Bureau of Forensic Ballistics
BFBPW: British Federation of Business and Professional Women
BFBS: British Forces Broadcasting Service; British and Foreign Bible Society
bfc: benign febrile convulsion
BFCA: British Federation of Commodity Associations
BFCF: Bremerton Freight Car Ferry
BFCS: British Friesian Cattle Society
BFCSD: Brewery, Flour, Cereal, Soft Drink and Distillery (Workers of America)
bfct: boiler feed compound tank
bfcy: beneficiary
BFDC: Bureau of Foreign and Domestic Commerce
bfe: beam-forming electrode
BFEA: Bureau of Far Eastern Affairs (U.S. Department of State)
BFEBS: British Far Eastern Broadcasting Society
BFFA: British Film Fund Agency
BFFC: British Federation of Folk Clubs
bfg: brute-force gyro
***Bfg:** Bank für Gemeinwirtschaft* (German—Bank for Municipal Management)
BFG: B.F. Goodrich
BFHMF: British Felt Hat Manufacturers' Federation
BFHS: Benjamin Franklin High School
BFI: British Film Institute; Business Forms Institute; Seattle, Washington (Boeing Field)
BFIA: British Flour Industry Association
bfl: back focal length
BFL: Barber Fern Line; Belgian Fruit Line; Blue Funnel Line (Holt's)
***BFM:** Ballet Folklorico de Mexico* (Spanish—Folklore Ballet of Mexico)
BFMA: Business Forms Management Association
BFMF: British Federation of Music Festivals; British Footwear Manufacturers' Federation
BFMIRA: British Food Manufacturing Industries Research Association
BFMP: British Federation of Master Printers
Bfn: Bloemfontein
BFN: British Forces Network
bfo: beat-frequency oscillator; blood-forming organs
Bfo: Buffalo
B.For.: Bachelor of Forestry
bform: budget formulation
B.For.Sci.: Bachelor of Forestry Science
bfp: biological false-positive (reactions); boiler feedpump
BFP: British Fishing Port (registration symbols appearing on the bows of British fishing vessels and indicating their home ports)—(*see* British Fishing Port appendix)
BFPA: British Film Producers Association
BFPC: British Farm Produce Council
BFPO: British Field Post Office
BFPPS: Bureau of Foods, Pesticides, and Product Safety (FDA)
bfpv: bona fide purchaser for value
bfr: biologic false reactor; blood flow rate; bone formation rate; buffer
***Bfr:** Belgische frank* (Dutch—Belgian franc)
B Fr: Belgian franc
BFRS: Bio-Feedback Research Society
bfR sol: buffered Ringer's solution
BFS: Belfast, Northern Ireland (airport); Board of Foreign Scholarships; Bureau of Family Services; Bureau of Federal Supply
B.F.S.: Bachelor of Foreign Service
***BFS:** Bundesanstalt für Flugsicherung* (German—Air-Traffic Control Authority)
BFSA: British Fire Services Association
BFSS: British and Foreign Sailors' Society
bft: bio-feedback training
BFT: Bentonite Flocculation Test
B.F.T.: Bachelor of Foreign Trade
BFTA: British Fur Trade Alliance
BFTC: Boeing Flight Test Center
BFUP: Board of Fire Underwriters of the Pacific
BFUSA: Basketball Federation of the United States of America
BFUW: British Federation of University Women
***BfV:** Bundesamt für Verfassungsschutz* (German—Federal Office for the Protection of the Constitution)—West German FBI roughly equivalent to the Special Branch in Britain
bfw: boiler feedwater
bg: back gear; bluish-green; buccogingival; business girl
b/g: bonded goods
bG: bluish green
bg (BG): background (behind tv performers)
Bg: Bengal; Bengalese; Bengali
***Bg:** Berg* (German—mountain)
BG: Benny Goodman; Birmingham Gage; British Guiana
B-G: Bach Gesellschaft; David Ben-Gurion
B & G: Barton and Guestier; Bing and Grondahl, buildings and grounds
bga: blue-green algae
BGA: Better Government Association; British Gliding Association
B-G b: Bordet-Gengou bacillus
BGB: Booksellers of Great Britain
bgc: blood group class
BGC: British Gas Corporation
BGCC: Bowling Green College of Commerce
B.G.E.: Bachelor of Geological Engineering
BG & E: Baltimore Gas and Electric
B.Gen.Ed.: Bachelor of General Education
BGF: Banana Growers' Federation; Black Guerrilla Family
BGFE: Boston Grain and Flour Exchange
bgg: booster gas generator; bovine gamma globulin
BGGRA: British Gelatine and Glue Research Association

bgh: bovine growth hormone
bght: bought
BGI: Bridgetown, Barbados (airport)
BGIRA: British Glass Industry Research Association
B-girl: bar girl
Bgk: Bangkok
bgl: below ground level
B.G.L.: Bachelor of General Laws
BGLA: Business Group for Latin America
bglb: brilliant-green lactose broth
bglr: burgler
bgl(s): bagel(s); beagle(s); bugle(s)
BGM: Bethnal Green Museum; Binghampton, New York (airport)
BGMA: British Gear Manufacturers' Association
bgmn: baggageman
Bgn: Bergen
BGN: Board on Geographic Names
BGNR: Barren Grounds Nature Reserve (New South Wales)
bgr: bombing and gunnery range
bgrv (BGRV): boost-glide reentry vehicle
bgs: bags
bg(s): back gear(s); bag(s)
Bgs: Brightlingsea
BGS: British Geriatrics Society
bgsa: blood-granulocyte specific activity
BGSC: Belfer Graduate School of Science (Yeshiva University); Boise-Griffin Steamship Company
BGSM: Bowman Gray School of Medicine
BGSU: Bowling Green State University
bgt: bought
BGT: Bender Gestalt Test; British Guiana Time
BGTT: Borderline Glucose Tolerance Test
B Gu: British Guiana
BGW: Baghdad, Iraq (airport)
bh: bloody hell (British expletive); boiler house; breast height (4 feet in U.S.); brinell hardness
bh: *bougie-heure* (French—candlehour)
Bh: Brinell hardness
BH: Base Hospital; Bath & Hammondsport (railroad); Benjamin Harrison (23rd President U.S.); Bill of Health; Brigade Headquarters; Brinell hardness; British Honduras; magnetization curve (symbol)
B/H: Bill of Health; Bordeaux-Hamburg (range of ports)
B&H: Bell and Howell; Breitkopf and Härtel
B of H: Board of Health
BH: *Bonne Humeur* (French—Good Humor); *Boston Herald; Thai bhat(s)*—monetary unit(s)
bha: base helix angle
bha (BHA): butylated hydroxyanisole
BHA: British Homeopathic Association; British Honduras Airways
bh ad: broach adapter
B.H.Adm.: Bachelor of Hospital Administration
BHAFRA: British Hat and Allied Feltmakers' Research Association
B'ham: Birmingham
Bharat: Republic of India
BHB: British Hockey Board
BHBNM: Big Hole Battlefield National Monument
B Hbr: boat harbor
BHBS: British Honduras Broadcasting Service
bhc: beaching cradle; benzene hexachloride (BHC)
BHC: Barbers, Hairdressers, Cosmetologists (and Proprietors' Union); Black Hawk College; British High Commissioner; British Hovercraft Corporation
BHCSA: British Hospitals Contributory Scheme Association
bhd: beachhead; bulkhead
BH$: British Honduras dollar
B.H.E.: Bachelor of Home Economics
B of HE: Board of Higher Education
B'head: Birkenhead
BHEW: Benton Harbor Engineering Works
Bhf: *Bahnhof* (German—station)
bhfx: broach fixture
B H & G: *Better Homes and Gardens*
bhi: brain-heart infusion
BHI: British Horological Institute; Bureau Hydrographique Internationale (International Hydrographic Bureau)
BHI: *British Humanities Index*
bhib: beef-heart infusion broth
BHISSA: Bureau of Health Insurance, Social Security Administration
BHK: type-B Hong Kong influenza virus
bhl: biological half-life
BHL: Borax Holdings Limited
Bhm: Birmingham, England
BHM: Birmingham, Alabama (airport)
BHMA: Bald-Headed Men of America
BHMC: Bell & Howell/Mamiya Company
BHMH: Benjamin Harrison Memorial Home (Indianapolis, Indiana)
BHMRA: British Hydromechanics Research Association
bhn: bephenium hydroynaphthoate
Bhn: Bremerhaven; Brinell hardness number
BHNWR: Bombay Hook National Wildlife Refuge (Delaware)
B Hond: British Honduras
B.Hort.: Bachelor of Horticulture
B.Hort.Sci.: Bachelor of Horticultural Science
bhp: brake horsepower
BHP: Broken Hill Proprietary
bhp hr: brake horsepower hour
Bhpric: Bishopric
BHQ: Brigade Headquarters
bhr: basal heart rate; biotechnology and human research
BHRA: British Hotels and Restaurants Association; British Hydromechanics Research Association
B & HRO: Biotechnology and Human Research Office (NASA)
bhs: betahemolytic streptococcus
Bhs: Bohus
BHS: Balboa High School; Boys High School; British Home Stores; British Horse Society; Bureau of Health Services; Burlesque Historical Society; Bushwick High School
B&HS: Bonhomie and Hattiesburg Southern (railroad)
B.H.Sci.: Bachelor of Household Science
BHSS: Bronx High School of Science
bht (BHT): butylated hydroxytoluene
BHTA: British Herring Trade Association
Bhu: Bhutan
bh/vh: body hematocrit/venous hemocrat (ratio)
bhw: boiling heavy water
BHW: Boston Hospital for Women
BHYC: Boothbay Harbor Yacht Club

B.Hyg.: Bachelor of Hygiene
bi: background investigation; bacteriological index; base ignition; base of prism in; burn index; bodily injury; buffer index
b/i: battery inverter
b & i: bankruptcy and insolvency; base and increment
b or i: brass or iron (cargo)
Bi: bismuth (symbol)
BI: Babson Institute; background investigation; Bahama Islands; Bermuda Islands; Braniff International; British India; Brookings Institution; Bureau of Investigation; National Biscuits (stock exchange symbol)
BI: *Banca d'Italia* (Bank of Italy)
BIA: Bicycle Institute of America; Braille Institute of America; Brazilian International Airlines; Bureau of Indian Affairs; Bureau of Insular Affairs
BI & A: Bureau of Intelligence and Research (US Department of State)
BIAA: Bureau of Inter-American Affairs (US Department of State)
BIAE: British Institute of Adult Education
bialy: bialystok roll (holeless onion-flaked bagel)
BIAS: Brooklyn Institute of Arts and Sciences
BIATA: British Independent Air Transport Association
bib.: bottled in bond
bib. (BIB): baby incendiary bomb
bib: *bibliothèque* (French—library)
bib.: *bibe* (Latin—drink)
Bib: Bible; Biblical
BIB: Biennale of Illustrations Bratislava (international exhibition of children's book illustrations)
BIB: *Berliner Institut für Betriebsführung* (German—Berlin Business Management Institute)
BIBA: Babson Institute of Business Administration
Bib Apo Vat: Biblioteca Apostolica Vaticana (Vatican Library)
bib b: *biblioteksbind* (Dano-Norwegian—library binding)
BIBC: British Isles Bowling Council
BIBF: British and Irish Basketball Federation
bibl: bibliotec-; bibliotek-; bibliothec-; bibliothek; bibliothèque
Bible Belt: rural areas of the southern United States where incredible biblical statements are taken literally
biblio: bibliographical imprint or note; biblioclasm (book destruction); biblioclast (book destroyer); bibliogenesis (book production); bibliognost (bibliographic expert or book expert); bibliogony (book production); bibliograph (bibliographer); bibliographee (the person the bibliography is concerned with); bibliographer (describer of books or a preparer of bibliographies); bibliographic(al); bibliography
biblioc: biblioclasm; biblioclast
bibliog: bibliographer; bibliographic(al); bibliography
bibliograph: bibliographer; bibliographee; bibliography
biblioklept: bibliokleptomania(c)
bibliol: bibliolater (person with excessive admiration or reverence for books); bibliolatrous characterized by bibliolatry); bibliolatry (book worship); bibliological; bibliologist; bibliology (scientific description and study of books)
bibliom: bibliomancy (divination by books such as the *Bible*); bibliomane (avid collector of books); bibliomania (mania for collecting books); bibliomaniac (person affected with the mania for book collecting); bibliomanist (synonym for bibliomaniac)
bibliop: bibliopegic (relating to book binding); bibliopegist (bookbinder); bibliopegy (bookbinder's art); bibliophagist (devourer of books); bibliophile (book lover); bibliophilia (love of books); bibliophobe (book hater); bibliophobia (aversion, dislike, or dread of books); bibliopole (bookdealer)
bibliopsy: bibliopsychology (study of authors, books, and readers as well as their interrelationships)
bibliothec: bibliotheca (bibliographer's catalog or a library); bibliothecal (belonging to the library); bibliothecar (librarian); bibliothecary (librarian or library)
bibliother: bibliotherapeutic; bibliotherapist; bibliotherapy
bibliothetic(al): arrangement or placement of books
bibliotrain: railroad car converted into a mobile library
bibl mun: *bibliothèque municipale* (French—city library; public library)
Bib Nac: Biblioteca Nacional (National Library, Madrid—or others so named)
Bib Nat: Bibliothèque Nationale (National Library—Paris)
Bib Naz Cen: Biblioteca Nazionale Centrale (Italian National Central Library—Florence, Naples, Rome, etc. International Business Operations)
BIBRA: British Industrial Biological Research Association
Bib Soc Am: Bibliographical Society of America
Bib Soc Can: Bibliographical Society of Canada
Bic: Societe Bic (ballpoint pen factory founded by Baron Marcel Bich)
BIC: Barrier Industrial Council; Bureau of International Commerce; Bureau International des Containers (International Bureau of Containers)
bicarb: sodium bicarbonate
bicarbonate (of soda): baking soda; sodium bicarbonate
BICC: British Insulated Callenders Cables
BICEMA: British Internal Combustion Engine Manufacturers Association
BICERA: British Internal Combusion Engine Research Association
BICERI: British Internal Combustion Engine Research Institute
bichloride of mercury: mercuric chloride
bichrome: sodium bichromate
BICS: British Institute of Cleaning Science
BICTA: British Investment Casters' Technical Association
bicv: biconcave
bicx: biconvex
bid. (BID): brought in dead
b.i.d.: *bis in die* (Latin—twice daily)
Bid: Bideford
BID: Banco Interamericano de Desarrollo (Interamerican Development Bank)
B.I.D.: Bachelor of Industrial Design

B. of I.D.: Bachelor of Interior Design
bidap: bibliographic data processing program
Biddy: Bridget
bidec: binary-to-decimal converter
BIE: Bureau International d'Education (International Bureau of Education); Bureau International des Expositions (International Bureau of Expositions)
B.I.E.: Bachelor of Industrial Engineering
Bieder: Biedermeier
BIEE: British Institute of Electrical Engineers
bien: biennial
Bien Aimé: (French—Well Beloved)—sobriquet of Louis XV
BIET: British Institute of Engineering Technology
BIF: Bombardier's Information File; British Industries Federation
BIFUS: Britain, Italy, France, United States
big.: best in group; biological isolation garment
BIG: Beneficial Insurance Group
BIG: *Bazak Israel Guide*
Big Apple: New York City's nickname
Big Ben: battleship USS *Franklin;* huge bell attached to clock in Parliament tower, Westminster district of London, named after Sir Benjamin Hall, commissioner of works in 1859 when bell was hung
Big Bend: big bend of the Rio Grande—bounding southern section of the Big Bend National Park on the Texas border of Mexico
Big Bill: William D(udley) Haywood
Big Board: New York City's Stock Exchange
Big Burg: New York City
Big Charlie: Charles de Gaulle
big D: (underground slang—hallucinogen such as diethyltryptamine, dimethyltryptamine, dipropylphyptamine, etc.)
Big-D: Dallas, Texas
Big Dan: Daniel Joseph Tobin
Big Ditch: Panama Canal's nickname
Big-E: aircraft carrier USS *Enterprise*
Big Eddy: Portland, Maine's skid-row area
Big Finger: Australia's Cape York Peninsula
Big Four: California railroad builders Charles Crocker, Mark Hopkins, Collis P. Huntington, and Leland Stanford; Cleveland, Cincinnati, Chicago, and St Louis; Great Britain, France, Italy, and the United States at the end of World War I or their representatives at the Peace Conference—Lloyd George, Georges Clemenceau, Vittorio Orlando, and Woodrow Wilson, respectively
Biggest Little City: Reno, Nevada's nickname
big H: big house (underground slang—penitentiary such as San Quentin or Sing Sing); heroin
Big Heart of Texas: Austin
Big Island: Hawaii (largest of the Hawaiians)
big J: big John (underground slang—policeman or other law-enforcement officer)
Big-J: battleship USS *New Jersey*
Big Jim: Postmaster General James Aloysius Farley
Big-M: battleship USS *Missouri*
Big Mac: Mac Donald hamburger; New York's Municipal Assistance Corporation (MAC)—Big Mac
Big Mamie: battleship USS *Massachusetts*
Big Miss: Mississippi River
Big Muddy: Missouri River
Big N: Vladimir Nabokov
Big Nail: translation of the Eskimo nickname for the North Pole
Big-O: attack aircraft carrier USS *Oriskany*
Big Red: racehorse Man-o'-War's nickname
bigs: biological isolation garments
Big Six: New York City's Typographical Union Number Six
Big Sky Country: Montana
Big Smoke: old nickname of London, England as well as Sydney, New South Wales
Big Sur: mountainous coastal resort area of California's Monterey County
Big Three: The Big Three (music publishers Robbins, Feist, Miller)—Robbins Music Corp; World-War-I peacemakers Georges Clemenceau, Lloyd George, and Woodrow Wilson; World-War-II peacemakers Winston Churchill, Franklin Roosevelt, and Joseph Stalin
Big Windy: Chicago, Illinois
bih: benign intracranial hypertension
BIH: Beth Israel Hospital
BIHA: British Ice Hockey Association
bihor.: *bihorium* (Latin—two hours)
BII: Biosophical Institute Incorporated
BIIA: British Institute of Industrial Art
Bij: Benjamin
bijb: *bijbelse term* (Dutch—biblical term)
bijv: *bijvoorbeeld* (Dutch—for example)
bike: bicycle
biki: bikini
bil: bilateral; billet
b-i-l: brother-in-law
Bil: Bilbao
BIL: Billings, Montana (airport); British India Line
bilat: bilateral
bildl: *bildeich* (German—figuratively)
BILG: Building Industry Libraries Group
bili: bilirubin
bilj: *biljarttern* (Dutch—billiards)
bil k: bilge keel
bill: *billede* (Dano-Norwegian—illustrations)
Bill: William; William F. Buckley, Jr; all other distinguished Williams nicknamed Bill
Bill Arp: Charles Henry Smith
Billie: William
billion: (American—a thousand million; 10^9); (British—a million million; 10^{12})
Bill of Rights: first ten amendments to the *Constitution of the United States*
Billtown: Williamstown, Kansas
Billy: William
Billy Sanders: (pseudonym—Joel Chandler Harris)
Billy the Kid: William Bonney alias William Wright
BILS: British International Law Society
Bim: Barbadan
bim: *bimensile* (Italian—semimonthly); *bimestrale* (Italian—bimonthly); *bimestre* (Italian—two-month period)
BIM: British Institute of Management
B.I.M.: Bachelor of Indian Medicine
bimac: bi-stable magnetic core

BIMCAN: British Industrial Measuring and Control Apparatus Manufacturers Association
Bimshire: Barbados
BIMT: Bahama Islands Ministry of Tourism
bin.: binary
BINA: *Bureau International des Normes de l'Automobile* (International Bureau of Automobile Standards)
binac: high-speed electronic digital computer
bind.: binding
B.Ind.: Bachelor of Industry
B.Ind.Ed.: Bachelor of Industrial Education
Bing Crosby: Harry Crosby
Binj: Benjamin
BINM: Buck Island National Monument, St. Croix, Virgin Islands
binocs: binoculars
bins: (Cockney contraction—binoculars)
BINWR: Blackbeard Island National Wildlife Refuge (Georgia)
bio: biographical; biography; biological; biology
BIO: Bedford Institute of Oceanography
BIOA: Bureau of International Organization Affairs (US Department of State)
biochem: biochemical; biochemist; biochemistry
biochron: biochronometry
bioclean: biologically clean
biocon: biocontamination
biocyb: biocybernetics
biodef: biological defense
biodeg: biodegradable
biodeg(s): biodegradable(s)
biodes: biodestructible
biodet: biodeterioration
bioeng: bioengineer(ing); biological engineer(ing)
bioex: bioexperiment(ation)
biog: biographer; biographical; biography
biogeo: biogeology
biogeog: biogeographer; biogeographic(al); biogeography
biol: biological; biologist; biology
Biol Abstr: *Biological Abstracts*
BIOLWPNSYS: Biological Weapon System (USA)
biomath: biomathematician; biomathematics
biomed: biomedical; biomedicine
bionics: biology + electronics
biophys: biophysical; biophysicist; biophysics
bior: business input-output rerun
BIOREP: Biological Attack Report
bios (BIOS): biological satellite
BIOS: Biological Investigations of Space
biosat: biosatellite
biosci: bioscience; bioscientific; bioscientist
BIOSIS: Biosciences Information Service of *Biological Abstracts*
biostat: biostatistic(s)
biostitutes: biologist prostitutes (biologists who prostitute themselves to the specious claims of ammunition and gun makers who with so-called sportsmen insist hunting and killing are essential in controlling wildlife on our planet although man has always been its principal predator)
BIOT: British Indian Ocean Territories
biotel: biotelemetric; biotelemetry
biowar: biological warfare
bip: bacterial intravenous protein; balanced in plane; bismuth iodoform paraffin; books in print; borough-interborough problem(s)
Bip: Marcel Marceau
BiP: *Books in Print*
BIP: British Industrial Plastics; British Institute of Physics
BIPAD: Bureau of Independent Publishers and Distributors
bipd: biparting doors
biphet: biphetamine (drug stimulant)
BIPL: Burmah Industrial Products Limited
BIPM: Bureau International des Poids et Mesures (International Bureau of Weights and Measures)
BIPO: British Institute of Public Opinion
bipp: bismuth, iodoform, paraffin paste
BIPP: British Institute of Practical Psychology
bipyr: bipyramidal
bir: basic incidence rate
Bir: *Birmania* (Italian or Spanish—Burma); *Birmânia* (Portuguese—Burma)
BIR: Board of Inland Revenue; British Institute of Radiology
Bird: Haydn's String Quartet in C (opus 33, no. 3)
BIRD: Banque Internationale pour la Reconstruction et le Développement (International Bank for Reconstruction and Development)
birdie: battery integration and radar display equipment
Birdofredum Sawin: (pseudonym—James Russell Lowell)
BIRE: British Institution of Radio Engineers
B.Ir.Eng.: Bachelor of Irrigation Engineering
BIRF: Brewing Industry Research Foundation
BIRF: *Banco Internacional de Reconstrucción y Fomento* (Spanish—International Bank for Reconstruction and Development)
birl: girlish boy (transvestite)
Birm: Birmingham
Birmingham notation: (*see* GKD-notation)
BIRMO: British Infra-Red Manufacturers' Association
BIRMPDis: Birmingham Procurement District (U.S. Army)
BIRS: British Institute of Recorded Sound
birt: bolt installation and removal tool
birthquake: population explosion
bis.: bissextile
Bis: Bismarck; Bissau
BIS: Bank for International Settlements; Bismarck, North Dakota (airport); Board of Inspection Survey (USN); British Information Service; British Interplanetary Society
BISAKTA: British Iron, Steel, and Kindred Trades Association
BisArch: Bismarck Archipelago
Bisc: Biscayan
BISCO: British Iron and Steel Corporation
bisett: *bisettimanale* (Italian—biweekly)
bisex: bisexual
BISF: British Iron and Steel Federation
BISFA: British Industrial and Scientific Film Association
Bish: Bishop
bishaw: bicycle rickshaw
Bish Mus: Bishop Museum
Bishop: Bishop Museum; Bishop Museum Press
Bishop of Rome: the Pope
bis in d.: *bis in dies* (Latin—twice daily)
bis in 7d.: *bis in septem diebus* (Latin—twice in seven days; twice weekly)
BISITS: British Iron and Steel Industry Translation Service

(BISRA)
BISL: British Information Service Library
Bismarcks: Bismarck Islands
BISN: British India Steam Navigation (company)
Bison City: Buffalo, New York
bisp: between ischial spines; bispinous (interspinous diameter)
BISPA: British Independent Steel Producers Association
BISRA: British Iron and Steel Research Associates
Bister: Bicester
bisw: *bisweilen* (German—sometimes)
bit.: binary digit
BIT: Bradford Institute of Technology; British Independent Television; Bureau International du Travail (International Labor Organisation)
BITA: British Industrial Truck Association
BITC: Bahamas International Trust Company
bite.: built-in test equipment
BITE: Base Installation Test Equipment
bitm: bituminous
BITM: Birla Industrial and Technological Museum
bito: burnishing tool
BITO: British Institution of Training Officers
bit(s).: binary digit(s)
Bitter Bierce: Ambrose Bierce
Bitterroot: Montana state flower
bitu: benzyl-thiourea
BITU: Bustamante Industrial Trade Union
bitum: bituminous
bituminous: soft coal
Bituminous City: Connellsville, Pennsylvania
BIU: *Bureau International des Universités* (French—International University Bureau)
biv: bivouac
BIW: Bath Iron Works; Boston Insulated Wire (and Cable Company)
BIWF: British Israel World Federation
BIWS: Bureau of International Whaling Statistics
Bix: Leon Bismarck Beiderbecke
biz: business
BIZ: Bank für Internationalen Zahlungsausgleich (Bank for International Settlements)
bizad: business administration
bizjet: business-type jet airplane
bizmac: business machine computer
bizman: business man
bj: back judge (football); biceps jerk; blow job (fellatio)
b & j: bone and joint
BJ: Benito Juarez; Byron Jackson (Borg-Warner)
B.J.: Bachelor of Journalism
B & J: Burke & James
B of J: Bank of Japan
BJA: Burlap and Jute Association
b/Jan: binding expected in January (for example)
BJC: Baltimore Junior College; Bismarck Junior College; Boise Junior College; Brevard Junior College
BJCEB: British Joint Communications-Electronics Board
B Jon: Ben Jonson
Bjørn Bjørn: Bjørnstjerne Bjørnson
BJOS: *British Journal of Occupational Safety*
BJp: Bence Jones protein
BJSM: British Joint Services Mission
BJTRA: British Jute Trade Research Association
BJU: Bob Jones University
B.Juris.: Bachelor of Jurisprudence
bk: bank; below the knee; black; book; brake
Bk: berkelium; Brook
B-K: Blaw-Knox
bka: below-knee amputation
bkble: bookable; bookmobile
bkbndg: bookbinding
bkbndr: bookbinder
bkc: benzalkonium chloride (BKC)
bkcy: bankruptcy
bkd: blackboard
bk di: brake die
bkfst: breakfast
bkg: banking; bookkeeping
bkgd: background
bkhs: blockhouse
BKII: *Vsesoyuenaya Kommunisticheskaya Partiya* (Russian—All-Union Communist Party)
BKK: Bangkok, Thailand (airport)
bklr: black letter
bklt: booklet
Bklyn: Brooklyn
Bklyn Brdg: Brooklyn Bridge
bkm: buckram
BKM: Moscow, USSR (Bykovo Airport)
bkn: broken
Bkn: Birkenhead
B. Kovner: Jacob Adler
bkpg: bookkeeping
bkpr: bookkeeper
bkpt: bankrupt
bkr: baker; beaker; breaker
bks: bunks; barracks; books; brakes
BKS: British Kinematograph Society
Bks for Libs: Books for Libraries
bk sh: bookshelves
bkt: basket; bracket
bkt(s): basket(s)
bktt: below knee to toe
bkw: breakwater
bkwp: below-knee walking plaster (cast)
bl: bank larceny; baseline; billet; bleed(ing); blood; blood loss; blue; bomb line; buccolingual; butt line; buttock line
Bl: Burkitt's lymphoma (BL)
BL: Bonanza Airlines: British Library
B-L: Belgium-Luxembourg
b/l: basic letter; bill of lading (B/L); blueline blueprint
b & l: ball and lever; business and loan
bl: *blad; blank* (Dano-Norwegian—leaf, sheet; blank)
Bl: *Blatt(er)* (German—leaf; leaves; page(s)); *Böluk* (Turkish—company)
BL: Bonanza Airlines
B.L.: Bachelor of Letters
B & L: Bausch & Lomb; Building and Loan (association or bank)
B es L: *Bachelier des Lettres* (French—Bachelor of Letters)
bl a: *blandt andet; blandt andre* (Danish—among other things)
Bla: Brasilia
BLA: Bangladesh Library Association; Black Liberation Army; British Library Association; Bombay Library Association
B.L.A.: Bachelor of Landscape Architecture; Bachelor of Liberal Arts
BLAC: British Light Aviation Center
BLACC: British and Latin American Chamber of Commerce
black.: blackmail
Blackbeard: Edward Teach—privateer-pirate also known as Edward Thatch
Blackberry Capital: McCloud, California
Black Castle of Opium: translation of Afyonkarahisar or Afyon in western Turkey where much of the world's opium is grown
Black Country: Midlands of En-

gland around smoke-blackened Birmingham
Black Dan: swarthy-complected Daniel Webster
Black Death: bubonic plague which devastated Asia, Africa, and Europe during the fourteenth century
black diamond: black or gray industrial diamond also called framesite bort; nickname for anthracite or hard coal
Black Diamond City: Wilkes-Barre, Pennsylvania
black diamonds: coal
black disease: anthrax of sheep; braxy
Black Explorer: modern sobriquet given Matthew Henson who in his day was called the Negro Explorer because he had accompanied Peary on all his Arctic expeditions and even pushed him to the North Pole as well as helping him survey the Nicaraguan canal route
Black-eyed Susan: Maryland state flower
black fever: kala-azar (Leishmaniasis)
black flag: symbol of death or emblem of piracy
Black Flower of Society: Nathaniel Hawthorne's nickname for any jail, penitentiary, or prison
black gold: petroleum
black jack: card game; licorice-flavored chewing gum; zinc blende or zinc sulfide
Black Jack: General John J. Pershing, USA
Black Key: Chopin's Piano Etude No. 5 in G-flat major
black lead: cerrusite (lead carbonate)
Black Messiah: Booker T. Washington
Black Nationalist: Marcus M(oziah) Garvey
Black Prince: Edward—Prince of Wales—son of Edward III; so nicknamed as he always wore black armor
Black Republic: Haiti originally and more recently applied to many emerging African nations
Black Rock: nickname of the Columbia Broadcasting System (CBS) situated in the black granite building at 51 West 52nd Street in New York City
Black Saturday: Commander's Internal Management Review (held on Saturdays)
Blackstairs: Blackstairs Mountains of Ireland
Black Stream: Japan Current
blackwater fever: malaria
black widow: nickname of the poisonous spider *Lactrodectus mactans*
blad: blotting pad
Blanca: Blanche
B.Land.Arch.: Bachelor of Landscape Architecture
Blaskets: Blasket Islands on Ireland's Atlantic coast
Blast: Blastoidea
BLAST: Black Legal Action for Soul in Television
BLB: Boothby-Lovelace-Bulbulian (oxygen mask)
blc: balance; boundary-layer control
BLC: British Lighting Council
bl cult.: blood culture
bld: blood; blood and lymphatic system; bloody; bold; boldface
BLEDCO: Brooklyn Local Economic Development Corporation
bldg: building
Bldg Engr: Building Engineer
bldi: blank die
bldr: builder
BLE: Brotherhood of Locomotive Engineers
B & LE: Bessemer and Lake Erie (railroad)
bleaching powder: calcium hypochlorite
BLESMA: British Limbless Ex-Service Men's Association
bleu: blind landing experimental unit
BLEU: Belgium-Luxembourg Economic Union
bleve: boiling-liquid expanding-vapor explosion
Blf: Bluff
BLF & E: Brotherhood of Locomotive Firemen and Enginemen
blg: betalactoglobulin
BLG: *Burke's Landed Gentry*
BLH: Baldwin-Lima-Hamilton
BLHA: British Linen Hire Association
BLI: Bliss & Laughlin Industries; Buyers Laboratory Incorporated
B.L.I.: Bachelor of Literary Interpretation
B.Lib.S.: Bachelor of Library Science
B.Lib.Sci.: Bachelor of Library Science
Blick: Blickensderfer (portable typewriter popular before World War I)
Blighty: (British slang—England)
Blind Bards: Homer and Milton
Blind Poet: John Milton
Blind Publisher: Joseph Pulitzer
Blind Tom: Thomas Bethune
BLIP: Big Look Improvement Program
B.Litt.: *Baccalaureus Literarum* (Latin—Bachelor of Literature)
Blitz: *Blitzkreig* (German—lightning war)
bliz: blizzard; blizzardly; blizzardous
blk: black; block; blocking
Blk: Block
blkd: bulkhead
blk lt: black light
blksh: blackish
blksmith: blacksmith
bll: below lower limit
BLM: British Leland Motor (corporation merging Austin, British Motor Moldings, Jaguar, Morris, Riley, Rover, Triumph, Wolseley); Bureau of Land Management (General Land Office and Grazing Service)
B.L.M.: Bachelor of Land Management
BLM: *Bonniers Literaray Magasin* (Bonnier's Literary Magazine)
blm: *besa la mano* (Spanish—a kiss to your hand)
BLMA: British Lead Manufacturers' Association
BLMC: British Leyland Motor Corporation
BLMRA: British Leather Manufacturers' Research Association
BLMS: Book-Library-Management System
bln: balloon; bronchial lymph nodes
Bln: Berlin
blnkt: blanket
BLNR: Benton Lake National Refuge (Montana)
BLNWR: Big Lake National Wildlife Refuge (Arkansas); Bitter Lake NWR (New Mexico); Buffalo Lake NWR (Texas)
BLNY: Booksellers League of New York
blo: blower
Bloater(s): inhabitant(s) of Yarmouth on the North Sea coast of England where herrings are salted and smoked
Bloch Pub: Bloch Publishing

Company
block.: blockade
Blockhousers: America's oldest Negro regiment whose gallant assault of a well-defended blockhouse won them this nickname during the Spanish-American War
Blondin: Charles Emile Gravele—the tightrope walker who crossed Niagara Falls in the mid-nineteenth century
Blood and Guts: General George S. Patton, USA
bloodstone: heliotrope plasma with red jasper inclusions
Bloody Mary: Mary I of England (Mary Tudor)
blooper: blunder and error
Blos: Blossom
blou: blouse
B-love: being love (unselfish accepting love of another person, according to Maslow)
blp: *besa los pies* (Spanish—a kiss to your feet)
BLP: British Labor Party
bl pr: blood pressure
blr: boiler; breech-loading rifle
BLR: Ballistic Research Laboratories (USA)
BLRA: British Launderers' Research Association
blrmkr: boilermaker
BLROA: British Laryngological, Rhinological, and Otological Association
blrp: boilerplate
bls: bales; barrels; binary light switch; blood sugar
BLS: Brooklyn Law School; Bureau of Labor Statistics
B.L.S.: Bachelor of Library Science; Bachelor of Library Service
B.L.S.: *Benevolenti Lectori Salutem* (Latin—Salutations to the Kind Reader)
BL & SA: Bank of London and South America
BLSGMA: British Lampblown Scientific Glassware Manufacturers' Association
blsh: bluish
blt: blood type; built
blstg pwd: blasting powder
blsw: barrels of load salt water
blswd: barrels of load salt water per day
b-l-t: bacon, lettuce, and tomato (sandwich)
BLT: Battalion Landing Team
Bltc: Baltic
bltn(s): built-in(s)
blu: blue
B-L u: Bessey-Lowry units
Blubo: *Blut und Boden* (German—blood and soil)
blue asbestos: crocidolite
Blue-backed Speller: nickname for *The American Spelling Book* by Noah Webster of dictionary fame
Bluebeard: nickname of any wife killer such as the Chevalier Raoul whose seventh wife discovered the bodies of his six previous wives
Bluebird: state bird of Nevada
Bluebonnet: Texas state flower
Bluebonnet Bowl: athletic stadium in Houston, Texas
Blue Grass Capital: Lexington, Kentucky
Blue Grass Country: Kentucky
Blue Grass State: Kentucky's official nickname
Blue Hen Chickens: nickname given Delawareans as their state bird is the Blue Hen Chicken
Bluehen(s): Delawarean(s)
Blue Hen State: Delaware (whose gamecocks were born of blue hens)
Blue Law State: Connecticut nickname
Bluenose: fisherman or sailor from Canada's Maritime Provinces
Bluenose Province: Nova Scotia
Bluenose(s): native(s) of Canada's Maritime Provinces, especially Nova Scotia; puritan(s)
blue ointment: mercurial ointment
blue peter: blue signal flag with a white rectangle in its center; flown when a ship is ready to sail; letter P or Papa in the international code
Blues: Blue Mountains
Blue Steel: air-to-surface nuclear missile
bluestone: blue vitriol (copper sulfate)
blue vitriol: bluestone (copper sulfate)
Bluff City: place-name nickname shared by Hannibal, Missouri; Memphis, Tennessee; and Natchez, Mississippi—all on bluffs above the Mississippi River
Bluff King Hal: nickname of Henry VIII
BLV: British Legion Village
Blvd: Boulevard
BLW: Baldwin-Lima-Hamilton
BLWA: British Laboratory Ware Association
Bly: Blyth
Blz: Belize (formerly British Honduras)
blz(n): *bladzijde(n)* ((Dutch—page(s))
Blz: Belize; Belizian
bm: basal metabolism; basement membrane; beam; board measure; body mass; bone marrow; book of the month; bowel movement; buccomesial
b/m (B/M): black male; bill of material; brown male; bill of material
bm: *bez mista* (Czech—no place of publication)
b.m.: *balneum maris* (Latin—bath in sea water)
Bm: beam; birthmark; board measure; bowel movement; Burma; Burmese
BM: Banco de México (Bank of Mexico); bench mark; Boatswain's Mate; Boston & Maine (railroad); Brigade Major; British Museum; Brooklyn Museum; Bureau of Medicine; Bureau of Mines; Bureau of the Mint
B.M.: Bachelor of Medicine; Bachelor of Music
B-M: Bolinder-Munktell; Bristol-Myers
BM: *Banca Mondiale* (Italian—World Bank); *Banco de México* (Spanish—Bank of Mexico); *Banco Mundial* (Portuguese or Spanish—World Bank); *Banque du Monde* (French—World Bank)
B & M: Beaufort & Morehead (railroad); Boston & Maine (railroad)
B de M: Banco de México (Bank of Mexico)
B of M: Bank of Montreal; Bishop(ric) of Münster; Bureau of Mines
BM: *Beata Maria* (Latin—Blessed Mary)
BMA: Baltimore Museum of Art; Bible Memory Association; Bicycle Manufacturers' Association; British Medical Association; British Military Authority; Stockholm, Sweden, airport (3-letter code)
B.Mar.E.: Bachelor of Marine Engineering
B.Mar.Eng.: Bachelor of Marine Engineering
B.Math.: Bachelor of Mathematics
BMB: Ballistic Missile Branch (USA); British Metrication Board

***BMB:** British Medical Bulletin*
***B-M B:** Baader-Meinhof Bande* (German—Baader - Meinhof Gang)—terrorist Red Army Group's nickname reflecting its West German leadership
***BMBW:** Bundesministerium für Bildung und Wissenscaft*—West German Ministry for Education and Science
bmc: blockhouse monitor console
BMC: Ballistic Missile(s) Center; Ballistic Missiles Committee; British Mountaineering Council; Bryn Mawr College
BMCC: Blue Mountain Community College
BMCS: Ballistic Missile Cost Study; Bureau of Motor Carrier Safety
bmd: births, marriages, deaths
BMD: Ballistic Missile Defense
B-M-D: Blow-Me-Down, Nova Scotia
BMDM: British Museum Department of Manuscripts
BMDMB: Ballistic Missile Defense Missile Battalion (USA)
bmdns: basic mission, design number, and series (aircraft)
bmdr: bombardier
BMD System: Ballistic Missile Defense System
bme: biomedical engineering
BME: Brotherhood of Marine Engineers
B.M.E.: Bachelor of Mechanical Engineering; Bachelor of Mining Engineering; Bachelor of Music Education
BMEC: British Marine Equipment Council
B. Med.: Bachelor of Medicine
B.M.Ed.: Bachelor of Music Education
B.Med.Sc.: Bachelor of Medical Science
BMEF: British Mechanical Engineering Federation
BMEG: Building Materials Export Group
BMEL: Barber Middle East Line
bmep: brake mean effective pressure
B.Met.: Bachelor of Metallurgy
B.Met.E.: Bachelor of Metallurgical Engineering
BMEWS: Ballistic Missile Early Warning System
BMFA: Boston Museum of Fine Arts
B.Mgt.Eng.: Bachelor of Management Engineering
bmi: ballistic missile interceptor (BMI)
BMI: Barley and Malt Institute; Batelle Memorial Institute; Book Manufacturers Institute; Broadcast Music Incorporated; Broadway Memorial Institute
B.Mic.: Bachelor of Microbiology
BMIC: British Music Information Centre (London); Broadcast Music Incorporated (Canada)
***BMIC:** Bureau of Mines Information Circular*
B.Min.E.: Bachelor of Mining Engineering
***BMJ:** British Medical Journal*
bmk: birthmark; bookmark(er)
BML: Belfast & Moosehead Lake (railroad); Bodega Marine Laboratory (University of California); British Museum Library (London)
B.M.L.: Bachelor of Modern Languages
B & M L: Belfast & Moosehead Lake (railroad)
BMLG: Branch and Mobile Libraries Group
BMM: Belfast, Mersey and Manchester Steamships
BMMA: British Mantle Manufacturers' Association
BMMO: Birmingham and Midland Motor Omnibus
Bmn: Bremen
BMN: British Merchant Navy
BMNH: British Museum (Natural History)
BMNP: Bale Mountains National Park (Ethiopia); Blue Mountains National Park (New South Wales)
BMNT: beginning morning nautical twilight
bmo: business machine operator
BMO: Ballistic Missile Office
bmoc: big man on campus
B'mouth: Bournemouth
bmp: brake mean power
BMP: Bricklayers, Masons and Plasterers' (Union)
BMPA: British Metalworking Plantmakers' Association
bmpp: benign mucous-membrane pemphigus
BMPS: British Medical Protection Society; British Musicians Pension Society
bmr: basal metabolic rate; bomber
BMR: Basal Metabolism Rate
BMRA: British Manufacturers' Representatives' Association
BMRB: British Market Research Bureau
BMRR: British Museum Reading Room
BMRS: Ballistic Missile Recovery System
BMs: Black Muslims; Boatswain's Mates
BMS: Boston Museum of Science; British Ministry of Supply; Buffalo Museum of Science; Bureau of Medical Services; Bureau of Medicine and Surgery
B.M.S.: Bachelor of Marine Science; Bachelor of Medical Science
BMSA: British Medical Students' Association
BMSE: Baltic Mercantile and Shipping Exchange
BMSS: British and Midlands Scientific Society
BMT: Basic Military Training; Boston & Maine Transportation (railroad); Brooklyn-Manhattan Transit (subway system)
B.M.T.: Bachelor of Medical Technology
BMTA: Boston Metropolitan Transit Authority
BMTFA: British Malleable Tube Fittings Association
***BMTP:** Bureau of Mines Technical Paper*
BMTS: Ballistic Missile Target System
B. Mus.: Bachelor of Music
bmv: bromegrass-mosaic virus
BMVM: British Military Volunteer Service
BMW: Bayerische Motoren Werke (Bavarian Motor Works)
BMWE: Brotherhood of Maintenance of Way Employees
BMWS: Ballistic Missile Weapon System
BMYC: Baltimore Motor Yacht Club
bn: battalion; branchial neuritis
Bn: beacon (daybeacon); bearing (as distinguished from bearing angle)
***bn:** bijvoeglijk naamwoord* (Dutch—adjective)
***Bn:** Bayan* (Turkish—Miss; Mrs.)
BN: Braniff; Bureau of Narcotics; Burlington Northern (merger of Chicago, Burlington, and Quincy; Great Northern; Northern Pacific; Spokane, Portland, and Seattle railways)
***BN:** Biblioteca Nacional* (Portuguese or Spanish—National

Library); *Biblioteca Nazionale* (Italian—National Library); *Bibliothèque National* (French—National Library)
B.N.: Bachelor of Nursing
B-N: Bloomington-Normal, Illinois
B & N: Barnes & Noble; Bauxite & Northern
B of N: Bureau of Narcotics
BNA: Brazil Nut Association; British Naturalists' Association; British North America; British North Atlantic; Bureau of National Affairs; Nashville, Tennessee (airport)
BNA: *Basle Nomina Anatomica* (Basel Anatomical Nomenclature)
B'nai B'rith: *Benai Berith* (Hebrew—Sons of the Covenant)
BNAF: British North Africa Force
BNAU: Bulgarian National Agrarian Union
B.Nav.: Bachelor of Navigation
BNB: British North Borneo
BNB: *British National Bibliography*
BNBC: British National Book Centre
BNC: Biblioteca Nacional de Chile; Biblioteca Nacional de Colombia
B.N.C.: Brasenose College (Oxford)
BNCC: Bay de Noc Community College
BNCF: *Biblioteca Nazionale Centrale Firenze* (Italian—National Central Library—Florence)
bnchbd: benchboard
BNCM: Bibliothèque Nationale du Conservatorie de Musique (National Library of the Conservatory of Music—Paris)
BNCOR: British National Committee for Oceanographic Research
BNCS: British Numerical Control Society
BNCSR: British National Committee for Space Research (Royal Society)
b/nd: binding—no date available
Bnd: Bend
BND: *Bundesnachrichtendienst* (German—Federal Intelligence Service)
BNDD: Bureau of Narcotics and Dangerous Drugs
Bndr: Bandmaster
Bndr S-L: Bandmaster—Sub-Lieutenant
bndy: bindery; boundary
bne: but not exceeding
BNE: Board of National Estimates (CIA); Brisbane, Australia (airport); Buffalo Niagara Electric Corporation
BNEC: British National Export Council; British Nuclear Energy Conference
BNES: British Nuclear Energy Society
BNE & SAA: Bureau of Near Eastern and South Asian Affairs (US Department of State)
bnf: bomb nose fuse
Bnf: Banff
BNF: Braniff International Airways
BNF: *British National Formulary*
BNFL: British Nuclear Fuels Limited
BNFMF: British Non-Ferrous Metals Federation
BNFMRA: British Non-Ferrous Metals Research Association
BNFSA: British Non-Ferrous Smelters' Association
Bng: Bangor
BNGA: British Nursery Goods Association
BNGM: British Naval Gunnery Mission
BNGS: Bomb Navigation Guidance System
bnh: burnish
BNHS: British National Health Service
BNHQ: Battalion Headquarters
BNI: Black Nation of Islam
BNIB: British National Insurance Board
BNJ: Bonn, Germany (Cologne-Bonn airport)
bnkg: banking
BNL: Brookhaven National Laboratory
BNM: Badlands National Monument (South Dakota); Biblioteca Nacional de México (National Library of México—Mexico City)
bno: barrels of new oil; bladder neck obstruction; but not over
BNO: Bank of New Orleans
BNOC: British National Oil Corporation; British National Opera Company
BNP: Bako National Park (Sarawak); Bahamas NP (West Indies); Banff NP (Alberta); Belair NP (South Australia); Bontebok NP (South Africa)
BNP: *Banque Nationale de Paris* (French—National Bank of Paris)
bnpa: binasal pharyngeal airway
bnr: burner
BNRDC: British National Research Development Corporation
BNS: Bathymetric Navigation System; British Nylon Spinners
B.N.S.: Bachelor of Natural Science; Bachelor of Naval Science
B of NS: Bank of Nova Scotia
B.N.Sc.: Bachelor of Nursing Science
BNSM: British National Socialist Movement
bnst: bassoonist
Bnt: Burntisland
BNTL: British National Temperance League
B-nut: B-shaped nut
BNW: Bureau of Naval Weapons
BNWR: Blackwater National Wildlife Refuge (Maryland); Bowdoin National Wildlife Refuge (Montana); Brigantine National Wildlife Refuge (New Jersey)
Bnx: Bronx
BNX: British Nuclear Export Executive
BNZ: Bank of New Zealand
bnzn: benzoin
bo: base (of prism) out; blackout; body odor; bowel obstruction; bowels open; bucco-occlusal
bo': boıe; brother
b/o: back order; boiloff; brought over
b & o: belladonna and opium
Bo: Bolivia; Bolivian
BO: Baltimore & Ohio (stock exchange symbol); Base Order; black oil (bunker oil fuel); Board of Ordnance; body odor; box office; branch office; broker's order; Bureau of Ordnance
B.O.: Bachelor of Oratory
B & O: Baltimore & Ohio Railroad; Bang & Olufsen
BO: *Boletin Oficial* (Spanish—Official Bulletin)
boa.: born on arrival; breakoff altitude
Boa: Balboa, CZ
BOA: Basic Ordering Agreement; British Optical Association; British Orthopedic Association; British Osteopathic Association; British Overseas Airways (BOAC)
BOAC: British Overseas Airways Corporation

BOAdicea: British Overseas Airways digital information computer for electronic automation
Boadbil: nickname of Abu Abdallah—last Moorish king of Granada
BOA (Disp): British Optical Association (Dispensing Certificate)
BOADS: Boston Air Defense Sector
BOAFG: British Order of Ancient Free Gardeners
BOAT/US: Boat Owners Association of the United States
Bob: Robert
BOB: Bureau of the Budget
BOBA: British Overseas Banks Association
Bobby: Robert(a); nickname for a London policeman and so named after Sir Robert Peel who organized the London police force
Bobbie: Robert
Bobbs: Bobbs-Merrill
b-o-b cult: ban-on-bathing cult (hippie subculture)
Bob Dylan: Robert Zimmermann
BOBMA: British Oil Burner Manufacturers Association
bobr: boring bar
boc: back outlet central; blowout coil; body on chassis
Boc: Boccaccio
BOC: Brooklyn Opera Company; Burmah Oil Company
BOCA: Building Officials Conference of America
boca(s): (Spanish—gulf(s); inlet(s); mouth(s))
B.Occu.Ther.: Bachelor of Occupational Therapy
bocd: barrels of oil per calendar day
BOCE: Board of Customs and Excise
BOCM: British Oil and Cake Mills
B & O—C & O: Baltimore and Ohio—Chesapeake and Ohio (merged railroad)
bod: beneficial occupancy date; biochemical oxygen demand; biological oxygen demand; blackout door
bod: *bodega* (Spanish—wineshop); *bodoniana* (Italian—Bodoni-style type)
Bod: Bodleian; Bodoni
Bodleian: Oxford University's superb library established in 1445
Bodl: Bodleian Library
Bodley: Bodley Head
Bod units: Bodansky units
boe: back outlet eccentric
BOE: *Boletín Oficial del Estado* (Spanish—Official State Bulletin)
bof: basic oxygen furnace; binary oxide film
bof: *beurre, oeufs, fromages* (French—butter, eggs, cheeses) —slang for a big butter-and-egg man
B-o-F: Books-on-File
Bog: Bogotá
BOG: Bogotá, Colombia (airport); Boston Opera Group
B o G: Board of Governors
boggan: toboggan
bogh: *boghandel* (Dano-Norwegian—bookstore; booktrade)
bogie: unidentified aircraft
Bogie: Maxwell Bodenheim; Humphrey Bogart
Bogside: Catholic workingclass district of Derry (Londonderry)
boh: breakoff height
Boh: Bohemia(n)
B O'H: Bernardo O'Higgins
BOHS: British Occupational Hygiene Society
boi: basis of issue; break of inspection
Boi: Boise
BOI: Boise, Idaho (airport)
BOIC: Boarding Officer in Charge
boil.: boiling
Bois: (French—woods)—short form for the Bois de Boulogne park, racetrack, and recreation area of Paris
boj: booster jettison
Bojangles: Bill (Bojangles) Luther Robinson
BOK: Book-of-the-Month Club
Boko: Bohner & Kohle
bol: bollard(s)
bol.: *bolus* (Latin—large pill)
Bol: Bolivia; Bolivian; boliviano
bol-148 (also BOL-148): d-2-bromolysergic acid tartrate (lsd-type hallucinogen)
BOLD: Bibliographic On-Line Display (document retrieval system)
bolo(s): bolshevik(s)
bolovac: bolometric voltage and current (voltage measurement)
bols: bolster
BOLSA: Bank of London and South America
bolshie(s): bolshevik(s)
Bolv: Bolivia; Bolivian
bom: business office must
Bom: Bombay
BoM: Bureau of Mines
BOM: Bombay, India (airport)
BOMAP: Barbados Oceanographic and Meteorological Analysis Project
Bomarc: interceptor missile produced by Boeing
BOMARC: Boeing-Michigan Research Center
bomb.: bombardment
Bomb: Bombardier
Bomba: (Italian—Bass Drum) —nickname of Ferdinand II—King of the Two Sicilies
Bom Com: Bomber Command
BOMC: Book of the Month Club
BOMEX: Barbados Oceanographic and Meteorological Experiment
bomst: bombsight
Bon: Bonin Islands
BON: Bonaire, Netherlands West Indies (airport)
Bonanza Land: Fort Smith, Arkansas area's nickname
bond.: bonding
boneblack: animal charcoal
bone(s): trombone(s)
Bo'ness: Borrowstounness
Boney: Napoleon Bonaparte
Bon Homme Richard: (French—Good Man Richard)—Benjamin Franklin
Boni: Boniface
Bonins: Bonin Islands (Ogasawaras)
Bonnie Prince Charles: Charles Edward Stuart—the Young Pretender
Bonny Johnny: John Adams—second President of the United States
Book: Bookman
bookie(s): bookmaker(s)
bookmobile: book + automobile (mobile branch library within a truck fitted with book-filled shelves and a book-issuing desk)
Boolist: *Booklist and Subscription Books Bulletin*
Boonie: Daniel W. Russell
boonies: boondocks
bop: basic oxygen process(ing); bebop (loud jazz accompanied by nonsensical lyrics); best operating procedure; buy our product(s)
Bop: Buffalo orphan prototype (virus)
BoPa: *Borgelige Partisaner* (Danish—Middleclass Partisans)—underground resistance against occupying German forces during World War II
BoPat: Border Patrol

bopd: barrels of oil per day
bops: blowout preventer stack(s)
B.Opt.: Bachelor of Optometry
BOQ: Bachelor Officers' Quarters; Base Officers' Quarters
bor: boring; bowels open regularly
Bor: Borough
BOR: Board of Review; Borg-Warner (stock exchange symbol); Bureau of Outdoor Recreation
boracic acid: boric acid
BORAD: British Oxygen Research and Development
boram: block-oriented random-access memories
borax: sodium tetraborate
Borax King: Francis Marion Smith of Death Valley, California
borazon: boron nitrogen compound harder than diamond; boron nitride heated and pressed with a catalyst
Borba: (Serbo-Croat—Struggle) —Yugoslavia's leading newspaper although under control of the Yugoslav Communist Party
Border Minstrel: Sir Walter Scott
Border States: former slave-holding states of Delaware, Maryland, Virginia, Kentucky, and Missouri; before the Civil War they divided the North from the South
boric acid: H_3BO_3
boricua(s): (Spanish-American slang —Puerto Rican(s)— slang truncation of *borinqueño(s)*
borino(s): *borinqueño(s)* [(Spanish-American slang derived from native name—Puerto Rican(s)]
Boris Karloff: William Henry Pratt
Boris Pilnyak: Boris Andreyevich Vogau
Boris Savinkov: (pseudonym—Vladimir Ropshin)
boro: borough
Borromeans: Borromean Islands in Lake Maggiore
Borscht Belt: Catskill Mountain resort area in New York State
bos: basic oxygen steel
Bos: Bosphorus; Boston
BoS: Bureau of Ships
BOS: Boston, Massachusetts (airport); British Oil Shipping
Boschaps: Boston Symphony Chamber Players
bo'sun: boatswain (pronounced as contracted)
Bo'sn: Boatswain
Bosna: (Yugoslav—Bosnia-Herzegovina)
Bosox: Boston Red Socks (baseball team)
BosPops: Boston Pops Orchestra
BOSS: Bioastronautic Orbital Space System
Boss Tweed: William Marcy Tweed
Bost: Boston
Boston Brahmin Historian: William Hickling Prescott
Boston Strong Boy: John L. Sullivan
Boston Tech: Boston Technical Publishers
BOSTPDis: Boston Procurement District (U.S. Army)
bo's'n: boatswain
Boswash: Boston-to-Washington (city complex)
bot: balance of time (to be served by a convict); botanic; botanical; botanist; botany; bottle; bottled; bottom; bottomed; bottoming
B o T: Board of Trade
BOT: Board of Trade; Board of Trade unit
B.O.T.: Bachelor of Occupational Therapy
BOTAC: Board of Trade Advisory Committee
bot & can: bottle and can
botel: boat hotel
both.: bombing over the horizon
botmg: bottoming
BOT-ohm: Board of trade ohm
bot(s): bottle(s)
Botswana: (formerly Bechuanaland)
Botticelli: Sandro di Botticelli—palette name of Alessandro Filipepi
BOTU: Board of Trade Unit
Bou: Boulogne-sur-Mer
BOU: Boat Operating Unit; British Ornithologists' Union
boul: boulevard
Boul' Mich': (contraction—Boulevard St Michel)—in the student quarter of Paris
bound.: boundaries; boundary
'bout: about
bov: bovine; bovril; brown oil of vitriol
Bov Eil: *Bovenwindse Eilanden* (Dutch—Windward Islands; Aruba, Bonaire, Curacçao)
bow.: bag of water (amniotic sac); blackout window; born out of wedlock
bowdler: bowdlerize
Bowker: R.R. Bowker Company
BOWO: Brigade Ordnance Warrant Officer
bo & w: barrels of oil and water
boyc: boycott (named for C. C. Boycott, a British army officer, and allegedly the first victim of this system of coercion and intimidation brought on by not having any dealings—commercial or social—with a company, a country, a person, or their products or services)
Boyhood Home of Mark Twain: Hannibal, Missouri
Boy Orator of the Platte: William Jennings Bryan
Boy's Town: Omaha, Nebraska; redlight sections of many Mexican border towns also bear this place-name nickname
Boz: Charles Dickens
Bozzy: James Boswell—biographer and friend of Dr Samuel Johnson
bp: back pressure; bandpass; baptized; bathroom privileges; beautiful people; bedpan; before present; behavior pattern; below proof; benzypyrene; between perpendiculars; bills payable; biotic potential; biparietal; birthplace; blood pressure; boiling point; bronchoplural; buccopulpal
bp (BP): back projection (tv slide-or-film background projection)
b/p: baking powder; bills payable; blueprint
b & p: bare and painted
bp: Bergstrom Paper Company; *buono per* (Italian—good for)
b.p.: *bonum publicum* (Latin—the public good)
Bp: Bishop
Bp: *Boerenpartij* (Dutch—Farmers' Party)
BP: Beach Party (amphibious military operation); Beschleunigter Personenzug (German—express train); Board of Parole; British Petroleum; British Pharmacopoeia; British Public; Bureau of Power; Bureau of Prisons; Burns Philp Lines
BP: *Biblioteca Publica* (Italian—Public Library); *Biblioteca Pública* (Portuguese or Spanish—Public Library); *British Pharmacopoeia*
B.P.: Bachelor of Pharmacy; Bachelor of Philosophy
B-P: Basses-Pyrénées; Bermuda

Plan (breakfast only)
B-P: Lord Robert S. Baden-Powell—founder of the Boy Scout movement
B de P: *Banque de Paris* (Bank of Paris)
B of P: Bishop(ric) of Passau
B of P: Bureau of Prisons
bpa: broadband power amplifier
Bpa: *Bahnpostampt* (German—railway post office)
BPA: Biological Photographers Association; Bonneville Power Administration; British Pediatric Association; Broadcasters Promotion Association; Brunswick Port Authority; Bureau of Public Assistance; Business Publications Audit (of circulation)
BPA: *Banco Portugués do Atlántico* (Portuguese Bank of the Atlantic)
B.P.A.: Bachelor of Professional Arts
BPAA: Bowling Proprietors' Association of America
BPAC: Budget Program Activity Code
B.Paed.: Bachelor of Paediatrics
BPAGB: Bicycle Polo Association of Great Britain
BPAO: Branch Public Affairs Office(r)
BPASC: Book Publishers Association of Southern California
bpay: bill(s) payable
bpb: bank post bills; bromophenol blue
BPBD: Bill Posters, Billers and Distributors (Union)
BPBF: British Paper Box Federation
BPBI: British Plaster Board Industries
BPBIRA: British Paper and Board Industry Research Association
BPBMA: British Paper and Board Makers Association
bpc: back-pressure control; book prices current; book and periodical circulation
BPC: British Pharmaceutical Codex; British Printing Corporation; British Purchasing Commission; Business and Professional Code
bpcd: barrels per calendar day
BPCF: British Precast Concrete Federation
BPCI: Bulk Packaging and Containerization Institute
BPCR: Brakes on Pedal Cycle Regulations
BPCRA: British Professional Cycle Racing Association
bpd: barrels per day; boxes per day
BPD: Bureau of the Public Debt
B. Pd.: Bachelor of Pedagogy
bpd & a: basic planning data and assumption
BPDC: Berkeley Particle Data Center
BPDP: Brotherhood of Painters, Decorators, and Paperhangers
bpe: bit-plane encoding
B.P.E.: Bachelor of Physical Education
BPE-LCA: Board of Parish Education—Lutheran Church in America
B.Pet.E.: Bachelor of Petroleum Engineering
bpf: bottom pressure fluctuation
bpf: *bon pour francs* (French—good for francs)
BPF: British Polio Fellowship
Bpge: bearing per gyro compass
bph: barrels per hour; benign prostatic hypertrophy
B.Ph.: Bachelor of Philosophy
B.P.H.: Bachelor of Public Health
B.Pharm.: Bachelor of Pharmacy
B.P.H.E.: Bachelor of Physical and Health Education
B.Phil.: Bachelor of Philosophy
B.Phys.: Bachelor of Physics
B.Phys.Ed.: Bachelor of Physical Education
B.Phys.Thy.: Bachelor of Physical Therapy
BP & HL: Brown Picton and Hornby Libraries (Liverpool)
bpi: bits per inch; bytes per inch
BPI: British Pacific Islands; Brooklyn Polytechnic Institute; Bureau of Public Information
BPICA: Bureau of Permanent Internationale des Constructeurs d'Automobiles (Permanent International Bureau of Automobile Manufacturers)
B picture: moving picture designed as a second or supporting feature in a cinema program
b-pid: book-physical inventory difference
BPISAE: Bureau of Plant Industry, Soils, and Agricultural Engineering
BP & JC FL: Birmingham Public and Jefferson County Free Library
BPKT: Basic Programming Knowledge Test
bpl: birthplace
Bpl: Barnstaple
BPL: Belfast Public Library; Binghamton Public Library; Birmingham Public Library; Boston Public Library; Brass Pounders League; Bridgeport Public Library; Brooklyn Public Library; Buffalo Public Library
bpm: barrels per minute; beats per minute
BPMA: British Photographic Manufacturers Association; British Printing Machinery Association; British Pump Manufacturers Association
BPMF: British Postgraduate Medical Federation; British Pottery Manufacturers' Federation
BPMS: Blood Pressure Measuring System
BPNHM: Banff Park Natural History Museum
BPNMA: British Plain Net Manufacturers' Association
BPO: Base Post Office; Base Procurement Office; Berlin Philharmonic Orchestra; Boston Pops Orchestra; British Post Office; Brooklyn Philharmonia Orchestra; Brooklyn Post Office
BPO: *Berliner Philharmonisches Orchester* (German—Berlin Philharmonic Orchestra)
BPOE: Benevolent and Protective Order of Elks
BPOEW: Benevolent and Protective Order of Elks of the World (Black, Chinese, and some White)
bp 120/80 lar: blood pressure 120 (systolic)/80 (diastolic) left arm reclining
BPP: Black Panther Party; Botswana People's Party
BPP: *British Parliamentary Papers*
BPPMA: British Power Press Manufacturers Association
BPR: Bureau of Public Roads
BPRA: Book Publishers' Representatives' Association
bprf: bulletproof
bprs: brief psychiatric rating scale
bps: bytes per second
bp's: beautiful people
BPS: Border Patrol Sector; Border Patrol Station; Bureau of Product Safety
B.Ps: Bachelor in Psychology
B_{psc}: bearing per standard com-

pass
bpsd: barrels per steam day
BPsS: British Psychological Society
Bp stg c: bearing per steering compass
B.Psych.: Bachelor of Psychology
bpt: boiling point
BPT: British Petroleum Tanker
B.P.T.: Bachelor of Physiotherapy
bptv: battleship propulsion test vehicle
bpu: base production unit
BPU: British Powerboating Union
bpwr: burnable poison water reactor
bpv: bovine papilloma virus
B-Pyr: Basses-Pyrénées
bq: beauty quotient
BQ: Bachelor's Quarters; Basic Qualification; Basically Qualified (member of USCG Aux)
BQLI: Brooklyn, Queens, Long Island
BQMS: Battery Quartermaster Sergeant
bque: barque
br: bank rate; bank robber(y); berth; bill of rights; branch; bread (underground slang—money); breath; breeder reactor; brown; builder's risk; butadiene rubber
b/r: bills receivable
b or r: bales or rolls (freight)
br: *bez roku* (Czech—no date; no year)
BR: bearing; branch; bridge; British; bromine; brown (buoy)
BR: Baton Rouge; Brazil (auto plaque); Breeder Reactor; British Railways; British Resident (commissioner); British United Airways; Bureau of Reclamation
Br: *Bachiller* (Spanish—Bachelor)—academic degree; *Bratsche* (German—viola)
B-R: Bas-Rhin; Business Route
B/R: Bordeaux or Rouen
BR: *Banco di Roma* (Italian—Bank of Rome)
B.R.: *Bancus Reginae* (Latin—Queen's Bench); *Bancus Rex* (Latin—King's Bench)
B-du-R: Bouches-de-Rhone
B of R: Bureau of Reclamation
bra: brassiere
BRA: Bee Research Association; Boston Redevelopment Authority; British Records Association; Building Renovating Association
BRAC: Brotherhood of Railway amah:Airline Clerks
brachycephs: brachycephalics (short-skulled people)
Bra Cur: Brazil Current
Brad: Bradford; Bradley
Bradshaw's: *Bradshaw's Railway Guide*
Brahmsburg: Hamburg, Germany—birthplace of Johannes Brahms
Bram: Abraham
Br.Am.: British America safety lock invented by Joseph Bramah
BRANCHHYDRO: Branch Hydrographic Office
Brandy Nan: Queen Anne so nicknamed because of her fondness for brandy
brane: bombing radar navigation equipment
Brangus: ⅜ths Brahman + ⅝ths Angus cattle
Brann the Iconoclast: William Cowper Brann, editor and publisher of *The Iconoclast*
bra(s): brassiere(s)
bras: ballistic rocket air suppression
Bras: Brasil; Brasileiro
Bras: *Brasil* (Portuguese or Spanish—Brazil); *Brasile* (Italian—Brazil)
BRAs: Bosom-Rehabilitation Associates
Bras Coll: Brasenose College—Oxford
b-r-a-s-s: breathe, relax, aim, squeeze, shoot (the marksman's acronym)
Brass: Butte, Montana
BRASS: Bottom Reflecting Active Sonar System
Brassai: Gyula Halàsz
Brass City: Waterbury, Connecticut
BRASTACS: Bradford Scientific, Technical, and Commercial Service
Bratwurst Capital: Sheboygan, Wisconsin
Bravo: code for letter B
braz: Brazil; Brazilian
Brazilian emerald: green variety of tourmaline
Brazilian Film Pioneer: Alberto Cavalcanti
Brazilian National Composer: Heitor Villa-Lobos
Brazilian ruby: topaz altered by heating so when cooling it turns purple-red to salmon-pink and hence passes for a ruby
Brazilian sapphire: blue tourmaline
Brazza: Brazzaville
Brb: *Borba* (Yugoslavia—Struggle)—leading newspaper in Communist-controlled Yugoslavia
BRB: British Railways Board
brbc: bovine red blood cells
BRBMA: Ball and Roller Bearing Manufacturers Association
brbzc: brass, bronze, or copper (cargo)
brc: business reply card
Br.C.: British Columbia
BRC: Balcones Research Center (University of Texas); Base Residence Course; Bolivia Railway Company; British Research Council; Broadcast Rating Council; Brotherhood of Railway Car men
BRCA: Brotherhood of Railway Carmen of America
Brch: Branch
BRCMA: British Radio Cabinet Manufacturers' Association
Br Col: British Columbia
BRCS: British Rail Catering Service; British Red Cross Society
brd: basic retirement date; board; bomb-release distance; broad
BRD: *Bundesrepublik Deutschland* (Federal Republic of Germany)—West Germany
BRDC: British Racing Drivers' Club
brdcst: broadcast
Brdw: Broadwood
Bre: Bremen; Bremerhaven
B.R.E.: Bachelor of Religious Education
Breadbasket of Canada: Saskatchewan with its tremendous wheat fields
Breadbasket of Sweden: southernmost province of Skåne given over to large-scale agriculture
Breakfast Food City: Battle Creek, Michigan
brec: bills receivable
breccia: pyroclastic volcanic rock
Breck: Breckinridge
Breck: Brecknockshire
Brecon: Breconshire (Brecknockshire)
brek: breakfast
BREL: British Rail Engineering Limited
'brella: umbrella
Brem: Bremen; Bremerhafen; Bremerhaven; Bremerton

BREMA: British Radio Equipment Manufacturers Association
Brennero: Brenner Pass
Br'er: Brother
Bres: Breslau
Bret: Brittany; Breton
brev: brevet; breviary; breviate; brevier
brev: *breveté* (French—patent); *brevetto* (Italian—patent)
brev.: *breviarium* (Latin—abridgement or breviary)
brew.: brewer; brewery; brewing
brew'd: brewed
Brewer's: *Brewer's Dictionary of Phrase and Fable*
brf: brief; briefing
BRF: British Road Federation
BRFC: British Record Fish Committee (of rod anglers)
brg: bearing
Brg: Bridge
BrG: British Guiana
brghd: bridgehead
brghm: brougham (pronounced *broom*)
Brgo Spgs: Borrego Springs
Br Gu: British Guiana
BrH: British Honduras
BRH: Brussels, Belgium (airport); Bureau of Radiological Health
BRHL: British Rail Hovercraft Limited
BrHon: British Honduras
BRHS: Bay Ridge High School; Betsy Ross High School
Br I: British Isles
BRI: Babson's Reports Incorporated; Banque des Réglements Internationaux (Bank of International Settlements); Biological Research Institute; Brain Research Institute; Building Research Institute; Burlington-Rock Island (railroad)
BRI: *Brand Rating Index*
BRICS: British Rail Inter-City Service
BRICSHST: British Rail Inter-City Service High-Speed Train
Bride of the Adriatic: Venice
Bride of the Sea: nearly inundated Venice on the Adriatic
brig: brigantine; slang for ship's prison
Brig: Brigade; Brigadier
Brig Gen: Brigadier General
brill: *brillante* (Italian—brilliant)
Brilliant Madman: nickname of Charles XII of Sweden
BRIMEC: British Mechanical Engineering Federation
BRINCO: British Newfoundland Corporation
Brisb: Brisbane
Brist: Bristol
Brit: Britain; Britannia; British
Brit: *Encyclopaedia Britannica*
Britain's Most Exclusive Club: the House of Commons
Britain's Premier Passenger Port: Southampton
Britannia: Britannia prima (England); Britannia secunda (Wales)—symbol of Great Britain including Scotland with England and Wales
Brit Book Centr: British Book Centre
Britic: Briticism
Brit Info: British Information Services
British Anatomist Extraordinary: Henry Gray
British lion: symbol of the British Commonwealth as well as of Great Britain
Brit J Surg: *British Journal of Surgery*
brit met: britannia metal (tin, copper, antimony alloy—sometimes bismuth, lead, and zinc)
Brit Mus: British Museum
Brit Pat: British Patent
BritRail: British Railways
Brit—Rail Hover: British Railways Hovercraft
Brit Sam: British Samoa
Britt.: *Britannorum* (Latin—of the Britons)
brk: brick
Brk: Brook
brkf: breakfast
brklyr: bricklayer
brkmn: breakman
brkt: bracket
brkwtr: breakwater
brl: bomb-release line
br/l: brown line positive
BRL: Babe Ruth League; Ballistic Research Laboratories; Beecham Research Laboratories; Bible Research Library; British Research Library
brlg: bomb radio longitudinal generator-powered
brlp: burlap
brl sys: barrier ready light system
BRL 1241: Beecham Research Laboratories formula 1241 (methicillan)
BRL 1341: Beecham Research Laboratories formula 1341 (penbritin)
BRM: British Racing Motors
BRMA: Board of Registration of Medical Auxiliaries; British Rubber Manufacturers' Association
BRMBR: Bear River Migratory Bird Refuge (Utah)
BRMCA: British Ready-Mixed Concrete Association
BRMF: British Rainwear Manufacturers' Federation
brn: brown
Brn: Bahrain
brng: bearing; browning; burning
BRNP: Blue Ridge National Parkway
brnsh: brownish; burnish
Brnx: Bronx
brnz: bronze; bronzing
bro: broach; bronchoscopy; brother
brO: brownish orange
Bro: Brother
BRO: Brigade Routine Order(s)
broast(ed): broil(ed) + roast(ed)
BROILER: Biopedagogical Research Organization on Intensive Learning Environment Reactions
brok: broker; brokerage
brom: bromide; bromidic; bromo; bromo-seltzer
bromo: bromidrosis; bromoform; bromo-seltzer
bromo-seltzer: (bromide + seltzer)
bronc: *bronco (Spanish—small half-wild horse)*
bronch: bronchial; bronchitis; bronchoscopic; bronchoscopist; bronchoscopy
Brontës: family of English writers including the sisters Charlotte, Emily, and Anne
Bronx Zoo: New York Zoological Gardens (Bronx Park)
bronze: 92% copper, 6% tin, 2% zinc
Bronzino: Agnolo di Cosimo
Brookings: Brookings Institution
Bros: brothers
brosch: *broschiert* (German—stitched)
Brose: Ambrose
brot: brought
brotel: brothel + hotel
Brother John: nickname for John Bull—long the personification of the British Empire as well as of Great Britain and its people
Brother Jonathan: British nickname for the United States and its citizens
BROU: Banco de la República Oriental del Uruguay (Bank of the Oriental Republic of Uruguay)
Brown Bomber: Joe Lewis
brown coal: lignite

browners: brown nosers
brownulated: granulated brown sugar
brp: bathroom privileges
BRPF: Bertrand Russell Peace Foundation
brph: bronchophony
brPk: brownish pink
BRPL: Baton Rouge Public Library
brpp: basic radio propagation prediction(s)
Br Rys: British Railways
brs: brass
Brs: Bristol
Br S: Bedroom Steward
BRS: Bertrand Russell Society; British Road Services; British Roentgen Society; Brotherhood of Railway Signalmen; Bureau of Railroad Safety; Business Radio Service; Buyers' Research Syndicate
BRSA: British Railway Staff Association
BR & SC: Brotherhood of Railway and Steamship Clerks
BRSCC: British Racing and Sports Car Club
br sounds: breath sounds
br snds: breath sounds
brst: burst
Br std: British standard
brstr: burster
brt: bright
Brt: Brest
BRT: Brotherhood of Railroad Trainmen
BRT: *Belgische Radio en Televisie* (Belgian Radio and Television); *brutto-Register-Tonnen* (German—registered gross tons)
BRTA: British Regional Television Association; British Road Tar Association
BR & TC: Bermuda Radio and Television Company
brt fwd: brought forward
Bru: Brunei; Bruno; Brutus
BRU: Brussels, Belgium (National Airport)
B.B.Ru.Eng.:Ru.Eng.: Bachelor of Rural Engineering
Brum: Brummagen (Birmingham, England's nickname)
Brum: *Brumaire* (French—Foggy Month)—beginning October 22nd—second month of the French Revolutionary Calendar
Brummagen: Birmingham (colloquial)
Brun: Brunei
brunch(eon): breakfast-lunch (eon)
Bruns: Brunswick
Bruno Walter: Bruno Walter Schlesinger
Brunsw: Brunswick
Brunsviga: (Latin—Brunswick)
B.Rur.Sci.: Bachelor of Rural Science
Brus: *Bruselas* (Spanish—Brussels); *Bruselle* (Italian—Brussels); *Brussel* (Dutch or Flemish); *Brüssel* (German—Brussels)
Brussels system: universal decimal classification
brut: (French—unadulterated) almost completely tart champagne or wine
BRUTE: British Universal Trolley Equipment
brux: bruxism; bruxitic
Brux: Brussels
Brux: *Bruxelas* (Portuguese—Brussels); *Bruxelles* (French—Brussels)
BRVMA (BVA): British Radio Valve Manufacturers' Association
Brw: Barrow
BRW: British Relay Wireless
Brx: Bronx
bry: bryology
Bry: Barry; Bryant
bryol: bryology
Bryth: Brythonic
brz: bronze
brzg: brazing
bs: blood sugar; bluestone; bomb service; bonded single-silk (insulation); bowel sound; both sides; breath sound; bullshit
bs (BS): backspace (data processing)
b/s (B/S): bill of sale
b & s: beams and stringers; bell and spigot; boosters and sustainers; brandy and soda
Bs: bolivares (Venezuelan currency); bolivianos (Bolivian currency)
BS: Battle Squadron; Battle Star; Bethlehem Steel; Berlin Sector; Birmingham Southern (railroad); British Standard; Bureau of Ships; Bureau of Standards
B.S.: Bachelor of Science
B & S: Brown and Sharpe; Butterfield and Swire
B$: bolivar(es)—Venezuelan monetary unit; boliviano(s)—Bolivian monetary unit
B de S: Baruch de Spinoza
B es S: *Bachelier es Sciences* (French—Bachelor of Science)
bsa: bismuth-sulphite agar; body surface area; bovine serum albumin; brown strain apparent
BSA: Bank Stationers Association; Bibliographical Society of America; Birmingham Small Arms; Blind Service Association; Botanical Society of America; Boy Scouts of America; Boy Scouts Association; British School of Athens; British South Africa; Bruckner Society of America; Bureau of Supplies and Accounts
B.S.A.: Bachelor of Agricultural Science
BSAA: British South American Airways
B.S.A.A.: Bachelor of Science in Applied Arts
BSAC: British South Africa Company; Brotherhood of Shoe and Allied Craftsmen
B.S.Adv.: Bachelor of Science in Advertising
B.S.A.E.: Bachelor of Science in Aeronautical Engineering; Bachelor of Science in Architectural Engineering
BSAF: British Sulphate of Ammonia Federation
B.S.Agr.: Bachelor of Science in Agriculture
B.S.A.M.: Bachelor of Suddha Ayurvedic Medicine
BSAP: British South Africa Police
B.S.Arch.: Bachelor of Science in Architecture
B.S.Arch. Eng.: Bachelor of Science in Architectural Engineering
B.S.Art Ed.: Bachelor of Science in Art Education
Bs As: Buenos Aires
BSAS: British Ship Adoption Society
BSAVA: British Small Animals Veterinary Association
bsb: body surface burned
Bsb: Brisbane
BSB: Brasilia, Brazil (airport)
BSBA: British Starter Battery Association
B.S.B.A.: Bachelor of Science in Business Administration
BSBC: British Social Biology Council
BSBI: Botanical Society of the British Isles
BSBSPA: British Sugar Beet Seed Producers' Association
B.S.Bus.: Bachelor of Science in Business

bsc: basic
B.Sc.: Bachelor of Science
BSC: Beltsville Space Center; Bemidji State College; Bethlehem Steel Corporation; Biological Stain Commission; Biomedical Sciences Corporation; Bloomsburg State College; Bluefield State College; Booth Steamship Company; British Society of Cinematographers; British Steel Corporation; British Supply Council
B.S.C.: Bachelor of Science in Commerce
BSCA: Bureau of Security and Consular Affairs (US Department of State)
B.Sc.Acc.: Bachelor of Science in Accounting
B.Sc.Ag(ri)(c): Bachelor of Science in Agriculture
B.Sc.Ag. & A.H.: Bachelor of Science in Agriculture and Animal Husbandry
B.Sc.Agr.Bio.: Bachelor of Science in Agricultural Biology
B.Sc.Agr.Eng.: Bachelor of Science in Agricultural Engineering
B.Sc.Agr.Eco.: Bachelor of Science in Agricultural Economics
B.Sc.Agr.Eng.: Bachelor of Science in Agricultural Engineering
B.Sc.Arch.: Bachelor of Science in Architecture
B.Sc.B.A.: Bachelor of Science in Business Administration
BSCC: British Society for Clinical Cytology
B.Sc.C.E.: Bachelor of Science in Civil Engineering
B.Sc.Chem.E.: Bachelor of Science in Chemical Engineering
B.Sc.Dent.: Bachelor of Science in Dentistry
B.Sc.Dom.Sc.: Bachelor of Science in Domestic Science
BSCE: Bank Street College of Education
B.S.C.E.: Bachelor of Science in Civil Engineering
B.S.Ch.: Bachelor of Science in Chemistry
B.S.Chm: Bachelor of Science in Chemistry
BSCorp: British Steel Corporation
B.Sc.Nurs.: Bachelor of Science in Nursing
B.S.Comm.: Bachelor of Science in Commerce
BSCP: Brotherhood of Sleeping Car Porters
BSCRA: British Steel Castings Research Association
BSCS: Biological Sciences Curriculum Study
B.Sc.S.S.: Bachelor of Science in Secretarial Studies
B.Sc.Vet.Sc.: Bachelor of Science in Veterinary Science
***BSCP:** British Standard Code of Practice*
bsd: beam-steering device; bit storage density; blast-suppression device; burst-slug detection
BSD: Ballistic Systems Division (USAF); British Space Development
B.S.D.: Bachelor of Science in Design
BSDA: British Spinners and Doublers Association
BSDC: British Space Development Company
B.S.Dent.: Bachelor of Science in Dentistry
B.S.D.H.: Bachelor of Science in Dental Hygiene
bsdl: boresight datum line
bse: base support equipment; breast self-examination (cancer control)
BSE: Base Support Equipment; Birmingham & Southeastern (railroad); Building Service Employees (Union); Bureau of Steam Engineering
B.S.E.: Bachelor of Sanitary Engineering; Bachelor of Science Education; Bachelor of Science Engineering
B & SE: Birmingham & Southeastern (railroad)
B.S.Ec.: Bachelor of Science in Economics
B.S.Ed.: Bachelor of Science in Education
B.S.E.E.: Bachelor of Science in Electrical Engineering; Bachelor of Science in Electrical Engineering
B.S.El.E.: Bachelor of Science in Electronic Engineering
B.S.Eng.: Bachelor of Science in Engineering
b's'er: bullshiter
BSES: British Schools Exploring Society
B7D: buyer has seven days to pay (for whatever was bought—usually securities)
bsf: back scatter factor; bulk shielding facilities
bsf (BSF): beta-s-fetoprotein
BSF: Basic Skill Films; British Shipping Federation
B.S.F.: Bachelor of Science in Forestry
BSFA: British Sanitary Fireclay Association; British Steel Founders' Association
bsfc: brake specific fuel consumption
BSFC: Baltic States Freedom Council
B.S.Fin: Bachelor of Science in Finance
BSFL: British Shipping Federation Limited
B.S.For.: Bachelor of Science in Forestry
B.S.F.S.: Bachelor of Science in Foreign Service
BSF & W: Bureau of Sport Fisheries and Wildlife
BSG: British standard gage
bsgg: *breveté sans garantie du gouvernement* (French—patented without government guarantee)
B.S.G.E.: Bachelor of Science in General Engineering; Bachelor of Science in Geological Engineering
B.S.Gen. Nur.: Bachelor of Science in General Nursing
B.S.Geog.: Bachelor of Science in Geography
B.S.Geol.: Bachelor of Science in Geology
B.S.Geol.Eng.: Bachelor of Science in Geological Engineering
B & S glands: Bartholin and Skene's glands
bsh: bushel
BSH: British Society of Hypnotherapists; British Standard of Hardness
B.S.H.A.: Bachelor of Science in Hospital Administration
B.S.H.E.: Bachelor of Science in Home Economics
B.S.H.Eco.: Bachelor of Science in Home Economics
B.S.H.Ed.: Bachelor of Science in Health Education
BSHS: British Society for the History of Science
bsi: bound serum iron
BSI: British Sailors' Institute; British Standards Institution
BSIA: Better Speech Institute of America
BSIB: Boy Scouts International Bureau; British Society for International Bibliography
bsic: binary-symmetric independent channel
BSIC: British Ski Instruction Council
B.S.I.E.: Bachelor of Science in Industrial Engineering

BSIHE: British Society for International Health Education
B.S.Ind.Art: Bachelor of Science in Industrial Art
B.S.Ind.Chem.: Bachelor of Science in Industrial Chemistry
B.S.Ind.Ed.: Bachelor of Science in Industrial Education
B.S.Ind.Eng.: Bachelor of Science in Industrial Engineering
BSIP: British Solomon Islands Protectorate
B.S.I.R.: Bachelor of Science in Industrial Relations
BSIRA: British Scientific Instrument Research Association
BSIU: British Society for International Understanding
BSIs: Baker Street Irregulars
bsj: balanced swivel joint; ball-and-socket joint
B.S.J.: Bachelor of Science in Journalism
BSJA: British Show Jumping Association
B.S.Jr.: Bachelor of Science in Journalism
BSMA: British Skate Makers' Association
bsk: basket(s)
bskt: basket
bsl: billet split lens
bs/l: bills of lading
BSL: Barber Steamship Lines; Behavioral Sciences Laboratory; Black Star Line; Blue Sea Line; Blue Star Line; Building Service League; Bull Steamship Lines
B.S.Lab.Rel.: Bachelor of Science in Labor Relations
bslb: ball-and-socket lower bearing
bsl(s): bushel(s)
B.S.L.S.: Bachelor of Science in Library Science; Bachelor of Science in Library Service
bsm: bi-stable multivibrator; bottom sonar marker
BSM: Birmingham School of Music; Bronze Star Medal
BSM: *beso sus manos* (Spanish—I kiss your hands)—respectfully yours
B.S.M.E.: Bachelor of Science in Mechanical Engineering; Bachelor of Science in Mining Engineering; Bachelor of Science in Music Education
B.S.Med.: Bachelor of Science in Medicine
B.S.Med.Rec.: Bachelor of Science in Medical Records
B.S.Med.Rec.Lib.: Bachelor of Science in Medical Records Librarianship
B.S.Med.Tech.: Bachelor of Science in Medical Technology
B.S.Met.: Bachelor of Science in Metallurgy
B.S.Met.Eng.: Bachelor of Science in Metallurgical Engineering
B.S.Mgt.Sci.: Bachelor of Science in Management Science
B.S.Min: Bachelor of Science in Minerology; Bachelor of Science in Mining
B.S.Min.Eng.: Bachelor of Science in Mining Engineering
BSMMA: British Sugar Machinery Manufacturers Association
bsmt: basement
B.S.Mus.Ed.: Bachelor of Science in Music Education
bsmv: barley-stripe-mosaic virus
bsn: bowel sounds normal
BSN: Baker School of Navigation
B.S.N.: Bachelor of Science in Nursing
BSN: *Bayerische Staatsoper—Nationaltheater* (German—National Theater—in Munich)
B.S.N.A.: Bachelor of Science in Nursing Administration
B.S.Nat.Hist.: Bachelor of Science in Natural History
BSNDT: British Society for Non-Destructive Testing
BSNH: Boston Society of Natural History; Buffalo Society of Natural History
B.S.Nurs.: Bachelor of Science in Nursing
B.S.Nurs.Ed.: Bachelor of Science in Nursing Education
bso: blue stellar objects
BSO: Baltimore Symphony Orchestra; Bamberg Symphony Orchestra; Birmingham Symphony Orchestra; Bombay Symphony Orchestra; Boston Symphony Orchestra; Bournemouth Symphony Orchestra; Budapest Symphony Orchestra
B.S.Occ.Ther.: Bachelor of Science in Occupational Therapy
B.Soc.Sci.: Bachelor of Social Science
B.Soc.St.: Bachelor of Social Studies
B.Soc.Wk.: Bachelor of Social Work
BSOIW: Bridge, Structural and Ornamental Iron Workers
B.S.Opt.: Bachelor of Science in Optometry
B.S.O.T.: Bachelor of Science in Occupational Therapy
bsp: bromosulphalein
Bsp: British Standard pipe
BSP: Bering Sea Patrol
BSP: *Bureau de Sécurité Publique* (French—Bureau of Public Security)
B-S-P: Bartlett-Snow-Pacific (foundry division)
B.S.P.: Bachelor of Science in Pharmacy
BSPA: Basic Slag Producers' Association
B.S.P.A.: Bachelor of Science in Public Administration
B.S.P.E.: Bachelor of Science in Physical Education
B-Specials: Belfast's special soldiers (attached to the Ulster Special Constabulary)—Protestant organization
B.S.Per. & Pub.Rel.: Bachelor of Science in Personnel and Public Relations
B.S.Pet.: Bachelor of Science in Petroleum
B.S.Pet.Eng.: Bachelor of Science in Petroleum Engineering
B.S.P.H.: Bachelor of Science in Public Health
B.S.Phar.: Bachelor of Science in Pharmacy
B.S.Pharm.: Bachelor of Science in Pharmacy
B.S.P.H.N.: Bachelor of Science in Public Health Nursing
B.S.Phys.Ed.: Bachelor of Science in Physical Education
B.S.Phys.Edu.: Bachelor of Science in Physical Education
B.S.Phys.Ther.: Bachelor of Science in Physical Therapy
bspl: behavioral science programming language
BSPM: Battlefield Systems Project Management
BSPMA: British Sewage Plant Manufacturers Association
B.S.P.T.: Bachelor of Science in Physical Therapy
B.Sp.Thy.: Bachelor of Speech Therapy
bspw: bare silver-plated wire
Bsq: Basque
BSQ: Bachelor Sergeant Quarters
bsr: backspace recorder; balloon-supported rockets (rockoons); basal skin resistance; battle short relay; blood sedimentation rate; blue-streak request; bore sight restricted
Bsr: Basra (Busreh)
BSR: British Society of Rheology

B.S.R.: Bachelor of Science in Rehabilitation
BSRA: British Ship Research Association
BSRC: Biological Serial Record Center
B.S.Rec.: Bachelor of Science in Recreation
B.S.Ret.: Bachelor of Science in Retailing
bsrf: brain stem reticular formation
BSRL: Boeing Scientific Research Laboratories
bss: balanced salt solution; basic shaft system; beam-steering system; black-silk suture; buffered saline solution
BSS: Bibliothèque Saint-Sulpice (Montreal); British Standard Specification; Bronze Service Star; Bureau of State Services
B.S.S.: Bachelor of Sanitary Science; Bachelor of Science in Science; Bachelor of Secretarial Science; Bachelor of Social Science(s)
Bssa: *Baronessa* (Italian—Baroness)
B.S.S.A.: Bachelor of Science in Secretarial Administration
B.S.Sc.: Bachelor of Sanitary Science
B.S.Sc.Eng.: Bachelor of Science in Science Engineering
B.S.Sec.Ed.: Bachelor of Science in Secondary Education
B.S.Sec.Sci.: Bachelor of Science in Secretarial Science
BSSG: Biomedical Sciences Support Grant
BSSO: British Society for the Study of Orthodontics
BSSR: Byelorussia Soviet Socialist Republic
BSSS: British Society of Soil Science
B.S.Soc.Serv.: Bachelor of Science in Social Service
B.S.Soc.St.: Bachelor of Science in Social Studies
B.S.Soc.Wk.: Bachelor of Science in Social Work
bssp: broadband solid-state preamplifier
BSSR: Bureau of Social Science Research
B.S.S.S.: Bachelor of Science in Secretarial Studies; Bachelor of Science in Social Science
B.S.S.Sc.: Bachelor of Science in Social Science
B.S.Struc.Eng.: Bachelor of Science in Structural Engineering
bssw: bare stainless-steel wire
bst: beam-steering transducer; blood serological test(ing); brief stimulus therapy
b s & t: blood, sweat, and tears
b/st: bill of sight
BST: Bering Standard Time; Blood Serological Test; British Summer Time
BSTA: British Surgical Trades Association
BSTC: Ball State Teachers College
bstd: bastard
B.S.Text.: Bachelor of Science in Textiles
bst lt: blue stern light
bstr: booster
B.S.Trans.: Bachelor of Science in Transportation
bstrk: bomb service truck
bstr rkt: booster rocket
BSU: Black Students Union; Boat Support Unit
bsub: ball-and-socket upper bearing
B.Sur.: Bachelor of Surgery
B.Surv.: Bachelor of Surveying
bsut: beam-steering ultrasonic transducer
bsv: Boolean simple variable
B.S.Voc.Ag.: Bachelor of Science in Vocational Education
bsw: barrels of salt water
bs & w: basic sediment and water
BSW: Boot and Shoe Workers (union); Botanical Society of Washington
B.S.W.: Bachelor of Social Work
bs & w: basic sediment and water
BSWB: Boy Scouts World Bureau
bswd: barrels of salt water per day
BSWE: Boy Scouts in Western Europe
BSWIA: British Steel Wire Industries Association
bt: bathtub; bathythermograph; bedtime; bent; blue tetrazolium (stain); bitemporal; boat; boat-tail; body temperature; bombing table; bought; brain tumor; brought
b & t: bacon and tomato sandwich
Bt: baronet
BT: basic trainer
B of T: Bank of Tokyo; Board of Trade
BT: *Berlingske Tidende* (Berling's Times—Copenhagen)
bta: better than average
bta (BTA): best time available (for tv broadcast)
BTA: Blood Transfusion Association; Board of Tax Appeals; Boston Transportation Authority; Brith Trumpeldor of America; British Travel Association; Brazilian Travel Agency
BTAM: Basic Telecommunications Access Method
BTAO: Bureau of Technical Assistance Operations (UN)
BTASA: Book Trade Association of South Africa
btb: braided tube bundle; bus tie breaker
BTB: Barbados Tourist Board; Belgian Tourist Bureau
BTBA: Blood Transfusion Betterment Association
BTBS: Book Trade Benevolent Society
btc: below threshold change; beryllium thrust chamber
BTC: Bankers Trust Company; Basic Training Center; Bethlehem Transportation Company; Board of Transport Commissioners
B.T.C.: Bachelor of Textile Chemistry
btca: *biblioteca* (Spanish—library)
BTCC: Bloom Township Community College; Board of Transportation Commissioners for Canada; Broome Technical Community College
B.T.C.P.: Bachelor of Town and Country Planning
BTCV: British Trust for Conservation Volunteers
btd: bomb testing device
BTDB: Bermuda Trade Development Board
btdc: before top dead center
bte: battery terminal equipment; blunt trailing edge; Boltzmann transport equation; bourdon tube element; Brayton turboelectric engine; bulk tape eraser
bte: *breveté* (French—patent)
B.T.E.: Bachelor of Textile Engineering
B.Tech.: Bachelor in Technology
Btee: Brayton turboelectric engine
BTEF: Book Trade Employers' Federation
B.Tel.E.: Bachelor in Telecommunications Engineering
BTEMA: British Tanning Extract Manufacturers' Association
B.Text.: Bachelor of Textiles
btf: barrels of total fluid; bomb

tail fuse
BTF: British Trawlers Federation
btg: ball-tooth gear; battery timing group; beacon trigger generator; burst transmission group
btgj: ball-tooth gear joint
bth: bath; bathroom; berth
B.Th.: Bachelor of Theology
BT-H: British Thompson-Houston
BTHS: Brooklyn Technical High School
B th u: British thermal unit (btu, Btu, BTU)
bti: bank-and-turn indicator; bridgetape isolator
BTI: Bandung Technical Institute
BTI:* *British Technology Index
BTIA: British Tar Industries Association
BTIPR: Boyce Thompson Institute for Plant Research
btj: ball-tooth joint
BTJ:* *Board of Trade Journals
btk: buttock
btk l: buttock line
btl: beginning tape label; bottle
BTL: Bell Telephone Laboratories
btm: bottom
btm (BTM): bromotrifluoromethane (fire extinguisher)
Btm: Bottom (postal abbreviation)
BTMA: British Typewriter Manufacturers Association
BTME: Babcock Test of Mental Efficiency
btn: button
BTN: Brussels Tariff Nomenclature
bto: big-time operator; bombing through overcast
bto: *bruto* (Spanish—gross weight); *bulto* (Spanish—bulk)
BTO: Branch Transportation Office(r); British Trust for Ornithology
bto(s): big time operator(s)
B-town: Bean Town (Boston—sailor's sobriquet)
btp: body temperature and pressure
BTP: Bush Terminal Piers
B.T.P.: Bachelor of Town Planning
btps: body temperature and pressure—saturated
btr: bus transfer
BTR: Baton Rouge, Louisiana (airport)
BTR:* *British Tax Review
B.T.R.A.: Bachelor of Town and Regional Planning
B.Traven: (pen name—Berick Traven Torsvan)
btry: battery
bts: base of terminal service (USAF); Boolean time sequence
BTS: Blood Transfusion Service; British Textile Society
BTSB: Bound-to-Stay-Bound Books
bttns: battens
btu (BTU, Btu): British thermal unit
BTU: Board of Trade Unit
btv: basic transportation vehicle
BTWHS: Booker T. Washington High School
btwn: between
btx: benzene, toluene, xylene
bty: battery
B-type: Basedow type
bu: base (of prism) up; base unit; base up; bromouracil; builder; bushel
Bu: Bulgaria; Bulgarian; Bureau (United States Navy); butyl
BU: Baker University; Baylor University; Bishop's University; Boston University; Bradley University; Brandeis University; Brown University; Bucknell University; Burma (symbol); Butler University
BU:* *Bollettino Ufficiale (Italian—Official Gazette)
BUA: Belfast Urban Area; British United Airways
BuAer: Bureau of Aeronautics (USN)
BUAF: British United Air Ferries
BUAV: British Union for the Abolition of Vivisection
bubbly: champagne
buc: buccal; buccaneer; buccinator
BUC: Bangor University College
bucc: buccal
Buchar: Bucharest
buck: buckram
Buckeye(s): Ohioan(s)
Buckeye State: Ohio's official nickname
Buck House: Buckingham House (Buckingham Palace—London residence of British royalty)
Buck Pal: Buckingham Palace
Bucks: Buckinghamshire
BUCOP:* *British Union Catalogue of Periodicals
bucu: burring cutter
bud.: budget
Bud: Buddha; Buddhism; Buddhist; Buddy; Budweiser
BUD: Budapest, Hungary (airport)
Buda: Budapest
Bud(dy): Brother
Buddy Rogers: Charles Rogers
budgie(s): budgerigar(s)
BuDocks: Bureau of Yards and Docks (USN)
Budpst: Budapest
budr: bromodeoxyuridine
budu: bromodeoxyuridine
bue: built-up edge
BUE: Buenos Aires, Argentina (Ezeiza airport)
Buen: Buenaventura
Buerger's disease: chronic inflammation of the blood vessels in a limb or limbs
Buf: Buffalo (city and port)
BUF: British Union of Fascists; Buffalo, New York (airport)
Buffalo Bill: Colonel William F. Cody
Buffalonians: people of Buffalo, New York
Bug: Bugatti; standard-model Volkswagen (also called the Beetle)
BUG: Brooklyn Union Gas (company)
Bugd Nyramdakh Mongol Ard Uls: (Mongolian People's Republic)—Outer Mongolia
Bughouse Square: square where cafeteria theoreticians and street people congregate to argue and to loaf—Pershing Square in Los Angeles, Union Square in New York, Washington Square in Chicago
Bugs Baer: Arthur Baer
BUH: Bucharest, Rumania (airport)
Buhl's disease: fatty degeneration associated with hemoglobinuria
BUIA: British United Island Airways
buic (BUIC): backup interceptor control
BUIC: Bureau (of Naval Personnel) Unit Identification Code (USN)
build.: building
buisys: barrier-up indicating system
bul: below upper limit; bulletin
BUL: Bombay University Library
Bulg: Bulgaria; Bulgarian
bull.: *bulla* (Latin—leaden seal; nickname for a papal pronouncement bearing such a seal)

Bull: bulletin
Bull Moose: Theodore Roosevelt—twenty-sixth President of the United States
bull(s): bulletin(s)
bulli.: *bulliat* (Latin—let it boil)
bull market: stock market short form indicating an upward trend in securities as if a bull were charging forward with uplifted horns; (*see* bear market)
buloga: business logistics game
BULVA: Belfast and Ulster Licensed Vintner's Association
BuMed: Bureau of Medicine and Surgery
Bu M & S: Bureau of Medicine and Surgery (USN)
B.U.M.S.: Bachelor of Urani Medicine and Surgery
BUN: blood urea nitrogen
buna: butadiene + natrium (synthetic rubber)
BUNAC: British Universities North America Club
bunsenite: nickel oxide
Buntline: Ned Buntline—nom de plume of Edward Z.C. Judson
Bunty: Barbara
bunwich: bun + sandwich (sandwich made in a bun)
BuOrd: Bureau of Ordnance (USN)
bup: backup plate; bull pup
BUP: British United Press
BUPA: British United Provident Association
Bupers: Bureau of Personnel (USN)
bup-bup-bup-bum: Beethovenian kettledrumming
BuPers: Bureau of Personnel (USN)
bupp: backup plate perforated
BuPubAff: Bureau of Public Affairs
bur: bureau
Bur: Burma; Burmese
BUR: Burbank, California (Lockheed Airport)
Buranello: Baldassare Galuppi
Burd suc: Burdick suction
BuRec: Bureau of Reclamation
Bur Eco Aff: Bureau of Economic Affairs (US Department of State)
Bur Eur Aff: Bureau of European Affairs (US Department of State)
burg: burgess; burgomaster
Burg: Burgos
burger(s): hamburger(s)
Burke's: *Burke's Peerage*
burl.: burlesque
Burlington Route: Chicago, Burlington and Quincy (railroad)
Burl Ives: Icle Ivanhoe Ives
buro: bureau
Bur Pub Aff: Bureau of Public Affairs (US Department of State)
Burs: Bursar
Burun: Burundi; Burundian
bus.: business; omnibus
BuSanda: Bureau of Supplies and Accounts (USN)
BUSARB: British-United States Amateur Rocket Bureau
busbar: omnibus bar
BUSF: British Universities' Sports Federation
BuS glands: Bartholin's, urethral, Skene's glands
bush.: bushing(s)
BuShips: Bureau of Ships (USN)
Bus Mgr: Business Manager
Busn Intl: Business International
Busta: Sir Alexander Bustamante
Buster Keaton: Joseph Francis Keaton
but.: butter; button
but.: *butyrum* (Latin—butter)
BUT: British United Traction
Butch: Fiorello H. La Guardia
Butter Capital: Owatonna, Minnesota
buv: backscatter ultraviolet
buvs: backscatter ultraviolet spectrometer
BuWeps: Bureau of Weapons (USN)
buy.: buyer; buying
buz: buzzer
bv: balanced voltage; bellows valve; biologic(al) value; blow valve; blood vessel; blood volume; bonnet valve; breviary; bronchovesicular
bv: *bijvoorbeeld* (Dutch—for example)
b.v.: *balneum vaporis* (Latin—steambath; vapor bath)
Bv: Benvenuto
B/v: book value
BV: Bureau Veritas (French ship-classification bureau)
B + V: Blohm und Voss (shipbuilders)
BV.: *Beata Virgo* (Latin—Blessed Virgin); *bene vale* (Latin—a good farewell); *bene vixit* (Latin—he lived a good life)
BVA: British Veterinary Association
B.V.A.: Bachelor of Vocational Adjustment; Bachelor of Vocational Agriculture
BVAL: Blackman's Volunteer Army of Liberation
bvbrf: blood vessel of bronchial filament
BVC: Buena Vista College
bvd: beacon video digitizer
BVD: Bradley, Vorhees & Day
BVD: *Binnenlandse Veiligheidsdienst* (Dutch—Internal Security Service)—FBI-type organization in the Netherlands
BVDs: suits of underwear (derived from BVD)
BVDT: Brief Vestibular Disorientation Test
B.V.E.: Bachelor of Vocational Education
B/ventura: Buenaventura, Colombia
B.Vet.Med.: Bachelor of Veterinary Medicine
B.Vet.Sci.: Bachelor of Veterinary Science
B.Vet.Sur.: Bachelor of Veterinary Surgery
BVG: *Berliner Verkehrs-Betriebe* (German—Berlin Traffic Carrier)—Berlin's transit system
bvh: biventricular hypertrophy
BVH: British Van Heusen
bvi: blood vessel invasion
BVI: Better Vision Institute; British Virgin Islands
BVJ: *British Veterinary Journal*
bvm: broncho-vascular markings
B.V.M.: Bachelor of Veterinary Medicine
B.V.M.: *Beata Virgo Maria* (Latin—Blessed Virgin Mary)
BVMA: British Valve Manufacturers Association
B.V.M.S.: Bachelor of Veterinary Medicine and Surgery
BVN: Bund der Verfolgten des Nazi Regimes (League of Persons Persecuted by the Nazi Regime)
BVNP: Bolusan Volcano National Park (Luzon, Philippines)
bvo: brominated vegetable oil
bvp: beacon video processor; booster vacuum pump; boundary value problem
BVP: British Volunteer Programme
BVPS: Beacon Video Processing System; Booster Vacuum Pump System
bvr: balanced valve regulator; black void reactor
BVR: British Vehicle Registration (symbols appearing on automotive vehicle license plates)—*see* British Vehicle Registration Symbols *in appendix*); Bureau of Vocational Rehabilitation

BVRO: Base Vehicle Reporting Officer
BVRR: Bureau of Veterans Reemployment Rights
BVRS: Breadboard Visual Reference System
BVS: Best Vested Socialists; Bevier & Southern (railroad)
B.V.S.: Bachelor of Veterinary Science; Bachelor of Veterinary Surgery
B-V S: Brisch-Vistem System (Visican punched-cards)
B.V.Sc.: Bachelor of Veterinary Science
B.V.Sc. & A.H.: Bachelor of Veterinary Science and Animal Husbandry
bvt: brevet; brevetted
bvv: bovine vaginitis virus
bvw: binary voltage weigher
bw: biological warfare (BW); birth weight; body water; body weight; both ways; braided wire (armor)
b/w: black-and-white
b & w: black and white; bread and water
bw: *bijwoord* (Dutch—adverb); *bitte wenden* (German—please turn over)
BW: Bendix-Westinghouse; Biological Warfare; Black Watch; Borg-Warner; Business Week
B-W: Bendix Westinghouse Automotive Air Brake; Borg-Warner
B & W: Babcock and Wilcox; Barker and Williamson; Burmeister and Wain
B of W: Bishop(ric) of Würzburg
BW: *Bitte Wenden* (German—please turn over); *Business Week*
bwa: backward-wave amplifier; bent-wire antenna
BWA: Baseball Writers Association; British West Africa; Building Waterproofers Association
BWAL: Barber West African Line
Bway: Broadway
BWB: British Waterways Board
bwc: basic weight calculator; broadband waveguide oscillator
BWC: British War Cabinet
BWCC: British Weed Control Conference
BWCI: Beauty Without Cruelty, Incorporated
bwcp: bench welder control panel
bw-cw: biological warfare—chemical warfare
bwd: bacillary white diarrhea; backward; barrels of water per day
BWD: Baldwin Wallace College; British War Cabinet
B & WE: Bristol and West of England
BWF: Baha'i World Faith
Bwg: Bowling
BWG: Birmingham Wire Gage
bwh: barrels of water per hour
BWI: British West Indies
bwia: better walk if able
BWIA: British West Indian Airways
BWIR: British West India Regiment
BWI$: British West Indian dollar
BWISA: British West Indies Sugar Association
bwk: brickwork; bulwark
bwl: belt work line
BWL: Biological War Laboratory
bwlt: bow light
bwm: barrels of water per minute
BWM: British War Medal; Broom and Whisk Makers (union)
BWMA: British Woodwork Manufacturers Association
BWMB: British Wool Marketing Board
BWN: Brown Company (stock-exchange symbol)
bwo: backward-wave oscillator
bwoc: big woman on campus
bwos: backward-wave oscillator synchronizer
bwot: backward-wave oscillator tube
bwp: ballistic wind plotter
BWP: Basic War Plan
bwpa: backward-wave parametric amplifier
BWPA: British Wood Preserving Association
bwpd: barrels of water per day
bwph: barrels of water per hour
bwr (BWR): boiling-water reactor
BWRA: British Water Research Association; British Welding Research Association
BWRC: Biological Warfare Research Center
BWRWS: Biological Warfare Rapid Warning System (USA)
bws: beveled wood siding
BWS: Bandipur Wildlife Sanctuary (India); Batch Weighing System; Battlefield Weapons System; Beaufort Wind Scale; Biological Weapons System; British Watercolour Society
BW & S: Boyd, Weir & Sewell
BWSF: British Water Ski Federation
BWSL: Battlefield Weapons Systems Laboratory
bwso: backward wave sweep oscillator
bwt: both-way trunk
BWT: Boeing Wind Tunnel
BWTA: British Women's Temperance Association
BWTP: Bureau of Work-Training Programs
bw-tv: black-and-white television
bwv: back-water valve
BWVA: British War Veterans of America
BWW: Bad Weather Watch (Coast Guard)
BWWA: British Water Works Association
bx: biopsy; box; electrical cable contained in flexible tubing (bx cable)
Bx: Beatrix; Box (post-office box); Brix; Bronx
BX: Base Exchange (USAF); Bellingham-Seattle Airways (2-letter code)
bx cable: insulated wires within flexible tubing
bxd: boxed
bxk: broadband X-band klystron
bx k: box keel
BXL: Bakelite Xylonite Limited
Bxm: Brixham
Bx Pk: Bronx Park
bxs: boxes
b-y: bloody
by.: brilliant yellow (litmus paper for testing alkalinity)
By: Buryat(ic); Byron(ic)
BY: blowing spray
BYC: Baltimore Yacht Club; Bayside Yacht Club; Bensonhurst Yacht Club; Beverley Yacht Club; Boston Yacht Club; Brewers Yeast Council; Bridgeport Yacht Club; Bronx Yacht Club; Buffalo Yacht Club
Bye: Byelorussia; Byelorussian
Byo: Bulawayo
byob: bring your own beer
byod: bring your own drinks
byog: bring your own girl
byp: bypass
Byp: Bypass
bypro(s): by-products(s)
Byron Janis: Byron Yanks
byt: bright young things (British younger set)
Byu: Bayou (postal place-name abbreviation)

BYU: Brigham Young University
Byz: Byzantine
bz: blank when zero; buzzer; (cartoonist's symbol—buzzing; sawing; snoring)
Bz: benzene; benzoyl; Brazil; Brazilian
Bz: *Beobachtungszimmer* (German—examining room)—hospital observation room
BZ: Air Congo (Brazzaville, Congo Republic); B'nai Zion
BZ: *Bild Zeitung* (German—Picture Newspaper)
B/Z: British Zone
Bza: Bizerta
BZA: Board of Zoning Adjustment
Bze: Belize
bzfx: brazing fixture
bzw: *beziehungsweise* (German—respectively)
bzz: cartoonist's symbol—buzzing; sawing; snoring
bzzz: same as bzz

C

c: calorie (large); candle; canine; capacity; carbon; cathode; caudal; cent; centavo; center; centi (prefix); centime; centimeter; central; certified; cervical; cervix; chest; child; chord length (symbol); cirrus; clearance; clonus; closure; coarse; cocaine; coefficient; color; colored; complement; conductor; contact; contraction; control; cortex; cranial; crystal(line); cube; cubic; cubical; cycle(s); cylinder(s); cytidine; cytochrome; cytosine; heat capacity per mole (symbol); see; speed of light (symbol)
c: *colón; colones* (currency in Costa Rica and El Salvador)
c.: *cibus* (Latin—meal); *circa* (Latin—about); *congius* (Latin—gallon); *cum* (Latin—with)
c/: *cargo* (Spanish—total; weight); *contra* (Spanish—against; versus)
C: calculated weight (symbol); candle; capacitance; capacitor; Cape; carat; carbon; Cardinal; cargo or transport airplane; cargo vessel; carton; case; cathode; cavalry; celestial; Celsius; Celtic; Centigrade; century; cervical; chairman; Charlie—code for letter C; Chief; Christ(ian); coast; cocaine (drug user's abbreviation); cold; college; colored; combat aircraft; commander; compliance; concentration; consul; control; Convair; copyright; Cosmopolitan Shipping; council; course; Curie's constant; Fraunhofer line characteristic of hydrogen (symbol); hundredweight (symbol); molecular heat (symbol); see (popular phonetic spelling)
C.: carbohydrates (dietary symbol); cocaine; Conservative (political party)
"C": Costa Line
C: *centum* (Latin—one hundred); (Latin—Gaius)
°C: degree Celsius; degree centigrade
C_1: first class
C^1: bacteriologic complement
C_1, C_2, C_3, etc.: cytochromes 1, 2, 3, etc.
$C^1$1, $C^1$2, $C^1$3, etc.: complements of complements
C I, C II, C III, etc.: cranial nerves I, cranial nerves II, cranial nerves III, etc.
C 1, C 2, C 3, etc.: cervical nerves or vertebrae 1, 2, 3, etc.
C^2: second class
C^3: third class
C-3: mentally or physically defective (British equivalent of American 4-F)
C^3: command, control, communications
C4: Convair 440 airplane; crown quarto (7-1/2 x 10 inches)
C5: Convair 580 turboprop airplane
C-5A: Lockheed military cargo transport airplane
C-6: hexamethonium
C8: crown octavo (5 x 7-1/2 inches)
C-10: decamethonium
C^{14}: radioactive carbon (used in determining age of objects by radioactivity measurement)
C 19 ster: steroids containing 19 carbon atoms
C 21 ster: steroids containing 21 carbon atoms
C 33: Oscar Wilde's identification number while incarcerated in Reading Gaol
C-123: Provider twin-engine assault transport
C-124: Globemaster heavy cargo four-engine transport airplane
C-130: Hercules medium-range cargo and troop transport airplane powered by four turboprop engines
C-133: Cargomaster heavy four-engine turboprop cargo transport airplane
C-140: Jet Star support-type transport aircraft powered by four turbojet engines
C-141: Starlifter large cargo transport airplane powered by four turbojet engines
ca: cable; calibrated altitude; cancer; capital asset; carbonic anhydrase; carcinoma; cardiac arrest; cathode; caudal; centare; cervoaxial; chronological age; civil affairs; civil authorities; clerical aptitude; cold agglutinin; common antigen; convening authority; coronary artery; council accepted; croup associated; current assets
ca': calf; call (Scottish contraction)
c/a: capital account; center angle; coated abrasive; current account
c & a: classification and audit
ca: *circa* (Latin—about); *corrente alternada* (Portuguese—alternating current); *corriente alterna* (Spanish—alternating current)
c^a^: *compañia* (Spanish—company)
ca (CA): cancer; carcinoma
Ca: calcium; Canada; Canadian

Ca: *Compagnia* (Italian—company)

C^a: *Companhia* (Portuguese—company); *Compañia* (Spanish—company)

Ca': *Casa* (Venetian—house)

CA: Capital Airlines; Central America; Certificate of Airworthiness; Charge d'Affaires; Chartered Accountant; Chemical Abstracts; Chief Accountant; Civil Affairs; Coast Artillery; Combat Aircrew; Combat Aircrewman; Commercial Agent; Companhia de Navegação Carregadores Açoreanos (Azore Line); Compensation Act; Comptroller of the Army; Confederate Army; Consular Agent; Convening Authority; County Attorney; Court of Appeals; Cranial Academy; heavy cruiser (naval symbol)

C.A.: Chartered Accountant

C & A: Clemens and August Breeninkmeyer's international house of fashion

C of A: College of Aeronautics

CA: *corriente alterna* (Spanish—alternating current)

caa: caging amplifier assembly; circular aperture antenna; computer amplifier alarm; crime aboard aircraft

CAA: Canadian Automobile Association; Canadian Authors' Association; Cantors Assembly of America; Caribbean Atlantic Airlines; Central African Airways; Chester Alan Arthur (21st President U.S.); Chief of Army Aviation; Civil Aeronautics Administration; Civil Aeronautics Authority; Clean Air Act; Collectors of American Art; Correctional Administrators Association; Cremation Association of America

C.A.A.: Civil Aviation Authority (United Kingdom)

CAAA: Canadian Association of Advertising Agencies; College Art Association of America; Composers, Authors, and Artists of America

CAAB: California Avocado Advisory Board

CAABU: Council for the Advancement of Arab-British Understanding

CAAC: Civil Aviation Administration of China

CAADRP: Civil Aircraft Airworthiness Data Recording Program (UK)

CAAE: Canadian Association for Adult Education

CAAIS: Computer-Assisted Action Information System(s)

caar: compressed-air-accumulator rocket

CAAR: Committee Against Academic Repression

CAARC: Commonwealth Advisory Aeronautical Research Council

CAAs: Community Action Agencies

CAAS: Ceylon Association for the Advancement of Science; Connecticut Academy of Arts and Sciences

CAAT: Canadian Academic Aptitude Test; College of Applied Arts and Technology

CA Att: Civil Air Attaché

CAAV: Central Association of Agricultural Valuers

cab: cabal; cabbage; cabin; cabinet; cable; cabochon; cabriolet; calibration; captured air bubble; cellulose acetate butyrate; taxicab

cab (CAB): cellulose acetate butyrate; coronary artery bypass

Cab: Cabell; Cabot

CAB: Charles A(ustin) Beard; Civil Aeronautics Board; Civil Aeronautics Bulletin; Commonwealth Agricultural Bureau; Contract Appeals Board (Veterans Administration)

CABA: Charge Account Bankers Association

cabal: *cabbala* (Hebrew—something secret)—(*see* also CABAL)

CABAL: Clifford of Chudleigh, Ashley (Lord Shaftesbury), Buckingham (George Villiers), Arlington (Henry Bennet), Lauderdale (John Maitland)—members of the cabal or secret cabinet of Charles II of England; by coincidence their initials spelled cabal

CABAS: City and Borough Architects Society

CABB: Captured Air-Bubble Boat (naval)

Cabbage Patch: Victoria, Australia

CABEI: Central American Bank for Economic Integration

CABLE: Computer-Assisted Bay Area Law Enforcement (San Francisco)

cablese: cablegram language (abbreviated, telegraphic, truncated style)

CABM: Commonwealth of Australia Bureau of Meteorology

CABMA: Canadian Association of British Manufacturers and Agencies

CABMS: Chinese-oriented Antiballistic Missile System

cabo: (Portuguese or Spanish—cape)

cabot: cabotage (coastal navigation)

CABRA: Copper and Brass Research Association

cabtmkr: cabinetmaker

cac: cardiac-accelerator center

Cac: Caceres

CAC: California Aeronautics Commission; Canadian Armoured Corps; Chief of Air corps; Civil Administration Commission; Coast Artillery Corps; College Admissions Center; Combat Air Crew; Commander Air Center; Consumer Advisory Council; Consumer Association of Canada; Continental Air Command; Corrective Action Committee; Corrective Action Commission

CAC: *Comité de Acción Cultural* (Spanish—Cultural Action Committee)

CACA: Canadian Agricultural Chemicals Association

cacc: cathodal closure contraction

CACC: Civil Aviation Communications Center; Corrective Action Control Section

CACCE: Council of American Chambers of Commerce in Europe

CACE: California Association for Childhood Education; Chicago Association of Consulting Engineers

CACEX: *Carteira do Comercio Exterior* (Portuguese—Foreign Commerce Department)—Bank of Brazil

CACF: Colombian-American Culture Foundation

cache.: computer-controlled automated cargo-handling envelope

CACHE: Computer Aids for Chemical Engineering Education

cachi: *cachivache* (Spanish—broken crockery; foolish or worthless person; poor quality; pots and pans; utensils)—dialect heard around Buenos Aires where it has many Ital-

ian, Portuguese, and Yugoslavian terms mixed with Spanish; dialect also called *porteño*
CACL: Canadian Association of Children's Librarians
CACM: Central American Common Market
Caco: *Cacoliche* (pidgin Argentine-Spanish including many Italian words)
CACO: Casualty Assistance Call Office(r)
$CaCO_3$: calcium carbonate (limestone)
cacoph: cacaphonic; cacophony
Cacos: (Spanish—Pickpockets; Poltroons)—nickname of a Guatemalan political party successful in the removal of Spanish authority from this Central American nation
cacp: cartridge-actuated compaction press
CACS: California Aqueduct Control System
CACSW: Citizens' Advisory Council on the Status of Women
CACTUS: *Capteur Accelerometrique Capacitif Triaxial Ultra-Sensible* (French—Ultra-Sensitive Triaxial Capacitive Accelerometric Detector)
Cactus Jack: Vice President John Nance Garner also called the Sage of Uvalde
Cactus State: New Mexico
CACUL: Canadian Association of College and University Libraries
CAC & W: Continental Aircraft Control and Warning
cad.: cadastral; cadaver; caddie; cadenza; cadet; cadmium; cartridge-activated device; cartridge-actuated device; cash against disbursements; cash against documents; contract award date
c.a.d.: cash against disbursements
cad: *cadenza* (Italian—solo passage near end of a concerto movement)
c-a-d: *c'est-à-dire* (French—that is to say)
Cad: Cadiz; Cadwallader
CAD: Civil Air Defense; Claude Archille Debussy; Combat Air Division; Crown Agents Department
cada: clean air dot angle
CADA: Centre d'Analyse Documentaire pour l'Archéologie *(Document Analysis Center—Archaeology)*
CADAN: Centre d'Analyse Documentaire pour Afrique Noir (Document Analysis Center—Africa)
cadav: cadaver(ous)
cadc: central air data computer
CADC: Continental Air Defense Command; Corrective Action Data Center
cadco: core and drum corrector
Caddie: Charlotte
Cad(dy): Cadillac
cade: computer-assisted data evaluation
cadet.: computer-aided design experimental translator
Cadet: old Russian acronym for Constitutional Democratic Party or one of its members
Cadets: Constitutional Democrats (in czarist Russia)
cadf: commutated antenna direction finder
CADF: Central Air Defense Force; Contract Administrative Data File
cadfiss: computation and data flow integrated subsystems
CADIG: Coventry and District Information Group
CADIN: Continental Air Defense Integration North
cadis: coronary artery disease
CADIZ: Canadian Air Defense Identification Zone
CADL: Christian Anti-Defamation League
CADM: CONUS (Continental United States) Air Defense Modernization
'cado(s): avocado(s)
CADO: Central Air Documents Office (USAF); Current Actions Duty Office(r)
Ca'd'Oro: Casa de Oro (Italian—House of Gold)
CADPIN: Customs Automatic Data Processing Intelligence Network (U.S. Bureau of Customs)
CADPOS: Communications and Data Processing Operation System
cadre.: current awareness and document retrieval for engineers
cads.: cellular-absorbed-dose spectrometer
CADS: Central Air Data System (USAF)
cadte: cathodal duration tetanus
Cadwal: Cadwallader
CAE: Canadian Aviation Electronics; Columbia, South Carolina (airport)
CAE: *Cóbrese al Entregar* (Spanish—cash on delivery)
CAEA: California Aviation Education Association; Chartered Auctioneers and Estate Agents
CAEAI: Chartered Auctioneers and Estate Agents Institute
Ca edta: calcium disodium ethylene diamine tetra-acetate
CAEM: *Conseil d'Assistance Economique Mutuelle* (French—Council for Mutual Economic Assistance)
Caern: Caernarvonshire
caerul.: *caeruleus* (Latin—cerulian)—sky blue
Caes: Caius Julius Ceasar
CAES: Canadian Agricultural Economics Society; Connecticut Agricultural Experiment Station
caesar: computerized automation by electronic system with automated reservations
CAET: Corrective Action Evaluation Team
caf: cafeteria; caffeine; clerical, administrative, and fiscal; cost and freight; cost, assurance, and freight
caf: *coût, assurance, fret* (French—cost, assurance, freight)
CAF: Canadian Armed Forces; Central African Federation; Ceylon Air Force
CAFA: Chicago Academy of Fine Arts
CAFB: Clark Air Force Base
CAFEA-ICC: Commission on Asian and Far Eastern Affairs—International Chamber of Commerce
cafetorium: cafeteria-auditorium
caff: caffeine
Caffarelli: Gaetano Majorano
CAFIC: Combined Allied Forces Information Center
CAFIT: Computer-Assisted Fault Isolation Test(ing)
cafm: commercial air freight movement
CAFMS: Continental Association of Funeral and Memorial Societies
CAFO: Command Accounting and Finance Office
C Afr Fed: Central African Federation
CAFSC: Control Air Force Specialty Code
CAFU: Civil Aviation Flying Unit
cag: chronic atrophic gastritis;

constant aerial glide; constant altitude glide
CAG: Carrier Air Group; Civil Air Guard; Composers-Authors Guild; Concert Artist Guild; Corrective Action Group; heavy guided-missile cruiser (naval symbol)
CAGA: California Asparagus Growers Association
CAGE: Convicts' Association for a Good Environment
cagel: consolidated aerospace ground equipment list
CAGI: Compressed Air and Gas Institute
Cagliostro: Giuseppe Balsamo
CAGS: Canadian Arctic Gas Study
cah: congenital adrenal hyperplasia
cahd: coronary atherosclerotic heart disease
CAHS: Comprehensive Automation of the Hydrometeorological Service
CAHT: Canadian Association for Humane Trapping
cai: computer-aided instruction; confused artificial insemination
Cai: Cairo
CAI: Computer Applications Incorporated; Configuration Audit Inspection (USA); Culinary Arts Institute
CAIB: Certified Associate of the Institute of Bankers
***CAI:** Club Alpino Italiano* (Italian Alpine Club)
C-a I: Computer-assisted Instruction
Cai Col: Gonville and Caius College—Cambridge
Caicos: Caicos Islands
CAIMAW: Canadian Association of Industrial, Mechanical, and Allied Workers
CAIN: CAtaloging-INdexing (National Agricultural Library data base)
caiop: computer analog input-output
CAIRA: Central Automated Inventory and Referral Activity (USAF)
CAirC: Caribbean Air Command
CAIRS: Central Automated Inventory and Referral System (USAF); Computer-Assisted Interactive Resources Scheduling System
CAIS: Canadian Association for Information Science; Central Abstracting and Indexing Service
Caith: Caithness
CAITS: Chemical Agent Identification Training Set
caj: calked joint
'cajun: Acadian (native of Louisiana)
cak: conical alignment kit; cube alignment kit
CAK: Akron, Ohio (airport)
cal: caliber; calorie (small); computer-assisted learning; conversational algebraic language
***cal:** calando* (Italian—calming); *carbine automatique légère* (French—light automatic carbine)—*CAL*
Cal: Calabar; Calabozo; Calabria; Calafat; Calahan; Calais; Calamar; Calcutta; Calder; Cale; Caleb; Caledonia(n); Calgary; Caliente; California; Calixto; Calkins; Call; Callao; Callcott; Callyhan; Calorie (large); Calpurnius; Calumet; Calvagh; Calvary; Calven; Calvin
CAL: China Airlines; Continental Airlines; Conversational Algebraic Language; Cornell Aeronautical Laboratory; Cyprus Airways; Point Arguello (California) tracking station
***cala:** calabozo* (Spanish—cell; dungeon; jail)
CALA: Civil Aviation Licensing Act
calamine: smithsonite (zinc carbonate)
Calamity Jane: Martha Jane Burke also known as Canary Jane whose activities resulted in the death of eleven of her twelve husbands
CALANS: Caribbean and Latin American News Service
calavo: California-grown avocado
C_{alb}: albumin clearance
calbr: calibration
calc: calculation; calculus
Calc: Calcutta
***Calç:** Calçada* (Portuguese—Street)
calcd: calculated
CALCOFI: California Cooperative Oceanic Fishery Investigation
Calcomp: California Computer Products
Calc Univ: Calcutta University
cald: calculated; caldera
CALDA: Canadian Air Line Dispatchers Association
CALDEA: California Driver Education Association
Calder: Cadwalader
CALE: Canadian Army Liaison Executive
CALEA: Canadian Air Line Employees Association
Caled: Caledonia
Caled Can: Caledonian Canal
***calef.:** calefactus* (Latin—warmed)
calen: calendar; calender
calendar: (*see* JFMAMJJASOND *and* French Revolutionary Calendar)
Calex: Calexico (California border city)
Cal Expo: California Exposition (permanent show at Sacramento)
Calg: Calgary
Calhan: Calahan
calib: calibrate; calibration
calibn: calibration
caliche: calcium carbonate crust (or) dust—$CaCO_3$
Caliente: Agua Caliente, Mexico
Calif: California; Californian
CALIF: California
Calif Cur: California Current
California Riviera: oceanside resorts ranging from San Diego to Santa Barbara
Caligula: Gaius Caesar
Calipuerto: Cali Aeropuerto (Cali, Colombia)
cal_{it}: calorie (International Table calorie)
CALIT: California Institute of Technology (also Caltech or CIT)
CALL: Canadian Association of Law Libraries; Community Action for Limited Learners; Composite Aeronautical Load List(ing); Counselling at the Local Level (SBA)
Calli: Callimachus of Alexandria (bibliographer-poet-scholar)
callig: calligrapher; calligraphic; calligraphy
calm.: collected algorithms for learning machines
CALM: Citizens Against Legalized Murder; Computer-Assisted Library Mechanization
CALMA: California Marine Associates
Calmex: California-Mexico
CALMS: Computer Automatic Line Monitoring System
caln: calculation
***calo:** calando* (Italian—softer and slower, bit by bit)
calogsim: computer-assisted logistics simulation
calomel: mercurous chloride (Hg_2Cl_2)

CALPA: Canadian Air Line Pilots Association
CALPIRG: California Public Interest Research Group
Cal Poly: California Polytechnic
CALRI: Central Artificial Leather Research Institute
CALS: Canadian Association of Library Schools
CALSO: California Transport
CalTec: California Institute of Technology
CALTEX: California-Texas Petroleum; Overseas Tankship Corporation
cal_{th}: calorie (thermochemical calorie)
Caltrans: California Department of Transportation
Calv: Calvin; Calvinism; Calvinist
Cal-VDAC: California Venereal Disease Advisory Council
Calvé: Emma Calvé—opera-house name of the soprano Emma de Roquer
Calypso Capital: Port-of-Spain, Trinidad
Calz: *Calzada* (Spanish—boulevard; highway)
cam.: camber; camouflage; circular area method; commercial air movement
C_{am}: amylase clearance
Cam: Camaguey; Cambodia; Cambodian; Cameroons; Campeche; Campechanos
CAM: Civil Aeronautics Manual; Civil Aviation Medicine; Composite Army-Marine; Contract Air Mail; Contract Audit Manual
cama: centralized automatic message accounting
CAMA: Civil Aerospace Medical Association
camal (CAMAL): continuous air borne missle alert
C'Amalie: Charlotte Amalie
Camb: Cambrian; Cambridge
Cambod: Cambodia; Cambodian
Cambrian: Cambrian Airways
Cambridge UP: Cambridge University Press
Cambs: Cambridgeshire
CAMC: Canadian Army Medical Corps
CAMDA: Car and Motorcycle Drivers Association
Camel-driver of Mecca: the Prophet Mohammed's nickname
Camellia: Alabama state flower
Camellia Capital: Sacramento, California
CAMEO: Capitol Area Motion Pictures Education Organization (D.C.)
camera.: cooperating agency method for event reporting and analysis
Cameroon: République Fédérale de Cameroun
CAMESA: Canadian Military Electronics Standards Agency
Cam High: Camden High School; Cameron Highlanders
CAMI: Columbia Artists Management, Incorporated
Camille Erlanger: Fréderic Regnal
CAMM: Canadian Association of Medical Microbiologists
CAMMIS: Command Aircraft Maintenance Manpower Information System
camof: camouflage
camp.: computer-assisted menu planning; cosmopolitan art—modern and personalized; cyclic adenosine monophosphate
Camp: Campeche (inhabitants—Campechanos
cAMP: cyclic adenosine 3', 5'-monophosphate
CAMP: Computer Applications of Military Problems; Continuous Air Monitoring Program
campan: campanological; campanologist; campanology
Camp Hall: Campion Hall—Oxford
campos: (Portuguese or Spanish—plains)
CAMPSA: Compañía Arrendataria del Monopolio de Petroleos
CAMP Test: Christie-Atkins-Munch-Peterson Test
CAMPUS: Comprehensive Analytical Methods for Planning in University Systems
cams.: cybernetic anthropomorphous machines
CAMS: Communication, Advertising, and Marketing Studies (System)
CAMSI: Canadian Association of Medical Students and Interns
Cam Soc: Camden Society
can.: canal; canalization; canalize; cancel; canceled; cancellation; cansiter; cannon; canon; canopy; canto; canvasback (duck)
can. (CAN): cancel character (data processing)
can: *canto* (Italian—melody; song)
Can: Canberra; Caen; Canada; Canadian; Cancer (constellation)
Can.: *Cantoris* (Latin—cantor's or preceptor's side of the choir)
CAN: Canberra, Australia (airport); Citizens Against Noise; Compagne Auxiliare de Navigation
CANABRIT: Canadian Navy Joint Staff in Great Britain
Canad: Canadian
Canada's Breadbasket: Saskatchewan
Canada's Doorstep: Nova Scotia
Canada's Heartland: The Province of Manitoba
Canada's Storied Province: Québec
Canada's Wonder City: Toronto—financial center and industrial headquarters
Canadian Gateway to the Pacific: British Columbia
Canadian Kaleidoscope: The Province of Ontario
Ca Na F: Campaña Nacional Fronterizo (National Frontier Campaign)
CANAIRDEF: Canadian Air Force Defense Command
CANAIRDIV: Canadian Air Force Division
CANAIRHED: Canadian Air Force Headquarters
CANAIRLIFT: Canadian Air Force Transport
CANAIRLON: Canadian Air Force Joint Staff—London, England
CANAIRMAT: Canadian Air Force Material Command
CANAIRNEW: Canadian Air Force—Newfoundland
CANAIRNORWEST: Canadian Air Force—Northwest, Edmonton
CANAIRPEG: Canadian Air Force—Winnipeg
CANAIRTAC: Canadian Air Force Tactical Command
CANAIRTRAIN: Canadian Air Force Training Command
CANAIRVAN: Canadian Air Force—Vancouver
CANAIRWASH: Canadian Air Force Joint Staff—Washington, D.C.
Canal Concessionaire: Vicomte Ferdinand Marie de Lesseps—original promoter of the Suez and the Panama Canal
Canaletto: Antonio Canale

Canal of Fire: Suez Canal's nickname as it was hot to dig, is hot to live along, and is hot to transit
canalimony: so-called $25-million-dollar alimony United States paid Colombia in 1922 for alienating and separating its province of Panama in 1903 so it could proceed unhindered in the task of controlling tropical disease and constructing the Panama Canal linking the Atlantic and the Pacific
Canal Zone Capital: Balboa Heights
Canar Cur: Canaries Current
Canaries: Canary Islands
CANAS: Canadian Naval Air Station
CANAVAT: Canadian Naval Attaché
CANAVCHARGE: Canadian Naval Officer in Charge
CANAVHED: Canadian Naval Headquarters
CANAVSTORES: Canadian Naval Stores
CANAVUS: Canadian Naval Joint Staff in United States
Canb: Canberra
canc: cancel; canceled; cancellation; cancelling
Canc.: *Cancellarius* (Latin—Chancellor)
CANCARAIRGRP: Canadian Carrier Air Group
CANCIRCO: Cancer International Research Cooperative
Can Cus: Canadian Customs
cand: candelabra; candidate
CANDEP: Canadian Naval Depot
cand sc: candelabra screw
Candu: Canadian deuterium uranium
Candy: Candice
CANDY: Cigarette Advertising Normally Directed to Youth
Canecutters: sugar-cane-cutting Queensland, Australians
CANEL: Connecticut Advanced Nuclear Engineering Laboratory
Can-End: Canton and Enderbury Islands
cane sugar: saccharose or sucrose
Cane Sugar State: Florida, Hawaii, and Louisiana share this nickname
CANF: Combined Allied Naval Forces
Can Fr: Canadian French
Can I: Canary Islands
Can Imm Cen: Canada Immigration Centre
canis: canister
CANLANT: Canadian Atlantic
Can Ltd: Canadair Limited (operating unit of General Dynamics Corporation)
Can Man Cen: Canadian Manpower Centre(s)
Can Met Ser: Canadian Meteorological Service (EAES)
Canned Salmon Capital: Ketchikan, Alaska
Cannery City: Seattle, Washington
Cannon City: Kannapolis, North Carolina where Cannon towels are made
Canoe City: Old Town, Maine
Can Pac: Canadian Pacific
Can Pen Ser: Canadian Penitentiary Service; Canadian Pension Commission
cans.: canvasbacks (ducks)
CANSAV: Canadian Save the Children Fund
CAN/SDI: Canadian Selective Dissemination of Information
CANSG: Civil Aviation Navigational Services Group
can't: can not; cannot
cant.: *canticum* (Latin—canticle or hymn of praise)
Cant: Canterbury; Canton; Cantonese
Cantab.: *Cantabrigiensis* (Latin—of Cambridge)
CANTAT: Canadian Transatlantic Telephones
Cantabrian Surge: Bay of Biscay
cant b: cantilever bridge
Can Telsat: Canadian Telecommunications Satellite System
Cantinflas: Mario Moreno
cantran: cancel(led) in transmission
Can Tran Comm: Canadian Transport Commission
cants: cantaloupes
Cantuar.: *Cantuaria* or *Cantuariensis* (Latin—of Canterbury)
Canuck: French-Canadian
CANUKUS: Canada—United Kingdom—United States
CANUS: Canada—United States
CANUSE: Canadian-United States Eastern (electric power interconnection)
CANUSPA: Canada, Australia, New Zealand, and United States Parents Association
canv: canvas
Canyon de Chelly: Canyon de Chelly National Monument (cliff-dweller ruins in northern Arizona)
canz: canzone; canzonetta
cao: chronic airway obstruction
CAO: Central Accounting Office(r); Chief Accounting Office(r); Civil Affairs Office(r); Crimean Astrophysical Observatory (USSR); Cultural Affairs Office(r)
caoc: cathodal opening contraction
CAOC: Consumers' Association of Canada
CAOGA: Crown Agents for Oversea Governments and Administrations
CAORB: Civil Aviation Operational Research Branch
CAORE: Canadian Army Operational Research Establishment
CAOSOP: Coordination of Atomic Operations—Standard Operating Procedures
CAOT: Canadian Association of Occupational Therapy
cap.: capacity; capital letter; capsule; caput
'cap: handicap
cap: capitolo (Italian—chapter); capitulo (Portuguese or Spanish—chapter); (French—cape)
cap.: *capiat* (Latin—take); *capsula* (Latin—capsule)
c/a/p: *codice di avviamento postale* (Italian—mailing code)—zip coding
Cap: capitol; captain; Charles A. Pearce
Cap.: Chapter—Number of Act of Parliament
CAP: Canadian Association of Pathologists; Certificat d'Aptitude Professionnelle (Certificate of Professional Aptitude); Civil Air Patrol; College of American Pathologists; Combat Air Patrol; Community Action Program
CAPA: California Association of Port Authorities
capac: cathodic protection
CAPAC: Composers, Authors, and Publishers Association of Canada
capal: computer-and-photographic-assisted learning
CAPC: Civil Aviation Planning Committee
capche: component automatic programmed checkout equipment
cap com: capsule communicator
CAPE: Classification and Place-

ment Examination; Confederation of American Public Employees
Cape-Cairo: Cape Town-to-Cairo Highway; Cape Town-to-Cairo Railway
Cape of the Californias: Cabo San Lucas (at the lower tip of Baja California)
Cape Cod turkey: codfish
Cape Colony: Cape of Good Hope Colony (South Africa)
capertsim: computer-assisted program evaluation review technique simulation
Cape Stiff: Cape Horn
Cape of Storms: Cape of Good Hope
Capital Island: Oahu, Hawaii
Capital Province: Ontario containing Canada's capital—Ottawa
Capital of the World: New York City—capital of the United Nations
CAPL: Controlled Assembly Parts List
CAPLOT: Canadians Against PLO Terrorism
cap. moll.: *capsula mollis* (Latin—soft capsule)
Cap^n: *Capitán* (Spanish—captain)
Cap'n: Captain
capo: (Italian—boss; cape (geog); chief; chief steward; foreman; overseer; ringleader; station master)—*capo*—boss or Cosa Nostra syndicate chief; cape (geog); *capobanda*—bandmaster; *capo cameriere*—chief steward; *capo fabbrica*—factory foreman or overseer; *caporione*—ringleader; *capo stazione*—station master)
CAPO: Canadian Army Post Office
CAPPA: Crusher and Portable Plant Association
capp^n: *capellán* (Spanish—chaplain)
CAPPS: Council for the Advancement of the Psychological Professions and Sciences
cap. quant. vult: *capiat quantum vult* (Latin—allow the patient to take as much as he will)
capri: computerized advance personnel requirements and inventory
Capric: Capricorn (constellation)
capris: capri pants
caps.: capital letters
caps.: *capsule* (Latin—capsule)
CAPs: Community Action Programs
CAPS: Clearinghouse on Counselling and Personnel Services; Computer-Aided Pipe Sketching System; Creative Artists Public Service
caps and lower case: capital letters and lower case letters
caps and small caps: upper case capital letters and small capital letters
capsep: capsule separation
CAPSS: Computer-Assisted Public Safety System
Capstone of Negro Education: Howard University
capt: caption
Capt: Captain
Capt.: Captain
Captain Kidd: William Kidd—privateer-pirate
Captive of History: Northern Ireland
Captn: old-style English abbreviation—Captain
car.: carat; carton; cloudtop altitude radiometer
Car: Carleton; Carlow; Caroline Islands
Car.: *Carolus* (Latin—Charles)
CAR: Canadian Association of Radiologists; Central African Republic; Chief Airship Rigger; Civil Air Regulation(s); Civil Air Reserve; Comité Agricole Régional (Regional Agricultural Committee); Contract Authorization Request; Corrective Action Request; US Army, Caribbean (area)
CAR: *Cadena Azul de Radiodifusión* (Spanish—Blue Broadcast Chain)
cara: combat air rescue aircraft
CARA: Chinese-American Restaurant Association
CARAC: Civil Aviation Radio Advisory Committee
Caran d'Ache: Emmanuel Poiré
Carat City: diamond-mining Kimberly, South Africa
Carav: Caravelle
Caravaggio, Michelangelo da: Michelangelo Merisio
Caravaggio, Polidoro da: Polidoro Caldara
carb: carbon; carbonacious; carbonate; carburetor; carburize
CARB: California Air Resources Board
carbecue: car + barbecue (device for melting waste out of junked automobiles)
carbo: carbohydrate
carbolic acid: phenol
carboloy: carbon-cobalt-tungsten alloy
carbonado: black or grayish-black industrial diamond; meat scored before grilling over charcoal
carbon dioxide: carbonic acid gas
Carbonif: Carboniferous
carbon monoxide: CO
carbontet: carbon tetrachloride
carbopol: carboxpolymethylene
carborundum: silicon carbide (SiC)
carb(s): carburetor(s)
Carcross: Caribou Crossing
card.: cardamom; cardinal
Card: Cardiganshire; Cardinal
CARD: Campaign Against Racial Discrimination; Civil Aeronautics Research and Development; Compact Automatic Retrieval Device (or Display)
CARDA: Continental Airborne Reconnaissance for Dammage Assessment (USAF)
cardamap: cardiovascular data analysis by machine processing
CARDE: Canadian Armament Research and Development Establishment
Cardinal: state bird of Illinois, Indiana, Kentucky, North Carolina, Ohio, Virginia, and West Virginia
Cardl: *Cardenal* (Spanish—Cardinal)
cardiol: cardiology
cardiov: cardiovascular
CARDIV: Carrier Division (naval)
Cards: Cardinals
CARDS: Combat Aircraft Recording and Data System
care.: continuous aircraft reliability evaluation
Care: Caretaker
CARE: Cooperative for American Remittances to Everywhere
CARES: Computer-Assisted Regional Evaluation System
CARF: Canadian Arthritis and Rheumatism Society; Central Altitude Reservation Facility
CARG: Corporate Accountability Research Group (Nader's)
Cargo Port of the Pacific: Vancouver, British Columbia
cargotainer: cargo container
CARI: Civil Aeromedical Research Institute
Carib.: Caribbean
CARIBAIR: Caribbean Atlantic Airlines

CARIBCOM: Caribbean Command
Carib Cur: Caribbean Current
Caribous: Caribou Mountains of British Columbia
CARIBSEAFRON: Caribbean Sea Frontier
caric: caricature; caricaturist
CARIC: Contractor All-Risk Incentive Contract (USAF)
Caricom: Caribbean Community: Anguilla, Antigua, Barbados, Belize, Dominica, Grenada, Guyana, Jamaica, Montserrat, St Kitts-Nevis, St Lucia, St Vincent, Trinidad and Tobago)
CARIFTA: Caribbean Free Trade Association
CARIH: Children's Asthma Research Institute and Hospital (Denver)
CARL: Chatfield Applied Research Laboratories
Carla: Carlotta; Caroline
Carleton Kendrake: Erle Stanley Gardner
Carm: Carmarthenshire
Carmen Silva: (pseudonym—Elisabeth Queen of Romania)
carmrand: civilian application of the results of military research and development
Carn: Caernarvonshire
Carnegie Inst: Carnegie Institution of Washington
Carnegie Tech: Carnegie Institute of Technology
Carnics: Carnic Alps
carnie(s): carnival(s); carnival workers
Caro: Carolina; Caroline
Carol: Carola; Carole; Carolina; Caroline; Carolyn
Carolinas: North and South Carolina
Carolines: Caroline Islands (Kusaie, Palau, Ponape, Truk, Yap) in the Western Pacific
carot: centralized automatic recording on trunks (Bell)
carp.: carpenter; carpentry; carpet(ing); computed air-release point; construction of aircraft and related procurement
Carp: Carpathian
CARP: computed air-release point
CARPAS: *Comisión Asesora Regional de Pesca el Atlantico Sud-Occidental* (Spanish—Regional Fisheries Advisory Commission for the Southwest Atlantic)
Carpet City: Amsterdam, New York
carp(s): stage carpenter(s)
Carps: Carpathian Mountains
carr: carrier
Carrie: Carolina; Caroline
Carrion's disease: Peruvian-sandfly enemia
CARRIS: *Companhia Carris de Ferro de Lisboa* (Portuguese—Lisbon Street Railway)
Carroll of Carrollton: Charles Carroll of Carrollton, Maryland—self-identified signer of the *Declaration of Independence*
cars.: community antenna relay service
CARS: Canadian Arthritis and Rheumatism Society; Community Antenna Relay Station; Computer-Aided Routing System
cart.: cartage; carton; collision-avoidance radar trainer
CARTB: Canadian Association of Radio and Television Broadcasters
Carth: Carthage; Carthaginian; Carthusian
cartobib: cartobibliographer; cartobibliography
cartog: cartographer; cartographic; cartography
Cary Grant: Archibald Leach
cas: calibrated airspeed; casual; casualty; close air support
cas (CAS): cooperative applications satellite
ca's: combat actions
Cas: Caracas; Casimir; Castle; Caslon
CAs: Consumers Associations; Cooperative Associations
CAS: California Academy of Sciences; Cambrian Airways (symbol); Casualty Actuarial Society; Change Analysis Section; Chemical Abstracts Service; Chicago Academy of Sciences; Chief of Air Staff; Civil Affairs Section; Civil Air Surgeon; Clean(er) Air System; Collision Avoidance System (aircraft); Commercial Air Service; Contract Administration Services; Courier Air Services; Customs Agency Service
C.A.S.: Certificate of Advanced Studies
ca.sa.: *capias ad satisfaciendum* (Latin—writ of execution)
CASA: Canadian Automatic Sprinkler Association; Catgut Acoustical Society of America; Contemporary Art Society of Australia
CASA: *Construcciones Aeronauticas, SA* (Spain)
Casanova: Giacomo Girolamo
Casa Pacifica: former President Nixon's Spanish-colonial seaside home at San Clemente, California
CASB: Cost-Accounting Standards Board
CASBS: Center for Advanced Study in the Behavioral Sciences (Stanford)
CASC: Council for the Advancement of Small Colleges
cascan: casualty cancelled
cascor: casualty corrected
CASCU: Cooperative Association of Suez Canal Users
casdac: computer-aided ship design and construction
CASDO: Computer Applications Support and Development Office (USN)
casdos: computer-assisted detailing of ships
case.: common-access switching equipment; computer-automated support equipment
CASE: Committee on the Atlantic Salmon Emergency; Coordinated Aerospace Supplier Evaluation; Council for the Advancement of Secondary Education
CASEA: Center for the Advanced Study of Educational Administration
Casey Stengel: Charles Dillon Stengel
CASF: Composite Air Strike Forces
cash.: cashier
Cash: Cassius
CASH: Commission for Administrative Services in Hospitals
CASI: Canadian Aeronautics and Space Institute
CASIG: Careers Advisory Service in Industry for Girls
Casl: Caslon
Ca S-L: Catering Sub-Lieutenant
CASLE: Commonwealth Association of Surveying and Land Economy
casm: cycling air sampling monitor
CASMT: Central Association of Science and Mathematics Teachers
casoff: control and surveillance of friendly forces
CASOS: Center for Advanced Study in Organization Science (U of Wisconsin)

Casp: Caspar
CASP: Capability Support Plan; Cape Arago State Park (Oregon); Country Analysis and Strategy Paper (U.S. State Department)
Caspar: Cambridge analog simulator for predicting atomic reactions
Cas Reps: Casualty Reports
Cass: Cassius
CASS: Command Active Sonobuoy System
CASSA: Continental Army Command Automated System Support Agency (USA)
CASSI: Chemical Abstracts Service Source Index
CASSIS: Communication and Social Science Information Service (Canada)
CASSR: Chuvash Autonomous Soviet Socialist Republic
Cast: Castel; Castile; Castilian; Castillon; Castle
CAST: Center for Application of Sciences and Technology
CAST: *Clearinghouse Announcements in Science and Technology*
CASTE: Collision-Avoidance System Technical Evaluation
CASTS: Canal Safe Transit System
CASW: Council for the Advancement of Science Writing
cat.: carburetor air temperature; catalog; catamaran; catapult; category; caterpillar tractor; clear air turbulence
Cat: Catalán; Catalina; Catalonia; Catalonian; Cataluña; Catalunya; Catamarca; Catania; Cataño; Catarina; Caterino; Catasauqua; Catawba; Caterpillar Tractor; Catesby; Catlett
CAT: California Achievement Test; Child's Apperception Test; Civil Air Transport; Civilian Actress Technician; Clerical Aptitude Test; Colleges of Advanced Technology; College Ability Test; Commercial Airlift Contract; Control and Assessment Team; Corrective Action Team
CAT: *Comisaría de Abastecimientos y Transportes* (Spanish—Commisariat of Supply and Transport)
CATA: Canadian Air Transportation Administration
catal: catalog; catalogue
Catal: Catalan; Catalonia; Cataluña
catawump: catawumpus (catamount; mountain lion)
CATC: Commonwealth Air Transport Council; Continental (Oil), Atlantic (Refining), Tidewater (Oil), and Cities (Service) (combined in mutual drilling)
CATCC: Canadian Association of Textile Colorists and Chemists
CATCO: Catalytic Construction Company
cate: comprehensive automatic test equipment
CATE: Current ARDC (Air Research and Development Command) Technical Efforts (program)
catec: catechism; catechist(ic)-(al)(ly)
Ca Test: Calcium Test (dental)
CATF: Canadian Achievement Test in French
cat gold: mica; yellowish mica
cath: cathartic; cathedral; catheter; catheterize
Cath: Catherine; Catholic; Cathedral
Cathay: China
CATHAY: Cathay Pacific Airways
Cathedral of Learning: University of Pittsburgh's 52-story building
Cathie: Catherine
cathol: catholic; catholically; catholicly; catholicalness; catholicness; catholicate; catholice; catholicity
Catholic Lib Assn: Catholic Library Association
Cathy: Catherine
CATIB: Civil Air Transport Industry Training Board
catk: counterattack
CATM: Canadian Achievement Test in Mathematics
CATOR: Combined Air Transport and Operations Room
CATRA: Cutlery and Allied Trades Research Association
CATRALA: Car and Truck Renting and Leasing Association
CATs: Civic Action Teams
CATS: Civil Affairs Training School (USN); Comprehensive Analytical Test System; Compute Air-Trans Systems; Computer-Assisted Test Shop; Computer-Automated Test System (AT & T)
cat's eye: chrysoberyl
catsie: cat's-eye playing marble; polished agate resembling a cat's eye
Catskills: Catskill Mountains of New York
CATSS: Cataloguing Support System
catt: conveyorized automatic tube tester
cattalo: cattle + buffalo—hybrid
CATTCM: Canadian Achievement Test in Technical and Commercial Mathematics
Catty: Catherine
catv: cabin air temperature valve; cable television; community antenna television
Cau: Caucasian
CAU: Congress of American Unions; Consumer Affairs Union; Consumer Affairs Unit
Caucasus: Caucasus Mountains between the Black Sea and the Caspian Sea
caud: caudal; caudate
cauli: cauliflower
caus: causation; causative
CAUSA: Compania Aeronautica Uruguay SA
causat: causative
'cause: because
CAUSE: Counselor Advisor University Summer Education
caust: caustic
caustic potash: potassium hydroxide (KOH)
caustic soda: sodium hydroxide (NaOH)
caut: caution
CAUT: Canadian Association of University Teachers
CAUTION: Citizens Against Unnecessary Tax Increases and Other Nonsense (St Louis citizens)
cav: cavalier; cavalry; cavitation; cavity; congenital absence of vagina; congenital adrenal uirilism; continuous airworthiness visit
cav (CAV): construction assistance vehicle
cav.: *caveat* (Latin—warning; writ of suspension)
c.a.v.: *curia advisare vult* (Latin—the court cares to consider)
Cav: *Cavaliere* (Italian—Knight)
Cavalier State: Virginia
Cavalleria española: nickname of Massenet's verismo opera *La Navarraise* also called *Calvélleria española* after the creatrix of its title role—Emma Calvé
cavd: completion, arithmetic, vo-

cabulary, directions (test)

cav. emp.: *caveat emptor* (Latin—let the buyer beware)—also appears as *c.e.*

CAVI: *Centre Audio-Visuel International* (French—International Audio-Visual Center)

caviol: caviology

ca virus: croup-associated virus

CAVN: Compañía Anonima Venezolana de Navegación (Venezuelan Steamship Line)

Cav-Pag: *Cavalleria Rusticana* and *I Pagliacci* (Italian operas frequently performed in succession)

cavu: ceiling and visibility unlimited

caw: cam-action wheel; channel address word

CAW: Cables and Wireless (company)

CAWA: Canadian-American Women's Association

CAWC: Committee on Air and Water Conservation (American Petroleum Institute)

CAWD: Canadian-American Wolf Defenders

cawg: coaxial adapter waveguide

CAWM: College of African Wildlife Management

CAWU: Clerical and Administrative Workers' Union

Caymans: Cayman Islands (Grand Cayman, Little Cayman, Cayman Brac)

cax: community automatic exchange (telephone)

Cay: Cayenne; Cayman

cayo: (Spanish—cay; key; shoal)

cb: cast brass; catch basin; cement base; center of buoyancy; chemical and biological; circuit breaker; common battery; continuous breakdown

c-b: circuit breaker

c/b: caught and bowled

c & b: collating and binding

c of b: confirmation of balance

Cb: columbium (symbol); cumulo-nimbus

CB: Cape Breton (island); Caribair (airline); Caribbean-Atlantic Airlines; Carte Blanche; Cavalry Brigade; Census Bureau; Chief Boilermaker; Children's Bureau; citizen's band (radiofrequency band for short-range two-way communication); Companion of the Bath; compass bearing; confidential book; confidential bulletin; confinement to barracks; Construction Battalions (hence the nickname "seabees"); Consultants Bureau; Control Branch; Counter Battery; Cumulative Bulletin; Currency Bond; large cruiser (naval symbol); William Cullen Bryant

C.B.: *Chirurgiae Baccalaureus* (Latin—Bachelor of Surgery); Companion of the Bath

C-B: (Sir Henry) Campbell-Bannerman

C & B: Clemens and Brenninkmeyer; Cleveland and Buffalo (steamship line)—*Seeandbee*

CB: *Carte Blanche* (French—white card indicating its holder can order as he or she pleases)

cba: cost-benefit analysis; chronic bronchitis with asthma

CBA: Canadian Booksellers Association; Caribbean Atlantic Airlines; Clydesdale Breeders Association; Community Broadcasters Association; Consumer Bankers Association

CBA: *Chemical-Biological Activities*

CBAA: Canadian Business Aircraft Association

CBAC: *Chemical-Biological Activities*

cbaf: cobalt-base alloy foil

CBAICP: Chemical and Biological Accident and Incident Control Plan (USA)

cbar: counterbore arbor

CBAT: Central Bureau of Astronomical Telegrams

CBB: Chesapeake Bay Bridge (Maryland)

CBB: *Centre Belge du Bois* (French—Belgian Forestry Research Center)

CBBA: Christian Brothers Boys Association

CBBB: Council of Better Business Bureaus

CBBI: Cast Bronze Bearing Institute

CBBII: Council of the Brass and Bronze Ingot Industry

CBBT: Chesapeake Bay Bridge-Tunnel (Maryland to Virginia)

cbc: combined blood count

CBC: Canadian Broadcasting Corporation; Caribbean Broadcasting Company; Ceylon Broadcasting Corporation; Children's Book Council; Columbia Basin Council; Contraband Control; Corset and Brassiere Council; Cyprus Broadcasting Corporation; large tactical-command ship (naval symbol)

cbcc: common bias—common control

CBCII: California Bureau of Criminal Identification and Investigation

CB Club: Citizen's-Band (radio) Club

cbcm: cheque book-charging method

CBCMA: Carbonated Beverage Container Manufacturers Association

CBCS: Commonwealth Bureau of Census and Statistics

cbct: circuit board card tester

cbcu: counterbore cutter

cbd: cash before delivery; closed bladder drainage; common bile duct

CBD: Central Business District; Construction Battalion Detachment

CBDNA: College Band Directors National Association

cbe: cesium bombardment engine; chemical binding effect; circuit board extractor; compression bonding encapsulation

CBE: Cheese Bureau of England; Conference of Biological Editors; Council of Basic Education

C.B.E.: Commander of the Order of the British Empire; Companion of the Order of the British Empire

CBEL: *Cambridge Bibliography of English Literature*

CBEMA: Canadian Business Equipment Manufacturers Association

cbf: cerebral blood flow; coronary blood flow

CBF: Children's Blood Foundation

cbg (CBG): corticosteroid-binding globulin; transcortin

CBG: Compagnie des Bauxites de Guinée

cbi: complete background investigation

CBI: Cape Breton Island; Carbonated Beverage Institute; Chesapeake Bay Institute; China-Burma-India (theater of war); Coffee Brewing Institute; Confederation of British Industry; Council of Burma Industries

CBI: *Cumulative Book Index*

CB & I: Chicago Bridge and Iron (company)

CBIS: Campus-Based Informa-

tion System (NSF); Computer-Based Instruction(al) System
cbit (CBIT): contract bulk inclusive tour (travel plan)
cbj: common bulkhead joint
CBJO: Coordinating Board of Jewish Organizations
cbk: checkbook
cbl: cable
cb/l: commercial bill of lading
c bl: *carte blanche* (French—white card)—full power to act
CBL: Configuration Breakdown List; Chesapeake Biological Laboratories
CB of L: Chartered Bank of London
cbm: chemical biological munitions; cubic meter(s)
cbm: *Kubikmeter* (German—cubic meter)
CBMA: Carbonated Beverage Manufacturers Association
CBMC: Corregidor-Bataan Memorial Commission
CBMIS: Computer-Based Management Information System
CBMM: Council of Building Materials Manufacturers
CBMPE: Council of British Manufacturers of Petroleum Equipment
CBMS: Conference Board of Mathematical Sciences
cbmu: current bit monitor unit
cbn: chemical, bacteriological, nuclear
CBN: Columbia Carbon Company (stock-exchange symbol)
CBNE: California Bureau of Narcotics Enforcement
CBNM: Custer Battlefield National Monument
Cbo: Colombo
CBO: Conference of Baltic Oceanographers
cboc: completion bed occupancy care
CBOE: Chicago Board Options Exchange
C-bomb: cobalt bomb
cbore: counterbore
cbp: ceramic beam pentode; constant boiling point
CBP: Centro de Biologia Piscatória (Piscatorial Biological Center—Lisbon)
CBPC: Canadian Book Publishers' Council
CB & PGNCS: Circuit Breaker and Primary Guidance Navigation Control System
CBPO: Consolidated Base Personnel Office
CBRI: Central Building Research Institute
CBT: *Centre Belge de Traductions* (French—Belgian Translations Center)
CBQ: Civilian Bachelor Quarters
C B & Q: Chicago, Burlington & Quincy (railroad)
cbr: chemical, biological, radiological
Cbr: Calabar
CBR: Canberra, Australia (airport); Center for Brain Research (University of Rochester)
CBRA: Chemical, Biological, Radiological Agency
CBRE: Chemical, Biological, and Radiological Element
CBRL: Chemical, Biological, and Radiation Laboratories (Ottawa)
cbrn: chemical, biological, radiological, and nuclear
CBRS: Child Behavior Rating Scale
cbrw: chemical, biological, Radiological warfare
cbs: chronic brain syndrome; concrete-block stucco
cBs: concerned Black students
CBS: Central Bureau of Statistics (Jerusalem); Columbia Broadcasting System; Currumbin Bird Sanctuary (Queensland)
CBSO: City of Birmingham Symphony Orchestra; City of Bournemouth Symphony Orchestra; Czechoslovak Broadcasting Symphony Orchestra
cbt: cesium beam tube
CBT: Chicago Board of Trade; Connecticut Bank and Trust (company)
CB & TC: Connecticut Bank & Trust Company
cbts: cesium beam time standard
cbu: cluster bomb unit
CBU: Chicago Board of Underwriters
cbv: central blood volume; circulating blood volume; corrected blood volume
CBVHS: Clara Barton Vocational High School
cbw: chemical-biological warfare
cby: carboy
cc: camp chair; carbon copy (or copies); centuries; chapters; close control; closing coil; color code; cubic centimeter(s)
Cc: cirrocumulus
c.c.: *corpora cardiaca* (Latin—cardiac body)—heart
c/c: *compte courant* (French); *conta corrente* (Portuguese); *conto corrente* (Italian); *cuenta corriente* (Spanish)—current account
cc (CC): chief complaint
Cc.: *Confessores* (Latin—Confessors)
CC: Calvin Coolidge (30th President U.S.)
CC: *corriente continua* (Spanish—direct current)
C & C: Command and Control
C-by-C: Come-by-Chance, Newfoundland
C de C (CDC): Canyon de Chelly
C of C: Count(y) of Cleves
cca: carrier-controlled approach; cellular cellulose acetate (plastic)
CCA: California Central Airlines; Chief of Civil Affairs; Circuit Court of Appeals; Citizens for Clean Air; Citizens' Councils of America; Comics Code Authority; Committee for Conventional Armaments; Community Concerts Association; Conquest of Cancer Act; Conservative Clubs of America; Consumers Cooperative Association; Container Corporation of America; Continental Control Area; Corduroy Council of America; Cruising Club of America
C & CA: Consumer and Corporate Affairs (Canada)
CCAB: Canadian Circulation Audit Board
CCAC: California College of Arts and Crafts
CCAD: Commerce and Consumer Affairs Department
CCAF: Commander-in-Chief—Atlantic Fleet
CCAHC: Central Council for Agricultural and Horticultural Cooperation; Central Council for Agricultural and Horticultural Cooperatives
CCAM: Colby College Art Museum
CCAP: Citizens Crusade Against Poverty
CCAQ: Consultative Committee on Administrative Questions (UN)
ccat: conglutinating complement absorption test
CCATS: Communications, Command, and Telemetry Systems
cca unit: chicken-cell agglutination unit
ccb: cubic capacity of bunkers

CCB: command-and-control boat (naval symbol); Configuration Control Board
cc black: conductive channel black
CCBM: Copper Cylinder and Boiler Manufacturers
CCBO: Cape Clear Bird Observatory (Ireland)
CCBS: California Canadian Banks
ccbv: central circulating blood volume
CCBW: Commission on Chemical and Biological Warfare
ccc: central computer complex
CCC: Canadian Chamber of Commerce; Central Control Commission; Chopin Cultural Center; Civilian Conservation Corps; Columbian Carbon Company; Commercial Credit Corporation; Commodity Credit Corporation; Corning Community College; Customs Cooperation Council; Cuyahoga Community College
CC & C: Command Control and Communications (USAF)
CCC: Consejo de Cooperación Cultural (Spanish—Council of Cultural Cooperation)—of the Council of Europe
CCCA: Classic Car Clubs of America; Conservative Christian Churches of America
CCCB: Component Change Control Board (DoD)
CCCC: Cape Cod Community College
CCCCO: Chicago Coordinating Council of Community Organizations
CCC-FID: Central Classification Committee—Fédération Internationale de Documentation
CCC Highway: Cleveland-Columbus-Cincinnati Highway
CCCJ: California Council on Criminal Justice
cccl: cathodal closure clonus
CC Co: Commercial Cables Company
CCCP: (Russian transliteration—USSR)—*Soyuz Sovetchikh Sotsialisticheckikh Respublik* (Union of Soviet Socialist Republics)
CCCPS: Chicago College of Chiropody and Pedic Surgery
ccd: charge-coupled device
CCD: Center for Curriculum Development; Cost Center Determination
CCDA: Commercial Chemical Development Association
CCDC: Central Citizens' Defence Committee
CCDN: Central Council for District Nursing
cce: carbon-chloroform extract
CCE: Casa de la Cultura Ecuatoriana (House of Ecuadorian Culture)
CCEBS: Committee for the Collegiate Education of Black Students
CCED: County Council Electoral Division
ccei: composite cost-effectiveness index
CCES: Catholic Church Extension Society
CCET: Carnegie Commission on Educational Television
ccf: cephalin-chlesterol flocculation; compound comminuted fracture; congestive cardiac failure; chronic cardiac failure; concentrated complete fertilizer
CCF: Canadian Commonwealth Federation; Citizens Council Forum; Combined Cadet Force; Common Cold Foundation; Cooperative Commonwealth Federation
CCFA: Combined Cadet Force Association
CCFC: Citizens Committee for a Free Cuba
ccfe: commercial customer-furnished equipment
ccfm: cryogenic continuous-film memory
ccfr: constant current flux reset
CCG: Choral Conductors Guild; Control Commission of Germany
CCGB: Cycling Council of Great Britain
CCGE: California Council for Geographic Education
ccgt: closed-cycle gas turbine
cch: cubic capacity of holds
Cch: Christchurch, New Zealand
CCH: Chaminade College of Honolulu; Commercial Clearing House
C of CH: Chief of Chaplains
CCHE: California Coordinating Council for Higher Education; Central Council for Health Education; Coordinating Council for Higher Education
CCHF: Children's Country Holidays Fund
cc/hr: cubic centimeters per hour
CCHS: Christopher Columbus High School
cci: chronic coronary insufficiency; circuit condition indicator; concentric coordinate incident; corrugated, cupped, or indented (cargo)
CCI: Community Concerts, Incorporated
CCI: Central Campesina Independiente (Spanish—Independent Peasant Central)—political party in Mexico
CCIAP: Cooperative Committee on Interstate Air Pollution (New Jersey-New York)
CCIB: Cook County Inspection Bureau
ccig: cold cathode ion gage
CCIL: Commander's Critical Item List (USA)
ccip: continuously computed impact point (USAF)
CCIR: Comité Consultatif International de la Radiodiffusion (French—International Consultative Committee on Broadcasting)
CCIs: Citizens Committee of Investigation members (investigating assassination of President Kennedy)
CCIS: Command Control Information System
CCITT: Consultative Committee in International Telephone and Telegraph
CCIW: Canada Centre for Inland Waters
CCJ: Circuit Court Judge; Cook County Jail (Chicago); County Court Judge
CCJC: Chicago City Junior College; Cook County Junior College; Custer County Junior College
CCJCA: California Community and Junior College Association
CCJO: Consultative Council of Jewish Organizations
cck (CCK): cholecystokinin
CCK: Centre College of Kentucky
cck-pz (CCK-PZ): cholecystokinin-pancreozymin
cckw: counterclockwise
CCL: Canadian Congress of Labour; Caribbean Cruise Lines
CCl_4: carbon tetrachloride
C-clamp: C-shaped clamp
cclkws: counterclockwise
CCLC: Cooperative College Library Center
c clef: alto clef (on the third line); soprano clef (on the first line); tenor clef (on the fourth line)
CC List: Critical Condition List

CCLM: Coordinating Council of Literary Magazines
CCLs: Court of Claims
CCLS: Canadian Council of Library Schools
ccm: cubic centimeter(s); counter-countermeasure(s)
ccm: *Kubikzentimeter* (German—cubic centimeter)
CCM: Canadian Cycle Manufacturers
CCMA: Canadian Council of Management Association
ccmc: coincident-current magnetic core
CCMC: College-Conservatory of Music of Cincinnati
ccmd: continuous-current monitoring device
CCMD: Chicago Contract Management District
cc/min: cubic centimeters per minute
CCMR: Central Contract Management Region
CCMS: California College of Mortuary Science; Chicago Chamber Music Society; Committee on the Challenges of Modern Society (NATO)
ccmt: catechol-O-methyl transferase
CCMTC: Crown Cork Manufacturers' Technical Council
ccn: coronary care nurse; coronary care nursing
CCN: Command Control Number; Companhia Colonial de Navegação (Colonial Navigation Company); Contract Change Notice; Contract Change Notification
CCNDT: Canadian Council for Non-Destructive Testing
CCNM: Chaco Canyon National Monument
CCNP: Callao Cave National Park (Luzon, Philippines); Carlsbad Caverns National Park (New Mexico)
CCNR: Citizens Committee on Natural Resources; Consultative Committee for Nuclear Research
CCNS: Cape Cod National Seashore (Massachusetts)
CCNSC: Cancer Chemotherapy National Service Center
CCNWR: Cross Creeks National Wildlife Refuge (Tennessee)
CCNY: Carnegie Corporation of New York; City College of the City University of New York
cco: current-controlled oscillator
Cco: Curaçao
CCO: Chicago College of Osteopathy; Clandestine Communist Organization; Comprehensive Certificate of Origin
CCOA: County Court Officers' Association
CCOC: Command Control Operations Center (USA)
CCOFI: California Cooperative Oceanic Fisheries Investigations
c conc: cast concrete
CCOS: Cabinet Committee on Opportunity for the Spanish Speaking
ccp: credit card purchase
ccp: *conto corrente postale* (Italian—current postal account)
CCP: Caribbean Conservation Program; Chinese Communist Party; Code of Civil Procedure; Consolidated Cryptologic Program
ccpa: cloud chamber photographic analysis
CCPE: Canadian Council of Professional Engineers
CCPF: Commander-in-Chief—Pacific Fleet
CCPG: Chemical Corps Proving Ground
cc-pill: compound-cathartic pill
CCPIT: China Commission for the Promotion of International Trade
CCPL: Corpus Christi Public Library
CCPO: Central Civilian Personnel Office
CCPO: *Comité Central Permanent de l'Opium* (French—Permanent Central Opium Committee)
ccpr: coherent cloud physics radar
CCPR: Central Council of Physical Recreation
CCPS: Consultative Committee for Postal Studies
ccr: closed-cycle refrigerator; combat crew; command control receiver; complex chemical reaction; computer character recognition; consumable case rocket; control circuit resistance; credit card reader; cross-channel rejection; crystal can relay; cube corner reflector
C_{cr}: creatinine clearance
CCR: Central Commission for the Navigation of the Rhine; Commission on Civil Rights; Contract Change Request
CCRDC: Chemical Corps Research and Development Command
CCRE: Canadian Council for Research in Education
CCRF: City College Research Foundation
C Cr P: Code of Criminal Procedure
CCR & R: covenants, conditions, restrictions, and reservations
CCRT: Check Collectors Round Table
ccru: complete crew
CCRU: Common Cold Research Unit
ccs: collective call sign; command, control, support (military function)
cc & s: central computer and sequencer
CCS: Cape Cod System; Caracas, Venezuela (Maiquetia Airport); Casualty Clearing Station; Center for Chinese Studies (University of California); Chief Commissary Steward; Church of Christ, Scientist; Combined Chiefs of Staff; Customer Conversion Statistics
CCSA: Canadian Committee on Sugar Analysis
CCSB: Credit Card Service Bureau
CCSC: Central Connecticut State College; Central Coordinating Staff, Canada
cc/sec: cubic centimeters per second
ccsep: cement-coated single epoxy
CCSF: City College of San Francisco
CCSL: Communications and Control Systems Laboratory
CCSO: Corpus Christi Symphony Orchestra
CCSS: Charles Camille Saint-Saëns; Cleveland-Cliffs Steamship (company)
CCSSO: Council of Chief State School Officers
CCST: Chelsea College of Science and Technology
cct: cathodal closing tetanus; chocolate-coated tablet; controlled cord traction
CCT: Clarkson College of Technology; Combat Control Team; Cumberland College of Tennessee
C & CT: Chemistry and Chemical Technology
CCTC: Chinese Cultural and Trade Center; Columbia

County Teachers College
ccte: cathodal closure tetanus
cctep: cement-coated triple epoxy
CC & TI: Community College and Technical Institute
cctks: cubic capacity of tanks
CCTP: Center City Transportation Program
CCTS: Canaveral Council of Technical Societies; Combat Crew Training School
cctv: closed-circuit television
CCTWg: Combat Crew Training Wing (USAF)
ccu: chart comparison unit
C-C u: Cherry-Crandall units
CCU: Calcutta, India (airport)
CCUL: California Credit Union League
CCUN: Collegiate Council for the United Nations
CCUS: Chamber of Commerce of the United States
ccv: closed-circuit voltage
ccw: counterclockwise
CCW: Caldwell College for Women
cc wr hdr: canvas-covered wire-rope handrail
ccws: counterclockwise
ccxd: computer-controlled X-ray diffractometer
cd: caesarean delivery; candela; canine distemper; cash discount; center door; certificate of deposit; civil defense; coin dimpler; cold drawn; communicable disease; confidential document; conjugate diameter (pelvic inlet); contagious disease; convulsive disorder; convulsive dose; cord; countdown; curative dose
c-d: countdown
c/d (C/D): carried down (bookkeeping); certificate of deposit
c & d: carpets and drapes; collection and delivery
cd_{50}: median curative dose (abolishing symptoms in 50 percent of all test cases)
cd: *cadde* (Turkish—street); *corriente directa* (Spanish—direct current)
c.d.: *conjugata diagonalis* (Latin—diagonal conjugate)—pelvic inlet diameter
c/d: cigarettes per day; cigars per day
Cd: cadmium; caudal
Cd_{115}: radioactive cadmium
Cd: *ciudad* (Spanish—city)
CD: Canadair turboprop airplane; Civil Defense; coastal defense radar (for surface-vessel detection); communicable disease; Community Development; confidential document; *Corps Diplomatique* (French—Diplomatic Corps); countdown
C.D.: Chancery Division
CD: *Centre Démocrate* (French—Democratic Center)
C $: cordoba (Nicaraguan monetary unit)
C & D: Chemist and Druggist; collection and delivery
C^2D^2 (ARDC): Command and Control Development Division
cda: command and data acquisition
cda (CDA): chenodeoxycholic acid
CDA: Canadian Dental Association; Canadian Dietetic Association; Catholic Daughters of America; Compañía Dominicana de Aviación (Dominican Aviation Company); Copper Development Association
CD Act(s): Contagious Diseases Act(s)
CDAE: Civil Defense Adult Education
Cd A Eng: Commissioned Air Engineer
Cd Airn: Commissioned Airman
CDAS: Civil Defense Ambulance Service
C. Day Lewis: Nicholas Blake
cdb: caliper disk brake; capacitance decode box; cast double base; central data bank; current data bit
Cd B: Commissioned Boatswain
CDB: Caribbean Development Bank; Combat Development Branch
cdba: clearance divers breathing apparatus
CDBA: California Dining and Beverage Association
cdbd: cardboard
Cd Bndr: Commissioned Bandmaster
cdc: calculated date of confinement; call direction code; career development course; command and data-handling console
CDC: Cadaver Disposal Center; California Debris Commission; California Democratic Council; Caribbean Defense Command(er); Center for Disease Control; Certificate of Disposition of Classified Documents; Cesspool Detergent Chemistry; Citizens' Defense Corps; Civil Defense Coordinator; Combat Development Command; Command Destruct Control; Commissioners of the District of Columbia; Communicable Disease Center; Configuration Data Control; Control Data Corporation; Control Distribution Center
C.D.C.: Commonwealth Development Corporation (formerly Colonial Development Corporation)
CDC: *Centro de Documentação Cientifica* (Portuguese—Scientific Documentation Center)
CDCA: chenodeoxycholic acid
cdcm: carbon-dioxide concentration module
Cd Cmy O: Commissioned Commissary Officer
Cd C O: Commissioned Communications Officer
Cd Con: Commissioned Constructor
CDCR: Center for Documentation and Communication Research; Control Drawing Change Request
CDCS: Civil Defense Countermeasures System; Construction Dollar Control System
CDCT: *Centro de Documentación Cientifica y Téchnica* (Spanish—Center of Scientific and Technical Documentation)—Mexico City
cdd: central data display; chart distribution data; coded decimal digit; color data display; command-destruct decoder; computer-directed drawing; cosmic dust detector; cratering demolition device
CDD: Certificate of Disability for Discharge
cddi: computer-directed drawing instrument
CDDP: Canadian Department of Defense Production
cde: carbon dioxide economizer; contamination - decontamination experiment
cde (CDE): canine distemper encephalitis
CDE: Cornell-Dubilier Electronics
CDEE: Chemical Defense Experimental Establishment
CDEG: Chicago District Electric Generating Corporation
CDEI: Control Data Education Institutes

C de J: *Compañía de Jesus* (Spanish—Company of Jesus)—Society of Jesuits
cdek: computer data entry keyboard
Cd El O: Commissioned Electrical (Electronic) Officer
Cd Eng: Commissioned Engineer
CDEOS: Civil Defense Emergency Operations System
cdf: command decoder film; command decoder filter; confined detonating fuse; constant current fringes
CDF: Campaign for Nuclear Disarmament; Canadian National Defence
CDFA: California Dried Fruit Association
CDFC: Commonwealth Development Finance Company
CDFGI: Charles Darwin Foundation for the Galápagos Islands
CD film: camouflage detection film
CDFRS: Charles Darwin Foundation Research Station (Academy Bay, Santa Cruz, Galápagos)
CDFSB: Canadian Dairy Foods Service Bureau
cd/ft^2: candela per square foot
cd fwd: carried forward
Cdg: Cardigan; Cardiganshire
CDG: Coder-Decoder Group (USA)
CDGA: California Date Growers Association
CD & GB TC: Chicago, Duluth and Georgian Bay Transit Company
Cd Gr: Commissioned Gunner
Cd Gr O: Commissioned Gunnery Officer
cdh: constant differential height
CDH: College Diploma in Horticulture
cdi: course deviation indicator
CDIC: Canada Deposit Insurance Corporation
Cd In O: Commissioned Instructor Officer
C Dip F & A: Certified Diploma in Finance and Accounting
c div: cum dividend
Cd J: Ciudad Juárez (inhabitants—Juaristas)
CDJ: *Comité de Défense des Juifs* (French—Committee of the Defence of Jews)
cdl: common display logic
Cdl: Cardinal
CDL: Central Dockyard Laboratory (UK); Citizens for Decent Literature
CDLC: Canadian Dental Laboratory Conference
cdm: contributing to the delinquency of a minor
cd/m^2: candela per square meter
CDM: Consolidated Diamond Mines (South Africa)
cdma: code division multiple access
Cd M-a-A: Commissioned Master-at-Arms
CDMB: Civil Defense Mobilization Board
CDMSWA: Consolidated Diamond Mines of South-West Africa
CDN: *Chicago Daily News*
CDNRA: Coulee Dam National Recreation Area (Washington)
CDNS: Chicago Daily News Service
Cd O: Commissioned Officer
CDO: California Disaster Office
Cd Ob: Commissioned Observer
Cd O E: Commissioned Ordnance Engineer
Cd O O: Commissioned Ordnance Officer
cdos: controlled date of separation
cdp: checkout data processor; communications data processor; contract definition phase
CDP: Centralized Data Processing; Certified Data Plan; Critical Decision Point
C.D.P.: Certificate in Data Processing
CDPC: California Delinquency Prevention Commission
CDPE: Continental Daily Parcels Express
cd pl: cadmium plate
cdr: command-destruct receiver; composite damage risk (audiometry)
Cdr: Commander
CDR: Countdown Deviation Request
CDRB: Canadian Defense Research Board
CDRBTE: Canadian Defense Research Board Telecommunication Establishment
CDRC: Civil Defense Regional Commission(er)
C d R: *Casa di Risparmio* (Italian—Savings Bank)
CDRA: Committee of Directors of Research Associations
Cdre: Commodore
CDRF: Canadian Dental Research Foundation
CDRI: Central Drug Research Institute
cdrill: center drill
Cdrngtn C: Codrington College
Cd R O: Commissioned Radio Officer
CDRS: Charles Darwin Research Station
cds: cards; cold-drawn steel; single cotton double silk (insulation)
cd's: certificates of deposit
C d S: *Circolo della Stampa* (Italian—Press Club); *Codice della Strada* (Italian—Highway Traffic Code); *Consiglio di Sicurezza* (Italian—Security Council)
CDS: climatological data sheet; commander destroyer squadron
Cd S B: Commissioned Signals Boatswain
cdse: computer-driven simulation environment
CdSh: Commissioned Shipwright
Cd S O: Commissioned Supply Officer
CDSO: Commonwealth Defense Service Organization
CDSP: *Current Digest of the Soviet Press*
CDSs: Civil Disobedience Squads
CDSS: Compressed Data Storage System
CDST: Central Daylight Saving Time
cdt: command-destruct transmitter; conduct; conductor
Cdt: Cadet; Commandant
CDT: Canadian Department of Transport; Central Daylight Time
C.D.T.: Certified Dental Technician
CDT (ADA): Council on Dental Therapeutics (American Dental Association)
Cdte: *Comandante* (Spanish—Commander)
Cdt Mid: Cadet Midshipman
cdts: constant-depth temperature sensor
cdu: cable distribution unit
CDU: Civil Disobedience Unit; coastal defense (radar) unit
CDU: *Christlich-Demokratische Union* (German—Christian Democratic Union)—political party
CDUEP: Civil Defense University Extension Program
cdv: cadaver; *carte de visite* (visiting card, sometimes with photograph)
CDV: Civil Defense Volunteer(s)
cdw: chilled drinking water

CDW: Civil Defense Warning
CD & W: Colonial Development and Welfare
Cd Wdr: Commissioned Wardmaster
Cd W O: Commissioned Writer Officer
c dwr: chest of drawers; chilled drinking water return
CDWS: Civil Defense Wardens Service
cdwt: cordwelt
cdx: control differential transmitter
Cdz: Cádiz
ce: carbon equivalent; center of effort (naval architecture); center entrance; constant error
c-e: communications-electronics
c & e: commission and exchange
c.e.: *curvée extra* (French—special sort)—special quality
Ce: Ceará; cerium; Ceylon
CE: Church of England; circular error; compass error; Corps of Engineers; Counselor of Embassy
C-E: communications electronics
C.E.: Civil Engineer
C_E: cost effectiveness
C of E: Church of England; Corps of Engineers
CE: Chemical Engineering
C.E.: Christian Era; Civil Engineer
cea: circular error average
cea (CEA): carcinoembryonic antigen
CEA: Childbirth Education Association; Correctional Education Association
CEA: *Commissariat à l'Energie Atomique* (French—Atomic Energy Commission)
CEAA: Center for Editions of American Authors; Council of European-American Associations
CEAC: Committee for European Airspace Coordination
CEAC: *Commission Européenne de l'Aviation Civile* (French—European Civil Aviation Commission)
CEANAR: Commission on Education in Agriculture and National Resources
CEAPD: Central Air Procurement District
CEARC: Computer Education and Applied Research Center
CEAT: Canadian English Achievement Test
ceb: cryogenic expulsive bladder
CEB: Central Electricity Board; Continuing Education Books
CEB: *Comité Electrotechnique Belge* (Belgian Electrotechnical Committee)
cebar: chemical, biological, radiological warfare
Ceb-Vis: Cebu-Visayan
CEC: Central Economic Committee; Ceramic Educational Council; Civil Engineer Corps; Coal Experts Committee; Commodity Exchange Commission; Commonwealth Economic Committee; Commonwealth Edison Company; Communications and Electronics Command; Consolidated Edison Company; Consolidated Electrodynamics Corporation; Consulting Engineers Council; Continental Entry Chart(s); Council for Exceptional Children
CECA: *Communauté Européenne du Charbon et de l'Acier* (French—European Coal and Steel Community); *Comunidad Europea del Carbon y del Acero* (Spanish—European Coal and Steel Community)
Cece: Cecil
CECEW: Catholic Education Council for England and Wales (often truncated to CEC—Catholic Education Council)
CECIL: Compact Electronic Components Inspection Laboratory
CECLA: *Comisión Especial de Coordinación Latinoamericana* (Special Commission for Latin American Coordination)
CECR: Central European Communication Region (USAF)
CECs: California Ecology Corpsmen
CECS: Church of England Children's Society; Communications Electronics Coordinating Section
CECS: *Comisión Especial de Consulta sobre Seguridad* (Spanish—Special Commission for Security Consultation)
ced: communications-electronics doctrine
c-e-d: carbon-equivalent-difference
c & ed: clothing and equipment development
CED: Committee for Economic Development; Communauté Européenne de Defense (European Defense Community); Communications-Electronics Doctrine (USAF manuals)
CEDA: California Economic Development Agency
CEDA: *Confederación Española de Derechas Autonomas* (Spanish—Spanish Confederation of Autonomous Rights)—right-wing Catholic-fascist party
cedac: central differential analyzer control; cooling effect detection and control
CEDAL: *Centro de Estudios Democráticos de America Latina* (Latin American Center of Democratic Studies)
CEDAM: Conservation, Exploration, Diving, Archeology, Museums (organization)
CEDI: *Centre Européen de Documentation et d'Information* (French—European Documentation and Information Center); *Centro Europeo de Documentación e Información* (Spanish—European Documentation and Information Center)
CEDIC: Church Estates Development and Improvement Company
CEDO: Centre for Educational Development Overseas (UK)
ced's: captured enemy documents
CEE: Central Engineering Establishment; Certificate of Extended Education; Common Entrance Examination; Cultural Environment Emergency
CEE: *Comunidad Económica Europea* (Spanish—European Economic Community)
CEEA: *Communauté Européenne de l'Energi Atomique* (European Atomic Energy Community)
CEEB: College Entrance Examination Board
CEEC: Council for European Economic Cooperation
CEECC: Consolidated-Edison Energy Control Center
CEEED: Council on Environment, Employment, Economy, and Development
CEEP: *Centre Européen d'Etudes de Population* (French—European Center for Population Studies)
CEev: Central European enceph-

alitis virus
cef: cellular-expansion factor; chicken-embryo fibroblasts
CEF: Canadian Expeditionary Force
C of EF: Count(y) of East Friesland Country
ceff: controlled energy flow forming
CEFTRI: Central Food Technological Research Institute
CEGGS: Church of England Girls' Grammar School
CEGB: Central Electricity Generating Board
CEGS: Church of England Grammar School
CEHHS: Charles Evans Hughes High School
CEHS: Civilian Employee Health Service
CEI: Cleveland Electric Illuminating Company; Commission Electrotechnique Internationale (International Electrotechnical Commission); Communications-Electronics Instruction
C & EI: Chicago & Eastern Illinois (railroad)
CEIF: Council of European Industrial Federations
c8^{va}: *coll'ottava* (Italian—in octaves)
cein: contract end-item number
CEIP: Carnegie Endowment for International Peace; Communications-Electronics Implementation Plan
C-E-I-R: Corporation for Economic and Industrial Research
CEIS: Cost and Economic Information System
cej: cement-enamel junction
cel: celluloid; cellulose
c-e-l: carbon-equivalent-liquid
Cel: Celeban; Celebes; Celsius
CEL: Constitutional Educational League; Cryogenics Engineering Laboratory
cel acet: cellulose acetate
CELADE: *Centro Latinoamericano de Demografía* (Latin American Demographic Center)
celeb: celebrate; celebration; celebrity
Celery City: Kalamazoo, Michigan
celebs: celebrities
Celestial City: John Bunyan's name for Heaven described in his *Pilgrim's Progress;* old traveller's name for China's capital city—Peking
Celestial Empire: Chinese Empire
Celia: Cecilia
Celine: Louis-Ferdinand Destouches
cell: celluloid
CELL: Continuing Education Learning Laboratory
celli: cellos (violoncellos)
'cellist(s): violoncellist(s)
cello: violoncello
cellulose: ($C_6H_{10}O_5$)
celnav: celestial navigation
cel nitr: cellulose nitrate
celo: chicken embryo lethal orphan (virus)
CELS: Continuing Education for Library Staffs
cel sheet: cellulose (plastic) sheet
celt: classified entries in lateral transposition
Celt: Celtic
Celtic Fringe: Celtic peoples of Cornwall, Ireland, Scotland, and Wales on the fringe of England
celtuce: celery-lettuce (lettuce-derived vegetable whose stalks taste like celery)
cem: cement; cement asbestos; cemetery; communication-electronics and meteorological
CEM: Council of European Municipalities
CEMA: Council for Economic Mutual Assistance; Council for the Encouragement of Music and the Arts; Conveyor Equipment Manufacturers Association
cemb: *cembalo* (Italian—harpsichord)
cem ab: cement asbestos board
CEMB: Communications-Electronic-Meteorological Board (USAF)
CEMCO: Continental Electronics Manufacturing Company
Cement City: Allentown, Pennsylvania
cemf: counter-electromotive force
cem fl: cement floor
CEMLA: *Centro de Estudios Monetarios Latinoamericanos* (Center of Latin American Monetary Studies)
c-e mix: chloroform-ether mixture
CEMO: Command Equipment Management Office
cem p: cement paint
cem plas: cement plaster
CEMR: Canadian Energy, Mines, and Resources
CEMS: Church of England Men's Society
CEMT: *Conferencia Europea de Ministros de Trasporte* (Spanish—European Conference of Ministers of Transport)
cen: center; central; centralization; centralize
Cen: Cenozoic
CEN: Central Airlines
CEN: *Comité Européen de Coordination des Normes* (European Committee of the Coordination of Standards)
Cenacolo: *Il Cenacolo* (Italian—Refectory; Supper Room)—another name for the tempera masterpiece of Leonardo da Vinci—*L'Ultima Cena*—The Last Supper
CENCOMMURGN: Central Communications Region
CENFAM: *Centro Nazionale di Fisica dell'Atmospera e Meteorologia* (Italian—National Center of Physics of the Atmosphere and Meteorology)
C Eng: Chartered Engineer; Chief Engineer
CENEUR: *Compañía Española de Navegación Maritima*
cens: censor; censorship
Censor of the Age: Thomas Carlyle
cent.: centrifugal; century
cent.: *centum* (Latin—hundred)
Cent: Century
CENTAG: Central European Army Group
centen: centennial
Centennial(s): Coloradan(s)
Centennial State: Colorado's official nickname recalling the state was admitted a century after the *Declaration of Independence* was signed.
Center of Austria: Salzburg
Center of the Copper Circle: Tucson, Arizona
Center of the Nation: Topeka, Kansas
Center of Scenic America: Utah
Center of the Sunshine State: Pierre, South Dakota
centi: 10^{-2}
CENTO: Central Treaty Organization (Great Britain, Iran, Pakistan, Turkey)
central: (French—middle)
Central Bureau: Amsterdam's old section (taken over by junkies, porn club owners, prostitutes, and criminals from Surinam) for illegal & illicit activities
centrale: (Italian—middle)

Central Prairie Province: Saskatchewan
centrex: central exchange
cént(s): céntimo(s); one-hundredth of a peseta
Century of Confusion: the 9th century when the Carolingian empire of Charlemagne disintegrated; European unity dismembered and divided—the 800s
Century of the Exodus: the 13th century before the Christian era when Moses lead the Israelites out of Egypt and across the Red Sea—the 1200s
ceo: chick embryo origin
CEO: Chief Executive Officer
CEOA: Central European Operating Agency
CEOAS: Corps of Engineers Office of Appalachian Studies (USA)
CEOs: Chief Executive Officers (conglomerate and multinational corporations)
CEOSL: *Confederación Centroamericana de Organizaciones Sindicales Libres* (Spanish—Central American Confederation of Free Trade Unions)
cep: circle of equal probability; circle of error probability
'cep': except
CEP: Color Evaluation Program; Council on Economic Priorities
CEPA: Chicago Educational Publishers Association; Civil Engineering Program Applications; Consumers Education and Protective Association
CEPAL: *Comisión Económica Para América Latina* (Spanish—Economic Commission for Latin America)—UNs ECLA
CEPC: City of Erie Port Commission
CEPC: *Comité Européen pour les Problemes Criminels* (French—European Committee on Crime Problems)
CEPE: Central Experimental and Proving Establishment; Corporación Estatal Petrolera Ecuatoriana (Ecuadorian State Petroleum Corporation)
CEPEX: Controlled Ecosystem Pollution Experiment
CEPG: Cambridge Economic Policy Group
ceph floc: cephalin flocculation (test)
CEPO: Corps of Engineers—Portland, Oregon
CEPS: Commonwealth-Edison Public Service; Cornish Engines Preservation Society
Cepsa: *Compañía Española de Petróleos* (Spanish Petroleum Company)
'cept: accept; except
'cepted: accepted; excepted
'ception: deception; exception; perception; reception
'cepting: accepting; excepting
CEPTA: Committee to End Pay Toilets in America
cept(s): concept(s); precept(s)
CEQ: Council on Environmental Quality (appointed by the President of the United States)
cer: ceramic; conditioned emotional response
c & er: combustion and explosives research
CER: Community Educational Resources
CERA/ACCE: Canadian Educational Researchers Association/Association Canadienne des Chercheurs en Education
ceram: ceramic; ceramicist; ceramics
ceramal: ceramic + alloy
CERB: Coastal Engineering Research Board (USA)
cerc: centralized engine-room control
CERC: Coastal Engineering Research Center; Coastal Engineering Research Council
CERCA: Commonwealth and Empire Radio for Civil Aviation
Cer.E.: Ceramic Engineer
Cereal City: Battle Creek, Michigan, and Cedar Rapids, Iowa, claim this title
CERI: Center for Educational Research and Innovation
CERL: Central Electricity Research Laboratories; Coastal Engineering Research Laboratory
cermet: ceramic-metallic (powders fused to form solid nuclear fuel elements)
CERN: Commission Européenne pour la Recherche Nucléaire (European Commission for Nuclear Research)
CERP: Current Economic Reporting Program
CERP: *Centre Européen des Relations Publiques* (French—European Center of Public Relations)
cerro(s): [Spanish—hill(s); mountain(s)]
cert: certificate; certify
certif: certificate(d)
cert inv: certified invoice
cerv: cervical
ces: central excitatory state; compressor end seal; constant elasticity of substitution
Ces: (German—C-flat)
CEs: Council of Europe members
CES: Closed Ecological System; Commercial Earth Station; Comprehensive Export Schedule; Conference on European Security; Cost-Effectiveness Study; Crew Escape System
CES: *Certificat d'Etudes Supérieures* (French—Advanced Studies Certificate)
CESA: Canadian Engineering Standards Association
CESAR: Capsule Escape and Survival Applied Research
CESAR: *Compagnie d'Etudes des Stations Air-Route* (French—Company for the Study of Airfields)
CESC: Calcutta Electric Supply Corporation
cesemi: computer evaluation of scanning electron microscopic image
cesi: closed-entry socket insulator
cesk: cable end-sealing kit
CESO-W: Council of Engineers and Scientists Organizations—West
c esp: *con espressione* (Italian—with expression)
CESP: Centrais Electricas de São Paulo
CESR: Canadian Electronic Sales Representatives
cess: assessment; cesspit; cesspool; success
Cess: Cecil
CESS: Council of Engineering Society Secretaries
CESSAC: Church of England Soldiers, Sailors, and Airmens Clubs
Cestr: Chester
Cestr.: *Cestrensis* (Latin—of Chester)
cet: capsule-elapsed time; controlled environmental test(ing); corrected effective temperature; cumulative elapsed time
CET: Central European Time; Certified Electrical Techni-

cian; Certified Electronics Technician
CET: *Collèges d'Enseignement Technique* (French—Technical Education Colleges)
CETA: Comprehensive Employment and Training Act
CETA: *Centre d'Études pour la Traduction* (French—Center for the Study of Automatic Translation)
CETAG: *Centre d'Études pour la Traduction, Grenoble* (French—Center for the Study of Translation, Grenoble)
CETAP: *Centre d'Études pour la Traduction, Paris* (French—Center for the Study of Translation, Paris)
CETDC: China External Trade Development Council
CETEC: Consolidated Engineering Technology Corporation
CETEKA: *Ceskoslovenská Tisková Kancelár* (Czechoslovakian Press Bureau)
CETEX: Committee on Contamination of Extra-Terrestrial Exploration (NASA)
ceti: communications with extraterrestrial intelligence
CETIS: Centre de Traitement de l'Information Scientifique (Center for Processing Scientific Information)
CETO: Center for Educational Television Overseas
cet. par.: *ceteris paribus* (Latin—other things being equal)
CETS: Church of England Temperance Society
CEU: Christian Endeavor Union
CEUSA: Committee for Exports to the U.S.A.
cev: cryogenic explosive valve
cevat: combined environmental, vibration, acceleration, temperature
cew: circular electric wire
cewrm: communications-electronics war-readiness materiel
cex: charge exchange; civil effects exercise
CEX: Corn Exchange Bank (stock-exchange symbol)
Cey: Ceylon; Singhalese
CEY: Century Electric (stock-exchange symbol)
CEYC: Church of England Youth Council
Ceyl: Ceylon
Ceylon: Sri Lanka
Cey Rs: Ceylon rupees
cf: calf binding; carried forward; carrier frequency; carry forward; cement floor; center of flotation; center forward; central files; central filing; centrifugal force; communication factor; complement fixation; conception formulation; cost and freight; counterfire; counting fingers; cystic fibrosis
c/f: carried forward
c & f: cost and freight
c-to-f: center-to-face
cf.: *confer* (Latin—compare)
c.f.: *cantus firmus* (Latin—fixed song)
Cf: californium
Cf.: *Confessor* (Latin—Confessor)
CF: Cape Fear (railroad); Chaplain to the Forces; Chief of Finance; Coastal Frontier; Colorado Fuel & Iron (stock-exchange symbol); Conservation Foundation; Corresponding Fellow
C/F: Contract Formulation
C de F: Collège de France (College of France)
C of F: Chief of Finance
CF: *Chemin de Fer* (French—Railroad)
cfa: complement-fixing antibody; cowl flap angle; crossed-field amplifier
cFa: complete Freund's adjunct
CFA: Chartered Financial Analyst; Colonies Françaises d'Afrique; Commission of Fine Arts; Community Facilities Administration; Council for Foreign Affairs
C & FA: Cookery and Foods Association
CF & A: Chief of Finance and Accounting (USA)
CFAA: Circus Fans Association of America
c factor: cleverness factor
cfae: contractor-furnished aerospace equipment
CFAE: Council for Financial Aid to Education
CFAE: *Centre de Formation en Aérodynamique Expérimentale* (French—Training Center for Experimental Aerodynamics)
cfar: constant false alarm rate
CFAL: Current Food Additives Legislation
CFAP: Canadian Foundation for the Advancement of Pharmacy
CFAT: Carnegie Foundation for the Advancement of Teaching
CFB: Canadian Forces Base; Consumer Fraud Bureau
cf black: conductive furnace black
CFBS: Canadian Federation of Biological Societies
CFBT: Canadian Forces Base Toronto
cfc: campus-free college; capillary filtration coefficient; colony-forming cells; complex facility console
CFC: Combined Federal Campaign (USA); Consolidated Freight Classification
CFCC: Canadian Forces Communications Command
CFCF: Central Flow Control Facility
cfd: cubic feet per day
CFD: Consumer Fraud Division
CFDC: Canadian Film Development Corporation
CFDTS: Cold-Flow Development Test System (AEC)
cfe: contractor-furnished equipment
CFE: Canadian Forces Europe; Central Fighter Establishment; College of Further Education
CFEME: Canadian Forces Environmental Medicine Establishment
cff: critical flicker frequency
Cff: Cardiff
CFF: *Chemin de Fer Fédéraux* (Swiss Federal Railroad)
cffc: counterflow film cooling
cfg: cubic feet of gas
CFG: Camp Fire Girls
cfgd: cubic feet of gas per day
cfgh: cubic feet of gas per hour
cfgm: cubic feet of gas per minute
cfh: cubic feet per hour
CFH: Council on Family Health
CFHS: Canadian Federation of Humane Societies
CFHQ: Canadian Forces Headquarters
cfi: cost, freight, and insurance
CFI: Canadian Film Institute
CF & I: Colorado Fuel and Iron
CFI: *Corporación Financiera Internacional* (Spanish—International Finance Corporation)—IFC
CFIA: Center for Independent Action
C-5A: heavy logistics transport airplane
cfl: context-free language
CFL: Canadian Football League; Carnegie Free Library; Chemins de Fer Luxembourgeois (Luxembourg State Railways)
cflg: counter flashing

cfm: confirm; confirmation; confirmed; cubic feet per minute; cubic feet per month
CFM: Council of Foreign Ministers
CFMC: Consumer-Farmer Milk Cooperative
CFN: Compagnie France-Navigation
cfo: calling for orders; coast for orders
CFO: Complex Facility Operator
CFOA: Chief Fire Officers Association
cfp: cold frontal passage; contractor-furnished property; cystic fibrosis of the pancreas
CFP: Consumer Fraud Protection
CEP:* *Colonies Française du Pacifique; Compagnie Française des Pétroles
CFPC: College of Family Physicians of Canada
CFPO: Compagnie Française des Phosphates de l'Océanie
cfr: chauffeur
CFR: Code of Federal Regulations; Contact Flight Rules; Coorong Fauna Reserve (South Australia); Council on Foreign Relations
CFRC: Canadian Forces Recruiting Centre
CFR engine: Cooperative Fuel Research (Council) engine (for measuring quality of fuels)
CFRPA: California Fire Rescue and Paramedic Association
CFRS: Central Fisheries Research Station
cfs: cubic feet per second
cf's: confessions of fornication (colonial-style abbreviation originating in Massachusetts and used before the American Revolution)
CFS: Canadian Forestry Service
CFS:* *Chemins de Fer Fédéraux Suisses (French—Swiss Federal Railways)
CFSA: College Food Service Association
CFSC: Canadian Forces Staff College
CFSR: Commission on Financial Structure and Regulation (White House)
CFSTI: Clearinghouse for Federal Scientific and Technical Information
cft: clinical full time; complement fixation test; craft; craftsman
CFT: California Federation of Teachers
CFT:* *Compagnie Française de Télévision (French Television Company)
CFTA: Cattle Food Trade Association
CFTAU: Canadian Friends of Tel Aviv University
cftb: controlled-flight test bed
CFTB: Commonwealth Forestry and Timber Bureau
CFTC: Commodity Futures Trading Commission
c-f tests: complement-fixation tests
CFTH: Compagnie Française Thomson-Houston
cftmn: craftsman
cfts: captive firing test set(s)
cfu: colony-forming units
cfvd: constant-frequency variable dot
CFWI: County Federation of Women's Institutes
cg: cardiogreen; center of gravity; centigram; choking gas (phosgene); chorionic gonadotropin; chronic glomerulonephritis; colloidal gold
cg:* *Zentigram (German—centigram)
CG: cargo glider aircraft (DoD symbol); Central of Georgia (railroad); Coast Guard; Commanding General; Connecticut General (Life Insurance Company); guided-missile cruiser (naval symbol)
C of G: Central of Georgia (railway); College of Guam (Agana)
CG:* *Consumer Guide
C G:* *cassa grande (Italian—bass drum)
C de G:* *Croix de Guerre (French—War Cross)
cga: cargo (proportion of) general average
CGA: Canadian Gas Association; Coat Guard Academy; Coast Guard Auxiliary; Compressed Gas Association; Corcoran Gallery of Art
CGAS: Coast Guard Air Station; Cornell Guggenheim Aviation Safety Center
CGB: Canadian Geographic Board
cgc: ceramic gold coating; critical grid current
CGC: Coast Guard Cutter; Continental Grain Company
cgd: chronic granulomatous disease
cge: carriage
CGE:* *Compagnie Générale d'Electricité (General Electric Company)
CG & E: Cincinnati Gas and Electric Company
cge fwd: carriage forward
CGEL & PB: Consolidated Gas, Electric Light and Power Company of Baltimore
cge pd: carriage paid; charge paid
C Gen: Consul General
cgf: chemotaxis-generating factor; coarse-glass frit
CGF: College of Great Falls
CGFA: Columbus Gallery of Fine Arts
cgfp: calcined gross fission product
CGFSA: Consolidated Gold Fields of South Africa
cgg: continuous grinding gage
cgh (CGH): chorionic gonadotrophic hormone
CGH: São Paulo, Brazil (Congonhas Airport)
C of GH: Cape of Good Hope
CGHB: Cape of Good Hope Bank
CGHSB: Cape of Good Hope Savings Bank
cgi: corrugated galvanized iron; cruise guide indicator
CGI: City and Guilds of London Institute
C-girl: call girl (prostitute); hundred-dollar girl
cgk: grid cathode capacitance
cgl: center-of-gravity locator; continuous-gas laser; controlled ground landing; corrected geomagnetic latitude (CGL)
cgl (CGL): chronic granulocytic leukemia
CGL: Canadian Gulf Line; Central Gulf Lines
CGLI: City and Guilds of London Institute
cg lkr: cleaning gear locker
cgm: centigram(s); ciliated groove to mouth
cgm (CGM): central gray matter
CGM: Conspicuous Gallantry Medal
CGMA: Covent Garden Market Authority
CGMW: Commission for the Geological Map of the World
cgn: chronic glomerulonephritis
CGN: Cologne, Germany (airport); nuclear-powered guided-missile cruiser (naval symbol)
CGNM: Casa Grande National Monument
cgo: cargo
Cgo: Chicago

CGO: Committee on Government Operations
cg/oq: cerebral glucose oxygen quotient
CGOT: Canadian Government Office of Tourism
CGOU: Coast Guard Oceanographic Unit
cgp: choline glycerophosphatide; chorionic growth hormone prolactin; circulating granulocyte pool; grid plate capacitance
CGP: College of General Practitioners
cgt: capital gains tax(ation); chorionic gonadotropin; combustible gas tracer
CGP: Current Geographical Publications
CGPM: Conférence Générale des Poids et Mesures (General Conference of Weights and Measures)
CGPS: Canadian Government Purchasing System
CGPSq: Cartographic and Geodetic Processing Squadron (USAF)
cgr: captured gamma ray; crime on government reservation
CGRA: Canadian Good Roads Association; Chinese Government Radio Administration (Taiwan)
CGRM: Commandant General—Royal Marines
cgs: centimeter gram second
CGS: Canadian Geographical Society; Central Gulf Steamship (corporation); Chief of General Staff; Coast and Geodetic Survey
C & GS: Coast and Geodetic Survey
CGSB: Canadian Government Specifications Board
C & GSC: Command and General Staff College
cgse: centimeter-gram-second electrostatic
cgsfu: ceramic glazed structural facing units
cgsm: centimeter-gram-second-electromagnetic
CGSS: Cryogenic Gas Storage System
CGSSC: Columbia Gas Service Corporation
CGSTC: Centro Giovanile Scambi Turistici e Culturali (Italian—Youth Center for Tourism and Culture)
cgsub: ceramic glazed structural unit base
CGSUS: Council of Graduate Schools in the United States
cgt: gains tax(ation); chorionic gonadotropin; combustible gas tracer
cgt (CGT): corrected geomagnetic time
CGT: Compagnie Générale Transatlantique (French Line); *Confederación General del Trabajo* (Spanish—General Confederation of Labor); *Confederation Générale du Travail* (French—General Confederation of Labor)
CGTA: Companie Générale de Transports Aériens (Air Algeria)
CGTB: Canadian Government Travel Bureau
CGTSF: Compagnie Générale de Télégraphie San Fils (French wireless company)
cgtt: cortisone glucose tolerance test (CGTT)
cgu: ceramic glazed units
CGUSCONARC: Commanding General United States Continental Army Command
CGUSFET: Commanding General United States Forces—European Theater
cgv: critical grid voltage
cgvs: ciliated groove to ventral sac
CGW: Chicago Great Western Railway
ch: case harden; chain; change; chapter; chest; chief; child; choke; choline; church; coat hook
c & h: cocaine + heroin; cold and hot
ch.: *chori* (Latin—choruses)
ch (CH): critical hours (when broadcast signals can cause interference)
ch: *chambre* (French—room); *cheque* (Portuguese or Spanish—check) *cheque* (French—check)
c & h: cocaine and heroin
Ch: Chile; Chilean; China; Chinese; choreographer; church
Ch.: *Chirurgiae* (Latin—Surgery)
CH: Carnegie Hall; Chicago Helicopter (airways); compass heading; concentration of hydrogen ions in moles per liter (symbol); Switzerland (autoplaque)
C.H.: Companion of Honour
C-H: Crouse-Hinds; Cutler-Hammer
CH: Confederatio Helvetico (Latin—Swiss Confederation)
CH_3COOH: acetic acid
cha: cable-harness analyzer; congenital hypoplastic anemia; cyclohexylamine
cha (CHA): cyclohexylamine
Cha: Charles
CHA: Catholic Hospital Association; Chattanooga, Tennessee (airport); Chicago Helicopter Airways; Community Health Association
CHABA: Committee on Hearing and Bio-Acoustics (US Army)
chabak: chabakano (Philippine Spanish dialect)
chacom: chain of command
chad: code to handle angular data
CHADS: Chicago Air Defense Sector
CHAFB: Chanute Air Force Base
Chagas-Cruz disease: South American sleeping sickness
Chagos: Chagos Archipelago
Chair: Chairman
Chairman Mao: Mao Tse-Tung
chal: challenge
chal: *chaleur* (French—heat; warmth)
Chald: Chaldean
chalk: calcium carbonate ($CaCO_3$)
cham: chamfer; champion
chamb: chamber
Chamb: Chamberlain
Chamb Ency: Chamber's Encyclopaedia
chammy: (English slang—champagne)
champ: champion(ship)
Champ: Beauchamp
champion.: compatible hardware and milestone program for integrating organizational needs
Champion of Darwin: Thomas Henry Huxley
Champion of Education: Horace Mann
Champions of Individualism: John Stuart Mill and Herbert Spencer
Champion of States Rights: John C. Calhoun—U.S. Senator from South Carolina
Champs: Champs Elysées (French—Elysian Fields)—main boulevard of Paris
CHAMPUS: Civilian Health and Medical Program of the Uniformed Services
chan: channel
Chanc: Chancellor; Chancery
CHANCE: Complete Help and Assistance Necessary for College Education

Chance Personified: Fortuna (Roman); Tyche (Greek)
CHANCOM: Channel Committee
Chandeleurs: Chandeleur Islands of Louisiana
'change: exchange; produce exchange; stock exchange
Channel City: Santa Barbara, California (on the Santa Barbara Channel)
Channels: Channel Islanders; Channel Islands
CHAP: Certified Hospital Admissions Program; Charring Ablation Program (NASA)
CHAOS: Committee for Halting Acronymic Obliteration of Sense
CHAOTIC: Computer-and-Human-Assisted Organization of a Technical Information Center (NBS)
chap.: chapter
Chap: Chaplain
CHAP: Charring Ablation Program (NASA)
Chappiequack: Chappaqua, New York's nickname
chaps.: *chaparajos* (Spanish—open backed leather overall pants worn by cowboys and charros when riding through thorny country)
CHAPS: Children Have A Potential Society; contractor-held Air Force property
Chapter 11, etc.: (legal euphemism—bankruptcy)—Chapter 11, etc., of the Bankruptcy Act of the U.S.
char: character; characteristic; charcoal; charwoman
char (CHAR): character (data processing)
Char: Charter
Char Amal: Charlotte Amalie
Charbray: Charolais-Brahman cattle
charc: charcoal
Charcot-Marie-Tooth disease: muscular atrophy
Charger: Convair multipurpose short takeoff-and-landing airplane
Charl: Charlottenburg
Charlemagne: (French—Charles the Great)
Charles Atlas: Angelo Siciliano
Charles J. Kenney: Erle Stanley Gardner
Charles the Bald: Charles I of France
Charles the Fat: Charles II of France
Charles the Simple: Charles III of France
Charley: Charles
Charley Car: St Charles Avenue trolleycar; one of America's oldest and the last in New Orleans where there was a streetcar named Desire
Charley South: Charleston, South Carolina
Charley West: Charleston, West Virginia
Charlie: Charles; code for letter C
Charlie Chaplin: Charles Spencer Chaplin
Charlot: (Spanish—Charlie)—Charlie Chaplin
Charm Spot of the Deep South: Mobile, Alabama
char reac: character reaction (sometimes simply cr)
chars: characters
char(s): charwoman; charwomen
chart.: *charta* (Latin—paper)
chart. bib.: *charta bibula* (Latin—blotting paper)
chart. cerat.: *charta cerata* (Latin—waxed paper)
Charter Oak City: Hartford, Connecticut, where the original charter was hidden in an oak tree to insure the liberty of the first settlers
chartul.: *chartula* (Latin—small paper)
chas: chassis
Chas: Charles
CHAS: Catholic Housing Aid Society
chase.: cut holes and sink 'em (navalese acronym for sinking old ammunition cases or obsolescent barges or boats)
Chasn: Charlestown
Chat Choo-Choo: Chattanooga Choo-Choo (restaurant)
chat mtg: chattel mortgage
Chat(ty): Charlotte
Chauc: Geoffrey Chaucer
chauf: chauffeur
chb: complete heart block
Chb: Cherbourg
Ch.B.: *Chirurgiae Baccalaureus* (Latin—Bachelor of Surgery)
ChBuAer: Chief of the Bureau of Aeronautics
ChBuDocks: Chief of the Bureau of Yards and Docks
ChBuMed: Chief of the Bureau of Medicine and Surgery
ChBuOrd: Chief of the Bureau of Ordnance
ChBuPers: Chief of the Bureau of Naval Personnel
ChBuSanda: Chief of the Bureau of Supplies and Accounts
ChBuShips: Chief of the Bureau of Ships
ChBuWeps: Chief of the Bureau of Weapons
chc: choke coil
CHC: Chicago House of Correction
ch cab: china cabinet
Ch Ch: Christ Church—Oxford
$CHCL_3$: chloroform
CHCMD: Chicago Contract Management District
chd: chaldron; childhood disease(s); congestive heart disease; coronary heart disease
Ch D: Charles Darwin
C-H d: Chediak-Higashi disease
Ch.D.: Chirurgiae Doctor (Latin—Doctor of Surgery)
CHD: Charles Halliwell Duell
Ch d'A: Chargé d'Affaires
chdm: cyclohexanedimethanol
che: cholinesterase
Che: *Chetverg* (Russian—Thursday); Ernesto (Che) Guevara (from Argentina where *Che* is a popular nickname)
Ch.E.: Chemical Engineer
CHE: Chete Game Reserve; Chewore Game Reserve; Chizarira Game Reserve—(all in Rhodesia
C-head: coke head (underground slang—cocaine addict)
CHEAR: Council on Higher Education in the American Republics
chec: checked; checkered
CHEC: Citizens Helping Eliminate Crime
Checkpoint Charlie: international frontier between East and West Berlin
Checo: *Checoslovaquia* (Spanish—Czechoslovakia)
cheesewich: cheese sandwich
Cheka: *Chrezvychainaya Kommissiya po Borbe s Kontrrevolutisiei i Sabotazhem* (Russian—Extraordinary Commission for Combating Counterrevolution and Sabotage)—original Soviet Secret Police founded December 20, 1917, at Lubianka Prison in Moscow (*q.v.—VOT*)
Chelm: (ancient Jewish town in Poland known in folklore as the Town of Fools); short form for Cheltenham
Chelmer: native of Chelm (ancient Jewish town in Poland known in folklore as the Town of Fools)
Chelt: Cheltenham
chem: chemical; chemist; chem-

istry
Chem.E.: Chemical Engineer
Chem Ed: Chemical Education Publishing Company
chem etch: chemically etched; chemical etching
Chem & Met Eng: *Chemical and Metallurgical Engineering*
chem mill: chemically milled; chemical milling
Chem Rubber: Chemical Rubber Company
CHEMTREC: Chemical Transportation Emergency Center
chem war.: chemical warfare
CHEN: *Chail Nashim* (Hebrew-Women's Force of the Israeli Army; *chen* is the Hebrew word for grace
CHEOPS: Chemical Operations System
Chequers: British prime minister's country home
Cherokee Rose: Georgia state flower
Cherv: Cherville; Chervin
chert: ironstone sedimentary rock
Ches: Cheshire
chesky: cherry-flavored whiskey
Chet: Chester
chev: chevron
Chev: *Chevalier* (French—Knight)
Chev(y): Chevrolet
Chewko: Chewing Tobacco Company
Chey: Cheyenne
chf: congestive heart failure; critical heart flux
Chf: Crimean hemorrhagic fever
Ch F: Chaplain of the Fleet
CHF: Carnegie Hero Fund
ch-factor: chutzpah factor (degree of guts or nerve)
CHFC: Carnegie Hero Fund Commission
Chf Engr: Chief Engineer
Chf M Sgt: Chief Master Sergeant
chg: change; charge
Chg: Chittagong
chgd: charged
Chgo: Chicago
chgph: choreographer; choreographic; choreography
chg pl: change plane
chgs: charges
chh: cartilage-hair hypoplasia
chi: specific magnetic susceptibility
Chi: Chicago; Chichester; China; Chinese
CHI: Crouse-Hinds (stock-exchange symbol)
chic: cermet hybrid integrated circuit
Chic: Chicago
Chickadee: state bird of Maine and Massachusetts
Chicagorican: Chicago Puerto Rican
Chicano: (diminutive nickname for *Mexicano* used by some Mexican-Americans in Arizona, California, Nevada, New Mexico, and Texas—formerly Mexican territory)
Chich: Chichester
Chick: Chickering
chick(s): chicken(s)
Chicom: Chinese communist
Chico Marx: Leonard Marx
Chicos: Chinese communists
Chidic: Chinese dictionary
Chief: Chief Engineer
Chih: Chihuahua (inhabitants—Chihuahuenses; chihuahua dogs characteristic of this area—chihuahueños)
chil: children('s)
Chil Cur: Chilean Current
child.: computer having intelligent learning and development
Chi$: Chilean peso
Children of Joseph: Israelites
Children of Pharoah: Egyptians
Chilton: Chilton Book Company
chim: *chimica* (Italian—chemistry)
Chimneyville: Jackson, Mississippi
chimponaut: chimpanzee astronaut (primate used in space travel experiments)
chimp(s): chimpanzee(s)
chin.: chinchilla
Chin: China; Chinese
china clay: kaolin (hydrous aluminum silicate)
Chinat: Chinese nationalist
Chinatown: Chinese quarter of any city outside mainland or offshore China
Chi Nats: Chinese Nationalists
Chinese Gordon: British general Charles George Gordon who suppressed the Taiping rebels; later named Gordon Pasha for similar services in the Sudan where he lost his life during the storming of Khartoum by the Mahdi
chinese white: zinc oxide (ZnO)
China Nac: *China Nacionalista* (Spanish—Nationalist China)—offshore China also known as Formosa or Taiwan
Chinook State: Washington where the warm Chinook wind blows from the Pacific to the Rockies
Chinsyn: Chinese-English synthesis-oriented machine translation system
Chip: *Chipre* (Portuguese or Spanish—Cyprus)
CHIPDis: Chicago Procurement District (US Army)
Chipitt: Chicago-to-Pittsburgh (complex of cities)
Chippy: Chipping Norton, England
Chips: ship's carpenter
CHIPS: Chemical Engineering Information Processing System
chir: chiropody
chir: *chirurgia* (Italian—surgery)
Chir. Doc.: *Chirurgiae Doctor* (Latin—Doctor of Surgery)
Chiricahuas: Chiricahua Mountains of Arizona
chiro: chirography; chiropractic; chiropractor
CHIRP: Community Housing Improvement and Revitalization Program
Chis: Chiapas (inhabitants—Chiapanecos)
Chisox: Chicago White Sox (baseball team)
chit: *chitty* (Hindustani—voucher signed to cover small debts for drinks, food, tobacco, etc.)
Chitlin Capital of the World: Salley, South Carolina
Chi-Trib: *Chicago Tribune*
chiv: chivalry
chix: chickens
Ch. J: Chief Justice
CHJM: Carnegie Hall—Jeunesses Musicales
CHJMKHK: *Chung-Hua Jen-Min Kung-Ho Kuo* (People's Republic of China—communist mainland China whose capital is Peking)
chk: check
chkr: checker
chl: chloroform; confinement at hard labor
CHL: Central Hockey League
chlb: chlorobutanol
Ch Lbr: Chief Librarian
ch-lkr: chiffonier-locker
chlor: chloride; chlorination; chlorine
chloride of lime: bleaching powder
chloro: chloroform; chlorophyll; chloroprene
chloroform: trichloromethane ($CHCl_3$)
chloroprene: synthetic rubber (C_4H_5Cl)

chm: chamber; checkmate
Chm: Chairman; Chairwoman; Choirmaster; Choirmistress
Ch.M.: *Chirurgiae Magister* (Latin—Master of Surgery)
CHM: Cleveland Health Museum
CHMC: Children's Hospital Medical Center (Boston)
ch-mir: chiffonier-mirror
CHMK: *Chung-Hua Min-Kuo* (Republic of China—offshore nationalist China whose capital is Taipei on the island of Formosa or Taiwan)
chmn: chairman
ChMNH: Chicago Museum of Natural History
CHN: College of the Holy Name
C-H-N: carbon, hydrogen, nitrogen, oxygen, phosphorus, sulfur (compounds)
chns: chains
CHNS: Cape Hatteras National Seashore (Buxton, North Carolina)
CHNSRA: Cape Hatteras National Seashore Recreational Area
Cho: Chosen (Korea)
CHO: carbohydrate (generalized formula)
choc: chocolate
choco: chocolate
Chocolate City: Hershey, Pennsylvania
Chocolate Coast: Ghana
chol est: cholesterol esters
chocs: chocolate candies; chocolate drops; chocolates
CHOKE: Care How Others Keep the Environment
chol: cholesterol
Chonos: Chonos Islands
CHOP: Change of Operational Control
chor: choral; choreographer; choreographist; choreography; chorus; choruses
Chord: Chordata
C Horn Cur: Cape Horn Current
chortle: chuckle and snort
Chotzie: Samuel Chotzinoff
Chou: Chou (pronounced *Joe*) En-lai
chovr: changeover
chow: (Chinese—small town)
chp: child psychiatry; comprehensive health plan(ning)
Chp: Chepstow
CHP: California Highway Patrol; Chihuahua Pacific (railroad—Ferrocarril de Chihuahua al Pacifico)
chpae: critical human performance and evaluation
CHPP: Cypress Hills Provincial Park (Saskatchewan)
ch ppd: charges prepaid
chpx: chickenpox
chr: chromobacterium; chronic
chq: cheque
CHq: Corps Headquarters
chr: chronic
c hr: candle-hour
Chr: Choir; Christ; Christian; Church
CHR: Connecticut Hard Rubber (company)
Chr Coll: Christ College—Cambridge
chrg: charge
CHRG: Citizens Health Research Group
Chris: Christian(a); Christopher
CHRIS: Cancer Hazards Ranking and Information System
Chrissie: Christina; Christine
Christ.: Christian; Christianity; Christmas
Christiania: Oslo's medieval name
christie: Christiania turn
Chrlstn: Charleston
chromite: iron chromate
chromo(s): chromolithograph(s); chromosome(s)
chron: chronogram; chronograph; chronology; chronometer; chronometry
Chron: *Chronicle(s)*—First Book of Chronicles; Second Book of Chronicles
Chrp. Chairperson
Chrs: Christians; Churches
Chrys: Chrysler
chrysanthemum: nationalist symbol of China and Japan; symbol of the Orient Overseas Line
chrysoberyl: beryllium aluminate
chrysocolla: hydrous copper silicate
chrysoprase: chalcedony gemstone
chs: chapters; crime on the high seas
Chs: Chambers
Ch of S: Chamber of Shipping
C-H s: Chediak-Higashi syndrome
CHS: Canadian Hydrographic Service; Charleston, South Carolina (airport); Chicago Historical Society; Childrens Home Society; Community Health Service (HEW); Cristobal High School; Curtis High School
ch'ship: championship
CHSM: China Service Medal
cht: cylinder head temperature
chtg: charting
CHTNP: Chittagong Hill Tracts National Park (Bangladesh)
Chu: Centigrade heat unit
CHU: *Christelijk-Historische Unie* (Dutch-Christian Historical Union)—political party
Chubu Nippon Shimbun: (Japanese—Central Japan Newspaper)
Chuck: Charles
Chuey: (Spanish-American nickname—Jesus)
Chugaches: Chugach Mountains of Alaska
Chumley: (British contraction—Chalmondeley)
Chung: Chungking
Chunnel: Channel Tunnel (under the English Channel where it will link England and France)
Chuqui: Chuquicamata
Churchill: Sir Winston Churchill—First Lord of the Admiralty during World War I and just before World War II when he became Great Britain's Prime Minister
chut: cable households using tv (audience survey)
'chute: parachute
ch v: check valve
chw: chilled water; cold-and-hot water; constant hot water
CHW: Charleston, West Virginia (airport)
CH & W: Canadian Health and Welfare
Chwdn: Churchwarden(ess)
chx: chiro-xylographic
chy: chimney
C Hy: Commission for Hydrology
chyd: churchyard
Chy Div: Chancery Division
ci: cardiac index; cardiac insufficiency; cast iron; cerebral infarction; chemotherapeutic index; clinical investigator (CI); clonus index; coefficient of intelligence; colloidal iron; color index; compression ignition; contamination index; coronary insufficiency; cost and insurance; counterintelligence; crystalline insulin
c.i. (C.I.): consular invoice
c/i (C/I): certificate of insurance
c & i: cost and insurance; cowboys and indians
Ci: cirrus; curie (unit of activity in radiation dosimetry)
Ci: *cerveau isolé* (French—isolated intellect; intellectual)
CI: Carnegie Institute; Channel Islands; Color Index; Com-

bustion Institute; Communist International; Cranberry Institute; Curtis Institute

C.I.: Lady of the Imperial Order of the Crown of India

C & I: Currier and Ives

cia: child(ren) in arms; computer interface adaptor

Cia: *Compagnia* (Italian—Company); *Companhia* (Portuguese—Company); *Compañía* (Spanish—Company)

C^{iac}: *Compania* (Spanish—company)

CIA: Caribbean International Airways; Central Intelligence Agency; Commerce and Industry Association; Cotton Insurance Association; Culinary Institute of America

CIA: *Comité International d'Auschwitz* (French—International Auschwitz Committee); *Conseil International des Archives* (French—International Council on Archives)

CIAA: Coordinator Inter-American Affairs

CIAB: Canadian Immigration Appeal Board

CIAC: Career Information and Counseling (USAF)

CIAL: *Communauté Internationale des Associations de la Librairie* (French—International Community of Booksellers' Associations)

CIAM: *Congreso Internacional de Arquitectura Moderna* (Spanish—International Congress of Modern Architecture)

CIANY: Commerce and Industry Association of New York

CIAO: Congress of Italian-American Organizations

CIAP: *Comite Interamericano de la Alianza para el Progreso* (Spanish—Inter-American Committee of the Alliance for Progress)—ICAP

CIAPS: Customer-Integrated Automated Procurement System

CIAS: California Institute of Asian Studies

CIASSR: Cecheno-Ingush Autonomous Soviet Socialist Republic

CIAT: *Centro Interamericano de Administradores Tributarios* (Inter-American Center of Revenue Administrators)

CIAW: Commission on Intercollegiate Athletics for Women

cib.: *cibus* (Latin—food)

CIB: Canadian International Bank; Central Intelligence Board; Criminal Intelligence Bureau; Criminal Investigation Bureau

CIB: *COBOL Information Bulletin* (USAF)

CIBC: Canadian Imperial Bank of Commerce

CIBG: Canadian Infantry Brigade Group

cibha: congenital inclusion body hemolytic anemia

cic: cardio-inhibitor center; cloud in cell

Cic: Marcus Tullius Cicero

CIC: Cedar Rapids & Iowa City (railroad); Center for Instructional Communications (Syracuse University); Central Inspection Commission; Chemical Institute of Canada; Combat Information Center; Combat Intelligence Center; Combined Intelligence Committee; Comité International de la Conserve (International Canning Committee); Commander-in-Chief; Command Information Center; Committee on Institutional Cooperation; Conseil International des Compositeurs (International Council of Composers); Continental Insurance Companies; Counter-Intelligence Corps; Critical Issues Council; Curaçao Information Center; Customer Identification Code

CIC: *Consejo Interamericano Cultural* (Spanish— Inter-american Cultural Council); *Cymdeithas yr Iath Cymraeg* (Welsh Language Society)

CICA: Canadian Institute of Chartered Accountants; Council of International Civil Aviation

CICAR: Cooperative Investigations of the Caribbean and Adjacent Regions (UNESCO)

Cicero: Marcus Tullius

Cicestr.: *Cicestrensis* (Latin—of Chichester)

CICJ: *Comité International pour la Coopération des Journalistes* (French—International Committee for the Cooperation of Journalists)

CICOM: *Centro de Comercialización Nacional e Internacional* (Spanish—Center of National and International Marketing)

CICP: Committee to Investigate Copyright Problems

CICRIS: Cooperative Industrial and Commercial Reference and Information Service

CICs: Community Improvement Corpsmen; Community Improvement Corpswomen

CIC's: Change Information Control (numbers)

CICS: Committee for Index Cards for Standards

CICT: *Conseil International du Cinéma et de la Télévision* (French—International Council of Cinema and Television)

cicu: cardiology intensive care unit (CICU); coronary intensive care unit (CICU)

CICU: Commission for Independent Colleges and Universities

CICYP: *Consejo Interamericano de Comercio y Producción* (Spanish—Interamerican Council of Commerce and Production)

cid: chick infective dose

cid (CID): cytomegalic inclusion disease

CID: Center for Industrial Development; Central Institute for the Deaf; Centre d'Information et de Documentation (Center for Information and Documentation—Belgium); Change in Design; Commission for International Development; Council for Independent Distribution; Criminal Investigation Department (Scotland Yard); Criminal Investigation Division

CID: *Colegio Interamericano de Defensa* (Spanish—Inter-American Defense College)

CIDA: Canadian International Development Agency

CIDC: Cryogenic Information and Data Section

CIDA: *Comite Interamericano de Desarollo Agricola* (Inter-American Committee of Agricultural Development)

CIDALC: *Comité International du Cinéma d'Enseignement et de la Culture* (French—International Committee of Film Education and Culture)

CIDC: Cryogenic Information and Data Section

CIDEM: *Consejo Interamericano de Música* (Spanish—Inter-American Music Council)

CIDG: Civil Indigenous Defense Group (Vietnam)

CIDH: *Comisión Interamericana*

de Derechos Humanos (Inter-American Commission of Human Rights)
cidi: crimping die
cidnp: chemically induced dynamic nuclear polarization
CIDOC: Centro Intercultural de Documentación (Intercultural Documentation Center)
cids: cellular immunity deficiency syndrome
CIDS: Chemical Information and Data System
cidstat: civil disturbance status (USA reporting activity)
cie: coherent infrared energy
Cie: *Compagnie* (French—company)
CIE: Cleveland Institute of Electronics
C.I.E.: Companion of the Order of the Indian Empire
CIE: *Comite Interamericano de Educación* (Inter-American Committee of Education)
CIEA: *Centro Internacional de Estudios Agricolas* (Spanish—International Center of Agricultural Studies)
CIEC: *Centre International d'Études Criminologiques* (French—International Center of Criminological Studies)
CIECC: *Consejo Interamericano para la Educación, la Ciencia, y la Cultura* (Inter-American Council for Education, Science, and Culture)
CIEE: Companion of the Institution of Electrical Engineers
Cie Gle Transatlantique: Compagnie Générale Transatlantique (French Line)
CIEM: Conseil International pour l'Exploration de la Mer (International Commission for the Exploration of the Sea)
CIEN: Comision Interamericana de Energia Nuclear (Inter-American Commission for Nuclear Energy)
ciénaga: (Spanish — swamp; marsh)
CIENES: *Centro Interamericano de Enseñaza de Estadística* (Inter-American Center for the Study of Statistics)
CIENT: Cambridge and Isle of Ely Naturalist Trust (England)
CIEP: Council on International Economic Policy
CIEO: Catholic International Education Office
CIER: *Centro Interamericano de Educación Rural* (Inter-American Center of Rural Education)
CIES: Comparative and International Education Society
CIES: *Consejo Interamericano Económico y Social* (Inter-American Economic and Social Council)
CIESMM: *Commission International pour l'Exploration Scientifique de la Mer Méditerranee* (French—International Commission for the Scientific Exploration of the Mediterranean Sea)
CIESPAL: *Centro Internacional de Estudios Superiores de Periodismo para América Latina* (International Center for Advanced Studies of Journalism in Latin America)
CIET: *Centro Interamericano de Estudios Tributarios* (Inter-American Center of Revenue Studies)
CIETA: Centre International de'Etude des Textiles Anciens (International Center for the Study of Antique Textiles)
cif: cost, insurance, and freight
CIF: California Interscholastic Federation; Canadian Institute of Forestry; Construction Industry Foundation
CIF: *Commission Interaméricaine des Femmes* (French—Interamerican Commission of Women); *Conseil International des Femmes* (French—International Council of Women)
CIFA: Courtauld Institute of Fine Arts
CIFAS: *Consortium Industriel Franco-Allemand pour Symphonie* (French—Franco-German Industrial Consortium for Symphonie)—communication satellite linking systems between points in Africa, the Americas, Europe, and the Middle East
CIFC: Council for the Investigation of Fertility Control
cifc & e: cost, insurance, freight, and exchange
cifci (CIF and C & I): cost, insurance freight (plus) commission and interest
CIFF: Cannes International Film Festival
cifLt: cost, insurance, and freight, London terms
cig: cigarette
CIG: *Comité International de Géophysique;* Commonwealth Industrial Gases
CIGA: *Compagnia Italiana dei Grandi Alberghi* (Italian Great Hotels Company)
Cigar City: Tampa, Florida
Cigarette: Josiah Flynt Willard
CIGS: Chief of the Imperial General Staff (Great Britain)
CIGTF: Central Inertial Guidance Test Facility
cih: carbohydrate-induced hyperglyceridemia
CII: Chartered Insurance Institute; Coffee Information Institute
CIIA: Canadian Institute of International Affairs
CIIB: Consumers Insurance Information Bureau
CIIC: Counter Intelligence Interrogation Center
CIIR: Central Institute for Industrial Research
CIIIA: *Soedinennye Shtaty Ameriki* (Russian—United States of America)—U.S.A.
CIJ: *Consejo Interamericano de Jurisconsultos* (Inter-American Council of Legal Consultants)
cil: current-inhibit logic
CIL: Canadian Industries Limited; Center for Independent Living
C/I/L: *Computer/Information/Library Sciences*
CILA: Centro Interamericano de Libros Académicos
Cilla: Priscilla
cim: capital investment model; communication-interface module(s); computer-input microfilm(ing); conductance-increase mechanism; continuous-image microfilm(ing)
CIM: California Institution for Men; Canadian Institute of Mining; Canadian Institute of Music; Commission for Industry and Manpower; Curtis Institute of Music
CIM: *Centro Italiano della Moda* (Italian Fashion Center); *Conseil International de la Musique* (French—International Music Council); *Consejo Internacional de Mujeres* (Spanish—International Council of Women)
C & IM: Chicago & Illinois Midland (railroad)
CIMA: Construction Industry Manufacturers Association
Cimabue: Cenni di Pepo
CIMBA: Contractor Installation

Make-or-Buy Authorization
CIMC: Commander's Internal Management Conference
cimco: card image correction
CIMCO: Congo International Management Corporation
CIME: Council of Industry for Management Education
cimm: constant-impedance mechanical modulation
CIMM: Canadian Institute of Mining and Metallurgy
CIMMS: Civilian Information Manpower Management System (USN)
CIMP: *Conseil International de la Musique Populaire* (French—International Folk Music Council)
CIMR: Commander's Internal Management Review
CIMTP: *Congrès International de Médecine Tropicale et de Paludisme* (French—International Congress of Tropical Medicine and Malaria)
cimu: compatibility-integration mockup
cin: cervical intra-epithelial neoplasia
c_{in}: insulin clearance
Cin: Cincinnati
CIN: Cooperative Information Network (linking libraries by twx)
CIN: *Chemical Industry Notes*
Cinc: Cincinnati
C-in-C: Commander-in-Chief
CINC: Commander-in-Chief
CINCAFLANT: Commander-in-Chief, Air Force Atlantic Command
CINCAFMED: Commander-in-Chief, Allied Forces Mediterranean
CINCAFSTRIKE: Commander-in-Chief, Air Force Strike Command
CINCAL: Commander-in-Chief, Alaskan Command
CINC ATL FLT: Commander-in-Chief, Atlantic Fleet
CINCEASTLANT: Commander-in-Chief, Eastern Atlantic
CINCENT: Commander-in-Chief, Central Europe
CINCEUR: Commander-in-Chief, Europe
CINCHAN: Commander-in-Chief—Channel (NATO)
Cinci: Cincinnati
Cincinnati oysters: pigs' feet
CINCLANT: Commander-in-Chief, Atlantic
CINCLANTFLT: Commander-in-Chief, Atlantic Fleet
CINCMEAFSA: Commander-in-Chief, Middle East, Southeast Asia, Africa South of the Sahara
CINCMED: Commander-in-Chief, Mediterranean
CINCNELM: Commander-in-Chief, U.S. Naval Forces in Europe, the Eastern Atlantic, and the Mediterranean
CINCNORAD: Commander-in-Chief, North American Defense Command
CINCNORTH: Commander-in-Chief, Northern Europe
CINCONAD: Commander-in-Chief, Continental Air Defense Command
CINCPAC: Commander-in-Chief, Pacific
CINCPACFLT: Commander-in-Chief, Pacific Fleet
CINCSOUTH: Commander-in-Chief, Southern Europe
CINCSTRIKE: Commander-in-Chief, United States Strike Command
CINCUNC: Commander-in-Chief, United Nations Command
CINCUSAFE: Commander-in-Chief, United States Air Forces in Europe
CINCUSAFLANT: Commander in Chief—United States Air Force Atlantic
CINCUSAFSTRIKE: Commander-in-Chief—United States Air Force Strike
CINCWESTLANT: Commander-in-Chief, Western Atlantic
Cincy: Cincinnati
Cindy: Cinderella; Cynthia
cine: cinema; cinematography
CINECA: Cooperative Investigation of the Eastern Central Atlantic
cinemactor: cinema actor
cinemactress: cinema actress
cinerama: cinematic panorama (three-dimensional film)
CINFAC: Counterinsurgency Information Analysis Center
CINFO: Chief of Information
CINM: Channel Islands National Monument (Southern California)
cinn: cinnabar
Cinn: Cincinnati
cinna: cinnamon
cinnabar: mercuric sulfide (H_gS)
cinnamon stone: hessonite
Cinn Sym Orch: Cincinnati Symphony Orchestra
CINOA: *Confédération International des Négociants en Oeuvres d'Art* (French—International Confederation of Art Dealers)
CINPDis: Cincinnati Procurement District (US Army)
CINS: CENTO Institute of Nuclear Science
CINTA: Compañía Nacional del Turismo (Chilean Airline)
Cinty: Cincinnati
CINVA: *Centro Interamericano de Vivienda y Planteamiento* (Inter-American Center of Housing and Planning)
CIO: Commission Internationale d'Optique (International Optical Commission); Congress of Industrial Organizations
Cio-Cio-San: (Japanese—Madame Butterfly)
CIOCS: Communications Input-Output Control System
CIOMS: Council for the International Organization of Medical Sciences
CIOSL: *Confederaciôn Internacional de Organizaciones Sindicales Libres* (Spanish—International Confederation of Free Trade Union Organizations)
cip: cast-iron pipe; cipher (zip is derived from this and is a slang shortcut for a cipher or zero—zero)
C i P: Cataloging in Publication (Library of Congress program)
CIP: Canadian International Paper; Civilian Institution Program; Composite Interface Program; Consolidated Intelligence Program; Cost Improvement Proposal
CIP: *Comisión Interamericana de Paz* (Inter-American Peace Commission)
CIPA: Canadian Industrial Preparedness Association; Chartered Institute of Patent Agents; Committee for Independent Political Action
CIPAC: Collaborative International Pesticides Analytical Council (UK)
CIPASH: Committee for an International Program in the Atmospheric Sciences and Hydrology
CIPCE: *Centre d'Information et de Publicité des Chemins de Fer Européens* (French—Information and Publicity Center of the European Railways)

CIPE: *Centro Interamericano para la Promoción de las Exportaciones* (Spanish—Inter-American Center for the Promotion of Exports); *Consejo Internacional de la Pelicula de Ensenañza* (Spanish—International Council for Educational Films)
ciph: cipher
CIPHER: Calculations of Patient and Hospital Education Resources
ciphony: enciphered telephony
CIPL: Canada India Pakistan Line
CIPL: *Comité International Permanent de Linguistes* (French—Permanent International Committee of Linguists)
CIPM: Council for International Progress in Management
CIPO: Conseil International pour la Préservation des Oiseaux (International Council for the Preservation of Birds)
CIPP: Cataloging-in-Publication Program (Library of Congress)
CIPP: *Conseil Indo-Pacifique des Pêches* (French—Indo-Pacific Fisheries Council)
CIPR: *Commission Internationale de Protection Contre les Radiations* (French—International Commission on Radiological Protection)
CIPRA: Cast-Iron Pipe Research Association
CIPS: Canadian Information Processing Society
cir: circle; circuit; circular
cir.: *circa* (Latin—about)
cIR: crime on Indian Reservation
Cir: Circle
CIR: Commission on Intergovernmental Relations; Commissioner of Internal Revenue; Cost Information Report; Court of Industrial Relations; Current Industrial Reports
CIRA: Committee on International Reference Atmosphere; Conference of Industrial Research Associations
CIRA: *Centro Interamericano de Reforma Agraria* (Spanish—Inter-American Center of Agrarian Reform)
CIRADS: Counter-Insurgency Research and Development System
cir ant.: circular antenna
cir bkr: circuit breaker
circ: circular; circulate; circumference; circumstance
circad: circadic; circadian; circadianly
circal: circuit analysis
circle: ancient symbol of annual, eternal, or female principle; Earth symbol if divided into four sectors by an erect cross or if bisected by a horizontal line; Full Moon (sometimes circle contains a cartoon face); Full Moon denoted by solid circle; rain represented by circle with vertical lines; solar corona if circle is divided by a vertical line; Sun if containing a central dot or if periphery contains radiating lines
circltr: circular letter
circs: circumstances
circum: circumference
Circumv Stz: Circumvesuviana Stazione (Neapolitan railroad station serving Herculaneum, Mt Vesuvius, and Pompeii)
Circus King: John Ringling
Ciren: Cirencester (Sisister)
CIRF: Corn Industries Research Foundation
CIRF: *Centre International d'Information et de Recherche sur la Formation Professionelle* (French—Vocational Training and Research Center)
CIRIA: Construction Industry Research and Information Association
CIRIS: Completely Integrated Range-Instrumentation System (NASA)
CIRJP: Commission on International Rules of Judicial Procedure
CIRM: Centro Internazionale Radio-Medico
CIRO: Consolidated Industrial Relations Office
CIRVIS: Communication Instructions for Reporting Vital Intelligence Sightings (of ufo's from aircraft)
cis: carcinoma in situ; cataloging in source; central inhibitory state
cis (CIS): cataloging in source
ci's: conflict indicators
Cis: Cecilia
Cis: (German—C-sharp)
CIS: Catholic Information Society; Center for International Studies (MIT); Central Instructor School; Chartered Institute of Secretaries; Cost Inspection Service; Cranbrook Institute of Science
CISA: Canadian Industrial Safety Association; Council for Independent School Aid
CISAC: Confédération Internationale des Auteurs et Compositeurs (International Federation of Authors and Composers)
Cisco: San Francisco
CISE: Colleges, Institutes, and Schools of Education (Library Association)
CISF: *Confédération Internationale des Sages-Femmes* (French—International Confederation of Midwives)
CISIR: Ceylon Institute of Scientific and Industrial Research
Cisister: Cirencester, England
cislun: cislunar; cislunarian; cislunarite
CISR: Center for International Systems Research
Cissie: Cecilia
Cissie Patterson: Eleanor Medill Patterson
Cissy: Cecilia
Cist: Cistercian
CISV: Children's International Summer Village
cit: citation; cited; citizen(ship); citrate
Cit: Citadel
CIT: Calcutta Improvement Trust; California Institute of Technology (Cal Tech); Carnegie Institute of Technology; Case Institute of Technology
CIT: *Compagnia Italiana di Turismo* (Italian Travel Bureau)
cit a: citric acid
CITB: Construction Industry Training Board
CITC: Canadian Institute of Timber Construction
cite.: compression ignition and turbine engine
CITE: Consolidated Index of Translations into English
CITEL: *Comisión Interamericana de Telecomunicaciones* (Inter-American Telecommunication Commission)
Citians: people of Minneapolis and St Paul also called Twin Citians
Citibank: First National City Bank
Cities of the Plain: Sodom and Gomorrah near Israel's Dead Sea
Citizen Composer: Dmitri Shos-

takovich
Citizen King: Louis Philippe of France
Citizen Louis Capet: Louis XVI
CITL: Canadian Industrial Traffic League
cito disp.: *cito dispensetur* (Latin—dispense rapidly)
CITP: Civilian Industrial Technology Program
citric acid: $C_8H_6O_7$
citricult: citriculture
citrine: false topaz (quartz with ferric iron)
citta: (Italian—city; town)
City: The City—business and financial section of the City of London within its historic bounds
City of Abraham: Hebron, Israel
City of Alexander the Great: Alexandria, Egypt
City of Angels: nickname shared by Bangkok and Los Angeles
City of the Apprentice Boys: Londonderry, Northern Ireland
City of the Arctic: Tromsø, Norway
City of Baked Beans: Boston, Massachusetts
City of Beaches: Montevideo, Uruguay
City of Beautiful Spires: Copenhagen
City of Bells: Strasbourg, France
City Beside the Broad Missouri: Bismarck, North Dakota
City Between Bridges: medieval Stockholm
City of Big Shoulders: Carl Sandburg's sobriquet for Chicago
City of Birches: Umeå, Sweden
City of Black Diamonds: Scranton, Pennsylvania
City of the Blues: Memphis, Tennessee (home of W.C. Handy)
City of Brotherly Love: Philadelphia (derived from the Greek *philos* (love) and *adelphos* (brother)
City of Canals and Bridges: sobriquet shared by Amsterdam, Copenhagen, Stockholm, and Venice
City of the Carmel: Haifa, Israel, on the slopes of Mount Carmel
City of Certainties: Des Moines, Iowa
City of Cheese: sobriquet shared by the Dutch cities of Alkmaar and Gouda
City of Cheese, Chairs, Children, and Churches: Sheboygan, Wisconsin
City of Churches: Brooklyn, New York
City of David: Jerusalem
City of the Doges: Venice
City of Dreadful Night: Kipling's nickname for Calcutta
City of Dreaming Spires: Oxford, England
City of the Dunes: Dunkerque, France
City of Elms: New Haven's nickname before Dutch-elm disease attacked her trees
City of Eternal Spring: Caracas
City of Five Seasons: Cedar Rapids, Iowa
City of Four Lakes: Madison, Wisconsin
City of Fun and Frolic: Atlantic City, New Jersey
City of Gardens and Beaches: Adelaide, Australia
City of Gold: Dawson, Yukon Territory
City by the Golden Gate: San Francisco
City of the Golden Horn: Istanbul
City of Good Neighbors: Arlington Heights, Illinois
City of Hans Christian Andersen: Copenhagen, Denmark
City of Heat: Thermopolis, Wyoming
City of a Hundred Towers: Italy's Pavia with its many towers and turrets
City of Illicit Love: Paphos on Cyprus in the Greek Isles
City of Jazz and Mardi Gras: New Orleans, Louisiana
City of Kielland and Bjelland: Stavanger, Norway
City of Light: Paris, France and Perth, Western Australia share this sobriquet
City of Lillies: Florence, Italy
City by the Lion's Gate: Vancouver, British Columbia
City of Magnificent Distances: Washington, D.C.
City of Manifold Advantages: Augusta, Maine
City of Mankind: Jerusalem
City of Masts: Port of London
City of Millionaires: Colorado Springs
City of Minarets: Miknès, Morocco
City of Money: Zurich, Switzerland (home of the Swiss bank account)
City of Monuments: Baltimore, Maryland and Florence, Italy, both claim this nickname
City in Motion: San Diego, California
City of Mozart: Salzburg, Austria
City on the Neva: Leningrad (formerly called Petrograd or St. Petersburg)
City of Notions: Boston, Massachusetts
City of Oaks: Raleigh, North Carolina
City of 1000 Lakes: Oklahoma City, Oklahoma
City of Palaces: Rome, Italy, and its Vatican City replete with papal palaces
City of Palms: Acajutla, El Salvador; Fort Myers, Florida; and Maracaibo, Venezuela, all claim this nickname
City of Peace: Brunei
City of Penn: Philadelphia, Pennsylvania founded by William Penn
City of Personality: Cincinnati, Ohio
City of Power: Peking, People's Republic of China
City of Presidents: Quincy, Massachusetts
City of the Prophet: Medina, Saudi Arabia, where Mohammed was protected after fleeing from Mecca
City of Quays and Grieg: Bergen, Norway
City of Razzle Dazzle: one of O Henry's nicknames for New York City he also called Bagdad on the Subway
City of Receptions: Washington, D.C.
City of Rocks: Nashville, Tennessee
City of Roses: Portland, Oregon
City of Ruins and Roses: Visby on Sweden's Gotland Island
City of Rum and Sugar: Georgetown, Guyana
City of Rumors: Washington, D.C.
City of St Michael: Dumfries, Scotland whose patron saint is St. Michael
City of Saints: Montreal where so many street names are saint names
City of Salt: Salzburg, Austria, and Syracuse, New York—both in salt-producing regions
City of the Sea: Venice
City of Seven Hills: Rome, Italy, as it is built on seven hills—Aventine, Caelian, Capitoline, Esquiline, Palatine, Quirinal, and Viminal
City of Shoes: Brockton, Massachusetts
City of the Silver Gate: San Diego
City of Sinbad: Basra, Iraq

City of the Slain: Arlington National Cemetery in Arlington, Virginia
City of Smokestacks: Everett, Washington
City of Soles: Lynn, Massachusetts
City of Sorrow: Buchenwald (concentration camp near Weimar, Germany)
City of the Straits: Detroit, Michigan, on the Straits of Belle Isle
City of the Sun: sobriquet shared by ancient Baalbec, Heliopolis, and Rhodes; Campanella's utopian republic also bore this title
City of Surprises: Amsterdam
City of Tamales: O Henry's sobriquet for San Antonio, Texas
City That Care Forgot: New Orleans
City That Knows How: San Francisco
City of the Thousand and One Nights: Baghdad, Iraq
City of Three Capitols: Little Rock, Arkansas
City of the Three Kings: Cologne, Germany, where it is reputed the Magi or Three Kings are buried; Lima, Peru
City of Trees: Christchurch, New Zealand; Saratoga Spring, New York
City of the Tribes: Galway, Ireland—home of the thirteen families or tribes—Athy, Blake, Budkin, Browne, Burke, d'Arcy, Ffont, Joyce, Kirwan, Lynch, Martin, Morris, Skerrett
City under Vesuvius: Naples
City of the Violet Crown: Athens
City on the Water: sobriquet shared by Amsterdam, Copenhagen, Stockholm, and Venice
City of Witches: Salem, Massachusetts
City without Clocks: Las Vegas, Nevada
CIU: Coopers' International Union
CIUS: Conseil International des Unions Scientifiques (International Council of Scientific Unions)
civ: civil; civilian; civilization; civilize
CIV: Commission Internationale du Verre (International Glass Commission)
Civ Air NM: Civil Aircraft National Marking(s)
civ eng: civil engineering
Civ Eng: Civil Engineer
civies: civilian clothes; civilians
Civil War Photographer: Matthew Brady
CIVIS: *Centro Italiano per i Viaggi d'Instruzione per Studenti* (Italian Center for Students' Educational Travel)
civvies: civilian clothes; civilians
CIW: California Institution for Women
cixa: constant infusion excretory urogram
cj: clip joint; conjectural; construction joint
CJ: Chief Justice
C of J: Collector of Junk
CJA: Carpenters and Joiners of America
CJB: Constructors John Brown (British shipbuilders)
CJC: Colby Junior College
CJC: *Corpus Juris Canonici* (Latin—Code of Canon Law)
CJCA: California Junior College Association
CJCiv: *Corpus Juris Civilis* (Latin—Code of Civil Law)
C-J disease: Creutzfeldt-Jakob disease (afflicting all primates)
cje: *corretaje* (Spanish—brokerage)
CJE: Citizens for Jobs and Energy
CJF: Carlos J. Finley
CJFWF: Council of Jewish Federations and Welfare Funds
CJI: Concrete Joint Institute
CJI: *Comite Jurídico Interamericano* (Inter-American Juridical Committee)
CJM: Congregation of Jesus and Mary
CJR: Cecil John Rhodes
CJR: *Columbia Journalism Review*
CJRL: Criminal Justice Reference Library (Austin)
cjs: cotton, jute, or sisal (cargo)
CJS: Canadian Joint Staff; College of Jewish Studies
CJS: *Corpus Juris Secundum*
CJTF: Commander Joint Task Force
ck: cask; certified kosher; check; coke; cork
ck: *ceekay* (Spanish-American slang—cocaine)
Ck: chalk
CK: cyanogen chloride (poison gas)
C K: Cape Kennedy
ckb: cork base
ckbd: cork board
CKC: Canadian Kennel Club
CKCL: Chicago-Kent College of Law
ckd: completely knocked down
ckf: cork floor
ckfm: checking form
ckga: checking gage
CKIC: Chemical Kinetics Information Center (NBS)
CKMTA: Cape Kennedy Missile Test Area
ck os: countersink other side
ckpt: cockpit
cks: casks; checks
ckt: circuit
CKT: *Chung-Kuo Kung-ch'an Tang* (Chinese Communist Party)
ckt bd: circuit board
ckt bkr: circuit breaker
ckt cl: circuit closing
ck tp: check template
ck ts: countersink this side
ck vlv: check valve
ckw: clockwise
cl: carload; center line; centiliter; chest and left arm (cardiology); chloride; class; clavicle; clear; clearance; climb; clinic; close; closure; corpus luteum; critical list
cl.: *classis* (Latin—class or collection)
cl (CL): control leader (data processing)
CL: chlorine; chlorine gas
CL.: *Clericus* (Latin—cleric or clergyman)
c/l (C/L): carload lot; cash letter
CL: Capital Airlines; Cooperative League; Critical List; Light cruiser (2-letter naval symbol)
C-L: Canadair Limited (Division of General Dynamics)
C/L: craft loss (insurance)
C of L: Count(y) of Lippe
cla: center line average; communication link analyzer
CLA: California Library Association; Canadian Library Association; Canadian Lumbermen's Association; Catholic Library Association; College Language Association; Connecticut Library Association; Conservative Library Association
CLAA: anti-aircraft light cruiser (4-letter naval symbol)
CLA-ACB: Canadian Library Association—l'Association Canadienne des Bibliothéques
Clack: Clackmannan(shire)
cl ad: collet adapter
CLAH: Conference of Latin

American History
CLAIRA: Chalk Lime and Allied Industries Research Association
clam (CLAM): chemical low-altitude missile
clam.: chemical low-altitude missile
clamato: clam-and-tomato juice
Clamcatcher(s): New Jerseyite(s)
Clamgrabber(s): Washingtonian(s)
Clam State: New Jersey and Washington both have claimed this nickname
Clam Town: Norwalk, Connecticut
cland lit: clandestine literature (underground)
cland press: clandestine press
CLAO: Contact Lens Association of Opthalmologists
clar: clarification; clarify; clarinet
Clar: Clarence
Clare: Clara; Clarita
Clar(en): Clarendon
Claribel: Charlotte Alington-Barnard
Clarin: (pseudonym—Leopoldo Alas y Urena)
clark: combat launch and recovery kit
CLARNICO: Clark, Nichols, and Coombes (confectioners)
Clarrie: Clarice; Clarissa
clas: classification; classify; congenital localized absence of skin
c-l-a-s: crowd-lift-actuate-swing (tractor backhoe control)
CLAS: Chartered Land Agents Society
CLASB: Citizens League Against the Sonic Boom
CLASC: *Confederación Latinoamericana de Sindicalistas Cristianos* (Spanish—Latin American Confederation of Christian Trade Unionists)
clasn: classification
clasp. (CLASP): computer liftoff and staging program
CLASP: Client's Lifetime Advisory Service Program; Computer Language for Aeronautics and Space Programming; Computer Launch and Separation Problem
class.: classification
CLASS: Class Action Study and Survey; Close Air-Support System; Closed-Loop Accounting for Store Sales; Computer-based Laboratory for Automated School Systems; Current Literature Alerting Search Service
class A's: class-A narcotics (addictive drugs such as opium and its derivatives)
class B's: class-B narcotics almost non-addictive drugs such as codeine and nalline)
Classical: Prokofiev's Symphony No. 1
classif: classification
Classifier and Compiler Extraordinary: Dr Peter Mark Roget
class M's: class-M narcotics (non-addictive drugs)
class X's: class-X narcotics (drugs containing small amounts of narcotics such as cough syrups with non-narcotic and almost non-addictive codeine)
CLAT: Confederation of Latin American Teachers
Claude Lorraine: Claude Gellée of Lorraine
clav: clavecin; clavichord; clavicle
clavicemb: *clavicembalo* (Italian—clavichord)
claw.: clustered atomic warhead
clayie: playing marble made of clay and often coated with enamel paint
Clb: Caleb
CLB: Church Lads' Brigade
clbbb: complete left bundle branch block
c & lc: capital and lower case letters
CLC: Canadian Labour Congress; Canners League of California; Chiriqui Land Company; Cost of Living Council; task-fleet command cruiser (naval symbol)
CLCB: City of Liverpool College of Building; Committee of London Clearing Banks
CLCMD: Cleveland Contract Management District
CL & Co: Cammell Laird and Company (shipbuilders)
clcr: controlled letter contract reduction
CLCT: City of Liverpool College of Technology
cld: cancelled; chronic liver disease; chronic lung disease; cleared; colored; cooled; cost laid down
CLD: Central Library and Documentation
CLDAS: Clinical Laboratory Data Acquisition System
cldwn: cooldown
cldy: cloudy
CLE: Cleveland, Ohio (Hopkins Airport)
Clea: Cleopatra
CLEAN: Committee for Leaving the Environment of America Natural; Commonwealth Law Enforcement Assistance Network (Pennsylvania)
CLEAPSE: Consortium of Local Education Authorities for the Provision of Science Equipment
CLEAR: Center for Lake Erie Area Research; Civic Leaders for Ecological Action and Responsibility; Closed-Loop Evaluation and Reporting (system); County Law Enforcement Applied Regionally
clec: closed-loop ecological cycle
Clem: Clemens; Clement; Clementina; Clementine
CLEMARS: California Law-Enforcement Mutual-Aid Radio System
Clemte: Clemente
CLENE: Continuing Library Education Network and Exchange
cleo: clear language for expressing orders
Cleo: Cleopatra
CLEP: College-Level Education Program; College-Level Examination Program
cler: clerical
cleric.: clerical(s); clerical error; clericalism; clericality; clerically
CLETS: California Law Enforcement Telecommunications System
CLEU: Coordinated Law Enforcement Unit
Cleve: Cleveland
Cleve Orch: Cleveland Orchestra
CLEVPDis: Cleveland Procurement District (US Army)
CLEW: Chicago Law Enforcement Week
clf: capacitive loss factor
CLF: Church of the Larger Fellowship (Unitarian Universalist)
Clfs: Cliffs
clg: calling; ceiling; clearing
Clg: College
CLG: light guided-missile cruiser (3-letter symbol)
CLGA: Composers and Lyricists Guild of America
clgsfu: clear glazed structural facing units
clgsub: clear glazed structural unit base
cl gt: cloth gilt

CLGW: Cement, Lime and Gypsum Workers (union)
CLH: *Croix de la Légion d'Honneur* (French—Cross of the Legion of Honor)
CLHU: Computation Laboratory of Harvard University
cli: coin-level indicator; cost-of-living index
CLI: Cost-of-Living Index
CLIA: Clinical Laboratory Improvement Act
C-library: circulating library
Cliff: Clifford; Clifton
Clifton Webb: Webb Parmalee Hollenbeck
clim: climatic
climat: climatological; climatologist; climatology
clin: clinic; clinical; clinicial; clinometer
clink: (generic nickname—prison)—also the nickname for brothels and in London, where it originated in Clink Prison, also stands for the Southwark Fair depicted by Hogarth
clin path: clinical pathology
clin proc: clinical procedures
Clint: Clinton
Clinton's Big Ditch: Erie Canal advocated by Governor De Witt Clinton of New York
clip.: compiler language for information processing; contused, lacerated, incised, and punctured (wounds)
CLIP: Cancel Launch in Progress (USAF); Country Logistics Improvement Program (USAF)
clips.: clippings
clit: clitoral; clitoridectomy; clitoris
C. Litt.: Companion of Literature
clj: control joint
CLJ: *Cambridge Law Journal*
CLJC: Copiah-Lincoln Junior College
clk: clerk; clock
CLK: hunter-killer cruiser (naval symbol)
clkg: caulking
clkws: clockwise
cll: cholesterol lowering lipid; chronic lymphatic leukemia; chronic lymphocytic leukemia; circuit load logic
CLL: Chief of Legislative Liaison
cllo: *cuartillo* (Spanish—fourth of a real; pint)
Cllr: Councillor
clm: column; culumnar
c-lm: common-law marriage
CLM: Canadian Liberation Movement
CLMA: Cigarette Lighter Manufacturers Association; Contact Lens Manufacturers Association
CLML: *Current List of Medical Literature*
CLMS: Clinical Laboratory Monitoring System
cln: colon
Cln: Colón
clnc: clearance
CLNP: Crater Lake National Park (Oregon)
clnr: cleaner
CLNS: Cape Lookout National Seashore (North Carolina)
clnt: coolant
CLNTS: China Lake Naval Test Station
CLNWR: Crescent Lake National Wildlife Refuge (Nebraska)
clo: closet; cloth; clothing; cod liver oil
Clo: Callao
CLO: Cali, Colombia (Calipuerto airport); Citizens for Law and Order; Cornell Laboratory of Ornithology
CLOB: Composite Limit Order Book
clora: closed-form ray analysis
clos: closure
clousy: cloudy—lousy (weather)
clp: criminal law and procedure
CLP: Carnegie Library of Pittsburgh
CLPA: Common Law Procedure Acts
cl pal: cleft pallet
clpr: caliper
clr: clear; clearing; cooler
CLR: Central London Railway; Council on Library Research; Council on Library Resources
CLRB: Canada Labour Relations Board
clrm: classroom
clr test: chloride test
CLRU: Cambridge Language Research Unit
CLS: Certificate in Library Science
CLSA: Conservation Law Society of America
CLSC: Chautauqua Literary and Scientific Circle
clsd: closed
clsg: closing
CLSG: Contact Lens Study Group
clsl: chronic lymphosarcoma leukemia
CLSP: Cape Lookout State Park (Oregon)
clsr: closure
clst: clarinettist
clt: communications line terminals
CLT: Charlotte, North Carolina (airport)
CLT: *Canadian Law Times*
CLTA: Chinese Language Teachers Association
C Lt-Cdr: Communication Lieutenant-Commander
cltgl: climatological
cltgr: climatographer
CLU: Chartered Life Underwriter
Clubland: Pall Mall clubhouse section of London
clurt: come let us reason together (mediator's motto)
CLUS: continental limits United States
CLUSA: Cooperative League of the USA
Clydebank: Scotland's shipyard city on the River Clyde northwest of Glasgow
clv: clevis
Clv: Cleveland
Clw: Collingwood
clwg: clear wire glass
Cly: Clydebank
clz: copper, lead, or zinc (cargo)
cm: centimeter(s); circular mil; circular muscle; contrast media; costal margin; countermortar; mechanic (symbol)
cm (CM): command module
cm: *carat métrique* (French—metric carat); *Zentimeter* (German—centimeter)
c.m.: *cras mane* (Latin—tomorrow morning)
c/m: color modulation (tv); communications multiplexer; control and monitoring
c'm': come
c & m: cocaine-morphine
cm^2: square centimeter
cm^3: cubic centimeter
Cm: curium
CM: absolute coefficient of pitching moments (symbol); Clyde-Mallory (steamship line); mine layer (naval symbol)
CM: *Correo Maritimo* (Spanish—sea mail)—appears on flags of Spanish mail ships
C-M: Charente-Maritime
C.M.: central meridian; *Chirurgiae Magister* (Latin—Master of Surgery)
C/M: Curtis/Mathes
C of M: Certificate of Merit; Count(y) of Mark

CM4: Comet 4 jet airplane
cma: civil-military affairs
Cma: Camilla
CMA: California Maritime Academy; Canadian Medical Association; Candle Manufacturers Association; Casket Manufacturers Association; Certified Medical Assistant; Chocolate Manufacturers Association; Cigar Manufacturers Association; Cleveland Metal Abrasive (company); Clothespin Manufacturers of America; Colorado Mining Association; Compania Mexicana de Aviacion (Mexican Aviation Company)—often called Mexicana; Confederate Memorial Association; Court of Military Appeals; Crucible Manufacturers Association
CMAA: Cleveland Musical Arts Association
CMAAC: Certified Medical Assistant Administrative and Clinical
cmab: clothing maintenance allowance, basic
CMAC: Capital Military Assistance Command; Catholic Marriage Advisory Council
cmai: clothing maintenance allowance, initial
CMAL: Clothing Monetary Allowance List
CMAR: Can't Manage A Rifle
C/marca: Cundinamarca, Colombia
CMAS: Confédération Mondiale des Activités Subaquatiques (World Confederation of Subaquatic Activities); Council for Military Aircraft Standards
CMAT: Canadian Mathematics Achievement Test
cmb: carbolic methylene blue; chloromercuribenzoate
Cmb: Colombo
CMB: Chase Manhattan Bank; coastal motor boat, Colombo, Ceylon (airport); Combat Maneuver Battalion(s); Compagnie Maritime Belge (Royal Belgian Lloyd Line)
***CMB:** Cuyas manos beso* (Spanish—whose hands I kiss)—very respectfully yours
CMBI: Caribbean Marine Biological Institute
cmbt: combat
cmc: contact-making clock; coordinated manual control
cmc (CMC): carboxymethyl cellulose
CMc: coastal mine layer (naval symbol)
CMC: Canadian Music Council; Commandant of the Marine Corps; Commercial Metals Company
CMCC: Canadian Memorial Chiropractic College; Classified Matter Control Center
cm-cellulose: carboxymethyl cellulose
cmcr: continuous melting, casting, and rolling
CMCR: Compagnie Maritime des Chargeurs Réunis
cmd: command; common meter double
CMD: California Moderate Democrats; Contract Management District
cmdg: commanding
Cmdr: Commander
Cmdre: Commodore
Cmdt: Commandant
cmdty: commodity
CME: California Motor Express; Chicago Mercantile Exchange (formerly Chicago Butter and Egg Board); Courtesy Motorboat Examination (U.S. Coast Guard)
***CME:** Conférence Mondiale de l'Energie* (French—World Power Conference)
CMEA: Council for Mutual Economic Assistance (also called CEMA or COMECON or by its founder's Russian name *Soviet Ekonomicheskoi Vzaimopomoshchi–SEV*)
CMERI: Central Mechanical Engineering Research Institute (India)
cmet: coated metal
cmf: calcium-and-magnesium-free
CMF: Commonwealth Military Forces; Composite Medical Facility
CMFNZ: Chamber Music Federation of New Zealand
CMFRI: Central Marine Fisheries Research Institute
cmfsw: calcium-and-magnesium-free seawater
cmg: control-moment gyroscope
C.M.G.: Companion of the Order of St Michael and St George
CMGH: Cleveland Metropolitan General Hospital
CMH: Columbus, Ohio (airport); Congressional Medal of Honor
cmha: confidential, modified handling authorized
CMHA: Canadian Mental Health Association
CMHC: Central Mortgage and Housing Corporation; Community Mental Health Center(s)
CMHPA: Cloves Memorial Hall for the Performing Arts (Indianapolis)
cmi: carbohydrate metabolism index; cellular-mediated immune (response)
CMI: Can Manufacturers Institute; Christian Michelson Institute (for Science and Free Thought—Bergen, Norway); Comité Météorologique Internationale (International Meterological Committee); Command Maintenance Inspection (US Army); Commission Mixte Internationale (International Mixed Commission for Experience Relative to the Protection of Telecommunication Lines and Underground Cables)
***CMI:** Cornell Medical Index*
CMIA: Coal Mining Institute of America; Cultivated Mushroom Institute of America
cmid: cytomegalic inclusion disease
***CMIK:** Choson Minjujuui In'min Konghwaguk* (North Korea)
cmil: circular mil
c/min: cycles per minute
CMIU: Cigar Makers' International Union
CMJ: Church's Ministry among the Jews
cml: chemical; circuit micrologic; commercial; current mode logic
cml (CML): chronic myelocytic leukemia
CML: Central Music Library; Container Marine Lines
***CML:** Camara Municipal de Lisboa* (Portuguese—Lisbon Town Council)
CMLA: Canadian Music Library Association
CmlC: Chemical Corps
cml def: chemical defense
cmlops: chemical operations
CMLS: Cleveland-Marshall Law School
CM/LSCNP: Cradle Mountain/Lake Saint Clair National Park (Tasmania)
cmm: cubic millimeter(s); cutaneous malignant melanoma
CMM: Chief Machinist's Mate (USN); Commission for Maritime Meteorology (WMO)

CMMA: Concrete Mixer Manufacturers Association
CMMBE: Comissaño Militar Mista Brasil-Estados Unidos (Mixed Brazilian-American Military Commission)
cmmch: combat Mach change
cmme: carcinogenesis of chloromethyl-methyl ether
CMMM: Chase Manhattan Money Museum (New York City)
cmmnd: command(ing)
CMMP: Commodity Management Master Plan
CMMS: Columbia Mental Maturity Scale
cmn: commission; cystic medial necrosis
CMN: Common Market Nationals; Common Market Nations
cmn-aa: cystic medial necrosis of the ascending aorta
cmnce: commence
CMNH: Cleveland Museum of Natural History
CMNM: Capulin Mountain National Monument; Craters of the Moon National Monument
cmnr: commissioner
cmo: cardiac minute output; computer microfilm output
CMO: Chief Medical Officer; Contract Management Office(r)
cmp: corrugated metal pipe; cost of maintaining product
CMP: Catoctin Mountain Park (Maryland); Church Music Publishers; Controlled Materials Plan; Cornell Maritime Press; Corps of Military Police
cmpd: compound; compounded; compounding
cm pf: cumulative preference; cumulatve preferred (shares)
cmpld: compiled
cmpnt: component
CMPO: Calcutta Metropolitan Planning Organisation
cmps: centimeters per second
cmpt: component
cmptr: computer
cmr: cerebral metabolic rate; common-mode rejection
CMR: Communications Monitoring Report; Consolidated Mail Room; Contract Management Region
CMRA: Chemical Marketing Research Association
cmrg: cerebral metabolic rate of glucose
CMRL: Chamber of Mines and Research Laboratories
CMRNWR: Charles M. Russell National Wildlife Range (Montana)
cmro: cerebral metabolic rate of oxygen
cmr0_2: cerebral metabolic rate for oxygen
CMRO: County Milk Regulations Office(r)
cmrr: common mode rejection ratio
c.m.s.: *cras mane sumendus* (Latin—to be taken tomorrow morning)
cm/s: centimeters per second
CMS: California Museum of Science; Center for Measurement Science (George Washington University); Chicago Medical School; Chief Master Sergeant; Christian Medical Society; Church Missionary Society; College Music Society; Compagnie Maritime de la Seine; Consumers and Marketing Service; Contemporary Music Society
CM & SA: Canning Machinery and Supplies Association
CMSC: Central Missouri State College
CMSER: Commission on Marine Science, Engineering, and Resources
CMSG: Canadian Merchant Service Guild
CMSgt: Chief Master Sergeant
CMSI: California Museum of Science and Industry
CMS & I: California Museum of Science and Industry
cm/sm: command module/service module
CMSN: China Merchants Steam Navigation (company)
CMSTP & P: Chicago, Milwaukee, St Paul and Pacific (railroad)
cmt: comment
CMT: California Mastitis Test; California Motor Transport; Camden Marine Terminals; Current Medical Terminology; Current Mortuary Tables
CMTA: Chinese Musical and Theatrical Association
CMTC: Citizens Military Training Camp
CMTCU: Communications Message Traffic Control Unit
cmte: committee
cmu: central markup unit; chlorophenyldimethylurea
CMU: Central Michigan University
C-M U: Carnegie-Mellon University
cmv: cytomegalovirus
CM von W: Carl María von Weber
CMVPB: California Motor Vehicles Pollution Board
CMZ: Compagnie Maritime du Zaire
CMZS: Corresponding Member of the Zoological Society
cn: cannon; coordination number
c/n (C/N): credit note
c.n.: *cras nocte* (Latin—tomorrow night)
Cn: contract number; cumulonimbus
CN: absolute coefficient of yawing moments (aerodynamic symbol); Carl Nielsen; Central Airlines; Chinese Nationalist; Code Napoléon; Commonwealth Nations; compass north; Confederate Navy; cosine of the amplitude (mathematical symbol)
CN: Canadian National-Grand Trunk Railways
C & N: communication and navigation
C-de-N: Côtes-de-Nord
cna: code not allocated
CNA: Canadian Nuclear Association; Canadian Numismatic Association; Canadian Nurses Association; Center for Naval Analyses(Franklin Institute); Central News Agency(Nationalist China); Central Northern Airways; Chemical Notation Association; Chief of Naval Air; Chief of Naval Aviation
CNAA: Council for National Academic Awards
CNAC: China National Aviation Corporation
CNADS: Conference of National Armaments Directors
CNAN: Compagnie Navale Afrique du Nord
CNAS: Chief of Naval Air Services; Civil Navigation Aids System
CNATra: Chief of Naval Air Training
CNAV: Canadian Naval Auxiliary Vessel
CNC: Christopher Newport College
Cncl(r): Council(or)
CNCMH: Canadian National Committee for Mental Hygiene
cncr: concurrent
cnd: conduit

CND: Campaign for Nuclear Disarmament; Commission on Narcotic Drugs (UN)
***CND:** Code Names Dictionary*
cn di: combination die
cnds: condensate
cne: chronic nervous exhaustion
CNE: Canadian National Exhibition
CNEL: community noise equivalent level
Cnel: Coronel (Spanish—Colonel)
C'nelia: Cornelia
CNEN: Comisión Nacional de Energia Nuclear (National Nuclear Energy Commission)
CNEngO: Chief Naval Engineering Officer
CNEP: Cable Network Engineering Program (Bell)
CNES: Centre National d'Etudes Spatiales (National Center for Space Studies)
CNET: Chief of Naval Education and Training
***CNET:** Centre National d' Etude des Télécommunications* (Telecommunication National Study Center)
***CNEXO:** Centre pour d'Exploitationdes Ocèans* (Center for the Exploitation of the Oceans)
cnf: confine
CNF: Caribbean National Forest (Puerto Rico)
CNG: Connecticut Natural Gas
CNGA: California Natural Gas Association
CN-gas: cyanide gas (deadly poisonous and forbidden by the Geneva Convention)
CNGB: Chief, National Guard Bureau
CN-GT: Canadian National Railways-Grand Trunk Western
CNH: Community Nursing Home
cnhd: congenital nonspherocytic hemolytic disease
CNHI: Committee for National Health Insurance
CNHM: Chicago Natural History Museum (Field Museum of Natural History)
CNI: Chief of Naval Information
CNIB: Canadian National Institute for the Blind
CNIPA: Committee of National Institutes of Patent Agents
CNJ: Central of New Jersey (railroad)
cnl: cancel(lation); cardiolipin natural lecithin
CNL: Canadian National Library (Ottawa); Commonwealth National Library (Canberra)
CNLA: Council of National Library Associations
CNM: Cabrillo National Monument; Chief of Naval Material; Chiricahua National Monument; Colombo National Museum; Colorado National Monument
CN-M: Certified Nurse-Midwife
CNN: Campagnie de Navigation Nationale
CNNR: Caerlaverock National Nature Reserve (Scotland); Cairngorms National Nature Reserve (Scotland)
CNO: Chief of Naval Operations
CNOBO: Chief of Naval Operations Budget Office
C-note: $100 bill
CNP: Canyonlands National Park (Utah); Caramoan NP (Philippines); Cleveland NP (South Australia; Colonial NP (Virginia); Compagnie Navale des Pétroles; Compagnie de Navigation Paquet; Corbett NP (India); Cyril Northcote Parkinson
cn/pnl: contractor's panel
CNPP: Centre National de Prévention et de Protection
CNPS: California Native Plant Society
cnr: carrier-to-noise ratio; composite noise rating; corner
CNR: Canadian National Railway; Civil Nursing Reserve; Coleford Nature Reserve (South Africa)
***CNR:** Consiglio Nazionale delle Ricerche* (Italian—National Research Council)
CNRA: Curecanti National Recreation Area (Colorado)
CNRN: Consiglio Nazionale delle Ricerche (National Research Council)
CNRS: Centre National de la Recherche Scientifique (National Center for Scientific Research)
cnrt: concrete
cns: central nervous system
***c.n.s.:** cras nocte sumendus* (Latin—to be taken tomorrow night)
CNS: Chief of the Naval Staff; Congress of Neurological Surgeons
***CNS:** Chubu Nippon Shimbun* (Central Japan Newspaper)
CNSA: Carl Nielsen Society of America
cnsg: consolidated nuclear steam generator
Cnst Pty: Constitution Party
cnstr: canister
cnt: celestial navigation trainer (CNT)
CNT: Canadian National Telegraphs
***CNT:** Confederación* Nacional de Trabajo (Spanish—National Confederation of Labor)—anarcho-syndicalist trades-union confederation; *Conselho Nacional de Telecommunicaoes* (Portuguese—National Telecommunications Council)—government controlled radio and television for all Brazil
CNTB: Colombia National Tourist Board
CNTCA: Canadian National Railway—Transcanada Airlines
cntn: contain
Cntr: Centaur (space vehicle)
cntr: container; contribute; contribution
Cnut: King Canute II of Denmark and England
cnv: contingent negative variation
CNV: Cape Canaveral, Florida (tracking station)
CNVA: Committee for Non-Violent Action
cnvc: conveyance
cnvr: conveyor
cnvt: convict
C & NW: Chicago and North Western (railway)
CNWDI: Critical Nuclear Weapons Design Information
CNWR: Camas National Wildlife Refuge (Idaho); Chassahowitzka NWR (Florida); Chatauqua NWR (Illinois); Chincoteague NWR (Virginia); Columbia NWR (Washington)
CNYP: Central New York Power (corporation)
co: carbon monoxide; cardiac output; castor oil; cervicoaxial; cleanout; coenzyme; conscientious objector; convenience outlet; corneal opacity; crossover(s); cutoff; cutout
***co.:** compositus* (Latin—compound(ed))
c-o: cutoff
c/o: care of; carried over; cash order; complains of
***co:** compagno* (Italian—company)
Co: cobalt; Colombia; Colombi-

an; Colombiano; Columbia; Columbian; Company; County
C/o: complained of
***C^o*:** *Comisario* (Spanish—Commisariat)
Co^{60}: radioactive cobalt
CO: carbon monoxide; Cleveland Orchestra; Commanding Officer; conscientious objector; Continental Airlines (2-letter code)
C/O: cash order
C & O: Chesapeake & Ohio (railroad)
C-d'O: Côte-d'Or
C of O: Count(y) of Oldenburg
co 1mo: *canto primo* (Italian—first treble)
CO_2: carbon dioxide
coa: condition on admission
coA: coenzyme A
COA: Canadian Orthopedic Association; Change Order Account; Chattanooga Opera Association; Connecticut Opera Association; Cordova Airlines
COA: *Comunidad Oriental Africana* (Spanish—East African Community)
CO(A): Change Order (Aircraft)
C o A: Committee on Accreditation (ALA)
coac: clutter-operated anti-clutter receiver
Coad: Coadjutor
coag: coagulant; coagulate; coagulation
coag time: coagulation time
Coah: Coahuila (inhabitants—Coahuileños or Coahuilenses)
Coal.: Coalition
Coaley: Samuel Coleridge-Taylor
coalit govt: coalition government
coam: coaming; customer-owned-and-maintained equipment
coam equip: customer-owned-and-maintained equipment (data processing)
CO-AMP: Cost Optimization-Analysis of Maintenance Policy
coas: crewman optical alignment sight
COAS: Council of the Organization of American States
Coastal Eastern: East-Coast-of-the-United-States; English reflecting cultural influences
Coast Line: Atlantic Coast Line Railroad
coax: coaxial
c-o-b: close of business
COB: Change Order Board
Cobbler Poet: Hans Sachs of Nuremberg also known as Prince of the Meistersingers
cobh: carboxyhemoglobin
C & O-B & O: Chesapeake and Ohio-Baltimore & Ohio (merged railroads)
cobol: common business-oriented language
cobra. (COBRA): coolant boiling in rod arrays
COBSI: Committee on Biological Sciences Information
coc: cathodal opening clonus; cathodal opening contraction; cocaine; coccygeal; combination-type oral contraceptive
COC: Canadian Opera Company; Combat Operations Center
coca: *cocaina* (Spanish—cocaine)
C & O Canal: Chesapeake and Ohio Canal
coca-colon: coca-colonization; coca-colonize; coca-colonizer
Cocaine Capital: Bogotá, Colombia
COCAST: Council for Overseas Colleges of Art, Science, and Technology
cocb: crossed olivochochlear bundles
cocc: coccyx
coccy: coccidioidomycosis
coch.: *cochleare* (Latin—spoonful)
coch. ampl.: *cochleare amplum* (Latin—tablespoonful)
coch. infant.: *cochleare infantis* (Latin—teaspoonful)
coch. mag.: *cochleare magnum* (Latin—tablespoonful)
coch. med.: *cochleare medium* (Latin—dessertspoonful)
coch. parv.: *cochleare parvum* (Latin—teaspoonful)
Coch: Cochin
COCI: Council on Consumer Information
cock.: cockney (dialect of London's East End and waterfront residents who by their own definition are born within sound of the bells of the Church of Saint Mary-le-Bow—Bow bells)
Cockade City: Petersburg, Virginia
cocl: cathodal opening clonus
C & OC NM: Chesapeake and Ohio Canal National Monument
Coco: (French—Little Pet)
Coco Chanel: Gabrielle Bonheur Chanel
COCOM: Coordinating Committee for Export to Communist Area(s)
COCOSEER: Coordinating Committee on Slavic and East European Library Services
cocp: closed olivocochlear potential
coct.: *coctio* (Latin—boiling)
COCU: Churches of Christ Uniting
cod.: cause of death; chemical oxygen demand; cleanout door; codeine
c-o-d: cargo-on-deck
c.o.d.: cash-on-delivery
Co D: Costume Designer
COD: coding
CODA: Committee on Drugs and Alcohol
codac: coordination of operating data by automatic computer
CODAC: Community Organization for Drug Abuse Control
CODAF: Commission on Border Development and Friendship (U.S.–Mexican)
codag: combined diesel and gas (turbine machinery)
codan: carrier-operated device anti-noise
CODAP: Client-Oriented Data-Acquisition Process
CODASYL: Conference on Data Systems Languages
CODC: Canadian Oceanographic Data Center
codd: codices
Codder(s): Cape Codder(s)
CODE: Committee on Donor Enlistment
coded.: computer-oriented design of electronic devices
codel(s): congressional delegation(s)
Code N: Code Napoléon
codic: computer-directed communication(s)
codiphase: coherent digital-phased array system
cod. memb.: *codex membranacius* (Latin—book printed or written on skin or vellum)
codog: combined diesel or gas
CODOT: Classification of Occupations and Directory of Occupational Titles (UK)
CODSIA: Council of Defense Space Industries Association
coe: cab over engine (truck); close of escrow (realty)
COE: Corps of Engineers
CO(E): Change Order (Electronic)
COE: *Conséil Aécuméniques des Eglises* (French—World

Council of Churches)
coed: coeducation(al); girl or woman student
co-ed: co-editor
COEDS: Char Oil Energy Development Systems
COEES: Central Office Equipment Engineering System (Bell)
coef: coefficient
Coel: Coelenterata
COENCO: Committee for Environmental Conservation
COEPS: Cortically-Originating Extra-Pyramidal System
COESA: Committee on Extension of the Standard Atmosphere (United States)
coxsec: coexsecant
cof: cause of failure
coff: cofferdam
C of F: Chief of Finance
COFI: (Committee on Fisheries (FAO)
COFO: Council of Federated Organizations (CORE, NAACP, SCLC, SNCC)
COFPHE: Capital Outlay Fund for Public Higher Education
COFRC: Chevron Oil Field Research Company
cofron: copper iron (patent medicine mixture)
cog.: cognate
COG: Change Our Gender; Change Our Goal; Council of Governments
cogag: combined gas and gas
CoGARD: Coast Guard
cogita: computerized general I.Q. test(ing)
cogn: cognomen
cognit: cognition(al)(ly); cognitive(ly)
cogn w: cognate with
cogo: coordinate geometry
cog/prsl: cognizant personnel
COGS: Continuous Orbital Guidance System
COGSA: Carriage of Goods by Sea Act
cogtt: cortisone-primed oral glucose tolerance test
coh: cash-on-hand; coefficient of haze
COH: carbohydrate (generalized formula)
COHATA: Compagnie Haitienne des Transports Aériens
cohb: carboxyhemaglobin
Co Hd: coral head
coher: cohere(d); coherence; coherency; coherer; cohering; coherent(ly)
coho: coherent oscillator
COHO: Council of Health Organization
Cohoun: Colquhoun
COHSE: Confederation of Health Service Employees
COI: Central Office of Information; Coordinator of Information
***COI:** Comite Olimpico Internacional* (Spanish—International Olympic Committee)
COIC: Canadian Oceanographic Identification Center
CoID: Council of Industrial Design
coif: coiffure
COIMS: Council for International Organizations of Medical Sciences
coin.: coinage; counterinsurgency—anti-guerrilla warfare
COIN: Counterinsurgency
coin gold: 90% gold, 10% copper
coin-op: coin-operated
COINS: Cooperative Intelligence Network System
coin silver: 50 to 92.5% silver with balance of copper or other metals
co-intel: counterintelligence
COINTELPRO: Counterintelligence Program (FBI)
COIR: Commission on Intergroup Relations (NYC)
Çois: François
COIT: Central Office of the Industrial Tribunal (UK)
COIU: Congress of Independent Unions
COJ: Court of Justice
COJO: Conference of Jewish Organizations
coke: coca drink; cocaine
Coke: Coca Cola
col: colon; colonial; colonic; colonist; colonization; colonize; colony; color; coloring; colorist; colors; column
***col.:** colatus* (Latin—strained, as through a filter); *collum* (Latin—collar); *colon* (Latin—large intestine)
c-o-l (COL): cost of living
co-L co-latitude
Col: Colima; College; Cologne; Colombia; Colombiano; Colon; Colonel; Colossians, Epistle to the; Columbia; Columbian; Coronel
Col: Lucius Iunius Moderatus Columella (Roman writer on agriculture)
COL: Computer Oriented Language
cola.: cost-of-living allowance
***cola:** colonia* (Spanish—colony)
COLA: Committee on Latin America; Committee on Library Automation (ALA)
Col Alb: College of the Albermarle
***colat.:** colatus* (Latin—strained)
col bh: collision bulkhead
***col C:** col canto* (Italian—follow the voice)
COLC: Cost of Living Council
Col$: Colombian peso
cold.: chronic obstructive lung disease
COLDEMAR: Compañía Colombiana de Navegación Maritima
***colen.:** colentur* (Latin—let them be strained; strain them)
***Col Ency:** Columbia Encyclopedia*
coleop: coleoptera; coleopterist
***colet.:** coleatur* (Latin—let it be strained; strain it)
Colette: Sidonie Gabrielle Claudine de Jouvenal
colidar: coherent light detection and ranging
Colin: Nicholas
colingo: compile online and go (data processing)
coll: collect(or); collection; colloid(al); colloquial(ism)
Coll: College; Collegiate
collab: collaboration; collaborator
coll agc: collection agency
collat: collateral
collect.: collection; collective; collectively
***Coll Ency:** Colliers' Encyclopedia*
Collier-Macmillan: Collier-Macmillan Library Service
Collins: Wm Collins Sons & Co
Coll L: Collection Letter
Collodi: (pseudonym—Carlo Lorenzini)
colloq: colloquial(ism); colloquium
***coll'ott:** coll'ottava* (Italian—play in octaves; with the octave)
collr: collector
***collun.:** collunarium* (Latin—nose wash)
***collut.:** collutorium* (Latin—mouthwash)
coll vol: collective volume
colly: colliery
***collyr.:** collyrium* (Latin—eyewash)
colm: column
colo: colophon (printer's or publisher's device, symbol, or trademark)
Colo: Colorado; Coloradan
colog: cologarithm

colograph: color lithograph
Colom: Colombia; Colombian
Colonels: natives of Kentucky
coloph: colophon
coloreds: colored persons (South Africans of mixed blood)
col p: color page
COLS: Communications for On-Line Systems
Col-Sgt: Colour-Sergeant
Col Sym: Columbia Symphony
Colt: Colt revolver (invented by Samuel Colt of Hartford, Connecticut)
COLT: Council on Library Technology
Columbine: Colorado's state flower—the Rocky Mountain Columbine
Columbus: Cristóbal Colón (Spanish); Cristoforo Colombo (Italian)
com: comedy; comma; command; commercial; commission; committee; common; complement; compliment
com (COM): computer-output microfilm(ing)
com.: *commemoratio* (Latin—commemoration)
Com: Comoro Islands
COM: Chief Operations Manager; Council of Ministers
COMA: Coke Oven Managers' Association
COMACH: *Confederación Marítima de Chile* (Spanish—Maritime Confederation of Chile)
COMAIRCENT: Commander, Allied Air Forces, Central Europe
COMAIRCENTLANT: Air Commander, Central Atlantic
COMAIRCHAN: Maritime Air Commander, Channel
COMAIRESTLANT: Air Commander, Eastern Atlantic
COMAIRLANT: Commander, Air Force, Atlantic
COMAIRNORLANT: Air Commander, Northern Atlantic
COMAIRNORTH: Commander, Allied Air Forces, Northern Europe
COMAIRSOUTH: Commander, Allied Air Forces, Southern Europe
Comalco: Commonwealth Aluminum Company (Australia)
COMANSEC: Computation and Analysis Section (Canadian Defense Research Board)
COMANTDEFCOM: Commander, United States Antilles Defense Command
COMARC: Cooperative Machine Readable Cataloging
COMART: Commander, Marine Air Reserve Training
comat: computer-assisted training
COMATS: Commander Military Air Transport Service
comb.: combat; combination; combine; combustion
COMBALTAP: Allied Command Baltic Approaches (NATO)
combi: combination
COMBISLANT: Commander, Bay of Biscay, Atlantic
combo: combination (of musicians, or of a safe)
COMBO: Combined Arts of San Diego
COMBQUARFOR: Combined Quarantine Force
Com Brit: *Comunidad Británica* (Spanish—British Commonwealth of Nations)—Great Britain and former colonies
combs.: combinations
combu: combustion
COMCANLANT: Commander, Canadian Atlantic
COMCENTLANT: Commander, Central Atlantic
ComCm: communications counter-measures and deception
COMCRUDESFLOT: Commander Cruiser-Destroyer Flotilla
COMCRUDESPAC: Commander Cruisers and Destroyers in the Pacific (USN)
COMCRULANT: Commander, Cruisers, Atlantic
comd: command
COMDEV: Commonwealth Development
comdg: commanding
Comdr: Commander
Comdt: Commandant
COME: Chief Ordnance Mechanical Engineer
comeas: countermeasures
COMECON: Council of Mutual Economic Assistance (of communist nations)
COMEINDORS: Composite Mechanized and Document Retrieval System
Comenius: John Amos Komensky
Com Err: *Comedy of Errors*
comet.: computer operated management evaluation technique
COMET: Committee for Middle East Trade
COMEXCO: Committee for Exploitation of the Oceans
Com Fran: *Comunidad Francesa* (Spanish-French Community of Nations)—France and former colonies
comfy: comfortable
Com-Gen: Commissary-General
COMIBOL: Corporación Minera de Bolivia (Bolivian Mining Corporation)
COMICEDEFOR: Commander, United States Iceland Defense Force
COMINCH: Commander-in-Chief, United States Fleet
Cominform: Communist Information Bureau (latter-day name for the Comintern)
comint: communications intelligence
Comintern: Communist International; Cominform
Com Int Sec: Committee on Internal Security (formerly House Committee on Un-American Activities—HUAC)
Com Isl: Comoro Islands
comis^{o}: *comisario* (Spanish—commissary; delegate; deputy; manager; police inspector)
comkd: completely knocked down
coml: commercial
COMLANDCENT: Commander, Allied Land Forces; Central Europe
COMLANDEAST: Commander, Allied Land Forces Southeastern Europe
COMLANDMARK: Commander, Allied Land Forces, Denmark
COMLANDNORWAY: Commander, Allied Land Forces, Norway
COMLANDSOUTH: Commander, Allied Land Forces, Southern Europe
COMLOGNET: Combat Logistics Network
comm: commerce; commercial; commission; committee; commonwealth; commune; communication; commutator
comm.: *commune* (Latin—all the people; the community)
Comm.: Commodore
Com Mat Cen: Communication Materials Center (Columbia University)
commd: command(ing); commissioned
commdg: commanding
Commdr: Commander
Commdt: Commandant
commem: commemoration; commemorative
Commerce: Department of Com-

merce
commfu: complete and utterly monumental foulup
commi: communism; communist
commie: commissary; communist
commies: communists
commn: commission
Commiss: Commissary
commo: communications
commod: commodity
Commoner: The Commoner—William Jennings Bryan
Commonwealth: free association of the United Kingdom, Australia, Bahamas, Bangladesh, Barbados, Botswana, Canada, Cyprus, Ghana, Grenada, Guyana, Fiji, India, Jamaica, Kenya, Lesotho, Malawi, Malaysia, Malta, Mauritius, Nauru, New Zealand, Nigeria, Sierra Leone, Singapore, Sri Lanka, Swaziland, Tanzania, The Gambia, Tonga, Trinidad and Tobago, Uganda, Western Samoa, Zambia, and their dependent territories
Commr: Commissioner
commun: communication
commun dis: communicable disease
commy: commissariat; commissary; communist
com: commission; communication(s)
ComNAB: Commander, Naval Air Bases
COMNAVCENT: Commander, Allied Naval Forces, Central Europe
COMNAVFORCESMARIANAS: Commander, Naval Forces, Marianas Islands
COMNAVFORJAPAN: Commander, Naval Forces, Japan
COMNAVNORTH: Commander, Allied Naval Forces, Northern Europe
COMNAVSUPPACT: Commander, Naval Support Activity
COMNORASDEFLANT: Commander, North American Anti-Submarine Defense Force, Atlantic
COMNORLANT: Commander, Northern Atlantic
comnr: commissioner
Como: Commodore; Comodoro Rivadavia (Argentine naval hero and seaport name); Comoro
comp a: compressed air
COMPAC: Commonwealth Pacific Telephone Cable (linking Australia, New Zealand, and Pacific Ocean islands with the rest of the world)
COMPACT: Computator Planning and Control Technique
compand: compress to expand (radio communication term describing compression followed by expansion)
compar: comparative
compare.: computerized performance and analysis response evaluator; console for optical measurement and precise analysis of radiation from electronics
COMPASS: Comprehensive Assembly System
comp case: compensation case
Comp Curr: Comptroller of the Currency
compd: compound
compdes: compensator design; competitive design
compen: compensate; compensation; compensatory
compend: compendious; compendium
***Compendex:** Computerized Engineering Index*
compf: composition floor
Comp Gen: Comptroller General
compl: complaint; complete; compilation; compiled
***Compl:** A Lover's Complaint*
complic: complications
complt: complaintant; complaint
comp mar: companionate marriage
COMPMR: Commander, Pacific Missile Range
compn: composition
compo: compensation; component; composer; composite; composition; compositor
compool: common pool
compos: components; composers; composites; compositions; compositors
compound A: 11-dehydrocorticosterone
compound B: corticosterone
compound E: cortisone
compound F: cortisol
compound S: 11-deoxycortisol
compr: compressor
compreg: compressed-impregnated (wood)
comp(s): complimentary ticket(s)
compt: catecholomethyltransferase; compartment; comptroller
Compt: Comptroller
***Comptes Rend.:** Comptes rendus de l'Académie des Sciences* (Proceedings of the Academy of Science)
compu: computable; computability; computation(al); computer; computerization; computerize
comput: computer
computes.: computers
computime: computer-computed time
Comr: Commissioner
COMRAC: Combat Radius Capability (DoD)
com rcm: command reconnaissance
COMS: College of Osteopathic Medicine and Surgery (Des Moines)
comsat(s): communications satellite(s)
Comsat: Communications Satellite (corporation)
ComSeaFron: Commander Sea Frontier (USN)
comsec: communications security
COMSER: Commission on Marine Science and Engineering Research
comsn: commission
comsoal: computer method of sequencing operations for assembly lines
comstock: comstockery
COMSTRIKFLTLANT: Commander, Striking Fleet Atlantic (USN)
COMSTRIKFORSOUTH: Commander, Naval Striking and Forces Support, Southern Europe
COMSTS: Commander Military Sea Transport Service
COMSUBEASTLANT: Commander, Submarine Force, Eastern Atlantic
COMSUBPAC: Commander, Submarines, Pacific
comsy: commissary
comsymp: communist sympathizer
comt: comptroller
comt (COMT): catechol-O-methyltransferase
comte: committee
com tech: communications technician
COMUSAFSO: Commander, United States Air Forces, Southern Command
COMUSFORAZ: Commander, U.S. Forces, Azores
COMUSJAPAN: Commander, U.S. Forces, Japan
COMUSKOREA: Commander, U.S. Forces, Korea
COMUSMACV: Commander

United States Military Assistance Command Vietnam
COMUSTDC: Commander, U.S. Taiwan Defense Command
Com Ver: Common Version (of the Bible)
com wc: command weapon carrier
Comy-Gen: Commissary-General
Com Z: Communications Zone
con: confidence (game; man; men); conned; conning; consolidated; control; conversation; convict
con.: *contra* (Latin—against)
con8va.: *con ottava* (Italian—with octaves)
Con: Concord; Conservative
CON: Conservative; Conservative Party
CONAC: Continental Air Command
CONAD: Continental Air Defense Command
CONADE: *Consejo Nacional de Desarrollo* (Spanish—National Development Council)
ConArC: Continental Army Command
conc: concentrate; concentration; concentric; concrete
concb: concrete block
conc c: concrete ceiling
concd: concentrated; concerned
concentr: concentrate(d)
Concertg: *Concertgebouworkest* (Dutch—Concertgebouw Orchestra)—Amsterdam's celebrated symphony orchestra
conc clg: concrete ceiling
conc f: concrete floor
conc fl: concrete floor
concg: concentrating
conch.: conchology
Concha: Maria de la Concepción
conchie: conscientious objector
concis.: *concisus* (Latin—cut)
concn: concentration
Concordance Cruden: Alexander Cruden—compiler of the *Complete Concordance of the Holy Scriptures* published in 1737
Concorde: Anglo-French supersonic airplane attaining normal cruising speeds of 1300 miles per hour
Con Cpt: Constructor Captain
concr: concrete
cond: condenser; condition; conductivity; conductor
condit: conditional
condiv: continental divide
condo(s): condominium(s)
condr: conductor
cond ref: conditioned reflex
cond resp: conditioned response
conductimetric: conductance + metric
CONE: Collectors of Numismatic Errors
CONEA: Confederation of National Educational Associations
Con Ed: Consolidated Edison (gas and electric light company)
conelrad: control of electromagnetic radiation
CONESCAL: *Centro Regional de Construcciones Escolares para America Latina* (Regional Center for Latin American Construction Students)
con esp: *con espressione* (Italian—with expression)
co-netic: high-permeability nonshock-sensitive (alloy developed for maximum attenuation at low flux density)
conex (CONEX): connection(s)
Coney: Coney Island
conf: confer; conference; confidential
conf.: *confer* (Latin—compare)
Conf: Confucian; Confucius
confab: confabulation; confabulate
confec.: *confectio* (Latin—confection)
Confed: Confederate
confer.: conference
Confederacy: Confederate States of America (Virginia, North and South Carolina, Georgia, Florida, Alabama, Mississippi, Louisiana, Texas, Arkansas, Tennessee)—and temporarily in Kentucky and Missouri
Confederate Raider: Rear Admiral Raphael Semmes, CSN
Confederation Province: Prince Edward Island
confi: confidant(e); confidence; confidential
confid: confidential
confr: confectioner
cong: congress(ional)
cong.: *congius* (Latin—gallon)
Cong: Congress
congal: *(cuarto) con gal* (Mexican-American—(room) with girl)—house of prostitution
con game: confidence game; confidence trick(ery)
Cong Christ: Congregational Christians
congen: congenital
Cong Fr: Congolese franc
Congl: Congregational
Cong Orat: Congregation of the Oratory
Congrats: congratulations
Cong Rec: *Congressional Record*
Congreg: Congregationalist
Cong U: Congregational Union (England and Wales)
CONGU: Council of National Golf Unions
conics: conic sections
conj: conjunction
Con Lt: Constructor Lieutenant
Con Lt-Cdr: Constructor Lieutenant-Commander
con man: confidence man; swindler
conn: connection; connective; connector
Conn: Connecticut; Connecticuter
CONN: Connellan Airways
CONNECT: Connecticut On-Line Enforcement Communication and Teleprocessing (computerized criminal file)
Connection City: Amsterdam, Netherlands or Marseilles, France (both European import-export stops in the hard-drug traffic from the Far East to Canada and the United States)
Connie: Conrad; Constance; Consuela; Cornelia; Cornelius
Connie Mack: Cornelius McGillicuddy
Conn Turn: Connecticut Turnpike
Conny: Constance
conobjtr: conscientious objector
CONOCO: Continental Oil Company
Conqueror of Suez: Ferdinand de Lesseps of Suez Canal fame
Conquering Lion of Judah and King of Kings: Emperor Haile Selassie of Ethiopia
Conquerors of Yellow Fever: Walter Reed and his colleagues Aristides Agramonte, James Carroll, and Jesse Lazear
Conr: Conrad
ConRail: Consolidated Rail Corporation (government-sponsored railroads including the Ann Arbor, Central Railroad of New Jersey, Erie-Lackawanna, Lehigh and Hudson River, Lehigh Valley, Penn Central, Reading)
con rod: connecting rod
cons: consider; consist
con(s): convict(s)
cons.: *conserva* (Latin—a preserve)

Cons: Conservative
CONSCIENCE: Committee on National Student Citizenship in Every National Case of Emergency
con sect: conic section
Cons Eng: Consulting Engineer
CONSER: CONversion of SERials (Council on Library Resources project)
conserv: conservation; conservationist; conservatoire; conservatory
Conserv: Conservatoire; Conservatory
cons. et prud.: *consilio et prudentia* (Latin—by counsel and prudence)
Cons Gen: Consul General
consgt: consignment
conshelf: continental shelf
Consc^{o}: *Consejo* (Spanish—Council)
consid: consideration
Con S-Lt: Constructor Sub-Lieutenant
consol: consolidated
consols: consolidated annuities
CONSORT: Conversation System with On-Line Remote Terminals
consperg.: *consperge* (Latin—dust; sprinkle)
conspic: conspicuous
const: constitution; constitutional; construction; constructor
Const: Constable; Constitution; Constructor
Const: *Constitution* (of the United States)
constab: constabulary
Constan: Constantine; Constantinople (Istanbul)
Constantia: Judith Sargent Murray
constit: constituent(s); constitution(al)
Constitution State: Connecticut's official nickname honoring its charter oak constitution of 1639
constn: construction
constr: construction; constructor
Const US: Constitution of the United States
consult.: consultant
consv: conservation; conserve
cont: contact; content(s); continent(al); continue(d); contract(or); control(ler)
cont.: *contra* (Latin—against); *contusus* (Latin—bruised; contused)
Cont: Continent; Continental
contag: contagious
contam: contaminant; contaminate; contamination
CONTAM: Committee on Nationwide Television Audience Measurement
contax: consumers and taxpayers
contbg: contributing
cont. bon. mor.: *contra bonos mores* (Latin—contrary to good manners)
contd: contained; continued
contemp: contemporary
contempo: contemporary
Contemporary Cassandra: Dorothy Thompson
conter.: *contere* (Latin—rub together)
conter US: conterminous United States (forty-eight states having common boundaries)
Cont Eur: Continental Europe
Cont Eur & Br I: Continental Europe and British Isles
contg: containing
Cont HH: continental range of ports from Havre to Hamburg
cont hp: continental horsepower
contig US: contiguous United States (fifty states having close proximity)
contin: continental; continuous
contin: *continuo* (Italian—continuous); *continuetur* (Latin—let it be continued)
Continental Nation: Australia
contin US: continental United States (Alaska plus the forty-eight conterminous states occupying much of the North American continent)
contl: continental
contr: contracted; contraction; contractor
contra: against; contra-indicated
contrail: condensation trail
contralat: contralateral
contran: control translator
contraprop: contra + propeller
contra(s): contraceptive(s)
contr. bon. mor.: *contra bonos mores* (Latin—contrary to good manners)
cont. rem.: *continuetur remedia* (Latin—let the remedy be continued)
contrib: contribution; contributor
contrit.: *contritus* (Latin—broken; ground; macerated)
CONTU: Commission on New Technological Uses of Copyrighted Works (Library of Congress)
contus.: *contusus* (Latin—bruised; contused)
cont w: continuous window
conurb(s): conurbation(s)
Con US (CONUS): Continental United States
CONUS Intel: Continental United States Intelligence (USA)
conv: convalescent; convention; conventional
Convair 600: Convair-Liner powered by Rolls-Royce turboprop engines
convce: conveyance
conv encl: convector enclosure
Convis Bur: Convention and Visitor's Bureau
convl: conventional
convn: convenient
convt: convert(ible)
conv^{te}: *conveniente* (Spanish—convenient)
CONWR: Crab Orchard National Wildlife Refuge (Illinois)
Coo: *Coo blimey* (Cockney contraction—God blind me)
COO: Chief Ordnance Officer
cooc: contact with oil or other cargo
COOH: (carboxyl group found in all organic acids)
cook.: cookery
Cooks: Cook Islanders; Cook Islands; Cook's Tours (Thomas Cook and Son, Ltd)
cool.: coolant
coon(s): coonhound(s)—contraction of racoon hounds
'coon(s): racoon(s)
coop.: cooperation
co-op: cooperative
Coop: Cooper
Co-op L: Cooperative League
COOPLAN: Continuity of Operations Plan (USN)
Co-op U: Co-operative Union
coord: coordinate; coordination; coordinator
COORS: Communications Outage Restoration Section
COOS: Chemical Orbit-to-Orbit Shuttle (NASA)
cop: capillary osmotic pressure; casing operating pressure; copper; copyright; customer owned property; policeman (slang)
c-o-p: change of plea
Cop: Copernican; Coptic
Cop: *Copenhague* (French, Portuguese, Spanish—Copenhagen)
COP: City of Prineville (railroad); Combat Outpost; Commissary Operating Program; Continuity of Operations Plan
Copa: Copacabana
COPA: Compañía Panameña de Aviacion

COPANT: *Comisión Panamericana de Normas Tecnicas* (Panamerican Commission for Technical Standards)
COPARS: Contractor-Operated Parts Stores (DoD)
copd: chronic obstructive pulmonary disease; coppered
COPDAF: Continuity of Operations Plan—Department of the Air Force
cope: chronic obstructive pulmonary emphysema
COPE: Committee for Original People's Entitlement (Canadian Eskimo's claim to Canadian land); Committee on Political Education (AFL-CIO); Congress on Optimum Population and Environment; Council on Population and Environment
COPEI: *Comité Organizador del Partido Electoral Independiente* (Spanish—Organization Committee of the Independent Electoral Party)—Venezuela's Social Christian Party
Copen: Copenhagen
Copernicus: Latinized name of the Polish astronomer Nikolaus Kopernicki
COPH: Congress of Organizations of the Physically Handicapped
copo: copolymer
copp: cobaltiprotoporphyrin
Copp: Copperplate
COPP: Conservation Organization Protesting Pollution
copperas: ferrous sulfate; green vitriol
Coppernose: Henry the VIII whose portrait exhibited a copper-colored nose on the so-called silver coins minted during his reign
copper pyrites: chalcopyrite (copper iron sulfide)
Copper State: Arizona's old nickname
COPPS: Committee on Power Plant Siting (Nat Acad Engineering)
COPR: Critical Officer Personnel Requirement (USAF)
cops: coppers; policemen (slang)
Copt: Coptic
copter(s): helicopter(s)
co-ptr: co-partner
COPUL: Council of Prairie University Libraries
copu: copulate; copulation; copulatory
copy.: copyright
coq.: *coque* (Latin—boil)
co Q: coenzyme Q
coq. in s.a.: *coque in sufficiente aqua* (Latin—boil in sufficient water)
coq. s.a.: *coque secundum artem* (Latin—boil correctly)
coq. sim.: *coque simul* (Latin—boil together)
cor: contactor, running; corner; cornet; correction
cor: *corno* (Italian—horn)
cor.: *corpus* (Latin—body)
Cor: Corinthians; Corona; Coronado; Coroner; Corsica; Coruña
Cor: *Corea* (Portuguese or Spanish—Korea)
COR: *Comisión(es) de Orientación Revolucionaria* (Spanish—Revolutionary Orientation Committee(s)—Cuba
cora: conditioned orientation reflex audiometry
cor bd: corner bead
Corbu: Le Corbusier (nickname of Edouard Jeanneret-Gris meaning the crow)
corbfus: copy of reply to be furnished us
Corc: Cornell computing (language)
Cor Chr Col: Corpus Christi College—Cambridge
CORCO: Commonwealth Oil Refining Company (Puerto Rico)
cord.: computer on-line devices
cord.: *cordillera* (Spanish—mountain range)
Cord: Cordelia; Córdoba
C of Ord: Chief of Ordnance
CORD: Commissioned Officer(s) Residency Deferment
Cordilleras: Cordillera Mountains of the Americas
CORDIPLAN: *Oficina Central de Coordinación y Planificación* (Spanish—Central Office of Coordination and Planning)
cordpo: correlated radar data printout
cords.: corduroy pants; corduroy trousers
CORDS: Civil Operations and Revolutionary Development Support
CORE: Competitive Operational Readiness Evaluation (Air Force); Congress of Racial Equality
corfam: (computer-devised word— not an acronym—microporous artificial leather)
corflu: correction fluid
CORG: Combat Operations Research Group
CORGI: Confederation for Registration of Gas Installers
corin: corinthian
Coriol: *Coriolanus*
CORL: Canadian Operations Research Society
cormant: cormorant
Cor Mem: Corresponding Member
Corn: Cornelius; Cornish; Cornwall
Corn Belt: midwestern United States where bumper corn crops are produced in Illinois, Indiana, Iowa, and Nebraska
Corncracker(s): Kentuckian(s)
Corncracker State: Kentucky
Cornell Maritime: Cornell Maritime Press
Corner House: Central Mining and Finance Corporation (South Africa)
Corney: Cornelia; Cornelius
Cornhusker(s): Nebraskan(s)
Cornhusker State: Nebraska's official nickname
Cornie: Cornelia; Cornelio; Cornelis; Cornelisz; Corneliu; Cornelius; Cornewall; Cornwall; Cornwallis
Corning Mus: Corning Museum of Glass
Cornish Riviera: English Riviera extending from Falmouth to the Isles of Scilly
Corns: Corn Islands in the Caribbean
Cornubian Shore: Cornwall, England
coroll: corollary
coron: coronary
Coron: Convair 990 Coronado (aircraft)
Coronation: Mozart's Mass in C or his Piano Concerto in D major (K 537)
Corp: Corporation
Corp Coll: Corpus Christi College—Oxford
Corpl: Corporal
Corpn: Corporation
CORPOANDES: *Corporación de los Andes* (Spanish—Andes Corporation)
Corporal John: early nickname of John Churchill who later became the first Duke of Marlborough; known to the Spaniards as Mambrú
corppin: corporeal pin (tuberculin testing)
corr: correction; correspondence; corrosion; corrugate
corr: *corregido* (Spanish—corrected); *corriage* (French—

corrected)
Corr: *Corriere della Sera* (Italian—Daily Courier)—Milan's leading newspaper
CORRA: Combined Overseas Rehabilitation Relief Appeal
corr case: corrugated case
Corregio: Antonio Allegri
correl: correlative
corres: correspondence; correspondent; corresponding
corresp: corresponding
Corridor State: New Jersey—serving as a corridor between New York and Pennsylvania
corrig: corrigenda
Corr Memb: Corresponding Member
corros: corrosive
corrosive sublimate: mercuric chloride
corr^{te}: *corriente* (Spanish—current month)
corrupt.: corruption
Cors: Corners; Corsica; Corsican
CORS: Canadian Operational Research Society
Cor Sec: Corresponding Secretary
Corsican Ogre: one of Napoleon's many nicknames
cort: cortex; cortical
cort.: *cortex* (Latin—bark)
corundolite: emery
corundum: aluminum oxide
CORT: Council On Radio and Television
Cory: Cornelia
cos: cash-on-shipment; contactor, starting; cosine; cosmic; cosmogany; cosmography; cosmology; cosmopolitan
co's: career officers
Cos: Consul; Counties
Cos: *Kosinus* (German—cosine)
COS: Canadian Ophthalmological Society; Chief of Section; Colorado Springs, Colorado (airport); Czechoslovak Ocean Shipping
cosa: combat operational support aircraft
co sa: *come sopra* (Italian—as above)
cosag: combined steam and gas (turbine machinery)
cosa nostra: (Italian—our thing)—nickname for international criminal syndicate network
COSA NOSTRA: Computer-Oriented System And Newly Organized Storage-To-Retrieval Apparatus
cosar: compression scanning-array radar
COSATI: Committee on Scientific and Technical Information (Federal Council for Science and Technology)
COSBA: Computer Services and Bureaus Association
COSD: Council of Organizations Serving the Deaf
Cos de Mar: *Costa de Marfil* (Spanish—Ivory Coast)
cosec: cosecant
COSEC: Coordinating Secretariat of National Unions of Students
COSFPS: Commons, Open Spaces, Footpaths Preservation Society
cosh: hyperbolic cosine (symbol)
COSI: Committee on Scientific Information
Cosie: Kathleen
COSINE: Committee on Computer Science in Electrical Engineering Education
COSIP: College Science Improvement Program
COSIRA: Council for Small Industries in Rural Areas
Co^{60}: radioactive cobalt
cosm: cosmetic; cosmetics; cosmetologist; cosmetology
COSMD: Combined Operations Signals Maintenance Department (Division)
COSMEP: Committee of Small Magazine Editors and Publishers
COSMIC: Computer Programmes Information Center (Univ of Georgia)
cosmo: cosmoline; cosmopolitan
cosmog: cosmogony; cosmographical; cosmography
cosmograph(s): composite photograph(s)
Cosmopolis of the Heartland: Kansas City
COSMOS: Coast Survey Marine Observation Station
co so: *come sopra* (Italian–as above)
COSPAR: Committee on Space Research (International Council of Scientific Unions)
COSPUP: Committee on Science and Public Policy (National Academy of Sciences)
cosr: cutoff shear
COSR: Committee on Space Research
coss.: *consules* (Latin—consuls)
COSSAC: Chief of Staff to the Supreme Allied Commander
cost.: contaminated oil settling tank; costume
COST: Cost-Oriented Systems Technique
costa: (Italian, Portuguese, Spanish—coast)
COSTEP: Commissioned Officer Student Training and Extern Program
coster: costermonger
COSTS: Committee on Sane Telephone Service
COSW: Citizen's Organization for a Sane World
COSY: Checkout Operating System
cot.: cathodal opening tetanus; cotangent; cotter; cotton
COT: Consecutive Overseas Tour
COTA: confirming telephone or message authority
COTAL: Confederación de Organizaciones Turísticas de la América Latina (Confederation of Touristic Organizations of Latin America)
CotB: Commonwealth of the Bahamas
COTC: Canadian Officers' Training Corps; Canadian Overseas Telecommunications Corporation
cote: cathodal opening tetanus
coth: hyperbolic cotangent (symbol)
cotics: narcotics
Coto: Cotopaxi
CotP: Captain of the Port
COTPAL: *Comité Tecnico Permanente sobre Asuntos Laborales* (Spanish—Permanent Technical Committee for Labor Matters)
COTR: Contracting Officers' Technical Representative
COTRANS: Coordinated Transfer Application System
cots.: cottages
'cot(s): apricot(s)
Cotswolds: Cotswold Hills of south-central England
COTT: Central Organization for Technical Training
Cotton Belt: cotton-growing areas of the southern United States; also known as the Cotton Kingdom
Cotton State: Alabama's nickname
Cottonwood City: Leavenworth, Kansas
couch: couchant
couldn't: could not
Coun: Council; Councillor; Counsellor; County
Count Basie: William Basie
COUP: Congress of Unrepre-

sented People
cour: *courant* (French—current)
Court: Courtenay; Courtland; Courtney
Cousin Jack: a Cornishman; a Cornish miner
Cousin Jenny: Cornish girl or woman
cov: concentrated oil of vitriol; cutout valve; cover
c-o v: cross-over value
Cov: Covenant
COVE: Citizens Opposed to the Violation of the Environment
covers.: coversed sine
covff: coverings, facing, or floor (cargo)
cov pl: coverplate
COWAR: Committee on Water Research
cowl.: cowling
Cowles: Cowles Education Corporation
COWRR: Committee on Water Resources Research
Cox: Coxwain
cox'n: coxswain (pronounced as contracted)
Coy: Company
Coyte: Coyte Lines
COYOTE: Call Off Your Old Tired Ethics (underworld organization urging legalization of just about every evil)
Coyote Cowboy: Pecos Bill
Coyote(s): South Dakotan(s)
Coyote State: South Dakota's official nickname
coz: cousin (colloquial contraction)
cozi: communication zone (indicator(s))
cp: camp; candlepower; capillary pressure; center of pressure; cerebral palsy; cesspool; chemically pure; chloropurine; chloroquinine and primaquine; chronic pyelonephritis; claw plate; closing pressure; cochlear potential; code of practice; cold-punch(ed); combination product; combining power; command post (CP); compare; compound; compressed; concrete-piercing; constant pressure; cor pulmonale; creatine phosphate
c/p: change package; control panel
c & p: carriage and packing
cP: polar continental air
cp (CP): carotid pulse; construction permit
Cp: Compline
CP: Caminhos de ferro Portuguese (Portuguese Railways); Canadian Press (news agency); cerebral palsy; charter party; chemically pure; Communist Party; Conservative Party; Constitution Party; copilot; Country Party
C-P: Colgate-Palmolive
C of P: Captain of the Port
CP: Crescendo Publishers
C & P: Compensation and Pension
cpa: closest point of approach; cost planning and appraisal
CPA: Canadian Pacific Airlines; Canaveral Port Authority; Cathay Pacific Airways; Certified Public Accountant; Civilian Production Administration; Consumer Protection Agency
CPA: *Community Planning Act*
CPAA: *Current Physics Advance Abstracts*
CPAB: California Prune Advisory Board
cpaf: cost plus award fee
CPAG: Collision Prevention Advisory Group
$\mathbf{C_{pah}}$**:** para-aminohippurate clearance
CPAI: Canvas Products Association International
CP Air: Canadian Pacific Air
C Pal: Crystal Palace
CPAM: Committee of Purchasers of Aircraft Material
CPAO: Country Public Affairs Office(r)
cpap: continuous positive airway pressure
cpb: cardiopulmonary bypass; casual payments book; cetyl pyridinium bromide; competitive protein-binding (clearance)
cpb: *cuyos pies beso* (Spanish—whose feet I kiss)
Cpb: Campbelltown
CPB: Consumer Protection Bureau; Corporation for Public Broadcasting
CPB: *Centraal Plan Bureau* (Dutch—Central Planning Bureau)
cpba: competitive protein-binding analysis
cpbl: capability; capable
CPBMP: Committee on Purchases of Blind-Made Products
cpc: chronic passive congestion; clinicopathological conference (CPC); computer-production control
CPC: California Polytechnic College; City Planning Commission; City Projects Council; Cogswell Polytechnical College; Communist Party of China; Consumers Power Company; Creole Petroleum Corporation
CPCC: Central Piedmont Community College
CPCGN: Canadian Permanent Committee on Geographical Names (Ottawa)
CPCU: Chartered Property and Casualty Underwriter
c-p cycle: constant-pressure cycle
CPCG: *Comite Panamericano de Ciencias Geofícicas* (Panamerican Committee of Geophysical Sciences)
cpd: charter pays dues; compound; contact potential difference; contagious pustular dermatitis; container-padded delivery
CPD: Consumer Protection Division
CPDL: Canadian Patents and Developments Limited
cpds: compounds
cpe: chronic pulmonary emphysema; circular probable error; compensation, pension, and education; customer-provided equipment; cytopathic effect; cytopathogenic effect
CPE: Certified Property Exchanger
CPEA: Cooperative Program for Educational Administration
CPEG: Contractor Performance Evaluation Group
CPEHS: Consumer Protection and Environmental Health Service
c pen: *code pénal* (French—penal code)
CPEP: Contractor Performance Evaluation Plan
CPEQ: Corporation of Professional Engineers of Quebec
cpf: conditional peak flow
CPF: Central Provident Fund
cpff (CPFF): cost plus fixed fee
CPFS: Council for the Promotion of Field Studies
cpg: controlled-pore glass; cotton piece goods
CPG: College Publishers Group
CPGB: Communist Party of Great Britain
Cpge: course per gyro compass
cph: cycles per hour
CPH: Certificate of Public Health; Copenhagen, Den-

mark (airport); Corps of Public Health
C-PH: Columbia-Presbyterian Hospital
CPHA: Canadian Public Health Association
CP & HA: Canadian Port and Harbour Association
cpi: characters per inch; commercial performance index; constitutional psychopathic inferior; consumer price index; crash position indicator
CPI: California Psychological Inventory; Chemical Processing Industries; Communist Party of India; Consumer Price Index
cpia: close-pair interstitial atom
CPIA: Chemical Propulsion Information Agency
cpiaf (CPIAF): cost-plus-incentive-award fee
cpib: chlorophenoxyisobutyrate
cpif (CPIF): cost plus incentive fee
CPJ: Communist Party of Japan (also called JCP)
CPILS: Correlation-Protected Integrated Landing System
CPIM: Curaçaosche Petroleum Industrie Maatschappij
cpin: crankpin
CPJI: *Cour Permanente de Justice Internationale* (French—Permanent Court of International Justice)
cpk (CPK): creatinine phosphokinase
cpl: cement plaster; characters per line; common program language
Cpl: Corporal
CPL: Calgary Public Library; Certified Parts List; Certified Products List; Charleston Public Library; Charlotte Public Library; Chattanooga Public Library; Chicago Public Library; Cincinnati Public Library; Civilian Personnel Letter; Cleveland Public Library; Columbus Public Library; Coronado Public Library
CPLA: California Palace of the Legion of Honor
cplg: coupling
cplmt: complement
cplr: center of pillar
cpm: cards per minute; commutative principle of multiplication; critical path method; cycles per minute
cpm (CPM): cost per thousand
CPM: Certified Property Manager; Communist Party of Malaya
CPMA: Computer Peripheral Manufacturers Association
CPMC: Columbia-Presbyterian Medical Center
CPMS: Computer Performance Monitoring System
cpn: chronic pyelonephritis; coupon
Cpn: Copenhagen
CPN: *Communistische Partij van Nederland* (Dutch Netherlands Communist Party)
CPNP: Cape Perth National Park (Western Australia)
CPNZ: Communist Party of New Zealand
cpo: cost proposal outline
CPO: Calgary Philharmonic Orchestra; Chief Petty Officer; Civilian Personnel Office(r); Czech Philharmonic Orchestra
cpp: critical path plan
CPP: Canada Pension Plan
CPP: *Civilian Personnel Pamphlet*
CPPA: Canadian Pulp and Paper Association
cppb: continuous positive-pressure breathing
CPPB: Canada Pension Plan Benefits
CPPCA: California Probation, Parole, and Correctional Association
cppd: calcium pyrophosphate dihydrate
CPPL: Canadian Pacific Princess Lines (Vancouver-Nanaimo run)
cpps: critical path planning and scheduling
CPPS: *Comisión Permanente para la Explotación y Conservación de las Riquezas Maritimas del Pacifico Sur* (Spanish—Permanent Commission for the Exploitation and Conservation of the Maritime Riches of the South Pacific)
cpr: cardiopulmonary resuscitation; copper
CPR: Canadian Pacific Railway; Carlos Peña Romulo; Cobourg Peninsula Reserve (Australian Northern Territory); Committee on Polar Research; Council for Public Responsibility
CPRA: Council for the Preservation of Rural America
CP Rail: Canadian Pacific Rail
CPRE: Council for the Preservation of Rural England
CPRF: Cancer and Polio Research Fund
CPRI: Council for the Protection of Rural Ireland
CPRS: Council for the Protection of Rural Scotland
CPRSA: Cape Peninsula Road Safety Association
CPRW: Council for the Protection of Rural Wales
cps: characters per second; constitutional psychopathic state; coupons; critical path scheduling; cycles per second
CP's: Command Posts
CPS: California Physician's Service; California Production Service; Canadian Pacific Steamships; Canadian Penitentiary Service; Catholic Pamphlet Society; Center for Population Studies (Harvard); Certified Professional Secretary; College Placement Council; Commission on Presidential Scholars; Congregational Publishing Society; Current Population Survey
C.P.S.: *Custos Privati Sigilli* (Latin—Keeper of the Privy Seal—Great Britain)
CPS: *Compendium of Pharmaceuticals and Specialities; Conseil Permanent de Sécurité* (French—Permanent Security Council)
CPSA: Canadian Political Science Association; Civil and Public Services Association (UK); Clay Pigeon Shooting Association
cpsac: cycles-per-second alternating current
CPSC: Consumer Product Safety Commission
CPSCU: College of Physicians and Surgeons—Columbia University
cpsd: cross-power spectral density
C_{pse}: course per standard compass
cpse: counterpoise
cpsi: causing pressure shut in
CPSL: Canadian Pacific Steamship Line
CPSP: Cove Palisade State Park (Oregon)
CPSS: Certificate in Public Service Studies
$C_{p\ stg\ c}$: course per steering compass
CPSU: Communist Party of the Soviet Union
cpt: casement-projected transom; chest physiotherapy;

cockpit procedure trainer; counterpoint
Cpt: Capitaine (French—Captain)
CPT: Canadian Pacific Telegraphs; Cape Town, South Africa (Malan Airport); Civilian Pilot Training
CPT: *Current Physics Titles*
C.P.T.: *Contador Público Titulado* (Spanish—Certified Public Accountant)
CPTB: Clay Products Technical Bureau
cptr: capture; carpenter; carpentry
CPTV: Connecticut Public Television
cpu: central processing unit
CPU: Canadian Paperworkers Union; Commonwealth Press Union
CPUSA: Communist Party USA
CPV: Combination Pump Valve; Compañía Peruana de Vapores (Peruvian Steamship Line)
cpvc: critical pigment volume concentration
CPVPL: Charles Patterson Van Pelt Library (University of Pennsylvania)
cpw: commercial projected window
cPw: polar continental air warmer than underlying surface
CPW: California Press Women
CPWH: Committee for the Preservation of the White House
CPX: Command Post Exercise
CPY: Communist Party of Yugoslavia
cpz: chlorpromazine
CPZ: Central Park Zoo
cq: chloroquine quinine; circadian quotient; come quick; conceptual quotient; copy correct; copy (spelled) correctly
CQ: call to quarters (radio signal meaning message following is intended for all receivers); Charge of Quarters; Conditionally Qualified
CQ: *Caribbean Quarterly; Congressional Quarterly*
CQC: Citizens for a Quiet City
CQs: Citizens for Quieter Cities
CQD: wireless distress signal
cqm: chloroquine mustard
CQM: Chief Quartermaster; Company Quartermaster
CQMS: Company Quartermaster Sergeant
CQR: Customer Quality Representative
CQSW: Certificate of Qualification in Social Work
CQT: College Qualification Test
CQU: College Qualification Test(s)
cr: calculus removal; calculus removed; cardiorespiratory; cathode ray; center; center of resistance; chest and right arm; clinical research; clot reaction; coefficient (of fat) retention; cold roll; cold-rolled; colon resection; complete remission; complete round; compression ratio; conditioned reflex; conditioned response; cranial; creatinine; credit; creek; cresyl red; crew; critical; critical ratio; crown; crown-rump; cruise
c/r: company risk
cr.: *crux* (Latin—cross)
c/r: *cuenta y riesgo* (Spanish—for account and risk of)
cr (CR): critical ratio
cr (CR): carriage return character (data processing); conditioned reflex; conditioned response
c & r: cops and robbers
Cr: creatinine; creditor; chromium
Cr.: *Credo* (Latin—I believe; the creed); *Ceskoslovensky rozhlas* (Czechoslovak Radio)
CR: Ceskoslovenska Republika (Czechoslovakian Republic); Change Recommendation; Combat Ready; Commonwealth Railways (Australia); Costa Rica; Costa Rican; cost reimbursement
C R: *comptes rendus* (French—proceedings; report)
C/R: Chicago Rawhide (manufacturing company)
C of R: Count(y) of Ravensberg
C-R: Crouse-Hinds; Cutler-Hammer
C & R: convoy and routing
CR: *Consumer Reports*
C.R.: *Carolina Regina* (Latin—Queen Caroline); *Carolus Rex* (Latin—King Charles); *Civis Romanus* (Latin—Citizen of Rome); *Custos Rotulorum* (Latin—Roll Keeper)
cra: central retinal artery
Cra: *Carretera* (Spanish—highway)
CRA: California Redwood Association; California Republican Assembly; Canadian Rheumatism Association; Cave Research Associates; Centres de la Recherche Appliqué (Applied Research Centers); Colorado River Aqueduct; Colorado River Authority; Community Redevelopment Agency; Continuing Resolution Authority; Convair Recreation Association
C.R.A.: Conzinc Riotinto of Australia (their periods as shown)
CRAC: Careers Research and Advisory Center
Crackers: rural Floridians and Georgians
Cracker State: Georgia
Cracovia: (Latin—Cracow)
CRAD: Committee for Research into Apparatus for the Disabled
CRAF: Civil Reserve Air Fleet
cram.: card random access memory
CRAM: Contractual Requirements Recording, Analysis, and Management
cran: cranial; craniology; cranium
cranapple: cranberry-and-apple juice
craniol: craniology
craniom: craniomitry
cran(s): cranberries; cranberry
CRAR: Critical Reliability Action Request
cras: coder and random access switch
CRASC: Commander—Royal Army Service Corps
CRASH: Citizens to Reduce Airline Smoking Hazards; Community Resource and Self Help
crast.: *crastinus* (Latin—of tomorrow)
C-rat(s): C-ration(s)
CRAW: Combat Readiness Air Wing (USN)
Crawfish Town: New Orleans, Louisiana
Crawthumper (s): Marylander(s)
cray(s): crayfish(es)
crb: central radio bureau; curb; curbing
crbbb: complete right bundle branch block
CRB: Civilian Review Board; Commission for Relief in Belgium; Cooper River Bridge (Charleston, South Carolina)
cr & br: crown and bridge (dental)
crc: complete round chart; cyclic redundancy check
CrC: control and reporting center; Crew Chief
CRC: Chemical Rubber Compa-

ny; Civil Rights Commission; Consolidated Railroads of Cuba; Control and Reporting Center; Coordinating Research Council

CRCC: Consolidated Record Communications Center (USA)

CRCE: Centaur Reliability Control Engineering

CRCNJ: Central Railroad Company of New Jersey

crcp: continuously reinforced concrete paving

CRCRS: Civil Rights Community Relations Service

CRCS: Canadian Red Cross Society

crd: chronic renal disease; chronic respiratory disease; complete reaction of degeneration

CRD: Community Relations Department; Crop Research Division (USDA)

CRDL: Chemical Research and Development Laboratories; Contractor Data Requirements List

Cr$: cruzeiro (Brazilian monetary unit)

CR & DP: Cooperative Research and Development Program

CRDSD: *Current Research and Development in Scientific Documentation*

cre: corrosion resistant

Cre: Crescent

CRE: Center for Radical Education

CREA: California Real Estate Association

C Real: Ciudad Real

cream of tartar: potassium acid tartrate ($KHC_4H_6O_6$)

creat: creatine

CREATE: Computational Requirements for Engineering, Simulation, Training, and Education (USAF time-sharing computer complex)

Creator God: *Viracocha* (Quechua—supreme god)—deity venerated in Incan and pre-Incan times

crectte: *creciente* (Spanish—crescent; growing)

cred: credit; creditor

Creek: The Creek—oilfields scattered along the creeks of western Pennsylvania

CREEP: Committee to Re-elect the President (Nixon's Watergate Gang)

CREFAL: Centro Regional de Educación Fundamental para la America Latina (Regional Center of Fundamental Education for Latin America—United Nations organization)

CREI: Capitol Radio Engineering Institute

crem: cremation

cremains: cremation remains

cremo: crematorium

Creole Country: southern counties of Alabama and Mississippi as well as coastal parishes of Louisiana where many people are of French or Spanish origin

Creole State: Louisiana

crep.: *crepitus* (Latin—crepitation)

cres: corrosion-resistant stainless steel; crescent; crescentic

cres: *crescendo* (Italian—expanding, swelling)

Cres: Crescent

CRES: Center for Research in Engineering Science (University of Kansas); Corrosion Resistant Stainless Steel

cresc: *crescendo* (Italian—increasing; swelling)

Crescendo: Crescendo Publishing Company

CRESS: Combined Reentry Effort in Small Systems

crest.: crew-escape and rescue techniques (USAF)

CREST: Committee on Reactor Safety Technology

Cret: Cretaceous

CrewTAF: Crew Training Air Force

crf: capital recovery factor; continuous reinforcements; cross-reference file

crf (CRF): corticotropin-releasing factor

CRF: Citizens Research Foundation

CRFA: Czechoslovak Rationalist Federation of America

crg: carriage

CRG: Cave Research Group; Cooperative Republic of Guyana (formerly British Guiana)

cri: chemical rust inhibitor; cold running intelligibility; criminal

CRI: Caribbean Research Institute; Coconut Research Institute; Committee for Reciprocity Information; Communications Research Institute; Composers Recordings Incorporated

CRI: *Croce Rossa Italiana* (Italian Red Cross)

CR & I: Chicago River and Indiana (railroad)

CRIC: Canon Regular of the Immaculate Conception

CRICAP: Carpet and Rug Industry Consumer Action Panel

CRIEPI: Central Research Institute of the Electrical Power Industry

CRIF: *Comité Represéntatif des Israélites de France* (Representative Committee of the Jews of France)

CRILC: Canadian Research Institute of Launderers and Cleaners

crim: criminal; criminalism; criminalist; criminologist; criminology

crim con: criminal conversation (British euphemism—adultery)

criminol: criminologist; criminology

criminotic: criminal neurotic

crip: cripple

CRI & P: Chicago, Rock Island and Pacific (railroad)

crips: cripples

CR & IR: Chicago River and Indiana (railroad)

Cris: Cristóbal

CRIS: Command Retrieval Information System

crisco: cream received in separating cottonseed oil

CRISP: Cosmic Radiation Ionization Spectrographic Program (NASA)

crit: critic; critical; criticality; criticism

criticalese: language and style of professional critics who delight in using such terms as value judgement

CRITICOMM: Critical Intelligence Communications System

crits: critical reactor experiments

Crk: Creek; Cork

crkc: crankcase

CRL: California Republican League; Cambridge Research Laboratory; Cardiac Research Laboratory; Center for Research Libraries

C.R.L.: Certified Record Librarian; Certified Reference Librarian

CRLA: California Rural Legal Assistance

CRLLB: Center for Research on Language and Language Behavior (Univ Mich)

crm: counter-radar missile; count rate meter; cross-react-

ing material; crucial reaction measure(ment)
cr/m: crew member
CRM: Certified Records Manager; Combat Readiness Medal; Communications/Research/Machines (publisher); Counter-Radar Missile
CRM: *Consumer Research Magazine*
CRMA: Cotton and Rayon Merchants Association
crmch: cruise Mach change
CRMD: Children with Retarded Mental Development
Crml: Carmel
crmn: crewman
crmnls: criminalism; criminalist; criminalistics; criminals
crmoly: chrome molybdenum
CRMP: Corps of Royal Military Police
CRMWD: Colorado River Municipal Water District
crn: crane
Crn: (The) Crown (The Monarchy)
CRNL: Chalk River Nuclear Laboratories (Canada)
CRNM: Capitol Reef National Monument
CRNP: Cape Range National Park (Western Australia)
CRNSS: Chief of the Royal Naval Scientific Service
CRNWR: Cape Romain National Wildlife Refuge (South Carolina); Clarence Rhode National Wildlife Range (Alaska)
cro: cathode-ray oscilloscope
CRO: Carnarvon, Australia (tracking station); Contractor's Resident Office; County Recorder's Office
Croat.: Croatia; Croatian
croc(s): Crocodile(s)
CROC: Committee for the Rejection of Obnoxious (tv) Commercials
crock.: crockery; crocks (English slang—broken-down animals or athletes)
cro'jack: crossjack
Cronian Sea: Arctic Ocean
cross.: crossing
CROSS: Committee to Retain Our Segregated Schools (Arkansas); Computerized Rearrangement of Special Subjects
'crosse: lacrosse; lacrosse stick
Cross of Geneva: emblem of the Red Cross (red cross on a white field) used to show the neutrality of ambulances, hospitals, and hospital ships during wartime
Crowell: Crowell Collier; Thomas Y. Crowell
Crown: Crown Publishers
Crozets: Crozet Islands in the South Indian Ocean
Crp: C-reactive protein
CrP: creatinine phosphate
CRP: Control and Reporting Post; Corpus Christi, Texas (airport); Cost Reduction Program
CRPD: Chicago Regional Port District
cr pl: chromium plate
CRPL: Central Radio Propagation Laboratory
Cr Pr: Criminal Procedure
crr: constant ratio roll
CrR: Croix-Rouge (French—Red Cross)
CRR: Cost Reduction Representative
CRRA: Component Release Reliability Analysis
CRRB: Centaur Reliability Review Board
CRRC: Costa Rica Railway Company
CRREL: Cold Regions Research and Engineering Laboratory (USA)
crrl: contour roller
CRRS: Combat-Readiness Rating System (USAF)
crs: coast radio station(s); cold-rolled steel; colon-rectal surgery; creditors; credits; crew reserve status
cr's: character reactions
Crs: Cristóbal, CZ
CRs: counter-revolutionaries (sometimes appears as KRs)
CRS: Career Service Status (USAF); Child Rearing Study; Community Relations Service; Congressional Research Service
CRS: *Conseil de la Recherché Scientifique* (French—Scientific Research Council)—Quebec; *Corps Républican de la Securite* (FRENCH—Republican Security Corps)—anti-riot squads
CRSA: Cold-Rolled Sections Association; Concrete Reinforcement Steel Association; Connecticut River Salmon Association
CRSG: Classification Research Study Group
CRSI: Concrete Reinforcing Steel Institute
crsp: criminally receiving stolen property
CRSP: Colorado River Storage Program
CRSR: Center for Radiophysics and Space Research (Cornell University)
CRSS: Collectors of Religion on Stamps Society
crst syndrome: calcification and clinical signs of Raynaud's phenomenon, scleroderma, and telangiectasis
crt: cathode-ray tube; cold-rolled and tempered
Crt: Court
CRT: Combat Readiness Training
cr tan lthr: chrome-tanned leather
CRTC: Canadian Radio-Television Commission; Cavalry Replacement Training Center
crtgc: cartographer
crtkr: caretaker
crtn: correction
crtog: cartographer; cartographic; cartography
cr tp: contour template
crt's: cathode-ray tubes
CRTS: Commonwealth Reconstruction Training Scheme
cru: clinical research unit; combined rotating unit; crucible
CRU: Cecil Rhodes University
Cru Base: Cruiser Base
CRUBATFOR: cruisers, battle force
CRUDESLANT: Cruiser-Destroyer Forces, Atlantic
CRUDESPAC: Cruiser-Destroyer Forces, Pacific
CRUDIV: cruiser division
CRUEL: Commission on Reform of Undergraduate Education and Living (Univ Ill)
cruis: cruiser; cruising
CRULANT: Cruiser Forces, Atlantic
CRUPAC: Cruiser Forces, Pacific
cru's: collective reserve units (international banking currency)
CRUSK: Center for Research on Utilization of Scientific Knowledge (Univ Mich)
Crust: Crustacea
crustas: ice-encrusted cocktails
cruz: *cruzeiro* (Brazilian currency)—also appears as *C, Cr, Cruz, Crz*
CRUZEIRO: Servicos Aéreos Cruzeiro do Sul (Southern Cross Air Service—Brazil)
crv: central retinal vein
CRV: Corvette aircraft
crvan: chrome vanadium

crvf: congestive right ventricular failure
CRWPC: Canadian Radio Wave Propagation Committee
cryolite: sodium aluminum fluoride
crypt.: cryptography
crypta: cryptanalysis; cryptanalyst
crypto: cryptographer; cryptographic; cryptography
crypton(s): cryptonym (s)
cryptos: cryptograms
crys: crystal; crystalline; crystallization; crystallize; crystallography; crystalloids
cryst: crystal; crystalline; crystallography
Crystal Hills: New Hampshire's White Mountains
crystd: crystallized
crystn: crystallization
cs: caesarean section; capital stock; carbon steel; cast steel; cast stone; center section; cerebrospinal; cirrostratus; close support; color stabilizer; common steel (projectile); concentrated strength; conditioned stimulus; corticosteroid; crucible steel; cryptographic system; current series; current strength; cutting specification(s); cycloserine
cs: céntimos (Spanish—centimes; hundredths)—coins worth a hundredth part of any unit; *come sopra* (Italian—as above); *cours* (French—course; currency; current price); *cuartos* (Spanish—apartments; fourths)—coins worth a fourth part of any unit
c/s: cases; cycles per second
c & s: clean and sober
c/s: *con safos* (Spanish-American slang—impervious to attack; the same to you; you're stuck with it)
cs (CS): central service; closeup shot (waist-up tv picture); conditioned stimulus
Cs: cesium; cirrostratus
C.S.: Custos Sigilli (Latin—Keeper of the Seal)
Cs^{137}: radioactive cesium
CS: Communications Station; Communications System; contract surgeon; Cryptographic System; current series; current strength; cutting specifications
C/S: call signal; certificate of service
C&S: Chicago and Southern (Delta Airlines); Citizens and Southern (bank); Colorado and Southern (railroad)
C del S: Corriere della Sera (Evening Courier—Milan)
C of S: Chief of Staff; Chief of Service
CSA: Canadian Standards Association; Ceskoslovenske Aerolinie (Czechoslovakian Airline); Chief of Staff, Army; Commercial Service Authorization; Communication Service Authorization; Community Services Administration; Confederate States of America; Confederate States Army
C & SA: Counterinsurgency and Special Activities (Joint Chiefs of Staff)
CSAA: Child Study Association of America
CSAC: Cameron State Agricultural College; Conners State Agricultural College
CSADC: Canadian—South African Diamond Corporation
CSAE: Canadian Society of Agriculture Engineering
CSAF: Chief of Staff, United States Air Force
CSAL: Central Scientific Agricultural Library (Moscow)
CSAP: Canadian Society of Animal Production
csar: communication satellite advanced research
CSAV: Compañía Sud America de Vapores (Chilean Line)
csb: chemical stimulation (of the brain); concrete splash block
Csb: Casablanca
CSB: Central Statistical Board; Christian Service Brigade; Committee for Safe Bicycling; Copra Stabilization Board
C.S.B.: Bachelor of Christian Science
CSBE: California State Board of Education
CSBs: Canada Savings Bonds
csc: cartridge storage case; change schedule chart; cosecant
c & sc: capital and small capital letters
CSC: Central Security Control; Child Safety Council; Citizens Service Corps; Civil Service Commission; Civilian Screening Center; Colorado State College; Combat Support Company; Command and Staff College (USAF); Communications Satellite Corporation; Computer Science Corporation; Consolidated Coal Company (stock exchange symbol); Conspicuous Service Cross; Continuous Service Certificate
CSCA: Civil Service Clerical Association
CSCAW: Catholic Study Circle for Animal Welfare
CSCC: Civil Service Commission of Canada
CSCD: Center for Studies of Crime and Delinquency
CSCFE: Civil Service Council for Further Education (UK)
csch: hyperbolic constant
CSCJ: Center for Studies in Criminal Justice
CScO: Chief Scientific Officer
CSCP: Christian Science Committee on Publications
CSCS: Cost, Schedule, and Control System
cscu: countersink cutter
csd: constant-speed drive; controlled-slip differentials; cortical spreading depression
CSD: Civil Service(s) Department; Consumer Service(s) Dividion; Convair San Diego (Division of General Dynamics Corporation)
CSD: Ceskolovenske Statne Draphy (Czechoslovak State Railway)
CSD-ALA: Children's Services Division—American Library Association
CSDE: Central Servicing Development Establishment
CSDI: Center for the Study of Democratic Institutions
CSDP: Coordinated Ship Development Plan (USN)
CSDPH: California State Department of Public Health
CSDS: Chicago Sewage Disposal System
cse: course
CSE: Calcutta Stock Exchange; Cincinnati Stock Exchange; Certificate of Secondary Education
CSEAA: Civil Service Employees Association of America
csed: coordinated ship electronics design
CSEIP: Center for the Study of the Evaluation of Instructional Programs
CSEPA: Central Station Electrical Protection Association
CSEU: Confederation of Shipbuilding and Engineering

Unions
csf: cerebrospinal fluid
CSF: Correctional Service Federation
CSF: Compagnie Générale de Télégraphie Sans Fil
CSFA: Canadian Scientific Film Association
CSFAC: Colorado Springs Fine Arts Center
CSFE: Canadian Society of Forest Engineers
CSFPA: Central Station Fire Protection Association
csf-Wr: cerebrospinal fluid-Wassermann reaction
csg: casing
CSG: Council of State Governments
CSG: Centre Spatial Guyanais (French-Guiana Space Center)
CSGA: Canadian Seed Growers Association; Central States Gas Corporation
CS-gas: civil(ian)-security or cyanide-simulating gas also called Mace or tear gas as it causes temporary blindness, burning, tearing, and I-can't-breathe sensations including choking, coughing, stinging, and vomiting; used to control unruly mobs
CSGBI: Cardiac Society of Great Britain and Ireland
CSGUS: Clinical Society of Genito-Urinary Surgeons
csh: calcium silicate hydrate; cash
cshaft: crankshaft
csi: contractor standard item
CSI: Campus Studies Institute; Construction Specification Institute
C.S.I.: Companion of the Order of the Star of India
CSIC: Consejo Superior de Investigaciones Cientificas (Spanish—Superior Council of Scientific Investigations)
CSICC: Canadian Steel Industries Construction Council
CSigO: Chief Signal Officer
csink: countersink
CSIR: Council for Scientific and Industrial Research (South Africa); Council of Scientific and Industrial Research (India)
CSIRA: Council for Small Industries in Rural Areas
CSIRO: Commonwealth Scientific and Industrial Research Organization (Australia)
CSISRS: Cross-Section Information Storage and Retrieval System (AEC)
CSIVP: California State Influenza Vaccine Program
CSJ: Christian Science Journal
csk: cask; countersink; countersunk
c$k: consumer's survival kit (consumer-oriented educational tv program)
CSK: Cooperative Study of the Kuroshio (UNESCO)
csko: countersink other side
csl: computer-sensitive language; console
CSL: Canada Steamship Lines; Chicago Short Line (railroad); Cinderella Softball League; Circle of State Librarians; Colorado State Library; Consumer Service Litigants
CSLA: Church and Synagogue Library Association
CSLATP: Canadian Society of Landscape Architects and Town Planners
CSLEA: Center for the Study of Liberal Education for Adults
CSLO: Canadian Scientific Liaison Office; Combined Services Liaison Office(er)
CSLP: Center for Short-Lived Phenomena (Smithsonian)
CSLS: Civil Service Legal Society (UK)
CSLT: Canadian Society of Laboratory Technologists
csm: cerebrospinal meningitis; combustion space monitor; command service module (CSM); corn-soya-milk (mixture)
CSM: Colorado School of Mines; Command and Service Module; Cosmopolitan School of Music
CSM: Christian Science Monitor
CSMA: Chemical Specialities Manufacturers Association
CSMC: Catholic Students' Mission Crusade
csmith: coppersmith
CSM-LM: Command Service Module—Lunar Module (Apollo spacecraft)
CSMMG: Chartered Society of Massage and Medical Gymnastics
CSMP: Continuous System Modeling Program
CSMPS: Computerized Scientific Management Planning System
CSMSW: Carver School of Missions and Social Work
CSN: Companhia Siderurgica Nacional (National Steel Company); Confederate States Navy; Contract Serial Number; Control Symbol Number
CSNAR: Charles Sheldon National Antelope Refuge (Nevada)
CSNH: Cincinnati Society of Natural History
CSNWR: Carolina Sandhills National Wildlife Refuge (South Carolina)
C^so^: Corso (Italian—Street)
CSO: Cairo Symphony Orchestra; Central Statistical Office; Charlotte Symphony Orchestra; Chattanooga Symphony Orchestra; Chicago Symphony Orchestra; Cincinnati Summer Opera; Cincinnati Symphony Orchestra; Clothing Supply Office(r); Columbia Symphony Orchestra; Columbus Symphony Orchestra; Montevideo, Uruguay (Carrasco airport)
CSOP: Commission to Study the Organization of Peace (UN)
CSOs: Community Service Officers; Community Service Organizations
csp: central switching point; concurrent spare parts
Csp: Caspar; Caspean
CSP: Certified Safety Professional
C.S.P.: Congregation of St Paul
CSPA: California State Psychological Association
CSPB: California State Personnel Board
CSPC: California State Polytechnic College
CSPCA: Canadian Society for the Prevention of Cruelty to Animals
CSPCo: Caledonian Steam Packet Company
C/SPCS: Cost-Schedule Planning Control Specification
CSPI: Center for Science in the Public Interest
CSPM: Communications Security Publications Memorandum
CSPP: Community Shelter Planning Program
cspr: chlorosulphonated polyethylene rubber
CSPR(s): Christian Science Practitioner(s)
crs: compulsive security ritual; corrected sedimentation rate
CSR: Certified Shorthand Reporter; Chartered Stenographic Reporter; Civil Service Requirement; Colonial

Sugar Refining; Commonwealth Strategic Reserve
CSRA: Central Savannah River Area (Planning and Development Commission)
CSRC: Communication Science Research Center (Batelle Memorial Institute—Columbus, Ohio)
CSRL: Center for the Study of Responsive Law
CSRO: Consolidated Standing Route Order (USA)
CSRP: Cognitive Systems Research Program
CSRS: Cooperative State Research Service
css: computer systems simulator
CSS: Calcutta School Society; Coded Switch System (to arm nuclear weapons); Combat Service Support (USA); Commit Sequence Summary; Confederate States Ship (C.S.S.); Contractor Storage Site
C^ssa^: *Contessa* (Italian—Countess)
CSSA: Cactus and Succulent Society of America
cssb: compatible single sideband
CSSB: Civil Service Supply Board
CSSC: California Seismic Safety Commission
C S-S Co: Cunard Steam-Ship Company
CSSD: Central Sterile Supply Department
CSSDA: Council of Social Science Data Archives
CSSDC: Canadian Society for the Study of Diseases in Children
cssm: compatible single-sideband modulation
CSSM: Council of State Supervisors of Music
CSSO: Consolidated Surplus Sales Office
CSSP: Center for Studies of Suicide Prevention
CSSRC: Canadian Social Science Research Council
CSSS: Canadian Soil Science Society
cst: convulsive shock therapy
CST: Council for Science and Technology
CSta: consolidating station
CSTA: Canadian Society of Technical Agriculturists; Canterbury Science Teachers Association
cs & tae: combat surveillance and target acquisition equipment (DoD)
CSTAL: *Confederación Sindical de Trabajadores de America Latina* (Spanish—Trade Union Confederation of the Workers of Latin America)
CSTC: Coppin State Teachers College
C'sted: Christiansted, St Croix
cstg: casting
CSTI: Chattanooga State Technical Institute
cstol: combined short takeoff and landing; controlled short takeoff and landing
cstr: canister
csts: combined systems test stand
CSTS: Combined Systems Test Stand
csu: catheter specimen of urine; central statistical unit; circuit switching unit(s)
CSU: Casualty Staging Unit; Colorado State University
CSU: *Christlich-Soziale Union* (German—Christian Social Union)—political party
CSUC: California State University at Chico; California State University and Colleges
CSUCA: Consejo Superior Universitaria Centroamericano (Superior Council of Central American Universities)
CSUF: California State University at Fresno
CSUH: California State University at Humboldt
CSULA: California State University at Los Angeles
CSULB: California State University at Long Beach
CSUS: California State University at Sacramento
CSUSA: Copyright Society of the U.S.A.
CSUSB: California State University at San Bernardino
CSUSD: California State University at San Diego
CSUSF: California State University at San Francisco
CSUSJ: California State University at San Jose
CSV: Community Service Volunteer
csw: continuous seismic wave
CSWE: Council on Social Work Education
CSWI: Commission for Synoptic Weather Information
Cswy: Causeway
csz: copper, steel, or zinc (freight)
ct: cellular therapy; cent; center; center tap; ceramic tile; coated tablet; coffee table; compressed tablet; compute topography; corrective therapist; corrective therapy
c/t: conference terms
c & t: classification and testing
ct.: *centum* (Latin—hundred)
Ct: celtium; Court
CT: Sir Charles Tupper (Canada's seventh Prime Minister)
C/T: California Terms
C of T: Count(y) of Tyrol
cta: call time adjustor; catamenia (menstruation)
cta (CTA): cyano-trimethyl-androsterone
cta: *communiquer à toutes adresses* (French—circulate to all addresses); *cuenta* (Spanish—account)
c.t.a.: *cum testamento annexo* (Latin—with the will annexed)
CTA: California Teachers Association; Canadian Tuberculosis Association; Caribbean Tourist Association; Chemical Toilet Association; Chicago Transit Authority; Compañía Transatlantica Española (Spanish Line); Council for Technical Advancement; Covered Threads Association
cta corr^te^: *cuenta corriente* (Spanish—current account)
cta cte: *cuenta corriente* (Spanish—current account)
CTAF: Crew Training Air Force
CTAL: *Confederación de Trabajadores de América Latína* (Spanish—Confederation of Latin American Workers)
CTAU: Catholic Total Abstinence Union
ctb: ceramic-tile base
CTB: Commercial Traffic Bulletin; Commonwealth Telecommunications Board; Corporation for Television Broadcasts
CTB: *Centre Technique de Bois* (French—Wood Research Center)
CTBA: California Toll Bridge Authority
ctbm: cetyl-trimethyl-ammonium bromide
ctbore: counterbore
CTBT: Comprehensive Test Ban Treaty
ctc: carbon tetrachloride
ctc (CTC): central train control; chlortetracycline
CTC: California Tankers Com-

pany; Canadian Tire Corporation; Catholic Teachers College; Central Test Control; Chicago Teachers College; Chicago Technical College; Citizens Training Camp; Citizens Training Corps; Concordia Teachers College; Curaçao Trading Company; Cyclists Touring Club
CTCP: Contract Task Change Proposal
ctd: coated; crated
CTD: Central Training Depot
ctdc: control track direction computer
CTDC: Chemical Thermodynamics Data Center (NBS)
ctdh: command and telemetry data handling
cte: coefficient of thermal expansion
cte: *corriente* (Spanish—current)
Cte: *Comte* (French—Count)
Cte: *Conte* (Italian—Count)—Earl
CTE: Car Tours in Europe; Compañía Transatlántica Espanola (Spanish Line)
CTEB: Council of Technical Examining Bodies
Cten: Ctenophora
Cteno: Ctenocephalides (fleas)
CTES: Computer Telex Exchange System (RCA)
Ctesse: *Comtesse* (French—Countess)
CTETOC: Council for Technical Education and Training for Overseas Countries
ctf: certificate; correction to follow; cytotoxic factor
CTF: Canadian Teachers Federation; Commander Task Force
CTFA: Cosmetics, Toiletry, and Fragrance Association
CTFE: Colleges of Technology and Further Education (subsection of the University and Research Section of the Library Association)
ctfm: continuous-transmission frequency-modulated (sonar)
ctg: cartage; cartridge; cutting
Ctg: Cartagena
CTG: Commander Task Group
ctge: cartage; cartridge; cottage
CTGI: Canadian Test of General Information
C3S: College Chemistry Consultants Service
CTH: Chalmers Techniska Högskola (Swedish—Chalmers Institute of Technology); Corporation of Trinity House
Cthse: Courthouse
cti: Container Transport International (trademark)
CTI: Central Technical Institute; Cooling Tower Institute
CTIC: Cable Television Information Center
cTk: tropical continental air colder than underlying surface
CTK: *Ceskoslovenska Tiskova Kancelar* (Czechoslovak Press Bureau)
ctl: castellate; cental; central; control
Ctl: central
CTL: Cincinnati Testing Laboratories
ctlo: constructive total loss only
ctm: communications terminal modules
CTM: *Confederacion de Trabajadores de México* (Spanish—Confederation of Workers of Mexico)
CTMA: Collapsible Tube Manufacturers Association
ctmdr: clamptop metal drum
ctn: carton; cotangent
C Tn: Cape Town (British maritime contraction)
CTN: Canton Island (tracking station)
CTNE: Compañía Telefonica Nacional de Espana (National Telephone Company of Spain)
ctn's: confectioners, tobacconists, newsagents
CTNS: Chicago Tribune News Service
cto: concerto
c^to: *conto* (Italian—account); *cuarto* (Spanish—fourth)
CTO: Central Treaty Organization; Cognizant Transportation Office; Courier Transfer Officer
CTOA: Creative Tour Operators Association
c-to-c: center-to-center
ctol: conventional takeoff and landing
ct ord: court order
ctp (CTP): cytidine triphosphate
ctpt: counterpoint
CTPTA: *Centro Tropical de Pesquisas y Tecnologías de Alimentos* (Tropical Center of Food Research and Technology)
ctptal: contrapuntal
ctptst: contrapuntist
ctr: center; contour; controlled thermonuclear reactor; counter; cutter
Ctr: Center
CTR: Controlled Thermonuclear Reactor
CTRA: Coal Tar Research Association
Ctr Appl Ling: Center for Applied Linguistics
CTRP: Controlled Thermonuclear Research Program
CTRU: Colonial Termite Research Unit
cts: cents; contralateral threshold shift (audiometry)
cts: *centavos* (Spanish—cents); *centimes* (French—cents); *centimos* (Spanish—cents)
Cts: courts
CTS: Canadian Thoracic Society
CTSA: Crucible and Tool Steel Association
ctsp: contract technical services personnel
CTSS: Compatible Time-Shared System
ctt: compressed tablet triturate
CTT: Columbia Technical Translations
CTT: *Correios e Telecommuniações de Portugal* (Postal and Telegraph Services of Portugal)
CTTB: Central Trade Test Board
Cttee: Committee
ctu: centigrade thermal unit
CTU: Commander Task Unit
CTU (AFL-CIO): Commercial Telegraphers' Union
CTUS: Carnegie Trust for the Universities of Scotland
C-tube: C-shaped tube
CTV: Canadian Television
ctvo: *centavo* (Spanish—cent)
ctw: counterweight
cTw: tropical continental air warmer than underlying surface
CTW: Children's Television Workshop
$C_{12}H_{22}O_{11}$: cane sugar
ctwt: counterweight
ctx: computer telex exchange (RCA system)
Ct X: Court Exhibit
Cty: City
ctz: chlorothiazide
CTZ: Corps Tactical Zone
ct zone: chemoreceptor trigger zone
cu: cleanup; clinical unit; close-up; container unit (CU); cube; cubic; cumulus
c-u: see you
c/u: *cada uno* (Spanish—each one)
C_u: urea clearance
Cu: Cuba; Cuban; cumulus; cup-

rum (Latin—copper)
CU: Cambridge University; Capital University; Carleton University; Clafkin University; Clark University; Colgate University; Columbia University; Cooper Union; Cornell University; Creighton University; Cumberland University
CUA: Canadian Underwriters Association; Catholic University of America; Council on Urban Affairs
CUAC: Cambridge University Athletic Club
cuad: *cuadrado* (Spanish—square)
CUAFC: Cambridge University Association Football Club
CUAS: Cambridge University Agricultural Society; Cambridge University Air Squadron
Cu b: copper band
CUB: advanced unit base
CUBANA: Compañía Cubana de Aviacion
cubanite: copper iron sulfide
CUBC: Cambridge University Boat Club; Cambridge University Boxing Club
CUBS: Congress for the Unity of Black Students
cuc: chronic ulcerative colitis
CUC: Canberra University College; Canadian Unitarian Council
CUCC: Cambridge University Cricket Club
cu cm: cubic centimeter
CUCNY: Citizens Union of the City of New York
'cuda(s): barracuda(s)
Cuddy: Cuthbert
CUDS: Cambridge University Dramatic Society
CUE: Center for Urban Education
CUEBS: Commission on Undergraduate Education in the Biological Sciences
Cuen: Cuenca
CUEW: Congregational Union of England and Wales
CUF: Canadian Universities Foundation
CUF: *Companhia Uniao Fabril* (Portuguese—United Manufacturing Company)—Iberian conglomerate whose company street in Barreiro is named Rua do Acido Sulfúrico (Sulfuric Acid Street) and is a constant source of air pollution
'cuffs: handcuffs
cu ft: cubic feet; cubic foot
cu ft min: cubic feet per minute
cu ft sec: cubic feet per second
cug: cystourethrogram
CUGC: Cambridge University Golf Club
CUHC: Cambridge University Hockey Club
cu in: cubic inch
cuis: *cuisine* (French—cookery; kitchen)
cuj.: *cujus* (Latin—of which)
cuj. lib.: *cujus libet* (Latin—of any you wish)
CUK: São Paolo, Brazil (Combica Airport)
cukes: cucumbers
CUKT: Carnegie United Kingdom Trust
cul: culinary
c-u-l: see you later
CUL: Cambridge University Libraries; China Union Lines; Columbia University Library; Cooper Union Library; Cornell University Library
cull.: cullage; cullboard; culling; cullion
cult.: cultural; culture
CULTC: Cambridge University Lawn Tennis Club
culv: culvert
cul vul(s): culture vulture(s)
cum: central unit memory; cumulative
cu m: cubic meter
Cumb: Cumberland
Cumberland River City: Nashville, Tennessee
Cumberlands: Cumberland Islands off Queensland, Australia
cum d(iv): cum dividend (with dividend)
cu mm: cubic millimeter
Cum Nursing Lit: *Cumulative Index to Nursing Literature*
cum pref: cumulative preference
CUMS: Cambridge University Musical Society
cu mu: cubic micron
cun: cuneiform
CUN: *Convent van Universiteits-bibliothecarissen in Nederland* (Dutch—Association of University Librarians in the Netherlands)
CUNA: Credit Union National Association
cuni: cupro-nickel (coin alloy)
cu-nim: cumulo-nimbus (clouds)
CUNSA: Canadian University Nursing Students Association
CUNY: City University of New York
CUOG: Cambridge University Opera Group
cup.: cupboard
CUP: Cambridge University Press; Columbia University Press
CUPA: College and University Personnel Association
CUPE: Canadian Union of Public Employees
Cupid: (Latin—Eros)—god of love and lust
cupper: cup-tie-er (athletic matches played for a trophy cup)
CUPR: Catholic University of Puerto Rico
cuprite: cuprous oxide
cupronic: copper-nickel alloy
CUPS: Consolidated Unit Personnel Section
cur.: curiosa; curiosity; currency; current
Cur: Curaçao (maritime abbreviation)
CUR: Curaçao, Netherlands West Indies (Plesman Airport)
CURAC: Coal Utilization Research Advisory Committee
curat: curative
curat.: *curatio* (Latin—dressing; wound dressing)
cure. (CURE): care, understanding, research (organization for the welfare of drug addicts)
CURE: Citizens United for Racial Equality
CURF: Citizens Union Research Foundation
CURFC: Cambridge University Rugby Football Club
curio: curiosa; curiosity
CURLS: College, University, and Research Libraries Section (California Library Association)
CURMCO: City Urban Renewal Management Corporation (NYC)
curr: currency; current
Currer Bell: pseudonym of Charlotte Brontë
curt.: current (Scottish—instant); curtain
Curt: Curtis
Curt: Quintus Curtius Rufus (Roman historian)
Curt Jurgens: Curd Jurgens
CURTS: Common-User Radio Transmission System
curv: cable-operated unmanned recovery vehicle
CURV: Cable-controlled Underwater Research Vehicle
Curzio Malaparte: pseudonym—

Curzio Suckert
Curzon: Lord Curzon (George Nathaniel Curzon)—Viceroy and Governor General of India
CUS: Cambridge Union Society
CUSA: Conservative United Synagogue of America
cusecs: cubic feet per second
Cu-7: copper-constructed 7-shaped intrauterine device
Cus Ho: Custom House
CUSM: Columbia University School of Medicine
CUSO: Canadian University Service Overseas
CUSP: Central Unit for Scientific Photography
CUSRPC: Canada-United States Regional Planning Committee
CUSRPG: Canada-United States Regional Planning Group
CUSS: Continental, Union, Shell, Superior (oil companies' deep-sea oil-drilling ship)
cust: custard; custodian; custody; custom(s)
custod: custodian
CUSW/NAS: Committee on Undersea Warfare—National Academy of Sciences
CUTF: Commonwealth Unit Trust Fund
CUTS: Computer-Utilized Turning System
Cu_2SO_4: copper sulfate
Cuu: Chihuahua
CUUS: Consumers Union of the United States
CUW: Committee on Undersea Warfare (DoD)
Cux: Cuxhaven
cu yd: cubic yard
cv: cardiovascular; check valve; coefficient of variation; collection voucher; concave; convertible; culture vulture
cv: *caballo de vapor* (Spanish), *cavallo vapore* (Italian), *cavalo vapor* (Portuguese), *cheval-vapeur* (French)—horsepower (also appears as *CV*)
c.v.: *conjugata vera* (Latin—true conjugate)—pelvic inlet diameter; *cras vespere* (Latin—tomorrow evening); *cursus vitae* (Latin—course of life)
Cv: Cove; molecular heat (symbol); specific heat at constant volume (symbol)
CV: aircraft carrier (2-letter naval symbol); Central Vermont (railroad); Chula Vista; collection voucher; combat vehicle; Convair
CV: *cheval-vapeur* (French—horsepower)
C-V: Convair (Division of General Dynamics)
cva: cerebrovascular accident (medical euphemism for a stroke); costovertebral angle
CVA: attack aircraft carrier (naval symbol); Columbia Valley Authority
CVA: Civilian Voluntary Agency
CVAA: Centre de Vulgarisation Aéro-Astronautique
CVAC: Consolidated Vultee Aircraft (now Convair)
CVAN: nuclear-powered aircraft carrier (naval symbol)
cvb: combined very-high-frequency band
CVB: large aircraft carrier (naval symbol)
c-v-c: consonant-vowel-consonant
CVC: Clinch Valley College; Consolidated Vacuum Corporation
cvcc: compound vortex-controlled combustion (Japanese automotive engine designed by Honda to reduce air pollution by reducing pollutant emissions)
cvd: cardiovascular disease; cash versus documents; coordination of valve development; coupled vibration dissociation; current-voltage diagram
CVDE: *Columbia-Viking Desk Encyclopedia*
cve (CVE): customer-vended equipment
CVE: aircraft carrier, escort (naval symbol)
CVF: Caravelle fan jet airplane; Corporation Venezolano de Fomento (Venezuelan Promotion Corporation)
CV4: Convair 440 airliner
CVG: Cincinnati, Ohio (Greater Cincinnati Airport)
CVG: Corporacion Venezolana de Guayana
cvh: combined ventricular hypertrophy
CVHS: Chelsea Vocational High School
cvi: cerebrovascular insufficiency
CVI: Cape Verde Islands; College of the Virgin Islands
C viruses: Coxsackie viruses
CVIS: Computerized Vocational Information System
cvk: centerline vertical keel
CVL: Caravelle jet airplane; small aircraft carrier (naval symbol)
CVM: Company of Veteran Motorists
CVMA: Canadian Veterinary Medical Association
cvn: convene
c.v.o.: *conjugata vera obstetrica* (Latin—conjugate obstetric diameter)
CVO: Chief Veterinary Office(r)
C.V.O.: Commander of the Royal Victorian Order
c voc: *colla voce* (Italian—with the voice)
cvp: central venous pressure
CVP: Corporación Venezolano del Petróleo (Venezuelan Petroleum Corporation)
cvr: cardiovascular renal; cardiovascular-respiratory; cerebrovascular resistance; continuous video recorder
cvrd: cardiovascular renal disease
cvs: cardiovascular surgery; cardiovascular system
CVS: antisubmarine warfare support aircraft carrier (3-letter symbol)
cvt: convertible
CVT: training aircraft carrier (naval symbol)
c/vta: *cuenta de venta* (Spanish—bill of sale)
Cvt Gdn: Covent Garden (Royal Opera House)
cvtr: charcoal viral transport medium
CVW: attack carrier air wing (naval symbol)
CVWS: Combat Vehicle Weapon System
cw: cardiac work; casework(er); chemical warfare (CW); chest wall(s); children's ward; clockwise; continuous wave; copperweld (copper-covered steel); cubic weight
c-w: chronometer time minus watch time
c/w: chainwheel; counterweight
c & w: country and western (music)
CW: Channel Airways; chemical warfare; continuous wave
C-W: Curtiss-Wright
C of W: College of Wooster (Ohio)
CWA: Civil Works Administration; Communication Workers of America; County Water Authority
CWAC: California Wildlife Advisory Committee
cwar: continuous-wave acquisition radar

cwas: contractor-weighted average share
CWB: Canadian Wheat Board; Central Wages Board; Child Welfare Board
cwbts: capillary whole blood true sugar
cw-bw: chemical warfare—biological warfare
CWC: Canadian Welfare Council; Central Wesleyan College
CWCC: Civil War Centennial Commission
c & w ck: caution and warning check
CWCO: China Wire and Cable Company
cwd: civilian war dead
cwe: current working estimate
CWE: Commonwealth Edison
C'wealth: Commonwealth
CWF: California Wildlife Federation; Cornell Word Form(ation)
CWFT: Cornell Word Form Test
cwg: corrugated wire glass
CWGC: Commonwealth War Graves Commission
cwi: cardiac work index; clear word identifier
cwik: cutting with intent to kill
CWINC: Central Waterways, Irrigation, and Navigation Commission
CWIS: Chaim Weizmann Institute of Science
cwit: concordance words in title
cwl: calm waterline
CWL: Catholic Women's League
CWLA: Child Welfare League of America
C & W Ltd: Cables and Wireless Limited
CWMTU: Cold Weather Materiel Test Unit
CWNA: Canadian Weekly Newspapers Association
cwo: cash with order
CWO: Chief Warrant Officer
cwp: childbirth with(out) pain; circulating water pump; community work plan
CWPEA: Childbirth Without Pain Education Association
CWPLs: Childbirth Without Pain Leagues
cwr: continuous welded rail
CWR: California Western Railroad
CWRA: California Water Resources Association
CWRSM: Case-Western Reserve School of Medicine
cws: clockwise; cold-water soluble; countersunk wood screw
Cws: Cowes
CWS: Canadian Welding Society; Canadian Wildlife Service; Chandraprabha Wildlife Sanctuary (India); Child Welfare Services; Cooperative Wholesale Society; Cunard-White Star (steamship line)
C-WS: Crop-Weather Service
CWSC: Central Washington State College
cw sig gen: continuous wave signal generator
CWSP: College Work-Study Program
Cwsy: Causeway
cwt: centum weight; hundredweight
CWT: Cooperative Wind Tunnel
CWTC: California World Trade Center
cwu: composite weighted work unit
CWU: California Western University
cwv: continuous-wave video
CWV: Catholic War Veterans
CWWC: Concerned Women in the War on Crime
cx: cervix; chest X-ray; complex; connection; convex; correct copy (instruction to the printer)
Cx: *Caixa* (Portuguese—Box)—post office box; also written *cx*
cxr: carrier
CXT: Common External Tariff
cy: calendar year; capacity; copy; currency; current year; cyanogen; cycle
Cy: City; cyanogen; Cyprus; Cyrus
cya: cover your ass (protect yourself)
CYA: California Youth Authority; Carded Yarn Association; Catholic Youth Adoration (Society); Covenant Youth of America
cyan: cyanamid; cyanic; cyanide; cyanogen; cyanotype
cyath.: *cyathus* (Latin—cup, ladle, glass)
cyath. vin.: *cyathus vinarius* (Latin—wineglassful)
cyb: cybernetic; cyberneticist; cybernetics
CYB: *Canada Year Book*
cyber: cybernetics
cyborg: cybernetic organism
cyc: cycle; cyclorama
CYC: Capital Yacht Club; Chicago Yacht Club; Cleveland Yacht Club; Columbia Yacht Club; Company of Young Canadians; Corinthian Yacht Club
CYCA: Clyde Yacht Clubs Association
Cycl: Cyclostomata
Cyclades: Cyclades Islands
cyclams: cyclamates
cyclaz: cyclazocine
cycle: bicycle; motorcycle
cycleade: bicycle or motorcycle parade
cyclo: cyclopedia; cyclopedic; cyclophosphamide; cyclopropane; cyclorama
cyclon: cyclonometer
Cyclone Coast: Australia's northwest coast
Cyclone State: Kansas
CYEE: Central Youth Employment Executive (UK)
CYFA: Club for Young Friends of Animals
CYHA: Canadian Youth Hostels Association
cyk: consider yourself kissed
cyke: cyclorama
cyl: cylinder; cylindrical; cylindroid
cyl l: cylinder lock
cyls: cylinders
cym: cymbal(s)
Cym: Cymric
CYMA: Catholic Young Men's Association
Cymb: Cymbeline
Cymr: *Cymric* (Welsh—Wales)
CYMS: Catholic Young Men's Society
cyn: cyanide
Cyn: Canyon; Cynthia
CYO: Catholic Youth Organization; Civic Youth Orchestra
Cyp: Cyprian; Cypriote; Cyprus
CYP: Cyprus Airways
Cypriot Apostle: Barnabas—Cyprus-born companion of Paul and Mark, according to the New Testament
cys: cysteine; cystoscopy
cys (CYS): cystine (amino acid)
CYS: Cheyenne, Wyoming (airport)
CYSA: Combed Yarn Spinners Association
cysto: cystoscope; cystoscopic examination
cyt: cytology
cytac: control of tactical aircraft
cytol: cytological; cytologist; cytology
cyto syst: cytochrome system
Cz: Czech; Czechoslovakia; Czechoslovakian
CZ: Canal Zone; combat zone; communications zone

C.Z.: Canal Zone
C-Z: Crown-Zellerbach
Cza: Constanza
CZA: Coastal Zone Authority
CZAG: Committee for Zero Automobile Growth
CZBA: Canal Zone Biological Area
CZC: Canal Zone College
CZC: *Canal Zone Code* (legal)
CZCA: Coastal Zone Conservation Act
Czech: Czechoslovakia, Czechoslovakian
Czech Phil: Czech Philharmonic
Czechoslovakian National Composer: Anton Dvořák
Czechoslovakian Operetta Composer: Rudolf Friml
CZF: Canadian Zionist Federation
CZG: Canal Zone Government
CZJC: Canal Zone Junior College
Cz kr: Czechoslovakian kronen (monetary unit)
czi (CZI): crystalline zinc insulin
CZI: Canal Zone Institute
CZm: compass azimuth
Czml: Cozumel
C-Zone: commercial zone
CZP: Chicago Zoological Park (Brookfield Park)
CZ Pen: Canal Zone Penitentiary
C-Z strain: Carr-Zilber (viral) strain
czy: crazy

D

d: angular deformation (symbol); date; daughter; day; declination; degree; depth; dextrorotatory; died; differentiation; dime; dinar; diopter; divorced; dorsal; drizzling; dyne; grating space in calcite (symbol); liter (symbol); pence (symbol); penny (symbol)
d: *decimus* (Latin—tenth); *der* (German—the); *denarii* (Latin—pennies); *denarius* (Latin—penny); *dexter* (Latin—right)
d_1: diffusing capacity—lung
'd: (contraction—could; did; had; would)
d': surname prefixes such as da, de, di, etc.— d'Acosta, d'Sola, d'Silva, etc.
da (DA): diphenylchlorasine (deadly gas); directional antenna
D: December; degree of curve (symbol); Delta—code for letter D; democracy; Democrat (ic); density; Denver; department; derivation; Detroit; deuterium; diameter; dielectric flux density (symbol); Dietzgen; dioptric power (symbol); director aircraft; disaster; disaster broadcasting; dollar; dose; Douglas; down; drag (symbol); drone-control version (symbol); Dublin; Dutch; Fraunhofer lines caused by sodium (symbol); propeller diameter (symbol)
D: *Damen* (German—ladies); *damas* (Spanish—ladies); *darin* (German—in); *Dauer* (German—bulb-type camera shutter stop); *dehors* (French—out); *départ* (French—departure); *derecha* (Spanish—right); *Deus* (Latin—God); *dexter* (Latin—right); *dun* (Danish—down)
D.: *Don* (Spanish—Sir)—Mr
D': surname prefixes such as Da, De, Di, Do, Du, etc.— D'Acosta, D'Sola, D'Silva, etc.
D_1, D_2, D_3, etc.: 1st dorsal vertebra, 2nd dorsal vertebra, 3rd dorsal vertebra, etc.
D_2O: deuterium oxide (heavy water)
D3: Douglas DC-3 airplane
D4: Douglas DC-4 airplane
D-5-HS: dextrose 5 percent in Hartman's Solution
D-5-S: dextrose 5 percent in saline (solution)
d_5w: 5 percent dextrose in water
D6: Douglas DC-6 airplane
D7: Douglas DC-7 airplane
D8F: Douglas D8F fan jet airplane
D8S: Douglas super DC-8 fan jet airplane
D9S: Douglas super DC-9 fan jet airplane
D 40: iopax (uroselectan)
D'66: Democrats 1966 (Dutch political party)
D-150: Dimension 150 (150-degree field of vision achieved by deeply curved motion-picture screen)
da: daughter; days after acceptance; delayed action; delayed arming; density altitude; deposit account; direct action; discharge afloat; district attorney; documents against acceptance; documents attached; do not answer; double acting; double aged; drift angle
d-a: direct-action (adjective)
d/a (D/A): deposit account
da: *dette ar* (Norwegian—this year)
dA: *dette Aar* (Danish—this year)
dA: *der Altere* (German—senior)
Da: Danish; Danmark
Dª: *Doña* (Spanish—lady, woman of rank)
DA: Daughters of America; Defense Aid; Dental Apprentice; Department of Agriculture; Department of the Army; direct action (DA as a noun; d-a as an adjective); District Attorney; Division Artillery; does not affect; Dominion Atlantic (railroad); Dragon Airways; drift angle (symbol)
DA: *Dissertation Abstracts*
D.A.: Diploma in Anesthetics
D of A: Defenders of Animals; Department of Agriculture
daa: data access arrangement
DAA: Danish Atlantic Association; Diploma of the Advertising Association; Direct Action Associates
DAAG: Deputy Assistant Adjutant General
DAA & QMG: Deputy Assistant Adjutant and Quartermaster General
dab.: daily audience barometer; dimethylaminoazobenzene
DAB: *Deutsches Aporthekerbuch* (German Pharmacopoeia); *Dictionary of American Biography*

DABPN: Diplomate American Board of Psychiatry and Neurology
DABS: Discrete Address Beacon System
dac: data assistance and control; deductible average clause; digital-to-analog converter; direct air cycle
Dac: Dacca
DAC: Daughters of the American Colonists; Defenders of the American Constitution; Douglas Aircraft Company; Durex Abrasives Corporation
DACAN: Douglas Aircraft Company of Canada
D.Acc.: Doctor of Accountancy
DACC: Dangerous Air Cargoes Committee
DACCC: Defense Area Communications Control Center
dachs: dachsbracke (Swedish basset); dachshund (underslung German hound)
dacks: slacks (sport pants) made of dacron
DACO: Douglas Aircraft Corporation Overseas
dacon: digital to analog converter
dacor: data correction
Da Costa's syndrome: soldier's heart
dacr: dacron (synthetic fiber)
DACRP: Department of the Army Communication Resources Plan
DACS: Data Acquisition and Correction System
dacty: dactylography; dactyloscopy
dactygram: dactylogram (fingerprint)
dad: daddy (father)
dad.: double-acting door
DAD: Directorate of Armament Development; Double Atmospheric Density (rocket)
D.Adm.: Doctor of Administration
DADS: Director Army Dental Service
D.Ae.: Doctor of Aeronautics
DAE: *Dictionary of American English*
daea: dimethyl aminoethyl acetate
DAEC: Danish Atomic Energy Commission
D.Ae.Eng.: Doctor of Aeronautical Engineering
DAEP: Division of Atomic Energy Production
DAER: Department of Aeronautical Engineering Research
D.Ae.Sc.: Doctor of Aeronautical Science
daf: delayed auditory feedback; described as follows
DAF: Department of the Air Force; *van Doorne Auto Fabriek* (Dutch autos and trucks made by van Doorne's auto factory)
dafa: data accounting flow assessment
dafc: digital automatic frequency control
DAFCCS: Department of the Air Force Command and Control System
DAFFO: *Dansk Forening til Fremme af Opfindelser* (Danish Society for Encouraging Inventions)
daffs: daffodils
daff(y): daffodil
DAFIE: Directorate for Armed Forces Information and Education
dafm: discard-at-failure maintenance
DAFO: Division Accounting and Finance Office
DAFS: Department of Agriculture and Fisheries (Scotland); Duty Air Force Specialty
DAFSC: Duty Air Force Specialty Code
DAFSO: Department of the Air Force Special Order
dag: decagram
Dag: Dagestan(i); Dag Hammarskjöld; Dagmar; Dagna
Dag: *Dagbladet* (Oslo's Daily Blade)
D.Ag.: Doctor of Agriculture
DAG: Deputy Adjutant General
DAG: *Deutsche Angestellten-Gewerkschaft* (German Employees Union)
dag(h): (Turkish—mountain)
daglari: (Turkish—mountain range)
dagmar: drift-and-ground-speed-measuring radar
Dag Nyh: *Dagens Nyheter* (Sweden's Daily News)
Dago: (navalese for San Diego, California)
D.Agr.: Doctor of Agriculture
D.Agr.Eng.: Doctor of Agricultural Engineering
D.Agr.Sc.: Doctor of Agricultural Science
dah: disordered action of the heart
Dah: Dahomey
DAH: disordered action of the heart
dai (DAI): death from accidental injuries
DAI: Dayton Art Institute; Drug Abuse Information
DAIR: Driver Aid Information and Routing (System)
DAIS: Defense Automatic Integrated Switching System
daisy.: data acquisition and interpretation system
DAJAG: Deputy Assistant Judge Advocate General
Dak: Dakota; Dakotan
Dakoming: Dakota + Wyoming
Dakotas: North and South Dakota
Dak Ter: Dakota Territory
Dak Zoo: Dakota Zoo (Bismarck, North Dakota)
dal: decaliter
d'AL: d'Amico Line
Dal: Dallas; Dalmatia; Dalmatian
DAL: Dallas, Texas (Love Field); Delta Air Lines; Department of Agriculture Library; Deutsche Afrika Linien (German Africa Line)
dala: delta-amino-levulinic acid
Dalarna: Swedish truncation of Dalecarlia the lake district of folklore
DALE: Drug Abuse Law Enforcement
Dalh: Dalhousie
Dall: *Dallas' Reports—U.S. Supreme Court*
dal s: *dal segno* (Italian—from the sign)
dal seg: *dal segno* (Italian—from the sign)
Dal Sym Orch: Dallas Symphony Orchestra
dalvp: delay enroute authorized chargeable as ordinary leave provided it does not interfere with reporting on date specified and provided individual has sufficient accrued leave
dam.: damage; degraded amyloid; diacetyl monoxime; divided and mashed
DAM: Damascus, Syria (airport); Dayton Art Museum; Denver Art Museum
Damaspo: (Latin—Damascus)
dame.: data acquisition and monitoring equipment
Dame Margot Fonteyn: Margot Hookham
DAMIS: Department of the Army Management Information System
DAMP: Down-Range Anti-Missile Measurement Project
DAMS: Defense Against Missiles System; Deputy Assistant Military Secretary

DAMWO: Department of the Army Modification Work Order
dan: dekanewton
Dan: Daniel (name); Daniel, Book of; Danish; Danmark (Denmark)
DAN: Dan-Air Service
DANBIF: *Danske Boghandleres Importrfrening* (Danish Booksellers Importation Association)
DANCOM: Danube Commission (Austria, Bulgaria, Czechoslovakia, Hungary, Romania, the USSR, Yugoslavia)
Dand(ie): Andrew
Dandy: Andrew
Dandy King: Joachim Murat—King of Naples
Danglish: Danish-English
Daniel Stern: pseudonym of Liszt's paramour, the Countess Marie d'Agoult
Danish Capital of the United States: Racine, Wisconsin
Danish Caribees: colonial name for what are now the U.S. Virgin Islands
Dani: Daniel
Danl W: Daniel Webster
Danm: Danmark (Denmark)
Danmark: (Danish—Denmark)
Dannebrog: (Danish—Danish cloth)—Denmark's flag reputed to be the oldest national symbol in western Europe
d'Annunzio: (Gabriel) Gaetano Rapagnetta
Danny: Daniel
Danny Kaye: Daniel Kominski
Dansker: Dane; Danish sailor
Dante: Dante (Durante) Alighieri
Dantiscum: (Latin—Danzig)
Danube Empire: Austro-Hungarian Empire
dao: duly-authorized officer, paldao (Philippine wood)
DAO: District Accounting Office(r); District Aviation Office(r); Division Air Office(r); Division Ammunition Office(r); Dominion Astrophysical Observatory (Victoria, British Columbia)
DAOT: Director of Air Organization and Training
dap: data automation proposal; direct-agglutination pregnancy (test); do anything possible
d-a-p: draw-a-person (psychological test)
dap (DAP): diaminopimelic acid; dihydroxyacetone phosphate
DAP: Division of Air Pollution (US Public Health)
DAP & E: Diploma in Applied Parasitology and Entomology
DAPM: Deputy Assistant Provost Marshal
dapon: diallyl phthalate resin
Da Ponte: Lorenzo Da Ponte (Mozart's librettist, born Emanuèle Conegliano—an Italian Jew)
D.App.Sci.: Doctor of Applied Science
dapr: digital automatic pattern recognition
DAPS: Direct-Access Programming System
dapt: daptazole; direct-agglutination pregnancy test (DAPT)
DAPT: Draw-a-Person Test
DAQMG: Deputy Assistant Quartermaster General
dar: (Arabic—land)
Dar: Dar-es-Salaam
Dar: *Dar-es-Salaam* (Arabic—There is the Peace)—capital and seaport of Tanzania; nickname for Dar-es-Salaam
DAR: Daughters of the American Revolution; Directorate of Atomic Research; Dominion Atlantic Railway
DARAS: Direction and Range Acquisition System
DARCEE: Demonstration and Research Center for Early Education (Peabody College)
D.Arch.: Doctor of Architecture
D.Arch.E.: Doctor of Architectural Engineering
DARD: Directorate of Aircraft Research and Development
DARE: Drug Abuse Research and Education (UCLAs neuropsychiatric institute); Drug Assistance, Rehabilitation, and Education
daren't: dare not
DARES: Data Analysis and Reduction System
DARF: Defense Atomic Research Facility
Dark Continent: Africa
DARPA: Defense Advanced Research Projects Agency
DARR: Department of the Army Regional Representative
Darren: Darwen, England
DARs: Design Assist Reports; Development Appraisal Reports
DARS: Digital Adaptive Recording System
dart.: development advanced rate techniques
DARTS: Dynamically-Actuated Road Transit System
darwin glass: queenstownite (silica glass)
darya: (Persian—salt lake)
das: delivered alongside ship
DAs: Design Assist Reports
DAS: Director of Administrative Services
DAS: *Dictionary of American Slang*
DASA: Defense Atomic Support Agency
DASC: Defense Automotive Supply Center; Direct Air Support Center
D.A.Sci.: Doctor of Agricultural Science
dasd: direct access storage device
DASD: Director of Army Staff Duties
dash.: drone antisubmarine helicopter
DASH: Delta Airlines Special Handling (of small packages)
dasm (DASM): delayed-action space missile
daso (DASO): development and shakedown operations
DASS: Direct Air Support Squadron (USAF)
DASSR: Dagestan Autonomous Soviet Socialist Republic
DAST: Division for Advanced Systems Technology
dastard.: destroyer anti-submarine transportable array detector
dat: dative; datum; delayed-action tablet; differential agglutination titer
DAT: Differential Aptitude Test; Docking Alignment Target (NASA)
DATA: Defense Air Transportation Administration; Development and Technical Assistance (UN); Draughtsmen's and Allied Technicians' Association
DATAC: Development Areas Treasury Advisory Committee
datacom: data communications
datacor: data correction; data correlator
datan: data analysis
datar: digital automatic tracking and ranging
Date Capital: Indio, California amidst date palms
datel: data + telecommunication
datico: digital automatic tape intelligence checkout
datin: data inserter
DATO: Disbursing and Transportation Office; Discover America Travel Organizations

dator: digital (data), auxiliary (storage), track (display), outputs (and) radar (display)
datran: data transmission
datrix: direct access to reference information
DATSC: Department of the Army Training and Support Committee
dau(s): daughter(s)
D.Au.Eng.: Doctor of Automobile Engineering
Dav: David
DAV: Disabled American Veterans
davc: delayed automatic-volume control
Dave: David
DAVI: Department of Audio-Visual Instruction (National Education Association)
David Frome: Zenith Jones Brown
davidite: uranium ferric ferrous iron titanate
David St John: E. Howard Hunt
Davie: David
DAVRS: Director of Army Veterinary and Remount Services
Davy: David
Davy Jones' Locker: seabottom grave of drowned sailors
DAW: Directorate of Atomic Warfare
DAWE: Daughters Already Well-Endowed
dawid: device for automatic word identification and discrimination
DAWS: Director of Army Welfare Services
Day: Dayton
DAY: Dayton, Ohio (airport)
db: day book; dead body; decibel(s); dextran blue; diameter baudelocque (external pelvic conjugate diameter); disability; distobuccal; distribution box; double bayonet-base (lamp); double-biased (relay); double braid(ed); double breasted; dry bulb
d & b: dead and buried
db (DB): delayed broadcast
dB: decibel
Db: dubhium (ytterbium symbol)
DB: Disciplinary Barracks; Dispersal Base; Dodge Brothers
DB: *Danmarks Biblioteksforening* (Danish Library Association); *Deutsche Bundesbahn* (German State Railways)
D.B.: *Divinitatis Baccalaureus* (Latin—Bachelor of Divinity)
D-B: Daimler-Benz
D & B: Dun & Bradstreet
D of B: Daughters of Bilitis
d b a: doing business as
dba (DBA): Dibenzanthracene
dBa: decibel A (unit of noise measurement)
DBA: Duke Bar Association
D.B.A.: Doctor of Business Administration
DBAP: Darien Book Aid Plan
dbb: detector back bias
db & b: deals, boards, and battens
dbc: diameter bolt circle; dye-binding capacity
DBC: Demerara Bauxite Company; Detective Book Club
D.B.C.: Doctor of Beauty Culture
DBCA: Du Bois Clubs of America
dbcl: dilute blood clot lysis
DBCM: De Beers Consolidated Mines
dbe: double-bell euphonium (marching band tuba)
D.B.E.: Dame Commander of the Order of the British Empire
dbed (DBED): dibenzyl-ethylene-diamine (penicillin)
D.B.Ed.: Doctor of Business Education
dbh: diameter breast high
dbhp: drawbar horsepower
dbi: development-at-birth index (DBI)
DBib: Douay Bible
D.Bi.Chem.: Doctor of Biological Chemistry
D.Bi.Eng.: Doctor of Biological Engineering
D.Bi.Phy.: Doctor of Biological Physics
D.Bi.Sc.: Doctor of Biological Sciences
DBIU: Dominion Board of Insurance Underwriters
DBJC: Daytona Beach Junior College
dbk: debark; drawback
DBK: Daiichi Bussan Kaisha (Japanese steamship line); Dobeckmun (company)
dbkn: debarkation
dbl: double; doubler
DBL: Displaced Business Loan (SBA)
dbl act.: double acting
dbl eleph fol.: double elephant folio—books about 50 inches high
dblr: doubler
dbm: decibels per milliwatt; diabetic management
dBm: decibel referred to one milliwatt
DBM: Division of Biology and Medicine (Atomic Energy Commission)
D.B.M.: Diploma in Business Management
db meter: decibel meter
DBMS: Director of Base Medical Services
Dbn: Durban
dbo: dead blackout; distobucco-occlusal; dreadful body odor
D-box: distribution box
dbp: diastolic blood pressure; distobuccopulpal; drawbar pull
DBP: Division of Beaches and Parks
db part: double-beaded partition
DBPO: Data Buoy Project Office
dbr: double book rack
D Br: Defendant's Brief
DBR: Division of Building Research
dbre: *diciembre* (Spanish—December)
DBRL: DeBeers Research Laboratory
dbrn: decibels above reference noise
db rts: debenture rights
dbs: despeciated bovine serum
dbs (DBS): direct broadcast satellite
db's: dirty books
DBS: Division of Biological Standards
DBST: Double British Summer Time
dbt: dry-bulb temperature
dbtt: ductile-brittle transmission temperature
dbv: decibel referred to 1 volt
DBV: *Deutscher Bund für Vogelschutz* (German Birdshooters Bund)
dbw: differential ballistic wind
dc: deck cargo; deposited carbon; deviation clause; digital computer; direct cycle; directional coupler; disorderly conduct; double cap; double column; double contact; down center
d-c: direct-chill (casting); direct-current (adjective)
d/c: deviation clause; double-column (bookkeeping)
d & c: dilation and curettage
dc: *da capo* (Italian—again)
d/c: *dinero contante* (Spanish—cash)
dc (DC): diagonal conjugate
dC: *dopo Cristo* (Italian—after the birth of Christ)
DC: Dana College; Dartmouth College; Davidson College;

decimal classification; Defiance College; Dental Corps; Department of Commerce; Dickinson College; Diners Club; direct current (when used as a noun); District of Columbia (D.C.); Doane College; Doctor of Chiropractic; Dominican College; Donnelly College; Dordt College; Drury College; Duchesne College; Dumbarton College; Dyke College; D'Youville College
D-C: Denver-Chicago (truck line); Dow-Corning (chemical products)
D/C: drift correction
D & C: Detroit and Cleveland (steamship line)
DC: *Democrazia Christiana* (Italian—Christian Democracy)— political party; *Distrito Capital* (Spanish—Capital District)
D C: *da capo* (Italian—from the beginning)
D of C: Daughters of the Confederacy; Department of Commerce; Department of Communications (DoC); District of Columbia (D.C.); Duchy (Duke) of Carinthia; Duchy (Duke) of Carniola
DC1, DC2, DC3, etc.: device-control characters (data processing)
DC-8: Douglas DC8 jet airplane
DC-9: Douglas twin-jet short-range airplane
DC-10: McDonnel-Douglas jumbo jetliner
dca: deoxycholate citrate sugar
DCA: Dachshund Club of America; Dalmatian Club of America; Damage Control Assistant; Defense Communications Agency; desoxycorticosterone acetate; Diamond Council of America; Diapulse Corporation of America; Digital Computers Association; Disassembly Compliance and Analysis; Disc Company of America; Distribution Contractors Association; Division of Consumer Affairs; Drug Control Agency; Dynamics Corporation of America; Washington, D.C. (national airport)
DCA: *Défense Contre Aéronefs* (French—anti-aircraft defense)
DCAA: Defense Contract Audit Agency
DCA/A: Disassembly Compliance and Analysis/Abbreviated
DCADA: District of Columbia Alley Dwelling Authority
D.C.Ae.: Diploma of the College of Aeronautics
DCAO: Deputy County Advisory Officer
DCAOC: Defense Communications Agency Operations Center
d cap: double foolscap (paper)
DCAR: Disassembly Compliance and Analysis Report
DCAS: Data Collection and Analysis System; Defense Contract Administration Services; Deputy Chief of Air Staff
DCASR: Defense Contract Administrative Service Region
DCATA: Drug, Chemical, and Allied Trades Association
DCB: Decimal Currency Board (British)
DCBRE: Defense Chemical, Biological, and Radiation Establishment
dcc: double concave; double cotton covered
DCC: Defense Concessions Committee; Dutchess Community College
DCCA: Design Change Cost Analysis
DCCB: Defense Center Control Building (USA)
DCCC: Domestic Coal Consumers Council
d & c color: drug and cosmetic color (synthetic dye)
DCCP: Directorate of Communication Components Production
DCCS: Digital Command Communications System
dcd: differential current density
DCD: Daitch Crystal Dairies; Directorate of Civil Disturbance
DCD: *Dansk Central för Dukumentation* (Danish Center for Documentation)
D.C.D.: Diploma in Chest Diseases
DCDMA: Diamond Core Drill Manufacturers Association
DCDPO: Directorate for Civil Disturbance Planning and Operations (USA)
dcdr: decoder
dcds: double cotton double silk
DCE: Division of Compensatory Education
D.C.E.: Doctor of Civil Engineering
D.C.E.P.: Diploma of Child and Educational Psychology
dcf: deal-cased frame; direct centrifugal flotation; discounted cash flow
dcfem: dynamic crossed-field electron multiplication
dcg: dancing; decigram
DCGS: Deputy Chief of the General Staff
dch: dicyclohexyl
DCH: Diploma in Child Health
D. Ch.: *Doctor Chirugiae* (Latin—Doctor of Surgery)
dcha: *derecha* (Spanish—right)
D.Ch.E.: Doctor of Chemical Engineering
DCHCL: Dropsie College for Hebrew and Cognate Learning
dchn: dicyclohexylamine nitrate
DChO: Diploma in Opthalmic Surgery
dci: dichloroisoprenaline; dischloroisoproterenol; double-column inch; driving car intoxicated
DCI: Department of Citizenship and Immigration; Des Moines and Central Iowa (railway); Director of Central Intelligence
DCIC: Defense Ceramic Information Center
DCIGS: Deputy Chief of the Imperial General Staff
DCII: Defense Central Index of Information
D.Civ.L.: Doctor of Civil Law
DCJ: District Court Judge
dcl: decaliter; declaration; declarative
DCL: Detroit College of Law; Deuterium of Canada, Limited; Distillers Company Limited
D.C.L.: Doctor of Canon Law; Doctor of Civil Law
DCLI: Duke of Cornwall's Light Infantry
dcls: deoxycholate citrate lactose saccharose (agar)
D.Cl.Sci.: Doctor of Clinical Science
dcm: decameter
DCM: Director of Civilian Marksmanship; Directorate of Classified Management; Distinguished Conduct Medal; District Court Martial; Dominican Campaign Medal
D.C.M.: Doctor of Comparative Medicine
DCMA: District of Columbia Manpower Administration; Dry Color Manufacturers Association

D.C.M.G.: Dame Commander of the Order of St Michael and St George
dcmi: disclosure of classified military information
DCMs: Deputy Chiefs of Missions
DCN: Design Change Notice
DCMS: Deputy Commissioner of Medical Services
dcn: delayed conditioned necrosis
DCNI: Department of the Chief of Naval Information
D.Cn.L.: Doctor of Canon Law
DCNO: Deputy Chief of Naval Operations
DCNS: Deputy Chief of Naval Staff
D_{co}: diffusing capacity—carbon monoxide
DCO: Dallas Civic Opera; Dominion, Colonial, and Overseas (Department of Barclays Bank)
d & coh: daughter and co-heiress
d col: double column
D. Com.: Doctor of Commerce
D.Com.L.: Doctor of Commercial Law
D. Comp. L.: Doctor of Comparative Law
DCOR: Defense Committee on Research (USAF)
dcp: discrete component parts
dcp (DCP): dicalcium phosphate
DCP: Department of Consumer Protection; Diploma in Clinical Pathology; Disaster Control Plan; Division of Consumer Protection
DCPA: Defense (Department's) Civil Preparedness Agency
DCPL: District of Columbia Public Library
dcr: decrease; decreasing; direct cortical response; division credit rebate
DCR: Design Characteristic Review; Design Change Request; Drawing Change Request
DCRE: Deputy Commandant—Royal Engineers
DCRLA: District of Columbia Redevelopment Land Agency
DCRO: Dyers and Cleaners Research Organization
dcs: dorsal column stimulator; double cotton silk
DCS: Damage Control School (USN); Defense Communications System; Deputy Chief of Staff; Digital Command System; Direct Coupler System; Distillers Corporation—Seagrams
D.C.S.: Doctor of Christian Science; Doctor of Commercial Science
DC of S: Deputy Chief of Staff
DCSAB: Distinguished Civilian Service Awards Board
DCSC: Defense Construction Supply Center
DCSL: District Cub Scout Leader
DCSO: Deputy Chief Scientific Officer
DCS/P: Deputy Chief of Staff for Personnel
DCS/P&O: Deputy Chief of Staff for Plans and Operations
DCS/P&R: Deputy Chief of Staff for Programs and Resources
DCS/R&D: Deputy Chief of Staff for Research and Development
DCS/S&L: Deputy Chief of Staff for Systems and Logistics
DCST: Deputy Chief of Supplies and Transport
dct: depth-charge thrower; distal convuluted (kidney) tubule; document(ary)
DCTC: District of Columbia Teachers College; Dodge County Teachers College
DCTD: Diploma in Chest and Tuberculous Diseases
dctl: direct-coupled transistor logic
DCTSC: Defense Clothing and Textile Supply Center
dcu: dynamic checkout unit
dcu (DCU): dichloral urea (herbicide)
dcutl: direct-coupled unipolar transistor logic
dcv: double cotton varnish
DCVO: Dame Commander of the Royal Victorian Order; Deputy Chief Veterinary Officer
dcw: dead carcass weight
DCW: Detroit Chemical Works
dcx: double convex
dd: days after date; day's date; deadline date; deep-drawn; deferred delivery; delayed delivery; delivered; development directive; differential diagnosis; digital display; discharged dead; double draft; drydock; due date; dutch door
d-d: dumb-dumb
d'd: deceased
d/d: dated; delivered at dock(s); demand draft; detergent dispersant; domicile to domicile; due date
d & d: deaf and dumb; drunk and disorderly
d.d.: *dono dedit* (Latin—he gave as a gift)
d 1/2 d: dispatch money payable at one-half demurrage rate
Dd: David
DD: Deputy Director; destroyer (naval symbol); Development Directive; Dishonorable Discharge; E.I. du Pont de Nemours & Company (stock exchange symbol)
DD: *Doctores* (Spanish—Doctors); *Dottores* (Italian—Doctors); *Doutores* (Portuguese—Doctors)
D.D.: Doctor of Divinity
DD-2: Second Development Decade (1971-1980)
D en D: *Docteur en Droit* (French—Doctor of Law)
dda (DDA): digital differential analyzer
DDA: Dangerous Drug Act
ddalv: days delay enroute authorized chargeable as leave
DDAS: Digital Data Acquisition System
D-Day: day of attack
ddc: direct digital control
DDC: corvette (naval symbol); Defense Documentation Center; Dewey Decimal Classification; Diamond Dealers Club; Digital Development Corporation
ddc's: deck decompression chambers
DDCs: Desk and Derrick Club members (petroleum professionals)
ddd: drink, drank, drunk (alcoholic's progress)
DDD: direct distance dialing
d.d. in d.: *de die in diem* (Latin—from day to day)
ddda: decimal digital differential analyzer
DDDS: Deputy Director of Dental Services
dde (DDE): dichlorodiphenyldichloroethylene
DDE: dichlorodiphenyldichloroethylene (insecticide less toxic than DDT); Dwight David Eisenhower (34th President U.S.)
D de l'U: *Docteur de l'Université* (French—Doctor of the University of Paris)—the Sorbonne
DDEM: Dwight D. Eisenhower Museum
DDEP: Defense Development Exchange Program
ddf: design disclosure format
DDF: Dental Documentary

Foundation
DDG: guided missile destroyer (naval symbol)
DDGSE: Deputy Director General—Signals Equipment
DDGSR: Deputy Director General of Signals Equipment
DDH: Diploma in Dental Health
ddi: depth deviation indicator
DDI: Deputy Director, Intelligence (CIA)
ddl: digital data link
DDL: Det Danske Luftfartsselskab (The Danish Airways)
D De L: Daniel De Leon
ddm: data demand module
DDM: Diploma in Dermatological Medicine
DDME: Deputy Director of Mechanical Engineering
DDMI: Deputy Director of Military Intelligence
DDMOI: Deputy Director of Military Operations and Intelligence
DDMS: Deputy Director of Medical Services
DDN: nuclear-powered destroyer (naval symbol)
DDNI: Deputy Director of Naval Intelligence
DDO: David Dunlap Observatory (Ontario)
D.D.O.: Diploma in Dental Orthopedics
DDOS: Deputy Director of Ordnance Services
DDP: Deputy Director, Plans (CIA)
DDPH: Diploma in Dental Public Health
DDPR: Deputy Director of Public Relations
DDPS: Discrimination Data Processing System
ddr: direct debit
DDr: Doktor, Doktor (Austrian-German—person with two doctor's degrees)
DDR: Deutsche Demokratische Republik (German Democratic Republic); radar picket destroyer (3-letter naval symbol)
D.D.R.: Diploma in Diagnostic Radiology
DDRA: Deputy Director—Royal Artillery
DDRD: Deputy Directorate of Research and Development
DD R & D: Department of Defense Research and Development
DDR&E: Defense Development Research and Engineering
DDRM: Deputy Director of Repair and Maintenance
ddrr: directional discontinuity ring radiator
dds: diaminodiphenysulfone; digital dynamics simulator
DDS: Deep-Diving System; Deployable Defense System
D.D.S.: Doctor of Dental Science; Doctor of Dental Surgery
D.D.Sc.: Doctor of Dental Science
DDSD: Deputy Director of Staff Duties
DDSG: Donau-Dampfschiffahrts- Gesellschaft (Danube Steamship Travel Service)
dd & shpg: dock dues and shipping
ddso: diamino-diphenyl sulphoxide
DDSR: Deputy Director of Scientific Research
DDST: Double Daylight Saving Time (two hours ahead)
DDSTs: Denver Developmental Screening Tests
ddt: deduct; drop dead twice (epithet)
DDAT: dichlorodiphenyl-trichloro-ethane (insecticide)
ddt & e: design, development, test, and evaluation
DDTV: Dry Diver Transport Vehicle (naval)
ddv: deck drain valve
ddvp (DDVP): dimethyldichlorovinylphosphate
DDVS: Deputy Director of Veterinary Services
DDWE&M: Deputy Director of Works, Electrical and Mechanical
DDx: differential diagnosis
DDY: Devlet Demiryollari (Turkish Railways)
de: diesel-electric; digestive energy; double end; double entry; dream elements; duration of ejection
de: det er (Norwegian—that is)
d & e: dilation and evacuation
DE: Deere (stock exchange symbol); Department of Education; Department of Employment; Department of the Environment; destroyer escort (naval symbol); District Engineer
D of E: Department of the Environment (UK)
dea (DEA): dehydroepiandrosterone
Dea: Deacon
DEA: Dance Educators of America; Department of External Affairs; Drug Enforcement Administration
deac: deacon
DEACONS: Direct English Access and Control System
dead President: slang for American paper money bearing the portrait of a dead President or an eminent statesman—$1—Washington, —$5—Lincoln, —$10—Hamilton, —$20—Jackson, —$50—Grant, —$100—Franklin
DEADS: Detroit Air Defense Sector
Deadwood Dick: Richard W. Clarke—English-born South Dakota frontier pioneer
DEAE-cellulose: diethylaminoethyl cellulose
Deaf Smith: General Erasmus Smith of Texas
deal: decision evaluation and logic
DEAN: Deputy Educators Against Narcotics
Dean Martin: Dino Crocetti
dear.: diamonds, emeralds, amethysts, rubies
Death Ride: Charge of the Light Brigade at Balaclava in Crimea
DEAUA: Diesel Engineers and Users Association
deb: debenture; debit; debut(ante); diethylbutanediol
DEB: Dental Examining Board
Debbie: Deborah
Deb(by): Deborah
de Bc: Honoré de Balzac
debk: debark; debarkation
deb(s): debenture(s); debutante(s)
deb. spis.: debita spissitudine (Latin—of the correct consistency)
deb stk: debenture stock
dec: decant; decanter; deceased; deciduous; decimal; decimeter; decision; declination; decompose(d); decorate; decoration; decorator; decrease(d)
dec.: décembre (French—December); *décor* (French—decoration; stage scenery); *decubitus* (Latin—lying down)
Dec: Decca; December
D.E.: Doctor of Economics
DEC: Detroit Edison Company; Digital Equipment Corporation
deca-: 10
DECA: Distributive Education Club of America
decad: decadence; decadency;

decadent(ly)
decaf: decaffeinated
decal: decalcomania
DECAL: detection and classification of an acoustic lens
decasyl: decasyllable; decasyllabic
DECCO: Defense Commercial Communications Office
decd: deceased
deci: 10^{-1}
decid: deciduous
decim: decimeter
decis: decision
decl: declension
declon: declaration
DECMD: Detroit Contract Management District
decn: decision; decontamination
deco: direct energy conversion operation
decoct: decoction
decomp: decomposition
decon: decontaminate; decontamination
D. Econ.: Doctor of Economics
decor: decorate; decoration; decorative
decr: decrease
decres: *decrescendo* (Italian—contracting; subsiding)
Decr: *Decreto* (Italian, Portuguese, Spanish—Decree)
DECS: Direct Evacuation Control System (air filtration)
Decuary: December and January
decub.: *decubitus* (Latin—lying down)
DECUS: Digital Equipment Users Society
ded: dedendum; dedicate; dedicated; deduct; deducted; deduction
D. Ed.: Doctor of Education
dedic: dedicate(d)(ly); dedicating; dedication; dedicative; dedicator(y)
de d. in d.: *de die in diem* (Latin—from day to day)
deduct.: deduction
dee: digital events recorder
DEE: Diploma in Electrical (Electronic) Engineering
Dee Cee: Washington, D.C.
dee-dee: deaf and dumb
Deedee: Dorothy
Dee High: Doctor of Hygiene
dee jay: disc jockey
deeks: duck decoys
Dee Pee: Doctor of Pharmacy
Deep North: Queensland, Australia
Deep South: South Carolina, Georgia, Florida, Alabama, Mississippi, Louisiana, and Texas; the conservative south coast of England
deep 6: burial at sea; disposing of anything unwanted in at least six fathoms of water
Dee R: doctor
Deeside: River Dee valley around Aberdeen
deet: diethyl toluamide (insecticide)
def: defecate; defecation; defect; defection; defective; defector; defendant; defense; defensive; defer; deferred; deficiency; deficient; define; definite; definition; deflagrate; deflagrating; deflagration; deflect; deflecting; deflection; defoliate; defoliating; defoliation; defrost; defroster; defrosting; defunct; defunction; defunctive
def.: *defunctus* (Latin—deceased)
def art.: definite article
defcon: defense condition
defec: defective
Defense: Department of Defense
defi: deficiency
defic: deficiency; deficit
defl: deflate; deflation; deflect; deflection
deflor: defloration
deform.: deformity
DEFREPNAMA: Defense Representative North Atlantic and Mediterranean
defs: definitions
DEFSIP: Defense Scientists Immigration Program
deft.: defendant; dynamic error free transmission (DEFT)
DEFY: Drug Education For Youth
deg: degenerate; degeneration; degree(s)
DEG: guided-missile escort ship (naval symbol)
D & EG: Development and Engineering Group
de ga: depth gage
degen: degeneration
deglut.: *deglutiatur* (Latin—let it be swallowed)
De Graff: John De Graff
DeHoCo: Detroit House of Correction
dei: double electrically isolated
DEI: Dutch East Indies
Deich Bib: *Deichmanske Bibliotek* (Norwegian—Deichman's Library)—Oslo
dej: dento-enamel junction
Dejerine's disease: infants' interstitial neuritis
Dek: *Dekabr* (Russian—December)
deka: 10
dekag: dekagram
dekal: decaliter
dekam: decameter
Deke: Deacon; Donald
del: delegate; delegation; delete; deletion; deliberate; deliberation; delineate; delineated; delineation
del.: *delineavit* (Latin—he or she drew it)
Del: Delaware; Delawarean; Delhi; Delphinus
del (DEL): delete character (data processing)
del acct: delinquent account
DELCO: Dayton Engineering Laboratory Company
deld: delivered
dele: delete
deleat.: *deleatur* (Latin—delete)
deleg: delegation
Delfi: (Latin—Delft)—also spelled Delphi
deli: delicatessen
delib: deliberate; deliberation
deli-market: delicatessen and market
DELIMCO: German-Liberian Mining Company
delin: delineate(d); delineating; delineation; delineative; delineator; delineatrix; delinquencies; delinquency; delinquent; delinquently; delinquents
delinq: delinquent
deliq: deliquescent
De L Isls: De Long Islands
Dell: Dell Publishing Company
Del-Mar-Va: Delaware-Maryland-Virginia (Eastern Shore peninsula)
D. Elo.: Doctor of Elocution
delphi: declaiming eclectic liberalism possessively, hotly, instantaneously
delpho: deliver by telephone
delt: delete; deletion
delt.: *delineavit* (Latin—he or she drew it)
de lt: deck edge light
delta.: detailed labor and time analysis
Delta: code for letter D
deltic: delay line time compression
delu: delusion
delv: deliver
Delv: Delvalle
delvd: delivered
dely: delivery
dem: demand; democracy; democrat; democratic; demodulate; demodulator; demonstrate; demonstration; de-

monstrative; demote; demotion; demur; demurrage; demy
dem (DEM): demerol
Dem: Demerera (British Guiana); democracy; Democrat; democratic; Democratic Party
DEMA: Diesel Engine Manufacturers Association
dem adj: demonstrative adjective
Demba: Demarara bauxite
Dembos: (Dutch truncation—'s-Hertogenbosch)
DEME: Director of Electrical (Electronic) and Mechanical Engineering
Demeter: (Greek—Ceres)—goddess of agriculture
demij: demijohn
demo: demolition; demonstration (model)
demob: demobilization; demobilize
democ: democracy; democrat; democratic; democratization; democratize; democratizer
demod: demodulator
demogr: demographer; demographic(al); demography
demon.: demonology; demonstrate; demonstration; demonstrator
Demon of Disease: Black Death (bubonic plague); hunger plague; murine plague (carried by rats); pneumonic plague; septicemic plague; sylvatic plague (carried by many species of rodents)
Demon of Misfortune and Ruin: the Sphinx
demonstr: demonstrative
demos: demonstrators
demo(s): demonstration(s); demonstrator(s)
Demos: Democrats
dem pro: demonstrative pronoun
dems: defensively-equipped merchant ship
demur: demurrage
den: denotation; dental; dentist; dentistry
den: *Denier* (German—denier)
Den: Denbighshire; Deniz; Denmark; Denver
Den: *Denizi* (Turkish—lake; sea)
D. En.: Doctor of English
DEN: Denver, Colorado (airport)
denat: denatured
Denb: Denbighshire
dend: dendrology
dendro: dendrometer
dendrol: dendrology
D. Eng.: Doctor of Engineering
D.Eng.Sc.: Doctor of Engineering Science
Denny: Denis; Dennis
denom: denomination
denot: denotation; denotative (ly); denote(ment)
dens: density
dent.: dental; dentist; dentistry; denture
dent.: *dentur* (Latin—give; let it be given)
Dent: J.M. Dent & Sons Ltd
D. Ent.: Doctor of Entomology
Dental Capital of Europe: Vaduz, Liechtenstein where artificial teeth are made
Dent Corps: Dental Corps
Dent Hyg: Dental Hygienist
dent. tal. dos.: *dentur tales doses* (Latin—give of such doses)
DEO: District Engineering Office; District Engineers Office; Divisional Education Office(r); Divisional Entertainment Office(r)—British Army
DEOR: Duke of Edinburgh's Own Rifles
dep: depart; department; departure; dependency; dependent; depilate; depilatory; depose; deposit; depositor; depot; depotize; deputy; do everything possible
dep.: *depuratus* (Latin—purify)
DEP: Defense Electronic Products (RCA); Department of Employment and Production
Dep: Deputy
Dep: *Département* (French—Department); *Député* (French—Deputy)
depa: diethylene phosphoramide
DEPA: Defense Electric Power Administration
depart.: department; departure
dep ctf: deposit certificate
Dep Dir: Deputy Director
depend.: dependent; dependency
dep inst: depot installed
depn: dependency; dependent
depon: deponent
depos: depositary
deposn: deposition
depr: depreciation; depreciative; depression
DEPS: Diploma in Economics and Political Science
DepSO: Departmental Standardization Office
dept: depart; department; departure; deponent; depot; deputy
dep't: (contraction—department)
DePU: De Paul University; De Pauw University
deputn: deputation
der: derivation; derivative; derived; dermatine
der: *derecha* (Spanish—right); *dernier* (French—last)
Der: Derringer
DeR: reaction of degeneration
DER: Development Engineering Review; radar picket escort ship (naval symbol)
DERAP: Development Economics Research and Advisory Service
Derb(s): Derby; Derbyshire
Derby.: Derbyshire
DERBY: Derby Aviation
Derbys: Derbyshire
Dercum's disease: subcutaneous connective-tissue dystrophy
Derek: Theodoric
Der Führer: (German—The Leader)—sobriquet of Adolf Hitler—dictator of Germany before and during World War II
deriv: derivation
derm: dermatitis; dermatology; dermatophyte
dermat: dermatology
Der Meister: (German—The Master)—Johann Wolfgang von Goethe
dernier(e): (French—last)
Derniers: Dernieres Islands
deros: date eligible for return from overseas; date of estimated return from overseas service
DERR: Duke of Edinburgh's Royal Regiment
Derrick: Theodoric
Derrick City: Oil City, Pennsylvania
Derry: Londonderry
derv: diesel-engine road vehicle
des: desert; design; designate; designation; designator; designer; desire; dessert
des (Des): diethylstrlbesterol (morning-after contraceptive)
de S: de Sola; De Solá
Des: Desmond
Des: *Desierto* (Spanish—desert); (German—D-flat)
De S: De Sola
DES: Department of Education and Science; destroyer (naval symbol); Director of Educational Services; Director of Engineering Stores
desat: desaturated
Des Base: Destroyer Base
desc: descendant
DESC: Defense Electronics Supply Center
Descendants of Eagles: the founders of Algeria, according to tradition

descron: description
descto: *descuento* (Spanish—discount)
Deseret: Salt Lake City, Utah
Desert Fox: Field Marshal Erwin Rommel
Desert and Prairie Painter: Georgia O'Keefe
desert roses: barytes or gypsum concretions whose shapes resemble roses
desg: designate; designation
desid: desiderata; desideratum
desider: desiderative
desig: designate; designer
DESLANT: Destroyer Forces—Atlantic
desp: despatch
DESP: Department of Elementary School Principals
DESPAC: Destroyer Forces—Pacific
DesRCA: Designer of the Royal College of Art
DESRON: destroyer squadron
dess: dessiatine
dest: destination; destroy; destroyer; destruction
dest.: *destilla* (Latin—distilled)
DEST: Diplôme de l'Ecole Supérieure Technique (Diploma of the Technical Institute)
destil.: *destilla* (Latin—distill)
destination SPPK: destination Singapore, Penang, and Port Klang (headed for far places; outward bound)
destn: destination
destr: destructor
destr fir: destructive firing
det: detach; detachment; detail; detective; detector; determine; detonator; double end trimmed
det (DET): diethyltryptamine (quick-acting hallucinogen drug)
det.: *detur* (Latin—let it be given)
det. in dup.: *detur in duplo* (Latin—let twice as much be given)
Det.: Detective; Detroit
DET: Design Evaluation Testing; Detroit, Michigan (Detroit City Airport)
DETA: Direcção de Exploração dos Transportes Aéreos (Mozambique airline)
Det Con: Detective Constable
detd: determined
det. in dup.: *detur in duplo* (Latin—give twice as much)
determin: determination
Det Insp: Detective Inspector
detm: determine
DETMAHOG: Deliver-the-Mail/Holy-Grail (dichotomous theory of problem protection practiced by adept bureaucracies worldwide)
detn: detention
detox: detoxification; detoxification center (for alcoholic and narcotic addicts)
detoxcen: detoxification center (for alcoholics and others addicted to imbibing, inhaling, injecting, or otherwise putting poisons into their bodies)
Detroit Inst: Detroit Institute of Arts
d. et s.: *detur et signatur* (Latin—let it be given and labelled)—dispense and label
Det Sgt: Detective Sergeant
Det Sup: Detective Superintendent
Det Sym Orch: Detroit Symphony Orchestra
deu: data exchange unit
DEUA: Diesel Engines and Users Association
deuce.: digital electronic universal computing engine
Deut: Deuteronomy
Deutschland: Germany
dev: develop; developer; development; deviate; deviation; deviator
dev (DEV): duck embryo vaccine
Dev: Devon; Devonian; Devonshire; Eamon De Valera's nickname
De V: De Vilbiss
Deva: (Latin—Chester)
devel: developer; development
Dev-Genc: *Devrimci-Gençler* (Turkish—Revolutionary Youth)—Maoist communists
Devil's Half Acre: Augusta, Maine's old slum
Devil's Island: generic nickname for the French Guiana penal colony in use up to 1950 and translated name of the Isle du Diable off its coast where Alfred Dreyfus was imprisoned from 1894 to 1899
Devin: Devin-Adair
dev^{mo}: *devotissimo* (Italian—devotedly yours)—yours truly
Devon: Devonshire
devp: develop
devpt: development
devs: developers; devotions
DEW: Distant Early Warning
dewat: deactivated war trophy
DEWIZ: Distant Early Warning Identification Zone
DEW Line: Distant Early Warning Line
dex: *dexter* (Latin—right)
Dex: Dexter
D. Ex.: Doctor of Expression
dexan: digital experimental airborne navigator
dexe: dexedrine
dexies: dexedrine tablets (stimulant drugs)
d. ex m.: *deus ex machina* (Latin—god from a machine)—introduction of a god-like device to resolve a play or problem
dext.: *dexter* (Latin—right)
dextrose: glucose ($C_6H_{12}O_6H_2O$)
dez: *dezembro* (Portuguese—December)
Dez: *Dezember* (German—December)
Dezhda: Nadezhda
df: decontamination factor; defensive fire; defogging; degree(s) of freedom; dense film; direction finder; double feeder; double fronted; drinking fountain; drive fit; drop forge
d & f: determination and finding
d/f: *días fecha* (Spanish—days from date)
Df: Douglas fir
DF: Dean of the Faculty; Defender of the Faith; Destroyer Flotilla
D-F: Dansk-Franske; deflection factor (symbol)
DF: *Distrito Federal* (Spanish—Federal District)
D.F.: *Defensor Fidei* (Latin—Defender of the Faith)
D of F: Department of Fisheries
DFA: Dairy Farmers Association; Department of Foreign Affairs; Drop Forging Association
D.F.A.: Doctor of Fine Arts
DFAC: Dried Fruit Association of California
dfb: distribution fuse board
dfc: dry-filled capsules
DFC: Distinguished Flying Cross
DFD: Dogs For Defense
DFDS: Det Forende Dampskibs-Selskab (United Steamship Company, Limited, Denmark)
DFDT: difluoro-diphenyl trichloroethane (insecticide)
dfg: diode function generator
DFGJPC: Daniel and Florence Guggenheim Jet Propulsion Center
DFH: Danmarks Fiskeri og Havundersøgelser
DFI: Director(ate) of Food Investigation

d/fing: direction finding
DFISA: Dairy and Food Industries Supply Association
D fl: Dutch florins
DFL: Deutsche Forschungsanstalt für Luft und Raumfahrt
DFLS: Day Fighter Leaders' School
DFM: Distinguished Flying Medal
DFMR: Dazian Foundation for Medical Research
DFMS: Domestic and Foreign Missionary Society
DFMSR: Directorate of Flight and Missile Safety Research
dfn: distance from nose
dfndt: defendant
DFNWR: Deer Flat National Wildlife Refuge (Idaho)
d forg: drop forging
dfp (DFP): diisopropyl phosphofluoridate
DFP: *Detroit Free Press*
DFPA: Douglas Fir Plywood Association
dfr: decreasing failure rate; dropped from rolls
D fr: Djibouti franc
DFRA: Drop Forging Research Association
dfs: distance finding station
D.F.Sc.: Doctor of Financial Science
DFSC: Defense Fuel Supply Center
dfsr: diffuser
dft: deaerating feed tank; defendant; draft
DFT: Diagnostic Function Test
dftmn: draftsman
dfu: dead fetus in uterus
DFW: Director of Fortifications and Works
dg: dark ground; decigram(s); deoxyglucose; diagnosis; diastolic gallup; diglyceride; disk grind; distogingival; double glass; double groove; durable gum
d/g: decomposed granite; displacement gyroscope
DG: Diego Garcia; Director General
DG: *Déclaration de Guerre* (French—Declaration of War)
D.G.: *Dei Gratia* (Latin—By the Grace of God)
DGA: Directors Guild of America
DGAA: Distressed Gentlefolk's Aid Association
DGAMS: Director General of Army Medical Services
DGB: *Deutscher Gewerkschaftsbund* (German Federation of Trade Unions)
DGC: Dangerous Goods Classification; Duty Group Captain
D.G.C.: Diploma in Guidance and Counseling
DGCA: Director General of Civil Aviation
DGCE: Director General of Communications Equipment
DGD: Director Gunnery Division
DGDC: Deputy Grand Director of Ceremonies
DGD & M: Director General Dockyards and Maintenance
DGE: Directorate General of Equipment
DGG: Deutsche Grammophon Gesellschaft (German Gramophone Record Company)
DGI: Date Growers Institute; Director General of Information; Director General of Inspection; Directorate of General Intelligence
DGI: *Directorio General de Inteligencia* (Spanish—Directorate General of Intelligence)—Cuban branch of the Soviet KGB
Dgls: Douglas
dgm: decigram
DGM: Diploma in General Medicine; Director General of Manpower; Director(ate) of General Mobilization
DGMS: Director General of Medical Services
DGMT: Director General of Military Training
DGMW: Director General of Military Works
Dgn: Dragoon(s)
dgnast (DGNAST): design assist
Dgo: Durango
DGO: Diploma in Gynecology and Obstetrics
DGP: Director General of Production
DGPS: Director General of Personnel Services
d Gr: *der Grosse* (German—the Great)
DGR: Director of Graves Registration
DGR: *Dirección General de Radiocomunicaciones* (Spanish—General Administration of Radio Communications)—Bolivian broadcasting control
DGRR: Deutsche Gesellschaft für Raketentechnik und Raumfahrt (German Society for Rocket Technique and Space Flight)
dgs: double green silk
DGS: Diploma in General Surgery; Director General of Ships
DGSC: Defense General Supply Center
DGSRD: Director(ate) General of Scientific Research and Development
DGSS: Director General Secret Service
DGT: Director General of Training
DGT: *Dirección General de Turismo* (Spanish—Administration of Tourism)
DGTA: Dry Goods Trade Association
DGW: Director General of Weapons
dgz: designated ground zero
dh: deadhead; dead heat; dehydrogenase (DH); delayed hypersensitivity; double hung
d & h: dressed and headed
dh: *das heisst* (German—that is to say)
Dh: Moroccan dirham(s)
DH: Declaration of Homestead; De Havilland (aircraft); Department of Health
D.H.: Doctor of Humanities
D & H: Delaware & Hudson (railroad)
D of H: Degree of Honor; Degree of Honour
dha: *dicha* (Spanish—good luck; happiness)
DHA: Dhahran, Saudi Arabia (airport)
D & HAA: Dock and Harbour Authorities Association
DHAC: De Havilland Aircraft of Canada Limited
D-handle: D-shaped handle
DHC: Detroit House of Correction
DH Canada: De Havilland Aircraft of Canada Limited
dhd: distillate hydrosulfurization
dh di: drophammer die
dhea (DHEA): dehydroepiandrosterone
DHEW: Department of Health, Education, and Welfare
DHF: Dag Hammarskjöld Foundation
D. Hg.: Doctor of Hygiene
DHI: *Deutsches Hydrographisches Institut* (German Hydrographic Institute)
dhia: dehydro-isoandrosterol (DHIA)
dhic: dihydro-isocodeine (DHIC)
D.H.L.: Doctor of Hebrew Letters; Doctor of Hebrew Literature
DHM: Detroit Historical Mu-

seum
dhma: dehydroxymandelic acid (DHMA)
DHMPGTS: Department of Her (His) Majesty's Procurator General and Treasury Solicitor
dho: *dicho* (Spanish—said)
DHO: deuterium hydrogen oxide; Downhill Only (ski club)
D.Hor.: Doctor of Horticulture
dhp: developed horsepower
DHP: *Diplome en Hygiène Publique* (French—Diploma in Public Health)
dhpg: dehydroxyphenylglycol (DHPG)
dhq: mean diurnal high water inequality
DHQ: Division Headquarters
dhr: delayed hypersensitivity reaction(s)
DHR: Division of Housing Research
dhs: dry heat sterilization
DHS: Detroit High School; Diploma in Horticultural Science; District High School; Dublin High School
D.H.S.: Doctor of Health Science(s)
dhsm: dihydrostreptomycin (DHSM)
DHSS: Department of Health and Social Security
dht: distillate hydrotreating
dht (DHT): dihydrotestosterone
DHUD: Department of Housing and Urban Development
D.Hum.L.: Doctor of Humane Letters
dhw: double-hung windows
D. Hy.: Doctor of Hygiene
di: daily inspection; de-ice; diameter; diametral; diplomatic immunity; document identifier
d i: *das ist* (German—that is)
di (DI): diabetes insipidus
Di: Diana; Diane; didymium; Dinorah
DI: Denizyollari Isletmesi (Turkish Maritime Lines); Department of the Interior; Director of Intelligence; District Inspector; Division Instruction; Drill Instructor
D-I: Dai-Ichi
D of I: Daughters of Isabella; Declaration of Independence; Department of Insurance; Department of the Interior
DI-5: Defense Intelligence (British agency)
dia: date of initial appointment; diagram; diameter; diathermy; due in assets
DIA: Defense Intelligence Agency; Design and Industries Association; Dulles International Airport (Washington, D.C.)
diab: diabetic
diac: di-iodothyroacetic acid (DIAC)
DIAC: Defense Industry Advisory Council
diacrit: diacritic(al)(ly)
di ad: die adapter
diag: diagnose; diagnosis; diagnostic; diagnostician; diagonal; diagram
dial.: dialect; dialectical; dialectician; dialectics
DIAL: Disc Interrogation and Loading (system)
dial-a-mation: dial-a-cremation (telephone service offering low-cost cadaver disposal)
dialec: dialect(al)(ly); dialectic(al)(ly); dialectician(s); dialectics; dialectologist(s); dialectological(ly); dialectology
dialgol: dialect of algol (*q.v.*)
diam: diameter
DIAMANG: *Companhia de Diamantes de Angola* (Portuguese—Angolan Diamond Company)
diamond: carbon
Diamond Jim: James Buchanan (Diamond Jim) Brady
Diamond Lil: Mae West
Diamond State: diamond-shaped Delaware's official nickname
Diamond Street: nickname of New York City's 47th Street between 5th and 6th avenues where so many diamond merchants maintain offices
dian: digital analog
Diana: (Latin—Artemis)—goddess of the hunt and the Moon; protectress of women
DIAND: Department of Indian Affairs and Northern Development (Canada)
diane: digital-integrated attack and navigation equipment (DIANE)
diap.: *diapason* (Greek—consonant harmony; octave)
diaph: diaphragm
dias.: defense-integrated automatic switch
DIAS: Dublin Institute for Advanced Studies
diath: diathermy
diat: diathermy
DIAT: Dundee Institute of Art and Technology
Diazpotism: despotism of Porfirio Diaz during his forty years as president of Mexico
dib: dead in bed (not physically but sexually)
DIB: Department of Information and Broadcasting
DIB: *Dictionary of International Biography*
DIBA: Domestic and Internal Business Administration
dibas: dibasic
dic: dictionary; disseminated intravascular coagulation
dic: *dicembre* (Italian—December); *diciembre* (Spanish—December)
DiC: diesel cargo vessel
DIC: Diplomate of the Imperial College (London)
DICASS: Directional Command Active Sonobuoy System
dicautom: automatic dictionary look-up
DIChem: Diploma of Industrial Chemistry
dichlorvos: dimethyldichlorovinyl phosphate (insecticide)
dicht: *dichterlijk* (Dutch—poetic)
Dick: Richard
Dickie: Dickman; Richard
DICNAVAB: *Dictionary of Naval Abbreviations*
Dickon: Richard(son)
dick(s): detective(s)
Dicky: Richard; Tricky Dicky
Dicky Sam(s): inhabitant(s) of Liverpool
dicot(s): dicotyledon(s)
dict: dictated; dictation; diction; dictionary
dicta: dictaphone
DICTA: Diploma of the Imperial College of Tropical Agriculture
Dict Amer Slang: *Dictionary of American Slang*
did.: dead of intercurrent disease; didactic
Did: Didot
DID: *Daily Intelligence Digest*
didac: didactic(al)(ly); didacticism; didactics
didad: digital data display
DIDAS: Dynamic Instrumentation Data Automobile (Automotive) System
didn't: did not
di/do: data input/data output
DIDS: Digital Information Display System
die.: died in emergency room (DIE)
DIE: Diploma in Industrial Engineering
dieb. alt.: *diebus alternus* (Latin—on alternate days)
dieb. tert.: *diebus tertius* (La-

tin—every third day)
Diedrich Knickerbocker: (pseudonym—Washington Irving)
Dief the Chief: John George Diefenbaker
diel: dielectrics
di el: diesel electric
DIEME: Director(ate) of Inspection of Electrical (Electronic) and Mechanical Equipment
Die Nullte: (German—The Zero)—Bruckner's Symphony No. 0 in D minor
DIEPO: Dieterich-Post
diet.: dietary; dietetic(s); dietician
dif: difference; differential
DIF: District Inspector(ate) of Fisheries
dif-amps: differential amplifiers
difce: difference
diff: difference; differential
diff calc: differential calculus
diff diag: differential diagnosis
diffr: diffraction
diffu: diffusion
DiFr: diesel fruit vessel
dig.: digest; digestion; digestive
dig.: *digeratur* (Latin—let it be digested)
DIG: Deputy Inspector General
digas: digastric
DIGEPOL: *Dirección General de Policías* (Spanish—General Directorate of Police)—Venezuela
digicom: digital communications (system)
digres: digression(al)(ly); digressionary; digressive(ly); digressiveness
dig r-o: digital readout
digs.: diggings (apartment; dwelling place; flat)
di-H: hydrogen
DIH: Diploma of Industrial health; Division of Indian Health
Dij: Dijon
dil: dilute; dissolve
dil.: *dilue* (Latin—dilute); *dilutus* (Latin—diluted)
dilat: dilatation; dilate; dilation (ed)
dild: diluted
dilet: dilettante
Dilmun: (Persian—Bahrain)
diln: dilution
diluc.: *diluculo* (Latin—at daybreak)
dilut.: *dilutus* (Latin—dilute)
dim: *dimanche* (French—Sunday); *dimidius* (Latin—one half); *diminuendo* (Italian—diminishing gradually)
dim.: dimension; dimensional; diminutive
DIM: Diploma in Industrial Management
DIMA: Detroit Institute of Musical Art
DIMD: *Dorland's Illustrated Medical Dictionary*
dime.: dual independent map encoding
DIME: Division of International Medical Education (Assn Amer Med Colleges)
dimin: diminish; diminution; diminutive
dimorph: dimorphous
dimple: deuterium-moderated pile low energy
din.: do it now
din: *dinar* (Yugoslavian monetary unit)
Din: *Dinsdag* (Dutch—Tuesday)
DIN: Data Identification Number; Deutsche Industrie-Norm (German Industrial Standard)
DIN: *Deutsche Industrie Norm* (German Industry Standard)—film rating sometimes written *din* and said to mean *das ist norm* (this is standard)
d in a: (found) dead in automobile (or) airplane
Dina: *Dinamarca* (Portuguese or Spanish—Denmark)
d in b: (found) dead in bed
diner: dining car
Ding: J.N. Darling
D.Ing.: *Doctor Ingeniariae* (Latin—Doctor of Engineering)
d. in p. aeq.: *divide in partes aequales* (Latin—divide into equal parts)
DINP: Dunk Island National Park (Queensland)
dio: diode
DIO: Director(ate) of Intelligence Operations; District Intelligence Office(r); Duty Intelligence Officer
dioc: dioceasan; diocese
Dion: Dionisio
Dionysus: (Greek—Bacchus)—god of revelry and wine
diop: diopter; dioptrics
dior: diorama
diox: dioxygen
dip.: diploma; diplomat; diphtheria; (slang for pickpocket)
DIP: Document Improvement Program (DoD)
DIPA: Diploma of the Institute of Park Administration
Dip AD: Diploma in Art and Design
Dip Agr: Diploma in Agriculture
Dip A Ling: Diploma in Applied Linguistics
Dip AM: Diploma in Applied Mechanics
Dip Amer Bd P & N: Diplomate of the American Board of Psychiatry and Neurology
Dip AMS: Diploma in Ayurvedic Medicine and Surgery
Dip Anth: Diploma in Anthropology
Dip App Sci: Diploma in Applied Science
Dip Arch: Diploma in Architecture
Dip Ars: Diploma in Arts
Dip Bac: Diploma in Bacteriology
Dip BMS: Diploma in Basic Medical Sciences
Dip CAM: Diploma in Communications, Advertising, and Marketing
Dip Card: Diploma in Cardiology
Dip Com: Diploma in Commerce
Dip DP: Diploma in Drawing and Painting
Dip DS: Diploma in Dental Surgery
DIPEC: Defense Industrial Plant Equipment Center
Dip Eco: Diploma in Economics
Dip Ed: Diploma in Education
Dip Eng: Diploma in Engineering
Dip FA: Diploma in Fine Arts
Dip For: Diploma in Forestry
Dip G & O: Diploma in Gynaecology and Obstetrics
Dip GT: Diploma in Glass Technology
diph: diphtheria
Dip HA: Diploma in Hospital Administration
Dip HE: Diploma in Highway Engineering
diph tet: diphtheria tetanus
diph tox: diphtheria toxin
diph tox ap: diphtheria toxin alum precipitated
Dip Hus: Diploma in Husbandry
dipj: distal interphalangeal joint
Dip J: Diploma in Journalism
dipl: diplomacy; diplomat; diplomatic
Dipl: *Diplom* (German—Diploma)
Dip L: Diploma in Languages
Dip Lib: Diploma in Librarianship
Dip Lib Sci: Diploma in Library Science
diplo: diploma; diplomacy; diplomat; diplomatic; diplomatics; diplomatism; diplomatist
Dip ME: Diploma in Mechanical Engineering
Dip MFOS: Diploma in Maxial,

Facial, and Oral Surgery
Dip Micro: Diploma in Microbiology
Dip Mus Edu: Diploma in Musical Education
Dip NA & AC: Diploma in Numerical Analysis and Automatic Computing
Dip NS Edu: Diploma in Nursery School Education
Dip NZLS: Diploma of the New Zealand Library Service
Dip OL: Diploma in Oriental Learning
Dip Phar: Diploma in Pharmacology
Dip Phys Edu: Diploma in Physical Education
Dip P & OT: Diploma in Physical and Occupational Therapy
Dip Pub Adm: Diploma in Public Administration
Dip RADA: Diploma of the Royal Academy of Dramatic Art
Dip RSAM: Diploma of the Royal Scottish Academy of Music
dips: dipsomaniacs
dipsey: deep-sea lead (line for measuring depths)
dipso: dipsomania(c); drunkard
Dip SS: Diploma in Social Studies
Dip SW: Diploma in Social Work
Dip T: Teachers Diploma
Dip T & CP: Diploma in Town and Country Planning
Dip Tec: Diploma in Technology
Dip TEFL: Diploma in Teaching English as a Foreign Language
dipth: diphthong (single sound as ae in aeolian)
Dip The: Diploma in Theology
Dip TP: Diploma in Town Planning
Dip VFM: Diploma in Valuation and Farm Management
dir: direct; direction; director
dir.: *directione* (Latin—directions); *direxit* (Latin—directed by)
Dir: Dirham(s)—Moroccan money
Dirceu: Tomaz Antonio Gonzaga
dir conn: direct-connect
dir coup: directional coupler
direct.: directory
D.Ir.Eng.: Doctor of Irrigation Engineering
Dir Gen: Director General
Dir Gen: *Direttore Generale* (Italian—General Manager)
Dirk: Derek; Everett McKinley Dirksen
diron: direction
dir. prop.: *directione propria* (Latin—with proper directions)
dis: disability; disable(d); disciple; discipline; disconnect(ed); discontinue(d); discount(ed); disease(d); distance; distant; distribute(d); distribution
Dis: Disney (Walt Disney); Disneyland; Disraeli (Benjamin Disraeli); Pluto
Dis: (German—D-sharp)
DIs: Department(al) Instructions
DIS: Dairy Industry Society; Defense Intelligence School; Defense Intelligence Service; Department of Industrial Services; Disney Productions (stock exchange symbol); Ductile Iron Society
disab: disable; disabled
disabl: disability
disac: digital simulator and computer
disap: disapprove
disassy: disassembly
disb: disburse; disbursement
disbmt: disbursement
disc.: discography; disconnect; discontinue; discophile
DISC: Defense Industrial Supply Center
disch: discharge; discharging
disco: discotheque
DISCO: Defense Industrial Security Clearance Office
discol: discolored
discon: disconnect; disorderly conduct
discontd: discontinued
discr: discriminator
discron: discretion
DISCs: Domestic International Sales Corporations
disct: discount
discus: (*see* DSSCS)
DISD: Data and Information System Division
disemb: disembark
disg: disagreeable
dishon: dishonest; dishonesty; dishonorable; dishonorably
DISI: Dairy Industries Society International
disk: *diskonto* (Norwegian—discount)
disloc: dislocation
dissem: disseminate
disin: disinfectant; disinfection
dism: dismiss; dismissal
dismal science: Carlyle's nickname for economics
Dismal Swamp City: (naval argot—Norfolk, Virginia)—less complimentary nicknames are usually used by sailors when referring to this port on the edge of the Dismal Swamp
dismd: dismissed
diso: die shoe
disod: disodium
disord: disorder
disp: dispensary; dispensatory; dispenser; disposition
disp.: *dispensa* (Latin—dispense)
dispen: dispensatories; dispensatory
displ: displacement
dispr: dispatcher
disr: disrated
diss: disassembly; dissent; dissenter; dissertation
dissd: dissolved
dissec: dissection
dissem: disseminated
dissert: dissertation(s)
disson: dissonance; dissonant(ly)
Dissonant: Mozart's String Quartet in C (K 465)
dissyl: dissyllable
dist: distance; distant; distribute; distribution; distributor; district
dist.: *distilla* (Latin—distill)
Dist: District
Dist Ad: District Administrator
Dist Atty: District Attorney
distb: distillable
Dist Ct: District Court
distil: distillation; distilled; distilling
Dist J: District Judge
distn: distillation
distng: distinguish; distinguishing
Dis TP: Distinction in Town Planning
distr: distribute; distribution
DISTRAMS: Digital Space Trajectory Measurement System
distran: diagnostic fortran
distrib: distribution; distributive; distributor
DISTRIPRESS: *Fédération International des Distributeurs de Presse* (French—International Federation of Wholesale Book, Newspaper, and Periodical Distributors)
DISUM: Daily Intelligence Summary (USAF)
disy: disyllabic
dit: domestic independent tour; dual input transponder
dit (DIT): diiodotyrosine
DIT: Detroit Institute of Technology; Drexel Institute of Technology; Durham Institute of Technology
DiTa: diesel tanker vessel
dithy: dithyramb(ic)(al)(ly); di-

thyrambs
diu: data interface unit
div: divergence; diverse; divide; divided; dividend; divisibility; division; divisor; divorce; divorced
Div: Divide (postal abbreviation); Divine; Divinity; Division
Div Arty: Division Artillery
divd: dividend
divde: *dividende* (French—dividend)
Div E: Division Engineer
divear: diving instrumentation vehicle for environmental and acoustic research
div. en p. aeq.: *divide in partes aequales* (Latin—divide into equal parts)
divi: divide; dividend
Divine Poet: John Donne
divine Sarah: the divine Sarah—Oscar Wilde's nickname for Sarah Bernhardt who began life as Rosine Bernard
div. in par. aeq.: *dividatur in partes aequales* (Latin—divide into equal parts)
Divio: (Latin—Dijon)
divi(s): dividend(s)
divn: division
divnl: divisional
divs: dividends
divvy: divide; dividend
diw: dead in the water
Dixie: southern United States; the South
diy: do it yourself
diz: *dizionario* (Italian—dictionary)
Dizzy: Benjamin Disraeli—British Prime Minister
Dizzy Dean: Jay Hanner (Dizzy) Dean
Dizzy Gillespie: John Birks (Dizzy) Gillespie
dj: disc jockey; dust jacket
Dj: *Djawa* (Indonesian—Java)
d J: *der Jüngere* (German—junior); *dieses Jahres* (German—of this year)
DJ: David Jones (Australian department store chain); Department of Justice; District Judge; Divorce Judge
D-J: Dow-Jones (average)
DJ: *Divehi Jumhuriyya* (Divehi Arabic—Republic of Maldives)—Maldive Islands
D.J.: *Doctor Juris* (Latin—Doctor of Law)
D of J: Department of Justice
Dja: Djakarta
DJAG: Deputy Judge Advocate General
djd: degenerative joint disease
djeziret: (Arabic or Turkish—island)
DJI: Dow-Jones Industrials (average)
DJIA: Dow-Jones Industrial Average
Djkta: Djakarta (Batavia), Java
Djl: *Djalan* (Malay—road or street)
Djokja: Djokjakarta, Java, Indonesia
D.Journ.: Doctor of Journalism
D.J.S.: Doctor of Juridical Science
D.Jur.: Doctor of Jurisprudence
dk: dark; decay; deck; diseased kidney(s); dock; dog kidney; duck; dusky
DKB: Dai-ichi Kangyo Bank; *Det Kongelige Bibliotek* (Danish—The Royal Library)—Copenhagen
DKC: De Kalb College
dk di: dinking die
dkg: decking; dekagram(s)
dk hse: deck house
DKI: *Det Kriminalistiriske Institute* (Danish—The Criminalistic Institute)—Copenhagen
dkl: dekaliter
dkm: dekameter
dkm²: square dekameter
dkm³: cubic dekameter
DKP: *Danmarks Kommunistiske Parti* (Danish Communist Party); *Deutsche Kommunistische Partei* (German Communist Party)
DKr: Danish krone(r)
DKR: Dakar, Senegal (airport)
dks: dekastere
DKS: Deputy Keeper of the Signet
dkt: docket
DKTC: Door-Kewaunee Teachers College
DKW: Deutsche Kraftfahrt Werks (German—German Power-drive Works)
DKW: *Dampf Kraft Wagen* (German—steam power vehicle); *Das Kleine Wunder* (German—The Little Wonder—automobile)
dkyd: dockyard
dl: data link; day letter; deadlight; dead load; deciliter; delay line; demand loan; difference limen (threshold); dog license; double acetate; drawing list; driver's license
d-l: -dextro-levo
d/l: data link; demand loan
Dl: Daniel
DL: Danger List; Delta Air Lines (2-letter symbol); Department of Labor; difference of latitude; Drawing List; frigate (naval symbol)
DL: *Danske Lov* (Danish Law)
D-L: Deputy-Lieutenant
D èn L: *Docteur èn Leyes* (French—Doctor of Law)
D es L: *Docteur es Lettres* (French—Doctor of Literature)
D.o.L.: Doctor of Oriental Learning
D of L: Department of Law; Department of Labor; Department of Labour; Duchy (Duke) of Lancaster; Duchy (Duke) of Lorraine; Duchy (Duke) of Lüneburg
dla: distolabial
DLA: Divisional Land Agent (UK)
dlai: distolabioincisal
D.Lang.: Doctor of Languages
D-L antibody: Donath-Landsteiner antibody
DLAS: Defence of Literature and the Arts Society
d lat: difference in latitude
DLAT: Defense Language Aptitude Test (USA)
dlb's: dead-letter boxes
dlc: direct lift control; down left center
DLC: Disaster Loan Corporation; Duquesne Light Company
dld: deadline date; delivered
dle: data link escape; disseminated lupus erythematosus (DLE)
dlea: double leg elbow amplifier
D.L.E.S.: Doctor of Letters in Economic Studies
D Lett: *Docteur en Lettres* (French—Doctor of Letters)
DLG: David Lloyd George; guided-missile frigate (naval symbol)
DLGA: Decorative Lighting Guild of America
DLGN: nuclear-powered guided-missile frigate (naval symbol)
DLH: *Deutsche Lufthansa* (German airline)
DLI: Defense Language Institute
DLIA: Dental Laboratories Institute of America
D-library: duplicating library
dlir: depot-level inspection and repair
DLIS: Desert Locust Information Service
D. Litt.: *Doctor Litterarum* (Latin—Doctor of Letters; Doctor of Literature)

dll: dial long line
DLL: Deutsche Levante-Linie (Levant Line); Donaldson Line Limited
dllf: design limit load factor
dlli: dulcitol lysine lactose iron (DLLI)
dlM: des laufenden Monats (German—this month)
DLM: Daily List of Mails
DLMA: Decorative Lighting Manufacturers Association; Downtown Lower Manhattan Association
DLNWR: Des Lacs National Wildlife Refuge (North Dakota)
dlo: difference in longitude; dispatch loading only; distolinguo-occlusal
D'Lo: The Lord (town in Mississippi)
DLO: Dead Letter Office; Difference of Longitude; District Legal Office(r)
D.L.O.: Diploma in Larygology and Otology
DLOC: Division Logistical Operation Center
DLOCA: Department of Law Office Consumer Affairs
d lock: dial-lock
d long: difference in longitude
D-love: deficiency love (exploitative and possessive love of another person)
DLOY: Duke of Lancaster's Own Yeomanry
dlp: distolinguopulpal; double-large post
DLP: Director of Laboratory Programs (USN)
dlq: deliquescent; mean diurnal low water inequality
dlr: dealers; dollar; double-lens reflex (camera)
DLR: Driving Licences Regulations
DLR: *Distrito de la Luz Roja* (Spanish—Red Light District)
DLRO: District Labor Relations Office(r)
DLRs: *Dominion Law Reports*
dls: debt liquidation schedule; dollars
dls: *dólares* (Spanish—dollars)
DLS: Debt Liquidation Schedule
D.L.S.: Doctor of Library Science; Doctor of Library Service
D.L.Sc.: Doctor of Library Science
DLSC: Defense Logistics Service Center
DLSEF: Division of Library Services and Educational Facilities (U.S. Office of Education)
dls/shr: dollars per share
dlt: deck landing training
dlt: *dans le texte* (French—in the text)
dlt (DLT): data-loop transceiver (data processing)
D-L T: Donath-Landsteiner Test
DLTS: Deck Landing Training School
dlu: digitizer logic unit
dlvr: deliver; delivery
dlvry: delivery
DLW: Diesel Locomotive Works
DL & W: Delaware, Lackawanna and Western (railroad)
dly: daily; delay; dolly
dlyd: delayed
dm: decimeter(s); demand meter; diabetes mellitus (DM); diabetic mother; diastolic murmur; diesel-mechanical; diphenylaminearsine chloride (Adamsite war gas); draftsman
d/m: density/moisture
dm²: square decimeter
dm³: cubic decimeter
d & m: dressed and matched
d M: *dieses Monats* (German—this month)
DM: Des Moines; Deutsche Mark (German mark—currency unit); Du Mont (television network); light minelayer, high-speed (naval symbol)
DM: *Daily Mail*
D.M.: Doctor of Mathematics; Doctor of Medicine; Doctor of Music; Doctor of Musicology
D & M: Detroit and Mackinac (railroad)
D en M: *Docteur en Médecine* (French—Doctor of Medicine)
D of M: Duchy (Duke) of Milan
DMA: Dance Masters of America; Defense Mapping Agency; Delicatessen Managers Association
DMAA: Direct Mail Advertising Association
dmac: dimethylacetamide (DMAC)
DMAC: Des Moines Art Center
D.Ma.Eng.: Doctor of Marine Engineering
DMAHC: Defense Mapping Agency Hydrographic Center
D.Math.: Doctor of Mathematics
Dmb: Dumbarton
dmba: dimethylbenzanthracene (DMBA)
DMBC: Detroit Motor Boat Club
dmbl: demobilization; demobilize; demobilized
dmc: digital microcircuit(ry); dimethylcarbinol (DMC)—insecticide; direct manufacturing cost(s); dough moulding compound
DMC: Del Mar College; District Materials Center
dmctc: dimethylchlortetracycline (DMCTC)
DM & CW: Diploma in Maternity and Child Welfare
dmd: diamond
Dmd: Duchenne's muscular dystrophy
D.M.D.: *Dentariae Medicinae Doctor* (Latin—Doctor of Dental Medicine)
dme: distance measuring equipment
DME: Director of Medical Education
DMEA: Defense Minerals Exploration Administration
D.Mech.: Doctor of Mechanics
D.Med.: Doctor of Medicine
D.M.Ed.: Doctor of Musical Education
D.Mec.E.: Doctor of Mechanical Engineering
D-men: drug-enforcement officers; narcotics officers
dmet: distance-measuring equipment and tacan
DMET: Director(ate) of Marine Engineering Training
D.Met.: Doctor of Metallurgy
D.Met.Eng.: Doctor of Metallurgical Engineering
D. Meteor.: Doctor of Meteorology
dmf: decayed, missing, or filled (teeth)
DMF: Decorative Marble Federation
DMFOS: Diploma in Maxillo-Facial and Oral Surgery
dmg: damage; damaged; damaging
DMG: Defense Marketing Group
D of M-G: Duchy (Duke) of Mecklenburg-Güstrow
DMGO: Division(al) Machine-Gun Officer
dmh: drop manhole
DMHS: Director of Medical and Health Services; Dolley Madison High School
dmi: defense mechanisms inventory
DMI: Director of Military Intelligence
DMIAAI: Diamond Manufacturers and Importers Association of America, Incorporated

DMIC: Defense Metals Information Center (Batelle Memorial Institute)
D.Mi.Eng.: Doctor of Mining Engineering
D.Mil.S.: Doctor of Military Science
DMIR: Duluth Mesabi and Iron Range (railroad)
DMJ: Diploma in Medical Jurisprudence
dml: demolish; demolition
D.M.L.: Doctor of Modern Languages
d mld: depth moulded
DMLT: Diploma in Medical Laboratory Technology
DMM: Directorate of Materiel Management
dmma: Direct Mail/Marketing Association (abbreviated trade mark)
DMMA: Direct Mail/Marketing Association (dmma)
dmmf: dry mineral matter free
dmn: dimension; dimensional
Dmn: Drammen
Dmn Fst: *Damnation of Faust*
DMNH: Denver Museum of Natural History
dmnstr: demonstrator
DMO: Director of Military Operations; District Medical Officer
DMO & I: Director of Military Operations and Intelligence
dmp: dimethylphthalate (insect repellent also abbreviated DMP)
DMP: Director of Manpower Planning
dmpa: depomedroxyprogesterone (DMPA)
DMPA: Dublin Master Printers' Association
DMPB: Diploma in Medical Pathology and Bacteriology
dmpi: desired mean point of impact
DMPL: Des Moines Public Library
DMPP: Duck Mountain Provincial Park (Manitoba and Saskatchewan)
dmpr: damper
DMPS: Deepwater Motion Picture System
DMR: Diploma in Medical Radiology
DMRC: Deering Milliken Research Corporation
DMRD: Diploma in Medical Radio-Diagnosis
DMRE: Diploma in Medical Radiology and Electrology
DMRT: Diploma in Medical Radio-Therapy
dms: dermatomyositis; diacritical marking system (DMS)
DMS: Data Management System; Decision Making System; Director of Medical Services; Disk Monitoring System; Display Management System
D.M.S.: Doctor of Medical Science
D of M-S: Duchy (Duke) of Mecklenburg-Schwerin
D.M.Sc.: Doctor of Medical Science
DMSC: Defense Medical Supply Center
DMSDS: Direct Mail Shelter Development System
DMSGR: Dowd's Morass State Game Reserve (Victoria, Australia)
DMSI: Directorate of Management and Support of Intelligence
dmso: dimethyl sulfoxide
DMSP: Defense Meteorological Satellite Program
DMSS: Director of Medical and Sanitary Services
dmst: demonstrate; demonstration
dmstn: demonstration
dmstr: demonstrator
dmt: dimethyltryptamine—DMT (dangerous hallucinogen)
DMT: Director(ate) of Military Training
DM & TS: Department of Mines and Technical Surveys
dmu: dual maneuvering unit
DMU: Des Moines Union (railway)
D.Mus.: Doctor of Music
D.Mus.A.: Doctor of Musical Arts
D.Mus.Ed.: Doctor of Musical Education
DMV: Department of Motor Vehicles
D.M.V.: Doctor of Veterinary Medicine
DmZ: demilitarized zone
dn: debit note; decinem; dekanem; delta amplitude (symbol); dibucaine number; dicrotic notch; died near; down; downward
d'n: damn
d/n (D/N): debit note
d/N: dextrose/nitrogen (ratio)
Dn: Dale; Daniel; Dragoon(s)
D^n: *Don* (Spanish—title equivalent to "Sir")
DN: Department of the Navy
D.N.: Diploma in Nursing; Diploma in Nutrition
D.N.: *Dominus Noster* (Latin—Our Lord)
D of N: Daughters of the Nile
dna: did not attend; does not answer
dna(s): *docena(s)* [Spanish—dozen(s)]
Dna: *Doña* (Spanish—Lady)—Mrs
DNA: Defense Nuclear Agency; desoxyribonucleic acid (chromosome and gene component)
DNA: *Deutscher Normenausschusz* (German Committee on Standards)
DNAD: Director of Naval Air Division
DNANR: Department of Northern Affairs and National Resources
D.N.Arch.: Doctor of Naval Architecture
DNase: deoxyribonuclease
dnb: dinitrobenzene
DNB: Distribution Number Bank
DNB: *Dictionary of National Biography*
D.N.B.: Diplomate of the National Board of Medical Examiners
DnC: *Det Norske Creditbank* (The Norwegian Credit Bank)—also shown as *DNC*
DNC: Democratic National Committee; Domestic National Committee; Director of Naval Construction
dncb: dinitrochlorobenzene (DNCB)
DNCCC: Defense National Communications Control Center
DNCMD: Dayton Contract Management Office
dnd: died a natural death
Dnd: Dunedin
DND: Department of National Defense; Division of Narcotic Drugs (UN)
DN & D: Director of Navigation and Direction
dne: *douane* (French—customs)
DNE: Director of Nursing Education
D.N.Ed.: Doctor of Nursing Education
D.N.Eng.: Doctor of Naval Engineering
DNES: Director of Naval Education Service
dnfb: dintrofluorobenzene
DNHW: Department of National Health and Welfare (United Kingdom)
DNI: Director of Naval Intelli-

gence

***DNI:** Dana Normalisasi Indonesia* (Indonesian Institute of Standards)

D of '98: Daughters of '98

***DNJ:** Det Norske Justervesen* (Norwegian Bureau of Weights and Measures)

***D.N.J.C.:** Dominus Noster Jesus Christus* (Latin—Our Lord Jesus Christ)

Dnk: Dunkirk

dnl: do not load

DNL: Det Norske Luftfartselkap (Norwegian Airlines)

DNM: Dinosaur National Monument

DNMS: Director(ate) of Naval Medical Services; Division of Nuclear Materials Safeguards

DNO: Director of Naval Ordnance; District Naval Office(r)

***DNO:** Den Norske Opera* (The Norwegian Opera)—Oslo

dnoc: dinitro-orthocresol DNO-C)

D-Note: $500 bill

D-Notices: Defense Notices

D-notice system: British defense-notice system for protecting state secrets with the cooperation of the press

DNP: 2, 4-dinitrophenol; Dinder National Park (Sudan)

dnpm: dinitrophenyl morphine (DNPM)

***D.N.P.P.:** Dominus Noster Papa Pontifex* (Latin—Our Lord the Pope)

dnr: does not run

D/N r: dextrose-to-nitrogen ratio

DNR: Department of National Revenue; Department of Natural Resources; Director(ate) of Naval Recruiting

d/n ratio: ratio of dextrose (glucose) to nitrogen in the urine

dns: dinoyl sebacate (DNS)

Dns: Downs

DNSA: Diploma in Nursing Administration

D.N.Sc.: Doctor of Nursing Science

DNSS: Defense Navigation Satellite System

dnt: dinitrotoluene

DNT: Director(ate) of Naval Training

DNTO: Danish National Travel Office

dntp: diethyl-nitrophenyl thiophosphate (DNTP)—insecticide

***Dnus.:** Dominus* (Latin—Lord)

DNV: Det Norske Veritas (Norwegian ship classifier)

DNWR: Darling National Wildlife Refuge (Florida); Delta NWR (Louisiana); Desert NWR (Nevada)

DNWS: Director(ate) of Naval Weather Service(s)

do: first tone in diatonic scale; *C* in fixed-do system

do.: day(s) off; diamine oxidase (DO); diesel oil; dissolved oxygen; ditto; dropout

d-o: dropout

d/o: delivery order

do: (Korean—island)

***do.:** dictum* (Latin—as before; the same); *ditto* (Italian—the same)

do': door

***d:o:** dito* (Swedish—ditto)

***d O:** der (die, das) Obige* (German—the aforementioned)

Do: Dominican; Dominican Republic; Dominican or Santo Domingan; Dornier

DO: Defense Order; Department of Oceanography; Director of Operations; Disbursing Office(r); District Office(r); Dominion Observatory; Dominion Office(r); Duty Officer

D.O.: Doctor of Optometry; Doctor of Osteopathy

D/O: Disbursing Officer

D_2O: deuterium oxide (heavy water)

doa: date of availability; dead on arrival

DoA: Department of the Army (DOA)

DOA: Dead on Arrival

Doac: Dubois oleic albumin complex

DOAE: Defence Operational Analysis Establishment (UK)

***DOAL:** Deutsche Ost Afrika Linie* (German East Africa Line)

DOARS: Donnelley Official Airline Reservations System

dob: date of birth; disbursed operating base

DoB: Daughters of Bilitis

DOB: Date of Birth; doctor's order book

***DOB:** Deutsche Oper Berlin* (German Opera of Berlin)

Dob(bin): Robert

'dobe: adobe

doc: desoxycorticosterone (DOC); died of other causes; doctor; doctoral; document; documentary; documentation

Doc: doctor

DoC: Department of Commerce

DOC: Department of Commerce; Department of Communications; District Officer in Command; District Officer Commanding

doca: data of current appointment; deoxycorticosterone acetate

DOCA: Deoxycorticosterone Acetate

doce: date of current enlistment

Doc.Eng.: Doctor of Engineering

docg: deosycroticosterone glucoside (DOCG)

DOCLINE: Document Delivery On-Line (computer service)

Doc.Pol.Sci.: Doctor of Political Science

***Doct.:** Doctor* (Latin—Doctor)

***Doct[a]:** Doctora* (Spanish—Doctor)—feminine

Doctor Angelicus: (Latin—Angelic Doctor)—Italian scholastic philosopher Thomas Aquinas also known as the *Princeps Scholasticorum* (Prince of Scholastics)

Doctor Charlie: Dr Charles Horace Mayo—co-founder of the Mayo Clinic (*see* Doctor Will)

Doctor Johnson: Doctor Samuel Johnson—critic, conversationalist, lexicographer

Doctor Mirabilis: (Latin—Admirable Doctor)—English savant Roger Bacon

Doctor Seuss: author-cartoonist Theodore S. Geisel

Doctor Singularis: (Latin—Singular Doctor)—William Occam

Doctor Subtilis: (Latin—Subtle Doctor)—Duns Scotus

Doctor Watson: Dr John B. Watson, M.D. of London; companion of the world-famous consulting detective Sherlock Holmes of 221-B Baker Street who with "My dear Watson" entered the mythology of almost modern times as literary creations of Sir Arthur Conan-Doyle

Doctor Will: Dr William James Mayo—co-founder with his brother Charles of the Mayo Foundation for Medical Education and Research at Rochester, Minnesota

docu: document(ary)

docum: document; documentary; documentation; documented

Documentary Photographer: Alfred Stieglitz

***documto:** documento* (Spanish—document)

DOCUS: Display-Oriented Computer Usage System

dod: date of death; died of disease
Dod: Dodecanese
Dod(dy): Dorothy
DoD: Department of Defense
DOD: Department of Defense; date of death; died of disease
DODAS: Digital Oceanographic Data Acquisition System
DoDCI: Department of Defense Computer Institute
Dodd: Dodd, Mead
DoDDAC: Department of Defense Damage Assessment Center
Dodecanese: Dodecanese Islanders; Dodecanese Islands
dodprt: date of departure
doe.: date of enlistment; dyspnea on exercise; dyspnea on exertion
DoE: Director of Education
DOES: Disk-Oriented Engineering System
doesn't: does not
dofab: damned old fool about books
dofic: domain-originated functional integrated circuit
DOFL: Diamond Ordnance Fuze Laboratories
dog.: disgruntled old graduate
dogm: dogmatic; dogmatism; dogmatist
Dogwood: state flower of North Carolina and Virginia
dohc: double overhead cam; dual overhead cam
doi: dead of injuries; descent orbit insertion
doi: (Thai—mountain)
DoI: Department of Industry; Director(ate) of Information
doin': doing
D of J: Dominion of Jamaica
D Ø K: Det Ostasiaatiske Kompagni (Royal Danish East Asiatic Company)
dol: dear old lady; dollar
dol: *dolce* (Italian—sweet); *dolor* (Latin or Spanish—pain)—the *dol* is the unit of pain; *dolore* (Italian—pain)
Dol: Dolph (Adolf); dolphin; Dorothea; Dorothy
dolciss: *dolcissimo* (Italian—very sweetly)
dolichocephs: dolichocephalics (long-skulled people)
Dolf: Adolph; Adolphus; Rudolph
Doll: Dorothy
Dolley (Dolly): Mrs Doreathea (Dolley) Payne Madison (wife of President James Madison); Dorothea; Dorothy
dollies: dolophine pills
dolo: dolophine (methadone hydrochloride used as a morphine substitute in withdrawing addicts from heroin)
dom: date of marriage; dirty old man; domestic; domicile; dominion; drawn over mandrel
dom: *domenica* (Italian—Sunday); *domingo* (Portuguese or Spanish—Sunday)
Dom: Domenico; Dominic; Dominican; Dominican Republic; Dominion
Dom.: *Dominicus* (Latin—of the Lord, as in *Dies Dominica*—the Lord's Day)
DOM: Date of Marriage; dimethoxyalpha methyl phenethylmine (dangerous psychedelic drug also called STP)
D.O.M.: *Deo Optimo Maximo* (Latin—to God the Best and the Greatest—inscription found on some cemetery cornerstones and on labels of some benedictine bottles
DOMAINS: Deep-Ocean Manned Instrument Station(s)
Dom Bk: *Domesday Book*
Dom Can: Dominion of Canada
dom econ: domestic economy (home economics)
dom ex: domestic exchange
domi: domicile
Dominican Republic: Santo Domingo
dom^o: *domingo* (Spanish—Sunday)
Dom^o: *Domingo* (man's name)
DOMO: Dispensing Opticians Manufacturing Organization
Dom.Proc.: *Domus Procerum* (Latin—House of Lords)
Dom Rep: Dominican Republic
DOMS: Diploma in Opthalmic Medicine and Surgery
domsat: domestic communication satellite; domestic satellite carrier
dom sci: domestic science
don.: *donec* (Latin—until)
Don: Donald; Donegal
Don: *Donderdag* (Dutch—Thursday); *Donnerstag* (German—Thursday); (Spanish—Lord and Master; from the Latin—dominus); *Don Quixote* (fantastic variations for cello and orchestra by Richard Strauss); The Don—Mozart's two-act comic opera—*Don Giovanni*
DoN: Department of the Navy
Donatello: Donato di Betto Bardi
donec alv. sol. fuerit: *donec alvus soluta fuerit* (Latin—until the bowels move)
Doneg: Donegal (sometimes Don)
Don Francisco: Francisco I. Madero—Mexican president
Donnie: Donald
Don Pepe: José Figueres Ferrer—democratic leader of Costa Rica
Don Porfirio: Don Porfirio Diaz — Mexican dictator-president
Don Q: Don Quixote
Don Quijote: (Spanish—Don Quixote)—central character in the novel of Cervantes—*Don Quijote de la Mancha*
Don Romulo: Romulo Betancourt—democratic leader and recent president of Venezuela
don't: do not
Don't Give Up The Ship: nickname of Captain James Lawrence, USN
do-nut: doughnut
Don Venus: Don Venustiano Carranza—Mexican general-president
doo: diesel oil odor
DOO: Director—Office of Oceanography
doom.: deep ocean optical measurement
Doorstep to Canada: Nova Scotia
dop: dermo-optical perception; developing-out paper
dopa (DOPA): dihydroxyphenylalanine
dopase: dopa oxidase
D. Oph.: Doctor of Opthalmology
dopl: *doplene* (Czech—enlarged)
d-o psychiatrists: directive-organic psychiatrists
D.Opt.: Doctor of Optometry
D.Opth.: Doctor of Opthalmology
dor: date of rank; dental operating room; doric; dormitory
Dor: Dorado; Doric; Dorothy
D. Or.: Doctor of Oratory
DOR: Director(ate) of Operational Research
Dora: Deborah; Dorothea; Dorothy; Eudora; Theodora
DORA: Defence of the Realm Act
doran: Doppler range and navigation
Dord: Dordogne
DORDEC: Domestic Refrigerator Development Council
Doric(k): Theodoric(k)
Dorie: Doris
Doris: Doreen; Dorothea; Dorothy; Eudora; Theodora

DORIS: Direct Order Recording and Invoicing System
Doris Day: Doris Kapelhoff
DORL: Developmental Orbital Research Laboratory
dorm: dormitories; dormitory
dorna: desoxyribose nucleic acid
Dorothy Dix: Elizabeth M. Gilmer
Dorothy Parker: Dorothy Rothchild
dorp: (Dutch—village)
Dors: Dorset; Dorsetshire
Dorset: Dorsethshire
D Orth: Diploma in Orthodontics; Diploma in Orthoptics
dos: date of separation; dosage; dose; dosimetric; dosimetry; dosiology
dos.: *dosis* (Latin—dose)
DoS: Department of State
DOS: Date of Separation; Department of State; Digital Operation System; Disk Operating System
D.O.S.: Doctor of Ocular Science; Doctor of Optical Science; Doctor of Optometric Science
Dosc: Dubois oleic serum complex
Dosh Univ: Doshira University
dosim: dosimetry (measurement of radiation doses)
dosv: deep ocean survey vehicle
dot.: deep-ocean technology; deep-oceanic turbulence
Dot: Dorothy; Dotty
D o T: Defense of the Territory; Department of Transportation
DOT: Deep Oil Technology (company); Department of Overseas Trade; Diploma in Occupational Therapy
DOT: *Dictionary of Occupational Titles*
DOTIPOS: Deep Ocean Test-in-Place and Observation System
Dott: *Dottore* (Italian—Doctor)
D o T & T: Dominion of Trinidad and Tobago
Dotty: Doreen; Dorothea; Dorothy; Eudora
double-B: double-backed; double-banked; double-barreled; double-bass; double-bedded; double-benched; double-bonded; double-bottomed; double-breasted; double-brooded
Double D: Doubleday
double-X: doublecross; double quality; double quantity; double thickness; doubleweight; two-X; XX
doubt.: doubtful
Doug: Douglas(s)
Doug fir: Douglas fir
Douglas Fairbanks: Douglas Ulman
dov: double oil of vitriol (sulphuric acid)
Dov: Dover; Dovid
dovap: Doppler velocity and position
Dover: Dover Publications
dow: died of wounds; dowager; dowel; dowelled
Dow: Dowager
DOW: Died of Wounds; Dow Chemical Company; Dow Chemicals
DoWaPO: *Dictionary of Word and Phrase Origins*
dowb: deep ocean work boat
Down East: Atlantic coast area extending from New York to Nova Scotia and particularly the coastal New England states
Down's syndrome: mongolism resulting from mental retardation due to extra chromosome-21 material
Down Under: Australia and New Zealand—both down under the Equator
Doyen of European Diplomacy: Prince Klemens Wenzel Nepomuk Lothar von Metternich
doz: dozen
dozer: bulldozer
dp: damp proof(ing); dash pot (relay); data processing; deck piercing; deep penetration; deep pulse; deflection plate; departure point; dewpoint; diametral pitch; diastolic pressure; diffusion pressure; digestible protein; diphosgene (deadly gas); diproprionate; disability pension; disphosphate; displaced person; distopulpal; distribution point; donar's plasma; double paper; double pole; drip-proof; drop point; dump; durable press; potential difference (symbol)
d & p: developing and printing
d.p.: *directione propria* (Latin—with proper direction)
d/p: delivery papers
d/p: *días plazo* (Spanish—pay days)
d. in p.: *divide in partes* (Latin—divide)
DP: by direction of the President; Democratic Party; Department of the Pacific; Detrucking Point; Director of the Port; Displaced Person
D-P: Data-Phone
D.P.: dementia praecox; Doctor of Pharmacy
D.P.: *Domus Procerum* (Latin—House of Lords)
D & P: Deberny and Peignot
D of P: Daughters of Pennsylvania; Daughters of Pocahontas; Director of Planning; Director of Plans; Duchy (Duke) of Prussia
dpa: deferred payment account
dpa (DPA): diphenylamine; dipicolinic acid
DPA: Deutsche Presse-Agentur (German Press Agency); Doulat i Padshahi ye Afghanistan (Kingdom of Afghanistan)
D.P.A.: Doctor of Public Administration
DPA: *Deutsche Press Agentur* (German news agency)
DPAS: Discharged Prisoners' Aid Society
dpb: deposit passbook
DPB: Department of Printed Books (British Museum Library)
dpbc: double pole both connected
dpc: data processing control; double paper single cotton
DPC: Daniel Payne College; Defense Plant Corporation; Defense Procurement Circular; Defense Production Chief; Desert Protective Council; Displaced Persons Commission; Duke Power Company
dpcm: differential pulse-code modulation
dpd: data project directive; diffuse pulmonary disease
DPD: Data Products Division (Stromberg-Carlson); Department of Public Dispensary; Diploma in Public Dentistry
dpdc: double paper double cotton
dp di: dimple die
dp dt: double pole, double throw
dpe: data processing equipment
Dpe: Dieppe
DPE: Diploma in Physical Education
D.P.E.: Doctor of Physical Education
D.Ped.: Doctor of Pedagogy
dpe service: developing-printing-enlarging service
dpf: deferred pay fund
DPf: Deutsche Pfennig (German—pfennig)
dpfc: double pole front connected
dpft: double-pedestal flat-top

(desk)
dpg (DPG): diphosphoglyceric acid
DPG: Dugway Proving Ground
dph: diamond pyramid hardness; (DPH) diphenylhydantoin
D. Ph.: *Doctor Philosophiae* (Latin—Doctor of Philosophy)
DPH: Department of Public Health; Diploma in Public Health
D.P.H.: Doctor of Public Health
D.Pharm.: Doctor of Pharmacy
DPHD: Diploma in Public Health Dentistry
D.Phil.: Doctor of Philosophy
DPHN: Diploma in Public Health Nursing
D.Ph.Sc.: Doctor of Physical Science
D Phys Med: Diploma in Physical Medicine
dpi: data processing installation
DPI: Department of Public Information; Distillation Products Industries
DPII: Dairy Products Improvement Institute
dp-ing: data processing; durable pressing
dpl: diploma; diplomat; dual propellant loading; duplex
DPL: Dallas Public Library; Dayton Power and Light; Dayton Public Library; Denver Public Library; Detroit Public Library; diplomatic corps (license plate)
DP & L: Dallas Power and Light
***DPL:** Den Polytekniske Laeranstalt* (Danish—The Polytechnic Institute)—Copenhagen
DP & LC: Dundee, Perth & London (shipping) Company
dplx: duplex
dpm: disintegrations per minute
DPM: Diploma in Psychological Medicine
D.P.M.: Doctor of Pediatric Medicine
DPMA: Data Processing Management Association
dpn: diamond pyramid number
dpn (DPN): diphosphopyridine nucleotide
dpnh (DPNH): reduced diphosphopyridine (same as nadh or NADH)
d pnl: distribution panel
DPNM: Devil's Postpile National Monument
Dpo: Depot (postal abbreviation)
DPO: Dayton Philharmonic Orchestra; Distributing Post Office
dpob: date and place of birth
D.Pol. Eco.: Doctor of Political Economy
D.Pol.Sci.: Doctor of Political Science
DPP: Director of Public Prosecutions; Disease Prevention Program
DPPS: Department of Public Printing and Stationery
dpr: day press rates; double lapping of pure rubber
DPR: Director(ate) of Public Relations
***DPRGR:** Dewan Perwakilan Ratjat-Gotong Rojong* (Indonesian—Mutual Cooperation House of Representatives)
DPRI: Disaster Prevention Research Institute
DPRK: Democratic People's Republic of Korea (North Korea)
dps: double-pole snap switch
DP's: displaced persons
DPS: Data Processing Station; Defense Printing Service; Division of Primary Standards
DPSA: Data Processing Supplies Association
DPSC: Defense Personnel Support Center; Defense Petroleum Supply Center
dpst: deposit
dp st: double pole, single throw
DPsy: Diploma in Psychiatry; Diploma in Psychology
D. Psych.: Doctor of Psychology
D.Psy.Sci.: Doctor of Psychological Science
dpt: department; deponent; deposition; depth
dpt (DPT): dipropylphytamine
DPT: Design Proof Test(ing)
dpt vaccines: diphtheria, pertussis, tetanus vaccines
dptw: double-pedestal typewriter (desk)
dpty: deputy
D.Pub.Adm.: Doctor of Public Administration
dpv: dry pipe valve
dp/w: drawbar pull/weight (ratio)
DPW: Department of Public Works
DPWO: District of Public Works Office
dpx: duplex
dq: definite quantity; deterioration quotient; direct question(s)
DQMG: Deputy Quartermaster General
DQMS: Deputy Quartermaster Sergeant
DQU: Deganawidah-Quetzalcoatl University (University of California at Davis)
dr: debit; differential rate; door; double-reduction; drachma; dram; draw; drawn; drill; drive; drum
d/r: deposit receipt
Dr: debtor; doctor; Drive; drachma (Greek monetary unit)
DR: Data Report; Date of Rank; Dead Reckoning; Deficiency Report; Dental Recruit; Design Requirements; Despatch Rider; Detailed Report; Development Report; Document Report; National Distillers and Chemical Corporation (stock exchange symbol); reaction of degeneration (symbol)
D/R: date of rank; dead reckoning
***DR:** Deutsche Reichsbahn* (German State Railway)
dra: dead-reckoning analyzer
***dra:** derecha* (Spanish—right)
dr & a: data reporting and accounting
***Dra:** Doctora* (Spanish—woman doctor)
***Dr^{a}:** Doctora* (Spanish—doctor)—feminine form; *Doutora* (Portuguese—doctor)— feminine form
DRAC: Director of the Royal Armoured Corps
dr ad: drill adaptor
***D^{ra} D^{na}:** Doctora Doña* (Spanish—Madam Doctor)
Dr.Ae.Sc.: Doctor of Aeronautical Science
dragon: symbol of China and the Chinese
Dragon Nation: Bhutan
Dr. Agr.: Doctor of Agriculture
drai: dead-reckoning analog indicator
drain.: drainage
dram.: drama; dramatic; dramatist
***dram. pers.:** dramatis personae* (Latin—cast of characters)
dr ap: dram, apothecaries'
drapes: draperies
***dras:** derechas* (Spanish—duties; fees; tariffs)
dr av: dram avoirdupois
Drav: Dravidian
draw.: drawing
Drb: Durban
DRB: Defense Research Board (Canada); Druggists' Research Bureau
DRBC: Delaware River Basin Commission
dr bg: drill bushing
Dr.Bi.Chem.: Doctor of Biologi-

cal Chemistry
Dr.Bus.Adm.: Doctor of Business Administration
drc: damage-risk criteria (noise-exposure limits); down right center (driving, lighting, or seating)
DRC: Dutch Reformed Church; Dynamics Research Corporation
drch: drachma
Dr. Chem.: Doctor of Chemistry
dr ck: drill chuck
DRCOG: Diploma of the Royal College of Obstetricians and Gynaecologists
Dr.Com.: Doctor of Commerce
Dr D: Doctor Don (Spanish—Sir Doctor)
DR & D: Defense Research and Development
DRDO: Defense Research and Development Organization
DRDT: Division of Reactor Development and Technology (AEC)
drdto: detection-radar data takeoff
dre: dead reckoning equipment
DRE: Defense Research Establishment (Canada)
D.R.E.: Doctor of Religious Education
DR & E: Defense Research and Engineering
DREA: Defense Research Establishment, Atlantic
Dream King: Ludwig II of Bavaria
drec: detection-radar electronic component
Dr.Ec.: Doctor of Economics
dred.: dredging
DREE: Department of Regional Economic Expansion (Canada)
Dr.Eng.: Doctor of Engineering
Dr.Ent.: Doctor of Entomology
DREO: Defense Research Establishment, Ottawa
DREP: Defense Research Establishment, Pacific
Dres: Doctores (Spanish—Doctors)
DRES: Defense Research Establishment, Suffield
Dresda: (Latin—Dresden)
DRET: Defense Research Establishment, Toronto
DREV: Defense Research Establishment, Valcartier
Drew: Andrew; Charles E. Drew Postgraduate Medical School
drews (DREWS): direct readout equatorial satellite
drf: differential reinforcement
DRF: Deafness Relief Foundation; Direct Relief Foundation
drftmn: draftsman
dr fx: drill fixture
drg: drawing(s)
DRGM: Deutsches Reichgebrauchsmuster (German registered design)
D & RGW: Denver and Rio Grande Western (railroad)
Dr. h.c.: Doctor honoris causa (Latin—honorary doctor)
dr hd: drill head
Dr.Hor.: Doctor of Horticulture
Dr.Hy.: Doctor of Hygiene
DRI: Defense Research Institute; Denver Research Institute; Direct Relief International
drib: deoxyribose
drill.: drilling
DRINC: Dairy Research Incorporated
D-ring: capital-D-shaped ring
Dr. Ing.: *Doktor-Ingenieur* (German—Doctor of Engineering)
drip.: digital ray and intensity projector
Drisheen City: Cork, Ireland
dr jg: drill jig
Dr Jinnah: Mohammed 'Ali Jinnah—president of All-India Moslem League and first governor-general of Pakistan
Dr.J.Sc.: Doctor of Judicial Science
Dr. Jur.: *Doctor Juris* (Latin—Doctor of Law)
DRK: Deutsches Rotes Kreuz (German Red Cross)
drl: data retrieval language
DRL: Design Report Letter; Diamond Research Laboratory
Dr. ès L.: Docteur ès Lettres (French—Doctor of Letters)
Dr.Lit.: Doctor of Literature
DRLS: Dispatch Rider Letter Service
drm: direction of relative movement
DRM: Drafting Room Manual
Dr Med: *Doktor der Medizin* (German—Doctor of Medicine)
Dr. Med.: *Doctor Medicinae* (Latin—Doctor of Medicine)
Dr.Mus.: Doctor of Music
drn: drawn
Drn: Darien
DRN: Daily Reports Notice; Detroit River Navigation
drna (DRNA): desoxyribose nucleic acid
Dr.Nat.Sci.: Doctor of Natural Science
drnt: diagnostic roentgenology
dro: destructive readout
dro: derecho (Spanish—custom duty; right)
DRO: Disablement Resettlement Office(r)
drod: delayed readout detector
DRO-LA: Defense Research Office—Latin America (USA)
Droll Breughel: Pieter Breughel the Elder
'drome: aerodrome; airdrome
'Drome: Hippodrome
dron: data reduction
dros: date returned from overseas
dros: derechos (Spanish—duties; fees; tariffs)
Drottningholm: (Swedish—Queen's Island)—Sweden's royal summer castle
drp: dead reckoning position
DRP: Deutsches Reichspatent (German—patent); Diebold Research Program
DRP: Deutsche Reichspartei (German Reich Party)
DRPA: Delaware River Port Authority
DRPC: Defense Research Policy Committee
Dr.P.H.: Doctor of Public Health
Dr. Phil.: *Doktor der Philosophie* (German—Doctor of Philosophy)
DRPL: Del Rio Public Library
Dr.Pol.Sc.: Doctor of Political Science(s)
DRPP: Director(ate) of Research Programs and Planning
drps: drapes
drq: discomfort relief quotient
Dr.Ra.Eng.: Doctor of Radio Engineering
DRRB: Data Requirements Review Board (DoD)
Dr.Rec.: Doctor of Recreation
Dr.Re.Eng.: Doctor of Refrigeration Engineering
DRRI: Defense Race Relations Institute (DoD)
d-r-r-r-r-r-um: snaredrum roll
drs: data reduction system; drawers
DRs: Discrepancy Reports
DRS: Data Reduction System
Dr. es S.: Docteur ès Sciences (French—Doctor of Sciences)
Dr Salazar: Antonio de Oliveira Salazar—dictator and prime minister of Portugal from 1932 to 1969
DRSAM: Diploma of the Royal Scottish Academy of Music
drsc: direct radarscope camera
Dr.Sc.: Doctor of Science

Dr.Sci.: Doctor of Science
D.Sc.Jur.: Doctor of the Science of Jurisprudence
DRSCS: Digital Range-Safety Command System
Dr Seuss: Theodor Seuss Geisel
dr sh: drill shell
drsmkr: dressmaker
DRSO: Danish Radio Symphony Orchestra
drsr: dresser
drt: dead reckoning tracer
dr t: dram troy
Drt: Dartmouth
DRT: Diagnostic Rhyme Test
DRTC: Documentation Research and Training Center
DRTE: Defense Research Telecommunications Establishment (Canada)
Dr.Tech.: Doctor of Technology
Dr.Theol.: Doctor of Theology
Dr. Theol.: *Doktor der Theologie* (German—Doctor of Theology)
dr tp: drill template
dru: digital remote unit
Dru: Drusila
drub: digital remote unit buffer
D.Ru.Eng.: Doctor of Rural Engineering
Druk Yul: (Tibetan—Realm of the Dragon)—Bhutan
Drum Roll: Haydn's Symphony No. 103 in E-flat major
Dr und Vrl: *Druck und Verlag* (German—printed and published by)
Dr.Uni.Par.: Doctor of the University of Paris
D.Rur.Sci.: Doctor of Rural Science
DRV: Democratic Republic of Vietnam (North Vietnam)
DRVN: Democratic Republic of Vietnam
dr vs: drill vise
DRW: Darwin, Australia (airport)
DRWW: Distillery, Rectifying, Wine Workers (union)
drx: drachma (Greek monetary unit)
dry.: drying
dry ice: solidified carbon dioxide
ds: days after sight; day's sight; dead-air space; decanning scuttle; density standard; detached service; dilute strength; dioptric strength; direct support; discarding sabot; document signed; domestic service; donar's serum; double-screened; double silk; doublestitch(ed); downspout; draft stop
ds: *destro* (Italian—right)
d.s.: document signed
d/s: dextrose in saline
d-s: dead slow (ship's engine signal)
d & s: demand and supply
d. et s.: *detur et signatur* (Latin—let it be given and labelled)
ds (DS): data set (data processing)
Ds: dysprosium (symbol)
Ds.: *Deus* (Latin—God)
d & s: dermatology and syphilology
DS: Date of Service; Delphian Society; Delta Society; Department of Sanitation; Department of State; Design Standard(s); Detached Service; Direct Support; Directing Staff; Director of Services; Drug Store; Durham & Southern (railroad)
DS: *Danske Standardiseringsraad* (Danish Standards Institute)
D-S: Deux-Sèvres; Ditlev-Simonsen Lines
D S: *dal segno* (Italian—return to the sign: *S:*)
D/S: *Dampskip* (Norwegian—steamer; steamship)
D & S: Durham & Southern Railway
D ès S: Dar ès Salaam
d ès S: *Docteur ès Science* (French—Doctor of Science)
D of S: Daughters of Scotia; Department of State; Duchy (Duke) of Savoy; Duchy (Duke) of Silesia; Duchy (Duke) of Styria
dsa: dial service assistance; dimensionally-stabilized anode; discrete sample analyzer
DSA: Danish Sisterhood of America; Dante Society of America; Defense Shipping Authority; Defense Supply Agency; Defense Supply Association; Department of Substance Abuse; Design Schedule Analysis; Division Service Area; Drum Seiners Association; Duluth, South Shore and Atlantic (railroad); Duodecimal Society of America
DSAA: Defense Security Assistance Agency
DSAB: *Dictionary of South African Biography*
dsabl: disable; disability
DSAM: *Defense Supply Agency Manual*
DSAO: Diplomatic Service Administration Office(r)
DSAP: Data Systems Automation Program
D/S A/S: *Dampskipaksjeselskap* (Norwegian—joint stock steamship company, limited)
dsasbl: disassemble
DSASO: Deputy Senior Air Staff Officer
dsb: double sideband
DSB: Danske Stats Baner (Danish State Railways); Drug Supervisory Body (UN)
dsbg: disbursing
dsbn: disband
dsc: downstage center
D.Sc.: Doctor of Science
DSC: Defense Supply Corporation; Delaware State College; Depot Supply Center; Die Casters' Conference; Distinguished Service Cross; Document Service Center
D.S.C.: Doctor of Christian Science; Doctor of Commercial Science; Doctor of Surgical Chiropody
D & SC: Defense and Space Center (Westinghouse)
DSCC: Deep Space Communications Complex
D.Sc.Com.: Doctor of Science in Commerce
D.Sc.Eco.: Doctor of Science in Economics
D.Sc.Eng.: Doctor of Science in Engineering
D.Sch.Mus.: Doctor of School Music
D.Sc.Hyg.: Doctor of Science in Hygiene
DSC (I): Die Sinkers' Conference (International)
D.Sc.I.: Doctor of Science in Industry
D.Sc.L.: Doctor of the Science of Law
DSCM: Diploma of the Sydney Conservatorium of Music
DSCMD: Dallas Contract Management District
D.Scn.: Doctor of Scientology
D. Sc. Os.: Doctor of the Science of Osteopathy
D.Sc.Pol.: Doctor of Political Science(s)
DSCS: Defense Satellite Communication System(s)
dsd: dry surgical dressing
DSD: Daily Staff Digest; Director of Signals Division
DSDP: Deep Sea Diving Project; Deep Sea Drilling Program; Deep Sea Drilling Project
DSDS: Deep Sea Diving School (USN)
DSE: *Departamento de Seguri-*

dad del Estado (Spanish—Department of State Security)—Cuba
D.S.E.: Doctor of Science in Economics
DSEA: Delaware State Education Association
dsf: day-second-feet (or foot)
Dsf: Dusseldorf
DSF: Dainippon Silk Foundation; Division of Sea Fisheries
dsg: designate; designation
DSG: *Deutsche Schlaf- und Speisewagen Gesellschaft* (German Sleeping-and-Dining-Car Company)
dsgl: *desgleichen* (German—ditto)
dsgn: design; designed; designer
DSI: Dairy Society International; Dalcroze Society Incorporated; Distilled Spirits Institute; Drinking Straw Institute
DSIA: Diaper Service Institute of America
DSIATP: Defense Sensor Interpretation and Application Training Program
DSIF: Deep-Space Instrumentation Facility
DSIR: Department of Scientific and Industrial Research
DSIs: Directorate of Service Intelligence members or operatives
DSIS: Directorate of Scientific Information Services
D-site: decoy site
dsj: differential space justifier
dsl: deep scattering layer; diesel
DSL: Deep Scattering Layer; Delta Steamship Lines; Dickinson School of Law; Dominican Steamship Line
DSL: *Directory of Special Libraries and Information Centers*
D & SL: Denver and Salt Lake (railroad)
DSLC: Defense Logistics Services Center
dsl elec: diesel electric
ds lt: deck surface light
d & sm: dressed and standard matched (lumber)
DSM: Des Moines, Iowa (airport); Distinguished Service Medal
DSM: *Diagnostic and Statistical Manual* (of mental disorders)
dsmd: dismissed
D.S.Met.Eng.: Doctor of Science in Metallurgical Engineering
DSM Project: Development of Substitute Materials (Manhattan Engineer District secret project from 1942 to 1947; responsible for development of A-bomb)
DSN: Deep Space Network
DSNWR: De Soto National Wildlife Refuge (Iowa)
D.So.: Doctor of Sociology
DSO: Dallas Symphony Orchestra; Denver Symphony Orchestra; Detroit Symphony Orchestra; Distinguished Service Order; District Security Office(r); District Service Officer(r); District Supply Office(r); Division Signal Officer; Duluth Symphony Orchestra
D.S.O.: Doctor of the Science of Oratory
D.Soc.Sci.: Doctor of Social Science
D.So.Se: Doctor of Social Service
d.s.p.: *decessit sine prole* (Latin—died without issue)
DSP: Detroit Steel Products; Division Standard Practice
DS & P: Duell, Sloan & Pearce
dspch: dispatch; dispatcher
d spec(s): design specification(s)
dspl: disposal
d.s.p.l.: *decessit sine prole legitima* (Latin—died without legitimate issue)
dspln: disciplinary; discipline
d.s.p.m.: *decessit sine prole mascula* (Latin—died without male issue)
d.s.p.m.s.: *decessit sine prole mascula superstite* (Latin—died without surviving male issue)
dspn: disposition
dspo: disposal; dispose; disposition
d.s.p.s.: *decessit sine prole superstite* (Latin—died without surviving issue)
DSPS: Dynamic Ship-Positioning System
d.s.p.v.: *decessit sine prole virile* (Latin—died without male issue)
dsq: discharged to sick quarters
DSR: Danmarks Radio (Danish radio and tv); Detroit Street Railways
ds & r: document search and retrieval
DSRC: David Sarnoff Research Center (RCA)
DSRD: Director(ate) of Signals Research and Development
d's & r's: dailies and rushes (motion-picture film editing)
DSRS: Data Storage and Retrieval System
dsrv (DSRV): deep-submergence rescue vehicle
dss: documents signed
DSS: Defense Supply Service; Directorate of Statistical Services
D.S.S.: Doctor of Sacred Scripture; Doctor of Social Science
DS & S: Data Systems and Statistics
D S S & A: Duluth, South Shore & Atlantic (railroad)
DSSc: Diploma in Sanitary Science
DSSC: Defense Subsistence Supply Center
DSSCS: Defense Special Security Communications System (spoken of as *discus*)
DSSN: Disbursing Station Symbol Number
DSSO: Defense Surplus Sales Office; Duty Space Surveillance Officer
dssp: deep-sea submergence project
DSSRG: Deep Submergence System Review Group
DSSV: Deep Submergence Search Vehicle
dst: door stop; drop survival time
DST: Daylight Saving Time; Defense et Sécurité du Territoire (French equivalent of FBI); Dermatology and Syphilology Technician; Desensitization Test (for allergies); Director of Supplies and Transport; Double Summer Time
D.S.T.: Doctor of Sacred Theology
d-std vehicle: driver-seated vehicle
D.St.Eng.: Doctor of Structural Engineering
d-stg vehicle: driver-standing vehicle
dstl: distill
dstn: destination
DSTP: Director, Strategic Target Planning
dstpn: dessert spoon
dstr: distribution; distributor
dsu: drum storage unit
DSUE: *Dictionary of Slang and Unconventional English*
dsuh: direct suggestion under hypnosis
dsuphtr: desuperheater
D.Sur.: Doctor of Surgery
D.Surg.: Dental Surgeon
dsv: double silk varnish
dsw: door switch
DSW: Department of Social Welfare

D.S.W.: Doctor of Social Welfare
D Sz: Diego Suarez
dt: dead time; delirum tremens; dinette; diphtheria tetanus; double throw; double time; drain tile; dual tires
d-t: double-throw
d/t: deaths (total ratio)
dt: *doit* (French—debit)
Dt: duration tetanus
DT: Daylight Time; Detroit Terminal (railroad); Department of Transportation; Department of the Treasury; Distance Test; Dylan Thomas
D.T.: Dental Technician; Doctor of Theology
DT: *Daily Telegraph* (London); *Danmarks Turistrad* (Danish Tourist Board)
DoT: Department of Telecommunications; Department of Transport(ation); Department of the Treasury
dta: development test article; differential thermal analysis; distributing terminal assembly; double tape armored cable
DTA: Defense Transportation Administration; Development Test Article; Differential Thermal Analysis; Diploma in Tropical Agriculture; Divisão de Exploração dos Transportes Aéreos
dtas: diffuse thalamic activating system
DTASW: Department of Torpedo and Anti-Submarine Warfare
dtc: direct-to-consumer
DTC: Department of Trade and Commerce
DTC: *Deutscher Touring Club* (German Touring Club)
DTCD: Diploma in Tuberculosis and Chest Diseases
D.T.Chem.: Doctor of Technical Chemistry
DTCS: Digital Test Command System
dt c sk: don't countersink
dtd: dated
d.t.d.: *detur talis dosis* (Latin—let such a dose be given)
DTD: Diploma in Tuberculosis; Director(ate) of Technical Development
DTD: *Dekoratie voor Trouwe Dienst* (Dutch—Decoration for Loyal Service)
D.Tech.: Doctor of Technology
D.T.Eng.: Doctor of Textile Engineering
dtf: daily transaction file
DTF: Dental Traders' Federation; Domestic Tariff Federation; Domestic Textiles Federation
dtg: date time group
Dtg: Dienstag (German—Tuesday)
dth: delayed-type hypersensitivity
D.Th.: Doctor of Theology
DTH: Diploma in Tropical Hygiene
D.Theol.: Doctor of Theology
D ThPT: Diploma in Theory and Practice of Teaching
dti: dial test indicator
DTI: Department of Trade and Industry (UK)
DT & I: Detroit, Toledo and Ironton (railroad)
d-time: dream time
dtl: detail; detailed; diode transistor logic
DTL: Detroit Testing Laboratory
dtm: duration time modulation
Dtm: Dortmund
DTM: Diocesan Travelling Mission; Diploma in Tropical Medicine
D.T.M.: Doctor of Tropical Medicine
DTMB: David Taylor Model Basin
DTMBAL: David Taylor Model Basin Aerodynamics Laboratory
DTMH: Diplomate of Tropical Medicine and Hygiene
DTMI: Dairy Training and Merchandising Institute
dt mld: draft moulded
DTMS: Defense Traffic Management Service
dtn: detain
dtn (DTN): diphtheria toxin, normal
DTN: Drug Trade News
DTNM: Devil's Tower National Monument
dto: *descuento* (Spanish—discount)
dt^{o}: *direito* (Portuguese—right)
DTO: Dental Therapists of Ontario; Director(ate) of Trade and Operations
DTO: *Dansk Teknisk Oplysningstjeneste* (Danish Technical Information Service)
d-to-a: digital-to-analog
d-to-d: dawn-to-dusk (daylight patrol); dusk-to-dawn (night patrol)—"when in doubt—spell it out"
dtp: diphtheria, tetanus, pertussis (whooping cough)—combined vaccination
DTP: distal tingling on pressure
dtps: diffuse thalamic projection system
dtr: deep tendon reflexes; double tax(ation) relief
dtr (DTR): distribution tape reel (data processing)
DTR: Diploma in Therapeutic Radiology
DTRA: Defense Technical Review Agency (USA)
DTRP: Diploma in Town and Regional Planning
Dtrt: Detroit
dt's: delerium tremens; dementia tremors
DTS: Defense Telephone Service; Defense Transportation System
D & TS: Detroit and Toledo Short Line (railroad)
Dtsch: Deutsch (German—German)
dtt: diphtheria tetanus toxin; duplicate title transferred
D of TT: Dominion of Trinidad and Tobago
dtu: data transformation unit
DTU: Delft Technical University
DTV: Deutsche Taschenbuch Verlag (German Pocketbook Publisher)
DTVM: Diploma in Tropical Veterinary Medicine
DTW: Detroit, Michigan (Detroit Metropolitan Airport)
d2s & cm: dressed two sides and center matched (lumber)
d2s & m: dressed two sides and matched (lumber)
d2s & sm: dressed two sides and standard matched (lumber)
Dtz: Dutzend (German—dozen)
DTZ: Division Tactical Zone (USA)
Dtzd: Dutzend (German—dozen)
du: diagnosis undetermined; density unknown; died unmarried; digital unit; dog unit; duodenal ulcer
Du: Ducal; Duchy; Duke; Dutch
DU: Dalhousie University; Denison University; diagnosis undetermined; Dillard University; Drake University; Drew University; Duke University; Duquesne University
dua: digital uplink assembly
DUA: Digitronics Users Association
DUADS: Duluth Air Defense Sector
DUAH: Department of Urban Affairs and Housing
DUAL: Data Use and Access

Laboratories
Dual Cities: Minneapolis and Saint Paul, Minnesota
Dual Protectorate: Andorra under the protection of France and Spain
dub.: double; dubber; dubbing; dubious
dub.: *dubius* (Latin—dubious)
Dub: Dublin
DUB: Dublin, Eire (airport)
Dubini's disease: rapid and rhythmic muscular contraction
Dubl: Dublin; Dubliner
DUBC: Durham University Boat Club
Dublinum: (Latin—Dublin)
duc: demonstration unity capsule
DUC: Distinguished Unit Citation; Durban University College
D.U.C.: Doctor of the University of Calgary
Duca Minimo: Gabriele D'Annunzio
Duchenne de Boulogne: Guillaume-Benjamin-Amand Duchenne—father of modern neurology
Ducky: Joe Medwick
DUCS: Deep Underground Communications System
duct.: ductile
Dud: Dudley
dudat: due date
Duff: Duffield; Duffle; Mc Duff
DUH: Duke University Hospital
dui: driving under the influence (of alcohol and/or drugs)
Duke: Marmaduke
Duke of the Abruzzi: Italian alpinist and arctic explorer Prince Luigi Amadeo Giuseppe Maria Ferdinando Francesco
Duke of Alba: Fernando Alvarez de Toledo
Duke Ellington: Edward Kennedy Ellington
Duke of Wellington: Arthur Wellesley
DUKW: amphibious truck
Dul: Duluth
DUL: Duke University Library
Dulag: *Durchgangslager* (German—prisoner-of-war transit camp)
dulc.: *dulcis* (Latin—sweet)
DUM: Dublin University Mission(aries)
Dumb: Dumbarton
DUMBO: seaplane used for rescue work (naval symbol) Duke University Medical Center
Dumf: Dumfries
Dumky: Dvõrák's Trio (opus 90) for violin, piano, and cello; name comes from a Czechoslovakian term meaning a musical lament
dums: deep unmanned submersibles
dun.: dunnage
Dun: Dunbar; Duncan; Dundalk; Dundas; Dundee; Dunedin; Dunellen; Dunelm; Dungarvan; Dungeness; Dunglas; Dunglison; Dun Laoghaire (Dunleary); Dunlap; Dunlop; Dunmore; Dunn; Dunnachie; Dunning; Dunnsville; Dunoon; Dunscore; Dunsmuir; Dunstable; Dunstan; Dunvegan; Dunwood; Dunwoody
Dunb: Dunbarton
dunc: deep underwater nuclear counter
Dunc: Duncan
Dun Edin: (Celtic—Edwin's burgh)—Edinburgh
Dunelm: *Dunelmensis* (Latin—of Durham)
Dungeness Crab Capital: Newport, Oregon
Dunk: Dunkerque (Dunkirk)
D.Univ.: Doctor of the University
Dunleary: (Gaelic Irish—Dun Laoghaire)
DUNS: Data Universal Numbering System
duo.: duodecimo
duod: duodenum
duodec: duodecimo
dup: duplicate; duplicating; duplication
DUP: Diplomate of the University of Paris
D.U.P.: *Docteur de l'Université de Paris* (French—Doctor of the University of Paris)—the Sorbonne
dup^{do}: *duplicado* (Spanish—duplicate)
dupe.: duplicate; duplicate copy
dupe. neg: duplicate negative
dupl: duplicate; duplication
dupli: duplicate; duplicated; duplication
DUPONT: E.I. du Pont de Nemours & Company
Dupont Town: Wilmington, Delaware (home of E.I. du Pont de Nemours & Co)
dur: duration
dur.: *duris* (Latin—hard)
Dur: Durango; Durban; Durham
Dur: (German—major musical key)
duralumin: durable aluminum-copper-magnesium-manganese alloy
dur. dolor.: *durante dolore* (Latin—as long as the pain lasts)
Durf: *Durfee's Reports*
Durh: Durham
Dur Mus: Durban Museum
Durocortorum: (Latin—Rheims)
Duroverum: (Latin—Canterbury)
DUS: Düsseldorf, Germany (airport)
DUSA: Defense Union of South Africa
DUSA: *Dispensatory of the United States of America*
DUSC: Deep Underground Support Center (USAF)
DUSW: Director(ate) of the Undersurface Warfare Division
Dut: Dutch
du 26 ct: *du 26 mois courant* (French—the 26th of this month)
Dutch Caribees: colonial name for the Netherlands Antilles
Dutch City: Holland, Michigan
Dutch Delight: Delft's nickname
Dutch East Indies: unofficial name for the Netherlands East Indies now known as Indonesia
Dutch Guiana: Netherlands Guiana or Surinam
Dutch New Guinea: West Irian, Indonesia formerly Netherlands New Guinea
Dutch Republic: the Netherlands sometimes called Holland although Holland is but one of its eleven provinces
Dutch-speaking Places: Flemish sections of Belgium; the Netherlands; colonies and former colonies of the Netherlands such as Aruba, Bonaire, Curaçao, Saba, Sint Eustatius, Sint Maarten—the Netherlands Antilles; Netherlands New Guinea now part of Indonesia formerly the Netherlands East Indies; Netherlands Guiana or Surinam and the Dutch-speaking community in and around Holland, Michigan
Dutch Ultramodernist: Pieter Cornelis Mondriaan
Dutch West Indies: the Netherlands Antilles
Dutch William: William III of Orange—Dutch-born British king
Dutz: *Dutzend* (German—dozen)
dv: dependent variable; device; dilute volume; direct vision; distemper virus; distinguished

visitor; dive; double vibrations
d.v.: dorsiventral
d/v: *días vista* (Spanish—days at sight)
DV: Diploma in Venereology; Douay Version
D/V: Discovery Vessel
D.V.: *Deo volente* (Latin—God willing)
dva: dynamic visual acuity
DVA: Distribuidora Venezolana de Azucareros (Venezuelan Sugar Growers Distributing Organization)
dva test: duration of voluntary apnoea test
DVC: Daiblo Valley College
DVCSA: Delaware Valley College of Science and Agriculture
dvd: direct-view device
DV & D: Diploma in Venereology and Dermatology
d Verf: *der Verfasser* (German—the author)
DVES: Defense Value Engineering Services
dvfr: defense visual flight rules
DVH: Diploma in Veterinary Hygiene
dvm: digital voltmeter
d.v.m.: *decessit vita matris* (Latin—he died during his mother's lifetime)
D.V.M.: Doctor of Veterinary Medicine
D.V.M.S.: Doctor of Veterinary Medicine and Surgery
DvN: D. Van Nostrand
DVNM: Death Valley National Monument
Dvnport: Devonport
DVO: Divisional Veterinary Office(r)
d.v.p.: *decessit vita patris* (Latin—he died during his father's lifetime)
DVPH: Diploma in Veterinary Public Health
dvr: driver
DVR: Division of Vocational Rehabilitation
dvs: *det vill säga* (Swedish—that is); *det vil si* (Norwegian—that is); *det vil sige* (Danish—that is)
D.V.S.: Doctor of Veterinary Surgery
D.V.Sc.: Doctor of Veterinary Science
DVSL: District Venture Scout Leader
DVSM: Diploma of Veterinary State Medicine
dvst: direct-view storage tube
DVTI: De Vry Technical Institute
dvtl: dovetail
Dvwp: Deo volente, weather permitting (God willing, weather permitting)
dynam: dynamic; dynamics; dynamo
dw: deadweight; dishwasher; distilled water; double weight; dumbwaiter; dust wrapper
d/w: dextrose in water; dock warrant
DW: Defenders of Wildlife; Department of Waters
dwa: double wire armor(ed)
DWA: Deadly Weapon Act
dwb: double with bath
dwc: deadweight capacity
DWCHS: De Witt Clinton High School
DWCP: Detroit-Wayne County Port
dwd: driving while drunk; dumbwaiter door
dw di: draw die
DWDL: Donald W. Douglas Laboratory
dwel: dwelling
Dwellers of the Field: the Poles
dwg: drawing
DWG: Diamond Walnut Growers
dwg-ho: dwelling house
DWGNRA: Delaware Water Gap National Recreation Area (New Jersey and Pennsylvania)
dwi: driving while intoxicated
DWI: Descriptive Word Index; Durable Woods Institute; Durham Wheat Institute; Dutch West Indies (Netherlands Antilles)
Dwig: Dwiggins
dwl: designed waterline; displacement waterline; dowel
DWM: Deutsche Waffen und Munitionsfabriken
dwn: down
DWOP: Denver War On Poverty
DWP: Department of Water and Power
D W & P: Duluth, Winnipeg & Pacific (railroad)
dwr: drawer
DWR: Duke of Wellington's Regiment
dws: drop wood siding; double white silk
DWS: Department of Water Supply
DWSG & E: Department of Water Supply, Gas, and Electricity
DWSO: Drainage and Water Supply Office(r)
dwt: denarius weight; pennyweight
dw tk: drinking water tank
dwv: drain, waste, and vent (pipe)
dwz: *dat wil zeggen* (Dutch—that is to say)
dx: distance (radio); double cash ruled; duplex; static (symbol)
dx (DX): defense exhibit
Dx: diagnosis (medical)
DX: distance radio reception or transmission; Sunray Mid-Continent Oil
DXC: Penn-Dixie Cement (stock exchange symbol)
dxd: discontinued
dxda-mc: ductile metals experimental diamond abrasive—metal clad
dxm: dexamethasone
dxr: deep X-ray
dxrt: deep X-ray therapy
dXt: deep X-ray therapy
dy: delivery; dockyard; duty; penny (nails)
Dy: Dylan; dysprosium
D-y: *Druk-yul* (Bhutanese—Bhutan)
DY: De Young Memorial Museum; Druk-Yul (Kingdom of Bhutan)
dyb: dynamic braking
dy bf hl: day before holiday
DYC: Detroit Yacht Club
dyd: dockyard
dye.: dyeing
dy fl hl: day following holiday
dyk: (Dutch—dam; dike)
dyke: bulldike
dykes: diagonal wire cutters
dymaxion: dynamic maximum
DYMM: M.H. De Young Memorial Museum
DYMM: (Malay—His Highness the Ruler or Her Highness the Ruler)
dyn: dynamic; dynamics; dynamo; dynamometer; dyne
dyna: dynamite
dynam: dynamic; dynamics; dynamite; dynamo
dynamo.: dynamic model
DYNAMO: Dynamic Action Management Operation
dynasoar: dynamic soaring (space flight)
dynmt: dynamite
dyno: dynamometer
dypso: dypsomania(c)
dysen: dysentery
dyslex: dyslexia; dyslexic
dysp: dyspepsia
dysphem: dysphemistic(al)(ly); dysphemism(s)—antonym(s)

for euphemism(s)

dystac: dynamic storage analog computer

dystal: dynamic storage allocation language

dysto: dystopia(n)

DX: Aerotaxi (Colombia); distance radio reception or transmission; Sun Ray Mid-Continent Oil (stock exchange symbol)

dz: dizygotic; dozen

dz: *deppelzentner* (German—100 kilograms); *distance zénithale* (French—zenith distance)

d Z: *der Zeit* (German—of the time)

Dz: *Deniz* (Turkish—sea)

DZ: Department of Zoology; Drop Zone

D.Z.: Doctor of Zoology

DZA: Drop Zone Area

DZF: *Deutsche Zentrale für Fremdenverhkehr* (German National Tourist Association)

dzg: dizygotic

Dzl: Delfzijl (Dutch port)

dzne: *douzaine* (French—dozen)

D.Zool.: Doctor of Zoology

D-Zug: *Durchgangszug* (German—express train; through train)

Dzun: Dzungaria

E

e: base for natural logarithms 2.7182818; coefficient of impact (symbol); electron; emulsifier; emulsion; error; errors; longitudinal strain per unit length (symbol); numerical value of electron charge in an electron or proton (symbol)

'e: he

e: angle of downwash (symbol); natural logarithmic (Napierian) base

e/: *envío* (Spanish—sent)

E: American Export-Isbrandtsen Lines; Eagle Airways; Earth; east; eccentricity of a curve (symbol); Echo—code for letter E; Edinburgh; efficiency; einsteinium; emmetropia; engineer; engineering; England; English; Equator; equatorial; erbium; estimated weight (symbol); excellent; exempt; eye; Fraunhofer line caused by iron (symbol); instantaneous value alternating current (symbol); modulus of elasticity (symbol)

E^1: Lhotse I (27,890-ft adjoining peak of Mount Everest, world's highest mountain—29,028 ft)

E^2: Lhotse II (27,560-ft adjoining peak of Mount Everest)

E$: Eurodollar (American dollar deposited in Europe)

E1, E2, etc.: East One, East Two, etc. (London postal zones)

E 107: tribromoethanol (anesthetic)

E: east; Einstein unit of energy (symbol); electromotive force (symbol); (Latin—Egregius); *en* (Dutch, Portuguese, Spanish—in); Envoy Extraordinary and Minister Plenipotentiary; *est* (French or Italian—east); *este* (Portuguese or Spanish—east); *etelä* (Finnish—south); experiment (symbol); voltage (symbol)

$E = mc^2$: Einstein's equation where energy *(E)* equals the atomic mass *(m)* and the speed of light *(c)* squared; the speed of light being 186,000 miles per second

ea: each; ends annealed; enemy aircraft; enlistment allowance

EA: East Africa(n); Eastern Air Lines; educational age; Egyptian Army; Electronic Associates; experimental aircraft

EA: *Ente Autonomo* (Italian—Autonomous Corporation)

E/A: Ecology Action; enemy aircraft

eaa: essential amino acid (EAA); ethylene acrylic acid (EAA)

EAA: Engineers and Architects Association; Equipment Approval Authority; Experimental Aircraft Association; Export Advertising Association

E.A.A.: Engineer in Aeronautics and Astronautics

EAA: *Encyclopedia of American Associations*

EAAA: European Association of Advertising Agencies

EAAC: East African Airways Corporation

EAAFRO: East African Agriculture and Forestry Research Organization

EAAP: European Association for Animal Production

EABn: Engineer Aviation Battalion

eabrd: electrically-actuated band-release device

eac: erythrocyte antibody complement

EAC: East African Community (Kenya, Tanzania, Uganda); East Asiatic Company; Eastern Air Command

eaca (EACA): epsilon-aminocaproic acid

eacd: eczematous allergic contact dermatitis

ea content: effective-agent content

EACSO: East African Common Services Organization

ead: equipment allowance document; estimated availability date; extended active duty

ead.: *eadem* (Latin—the same)

EAD: Employer Association of Detroit

EADB: East African Development Bank

EADF: Eastern Air Defense Force

eae: experimental allergic encephalomyelitis

EAEC: East African Economic Community; European Atomic Energy Community

EAEG: European Association of Exploration Geophysicists

EAEI: Ecology Action Educational Institute

EAES: Environment-Atmospheric Environment Service (Cana-

da); European Atomic Energy Society
eaf: emergency action file
EAFC: Eastern Association of Fire Chiefs
EAFFRO: East African Freshwater Fisheries Research Organization
EAG: Edmonton Art Gallery
EAGGF: European Agricultural Guidance and Guarantee Fund
Eagle: *(see Columbia)*
Eagle of the North: Swedish statesman Count Axel Oxenstierna
EAHC: East African Harbours Corporation; East African High Commission
eahf: eczema, asthma, and hay fever
EAI: East Asian Institute (Columbia University); Education Audit Institute
EAIC: East African Industrial Council
EAID: Equipment Authorization Inventory Data
EAJC: Eastern Arizona Junior College
EAL: East Asiatic Line; Eastern Air Lines; Ethiopian Airlines
EALA: East African Library Association
eam (EAM): electrical accounting machine
EAM: Eastern Atlantic and Mediterranean
EAM: *Ethniko Apelevtherotiko Metopo* (Greek—National Liberation Front)
EAME: European, African, Middle Eastern
EAMECM: European-African Middle Eastern Campaign Medal
EAMF: European Association of Music Festivals
EAMFRO: East African Marine Fisheries Research Organization
EAMPA: East Anglian Master Printers' Alliance
EAMS: Empire Air Mail Scheme
EAMTC: European Association of Management Training Centers
EAN: Emergency Action Notification
EANA: Esperanto Association of North America
EANDC: Edgewood Arsenal Nuclear Defense Center; European American Nuclear Data Center
EANS: Emergency Action Notification System (radio broadcasting)
eaon: except as otherwise noted
eap: eye artifact potential
EAP: Edgar Allan Poe
EAPA: Employment Aptitude Placement Association
EAPD: Eastern Air Procurement District
EAPR: European Association for Potato Research
EAPTC: East African Posts and Telecommunications Corporation
ear.: electronic analog resolver
Ea-R: *Entartungs-Reaktion* (German—degeneration reaction)
EAR: East African Railways; Edwin Arlington Robinson
EARC: East African Railways Corporation; Eastern Air Rescue Center
EAR & H: East African Railways and Harbours
Earnie: Ernest; Ernestine; Ernesto
EARS: Emergency Airborne Reaction System
eas: equivalent airspeed
EAs: East African shilling
EAS: Early American Society
EASA: Electrical Apparatus Service Association
EASE: Emigrant's Assured Savings Estate
easemt: easement
EASEP: Early Apollo Scientific Experiments Payload
EA sh: East African shilling
easl: engineering analysis and simulation language
east.: easterly; eastern
EAST: Eastern Australian Standard Time
EASTAF: Eastern Transport Air Force
East African Community: Kenya, Tanzania, Uganda
Eastcommrgn: Eastern Communications Region
East End: congested and depressed eastern section of London
easter: storm from the east
Eastern Desert: Arabian Desert
Eastern Empire: Byzantine Empire
Eastern Europe: Czechoslovakia, Hungary, Poland, the Soviet Union
Eastern Samoa: American Samoa
Eastern Sea: East China Sea
Eastern Shore: eastern shore of Delaware, Maryland, and Virginia comprising the Del-Mar-Va Peninsula
Eastern States: states east of the Mississippi
East Germany: communist-controlled Soviet sector of Germany
East L: East Lothian
EASTLANT: Eastern Atlantic Area
East Phil: Eastman Philharmonia
EASTROLANT: Eastern Tropical Atlantic
EASTROPAC: Eastern Tropical Pacific
easy.: expense-account spending ? yes !
EASY: Early Acquisition System (USA); Engine Analyzer System
eat.: earliest arrival time; estimated arrival time (both shown as EAT on some timetables)
EAT: earliest arriving time; Experiments in Art and Technology
EATRO: East African Trypanosomiasis Research Organization
EATS: Equipment Accuracy Test Station
EATTA: East Africa Tourist Travel Association
EAVRO: East African Veterinary Research Organization
eaw: equivalent average words
eaw: Electrical Association for Women
EAWS: East African Wildlife Society
eax: electronic automatic exchange
eb: electron beam; elementary body
e-b: estate-bottled
eb: *point d'ébullition* (French—boiling point)
Eb: Ebenezer; erbium (symbol)
EB: Avitour Airlines; Eesti Vabariik (Estonian Republic)
E-B: Electric Boat (Division of General Dynamics)
E & B: Ellerman and Bucknall (Ellerman Lines)
EB: *Encyclopaedia Britannica; Engineering Bulletin*
EBA: English Bowling Association
EBAA: Eye-Bank Association of America
ebar: edited beyond all recognition
EBAR: E.B. Aabys Rederi (Norwegian freight line)
EBB: Elias Baseball Bureau; Elizabeth Barrett Browning
ebc: enamel bonded single cotton

EBC: Educational Broadcasting Corporation; European Bibliographical Center (Oxford, England)
ebcdic: extended binary-coded decimal interchange code
ebd: effective biological dose
ebd: *ebenda* (German—in the same place)
ebds: enamel bonded double silk
EBEC: Encyclopedia Britannica Educational Corporation
Eben: Ebenezer
ebf: erythroblastosis foetalis
EBF: Encyclopedia Britannica Films
ebi: emetine bismuth iodide
EBI: Emerson Books, Incorporated
EBIC: European Banks International Corporation (lowercase logotype appears as *ebic*)
ebicon: electron-bombardment-induced conductivity
eb 1 s: edge bead one side (lumber)
ebk: embryonic bovine kidney
EBL: Eastern Basketball League
Eblana: (Latin—Dublin)
ebm: expressed breast milk
EBM: *Empresa Bacaladera Mexicana* (Mexican Codfishing Enterprise)
EBMC: English Butter Marketing Company
EBNI: Electricity Board for Northern Ireland
Ebnr: Ebenezer
E-boat: enemy boat
Ebor.: *Eboracensis* (Latin—of York); *Eboracum* (Latin—York)
ebp: enamel single paper bonded
ebr: electron-beam recorder
EBR: Emu Bay Railway
EBRA: Engineer Buyers' and Representatives' Association
EBRD: Export Business Division (U.S. Department of Commerce)
'Ebrides: (Cockney contraction—Hebrides)
ebs: enamel single cotton
eb(s): eager beaver(s)
EBS: Emergency Bed Service; Emergency Broadcast System; English Bookplate Society; Ethiopian Broadcasting Service
EBSR: Eye-Bank for Sight Restoration
ebt: earth-based tug (NASA); electron-beam technique
eb 2 s: edge bead two sides (lumber)
EBU: European Broadcasting Union
ebul: ebullition
EBv: Epstein–Barr virus
ebw: exploding bridge wire
ebwr (EBWR): experimental boiling-water reactor
EBYC: European Bureau for Youth and Childhood
ec: economics; electric(al) coding; emergency capability; enamel coated; enteric coated; entering complaint; error correcting; expansive classification; expiratory center; extended coverage; extension and conversion; extension course
e/c: estrogen-to-creatinine (ratio)
E-in-C: Engineer-in-Chief
ec: *en cuento* (Spanish—on account)
e.c.: *exempli causa* (Latin—for example)
Ec: Ecuador; Ecuadorian
EC: Earlham College; East African Airways; East Carolina (railroad); East Central; Eastern College; Eastern Command; Edgewood College; Elizabethtown College; Elmhurst College; Elmira College; Elon College; Emergency Coordinator; Emerson College; Emmanuel College; Engineer Captain; Engineering Change; Engineering Construction; Episcopal Church; Erskine College; Essex College; Established Church; Eureka College; Evangel College; Evansville College; Explorers Club
E-C: Erckmann-Chatrian (combined name for two friendly collaborators: Emile Erckmann and Alexandre Chatrian)
EC1, EC2, etc.: East Central One, East Central 2, etc. (London postal zones)
EC (followed by numbers): Enzyme Commission (numbers indicate enzyme classification)
E & C: Engineering and Construction
EC: *Encyclopedia Canadiana*
eca: electronics control assembly
ECA: Economic Commission for Africa (UN); Economic Control Agency; Economic Cooperation Administration; European Confederation of Agriculture
ECAC: Eastern College Athletic Conference; Electromagnetic Compatibility Analysis Center
ECAFE: Economic Commission for Asia and the Far East (UN)
ecan: excitation, calibration, and normalization
ECAP: Electronic Circuit Analysis Program; Environmental Compatability Assurance Program (USN)
ECAS: Electrical Contractors Association of Scotland
ECB: E(benezer) Cobham Brewer
ecbo: enteric cytopathogenic bovine orphan (virus)
e & cb 1 s: edge and center bead one side (lumber)
e & cb 2 s: edge and center bead two sides (lumber)
ecc: eccentric; electrically-continuous cloth; emergency combat capability
ecc (ECC): electrocorticogram
ECC: Economic Council of Canada; Educational Cultural Complex; Electronics Capital Corporation; Emergency Conservation Committee; Employees Compensation Commission; European Coordinating Committee; European Coordinating Council; European Cultural Center; European Cultural Commission
ecc: *eccetera* (Italian—et cetera)
Ecc: *Eccellenze* (Italian—Excellency)
ECCA: East Caribbean Currency Authority
ECCA: *Empresa Consolidada Cubana de Aviación* (Spanish—Consolidated Cuban Aviation Enterprise)
ECCAA: Executive Chefs de Cuisine Association of America
ECCC: English Country Cheese Council
ECCDA: Eastern Connecticut Clam Diggers Association
eccen: eccentric; eccentrics
Eccentric Naturalist: Constantine Rafinesque
Ecc. Hom: *Ecce Homo* (Latin—Behold the Man)
ECCI: Executive Committee Communist International
eccl: ecclesiatic(al)
Eccl: *Ecclesiastes*
eccles: ecclesiastic; ecclesiastical
Ecclus.: *Ecclesiasticus*
eccm: electronic counter-counter-measures
ec^co: *eclesiástico* (Spanish—cler-

gyman; ecclesiastic; ecclesiastical; priest)
ECCP: East Coast Coal Port
ECCS: Emergency Core Cooling Systems (AEC)
eccsl: emitter-coupled-current steered logic
ECCU: English Cross-Country Union
ecd: endocardial cushion defect; estimated completion date
EC & D: Electronic Components and Devices
ecdn: electrical cables down
ece: extended coverage endorsement
ECE: Early Childhood Education; Economic Commission for Europe (UN)
ecf: extracellular fluid
ECF: European Cultural Foundation
ECFI: Eastern Caribbean Farm Institute
ECFMG: Educational Council for Foreign Medical Graduates
ECFMS: Educational Council for Foreign Medical Students
ecg: electrocardiogram; electrocardiography
ECG: electrocardiogram
ECGB: East Coast of Great Britain
ECGC: Empire Cotton Growing Corporation
ECGD: Export Credit Guarantee Department
ech: echelon
echo.: enteric cytopathogenic human orphan (virus)
Echo: code for letter E
ECHO: Experimental Contract Highlight Operation
ECHS: Evander Childs High School
eci: extracorporeal irradiation
ECI: Electronic Communications Incorporated; Extension Course Institute (Air University)
ECIC: Export Credits Insurance Corporation (Canada)
ECITO: European Central Inland Transport Organization
ECIUSAF: Extension Course Institute, USAF
ECJ: Erie County Jail (Buffalo)
eck: embryonic chicken kidney
Eck(ie): Alexander; Alexandra; Alexis; Hector; Hecuba
ecl: eclipse; electrocardiograph log; electronic crash locator (aircraft)
ecl: *eclairage* (French—lighting)
ECL: Equipment Component List; Europe-Canada Line
ECLA: Economic Commission for Latin America (UN)
eclec: eclectic; eclecticism
ecli: eclipse; ecliptic
eclo: emitter-coupled logic operator
ecm: electric coding machine; electrochemical machining; electronic countermeasure(s); ends matched, center (lumber)
ECM: Engineering Change Management; European Common Market
EC & M: Electric Controller and Manufacturing (company)
ECMA: Engineering College Magazines Associated; European Computer Manufacturers Association
Ecmalgol: European Computer Manufacturers Association Algorithmic Language
ECME: Economic Commission for the Middle East (UN)
ECMF: Electric Cable Makers' Federation
ECM & FS: East Coast Marine and Ferry Service
e-c mix.: ether-chloroform mixture
ECMR: Eastern Contract Management Region
ECMRA: European Chemical Market Research Association
ECMSA: Electronics Command Meteorological Support Agency (USA)
ECN: Engineering Change Notice
eco: ecological; ecologist; ecology; economic; economist; economics; electron-coupled oscillator; exempted by commanding officer
ECO: East Coast Overseas; Economic Corporation Organization; Effective Citizens Organization; Engineering Change Order; Environmental Control Organization; European Coal Organization
ECOA: Equipment Company of America
ecog: electrocorticogram
ecol: ecology
E coli: *Escherichia coli* (intestinal bacillus)
Ecol Soc Am: Ecological Society of America
ECOM: Electronics Command (USA)
econ: economic; economics; economist; economy
e con.: *e contrario* (Latin—on the contrary)
Econ Jrnl: *Economic Journal*
economan: effective control of manpower
economet: econometric
Econ Rev: *Economic Review*
ECOPETROL: *Empresa Colombiana de Petróleos* (Spanish—Colombian Petroleum Enterprise)
ecopow(s): economic superpower(s)—U.S.A., USSR, Japan, West Germany
ECOR: Engineering Committee on Ocean Resources
EcoSoc: Economic and Social (Council)
ecosupow(s): economic superpower(s)—U.S.A., USSR, Japan, West Germany
eco system: ecological system; economic system
ecpo: enteric cytopathogenic procine orphan (virus)
ecp(s): external casing packer(s)
ECP: Engineering Change Proposal
ECPD: Engineers Council for Professional Development
ecpog: electrochemical potential gradient
ECPS: European Center for Population Studies
ECPTA: European Conference of Postal and Telecommunication Administrations
ECQAC: Electronic Components Quality Assurance Committee
ecr: external channels ratio
ECR: Engineering Change Request
ECRB: Export Control Review Board
ECRC: Electronic Component Reliability Center; Engineering College Research Council
ECRL: Eastern Caribbean Regional Library
ecs: electroconvulsive shock; emperor's clothes syndrome; extended core storage
ECS: Electrochemical Society; Environmental Control Systems; Etched Circuit Society
ECSA: East Coast of South America; European Communication Security Agency; Expanded Clay and Shale Association
ECSC: European Coal and Steel Community
ECSIL: Experimental Cross-Section Information Library (University of California—Livermore)

ECSTC: Elizabeth City State Teachers College
ect: electroconvulsive therapy; engine cutoff time; enteric coated tablet
ect (ECT): electroconvulsive treatment
ECTA: Electrical Contractors' Trading Association
ectl: emitter-coupled transistor logic
ecu: ecumania(c); ecumenism; environmental control unit; extra closeup; extreme close-up
ecu (ECU): extra closeup; extreme closeup
Ecu: Ecuador; Ecuadorean
ECU: English Church Union
Ecua: Ecuador; Ecuadorean
Ecu Con: Ecumenical Conference; Ecumenical Council
ECUK: East Coast of United Kingdom
ecumen: ecumenical
e & cV 1 s: edge and center-V one side (lumber)
e & cV 2 s: edge and center-V two sides (lumber)
ecw: extracellular water
ECWA: Economic Commission for Western Asia (UN)
ECY: European Conservation Year
ed: edge distance; edit; edited; edition; editor; editorial; educate; educated; education; educational; educator; effective dose; enemy dead; error detecting; erythema dose; excused from duty; existence doubtful; extra duty
ed: *edición (Spanish—edition), édition* (French—edition); *edizione* (Italian—edition)
ed_{50}: median effective dose
Ed: Edgar; Editor; Edmond; Edmund; Edson; Edward; Edwin
Ed.: Editor
ED: Consolidated Edison Company (stock exchange symbol); Eastern District; Economics Division; Efficiency Decoration; Elder Dempster Line; Electric Dynamic; Engineering Data; Engineering Depot; Engineering Design; Engineering Draftsman
E-D: Electro Dynamics (Division of General Dynamics)
E.D.: Doctor of Engineering
eda: early departure authorized
EDA: Economic Development Administration (Puerto Rico); Environmental Development Agency
EDARR: Engineering Drawing and Assembly Release Record
edb: ethene dibromide (EDB)
Ed.B.: Bachelor of Education
EDB: Economic Development Board
edbiz: educational business
edc: electronic digital computer; engine-driven compressor; estimated date of completion; estimated date of confinement
EDC: Eastern Defense Command; European Defense Community; Export Development Corporation
edcn: education
EDCPF: Environmental Data Collection and Processing Facility (USA)
EDCs: Economic Development Committees
edcsa: effective date of change of strength accountability
edcv: enamel double cotton varnish
edd: electronic data display; expected date of delivery
edd: *ediderunt* (Latin—published by)
edd.: *editiones* (Latin—editions)
Ed. D.: Doctor of Education
EDD: Eastman Dental Dispensary
EDD: English Dialect Dictionary
eddf: error detection and decision feedback
Eddie: Edgar; Edmund; Edoardo; Edouard; Edsel; Eduard; Eduardo; Edvard; Edward; Edwin; Edwina
Eddie Cantor: Izzie Itskowitz
EDDS: Electronic Devices Data Service
Eddy: Edgar; Edmund; Edward; Edwin; Edwina
ede: electronic defense evaluator
Eden of the Orient: Thailand
edent: edentate; edentulous
EDF: Environmental Defense Fund; European Development Fund; Everyman Defense Fund
Edg: Edgar
edhe: experimental data-handling equipment
EDI: Economic Development Institute; Edinburgh; Scotland (airport); Engineering Department Instruction
edict.: engineering document information collection technique
Edie: Edith
Edim: *Edimburgo* (Portuguese or Spanish—Edinburgh)
Edin: Edinburgh
Edin(a): Edinburgh's poetical name
Edinburgum: (Latin—Edinburgh)— also known as Edinbruchium or Edinum
Ed-in-Ch: Editor-in-Chief
Edinglassie: Edinburgh + Glasgow (early name of the Moreton Bay Settlement now called Brisbane)
EDIP: European Defence Improvement Program (NATO)
EDIS: Engineering Data Information Service; Engineering Data Information System
edit.: editing; edition; editor; editorial
EDIT: Estate Duties Investment Trust
EDITS: Experimental Digital Television System
edl: edition de luxe
EDL: Elder Dempster Lines
EDLNA: Exotique Dancers League of North America
edm: electrical-discharge machining
Edm: Edmund
Ed. M.: Master of Education
EDMICS: Engineering Data Management Information Control System
Edm & Ips: St Edmundsbury and Ipswich
Edmn: Edmonton
Edmond Adam: French author-editor Juliette Lamber
edn: electrodesiccation
Edn: Edwin
edo: effective diameter of objective; error demodulator output; error detector output
EDO: Employee Development Officer; Engineering Duty Officer; Engineering Duty Only
edoc: effective date of change
EDOPAC: Enlisted Personnel Distribution Office Pacific Fleet
edp (EDP): electronic data processing
edpe: electronic data processing equipment
ed-ped-psych-soc: education-pedagogy-psychology-sociology
edpm: electronic data processing machine(s)
edr: electrodermal response
EDPS: Electronic Data Processing System
EDPT: Electronic Data Processing Test
edrl: effective damage risk level

EDRs: European Depository Receipts
EDRS: Education Document Reproductive Service
edrt: effective date of release from training
eds: editors; enamel double silk; estimated date of separation
EDs: Explosive Disposal specialists
EDS: English Dialect Society; Environmental Data Service
edsac: electronic delayed-storage automatic computer
edsat: educational television satellite (EDSAT)
Ed. Spec.: Educational Specialist
edst: elastic diaphragm switch technology
EDST: Eastern Daylight Saving Time
edsv: enamel double silk varnish
edt: effective date of training
EDT: Eastern Daylight Time
edta: ethylene diamine tetra-acetic (acid)
edtr: experimental, developmental, test, and research
edu: experimental diving unit
EDU: European Democratic Union
Eduardo: E. Howard Hunt
educ: education; educational
Educational Film: Educational Film Library Association
educom: education communication(s)
Educ Pr: Educational Press; Educational Press Association of America
Educ Pub: Educational Publications Services; Educational Publishers
educrat: educational bureaucrat
EDUPLAN: *Oficina de Planeamiento Integral de Educación* (Spanish—Office of Integral Planning in Education)
edutherap: educational therapist; educational therapy
edv: end-diastolic volume
Edw: Edward
Edward G: Edward G. Robinson (Emmanuel Goldberg)
Edward Longshanks: Edward I of England
eDx: electrodiagnosis
ee: eased edges (lumber); embryo extract; equine encephalitis; errors excepted; expriation of enlistment; eye and ear
'ee: thee
e & e: evacuation and evasion; evasion and escape; eye and ear
e-to-e: end-to-end
EE: Early English; Electrical Engineer(ing); Electronics Engineer(ing); Envoy Extraordinary; Estado Español (The Spanish State)
E.E.: Electrical Engineer
EE: *Euer Ehrwürden* (German—Your Reverence)
EEA: Electronic Engineering Association; Ethical Education Association
EEAIE: Electrical, Electronic, and Allied Industries of Europe
EEB: Eastern Electricity Board; Educational Employees Board
EEB: *Enosis Ellenon Bibliotekarion* (Modern Greek—Greek Library Association)
EEC: East Erie Commercial (railroad); European Economic Community
EECA: Engineering Economic Cost Analysis
eecom: electrical, environmental, and communications
e.e. cummings: Edward Estlin Cummings' lowercase way of writing his name
eed: electrical explosive device
eee: eastern equine encephalitis
EEF: Egyptian Expeditionary Force
eefi: essential elements of friendly information
eeg (EEG): electroencephalogram; electroencephalograph
EEI: Edison Electric Institute; Environmental Equipment Institute; Essential Elements of Information
EEIBA: Electrical and Electronic Industries Benevolent Association
EEL: Ecology and Epidemiology Laboratory; English Electric Limited; Evans Electroselenium Limited
eem: *Electronic Engineers Master* (catalog)
EE & MP: Envoy Extraordinary and Minister Plenipotentiary
e'en: even; evening
E Eng: Early English
EENT: end, evening nautical twilight; eye, ear, nose, and throat
EENWR: Exe Estuary National Wildlife Refuge (England)
eeo: equal employment opportunity
EEOC: Equal Employment Opportunity Commission
eep: electronic evaluation and procurement; electronic event programmer(s); emergency essential personnel
eepnl: estimated effective-perceived noise level
e'er: ever
EERI: Earthquake Engineering Research Institute
EERL: Electrical Engineering Research Laboratory (University of Texas)
EETU: Electrical Electronic Telecommunication Union
ees: electronic environment simulator
EES: Engineering Experiment Station; Enlisted Evaluation System; European Exchange System
EESS: *Encyclopedia of Engineering Signs and Symbols*
EET: Eames Eye Test; Eastern European Time; Education Equivalency Test
EETS: Early English Text Society
EEUA: Engineering Equipment Users Association
EEUU: *Estados Unidos* (Spanish—United States)
EEV: English Electric Valve (company)
EEVC: English Electric Valve Company
eex: electronic egg exchange (computer program)
ef: each face; elevation finder; equivalent focal length; expectant father; experimental flight; extra fine
EF: Educational Foundation; Emergency Fleet; Expeditionary Force
E & F: Elders and Fyffes (steamship line)
efa: essential fatty acids
EFA: Environmental Financing Authority; Epilepsy Foundation of America; European Free Associations
efc: earth fixed coordinate; Evergreen Fir Corporation (initials)
EFC: European Forestry Commission
EFCX: Evergreen Freight Car Express
efd: excused from duty
EFDSS: English Folk Dance and Song Society
efe: endocrinal fibro-elastosic
EFEA: Empresa Ferrocarriles del Estado Argentino (Argentine State Railways)
eff: effect; effective; efficiency
eff: *effeto* (Italian—bill; promissory note)

EFF: European Furniture Federation
effcy: efficiency
effect.: effective; effectivity
effer: efferent
Effie: Euphemia
effl: efflorescent
eff wd: effective wind
EFG: Edward FitzGerald
ef & i: engineer, furnish, and install
EFINS: Enrico Fermi Institute for Nuclear Studies (Univ of Chicago)
efl: effective focal length
EFLA: Educational Film Library Association
EFLC: Engineers Foreign Language Circle
EFM: European Federalist Movement
EFMG: Electric Fuse Manufacturers Guild
EFNS: Educational Foundation for Nuclear Science
efp: effective filtration pressure; electric(al) fuel propulsion
EFPA: Educational Film Producers Association
EFPW: European Federation for the Protection of Waters
efr: effective filtration rate
EFRC: Edwards Flight Research Center
E Fris: East Frisian
EFS: Edinburgh Festival Society; Emergency Feeding Service
EFSA: European Federation of Sea Anglers
EFSC: European Federation of Soroptimist Clubs
eft: earliest finish time
eft (EFT): electronic funds transfer
EFT: Embedded Figures Test; Engineering Flight Test
EFTA: European Free Trade Association
EFTC: Electrical Fair Trading Council
eftf: *efterfölger* (Dano-Norwegian—successor)
Eftf(lg): *Efterfölgere* (Dano—Norwegian—successor)
EFTI: Engineering Flight Test Instrumentation
eftm: *eftermiddag* (Norwegian—after noon)—p.m.
efto: encrypt for transmission only
EFTS: Elementary Flying Training School
efu: energetic feed unit
EFU: European Football Union
EFU: *Europäische Frauenunion* (German—European Women's Union)
EFVA: Education Foundation for Visual Aids
e.g.: *exempli gratia* (Latin—for example)
Eg: Egypt; Egyptian
EG: Equatorial Guinea (formerly Spanish Guinea); grid voltage (symbol)
EGA: European Golf Association
egad.: electronegative gas detector
egads: electronic ground automatic destruct sequencer (system for destroying malfunctioning missiles)
egal: egalitarian(ism)
Egb: Egbert
e-g-b-d-f: (musical menemonic—every good boy does fine)—treble clef note names of the five lines (e-g-b-d-f)
egcr: experimental gas-cooled reactor
EGCRNR: Eilat Gulf Coral Reef Nature Reserve (Israel)
EGCS: English Guernsey Cattle Society
egd: electrogasdynamics
egdg: electrogasdynamic generator
ege: *eau, gaz, electricite* (French—water, gas, electricity)
E Ger: East Germany
egg.: electrogastrogram
EG & G: Edgerton, Germeshausen & Grier
Egg Basket of California: Petaluma
eggler: egg + dealer (an egg dealer)
eggwich: egg sandwich
EGIFO: Edward Grey Institute of Field Ornithology
Egip: *Egipto* (Portuguese or Spanish—Egypt)
Egit: *Egitto* (Italian—Egypt)
EGL: Eglin, Florida (tracking station)
egm: extraordinary general meeting
EGM: Extraordinary General Meeting (of shareholders)
EGmc: East Germanic
EGMRSA: Edible Gelatin Manufacturers Research Society of America
EGNR: Ein Gedi Nature Reserve (Israel's Dead Sea oasis)
EGO: Ankara Elektrik, Havagazi ve Otobüs Isletme Müessesesi (Ankara Electricity, City-Gas, and Bus Traffic Department); Eccentric-Orbiting Geophysical Observatory; Educational Growth Opportunities
egp: embezzlement of government property; exhaust gas pressure
EGPC: Egyptian General Petroleum Corporation
egr: egress; exhaust gas recirculation
egr (EGR): erythrocyte glutathione reductase
egt: exhaust gas temperature
Egyp: Egypt; Egyptian; egyptology
Egyptian: Piano Concerto No. 5 by Saint-Saëns
egyptol: egyptology
e & h: environment and heredity
eH: oxidation-reduction potential (symbol)
EH: *Enciclopedia Hoepli* (Italian—Hoepli's Encyclopedia)
EHA: Economic History Association
EHB: Environmental Hearing Board
ehbf: extrahepatic blood flow
ehc: enterohepatic circulation; enterohepatic clearance
E & HC: Emory and Henry College
ehd: electrohydrodynamics
ehd (EHD): epizootic hemorrhagic disease
ehf: extreme high-frequency—30,000-300,000 mc
ehf (EHF): epidemic hemorrhagic fever
EHF: Experimental Husbandry Farm
EHG: Edvard Hagerup Grieg
EHH: Ernst Heinrich Haeckel
EHHS: Erasmus Hall High School
EHI: Emergency Homes, Incorporated
ehl: effective half life
EHL: Eastern Hockey League
e/h/m: eggs per hen per month
EHMA: Electric Hoist Manufacturers Association
ehp: effective horsepower; electric horsepower; extra-high potency
EHPT: Eddy Hot-Plate Test
EHS: Emergency Health Service; Environmental Health Services; Experimental Horticultural Station (UK)
eht: extra-high tension
EHTRC: Emergency Highway Traffic Regulation Center
ehv: extra-high voltage
EHV: Empresa Hondureña de

Vapores (Honduran Steamship Line)
ehw: extreme high water
ehws: extreme-high-water-level spring tides
e/h/yr: eggs per hen per year
e-i: extraversion-introversion
e/i: endorsement irregular
Ei: Eire (Irish Free State)
Ei: *encéphale isolé* (French—isolated intellectual)
EI: East Indies; Electro Institute; Essex Institute; Eunice Institute
EI: *Engineering Index*
EIA: East Indian Association; Electronic Industries Association; Empire Industries Association; Engineering Institute of America
EIAJ: Electronics Industry Association of Japan
EIAR: Environmental Impact Analysis Report
EIB: Ernst Ingmar Bergman; European Investments Bank; Export-Import Bank
EIB: *Economisch Instituut voor de Bouwuijverheid* (Dutch—Economics Institute of the Building Industry)
EIBA: Electrical Industries Benevolent Association
EIBUS: Export-Import Bank of the United States
EIBW: Export-Import Bank of Washington
eic: emotional inertia concept
EIC: Engineering Institute of Canada
EICF: European Investment Casters' Federation
eicm: employer's inventory of critical manpower
EICR: Eppley Institute for Cancer Research (Omaha)
EICS: East India Company's Service
eid: end item description
EID: End Item Delivery; End Item Description; Engineering Item Description
EIDEBOEWABEW: Economic Intelligence Division of the Enemy Branch of the Office of Economic Warfare Analysis of the Board of Economic Warfare
Eidg: *Eidgenössisch* (Swiss—federal)
eid lt: emergency identification light
EIDs: East India Docks (London)
EIF: Elderly Invalids Fund
EIFAC: European Inland Fisheries Advisory Committee (FAO)
eiff: enemy identification—friend or foe
eig: *eigenlijk* (Dutch—proper)
eiii: Electrical Industry Information Institute
eil: electron injection laser
EIL: Electronic Instruments Limited; Experiment in International Living
Eimac: Eitel-McCullough
EIMO: Electronic Interface Management Office
EIN: *Empresa Insulana de Navegacão* (Island Navigation Line)
EINP: Elk Island National Park (Alberta)
Ein Heldenleben: (German—A Hero's Life)—autobiographical symphonic poem by Richard Strauss
E Ind: East Indian; East Indies
Eine Kleine Nachtmusik: (German—A Little Night Music)—Mozart's Serenade for String Orchestra (K 525)
EINP: Elk Island National Park (Alberta)
einschl: *einschliesslich* (German—including)
Einw: *Einwohner* (German—inhabitants; population)
EIO: Emergency Information Office(r)
EIP: Environmental Improvement Program; Experiment Implementation Plan
EIPC: European Institute of Printed Circuits
eir: earned income relief (tax)
EIR: East Indian Railway; Emergency Information Readiness; Environmental Impact Report
Eire: (Gaelic—Ireland)
EIRMA: European Industrial Research Management Association
eirnv: extra incidence rate in non-vaccinated groups
eirv: extra incidence rate in vaccinated groups
eis: electrical intersection splice
Eis: (German—E-sharp)
EIS: Economic Information Systems; Epidemic Intelligence Service (HEW)
Eisted: *(Welsh*—Eisteddfod—annual meeting of Welsh bards)
eit: engineer in training
ei & t: emplacement, installation, and test(ing)
EIT: Electrical Information Test
EITA: Electric Industrial Truck Association
EITB: Engineering Industry Training Board
EITS: Educational and Industrial Testing Service
eiu: economist intelligence unit
EIVT: European Institute for Vocational Training
ej: elbow-jerk
ej: *ejemplo* (Spanish—example)
EJA: Executive Jet Aviation
EJC: Edison Junior College; Engineers Joint Council; Engineers Junior College; Everett Junior College
eject.: ejector
EJ & E R Y: Elgin, Joliet & Eastern Railway
EJMA: Educational Jewelry Manufacturers Association; Expansion Joint Manufacturers Association
EJN: Edicott Johnson (stock exchange symbol)
ejp: excitatory junction potential
EJT: Engineering Job Ticket
ejusd.: *ejusdem* (Latin—of the same)
ek: single enamel single cellophane (insulation symbol)
eK: *etter Kristi* (Norwegian—after Christ)
EK: Eastman Kodak
EK: *Eisernes Kreuz* (German—Iron Cross)—military decoration
ekc: epidemic keratoconjunctivitis
EKCO: E.K. Cole (Limited)
EKD: *Evangelische Kirche in Deutschland* (Protestant Church in Germany)
Eken: (Swedish slang—Stockholm)
ekg: electrokardiogram (electrocardiogram); electrocardiography
EKG: Electrokardiogram
eks: *eksempel* (Danish—example)
EKSC: Eastern Kentucky State College
ekv: electron kilovolt
el: each layer; educational level; elastic level; elevation; elongation
El: Elbert; Elevated Railroad; Elias; Elvie; Elvira
EL: Eastern League; Electrical Laboratory; Electronics Laboratory; Empresa do Limpopo (Limpopo Line); Engineer Lieutenant; Epworth League; Erie-Lackawanna (railroad)
E-L: Erie-Lackawanna (railroad)

E-et-L: Eure-et-Loire
elab: elaborate(d); elaborately; elaborating; elaboration; elaborative
ELAC: East Los Angeles College
e lacte.: *e lact* (Latin—with milk)
EL AL: El Al Israel Airlines
ELAM: *Escuela Latinoamericana de Matemáticas* (Latin American School of Mathematics)
ELAPR: *Estado Libre Asociado de Puerto Rico* (Spanish—Associated Free State of Puerto Rico)—the Commonwealth of Puerto Rico's official name
elas: elastic; elasticity; emergency logistical air support
ELAS: *Ethnikos Laikos Apelephterotikos Stratos* (Greek—Hellenic Peoples' Army of Liberation)
Elasm: Elasmobranchia
elasmobranchs: elasmobranch fishes (cartilaginous fishes such as chimaeras, dogfishes, rays, and sharks)
El-ay: Los Angeles, California
El of B: Elector(ate) of Bavaria; Elector(ate) of Brandenburg
E.L.B.: Bachelor of English Literature
El Banco: (Spanish—The Bank)—World Bank for Reconstruction and Development
ELBS: English Language Book Society
elc: extra-low carbon (electrodes)
ELC: Electronic Location Center
elcar: electric car
El Caudillo: (Spanish—The Chief)—sobriquet of General Francisco Franco-Bahamonde
El Cid: *El Cid Campeador* (Spanish—The Lord Champion)—Rodrigo Díaz de Bivar
elct: electronics
eld: eldest
Eldercare: plan providing medical care for the elderly
Elder Pitt: William Pitt the Earl of Chatham also called the Great Commoner
ELDO: European Launcher Development Organization
El Dorado State: California
ELDS: Editorial Layout Display System
Elean: Eleanor
Eleanor: Mrs Anna Eleanor Roosevelt—wife of President Franklin Delano Roosevelt
elec: electric; electrical; electrician; electricity; electro-; electuary
Elec: Elector; Electorate; Electra
ELEC: European League for Economic Cooperation
elect.: election; elector; electoral; electrolyte; electrolytic
elect.: *electuarium* (Latin—electuary)—confectioned drug; lollipop
electn: electrician
ELECTRA: Electrical, Electronics, and Communications Trades Association; trademark of the London Electricity Board
electraac: electronic auto analysis clinic
electro: electrocute; electrocution; electrotype
electrochem: electrochemistry
electroenceph: electroencephalography
electrogas: electrogasdynamic(s)
electrohyd: electrohydraulic(s)
electrol: electrolysis
electromusic: electronic music
electron.: electronic(s)
electrophys: electrophysics
electro(s): electrotype(s)
electrum: 50% gold, 50% silver
Elekt: *Elektrizität* (German—electricity)
elektr: *elektriciteit* (Dutch—electricity)
elem: element; elementary
eleph fol: elephant folio—books about 23 inches high
El Español: (Spanish—The Spaniard)—Giuseppe Maria Crespi—Italian painter's nickname
El Españoleto: Spanish painter José Ribera
elev: elevated; elevation; elevator
elf.: early lunar flare; extra low frequency
elf: (Swedish—river)
ELF: Early Lunar Flare
ELFA: Electric Light Fittings Association
El Fatah disease: virulent antisemitism
elfc: electroluminescent ferroelectric cell
El Fondo: (Spanish—The Fund)—International Monetary Fund—IMF
El G: El Paso Natural Gas Company
ELG: European Liaison Group (USA)
elgas: electricity and gas
El Gran Libertador: (Spanish—The Great Liberator)—Simón Bolívar—liberated Venezuela, Colombia, Ecuador, Peru, and Bolivia from Spanish rule
El Greco: (Spanish—The Greek)—Kryaikos Theotokopoulos (Domingo Theotocopuli)
elhi: elementary and high school (textbooks)
Eli: Elias; Elihu; Elijah; nickname for a student or alumnus of Yale University
ELI: English Language Institute; Environmental Law Institute
ELIA: English Language Institute of America
Elia: Charles Lamb
ELIC: Electric Lamp Industry Council
Elien.: *Eliensis* (Latin—of Ely)
elig: eligible
Elij: Elijah
elim: eliminate; eliminated; elimanation
ELIM: Evangelical Lutherans in Mission
El Inca: (Spanish—The Inca)—Garcilaso de la Vega
elint: electronic intelligence
elints: electronic intelligence-gathering vessels
elip: electrostatic latent image photography
Elis: Elisabeth
Elise: Elizabeth
elix: elixir
Eliz: Elizabeth(an)
Eliza: Elizabeth
Elizabeth Arden: Florence N. Graham
Elizabeths: Elizabeth Islands; queens named Elizabeth
ell.: elbow; ellipsoid(al); elliptic(al)
ell: *eller* (Spanish—or)
Ella: Eleanor; Eleanora; Eleanore; Isabella
ELLA: European Long Lines Agency
Ellen: Eleanor(a)(e)
Ellerman: Ellerman Lines Ltd
Ellery Queen: Frederic Dannay and Manfred B. Lee
El Libertador: (Spanish—The Liberator)—Simón Bolívar
Ellices: Ellice Islands
Ellie: Alice
ellip: elliptic; elliptical; elliptically
ELLIS: Ellis Air Lines
Ellis Bell: pseudonym of Emily Brontë
el lt: electric light; electric light-

ing
elm.: element; energy-loss meter
ELM: Eastern Atlantic and Mediterranean; Edgar Lee Masters
elma: electromechanical aid
Elma: Elizabeth Mary; Wilhelmina
ELMA: Empresa Lineas Maritimas Argentinas (Argentine Lines)
El Manco de Lepanto: (Spanish—The One-handed Man of Lepanto)—Cervantes whose left hand was maimed at the Battle of Lepanto
Elmer R. Rice: Elmer Reizenstein
elmint: electromagnetic intelligence
elmobile: electric automobile
ELMS: Experimental Library Management System
El Mus: East London Museum
E Ln: East London
ELN: *Ejército de Liberación Nacióinal* (Spanish—Army of National Liberation)—Bolivian and Colombian underground group
ELNA: Esperanto League of North America
El Niño: El Niño Current
ELNM: Edison Laboratory National Monument (West Orange, New Jersey)
elo: elocution; eloquence
Elo: Eloheimo
eloc: elocution(ary); elocutionist(ic)(al)(ly)
ELOI: Emergency Letter of Instruction
Eloise: European large-orbiting instrumentation for solar experimentation
elong: elongate; elongation
E long: east longitude
eloq: eloquence; eloquent(ly)
E Loth: East Lothian
elox: electrical spark erosion
ELP: El Paso, Texas (airport)
elpc: electroluminescence photo conductor
El Precursor: (Spanish—the Precursor)—Francisco Miranda—fighter for Venezuelan freedom from Spanish rule; Antonio Nariño—fighter for Colombian freedom from Spanish rule
ELR: Engineering Laboratory Report
elra: electronic radar
ELRO: Electronics Logistics Research Office (USA)
Elroy: American country-boy name derived from the French for king—*Le Roi* or the Spanish equivalent—*El Rey*—or their combination
Els: Elsinore (Helsingör)
El of S: Elector(ate) of Saxony
ELS: Escabana and Lake Superior (railroad)
Elsa: Elizabeth
El Salv: *El Salvador* (Spanish—Republic of El Salvador)
elsec: electronic intelligence
Elsev: Elsevier (family of Dutch printers and publishers dating from the 16th century)—also spelled Elzevir like the typeface named for this family
Elshender: (Scottish—Alexander)
elsie: emergency life-saving instant exit
Elsie: Elizabeth
El Silencio: (Spanish—The Silence)—downtown Caracas where bus routes start and automotive traffic is at its noisiest
Elspet(h): (Scottish—Elizabeth)
ELSS: Emplaced Lunar Scientific Station
Elt: European letter telegram
E Lt: Engineer Lieutenant
ELT: *English Language Teaching*
E Lt-Cdr: Engineer Lieutenant-Commander
el2: elongation in 2 inches
ELU: English Lacrosse Union
elv: extra-low voltage
elv: (Dano-Norwegian—river)
elw: extreme low water
El Wld: *Electrical World*
elws: extreme-low-water-level spring tides
Ely: easterly
Elz: (*see* Elsev)
em: emanation; emergency mobilization; enlisted man; expanded metal
e/m: specific electronic mass
'em: them
e of m: error of measurement
e & m: endocrine and metabolism; erection and maintenance
em (EM): electron microscope; electron microscopy; end of medium character (data processing)
em: *eftermiddag* (Danish—afternoon)—p.m.
Em: Emily; Emma; Emmanuel; Emy
EM: Earl Marshal; Education Manual; Electrician's Mate; electromagnetic (symbol); Engineer Manager; Engineering Memorandum; Enlisted Man (Men); Etna & Montrose (railroad); European Movement; External Memorandum
E-M: Electric Machinery (company); Electro-Motive (corporation); Embden-Meyerhof (glycolitic path)
E.M.: Engineering of Mines; Engineer of Mining
EM: *Estado-Maior* (Portuguese—general staff; headquarters); *Estado Mayor* (Spanish—general staff; headquarters)
E.M.: *Equitum Magister* (Latin—Master of Horse)
E da M: *Escuatrão da Morte* (Portuguese—Death Squad)—Brazilian right-wing terrorists
E-M: *Etat-Major* (French—Headquarters)
EM 1 C: Electrician's Mate First Class (USN)
EMA: Electronics Manufacturers Association; Envelope Manufacturers Association; European Monetary Agreement; Evaporated Milk Association; Exposition Management Association; Extended Mission Apollo
E MacD: Edward MacDowell
EMAD: Engine Maintenance Assembly and Disassembly
EMAIA: Electrical Meter and Allied Industries Association
Emancipator of the Serfs: Czar Alexander II of Russia
Emancipator of the Slaves: William Wilberforce
Em Ar Un: *Emiratos Arabes Unidos* (Spanish—United Arab Emirates)
EMAS: Emergency Message Authentication System; Employment Medical Advisory Service (UK)
EMATS: Emergency Message Automatic Transmission System
emb: embankment; embargo; embark; embarkation; embassy; embroidered; embroidery; embryo; embryology
emball: *emballasje* (Norwegian—packing)
Emb: Embassy
embk: embark
embkn: embarkation
EMBL: Eniwetok Marine Biological Laboratory
EMBO: European Molecular Biology Organization
embr: embroider(y)

embry: embryology
embryol: embryology
emc: engineered military circuit; equilibrium moisture content
emc (EMC): encephalomyocarditis
EMC: Education Media Council; Einstein Medical Center; Electronic Material Change; End Mollycoddling in America; Engineering Maintenance Center; Engineer(ing) Maintenance Control; Engineering Manpower Commission
EMCC: European Municipal Credit Community
EMCCC: European Military Communications Coordinating Committee
EMCE: Eastern Montana College of Education
emcee: master of ceremonies
emcees: masters of ceremony
emcon: emission control
emcv: encephalomyocarditis virus
emd: electric-motor-driven
Emd: Emden
E-MD: Electro-Motive Division (General Motors)
emdp: electromotive difference of potential
EMEA: Electrical Manufacturers Export Association
EMEB: East Midlands Electricity Board
EMEC: Electronics Maintenance Engineering Center
EMELEC: trademark of East Midlands Electricity Board
emend.: emendate(d); emendating; emendation(s); emendator(s); emendatory; emender(s)
emend.: *emendatis* (Latin—corrected; edited; emended)
emer: emergency
Emer: Emeritus
emerald: beryllium chromium aluminum silicate (gemstone variety of beryl)
Emerald Empire: Idaho's panhandle
Emerald Isle: Ireland
Emerald Necklace: 18,000 acres of parks surrounding Cleveland
emerald nickel: zaratite (basic hydrated nickel carbonate)
emerg: emergency
E-meter: electrical-resistance galvanometer
emergcons: emergency conditions
emerit.: *emeritus* (Latin—retired with honor)
emery: aluminum oxide (Al_2O_3)
E.Met.: Engineer of Metallurgy
EMETF: Electromagnetic Environment Test Facility (USA)
EMEU: East Midlands Educational Union
emf: electromotive force; erythrocyte maturing factor; every morning fix (your old automobile)
EMF: European Motel Federation; Excerpta Medica Foundation
E.M.F.: E(dward) M(organ) Foster
emg: electromyogram; electromyography
EMG: *Estado-Maior General* (Portuguese—Staff General); *Estado Mayor General* (Spanish—Staff General)
emi: electromagnetic interference
EMI: Electrical and Musical Industries; Equipment Manufacturing Incorporated
EMI: *Edizioni Musicali Italiane* (Italian Musical Publications)
emic: emergency maternity and infant care
E Midl: East Midland
emig: emigrant; emigration
Emil Ludwig: Emil Cohn
Emin: Eminence
emis: emission
EMJC: East Mississippi Junior College
Emjo: Emmanuel Jobe
emK: *elektromotorische Kraft* (German—electromotive force)
eml: electromagnetic levitation
Eml: Emily
EML: Equipment Modification List
EML: *Everyman's Library*
em log: electromagnetic log
EMLTS: Electromagnetic Levitation Transportation System (wheelless railway)
emm: electromagnetic measurement
Emm: Emmanuel
emma: electron microscopy and microanalysis
Emma Calvé: Rosa Calvet
Emm Coll: Emmanuel College—Cambridge
Emmie: Emma; Emy; Emmy
EM^{MO}: *Eminentísimo* (Spanish—Most Eminent)—masculine ecclesiastical title applied to cardinals
EMMSA: Envelope Makers and Manufacturing Stationers Association
Emmy: award given for outstanding television performances in the United States; statuette named after tv entertainer Faye Emerson
Emmy Destinn: Ema Kittl
EMNM: El Morro National Monument
EMO: Emergency Services Organization
emol: *emolumentos* (Portuguese or Spanish—emoluments; official fees)
emos: earth's mean orbital speed
Emos: Earth's mean orbital speed
emot: emotion(al)
E-motor(s): electric motor(s)—submarine
emp: electromagnetic pulses; empennage
emp.: *emplastrum* (Latin—adhesive; a plaster)
e.m.p.: *ex modo prescripto* (Latin—in the manner prescribed)
Emp: Emperor; Empire; Empress
emp agcy: employment agency
empath: empathetic; empathy
empd: employed
Emperor: Beethoven's Piano Concerto No. 5 in E flat; Haydn's String Quartet in C (opus 76, no. 3)
Emperor of Europe: Napoleon Bonaparte's self-imposed but short-lived title
emph: emphasis
emphy: emphysema; emphysematous; emphyteusis; emphyteuta; emphyteutic
EMPI: European Motor Products Incorporated
EMPIRE: Early Manned Planetary Interplanetary Round-Trip Experiment
Empire City: New York
Empire State: New York's official nickname
Empire State of the South: Georgia's official nickname
empl: emplace; emplacement; employ; employee; employer; employment
empld: employed
EMPOCOL: Empresa Puertos de Colombia (Colombian Port Works)
EMPPO: European and Mediterranean Plant Protection Organization
Empress Carlota: Marie Charlotte Amélie Augustine Victoire Clémentine Léopoldine—empress of Mexico un-

der Maximilian
Empress Eugénie: Eugénie Marie de Montijo de Guzman—empress of the French under Napoleon III
Empress of India: Queen Victoria
emp. vesic.: *emplastrum vesicatorium* (Latin—a blistering plaster)
emq: electromagnetic quiet
emr: educable mentally retarded; electromagnetic resonance
EMR: Emerson Electric (stock exchange symbol); Engineering Master Report; Enlisted Manning Report
EM & R: Equipment Maintenance and Readiness
EMRIC: Educational Media Research Information Center
EMRS: East Malling Research Station
ems: emergency medical services
Ems: Bad Ems
EMS: Econometric Society; Emergency Medical Service; Export Marketing Service
EMSA: Electron Microscope Society of America
EMSC: Educational Media Selection Center
emt: electrical metallic tubing; equivalent megatonnage
EMTA: Electro-Mechanical Trade Association
EM 2 C: Electrician's Mate Second Class (USN)
EM 3 C: Electrician's Mate Third Class (USN)
EMSO: European Mobility Service Office (USA)
EMSU: Environmental Meteorological Support Unit
emu.: electromagnetic unit
Emu: European monetary unit
EMU: Eastern Michigan University
EMU: *Europese Monetaire et Economische Unie* (Dutch—European Monetary and Economic Union
emul: emulsion
emuls.: *emulsio* (Latin—emulsion)
emv: electron megavolt
Emy: Emilia; Emily
en: enema; exceptions noted
En: English
EN: *Emissora Nacional* (Portuguese—National Broadcast); *Estrada Nacional* (Portuguese or Spanish—National Highway); *Evening News*
ENA: English Newspaper Association
ENA: *L'Ecole Nationale d'Administration* (French— National Administration School) —France's civil-service academy
ENAB: Evening Newspaper Advertising Bureau
enam: enamel; enameled; enamels
ENAMI: *Empresa Nacional de Minería* (Spanish—National Mining Enterprise)—Chile
ENAP: Empresa Nacional del Petroleo (Chile)
ENBPS: *Ente Nazionale per le Biblioteche Popolari e Scolastiche* (Italian—National Organization of Popular and Scholastic Libraries)
enc: enclosed
ENCA: European Naval Communications Agency
encap: encapsulate(d); encapsulation
Enc Can: *Encyclopedia Canadiana*
encl: enclose; enclosed; enclosure
enclit: enclitic
ENCO: Energy Company (Humble Oil & Refining)
encom: encomiast(ic); encomium(s)
ency: encyclopedia
Ency Assn: *Encyclopedia of Associations*
Ency Brit: *Encyclopaedia Britannica*
end.: endorsement
END: Environment Near Death
endo: endocrine; endocrinology
endocrin: endocrinological; endocrinologist; endocrinology
EndocSoc: Endocrine Society
endor: electron nuclear double resonance
endow.: endowment
endp: endpaper(s)
ends.: endpapers
ENDS: Euratom Nuclear Documentation System
end tel: *endereço telegráfico* (Portuguese—cable address)
ENE: east northeast
ENEA: European Nuclear Energy Association
ENEL: Ente Nazionale per l'Energia Elettrica (National Electric-Power Company of Italy)
enem.: *enema* (Greek—injection)
ener: energize
energ: *energicamente* (Italian—energetically)
ENF: European Nuclear Force
en fav de: *en faveur de* (French—in favor of)
En 1c: Engineman, first class
eng: engine
Eng: England; English
Eng: *Engineering* (British periodical)
Eng. D.: Doctor of Engineering
eng fnd: engine foundation
engin: engineering
Engineer of Fantasy: Walt Disney
Engineer-Humanitarian-Statesman: Herbert Hoover
Engineers' Town: Coulee City, Washington
engitist: engineer + scientist
Engl: England; English
English Caribees: colonial name for the British West Indies
English Lit: English literature
English Opium Eater: Thomas De Quincey
English Polynesia: jocular nickname for the Seychelles Islands in the Indian Ocean far from Polynesia in the South Pacific
English Riviera: (*see* Cornish Riviera)
English Symphonist: Ralph Vaughan Williams
Eng Lit: English Literature
Eng News-Rec: *Engineering News-Record*
eng^o: *engenheiro* (Portuguese—engineer)
engr: engineer
eng rm: engine room
engrv: engraver; engraving
Eng. Sc. D.: Doctor of Engineering Science
ENI: Ente Nazionale Idrocarburi (National Fuel Agency)
eniac: electronic numerical integrator and computer
ENIC: *Ente Nazionale Industrie Cinematografiche* (Italian—National Association of Film Producers); *Ente Nazionale della Cinofilia Italiana* (National Organization of Italian Dog Lovers)
Enigma: Elgar's *Enigma* Variations for Orchestra with an enigmatic program wherein the composer dedicates its movements to his friends described by their initials
ENIM: *Ente Nazionale dell'Istruzione Media* (Italian—National Organization for Intermediate Instruction)
ENIT: Ente Nazionale Industrie Turistiche (Italian—National Tourist Industry)
enk: *enkelvoud* (Dutch—singular)
enl: enlist

enlgd: enlarged
Enlightenment: (*see* The Enlightenment)
en ml: end mill
ENMU: Eastern New Mexico University
ENNWR: Eastern Neck National Wildlife Refuge (Maryland)
eno: *enero* (Spanish—January)
en^o: *enero* (Spanish—January)
E/no: *estacionamiento no* (Spanish—no parking)
enol: enology
En 1 c: Engineman, first class
ENP: Egmont National Park (North Island, New Zealand); Etosha NP (South-West Africa); Everglades NP (Florida)
ENPA: Ente Nazionale Protezione Animali (National Society for the Protection of Animals—Italy)
ENPI: *Ente Nazionale Prevenzione Infortuni* (Italian—National Institution for the Prevention of Accidents)
E Lt-Cdr: Engineer Lieutenant-Commander
Enn: Quintus Ennius (Roman poet)
Enoch Pratt: Enoch Pratt Free Library
ENPMA: Eastern National Park and Monument Association
enr: en route; equivalent noise resistance
enr (ENR): extrathyroidal neck radioactivity
ENR: Emissora Nacional de Radiodifusão (Radio Portugal)
E & NR: Esquimalt and Nanaimo Railway
enrt: enroute
Ens: Ensign
ENSA: Entertainments National Service Association
Ensen: Ensenada
ensi: equivalent—noise sideband input
ENSIDESA: *Empresa Nacional Siderurgica SA* (Spanish—National Steel Works)
ent: ear, nose, and throat; enter; entrance
ENT: Aerolineas Argentinas (Argentine Airlines); Ear, Nose, and Throat (clinic or hospital department)
entd: entered
ENTE: Ente Nazionale per l'Energia Elettrica (National Electric Energy Enterprise)
entl: entitle
entom: entomology
entr: entrance
entspr: *entsprechend* (German—corresponding)
Ent Sta Hall: Entered at Stationers' Hall
ent-vio: entero-vioform (antidiarrhetic)
enur: enuresis
env: envelop; envelope; environ; envoy
Env: Envoy
Env Ext: Envoy Extraordinary
environ.: environment; environmental; environmentalism; environmentalist
ENWR: Erie National Wildlife Refuge (Pennsylvania); Eufaula National Wildlife Refuge (Alabama)
enz: *enzovoort(s)* (Dutch—and so on)
enza: influenza
En Zed(er)(s): New Zealand (er)(s)
eo: engine oil
e-o: even-odd
e.o.: *ex officio* (Latin—by virtue of office)
Eo: Ecuadorian escudo(s); escudo(s) (Portuguese currency)
E_0: electric affinity (symbol)
EO: Eastern Orthodox; Education Officer; Engineering Order; Entertainments Office(r); Executive Office(r); Executive Order
E & O: Eastern and Oriental
eoa: effective on or about; examination, opinion, advice (medical)
EOA: Economic Oil Association; Essential Oil Association
EOARDC: European Office of the Air Research and Development Command (USAF)
EOB: Executive Office Building
eoc: electric overhead crane; emotional-organic combination
Eoc: Eocene
EOC: Economic Opportunity Commission; Electronic Operations Center; Enemy Oil Committee; Executive Officers Council
EOCI: Electric Overhead Crane Institute
eod: entry on duty; every other day; explosive ordnance disposal
EODP: Engineering Order Delayed for Parts
eoe: earth orbit ejection
e & oe: errors and omissions excepted
EOE: Enemy-Occupied Europe
eof (EOF): end of file
EOF: Earth Orbital Flight
eog: effect on guarantees; electro-oculogram
EOGs: Educational Opportunity Grants
EOH: Emergency Operation Headquarters
eohp: except otherwise herein provided
Eol: Eolic
EOL: Ex Oriente Lux (The Light of the Orient—The Oriental Society)
eolm: electro-optical light modulator
eom: end of month; extra-ocular movements
eom (EOM): end of message (data processing)
EONR: European Organization for Nuclear Research
eooe: error or omission excepted
eop: earth orbit plane; end of part
EOP: Equipment Operations Procedure; Executive Office of the President
EOPs: Extended Opportunity Programs
eoq: economical ordering quantity; end of quarter
EOQC: European Organization for Quality Control
eor: earth orbital rendezvous; explosive ordnance reconnaissance
EOR: Earth Orbit Rendezvous
EORSA: Episcopalians and Others for Responsible Social Action
EORTC: European Organization for Research on the Treatment of Cancer
eos: eligible for overseas service
EO's: Engineering Orders
EOS: Earth Orbiting Shuttle (NASA); European Orthodontic Society
eosins: eosinophils
eosp: economic order and stocking procedure
EOSS: Earth Orbital Space Station
eot: end of transmission; enemy-occupied territory
EOT: Eagle Ocean Transport
EOTP: European Organization for Trade Promotion
ep: electrically polarized; electric primer; electroplate; electroplated; electroplating; electropneumatic; endpaper(s); estimated position; exit pupil; experienced playgoer; explosion-proof; external publication; extreme pressure

e/p: endpaper
e & p: exploration and production (area)
ep (EP): extended play (45 rpm phonograph disc)
e p: *en passant* (French—in passing)
e.p.: *editio princeps* (Latin—first edition)
Ep.: *Episcopus* (Latin—Bishop or overseer)
EP: Eagle-Picher; Ecole Polytechnique (Polytechnic School); engineering personnel; Engineering Publications; entrucking point; estimated position; exceptions passed
E-P: European Plan (no meals)
E & P: Extraordinary and Plenipotentiary
EP: *Environmental Pollution*
E & P: *Editor & Publisher*
epa: estimated profile analysis
EPA: Emergency Powers Act; Empire Parliamentary Association; Empire Press Agency; Environmental Protection Agency; European Productivity Agency; Evangelical Press Association
EPAA: Educational Press Association of America; Employing Printers Association of America
EPAC: Electronic Parts Advisory Committee
EPACCI: Economic Planning and Advisory Council for the Construction Industries
epam (EPAM): elementary perceiver and memorizer
epaq: electronic parts of assessed quality
epc: electroplate on copper
EPC: Economic and Planning Council; Educational Publishers' Council; Environmental Policy Center; Esso Petroleum Company; European Planning Council
EPCA: European Petro-Chemical Association
epc black: easy-processing channel black
ep cells: epithelial cells
epcg: endoscopic pancreaticholangiography (EPCG)
EPCOT: Experimental Prototype Community of Tomorrow
EPCS: Equitable Pioneers Cooperative Society
epd: earliest practicable date; excess profits duty
epd: *en paz descanse* (Spanish—may he rest in peace)
EPDA: Exhibit Producers and Designers Association
ep disc: extended-play (45 rpm) disc
epdm: epidemiological; epidemiologist; epidemiology
EPE: Editorial Projects for Education
EPEA: Electrical Power Engineers Association
epedemiol: epedemiology
epf: exopthalmos-producing factor
EPF: European Packaging Federation
EPF: *Empresa Petrolera Fiscal* (Spanish—State Petroleum Enterprise)—Peru
EPFL: Enoch Pratt Free Library (Baltimore)
epg: eggs per gram (parasitology)
EPG: Electronic Proving Ground (US Army)
EPGA: Emergency Petroleum and Gas Administration
Eph: Ephraim
ephmer: ephemeral; ephemerides; ephemeris
epi: electronic position indicator; emotional-physiologic illness
EPI: Emergency Public Information
EPIC: Electronic Properties Information Center; El Paso Intelligence Center; End Poverty in California
Epict: Epictetus
epid: epidemic
epig: epigastric; epigeal; epigeous; epigenesis; epigenetic; epigenic; epiglottal; epiglottic; epiglottis; epigone; epigonic; epigonism(s); epigonus; epigram; epigrammatic(al)(ly); epigrammatism; epigrammatist(s); epigrammatize; epigrammatized; epigrammatizing; epigraph(er); epigraphic(al)(ly); epigraphist(s); epigraphy; epigynous; epigyny
epil: epilogue
epineph: epinephrine
Epiph: Epiphania; Epiphany
epirb: emergency position-indicating beacon
epis: episiotomy
Epis: Episcopal(ian)
Epist.: *Epistola* (Latin—epistle or letter)
epistem: epistemic(al(ly); epistemological (ly); epistemologist(s)
epithal: epithalamic; epithalamion
epistom.: *epistomium* (Latin—stopper)
epit: epitaph; epitome
epith: epithelial; epithelium
epivag: epivaginitis
epl: extreme pressure lubricant
EPL: Erie Public Library; Evansville Public Library
EPL: *Ecole Polytechnique de Lausanne* (French— Polytechnic School of Lausanne)
epm: explosions per minute
epm: *en propia mano* (Spanish—in good hands; the right way)
EPMS: Engine Performance Monitoring System; Engineering Project Management System
epn: effective-perceived noise
epnd: effective-perceived noise decibels
epndbl: effective-perceived noise decibel level
EPNG: El Paso Natural Gas
epns: electroplated nickel silver
EPNS: English Place-Name Society
epo: experimental processing operation
epon: eponym(s) [(designation(s) derived from proper names of families, places, or persons such as Hapsburg dynasty, Paris of America (Montreal), or Raynaud's disease)]
epp: end plate potential
epp: *edellä puolenpäiven* (Finnish—before noon)
Epp.: *Episcopi* (Latin—Bishops or overseers)
EPP: Earth Physics Program; European Pallet Pool
EPPL: El Paso Public Library
EPPO: European and Mediterranean Plant Protection Organization
epr: electronic paramagnetic resonance; engine pressure ratio
EPRA: Eastern Psychiatric Research Association
eps: earnings per share
ep's: epithelial cells
eps (EPS): energetic particles satellites
EPS: El Paso Southern (railroad); Emergency Procurement Service; Engineering Purchase Specification; Escape Propulsion System
epsom salt: magnesium sulfate ($MgSO_4 \cdot 7H_2O$)
epsp: excitatory postsynaptic potential
ept: ethylene-propylene terpolymer; excess profits tax; external pipe thread
EPT: Excess Profits Tax

EPTA: Expanded Program of Technical Assistance (UN)
epte: existed prior to entry
epts: existed prior to service
EPU: Empire Press Union; European Payment Union
EPUL: Ecole Polytechnique de l'Université de Lausanne (Polytechnic School of the University of Lausanne)
Epus: *Episcopus* (Latin—Bishop)
eput: events-per-unit-time
epw: enemy prisoner of war
epwm: electroplated white metal
EPZ: Ecole Polytechnique de Zürich (Polytechnic School of Zurich)
eq: encephalization quotient; equal; equalization quotient; equation; equivalent; (*also see* EQ)
Eq: Equator
EQ: educational quotient; enthusiasm quotient; ethnic quotient
EQA: Environmental Quality Act (California)
EQAA: Environmental Quality Advisory Agency
EQAD: Electrical (Electronic) Quality-Assurance Directorate
EQB: Environmental Quality Board
EQC: Environmental Quality Council
eqi: environmental quality index
eqn: equation
eqp: equip; equipment
eqpt: equipment
eqq: electric quadripole-quadripole
EQSC: Environmental Quality Study Council
Eq T: equation of time
eq tr: equipment trust
Equ: Equerry
Equa: Equator; Equatorial
Equa C Cur: Equatorial Countercurrent
Equality State: Wyoming's official nickname reminding all it was the first state to guarantee women's suffrage (1869) and the first state to have a woman governor (1924)
equat: equator; equatorial
equil: equilibrium
equin: equinox
equip.: equipment
equipt: equipment
Equity: Actors' Equity Association
equiv: equivalent
er: echo ranging; electronic reconnaissance; emergency rescue; external resistance
e/r: en route
'er: her
Er: erbium; Eritrea; Eritrean
ER: East Riding; East River; Edwardus Rex (King Edward); Effectiveness Report; Elizabeth Regina (Queen Elizabeth); Emergency Request; Emergency Rescue; Emergency Reserve; Emergency Room; Engine Room; Engineering Report; Equipment Requirement; Evaluation Report; Expert Rifleman; Explosives Report; External Report; Express Route
E.R.: *Elizabeth Regina* (Queen Elizabeth)
ERA: Electrical Research Association; Electronic Representatives Association; Engineering Research Associates; Engineering Research Association; Equitable Reserve Association
ERA: *Equal Rights Amendment*
ERAA: Equipment Review and Authorization Activity
Era of Good Feeling: (administration of James Monroe—fifth President of the United States)
ERAI: Embry-Riddle Aeronautical Institute
ERAP: Economic Research and Action Project
ERAP: *Entreprise de Recherches et d'Activités Petrolienes* (Petroleum Research Development Enterprise—French)
Eras: Erasmus
eraser. (ERASER): elevated radiation seeker rocket
Erasmus: Desiderius Erasmus (Geert Geerts)
erb: electron beam recording
'Erb: Herbert
Erb: *Erbitten* (German—ask for; beg for; request)
ERB: Educational Records Bureau; Equipment Review Board
er bh: engine room bulkhead
erbm (ERBM): extended-range ballistic missile
erc: en-route chart; equatorial ring current
ERC: Economic Resources Corporation; Electronics Research Center (NASA); Enlisted Reserve Corps
Erckmann-Chatrian: Emile Erckmann + Alexandre Chatrian
ERC & I: Economic Reform Club and Institute
ERCO: Electric Reduction Company
Ercoli: Palmiro Togliatti
ercp: endoscopic retrograde cholangiopancreatography
ERCS: Emergency Rocket Communications System
erd: equivalent residual dose
ERD: Emergency Reserve Decoration
ERDA: Electronics Research and Development Agency; Energy Research and Development Administration
ERDE: Explosives Research and Development Establishment
ERDL: Engineering Research and Development Laboratory
'ere: here
erect.: erection
'Ereford(shire): [(Cockney contraction—Hereford(shire)]
Eretz Israel: (Hebrew—Land of Israel)
erf: error function
ERF: Education and Research Foundation; Eye Research Foundation
ERFA: European Radio-Frequency Agency
erg: unit of mechanical energy or work (derived from the word *energy*)
erg.: electroretinogram
ERGOM: European Research Group on Management
ergon: ergonomic; ergonomical; ergonomics
Erh: Erhard
E & R: Hist Soc: Evangelical and Reformed Historical Society
ERI: Earthquake Research Institute (Tokyo University); Environmental Research Institute; Erie, Pennsylvania (airport)
E.R.I.: *Edwardus Rex et Imperator* (Latin—Edward, King and Emperor)
eric: electronic remote and independent control
ERIC: Educational Resources Information Center (US Office of Education)
ERIC/AE: Educational Resources Information Center/ Adult Education
ERIC/CEA: Educational Resources Information Center/ Clearinghouse on Educational Administration
ERIC CLS: Educational Resources Information Center/

Clearinghouse for Library and Information Sciences
ERIC/CRIER: Educational Resources Information Center / Clearinghouse on Retrieval Information and Evaluation on Reading
Eric Evergood: King Eric I of Denmark
Erich Maria Remarque: Erich Maria Kramer
ERIC/IRCD: Educational Resources Information Center/ Information Retrieval Center on the Disadvantaged
Ericofon: Ericsson telephone
Eric the Lamb: King Eric III of Denmark
Eric the Memorable: King Eric II of Denmark
Erie: Erie-Lackawanna (railroad)
ERiEI: Eastern Regional Institute for Education
ERISA: Employee Retirement Income Security Act
Erit: Eritrea
Erl: *Erläuterung* (German—explanatory note)
ERL: Environmental Research Laboratories
erm: ermine
erma: electronic recording machine accounting
Ern: Ernest; Ernst
Ernie: Ernest
ERNIE: Electronic Random Number Indicator Equipment
Ernie Pyle: Ernest Taylor Pyle
ERO: Eastman-Rochester Orchestra
eroduction(s): erotic production(s)
Eroica: Beethoven's Symphony No. 3 in E-flat major *(Sinfonia eroica)*
EROPA: Eastern Regional Organization for Public Administration
Eros: (Greek—Cupid)—god of love and lust
EROS: Earth Resources Observation Satellite; Eliminate Zero Range System (for collision avoidance); Experimental Reflector Orbital Shot (space probe)
erot: erotic; erotica; erotical(ly); eroticism; eroticist; eroticization; eroticize; eroticizing; erotism(s); erotogenic(s)
erotol: erotologist; erotology
erp: effective radiated power
ERP: Easy Revolving Plan; Emerson Radio & Phonograph (stock exchange symbol); European Recovery Program
ERP: *Ejército Revolucionario del Pueblo* (Spanish—People's Revolutionary Army)— Argentine Trotskyist combat wing
ERPC: Eastern Railroads Presidents Conference
erpf: effective renal plasma flow
err.: error; erroneous
ERR: Engineering Release Record
err & app: error and appeals (legal)
errc: expandability, recoverability, repairability cost
erron: erroneous(ly)
ers (ERS): environmental research satellite
ERS: Economic Research Service; Edwards Rocket Site; Emergency Relocation Site; Experimental Research Society
E-R S O: Eastman-Rochester Symphony Orchestra
ERSP: Earth Resources Survey Program (NASA)
ERSR: Equipment Reliability Status Report
ERTS: Earth Resources Technology Satellite; European Rapid Train System
ERU: English Rugby Union
erv: expiratory reserve volume
ERV: English Revised Version
erw: electro-resistance welding
erw: *erweiterte* (German—enlarged; extended)
ery: erysipelothrixia
ER Yorks: East Riding, Yorkshire
es: echo sounding; eldest son; electrostatic; enamel single silk (insulation); engine-sized (paper); equal section
es (ES): ejection sound
es: *esempio* (Italian—example)
Es: einsteinium; Essen
ES: Econometric Society; Educational Specialist; Electrochemical Society; Ellis Air Lines; El Salvador; Endocrine Society; Engineering Study; Espirito Santo; Experiment(al) Station
ESA: Ecological Society of America; Economic Stabilization Agency; Electrolysis Society of America; Employment Standards Administration; Engineers and Scientists of America; Entomological Society of America; Epiphyllum Society of America; European Space Agency: Euthanasia Society of America; Exceptional Service Award; Export Screw Association
ESAB: Energy Supplies Allocation Board (Canada)
ESAC: Environmental Systems Applications Center
E Sam: Eastern Samoa (American Samoa)
ESANZ: Economic Society of Australia and New Zealand
esar: electronically-steered array radar
ESARS: Employment Service Automated Reporting System
ESAWC: Evaluation Staff, Air War College
esb: electrical stimulation (of the) brain; electric storage battery
ESB: Economic Stabilization Board; Electric Storage Battery (company); Empire State Building
ESBA: English Schools' Badminton Association
ESBBA: English Schools' Basket Ball Association
esc: escadrille; escape; escort; escrow; escutcheon
esc (ESC): escape character (data processing)
esc: *escompte* (French—discount)
Esc: escudo (Portuguese currency)
ESC: Economic and Social Council (UN); Electronics Systems Center; Electronic Systems Command (USN); Executive Service Corps
ESCA: English Schools' Cricket Association; English Schools' Cycling Association
escap: escapologist; escapology
ESCAP: Economic and Social Commission for Asia and the Pacific (UN)
Escape King: Harry Houdini
eschat: eschatology
ES/CIP: Employee Suggestion/ Cost Improvement Proposal
escl: *esclamazione* (Italian—exclamation); *esclamativo* (Italian—exclamative); *esclusivo* (Italian—exclusive)
ESCL: Evans Signal Corps Laboratory
ESCMA: Electric Steel Conduit Manufacturers' Association
escn: electrolyte-and-steroid-produced cardiopathy characterized by necrosis
esc^o: *escudo* (Portuguese or Spanish—coat of arms; Por-

tuguese monetary unit; shield)
Esco: *Escocia* (Spanish—Scotland); *Escócia* (Portuguese—Scotland)
ESCO: Educational, Scientific, and Cultural Organization (UN)
Escom: Electrical Supply Commission
ESCORTDIV: escort division
escr: escrow
escrit^{a}: *escritura* (Portuguese or Spanish—assignment; contract; deed; writ)
escrnía: *escribanía* (Spanish—notary's office)
escrno: *escribano* (Spanish—notary)
escr^{no}: *escribano* (Spanish—court clerk; notary; scribe)
escs: *escudos* (Portuguese or Spanish—coats of arms; Portuguese monetary units; shields)
esd: estimated shipping date; extended school day
esd (ESD): external symbol dictionary (data processing)
ESD: Electronic Systems Division (USAF)
ESDAC: European Space Data Analysis Center (Darmstdat)
Esdr: *Esdras* (The Book of Esdras)
esE: *electrostatische Einheit* (German—electrostatic unit)
ESE: east southeast
ESEA: Elementary and Secondary Education Act
ESEF: Electrotyping and Stereotyping Employers Federation
esf: electrostatic focusing; erythropoietic stimulating factor
ESF: Eastern Sea Frontier; Engineering Specification Files
e sg: *e seguente* (Italian—and the following one)
Esg: English standard gage
esh: equivalent solar hour(s)
ESH: European Society of Haematology
eshp: equivalent shaft horsepower
ESIS: Executive Selection Inventory System
E 605: parathion (deadly insecticide)
Esk: Eskimo
Eskie(s): Eskimo(s)
Eskimo Village: Kotzebue, Alaska
esl: expected significance level
ESL: Eastern Steamship Lines; Engineering Societies Library
E S-L: Engineer Sub-Lieutenant
ESL: *Endangered Species List*
ESLAB: European Space Laboratory (Delft)
ESLO: European Satellite Launching Organization
esm: ends standard matched (lumber)
ESM: Eastman School of Music; Engineering Services Memo; Engineering Shop Memo
ESMA: Electronic Sales-Marketing Association; Engraved Stationery Manufacturers Association
ESMRI: Engraved Stationery Manufacturers Research Institute
esn: essential
esn (ESN): educationally subnormal
ESN: Elastic Stop Nut (corporation); English-Speaking Nations (NATO)
ESNA: Elastic Stop Nut Corporation of America; Empire State Numismatic Association
ESNE: Engineering Societies of New England
esntl: essential
ESNZ: Entomological Society of New Zealand
ESO: Educational Services Office(r); Electronic Supply Office(r); Embarkation Staff Office(r)
ESOC: European Space Operations Center
ESOMAR: European Society for Opinion Surveys and Market Research
ESOP: Employees Stock Ownership Plan
esoph: esophageal; esophagus
esot: esoteric; esoterica; esoterical(ly); esotericism(s)
esp: electro-sensory panel; especially; extrasensory perception
e & sp: equipment and spare parts
Esp: Esperanto
Esp: *Espagne* (French—Spain); *España* (Span—Spain); *Español* (Spanish—Spanish)
ESP: Ecole des Sciences Politiques (School of Political Science); Extrasensory Perception
ESPA: Evening Student Personnel Association
España: (Spanish—Spain)
espec: especial(ly)
Esper: Esperanto
Esperanto: pseudonym of Dr L.L. Zemenhoff—inventor of Esperanto—his artificially-contrived universal language
espg: espionage
express: *espressivo* (Italian—expressive)
esq: *esquerdo* (Portuguese—left)
Esq: Esquire
ESQA: English Slate Quarries Association
esq^{o}: *esquerdo* (Portuguese—left)
Esqrr: Esquire
esr: effective signal radiated; electrical skin resistance; electronically-scanned radar; electron skin resonance; equivalent series resistance; erythrocyte sedimentation rate
ESR: Engineering Summary Report
ESRANGE: European Space Research (northern rocket range)—Kiruna
ESRIN: European Space Research Institute
ESRO: European Space Research Organization
ess: essence; essences; essential
Ess: Essex
ESS: Educational Services Section; Electronic Switching System; Employment Security System; Evaluation SAGE Sector; Experimental SAGE Sector
ESS: *Encyclopedia of the Social Sciences*
essa: environmental survey satellite (weather satellite)
ESSA: Environmental Science Services Administration—Central Radio Propagation Laboratory, Coast and Geodetic Survey, Weather Bureau (Department of Commerce); environmental survey satellite
Essandess: Simon and Schuster
Essie: Esther
ESSO: Esso Shipping; Standard Oil
ESSPO: Electronic Support System Project Office
ESSR: Estonian Soviet Socialist Republic
est: establish; established; establishment; estimate; estimated; estimation; estimator; estuary
est (EST): electroshock therapy
est: *estación* (Spanish—station)
Est: The Book of Esther; Estates (postal abbreviation); Estonia(n)
Est: (French—east)
EST: Eastern Standard Time; Eastern Summer Time; En-

listment Screening Test; Enroute Support Team; Epidemiology and Sanitation Technician
estab: established
Established Church: Established Church of England
estab tip: *establecimiento tipografico* (Spanish—publishing company)
estar: estimated arrival
estb: establish
estbl: establishment
este: (Italian, Portuguese, Spanish—east)
ESTEC: European Space Technology Center
estero: (Spanish—estuary)
estg: estimating
esth: esthetics
Esth: Esthonia; Esthonian
Esther: Hester
Esthr: Apocryphal Book of Esther
ESTI: European Space Technology Institute
estn: estimation
Estoc: *Estocolmo* (Portuguese or Spanish—Stockholm)
ESTRACK: European Space Satellite Tracking and Telemetry Network
Estr B: Estero Bay
estrecho: (Spanish—strait)
est wt: estimated weight
esu: electrostatic unit
ESU: English-Speaking Union
E-SU: English-Speaking Union
e sub: excitor substance
E Suffolk: East Suffolk
E Sussex: East Sussex
E-SUUS: English-Speaking Union of the United States
esv: earth satellite vehicle; enamel single varnish (insulation code)
ESV: Earth Satellite Vehicle; Experimental Safety Vehicle
Esx: Essex
et: edge thickness; educational therapy; educational training; effective temperature; electrical time; electric telegraph; electrical transcription; electronic tests; engineering test; engineering testing
e t: *en titre* (French—in the title)
e/t (E/T): ergotamine tartrate; ergotin tartrate
Et: Ethyl; Etienne
ET: Eastern Time; East Texas (Pulp & Paper Company); Electronics Technician; English translation; Ethiopian Airlines; European Theater (of war)
eta: estimated time of arrival; expect to arrive
ETA: European Teachers Association
ETA: *Euzkadi ta Azkatasuna* (Basque Nation and Liberty)
Etab: *Etablissement* (French—business establishment or factory)
ETAB: Environmental Testing Advisory Board (Dow)
ETAC: Environmental Technical Applications Center
et al.: *et alibi* (Latin—and elsewhere); *et alia* (Latin—and others)
etang: (French—lake; pond)
ETAP: Expanded Technical Assistance Program
etat: (French—state)
etb: early to bed
etb (ETB): end of transmission block character (data processing)
etc: estimated time of completion
etc.: *et cetera* (Latin—and so forth)
e t c: *en tout cas* (French—in any case)
ETC: Electro Tech Corporation; Emergency Training Center; Engine Technical Committee; European Translations Center; European Travel Commission
ETC.: *A Review of General Semantics* (Official Organ of the International Society for General Semantics)
etcg: elapsed-time code generator
etd: estimated time of departure
ete: estimated time enroute
ete: *este* (Spanish—east)
ETE: Experimental Tunnelling Establishment
Eternal City: Rome
etf: electron-transferring flavorprotein
eth: ether; ethical; ethics; ethmoid; ethmoidal
Eth: Ethiopia; Ethiopian; Ethiopic
ETH: Eidgenössiche Technische Hochschule (Swiss Federal Institute of Technology)
ethanol: ethyl alcohol or grain alcohol C_2H_5OH)
eth dat: ethic dative
Eth$: Ethiopian dollar
Ethel Leginska: Ethel Liggins
Ethelred the Unready: Ethelred II of England
ether: ethyl ether $(CH_2H_5)_2O$
Ethical Culturist: Felix Adler
Ethiop: Ethiopia; Ethiopian
ethno: ethnology
ethnog: ethnography
ethnol: ethnology
ethnomus: ethnomusicologist; ethnomusicology
etho: ethylene oxide
eti: elapsed-time indicator; estimated time of interception
Eti: *Etiopia* (Italian—Ethiopia); *Etíopia* (Portuguese—Ethiopia); *Etiopia* (Spanish—Ethiopia)
ETI: Electric Tool Institute; Electronic Technical Institute; Equipment and Tool Institute
ETIC: English Training Information Centre (London)
etio: etiocholandone
etiol: etiology
etk (ETK): erythrocyte transketolase
etkm: every test known to man
etl: ending tape label
ETL: Essex Terminal (railroad)
ETM: Electronic Technician's Mate
ETMA: English Timber Merchants Association
ETMWG: Electronic Trajectory Measurements Working Group
etn: equipment table nomenclature
ETN: Eastern Technical Net (USAF)
eto: estimated time off
ETO: European Theater of Operations; European Transport Organization
Et OH: ethyl alcohol
Etona: (Latin—Eton)
etp: estimated turnaround point; estimated turning point
etp (ETP): electron transfer particle
ETP: Effluent Treatment Plant
et-pnl: engine test panel
ETPS: Empire Test Pilots School
etr: effective thyroid ratio; estimated time of return
Etr: Etruscan
Etr: *entrada* (Spanish— entrance)
ETR: Eastern Test Range; Engineering Test Reactor; Export Traffic Release; External Technical Report
etra: estimated time to reach altitude
ETRC: Educational Television and Radio Center; Engineering Test Reactor Critical Facility
etro: estimated time of return to operation

ets: electronic telegraph system; expiration term of service
Ets: *Etablissements* (French—establishments)
ETS: Educational Television Stations; Educational Testing Service; Engineering Task Summary; Engine Test Stand
ETSA: Electricity Trust of South Australia
ETSC: East Tennessee State College; East Texas State College
et seq.: *et sequens* (Latin—and following)
etsp: entitled to severance pay
etsq: electrical time superquick
Etta: Henrietta
ETTA: English Table Tennis Association
et to: extractor tool
ETTU: English Table Tennis Union
etu: electron tube
ETU: Electrical Trades Union
ETUC: European Trade Union Confederation
et ux.: *et uxor* (Latin—and wife)
etv (ETV): educational television
etv: educational television; engine test vehicle
ETV: Educational Television; Electrotechnischer Verein (Electrotechnical Society); Engine Test Vehicle
etw: *etwas* (German—something)
ETWN: East Tennessee & Western North Carolina (railroad)
etx (ETX): end of text character (data processing)
etym: etymology
Eu: entropy unit (symbol); Euler unit; Europe; European; europium; Eustace; Eustatia
EU: Emory University; Estados Unidos (Spanish—United States); Evacuation Unit
E-U: Etats-Unis (French—United States)
EU: *Europa Unie* (French—United Europe)
eua: examination under anesthetic
EUA: Eastern Underwriters Association; Estados Unidos de America (Spanish—United States of America); Etats-Unis Amérique (French—United States of America)
EUB: Estados Unidos do Brasil (Brazil)
EUC: Euclid (railroad)
Eucl: Euclid
EUCOM: European Command
euc(s): eucalyptus tree(s)
euf: *eufemismo* (Italian, Portuguese, Spanish—euphemism)
EUF: European Union of Federalists
EUFTT: European Union of Film and Television Technicians
Eug: Eugene; Eugenia
eugen: eugenics
Eug^{o}: Eugenio
EUI: *Enciclopedia Universal Ilustrada* (Spanish—Universal Illustrated Encyclopedia)
EUL: *Everyman's University Library*
Eulenberg's disease: congenital muscular spasms
EUM: Estados Unidos Mexicanos (Spanish—Mexican United States—Mexico); European Mediterranean
EUM-AFTN: European-Mediterranean Aeronautical Fixed Telecommunications Network
Euni: Eunice
EUP: Edinburgh University Press; English Universities Press
euphem: euphemism; euphemistic(al)
euphém: *euphémique* (French—euphemistic); *euphémisme* (French—euphemism)
Euphie: Euphemia
euphon: euphonic; euphonically; euphony
Eur: Europe; European
Eurafrica: Europe and Africa
EURATOM: European Atomic Energy Community
Eurailpass: European tourist railroad pass
Eurasafrica: Europe, Asia, and Africa
Eurasia: Europe and Asia
Eurasian(s): person(s) of European and Asian parents such as Euro-Chinese, Euro-Indian, Euro-Japanese, etc.
Euratom: six-nation atomic energy pool consisting of France, Germany, Italy, and the three Benelux countries: Belgium, Netherlands, and Luxembourg
eurex: enriched uranium extraction
Eurip: Euripides
EURO: European Regional Office (FAO)
EUROCAE: European Organization of Civil Aviation Electronics
EUROCEAN: European Oceanographic Association
Eurochemic: European chemical processing of irradiated fuels
EUROCOM: European Coal Merchants Union
Eurodol(s): European dollar(s)
Eurofima: European Company for the Financing of Rolling Stock
Eurofinance: Union International d'Analyse Economique et Financière
EUROFINAS: European Financial Houses
Euromart: European Common Market
Europ: European railway car pool
Europhot: European professional photographers
Eurosac: European paper sack manufacturers
Eurosat: European application satellite systems
EUROSPACE: European Space Study Group
Euseb: Eusebius Pamphili
Eurotox: European Committee on Toxicity Hazards
Eurovision: European Television
EUS: Eastern United States
EUSIDIC: European Association of Scientific Information Dissemination Centers
euv: extreme ultraviolet
eutec: eutectic; eutectoid
euvsh: equivalent ultraviolet solar hour
EUW: European Union of Woman
Eux: Euxine
Euxine Sea: Black Sea
ev: electric vehicle; electron volt; enclosed and ventilated; escort vessel; evangelical; exposure value
ev: *electrón-voltio* (Spanish—electron volt)—also appears as *eV; en ville* (French—local); *evangelisch* (German—Protestant)
eV: electronvolt
eV: *eingetragener Verein* (German—registered society)
Ev: Evenkian; Everest; Everett
Ev: *Eingang vorbehalten* (German—rights reserved)
Ev.: *Evangelium* (Latin—the Gospel)
EV: Elivie (Italian Heliways); English Version; Erne Valley; Everett (railroad)
eva: ethyl-vinyl acetate; extravehicular activity
EVA: Electrical Vehicle Association; Engineer Vice Admiral

evac: evacuate; evacuation
eval: evaluate; evaluation
Evan: Evangelical; Evangelist
evap: evaporate; evaporation; evaporator; evaporize
evapd: evaporated
EVC: Educational Video Corporation
evce: evidence
EVCS: Extravehicular Communications System
EVDF: Eugene V. Debs Foundation
eve: evening
Eve: Eveleen; Evelina
evea: extravehicular engineering activities
event.: *eventuell* (German— possibly)
Everglade State: Florida
Evergreen State: Washington's official nickname
Every Good Boy Does Fine: (mnemonic for remembering the line notes of the treble clef—E, G, B, D, F)
Eve Trib: *Evening Tribune*
evg: evening
EVG: Europäische Verteidigungsgemeinschaft (European Defense Community)
evid: evidence
Evil Florist: Charles Pierre Baudelaire—famous for his *Les Fleurs du Mal* (Flowers of Evil)—drug-addicted leader of French decadents
e viv. disc.: *e vivis discessit* (Latin—departed from life)
EVL: E(dward) V(errall) Lucas
evln: evolution
ev-luth: *evangelisch-luterisch* (German—Evangelical Lutheran)
evmu: extra-vehicular material unit
evng: evening
evol: evolution; evolutionary; evolutionist
evop: evolutionary operation
eV 1 s: edge-V one side (lumber)
eV 2s: edge-V two sides
evr: electronic video recording
EVRS: Electronic Video Recording System
evs (EVS): extravehicular system
evss: extravehicular space suit
evstc (EVSTC): extravehicular suit telemetry and communications
evt: educational and vocational training; equiviscous temperature; eventually
E v T: E van Tongeren
EVT: *Europäische Vereinigung für Tierzucht* (German—European Association for Animal Production)
evtl: *eventuell* (German—eventually; perhaps; possibly)
EVV: Evansville, Indiana (airport)
EVW: European Voluntary Workers
ew: effective warmth; electronic warfare; extensive wound
Ew: Ewart; Ewbanke; Ewell; Ewen; Ewing
Ew: *Euere* or *Eure* or *Eurer* (German—your)—abbreviation used in titles
EW: early warning; electronic warfare; enlisted woman; enlisted women
E & W: England and Wales
EWA: East-West Airlines; East and West Association; Education Writers Association
EWAS: Economic Warfare Analysis Section
ewc: electric water cooler
EWC: East-West Center (University of Hawaii)
EWCRP: Early Warning Control and Reporting Post
EWD: Economic Warfare Division
EWES: Engineering Waterways Experiment Station
ewf: equivalent weight factor
EWF: Electrical Wholesalers Federation
EWG: *Europäische Wirtschaftsgemeinschaft* (German—European Common Market)
EWHS: Eli Whitney School
ewi: education with industry; entered without inspection
ewl: evaporative water loss
EWL: Ellerman's Wilson Line
EWMC: Eli Whitney Metrology Center
EWO: Electrical and Wireless Operators; Electronic Warfare Officer; Emergency War Order; Engineering Work Order; Essential Work Order
EWOS: Electronic Warfare Operational System (USAF)
EWP: Emergency War Plan
ewr: early-warning radar
EWR: Newark, New Jersey (airport)
EWRC: European Weed Research Council
EWS: Emergency Water Supply; Emergency Welfare Service; European Wars Survey
EWSC: Eastern Washington State College; Electric Water Systems Council
EWSF: European Work Study Federation
EWT: Eastern War Time (advanced time)
EWWS: Electronic Warfare Warning System
ex: examination; examine; examined; examiner; example; excess; exercise; experiment(al's)
ex: (Latin—from)
Ex: Excelsior; Exchange; Exchequer; Exeter; Exmoor; Exmouth; Extremadura; Exuma
Ex: *Exodo* (Spanish—The Book of Exodus); ***Exodus***
EX: experimental broadcasting
exacct: expense account
ex af.: *ex affinis* (Latin—of affinity)
exag: exaggerate; exaggerated; exaggeration
Ex Agt: Executive Agent
exam: examination; examine; examiner
examd: examined
exametnet: experimental meteorological sounding rocket network
examg: examining
examn: examination
exams: examinations
ex aq.: *ex aqua* (Latin—out of water)
exbedcap: expanded bed capacity
Ex B/L: exchange bill of lading
exc: excavate; excellent; exciter
exc.: *excudit* (Latin—he engraved it)
Exc: Excelencia (Spanish—Excellency); Excellency
Exc: *Excélsior* (Mexico City); *Exelencia* (Spanish—Excellency)
Exc^a: Excelencia (Spanish—Excellency)
ex cath.: *ex cathedra* (Latin—from the seat of authority)
Excel: Excelsior
Excelsior State: New York whose motto is Excelsior
exch: exchange
ex champ: ex-champion; former champion
Excheq: exchequer
excl: exclude; exclusion; exclusive; exclusivity
exclam: exclamation; exclamatory
Exc^ma: *Excelentísima* (Spanish—Most Excellent)—feminine
Excmo: Excelentísimo (Spanish—Most Excellent)
Exc^mo: *Excelentisimo* (Span-

ish—Most Excellent)—masculine
Ex Com: Executive Committee
ex-con(s): ex convict(s); former convict(s)
ex cp: ex coupon
exd: examined
EXDAMS: Extendable Debugging and Monitoring System
Ex Doc: Executive Document
ex div: ex dividend
Ex Div: Experimental Division
Exe: Exeter
exec (EXEC): execute statement (data processing)
Exec: execute; executed; execution; executive; executive officer; executor
Exec Dir: Executive Director
execs: executives
Exec Sec: Executive Secretary
Executive City: Washington, D.C.
exer: exercise
exes: expenses
Exet Coll: Exeter College—Oxford
ex f: extremely fine
ex fy: extra fancy
ex ga: external gage
ex gr.: *exempli gratia* (Latin—for example)
exh: exhaust
exhib: exhibit; exhibition; exhibitor
exhib.: *exhibeatur* (Latin—let it be shown)
exh t: exhaust turbine
exh v: exhaust vent
ex hy: extra heavy
Ex-Im: Export-Import Bank
EXIMBANK: Export-Import Bank
ex int: ex interest
exis: existential; existentialism; existentialist
exist.: existing
exkl: *exklusiv* (German—excepted; not included)
ex lib.: *ex libris* (Latin—from the library of)
Ex^{ma}Sr^{a}D: *Excelentissima Senhora Dona* [Portuguese—Mrs (precedes full name in formal style)]
ex-mer: ex-meridian
Ex^{mo}Sr: *Excelentissimo Senhor* [Portuguese—Mr (precedes full name in formal style of address)]
exmr: examiner
ex n(ew): excluding new shares
ExO: executive officer; executive order
Ex O: Experimental Office(r)
Exod: *Exodus*
ex off.: *ex officio* (Latin—by authority of his office)
Exon.: Exonia (Latin—Exeter)
exor: executor
exot: exotic
exp: expansion; expense; experiment(al); exponential; export; Exposition; express; expulsion
exp: *expreso* (Spanish—express)
ex p.: *ex parte* (Latin—on one side only)
EXP: Exchange of Persons (UNESCO office)
expdivun: experimental diving unit
expdn: expedition
exped: expedite; expedition
exper: experiment; experimental
Expert: Expanded Pert (program evaluation and review technique)
expir: expiratory; expiration
expl: explain; explanation; explanatory; explosimeter; explosimetric; explosion; explosive(s)
expl: *exemple* (French—example)
explo: explosion; explosive
exploit.: exploitation
explor: exploration
explos: explosive
expn: exposition
expnd: expenditure
expo: expose; exposition
exp o: experimental order(s)
expol: expanded polysterene (light-weight packing moulding)
Expo 70: 1970 exposition at Tokyo
Expo 67: 1967 exposition in Montreal
expr: expiration; expire
ex-Pres: ex-President
EXPRESO: Expreso Aéreo Interamericano
expt: experiment
exptl: experimental
exptr: exporter
expul: expulsion
expur: expurgate(d)
Expwy: Expressway
Expy: Expressway
ex-quay: free on quay
exr: executor
exrx: executrix
exs: expenses; expropriations
exsec: exsecant
Ex Sta: Experimental Station
ext: extend; extension; exterior; external; extinguish; extinguisher; extra
ext.: *extend* (Latin—spread); *extractum* (Latin—extract)
ext (EXT): extraction (dental)
Ext: Extended; Extension
extal: extra time allowance
extd: extracted
ext d & cc: external drug and cosmetic color
Extel: Exchange Telegraph (press agency)
EXTEL: Exchange Telegraph (British news agency)
extemp: extemporaneous(ly)
exten: extension
extend.: *extensus* (Latin—spread)
extern: external; externally
EXTERRA: Extraterrestrial Research Agency (USA)
ext fl: extract fluid (fluid extract)
extg: extinguish(er)
exting: extinguished
ext. liq.: *extractum liquidum* (Latin—liquid extract)
ex tm.: *ex testamento* (Latin—in accord with the testament)
extn: extraction
extr: extract; extrude; extruded; extrusion
Extr: Extremadura
extra: extraordinary
extrad: extradition
extradop: extended range doppler
extrap: extrapolate; extrapolated; extrapolating; extrapolation; extrapolative; extrapolator
extra sess: extra session (legislature)
extrd: extruded
extrem: extremity
extro: extroversion; extrovert
extrx: executrix
exurb: exurban; exurbanite; exurbia; exurbian
exx: examples; executrix
Exxon: (formerly ESSO)—Standard Oil
Exz: Exzellenz (German—Excellency)
eyawtkas: everything you always wanted to know about sex
EYC: Eastern Yacht Club; Encinal Yacht Club; European Youth Campaign
Eye of the Baltic: Gotland
Eye of England: London
Eye of Greece: Athens
Eye of Italy: Rome
Eyetie(s): [(Cockney—Italian(s)]
Eyety: (Cockney—Italian)
Eyety Navy: (Cockney—Italian Navy)
EYOA: Economic and Youth Opportunities Agency
EYR: East Yorkshire Regiment
EYW: Key West, Florida (air-

port)
ez: easy; electrical zero
e-z: easy
Ez: Ezekiel; Ezra; The Book of Ezra
EZ: Eastern Zone; Emile Zola; Extraction Zone
EZ Duzit: Easy Does It
Ezek: The Book of Ezekiel
Ezi: Ezias; Eziel; Eziongaber
Ezr: Ezra
EZU: Europäische Zahlungsunion (European Payment Union)

F

f: farthing; fast; father (capitalized in religious orders); fathom; female; feminine; filment; final target; fine; flat; focal length; fog; folio; following; following page; force; forecastle; franc(s); frequency; freshwater; fugacity; function; latitude factor (symbol); relative humidity (symbol)
f°: folio
f/: relative aperture of a lens (also shown as *f:*)
f: *fecit* (Latin—he did); *filius* (Latin—son); *forte* (Italian—loud); *für* (German—for)
f/: *fardo(s)* [Spanish—bale(s); bundle(s); package(s)]
F: Fahrenheit; Fairchild; farad; Faraday; Faraday constant (symbol); Farrell Lines; fathom(s); February; Fellow; field of vision (symbol); fighter; fire; fixed; fixed broadcast; fixed broadcasting; flagship; florin; fluorine; formal(ity); formula; Foxtrot—code for letter F; France; franc(s); Fraunhofer line (caused by hydrogen); freedom; freedom, degree of (symbol); free energy (symbol); French; Friday; fuel; furlong(s); Furness Lines; Grumman; longitude factor
F.: fats (dietary symbol)
F: *feria* (Latin, Portuguese, Spanish—fair or market); *fora* (Portuguese—out); *framkomst* (Swedish—arrival); *Frauen* (German—women); *freddo* (Italian—cold); *frio* (Portuguese, Spanish—cold); *froid* (French—cold); *fuera* (Spanish—out); *fuori* (Italian—out); (Latin—Filius)
°F: degree Fahrenheit
F_0: pure parental type
F_1: first filial generation
F-1: Fury single-engine jet fighter-bomber flown from aircraft carriers
F1S: finish one side
F^2: prostaglandin alpha (abortion-producing hormone)
F_2: second filial generation
F2S: finish two sides
F-3: Demon single-engine supersonic all-weather jet fighter
F-4: Phantom II twin-engine all-weather supersonic jet fighter-bomber
F-6: Skyray single-engine supersonic all-weather jet fighter
F-8: Crusader single-engine all-weather supersonic jet fighter
F_{10}: decimetric solar flux (symbol)
F-11: Tiger single-engine supersonic jet fighter
f-12: freon (refrigerant)
F-16: high-performance low-cost air-combat fighter aircraft produced by Convair's Fort Worth Division for the U.S. Air Force and the air forces of Belgium, Denmark, the Netherlands, and Norway—NATO allies
F-27: Fokker Friendship (aircraft)
F-28: Fokker turbojet aircraft
F-89: Scorpion all-weather interceptor with twin turbojet engines
F-100: Super Sabre supersonic turbojet fighter
F-101: Voodoo supersonic twin-engine turbojet aircraft
F-102: Delta Dagger single-engine supersonic turbojet interceptor
F-104: Starfighter supersonic single-engine turbojet fighter
F-105: Thunderchief supersonic single-engine turbojet tactical fighter
F-106: Delta Dart supersonic single-engine turbojet interceptor aircraft
F-111: twin-engine turbojet tactical fighter-bomber all-weather interceptor aircraft (TFX)
F-111A: variable-geometry supersonic fighter-bomber (TFX)
fa: family allowance; fatty acid; filterable agent; fire alarm; first aid; first attack; folic acid; fortified aqueous; free aperture; frequency agility; friendly aircraft; field activities; fuel-air (ratio)
f/a: fuel-air ratio
f & a: fore and aft
fa (FA): fatty acid
fa: (Italian—fourth tone; *D* in diatonic scale; *F* in fixed-do system)
fA: *forrige Aar* (Danish—last year)
f^a: *factura* (Spanish—invoice)
Fa: Faeroes
Fa: *Firma* (German—firm; business)
FA: Farm Advisor; Field Ambulance; Field Artillery; Fireman Apprentice; Flota Argentina (de Navegación Fluvial)—Argentine River Navigation Line; Football Association; Frankford Arsenal
F/A: friendly aircraft
F & A: Finance and Accounting
F of A: Foresters of America; Freethinkers of America
FA: *Forze Armate* (Italian—Armed Forces)
faa: field artillery airborne; formalin, acetic acid, alcohol (mixture); free of all average
FAA: Federal Aviation Administration; Fifth Avenue Association; Film Artists' Association; Finska Angpartygys (Finnish Steamship Line); Fleet Air Arm; Foreman's Association of America; Foundation for American Agriculture; Fraternal Actuarial As-

sociation
FAAAS: Fellow of the American Academy of Arts and Sciences; Fellow of the American Association for the Advancement of Science
FAABMS: Forward Army Anti-Ballistic Missile System
FAAG: First Advertising Agency Group
FAAN: First Advertising Agency Network
FAAO: Finance and Accounts Office (US Army)
FAAOS: Fellow of the American Academy of Orthopaedic Surgeons
FAAP: Federal Aid to Airports Program
faar: forward area alerting radar
fab: fable; fabric; fabricate; fabrication; fabulist; fabulous
fab: *fabrique* (French—factory); *franco à bord* (French—free on board); *frei an bord* (German—free on board)
Fab: Fabrian; Fabio; Fabius; Fabre; Fabrice; Fabrizio
FAB: Fleet Air Base; Força Aérea Brasileira (Brazilian Air Force); Frédéric Auguste Bartholdi
FABAS: Farm Amalgamations and Boundary Adjustment Schemes
fabbr: *fabbrica* (Italian—factory)
FABI: Fédération Royale des Associations Belges d'Ingénieurs (Royal Federation of Belgian Engineering Associations)
Fabien Sevitzky: Fabien Koussevitzky
fabl: fire alarm bell
FABMDS: Field Army Ballistic Missile Defense System
FABMIDS: Field Army Ballistic Missile Defense System
fabr: fabricate; fabrication
Fab Soc: Fabian Society
FABSS: Fellow of the Architectural and Building Surveyors' Society
FABU: Fleet Air Base Unit
fabx: fire alarm box
fac: façade; facial; facility; facsimile; factor; factory; faculty; fast as can; field accelerator
fac: façade
fac.: *factum similie* (Latin—facsimile)
Fac: Faculty
FAC: Factor (Max; stock exchange symbol); Federal Advisory Council; Federal Aviation Commission; Financial Administrative Control; Fleet Air Control; Forward Air Controller; Frequency Allocation Committee
FACA: Fellow of the American College of Anaesthetists; Fellow of the American College of Angiology; Fellow of the Association of Chartered Accountants
FACA: *Federación Argentina Cooperative Agrarias* (Spanish—Argentine Agrarian Cooperative Federation)
FACAI: Fellow of the American College of Allergists
FACAn: Fellow of the American College of Anesthesiologists
FACC: Fellow of the American College of Cardiology
FACCA: Fellow of the Association of Certified and Corporate Accountants
FACD: Fellow of the American College of Dentistry
FACDS: Fellow of the Australian College of Dental Surgeons
face.: field artillery computer equipment
FACE: Facilities and Communications Evaluation (USA); (mnemonic for remembering the space notes of the treble clef—F, A, C, E)
FACEM: Federation of Associations of Colliery Equipment Manufacturers
facet: facetious(ly)
FACFO: Fellow of the American College of Foot Orthopedics
FACG: Fellow of the American College of Gastroenterology
FACI: First Article Configuration Inspection
facil: facility
FACMTA: Federal Advisory Council on Medical Training Aids
FACOG: Fellow of the American College of Obstetricians and Gynecologists
facp: forward air control point
FACP: Fellow of the American College of Physicians
FACPM: Fellow of the American College of Preventive Medicine
fac pwr ctl: facility power control
fac pwr mon: facility power monitor
fac pwr pnl: facility power panel
FACR: Fellow of the American College of Radiology
facs: facsimile(s)
FACS: Fellow of the American College of Surgeons
FACSFAC: Fleet Air Control and Surveillance Facility
facsim: facsimile(s)
facsim(s): facsimile(s)
fact: *factura* (Spanish—bill of lading; invoice)
fact.: factory; fully-automatic compiler translator
FACT: Flanagan Aptitude Classification Test; Flight Acceptance Composite Test(-ing); Fully-Automatic Compiler Translator; Fully-Automatic Compiling Technique
fact^a: *factura* (Spanish—invoice)
facty: fact filled; factory
fad. (FAD): flavine adenine dinucleotide
FAD: Fleet Air Defense
fadac: field artillery digital automatic computer
F Adm: Fleet Admiral
FADO: Fellow of the Association of Dispensing Opticians
FAE: Federación de Amigos de la Enseñanza (Federation of the Friends of Teaching); Fund for the Advancement of Education
Faer: Faeroe Islands
Faeroes: Faeroe Islands in the North Atlantic
FAETUA: Fleet Airborne Electronic Training Unit, Atlantic
FAETUP: Fleet Airborne Electronic Training Unit, Pacific
faf: forage acre factor; flyaway factory
FAF: Fafnir Bearings (stock exchange symbol); Financial Analysts Federation; Fine Arts Foundation
fag(s): faggot(s)
fag: *fagotto* (Italian—basson)
FAG: Failure Analysis Group; Fine Arts Gallery
fagms (FAGMS): field artillery guided missiles
FAGO: Fellow of the American Guild of Organists
fags: *fagottos* (Italian—bassoons)
FAGS: Federation of Astronomical and Geophysical Permanent Services; Fellow of the American Geographical Society
fagt: first available government transportation
fagtrans: first available government transportation
FAGU: Fleet Air Gunnery Unit
fah: failed to attend hearing

FAHA: Finnish-American Historical Archives
fahqmt: fully automatic high-quality machine translation
Fahr: Fahrenheit
fai: frequency-azimuth intensity; fresh air intake
FAI: Fairbanks Alaska (airport); Fédération Aéronautique Internationale
FAI: *Fédération Abolitionniste Internationale* (French— International Abolitionist Federation); *Federación Anarquista Iberica* (Spanish—Iberian Anarchist Federation)
FAIA: Fellow of the American Institute of Architects
FAIAS: Fellow of the Australian Institute of Agricultural Science
FAIC: Fellow of the American Institute of Chemists
FAIEx: Fellow of the Australian Institute of Export
FAIHA: Fellow of the Australian Institute of Hospital Administration
FAII: Fellow of the Australian Insurance Institute
FAIM: Fellow of the Australian Institute of Management
FAIME: Foreign Affairs Information Management Effort (Dept State)
FAIO: Field Army Issuing Office(r)
FAIP: Fellow of the Australian Institute of Physics
FAIPM: Fellow of the Australian Institute of Personnel Management
fair.: fairing; fast-access information retrieval
FAir: fleet air
FAIR: Fair Access to Insurance Requirements; Fleet Air (Wing); Friends in America for Independence of Rhodesia
Fair City: Perth, Scotland
Fair Deal: (administration of Harry S. Truman—thirty-third President of the United States)
FAIRS: Fair and Impartial Random Selection System (military draft)
fairships: fleet airships
Fairytale Land: Denmark—home of Hans Christian Andersen
FAIS: Fellow of the Amalgamated Institute of Secretaries
fak: freights all kinds
Fak: *Faktura* (German—invoice)
FAK: *Federasie van Afrikaanse Kultuurverenigingе* (Afrikaans—Federation of Afrikaans Cultural Societies)
fak-pak: freight all kinds (in a box on wheels)
faks: *faksimile* (Dano-Norwegian—facsimile)
Fakt: *Faktura* (German—invoice)
Fal: Falmouth
fal: *fusil automatique légère* (French—light automatic rifle)—*FAL*
F a L: Fathers-at-Large
FAL: Frequency Allocation List; Frontier Airlines
FAL: *Frente Argentino de Liberación* (Spanish—Argentine Liberation Front) — pro-Cuban
FALA: Federation of Asian Library Associations
falcons of the sea: clipper ships
'falfa: alfalfa
Falk Cur: Falkland Current
Falk Isl: Falkland Islands (Islas Maldivas)
Falklands: Falkland Islands and Dependencies (South Georgia, South Sandwich Islands, South Shetlands)
Falls City: Louisville, Kentucky
fallwarn: fallout warning
FALN: *Fuerzas Armadas de Liberación Nacional* (Armed Forces of National Liberation—Communist paramilitary organization)
FALS: Ford Authorized Leasing System
false topaz: citrine (quartz with ferric iron)
fam: familiar; family; foreign air mail; free at mill
FAM: foreign airmail; Free and Accepted Masons
F & AM: Free and Accepted Masons
FAMA: Fellow of the American Medical Association; Fire Apparatus Manufacturers Association
fame.: fatty-acid methyl ester(s)
FAME: Farmers Allied Meat Enterprises Cooperative; Future American Magical Entertainers
FAMEM: Federation of Associations of Mining Equipment Manufacturers
FAMEME: Fellow of the Association of Mining, Electrical, and Mechanical Engineers
FAMHEM: Federation of Associations of Materials Handling Equipment Manufacturers
FAMOS: Fleet Applications of Meteorological Observations from Satellites
FAMOUS: French-American Mid-Ocean Undersea Study (of an Atlantic reef off the Azores on the line of an undersea rift extending from the Arctic to Antarctica)
fam per para: familial periodic paralysis
fam phys: family physician
FAMS: Fellow of the Ancient Monuments Society
fan.: fanatic (usually in sense of enthusiast); fantasia; fantasy
Fanguito: (Spanish—Little Muddy)—San Juan, Puerto Rico's most notorious slum
Fan(ny): Frances; Francisca; Frasquita
FANK: *Forces Armées Nationales Khmères* (French—Khmer National Armed Forces)—Cambodian armed forces
Fannie Mae: Federal National Mortgage Association
Fanshaw: Featherstonehaugh
fant: fantasia; fantasy
fantabulous: fantastic + fabulous
fantac: fighter analysis tactical air combat
FANU: Flota Argentina de Navegación de Ultramar (Argentine High Seas Navigation Line)
FANY: First-Aid Nursing Yoemanry
FANZAAS: Fellow of the Australian and New Zealand Association for the Advancement of Science
fanzines: fan + magazines
fao: finish all over
FAO: Field Audit Office(r); Finance and Accounts Office(r); Fleet Accountant Officer; Fleet Administration Office(r); Food and Agriculture Organization (UN); Free Albania Organization
F & AO: Finance and Accounts Office (US Army)
fap: final approach; floating arithmetic package
fap (FAP): fixed action pattern
FAP: Family Assistance Plan; Family Assistance Program(ming); First Aid Post; Frequency Allocation Panel
FAP: *Forca Aérea Portuguesa* (Portuguese Air Force); *Fuerzas Armadas Peronistas* (Spanish—Peronist Armed

Forces)—right-wing Argentine guerrilla group
FAPA: Filipino-American Political Association
FAPHA: Fellow of the American Public Health Association
FAPHI: Fellow of the Association of Public Health Inspectors
FAPI: First Article Production Inspection
FAPIG: First Atomic Power Industry Group
FAPR: Federal Aviation Procurement Regulations
FAPS: Fellow of the American Physical Society
FAPT: Fellow of the Association of Photographic Technicians
faq: fair average quality; free at quay
FAQ: Free at Quay
faqs: fair average quality of season
far.: false alarm rate; farad; Faraday; faradic; farthing; finned air rocket; forward-acquisition radar
Far: Faraday
FAR: Failure Analysis Report; Federal Aviation Regulations; finned air rocket; flight aptitude rating
FAR: *Fuerzas Armadas Rebeldes* (Spanish—Rebel Armed Forces)—Guatemala; *Fuerzas Armadas Revolucionarias* (Spanish—Revolutionary Armed Forces)—Cuba
FARA: Foreign Agents Registration Act
FARADA: Failure Rate Data (BuWeps Program
Farallones: Farollon Islands off San Francisco
FARC: Federal Addiction Research Center
FARC: *Fuerzas Armadas Revolucionarias de Colombia* (Spanish—Armed Revolutionary Forces of Colombia)—pro-Soviet communists
FARELF: Far East Land Forces
Far East: countries and islands of East Asia or in the Pacific—eastern Siberia, China, Japan, Taiwan, Korea, Indochina, the Philippines, the Malay Peninsula
faret: fast reactor test
Farewell: Beethoven's Piano Sonata No. 32 in C minor (opus 111); Haydn's Symphony No. 45 in F-sharp minor
Farinelli: Carlo Broschi
FARL: Frick Art Reference Library
farm: *farmacia* (Spanish—pharmacy)—drugstore
farmobile: farm automobile
Farmer President: sobriquet shared by William Henry Harrison and George Washington
faro.: flow(ed; ing) at rate of
FARP: *Fronte Antifascista e di Rinascita Populare* (Italian—Antifascist Front and Popular Revival)—left-wing group
Far Pom: Farther Pomerania (coastal Poland)
Farrar: Farrar, Straus and Giroux
Fars: Faristan
Far West: the Rocky Mountain States
fas: fetal alcohol syndrome; first and seconds; free alongside ship
FAS: Federal Agricultural Service; Federal Air Surgeon; Federation of American Scientists; Fellow of the Society of Arts; Food Advice Service; Foreign Agricultural Service; Free Alongside Ship; Frequency Assignment Subcommittee
FASA: Fellow of the Acoustical Society of America
FASAP: Fellow of the Australian Society of Animal Production
fasc: *fascicule* (French—part); *fasciculus* (Latin—little bundle)
FASCE: Fellow of the American Society of Civil Engineers
fase: fundamentally-analyzable simplified English
FASE: Fellow of the Antiquarian Society—Edinburgh
FASEB: Federation of American Societies of Experimental Biology
FASL: Florida Association of School Librarians
FASPM: Flotte Administrative des Iles Saint Pierre et Miquelon
FAST: First Atomic Ship Transport
fastnr: fastener
fat.: final assembly test(ing); fixed asset transfer; full annual toll
FAT: Fresno, California (airport)
Fatah: *Harakat-Tahrir Falastin* (Arabic—Palestinian terrorist underground organization)—Arabic acronyms such as this have inverted initials
fatdog: fatty hotdog (fat-filled frankfurter)
Fate: American nickname for Lafayette and one adorning many country boys
Fate: Beethoven's Symphony No. 5 in C minor (see *Victory*)
fa technique: fluorescent antibody technique
fatfurters: fat-filled frankfurters
fath: fathom
Father of Abolition: Samuel Hopkins
Father Abraham: Abraham Lincoln
Father of Algebra: Diophantus of Alexandria
Father of America: Sam(uel) Adams
Father of American Anthropology: Lewis Henry Morgan
Father of American Baptists: John Clarke
Father of American Botany: John Bartram
Father of American Boxing: William Muldoon
Father of American Conchology: Thomas Say
Father of American Football: Walter Camp
Father of American Freethought: Thomas Paine
Father of American Geography: Jedidiah Morse
Father of American Geology: William Maclure
Father of American History: George Bancroft and William Bradford—both have backers for this title
Father of American Horticulture: Peter Henderson
Father of American Independence: John Adams
Father of American Lexicography: Noah Webster
Father of American Literature: Washington Irving
Father of the American Medical Association: Dr Nathan Smith Davis
Father of American Medical Botany: Jacob Bigelow
Father of American Mineralogy: Parker Cleaveland
Father of American Naval Architecture: William A. Webb
Father of American Navigation: Nathaniel Bowditch
Father of American Oceanography: Matthew Fontaine Maury
Father of American Orchestral Music: Johann Christian Gottlieb Graupner
Father of American Ornithology:

appelation shared by John James Audubon and Alexander Wilson
Father of American Photo-Journalism: Matthew Brady
Father of American Poets: William Cullen Bryant
Father of American Pragmatism: Charles Sanders Peirce
Father of American Prison Reform: George O. Osborne
Father of American Psychiatry: Dr Benjamin Rush
Father of American Psychobiology: Adolf Meyer
Father of American Psychology: William James
Father of American Railroads: Peter Cooper
Father of the American Revolution: Sam(uel) Adams
Father of American Rocketry: Robert H. Goddard
Father of American Surgery: Dr William Halsted or Dr Philip Syng Physick, depending on whose doing the nicknaming
Father of American Universalism: nickname shared by Hosea Ballou and John Murray
Father of American Zoology: Thomas Say
Father of Anatomical Dissection: Andreas Vesalius
Father of Angling: Izaak Walton
Father of Annapolis: George Bancroft
Father of the Atomic Submarine: Admiral Hyman Rickover, USN
Father of the Automobile: Gottlieb Daimler
Father of Baseball: Henry Chadwick, Alexander Cartwright, and Abner Doubleday share this sobriquet
Father of Basketball: James Naismith
Father of Belgian Opera: Andri Ernest Modeste Grétry
Father of Believers: Mohammed
Father of the Bill of Rights: James Madison
Father of Blood Banks and Blood Plasma: Charles R. Rich
Father of the Blues: W(illiam) C(hristopher) Handy
Father of Brazilian Opera: Antonio Carlos Gomes
Father of Buffalo: Joseph Ellicot
Father of Chemistry: Robert Boyle
Father of Chemurgy: George Washington Carver
Father of Church History: Eusebius
Father of Civil Service Reform: George Hunt Pendleton
Father of Comedy: Aristophanes
Father of Confederation: John A. Macdonald—Canada's first prime minister
Father of the Constitution: James Madison—fourth President of the United States
Father of the Continental Congress: Benjamin Franklin
Father of the Cotton Gin: Eli Whitney
Father of Courtesy: Richard Beauchamp—Earl of Warwick
Father of the Cowboys: Charles Goodnight
Father Christmas: Santa Claus; Snow King
Father Damien: Joseph Damien de Veuster
Father of Danish Opera: Friedrich Kuhlau
Father of Dano-Norwegian Literature: Ludvig Holberg
Father of the Declaration of Independence: title many historians agree must be shared by Thomas Paine who wrote the first rough draft and Thomas Jefferson who wrote the final draft with John Adams and Benjamin Franklin lending support
Father Divine: Morgan J. Divine born George Baker
Father of Dutch Poetry: Jakob van Maerlant
Father of the Dutch Reformed Church in America: John Henry Livingston
Father of Ecclesiastical History: Eusebius Pamphili
Father of Embryology: Carl Ernst von Baer
Father of English Lexicography: Dr Samuel Johnson also celebrated as the leading conversationalist of his era, according to his biographer James Boswell called Bozzy
Father of English Poetry: Geoffrey Chaucer
Father of English Printing: William Caxton
Father of English Song: Caedmon
Father of English Unitarianism: John Biddle
Fathers of the Enlightenment: Diderot, Rousseau, Voltaire
Father of Epic Poetry: Homer
Father of Ethical Culture: Felix Adler
Father of Experimental Physiology: Galen
Father of the Faithful: Abraham
Father of Fascism: Italian bully-boy tyrant Benito Mussolini
Father of the Federal Reserve System: George Carter Glass
Father of the Film Industry; D(avid) W(ark) Griffith
Father of Fingerprinting: Alphonse Bertillon
Father of the Flivver: Henry Ford
Father of the Free School System: Governor James Edward English of Connecticut
Father of Free Trade: Adam Smith
Father of French-Canadian Poetry: Octave Cremazie
Father of French Opera: Jean-Baptiste Lully
Father of the French School of Neurology: Jean-Martin Charcot
Father of French Surgery: Ambroise Paré
Father of Geography: Strabo the Greek Stoic who wrote seventeen books about Asia, Egypt, Libya, and Europe
Father of Geometry: Pythagorus
Father of German Literature: Gotthold Ephraim Lessing
Father of German Opera: Christoph Willibald von Gluck
Father of the German Reformation: Martin Luther
Father of German Unification: Prince Otto von Bismarck
Father of Gods and Men: Odin or Wotan, according to the Norse; Jove or Jupiter, according to the Romans; Zeus, according to the Greeks; etc.
Father of Greater Philadelphia: John Christian Bullitt
Father of Greek Didactic Poetry: Hesiod whose poem *Theogony* describes the beginning of the world, its gods, and the five Ages of Mankind (*see entry*)
Father of Greek Music: Terpander of Lesbos
Father of Greek Sculpture: Phidias
Father of Greek Tragedy: Aeschylus
Father of Greenbacks: Salmon Portland Chase
Father of His Country: Cicero and several Roman caesars; George Washington—Commander-in-Chief of the Continental Army and first President of the United States
Father of History: Herodotus
Father of Homeopathy in Ameri-

ca: Dr Constantine Hering
Father of the Household Heater: Benjamin Franklin
Father of Hypnotism: Friedrich Anton Mesmer
Father of Individual Psychology: Alfred Adler
Father of Italian Landscape Painting: Andrea del Verrocchio (Andrea di Michele Cione)
Father of Italian Opera: Claudio Monteverdi
Father of Japanese Caricature: Toba Sojo
Father of Japanese Shipbuilding: Thomas Glover known to the Japanese as Kuraba
Father of Jests: Joseph Miller
Father of the Juvenile Court: Judge Benjamin Barr Lindsey
Father of the Kindergarten: Friedrich Froebel
Father of Latin Song: Ennius (239–169 BCE)
Father of the Legal Code: David Dudley Field
Father of Lies: Satan
Father of Massachusetts: Governor John Winthrop
Father of Medicine: Hippocrates
Father of Mexican Independence: Miguel Hidalgo y Costilla
Father of Mineralogy: Agricola
Father of Modern Art: Masaccio (Tommaso Guidi)
Father of Modern Baseball: Alexander Joy Cartwright
Father of Modern Conservative Thought: Edmund Burke
Father of Modern Democratic Philosophy: John Locke
Father of Modern Genetics: Gregor Mendel
Father of Modern Geology: Sir Charles Lyell
Father of Modern Medicine: Canadian-born Sir William Osler
Father of Modern Music: Mozart
Father of Modern Navies: Captain Alfred T. Mahan author of *The Influence of Sea Power upon History* published in 1890
Father of Modern Neurology: Guillaume-Benjamin-Amand Duchenne
Father of the Modern Novel: Lion Feuchtwanger
Father of Modern Painters: Giovanni Cimabue (Cenni di Pepo)
Father of Modern Pedagogy: Heinrich Pestalozzi
Father of Modern Physiology: William Harvey
Father of Modern Surgery of the Brain: Paul Broca
Father of the Modern Zoo: Carl Hagenbeck
Father of Moral Philosophy: Thomas Aquinas
Father of the Mormons: Joseph Smith
Father of Muckrakers: Upton Sinclair, Lincoln Steffens, and Joseph Flynt Williard share this unattractive sobriquet attesting to their success as reporters revealing corruption and graft
Father of Negro History: Carter G(odwin) Woodson
Father of the Neighborhood Settlement House: Jacob August Riis
Father of Neurosurgery: American-born Canadian Doctor Wilder Penfield
Father of New England: John Endicott—its first governor
Father of Niagara Power: William Birch Rankine
Father of Organic Architecture: Frank Lloyd Wright
Father of Osteopathy: Dr Andrew T. Still
Father of the Patent Office: John Ruggles
Father of Pennsylvania: William Penn—its founder
Father of Philippine Independence: Emilio Aguinaldo
Father of the Phonograph: Thomas A. Edison
Father of Physiography: William Morris Davis
Father of Pittsburgh: George Washington who proposed the location and the name during the French and Indian War
Father of the Potteries: Josiah Wedgwood
Father of Psychoanalysis: Sigmund Freud
Father of Radio: Lee De Forest
Father of Radio Broadcasting: Harry P(hillips) Davis
Father of the Reformed Church: John Henry Livingston
Father of the Republic of China: Sun Yat Sen
Father of Ridicule: Rabelais
Father of the Royal Navy: King Alfred
Father of Rural Free Delivery: Marion Butler of North Carolina
Father of Russian Literature: Alexander Pushkin
Father of Russian Opera: Michael Glinka
Father of Science Fiction: Jules Verne *(see entry)*
Father of the Sewing Machine: Elias Howe
Father of the Skyscraper: Cass Gilbert
Father of South African Poetry: Thomas Pringle
Father of the Soviet Hydrogen Bomb: Nobel-Peace-Prize-winner Andrei D. Sakharov
Father of Spanish Drama: Lope de Vega
Father of States' Rights: John Caldwell Calhoun
Father of State Universities: Manasseh Cutler
Father of Steam Navigation: Robert Fulton
Father of the String Quartet and the Symphony: Franz Joseph Haydn—his 85 string quartets and 104 symphonies set the style for such works up to the end of the 19th century
Father of the Submarine: John Philip Holland
Father of Supersonic Flight: Theodor von Karman
Father of Swedish Music: Johan Helmich Roman
Father of Swedish Opera: Ivar Hallström
Father of Swiss Reformation: Huldreich Zwingli
Father of the Tablet Triturate: Dr Robert Mason Fuller
Father of the Tariff: Secretary of the Treasury Alexander Hamilton
Father of the Telegraph: S(amuel) F(inley) B(reese) Morse
Father of the Telephone: Alexander Graham Bell
Father of Television: John Logie Baird
Father of Texas: sobriquet shared by Stephen F. Austin and Sam(uel) Houston
Father of Theoretical Chemistry: Antoine Laurent Lavoisier
Father Time: time personified and symbolized by a bearded elder wielding a scythe
Father of Tragedy: Aeschylus
Father of Tropical Medicine: Sir Patrick Manson
Father of the Typewriter: Christopher Latham Sholes
Father of the United States Navy: nickname shared by President John Adams and Commodore John Barry
Father of the United States Lighthouse Service: President John

Quincy Adams
Father of the United States Military Academy: Brigadier General Sylvanus Thayer, USA
Father of the United States National Museum: John Quincy Adams who when President advocated the founding of what became the Smithsonian Institution
Father of the United States Naval Academy: Secretary of the Navy George Bancroft
Father of the United States Naval War College: Rear Admiral Stephen Bleecker Luce
Father of Universalism in the United States: Hosea Ballou
Father of the University of Virginia: Thomas Jefferson—third President of the United States
Father of the U.S. Navy: John Adams—second President of the United States
Father of the U.S. Post Office: Benjamin Franklin—author, inventor, patriot, printer, philosopher, scientist, statesman
Father of Vaccination: Edward Jenner
Father of Vasectomy: Sir Astley Paston Cooper
Father of the Viennese Operetta: Franz von Suppé
Father of Virginia: Captain John Smith
Father of the Waters: sobriquet shared by great rivers such as the Amazon, Amur, Congo, Euphrates, Huang, Irrawaddy, Lena, Mackenzie, Mekong, Mississippi, Niger, Nile, Ob, Volga, Yangtze, Yenisei
Father of the Western Story: Zane Grey
Father of West Point: Sylvanus Thayer
Father of Zionism: Theodor Herzl
Fathers of Canadian Confederation: Sir John A. Macdonald and George Brown of Ontario, Sir George S. Etienne Cartier and Sir Alexander Galt of Quebec, Sir Charles Tupper of Nova Scotia, Sir Samuel Leonard Tilley of New Brunswick
Fathers of Italian Unification: Camillo Cavour, Giuseppe Garibaldi, Giuseppe Mazzini
FATIS: Food and Agriculture Technical Information Service
fatt: *fattura* (Italian—invoice)
fau: faucet; field action units; forced air unit
FAU: Florida Atlantic University; Friends' Ambulance Unit
FAUL: Five Associated University Libraries (Binghampton, Buffalo, Cornell, Rochester, Syracuse)
Faulkner's County: Yoknapatawpha (an invention of novelist William Faulkner)
Faunty: Fauntleroy
FAUSST: French-Anglo-U.S. Supersonic Transport
faustite: basic hydrated zinc aluminum phosphate (zinc-rich form of turquoise)
Faustus Socinus: Fausto Sozzini
Fauvist Painter: Raoul Dufy
fav: favor; favorable; favorite
Favelas: Rio de Janeiro's hillside slums
FAVO: Fleet Aviation Officer
Favorite Island of Columbus: Jamaica
FAWA: Factory Assist Work Authorization; Federation of Asian Women's Associations
Fawcett: Fawcett World Library
FAWCO: Federation of American Women's Clubs Overseas
FAWS: Flight Advisory Weather Service
fax: facilities (tv technical equipment such as cameras, lights, microphones); facsimile; facts
FAX: fixed aeronautical station
Faxon: Fetherstoneaugh
Fay: Fagele; Faith; Fanny
FAZ: *Frankfurter Allgemeine Zeitung* (Frankfurt's Universal Newspaper)
fb: film bulletin; flat bar; fog bell; foreign body; freight bill; fullback
f-b: full-bore (greater than 22 caliber)
f & b: fire and bilge; fumigation and bath
f/B: female Black
FB: Fenian Brotherhood; Film Bulletin; Fire Brigade; Fisheries Board; Flying Boat; Forth Bridge; Free Baptist
FBA: Federal Bar Association; Fellow of the British Academy; Fibre Box Association; Fur Brokers Association
FBAA: Fellow of the British Association of Accountants and Auditors
f'ball: football
fbc: fallen building clause
FBC: Federal Broadcasting Corporation
FBCM: Federation of British Carpet Manufacturers
FBCP: Fellow of the British College of Physiotherapists
FBCS: Fellow of the British Computer Society
fbcw: fallen building clause waiver
fbd: freeboard
FB & D: Ford, Bacon and Davis
FBEA: Fellow of the British Esperanto Association
FBF: Frankfurt Book Fair
fbfm: frequency feedback frequency modulation
FBFM: Federation of British Film Makers
FBG: Federation of British Growers
fbh: fire-brigade hydrant
FBHI: Fellow of the British Horological Institute
FBHTM: Federation of British Hand Tool Manufacturers
FBI: Federal Bureau of Investigation; Federation of British Industries; Food Business Institute
FBIA: Fellow of the Bankers' Institute of Australasia
FBIM: Fellow of the British Institute of Management
FBIRA: Federal Bureau of Investigation Recreation Association
FBIs: Forgotten Boys of Iceland (American armed forces personnel stationed in Iceland)
FBIS: Fellow of the British Interplanetary Society
fbk: flat back (lumber); fast buck
FBKS: Fellow of the British Kinematograph Society
fbl: forged billet
FBL: Federal Barge Lines; Furness Bermuda Line
FBLA: Future Business Leaders of America
fbm: feet board measure; fleet ballistic missile
FBM: Fleet Ballistic Missile
FBN: Federal Bureau of Narcotics
fbo: fixed-base operation; foreign building office
FBOA: Fellow of the British Optical Association
FBOU: Fellow of the British Ornithologists' Union
fbp: final boiling point
FBP: Federal Bureau of Prisons; Federation of Podiatry Boards
FBPI: Franklin Book Programs, Incorporated
FBPS: Fellow of the British Psychological Society

fbr: fast burst reactor; fiber
FBRAM: Federation of British Rubber and Allied Manufacturers
fbrk: firebrick
fbrl: final bomb release line
fbro: *febrero* (Spanish—February)
FBRS: Farm Business Recording Scheme
fbs: fasting blood sugar
FBS: Fellow of the Botanic(al) Society; Fighter Bomber Squadron; Forward-Base System(s)
FBSE: Fellow of the Botanical Society—Edinburgh
FBSM: Fellow of the Birmingham School of Music
FBTT: Federal Board of Tea Tasters
FBu: Burundi Franc(s)
FBU: Oslo, Norway (Fornebu Airport)
FBUI: Federation of British Umbrella Industries
fbw: full bandwidth
FBW System: Fly-by-Wire System
fby: future budget year
fc: file cabinet; filter center; fire clay; fire-control; follow copy; foot-candle; franc; front-connected; functional code; fund code
f/c: flight control; for cash; free and clear
f & c: fire and casualty (insurance); full and change (tides)
fc: *ferrocarril* (Spanish—railroad; railway)
Fc: fractocumulus
FC: Fairbury College; Fenn College; Finch College; Findlay College; fire control; Fontbonne College; Foothill College; Franconia College; Frederic Chopin; Frederick College; Free Church (Scotland)
F-C: Franche-Comté
FC: *Ferrocarril(es):* [Spanish railroad(s)]
fca: frequency control and analysis
FCA: Farm Credit Administration; Fellow (of the Institute) of Chartered Accountants
FCAA: Federal Clean Air Act; Florence Crittenton Association of America
FCACS: Federal Civil Agencies Communications System
f cant.: forward cant frames
fcap: foolscap
FCAP: Fellow of the College of American Pathologists
fcb: free-cutting brass
FCB: Facility Clearance Board; Flight Certification Board; Foundation for Commercial Banks; Freight Container Bureau
FCBA: Federal Communications Bar Association
fcc: fluid catalytic cracking
fcc (FCC): first-class certificate
FCC: Farm Credit Corporation (Canada); Federal Communications Commission; Federal Council of Churches; Federal Court of Canada; First-Class Certificate; Flight Coordination Center; Florida Citrus Commission
FCCA: Four Cylinder Club of America
FCCCA: Federal Council of Churches of Christ in America
FCCO: Fellow of the Canadian College of Organists
fccp (FCCP): carbonylcyanide p-trifluoromethoxyphenylhydrazone
FCCP: Fellow of the College of Chest Physicians
FCCS: Fellow of the Corporation of Certified Secretaries
fcd: failure-correction coding
FCDA: Federal Civil Defense Administration
F & CD—IR: Failure and Consumption Data—Inspector's Report
FCE: Florida Citrus Exchange; Foreign Currency Exchange; French-Canadian Enterprises
FCECA: Fishery Committee for the Eastern Central Atlantic
FCGB: Forestry Committee of Great Britain
FCEX: Fruit Growers Express
fcg: facing
FCG: Foreign Clearance Guide
FCGI: Fellow of the City and Guilds of London Institute
FCGP: Fellow of the College of General Practitioners
FChS: Fellow of the Society of Chiropodists
FCI: Fellow of the Clothing Institute; Federal Correctional Institution; *Federazione Ciclista Italiana* (Italian Cycling Association); *Federazione Calcistica Italiana* (Italian Football Association); *Federazione Colombotila Italiana* (Italian Carrier-pigeon Fanciers' Association); Fluid Controls Institute; Franklin College of Indiana
FCIA: Fellow of the Corporation of Insurance Agents; Foreign Credit Insurance Association; Friends of Cast-Iron Architecture
FCIB: Fellow of the Corporation of Insurance Brokers
FCIC: Fairchild Camera and Instrument Corporation; Farm Crop Insurance Corporation; Fellow of the Chemical Institute of Canada
FCIF: Flight Crew Information File
FCII: Fellow of the Chartered Insurance Institute
fcim: farm, construction, and industrial machinery
FCIPA: Fellow of the Chartered Institute of Patent Agents
FCIS: Fellow of the Chartered Institute of Secretaries
FCIT: Fellow of the Chartered Institute of Transport
FCIV: Fellow of the Commonwealth Institute of Valuers
FCJC: Flit Community Junior College
f clef: bass clef
fclty: facility
fcly: face lying
FCM: Ferrocarril Mexicano (Mexican Railway); Firestone Conservatory of Music (Akron)
FCM: *Ferrocarril Mexicano* (Spanish—Mexican Railway)
FCMA: Finch College Museum of Art
FCMI: Federation of Coated Macadam Industries
FCMIE: Fellow of the Colleges of Management and Industrial Engineering
FCMSBR: Federal Coal Mine Safety Board of Review
FCNA: Fellow of the College of Nursing—Australia
fco: cleanout flush with finished floor; fair copy; franking privilege; free postage
fco: *franco* (Italian—free)
F^{co}: Francisco (Spanish—Francis)
FCO: Fire Control Officer; Fleet Constructor Officer; Rome, Italy (Leonardo da Vinci airport, formerly Fiumicino—hence FCO)
F & CO: Foreign and Commonwealth Office
fcos: francos (Spanish—francs)
fcp: final common pathway; foolscap
FCP: Fellow of the College of

Preceptors; Ferrocarril de Chihuahua al Pacifico (Chihuahua Pacific Railroad)
FCPA: Fellow of the Canadian Psychological Association
FCPC: Federal Committee on Pest Control
fc pl: face plate
FCPO: Fleet Chief Petty Officer
FCPS: Fellow of the College of Physicians and Surgeons
fcr: forward contactor; full cold rolled (steel sheeting)
FCR: Fire Control Room; First City Regiment; Flinders Chase Reserve (South Australia)
FCRA: Fellow of the College of Radiologists of Australia; Fellow of the Corporation of Registered Accountants
FCRLS: Flight-Control Ready Light System
fcs: francs
fc & s: free of capture and seizure (insurance)
FCS: Farmer Cooperative Service; Fellow of the Chemical Society; Fire Control School; Fire Control Station; Fire Control System
F/CS: Flight-Control System
fcsad: free of capture, seizure, arrest or detainment (shipping insurance)
FCSBC: Ferrocarril Sonora-Baja California (Sonora-Baja California Railroad)
FCSC: Foreign Claims Settlement Commission
FCSCUS: Federal Claims Settlement Commission of the United States
fcsle: forecastle
fcsrcc: free of capture, seizure, riots and civil commotion (shipping insurance)
fc & s and r & cc: free of capture, seizure, riots, and civil commotion
fcst: forecast
FCST: Federal Council for Science and Technology (Executive Office of the President)
fct: filament center tap; fraction thereof; function
FCT: Federal Capital Territory
FCTB: Fellow of the College of Teachers of the Blind
fcty: factory
fcu: fire-control unit
FCU: Federal Credit Union(s)
FCUS: Federal Credit Union System
FCWA: Fellow of the Chartered Institute of Cost and Works Accountants
fcy: fancy
fcy pks: fancy packs
FCZ: Ferrocarril de Coahuila y Zacatecas (Coahuila and Zacatecas Railroad)
fd: fan douche; fatal dose; field; flight deck; floor drain; focal distance; forced draft; framed; free discharge; free dispatch; freeze-dried; front of dash; fund
f/d: father and daughter
f & d: faced and drilled; fill and drain; findings and determination; fire and flushing; freight and demurrage
fd_{50}: median fatal dose
fd (Fd): ferredoxin
Fd: Ferdinand; Fiord (Fjord)
FD: field drum; Finance Department; Fire Department
fda: flight-direction attitude; fronto-dextra anterior
FDA: Food and Drug Administration
FDATC: Flying Division, Air Training Command
fdb: field dynamic braking; forced-draft blower
fdc: fire-direction center (FDC)
***F.D.:** Fidei Defensor* (Latin—Defender of the Faith
FD & C: Food, Drug, and Cosmetic (Act)
***fdc:** fleur de coin* (French—mint condition)
FDC: Fire-Detection Center; Forsyth Dental Center (Harvard)
FDCC: Fort Dodge Community College
F D & C-color: Food, Drug, and Cosmetic (Act) color
***fdd:** franc de droits* (French—free of charge)
FDD: Fondation Documentaire Dentaire (Dental Documentation Foundation)
fddc (FDDC): ferric dimethyl dithiocarbonate
fddl: frequency division data link
fddlp.: frequency division data link printout
fde: field decelerator
F del P: Ferrocarril del Pacifico (Pacific Railroad)
Fdez: Fernández
FDF: Footwear Distributors' Federation
FDFU: Federation of Documentary Film Units
fdg: funding
FDH: Federal Detention Headquarters
FDHO: Factory Department—Home Office
fdi: field discharge
FDI: Federal Department of Information (Malaysia); Federation Dentaire Internationale (International Dental Federation); Fir Door Institute
FDIC: Federal Deposit Insurance Corporation
***FDIF:** Fédération Démocratique Internationale des Femmes* (French—International Democratic Federation of Women)
FDIT: Federal Daily Income Trust
***FDJ:** Freie Deutsche Jugend* (Free German Youth)—communist youth organization in East Germany
FDL: Fast Deployment Logistic(s)—naval Logistic(s)—naval cargo carrier(s); fleet deployment logistic ship (naval symbol); Flight Dynamics Laboratory; Foremost Defended Localities
F & DL: Food and Drug Laboratory
fd ldg: forced landing
FDLI: Food and Drug Law Institute
FDLS: Fast Deployment Logistics Ship
fdm: frequency division multiplexing
***FDM:** Forenede Dansk Motorejere* (Federation of Danish Motorists)
FDMA: Fibre Drum Manufacturers Association
FDMHA: Frederick Douglass Memorial and Historical Association
fdn: foundation
FDN: Field Designator Number
fdnb (FDNB): fluorodinitrobenzene
Fdo: Ferdinando
FDO: Fleet Dental Officer
***F do I:** Foz do Iguaçu* (Portuguese—Mouth of the Iguazu)—three miles above the gigantic Iguazu Waterfalls shared by Argentina, Brazil, and Paraguay at their juncture
fdp: foreign duty pay
fdp (FDP): fructose 1,6-diphosphate
FDP: foreign duty pay; fronto-dextra posterior
***FDP:** Freie Demokratische Partei* (German—Free Democratic Party)
FDPA: Fogg Dam Protected Area (Australian Northern

Territory)
FDPC: Federal Data Processing Center(s)
Fd PO: Field Post Office
fdr: feeder
f dr: fire door
Fdr: Founder
FDR: Franklin Delano Roosevelt—thirty-second President of the United States
FDRHS: Franklin Delano Roosevelt High School
FDRL: Franklin D. Roosevelt Library (Hyde Park, New York)
FDRMC: Franklin Delano Roosevelt Memorial Commission
FDRS: Fire Department Rescue Squad
fdry: foundry
FDS: Fellow in Dental Surgery; fighter-director ship
FDSRCS: Fellow in Dental Surgery of the Royal College of Surgeons
fdt: first destination transportation; fronto-dextra transverse
FDU: Fairleigh Dickinson University
f/d vlv: fill-and-drain valve
fdw: feed water
fdx (FDX): full duplex (data processing)
FD-Zug: *Fernschnellzug* (German—long-distance express train)
fe: fighter escort; fire extinguisher; first edition; flanged ends
f & e: facilities and equipment
fe (FE): format effective character (data processing)
Fe: *ferrum* (Latin—iron)
$Fe^{52/3}$: radioactive iron
FE: Far East; Fighter Escort; Flight Engineer
FE: ***Fonetic English*** (for spelling words as they sound)
F of E: Friends of the Earth
F & E: Fearnley & Eger (Fern-Ville [steamship] Lines)
FEA: Failure Modes and Effects Analysis; Federal Energy Administration; French Equatorial Africa
FEAD: *Fondo Especial de Asistencia para el Desarrollo* (Spanish—Special Assistance Fund for Development)
FEAF: Far East Air Force
FEA(I): Federal Employees Association (Independent)
FEANI: Fédération Européenne d'Associations Nationales d'Ingénieurs (Federation of European National Associations of Engineers)
feath: feather(ed); r(ed; ing)
Fearkar: Farquhar
feb: functional electronic block
Feb: February
FEB: Flying Evaluation Board
feba (FEBA): forward edge of battle area
Febarch: February and March
febb: *febbraio* (Italian—February)
feb.dur.: *febre durante* (Latin—as long as fever lasts)
feb^{o}: *febrero* (Spanish—February)
FEBs: Federal Executive Boards
FEBS: Federation of European Biochemical Societies
fec: feckless; forward error correction
fec: *foi, espérance, charité* (French—faith, hope, charity)
fec.: *fecit* (Latin—he made)
FEC: Facilities Engineering Command; Far East Command; Federal Election Commission; Federal Electric Corporation; Florida East Coast (railway); Free Europe Committee
FECA: Facilities Engineering and Construction Agency
FECB: Foreign Exchange Control Board
FECIT: *Federación Española de Centros de Iniciativas y Turismo* (Spanish Federation of Centers of Initiative and Tourism)
feck: (Scottish abbreviation—effect; efficacy; value)
FECM: Fellowship of the Elder Conservatorium of Music
FECUA: Farmers Educational and Cooperative Union of America
fed.: federal; federated; federation
Fed: Federal; Federalist (Party); Federation; The Fed—The Federal Reserve Board
FED: Fuel Element Design
FEDC: Federation of Engineering Design Consultants
FEDECAME: *Féderación Cafetalera de America* (Spanish—Coffee-Growers' Federation of America)
federalese: the jargon of bureaucrats on the federal payroll (*see* Watergab)
Federal Hill: Providence, Rhode Island's slum section
fedja: (Arabic—pass)
Fed Mal: Federation of Malaya; Federation of Malay States; Malaysia
Fed Mal Sta: Federated Malay States
fedn: federation
fed narc: federal narcotics agent
Fed Ref: Federal Reformatory
Fed Reg: Federal Register
Fed Rep: Federal Reporter
Feds: federal excise tax collectors; federal law-enforcement officers
Feds: *Federales* (Spanish—federal police; federal troops)
FEDS: Foreign Economic Development Service
Fed-Spec: Federal Specification(s)
Fed-Std: Federal Standard
FEE: Foundation for Economic Education; Foundation for Environmental Education
feeb: feeble; feebleminded
FEEB: Fleet Electronic Effectiveness Branch (USN)
Feebie: (American slang—member of the Federal Bureau of Investigation)
FEER: *Far Eastern Economic Review*
FEF: Foundry Educational Foundation
FEFC: Far Eastern Freight Conference
FE & FO: Francis E. and Freeland O. Stanley of Stanley Steamer fame
FEGLI: Federal Employees Group Life Insurance
FEHB: Federal Employees Health Benefit
FEI: Farm Equipment Institute; Financial Executives Institute; Flight Engineers International; Free Enterprise Institute
FEIA: Flight Engineers International Association
FEIS: Fellow of the Educational Institution of Scotland
feks: *for eksempel* (Dano-Norwegian—for example)
fel: fellow
Fel: Felicita; Felix
feldspar: barium, calcium, potassium, or sodium silicates (mineral mixtures such as orthoclase)
Fels: (German—rock)
FELL: Finland, Estonia, Latvia, and Lithuania (the first country—Finland—fell under Soviet domination whereas the others named were absorbed into the Soviet Union during World War II)
fella: *fellaheen* (Arabic—tillers)—peasant farmers of

Egypt, Syria, and nearby lands
Felsina: (Latin—Bologna)
felv: feline complex leukemia virus(es)
fem: female; feminine; fermoral; femur
fem.: *feminea* (Latin—female); *femoris* (Latin—femur; thigh)
f.e.m. (fem or FEM): *fuerza electromotriz* (Spanish—electromotive force)
FEMA: Farm Equipment Manufacturers Association; Fire Equipment Manufacturers Association; Foundry Equipment Manufacturers Association
Female Seminary: Mount Holyoke College
fem. ext.: *femur externum* (Latin—external thigh)
FEMIC: Fire Equipment Manufacturers Institute of Canada
Feminist Revolutionist: Mary Wollstonecraft also known as Mary Godwin
fem.int.: *femur internum* (Latin—inner thigh)
femlib: feminine liberation (women's liberation); feminine liberationist
femm: *femminile* (Italian—feminine)
femo: femoral
FEMSA: Fire Equipment Manufacturers and Suppliers Association
fem-sem: feminine seminary (woman's college)
femto: 10^{-15}
fenc: fencing
F/Eng: Flight Engineer
FENSA: Film Entertainment National Service Association
Fen-Scan: Fenno-Scandia; Fenno-Scandinavian
FEO: Federal Energy Office; Federal Executive Office; Federation of Economic Organizations; Fleet Engineer(ing) Office(r)
fep: fore edges painted
FE al P: Ferrocarril Eléctrico al Pacífico (Costa Rican electric railway)
FEPC: Fair Employment Practices Commission
FEPE: Fédération Européenne pour la Protection des Eaux (European Federation for the Protection of Waters)
FEpow: Far East prisoner of war
fer: forward engine room
Fer: Ferdinand; Fermanagh; Ferris
FERA: Federal Emergency Relief Administration
Fer. Aet.: *Ferrea Aetas* (Latin—Iron Age)—last of the four ages of the human race—the Plutonian period marked by avarice, crime, and cunning in the absence of honor, justice, or truth
FERC: Franco-Ethiopian Railway Company
fer con: ferrule-contact
Ferd: Ferdinand
Ferdie: Ferdinand
Fergie: Fergus
Ferm: Fermanagh
fermentol: fermentology
Fernandel: Fernand Contandin
Fern^{do}: Fernando (Spanish—Ferdinand)
Fernspr: *Fernsprecher* (German—telephone)
ferp: family educational rights and privacy
FERPC: Far Eastern Research and Publications Center
ferr: *ferrovia* (Italian—railroad)
Ferraria: (Latin—Ferrara)
fert: fertility; fertilization; fertilizer
fertd: fertilized
fertz: fertilizer
ferv.: *fervens* (Latin—boiling)
Ferv: *Fervidor* (French—Glowing Month)—synonym sometimes used for *Messidor* (see *Mess*)
fes: festival(s); fundamental electrical standards
Fes: (German—F-flat)
FES: Fellow of the Entomological Society; Fellow of the Ethnological Society; Fisheries Experiment Station; Florida Engineering Society
FESA: Fonetic English Spelling Association
FESO: Federal Employment Stabilization Office
fest: festival; festive; festivities; festivity
fest.: *festivus* (Latin—festive or gay)
FEST: Federation of Engineering and Shipbuilding Trades (British)
fesv: feline sarcoma virus
fet: field-effect transistor
FET: Federal Estate Tax; Federal Excise Tax
FET: *Falange Española Tradicionalista* (Spanish Traditional Falange)—fascist organization
FETF: Flight Engine Test Facility (National Reactor Test Station, Idaho)
fetol: fetological; fetologist; fetology
fets: field-effect transistors
$Fe_2O_3 \cdot H_2O$: rust
FEU: Federated Engineering Union
FEU: *Federación de Estudiantes Universitarios* (Spanish—Federation of University Students)
feud.: feudal; feudalism; feudalistic
fev: fever(ish); forced expiratory volume
fev: *fevereiro* (Portuguese—February)
fev: *février* (French—February)
fev 1 : forced expiratory volume in 1 second
FEVA: Federal Employees Veterans Association
Fevr: *Fevral'* (Russian—February)
FEW: Federally-Employed Women
fex: fleet exercise
fey: forever yours
ff: fat-free; file finish; fixed focus; folded flat; following folios; fortissimo; french fried; front focal (length); front focus; full fashioned; full field
f/f: flip-flop
f & f: fire and flushing; furniture and fixtures
f to f: face to face; foe to foe; friend to friend
ff: *følgende* (Danish—following); *folgende Seiten* (German—following pages); *fortissimo* (Italian—very loud)
ff (FF): form feed character (data processing); folios
Ff: *Fortsetzung folgt* (German—to be continued)
FF: Field Foundation; fleet flagship (naval symbol); Ford Foundation
FF: *Faith and Freedom; Fianna Fail* (Irish—Republican Party); fratres (Latin—brothers); *frères* (French—brothers)
F of F: field of fire; Firth of Forth
F & F: Faber & Faber
ffa: for further assignment; free of fatty acid; free from alongside
FFA: Fellow of the Faculty of Actuaries; Foreign Freight Agent; Foundation for Foreign Affairs; Future Farmers of America
ffar: folding-fin aircraft rocket; forward-fighting aircraft rock-

et

FFARACS: Fellow of the Faculty of Anaesthetists of the Royal Australasian College of Surgeons

FFAS: Fellow of the Faculty of Architects and Surveyors

ffb: fat-free body

FFB: Fellow of the Faculty of Building

ff black: fine furnace black

ffc: free from chlorine

FFC: Farmers Federation Cooperative; Federal Facilities Corporation; Federal Fire Council

ff cc: *ferrocarriles* (Spanish—railroads)

FFCC Nales: Ferrocarriles Nacionales (Colombian National Railways)

FFCDPA: Federal Field Committee for Development Planning in Alaska

FFCSA: Florida Fresh Citrus Shippers Association

ffd: focus film distance; fuel failure detection

FFDA: Flying Funeral Directors of America

FFDRCS: Fellow of the Faculty of Dental Surgery of the Royal College of Surgeons

FFE: Fight for Free Enterprise

fff: fat, forty, and female

fff: *forte fortissimo* (Italian—very, very loud)

FFF: Frozen Food Foundation

ffff: *forte forte fortissimo* (Italian—very, very, very loud)

ffft: (not an abbreviation but the symbol for the sound of a pump spray)—see *ssst*

ffgt: firefighter; firefighting

ffh: formerly-fat housewife; formerly-fat husband

FFHC: Freedom from Hunger Campaign

FFHMA: Full-Fashioned Hosiery Manufacturers of America

FFHom: Fellow of the Faculty of Homeopathy

ffi: free from infection

FFI: Flanders Filters Incorporated; Freight Forwarders Institute; Frozen Food Institute

FFI: *Forces Françaises de l'Intérieur* (French Forces of the Interior)—underground soldiers fighting against the Germans in occupied France during World War II

ffl: field failure; fixed and flashing

F Fl: fixed and flashing (light)

ff ind: fact-finding index

FFL: Forces Françaises Libres (Free French Forces)

FFLA: Federal Farm Loan Association

FFLI: Frozen Food Locker Institute

ffly: faithfully

FFMC: Federal Farm Mortgage Corporation

FFNM: Fort Frederica National Monument (Georgia)

ffp: firm fixed price

FFP: Forest Fires Prevention

F & FP: Force and Financial Program

FFPS: Fellow of the Faculty of Physicians and Surgeons

FFPSG: Fellow of the Faculty of Physicians and Surgeons

FFR: Fellow of the Faculty of Radiologists; Fleay's Fauna Reserve (Queensland)

ffrr: full frequency range recording

ffs: fat-free solids

FFs: first families

FFS: Ferrovie Federali Svizzere (Swiss Federal Railways); Fruit-Frost Service

ffss: full-frequency stereophonic sound

FFSS: *Ferrovie dello Stato* (Italian—State Railways)

fft: for further transfer

FFTF: Fast Flux Test Facility

fftr: firefighter

FFU: Feminist Free University; Fire Fighters Union

FFV: First Families of Virginia

ffwm: free-floating wave meter

Ffy: Faithfully

FFY: Fife and Forfar Yeomanry

FFZ: Free Fire Zone (USA)

fg: fine grain; fire glaze; flat grain; friction glaze; frog; fuel gas; fully good

fg: *faubourg* (French—suburb)

FG: Fitzroy Gardens

FG: *Fine Gael* (Irish—United Ireland Party)

fga: foreign general average; free of general average

FGA: Freer Gallery of Art

FGAA: Federal Government Accountants Association

FGAJ: Fellow of the Guild of Agricultural Journalists

fgc: facility group control

f & gc: failure and guilt complex

FGC: Fish and Game Code

FGCM: Field General Court Martial

FGCSO: Florida Gulf Coast Symphony Orchestra

FGCSSWA: Federation of Glass, Ceramic, and Silica Sand Workers of America

FGDS: *Fédération de la Gauche Démocrate et Socialiste* (French—Federation of the Democratic and Socialist Left)

FGEX: Fruit Growers Express

fgf: fully good, fair

FGL: Federico García Lorca

FGMD: Fairchild Guided Missile Division

fgn: foreign; foreigner

FGNRA: Flaming Gorge National Recreation Area (Utah and Wyoming)

FGO: Fellow of the Guild of Organists; Fleet Gunnery Officer

FGR: Franklin Game Reserve

f & g's: folded-and-gathered signatures

FGS: Fellow of the Geological Society

FGSA: Fellow of the Geological Society of America

FGSM: Fellow of the Guildhall School of Music

fgt: freight

FGT: Federal Gift Tax

FGTO: French Government Tourist Office

fh: firehose; flathead; forehatch

f/h: freehold(er)

f.h.: *fiat haustus* (Latin—make a draft)

FH: Fair Haven; Family History; Far Hills; Fashion Hills

fha: filterable hemolytic anemia

fha: *fecha* (Spanish—date)

FHA: Farmers Home Administration; Federal Highway Administration; Federal Housing Administration; Fine Hardwoods Association; Friends Historical Association; Future Homemakers of America

FHAA: Field Hockey Association of America

FHAS: Fellow of the Highland and Agricultural Society (Scotland)

FHASA: Forces Hydroelectriques de l'Andorre (Andorra Hydroelectric Power)

fhb: family hold back

FHBC: Federation of Historical Bottle Clubs

FH/B USA: Freedom House/ Books USA

fhc: fire-hose cabinet

FHC: Freed-Hardeman College

FHCI: Fellow of the Hotel and Catering Institute

fhdo: *fechado* (Spanish—dated)

FH_4: tetrahydrofolic acid

FH_5: Firehouse Five

fhh: fetal heart heard

FHI: Fraser-Hickson Institute; Fuji-Hakone-Izu (national park on Honshu, Japan)
FHIP: Family Health Insurance Plan
FHKSC: Fort Hays Kansas State College
FHL: Friends Historical Library (Swarthmore)
FHLB: Federal Home Loan Bank
FHLBB: Federal Home Loan Bank Board
FHLBS: Federal Home Loan Bank System
fhld: freehold
FHNWR: Flint Hills National Wildlife Refuge (Kansas)
f-holes: f-shaped sound holes in tops of stringed instruments such as violins, violas, cellos, double basses
fhp: fractional horsepower
FHPRP: Family Housing Program Review Panel
fhr: fire-hose rack
FHR: Federal House of Representatives (Australian)
fhs: fetal heart sounds
FHS: Fellow of the Heraldry Society; Forest History Society
fhsg: family housing
fht: fetal heart tone
FHT: Fellowship Houses Trust
FHTA: Federated Home Timber Association
FH_2: dihydrofolic acid
FHWA: Federal Highway Administration
fhws: flat-headed wood screw
fhy: fire-hydrant
fi: fixed interval; for instance
Fi: Fidel; Finland; Finnie; Finnish
FI: Falkland Islands; Faeroe Islands; Fiji Islands; Franco-Iberian; Franklin Institute
F of I: Fruit of Islam (Black Muslim storm-troop disciplinary corps)
fia: financial inventory accounting; full interest admitted
FIA: Factory Insurance Association; Federal Insurance Administration; Federal Intelligence Agency; Fellow of the Institute of Actuaries; Flatware Importers Association; Flight Information Area
***FIA:** Féderation Internationale de l'Automobile* (French—International Automobile Federation); *Federazione Internazionale Automabilistica* (Italian—International Automobile Association)
FIAB: Fédération Internationale des Associations de Bibliothécaires (International Federation of Librarian Associations)
FIAJY: Fellowship in Israel for Arab-Jewish Youth
FIAL: Fellow of the Institute of Arts and Letters
FIAM: Fellow of the International Academy of Management
FIAMA: Fellow of the Incorporated Advertising Managers' Association
FIAMS: Fellow of the Indian Academy of Medical Sciences
FIANZ: Fellow of the Institute of Actuaries of New Zealand
FIAP: Fédération Internationale de l'Art Photographique (International Federation of the Photographic Art)
FIAR: Fabbrica Italiana Apparecchi Radio (Italian Radio Apparatus Factory)
FIArb: Fellow of the Institute of Arbitrators
FIAT: Fabrica Italiana Automobili, Torino (Italian Automobile Factory—Turin)
FIAV: Fédération Internationale des Agences de Voyage (International Federation of Travel Agencies)
fib.: fibula; free into barge; free into bond; free into bunkers
FIB: Fellow of the Institute of Bankers; Franklin Institute of Boston
***FIB:** Fédération des Industries Belge* (French—Federation of Belgian Industries); *Félag Islenzkra Bifreidaeigenda* (Icelandic Automobile Association)
FIBM: Fellow of the British Institute of Management
FIBP: Fellow of the Institute of British Photographers
fibril: fibrillation
FIBST: Fellow of the Institute of British Surgical Technicians
fic: fiction; freight, insurance, carriage; frequency interference control
FIC: Federal Information Center(s); Federal Insurance Corporation; Fellow of the Institute of Chemistry; Flight Information Center; Forest Industries Council
***FIC:** Federación Internacional de Carreteras* (Spanish—International Highway Federation)
F 1C: Fireman 1st Class (USN)
FICA: Federal Insurance Contributions Act; Ferrocarriles Internacionales de Centro America (International Railways of Central America); Food Industries Credit Association
FICCI: Federation of Indian Chambers of Commerce and Industry
FICD: Fellow of the International College of Dentists
FICeram: Fellow of the Institute of Ceramics
FICO: Ford Instrument Company
FICE: Fellow of the Institute of Civil Engineers
***fic(s):** aficionado(s)* [Spanish—devotee(s)]
FICS: Fellow of the International College of Surgeons; Fellow of the Institute of Chartered Shipbrokers
FICSA: Federation of International Civil Servants Associations
fict: fiction; fictitious
***fict.:** fictilis* (Latin—made of pottery)
FICWA: Fellow of the Institute of Cost and Works Accountants
fid: fiduciary
***Fid:** Fidji:* (Spanish—Fiji)
FID: Falkland Island Dependencies; Federation of International Documentation; Fellow of the Institute of Directors
FIDA: Federal Industrial Development Authority
fidal: fixed-wing insecticide-dispersal apparatus, liquid (USNs defoliant spraying system)
FIDE: Fédération Internationale des Echecs (International Chess Federation)
Fidel: Fidel Castro
***FIDEL:** Frente Izquierda de Liberación* (Spanish—Leftist Liberation Front)
fido: fog investigation dispersal operation
FIDO: Flight Dynamics Officer
FIDOR: Fibre Building Board Development Organisation
FIDP: Fellow of the Institute of Data Processing
FIDS: Foolproof Identification System
FIED: Fellow of the Institution of Engineering Designers
FIEE: Fellow of the Institution of Electrical Engineers
***FIEN:** Forum Italiano dell'Energia Nucleare* (Italian

Nuclear Energy Forum)

FIER: Foundation for Instrumentation Education and Research

FIERE: Fellow of the Institute of Electronic and Radio Engineers

FIES: Fellow of the Illuminating Engineering Society

fif: ferric ion free

FIF: First Investment Fund; Friends of Irish Freedom

fi. fa.: *fieri facias* (Latin—see it done)

Fife: Fifeshire

FIFE: Fellow of the Institution of Fire Engineers

fifo: first in, first out (inventory)

FIFO: Flight Inspection Field Office(r)

FIFRA: Federal Insecticide, Fungicide, and Rodenticide Act

Fifth Avenue: famous New York City shopping street extending from Washington Square Park to upper Harlem

Fifth Estate: The Underworld of Organized Crime—international conglomerates and syndicates aided by corrupt public officials, unlawful labor leaders, and bribable politicians

Fiftieth State: Hawaii

fig.: figuratively; figure

Fig.: *Figur(en)* [German—figure(s)]; *Le Figaro* (Paris' oldest daily newspaper)

FIG: Farmers Insurance Group

FIG: *Federazione Italiana Golf* (Italian Golf Association)

FIGA: Fretted Instrument Guild of America

Figaro: Mariano José de Larra's pseudonym

FIGB: *Federazione Italiana Gioco Bocce* (Italian Bocce Ball Association)

FIGCM: Fellow of the Incorporated Guild of Church Musicians

Fighting Bob: Rear Admiral Robley Evans; English prizefighter Robert P. Fitzsimmons; Senator Robert M. La Follette, Sr

FIGM: Fellow of the Institute of General Managers

fig(s).: figure(s); finger-sized banana(s)

figs (FIGS): figures shift (data processing)

fih: fat-induced hyperglycemia

FIH: Fédération Internationale des Hôpitaux (International Federation of Hospitals)

FIHVE: Fellow of the Institution of Heating and Ventilating Engineers

FII: Fellow of the Imperial Institute

FIIA: Fellow of the Institute of Industrial Administration

FIIAL: Fellow of the International Institute of Arts and Letters

fiigmo: forget it, I've got my orders

FIIM: Fellow of the Institute of Industrial Management

FIIN: Federal Item Identification Number

FI Inf Sc: Fellow of the Institute of Information Scientists

FIIP: Fellow of the Institute of Incorporated Photographers

FIIT: Federal Individual Income Tax

FIJ: Fellow of the Institute of Journalists

FIJ: *Fédération Internationale des Journalistes* (French—International Federation of Journalists)

Fijis: Fiji islanders; Fiji Islands

fil: filament; fillet; fillister; filter; filtrate

f-i-l: father-in-law

Fil: Filbert; Filemón; Filiberto; Filinto; Filipp; Filippino; Filippo; Filley; Fillmore; Filmore; Filpot; Filpotts

FIL: Fellow of the Institute of Linguists

FILA: Fellow of the Institute of Landscape Architects

Filatov's disease: scarlatina-like exanthematous affection

Filbert Center: Hillsboro, Oregon

File: *Filemón* (Spanish—The Book of Philemon)—The Epistle of St Paul to the Philippians

FILE: Fellow of the Institute of Legal Executives

file 13: trashcan; wastebasket

fil h: fillister head

Fili: *Filipinas* (Portuguese or Spanish—Philippines)

Filipino Libertarian: Emilio Aguinaldo

fill.: filling

filo: first in, last out

filos: *filosofia* (Italian or Portuguese—philosophy); *filosofía* (Spanish—philosophy)

filt: filter; filtrate; filtration

filt.: *filtra* (Latin—filter)

fim: field ion microscope

FIM: Fellow of the Institute of Metallurgists; Flight Information Manual

FIMA: Fellow of the Institute of Municipal Administration; Forging Ingot Makers' Association; Friendly International Males' Association

FIMI: Fellow of the Institute of the Motor Industry

FIMIT: Fellow of the Institute of Musical Instrument Technology

FIMLT: Fellow of the Institute of Medical Laboratory Technology

FIMT: Fellow of the Institute of the Motor Trade

FIMTA: Fellow of the Institute of Municipal Treasurers and Accountants

fin.: finance; financial; financier; finish

fin.: *finis* (Latin—the end)

Fin: Finistère; Finland; Finnic; Finnish

FIN: Fellow of the Institute of Navigation

fina: following items not available

FINAC: Fast Interline Non-Active Automatic Control (automatic teletype service)

FINAST: First National Stores

FINCANTIERI: *Società Finanziaria Cantleri Navali* (Italian—Dockyards Finance Company)

FIND: Friendless, Isolated, Needy, Disabled (older people)

fin dec: final decree

FINEBEL: France, Italy, Netherlands, Belgium, and Luxembourg (economic agreement)

FINELETTRICA: *Società Finanziaria Elettrica* (Italian—Electric Power Finance Company)

fines.: fine particulates

fin fl: finished floor

F-ing: fucking (slang—copulating)

Finlan: *Finlandia* (Italian or Spanish—Finland); *Finlândia* (Portuguese—Finland)

Finn: Finnish

FINNAIR: Aero O/Y (*q.v.*; Finish Airlines)

FINMARE: *Società Finanziaria Marittima* (Italian—Maritime Shipping Finance Company)

Finnglish: Finnish + English

Finnish National Composer: Jan Sibelius

Fi-No-Tro: Finmark-Nord-Troms

(fish processing)
FINS: Fire Island National Seashore
Fin Sec: Financial Secretary
FINSINDER: Società Finanziaria Siderurgica (Stell Financing Society)
F Inst F: Fellow of the Institute of Fuel
F Inst P: Fellow of the Institute of Physics
F Inst Pet: Fellow of the Institute of Petroleum
F Inst SP: Fellow of the Institute of Sewage Purification
f insulin: fibrous insulin
Fin-Ug: Finno-Ugric
fio: for information only; free in and out
FIO: Fleet Information Office
Fiona Macleod: William Sharp's pseudonym
Fiordland: southernmost west coast of New Zealand's South Island
fip: fi'pence (fivepence); fi'penny (fivepenny); fire insurance policy
FIP: Flight Instruction Program
FIP: *Fédération Internationale des Phonothèque* (International Federation of Record Libraries)
FIPA: Fellow of the Institute of Practitioners in Advertising
FiPo: Fire and Police (Research Association)
FIPS: Federal Information Processing Standards
FIQS: Fellow of the Institute of Quantity Surveyors
fir.: firkin; flight information region; floating in rate(s); fuel indicator reading
FIRA: Foreign Investments Review Agency; Furniture Industry Research Association
FIRAA: Fire Insurance Research and Actuarial Association
FIRB: Fire Insurance Rating Bureau; Florida Inspection and Rating Bureau
FIRE: Fellow of the Institution of Radio Engineers
Firebrand of the Navy: Lieutenant Stephen Decatur, USN
Firebrand of the World: Tamerlane (Timur Lenk or Timur the Lame)
FIREBRICK: Federal Inter-Agency River Basin Committee
fireclay: sedimentary rock containing chlorite-kaolinite with illite
Fireclay Capital: Mexico, Missouri
fire damp: methane
Firenze: (Latin—Florence)
Firestreak: air-to-air missile
FIRFLT: First Fleet
FIRI: Fellow of the Institute of the Rubber Industry; Fishing Industry Research Institute
FIRME: *Fondo de Inversiones Rentables Mexicanas* (Spanish—Mexican Rental Investments Fund)
FIRST: Financial Information Reporting System
First American Advertiser: William Penn
First Citizen of Ghana: Dr W.E.B. Du Bois
First City of the South: Savannah, Georgia
First Estate: The Clergy
First Foreign Enclave: Macao, Portuguese China
First Gentleman of the Land: charming President Chester A. Arthur
First Great Cheerful Giver: George Peabody
First International: First International Workingmen's Association (of anarchists, communists, and socialists convening in Paris in 1864)
First Lady of the Air: Amelia M(ary) Earhart
First Lady of America: Pocahontas
First Lady of the American Revolution: Mercy Otis Warren also known as Philomela
First Lady of Liberty: sobriquet of Abigail Adams—wife of President John Adams
First Lady of the Library: President Millard Fillmore's wife Abigail—founder of the first library in the White House
First Lady of Song: Ella Fitzgerald
First Lady of the World: sobriquet of Anna Eleanor Roosevelt—wife of President Franklin D. Roosevelt
First Lawyer of the Land: U.S. Attorney General
First Mayor of Chicago: William Butler Ogden
First Perspective Painter: Paolo Uccello (Paolo di Dono)—known for his studies in foreshortening and linear perspective
First Poet Laureate: Ben Jonson
First Romantic Artist: Giambattista Piranesi
First State: Delaware's official nickname recalling it was first of the original thirteen states to ratify the *Constitution*
First Street in Europe: Disraeli's nickname for London's Strand
First University: Plato's Academy
First Woman Physician: Dr Elizabeth Blackwell
First Woman Reporter: Anne Royale of Virginia (publisher of *Paul Pry*) and Nellie Bly of Pennsylvania (reporter for the *New York World*) share this nickname
First Zen: First Zen Institute of America
fis: family income supplement
fis: *fisica* (Italian—physics)
fís: *física* (Portuguese or Spanish—physics)
Fis: (German—F-sharp)
FIS: Fighter Interceptor Squadron; Flight Information Service
FISA: Fellow of the Incorporated Secretaries Association
FISAR: Federal Institute for Snow and Avalanche Research
FISC: Financial Industries Service Corporation
fisc irre: fiscal irresponsibility
FISD: *Fédération Internationale de Sténographie et de Dactylographie* (French—International Federation of Stenography and Typewriting)
FISE: *Fédération Internationale Syndicale de l'Enseignement* (French—International Federation of Teachers' Unions)
fish.: fishery; fishes; fishing
FISH: Friends in Service Here
fishwich: fish sandwich
fit.: foreign independent traveler; foreign independent trip; free of income tax; free in truck
FIT: Fashion Institute of Technology; Federal Income Tax; Fédération Internationale des Traducteurs (International Federation of Translators)
fitw: federal income tax withholding
Fitz: Fitzedward; Fitzgerald; Fitzgreen(e); Fitzhugh; Fitzjames; Fitzjohn; Fitzmaurice; Fitzrandolph; Fitzroy; Fitzsim(m)ons; Fitzwilliam(s)
Fitzw: Fitzwilliam Library (Cambridge)
Fitzw Coll: Fitzwilliam College—Cambridge

FIU: Forward Interpretation Unit (US Army)
Five Nations: Cayugas, Oneidas, Onondagas, Mohawks, and Senecas (American Indian tribes on the English side in the French and Indian Wars)
fiw: free in wagon
fix.: fixture
Fj: Fjord
FJ: Fiji Airways
F-J: Fisher-John
FJA: Future Journalists of America
FJC: Fullerton Junior College
Fjd: Fjord
FJH: Franz Josef Haydn
FJI: Fellow of the Institute of Journalists
FJIC: Federal Job Information Center
FJNM: Fort Jefferson National Monument
Fjord Land: Norway with its more than 365 arms of the sea indenting its shoreline
FJS: Fulton J. Sheen
fk: flat keel; fork
Fk: Frank
FK: Fluid Kinetics; Fujita Airways
FK: *Frankfurt Kassenverein* (German—Frankfurt Clearinghouse)
FKBD: Fort Knox Bullion Depository
FKBI: Fourdrinier Kraft Board Institute
FKC: Fellow of King's College
Fkd: Frankford
FKJC: Florida Keys Junior College
FKL: *Frauen Konzentrationslager* (German—Women's Concentration Camp)
Fkn: Franklin; Frederikshavn
Fks: Fredrikstad
FKSNS: Fort Kent State Normal School
FKWR: Florida Keys Wildlife Refuges
fl: flash(ing); flight level; flood(ing); floor(ing); flow(ing); flow line; fluid(s); flush(ing); follow(ing); foot-lambert
fl: *flauto; flauti* (Italian—flute, flutes); *flores* (Latin—flowers) *floruit* (Latin—he flourished)
f.l.: *falsa lectio* (Latin—false reading)
fL: foot-lambert
Fl: Fall (postal abbreviation); Flemish; fluorine
FL: Flag Lieutenant; Flight Lieutenant; focal length; foreign language; Frontier Airlines (2-letter code)
F.L.: Franz Liszt
F for L: Feminists for Life
FL: *Fürstentum Liechtenstein* (Principality of Liechtenstein)
fla: fronto-laeva anterior
f.l.a.: *fiat lege artis* (Latin—according to the rules of art)
Fla: Florida; Floridian
FLA: Federal Loan Administration; Federal Loan Agency; Fellow of the Library Association; Florida; Florida East Coast Railway (symbol); Foam Laminators Association
FLA: *Frente de Libertação Açoriana* (Portuguese—Azorian Liberation Front)
FLAA: Fellow of the Library Association of Australia
fl abwth: flush armor balanced watertight hatch
Fla Cur: Florida Current
flag.: flageolet
Flagellum Dei: (Latin—Scourge of God)—Attila the king of the Huns
FLAI: Fellow of the Library Association of Ireland
FLAIR: Floating Airport
flak: *Fliegerabwehrkanone* (German—anti-aircraft cannon; anti-aircraft shrapnel)
flam(s): flamenco (songs); flaming(s); flammable(s)
FLAME: Facility Laboratory for Ablative Materials Evaluation
flar: florward-looking airborne radar
FLAS: Fellow of the Land Agents Society
Flats: Durango, Colorado's slums
flav: flavor(ing)
flav.: *flavus* (Latin—yellow)
FLB: Federal Land Bank
FLC: Foundation Library Center
FLCM: Fellow of the London College of Music
FLCO: Fellow of the London College of Osteopathy
fld: field; flowered; fluid
Fld: Field (postal abbreviation)
FLD: Friends of the Lake District
fldec: floating-point decimal
fldg: folding
fldg chr: folding chair(s)
fl di: flare die
FL & DI: Food Law and Drug Institute
fldo: final limit, down
fldop: field operations
fl dr: fluid dram
Flds: Fields
fldxt: fluid extract
Fl e: Flemish ell (unit of measure)
flea.: flux logic element array
FLEEC: Federal Libraries' Experiment in Cooperative Cataloging
Fleet Street: London's street of periodical publishers
Flem: Flemish
fleming(s): fleming-gear hand-propelled lifeboat(s)
Flemish Colorist: Peter Paul Rubens
Flemish Primitive Painter: Gheeraert David long accorded this title
fles: foreign language in elementary school
FLES: Foreign Languages in Elementary Schools (linguistic teaching program)
FLETC: Federal Law Enforcement Training Center
FLETRABASE: Fleet Training Base (USN)
fleur-de-lis: symbol of France and the French
flex.: flexible
flexo: flexographic
flf: final limit, forward
flg: flagging; flange; flooring; flying
FLGA: Fellow of the Local Government Association
flgd: flanged
flgstn: flagstone
flh: final limit, hoist
fl hd: flathead
flhls: flashless
FLIC: Film Library Information Council
Flickertail(s): North Dakotan(s)
Flickertail State: North Dakota
flick(s): flicker(s; motion picture[s])
flicon: flight control
flicr: fluid-logic industrial control relay
flint: variety of chalcedony
Flint: Flintshire
Flints: Flintshire
flip.: film library instantaneous presentation
FLIP: Flight Information Publication; Floated Lightweight Inertial Platform; Floating Instrument Platform
Flip(s): Filipino(s)
flir: forward-look infrared
FLIRT: Federal Librarians Round Table
fliv: flivver
Flivver King: Henry Ford
fll: final limit, lower
FLL: Fort Lauderdale, Florida

(airport); Friends Library, London
fllar: forward-looking light attack radar
fl ld: floor load
Flli: *fratelli* (Italian—brothers)
FLM: *Fédération Luthérienne Mondiale* (French—Lutheran World Federation)
FLMI: Fellow of the Life Management Institute
fl/mtr: flow meter
fln: following landing numbers
Fln: Flensburg
FLN: *Frente de Liberación Nacional* (Spanish—National Liberation Front); *Front de Liberation Nationale* (French—National Liberation Front)—official Algerian party
FLNM: Fort Laramie National Monument
Flo: Florence
Fl O: Flight Officer
floatel: floating motel
floc: floccule; flocculent; floccus
FLOC: For Love of Children
flod: (Danish or Swedish—river)
Fl Offr: Flying Officer
FLOG: Fleet Logistics Air Wing
FLOOD: Fleet Observation of Oceanographic Data (USN)
flor: floriculture
flor: *flores* (Latin—flowers); *floruit* (Latin—he flourished)
Flor: *Floréal* (French—Flowery Month)—beginning April 20th—eighth month of the French Revolutionary Calendar
Flor(a): Florence
Floral Watercolorist: William Demuth
Florence Austral: Florence Wilson
Florentia: (Latin—Florence)
Floribbean: Floridian-Caribbean (resort area)
Florrie: Flora; Florence
floss.: flossing (dental care)
Floss(ie): Florence
flot: flotation; flotilla; flotsam
Flour City: nickname shared by Buffalo or Rochester as both New York State cities are proud of their flour mills
Flower City: Rochester, New York
Flower Garden of England: The Sorlings or Isles of Scilly off Land's End
Flower of Quakerism: abolitionist Lucretia Mott
Flower Seed Capital of the West: Santa Maria, California
Flowery Kingdom: China
fl ovth: flush oiltight ventilation hole
flox: fluorine + liquid oxygen
Floy: Florence
fl oz: fluid ounce
flp: fault location panel; fronto-laeva posterior
fl pl.: *flore pleno* (Latin—in full bloom)
fl prf: flameproof
fl pt: flashpoint
FLQ: *Front de Libération Quebecois* (French—Front for the Liberation of the people of Quebec)—radical terrorist separatists
flr: final limit, reverse; floor; florin
FLR: Florence, Italy (Firenze Airport)
flrg: flooring
flrng: flash ranging
flrs: flowers
fl/rt: flow rate
Fls: Falls (postal abbreviation); Flushing
FLS: Fellow of the Linnaean Society
FLSA: Fair Labor Standards Act
flsc: flight shape charge
FLSEP: Family Life and Sex Education Program
FLSO: Fort Lauderdale Symphony Orchestra
FLSP: Fort Lincoln State Park (North Dakota)
flst: flautist; flutist
flt: filter; fleet; flight; float; flotation; fronto-laeva transverse
Flt: Flats (postal abbreviation); Fleetwood
Flt Adm: Fleet Admiral
Fltcher C: Fletcher College
Flt Cmdr: Flight Commander
fltg: floating
Flt Sgt: Flight Sergeant
Flt Lt: Flight Lieutenant
flt/pg: flight programmer
flt pln: flight plan
fltr: floater
Flt Sgt Nav: Flight Sergeant Navigator
flu: final limit, up; influenza
fluc: fluctuant; fluctuate; fluctuating; fluctuation
FLUG: Flugfelag Islands (Iceland Airways)
flummery: foolish humbeggery (named after British custard made of flour or oatmeal boiled with water until almost too thick to swallow)
fluor: fluor-apatite; fluorescence; fluorescent; fluorite; fluorspar; fluotaramite—generally fluor is the synonym of fluorite although the abbreviation for the foregoing so when in doubt—spell it out
fluorspar: calcium fluoride (CaF2)
flüss: *flüssig* (German—fluid)
FLW: Frank Lloyd Wright
flx: flexible
fly.: flinty; flying; flyweight
FLY: Flying Tiger Line
Flying Dutchman: mythical character immortalized in Richard Wagner's opera *Der Fliegende Holländer*; nickname of the baseball batting champion of the early 1900s—Honus Wagner
FlyTAF: Flying Training Air Force
FLZO: Farband-Labor Zionist Order
fm: face measurement; facial measurement; fan marker; farm; farmer; fathom; fathometer; fine measurement; form; frequency modulation; from; fumigation
fm: *formiddag* (Dano-Norwegian—before noon)—a.m.; *formiddagen (Swedish—before noon)—a.m.*
f.m.: *fiat mistura* (Latin—make a mixture)
f/M: female Mexican
F/m: unit of permittivity
Fm: fermium
FM: Fed Mart; Ferrocarril Mexicano (Mexican Railroad); Field Manual; Field Marshal; Flight Mechanic; Foreign Minister; frequency modulation
F-am-M: Frankfurt-am-Main (Frankfurt-on-Main)
F & M: Franklin and Marshall College
FMA: Felt Manufacturers Association; File Manufacturers Association; Flour Mills of America; Forging Manufacturers Association
FMACC: Foreign Military Assistance Coordinating Committee
FMAI: Financial Management for Administrators Institute
fman: foreman
FMANA: Fire Marshals Association of North America
FMAO: Farm Machinery Advisory Office(r)
FMAS: Foreign Marriage Advisory Service
FMB: Federal Maritime Board; Felix Mendelssohn Bartholdi
FMBRA: Flour Milling and Bak-

ing Research Association
FMBSA: Farmers and Manufacturers Beet Sugar Association
FMC: Failure Mode Center (Reliability Laboratory); Federal Maritime Commission; Felt Manufacturers Council; Food Machinery Corporation; Ford Motor Company
FMC: *Federación* de Mujeres Cubanas (Spanish—Federation of Cuban Women)
FM Can: Ford Motor of Canada
FMCC: Fulton-Montgomery Community College
F McH NM: Fort McHenry National Monument
FMCS: Federal Mediation and Conciliation Service
fm cu: form cutter
fmcw: frequency-modulated continuous wave
fmd: foot-and-mouth disease
FMD: Federated Metals Division—American Smelting and Refining; Fixtures Manufacturers and Dealers; Flota Mercante Dominicana (Dominican Steamship Line); Forward Metro Denver
fm di: form die
FMEA (FEA): Failure Modes and Effects Analysis
FMECA: Failure Mode, Effects, and Criticality Analysis
fMf (FMF): familial Mediterranean fever
FMF: Fleet Marine Force
FMF-A: Fleet Marine Force—Atlantic
fmfb: frequency-modulation feedback
FMFIC: Federation of Mutual Fire Insurance Companies
FMF-P: Fleet Marine Force—Pacific
FMFPAC: Fleet Marine Forces—Pacific
fmg: foreign medical graduate
FMG: Flota Mercante Grancolombiana (Colombian national steamship lines); franc(s) Malagasy
FMGJ: Federation of Master Goldsmiths and Jewelers
fmh (FMH): fat-mobilizing hormone
FMH: Friends Meeting House
FmHA: Farmers Home Administration
FMHHS: Fort McHenry Historic Shrine (Baltimore)
FMI: *Fondo Monetario Internacional* (Spanish—International Monetary Fund)
FMI: FM Intercity (relay broadcasting); Fonds Monétaries Internationals (International Monetary Fund)
FMIG: Food Manufacturers' Industrial Group
Fmk: Finnmark; Finnish markka (currency unit)
FML: Factory Mutual Laboratories
fmly k a: formerly known as
FMMA: Floor Machinery Manufacturers Association
fmn: formation
fmn (FMN): flavin mononucleotide
FMN: Ferrocarril Mexicano del Norte (Northern Mexican Railroad)
FMNH: Field Museum of Natural History
FMNM: Fort Matanzas National Monument
FMO: Fleet Mail Office; Fleet Medical Officer; Flight Medical Officer
FMP: Fairbanks Morse Pump
FMPA: Fellow of the Master Photographers' Association
FMPE: Federation of Master Process Engravers
fm prot: fine-mesh (cover) protected
FMPS: Fairbanks Morse Power Systems
fmr: former
fm rl: form roll
fmrly: formerly
FMRS: Federal Mediation and Reconciliation Service
fms: fathoms; flush metal saddle; free-machining steel
fm's: formerly-married persons
FMS: Federal Mining and Smelting (company); Federated Malay States; Field Music School; Financial Management System; Floating Machine Shop; Fort Myers Southern (railroad); Friends Mission Society
fmsa: frequency measuring spectrum analyzer
FMSI: Friction Materials Standards Institute
FMSL: Fort Monmouth Signal Laboratory
FMSM: Fédération Mondiale pour la Santé Mentale (World Mental Health Federation)
fmt: flush metal threshold
fm to.: form tool
FMTS: Field Maintenance Test Station
F & MTVHS: Food and Maritime Trades Vocational High School
fmu: force measurement unit
FMVSS: Federal Motor Vehicle Safety Standard
FMWC: Federation of Medical Women of Canada
FMWS: Fairbanks Morse Weighing Systems
fmk: full-mouth radiograph
fn: flatnose (projectile); footnote; fusion
fn: *fête nationale* (French—national holiday)
fmx: full-mouth radiography
Fn: Factonimbus
FN: Flight Nurse; Fridtjof Nansen
FN: *Fabrique Nationale* (French— National Factory)—Belgian arms firm's initials appearing on all its products
FNA: following named airmen; French North Africa
FNAA: Fellow of the National Association of Auctioneers
FNAL: Fermi National Accelerator Laboratory
FNB: First National Bank; Food and Nutrition Board
FNBP: Far North Bicentennial Park (Anchorage)
FNC: Federación Nacional de Cafeteros (National Federation of Coffee Growers—Colombia); Ferrocarriles Nacionales de Colombia (National Railroads of Colombia)
FNCB: First National City Bank
FNCR: Ferrocarril del Norte de Costa Rica (Northern Railway of Costa Rica)
fnd: found; foundered
fndd: founded
fndg: founding
fndn: foundation
fndr: founder
fndry: foundry
fne: fine
fnf: flying needle frame
fnh: flashless nonhygroscopic (gunpowder)
FNH: Ferrocarril Nacional de Honduras (National Railway of Honduras)
FNIF: Florence Nightingale International Foundation
FNIMC: Florida Normal and Industrial Memorial College
FNL: Friends of the National Libraries
FNLA: *Frente Nacional de Libertação de Angola* (Portuguese—Angolan National Liberation Front)
FNM: Ferrocarriles Nacionales de México (National Railroads of Mexico)

FNMA: Federal National Mortgage Association
FNNWR: Fort Niobrara National Wildlife Refuge (Nebraska)
FNO: following-named officers
FNOA: following-named officers and airmen
fnp: fusion point
FNP: Fiordland National Park (South Island, New Zealand); Fundy National Park (New Brunswick, Canada)
FNRJ: Federationa Narodna Republika Jugoslavija (Yugoslavia)
FNS: Food and Nutrition Service; Frontier Nursing Service
fnshr: finisher
FNTO: Finnish National Travel Office
fnu: first name unknown
FNU: Forces des Nations Unies (United Nations Forces)
f number: focal length of a lens
FNWF: Fleet Numerical Weather Facility
FNZLA: Fellow of the New Zealand Library Association
fo: faced only; fast operating; firm offer; flat oval; folio; for orders; free overside; fuel oil; full out terms
fo': for; four
f^o: *firmato* (Italian—signed)
f/O: female Oriental
FO: Field Order; Finance Officer; Foreign Office; Forward Observer
F.O.: Foreign Office
F/O: Flight Officer; Flying Officer
fo^o: *folio* (Spanish—folio)
FOA: Football Officials Association; Foreign Operations Administration; Foresters of America; Friends of Animals
Foam City: Milwaukee, Wisconsin famous for its beers
fob: feet out of bed
f.o.b.: free on board; fuel on board
fo & b: fuel oil and ballast
FOB: Federal Office Building; Forward Operating Base; Free on Board
FOBS: Fractional-Orbit Bombardment System
foc: final operational capability; focal; focus; focusing
f.o.c.: free of charge; free on car
FoC: Father of the Chapel (printer's union)
FOC: Ferrocarriles Occidentales de Cuba (Western Railroads of Cuba); Flight Operations Center
FOCA: Federation of Citizens Associations
FOCOL: Federation of Coin-Operated Launderettes
FOCI: Farrand Optical Company, Incorporated
FOCSL: Fleet-Oriented Consolidated Stock List
fo'c's'le: forecastle
FOCT: Flag Officer Carrier Training
FOCUS: Federation of Community United Services
fod: fodder; foreign object damage; free of damage
f.o.d.: free of damage
FOE: Fraternal Order of Eagles; Friends of the Earth
F of F: Firth of Forth
FOF: *Facts On File*
fog.: flow of gold
FOG: Florida Orange Growers
FOGA: Fashion Originators Guild of America
Foggy Bottom: nickname of the U.S. State Department
Fog Sig: fog signal (station)
foh: front of house
foi: freedom of information
FOI: (station) Operations Intelligence; Fighter Officer Interceptors; Fruit of Islam (Black Nationalists)
FOIC: Flag Officer in Charge
FOIR: Field-of-Interest Register
f.o.k.: free of knots
fol: folio; folios; follow; following; follows
fol.: *folium* (Latin—leaf); *folia* (Latin—leaves)
FOL: Foreign Office Library; Friends of the Land
fold.: folding
folg: *folgend* (German—following)
foll: followed by
folnoaval: following (items) not available
fomm: functionally-oriented maintenance manual(s)
FoMoCo: Ford Motor Company
Fondo: *El Fondo* (Spanish—The Fund)—International Monetary Fund—IMF
fonecon: telephone conversation
fonét: *fonética* (Italian—phonetics)
fonet: *fonetica* (Portuguese or Spanish—phonetics)
F on F: *Facts on File*
fono: photograph
fonoff: foreign office
FOO: Forward Observation Officer
foob (FOOB): firing out of the battery (artillery project)
fool's gold: pyrites (copper, iron, tin, etc.)
Football Capital of the South: Birmingham and New Orleans vie for this title as each supports a tremendous stadium
foot(s): footnote(s)
fop.: forward observation post
FOP: Fraternal Order of Police
fopt: fiber-optics photon transfer
f.o.q.: free on quay
for.: foreign; foreigner; forensic; forest; forester; forestry; forint (Hungarian monetary unit); free on rail; free on road
f.o.r.: free on rail
For: Formosa; Formosan
FOR: Fellowship of Reconciliation
forac: for action
FORACS: Fleet Operational Readiness Accuracy Check Site
FORATOM: *Forum Atomique Européen* (French—European Atomic Forum)
for. bal: forensic ballistics
FORBID: *Federatie van Organisaties op het gebied van Bibliotheek—Informatieen Dokumentatiewezen* (Dutch—Federation of Organizations on Libraries, Information, and Documentation Services)
Forbidden City: Lhasa, Tibet
forbloc: fortran-compiled block-oriented (simulation programme)
for. bod: foreign body
for'd: forward
FORD: Families Opposed to Revolutionary Destruction
Fordham Flash: Frank Frisch
Ford Madox Ford: Ford Madox Hueffer
FORDS: Floating Ocean Research and Development Station
Fordtown: Detroit, Michigan
'fore: before
Forellen Quintet: (see *Trout*)
foren: forensic(ally); forensic medicine
Forensic Psychiatrist: Richard von Krafft-Ebing
Forerunner of the Reformation: John Huss who denounced the abuses of the Roman Catholic hierarchy and was burned at the stake
fores'l: foresail
Forest Cantons: Swiss cantons of Lucerne, Schwyz, Unterwalden, and Uri
Forest City: Cleveland, Ohio and

London, Ontario compete for this sobriquet
forf: forfeit; forfeiture
förf: *forfatter* (Dano-Norwegian—author)
forf: *forfattare, författarinna* (Swedish—author, authoress)
forg: forger; forgery; forging
Forget-Me-Not: Alaska's state flower
fork: *forkortning* (Swedish—abbreviation)
fork.: *forkortelse* (Danish—abbreviation)
form.: format; formation; former(ly)
form: *formiddag* (Norwegian—before noon)—a.m.
forma: fortran matrix analysis
formac: formula manipulation compiler
formal.: formaldehyde; formalin
formalin: HCHO
format.: fortran matrix abstraction technique(s)
for med: forensic medicine
For Min: Foreign Minister; Minister of Foreign Affairs
formn: foreman
for'm'st: foremast
formul: formulary
forpac: forecasting passengers and cargo
for'rd: forward
for. rts: foreign rights
Forsch: *Forschung* (German—research)
for's'l: foresail
fort.: fortification; fortify; fortress; full-out rye terms (grain trade)
fort.: *fortis* (Latin—strong)
for. tox: forensic toxicology
fortran: formula translation
FORTRANS: Formula Translating System
Forts: *Fortsetzung* (German—continuation)
fort. twn: fortified town
Fortunate Island: Monhegan, Maine
Fortunate Islands: Canary Islands
Forty Immortals: collective nickname of the forty members of the French Academy
Forty-ninth State: Alaska
forwn: forewoman
'forz: *sforzando* (Italian— emphasized forcefully)
fos: fossil; fuel-oxygen scrap
fos: (Dano-Norwegian—waterfall)
f.o.s.: free on steamer
FOS: Fisheries Organization Society; Fuel Oil Supply (company)
fosdic: film optical sensing device for input to computers
fos fls: fossil fuels (coal, natural gas, oil, etc.)
FOSH: Foshing (airlines)
Foster Mother of the Sciences: Medicine
fot: frequency optimum traffic; fuel-oil transfer
fot: *fotographie* (Dutch—photography)—plus all derivatives
f.o.t.: free on truck
FOT: Fraternal Order of Police
F o t L: Friends of the Library
FOTM: Friends of Old-Time Music
foto: photograph(ic)
foto: *fotografia* (Italian or Portuguese—photography); *fotografía* (Spanish—photography)—plus all derivatives in all three languages
fotog: *fotografia* (Italian or Portuguese—photography); *fotografía* (Spanish—photography)
fo'ty: forty
found: foundation; foundling; foundling; foundry
Found Econ Educ: Foundation for Economic Education
Founder of Agnosticism: Thomas Henry Huxley
Founder of Agricultural Chemistry: Justus von Liebig
Founder of Antiseptic Surgery: Lord Lister (Joseph Lister—first Baron Lister of Lyme Regis
Founder of Art History and Criticism: Giorgio Vasari
Founder of Behaviorism: John Watson
Founder of the Birth Control Movement: Margaret Sainger
Founder of Brazil: Pedro Alvares Cabral
Founder of Buenos Aires: Pedro de Mendoza
Founder of Cellular Pathology: Rudolf Virchow
Founder of Chicago: Jean de Sable whose pioneer trading post at the portage between the Chicago and Des Plaines rivers became the site of present-day Chicago in 1775
Founder of Cleveland, Ohio: Moses Cleaveland
Founder of the Columbia University School of Journalism: Joseph Pulitzer
Founder of Comparative Anatomy: Baron Georges Cuvier
Founder of Conservative Surgery: Sir William Fergusson
Founder of Continental Rationalism: René Descartes
Founder of Cubism: George Braque, Pablo Picasso, and others claim this title
Founder of Electrophysiology: Emil du Bois Reymond
Founder of English Empiricism: Sir Francis Bacon
Founder of Experimental Hygiene: Max von Pettenkofer
Founder of the Faculty of Physicians and Surgeons of Glasgow: Peter Lowe
Founder of Fauvism: Henri Emile Benoit Matisse
Founders of Flemish Painting: the van Eyck brothers— Hubrecht and Jan
Founders of French Romantic Painting: Delacroix, Géricault, and Gros
Founder of French Socialism: Compte Claude Henri de Rouvroy de Saint-Simon
Founder of the Friends: George Fox of Quaker fame
Founder of Functionalism: Louis Sullivan
Founder of Gestalt Therapy: Fritz Perls
Founder of Histology: Marcello Malpighi
Founder of Humanistic Psychology: Abraham Maslow
Founder of Hungary: Arpad
Founder of Iconographic and Physiologic Anatomy: Leonardo da Vinci
Founder of Impressionism: Claude Monet
Founder of Islam: Mohammed
Founder of Jainism: Mahavira also known as Vardhamana
Founder of Japanese Color-Print Making: Iwasa Matabei
Founder of the Kelmscott Press: William Morris
Founder of the Lutheran Church: Martin Luther
Founder of the Methodist Church: John Wesley
Founder of Modern Military Medicine: Sir John Pringle
Founder of Medical Statistics: Pierre-Charles Alexander Louis
Founder of Modern Chemistry: Antoine Lauret Lavoisier
Founder of Modern Existentialism: Sören Kierkegaard
Founder of Modern German Sculpture: Johann Gottfried Schadow
Founder of Modern Sculpture:

Donatello (Donato di Niccolo di Betto Bardi)

Founder of Mormanism: Joseph Smith who founded the Church of Jesus Christ of the Latter-Day Saints

Founder of Oklahoma: Jean Pierre Chouteau

Founder of Optics: Giovanni Battista della Porta

Founder of Pennsylvania: William Penn

Founder of Phenomenology: Edmund Husserl

Founder of Positivism: Auguste Compte

Founder of Postimpressionism: Paul Cézanne

Founder of Providence, Rhode Island: Roger Williams

Founder of Psychoanalysis: Sigmund Freud

Founder of Psychology: Wilhelm Wundt

Founder of Québec: Samuel de Champlain

Founder of Rhode Island: Roger Williams

Founder of Rome: Romulus, according to legend

Founder of Russian Literature: Alexander Pushkin

Founder of Salt Lake City: Brigham Young

Founder of Scottish Presbyterianism: John Knox

Founder of Secularism: George Holyoake who in 1846 gave it its name as an ethical system based on natural morality

Founder of Sociology: Auguste Compte

Founder of Taoism: Lao-tse

Founder of Transcendentalism: Ralph Waldo Emerson who believed in the mystical unity of nature

Founder of Troy: Tros, according to Greek mythology, who was the father of Assaracus, Cleopatra, Ganymede, and Ilus

Founder of the University of Pennsylvania: Benjamin Franklin

Founder of the University of Virginia: Thomas Jefferson

Founder of Unitarianism: John Biddle

Founder of the U.S. Navy: Captain John Paul Jones

Founder of the Venetian School of Painting: Giovanni Bellini

Founder of Vermont: Ira Allen

Founder of Zoroastrianism: Zoroaster also known as Zarathustra

Founders of Cubism: Georges Braque and Pablo Picasso

Founders of the Hudson River School (of painting): Thomas Cole and Asher Brown Durand

Founders of Neo-Impressionism: Georges Seurat and Paul Signac

Founders of Scientific Socialism: Karl Marx and Friedrich Engels

Foundress of Swarthmore College: Martha Ellicott Tyson and a few concerned Friends

fount: fountain

FOUO: For Official Use Only

Four Corners: any highway or street intersection bearing this name; boundary-line junction of Arizona, Colorado, New Mexico, and Utah

Four Lakes City: Madison, Wisconsin

Four Mountains: Islands of the Four Mountains

Four Seasons Crossroad of New England: Manchester, New Hampshire

Four Temperaments: Nielsen's Symphony No. 2

Fourth Bureau: Red Army bureau in charge of overseas intelligence-gathering activities of the Soviet Union

Fourth Estate: The Media—press, radio, television

Fourth International: Trotsky-oriented organization rejecting the Second and Third Internationals in the direction of the class struggle

Four Winds: Boreas (north), Eurus (east), Notus (south), Zephyrus (west)

FOUSA: Finance Office(r), United States Army

f.o.w.: first open water (shipping term); free on wagon

Foxardo: (naval argot—Fajardo, Puerto Rico)

Foxes: Fox Islands off southwestern tip of Alaska

Foxtrot: code for letter F

Foy: Fowey

fp: fireplace; fixed price; flameproof; flat point; flight pay; flower people; foot pound; forward perpendicular; freezing point

f/p: flat pattern

f.p.: *fiat potio* (Latin—make a potion)

fp (FP): flavoprotein

FP: Ferrocarril del Pacífico (Pacific Railroad); former pupil; Franklin Pierce (14th President U.S.)

FP: *Freiheitliche Partei* (German—Freedom Party)—Austrian party with neo-Nazi orientation

F del P: Ferrocarril del Pacífico (formerly Southern Pacific of Mexico)

fpa: free of particular average

FPA: Family Planning Association; Flying Physicians Association; Foreign Policy Association; Franklin Pierce Adams; Freethought Press Association

fpaAc: free of particular average, American conditions

FPAD: Fund for Peaceful Atomic Development

fpaEc: free of particular average, English conditions

fpaf: fixed-price award fee

FPAS: Fellow of the Pakistan Academy of Sciences

FPBA: Folding Paper Box Association

FPBAI: Fellow of the Publishers' and Booksellers' Associations in India

fpc: fish protein concentrate; fixed-price call; for private circulation

FPC: Family Planning Center; Federal Pacific Electric (stock exchange symbol); Federal Power Commission; Federal Prison Camp; Food Packaging Council; Friends Peace Committee; Frozen Pea Council

FPCA: Federal Post Card Application (for absentee ballot)

FPCC: Fair Play for Cuba Committee

FPCE: Fission Products Conversion and Encapsulation (AEC plant)

FPD: *Fundación Panamericana de Desarrollo* (Pan-American Development Foundation)

FPDA: Finnish Plywood Development Association

fpdi: flight path deviation indicator

fpe: fixed price with escalation

FPE: Foundation for Personality Expression; Full Personality Expression

FPEBT: Fire Prevention and Engineering Bureau of Texas

FPED: Farm Production Economics Division (USDA)

FPF: French Protestant Federation

FPHA: Federal Public Housing Authority

F Pharm S: Fellow of the Pharmaceutical Society
fphs: fallout protection in homes
F Ph S: Fellow of the Philosophical Society
F Phy S: Fellow of the Physical Society
fpi: faded prior to interception; family pitch in; fixed price incentive
FPI: Federal Prison Industries; Fellow of the Plastics Institute
FPI: *Fédération Prohibitionniste Internationale* (French—International Prohibitionist Federation)
fpif: fixed-price-incentive firm
fpil: full premium if lost
f. pil.: *fiat pilulae* (Latin—make pills)
fpis: fixed-price incentive successive
fpl: final protective line; fire plug
FPL: Forest Products Laboratory
fpm: feet per minute
FPML: Forest Products Marketing Laboratory
FPMR: Federal Property Management Regulation(s)
FPMSA: Food Processing Machinery and Supplies Association
FPMT: Filter Paper Microscopic Test
FPNM: Fort Pulaski National Monument
fpo: fixed price open
FPO: Field Post Office; Field Project Office; Fleet Post Office; Fleet Postal Organization
FPP: Family Planning Program; Foster Parents Plan; Foster Parents Program; Friendly Peoples Proviso
FPPC: Fair Political Practices Commission
FPPS: Flight Plan Processing System
fpr: fixed price redeterminable
FPR: Factory Problem Report; Field Personnel Record
FPRC: Fair Play for Rhodesia Committee
fprf: fireproof
FPRI: Foreign Policy Research Institute (University of Pennsylvania)
FPRL: Forest Products Research Laboratory
FPRS: Forest Products Research Society
fps: feet per second; foot per second; foot-pound-second; frames per second
f'ps: former priests
FPS: Farm Placement Service; Fauna Preservation Society; Fellow of the Pharmaceutical Society; Fellow of the Philharmonic Society; Fellow of the Philological Society; Fellow of the Philosophical Society; Fluid Power Society
FPSA: Fellow of the Photographic Society of America
FPSL: Fellow of the Physical Society of London
fpsps: feet per second per second
fpt: female pipe thread; full power trial
fpts: forward propagation tropospheric scatter
FPTU: Federation of Progressive Trade Unions
fq: fiscal quarter
FQ: French Quarter (New Orleans)
fqawt: flush quick-acting watertight
fqcy: frequency
FQL: Food Quality Laboratory
FQO: Federation of Quarry Owners
FQS: Federal Quarantine Service
fr: fast release (relay); field relay; fixed response; frame; front
f/r: fixed response; freight release
f & r: feed and return (plumbing); force and rhythm (pulse)
fr.: *folio recto* (Latin—front of the sheet)
Fr: France; Franco-; francium; Frau (German—Missus); French; Froude number
Fr: *Frau* (German—Misses); *Fray* (Spanish—Friar); *Fredag* (Danish—Friday)
FR: Feather River (railroad); Federal Register; Federal Reserve; Field Report; fighter reconnaissance (aircraft); Final Report; Fireman Recruit; flash red—enemy aircraft nearby; Fleet Reserve; Friden (stock exchange symbol)
F.R.: *Forum Romanum* (Latin—Roman Forum)
F of R: Fellowship of Reconciliation
fra: factura (Spanish—invoice)
Fra: Francis
Fra.: *frater* (Latin—brother; monk)
FRA: Federal Railroad Administration; Fleet Reserve Association; Footwear Research Association; Frankfurt-am-Main (airport)
Fra Angelico: Giovanni da Fiesole
FRAC: Food Research and Action Center
FRACI: Fellow of the Royal Australian Chemical Institute
FRACP: Fellow of the Royal Australian College of Physicians
FRACS: Fellow of the Royal Australian College of Surgeons
fract: fraction; fracture
fract. dos.: *fracta dosi* (Latin—in divided doses)
FRAD: Fellow of the Royal Academy of Dancing
Fra Elbertus: Elbert Hubbard
FRAeS: Fellow of the Royal Aeronautical Society
frag: fragile; fragment; fragmentary; fragmentation; fragmented
FRAgS: Fellow of the Royal Agricultural Societies
FRAHS: Fellow of the Royal Australian Historical Society
FRAI: Fellow of the Royal Anthropological Institute
FRAIA: Fellow of the Royal Australian Institute of Architects
FRAIC: Fellow of the Royal Architectural Institute of Canada
'fraid: afraid
FRAM: Fellow of the Royal Academy of Music; Fleet Rehabilitation and Maintenance (USN)
FRAME: Fund for the Replacement of Animals in Medical Research
Framer of the *Declaration of Independence:* Thomas Jefferson who rewrote Thomas Paine's first rough draft with the aid of John Adams and Benjamin Franklin
fran: framed-structure analysis
Fran: Frances; Francis; Franciscan
Frances Alda: Frances Davis
Francine: Frances
Franc^{o}: Francisco (Spanish—Francis)
Franco: Francisco Paulino Hermenegildo Teodulo Franco-Bahamonde—Spanish dictator
Françoise Sagan: (pseudonym—Françoise Quoirez)
Francophone Africa: Afars and Issas, Algeria, Burundi, Cam-

eron, Central African Republic, Chad, Congo, Dahomey, Gabon, Guinea, Ivory Coast, Madagascar, Mali, Mauritania, Mauritius, Niger, Reunion, Rwanda, Senegal, Seychelles, Togo, Tunisia, Upper Volta, Zaire
Francophone America: French Guiana; Guadeloupe; Haiti; coastal parishes of Louisiana; Martinique; some places in northern New York, Vermont, New Hampshire, Maine, and New Brunswick close to Québec; Québec; St Pierre and Miquelon Asia: Cambodia, Laos, Vietnam
Francophone Europe: Andorra, French-speaking parts of Belgium, France, Luxembourg, Monaco, French-speaking cantons of Switzerland
Francophone Pacific: French Polynesia, New Caldonia, New Hebrides, Wallis and Fatuna Islands
Francophone Province: Québec
Franglais: *français* + *anglais* (French + English)—English-filled French heard around airports, travel agencies, and many French resorts visited by American and British travelers
Frank: Frank; Frankish; Franklin
Frank Leslie: business name of Henry Carter
franklinite: ferric iron and zinc crystalline compound
Frank Richards: Charles Hamilton's pen name
frank(s): frankfurter(s)
FRAP: *Frente Revolucionario de Acción Popular* (Spanish—Revolutionary Popular Action Front)—Chile
FRAS: Fellow of the Royal Asiatic Society; Fellow of the Royal Astronomical Society
Frasca: Francesca
Frasco: Francisco
frat: fraternity
frat: *fratello* (Italian—brother)
FRAT: Free Radical Assay Technique (heroin-morphine test)
frate: formula for routes and technical equipment
frater: fraternity brother
fratting: fraternizing
fraud.: fraudulent
FRB: Federal Reserve Bank; Federal Reserve Board
FRBC: Fisheries Research Board of Canada
fr bel: from below
FRBk: Federal Reserve Bank
FRBS: Fellow of the Royal Botanic Society; Fellow of the Royal Society of British Sculptors
frc: functional residual capacity
FRC: Facility Review Committee; Fasteners Research Council; Federal Radiation Council; Federal Radio Commission; Federal Records Center; Federal Republic of Cameroon; Filipino Rehabilitation Commission; Flight Research Center; Foreign Relations Committee; Foreign Relations Council; Fuels Research Council
FRCA: Fellow of the Royal College of Art
FRC—AAP: Freedom-to-Read Committee—Association of American Publishers
Fr-Can: French-Canadian
fr & cc: free of riots and civil commotion
FRCGP: Fellow of the Royal College of General Practitioners
FRCI: Fellow of the Royal Colonial Institute
FRCM: Fellow of the Royal College of Music
FRCO: Fellow of the Royal College of Organists
FRCOG: Fellow of the Royal College of Obstetricians and Gynaecologists
FRCP: Fellow of the Royal College of Physicians
FRCPath: Fellow of the Royal College of Pathologists
FRCP(C): Fellow of the Royal College of Physicians of Canada
FRCPE: Fellow of the Royal College of Physicians of Edinburgh
FRCPGlas: Fellow of the Royal College of Physicians of Glasgow
FRCPI: Fellow of the Royal College of Physicians of Ireland
FRCS: Fellow of the Royal College of Surgeons
FRCSc: Fellow of the Royal College of Science
FRCS(C): Fellow of the Royal College of Surgeons of Canada
FRCSE: Fellow of the Royal College of Surgeons of Edinbrugh
FRCPSG: Fellow of the Royal College of Physicians and Surgeons of Glasgow
FRCs: Federal Regional Councils
FRCSGlas: Fellow of the Royal College of Surgeons of Glasgow
FRCSI: Fellow of the Royal College of Surgeons of Ireland
FRCSL: Fellow of the Royal College of Surgeons of London
FRCTS: Fast Reactor Core Test Facility
FRCVS: Fellow of the Royal College of Veterinary Surgeons
frd: formerly restricted data; friend; friendly
Frd: Ford (postal abbreviation)
FR Dist: Federal Reserve District
Frdn: Friedenau
fre: free energy region
fre: *fracture* (French—invoice)
Fre: Freemantle; French
Fre: *Freitag* (German—Friday)
FREB: Federal Real Estate Bord
FR Econ Soc: Fellow of the Royal Economic Society
Fred: Alfred; Alfredo; Freddie; Frederic; Frederick; Fredric; Fredrick; Wilfred
Freda: Winifred
Fred Astaire: Frederick Austerlitz
Fred(die): Frederica; Fredrica
Fred(dy): Alfred; Frederick; Wilfred
Frederick Douglass: Frederick Augustus Washington Bailey
Frederick the Great: Frederick II of Prussia
Fredk: Frederick
Fredk D: Frederick Douglass
Free: Freeway
freebd: freeboard
freebies: free services; free things; free tickets
Freedman's Bureau: Bureau of Refugees, Freedmen, and Abandoned Lands (set up after the Civil War in the United States)
Free Lib Phila: Free Library of Philadelphia
Free State: Maryland whose constitution guarantees religious freedom—the right to believe or to disbelieve, to worship or not to worship
Freestone State: Connecticut with its many freestone quarries
freeway: toll-free express highway

Freeway City: Los Angeles bisected and surrounded by automotive freeways also known as smogways
FREI: Fellow of the Real Estate Institute
Freib: Freiburg (Germany)
FRELIMO: *Frente de Libertação de Moçambique* (Portuguese—Mozambique Liberation Front)
frem. voc.: *fremitus vocalis* (Latin—vocal fremitus)
French Antilles: French West Indies
French Canada: French-speaking Canada but mainly the Province of Québec
French Caribees: colonial name for the French West Indies
French disease: pejorative nickname for syphilis also known as the Italian disease or the Spanish disease as well as *morbus gallicus* (Latin—Gallic disease)—the French disease
french fries: french fired potatoes
French Indo-China: former name of area comprising Annam, Cambodia, Chochin China, Laos, Tonkin, and Vietnam
French Polynesia: Polynesian Islands under French control
French Quarter: oldest and most picturesque section of New Orleans
French Revolutionary Calendar: (see *Vend, Brum, Frim, Niv, Pluv, Vent, Germ, Flor, Prair, Mess, Therm, Fruc,* entries)
French Riviera: resort areas along the Mediterranean from Marseilles to Menton, including Cannes, Monaco, and Nice
French Shore: Newfoundland's northern and western coasts where the French have certain fishing rights
French Somaliland: Afars and Issas Territory
French-speaking Places: (*see entries under* Francophone)
French Switzerland: French-speaking areas of Switzerland
French West Africa: Afrique Occidentale Française—AOF
French West Indies: St. Martin, St. Barthelemy, Guadeloupe, Desirade, Les Saintes, Marie-Galante, Martinique and at one time the French-speaking section of Hispaniola—Haiti
FREntS: Fellow of the Royal Entomological Society
freon tf: trifluorotrichloroethane (solvent)
freq: frequency; frequent
FrEqAfr: French Equatorial Africa
freq m: frequency meter
fres: fire-resistant
fres: *frères* (French—brothers)
FRES: Fellow of the Royal Entomological Society
frescanar: frequency scan radar
fresh.: freshman; freshmen
Freud.: Freudian
frf: flight-readiness firing; frequency response function
fr-f: french-fried (potatoes)
FRFPS: Fellow of the Royal Faculty of Physicians and Surgeons
Frg: Forge (postal abbreviation)
FrG: Federal Republic of Germany (West Germany)
FRGS: Fellow of the Royal Geographical Society
frgt: freight
FRHB: Federation of Registered House Builders
frhgt: free height
FR Hist S: Fellow of the Royal Historical Society
FR Hort S: Fellow of the Royal Horticultural Society
Fr hr: French horn
Frhr: *Freiherr* (German—Baron)
FRHS: Fellow of the Royal Horticultural Society
fri: feeling rough inside
Fri: Friday
FRI: Fellow of the Royal Institution; Fels Research Institute; Friends of Rhodesian Independence
FRIA: Fellow of the Royal Irish Academy
FRIAI: Fellow of the Royal Institution of Architects of Ireland
FRIAS: Fellow of the Royal Incorporation or Architects of Scotland
Frib: Fribourgh (Switzerland)
FRIBA: Fellow of the Royal Institute of British Architects
fric: frication; fricative; fricatruce; fricatrix; friction; frictional
FRIC: Fellow of the Royal Institute of Chemistry
Frick: Frick Collection (New York City)
FRICS: Fellow of the Royal Institution of Chartered Surveyors
frict: friction
fridg: frigidaire (refrigerator)
fridge(s): refrigerator(s)
Friedrh: Friedrichshafen
Fried Test: Friedman Test (for pregnancy)
Friend of the American Revolution: Caron de Beaumarchais
Friend of Helpless Children: Herbert Clark Hoover—thirty-first President of the United States
Friendly Island: Molokai, Hawaii in the North Pacific
Friendly Islands: Tonga Islands in the South Pacific
Friendly Kingdom: Tonga Islands
Friends: Society of Friends (Quakers)
Friends Meet: Friends Meeting
Fries: Friesic
frig: refrigerator
frig.: *frigidus* (Latin—cold)
FRIGS: Fellow of the Royal Imperial Geographical Society
FRIIA: Fellow of the Royal Institution of International Affairs
Frim: *Frimaire* (French—Sleety Month)—beginning November 21st—third month of the French Revolutionary Calendard
FRINA: Fellow of the Royal Institution of Naval Architects
Fringlish: French + English (English interlarded with French expressions and words)
FRIPA: Fellow of the Royal Institution of Public Administration
FRIPHH: Fellow of the Royal Institute of Public Health and Hygiene
Fris: Friesland; Frisia; Frisian
frisco: fast-reaction integrated submarine control
Frisco: (navalese—San Francisco)—but no San Franciscan will use this nickname
FRISCO: St. Louis-San Francisco Railway
Frisco Bay: (sailor's slang—San Francisco Bay)
Frisians: Frisian islanders or the Frisian Islands in the North Sea where they are under Dutch, German, or Danish control as some belong to the Netherlands, to Germany, and to Denmark
Fritalux: France, Italy, and Benelux nations
frits: fritters
Fritz: Friedrich
frjm: full-range joint movement
frk: *fröken* (Swedish—Miss)
Frk: Fork (postal abbreviation);

Frankfort
Frk: *Fröken* (Dano-Norwegian—Miss)
Frks: Forks (postal abbreviation)
frl: fractional
Frl: El Ferrol
Frl: *Fräulein* (German—Miss)
FRL: Fuel Research Laboratory
frm: fireroom; framing
FRM: Federal Reformatory for Men
FRMA: Floor Rug Manufacturers Association
FRMCM: Fellow of the Royal Manchester College of Music
FR Met Soc: Fellow of the Royal Meteorological Society
FRMIT: Fellow of the Royal Melbourne Institute of Technology
frmn: formation
frmr: former
Frms: Farms (postal abbreviation)
FRMS: Fellow of the Royal Microscopical Society
FRN: Federal Republic of Nigeria
FRNHS: Fort Raleigh National Historic Site
FRNS: Fellow of the Royal Numismatic Society
FRNSA: Fellow of the Royal Navy School of Architects
Frnz: Fernandez
FRNZIH: Fellow of the Royal New Zealand Institute of Horticulture
'fro: Afro
FRO: Fellow of the Register of Osteopaths; Fire Research Organization; Friends Religious Order
FROC: Federated Russian Orthodox Clubs
frof: fire risk on freight
frog.: free rocket over ground
Frog: Haydn's String Quartet in D (opus 50, no. 6)
Frogner Park: Oslo's public park filled with the surpassing nude statuary of Vigeland
from: full range of movement
From My Life: Smetana's String Quartet No. 1 in E minor (transcribed for orchestra by George Szell)
From the New World: Dvŏrák's Symphony No. 9 (formerly No. 5)
fron: frontal; frontalis
FRONAPE: Frota Naccional de Petroleiros (National Petroleum Fleet—Brazil)
front.: frontispiece
FRONT BC: *Frontera (Fronteriza) Baja California* (Spanish—Baja California Frontier)—appears on Mexican border city and town license plates
Frontier Fighter: Davy Crockett
Frontier States: last states to be admitted to the United States; the 49th and the 50th were Alaska and Hawaii
frosh: freshman; freshmen
Frostbite: nickname of Fairbanks, Alaska
frp: fiberglass reinforced plastic
frpf: fireproof
frpng: fireproofing
FRPS: Fellow of the Royal Photographic Society
FRPSL: Fellow of the Royal Philatelic Society of London
frs: francs
Frs: Frisian
Fr S: French Somaliland (French Territory of the Afars and the Issas)
FRS: Federal Reserve System; Fellow of the Royal Society; Fisheries Research Society
FRSA: Fellow of the Royal Society of Arts
FRSAI: Fellow of the Royal Society of Antiquaries of Ireland
FRSC: Fellow of the Royal Society of Canada
FRSE: Fellow of the Royal Society of Edinburgh
FRSGS: Fellow of the Royal Scottish Geographical Society
FRSH: Fellow of the Royal Society of Health
FRSI: Fellow of the Royal Sanitary Institute
FRSL: Fellow of the Royal Society of Literature; Fellow of the Royal Society—London
FRSM: Fellow of the Royal Society of Medicine
FRSNA: Fellow of the Royal School of Naval Architecture
FRSNZ: Fellow of the Royal Society of New Zealand
Fr Som: French Somaliland
FRSPS: Fellow of the Royal Society of Physicians and Surgeons
FRSS: Fellow of the Royal Statistical Society
FRSSA: Fellow of the Royal Scottish Society of Arts
FRS(SA): Fellow of the Royal Society of South Africa
FRSSI: Fellow of the Royal Statistical Society of Ireland
FRSSS: Fellow of the Royal Statistical Society of Scotland
Frst: Forest (postal abbreviation)
FRSTM & H: Fellow of the Royal Society of Tropical Medicine and Hygiene
frt: free return trajectory; freight; fruit
Fr To: French Togoland
frt ppd: freight prepaid
fru: fructose; fruit sugar
fruat.: *frustrillatum* (Latin—in small bits)
fruc.: *fructus* (Latin—fruit)—sometimes abbreviated *fr.*
Fruc: *Fructidor* (French—Fruitful Month)—beginning August 18th and extending through September 16th—twelfth month of the French Revolutionary Calendar whose remaining five days—September 17th through the 21st—were called Sansculottides and named respectively for the Virtues, Genius, Labor, Reason, and Rewards
frugal.: fortran rules used as a general applications language
Fruit Bowl of the Nation: Yakima, Washington
frust.: *frustillatim* (Latin—in small portions)
FRVIA: Fellow of the Royal Victorian Institute of Architects
FRW: Federal Reformatory for Women (Alderson, West Virginia)
frwk: framework
Frwy: Freeway
frx: firex
Fry: Ferry (postal abbreviation); Freeway (highway abbreviation)
FRYC: Fall River Yacht Club
FRZS: Fellow of the Royal Zoological Society
FRZS (NSW): Fellow of the Royal Zoological Society of New South Wales
FRZS(Scot): Fellow of the Royal Zoological Society of Scotland
fs: factor of safety; far side; film strip; fin stabilized; fire station; flight service; flying status; foot second; foreign service; foresight; freight supply; front spar; sulfur trioxide chlorsulfonic acid (commercial short form or symbol)
f/s: first-stage
fs (FS): file separator character (data processing)
fs: *faites suivre* (French—please forward)
f^s: *francos* (Spanish—francs)
Fs: fractostratus
FS: Faraday Society; Feasibility

Study; Federal Specification(s): Field Security; Field Service; Fighter Squadron; Fire Station; Flight Sergeant; Fog Signal (Station); Foreign Service; Forest Service; Franz Shubert; Freedom School; Free State; freight supply (vessel); small freighter (naval symbol)

F.S.: Father of Sion

F-S: Fenno-Shipping

F/S: Financial Statement

FS: *Filharmonisk Selskap* (Norwegian—Philharmonic Orchestra); *Forente Staterna* (Swedish—United States)

F de S: Ferrovie dello Stato (Italian State Railways

F del S: Ferrocarril del Sureste (Southeast Railway—Tabasco, Campeche, Veracruz, Yucatan)

fsa: family separation allowance; fuel storage area

f.s.a.: *fiat secundum artem* (Latin—let it be done skilfully)

fsa (FSA): fetal sulfoglycoprotein

FSA: Farm Security Administration; Federal Security Administration; Federal Security Agency; Federal Supply Classification; Federation of South Arabia; Fellow of the Society of Antiquaries; Fellow of the Society of Arts; Finance Service—Army; Fire Support Area; Fraternal Scholastic Association; Free Society Association; Freethinkers Society of America; Future Scientists of America

FSAA: Family Service Association of America

FSAG: Fellow of the Society of Australian Genealogists

fsaga: first sortie after ground alert

FSAICU: Federation of State Associations of Independent Colleges and Universities

FSAL: Fellow of the Society of Antiquaries of London

FSALA: Fellow of the South African Library Association

f.s.a.r.: *fiat secundum artem regulas* (Latin—let it be prepared according to the rules of the art)

FSAS: Fellow of the Society of Antiquaries of Scotland

FSAScot: Fellow of the Society of Arts of Scotland

FSASM: fellow of the South African School of Mines

fsd (FSD): focus skin distance

FSB: Federal Specifications Board; Field Selection Board

FSBC: Ferrocarril Sonora—Baja California (Sonora—Baja California Railway)

fsc: foreign service credit

FSC: Family Services Bureau; Federal Safety Council; Federal Stock Catalog; Federal Supply Classification; Federal Suppy Code; Flight Service Center; Flying Status Code; Foreign Service Credits; Foundation for the Study of Cycles

FSC: *Federal Supply Catalog*

FSCC: Federal Surplus Commodities Corporation; Fire Support Coordination Center; Food Surplus Commodities Corporation

fscl: fire-support coordination line

fscp: foolscap

FSCS: Fire Support Coordination Section; Flight Service Communications System

fsd: flying spot digitizer; foreign sea duty

FSD: Federal Systems Division; Fuel Supply Depot; Sioux Falls, South Dakota (airport)

FSDC: Fellow of the Society of Dyers and Colourists

fse: field-support equipment

FSE: Federation of Stock Exchanges; Fellow of the Society of Engineers

FSEA: Food Service Executives Association

FSES: Federal-State Employment Service

FSF: Flight Safety Foundation

FSFA: Federation of Specialized Film Associations

FSG: Federal Supply Group; Fellow of the Society of Genealogists; Friends School Group

FSGB: Foreign Service Grievance Board

FSgt: Flight Sergeant

FSGT: Fellow of the Society of Glass Technology

FSH (fsh): follicle-stimulating hormone

FSHM: Fellow of the Society of Housing Managers

fshrf (FSHRF): follicle-stimulating hormone releasing factor

fshrh (FSHRH): follicle-stimulating hormone releasing hormone

fsh stk: fish steak

FSI: Federal Stock Item; Fellow of the Sanitary Institute; Fellow of the Surveyors' Institution; Foreign Service Institute; Free Sons of Israel

FSIA: Fellow of the Society of Industrial Artists

FSIC: Federal Savings Insurance Corporation; Foreign Service Inspection Corps (US Department of State)

FSJC: Fort Smith Junior College

fsk: frequency shift keying

fsl: formal semantic language

FSL: First Sea Lord; Folger Shakespeare Library

FSLIC: Federal Savings and Loan Insurance Corporation

fsm: flying-spot microscope

FSM: Fédération Syndicale Mondiale (World Federation of Trade Unions); Fort Smith, Arkansas (airport); Free Speech Movement

FSMC: Flora Stone Mather College

FS Method: Federal Standard Method

FSMWO: Field Service Modification Work Order

FSN: Federal Stock Number

FSNA: Fellow of the Society of Naval Architects

FSNC: Federal Steam Navigation Company

FSNM: Fort Sumter National Monument

FSNP: Fuyot Spring National Park (Philippines)

FSNWR: Fish Springs National Wildlife Refuge (Utah)

FSNY: Free Synagogue of New York

FSO: Flint Symphony Orchestra; Florida Symphony Orchestra; Flying Safety Officer; Foreign Safety Officer; Fuel Supply Office(r)

FSOs: Foreign Service Officers

FSOTS: Foreign Service Officers Training School

fsp: foreign service pay

FSP: Field Security Police; Food Stamp Program

FSPB: Field Service Pocket Book

FSPT: Federation of Societies for Paint Technology

fsr: flight safety research

FSR: Fellow of the Society of Radiographers; Field Service Representative; Foreign Service Reserve

FSRA: Federal Sewage Research Association

FSRJ: Federativna Socijalisticka Republika Jugoslavija (Republic of Yugoslavia)

FSS: Fellow of the Statistical Society; Federal Supply Schedule; Federal Supply Service; Flight Service Station; Flight Standard Service
FSSC: Federal Standard Stock Catalog
fssd: foreign service selection date
FSSU: Federated Superannuation Scheme of Universities
fst: forged steel; full-scale tunnel
Fst: *Funkstation* (German—radio station)
FSTC: Farmington State Teachers College; Fayatteville State Teachers College
FS & TC: Foreign Science and Technology Center (US Army)
FSTD: Fellow of the Society of Typographic Designers
F'sted: Frederiksted, St Croix
FSTMB: *Federación Sindical de Trabajadores Mineros de Bolivia* (Spanish—Syndicalist Federation of Bolivian Miners)
FSTWP: Fellow of the Society of Technical Writers and Publishers
fsu: freak student union
FSU: Florida State University; Friends of the Soviet Union
fsv: final-stage vehicle
FSVA: Fellow of the Society of Valuers and Auctioneers
FSWA: Federation of Sewage Works Associations
F & SWMA: Fine and Specialty Wire Manufacturers Association
fswt: free-surface water tunnel
ft: feet; flush threshold; firing table; formal training; fumetight
ft²: square feet; square foot
ft³: cubic feet; cubic foot
f-t: follow through
f & t: fire and theft
ft.: *fiat* (Latin—let it be made)
Ft: Fort; forint (Hungarian currency unit)
Ft: *Folyoirat* (Hungarian—journal; review)
FT: Flying Tiger Lines (2-letter coding)
FT: *Financial Times* (London)
F de T: *Fulano de Tal* (Spanish—So-and-So)
fta: fluorescent treponemal antibody
FTA: Finnish Travel Association; Free Trade Association; Future Teachers of America
fta-abs: fluorescent treponemal antibody absorption (test for syphilis)
FTAF: Flying Training Air Force
ftb: fails to break
FTB: fleet torpedo bomber
ft black: fine thermal black
ftbrg: footbridge
ftc: fast time constant; final turn collision
ft c: foot-candle
FTC: Federal Telecommunications Laboratories; Federal Trade Commission; Flight Test Center; Flying Training Command
FTCA: Federal Tort Claims Act
ft. cata.: *fiat cataplasma* (Latin—make a poultice)
FTCC: Flight Test Coordinating Committee
FTCD: Fellow of Trinity College—Dublin
ft. cerat.: *fiat ceratum* (Latin—make a cerate)
ft. chart.: *fiat chartulae* (Latin—let powders be made)
FTCL: Fellow of Trinity College of Music—London
ft. colly.: *fiat collyrium* (Latin—make an eyewash)
ftd: fails to drain
FTD: Field Training Detachment; Florists' Telegraph Delivery; Foreign Technology Division
FTDA: Fellow of the Theatrical Designers and Craftsmens Association
FTDC: Fellow of the Society of Typographic Designers of Canada
ft di: flattening die
ftdr: friction-top drum
ft. emuls.: *fiat emulsio* (Latin—make an emulsion)
ft. enem.: *fiat enema* (Latin—make an enema)
FTESA: Foundry Trades Equipment and Supplies Association
FTF: Flygtekniska Forsoksantalten (Aeronautical Research Institute of Sweden)
ftfet: four-terminal field-effect transistor
ftg: fitting; footing
FTG: Fuji Texaco Gas
ft. garg.: *fiat gargarisma* (Latin—make a gargle)
fth(m): fathom
ft/hr: feet per hour
fti: federal tax included; frequency time indicator; frequency time intensity
FTI: Facing Tile Institute; Federal Tax Included; Fellow of the Textile Institute
FTII: Fellow of the Taxation Institute Incorporated
FTIMA: Federal Tobacco Inspectors Mutual Association
FT Index: *Financial Times Index*
ft. infus.: *fiat infusum* (Latin—make an infusion)
ft. injec.: *fiat infectio* (Latin—make an injection
FTIT: Fellow of the Institute of Taxation
ftk: forward track kill
ftl: faster than light
ft l: foot -lambert
FTL: Federal Telecommunications Laboratory; Flying Tiger Line
ft lb: foot pound
ft-lbf: foot-pound force
ft. linim.: *fiat linimentum* (Latin—make a liniment)
FTM: Flying Training Manual
ft. mas.: *fiat massa* (Latin—make a mass)
ft. mas. div. in pil.: *fiat massa dividenda in pilulas* (Latin—make a mass and divide into pills)
ft md: flattening mandrel
ft/min: feet (foot) per minute
ft³/min: cubic feet per minute
ft. mist.: *fiat mistura* (Latin—make a mixture)
ftn: fortification
Ftn: Fountain (postal abbreviation); Freetown (maritime abbreviation)
FTN: Facsimile Transmissión *Network*
f^to: *firmato* (Italian—signed)
FTO: Fleet Torpedo Officer
ftp: final-turn pursuit (aircraft); folded, trimmed, and packed (books); full-time personnel (civil service)
FTP: Fleet Training Publication; Flight Test Program
ft-pdl: foot poundal
ft. pil.: *fiat pilulae* (Latin—make pills)
FTPR: *Federación del Trabajo de Puerto Rico* (Spanish—Federation of Labor of Puerto Rico)
FTPS: Fellow of the Technical Publishing Society
ft. pulv.: *fiat pulvis* (Latin—make a powder)
ftr: fighter; fixed-transom; flat-tile roof
F Tr: flag tower
FTR: Final Technical Report; flag tower (chart and map designation); Flight Test Report; Fruehauf (stock exchange symbol); Functional Test Re-

port; Functional Test Request
ftrac: full-tracked (vehicle)
FTRF: Freedom-to-Read Foundation
ft/s: feet (foot) per second
ft/s²: foot per second squared
ft³/s: cubic feet per second
FTS: Federal Telecommunications System; Flying Traffic Specialist; Flying Training School; Forged Tool Society; Funeral Telegraph Service
ft sec: foot second
ft. so.: *fiat solutio* (Latin—make a solution)
ft. suppos.: *fiat suppositorium* (Latin—make a suppository)
ftt: full-time temporary (civil-service employee)
FTT: Fever Therapy Technician
fttr: fitter
ft & tw: combination flat top and typewriter (desk)
ftu: fuel tanking unit
Ftu: Freeman time unit
FTU: Field Torpedo Unit; First Training Unit
ft. ung.: *fiat unguentum* (Latin—make an ointment)
FTV: Flight Test Vehicle
ftw: free-trade wharf
Ft W: Fort Worth
FTZ: Foreign Trade Zone
FTZB: Foreign Trade Zones Board
fu: Farmers Union
Fu: Finsen unit
F-u: fuck you (underground slang—very insulting epithet)
FU: Fairfield University; Fisk University; Fordham University; Franklin University; Freie Universität (Berlin Free University); Friends University; Furman University
FUB: Freie Universität Berlin (Free University, Berlin)
fubar: fouled up beyond all recognition
fubb: fouled up beyond belief
FUC: Ferrocarriles Unidos de Yucatan (United Railroads of Yucatan)
fuchsite: chrome mica
FUDR: Failure and Usage Data Report
FUEN: Federal Union of European Nationalities
Führer: (German—Leader)—Hitler's title
FUIB: Fire Underwriters Inspection Bureau
Fujita: Leonardo Fujita
Ful: Fulcran; Fulgence; Fulgencio; Fulke; Fuller; Fullerton; Fulton; Fulvia; Fulvius
FULICO: Fidelity Union Life Insurance Company
fum: fuming
FUM: Friends United Meeting
Fum the Fourth: nickname of George IV
fumi: fumigant; fumigate; fumigation
fumtu: fouled up more than usual
fun.: funeral; funerary
funamb: funambulation; funambulist (tightrope or tightwire walker)
func: function(al)
Fun Capital of Scandinavia: Copenhagen, Denmark
Fun City: New York
funct: function; functional; functionally
fund.: fundamental; fundamentalism; fundamentalist
fund.: *fundador* (Spanish—founder)
FUND: International Monetary Fund
Fundador de Nueva Granada: (Spanish—Founder of New Granada)—Francisco de Paula Santander—founder of Colombia (Nueva Granada)
Fundador de la República: (Spanish—Founder of the Republic)—José Nuñez Cáceres—founder and first president of the Dominican Republic (Spanish Haiti)
Funeral March Sonata: Piano Sonata in B-flat minor by Chopin (contains his celebrated funeral march)
fungi.: fungicide
Fungus Corners: (naval argot—Bremerton, Washington)—a rainy port
Funk: Funk & Wagnalls
FUNK: *Front Uni National du Kampuchea* (French—Khmer National United Front)—Cambodia and Khmer forces
FUNM: Fort Union National Monument
FUNNs: For Your Nieces and Nephews
FUNU: *Force d'Urgence de Nations Unies* (French—United Nations Emergency Force)
fuo: fever (of) unknown origin
fup: fusion point
fuposat: follow-up on supply action taken
fur.: furlong
furl.: furlough
furlong: furrow long (one eighth mile or 220 yards—201.17 meters), originally the average length of a plowman's furrow
furn: furnace; furnish(es; ed; ing; ings); furniture
Furn: Furnace (postal abbreviation)
furngs: furnishings
furnit: furniture
Fur Seal Islands: Probilov Islands off Alaska
Furt: (German—ford)
fus: fuselage
FuSf: *Fortsetzung und Schluss folgen* (German—to be concluded in the next issue)
Fuss and Feathers: General Winfield Scott, USA
fut: future
Fut: Futura
FUTC: Fidelity Union Trust Company
FUW: Farmers' Union of Wales
fv: flush valve; forward visibility; fire vent
fv.: *folio verso* (Latin—back of the sheet)
FV: Falck's Flyvetjeneste (Copenhagen); fishing vessel; Fruit and Vegetable (US Department of Agriculture)
FVA: Fellow of the Valuers Association
fvc: forced vital capacity
FVCQFRA: Fruit and Vegetable Canning and Quick Freezing Research Association
FVDE: Fighting Vehicles Design Establishment
FVI: Fellow of the Valuers' Institution
FVMMA: Floor and Vaccum Machinery Manufacturers Association
FVNM: Fort Vancouver National Monument
FVPA: Flat Veneer Products Association
FVPRA: Fruit and Vegetable Preservation Research Association
FVRDE: Fighting Vehicles Research and Development Establishment
fv's: fashion victims
f. vs.: *fiat venaesectio* (Latin—perform a venesection)
FVSC: Fort Valley State College
fvt: family vewing time
fw: fire wall; fixed wing; formula weight; fresh water
f & w: feed and water; feeding and watering
fw: Funk & Wagnalls
f/W: female White
FW: Fairbanks Whitney (stock exchange symbol); Focke-Wulf; Fog Whistle; Fort Worth; Foster Wheeler

fwa: first word address; fluorescent whitening agent
FWA: Family Welfare Association; Federal Works Agency; French West Africa; Future Weapons Agency
FWAA: Football Writers Association of America
FWAS: Fort Wayne Art School
fwb: four-wheel brake; four-wheel braking; free-wheel bicycle; front-wheel bicycle; furnished with bed
FWB: Fort Worth Belt (railroad); Free-Will Baptists
FWC: Foster Wheeler Corporation
FW & C: Furness, Withy & Company
FWCC: Friends' World Committee for Consultation
fwd: forward; forwarding; four-wheel drive; freshwater damage
F W & D: Fort Worth & Denver (railroad)
FwdBL: forward bomb line
fwdct: fresh water drain collecting tank
fwdg: forwarding
fwdr: forwarder
f-w-e: finished with engine(s)
FWeldI: Fellow of the Welding Institute
FWGE: Fort Worth Grain Exchange
FWHF: Federation of World Health Foundations
FWI: Federation of West Indies; French West Indies
fwl: foilborne waterline
FWL: Foundation for World Literacy
FWO: Facilities Work Order; Fleet Wireless Officer
FWOA: Fort Worth Opera Association
fwop: furloughed without pay
FWP: Federal Writers' Project
FWPCA: Federal Water Pollution Control Administration
FWPO: Fort Wayne Philharmonic Orchestra
FWQA: Federal Water Quality Administration; Federal Water Quality Association
fwr: full-wave rectifier; full-wave reflector
FWRC: Federal Water Resources Council
FWRM: Federation of Wire Rope Manufacturers
fws: filter wedge spectrometer
FWS: Fighter Weapons School
F & WS: Fish and Wildlife Service
FWSG: Farm Water Supply Grant
FWSO: Fort Worth Symphony Orchestra
FWSSUSA: Federation of Worker's Singing Societies of the U.S.A.
fwt: fair wear and tear; featherweight
FWT: Free World Trade
fwth: flush watertight hatch
FWWS: Fire-Weather Warning Service
Fwy: Freeway
fx: extraneous (television) effects; fixed; foreign exchange; foxed; fractured
Fx: fracture (bone)
FX: Foreign Exchange
F.X.: Francis Xavier
fxd: fixed; foxed
fxg: fixing
fxle: forecastle
fy (FY): fiscal year
Fy: Ferry
FY: fiscal year; Ferdinand(e) Ysabella
FYC: Federal Youth Center; Florida Yacht Club
fyi: for your information
fyig: for your information and guidance
fym: farmyard manure
FYP: Five-Year Plan; Four-Year Plan; etc.
FYPB: Five-Year Planning Base (USA)
FYPP: Five-Year Procurement Program (USA)
fz: fuze (ordnance explosive device)
fz: *forzando* (Italian—accented strongly)
Fz: Fernández; Franz
FZ: Franc Zone; Free Zone; French Zone
FZA: Fellow of the Zoological Academy; Fellow of the Zoological Association
FZGBI: Fellow of the Zoological Gardens of Great Britain and Ireland
FZIA: First Zen Institute of America
FZS: Fellow of the Zoological Society
FZSL: Fellow of the Zoological Society, London
FZSScot: Fellow of the Zoological Society of Scotland

G

g: gage; gender; gilbert; gold; gram; gravitational acceleration (symbol); great; green; grey; gross; gyromagnetic ratio (symbol); Lande factor (symbol)
g: acceleration of gravity (symbol); gloom (gloomy weather symbol)
g/: *giro* (Spanish—bank check)
g (G): glucose
G: conductance (symbol); control grid (symbol); Fraunhofer line caused by iron (symbol); gap; gear; German(ic); Germany; Gibbs function (free energy symbol); glider; go; God (on Masonic emblems); Golf—code for letter G; good; Goodyear; gourde (Haitian unit of currency); government (broadcasting); Grace (steamship line); Green Line; Greene Line; Greenwich; Greyhound (bus line); guineas; gulden (Netherlands guilder); gulf; Gulf Oil (stock exchange symbol); Newtonian gravitational constant (symbol); specific gravity (symbol)
G: *Gade* (Danish—Street); *Gasse* (German—Street); *Gata* (Swedish— Street); *Gate* (Norwegian— Street); (Latin—Gallica; Germania)
G-1: Army or Marine Corps personnel section; personnel officer

G-2: military intelligence section of Army or Marine Corps; military intelligence officer
G-3: operations and training section of Army or Marine Corps; operations and training officer
G3P: glyceraldehyde 3-phosphate
G-4: logistics section of Army or Marine Corps; logistics officer
G-5: civil affairs section of Army; civil affairs officer
G6PD: glucose-6-phosphate dehydrogenase
G_4: dichlorophen (bactericide and fungicide)
G_{11}: hexachlorophene (antibacterial agent)
ga: gage; gas amplification; gastric analysis; general average; glide angle; go ahead; ground to air
g/a: general average; ground-to-air
Ga: gallium; Georgia; Georgian; Ghana (tribe)
G^a: García
GA: Gage Man; Garrison Adjutant; General Agent; General Assembly (UN); Georgia (railroad); Glen Alden (stock exchange symbol); Gypsum Association
G-A: General Atomic (Division of General Dynamics)
GAA: Gaelic Athletic Association; Gay Activists Alliance
GAAC: Graphics Arts Advisers Council
GAATV: Gemini-Atlas-Agena Target Vehicle
gab: gabardine; gabbing; gabble; gable
Gab: Gabon Republic (République Gabonaise); Gabriel
GABA: gamma-aminobutyric acid
Gabba: Wollongabba, Brisbane
Gabby: Gabriel; Gabriella; Gabrielle
Gabe: Gabriel
Gabl: Gabriel
Gabr: Gabriel; Gabriella; Gabrielle
Gabriela Mistral: Lucila Godoy de Alcayaga
Gabriel Padecopeo: Lope de Vega
Gaby: Gabrielle Dupont
gac: grilled American cheese (sandwich)
GAC: General Acceptance Corporation; Geological Association of Canada; Goodyear Aircraft Corporation; Gustavus Adolphus College
GACHAL: *Gush Herut Liberalim* (Hebrew—Herut-Liberal Bloc)—right-wing party
g/a con: general average contribution
GAD: Great American Desert
g/a dep: general average deposit
GADNA: *Gdud Noar* (Hebrew—Youth Corps)
GADO: General Aviation District Office
GADS: Goose Air Defense Sector
Gae: Gaelic
GAE: General American English
GAEC: Goodyear Aircraft and Engineering Corporation; Grumman Aircraft Engineering Corporation
Gael: Gaelic
Gaet: Gaetano
gaf: General Aniline & Film Corporation (trademark)
GAFB: Goodfellow Air Force Base
GAFD: Guild of American Funeral Directors
gaffer: (motion-picture and tv slang—chief electrician)
gaffer and gammer: grandfather and grandmother
GAFLAC: General Accident Fire and Life Assurance Corporation
gag.: gaging
g/a/g: ground-air-ground
gai: guaranteed annual income
GAI: Government Affairs Institute
GAIA: Graphic Arts Information Association
Gail: Abigail
GAJ: Guild of Agricultural Journalists
GAK: Garlock (stock-exchange symbol)
Gaku Univ: Gakushuin University
gal: galileo (unit of acceleration); gallon (unit of capacity)
Gal: Epistle to the Galatians; Galacia; Galway
Gal: *Général* (French—General)
GAL: Gdynia America Line; Guggenheim Aeronautical Laboratory; Guinea Airways
G A & L: General Aircraft and Leasing (Division of General Dynamics Corporation)
Galáp: Galápagos Islands
Galápagos: Galápagos Islands
galaxy.: general automatic luminosity and x y (measuring machine)
gal cap: gallon capacity
GALCIT: Guggenheim Aeronautical Laboratory, California Institute of Technology
Gale: Gale Research Company
galena: lead sulfide (Germans call it Bleischweif)
gall.: gallery
Gall: *Galleria* (Italian—gallery or tunnel)
Gallo-Rom: Gallo-Romance
Gallup: Dr George Horace Gallup of Gallup Poll fame
gal per min: gallons per minute
gal(s): girl(s)
gals: gallons
galt: gut-associated lymphoid tissue
Galtees: southern Ireland's Galty Mountains
galumphing: galloping and triumphing
galv: galvanic; galvanism; galvanize(d); galvanometer
Galv: Galveston
galv i: galvanized iron
galvnd: galvannealed
galvo(s): galvanometer(s)
Galw: Galway
gam: gammon (sailor's gossip; seamen's talkfest); gamut; guided-aircraft missile
Gam: Gamaliel; Gambia
GAM: Guest Aerovías Mexico; Guided-Aircraft Missile
GAMA: Gas Appliance Manufacturers Association
GAMAA: Guitar and Accessories Manufacturers Association of America
Gambiers: Gambier Islands in the South Pacific
Gambling Capital of the Far East: Macao, Portuguese China
Gambling Capital of the Far West: Las Vegas, Nevada
Gamerco: (acronymic placename—Gallup American Coal Company)—coal-mining town near Gallup in northwestern New Mexico
GAMIS: Graphic Arts Marketing Information Service
GAMM: Gesellschaft für Angewante Mathematik und Mechanik
GAMMA: Guns and Magnetic Material Alarm (anti-hijacking device)
GAN: Generalized Activity Network
Gandhi: *Mahatma* (Hindustani—Great Souled)—Mohandas Karamchand Gandhi
gang.: ganglia; ganglion
Ganga: (Hindi or Sanskrit—Ganges)

ganzl: *gänzlich* (German—complete, entire)
GAO: General Accounting Office; General Administrative Order; General American Oil (company); General American Overseas (corporation)
GAO: *Glavnaya Astronomicheskaya Observatoriya* (Russian—Main Astronomical Observatory)
gap.: guidance autopilot
Gap: Delaware Water Gap; Pennington Gap
GAP: Government Aircraft Plant; Great American Public; Great Atlantic & Pacific (Tea Company); Group for the Advancement of Psychiatry
GAP: *Gruppo d'Azione Partigiana* (Italian—Partisan Action Group)
gapa: ground-to-air pilotless aircraft
GAPAN: Guild of Air Pilots and Air Navigators
GAPCE: General Assembly of the Presbyterian Church of England
GAPL: Group Assembly Parts List
gar.: garage; garrison; guided aircraft rocket
GAR: Gioacchino Antonio Rossini; Grand Army of the Republic; Guided Aircraft Rocket; Gustavus Adolphus Rex (King Gustav II of Sweden)
Gara: Garamond
garb.: garbage; green, amber, red, blue (airway priority color code)
garbd: garboard
garbz: *garbanzos* (Spanish—chickpeas)
GARC: Graphic Arts Research Center
G.Arch.: Graduate in Architecture
Garcia: Diego Garcia (Anglo-American naval base in the Chagos Archipelago or Oil Islands of the Indian Ocean)
gard: gamma atomic radiation detector; garden; gardener; gardening; general address reading device; guard
GARD: Gamma Atomic Radiation Detector
Garden of the Andes: Mendoza, Argentina
Garden of Canada: Ontario
Garden of the Caribbean: Puerto Rico
Garden City of Georgia: Augusta
Garden of Denmark: Fyn or Funen—home of Hans Christian Andersen
Garden of England: Kent and Worcester share this sobriquet
Garden of France: Amboise and Touraine share this nickname
Garden of God: ancient eponym of Lebanon just north of the Holy Land
Garden of the Gulf: rural Prince Edward Island in the Gulf of St Lawrence
Garden of Ireland: Carlow
Garden Island: Kauai, Hawaii
Garden of Italy: Sicily
Garden of Maine: Aroostook County
Garden of Paradise in the Sea: Madeira
Garden Province: Canada's Prince Edward Island
Garden of Spain: fields of Andalucía and Valencia
Garden State: New Jersey's official nickname
Garden of the Sun: Indonesia
Garden of Sweden: Blekinge
Garden of Switzerland: Thurgau
Garden of the World: Mississippi River Valley
gards: gardenias
garg.: *gargarisma* (Latin—gargle)
garioa: government and relief in occupied areas
GARP: Global Atmospheric Research Program
G.A.R.S.: Gustavus Adolphus Rex Sueciae (Gustavus Adolphus King of Sweden)
gar str: garboard strake
Gart: Garrett
GARUDA: Garuda Indonesia Airways
Gary: Gareth; Garvey
gas: gasoline
g-a s: general-adaptation syndrome
ga & s: general average and salvage
GAs: Gamblers Anonymous
GAS: Georgia Academy of Science; Ghana Academy of Sciences; Government of American Samoa
GASC: German-American Securities Corporation
gasid: gas-acid (indigestion)
GASL: General Applied Science Laboratories
gaso: gasoline
gasp.: gravity-assisted space probe
Gasp: Gaspar(o)
GASP: Greater (Washington, D.C.) Alliance to Stop Pollution (air and water); Group Against Smog and Pollution
Gaspar: Jasper
Gasparilla: (Spanish — Little Gaspar)—nickname of José Gaspar—pirate active along west coast of Florida around 1750
gast: gastric
Gast: Gaston
Gastown: waterfront area of Vancouver, BC
gastro: gastronomy
gastroc: gastrocnemius
gastroenterol: gastroenterology
gat: gatling gun; gun; revolver
gat: *gata* (Swedish—Street); (Dano-Norwegian—channel)
GAT: Georgetown Automatic Translation; Greenwich Apparent Time
GATA: Graphic Arts Technical Association
gatac: general assessment tridimensional analog computer
GATB: General Aptitude Test Battery
GATCO: Guild of Air Traffic Control Officers
GATE: Group to Advance Total Energy (American Gas Association)
Gate City of the South: Atlanta, Georgia
Gate of Tears: Bab-el-Mandeb Strait linking Gulf of Aden and Indian Ocean with the Red Sea; Arabic name means Gate of Tears although many sailors call it Gate of Hell because of its desert-heated hot winds
Gateway to Alaska: Seattle, Washington
Gateway to America: New York City
Gateway Arch City: St Louis, Missouri
Gateway to the Big Bend National Park: Marfa, Texas
Gateway City: old nickname of Pittsburgh, Pennsylvania, after the Revolutionary War
Gateway to the Dakotas: Sioux Falls, South Dakota
Gateway to the East: Port Said, Egypt
Gateway to Eastern India: Calcutta
Gateway to the Great Seaway: Green Bay, Wisconsin
Gateway to India: Bombay
Gateway to Israel: Haifa
Gateway to Japan: Yokohama

Gateway to Latin America: Miami, Florida
Gateway to Mount Rainier: Tacoma, Washington
Gateway to the Negev: Beersheba, Israel
Gateway to the North: North Bay, Ontario
Gateway to Northern Europe: Göteborg (Gothenburg), Sweden
Gateway to the NY-NJ Market: Bayonne, New Jersey
Gateway to the Smokies: Knoxville, Tennessee
Gateway to Southwest Japan: Kobe
Gateway to the West: sobriquet shared by Pittsburgh, Pennsylvania, and St Louis, Missouri
Gateway to Western India: Bombay
GATF: Graphic Arts Technical Foundation
'gator(s): alligator(s)
GATT: General Agreement on Tariffs and Trade
Gatti: Guilio Gatti-Casazza
GATX: General American Transportation Corporation (tank car marking)
GAUFCC: General Assembly of Unitarian and Free Christian churches
Gaul.: Gaulish
gav: gross annual value
Gavin Ogilvy: Hames M. Barrie
gaw: guaranteed annual wage
gawam: great American wife and mother
gawr: gross axle weight rating
Gay: Gaylord
Gay White Way: New York City's Broadway in the 42nd Street and Times Square area
gaz: gazette; gazetteer
GAZ: (Russian—*Gorki Avtomobilnii Zavod)*—Gorki Automobile Factory producing the Volga sedan-type auto
gb: gall bladder; glide bomb; goodbye; grid bearing; gun bed
g-b: goof-ball (barbiturate pill)
g/b: ground based
gB: greenish blue
Gb: gilbert
GB: General Board; General Bronze(corporation);Georges Bizet; Great Books; Great Britain; gunboat (naval symbol)
gba: give better address
GBAD: Great Britain Allied and Dominion
GBBA: Glass Bottle Blowers Association
GBC: General Binding Corporation; Gibraltar Broadcasting Company; Greenland Base Command
GB & C: General Battery and Ceramic (corporation)
GB COLL: George Brown College
gb'd: goofballed (underground slang—drugged)
GBDC: Grand Bahama Development Company
g-b-d-f-a: (musical mnemonic—good boys do fine always)—bass clef note names of the five lines (g-b-d-f-a)
GBDO: Guild of British Dispensing Opticians
gbe: gilt bevelled edge
G.B.E.: Dame or Knight of the Grand Cross of the British Empire
GBF: Gakujitsu Bunken Fukyukai (Japanese Society of Scientific Documentation and Information); Great Books Foundation
GBG: General Baking (Stock exchange symbol)
gb gas: US Army symbol for a colorless and odorless nerve gas of extreme lethality as a one-milligram dose can kill in a few minutes; as a token of its lethality it is also referred to as general biological gas, goodbye gas, or gruesome business gas
GBGB: Gaming Board for Great Britain
gbh (GBH): gamma benzene hydrochloride
GBHC: Governor Bacon Health Center
GBI: Grand Bahama Island (tracking station)
GB & I: Great Britain and Ireland
g/bl: government bill of lading
GBL: Georgian Bay Line; government bill of lading
gbm: glomerular basement membrane
GBMA: Golf Ball Manufacturers Association
GBNE: Guild of British Newspaper Editors
GBNM: Glacier Bay National Monument
gbo: goods in bad order
G-bomb: gravitational bomb
GBPA: Grand Bahama Port Authority
gbr: give better reference; gun, bomb, rocket
gbr: *gebräuchlich* (German—usual)
gbs: gall-bladder series
gb's: goofballs (barbiturates)
GBS: George Bernard Shaw; Guyana Broadcasting Service
GBSM: Guild of Better Shoe Manufacturers
GBSTC: General Beadle State Teachers College
GBV: Gustahlwerk Bochumer Verein (Krupp Steel)
GB & W: Green Bay & Western (railroad)
g'bye: goodbye
gc: gas check; gigacycle; glucocorticoid; gonorrhea case; great circle; grid course; ground control; guidance control; gun control
Gc: great tropic range
GC: Gallaudet College; Gannon College; Gaston College; Geneva College; Georgetown College; Gettysburg College; Glendale College; glucorticoid; Goddard College; Gordon College; Goshen College; Goucher College; Graceland College; Grambling College; Greensboro College; Greenville College; grid course (symbol); Grinnell College; Grover Cleveland (22nd and 24th President U.S.); Guilford College; Gustave Charpentier
G.C.: George Cross; gonorrhea case
gca (GCA): ground-controlled approach
GCA: Girls' Clubs of America; Green Coffee Association; Greeting Card Association; Government Contract Committee; Ground Control Center
GCAHS: Guggenheim Center for Aviation Health and Safety
g cal: gram calorie
G-Cass: Gomes-Cásseres;Gomez-Cásseres
GCB: Glen Canyon Bridge
G.C.B.: Knight of the Grand Cross, Order of the Bath
GCC: Grand Canyon College; Gulf Coast College
G & CC: Gonville and Caius College—Cambridge
GCCC: Goshen County Community College
gcd: general and complete disarmament; greatest common divisor
GCD: Grand Coulee Dam
GCE: Gas City Empire; General

Certificate of Education; General College Entrance (diploma or examination)
gcf: greatest common factor
GCFI: Gulf and Caribbean Fisheries Institute
gcfr: gas-cooled fast reactor
GCFT: Gonorrhea Complement Fixation Test
GCGR: Giant's Castle Game Reserve (South Africa)
GCHQ: Government Communications Headquarters
gci: gray cast iron; ground-controlled interception
GCI: Grand Canary Island (tracking station); ground-controlled interception
GCIA: Granite Cutters' International Association
G. C. I. E.: Knight Grand Commander of the Order of the Indian Empire
GCIS: Ground Control Interception Squadron
GCJC: Gulf Coast Junior College
gcl (GCL): ground-controlled landing
GCL: Gulf Caribbean Lines
G clef: treble clef
GCLH: Grand Cross of the Legion of Honour
gcm: greatest common measure
GCM: General Court-Martial; Gian Carlo Menotti; Good Conduct Medal; Grand Cayman, Cayman Islands (airport)
G.C.M.G.: Knight Grand Cross of the Order of Saint Michael and Saint George
GCMI: Glass Container Manufacturers Institute
GCN: Greenwich Civil Noon
GCNA: Guild of Carillonneurs in North America
GCNM: Grand Canyon National Monument
GCNP: Grand Canyon National Park (Arizona)
GCNRA: Glen Canyon National Recreation Area (Arizona and Utah)
GCO: Greater Coin Operators; Guidance Control Officer
GCOS: Great Canadian Oil Sands
GCPL: Glasgow Corporation Public Libraries
gcr (GCR): gas-cooled graphite-moderated reactor; ground-controlled radar
g crg: gun carriage
GCRI: Gilette Company Research Institute
GCRO: Grand Council and Register of Osteopaths
gcs: gate-controlled switch; gram-centimeter-second
gc/s: gigacycles per second
gc's: genetic girls (real girls)
Gc/s: gigacycle per second
GCS: Game Conservation Society; Georgia Consumer Services
GCSCO: Göta Canal Steamship Company
G.C.S.G.: Knight Grand Commander of the Order of Saint Gregory the Great
G.C.S.I.: Dame or Knight Grand Commander of the Star of India
gct: ground-control unit
GCT: General Classification Test; Glamorgan College of Technology; Greenwich Civil Time
GCTC: Green County Teachers College
GCTS: Ground Communication Tracking System
GCU: Glasgow Choral Union
G.C.V.O.: Dame or Knight of the Grand Cross of the Victorian Order
gcw: gross combination weight (of tractor and loaded trailer)
gd: good; good delivery; granddaughter; gravimetric density; ground; guard; guardian
g-d: god-damned
g/d: gallons per day
g & d: galvanized and dipped
gd: *gade* (Danish—street)
Gd: gadolinium
G-d: God (Hebraic contraction)
GD: General Discharge; General Dispensary; General Dynamics (corporation); George Dewey; Grand Duchy; Gudermannian or hyperbolic amplitude (symbol)
G-D: General Dynamics Corporation
G & D: Garcia & Diaz (steamship line)
GD: *Globe-Democrat*
gda: gun-defended area
GDA: General Dynamics Ardmore
GD/A: General Dynamics/Astronautics
GDBA: Guide Dogs for the Blind Association
gdc: geocentric dust cloud
GDC: General Dynamics Convair; Gesellschaft Deutscher Chemiker (Society of German Chemists)
Gd Ch: *Grand Choeur* (French—full choir; full organ)
GDCL: General Dynamics Canadair Limited
GD/Convair: General Dynamics/Convair
GD/D: General Dynamics/Daingerfield
gde: gilt deckle edging
Gde: gourde (Haitian monetary unit)
GDE: General Dynamics Electronics
GD/EB: General Dynamics/Electric Boat
GDED: General Dynamics Electro Dynamic
GDFB: Guide Dog Foundation for the Blind
GD Fort Worth: General Dynamics Fort Worth
GDFW: General Dynamics Fort Worth
GDGA: General Dynamics General Atomic
gdh: growth and development hormone
gdh (GDH): glutamate dehydrogenase
GDHS: Ground Data Handling System
GDIFS: Gray and Ductile Iron Founders' Society
Gdk: Gdansk (Danzig)
Gdl: Guadalajara; Guadalajareños (inhabitants)
GDL: Grand-Duche de Luxembourg (Grand Duchy of Luxemburg); Guadalajara, Mexico (airport)
GDLC: General Dynamics Liquid Carbonic
gdling: good looking
GDMO: General Duty Medical Officer
GDMS: General Dynamics Material Service
gdn: garden
Gdn: Gardener; Guardian
GDNA: Gesellschaft Deutscher Naturforscher und Ärzte (Society of German Naturalists and Physicians)
gdnce: guidance
gdnr: gardener
Gdns: Gardens
gdp: gross domestic product; guanosine diphosphate; gun director pointer
GDP: General Dynamics Pomona; Guanosine diphosphate
GDP(D): General Dynamics Pomona (Daingerfield)
gdr: guard rail
GDR: German Democratic Republic
gds: goods

Gdsk: Gdansk (Danzig)
Gdsm: Guardsman; Guardsmen
gdsob: god-damned son of a bitch
gdu: graphic display unit
Gdy: Gdynia
ge: gas ejection; gastroenterology; gilt edge(s); good evening; gyroscope error
Ge: German; Germanic; germanium; Germany
GE: General Electric; Great Exuma; Group Engineer
GEA: Gravure Engravers Association; Greater East Asia
GEACS: Great East Asia Coprosperity Sphere
GE-ANPD: General Electric Aircraft Nuclear Propulsion Development
gear.: gearing
geb: *geboren* (German—born); *gebunden* (German—bound)
GEB: General Education Board; Gerber Products (stock exchange symbol); Guiding Eyes for the Blind
gebco: general bathymetric chart of the oceans
GEBECOMA: Groupement Belge des Constructeurs de Matériel Aérospatial
Gebr: *Gebroeders* (Dutch—brothers); *Gebrüder* (German—brothers)
gec: *gecartonneerd* (Dutch—bound in boards)
GEC: General Electric Company
GECOMIN: General Congolese Ore Company
gecref: geographic reference (worldwide geographic reference system; also appears as GECREF)
ged: *gedämpft* (German—muted)
GED: General Educational Development (testing service)
Geda: Goodyear electronic differential analyzer
GEDP: General Educational Development Program (USA)
gedr: *gedrukt* (Dutch—printed)
GEDT: General Educational Development Test
GEEIA: Ground Electronics Engineering Installation Agency
geek: geomagnetic electrokinetograph
Ge. Eng.: Geological Engineer
gef: gonadotrophin enhancing factor
GEG: Spokane, Washington (airport)
gegr: *gegründet* (German—founded)
GEHP: George Eastman House of Photography (Rochester)
Geh Rat: *Geheimrat* (German—Privy Councillor)
GEI: *Giovani Esploratori Italiani* (Italian Boy Scouts)
GEIA: Ground Equipment Electronics Installations Agency
GEIC: Gilbert and Ellice Islands Colony
GEICO: Government Employees Insurance Company
geistl: *geistlich* (German—spiritual)
gek: geomagnetic electrokinetograph
gek: *gekürzt* (German— abbreviated)
GEKTUSA: Grand Encampment of the Knights Templar of the United States of America
gel: gelatine; gelatinous
GEL: General Electric Laboratory; Great Eastern Line
gelat: gelatinous
Gell: Aulus Gellius (Roman grammarian)
gel. quav.: *gelatina quavis* (Latin—in some jelly)
gem.: ground-effect machine; guidance evaluation missile
Gem: Gemini
GEM: Gas Equipment Manufacturers
GEMA: Gymnastic Equipment Manufacturers Association
Gem Beside the Amstel: Amsterdam on the Amstel River
Gemini: two-man spacecraft
GEMMWU: General, Electrical, Mechanical, and Municipal Workers' Union
gem's: ground-effect machines
Gem State: Idaho's official nickname
Gemy: General Motors Corporation
gen: gender; genealogy; genera; general; generator; generic; genetic(s); genital; genitive; gentian; genus
Gen: General; Genoa; Genoese
Gen: *Genesis*
GEN: Oslo, Norway (Gardermoen Airport)
gen av: general average
Gend: *Gendarme* (French—Policeman)
genda: general data analysis and simulation
Gene: Eugene; Eugenia
geneal: genealogy
General Douglas: pseudonym of Soviet corps commander Yakov Smuskevich while leading the Spanish Republican air force in 1936–37
General John: nickname of the first Duke of Marlborough—John Churchill
General Kleber: pseudonym of Soviet general Grigory Shtern while serving as chief advisor to the Spanish Republican army in 1936–37
General's Lady: Martha Washington—wife of General George Washington
General Tom Thumb: Charles S. Stratton
General Tubman: Harriet Ross Tubman of Underground Railroad fame
genet: genetic; geneticist; genetics
Genet: Janet Flanner's pen name
gen. et sp. nov.: *genus et species nova* (Latin—new genus and species)
Geneva Cross: (*see* Cross of Geneva)
Gen Hosp: General Hospital
genit: genitive
genl: general
Gen[1]: General (Spanish—General)
Gen Mgr: General Manager
genn: *gennaio* (Italian—January)
gen. nov.: *genus novum* (Latin—new genus)
gen prac: general practice
gen proc: general procedure
gen pub: general public
genr: generate; generation; generator
genrl: general
Gensek: *Generalnyi Sekretar* (Russian—Secretary General)—leader of the secretariat of the Central Committee of the Communist Party—post held by Stalin
Gen Supt: General Superintendent
gent: gentleman
Gentleman Jim: prizefighter James John Corbett
Gentleman Johnny: General John Burgoyne, also a noted British playwright
gents: gentlemen; gentlemen's
Geo: George
GEO: Georgetown, Guyana (Atkinson Field)
GEOC: General Estate and Orphan Chamber (trust company)
geod: geodesic; geodesist; geodesy; geodetic; geodynamic(s)
Geod. E.: Geodetic Engineer
Geof: Geoffrey; Geoffroy
Geoffrey: Jeffrey
Geoffrey Crayon: Washington

Irving
geog: geographer; geographical; geography
Geographical Center of North America: Rugby, North Dakota
geohy: geohygiene
GEOIS: Geographic Information System
geol: geologic; geological; geologist
Geol.E.: Geological Engineer
Geol Surv: Geological Survey
geom: geometry
geomorph: geomorphologic(al); geomorphologist; geomorphology
geon (GEON): gyro-erected optical navigation
geoph: geophysics
geophy: geophysical; geophysics
geopol: geopolitical; geopolitics
geor: Georgian
Geordie: George; Newcastle-on-Tyne, England
Geordieland: Newcastle-on-Tyne area of northeastern England
Geordies: people from the coal-mining and industrial area of Newcastle-on-Tyne and its satellite cities
Georef: World Geographic Reference System
George: George Jefferson (black counterpart of white bigot Archie Bunker and central character of the television serial called *The Jeffersons*)
George Burns: Nathan Birnbaum
George Eliot: Mary Ann Evans Cross
George Gissing: J. Storer Glouston
George London: George Burnstein
George Orwell: Eric Blair
George Sand: Amandine Aurore Lucie Dupin (Baroness Dudevant)
Georges Duhamel: Denis Thevenin
George Spelvin: John Chapman
Georges Simenon: (pen name—Georges Sim)
Georgia's Oldest City: Savannah
Georgie: George
Georgies: one-dollar bills bearing the portrait of President George Washington
Georgy: George
geos: generator, earth orbital scene; geodetic orbiting satellite
GEOS: Geodetic Orbiting Satellite; Geodynamics Experimental Ocean Satellite
GEOSECS: Geochemical Ocean Sections Study
Geph: Gephyra
GEPI: *Gestioni e Partecipazioni Industriali* (Italian—Industrial Management and Participation)
ger: gerund; gerundial; gerundival; gerundive
Ger: German; Germanic; Germany
GER: Great Eastern Railway
Gerard de Nerval: (pseudonym—Gerard Labrunie)
ger grndng: gerund grinding (pedagogic pedantry)
geriat: geriatrics
Germ: *Germinal* (French—Seedy Month)—beginning March 21st—seventh month of the French Revolutionary Calendar and also title of a novel by Zola
German Ocean: North Sea
Germanophone Countries: Austria, Germany, Liechtenstein, Luxembourg, German-speaking cantons of Switzerland, and many places in the United States where German or German dialects such as Pennsylvania German (Pennsylvania Dutch) are spoken
Germans: the Germans [Former President Nixon's Chief of Staff—H.R. (Bob) Haldeman and Domestic Adviser John Erlichman]
german silver: 50% copper, 30% nickel, 20% zinc
German-speaking Places: (*see* Germanophone Countries)
germi: germicide
Geron: Geronimo
gerontol: gerontology
Gerry: Gerald; Gerard; Gerhard
Gersis: General Electric range safety instrumentation system
gert: graphical evaluation and review technique
Gert: Gertie; Gertrude
Geru: *Gerusalemme* (Italian—Jerusalem)
ges: *gesetzlich* (German—registered)
Ges: (German—G-flat); *Gesellschaft* (German—association; company; society)
GES: Great Eastern Shipping
GESAMP: Group of Experts on the Scientific Aspects of Marine Pollution
gesch: *geschützt* (German—registered)
Gesch: *Geschichte* (German—history)
GESCO: General Electric Supply Corporation
gespeg: (Micmac Indian—end of the earth)—Quebec's Gaspé Peninsula
gest: *gestorben* (German—dead; deceased)
Gestapo: Geheime Staatspolizei (German—State Secret Police)
get.: ground-elapsed time
GET: Getty Oil (stock exchange symbol)
getlo: get locally
getma: get from local manufacturer; purchase for local manufacturer
getol: ground-effect takeoff and landing
Gettysburg Battlefield Painter: Henri Emmanuel Félix Philippoteaux
gev: giga electron volt (10^9 electron volts)
Gew: *Gewehr* (German—rifle)
gez: *gezeichnet* (German—signed)
GEZ: Gosudarstvennoe knigoisdatelstvo (Russian—State Publishing House)
gf: gap filler; generator field; girl friend; globular fibrous; glomerular filtrate; goldfield; ground fog; growth fraction; guiltfree
g-f: globular-fibrous
Gf: Gottfried
GF: General Fireproofing; General Foods; Georgia & Florida (railroad)
G & F: Georgia & Florida (railroad)
gfa: good fair average; gunfire area
GFA: Gardens For All
GFA: *Générale Française (de Construction) Automobile*
g factor: general factor
gfae: government-furnished aerospace equipment
gfci: ground fault circuit interrupter
GFCM: General Fisheries Council for the Mediterranean (FAO)
GFDL: Geophysical Fluid Dynamics Laboratory
gfe: government-furnished equipment
gff: granolithic finish floor
GFG: *Good Food Guide*
GFH: George Frideric Handel
gfi: ground-fault interrupter
Gfk: Gustafsvik
gfm: government-furnished

material
GFMVT: General Foods Moisture Vapor Test
G forces: acceleration forces
gfp: government-furnished property
gfr: gap-filled radar; glomerular filtration rate
GFR: German Federal Republic
gfrc: glass-fiber reinforced cement; glass-fiber reinforced concrete
gfrp: glass-fiber reinforced plastic
GFS: Girls Friendly Society
gfst: ground fuel start tank
GFTU: General Federation of Trade Unions
gfu: glazed facing units
gfut: ground fuel ullage tank
GFWC: General Federation of Women's Clubs
gg: gamma globulin; gas generator; great gross
g-g: ground-to-ground
Gg: Georgian
G-G: Goodrich-Gulf (chemicals)
GGA: Girl Guides Association; Gulf General Atomic
GGAC: Gulf General Atomic Company (formerly General Atomic division of General Dynamics)
GGB: Golden Gate Bridge
GGB & HD: Golden Gate Bridge and Highway District
ggc: ground guidance computer
GGC: Golden Gate College
ggd: great granddaughter
gge: generalized glandular enlargement
g.g.g.: *gummi guttae gambiae* (Latin—gamboge)—cathartic
GGHNP: Golden Gate Highlands National Park (South Africa)
g gl: ground-glass
ggm (GGM): ground-to-ground missile
GGNRA: Golden Gate National Recreation Area (San Francisco)
Ggo: Gallego
GGOC: Goldovsky Grand Opera Company
g gr: great gross
GGR: Gambill Goose Refuge (Texas); Ground Gunnery Range
ggs: great grandson
g-g's: go-go girls
GGS: Ground Guidance System
GGSM: Graduate of the Guildhall School of Music
ggts: gravity-gradient test satellite
gh: grid heading; growth hormone; guardhouse
gh (GH): growth hormone
Gh: Ghana, Commonwealth of
GH: General Hospital; Grosvenor House
GH: *Good Housekeeping*
GHA: Greenwich Hour Angle
GHAA: Group Health Association of America
GhAF: Ghanian Air Force
GHANA: Ghana Airways
GHC: Gray Harbor College
GHDVHS: Grace H Dodge Vocational High School
ghe: ground handling equipment
G H & H: Galveston, Houston & Henderson (railroad)
GHI: Good Housekeeping Institute
Ghirlandaio: Domenico di Tomaso Bigordi
GHMS: Graduate in Homeopathic Medicine and Surgery
GhN: Ghana Navy
ghost.: global horizontal sounding technique
GHQ: General Headquarters
g/hr: gallons per hour
ghrf: growth hormone-releasing factor
ghrh: growth hormone releasing hormone
GHS: Galileo High School; Girls High School
Ght: Ghent
GHz: gigahertz (gigacycle per second)
gi: galvanized iron; gastrointestinal; general issue; gill; globulin insulin; government issue; gross inventory
g-i: granuloma inguinale
Gi: Giles; Guy
GI: Air Guinée; American Soldier (from *gi*—general issue or government issue); Gideons International; Gimbel Brothers (stock exchange symbol); Government of India; Gunner Instructor
gia: grant-in-aid (diplomatese—handout)
GIA: Garuda Indonesian Airways; Gemological Institute of America; Goodwill Industries of America; Gregorian Institute of America; Gummed Industries Association
Giacomo Meyerbeer: Jakob Liebmann Beer
GIAHA: Gilcrease Institute of American History and Art (Tulsa)
Giant of Danish Literature: Hans Christian Andersen
gib: guy in the back
Gib: Gibraltar; Gibraltarian
GIB: Gibraltar, British Crown Colony (airport)
GIBAIR: Gibraltar Airways
Gib(bie): Gilbert
Gibfo: Gibraltar for orders
gibs: guy in the back seat
Gibs: Gibraltarians
Gib-tv: Gibraltar television
GIC: General Investment Corporation
GICA: Green Island Coral Atoll (Queensland)
gi'd: prepared for military-type inspection
Gid: Gideon
GID: General Intelligence Division
gi distress: gastro-intestinal distress
gidp: grounded into double plays
GIEE: Graduate of the Institution of Electrical Engineers
gif (GIF): growth hormone-inhibiting factor
GIF: Rio de Janeiro, Brazil (Galeo Airport)
giga: 10^9
gigo: garbage in, garbage out (acronym describing a computer whose operation is suspect because input is suspect)
GIIS: Graduate Institute of International Studies (Geneva)
GIJ: Guild of Irish Journalists
Gil: Gilbert; Giles
Gilberts: Gilbert Islands
Gilded Age: opulent post-Civil War period in the United States
Gill(y): Gillian
gim: gimmick
GI Mech Eng: Graduate of the Institution of Mechanical Engineers
GIMPEX: Guyana Import-Export
GIMRADA: Geodesy, Intelligence and Mapping Research and Development Agency (US Army)
gin: *giugno* (Italian—June)
Gin: *Ginebra* (Spanish—Geneva)
ging: gingival; gingivitis
ging.: *gingiva* (Latin—gum)
Ginny: Virginia
gins: aborigine girls
G Inst T: Graduate of the Institute of Transport
GI Nuc Eng: Graduate of the Institution of Nuclear Engineers
Ginza: center of downtown Tokyo
gio: *giovedi* (Italian—Thursday)
GIO: Government Information

Organization
g ion: gram ion
Giorgione: Giorgio Barbarelli
giorn: *giornaliero* (Italian—daily); *giornalist* (Italian—journalist)
Giov: Giovanna; Giovanni
gip: get(ting) into publication(s); get(ting) into publishing
GIP: Great Indian Peninsular (railway)
Gippsland: not a country but Victoria—Australia's best-endowed province and holiday paradise for surfers and others
GIPR: Great Indian Peninsula Railway
GIPSY: General Information Processing System
giq: giant imperial quart (of beer)
gir: girder
GIRB: Georgia Inspection and Rating Bureau
GIRLS: Generalized Information Retrieval and Listing System
giro: autogiro
gis: gastrointestinal series
Gis: (German—G-sharp)
GI's: enlisted men; enlisted soldiers in the US Army
GIS: General Mills (stock exchange symbol)
Gisep: Giuseppe
gi spasm: gastro-intestinal spasm
GISS: Goddard Institute of Space Studies (NASA)
git: guitar
GIT: General Information Test; Georgia Institute of Technology
git (GIT): group insurance tour (travel plan)
Gita: *Bhagavad-Gita*
Gitmo: Guantánamo Naval Base (Guantánamo Bay, Cuba)
GIUK: Greenland, Iceland, United Kingdom
Gius: Giuseppe
GIW: Gulf Intracoastal Waterway
gj: grapefruit juice
GJC: Galdhöppigen Jotunheimen Climbers; Gibbs Junior College; Grand Junction Canal
GJD: Grand Junior Deacon
Gjn: Gijon
Gk: Greek
GK: Gaol Keeper
GKC: Gilbert Keith Chesterton
GKD-notation: Gordon-Kendall-Davison notation for chemical formulas (sometimes called Birmingham notation)
Gk I: Greek Isles
GKIAE: *Gossurdarstveinny Komitet po Ispolzovaniyu Atomnoi Energi* (Russian—State Committee for the Use of Atomic Energy)
GKN: Guest, Keen, and Nettlefold
GK & N: Guest, Keen & Nettleworth
gkw: god knows what
gl: glass; glazed; gloss
g/l: grams per liter
Gl: Glagolitic; glucinium
Gl.: *Gloria in excelsis Deo* (Latin—Glory be to God in the highest)
GL: Germanischer Lloyd's (German ship classifier); Great Lakes (load line mark); Greek line
G.L.: Graduate in Law
gla: gingiovolinguo—axial
GLA: General Laboratory Associates; Georgia Library Association; Glasgow, Scotland (airport)
glab: glabrous
glac: glacial
GLAC: Greek Library Association of Cyprus
Glad: Gladstone; Gladwin; Gladys
glads: gladiolas
Glam: Glamorganshire
Glamorgan: Glamorganshire
gland.: glandular
gland.: *glandula* (Latin—gland)
Glas: Glasgow; Glaswegian
GLASLA: Great Lakes—St Lawrence Association
glasphalt: glass + asphalt (paving)
glass: silicon dioxide—SiO_2
glass.: glassware
Glass Capital of Massachusetts: Boston
Glass Capital of New York: Corning
Glass Capital of Ohio: Toledo
Glass Capital of Pennsylvania: Pittsburgh
Glass Center: Toledo, Ohio
glassie: glass playing marble
Glass Menagerie on the East River: United Nations headquarters facing New York City's East River
glassteel: glass + steel (skyscrapers)
glau: glaucous
glauberite: calcium sodium sulfate
glauber's salt: sodium sulfate
glauc: glaucoma
Glav Red: *Glavnyi Redaktor* (Russian—Editor-in-Chief)
glb: glass block
GLB: Greater London Borough (City of London)
GLBA: Great Lakes Booksellers' Association
glc: gas-liquid-chromatographic; global loran (navigation) chart(s)
GLC: Greater London Council; Great Lakes Carbon; Great Lakes Commission
GLCA: Great Lakes College Association
GLCM: Graduate of the London College of Music
gld: guilder
Gld Cst: Gold Coast
gldr: guilder
GLDP: Greater London Development Plan
GLe: *Grand Larousse encyclopedie* (French—Great Larousse Encyclopedia)
gleep: graphite low-energy experimental pile
Glenard's disease: prolapse of one or more internal organs
GLF: Gay Liberation Front
GLFB: Greater London Fund for the Blind
GLFC: Great Lakes Fisheries Commission
Glf Mex: Gulf of Mexico
Glf Str: Gulf Stream
GLHA: Great Lakes Harbor Association
gli: glider
gli (GLI): glucagon-like immunoreactive factor from gastrointestinal mucosa
GLI: General Time (stock exchange symbol); Great Lakes Institute (University of Toronto)
Glimmerglass: James Fenimore Cooper's nickname for Lake Otsego in New York State
GLIS: Greater London Information Service
glit: glittering
glitch: unexpected transient
Glitter Gulch: Reno, Nevada's nickname
Glitz: *Galitzianer* (Yiddish—Galician)—person of Judaic origin from Austrian or Polish Galicia
GLLO: Great Lakes Licensed Officer's Organization
glm: graduated length method
glm: *grand livre du mois* (French—great book of the month)—best-seller
GLM: Gay Liberation Movement
GLMI: Great Lakes Maritime Institute

gln (GLN): glutamine (amino acid)
Gln: Glen (postal abbreviation)
GLNTC: Great Lakes Naval Training Center
GLO: General Land Office; Goddard Launch Operations (NASA); Ground Liaison Office(r); Gunnery Liaison Office(r)
glob: globular; globule
globecomm: global communications
glock: glockenspiel
glomb: glide bomb
glomex: global oceanographic and meteorological experiment (GLOMEX)—1975–1980
Gloria: Gloria Swanson
Glorious Fifty: Glorious fifty states comprising the United States of America
Glos: Gloucestershire
gloss.: glossary
glossies: slick-paper magazines
Gloster: Gloucester
Glostr: Glostrup
glotrac: global tracking
Glou: Gloucester(shire)
Gloucestr: Gloucester
glow.: gross liftoff weight
GLP: Greater London Plan
GLP: Great Lakes Pilot
GLPA: Great Lakes Pilotage Administration
glq: greater than lot quantities
Glr: Gloucester
Gls: Glasgow
GLS: Georgetown Law School; Graduate Library School (University of Chicago); Greene Line Steamers (Mississippi); Gypsy Lore Society
glt: gilt; guide light
glu: glutamic acid
Glubb Pasha: John Bagot Glubb
glv: globe valve
GLV: Gemini Launch Vehicle
GLW: Corning Glass Works (stock exchange symbol)
glwb: glazed wallboard
GLWQB: Great Lakes Water Quality Board (Canada-U.S.)
gly: glycerine; glycerol glycogen
gly (GLY): glycine (amino acid)
glycerol: glycerine—$C_3H_5(OH)_3$
glyp: glyphography; glyptics; glyptography
GLZ: General Bronze Corporation (stock exchange symbol)
gm: general medicine; general mortgage; good morning; gram; guard mail; guided missile; mutual conductance (symbol)
g/m: gallons per minute
gm (GM): group mark (data processing)
gm/1: grams per liter
GM: General Manager; General Medicine; General Motors; Grand Master; Guided Missile; Gunner's Mate; Gustav Mahler
GM: metacentric height (symbol)
G.M.: George Medal
G & M: Globe and Mail (Toronto)
GMA: Gallery of Modern Art; Government Modification Authorization; Grocery Manufacturers of America
GMAA: Gold Mining Association of America
gmac: gaining major air command
GMAC: General Motors Acceptance Corporation
GMAIC: Guided Missile and Aerospace Intelligence Committee
G-man: FBI law-enforcement officer also known as a special agent
GMAT: Greenwich Mean Astronomical Time
GMATS: General Motors Air Transport Section
gm-aw: gram atomic weight
gmb: good merchandise brand
GMB: Georg Morris Brandes (originally Cohen)
GMBE: Grand Master (of the Order of the) British Empire
GmbH: Gesellschaft mit beschränkter Haftung (German—incorporated, limited liability company)
gmbl: gimbal
gmc: gun motor carriage
Gmc: Germanic
GMC: General Medical Council; General Motors Corporation; George Mason College; Guggenheim Memorial Concerts; Guided Missile Command; Guided Missile Committee
g-m counter: Geiger-Müller counter for measuring cosmic rays and radioactivity
GMDRL: General Motors Defense Research Laboratories
G-men: FBI law-enforcement officers
g met: gun-metal
GMF: Glass Manufacturers Federation
GMFC: General Mining and Finance Corporation
Gmh: Grangemouth
GM-H: General Motors-Holden (Australia)
GMI: General Motors Institute
GMIA: Gelatin Manufacturers Institute of America
gmk: grand master keyed
GML: Gold Mining Lease
gmldg: garnish molding
GMNNR: Glasson Moss National Nature Reserve (England)
GMNP: Guadalupe Mountains National Park (Texas)
Gmo: Guillermo (Spanish—William)
GM & O: Gulf, Mobile & Ohio (railroad)
g mol: g molecule
GMOO: Guided Missile Operations Office(r)
gmp (GMP): guanosine monophosphate
GMP: Green Mansion Properties
gmq: good merchantable quality
gmr: ground mapping radar
GMRD: Guided Missiles Range Division (Pan American World Airways)
gms: guidance monitor set
gm & s: general, medical, and surgical
Gms: Grimsby
GMS: General Medical Services
GMST: General Military Subjects Test
GMT: General American Transportation (stock exchange symbol); Greenwich Mean Time; Greenwich Meridian Time
GMT: Geo Marine Technology
GMTC: General Motors Technical Center; Glutamate Manufacturers Technical Committee
GMTL: Goudy Memorial Typographic Laboratory (Newhouse Communications Center—Syracuse University)
gmts: guided missile test set
g-m tube: geiger-müller tube
gmv: gram molecular volume
gmw: gram molecular weight
GMWU: General and Municipal Workers Union
gn: general; green; golden number; good night; guinea (21 shillings); gun
g:n: glucose-nitrogen (ratio)
GN: Great Northern (railroad); great novel (in sense of great American novel as discussed in World-War-I days by e.e. cummings, John Dos Passos, Gilbert Seldes, and their generation of writers)
GN: Gas Natural (Spanish—natural gas)

G.N.: Graduate Nurse
GN_2: gaseous nitrogen
GN_2 s/a: gaseous nitrogen storage area
GNAL: Georgia Nuclear Aircraft Laboratory
GNAS: Grand National Archery Society
gnc: general nuclear war
gn & c: guidance, navigation, and control
GNC: General Nursing Council
gnd: ground
gne: gross national effluent
gni (GNI): gross national income
gnl: general
GNL: Georgia Nuclear Laboratory
GNM: Ghana National Museum
GNMA: Government National Mortgage Association
GNN: Great Northern Nekoosa
g noz: grease nozzle
g np: gas, nonpersistent
gnp (GNP): gross national product
GNP: Glacier National Park (one in British Columbia and another in Montana); Gombe National Park (Tanzania); Gorongoza National Park (Mozambique); gross national product
GNP & BL: Great Northern Pacific & Burlington Lines (merger of Chicago, Burlington & Quincy; Great Northern; Northern Pacific; Pacific Coast Railroad; Spokane, Portland & Seattle Railway)
GNPC: Great Northern Paper Company
gnr: gunner; gunnery
GNR: Great Northern Railway
GNRA: Gateway National Recreation Area (New York City's designation by the Department of the Interior)
g/n ratio: glucose-nitrogen ratio
gnrl: general
gnry: gunnery
gns: guineas
Gns: Guernsey
GNSRA: Great North of Scotland Railway Association
GNTC: Girls' Nautical Training Corps
gnte: *gerente* (Spanish—manager)
GNTO: Greek National Tourist Organization
Gny Sgt: Gunnery Sergeant
Go: gadolinium; Gothic
G^o: Gonzalo (Spanish)
GO: General Office; general order(s); Gulf Oil (stock exchange symbol)
GO_2: gaseous oxygen
go': gore
gob.: gobbledygook; good ordinary brand
gob: *gobierno* (Spanish—government)
Gob: *Gobernador* (Spanish—Governor)
G o B: Government of Belize (formerly British Honduras)
GObC: Ground Observers Corps (Canada)
gob^o: *gobierno* (Spanish—government)
Gobr: *Gobernador* (Spanish—Governor)
GOC: General Officer Commanding; Ground Observer Corps; Gulf Oil Company
GOC in C: General Officer Commanding in Chief
goco: government-owned contractor-operated
g.o.d.: good old days
god. (GOD): government observing device (acronym suggesting big brother is watching)
God of Animals, Crops, Fertility, Prophecy, and Rural Life: Faunus (Roman); Pan (Greek)
God of Blacksmithing and Forges: Hephaistos (Greek); Vulcan (Roman)
God of Bloodshed and War: the Greek god Ares; the Roman god Mars
God of Boundaries: Terminus (Roman) whose name in Latin means boundary
God of the Christians and Jews: Jehovah
God of Corn and Grain: Robigus (Roman)
God of Creation and Destruction: Siva (Hindu)
God of Cunning Dexterity: Hermes (Greek); Mercury (Roman)
God of the Dead and the Underworld: Dis (Roman); Hades or Hiades (Greek); Mantus (Etruscan); Pluto (Roman)
God of Death: Mors (Roman); Thanatos (Greek)
God of Dreams: Morpheus—Greek god of dreams and sleep
God of Earth: Tellumo (Roman)—his name is derived from the Latin *tellus* meaning earth
God of Eloquence and Oratory: Hermes (Greek); Mercury (Roman)
Godfather of American Liberty: Thomas Paine
God of Fertility: Priapos (Greek); Priapus (Roman)
God of Fields, Pastures, Shepherds, and Woods: Faunus (Roman); Pan (Greek)
God of Fire: Agni, according to the Hindus
God of Fire and Forges: Hephaestus (Greek); Vulcan (Roman)
God of Forests, Herds, Plants, and Trees: Silvanus (Roman) from whose name is derived *silva*—Latin for wood
God of Gods and Ruler of Heaven and Earth: Zeus (Greek); Jove or Jupiter (Roman)
God of Good Harvests and Successful Undertakings: *Eventus Bonus* (Latin—Good Results)—a Roman god
God of the Greeks: Panhellenius or Zeus
God of Healing and Medicine: Asclepius (Greek); Aesculapius (Roman)
God of Heaven: Uranus (Greek); Coleus (Roman)
God of Heaven, Lightning, Rain, Storm, and Thunder: Indra, according to the Hindus
God of Inanimate Dreams: Phantastus (Greek)
God of the Infernal Regions: Dis (Greek); Pluto (Roman); Yama (Hindu); etc.
God-Intoxicated Man: Benedictus de Spinoza
God of Landmarks: Terminus (Roman)
God of Light: Mithra (Aryan, Indian, Persian)
God of Love: Cupid (Roman); Eros (Greek); Krishna (Hindu)
God of Marriage: Hymen, according to Greek mythology, also leader of the nuptial chorus and personification of the wedding feast
God of the Mohammedans: Allah
God of Music, Poetry, and the Sun: Apollo (Roman) or Apollon (Greek)
God of the Nile and Vegetation: Osiris (Egyptian)
God of Purification: (Februus (Roman)
God of Revelry and Wine: Dionysus (Greek); Bacchus (Roman)
God of the Romans: Jupiter—supreme god
God of the Sea: Neptune (Roman); Poseidon (Greek)

God of Skill: Hermes (Greek); Mercury (Roman)—the winged cap-and-shoes messenger of Jove or Jupiter (Zeus) presided over anything requiring dexterity and skill—commerce, gymnastics, medicine, thieving, wrestling, et cetera; in one hand he bore a rod entwined by two serpents (the caduceus)—symbol of the medical profession

God of Sleep: Hypnos (Greek); Somnus (Roman)

God of Soil Fertilization: Saturn or Stercutus (Roman)—*stercus* is Latin for dung

God of Springs: Fons (Roman)

God of the Sun: Adonis (Syrian); Apollo (Roman); Apollon (Greek); Baal (Chaldean); Helios Hyperion (Greek in Homer's time); Horus (symbolized in Upper Egypt by a hawk); Mithras (Persian); Moloch (Canaanite); Osiris (Egyptian); Ra or Re (symbolized in Egypt's Old Kingdom by an obelisk); Sol Invictus (Latin—Sun Invincible)—Romans shortened this to Sol and to this day Old Sol is the sun's nickname; Surya (Hindu)

God of Time: Cronus (Greek); Saturn (Roman)

God of Trade and Travelers: Hermes (Greek); Mercury (Roman)

God of the Underworld: (Dis (Roman); Hades or Haides (Greek); Mantus (Etruscan); Pluto (Roman)

God of Vineyards and Wine: Bacchus (Roman); Dionysus (Greek)

God of War: Ares (Greek); Mars (Roman)

God of Wine: Bacchus (Roman); Dionysus (Greek)

Goddess of Agriculture: Ceres or Vacuna (Roman); Demeter (Greek)

Goddess of Animals, Crops, Fertility, Prophecy, and Rural Life: Bona Dea or Bona Mater or Fauna (Roman)

Goddess of Arts, Crafts, and Sciences: Athena (Greek); Minerva (Roman)

Goddess of Avenging Justice: Nemesis (Greek)

Goddess of Beauty and Love: Aphrodite (Greek); Venus (Roman)

Goddess of Birth: the Roman goddess Carmenta also known as Carmentis

Goddess of the Breeze: Aura (Greek)

Goddess of Bridesmaids: Juno Pronuba (Roman)

Goddess of Burials, Corpses, and Funerals: Libitina (Roman)

Goddess of Cattle and Pastures: Pales (Roman)

Goddess of Chance: Fortuna (Roman)

Goddess of Chaos, Sickness, and Death: Kali (Hindu)

Goddess of Childbirth and Prophecy: Roman names include those of Carmenta, Juno Lucina, and Postverta

Goddess of the Crops: the Greek goddesses Auxesia and Demeter share this appellation

Goddess of the Dead: Mania (Roman)

Goddess of Destiny or Fate: Necessitas (Roman)

Goddess of Discord and Strife: Discordia (Roman) or Eris (Greek); each credited with throwing the apple of discord and strife in revenge for not being invited to a wedding

Goddess of Domestic Animals: Bubona (Roman)

Goddess of Earth: Gaea or Rhea (Greek); Cybele, Tellus, or Terra (Roman)

Goddess of Faith, Honesty, and Oaths: Fides (Roman)

Goddess of Fame: Fama (Roman); Pheme (Greek)

Goddess of Family Harmony: Verplaca (Roman) also spelled Virplaca

Goddess of Famine: Fames (Roman goddess whose Latin name means famine or hunger)

Goddess of the Fertile Earth: Opalia or Ops (Roman)

Goddess of Fertility, Love, Lust, and War: Ishtar (Assyrian and Babylonian)

Goddess of Fertility and Procreation: Aphrodite (Greek); Isis (Egyptian); Mylitta (Assyrian); Venus (Roman)

Goddess of Fertility and Purity: Bona Dea (Roman)

Goddess of Fire: Hestia (Greek); Vesta (Roman)

Goddess of Flowers, Gardens, and Love: Flora (Roman)

Goddess of Freedom: Libertas (Roman)

Goddess of Fruit Trees: Pomona (Roman)

Goddess of Funerals: Naenia (Roman)

Goddess of the Future: Antevorta (Roman)

Goddess of Gardens and Fruit Trees: Pomona (Roman)

Goddess of Good Faith: Fides (Roman goddess whose Latin name means faith)

Goddess of Groves, Orchards, and Woods: Feronia (Roman)

Goddess of Harmony: Concordia (Roman)

Goddess of Healing: Iaso (Greek)

Goddess of Health: Hygeia (Roman); Hygieia (Greek)

Goddess of the Hearth: Hestia (Greek); Vesta (Roman)

Goddess of Heaven: Hera (Greek); Juno (Roman)

Goddess of the Home: Hera (Greek); Juno (Roman)

Goddess of Home Security: the Roman goddess Cardea or Carna who guarded the door hinges and locks

Goddess of Horses: Epona (Gallic); Hippona (Roman)

Goddess of Hunting and the Moon: Artemis (Greek); Diana (Roman)

Goddess of Imposters and Thieves: Laverna (Roman)

Goddess of Law and Order: Eunomia or Themis (Greek); Justitia (Roman)

Goddess of Leisure and Repose: Vacuna (Roman)

Goddess of Lightning: Fulgora (Roman)

Goddess of Love and Lust: Aphrodite (Greek); Venus (Roman)

Goddess of Magic, Sorcery, and the Underworld: Hecate or Hekate (Greek—working afar); Trivia (Latin—of the three ways) and hence the Romans placed her wherever three roads met

Goddess of Married Women: Juno Matronalis (Roman)

Goddess of Memory: Mnemosyne (Greek)—mother of the muses; her name gives rise to mnemonic—an aid to memory such as the lines beginning *Thirty days hath September, April, June, and November*

Goddess of Menstruation: Mena (Roman)

Goddess of Midwives: Deverra (Roman); Eileitia (Greek)

Goddess of the Moon: Luna (Roman); Selene (Greek)

Goddess Mother of the World:

Mount Everest
Goddess of Nature: Cybele (Roman) or Kubele (Greek)—sometimes called Mistress of the Animals
Goddess of Newborn Babes: Levana (Roman)
Goddess of Night: Nux (Greek) sometimes spelled Nyx
Goddess of Nursing Mothers: Rumina (Roman)
Goddess of Passion: Stimula (Roman)—her name, translated from Latin, means she who excites
Goddess of the Past: Postvorta (Roman)
Goddess of Peace: known to the Romans as Concordia, Irene, or Pax, and to the Greeks as Eirene
Goddess of Profit: Laverna (Roman)
Goddess of Public Welfare: Salus (Roman) whose Latin name means health
Goddess of the Rainbow: Iris (Roman)
Goddess of Robbers: Furina (Roman)
Goddess of Rome: Roma
Goddess of the Sea and Seaports: Matuta (Roman)—originally goddess of the dawn
Goddess of Sensual Pleasure: Voluptas (Roman)
Goddess of Shepherds: Pales (Roman)
Goddess of Silence: Muta (Roman)
Goddess of Storms and Winds: Tempestes (Roman)
Goddess of Suckling Infants: Rumina (Roman)
Goddess of Treachery: Fraus (Roman)
Goddess of Truth: Alethia (Greek); Veritas (Roman)
Goddess of the Underworld: Persephone (Greek); Proserpina (Roman)
Goddess of Vice: Kakia (Greek)
Goddess of Virgins: Juno Virginalis (Roman)
Goddess of War: Bellona (Roman); Enyo (Greek)
Goddess of Wisdom: Athena (Greek); Minerva (Roman)
Goddess of Youth: Hebe (Greek); Juventus (Roman)
godsd: *godsdienst* (Dutch—religion)
goe: gas, oxygen, ether (mixture)
GOES: Geostationary Operational Environmental Satellite
gof: good old Friday
GOFAR: Global Ocean Floor Analysis and Research
gogo: government-operated government-owned
gogs: goggles
Goi: Goidelic
GoI: Government of Indonesia
GOI: Gallup Organization Incorporated
goin': going
GOIN: *Gossudarstvienny Okeanograficheskiy Institut* (Russian—State Oceanography Institute)
Golda: Golda Meir (Israel's first woman prime minister)
Gold Coast: Africa's Ghana—formerly the Gold Coast; Australia's beach-fronted resort area extending from Coolangatta to Southport near Brisbane; Florida's resort coast extending from Key West to Palm Beach
Golden Age: mankind's age of innocence where there was springtime all the time and happiness, right, and truth prevailed; there were no bodily ailments and nobody had to work as the earth gave men all they needed, according to Greek and Roman mythology; (see *Siglo de Oro*)
Golden Age of Greece: 5th and 4th centuries before the Christian era when Aristotle, Euripides, Plato, and Sophocles were contemporaries or near contemporaries
Golden Age of Opera: late 1800s and early 1900s
Golden Age of Rome: the reign of Augustus from 27 B.C.E. to 14 A.D.
golden beryl: heliodor
Golden Century: Nineteenth Century
Golden City of a Hundred Spires: Prague
Golden Flutist: Georges Barrère
Golden Gate: entrance to San Francisco Bay
Golden Gate City: San Francisco
Golden Horn: Istanbul's harbor formed by the curved arm of the Bosporus
Golden Horseshoe: Hamilton-Toronto-Oshawa industrial complex along Lake Ontario
Golden Hyphen: Winston-Salem, North Carolina
Golden Isles: Jekyll, Saint Simons, and Sea Island off Brunswick, Georgia
Golden Key to the Fjords: Stavanger, Norway
Golden Peninsula: Malay Peninsula
Golden Poppy: California's state flower
Golden Province: Canada's Ontario
Golden Rock: Sint Eustatius (Netherlands Antilles)
Goldenrod: state flower of Kentucky and Nebraska
Golden State: California's official nickname
Golden Triangle: point of downtown Pittsburgh where the three rivers meet: the Allegheny, Monongehala, and Ohio rivers; industrialized northern Europe where the three points are Birmingham, Paris, and the Ruhr; opium-productive fields where Burma, Laos, and Thailand meet near southern Yunnan, China
Goldhunter(s): Californian(s)
Goldie: Gold; Golden; Goldilocks; Goldsborough; Goldsmith; Goldsworthy; Goldwin; Goldwyn
Gold Rush Town: Nome, Alaska
Golf: code for letter G
Golftown: Pinehurst, North Carolina
Gollancz: Victor Gollancz Ltd
gom (GOM): government-owned material
Gom: God's own medicine (opiates)
G.O.M.: Grand Old Man (sobriquet for William Ewart Gladstone)
GOMA: Good Outdoor Manners Association
gon: *goniff* (Yiddish—thief)
go'n': going
gond(s): gondola(s); railroad car(s); car(s)
GONP: Gal Oya National Park (Ceylon)
Gonz: Gonzáles
Goo: Goole
GOO: Get Oil Out (of Santa Barbara, California)
Goober(s): nickname for peanut (goober) grower(s) and particularly natives of Alabama, Georgia, and North Carolina where so many goobers are grown
Good Gray Poet: Walt Whitman
Good Queen Bess: Queen Elizabeth I of England (1558 to 1603)
Good Richard: (pseudonym—Benjamin Franklin)
goof.: general on-line oriented

function
googol: 10 raised to the 100th power (10^{100})
GOP: Grand Old Party (Republican)
GO & P: Griffith Observatory and Planetarium
Gopher(s): Minnesotan(s)
Gopher State: Minnesota
Gor: Gorki
GOR: General Operating Room; General Operational Requirements
GORA: Government Oil Refineries Administration
Gordie: Gordon
Gordon Pasha: Charles George Gordon
GORF: Goddard's Optical Research Facility
g org: great organ
gorill(s): gorilla(s)
gorm: gormandize(r)
gos: *gosudarstvo* (Russian—state)—as in *gosplan*—state plan
Gos: *Gossudarstvo* (Russian—State)
GOS: General Operating Specification(s); Global (weather) Observing Systems
GOSS: Ground Operational Support System
GOST: Goddard Satellite Tracking
got. (GOT): glutamic oxaloacetic transaminase
Goten: (German naval contraction—Gotenhafen)—Gdynia's name during World-War-II Nazi occupation
goth.: gothic type
Goth.: Gothic
Göt(h): Göteborg (Gothenburg)
Gotham: New York City
Gothamite(s): native(s) of New York City; nickname derived from *The Three Wise Men of Gotham* by Washington Irving
Gothoburgum: (Latin—Göteborg) — Gothenburg
Gotorum: (Latin—Lund)
Gott: Gottingen
gou: *gourde* (Haitian currency)
Gou: Goudy
Gouv: Gouverneur
gov: government
Gov: Governor
govg: governing
Gov Gen: Governor General
Gov Is: Governor's Island
govt: government
govtalk: government talk
gox: gaseous oxygen
gp: gas, persistent; general paralysis; general practice; general practitioner; general purpose; geographic position; grateful patient; gratitude patient; guinea pig; gun pointer
g-p: general purpose
g/p: *giro postal* (Spanish—money order)
G6P: glucose 6-phosphate
GP: Gaspesian Park (Quebec); general public; Georgia-Pacific (stock exchange symbol); Giacomo Puccini
G-P: Georgia-Pacific (forest products); Gunier-Preston zone
GP: *Generalpause* (German—general pause (musical term))
gpa: grade-point average
GPA: General Practitioners' Association
gpad: gallons per acre per day
GPATS: General-Purpose Automatic Test System
gpb: glossopharyngeal breathing
gpc: gallons per capita; general purpose computer; gypsum-plaster ceiling
GPC: Georgia Power Company; Gulf Park College
Gp Capt: Group Captain
gpcd: gallons per capita per day
Gp Cmdr: Group Commander
Gp Comdr: Group Commander
GPCT: George Peabody College for Teachers
gpd: gallons per day
GPDA: Gypsum Plasterboard Development Association
GPDS: General-Purpose Display System
GPDST: Girls' Public Day School Trust
GPE: General Precision Equipment
Gp. Eng.: Geophysical Engineer
gperf: ground passive electronic reconnaissance facility
GPES: Ground Proximity Extraction System
gpf: gasproof
Gp Fl: group flashing (light)
gpg: grains per gallon
gph: gallons per hour
G.Ph.: Graduate in Pharmacy
GPHI: Guild of Public Health Inspectors
gpi: general paralysis of the insane (symptom of tertiary syphilis); ground-position indicator (aviation)
gpi (GPI): glucosephosphate isomerase
gpl: geographic position locator; grams per liter
GPI: General Printing Ink
GPII: Geist Picture Interest Inventory
gpl: geographic position locator
GPL: General Precision Laboratory
GPLC: Guild of Professional Launderers and Cleaners
gply: gingivoplasty
gpm: gallons per minute
GPM: General Preventive Medicine; Grand Past Master
GPMS: Gross Performance Measuring System (USAF)
GPNITL: Great Plains National Instructional Television Library
GPO: General Post Office; Government Printing Office
Gp Occ: group occulting (light)
GPR: Glider Pilot Regiment
GPRA: General Practice Reform Association
gps: gallons per second
gp's: galley proofs
g-p's: general practitioners (GPs)
Gps: general-parents motion pictures (for youngsters only with parent's consent)
GPS: Graduated Pension Scheme
gpt (GPT): glutamic pyruvic transaminase
GPT: Guild of Professional Toastmasters
gp th: group therapy
GPU: General Postal Union
GPU: *Gosudarstvennoe Politicheskoe Upravlenie* (Russian—State Political Administration)—secret police—*Gay-Pay-Ooo*
GPV: *Gereformeerd Politiek Verbond* (Dutch—Reformed Political Union)—Calvinist party
gpw: gross plated weight; gypsum-plaster wall
GPW: Geneva (Convention Relative to Treatment of) Prisoners of War
GPX: Greyhound Package Express
GQ: general quarters
GQNM: Gran Quivira National Monument
gr: gear; grab rod; grade; grain; gram; grammar; gross; group
Gr: Great (postal abbreviation); Grashof number; Grecian; Greece; Greek
GR: B.F. Goodrich (stock exchange symbol); General Radio; General Reconnaissance; General Reserve; Georgius Rex (King George); Grand Recorder; Grasse River (railroad); Graves Registration;

Group Report; Gunnery Range
GRA: Governmental Research Association; Grass Roots Association; W.R. Grace & Company (stock exchange symbol)
gr ab: grade ability
GRAB: Group Rooms Availability Bank (hotel-motel convention service)
GRACE: Grace Agencies; Grace Chemicals; Grace Line; W.R. Grace and Company (stock exchange symbol); graphic arts composing equipment; group routing and exchange equipment (telephone)
Grace Greenwood: Sara Jane Clarke Lippincott's pseudonym
grad: gradient; grading; graduate
grad.: *graditim* (Latin—by degrees)
Grad IAE: Graduate of the Institution of Automobile Engineers
Grad IM: Graduate of the Institution of Metallurgists
Grad Inst BE: Graduate of the Institution of British Engineers
Grad Inst P(hys): Graduate of the Institute of Physics
Grad Inst R(frg): Graduate of the Institute of Refrigeration
Grad IRI: Graduate of the Institution of the Rubber Industry
grad(s): gradient(s); graduate(s)
GRADS: Great Falls Air Defense Sector
Grad SE: Graduate of the Society of Engineers
Grad Soc Eng: Graduate of the Society of Engineers
Graduate of Oxford: John Ruskin's pseudonym
Graffiti Capital: defaced buildings, buses, streets, and subways of New York City
gral: *general* (Spanish—general)
Gral: General (Spanish—General)
gram.: grammar; gramophone
'gram: cablegram; radiogram; telegram
Grampians: Grampian Hills of Scotland or the Grampian Mountains of Australia
gran: granite
gran.: *granulatus* (Latin—granulated)
Gran: Granada; Granjon
Granary of Canada: Saskatchewan
Granary of Russia: Ukraine's vast wheat fields
Granary of Sweden: Skåne
Gran Colombia: (Spanish—Great Colombia) — post-colonial consolidation of Colombia, Ecuador, and Venezuela
Grand Canyon State: Arizona's official nickname
Grand Cham of Literature: Dr Samuel Johnson
Grand Divide: Continental Divide
Grand Duke: Duke of Wellington
Grand Inquisitor: Tomás de Torquemada
Grandma Moses: Anne Mary Moses
Grandmother of Boston: preacher-reformer-teacher Elizabeth Palmer Peabody
grando: *grandioso* (Italian—grandiose)
Grand Old Lady of Fifty-seventh Street: Carnegie Hall
Grand Old Lady of Opera: Ernestine Schumann-Heink
Grand Old Man: William Ewart Gladstone—four times Prime Minister of Great Britain
Grand Old Man of American Labor: Samuel Gompers
Grand Old Party: Republican Party of the United States—the GOP
Grandsire of American Painting: Benjamin West
Grand Zohra: General Charles de Gaulle
Granger States: farm-filled Illinois, Iowa, Minnesota, and Wisconsin
Granite boy(s): New Hampshirite(s)
Granite Center: Barre, Vermont
Granite City: Aberdeen, Scotland
Granite Island: Corsica
Granite State: New Hampshire's official nickname
Gran Libertador: (Spanish—Great Liberator—Simón Bolivar)
Granny: Grandmother
grape sugar: glucose ($C_6H_{12}O_6$)
graph.: graphology
grapheme: written language sym bol representing an oral language code
graphite: carbon
gr ar: grinding arbor
gras: generally recognized as safe (beverage or food additives)
grat: graticule
grats: congratulations
grav: gravimetric; gravitation; gravity
Graveyard of the Atlantic: nickname shared by Cape Hatteras, North Carolina and Sable Island off Nova Scotia
grazo: *grazioso* (Italian—gracious)
grb: granolithic base
GRBI: Gardeners' Royal Benevolent Institution
grbm (GRBM): global-range ballistic missile
Gr Br: Grande Bretagne (French—Great Britain); Great Britain
Gr Brit: Great Britain
GRBS: Gardeners' Royal Benevolent Society
GRC: *Gendarmarie Royale du Canada* (French—Royal Gendarmarie of Canada)—Royal Canadian Mounted Police
GRCM: Graduate of the Royal College of Music
Gr Cpt: Group Captain
grd: grind; ground; ground detector; guard
Grd: Ground (postal abbreviation)
Gr D: Grand Duchy
GRD: Geophysics Research Directorate
GRDC: Gulf Research and Development Company
Grdn: *The Guardian* (London and Manchester)
GRE: Graduate Record Examination; Guardian Royal Exchange
Great: *The Great* Symphony No. 9 in C major by Schubert (formerly No. 7)
Great Agnostic: Colonel Robert G. Ingersoll
Great American Pastime: baseball, basketball, and football vie for this nickname
Great Britain: England, Scotland, and Wales—GB
Great Cham of Literature: Dr Samuel Johnson
Great Charter: Magna Charta
Great Commoner: Henry Clay, William Ewart Gladstone, William Pitt (the Elder Pitt also known as the Earl of Chatham), and Thomas Paine have all borne this nickname
Great Compromiser: Henry Clay—U.S. Senator from Kentucky
Great Debunker: H(enry) L(ouis) Mencken—editor of *The American Mercury*
Great Destroyer: syphilis
Great Dissenter: Supreme Court

Justice Oliver Wendell Holmes, Jr
Great Divide: Rocky Mountains
Great Duke: Duke of Wellington
Great Emancipator: Abraham Lincoln—sixteenth President of the United States and author of the *Emancipation Proclamation*
Great Engineer: Herbert Hoover—thirty-first President of the United States
Greater Antilles: Cuba, Hispaniola (Dominican Republic and Haiti), Jamaica, Puerto Rico
Greatest American Jurist: John Marshall—Chief Justice of the Supreme Court from 1801 to 1835
Greatest Artist of the South Seas: Paul Gauguin
Greatest Composer: Haydn's name for Mozart
Greatest Heavyweight Boxer: Jack Johnson
Greatest Show on Earth: Barnum and Bailey—Ringling Brothers Circus
Great Lakes: (east to west) Ontario, Erie, Huron, Michigan, Superior
Great Lakes Province: Ontario on lakes Ontario, Erie, Huron, and Superior
Great Lake State: Michigan
Great Lakes States: New York, Pennsylvania, Ohio, Michigan, Indiana, Illinois, Wisconsin, Minnesota
Great Land: The Great Land—Alaska
Great Moralist: Dr Samuel Johnson
Great Plains: plains and prairies of Canada and the United States east of the Rockies
Great Sea: Biblical name for the Mediterranean
Great Smoke: London's unenviable nickname before air-pollution control was enforced
Great Smoky: Great Smoky National Park
Great Society: (administration of Lyndon Baines Johnson—thirty-sixth President of the United States)
Great Stink: nickname of the Thames River before English conservationists set out to clean up its pollution
Great Stone Face: Daniel Webster; Old Man of the Mountain also known as Profile Mountain in New Hampshire's White Mountains
Great Wet Ditch: British nickname for the English Channel
Great White Father: (American Indian term—the President of the United States)
Great White Way: New York City's brightly-illuminated theatrical section of midtown Broadway
Grec: *Grécia* (Italian or Spanish—Greece); *Grécia* (Portuguese—Greece)
Greek Isles: Cyclades, Dodecanese, Ionian, Sporades
Greek Muses: (*see* Nine Muses)
Greeks: Greek Islands; Greek people
Green.: Greenland
green flag: all-clear signal; express; go-ahead
Green Isle: Ireland
green light: all-clear signal; go-ahead signal; safety signal; starboard side of aircraft, ships, or other vessels
Green Mountain boy(s): Vermonter(s)
Green Mountain City: Montpelier, Vermont
Green Mountain State: Vermont's official nickname
green vitriol: copperas, ferrous sulfate ($FeSO_4 \cdot 7H_2O$)
Grefco: General Refractories
Greg: Gregorian; Gregory
Greg°: Gregorio (Spanish — Gregory)
Gren: Grenada
Grenadines: Grenadine Islands
Grepo: *Grenzpolizei* (German—border-control police)
Greta: Greta Garbo; Margaret
Greta Garbo: Greta Gustafson
Gretchen: Marguerite
grf (GRF): growth hormone-releasing factor
GRF: Gerald Rudolph Ford—thirty-eighth President of the United States; Grassland Research Foundation; Gravity Research Foundation
gr Fl: *grosse Flöte* (German—full-size flute)
GRFMA: Grand Rapids Furniture Market Association
gr fx: grinding fixture
GRI: Geothermal Resources International; Government of the Ryukyu Islands
G.R.I.: *Georgius Rex et Imperator* (Latin—George, King and Emperor)
grif (GRIF): growth hormone-inhibiting factor
Grif: Griffin; Griffith; Griffiths
griff: griffin
grip: (motion-picture and tv slang—stage hand delegated to move camera and sound equipment)
GRIP: Grass Roots Improvement Program
grit.: gradual reduction in tensions
GRITS: Goddard Range Instrumentation Tracking System (NASA)
GRJC: Grand Rapids Junior College
Grk: Greenock
Gr-L: Graeco-Latin
gr lp: ground lamp
Gr Lt: Gunner Lieutenant
grm: gram
grn: green
g/r/n: goods received note
Gr.N.: Graduate Nurse
Grnd: Grand (postal abbreviation)
grnl: *giornalista* (Italian—newspaperman)
Grnld: Greenland
grnsh: greenish
grnt: guarantee
gro: gross
Gro: Guerrero
GRO: Greenwich Royal Observatory
GROBDM: General Register Office of Births, Deaths, and Marriages
groc: grocer(y)
Groen: *Groenlandia* (Italian or Spanish—Greenland); *Groenlândia* (Portuguese—Greenland)
GROIN: Garbage Removal Or Income Now
Grolier: Grolier Society
grom: grommet
Gron: Groningen
Gronaicum: (Latin—Greenwich) —also known as Gronvicum
groot: (Dutch—great)
gros.: *grossus* (Latin—coarse; gross)
Grosset: Grosset & Dunlap
Grotius: Hugo de Groot
Groucho Marx: Julius Marx
Grove's: Sir George Grove's *Dictionary of Music and Musicians*
grp: ground relay panel
Grp: Group
grp's: gross rating points
GRR: Grand Rapids, Michigan (airport)
grreg: graves registration
GrReg: graves registration
grs: grains; grass; greens
gr-s: government rubber plus styrene (buna-S synthetic rub-

ber)
GRS: General Railway Signal; Graves Registration Service
GRSE: Guild of Radio Service Engineers
Gr S-Lt: Gunner Sub-Lieutenant
GRSM: Graduate of the Royal Schools of Music (Royal Academy of Music and the Royal College of Music)
grt: gross register(ed) tonnage (tons)
grtg: grating
gr tons: gross tons
gr tr: graphite treatment
gr Tr: *grosse Trommel* (German-bass drum)
GRU: *Glavnoye Razvedyvatelnoye Upravlenie* (Russian—Intelligence Directorate of the Red Army)—(*q.v. VOT*)
grub.: grubby; grubstreet (Grubstreet, according to Dr Johnson—"Originally the name of a street in Moorfield in London, much inhabited by writers of small histories, dictionaries, and temporary poems; whence any mean production is called *grubstreet*."
Grv: Grove
Grwd: Grunewald
gr wt: gross weight
gry: grocery; gross redemption yield
gs: galvanized steel; gauss; german silver; glide slope; grandson; ground speed; guardship; guineas
g/s: gallons per second
gs (GS): group separator character (data processing)
Gs: general motion pictures (for the general public); Gomes
GS: General Schedule (civil service classification system); General Secretary; General Service; General Staff; General Support; Geochemical Society; Geological Survey; Gerontological Society; Gillette (stock exchange symbol); Girl Scouts; Grand Secretary; Gunnery School; Gunnery Sergeant
G-S: Gallard-Schlesinger
gsa: gross soluble antigen
GSA: Garden Seed Association; General Services Administration; Genetics Society of America; Geological Society of America; Girl Scouts of America; Gourd Society of America
G & SA: Gulf and South American (steamship line)
GSAI: General Services Administration Institute
gsb: gypsum sheathing board
GSB: Government Savings Bank
GSBAA: General Service Board of Alcoholics Anonymous
gs bot: glass-stoppered bottle
gsbr: gravel-surface built-up roof
gsc: geodetic spacecraft
GSC: General Staff Corps; Geological Survey of Canada; Group Study Course
GSCBA: Georgia State College of Business Administration
GSCW: General Society of Colonial Wars
GSD: General Supply Depot
GSDFJ: Ground Self-Defense Force Japan
GSDNM: Great Sand Dunes National Monument
gse (GSE): ground-service equipment; ground-support equipment
GSE: Graduate School of Education (Harvard University)
GSED: Ground Support Equipment Division (USN)
gsf: general scientific framework
GSF: General Support Force (USAF)
GSFC: Goddard Space Flight Center
GSFLT: Graduate School Foreign Language Test
gsfu: glazed structural facing units
GSGB: Geological Survey of Great Britain
GSGS: Geographical Section—General Staff
GSGS maps: General Staff, Geographical Section (British War Office) maps covering Africa, Asia, the East Indies, and Europe
GSH: glutathione
gshr: grand-slam home run(s)
gshv: globe stop hose valve
gsi: ground speed indicator
GSI: General Safety Inspection; General Safety Inspector; General Service Infantry; General Steel Industries; Geological Survey of Israel; Geophysical Services International; Government Source Inspection
G & SI: Gulf and Ship Island (railroad)
g sil: german silver
gskt: gasket
GSL: Geological Society of London
GS & LA: Guam Savings and Loan Association
gslcv: globe stop lift check valve
gsm: good sound merchantable; grams per square meter; gross sales monthly
GSM: Guildhall School of Music
GSMD: General Society of Mayflower Descendants; Guildhall School of Music and Drama
GSMNP: Great Smoky Mountains National Park (Tennessee and North Carolina)
GSMS: Graduate Student of the Management Society
GSNC: General Steam Navigation Company
GSNWR: Great Swamp National Wildlife Refuge (New Jersey)
GSO: General Staff Officer; Girls Service Organization; Greensboro, North Carolina (airport); Ground Safety Officer
GSPA: Gulfport State Port Authority
gsr: galvanic skin reflex; galvanic skin response
GSRI: Gulf South Research Institute
gsrv: globe stop radiator valve
GSS: General Service School; General Supply Schedule; Geo-Stationary Satellite; Gilbert and Sullivan Society; Global Surveillance System
GSSF: General Supply Stock Fund
GSSH: Grand Street Settlement House
GSSR: Georgian Soviet Socialist Republic
gst: garter stitch (knitting)
GST: Greenwich Sidereal Time; Guamanian Standard Time
GSTC: Gorham State Teachers College
G-string: capital-G-shaped string-like genital covering worn by exotic entertainers
gsu: glazed structural units
GSU: General Service Unit; Gulf States Utilities
gsub: glazed structural unit base
g-suit: antigravity suit worn during supersonic flight
GSUSA: Girl Scouts of the USA
gsv: globe stop valve
GSV: Guided Space Vehicle
gsw: gunshot wound
GSW: Fort Worth, Texas (Greater Southwest International Airport)
GSW 1812: General Society of the War of 1812
gt: gastight; gilt top; grease trap; great; gross tonnage; gross ton(s); ground transmit

g/t: granulation time; granulation tissue
***gt:** gate* (Norwegian—street)
***gt.:** gutta* (Latin—drop)
GT: Good Templar; Goodyear Tire & Rubber (stock exchange symbol); Grand Tiler; Gran Turismo; Grupo de Transportes (Transport Group)
***GT:** Gran Turismo* (automobile)
G/T: Gas Turbine (vessel)
gta: graphic training aid
GTA: Gun Trade Association
GTBC: Guild of Teachers of Backward Children
Gt Br: Great Britain
Gt Brit: Great Britain
gtc: gain time control; good till cancelled
GTC: Guam Territorial College; Gulf Transport Company (railroad)
GTCs: Government Training Centres (UK)
gtd: geometrical theory of diffraction; guaranteed
GTDS: Goddard Trajectory Determination System (NASA)
gte: gilt top edge
***gte:** gerente* (Spanish—manager)
GT & E: General Telephone and Electronics (Corporation)
GT & EA: Georgia Teachers and Education Association
gtee: goatee; guarantee
GT & EL: General Telephone and Electronics Laboratories
gtf: glucose tolerance factor
GTF: Great Falls, Montana (airport)
gth: go to hell
gth (GTH): gonadotrophic hormone
GTI: Grand Turk Island (tracking station)
GTIL: Government Technical Institute Library
GTIO: German Tourist Information Office
GTL: Glass Technology Laboratories
gtm: good this month
GTM: General Traffic Manager
GTMA: Gauge and Tool Makers Association
Gtmo: Guantánamo Bay
gtn: glomerulo-tubulo nephritis
GTNP: Grand Teton National Park (Wyoming)
gto: gate turnoff
Gto: Gunajuato
***GTO:** Gran Turismo Omologato* [hard-top type of high-performance auto certified (*omologato*) to enter Gran Turismo automobile race]
gtol: ground takeoff and landing
gtp (GTP): guanosine triphosphate
gtr: gantry test rack
g/t/s: gas-turbine ship
GTR: Grand Trunk Railway
Gtr Ant: Greater Antilles
Gts: Gateshead
GTS: gas turbine vessel (3-letter code); General Telephone System
gtss: gas turbine self-contained starter
***gtt.:** guttae* (Latin—drops)
gtt (GTT): gelatin-tellurite-taurocholate
gtT: gone to Texas (one jump ahead of the sheriff)
GTT: Glucose Tolerance Test
GTU: Graduate Theological Union
gtv: gate valve
gtw: good this week
GTW: Grand Trunk Western (railroad)
Gtwy: Gateway (postal abbreviation)
gty: gritty
Gtz: Galatz
gu: gastric ulcer; genitourinary; glycogenic unit
Gu: Gujarat; Gujarati
GU: genito-urinary; Georgetown University; Gonzaga University
GUA: Guatemala City, Guatemala (airport)
Guad: Guadeloupe
Guadal: Guadalajara
Guam ST: Guamanian Standard Time
'Guana: Iguana Island, British Virgin Islands
guar: guarantee
Guar: Guarani (Brazil)
GUARD: Government Employees United Against Discrimination
***Guardian:** The Guardian* (a leading British newspaper published simultaneously in London and Manchester)
Guat: Guatemala(n)
Guay: Guayaquil
guba: (Russian—bay; gulf)
GUBC: Guyana United Broadcasting Company (Radio Demerara)
gubernalection: gubernatorial election
Gui: Guinea
GUI: Golfing Union of Ireland
Gui-Bis: Guinea-Bissau (formerly Portuguese Guinea)
Gui Cur: Guinea Current
guid: guidance
guide.: guidance for users of integrated data equipment
guil: guilder(s)
Guil: Guillaume
Guill°: Guillermo (Spanish—William)
guin: guinea(s)
Guinea-Bissau: (formerly Portuguese Guinea)
Guinea Ecuatorial: (Spanish—Equatorial Guinea)—formerly Spanish Guinea
Guinée: (French—Guinea)
Guip: Guipuzcoa
Guj: Gujarat; Gujarati
GULAG: Chief Administration of Corrective Labor Camps, Prisons, Labor, and Special Settlements of the Soviet Secret Police (*q.v. VOT*)
Gulag Archipelago: Solzhenitsyn's title for the thousands of prisons found from the Bering Strait almost to the Bosporus and all within his former country, the USSR
GULC: Georgetown University Law Center
Gulf: Arabian or Persian Gulf; Gulf of Aden, Alaska, Anadyr, Bothnia, California, Cambay, Campeche, Chiriqui, Darien, Gabes, Guinea, Honduras, Kutch, Mannar, Martaban, Mexico, Oman, Panama, Papua, Riga, Saint Lawrence, Siam or Thailand, Sidra, Tehuantepec, Tonkin, Venezuela; Gulf Oil; Spencer Gulf; all other gulfs referred to as The Gulf
GULF: Gays United for Liberty and Freedom (street-people subculture society)
Gulf City: Mobile, Alabama
Gulf States: Florida, Alabama, Mississippi, Louisiana, and Texas—all along the Gulf of Mexico
Gull's disease: myxedema resulting from atrophy of the thyroid gland
gulp: (data-processing slang—a succession of bytes)
GUM: Gosudarstvennoe Universalny Magasin (Russian—State Universal Store); Guam (airport)
gun.: guncotton; guncrete; gunnery; gunpowder
***gun:** gunung* (Malay—mountain)
Gunflint(s): Rhode Islander(s)
gun'l: gunwale
Gun Sgt: Gunnery Sergeant
gup: guppy

guppy.: greater underwater propulsive-powered (guppy-shaped) submarine
gups: guppies
GURC: Gulf Universities Research Corporation
Gus: August; Augustus; Gustaf; Gustave; Gustavus
GUS: Globe Universal Services; Great Universal Stores
Gussie: Augusta; Augustina; Augustine
Gussies: Great Universal Stores
Gustus: Augustus
gut.: gutter
Gut: Gutenberg
Gutenberg: Johannes Gensfleisch (German—John Gooseflesh)—the inventor of movable type
GUTS: Georgians Unwilling to Surrender
gutt.: *gutta* (Latin—drop)
guttat.: *guttatim* (Latin—drop by drop)
gutt. quibus.: *guttis quibusdam* (Latin—a few drops)
guv: governor
GuV: *Gerecht und Volkommen* (German—correct and complete)
guv'nor: governor
Guy: Guido; Guyana; Guyon
Guyane Française: French Guiana
Guybau: Guyana Bauxite
Guy d'Hardelot: Mrs W.I. Rhodes (Helen Guy)
gv: gate valve; gentian violet; gravimetric volume; grid variation; ground visibility
gv: *grande vitesse* (French—fast-freight train); *gran velocidad* (Spanish—high velocity)
Gv: Gustav
GV: Giuseppe Verdi; Göta Verken (steel company); grid variation
gva: general visceral afferent
GVA: Geneva, Switzerland (airport)
GVC: Grand View College
gve: general visceral efferent
Gve: Gustave
GVF: *Grazhodanskii Vozdushnyi Flot* (Russian—Civil Air Fleet)
gvhd: graft versus host disease(s)
gvhr: graft versus host reaction(s)
GVI: Gas Vent Institute
GVL: Global Van Lines
GVP: General Vice President
GVP: *Gereformeerd Politiek Verbond* (Dutch—Reformed Political Union)
GVRD: Greater Vancouver Regional District
GVS: Government Vehicle Service
gvt: government
gvty: gingivectomy
gvw: gross vehicle weight
gw: guerrilla warfare
GW: George Washington—first President of the United States; Great Western (savings)
G-W: Globe-Wernicke
G & W: Gulf and Western
GWA: Girl Watchers of America
GWA: *Goode's World Atlas*
GWB: George Washington Bridge
GWCHS: George Washington Carver High School
GWCM: George Washington Carver Museum
Gwen: Gwendolyn
Gwenda: Gwendolen
Gwennie: Gwendolen
GWHNWR: Great White Heron National Wildlife Refuge (Florida)
GWHS: George Washington High School; George Westinghouse High School
GWI: Grinding Wheel Institute; Ground Water Institute
G'wich Village: Greenwich Village
Gwin: Gwinett
GWMNP: George Washington Memorial National Parkway
GWOA: Guerrilla Warfare Operational Area
gwp (GWP): gross world product
GWP: *Government White Paper*
GWPA: *Grote Winkler Prins Atlas* (Dutch—Great Winkler Prins Atlas)—Elsevier publication printed in Amsterdam
GWR: General War Reserves; Great Western Railway
GWRI: Ground Water Resources Institute
GWS: Geneva (Convention for the Amelioration of the) Wounded and Sick (in Armed Forces in the Field); George Washington School; Gir Wildlife Sanctuary (India)
gwt: glazed wall tile
GWTA: Gift Wrappings and Tyings Association
GWU: George Washington University
GWVA: Great War Veterans Association
Gwyn: Gwynne
gx (GX): government exhibit
gxmtr: guidance transmitter
gy: gray; gunnery; gyro; gyrocar; gyrocompass; gyrodyne; gyroscope
gY: greenish yellow
GYE: Guayaquil, Ecuador (airport)
gym: gymnasium; gymnastics
GYM: General Yard Master; Guyamas, Mexico (tracking station)
gyn: gynecology
G.Y.N.: gynecologist
gynae(col): gynaecological; gynaecologist; gynaecology
gynecol: gynecology
gyp: gypsum; gypsy; cheat or swindle (slang)
GYP: Guild of Young Printers
Gyppy: (British slang—Egyptian)
gypsum: calcium sulfate ($CaSO_4 \cdot 2H_2O$)
'gyptian(s): Egyptian(s)
gyro: gyrocompass; gyroplane; gyroscope
gyrocop: gyrocopter
GYS Co: Great Yarmouth Shipping Company
gywp: gee you're wonderful, professor
gz: ground zero
Gz: Gomez
GZn: grid azimuth
GZT: Greenwich Zone Time

H

h: hard; hardening; hardness; hazy; hecto; height; hit(s); hour(s); hundred(s); husband; hydrant; hydrodynamic head (symbol); hydrolysis; Planck's constant (symbol); Planck's element of action- (symbol)
h: altitude (symbol); atmospheric head (symbol)
(h): per hypodermic
H: amateur broadcasting (symbol); ceiling (symbol); Fraunhofer line produced by calcium (symbol); Hamiltonian function (symbol); hard; hardness; hatch; headlines; heat; heater; helicopter; henry; heroin (drug-user's abbreviation); Hindu; Hinduism; horizontal component of the earth's magnetism (symbol); hot; Hotel—code for letter H; humidity; hydrogen; hyperopia; intensity of magnetic field (symbol); maximum altitude (symbol); McDonnel Aviation; Minneapolis-Honeywell (trademark); very hazy (symbol)
H: *hacienda* (Spanish—customs service; treasury); *haut* (French—up); *heet* (Dutch—hot); *Herren* (German or Swedish—gentlemen); *herrer* (Norwegian—gentlemen); *het* (Norwegian—hot); *hinaus* (German — out); *hombres* (Spanish—men); *Hoyre* (Norwegian—Right)— Conservative Party
H^1: protium
H^1+: proton
H^2: deuterium (heavy hydrogen symbol)
H24: hard rolled and partially annealed (half hard)
H_2O: water
H_2O_2: hydrogen peroxide
H_2SO_4: sulfuric acid
H^3: tritium
H_3: procaine hydrochloride (symbol)
H_3BO_3: boric acid
ha: hectare; high altitude; high angle; home address; hour angle; hour aspect
h.a.: *hoc anno* (Latin—in this year)
Ha: hahnium (element 105); Haiti(an)
Ha: (German pronunciation for B sharp)
HA: Hawaiian Airlines; Headquarters Administration; Heavy Artillery; Horse Artillery; Hospital Apprentice
HA: *Hardware Age*
H-A: Hautes-Alpes
H/A: Havre–Antwerp (range of ports)
haa: heavy antiaircraft artillery
haa (HAA): hepatitis-associated antigen
HAA: Helicopter Association of America; Hotel Accountants Association
haaat: height of (transmission) antenna above average terrain
HAAC: Harper Adams Agricultural College
HAAFE: Hawaiian Army and Air Force Exchange
Haakon the Good: King Haakon I of Norway
Haakon Jarl: (Norwegian–Earl Haakon)
Haakon the Old: King Haakon IV of Norway
haandb: *haandbog* (Dano–Norwegian—handbook)
Ha'aretz: (Hebrew—The Land)— Israel's leading daily newspaper both independent and non-partisan
haat: height (of tv transmission antenna) above average terrain
haatc: high altitude air traffic control
haaw: heavy anti-tank assault weapon
hab: high-altitude bombing; habitat; habitation
hab: *habitantes* (Spanish–inhabitants)—often seen on road signs
Hab: Habana (Spanish—Havana); The Book of Habakkuk
HAB: Hazards Analysis Board (USAF)
HABA: Hardwood Agents and Brokers Association
Hab(bie): Albert; Alberta; Halbert
hab. corp.: *habeas corpus* (Latin—may you have the body)—prisoner's right to be brought before the court so its judge may decide on the legality of the detention
Habeas Corpus Howe: William Frederick Howe also nicknamed Criminal Bar Howe
habit.: *habitat* (Latin—it inhabits)
Habitants: (French—Inhabitants)—Canadian farmers and fishermen of French descent
habt.: *habeat* (Latin—let him have)
HAc: acetic acid
HAC: Hines Administrative Center; Honourable Artillery Company; Hughes Aircraft Company
HACC: Harrisburg Area Community College
hack: hackney coach; hackney horse; taxicab
had.: heat-actuated device (thermostat); hereinafter described
H/A or D: Havre-Antwerp or Dieppe (grain trade)
HADA: Hawaiian Defense Area
HADC: Holloman Air Development Center
Hades: (Greek—invisible)—equivalent to the Roman god Pluto who was god of the dead and the invisible underworld
HADES: Hypersonic Air Data Entry System
HADIS: Huddersfield and District Information Service
HADIZ: Hawaiian Air Defense Identification Zone
hadn't: had not
hads: hypersonic air data sensor
hads.: hypersonic air data sensor
ha'e: (Gaelic contraction—have)
Haeck: Ernst Heinrich Haeckel; Haeckelian; Haeckelism
haf: high-abrasion furnace; high-altitude fluorescence
HAF: Hebrew Arts Foundation; Helms Athletic Foundation; Helvetia-America Federation
haf black: high-abrasive furnace black

Haffner: Mozart's Serenade Suite in D or his Symphony No. 35 in D major; both honor the Burgomeister of Salzburg—Sigmund Haffner
HAFMED: Headquarters—Allied Forces Mediterranean
HAFO: Home Accounting and Finance Office (USAF)
HAFRA: Hat and Allied Feltmakers Research Association
HAFTB: Holloman Air Force Test Base
Hag: The Book of Haggai; The Hague
HAG: Hardware Analysis Group
HAGB: Helicopter Association of Great Britain
hagiol: hagiology
HAI: Hospital Audiences Incorporated
HAIA: Hearing Aid Industry Association
HAIL: Hague Academy of International Law
H&A Ins: Health and Accident Insurance
hairdrsr: hairdresser
hairies: long-haired hippies
HAJ: Hanover, Germany (airport)
Hak: Hakka
HAKASH: *Hayl Kashish* (Hebrew—Army of Elders)—Israel's senior-citizen corps
Hak Soc: Hakluyt Society
Hal: Halogen
Hal: Halensee; Harold
HAL: Hamburg-Amerika Linie (Hamburg-America Line); Hamburg-Atlantic Line; Hawaiian Airlines
HALDIS: Halifax and District Information Service
Halebum: (Latin—Aleppo)
Halévy: Jacques Fromental Elie Lévy
Halifax: (named for the second Earl of Halifax)
halite: rock salt (sodium chloride)
Halle a/S: *Halle an der Saale* (German—Halle on the Salle River)
hallu: hallucinant; hallucinate; hallucination; hallucinogen; hallucinogenic
halluc: hallucination
halo.: high-altitude low opening
Hal Orch: Hallé Orchestra
Halstern's disease: endemic syphilis
haltata: high-and-low-temperature-accuracy testing apparatus
halv: hamster leukemia virus
ham.: hardware-associated memory
Ham: Hamburg; Hamilton; Hamitic; Hamlet; Hammerfest
HAM: Hamburg, Germany (airport)
HA & M: *Hymns Ancient and Modern*
ham and: ham and eggs
Hamb: Hamburg
Hamburg Bach: Karl Philipp Emanuel Bach—also nicknamed Berlin Bach
Haml: *Hamlet, Prince of Denmark*
hamlet: ham omelet
Hamlet: funeral march by Berlioz; fantasy overture by Tchaikovsky; five-act opera by Thomas—all based on Shakespeare's character in his play of the same name
hamletom: ham, lettuce and tomato (sandwich)
Hamlet's Town: Helsingør, Denmark (called Elsinore by the English)
Hammerfestinger: native of Hammerfest, Norway
Hammering Hank: Henry Aaron
Hammerklavier: Beethoven's Piano Sonata No. 29 in B flat (opus 106)
Hammerman: John Henry
Hammer of Scotland: Edward I
hammer and sickle: communist symbol appearing wherever communists are found; the crossing of the proletarian hammer and the agrarian sickle also appears on the flags of the Congo and the USSR
Ham 'n' Eggs: musician's nickname for *Cavalleria Rusticana* and *Pagliacci* as these two operas seem to go well together and are usually billed together
Hamp: Hampton Roads
Hampton Roads Ports: Newport News, Norfolk, Portsmouth
HAMTC: Hanford Atomic Metal Trades Council
hamwich: ham sandwich
Han: Handel Society
han': hand
hand.: handling
Handcuff King: Harry Houdini
Hand of Fatima: five-fingered heraldic symbol topping the emblem of Algeria
Handl: *Handlingar* (Swedish—transactions)
hane: high-altitude nuclear effects
Hanging Judge: Judge Roy Bean of Langtry, Texas—Law West of the Pecos, and many other judges who earned this nickname from the number of criminals they eliminated by hanging
Hangtown: El Dorado, California's nickname recalling when so many bandits were hanged during the Gold Rush
Hank: Henry
hanki: handkerchief
Hanot's disease: cirrhosis of the liver accompanied by jaundice
Hans: Johann(es)
Hansa Ports: Hanseatic League ports—Bremen and Hamburg on the North Sea, Danzig and Lübeck on the Baltic, Visby on Gotland Island in the Baltic
Hansard: official verbatim reports of debates of both Houses of Parliament
Hansen's disease: leprosy
Hans Fallada: (pseudonym—Rudolf Ditzen)
han't: has not; have not (British contraction)
Hants: Hampshire
Hanuk: *Chanukkah* (Hebrew—Feast of Lights)
HAO: High Altitude Observatory
hap: happening
HAPAG: Hamburg-American Line
Hap Arnold: General Henry Harley Arnold, USA and USAF
hapdar: hardpoint demonstration array radar
hapdec: hard point decoy
ha'penny: halfpenny
ha'p'orth: halfpennyworth
Happy Chandler: High Commissioner of Baseball Albert Benjamin Chandler
Happy Land: Burma's sobriquet
Happy Warrior: Franklin D. Roosevelt's nickname for Al Smith (New York State's Governor Alfred E. Smith)
haps: happenings
Happy Home of the Bulldozer: Los Angeles or any other fast-growing metropolis
har: harbor; harmonic
Har: Harbin; Harold
HAR: Harrisburg, Pennsylvania (airport)
Harald Hårdråde: (Norwegian—Harold Hardruler)—viking king and founder of Oslo
HARAO: Hartford Aircraft

Reactor Area Office
harb: harbor
Harbrace: Harcourt Brace Jovanovich
harcft: harbor craft
Harcourt: Harcourt Brace Jovanovich
hard.: hardware
Harden: (British contraction—Harwarden)
Hard Heart of Hickland: Cleveland, Ohio, according to authors Jack Lait and Lee Mortimer—*U.S.A. Confidential*
Hard Rock: nickname of the American Broadcasting Company (ABC)
Hardware City: New Britain, Connecticut
harm.: harmonic; harmony
HARM: Humans Against Rape and Molestation
harn: harness
harn lthr: harness leather
Harold Haardraade: (Norwegian—Harold the Hard Ruler)—King Harold III of Norway
Harold Bluetooth: King Harold of Denmark
Harold Harefoot: Harold I of Denmark and England
harp: symbol of Ireland and the Irish
harp.: harpoon; harpsichord; harpsichordist; high-altitude relay point
Harp: Halpern's anti-radar point
Harp: Beethoven's String Quartet in E-flat major (opus 74) for two violins, viola, and cello with harplike arpeggio passages for all the instruments; Chopin's Piano Etude in A flat (opus 25, no. 1)
HARP: Honeywell Acoustic Research Program
Harper: Harper & Row
Harpo Marx: Arthur Marx
harps.: harpsichord
Harry: Harold; Henry
Harry Golden: Herschel Goldhirsch
Harry Houdini: Ehrich Weiss
Hart: Hartford
Hartran: Hartwell Atlas fortran
Hart Sym Orch: Hartford Symphony Orchestra
Harv: Harvard; Harvey
Harvard's Heroic Historian: John Lothrop Motley
Harw: Harwarden (*Harden*)
HARYOU: Harlem Youth Opportunities Unlimited
has.: high-altitude sample
Has: Haselhorst
HAS: Helicopter Air Service
HASC: House (of Representatives) Armed Services Committee
HASCO: Haitian-American Sugar Company
hash.: hashish
Hashbury: Haight-Ashbury (district of San Francisco)
Hashemite Kingdom: Jordan
Hashish: Hasan-ibn-al-Sabbah (11th-century Persian founder of the Assassins)
Hashish Trail: extends from the Balkans to India; trail filled with narcotic addicts searching for something cheaper but stronger; many go but few return to tell the tale of the Hashish Trail
Hasid: Hasidim (Hebrew—godly pious people)
HASL: Health and Safety Laboratory (Atomic Energy Commission)
hasn't: has not
hasp.: hardware-assisted software polling; high-altitude sampling program; high-altitude space platform
HASP: Hawaiian Armed Services Police
hasr: high-altitude sounding rocket
hast: high-altitude supersonic target
Hastings: Hastings House; Hastings-on-Hudson
Ha strain: Harris (viral) strain
hasvr: high-altitude space-velocity radar
hato: handling tool
HATRA: Hosiery and Allied Trades Research Association
HATRICS: Hampshire Technical Research Industrial and Commercial Service
hats.: hour angle of the true sun
HATS: Helicopter Advanced Tactical System
Hattie: Harriet
Hau: Hausa
Haunt of Yachtsmen: British Virgin Islands
Hauptw: *Hauptwerk* (German—great or chief work)
haust.: *haustus* (Latin—a draught)
haut: hautboy (oboe)
hav: haversine
hAv: hepatitis A virus
HAV: Havana, Cuba (airport)
Havana High: Miami High School's nickname reflecting the overwhelming number of Cuban students
HAVEN: Help Addicts Voluntarily End Narcotics
haven't: have not
Havercake(s): native(s) of Lancashire
havoc.: histogram average ogive calculator
haw. (HAW): heavy anti-tank assault weapon
Haw: Hawaii; Hawaiian (unauthorized abbreviations)
HAW: Kauai, Hawaii (tracking station)
HAWA: Hammond Ambassador World Atlas
Hawaiian Pineapple King: James Drummond Dole
Hawaiians: Hawaiian Islanders; Hawaiian Islands
HAWE: Honorary Association for Women in Education
hawk. (HAWK): homing-all-the-way kill (missile)
Hawkeye(s): Iowan(s)
Hawkeye State: Iowa's official nickname
Haw'n: Hawaiian
Hawthorn: Hawthorn Books; Missouri state flower
hax: hrir/apt interface (high-resolution infrared radiometer/automatic picture transmission)
haystaq: have you stored answers to questions?
haz: hazard; hazardous
hb: halfback; halfbound; hard black; heavy barrel; heavy bombardment; heavy bombing; hemoglobin; homing beacon; horizontal bands; horizontal bombing; hose bib; human being
h/b: handbook
Hb: hemoglobin; herbarium
Hb: *Hoboe* (German—oboe)
H^b: deuterium (heavy hydrogen symbol)
HB: Hawthorn Books; Hector Berlioz; High Bridge
HB: *Hindi Bharat* (Hindustani—Republic of India)
H & B: Humboldt and Bonpland
Hba: Habana (Spanish—Havana)
HBA: Hoist Builders Association; Hollywood Bowl Association; Honest Ballot Association
h B ag: hepatitis B antigen
H-bar: capital-H-shaped bar
HBAVS: Human Betterment Association for Voluntary Sterilization
HBC: Hudson's Bay Company
HbCO: carbon monoxide hemo-

globin
hbd: has been drinking; hereinbefore described
hbd (HBD): hydroxybutyrate dehydrogenase
hbe: hard-boiled egg(s)
H-beam: capital H-shaped beam
hbf: hepatic blood flow
Hbf: fetal hemoglobin
Hbf: Hauptbahnhof (German—depot; main station)
Hbg: Hamburg; Harrisburg
HBG: Henry B(arbosa) Gonzalez; Hongkong Bank Group; Huntington Botanical Gardens
HBJ: Harcourt Brace Jovanovich
hbk: hollow back (lumber)
Hbk: Hoboken
HB & K: Humboldt, Bonpland, and Kunth (botanists)
HBM: His (Her) Britannic Majesty
HBNNR: Hickling Broad National Nature Reserve (England)
HBNWR: Holla Bend National Wildlife Refuge (Arkansas)
HBOG: Hudson's Bay Oil and Gas
H-bomb: hydrogen bomb
HBO_2; oxyhemoglobin
hbp: high blood pressure; hit by pitcher (baseball)
Hbr: Harbor
HBR: Hudson Bay Railway
HBR: Harvard Business Review
Hbs: sickle-cell hemoglobin
HBS: Harvard Business School; Hawaiian Botanical Society; Hope Botanic Gardens
Hbt: Hobart
HB & T: Houston Belt and Terminal (railroad)
hBv: hepatitis B virus
H&BV: Houston and Brazos Valley (railroad)
Hbwr: Halden boiling heavy water reactor
hby: hereby
hc: hand control; heating cabinet; hexachlorethane; high-capacity; high carbon; screening smoke
h/c: held covered
h & c: heroin + cocaine; hot and cold; (running water)
h.c.: hac nocte (Latin—tonight); *honoris causa* (Latin—out of respect for); *hors commerce* (French—not for sale; privately printed)
Hc: computed altitude
HC: Hagerstown College; Hamilton College; Hamline College; Hanover College; Harding College; Harpur College; Hartford College; Hartnell College; Hartwick College; Hastings College; Haverford College; Heidelberg College; Helicopter Council; Hendrix College; Hershey College; Hesston College; Hillsdale College; Hiram College; Hood College; Hope College; Hospital Corps; House of Commons; Howard College; Humphreys College; Hunter College; Huntingdon College; Huntington College; Huron College; Hussan College; Hutchinson College
H C: Holy Communion
H.C.: High Commission
H-C: Harbison-Carborundum
HC: Hartford Courant
H of C: House of Commons; House of Correction
hca: held by civil authorities
HCA: High Conductivity Association; Hobby Clubs of America; Hotel Corporation of America; Hunting-Clan Air Transport
HCAAS: Homeless Children's Aid and Adoption Society
hcap: handicap
H-caps: heroin capsules
HCB: House of Commons Bill
hcc: hydraulic cement concrete
hcc (HCC): 25-hydroxycholecalciferol (vitamin D^3 metabolite)
HCC: Hebrew Culture Council; Holyoke Community College
hcd: high current density
hcd (HCD): human chorionic gonadotropin
HC Deb: House of Commons Debates
hce: human-caused error
HC & ES: Hull Chemical and Engineering Society
hcf: height-correction factor; highest common factor; hundred cubic feet
HCF: Hungarian Cultural Foundation
hcg: horizontal location of center of gravity; human chorionic gonadotropin pregnancy test
hch (HCH): hexachlorocyclohexane (insecticide)
HCH: Herbert Clark Hoover (31st President U.S.)
HCHI: Hand Chain Hoist Institute
HCI: Hotel and Catering Institute
HCIL: Hague Conference on International Law
HCIS: House Committee on Internal Security
HCITB: Hotel and Catering Industry Training Board
HCJ: High Court of Justice
HCJC: Howard County Junior College
hcl: high cost of living; horizontal center line
h cl: hanging closet
HCl: hydrochloric acid (muriatic acid)
HCL: Hod Carriers, Building and Common Laborers (union)
HCM: Ho Chi Minh (Chinese—He Who Shines)
HCMC: Ho Chi Minh City (Saigon's new name imposed upon its surrender to Vietcong communist guerrillas wishing to honor the founder of their forces—Ho Chi Minh)
HCMT: Ho Chi Minh Trail
HCMW: Hatters, Cap and Millinery Workers (union)
hcn: hydrocyanic acid
HCn: hydrocyanic acid
HCO: Harvard College Observatory
HCO_3: bicarbonate ion
hcp: handicap; hexachlorophene
HCP: Honors Cooperative Program
HCP: House of Commons Proceedings
HCPNI: Hardware Cloth and Poultry Netting Institute
HCPT: Historic Churches Preservation Trust
hcptr: helicopter
HCR: High Chief Ranger
HCRAO: Hat Creek Radio Astronomy Observatory (University of California)
hcrit: hematocrit
hcrw: hot and cold running water
hcs: high-carbon steel
hc's: hard cover books
hcs (HCS): human chorionic somatomammotropin
HCS: Hallé Concerts Society; Harvey Cushing Society; Home Civil Service
HCSA: House (of Representatives) Committee on Space and Astronautics
hcsht: high-carbon steel heat treated
hct: hematocrit
HCT: Huddersfield College of Technology
HCTBA: Hotel and Catering Trades Benevolent Association
hcu: homing comparator unit;

hydraulic cycling unit
HCVC: Historic Commercial Vehicle Club
hcvd: hypertensive cardiovascular disease
hd: hard-drawn; head; hearing distance; high density; hourly difference; hurricane deck
h-d: high-density
h/d: holddown
h.d.: *hora decubitus* (Latin—at bedtime)
hd (HD): half duplex (data processing)
Hd: Head
Hd: *Hochdruck* (German—high pressure)
HD: Hansen's Disease (leprosy); Harbor Defense; Harbor Drive; Historical Division; Home Defense; Honorable Discharge; Hoover Dam
H.D.: Hilda Doolittle
H/D: Havre-Dunkirk (range of ports)
H & D: Hurter & Driffield (photo emulsion speed)
HDA: High Duty Alloys
hdatz: high-density air traffic zone
HDB: Housing Development Board
hdbk: handbook
hdc: holder in due course
HDC: Housing Development Corporation
HD Clinic: Hansen's Disease Clinic (for lepers)
hd cr: hard chromium
hdd: heavy-duty detergent
HDD: Higher Dental Diploma
hddr: high-density digital recording
HDDS: High-Density Data System
HDE: Higher Diploma in Education
hded: heavy-duty enzyme detergent
hdg: heading
HDGA: Hot Dip Galvanizers Association
HDHD: Hawaiian District Harbors Division
HDI: Humane Development Institute
H Dip E: Higher Diploma in Education
H disease: Hart's disease
hdk: husbands don't know
h dk: hurricane deck
hdkf: handkerchief
hdl: handle
HDL: Harry Diamond Laboratory (US Army Diamond Ordnance Fuze Laboratory)
hdlg: handling
hdls: headless
hdlw: hearing distance, watch at left ear
hdm: high-duty metal
hdmr: high-density moderated reactor
hdn: harden
hdn (HDN): hemolytic disease of the newborn
H Doc: House Document
hdp (HDP): hexose diphosphate
hdpe: high-density polyethylene
hdqrs: headquarters
hdr: handrail
HDRI: Hannah Dairy Research Institute
HDRSS: High-Data-Rate Storage System(s)
hdrw: hearing distance, watch at right ear
hds: hydrodesulfurization
Hds: Holidays (of Obligation)
HDS: Hospital Discharge Survey
hdsp: hardship
hdst: high-density shock tube
HDST: Hawaiian Daylight Saving Time
HDT: Henry David Thoreau
HDTMA: Heavy-Duty Truck Manufacturers Association
HDTS: Harbor Drive Test Site (Convair Ramp)
hdu: hemodialysis unit
hdv: heavy-duty vehicle
hdw: hardware
Hdwbch: *Handwörterbuch* (German—pocket dictionary)
hdw c: hardware cloth (wire screen)
hdwd: hardwood
hdwe: hardware
hd whl: hand wheel
hdx (HDX): half duplex (data processing)
he.: heat engine; heavy enamel; height of eye; high explosive; hub end; human enteric
h&e: hemotoxylin and eosin; heredity and environment
h.e.: *hic est* (Latin—this is)
He: Hebraic; Hebrew; helium; Hertz
HE: high explosive; His Eminence; His Excellency; Hollis & Eastern (railroad); Human Engineering; Hydraulics Engineer(ing)
H.E.: His Eminence; His Excellency
HEA: Higher Education Act; Horticultural Education Association
heaa: high-explosive anti-aircraft (shell)
Head of the Adriatic: Trieste
Head of the Commonwealth: Her (His) Most Excellent Majesty the Queen (King) of the United Kingdom of Great Britain and Northern Ireland and of Her (His) other Realms and Territories Queen (King)
head(s).: headache(s)
heaf: heavy end aviation fuel
HEAO: High-Energy Astronomical Observatory
heap.: high-explosive armor-piercing (shell)
HEAR: Hospital Emergency Administrative Radio
Hearst's Castle: (see *La Casa Grande*)
Heart of America: Kansas City
Heartland of America: the Midwest
Heart of California: Sacramento
Heart of Central Alaska: Fairbanks
Heart of Dixie: Alabama's official nickname
Heart of England: Warwickshire
Heart of Historic Virginia: Charlottesville
Heart of Kentucky: Frankfort
Heart of Canada: Ontario
Heartland City: Kansas City
Heartland of Monarchy: Grand Duchy of Luxembourg
Heart of Midlothian: Tolbooth Prison in Edinburgh—an old jail commemorated in Scott's novel of the same title
Heart of Polynesia: American Samoa
Heart of Portugal: Mondego Valley
Heart of the Roman Empire: Italy
Heart of South America: Bolivia
Heart of Sweden: Dalarna Province formerly called Dalecarlia
heat.: heating; high-explosive anti-tank (projectile)
Heb: Epistle of Paul the Apostle to the Hebrews: Hebraic; Hebrew
hebc: heavy enamel bonded single cotton
hebd: hebdomadal (weekly)
hebdom.: *hebdomas* (Latin—week)
hebdp: heavy enamel bonded double paper
hebds: heavy enamel bonded double silk
Hebr: Hebrides
Hebrides: Hebrides Islands off Scotland's west coast
hec: heavy-enamel single-cotton (insulation)
HEC: Hydro-Electric Commis-

sion
HECO: Hydro-Electric Commission of Ontario
hect: hectare; hectoliter
Hect: Hector
hecto: 10^2
hectog: hectogram
hectol: hectoliter
hectom: hectometer
hector.: heated experimental carbon thermal oscillator reactor (HECTOR)
hed: horizontal electric dipole
he'd: he had; he would
HED: *Haupt-Einheits Dosis* (German—unit skin dose)—X—rays
HEDCOM: Headquarters Command
hed sked: headline schedule
hedsv: heavy-enamel double-silk varnish (insulation)
Hedy: Hedvig; Hedwig
Heel of Italy: Salentine Peninsula
heent: head, ears, eyes, nose, throat
hef: heifer; high-energy fuel
HEF: High-Energy Fuel
heg: heavy-enamel single-glass (insulation)
HEH: Her (His) Exalted Highness
HEHF: Hanford Environmental Health Foundation (AEC)
HEHL: Henry E. Huntington Library
hei: high-explosive incendiary
HEI: Hotel Enterprises Incorporated
HEI: *H/F Eimiskipafelag Islands* (Icelandic Steamship Company)
HEIAS: Human Engineering Information and Analysis Service (Tufts U)
HEIC: Honourable East India Company
HEICN: Honourable East India Company Navy
HEICS: Honourable East India Company Service
Heide: Adelaide
Heidel: Heidelberg
Hein: Heinersdorf
Heine-Medin disease: muscular atrophy sometimes followed by permanent deformity
heir app: heir apparent
heir pres: heir presumptive
heit: high-explosive incendiary with tracer
hek: heavy-enamel single-cellophane (insulation)
hek (HEK): human embryo kidney
hel: helicopter
hel (HEL): hen's egg-white lysozyme; human embryonic lung
Hel: Helen; Helena; Helvetia (Switzerland)
HEL: Hartford Electric Light; Helsinki, Finland (airport)
HeLa: Helen Lake (tumor cells)
Helena Modjeska: Helena Modrejewska
Helen Hayes: Helen Hayes Brown
heli: helicopter; heliport
helio: heliochrome; heliodon; heliodor; helioelectric; helioengraving; heliogram; heliograph; heliogravure; heliology; heliostat; heliotherapy; heliotrope; heliotype
helipad: helicopter landing pad
Hell: Hellerup
HELL: Higher Education Learning Laboratory
he'll: he will
Hell Breughel: Pieter Breughel the Younger who painted hellish scenes
Hellen: Hellenic; Hellenism; Hellenistic
Hell in the Hills: Pittsburgh, Pennsylvania
Hell's Forty Acres: San Carlos, Arizona
Hell on Wheels: Cheyenne, Wyoming
helminthol: helminthology
helo: helicopter; heliport
HELP: Helicopter Electronic Landing Path; Help Establish Lasting Peace; Highway Emergency Locating Plan
HELPR: Handbook of Electronic Parts Reliability
hel rec: health record
Hel San: *Helsingin Sanomat* (Helsinki's News)
Helv: Helvetia; Helvetica
hem.: hemoglobin; hemorrhage; hemorrhoid
HEM: Ernest Hemingway
hematol: hematology
hemi engine: hemispherical combustion chamber engine
hemolysis: hemocytolysis
Hen: Henrietta; Henry
Hence: Henderson
Hen V: *King Henry V*
Hen VIII: *King Henry VIII*
H'english: Limey English
Henk: Hendrik
Henriqz: Henriquez
Henry B: Henry B. Gonzalez of San Antonio, Texas
Henry Bolingbroke: Henry IV of England
Henry the K: Henry Kissinger
heos (HEOS): high eccentric orbiting satellite
hep: high-energy phosphate; high-explosive plastic
Hep: Hepburn; Hepple; Hepworth
HEP: Have Error-free Product
HEPC: Hydro-Electric Power Commission
HEPCAT: Helicopter Pilot Control and Training (educational program)
HEPCC: Heavy Electrical Plant Consultative Council
HEPL: High Energy Physics Laboratory
her.: heraldry
her.: *heres* (Latin—heir)
Her: Hereford; Herefordshire
hera: high explosive rocket assisted
Hera: (Greek—Juno)—goddess of the heavens
HERALD: Highly-Enriched Reactor—Aldermaston
herb.: herbarium
Herb: Herbert
Herblock: Herbert Lawrence Block
HERC: Humber Estuarial Research Committee
Herdez: (Spanish contraction—Hernandez)
herd^o: *herdeiro* (Portuguese—heir)
herdr: *herdruk(ken)* (Dutch—reprint(s))
hered: heredity
hereds: *herederos* (Spanish—heirs)
Heref: Herefordshire
Herefs: Herefordshire
here's: here is
herf: high-energy rate forging
herfs: high-energy-rate forging systems
herj: high explosive ramjet
Herkimer diamond: gem-quality quartz from New York State's Herkimer County
herm: hermetically
Her Majesty: the Queen
hermes: heavy element and radioactive material electromagnetic separator (HERMES)
Hermes: (Greek—Mercury)—the messenger
Hermit of Slabsides: John Burroughs
Hermitage: Andrew Jackson's home in Nashville, Tennessee
hero.: hot experimental reactor of 0 (zero power)—also appears as HERO
Hero: *heroina* (Spanish-American slang shortcut—heroin)
HERO: Historical Evaluation

and Research Organization
Hero of Antiquity: Heracles or Herakles (Greek); Hercules (Roman)
Hero of Appomattox: General Ulysses Simpson Grant, USA
Hero of the Cities: Alfred E(manuel) Smith—usually called Al Smith
Herod.: Herodotus
Hero of Fort Sumter: Confederate General Pierre Gustave Toutant Beauregard (known to his soldiers as Old Alphabet or Old Bore)
Hero of the Frontier: George Rogers Clark
Hero of a Hundred Fights: Admiral Horatio Nelson
Hero of Lake Erie: Commodore Oliver Hazard Perry, USN
Hero of Manila Bay: Commodore George Dewey, USN
Hero of Mobile Bay: Admiral David Glasgow Farragut
Hero of New England: Captain Miles Standish
Hero of New Orleans: General Andrew Jackson
Hero of the Nile: Lord Horatio Nelson
Hero of San Juan Hill: Lt Col Theodore Roosevelt, USV
Hero of Tampico: General Antonio López de Santa Anna
Hero and Traitor: Benedict Arnold
Hero of Upper Canada: Sir Isaac Brock
herp: herpetologist; herpetology
HERPOCO: Hercules Powder Company
herps: herpetologists
Herring Pond: Atlantic Ocean
Herr Kaleun: *Herr Kapitänleutnant* (German—Mr Captain Lieutenant)—U-boat commander
HERS: Home Economics Reading Service
Hersch: Herschel
herst: *herstellung* (German—manufacture)
HERTIS: Hertfordshire County Council Technical Information Service
Herts: Hertfordshire
HERU: Higher Education Research Unit
Hervey Allen: William Hervey Allen
hes: heavy enamel single silk (insulation)
he's: he has; he is
Hes: Hesba; Hesketh; Hessels; Hessin; Hester
HES: Hawaiian Entomological Society
Hesperus: the evening star—Venus, son of Aurora and Cephalus/ (see *Lucifer)*
hest: heavy-end aviation fuel emergency service tanks
h'est: highest
HEST: High-Explosive Simulation Test
Hestia: (Greek—Vesta)—goddess of hearth and home
hesv: heavy-enamel single-silk varnish (insulation)
het: heavy equipment transporter
heterocl: heteroclite
heterog: heterogeneous
HETS: Hyper-Environmental Test System
Hetty: Hester
heu: hydroelectric units
Heung Kong: (Chinese—Fragrant Harbor)—Aberdeen Anchorage's original name now applied to all Hong Kong
heur: heuristic (problem solution by trial and error)
HEVAC: Heating, Ventilating, and Air Conditioning Manufacturers Association
Hew: Heward; Hewett; Hewitt; Hewlett; Hewson; Hugh; Hugo
HEW: Health, Education, and Welfare (US department)
hex: hexagon(al); uranium hexafluoride
hexa: hexamethylene tetramine
hexag: hexagon(al)
hex hd: hexagonal head
Hez: Hezekiah
hf: hageman factor; half; hard firm; height finding; high frequency (3000 to 30,000 kc); hold fire; hook fast; horse and foot (cavalry and infantry); hyperfocal
h/f: held for
Hf: hafnium
HF: Handwriting Foundation; Home Fleet; Home Forces; hydrofluoric acid
H/F: *Hlutafjelagid* (Icelandic—limited company)
H of F: Hall of Fame
Hfa: Haifa
HFAA: Holstein-Friesian Association of America
HFARA: Honorary Foreign Associate of the Royal Academy
hf bd: half-bound
hf bd cf: half bound in calfskin (calf leather back and corners)
hf bd cl: half bound in cloth (cloth back and corners or cloth sides)
hf bd mor: half bound in morocco (morocco leather back and corners)
hfbr: high flux beam reactor
hfc: hard-filled capsules; high-frequency current
HFC: Household Finance Corporation
HFCC: Henry Ford Community College
hf cf: half-calf
hf cl: half-cloth (binding)
hf-df: high-frequency direction finder
hfe: human factors (in) electronics; human factors engineering
HFFF: Hungarian Freedom Fighters Federation
hfg: heavy free gas
HFGA: Hall of Fame for Great Americans
hfh: half-hard (steel)
HFIA: Heat and Frost Insulators and Asbestos Workers Union
hfim: high-frequency instruments and measurements
hfir: high flux isotope reactor
HFL: Human Factors Laboratory (NBS)
hfm: hold for money
HFM: Henry Ford Museum
hfmf: home-furnish monolithic floor
hf mor: half-morocco
hfo: high-frequency oscillator; hole full of oil
HFORL: Human Factors Operations Research Laboratory
hfp: hostile fire pay
h&f pool: heated and filtered (swimming) pool
HFPS: Home Fallout Protection Survey
hfr: high-frequency range; high-frequency recombination; hold for release
HFR: (Sir Edward) Hallstrom Faunal Reserve (New South Wales)
HFRA: Honorary Fellow of the Royal Academy
HFRB: Hawaii Fire Rating Bureau
Hfrz: *Halbfranzband* (German—halfbound in calf)
hfs: hyperfine structure
Hfs: Helsinki (Helsingfors)
HFS: Human Factors Society
hft: *hefte* (Dano-Norwegian—part; issue)
Hft: *Heft* (German—part; issue)
HFT: Human Factors Team
HFTS: Human Factors Trade

Studies (USU)
hfw: hole full of water
Hfx: Halifax
hg: hand generator; hectogram; heliogram
Hg: *hydrargyrum* (Latin—mercury)
h & g: harden and grind
HG: Haute-Garonne; Her (His) Grace; H(erbert) G(eorge) (Wells); High German; Home Guard; Horse Guards
H-G: Haute-Garonne
HGA: Heptagonal Games Association, Hobby Guild of America; Hop Growers of America; Hotel Greeters of America; Hungarian Gypsy Association
h-galv: hot-galvanize
hgb: hemoglobin
HGCA: Home-Grown Cereals Authority
$HgCl_2$: bichloride of mercury; mercuric chloride
hge: hogshead
HGD: Hourglass Device
hgf (HGF): hyperglycemic-glucogenolytic factor
HGF: Human Growth Foundation
hg ga: height gage
HGH: human growth hormone
HGJP: Henry George Justice Party
Hglds: Highlands
HGMM: Hereditary Grand Master Mason
hgo: hepatic glucose output
Hgo: Hidalgo
HGOA: Houston Grand Opera Association
hgor: high gas-oil ratio
hgps: high-grade plow steel
hg pt: hard-gloss paint
hgr: hangar; hanger
HGR: Hluhluwe *(shloosh-loo-way)* Game Reserve (northern Zululand)
hgs: hangars; hangers
Hgs: Haugesund
hgsw: horn gap switch
hgt: height
HGTAC: Home Grown Timber Advisory Committee
HGTB: Haiti Government Tourist Bureau
hgv: heavy goods vehicle
HGW: Herbert George Wells
Hgy: Highway
hh: half-hard; handhole; heavy hydrogen
h/h: hard of hearing
hh: *hojas* (Spanish—leaves)
h to h: heel-to-heel
hH: heavy hydrogen
HH: Harry Hansen; Helen Hunt Jackson; Her (His) Highness; His Holiness; Howard Hanson; Huntington Hartford
H/H: Havre-Hamburg (range of ports)
H & H: Handy & Harman; Holland & Holland
HH: *Herren* (German—Gentlemen)
hha: half-hardy annual
hhb: half-hardy biennial
HHBS: Hereford Herd Book Society
hhd: hogshead
HH. D.: *Humanitatis Doctor* (Latin—Doctor of Humanities)
hhdws: heavy handy deadweight scrap
hhf: household furniture
HHFA: Housing and Home Finance Agency
hhg: household goods
hhh: triple hard
HHH: Hubert Horatio Humphrey
HHHC: Hunt the Hunters Hunt Club (Amory Foundation funded)
HHI: Hellenic Hydrobiological Institute
H-hinge: capital-H-shaped hinge
hhld: household
HHMS: His Hellenic Majesty's Ship
hhmu: hand-held maneuvering unit
HHNSR: Hudson Highlands National Scenic Riverway
H-hour: hostile operations commencement hour
hhp: half-hardy perennial
HHPL: Herbert Hoover Presidential Library
HHS: Haaren High School; Hunter High School
HHSP: Highland Hammock State Park (Florida)
HHUMC: Hadassah-Hebrew University Medical Center
HHW: higher high water
HHWI: higher high water interval
hi: contracted form of "hail"; high; high intensity; humidity index
h.i.: *hic iacet* (Latin—here lies)—also appears on tombstones as H.I.
h & i: harassing and interdictory (artillery fire)
hi (HI): hyperglycemic index
Hi: Hering illusion; High (postal abbreviation); Hindi; Hiram
HI: Harris Intertype; Hat Institute; Hawaiian Islands; Heat Index; Henrik Ibsen; Humidity Index; Hydraulic Institute
hia: hold in abeyance
HIA: Handkerchief Industry Association; Horological Institute of America; Hospital Industries Association; Hungarian Imperial Association
HIAA: Health Insurance Association of America
hi-ac: high accuracy
HIAD: Handbook of Instructions for Airplane Designers
HIAG: *Hilfsorganisation auf Gengenseitigkeit* (German—Mutual Aid Organization)
HIAGSED: Handbook of Instruction for Aircraft Ground Support Equipment Designers
HIAS: Hebrew Sheltering and Immigrant Aid Society
Hib: Hibernia (Ireland); Hibernian (Irish)
HIB: Herring Industry Board
Hibbd: *Halbband* (German—half binding)
hibex: high-acceleration booster experiment
Hibiscus: Hawaii state flower; Hawaiian girl's nickname
HIC: Heart Information Center; Herring Industries Council
hicapcom: high-capacity communications
hicat: high-altitude clear-air turbulence
hic jac: *hic jacet* (Latin—here lies)
hiclass: hierarchical classification
Hi Com: High Command; High Commission; High Commissioner
hid.: hallucinations, illusions, and delusions; headache, insomnia, depression (syndrome); high-intensity discharge (lamps)
Hid: Hidalgo
hidal: helicopter insecticide-dispersal apparatus, liquid
hidalgo: *hijo de algo* (Spanish—son of someone)
Hidalgo: Miguel Hidalgo y Costilla (Padre Hidalgo)
HIDB: Highlands and Islands Development Board (Scotland)
Hidden Empire: Ethiopia
HIE: Hibernation Information Exchange; Histrionic Instruction Education
hier: hieroglyphics
Hier.: *Hierosolma* (Latin—Jerusalem)
Hieronymus Bosch: palette name

of Hieronymus van Aeken
HIES: Hadassah Israel Education Services
HIF: Health Information Foundation
hifar: high-flux Australian reactor (HIFAR)
hifc: hog intrinsic factor concentrate
hi-fi: high-fidelity
hiflex: high flexibility
HIFNY: Hospitality Industry Foundation of New York
hifor: high-level forecast
hig: hermetically sealed integrating gyroscope; higgler
Hig: Higgins; Higginson
HIG: Hartford Insurance Group
higashi: (Japanese—east)
HIGED: *Handbook of Instruction for Ground Equipment Designers*
Highlands: Highlands of the Hudson; Highlands of the Navesink close to where Henry Hudson first landed in 1609 before entering New York Bay and sailing up the Hudson River; Highlands of Scotland—hills and mountains of northern Scotland
High Priestess of Transcendentalism: Margaret Fuller
high-Q: high quality
High Sierras: higher Sierra Nevada Mountains of California
High Tatras: high Tatra Mountains of Czechoslovakia's Carpathians
High-Tide Province: Canada's New Brunswick
HIH: Her (His) Imperial Highness
HII: Health Insurance Institute
hijack: hijacked; hijacker; hijacking
hik: hiking
hil: high intensity lighting
Hil: Hilary
hilac: heavy-ion linear accelerator
HILC: Hampshire Inter-Library Center (Amherst, Mount Holyoke, and Smith colleges)
Hildegarde Neff: stage name of Hildegard Knef
Hill: The Hill (Capitol Hill in Washington, D.C. where the Congress meets within the Capitol)
Hillbilly Country: mountainous parts of the Carolinas, Georgia, Tennessee, Kentucky, and West Virginia
Hill District: Pittsburgh's worst slum recently redeveloped into a low-rent housing area
hi-lo: high-low
Hil-Vis: Hiligaynon-Visayan
HIM: Her (His) Imperial Majesty
Himalaya: (Sanskrit—Home of the Snow)
Himalayas: Himalaya Mountains between India and Tibet
hi mi: high mileage
HIMS: Heavy Interdiction Missile System
Hinck: Hinckley
Hind: Hindi; Hindu; Hindustani
Hindu Monarchy: Nepal
Hinglish: Hindi + English (English interlarded with Hindi expressions and words)
HINP: Hundred Islands National Park (Philippines)
Hint: Hinton; Hinton Test (for syphilis)
HINWR: Hawaiian Islands National Wildlife Refuge
hio: hypoiodite
hiomt (HIOMT): hydroxyindole-O-methyltransferase
H-ion: hydrogen ion
hip.: high-impact pressure
Hip: Hippolyte
HIP: Health Insurance Plan
hipar: high-power acquisition radar
hipdom: hippiedom
HIPERNAS: High-Performance Navigation System
hipoe: high-pressure oceanographic equipment
hipot: high potential
Hippiedam: hippie-infested Dutch city such as Amsterdam or Rotterdam
Hipp: Hippocrates
Hippocrates of Pennsylvania: Benjamin Rush
hippo(s): hippopotamus(es)
hips.: hippies
HIR: Heron Island Resort (Queensland)
hiran: high-precision shoran
HIRB: Health Insurance Registration Board
hirel: high reliability
HIRI: Hawaiian Independent Refinery Incorporated
Hirohito: Emperor Hirohito Showa (Japan's 124th emperor in direct lineage)
Hiroshige: Ando Hiroshige (19th-century Japanese landscape painter)
HIRS: High-Impulse Retrorocket System
Hirschsprung's disease: congenital colonic dilatation
HIRS/smrd: High-Impulse Retrorocket System/spin-motor rotation detector
Hirt: Aulus Hirtius (Roman historian)
his. (HIS): histidine (amino acid); history
h.i.s.: *hic iacet sepultus* (Latin—here lies buried)—also appears as h.i.s.
Hi-S: Hi-Standard (firearms)
HIS: Health Interview Survey; Hospital Information System
HISC: House Internal Security Committee (formerly House Un-American Activities Committee—HUAC)
His Holiness: the Pope
His Majesty: the King
Hisp: Hispaniola
Hispan: Hispanic
Hispania: (Latin—Hispanic Peninsula)—Portugal and Spain
Hispanic Places: Andorra, Argentina, Azores, Balearic Islands, Bolivia, Brazil, Canary Islands, Cape Verde Islands, Ceuta and Melilla, Chile, Colombia, Costa Rica, Cuba, Dominican Republic, Ecuador, El Salvador, Equatorial Guinea, Guam, Guatemala, Honduras, Macao, Madeira, Mexico, Morocco, Nicaragua, Panama, Paraguay, Peru, Philippines, Portugal, Puerto Rico, Spain, Spanish Sahara, Uruguay, Venezuela
Hispanics: people of Portuguese or Spanish descent or a study of their culture and language
Hispaniola: (Spanish—Little Spain)—large West Indian island containing the Dominican Republic and Haiti
Hispano: Hispanoamericano (Spanish American); Hispano-Suiza (automobile)
hist: historical; history
Histadrut: (Hebrew—General Federation of Labor)
histo: histoplasmosis
histol: histology
Historian of the American Forest: Francis Parkman
Historian With A Camera: Mathew B. Brady
Historic Center of North Carolina: New Bern
Hit: Holtzman inkblot technique
hi-T: high torque
HIT: Health Indication Test
Hitch: Hitchborn(e); Hitchcock
hi-temp: high temperature
Hit Pom: Hither Pomerania (coastal East Germany)
Hitler: Adolph Schickelgruber

Hitt: Hittite
HIUS: Hispanic Institute of the United States
hiv: *hiver* (French—winter)
hivos: high-vacuum orbital simulator
hi wat: high water
Hiwi: *Hilfsfreiwilliger* (German—auxiliary volunteer)
HIWRP: The Hoover Institution on War, Revolution and Peace
HJ: Hitler Jugend (German—Hitler Youth); Honest John (short-range unguided missile); Howard Johnson (stock exchange symbol)
H. J.: *hic jacet* (Latin—here lies)
HJBS: Hashemite Jordan Broadcasting Service
HJC: Hershey Junior College
HJPA: Holmes Junge Protected Area (Australian Northern Territory)
H J Res: House Joint Resolution
H.J.S.: hic jacet sepultus (Latin—here lies buried)
h-k: hand to knee
HK: Hong Kong
HK: Helsingin Kaupunginorkesteri (Finnish—Helsinki City Symphony Orchestra)
HKA: Hong Kong Airways
HKCEC: Hong Kong Catholic Education Council
hk cells: human kidney cells
HK$: Hong Kong dollar
hkf: handkerchief
H Kg: Hong Kong
HKG: Hong Kong, British Crown Colony (airport)
HKJ: Hashemite Kingdom of Jordan
HKL: Halldor Kilyan Laxness
HKLA: Hong Kong Library Association
hkm: high-velocity kill mechanism
HKMA: Hong Kong Management Association
HKPO: Hong Kong Philharmonic Orchestra
HKTA: Hong Kong Tourist Association
HKTDC: Hong Kong Trade Development Council
HK virus: Hong-Kong type of influenza virus
hl: hand lantern; hectoliter; hinge line; holiday
h&l: door hinge resembling ligature of capital H and capital L
h.l.: *hoc loco* (Latin—in this place)
H: Hill (postal abbreviation); latent hypermetropia (symbol)
HL: Haute-Loire; Herpetologists League; Home Lines; Honours List; House of Lords; Hygienic Laboratories; Hygienic Laboratory
H-L: Haute-Loire
H of L: House of Lords
hla (HLA): homologous leucocytic antibodies
HL&AG: Henry E. Huntington Library and Art Gallery
hlb: hydrophile-lipophile balance
HLBB: Home Loan Bank Board
HLC: Hospital Library Council (Dublin)
HLD: Harold Handley Page (aircraft)
hl di: hole die
hlg: halogen
HLH: Haroldson Lafayette Hunt
HLHS: Heavy-Lift Helicopter System
HLI: Highland Light Infantry
HLL: Hellenic Lines Limited
h/l number: hydrophile/lipophile number
HLNP: Hattah Lakes National Park (Victoria, Australia)
HLNWR: Havasu Lake National Wildlife Refuge (California); Hutton Lake National Wildlife Refuge (Wyoming)
hlp (HLP): hyperlipidemia
hlpr: helper
HLPR: Howard League for Penal Reform
hlr: heart-lung resuscitation
HLRS: Homosexual Law Reform Society
hls: heavy logistics support; hills
hl S: heilige Schrift (German—holy scripture)
Hls: Hills (postal abbreviation)
HLS: Harvard Law School; Heavy Logistics Support
hl sa: hole saw
hlv: herpes-like virus
hlw: higher low water; high-level waste
Hlw: Halbleinwand (German—half-bound cloth)
HLW: higher low water
HLWI: higher low water interval
hlwn: highest low-water neap tides
HLWRP: Hoover Library on War, Revolution, and Peace (Stanford University)
Hlzbl: Holzbläser (German—woodwinds)
hm: hallmark; harmonic mean; hectometer; hollow metal
h.m.: *hoc mense* (Latin—in this month)
h & m: hit and miss; hull and machinery
hm^2: square hectometer
hm^3: cubic hectometer
Hm: manifest hypermetropia
HM: Harbour Master; Haute-Marne; Head Master; Head Mistress; Her (His) Majesty; Herman Melville; Home Missions
H-M: Haute-Marne
Hma: Hiroshima
HMA: Her (His) Majesty's Airship; Hoist Manufacturers Association; Home Manufacturers Association
H & MA: Hotel and Motel Association
HMAA: Horse and Mule Association of America
HMAC: Her (His) Majesty's Aircraft Carrier
HMARC: Houston Metropolitan Archives and Research Center
HMAS: Her (His) Majesty's Australian Ship
hmb: homatropine methyl bromide (HMB)
HMB: Hops Marketing Board
HMBDV: Her (His) Majesty's Boom Defence Vessel
HMBI: Her (His) Majesty's Borstal Institution
hmc: howitzer motor carriage
hmc (HMC): hydroxymethyl cystosine
HMC: Harvey Mudd College; Her (His) Majesty's Customs
HMCG: Her (His) Majesty's Coastguard
HMC & H: Hahnemann Medical College and Hospital
HMCIF: Her (His) Majesty's Chief Inspector of Factories
HMCN: Her (His) Majesty's Canadian Navy
HM Comm: Historical Manuscripts Commission
HMCS: Her (His) Majesty's Canadian Ship
HMCSC: Her (His) Majesty's Civil Service Commissioners
HMCyS: Her (His) Majesty's Ceylonese Ship
hmd: hollow metal door; humid; hydraulic mean depth
hmd (HMD): hyaline membrane disease
HMD: Her (His) Majesty's Destroyer
HMDBA: Hollow Metal Door and Buck Association
hmdf: hollow metal door and frame
hmf: hollow metal frame
HMF: Her (His) Majesty's Forces

hmf black: high-modulus furnace black
HMFI: Her (His) Majesty's Factory Inspectorate
hmg (HMG): human menopausal gonadotrophin
HMG: heavy machine gun; Her (His) Majesty's Government
HMHS: Horace Mann High School
HMI: Her (His) Majesty's Inspector; Hughes Medical Institute
HMIS: Her (His) Majesty's Indian Ship; Her (His) Majesty's Inspector of Schools
HMIT: Her (His) Majesty's Inspector of Taxes
HML: Harper Memorial Library (University of Chicago)
HMLI: Horace Mann—Lincoln Institute
HMLR: Her (His) Majesty's Land Registry
hmlt: hamlet
HMM: Her (His) Majesty's Minister
hmma (HMMA): 4-hydroxy-3-methodxy-mandelic acid
HMML: Her (His) Majesty's Motor Launch
HMMS: Her (His) Majesty's Motor Mine Sweeper
HMNAO: Her (His) Majesty's Nautical Almanac Office
HMNAR: Hart Mountain National Antelope Refuge (Oregon)
hmo: heart minute output
HMO: Health Maintenance Organization
HMOCS: Her (His) Majesty's Overseas Civil Service
H moll: (German—B minor)
HMOW: Her (His) Majesty's Office of Works
hmp: handmade paper
hmp (HMP): hexose monophosphate
HMP: Her (His) Majesty's Penitentiary; Her (His) Majesty's Prison
H.M.P.: *hoc monumentum posuit* (Latin—he erected this monument)
HMPMA: Historical Motion Picture Milestones Association
HMRC: Heineman Medical Research Center
HMRCS: Her (His) Majesty's Royal Canadian Ship
HMRT: Her (His) Majesty's Rescue Tug
hms: hours, minutes, seconds
HMS: Harvard Medical School; Her (His) Majesty's Service, Ship, or Steamer
HMS: *Hotel and Motel Systems*
HMSO: Her (His) Majesty's Stationery Office
hmstd: homestead
HMT: Her (His) Majesty's Trawler; Her (His) Majesty's Treasury; Her (His) Majesty's Tug
hmu (HMU): hydroxymethyl uracil
HMV: His Master's Voice (phonograph records)
hmy: too little
h.n.: *hac nocte* (Latin—tonight)
Hn: Herman(n)
HN: Head Nurse
Hna: Habana
HNBI: Hellenic National Broadcasting Institute
hnc: hypothalamic-neurohypophysical complex
HNC: Harbors and Navigation Code
Hnd: *The Hindu* (Madras)
HND: Higher National Diploma
hndbk: handbook
hndlr: handler
hn fm: hand form
HNG: Houston Natural Gas
HNL: Honolulu, Hawaii (airport)
HNNNR: Herma Ness National Nature Reserve (Scotland)
Hno: Hanover
HNO_3: nitric acid
Hnos: *Hermanos* (Spanish—brothers)
hnp: high needle position
HNP: Haleakala National Park (Maui, Hawaii)
hnrs: honors
hn(s): horn(s)
HNWR: Hagerman National Wildlife Refuge (Texas); Horicon National Wildlife Refuge (Wisconsin)
ho: hoist
ho: (Chinese—river)
'ho': whore
Ho: Ho Chi Minh
Ho: holmium; Honduran; Honduras; Hondureño
HO: Hydrographic Office (USN)
HO: *Handelsorganisation* (German—trade organization)
hoa: hands off—automatic
HOA: Home Owners Association
hoax: (Contraction—hocus pocus)
hob.: height of burst
Hob: Anthony van Hoboken (Dutch chronologist-enumerator of Haydn's music); Hoboken (Belgian seaport near Antwerp; place near Waycross, Georgia; port city in New Jersey opposite lower Manhattan)
Hoban: Holborn
Hob(bie): Albert
hobe: honeycomb before expansion
hobgob(s): hobgoblin(s)
Hob-Job: Hobson-Jobson (similar-sounding words to those of other languages with some or complete loss of meaning; e.g., Hobson—Jobson supposedly equivalent to Arabic cry of mourning for grandsons of Mohammed—*ya Hasan!—o Husain!;* Key West believed same as *Cayo Hueso* (Spanish—Bone Key); Leghorn invented by British sailors who thought it equivalent to *Livorno;* Coromuel—beach in Baja California—named after English pirate—*Cromwell;* white rhino really the Dutch *weid rhino*—a wide-mouthed rhinoceros and really not white)
Hobo: Hoboken
Hobohemia: Hobo bohemia (skid-row areas such as Brooklyn's Park Slope or Manhattan's Bowery or its East Village, to name but three New York Hobohemias)
hoc: heavy organic chemical(s)
HoC: House of Commons
hoch: (German—high)
Ho Chi Minh: Nguyen That Thanh
Ho Chi Minh City: Saigon's new name imposed upon its surrender to Vietcong communist guerrillas wishing to honor the founder of their forces liberating French Indo-China—Ho Chi Minh
hock.: Hockheimer (Rhine wine)
H.O.C.S.: *Hostem Occidit, Civem Servavit* (Latin—A foe he slew, a citizen he saved)—inscription found on Roman civic crowns
hoc vesp.: *hoc vespere* (Latin—this evening)
hod.: hyperbaric oxygen drenching
H o D: Head of Department
Hodara's disease: hair splitting
Hodge: (nickname for the typical English farmer)
Hodgkin's disease: progressive enlargement of the lymph nodes
HOD Test: Hoffer, Osmond, and Desmond Test (for schizo-

phrenia)
HoF: Hall of Fame
Hoff: Hoffman; Hoffmann; Hofman reflex
HO-gage: 5/8-inch track gauge (model railroads)
Hog Butcher for the World: Chicago's nickname in the early 1900s
ho & gem: heavy oil and gas-cut mud
Hog and Hominy State: Tennessee
HOI: Headquarters Operating Instruction
hoj: home on jamming
HoJo: Howard Johnson (roadside restaurants)
H o K: House of Keys
hoke: hokum
hoku: (Japanese—north)
Hokusai: Katsushika Hokusai (19th-century Japanese engraver-illustrator-teacher)
hol: holiday; hollow; holly
Hol: Holland; Hollander
Hol: *Holanda* (Portuguese or Spanish—Holland)
HoL: House of Lords
holidaze: alcohol-or-drug-induced daze characterized by incidence of over-the-holidays accidents and fatalities
HOLC: Home Owners Loan Corporation
holl: *hollandais* (French—Dutch)
Holl: Holland; Hollander
Holland in the Caribbean: Netherlands Antilles (Aruba, Bonaire, Curaçao, Saba, Sint Eustatius, Sint Maarten)
Hollie: Holladay; Holiday; Hollingsworth; Hollis; Hollister; Hollway
Hollyw'd: Hollywood
holo: holograph
Holocaust: Hitler's extermination, humiliation, and torture of the Jews and others he and his Nazi minions persecuted
hol-ry: whole rye
hols: holidays
Holt: Holt, Rinehart & Winston
Holw: Hollow (postal abbreviation)
Holy Cities: Mecca and Medina in Saudi Arabia; Mohammed was born in Mecca and died in Medina
Holy Horatio: Horatio Alger, Jr
Holy Land: Israel
hom: homonym
Hom: Homer
Hom.: *Homilia* (Latin—homily; sermon)
Home: Home Office (England and Wales)
HOME: Home Ownership Made Easy
Home of Abraham Lincoln: Springfield, Illinois
Home of the Alamo: San Antonio, Texas
Home of Baseball: Cooperstown, New York
Home of the Blues: Memphis, Tennessee
Home of Casey Jones: Jackson, Tennessee
Home of Contented Cows: Carnation, Washington
Home of the Cotton Carnival: Memphis, Tennessee
Home of Diamond Walnuts: Stockton, California
home ec: home economics
Home of Franklin Delano Roosevelt: Hyde Park, New York
Home of George Washington: Mount Vernon, Virginia
Home of the Giants: Jotunheimen Mountains in Norway
Home of the Kentucky Derby: Louisville
Homeland of the Bengalis: Bangladesh
homeo: homeopath; homeopathic; homeopathy
Home of Old Miss: Oxford, Mississippi—the home of Ole Miss—The University of Mississippi
Home of the Snow: Himalaya Mountains
Home of Storms: Gulf of Alaska
Home of Theodore Roosevelt: Oyster Bay, Long Island, New York
Home of Thomas Jefferson: Monticello, Virginia
Home of the Waltz: Vienna
Homer.: Homeric
Homer Wilbur: (pseudonym—James Russell Lowell)
HOMES: mnemonic for remembering the five Great Lakes—Huron, Ontario, Michigan, Erie, Superior
homo: homeopath; homeopathic; homeopathy; homosexual; homosexuality
homolat: homolateral
homosex: homosexual; homosexuality
hon: honey; honor; honorable; honorarium; honorary; honored
Hon: Honduran; Honduras; Hondureño; Honorable
Hon'ble: Honourable
Hon Consul: Honorary Consul
Hond: Honduran; Honduras
Honest Abe: Abraham Lincoln
Honest John: solid-sustainer motor surface-to-surface ballistic missile produced by Douglas Aircraft
Honest Harold: Secretary of the Interior Harold Le Claire Ickes also called the Old Curmudgeon
Honey Capital: Uvalde, Texas
Honey Fitz: John F. (Honey Fitz) Fitzgerald
Honeymoon City: Niagara Falls, New York
Hono: Honolulu
hons: honors
Hon Sec: Honorary Secretary
hood.: hoodlum
Hook: Hooker; The Hook—Hook of Holland *(Hoek van Holland)*; Hook Point, Ireland; Sandy Hook, New Jersey; Hooky Nail
Hoosier Capital: Indianapolis, Indiana
Hoosier Poet: James Whitcomb Riley
Hoosier(s): native(s) of Indiana; name believed to be a frontier-era contraction of *Who's there?*—pronounced *hoosier*
Hoosier State: Indiana's official nickname
Hoover: Hoover Institution (Stanford University)
hop.: high oxygen pressure; holding procedures
Hop: Hopkin; Hopkins; Hopkinson; Hopwood
HOPE: Health Opportunity for People Everywhere
HOPEG: Hotel and Public Building Equipment Group
hoppers: grasshoppers
hor: home of record; horizon; horizontal
Hor: Horace; Horatio
H o R: House of Representatives
Horace: Quintus Horatius Flaccus
hora decub.: *hora decubitus* (Latin—at bedtime)
hora interm.: *hora intermedius* (Latin—at the intermediate hours)
hora som.: *hora somni* (Latin—at bedtime)
HO & RC: Humble Oil and Refining Company
HoReCa: Hotel, Restaurant, and Cafe Keepers
horiz: horizontal
Horn: (German—peak)
Horn: Hornblower (Midshipman, Lieutenant, Captain, Commodore, Lord, or Admi-

ral—indomitable naval character created by C.S. Forester)
horo: horoscope
horol: horology
Hor Q: Horatius Quintus Flaccus (Roman poet)
HORSA: Hut Operation Raising School-leaving Age
Horseman: Haydn's String Quartet in G minor (opus 74, no. 3)
Horseshoe Curve: Altoona, Pennsylvania's nickname as it is a railroad town close to the celebrated Horseshoe Curve built by the Pennsylvania Railroad to cross the Alleghenies and traverse the valley of the Juniata River
Horse Thief Hollow: Oak Lawn, Michigan's original name and now a nickname
hort: horticulture
hortic: horticultural; horticulture; horticulturist
HORU: Home Office Research Unit
hor. un. spatio: *horae unius spatio* (Latin—at the end of an hour)
'ho's: whores
Hos: The Book of Hosea
HOS: Hawaiian Orchid Society
hose.: hosiery
Hosea Biglow: (pseudonym—James Russell Lowell)
Hosp: Hospital (postal abbreviation)
hosp ins: hospital insurance
Hostess to the Nation: Dolley Madison—wife of President James Madison
hot.: human old tuberculin
HOT: Hamilton-Oshawa-Toronto (industrial complex); Hot Springs, Arkansas (airport)
HOTAC: Hotel Accommodation (London hotel service)
Hotel: code for letter H
HOTLIPS: Honorary Order of Trumpeters Living in Possible Sin
Hot Potato: Luke Hamlin
Hotspur: Sir Henry Percy
Hottest Town in Texas: Presidio—on the Rio Grande opposite Ojinago in Mexico
Hot Water State: Arkansas
Hou: Houston
HOU: Houston, Texas (airport)
Houdini: Harry Houdini (real name Ehrich Weiss)—America's foremost escapologist-magician
Houghton: Houghton Mifflin
Hounds: Houndsditch
Hous: Houston
House: The House—House of Commons in England; House of Representatives in the United States; London's Stock Exchange; Oxford University's Christ College
House of the Book: (see *LCL*)
House of D: (Women's) House of Detention (NYC)
household coal: bituminous coal; soft coal
House Ruth Built: New York City's Yankee Stadium in the Bronx where Babe Ruth hit so many home runs
Hou Sym Orch: Houston Symphony Orchestra
houv: *houvere* (Finnish—charity)
hoved: (Dano-Norwegian—cape)
how.: howitzer
How: *Howard (U.S. Supreme Court Reports)*
HoW: Happiness of Womanhood
HOW: Home-Owners' Warranty
Howie: Howard; Howarth; Howe; Howell; Howland
howtar: howitzer-mortar
HOW-TO: Housing Operation with Training Opportunity (OEO)
Hox: Hoxie
Hoxford(shire): (Cockney—Oxford(shire))
hp: highpass; high potency; high pressure; hollowpoint; horizontal parallax; horizontally polarized; horsepower; hot press(ed)
h & p: history and physical (examination)
HP: Haute-Pyrénées; House Physician; Houses of Parliament
H-P: Handley-Page; Haute-Pyrénées; Hewlett-Packard
HP: *Homeopathic Pharmacopoeia*
HPA: Hospital Physicists Association
HPAAS: High-Performance Aerial Attack System
hpac: hydropress accessor
HPAL: Holland Pan-American Line
hpb: hinged plotting board
HPC: Hercules Powder Company; Highland Park College
hpc black: hard-processing channel black
HPCC: High-Performance Control Center
hpchd: harpsichord
hpchdst: harpsichordist
hp cyl: high-pressure cylinder
H-P d: Hough-Powell digitizer
HPD: Hawaii Police Department
hpf: highest possible frequency; high-powered field; hydropress form
HPF: Horace Plunkett Foundation
hpg (HPG): human pituitary gonadotrophin
H_{pge}: heading per gyro compass
hp hd: high-pressure high-density
hp hr: horsepower hour
hpi: history of present illness
hpl: high(est) point level; human parotid lysozyme; human placental lactogen
Hpl: Hartlepool
HPL: Halifax Public Library; Hamilton Public Library; Hartford Public Library; Houston Pipe Line; Houston Public Library
hplr: hinge pillar
HPM: Human Potential Movement
HPMA: Hardwood Plywood Manufacturers Association
hpn: horsepower nominal
hpo: high-pressure oxygenation
HPO: Hamilton Philharmonic Orchestra; Highway Post Office
H-pole: H-shaped telegraph or telephone pole
hpox: high-pressure oxygen
HPPA: Horses and Ponies Protection Association
h-p plan: hire-purchase plan (British equivalent of American installment-plan purchasing)
HPR: House of Pacific Relations
HPRF: Hypersonic Propulsion Research Facility
hps: high-pressure steam; high protein supplement; hot-pressed sheet
HPS: Harlem Preparatory School; Health Physics Society; High Protestant Society
H_{psc}: heading per standard compass
hpst: harpist
H_{pstgc}: heading per steering compass
hpt: high point; high-pressure test
HPTA: High Purchase Trade Association
hptn: hypertension
Hptw: *Hauptwerk* (German—great work)
hpu: hydraulic pumping unit
hpv: high-passage virus
hpv-de: high-passage virus (grown in) duck embryo

hpv-dk: high-passage virus (grown in) dog kidney
hq: headquarters
h.q.: *hoc quaere* (Latin—see this)
H-Q: Hydro-Quebec
HQBA: Headquarters Base Area
hqc: hydroxyquinoline citrate
HQ COMD USAF: Headquarters Command, USAF
HQMC: Headquarters—Marine Corps
HQ USAF: Headquarters, USAF
hr: hairspace; handling room; heat resisting; height range; home run; hook rail; hoserack; hour; relative humidity (symbol)
hr: *herr* (Swedish—Sir)—Mr
h(r): hail and rain (meteorological symbol)
Hr: *Herr* (Danish or German—Mr; Sir)
HR: Hospital Recruit; House of Representatives; International Harvester (stock exchange symbol)
H-R: Haut-Rhin
H & R: Harper & Row; Harrington & Richardson; Herweg & Romine
Hra: Herra (Finnish—Mister)
HRA: Health Resources Administration; Human Resources Administration; Hunters' Rights Association
HRA: *Historical Records of Australia*
HRAG: Helena Rubinstein Art Gallery
HRB: Highway Research Board; Highway Research Bureau; Housing and Redevelopment Board
hrc: high rupturing capacity
HRC: Humacao Regional College; Humanities Research Council
hrd: hard
HRD: Human Resources Development
HRDA: Human Resources Development Agency
HRDL: Hudson River Day Line
hrdwd: hardwood
hrdwr: hardware
hre: hypersonic research engine
hre (HRE): high-resolution electrocardiography
HRE: Holy Roman Empire
H reflex: Hoffmann reflex (of the tibial nerve)
H Rept: House Report
HRes: House Resolution (US House of Representatives)
HREU: Hotel and Restaurant Employees Union
Hrf: *Harfe* (German—harp)
HRF: Hat Research Foundation
HRFA: Hudson River Fishermen's Association
HRG: Halford, Robins, and Godfrey
HRH: His (Her) Royal Highness
hri: height-range indicator
HRIP: Highway Research in Progress
H.R.I.P.: *hic requiescit in pace* (Latin—here rests in peace)
hrir: high-resolution infrared radiometer
HRIS: Highway Research Information Service
hrl: horizontal reference line
Hrl: Harlingen
HRL: Hughes Research Laboratories; Human Resources Laboratory
Hrm: Herman
HRMA: Hampton Roads Maritime Association
Hr Ms: Haar Majesteits Schip (Dutch—Her Majesty's Ship)
Hrn: Herren (German—gentlemen)
HRO: Housing Referral Office (USAF)
HRP: Hampton Roads Ports; Human Reliability Program; Huntsville Research Park
hrr: higher reduced rate (taxation)
HRRC: Human Resources Research Center
HRRL: Human Resources Research Laboratory
HRRO: Human Resources Research Office
hrs: hot-rolled steel; hours
HRS: Hydraulics Research Station
HRSA: Honorary Member of the Royal Scottish Academy
hrsg: *herausgegeben* (German—edited or published)
Hrsg: *Herausgeber* (German—editor)
HRSRS: Hartbeestehoek Radio Space Research Station
HRT: Honolulu Rapid Transit
hrts: high risk test site
hrtwd: heartwood
Hrtz: *Ha'aretz* (Hebrew—The Land)—Israel's leading newspaper
HRU: Hydrological Research Unit
hrv: hypersonic research vehicle
HRVC: Hudson River Valley Commission
HRWMC: House of Representatives Ways and Means Committee
Hry: Henry
HRYC: Halifax River Yacht Club; Hampton Roads Yacht Club
HRZ: Hertz Corporation (stock exchange symbol)
hs: half strength; hardstand; high-speed; hinged seat; horizontal shear; horizontal stripe(s); hot stuff; hypersonic
h.s.: *hoc sensu* (Latin—in this sense)
Hs: Henriques
Hs: *Handschrift* (German—manuscript)
HS: Hakluyt Society; Haute-Saône; Haute-Savoie; High School; Home Secretary; House Surgeon; Hunterian Society; hydrofoil ship (naval symbol)
H.S.: *hic sepultus* or *hic situs* (Latin—here lies buried)
H-S: Haute-Saône; Haute-Savoie
H & S: Home & School
hsa: human serum albumin; hypersonic aircraft (HSA)
HSA: Health Services Administration; Herb Society of America; Hispanic Society of America; Holly Society of America; Hospital Savings Association; Hunt Saboteurs Association
HSAA: Health Sciences Advancement Award
HSAC: House (of Representatives) Science and Astronautics Committee
HSA & D: High School of Art and Design
hsb: human sexual behavior
hsbr: high-speed bombing radar
HSC: Health and Safety Code
HSCC: Historical Society of Southern California
H Sch: High School
Hschonhsn: Hohenschonhausen
HS-Co A: reduced coenzyme A
hscp: high-speed card punch
hscr: high-speed card reader
hsd: hard-site defense
HSD: Hawker Siddeley Dynamics
hsda: high-speed data acquisition
HSDG: Hamburg-Südamerika DampfschiffahrtsGesellschaft (Columbus Line)
HSDM: Harvard School of Dental Medicine
hse: house
Hse: House (postal abbreviation)
H.S.E.: *hic sepultus est* or *hic situs est* (Latin—here lies buried)

HSFI: High School of Fashion Industries
hsg: housing
Hsg: Helsingör (Elsinore)
HSG: Hawker Siddeley Group
hsgt: high-speed ground transport
HSGTP: High-Speed Ground Transportation Program
HSH: Her (His) Serene Highness
h & s hole: hellhole and smellhole (epithet applied to many African, Asian, Latin American, and Levantine places)
hsi: horizontal situation indicator
hsien: (Chinese—district; district capital)
Hsinhua: New China News Agency
HSK: Honorary Surgeon to the King
hskpg: housekeeping
hskpr: housekeeper
hsl: herpes simplex labialis (HSL)
HSL: Huguenot Society of London
HSLA: Home and School Library Association
HSLWI: Helical Spring Lock Washer Institute
hsm: high-speed memory
hsm (HSM): holosystolic murmur
HSM: Historical Society of Montana
HSMB: Hydronautics Ship Model Basin
HSNP: Hot Springs National Park
HSNR: Huleh Swamp Nature Reserve (Israel)
HSO: Haifa Symphony Orchestra; Hamburg Symphony Orchestra; Hartford Symphony Orchestra; Hitachi Symphony Orchestra; Honolulu Symphony Orchestra; Houston Symphony Orchestra
hsp: high-speed printer
h of sp: hybrid of species
HSP: Historical Society of Pennsylvania
HSP:* *Haute Société Protestant (French—High Protestant Society)
HSPA: Hawaiian Sugar Planters' Association; High School of the Performing Arts
HSPG: Hansard Society of Parliamentary Government
HSPH: Harvard School of Public Health
hsptp: high-speed paper-tape punch
HSQ: Honorary Surgeon to the Queen
hsr: high-speed reader
hsrc: high-speed rail concept
HSRI: Highway Safety Research Institute
hss: high-speed steel
HSS: History of Science Society; Hungarian State Symphony
HSSA: History of Science Society of America
HSSO: Hungarian State Symphony Orchestra
hst: hoist; hypersonic transport
H St: Hugo Stinnes (steamship line)
HST: Harry S. Truman—thirty-third President of the United States; Hawaiian Standard Time; hypersonic transport
HSTC: Henderson State Teachers College
HSTS: House Subcommittee on Traffic Safety
HSTI: Hartford State Technical Institute
HSTL: Harry S. Truman Library
hsts: horizontal stabilizer trim setting(s)
HSU: Hardin-Simmons University
H substance: histamine-like capillary vasodilator
H-substance: histamine-like substance
HSUNA: Humanist Student Union of North America
HSUS: Humane Society of the United States
hsv: heat-suppression valve
hsv (HSV): herpes simplex virus
HSV: Huntsville, Alabama (airport)
hswf: housewife
hszd: hermetically-sealed zener diode
ht: halftime; halftone; heat; heat treat; heat-treated; heat treatment; heavy formex; heavy tank; height; height telling; high temperature; high tension; hollow tile; hydrotherapy; hypertropia; hypodermic tablet
h & t: harden(ed) and temper(ed); hospitalization and treatment; hospitalize and treat
h.t.: *hoc tempore* (Latin—at this time); *hoc titulo* (Latin—under this title)
ht (HT): horizontal tabulation (data processing)
Ht: total hypermetropia
HT: Hawaiian Telephone; Hawaiian Territory; Hawaiian Theater; Hawaiian Time; Height Technician; Horsed Transport; Hospital Train
hta: heavier than air
htb: high-tension battery
HTB: Horserace Totalisator Board
htc: hydraulic temperature control
htd: heated
HTD: Hospital for Tropical Diseases
htd pl: heated pool
htd rm: heated room
Hte-Gar: Haute-Garonne
Hte-L: Haute-Loire
Hte-M: Haute-Marne
Hte-Sao: Haute-Saône
Hte-Sav: Haute-Savoie
Htes-Pyr: Hautes-Pyrénées
htfc: high-temperature fuel cell
ht fx: heat treat fixture
htg: heating
htgr (HTGR): high-temperature gas-cooled reactor
Htg & Vent: Heating & Ventilating
HTI: High Twelve International
htk: headline to come
htm: high-temperature metallography
HTMC: High Temperature Materials Corporation
Htn: Hamilton, Bermuda
hto: high-temperature oxidation; horizontal takeoff
htofore: heretofore
htol (HTOL): horizontal-take-off-and-landing
htp: high-test peroxide
h-t-p: house-tree-person (psychological drawing test)
HTP: House-Tree-Person (test)
htr: heater
htr (HTR): high-temperature reactor
HTR: Highway Traffic Regulations(s)
htrac: half-track
HTRDA: High-Temperature Reactor Development Associates
H Trin: Holy Trinity
hts: half-time survey; heights; high-tensile steel
Hts: Heights
HTS: Huntington, West Virginia (airport)
HTSA: Highway Traffic Safety Administration
htst: high-temperature short-time (pasteurization)
htt (HTT): heavy tactical transport
htu: heat transfer unit
htv (HTV): hypersonic test vehicle

htvt: heating and ventilating
htw: high-temperature water
HT&W: Hoosac Tunnel & Wilmington (railroad)
ht wkt: hit wicket
hu: hyperemia unit
Hu: Hungarian; Hungary
HU: Harvard University; Hebrew University; Howard University
HUA: Housing and Urban Affairs
HUAC: House Un-American Activities Committee
Hub: The Hub—Boston, Massachusetts also called Hub of American Culture, Hub of New England, and even Hub of the Universe
hubby: husband
Hub of Empire: London
Hubey: Hubert
Hub of New England: Boston
Hub of New York City: Columbus Circle
Hub of the Universe: nickname given by Oliver Wendell Holmes to the statehouse in Boston and later by others to the entire city
HUC: Hebrew Union College
HUCIA: Harvard University Center for International Affairs
HUCJIR: Hebrew Union College Jewish Institute of Religion
hucks: huckleberries
hucr: highest useful compression ratio
hud: head-up display
Hud: Huddleston; Hudson
HUD: Housing and Urban Development
Huel: Huelva
Hues: Huesca
huff-duff: high-frequency direction finder
HUFSM: Highway Users Federation for Safety and Mobility
Huggin: Hugh; Hugo
HUGHES: Hughes Aircraft Company
Hughie: Hugh
hugo: highly unusual geophysical operations
Hugo Wast: Gustavo Martínez Zuviría
Hugues Capet: Hugh Capet
HUJ: Hebrew University of Jerusalem
huk (HUK): hunter-killer
HUKFORLANT: Hunter-Killer Forces—Atlantic (USN)
HUKFORPAC: Hunter-Killer Forces—Pacific (USN)
huks (HUKS): hunter-killer submarine(s)—USN
Huks: *Hukbong Mapgapalayang Bayan* (Philippine Communist Armed Forces)
Hul: Hulbert; Huldreich; Hulton
HUL: Harvard University Library; Helsinki University Library
Hull: Kingston-upon-Hull
Hully: Hulbert
HULTIS: Hull Technical Interloan Scheme
hum: human; humane; humanism; humanities
hum.: *humaniora* (Latin—humanities)—also appears as *H.U.M.*
Hum: Humbert; Hummel; Humphrey; Humphreys; Humphry
Huma: *L'Humanité* (French-communist daily paper)
human eng: human engineering
Humanitarian Scientist: Louis Pasteur
HUMBLE: Humble Oil (Company)
humer: humerus
humi: humidity
Humph: Humphrey
HUMRRO: Human Resources Research Office
hums: humanitarian reasons
hun: hundred
Hun: Hungarian; Hungary
Hun: *Hungria* (Portuguese—Hungary); *Hungria* (Spanish—Hungary)
hund: hundred
Hung: Hungaria; Hungarian; Hungarica; Hungary
Hungarian Ocean: Lake Balaton—largest lake in central Europe
Hunt: Hunter; Huntington; Huntley; Huntly
Hunter's Point: San Francisco slum section
hunth: hundred thousand
Hunting: Mozart's String Quartet in B flat (K 458)
Hunts: Huntingdonshire
HUP: Harvard University Press
HUPAS: Hofstra University Pro Arte Symphony
hur: hurricane
hur (HUR): homes using radio
HURRAH: Help Us Reach and Rehabilitate America's Handicapped (HEW program)
hus: hemolytic uremic syndrome (HUS)
husb: husbandry
Husky Territory: the Yukon
Huss: Jan Huss (Johannes Hus von Husinetz)
hustle.: helium-underwater speech-translating equipment
hut. (HUT): homes using television
Hutch: Hutcheson; Hutchings; Hutchins; Hutchinson; Hutchison
hutv: home(s) using television
hv: heavy; high velocity; high voltage
h.v.: *hoc verbum* (Latin—this word)
h-v: high-voltage
h & v: heating and ventilating
HV: Health Visitor
Hva: Huelva
HVA: Health Visitors' Association
hvac: heating, ventilating, and air conditioning
hvar (HVAR): high-velocity aircraft rocket
HVB: Hawaii Visitors Bureau
hv & c: heating, ventilating, and cooling
HVCA: Heating and Ventilating Contractors' Association
HVCC: Hudson Valley Community College
hvd: high-velocity detonation; hypertensive vascular disease
hvdc: high-voltage direct current
HVEC: High Voltage Engineering Corporation
hvem: high-voltage transmission electron microscopy
hvh: herpsevirus hominis
Hvh: *Herpesvirus hominus* (Latin—herpes simplex virus)
H v H: *Hoek van Holland* (Dutch—Hook of Holland)
HVI: Home Ventilating Institute
H'ville: Huntsville, Alabama
hvJ: hemagluttinating virus of Japan
hvl: half-value layer
HVL: Hanseatic Vaasa Line; Heitor Villa-Lobos
Hvn: Haven
HVNP: Hawaii Volcanoes National Park
HVO: Hawaiian Volcano Observatory
HVP: Hudson Vitamin Products
HVPO: Hudson Valley Philharmonic Orchestra
hvps: high-voltage power supply
hvr: high-vacuum rectifier
HVRA: Hawaiian Volcano Research Association
hvsa: high-voltage slow activity
hvss: horizontal volute spring suspension
hvtp: high-velocity target-practice
HVWS: Hebrew Veterans of the War with Spain

hvy: heavy
hw: headwaiter; headwind; herewith; high water; hot water
Hw: *Hauptwerk* (German—great work)
h/w: husband and wife
H-W: Harbison-Walker (refractories)
H & W: Harland and Wolff (Belfast shipbuilders)
hwang: (Chinese—yellow, as in Hwang Ho)
Hwb: *Handwörterbuch* (German—pocket dictionary)
hwc: hot-water circulating
HWC: Heriot-Watt College
hwctr: heavy-water components test reactor
H'w'd: Hollywood
hwf & c: high water full and change
hwi: high water interval
HWI: Helical Washer Institute
hwl: high-water line
HWL: Henry Wadsworth Longfellow
hwLB: high water London Bridge
hwlwr (HWLWR): heavy-water-moderated boiling light-water-cooled reactor
hwm: high-water mark
HWM: Hiram Walker Museum (Windsor, Ontario)
HWMC: House Ways and Means Committee
hwmnt: high-water mark neap tide
hwmont: high-water mark ordinary neap tide
hwmost: high-water mark ordinary spring tide
hwmst: high-water mark spring tide
HWO: Homosexual World Organization
hwocr (HWOCR): heavy-water (moderated) organic-cooled reactor
hwost: high-water ordinary spring tides
hwq: high-water quadrature; tropic high-water inequality
hwr (HWR): heavy water reactor (AEC)
hws: hot-water soluble
HWS: Hurricane Warning Service
H & WSC: Hobart and William Smith Colleges
HWW: Hochschule für Welthandel, Wien (School for World Trade—Vienna)
Hwy: Highway
hx: hexode; history
Hx: history (medical case)
Hxd: Hardinxveld
hy: henry
Hy: Highway; Hiram; Hyman
HY: Helsingin Yliopisto (University of Helsinki)
hyb: hybrid
HYC: Harlem Yacht Club; Hartford Yacht Club; Haverhill Yacht Club
hyball: hydraulic ball
hycol: hybrid computer link
hycon: hydraulic control
hycotran: hybrid computer translator
hyd: hydrate; hydraulic(s); hydrostatics
Hyd: Hyderabad
hydac: hybrid digital-analog computer
hydapt: hybrid digital-analog pulse time
Hyde Park: Franklin Delano Roosevelt's home and library on the banks of the Hudson at Hyde Park, New York
hydr: hydrographer
hydrarg.: *hydrargyrum* (Latin—mercury)
HYDRAS: Hydrographic Digital Positioning and Depth Recording System
hydraul: hydraulic(s)
hydraweld: hydraulic-drawn welded (steel tubing)
hydro: hydrodynamic group of hydrodynamics (slang); hydroelectric; hydroelectrical; hydrographic; hydrology; hydrostatic
HYDRO: Hydrographic Office
hydrodyn: hydrodynamics
hydroelec: hydroelectric
hydrog: hydrography
hydrol: hydrology
HYDROIND: Hydrography of the Indian Ocean
HYDROLANT: Hydrography of the Atlantic Ocean
hydrom: hydromechanics
hydromagnetics: magnetohydrodynamics
HYDROPAC: Hydrography of the Pacific Ocean
hydros: hydrostatics
hydrot: hydrotherapy
hydrox: hydroxyline
HYDRSS: High Data Rate Storage System (NASA)
hydt: hydrant
hydx: hydroxide(s)
hyfes: hypersonic flight environmental simulator
hyg: hygiene; hygienic; hygroscopic
hygas: hydrogen gasification
hyl (Hyl): hydroxylysine
hyla: hybrid language assembler
HYMA: Hebrew Young Men's Association
hymnol: hymnologist; hymnology
hyp: hyperbola; hyperbolic; hyphen; hyphenate; hyphenation; hypochondria(c); hypothesis; hypothetical
hyp (Hyp): 4-hydroxyproline
Hyp: Hypolite
HYP: Harvard, Yale, and Princeton
hype: hypodermic (underground slang—person who injects drugs with a hypodermic syringe)
hyper: hypercritical
hyperdop: hyperbolic doppler
hypn: hypertension
hypno: hypnotism
hypnot: hypnotic; hypnotism; hypnotist
hypo: hypochondria; hypochondriac; hypochondriacal; hypodermic (injection or needle); hyposulfite of soda (sodium thiosulfate—$NaS_2O_3 + 5H_2O$)
hypoth: hypothesis
hypro: hydroxyproline
Hyrcanian: Caspian
hys: hysteria; hysteric; hysterical; hysterics
hyst: hysteresis; hysteria
hystad: hydrofoil stabilizing device
HYSURCH: Hydrographic Survey and Charting System
hytemco: high-temperature coefficient nickel-iron alloy
hy tr: heat treat
hz (Hz): hertz (one cycle per second); hertzian
Hz: Henriquez; hertz (cycles per second)
Hzk: Hezekiah
hzy: hazy

I

i: angle of incidence (symbol); incisor; indigo; infant; instantaneous current (symbol); interest; intransitive; isotopic fine structure (symbol); moment of photographic plate (symbol); optically inactive (symbol); rate of interest (symbol); Van't Hoff factor (symbol); vapor pressure constant (symbol)

i': in

i: Imperial Savings

i.: *id* (Latin—that)

I: acoustic intensity (symbol); candlepower or intensity of luminosity (symbol); conduction current (symbol); convection current (symbol); Ido (artificial language); in; inclination; India—code for letter I; Indian; industrial broadcasting; inertia; infantry; iodine; ionic strength (symbol); Ireland; Irish; Island; Isthmian Line; Italian Line; Italy—auto plaque; izzard

I: *in* (German or Italian—in); *inde* (Danish—in); *Isle* (French— island); *itä* (Finnish—east); *izquierda* (Spanish—left)

I: *Ile* (French—Island; Isle)

I^{128}: radioactive iodine

I^{130}: radioactive iodine

I^{131}: radioactive iodine

ia: immediately available; impedance angle; indicated altitude; infra-audible; initial appearance; international angstrom; intra-arterial; intra-articular

i.a.: *in absentia* (Latin—in the absence of)

i A: *im Auftrage* (German—by order; for; under instruction)

Ia: Ingegerd

IA: Indian Army; Industrial Arts; Inspection Administration; International Angstrom; Iraqi Airways

I/A: Isle of Anglesey

IA: *International Atlas* (Rand McNally)

I of A: Instructor of Artillery

IAA: Independent Airlines Association; Indian Association of America; Inspector Army Aircraft; Insurance Accountants Association; Interment Association of America; International Academy of Astronautics; International Acetylene Association; International Advertising Association; International Apple Association; International Association of Allergology; Intimate Apparel Associates

IAA: *International Aerospace Abstracts*

IAAA: Institute of Air Age Activities

IAAAA: Intercollegiate Association of Amateur Athletes of America

IAAB: Inter-American Association of Broadcasters

IAAC: International Agriculture Aviation Center

IAACC: Inter-Allied Aeronautical Control Commission

IAAE: Institution of Automotive and Aeronautical Engineers

IAAF: International Amateur Athletic Federation

IAAFA: Inter-American Air Force Academy

IAAI: International Association of Arson Investigators

IAALD: International Association of Agricultural Librarians and Documentalists

IAAM: International Association of Auditorium Managers; International Association of Automotive Modelers

IAAO: Interlochen Arts Academy Orchestra; International Association of Assessing Officers

IAAP: International Association of Applied Psychology

IAAS: Institute of Advanced Arab Studies

IAASE: Inter-American Association of Sanitary Engineering

IAASS: International Association of Applied Social Science

IAB: Inter-American Bank; International Air Bahama

IABA: Inter-American Bar Association

IABC: International Association of Business Communicators

IABG: International Association of Botanic Gardens

IAB-ICSU: International Abstracting Board—International Council of Scientific Unions

IABLA: Inter-American Bank for Latin America; Inter-American Bibliographical and Library Association

IABO: International Association of Biological Oceanography

IABPAI: International Association of Blue Print & Allied Industries

IABPC: International Association of Book Publishing Consultants

IABSE: International Association for Bridge and Structural Engineering

iac: intergration, assembly, checkout; interview after combat

IAC: Indian Airlines Corporation; Industry Advisory Commission; Information Analysis Center; Insurance Advertising Conference; Intermediate Air Command; Interview After Combat; Irish Air Corps

IACA: Independent Air Carriers Association; Inter-American College Association

IACB: Indian Arts and Crafts Board; International Advisory Committee on Bibliography (UNESCO); International Association of Convention Bureaus

IACC: Italy-America Chamber of Commerce

IACCP: Inter-American Council of Commerce and Production

IACD: International Association of Clothing Designers

IACE: International Air Cadet Exchange

IACES: International Air Cushion Engineering Society

IACHR: Inter-American Commission on Human Rights

IACI: Irish-American Cultural Institute

IACID: Inter-American Center

for Integral Development
IACM: International Association of Concert Managers
IACOMS: International Advisory Committee on Marine Sciences (FAO)
IACP: International Association of Chiefs of Police
IACP & AP: International Association for Child Psychiatry and Allied Professions
IACRL: Italian-American Civil Rights League
IACS: International Annealed Copper Standard
IACT: Illinois Association of Classroom Teachers
iad: intergrated automatic documentation
IAD: International Astrophysical Decade—1965–1975
IADB: Inter-American Defense Board; Inter-American Development Bank
IADC: Inter-American Defense College
IADF: Inter-American Association for Democracy and Freedom
IADIS: Irish Association for Documentation and Information Services
IADL: Italian-American Defense League
IADPC: Inter-Agency Data Processing Committee
IADR: International Association for Dental Research
IADS: International Association of Dental Students; International Association of Department Stores
iae: integral absolute error
IAE: Institution of Automobile Engineers
***IAE:** Institut Atomnoi Energii* (Russian—Atomic Energy Institute)
IAeA: Institution of Aeronautical Engineers
IAEA: International Atomic Energy Agency
IAEC: Israel Atomic Energy Commission
IAECOSOC: Inter-American Economic and Social Council
IAEE: International Association of Earthquake Engineers
IAEI: International Association of Electrical Inspectors
IAEL: International Association of Electrical Leagues
IAES: International Association of Electrotypers and Stereotypers
IAESTE: International Association for the Exchange of Students for Technical Experience
IAEWP: International Association of Educators for World Peace
iaf: interview after flight
IAF: Industrial Areas Foundation; International Abolitionist Federation (for abolition of prostitution); International Astronautical Federation; Israeli Air Force
I-AF: Inter-American Foundation
IAFAE: Inter-American Federation for Adult Education
IAFC: International Association of Fire Chiefs
IAFD: International Association of Food Distribution
IAFE: International Association of Fairs and Expositions
IAFF: International Association of Fire Fighters
iafi: infantile amaurotic family idiocy
IAFMM: International Association of Fish Meal Manufacturers
IAFWNO: Inter-American Federation of Working Newspapermen's Organizations
IAG: Interagency Advisory Group; International Association of Geodesy; International Association of Gerontology
IAGA: International Association of Geomagnetism and Aeronomy
IAGB & I: Ileostomy Association of Great Britain and Ireland
iagc: instantaneous automatic gain control
IAGC: International Association for Geochemistry and Cosmochemistry
IAGFCC: International Association of Game, Fish, and Conservation Commissioners
IAGM: International Association of Garment Manufacturers
I Agr E.: Institution of Agricultural Engineers
IAGS: Inter-American Geodetic Survey
IAH: Inter-American Highway; International Asian Highways; International Association of Hydrology
IAHA: Inter-American Hotel Association
IAHF: International Aerospace Hall of Fame
IAHM: International Association of Head Masters
IAHP: Institutes for the Achievement of Human Potential; International Association of Horticultural Producers
IAHR: International Association for Hydraulic Research
IAI: Icelandic Airlines Incorporated; International African Institute; International Association for Identification
IAIAS: Inter-American Institute of Agricultural Sciences
IAICM: International Association of Ice Cream Manufacturers
IAIE: Inter-American Institute of Ecology
IAIs: Israeli Aircraft Industries
IAL: Icelandic Airlines; Imperial Airways Limited; International Algebraic Language; International Arbitration League; International Association of Limnology; Irish Academy of Letters
***IAL:** Icelandic Airlines-Loftleider*
IALA: International Association of Lighthouse Authorities
IALC: International Association of Lions Clubs; International Association of Lyceum Clubs
IALL: International Association of Law Libraries
***i allg:** im allgemeinen* (German—generally; in general)
IALS: International Association of Legal Science
IAM: Institute of Appliance Manufacturers; Institute of Aviation Medicine; International Academy of Medicine; International Association of Machinists; International Association of Meteorology
IAMA: International Abstaining Motorists Association
IAMAM: International Association of Museums of Arms and Military History
IAMAP: International Association of Meteorology and Atmospheric Physics
IAMAT: International Association for Medical Assistance to Travelers
IAMB: International Association of Microbiologists
IAMC: Institute for Advancement of Medical Communication; Inter-American Music Council
IAMCA: International Association of Milk Control Agencies

IAMCL: International Association of Metropolitan City Libraries
IAMCR: International Association for Mass Communication Research
IAMFS: International Association of Milk and Food Sanitarians
IAML: International Association of Music Libraries
IAMLT: International Association of Medical Laboratory Technologists
IAMM: International Association of Medical Museums
IAMO: Inter-American Municipal Organization
IAMP: Inter-Agency Motor Pool
IAMR: Institute of Arctic Mineral Resources
IAMS: International Association of Microbiological Societies
IAMTCT: Institute of Advanced Machine Tool and Control Technology
IAMTF: Inter-Agency Maritime Task Force
IAMWF: Inter-American Mine Workers Federation
Ian: (Gaelic—John)
IAN: Instituto Agrario Nacional (National Agrarian Institute—Venezuela)
IANA: Inter-African News Agency
IANAP: Interagency Noise Abatement Program
IANC: International Airline Navigators Council
IA & ND: Indian Affairs and Northern Development (Canada)
IANEC: Inter-American Nuclear Energy Commission
iao: intermittent aortic occlusion
IAO: Incorporated Association of Organists
IAOC: Indian Army Ordnance Corps
IAOL: International Association of Orientalist Libraries
IAOR: International Abstracts in Operations Research
IAOS: Irish Agricultural Organization Society
IAP: Institute of Agricultural Parasitology; International Academy of Pathology; International Academy of Proctology
IAPA: Inter-American Parliamentary Organization; Inter-American Police Academy; Inter-American Press Association
IAPB: International Association for the Prevention of Blindness
IAPC: International Association for Public Cleansing
IAPG: Interagency Advanced Power Group; International Association of Physical Geography
IAPH: International Association of Paper Historians; International Association of Ports and Harbors
IAPHC: International Association of Printing House Craftsmen
IAPI: Institute of American Poultry Industries; Instituto Argentino de Producción Industrial (Argentine Industrial Production Institute)
IAPIP: International Association for the Protection of Industrial Property
IAPM: International Association of Progressive Montessorians
IAPN: International Association of Professional Numismatists
IAPO: International Association of Physical Oceanography
IAPP: International Association of Police Professors
IAPR: Indian Air Patrol Reserve
IAPS: Incorporated Association of Preparatory Schools
IAPSC: Inter-African Phytosanitary Commission
IAPSO: International Association of Physical Sciences of the Oceans
IAPT: International Association for Plant Taxonomy
IAPTA: International Allied Printing Trades Association
IAPW: International Association of Personnel Women
IAR: Institute for Air Research
IARA: Inter-Allied Reparations Agency
I Arb: Institute of Arbitrators
IARC: International Agency for Research on Cancer
IARF: International Association for Liberal Christianity and Religious Freedom
IARI: Industrial Advertising Research Institute
IARIGAI: International Association of Research Institutes for the Graphic Arts Industry
IARIW: International Association for Research into Income and Wealth
IARS: International Anesthesia Research Society
IARU: International Amateur Radio Union
ias: immediate access storage; indicated airspeed; instrument approach system
IAS: Institute for Advanced Study; Institute of the Aeronautical Sciences; Institute of Aerospace Sciences; Institute of American Strategy; Institute of Andean Studies; Instrument Approach System; International Accountants Society; International Association of Siderographers; International Aviation Service
IASA: International Air Safety Association; International Association of Sound Archives
IASC: Inter-American Safety Council
IASCH: Institute for Advanced Studies in Contemporary History (formerly Wiener Library)
iasd: interatrial septal defect
IASDI: Inter-American Social Development Institute
IASH: International Association of Scientific Hydrology
IASI: Inter-American Statistical Institute
IASL: International Association of School Librarians; Irish Association of School Librarians
IASLIC: Indian Association of Special Libraries and Information Centers
iasor: ice and snow on runway
IASP: International Association for Social Progress; International Association for Suicide Prevention
IASPEI: International Association of Seismology and Physics of the Earth's Interior
IASPO: International Association of Senior Police Officers
IASS: International Association for Shell Structures
IASSW: International Association of Schools of Social Work
iasy: international active sun years
iat: inside air temperature
IAT: Individual Acceptance Test-(ing); Institute for Applied Technology; Institute of Atomic Physics (Peking); International Academy of Tourism
IATA: International Air Transport Association
IATC: International Association of Tool Craftsmen

iatd: is amended to delete
IATE: International Association for Temperance Education
IATL: International Association of Theological Libraries
IATM: International Association for Testing Materials
IATME: International Association of Terrestrial Magnetism and Electricity
iatr: is amended to read
IATSE: International Alliance of Theatrical Stage Employees
IATTC: Inter-American Tropical Tuna Commission
IATUL: International Association of Technical University Libraries
iau: intrusion alarm unit
IAU: International Association of Universities; International Astronomical Union
IAUPL: International Association of University Professors and Lecturers
IAUPR: Inter-American University of Puerto Rico
IAV: International Association of Volcanology
IAVA: Industrial Audio-Visual Association
IAVFH: International Association of Veterinary Food Hygienists
IAVG: International Association for Vocational Guidance
iaw: in accordance with
IAW: International Alliance of Women
IAWA: International Association of Wood Anatomists
IAWMC: International Association of Workers for Maladjusted Children
IAWPR: International Association on Water Pollution Research
IAWS: Irish Agricultural Wholesale Society
IAWWW: *International Authors and Writers Who's Who*
IAZ: Inner Artillery Zone
ib: incendiary bomb; inclusion body; index of body build; infectious bronchitis; inner bottom; instruction book; instructional brochure
i b: *im besonderen* (German—in particular)
ib.: *ibidem* (Latin—in the same place)
Ib: Ibadan
IB: Iberia Líneas Aéreas de España (Iberian Airlines of Spain); incendiary bomb; Infantry Battalion; Information Bulletin; Intelligence Branch; international broadcast(ing)
IB: *Istanbul Bankasi* (Turkish—Istanbul Bank)
I o B: Institute of Bakers; Institute of Bankers; Institute of Bookkeepers; Institute of Brewers; Institute of Builders
IBA: Independent Bankers Association; Independent Bar Association; Institute for Bioenergetic Analysis; Institute of British Architects; Independent Broadcasting Authority; International Bar Association; International Briqueting Association; Investment Bankers Association; Investing Builders Association
IBAA: Investment Bankers Association of America; Italian Baptist Association of America
IBAE: Institution of British Agricultural Engineers
IBAHP: Inter-African Bureau for Animal Health and Protection
IBAM: Institute of Business Administration and Management
IBAP: Intervention Board for Agricultural Produce
I-bar: capital-I-shaped metal bar
IBAU: Institute of British-American Understanding
ibb: intentional bases on balls (baseball)
IBB: Illinois Inspection Bureau; International Bowling Board; International Brotherhood of Bookbinders
IBBD: *Instituto Brasileiro de Bibliografía e Documentaçao* (Brazilian Institute of Bibliography and Documentation)
ibbm: iron body bronze (or brass) mounted
IBBY: International Board on Books for Young People
IBC: International Broadcasting Corporation
IBC: *Instituto Brasileiro do Café* (Portuguese—Brazilian Coffee Institute)
IBCS: Integrated Battlefield Control System (USA)
IBD: Institute of British Decorators
IBE: Institute of British Engineers; International Bureau of Education
I-beam: capital-I-shaped metal beam
IBEC: International Bank for Economic Cooperation; International Basic Economy Corporation
IBECC: Instituto Brasileiro de Educação Ciencia e Cultura
IBEG: International Book Export Group
iben: incendiary bomb with explosive nose
IBERIA: Líneas Aéreas de España (Iberian Airlines of Spain)
Iberia: (Greek—Spain)
IBES: Illinois Bureau of Employment Security
IBEW: International Brotherhood of Electrical Workers
IBF: Institute of British Foundrymen
IBFD: International Bureau of Fiscal Documentation
IBFMP: International Bureau of the Federations of Master Printers
IBFO: International Brotherhood of Firemen and Oilers
IBG: Institute of British Geographers
IBHA: Insulation, Building, and Hardwood Association
IBhd: initial beachhead
ibi: invoice book, inward
IBI: Illinois Bureau of Investigation; Indiana Bureau of Investigation; Insulation Board Institute
ibid.: *ibidem* (Latin—in the same place)
IBI: *Instituto Bancario Italiano* (Italian Banking Institute)
ibid.: international bibliographical description
IBiol: Institute of Biology
IBK: Institute of Bookkeepers
IBL: Institute of British Launderers; Irish Biscuits Limited
ibm (IBM): intercontinental ballistic missile
IBM: International Business Machines
IBMR: International Bureau for Mechanical Reproduction
IBN: *Institut Belge de Normalisation* (French—Belgian Standards Institute)
ibo: invoice book, outward
IBOP: International Brotherhood of Operative Potters
ibp: initial boiling point
IBP: Institute of British Photographers; International Biological Program
IBPOEW: Improved Benevolent and Protective Order of Elks of the World
ibr: integral boiling reactor
IBR: Institute of Behavioral Re-

search
IBRD: International Bank for Reconstruction and Development (World Bank)
ibrl: initial bomb-release line
IBRM: Institute of Boiler and Radiator Manufacturers
IBRO: International Bank Research Organization; International Brain Research Organization; International Brewers' Research Organization
IBS: Indian Boy Scouts; Institute of Basic Standards; International Bach Society; Israel Broadcasting Service
IBSA: International Barber Schools Association
IB Scot: Institute of Bankers in Scotland
IBSGR: Isiolo Buffalo Spring Game Reserve (Kenya)
IBSS: Imperial Bureau of Soil Science
IBST: Institute of British Surgical Technicians
IBSTP: International Bureau for the Suppression of Traffic in Persons
IBT: International Brotherhood of Teamsters
IBTA: International Baton Twirlers Association
IBTCWH: International Brotherhood of Teamsters, Chauffeurs, Warehousemen, and Helpers
ib test: inkblot test (Rorschach test)
IBTS: International Bicycle Touring Society
IBTTA: International Bridge, Tunnel, and Turnpike Association
ibu: imperial bushel
IBU: International Broadcasting Union
ibv: infectious bronchitis vaccine
ibw: information bandwidth
IBW: International Boiler Works
IBWM: International Bureau of Weights and Measures
IBWS: International Bureau of Whaling Statistics
ibx (IBX): intermediate branch exchange
IBY: International Book Year (1972)
Ibz: Ibiza
ic: ice crystals; in charge of; index correction; informal communication; inspected and condemned; inspiratory capacity; inspiratory center; instruction counter; instrument correction; integrated circuit; intermediate language; internal combustion; internal connection; international control; interstitial cells; intracerebral; intracutaneous
i-c: integrated circuit
i/c: in charge; in command
i & c: installation and construction
ic.: *icon* (Latin—figure; woodcut)
i.c.: *inter cibos* (Latin—between meals)
Ic: Iceland; Icelander; Icelandic
IC: Idaho College; Ignatius College; Illinois Central (railroad); Illinois College; Immaculata College; Information Center; Interchemical Corporation; International Control; Iola College; Iona College; Itaska College; Itawamba College; Ithaca College
I.C.: Institute of Charity (Rosminian)
I-C: Indo-China; Indo-Chine; Indo-Chinese
I & C: Ictinus and Callicrates (designers of the Parthenon)
I de C: Islas del Cisne (Spanish—Swan Islands)
I.C.: *Iesus Christus* (Latin-Jesus Christ)
ica: Imperial Corporation of America; Institute of Contemporary Arts
ICA: Industrial Communication Association; Institute of Contemporary Arts; Intermuseum Conservation Association; International Chefs' Association; International Chiropractors Association; International Claims Association; International Communication Association; International Cooperative Administration; International Cooperative Alliance; International Council on Archives
I of CA: Institute of Chartered Accountants
ICAA: Invalid Children's Aid Association; Investment Counsel Association of America
ICAAAA: Intercollegiate Association of Amateur Athletes of America
ICAB: International Council Against Bullfighting
icad: integrated control and display
ICADS: Integrated Control and Display System
ICAE: International Commission on Agricultural Engineering
ICAESD: International Center for African Economic and Social Documentation
ICAF: Industrial College of the Armed Forces; International Committee on Aeronautical Fatigue
ICAI: International Commission of Agricultural Industries
ICAITI: Instituto Centroamericano de Investigación y Technológica Industrial (Central American Institute of Investigation and Industrial Technology)
ICAM: Institute of Corn and Agricultural Merchants
I Can: Information Canada
ICAN: International Commission for Air Navigation
ICAO: International Civil Aviation Organization
ICAP: Institute of Certified Ambulance Personnel; Inter-American Committee of the Alliance for Progress
ICAP: *Instituto Cubano de Amistad con los Pueblos* (Spanish—Cuban Institute for Friendship with Peoples)—Castro-controlled
icas: intermittent commercial and amateur service
ICAS: Interdepartmental Committee for Atmospheric Sciences; Intermittent Commercial and Amateur Service; International Council of the Aeronautical Sciences; International Council of Aerospace Sciences
ICASALS: International Center for Arid and Semi-Arid Land Studies
icav: intracavity
ICB: International City Bank; Indian Coffee Board; Institute of Comparative Biology; International Container Bureau
ICBA: International Community of Booksellers Associations
ICBC: Insurance Corporation of British Columbia; International Commercial Bank of China
icbm (ICBM): intercontinental ballistic missile
ICBO: Interracial Council for Business Opportunities
icbp: intracellular binding proteins
ICBP: International Council for Bird Preservation
ICBS: Interconnected Business

System
icbt: intercontinental ballistic transport
icc: integrated circuit computer; international catalog card (3 x 5 inches or 7.5 x 12.5 centimeters)
ic & c: invoice cost and charges
ICC: Indian Claims Commission; International Chamber of Commerce; International Control Commission; International Correspondence Course(s); Interstate Commerce Commission
icca: initial cash clothing allowance
ICCA: Infants' and Children's Coat Association; International Corrugated Case Association; International Consumer Credit Association
ICCAT: International Commission for the Conservation of Atlantic Tunas
ICCF: International Correspondence Chess Federation
ICCP: International Conference on Cataloguing Principles
ICCR: Indian Council for Cultural Relations; International Charge Card Registry
ICCS: International Center of Criminological Studies
ICCSL: International Commission of the Cape Spartel Light
IC & CY: Inns of Court and City Yeomanry
icd: immune complex disease; investment certificate of deposit (ICD)
ICD: Industrial Cooperation Division; Industry Cooperation Division; Institute for the Crippled and Disabled; International College of Dentists; International Cooperative Distributors
***ICD:** International Classification of Diseases*
***ICDA:** International Classification of Diseases, Adapted for Use in the United States*
icdh (ICDH): isocitric dehydrogenase
ICDO: International Civil Defense Organization
icd's: investment certificates of deposit
ice.: increased combat effectiveness; internal combustion engine
Ice: Iceland; Icelander; Icelandic
ICE: Institution of Civil Engineers; Instituto Costarricense de Electricidad (Costa Rican Electric Institute); International Cultural Exchange
Iceberg Alley: North Atlantic Ocean between Greenland and Labrador where icebergs float down from the Arctic and endanger ships
ICEF: International Children's Emergency Fund; International Council for Educational Films
ICEG: Insulated Conductors' Export Group
ICEI: International Combustion Engine Institute
Icel: Icelandic
ICEL: International Committee on English in the Liturgy
Iceland spar: calcite (calcium carbonate)
ICEM: International Commission for European Migration
Ice Mine City: Coudersport Pennsylvania
ICER: Information Centre of the European Railways
I Ceram: Institute of Ceramics
ICES: Integrated Civil Engineering Systems; International Council for the Exploration of the Sea
ICESC: Industry Crew Escape Systems Committee
ICET: Institute for the Certification of Engineering Technicians; International Center of Economy and Technology
ICETT: Industrial Council for Educational and Training Technology
ICEWATER: Inter-Agency Committee on Water Resources
icf: intracellular fluid; intermediate care facilities
ICF: Ingénieur Civil de France (Civil Engineer of France); Inter-bureau Citation of Funds; International Canoe Federation
ICFC: Industrial and Commercial Finance Corporation
IC 4-A: Intercollegiate Amateur Athletic Association of America
ICFPW: International Confederation of Former Prisoners of War
ICFR: Intercollegiate Conference of Faculty Representatives (Big Ten)
ICFTU: International Confederation of Free Trade Unions
icg: icing
ICG: International Commission on Glass; International Congress of Genetics; Interviewers Classification Guide
ich: ichthyology
ich (ICH): infectious canine hepatitis
ICHAM: Institute of Cooking and Heating Appliance Manufacturers
ICHCA: International Cargo Handling Coordination Association
IChemE: Institute of Chemical Engineers
ICHEO: Inter-University Council for Higher Education Overseas
ichnol: ichnolite; ichnologist; ichnology
ICHPER: International Council for Health, Physical Education, and Recreation
ichs: ichthyologists
ICHS: International Committee of Historical Sciences
ichth: ichthyology
ichthyol: ichthyology
ICI: Imperial Chemical Industries; Institution of Chemistry in Ireland; International Commission on Illumination; Investment Casting Institute; Investment Company Institute
ICIA: Interagency Committee on International Athletics; International Credit Insurance Association; International Crop Improvement Association
ICIANZ: Imperial Chemical Industries of Australia and New Zealand
ICIAP: Interagency Committee on International Aviation Policy
ICID: International Commission on Irrigation and Drainage
ICIE: International Council of Industrial Editors
ICIECA: Interagency Council on International Educational and Cultural Affairs
ICIMP: Interagency Committee for International Meteorological Programs
ICIPE: International Center for Insect Physiology and Ecology
ICITA: International Cooperative Investigation of the Tropical Atlantic
ICITO: Interim Commission for the International Trade Organization
ICJ: Institute of Criminal Justice; International Commission of Jurists; International Court of Justice

ICJW: International Council of Jewish Women
icky: sticky
ICL: Institut de Chimie de Lyon; International Computers Limited
ICLA: International Committee on Laboratory Animals
Iclnd: Iceland
ICLP: Institute of Criminal Law and Procedure (Georgetown University)
ICLS: Irish Central Library for Students
icm: increased capability missile; intercostal margin
ICM: Increased Capability Missile; Indian Campaign Medal; Institute of Computer Management
ICMA: International City Manager's Association
ICMPH: International Center of Medical and Psychological Hypnosis
ICMR: Indian Council of Medical Research
ICMREF: Interagency Committee on Marine Science, Research, Engineering, and Facilities
ICMS: International Commission on Mushroom Science
ICN: International Chemical and Nuclear (corporation); International Council of Nurses
ICNAF: International Commission for the Northwest Atlantic Fisheries
ICNV: International Committee on Nomenclature of Viruses
ico: iconology
ICO: Immediate Commanding Officer; Interagency Committee on Oceanography; International Coffee Organization; International Commission for Optics
ICOA: International Castor Oil Association
ICOGRADA: International Council of Graphic Design Associations
ICOM: International Council of Museums
icon.: iconic; iconoclasm; iconoclast; iconography
ICONS: Information Center on Nuclear Standards; Isotopes of Carbon, Oxygen, Nitrogen, and Sulfur (AEC)
ICOPA: International Conference of Police Associations
ICOR: Intergovernmental Conference on Oceanic Research (UNESCO)
I Corr Tech: Insitution of Corrosion Technology
ICOT: Institute of Coastal Oceanography and Tides
icp: inventory control point
ICP: Institut de Chimie de Paris (Chemical Institute of Paris); International Center of Photography; International Council of Psychologists
ICPA: International Commission for the Prevention of Alcoholism; International Conference of Police Associations
ICPC: International Criminal Police Commission (Interpol)
ICPHS: International Council for Philosophical and Humanistic Studies
ICPI: Insurance Crime Prevention Institute
i/c/pm/m: incisors, canines, premolars, molars (dentition formula, *e.g.* . i 4/4 means 4 upper and 4 lower incisors, c 2/2 means 2 upper and 2 lower canines, etc.)
ICPO: International Criminal Police Organization (Interpol)
ICPP: Idaho Chemical Processing Plant (AEC)
icr: increase; increment; instrumentation control rack; ion cyclotron resonance
ICR: Independent Congo Republic; Institute of Cancer Research; Institute for Cooperative Research
ICRA: International Copper Research Association
ICRC: International Committee of the Red Cross
ICRF: Imperial Cancer Research Fund
ICRH: Institute for Computer Research in the Humanities (NYU)
icrm: intercontinental reconnaisance missile (ICRM)
ICRM: Institute of Certified Records Managers
ICRO: International Cell Research Organization
ICRP: International Commission on Radiological Protection
ICRSC: International Council for Research in the Sociology of Cooperation
ICRU: International Commission on Radiological Units and Measurements
ics: intercostal space
ic's: immediate constituents; integrated circuits
ICS: Indian Civil Service; Inner Continental Shelf; Integrated Command System; Interagency Communications System; International Chamber of Shipping; International College of Surgeons; International Correspondence Schools
ICSAC: International Confederation of Societies of Authors and Composers
ICSB: International Center of School Building
ICSC: Independent Colleges of Southern California; Interoceanic Canal Study Commission
ICSDW: International Council of Social Democratic Women
icse: intermediate current stability experiment
ICSEMS: International Commission for the Scientific Exploration of the Mediterranean Sea
icsh (ICSH): interstitial cell-stimulating hormone
ICSI: International Conference on Scientific Information
ICSLS: International Convention for Safety of Life at Sea
ICSOM: International Conference of Symphony and Opera Musicians
ICSPE: International Council of Sport and Physical Recreation
ICSPRO: International Calcium Silicate Products Research Organization
ICSSD: International Committee for Social Sciences Documentation
ICS & T: Imperial College of Science and Technology
ICSTA: International Cooperative Study of the Tropical Atlantic
ICSTS: Intermediate Combined System Test Stand
ICSU: International Council of Scientific Unions
ICSW: Interdepartmental Committee on the Status of Women
ict: icterus; inflammation of connective tissue; insulin coma therapy (ICT)
ICT: International Computers and Tabulators; Wichita, Kansas (airport)
ICT: International Critical Tables
ICTA: Imperial College of Tropical Agriculture; International Center for the Typographic Arts
ICTMM: International Congresses of Tropical Medicine

and Malaria
ICTP: International Center for Theoretical Physics
ICTR: International Center of TheatreResearch
Ictus.: *Iurisconsultus*—Latin-attorney; counsellor-at-law)
ic tv: integrated-circuit television
icu: intensive care unit (medical)
ICU: International Code Use
ICUMSA: International Commission for Uniform Methods of Sugar Analysis
ICUS: inside continental United States
ICVA: International Council of Voluntary Agencies
icw: interrupted continuous wave; intracellular water
ICW: India-China Wing (World War II); Institute of Child Welfare; Inter-American Commission of Women; International Chemical Workers; International Commission on Whaling; International Council of Women
ICWA: Institute of Current World Affairs
ICWG: International Cooperative Women's Guild
ICWM: International Committee on Weights and Measures
ICWP: International Council of Women Psychologists
ICY: International Cooperation Year (1965)
ICZN: International Commission on Zoological Nomenclature
id: idea; identification; induced draft; infectious disease; infective dose; inside diameter; intradermal; island; islander
id.: *idem* (Latin—the same)
id50: median infective dose
i & d: incision and drainage
Id: Iraqi dinar (monetary unit of Iraq)
I'd: I could; I had; I should; I would
ID: Interior (US department); Institute of Distribution; Intelligence Department; Iraqi dinar (currency unit)
IDA: Industrial Diamond Association; Institute for Defense Analyses; Institute for Design Analysis; Intercollegiate Dramatic Association; International Development Association; International Dredging Association
IDAA: International Doctors in Alcoholics Anonymous
id. ac: *idem ac* (Latin—the same as)
IDAC: Import Duties Advisory Committee
IDAI: Industrial Development Authority Ireland
Idaho Lion: Senator William E. Borah
IDA Ireland: Industrial Development Authority of Ireland
idast: interpolated data and speech transmission
idb: illicit diamond buyer; illicit diamond buying; intercept during burning
IDB: Industrial Development Board; Inter-American Development Bank; Israel Diamond Building (Ramat Gan)
IDBT: Industrial Development Bank of Turkey
id card: identification card
idc: interest during construction
IDC: Imperial Defense College; Industrial Development Corporation; Intercontinental Dynamics Corporation; Interdepartmental Committee; Interdepartmental Communication; International Danube Commission; Iowa Development Commission
ID-card: identification card
IDC(orp): International Disposal Corporation
IDCSP: Initial Defense Communications Satellite Program
i-d curve: intensity-duration curve
IDD: Island Development Department
IDDD: International Direct Distance Dialing
IDE: Industrial Development Executive
IDEA: Institute for the Development of Educational Actinities
ideffi: intercept during exo-atmospheric fall
iden: identification; identify
ident: identification; identify; identity
IDEP: Interagency Data Exchange Program; Interservice Data Exchange Program
idex: initial defense experiment
idf: intermediate distribution frame; international distress frequency
IDF: International Dairy Federation; International Democratic Fellowship; International Diabetes Federation
IDFF: *Internationale Demokratische Frauenfederation* (German—Women's International Democratic Federation)
ID grinding: internal grinding
id he.: index head
IDHEC: *Institut des Hautes Études Cinématographiques, Paris* (Paris Institute of Higher Cinematographic Studies)
IDHS: Intelligence Data Handling System
idi: improved data interchange
IDI: Industrial Designers' Institute
IDI: *Institut de Droit International* (French—International Law Institute)
IDIA: Industrial Design Institute of Australia
IDIB: Industrial Diamond Information Bureau
idiot.: instrumentation digital on-line transcriber
IDIU: Interdivisional Information Unit; Interdivisional Intelligence Unit
IDL: New York, New York (Kennedy International Airport—Idlewild); International Date Line
IDLIS: International Desert Locust Information Service
id lt: identification light
idm: illicit diamond mining
IDMA: Isaac Delgado Museum of Art
IDNL: Indiana Dunes National Lakeshore (Indiana)
IDO: Intelligence Division Office; International Disarmament Organization
idoc: inner diameter of outer conductor
IDOE: International Decade of Ocean Exploration—1970–1980
idon. vehic.: *idoneo vehiculo* (Latin—in a suitable vehicle)
idp: integrated data processing
IDP: Independent Development Project; Industrial Development Bank; Integrated Data Processing; International Driving Permit
idr: intercept during reentry
idr: *idraulica* (Italian—hydraulics)
IDR: Infantry Drill Regulations; Institute for Dream Research
IDRC: International Drycleaning Research Committee
ids: illicit diamond smuggling; inadvertent destruct
IDS: International Development Services; Internatonal Documents Service; Investigative Dermatological Society
IDSA: Industrial Designers Society of America

IDSCS: Initial Defense Satellite Communication System
IDSO: International Diamond Security Organization
idt: *in de text* (Dutch—in the text)
IDT: Industrial Detergents Trade
IDTA: International Dance Teachers Association
IDTS: Instrumentation Data Transmission System
idu: intermittent drive unit; iododeoxyuridine
IDU: idoxuridine; International Dendrology Union
idur: intercept during unpowered rise
i Durchshn: *im Durchschnitt* (German—on an average)
IDV: International Distillers and Vinters
IDX: *Index to Dental Literature*
ie: index error; initial equipment; inside edge
i/e: ingress/egress
i-e: internal-external
i & e: identification and exposition (lines)
i.e.: *id est* (Latin—that is)
IE: Indo-European; Industrial Engineering; Industrial Espionage; Information and Education
I.E.: Industrial Engineer
I & E: Information and Education
IE: *Immunitäts Einheit* (German—immunizing unit)
I o E: Isle of Ely
I of E: Institute of Export
iea: intravascular erythrocyte aggregation
IEA: Institute of Economic Affairs; International Economic Association
IEAF: Imperial Ethiopian Air Force
IEB: International Energy Bank
iec: injection electrode catheter; intra-epithelial carcinoma
IEC: Institut d'Études Centrafricaines (Institute of Central African Studies); International Education Center; International Electrochemical Commission; International Electrotechnical Commission
iec's: integrated electronic components
ied: individual effective dose
IED: Institution of Engineering Designers; Integrated Electronics Division (USA Electronics Command)
iee: inner enamel epithelium
IEE: Institute of Environmental Engineers; Institution of Electrical Engineers
Ieee: I expect everything eventually
IEEE: Institue of Electrical and Electronics Engineers
IEETE: Institution of Electrical and Electronics Technician Engineers
IEF: International Eye Foundation
IEG: Information Exchange Group
IEHA: International Economic History Association
iei: indeterminate engineering items
IEI: Industrial Education Institute; Industrial Engineering Institute
IEIC: Iowa Educational Information Center
iem: *iemand* (Dutch—a man; somebody; someone)
IEME: Inspectorate of Electrical and Mechanical Engineering
IEMS: Institute of Experimental Medicine and Surgery
IEN: Imperial Ethiopian Navy
IEO: Instituto Español de Oceanografía (Spanish Oceanographic Institute)
iep: iso-electric point
IEP: Institut d'Études Politiques (Institute of Political Studies); Institute of Experimental Psychology
IEPA: International Economic Policy Association
ieq: index of environmental quality
IER: Industrial Equipment Reserve; Institute of Educational Research; Institute of Engineering Research; Interim Engineering Report
IERC: International Electronic Research Corporation
IERE: Institution of Electronic and Radio Engineers
IERT: Institute for Education by Radio-Television
IER Test: Institute of Educational Research Test (intelligence)
IES: Illuminating Engineering Society; Indian Educational Service; Information Exchange Service; Institute of Environmental Sciences; Institution of Engineers and Shipbuilders
IESC: International Executive Service Corps
IESS: Institution of Engineers and Shipbuilders in Scotland
iet: interest equalization tax
IET: Initial Engine Test; Institute of Educational Technology
I-et-L: Indre-et-Loire
if.: ice fog; intermediate frequency; interstitial fluid; intrinsic factor
i-f: in-flight; intermediate frequency
if: *iflge* (Danish—according to)
i.f.: ipse fecit (Latin—he did it himself)
If: Ifni; Sidi Ifni (Spanish West Africa)
IF: grid current (symbol)
I-F: Isotta-Fraschini
I de F: Institut de France (Institute of France)
I f A: *Institutt for Atomenergi* (Norwegian—Atomic Energy Institute)
IFA: Industrial Forestry Association; Industry Film Association; Intercollegiate Fencing Association; International Federation of Actors; International Fertility Association; International Fiscal Association; International Footprints Association; International Franchise Association
IFA: *Institut Fiziki Atmosfery* (Russian—Atmospheric Physics Institute)
IFAC: International Family Association of Canada
IFALPA: International Federation of Air-Line Pilots' Associations
Ifan: (Welsh—John)
IFAN: Institut Français d'Afrique Noire (Dakar, Ivory Coast)
IFAP: International Federation of Agricultural Producers
IFAPA: International Federation of Airline Pilots Association
IFAS: Institute for American Strategy; International Federation of Aquarium Societies
IFATCA: International Federation of Air Traffic Controllers Associations
IFATCC: International Federation of Associations of Textile Chemists and Colourists
IFAW: International Fund for Animal Welfare
IFB: Invitation for Bid(s)
IFBPW: International Federation of Business and Professional Women
IFBWW: International Federation of Building and Woodworkers

ifc: integrated fire control
IFC: International Finance Corporation; International Fisheries Commission; International Freighting Corporation
IFC-ALA: Intellectual Freedom Committee—American Library Association
IFCATI: International Federation of Cotton and Allied Textile Industries
IFCC: International Federation of Camping and Caravanning
IFCCTE: International Federation of Commercial, Clerical, and Technical Employees
IFCJ: International Federation of Catholic Journalists
IFCL: International Fixed Calendar League
IFCO: Interreligious Foundation for Community Organization
IFCS: International Federation of Computer Sciences
IFD: International Federation of Documentation
IFDA: Institutional Food Distributors of America
IFE: Industrial Foundation on Education; Institution of Fire Engineers
IFEMS: International Federation of Electron Microscope Societies
IFEP: *Instituttet for Elektronikmateriels Pålideliged* (Danish—Electronic Materials Reliability Institute)
iff (IFF): identification friend or foe
IFF: Institute for the Future; International Flavors and Fragrances (corporation)
IFFA: International Federation of Film Archives
IFFNM: *Internationale Ferienkurse für Neue Musik* (German—International Vacation Courses for New Music)—held in Darmstadt
IFFJ: Independent Federation of Free Journalists
IFFJP: International Federation of Fruit Juice Producers
IFFPA: International Federation of Film Producers Associations
IFFS: International Federation of Film Societies
IFFTU: International Federation of Free Teachers' Unions
IFGO: International Federation of Gynecology and Obstetrics
IFHE: International Federation of Home Economics
IFHP: International Federation for Housing And Planning
IFI: Industrial Fasteners Institute
IFIA: International Federation of Ironmongers' and Iron Merchants' Associations
IFIF: International Foundation for Internal Freedom (hallucinogenic experimenter's society found by former Harvard professors Richard Alpert and Timothy Leary)
IFIP: Iguazu Falls International Park (shared by Argentina, Brazil, and Paraguay)—Argentinians spell it Iguazu, Brazilians—Igauçu, Paraguayans—Iguassu; International Federation of Information Processing
IFIPS: International Federation of Information Processing Societies
I Fire E: Institution of Fire Engineers
IFIS: Integrated Flight Instrument System
IFJ: International Federation of Journalists
IFKM: *Internationale Föderation für Kurzschrift und Maschinenschreiben* (German—International Federation of Short hand and Typewriting)
IfL: *Institut für Landeskunde* (German—Geographical Institute)—at Bad Godesberg
IFL: Imperial Fascist League
IFLA: International Federation of Landscape Architects; International Federation of Library Associations
IFLWU: International Fur and Leather Workers Union
IFM: Institute for Forensic Medicine
IFMA: International Federation of Margarine Associations
IFMC: International Folk Music Council
IFME: International Federation of Medical Electronics
IFMEO: International Fish Meal Exporters Organization
IFMP: International Federation of Medical Psychotherapy
IFMSA: International Federation of Medical Students Associations
IFNE: International Federation for Narcotic Education
if nec: if necessary
IFOFSAG: International Fellowship of Former Scouts and Guides
Ifor: (Welsh—Ivo; Ivor)
IFOR: International Fellowship of Reconciliation
IFORS: International Federation of Operational Research Societies
IFOSA: International Federation of Stationers' Associations
ifp: international fixed public broadcast band
IFP: Imperial and Foreign Post; Institut Français du Pétrole (French Petroleum Institute)
IFPA: Industrial Film Producers Association
IFPCW: International Federation of Petroleum and Chemical Workers
IFPI: International Federation of the Phonographic Industry
IFPM: International Federation of Physical Medicine
IFPP: Imperial and Foreign Parcel Post
IFPW: International Federation of Petroleum Workers
ifr: infrared; inflight refueling
i-f-r: image-to-frame ratio
IFr: *Internationaler Frauenrat* (German—International Council of Women)
IFR: Instrument Flight Rules
IFRA: International Foundation for Research in the Field of Advertising
IFRB: International Frequency Registration Board
IFRF: International Flame Research Foundation
IFS: International Federation of Surveyors; Irish Free State
IFS: *International Financial Statistics*
IFSA: International Federation of Sound Archives
IFSP: International Federation of Societies of Philosophy
IFSPO: International Federation of Senior Police Officers
IFSPS: International Federation of Students in Political Sciences
IFSS: Instrumentation Flight Safety System
IFSSO: Irish Free State Stationery Office
IFST: International Federation of Shorthand and Typing
IFSTA: International Fire Service Training Association
IFSW: International Federation of Social Workers
ift: inflight text
IFT: Institute of Food Technologists; International Federation of Translators; International Foundation for

Telemetering; International Frequency Tables
IFTA: International Federation of Travel Agencies
IFTC: International Film and Television Council
IFTF: Inter-Faith Task Force
IFTR: International Federation for Theatre Research
IFUW: International Federation of University Women
IFVME: Inspectorate of Fighting Vehicles and Mechanical Equipment
IFWL: International Federation of Women Lawyers
ig: immunoglobulin; inertial guidance
ig (Ig) (IG): immunoglobulin
IG: Indo-Germanic; Inspector General
IG: *Interessengemeinschaft* (German—pool; trust)
IGA: Independent Grocers' Alliance; International Geneva Association; International Geographical Association; International Golf Association; International Graduate Achievement
i gal: imperial gallon
IGAS: International Graphic Arts Society
I Gas Eng: Institution of Gas Engineers
IGB: International Gravimetric Bureau
IGB: *International Geophysics Bulletin*
igc: intellectually gifted children
IGC: Intergovernmental Copyright Committee; International Geophysical Cooperation
IGCC: Inter-Governmental Copyright Committee
IGCI: Industrial Gas Cleaning Institute
IGCM: Incorporated Guild of Church Musicians
i/g/d: illicit gold dealer
IGD: Inspector General's Department
ige: instrumentation ground equipment
IGE: International General Electric
IGF: International Grieg Festival
IGFA: International Game Fish Association
I.G. Farben: Interessengemeinschaft der Farbenindustrie (German Dye Trust)
ig. fat.: *ignis fatuus* (Latin—foolish fire)—will-o'-the- wisp; marsh gas
igfet: insulated gate field-effect transistor
IGH: Incorporated Guild of Hairdressers
IGIA: Interagency Group on International Aviation
IGIS: International Guild for Infant Survival
igl: information grouping logic
igl: *iglesia* (Spanish—church)
igla: *iglesia* (Spanish—church)
igl[a]**:** *iglesia* (Spanish—church)
ign: ignite; ignition
ign.: *ignotus* (Latin—unknown)
Ign: Ignacio; Ignatius; Ignatz; Ignazio
IGN: International Great Northern (railroad)
Ignatius Loyola: Iñigo López de Recalde
Ignazio Silone: (pseudonym—Secondo Tranquilli)
Ign[o]***:*** *Ignacio* (Spanish—Ignatius)
IGO: Independent Garage Owners; Intergovernmental Organization
igor: injection gas-oil ratio
igortt: intercept ground optical recorder tracking telescope
IGOSS: Integrated Global Ocean Station System
IGP: Industrial Government Party
IGPP: Institute of Geophysics and Planetary Physics (UCLA)
igr.: *igitur* (Latin—therefore)
igrf: international geomagnetic reference field
IGROF: *Internationale Rorschach Gesellschaft* (German—International Rorschach Society)
IGRS: Irish Geneological Research Society
IGS: Imperial General Staff; Inertial Guidance System; Institute of General Semantics; International Geranium Society
IGSESS: International Graduate School for English-Speaking Students
IGT: Institute of Gas Technology
IGTO: India Government Tourist Office; Israel Government Tourist Office; Italian Government Tourist Office
IGU: International Gas Union; International Geographical Union
IGWF: International Garment Workers Federation
IGWUA: International Glove Workers Union of America
IGY: International Geophysical Year (July 1957 through December 1958)
ih: inside height
i.h.: *iacet hic* (Latin—here lies)
ih (IH): infectious hepatitis
IH: International Harvester
iha (IHA): idiopathic hyperaldosteronism
IHA: International Hahnemannian Association; International Hotel Association; International House Association
IHAR: Institute for Human-Animal Relationships
IHAS: Integrated Helicopter Avionics System
IHB: International Hydrographic Bureau (Monaco)
IHBR: Indiana Harbor Belt Railroad
ihc: interstate highway capability
IHC: Intercontinental Hotels Corporation
IHCA: International Hebrew Christian Alliance
ihd (IHD): ischemic heart disease
IHD: Institute of Human Development; International Health Division (Rockefeller Institute for Medical Research); International Hydrological Decade (1965–1974)
IHE: Institute of Highway Engineers; Institute of Home Economics
I-head: capital-I-shaped head (gasoline engine)
IHEU: International Humanist and Ethical Union
ihf: interesting historic figure
IHF: Industrial Hygiene Foundation; Institute of High Fidelity; International Hockey Federation; International Hospital Federation
IHFA: Industrial Hygiene Foundation of America
IHFAS: Integrated High-Frequency Antenna System
IHHA: International Halfway House Association
IHI: Ishikawajima-Harima Heavy Industries
IHK: *Internationale Handelskammer* (German—International Chamber of Commerce)
IHL: International Homeopathic League
I.H.M.: *Jesus Mundi Salvator* (Latin—Jesus, Savior of the World)
iho: in-house operation
IHOP: International House of Pancakes
IHOU: Institute of Home Office

Underwriters
ihp: indicated horsepower; ischemic heart disease
IHPA: Imported Hardwood Plywood Association
ihph: indicated horsepower hour
IHR: Institute of Human Relations
IHRB: International Hockey Rules Board
ihrd: international rubber hardness degree(s)
ihs: independent hemopathic syndrome
IHS: Immigration Historical Society; Irish Hospitals Sweepstakes
I.H.S.: *Iesus Hominum Salvator* (Latin—Jesus Savior of Men); *In Hoc Signo* (Latin—In This Sign)
ihsa: iodinated human serum albumin
IHSA: Italian Historical Society of America
ihsbr: improved high-speed bombing radar
ihss: idiopathic hypertrophic subaortic stenosis (IHSS)
IHT: Institute of Handicraft Teachers
IHT: *International Herald Tribune*
IHU: Interservice Hovercraft Unit
ihv: intravenous hyperalimentation
IHVE: Institute of Heating and Ventilating Engineers
ihx: intermediate heat exchanger
IHYC: Indian Harbor Yacht Club; Indian Harbour Yacht Club
ii: ingot iron; initial issue; inventory and inspection
II: Ikebana International; Instituto Interamericano (Interamerican Institute); Irish Institute
I/I: Inventory and Inspection (Report)
I & I: instruction and inspection
iia: if incorrect advise
IIA: Aerlinte Eireann (3-letter symbol for Irish Airlines); Incinerator Institute of America; Institute of Internal Auditors; Insurance Institute of America; International Information Administration; Invention Industry Association
IIAA: Independent Insurance Agents Association
IIAF: Imperial Iranian Air Force
IIAL: International Institute of Arts and Letters
IIAPCO: Independent Indonesian-American Petroleum Company
IIAS: International Institute of Administrative Services
IIASA: International Institute of Applied Systems Analysis
IIB: Institut International de Bibliographie
IIC: International Institute for the Conservation of Historic and Artistic Works
IICA: *Instituto Interamericano de Ciencias Agrícolas* (Inter-American Institute of Agricultural Sciences)
IICLRR: International Institute for Children's Literature and Reading Research
IID: Internal Investigation Division
IID: *Institut International de Documentation* (French—International Documentation Institute)
IIDA: Irish Industrial Development Authority
IIE: Institute for International Education; International Institute of Embryology
IIE: *Instituto Interamericano de Estadistica* (Inter-American Institute of Statistics)
IIEA: International Institute for Environmental Affairs
IIEP: International Institute of Educational Planning
IIET: Inspection Instructions for Electron Tubes
IIF: Institute of International Finance; Institut International du Froid (International Institute of Refrigeration)
IIFA: International Institute of Films on Art
IIHCEHV: International Institute of Health Care, Ethics, and Human Values
IIHF: International Ice Hockey Federation
IIHS: Insurance Institute for Highway Safety
III: International Institute of Interpreters (UN); International Isostatic Institute
III: *Instituto Indigenista Interamericano* (Inter-American Indigenist Institute); *International Intertrade Index*
IIJR: Illinois Institute of Juvenile Research
IILC: International Instituut voor Landaanwinning en Cultuurtechniek (International Institute of Land Reclamation and Cultivation)
IILS: International Institute for Labour Studies
IIM: Indian Institute of Management
IIMSD: International Institute for Music Studies and Documentation
IIN: Item Identification Number
IIN: *Instituto Interamericano del Niño* (Inter-American Children's Institute)
IInfSc: Institute of Information Scientists
IIOE: International Indian Ocean Expedition
IIOOF: International Independent Order of Odd Fellows
IIOS: International Indian Ocean Survey
iip: index of industrial production
IIP: Institute International de la Presse (International Institute of the Press); International Ice Patrol; International Institute of Philosophy
IIPER: International Institution of Production Engineering Research
iir: isobutylene isoprene rubber
IIR: International Institute of Refrigeration
IIRA: International Industrial Relations Association
IIRS: Institute for Industrial Research and Standards (Erie)
ii's: illegal immigrants
IIS: Institut International de la Soudure (International Institute of Welding); Institut International de la Statistique (International Institute of Statistics)
IIS & EE: International Institute of Seismology and Earthquake Engineering
IISL: International Institute of Space Law
IISO: Institution of Industrial Safety Officers
IISR: International Institute for Submarine Research
IISRP: International Institute of Synthetic Rubber Producers
IISS: International Institute of Strategic Studies
IISWM: International Institute of Iron and Steel Wire Manufacturers
IIT: Illinois Institute of Technology; Israel Institute of Technology
IIT: *Institut International du Théâtre* (French—International Institute of the Theater)
IITB: Indian Institute of Tech-

nology—Bombay
IITM: Indian Institute of Technology—Madras
IITRAN: Illinois Institute of Technology Translators
IIIRI: Illinois Institute of Technology Research Institute
IITYWYBAD?: If I tell you will you buy a drink?
IIW: International Institute of Welding
iiwfm: if it weren't for me
iiwfy: if it weren't for you
iJ: *im Jahre* (German—in the year)
IJ: Institute of Journalists
I of J: Institute of Jamaica
IJA: Institute of Jewish Affairs; International Judiciary Association
IJC: International Joint Commission (Canada—U.S.); Itawamba Junior College
IJF: International Judo Federation
I-J FC: Iselin-Jefferson Financial Company
IJISID: Imperial Japanese Institute for the Study of Infectious Diseases
IJK: *Internationale Juristen Kommission* (German—International Jurists Commission)
ijp: inhibitory junction potential
IJR: Institute for Juvenile Research
ik: inner keel
ik: *ikke* (Danish—not)
Ik: Ichabod
IK: *Immune Korper* (German—immune bodies)
IKB: Isambard Kingdom Brunel
ike: iconoscope
Ike: Dwight David Eisenhower (nickname)—thirty-fourth President of the United States; Isaac
Ikey: (*see* Ikie)
Ikie: Isaac; Isaak; Isack; Izaak; Isaque
IKPK: International Kriminal-Polizei-Kommission (International Criminal Police Commission)
I kr: Icelandic krona (monetary unit)
ik unit: infusoria killing unit
il: illustrate; illustrated; illustration; illustrator; including loading; incoming letter; inside layer; inside left; inside length; instrument landing; interline; interlinear; interlinearly
Il: illinium
Il: *Illiad*
IL: Incres Line; Interocean Line; Israel (auto plaque)
IL: *Institut Littéraire*
I & L: Installations and Logistics
I-et-L: Indre-et-Loire
I of L: Institute of Linguists
ila (ILA): instrument landing approach
ILA: Indian Library Association; Indonesian Library Association; International Laundry Association; International Law Association; International Leprosy Association; International Longshoremen's Association; Iranian Library Association; Iraq Library Association; Israel Library Association
ILAA: International Legal Aid Association
ILAAS: Integrated Light Aircraft Avionics System; Integrated Light Attack Avionics System
ILAB: International League of Antiquarian Booksellers
ILAFA: Instituto Latinamericano del Fierro y del Acero (Latin American Institute of Iron and Steel)
ILAR: Institute of Laboratory Animal Resources
ilas: interrelated logic accumulating scanner
ilc: irrevocable letter of credit
ILC: International Law Commission (UN)
Il Cieco: (Italian—The Blind One)—Italy's blind poet—Luigi Groto who lived and wrote in the mid-sixteenth century
ILCOP: International Liaison Committee of Organizations for Peace (UN)
ILCW: Inter-Lutheran Commission on Worship
Ildef^{o}: Ildefonso (Spanish)
Il Duca di Spoleto: (Italian—The Duke of Spoleto)—composer-impresario Gian Carlo Menotti's nickname as he directs the Spoletto Festival
Il Duce: (Italian—The Leader)—sobriquet of Benito Mussolini—dictator of Italy before and during World War II
Il^{e}: Illustre (Spanish—illustrious)
Il^{mo}: Illustrísimo (Spanish—Most Illustrious)
ile: isoleucine
île: (French—island)
ile (ILE): isoleucine (amino acid)
ILE: Institution of Locomotive Engineers
ILEA: Inner London Education Authority
ILEI: *Internacia Ligo de Esperantistaj Instruistoj* (International League of Esperanto Instructors)
ileu: isoleucine
ilf: inductive loss factor
Ilf: Ilya Arnoldovich FeislibER
ILF: International Landworkers Federation
ILFI: International Labor Film Institute
ILFO: International Logistics Field Office (USA)
Il Furioso: (Italian—the Furious One)—nickname of Tintoretto who painted at a furious rate
ILGA: Institute of Local Government dministration
ILGWU: International Ladies' Garment Workers' Union
ILH: Imperial Light Horse
ILI: Indiana Limestone Institute; Institute of Life Insurance
Ilia Mourometz: Gliere's Symphony No. 3
ILIC: International Library Information Center
ill.: illusion; illusionary; illusionist; illustrate; illustrated; illustration; illustrator
ill.: *illustrissimus* (Latin—most illustrious)
Ill: Illinois; Illinoisan
I'll: I shall; I will
ILLC: Inner London Library Committee
illegit: illegitimate
Illinois River City: Peoria
ILLRI: Industrial Lift and Loading Ramp Institute
illum: illuminant; illuminate; illumination
illus: illustrated; illustration; illustrator
Illusion Factory: Hollywood
Illustrator of Early Twentieth-Century America: Norman Rockwell
Illustrator of the Russian Underground: Ilya Efimovich Repin
Illustrious Infidel: Colonel Robert G. Ingersoll
ILM: International Literary Management
ILMA: Incandescent Lamp Manufacturers Association
Ilmo: *Illustrissimo* (Italian—Most Illustrious)
ILMP: *International Literary Market Place*
ILN: *Illustrated London News*
ilo: in lieu of
Ilo: Iloilo

I lo: iodine lotion
ILO: International Labour Office (UN); International Labor Organization
ILOA: Industrial Life Officers Association
I Loco E: Institution of Locomotive Engineers
I Loco Eng: Institution of Locomotive Engineers
iloue: in lieu of until exhausted
ILP: Independent Labour Party
ILPA: Independent Labor Press Association
ILPES: *Instituto Latinoamericano de Planificación Econó mica y Social* (Latin American Institute for Economic and Social Planning)
ILR: Institute of Library Research; International Luggage Registry
ILRA: International Log Rolling Association
ILRI: Indian Lac Research Institute
ILRM: International League for the Rights of Man
ILS: Instrument Landing System; International Latitude Service; International Lunar Society
ILSR: Institute for Law and Social Research
ILSA: Insured Locksmiths and Safemen of America
ILSC: International Learning Systems Corporation
IL-62: Ilyushin 62 aircraft
ilt: in lieu thereof
ILT: Illinois Terminal (railroad)
ILTF: International Lawn Tennis Federation
ILU: Institute of Life Insurance
ilv: induced leukemia virus(es)
Ilyusha: (Russian nickname—Ilya)
ilw: intermediate-level wastes
ILWU: International Longshoremen's and Warehousemen's Union
ILZ: Illinois Zinc (company)
im: immature; imperial measure; impulse modulation; infectious mononucleosis; inner marker; intensity modulation; intermodulation; intramuscular
im: *in dem* (German—in the)
'im: him
Im: Imperial
I'm: I am
IM: impulse modulation; intermediate modulation; Inventory Manager
IM: *Index Medicus*
IoM: Isle of Man
I of M: Institute of Medicine
Ima: *prima* (Italian—first)
IMA: Ignition Manufacturers Institute; Indian Military Academy; Industrial Marketing Association; Industrial Medical Association; Institute for Mediterranean Affairs; Instituto Mobiliare Italiano; International Management Association; International Mineralogical Association; Islamic Mission of America
imag: imaginary
Image Maker: Thomas Nast
Imamu Amiri Baraka: Le Roi Jones
IMAR: Inner Mongolia Autonomous Region (of the People's Republic of China)
IMarE: Institute of Marine Engineers
IMARS: Institutional Management for Accountability and Renewal System
IMAU: International Movement for Atlantic Union
IMB: Institute of Marine Biology
IMBE: Institute for Minority Business Education
IMBO: Institutt for Marin Biologi (Oslo)
imc: image motion compensation; instrument meteorological condition
IMC: Industrial Management Center; International Maritime Committee; International Meteorological Committee; International Minerals & Chemical; International Mining Corporation; International Missionary Council; International Music Council
IMCC: Integrated Mission Control Center
IMCE: *Instituto Mexicano de Comercio Exterior* (Spanish—Mexican Institute of Foreign Commerce)
IMCI: Interracial Music Council, Incorporated
imco: improved combustion
IMCO: Inter-Governmental Maritime Consultative Organization
IMCOS: International Meteorological Consultant Service
IMCOV: Iron Mines Company of Venezuela
IMD: Indian Medical Department
imdtty: it's my duty to tell you
IME: Institute of Makers of Explosives; Institution of Mechanical Engineers
I&ME: Indiana and Michigan Electric Company
I of ME: Institution of Mining Engineers
I Mech E: Institution of Mechanical Engineers
IMEG: International Management and Engineering Group
imep: indicated mean effective pressure
IMER: Institute for Marine Environmental Research
I Met: Institute of Metals
IMF: International Metalworkers Federation; International Monetary Fund; International Motorcycle Federation; Interstate Motor Freight (stock exchange symbol); Israel Music Foundation
IM FI: International Mineral Fiber Institute
img: informational media guarantee
IMG: International Marxist Group
IMH: Institute of Materials Handling
IMHT: Institute for Material Handling Teachers
imi: improved manned interceptor
IMI: Ignition Manufacturers Institute; International Masonry Institute; Irish Management Institute; Israel Military Industries
IMI: *Instituto Mobiliare Italiano* (Italian Assets Institution)—credit bank
IMIB: Inland Marine Insurance Bureau
imieo: initial mass in earth orbit
IMIMI: Industrial Mineral Insulation Manufacturers Institute
IMinE: Institute of Mining Engineers
imit: imitate; imitation
IMIT: Institute of Musical Instrument Technicians
imit lea: imitation leather
iml: inside mold line
Iml: Imanuel
IML: International Music League; Irradiated Materials Laboratory
IMLT: Institute of Medical Laboratory Technology
imm: immune; immunization; immunologist; immunology
Imm: Immingham
IMM: Institute of Mining and Metallurgy; Integrated Maintenance Management; International Mercantile Marine

immac: inventory management and material control
immat: immature; immaturity
immed: immediate
immie: immitation marble; low-grade playing marble
immig: immigrant; immigration
immob: immobilization; immobilize
Immortal Dreamer: John Bunyan
Immortal Tinker: author-tinker John Bunyan
Immortal Four: Italian poets Dante Alighieri, Ludovico Ariosto, Francesco Petrarca (Petrarch), Bernardo Tasso
IMMS: International Material Management Society
IMMTS: Indian Mercantile Marine Training Ship
immun: immunity; immunization
immunol: immunology
immy: immediately
IMNS: Imperial Military Nursing Service
imo: imitation (slang short form)
IMO: Inter-American Municipal Organization; International Meteorological Organization (World Meteorological Organization)
imp.: imperative; imperfect; imperial; implement; implementation; import; imprint; improve; improvement
imp.: *imprenta* (Spanish—printing office; printing press); *imprimatur* [Latin—let it be printed (R.C. Church)]; *imprimé* (French—printed); *imprimis* (Latin—especially; particularly)
Imp.: *Imperator* (Latin—Emperor); *Imperatrix* (Latin—Empress)
IMP: Instrumented Mobile Platform (oceanographic drone boat); International Monitoring Probe (space instrument); Interplanetary Monitoring Platform (space vehicle)
impact.: implementation planning and control technique
IMPACT: Improving Public Awareness of Concepts of Telecommunications
Imp B: Imperial Beach
impce: importance
imper: imperative
imperf: imperfect
Imperial: Haydn's Symphony No. 99 in E flat
Imperial City: Rome
Imperial Impersonation of Force and Murder: Napoleon
Imperialist Poet-Writer: Rudyard Kipling
impers: impersonal
impf: imperfect
impg: impregnnate
imp. gal: imperial gallon
IMPI: International Microwave Power Institute
impig: impignorate; impignorated; impignorating; impignoration
impl: imperial; implement
imposs: impossible
impr: improvement
impr: *impresión; imprenta (Spanish—edition; printing office)*
impreg: impregnate(d); impregnation
imprim.: *imprimatur* (Latin—let it be printed)
Impr Nat: *Imprimerie Nationale* (French—National Printing Office of France)
improp: improper(ly)
improv: improvement
imps.: interplanetary measurement probes
Imps: Imperial Tobacco Company
impt: important
Imptypco: Imperial Typewriter Company (also appears as ITC)
imptr: importer
impv: imperative
impx: impaction
IMR: Individual Medical Report; Institute of Marine Resources; Institute of Masonry Research; Institute for Materials Research; Institute for Medical Research; Institute for Mortuary Research; Institute for Motivational Research; Institute for Muscle Research; International Medical Research
IMRA: Industrial Marketing Research Association
imran: international marine radio aids to navigation
IMRC: International Marine Radio Company
IMRO: Interior Macedonian Revolutionary Organization
IMS: Indian Medical Service; Industrial Management Society; Industrial Mathematics Society; Institute of Management Sciences; Institute of Marine Science; Institute of Mathematical Statistics; International Musicological Society; International Mythological Society
IMSA: International Municipal Signal Association
IMSM: Institute of Marketing and Sales Management
IMSO: Institute of Municipal Safety Officers
IMSR: Isle of Man Steam Railway
IMSS: Integrated Manned Systems Simulator
IMT: International Military Tribunal
IMTA: Institute of Municipal Treasurers and Accountants
IMTD: Inspectors of the Military Training Directorate
IM Tech: Institute of Metallurgists Technician
IMTFE: International Military Tribunal for the Far East
IMTP: Industrial Mobilization Training Program
imu: inertial measurement unit
IMU: International Mailers Union; International Maritime Union
IMUA: Inland Marine Underwriters Association
I Mun E: Institution of Municipal Engineers
imv: imperative; improve
IMVS: Institute of Medical and Veterinary Science
imw: international map of the world
IMW: Institute of Masters of Wine
Im Yem: Imamate of Yemen
in.: inch(es)
in. (In): inulin
in.^{2}: square inch(es)
in.^{3}: cubic inch(es)
In: India; Indian; indium; Indus
IN: Institute of Neurobiology (Göteborg); Interested Negroes
I of N: Institute of Navigation
I & N: Immigration and Naturalization
ina: international normal atmosphere
INA: Indian National Army; Inspector Naval Aircraft; Institution of Naval Architects; Insurance Company of North America; Iraqi News Agency; Israeli News Agency
inacdutra: inactive duty training
inactv: inactivate; inactivation; inactive
INAEA: International Newspaper Advertising Executives Association
InAF: Indian Air Force
inah (INAH): isonicotinic acid hydrazide
INAH: *Instituto Nacional de An-*

tropología e Historia (National Institute of Anthropology and History)—Mexico
inanim: inanimate: inanimative
INAS: Inertial Navigation and Attack System(s)
inaud: inaudible
inaug: inaugurate; inaguration
inaug diss: inaugural dissertation (thesis for doctor's degree)
in bal.: in ballast
inbd: inboard
INBUCON: International Business Consultants
inc: inclosure; include; increase
Inc: Incorporated
In C: Instructor Captain
INC: Indian National Congress; Industrial National Corporation; Island Navigation Company (tankers)
Inca: Incahuasi
INCA: Information Council of the Americas
incair: including air
incalz: *incalzando* (Italian—increasing dynamics and tone)
incan: incandescent
Incan and Aztecan Century: the 1000s — great monuments standing in the highlands of Peru and Mexico attest to these astounding American cultures—the 11th century
incap: incapacitant; incapacitating
INCAP: Institute of Nutrition of Central America and Panama
incaps: incapacitating agents
incb: inclusion body
INCB: International Narcotics Control Board (Geneva, Switzerland)
incd: incendiary; incident
incdt: incident
ince: insurance
inch.: inchoative
In-Ch: Indo-China
inchoat: inchoative
incid: incidence; incident; incidental
incid mus: incidental music
incl: inclose; inclosure; include; including; inclusive
incl: *inclusivement* (French—inclusively)
incln: inclusion
inclr: intercooler
INCMD: Indianapolis Contract Management District
INCO: International Nickel Company
incog: incognito
incomp: incomplete
Incomparable Infidel: Voltaire
incompat: incompatible; incompatibility
incompl: incomplete
incor: incorrect
Incorp: Incorporated
Incorruptible: The Incorruptible—sobriquet given Robespierre by his followers
inco(s): incorrigible(s)
incpt: intercept
incr: increase; increased; increasing; increasingly; increment; incremental
INCRA: International Copper Research Association
INCREF: International Children's Rescue Fund
incun: incunabula
incur.: incurable
ind: independent; index; indicate; indicative; indicator; indigo; indorse; indorsement; industrial; industry
in d.: *in diem* (Latin—daily)
Ind: India; Indian; Indiana; Indianapolis; Indianian; Indo-
Ind: *Indiano* (Italian—Indian; Indian Ocean); *Indien* (French—Indian; Indian Ocean)
Ind: *Indico* (Portuguese or Spanish—Indian; Indian Ocean)
IND: India (auto plaque); Indianapolis, Indiana (airport)
indecl: indeclinable
INDECO: Industrial Development Corporation
Ind Dem: Independent Democrat
Ind. E.: Industrial Engineer
indef: indefinite
indef art.: indefinite article
indem: indemnify; indemnity
inden: indenture; indentured; indenturing
Ind Eng: Industri l Engineer(ing)
Ind & Eng Chem: *Industrial and Engineering Chemistry*
indep: independent
Independence Day: July Fourth
Ind-et-L: Indre-et-Loire
Index: *Index Librorum Prohibitorum [Latin—Index of Forbidden Books (RC Church)]*
India: code for letter I
Indian: MacDowell's Suite No. 2 for Orchestra introducing American Indian themes
Indian Film Pioneer: Satyajit Ray
Indian Girl Guide: Sacajawea who guided Lewis and Clark; both Idaho and South Dakota claim her as a native daughter
Indian Princess: Pocahontas
Indian Territory: old name of Oklahoma
Indian's Friend: Roger Williams
indic: indicative; indicator
indic: *indicateur* (French—informer)
indicolite: blue tourmaline
Ind. Imp.: *Indiae Imperator* (Latin—Emperor of India)
Indira: Indira Ghandi (India's first woman prime minister)
indiv: individual
indiv psychol: individual psychology
Ind L: Independent Liberal
indm: indemnity
Ind Med: Index Medicus
Ind Mgr: Industrial Manager
Indo: Indonesia; Indonesian
Ind O: Indian Ocean
Indo-Afr: Indo-African
Indo-Austral: Indo-Australasian
indoc: indoctrinate; indoctrination
Indoc: Indochina; Indochinese
Indo-Chi: Indo-China; Indo-Chinese
indocin: indomethacine
Indo-Eur: Indo-European
Indo-Ger: Indo-German(ic)
Indo-Mal: Indo-Malayan
Indon: Indonesia
Indonesia: East Indies
Indonesias: Indonesian Islands
Indo-Pak: India-Pakistan; Indo-Pakistan(i)
indre: indenture
ind reg: induction regulator
Ind Rep: Independent Republican
In Res: Indian Reservation
Ind Ter: Indian Territory (now Oklahoma)
induc: inductance; induction
indus: industrial; industry
indust: industrial; industrialization; industrialize; industrialized; industry
Industrial Capital of Connecticut: Bridgeport
Indy: Indianapolis; Indianapolis Speedway
ined.: *ineditus* (Latin—unpublished)
INEOA: International Narcotic Enforcement Officers Association
Iness: Inverness-shire
in ex.: *in extenso* (Latin—at length)
Inextinguishable: Nielsen's Symphony No. 4
inf: infantry; infectious; infinitive
inf.: *infra* (Latin—below; beneath); *infunde* (Latin—pour into)
Inf: Infirmary
INF: International Naturist Federation; International Nudist Federation

Inf: *Inférieure* (French—Inferior; Lower)
INFA: *Institut pour l' Étude du Fascisme* (French—Institute for the Study of Fascism)
infect.: infection; infectious
infin: infinitive
infirm.: infirmary
infl: inflammable
influ: influence; influential
infm: information
infmry: infirmary
INFN: Istituto Nazionale di Fisica Nucleare (National Institute of Nuclear Physics)—Italy
info: inform; information
Info Can: Information Canada
INFORFILM: International Information Film Service
Informbureau: Communist Information Bureau (Cominform)
Informburo: (Soviet) Information Bureau
Informex: *Informaciones Mexicanas* (Mexican Information Service)
info theory: information theory
infra: below
infra dig.: *infra dignitatem* (Latin—beneath one's dignity; undignified)
infral: information retrieval atuomatic language
infraptum.: *infrascriptum* (Latin—written below)
infric.: *infricetur* (Latin—let it be rubbed in)
inft: infant
infus: infusible
infx: inspection fixture
ing: inguinal
ing: *ingégnere* (Italian—engineer); *ingegneria* (Italian—engineering)
Ing: Ingmar
Ing: *Ingénieur* (French—engineer); *Ingenieur* (German—engineer)
inga: inspection gage
Ingl: *Inghilterra* (Italian—England); *Inglaterra* (Portuguese or Spanish—England)
Ingm Berg: Ingmar Bergman
INGO: International Non-Governmental Organization
ingred(s): ingrediient(s)
Ingria: Ingermanland
inh (INH): isonicotinic hydrazide
Inh: *Inhaber* (German—proprietor)
inhab: inhabitant(s)
inhal: inhalation
in. Hg: inch of mercury
inhib: inhibition; inhibitory
INHP: Independence National Historical Park
INHS: Indian Naval Hospital Ship
INI: Indianapolis Newspapers Incorporated; Industrial Nurses Institute; Institut National De l'Industrie (National Institute of Industry)
INI: *International Nursing Index*
INIBP: Instituto Nacional de Investigaciones Biológico-Pesqueras
in./in.: inch per inch
in init.: *in initio* (Latin—in the beginning)
INIS: International Nuclear Information System
init: initial
inj: inject; injection; injections; injure; injury
inj.: *injectio* (Latin—inject; injection)
inj. enema: *injiciatur enema* (Latin—inject an enema)
inj. hyp.: *injectio hypodermica* (Latin—hypodermic injection)
inkl: *inklusiv* (German—inclusive)
inl: initial
In L: Instructor Lieutenant
Inland Empire: official nickname of Illinois
in.-lb: inch-pound
In L-Cdr: Instructor Lieutenant-Commander
in lim.: *in limine* (Latin—at the outset)
in litt.: *in litteris* (Latin—in correspondence)
in loc.: *in loco* (Latin—in the place)
in. loc. cit.: *in loco citato* (Latin—in the place cited)
Inlt: Inlet (postal abbreviation)
in mem.: *in memoriam* (Latin—in memory of)
i n mi: international nautical mile(s)
inn.: inning
Inn.: Innoshima
innerv: innervated; innervation
Innis: Inniskilling
Innisfail: (Gaelic—Isle of Destiny)—Ireland
inns.: innings
INO: Inspectorate of Naval Ordnance
inoc: inoculation; inoculate
INOC: Iraq National Oil Company
inop: inoperative
inorg: inorganic
INOS: Instituto Nacional de Obras Sanitarias (National Institute of Sanitation—Venezuela)
in-out: input-output
inp: inert nitrogen protection
INP: Inyanga National Park (Rhodesia)
INPA: International Newspaper Promotion Association
in partibus: *in partibus infidelium* (Latin—in the region of the unbelievers)
INPFC: International North Pacific Fisheries Commission
inph: interphone
in p. inf.: *in partibus infidelium* (Latin—in the region of the unbelievers)
in pr.: *in principio* (Latin—in the first place)
Inprecorr: *International Press Correspondence*
in prep: in preparation
in pro: in proportion
inprons: information processing in the central nervous system
in pulm.: *in pulmento* (Latin—in gruel)
inq: inquiry
Inq: *Inquisidor* (Spanish—inquisitor; investigator)
INQUA: International Association on Quaternary Research
inr: impact noise rating
in'r: inner
INR: Institut National de la Radio (National Radio Institute); Intelligence and Research
INRA: Instituto Nacional de la Reforma Agraria (National Institute of Agrarian Reform)—exercises economic control of Cuba
I.N.R.I.: *Iesus Nazarenus Rex Iudaeorum* (Latin—Jesus of Nazareth, King of the Jews)
ins: insulate; insulated; insulation; insurance; insure; insured
in's: in his
in./s: inch(s) per second
Ins: Insecta
INS: Indian Naval Ship; Institute of Naval Studies; Institute of Nutritional Sciences; Integrated Navigation System; International News Service
I & NS: Immigration and Naturalization Service
InsACS: Interstate Airway Communication Station
INSAIR: Inspector of Naval Aircraft
INSCAIRS: Instrumentation Calibration Incident Repair Service
insce: insurance

INSCO: Intercontinental Shipping Corporation
inscr: inscribed; inscription
INSDC: Indian National Scientific Documentation Center
INSDOC: Indian National Scientific Documentation Center
insd val: insured value
INS & E: Institute of Nuclear Science and Engineering
INSEA: International Society for Education Through Art
in./sec: inches per second
INSEL: International Nickel Southern Exploration Limited
INSENG: Inspector of Naval Engineering Material
insep: inseparable
Ins Gen: Inspector General
insh: inspection shell
insinuendo: insinuate + innuendo
INSMACH: Inspector of Naval Machinery
INSMAT: Inspector of Naval Material
INSNAVMAT: Inspector of Navigational Material (USN)
insol: insoluble
insolv: insolvent
insoly: insolubility
INSORD: Inspector of Naval Ordnance
insp: inspect; inspected; inspection; inspector; inspiration; inspire; inspired
Insp: Inspector
in-spec: within specifications
***INSPEL:** International Journal of Special Libraries*
INSPETRES: Inspector of Petroleum Resources
Insp Gen: Inspector General
***inspir.:** inspiretur* (Latin—let it be inspired)
INSPIRE: Institute for Public interest Representation
Inspired Innovator: Edgar Allan Poe
INSRADMET: Inspector of Radio Materials
inst: instant; instantaneous; institute; institution; instruct; instruction; instructor; instrument; instrumentation; instrumented
inst.: instant; this month
Inst: Institute; Institution
INSTAAR: Institute of Arctic and Alpine Research
INSTAB: Information Service on Toxicity and Biodegradability
insta-cam: instant camera (tv)
Instant Asia: polyglot Singapore with its Chinese, Indian, Malay, Pakistani, and Singhalese mixtures and tongues making this seaport nation a global crossroads
Instant Orient: Singapore
instar: inertialess scanning, tracking, and ranging
INSTARS: Information Storage and Retrieval System
Inst CE: Institute of Civil Engineers
Inst Ceram: Institution of Ceramics
Inst Dirs: Institute of Directors
Inst EE: Institute of Electrical Engineers
Inst F: Institute of Fuel
Inst Gen Sem: Institute of General Semantics
Inst Gas Eng: Institute of Gas Engineers
Inst HE: Institute of Highway Engineers
Inst Int Educ: Institute of International Education
inst: install; installation; installment
instm: instrument; instrumentation; instrumented
Inst ME: Institute of Mechanical Engineers
Inst Met: Institute of Metals
instn: institution(al)
INSTN: Institut National des Sciences et Techniques nucléaires (National Institute of Science and Nuclear Techniques)
instns: instructions
Inst P: Institute of Physics
Inst Pat: Institute of Patentees
Inst Pckg: Institute of Packing
Inst Pet: Institute of Petroleum
instr: instruct; instruction; instructor; instrument(s)
instru: instrumentation
instruct.: instruction; instructor
Inst W: Institute of Welding
Inst WE: Institute of Water Engineers
insuf: insufficient
Insurance Capital: Hartford, Connecticut and Omaha, Nebraska both claim this nickname
Insurance City: place-name nickname shared by Atlanta, Georgia and Hartford, Connecticut
INSURV: Board of Inspection and Survey
in sync: in synchronization; perfectly synchronized
int: intake; integer; integral; interest; interior; interjection; internal; international; intersection
INT: Air Inter (Lignes Aériennes Intérieures)
***int. al.:** inter alia* (Latin—among other things)
INTAMEL: International Association of Metropolitan City Libraries
***int. cib.:** inter cibos* (Latin—between meals)
intcl: intercoastal
int comb.: internal combustion
Int Com Illum: International Commission on Illumination
intcp: intercept; interception; interceptor
int dec: interior decorator
Int Doc Serv: International Documents Service (Columbia University)
INTECOM: International Council for Technical Communication
intel: intelligence
Intellectual Emperor of Europe: Voltaire
Intellectual Seed Pod of the Nation: Emerson's nickname for Concord, Massachusetts where he lived with such neighbors as the Alcotts, Hawthorne, and Thoreau
intelsat: international telecommunications satellite
INTELSAT: International Telecommunications Satellite Consortium
***INTEM:** Instituto Interamericano de Educacion Musical* (Inter-American Institute of Musical Education)
***Intend:** Intendente* (Spanish—manager; police commissioner; provincial governor; superintendent; supervisor)
intens: intensive
inter: intermediate; interrogation; intercalation
Interarmco: International Armament Corporation
INTERASMA: Association Internationale d'Asthmologie (International Association for the Study of Asthma)
***Interavia:** World Review of Aviation and Astronautics*
Interchem: Interchemical Corporation
intercom: intercommunication system
interdict.: intelligence detection and interdiction countermeasures
INTEREXPO: International Expositions
interf: interference
INTERFILM: International

Church Film Center
interi: (Japanese short form—intellectual)
Interior: US Department of the Interior
Interior Plains: Canada's great plains
interj: interjection
Intermex: International Mexican Bank
InterMilPol: International Military Police (NATO)
intern.: internal
internat: international; internationalism; internationalist
International Capital: New York City—headquarters of the United Nations
International Functionalists: Walter Gropius and Mies van der Rohe
International Prizegiver: Alfred Nobel
interp: interpolation
Interpace: International Pipe and Ceramics
Interpol: International Criminal Police Commission
Interpreter of the Sea: Winslow Homer
interr: interrogative
interrog: interrogation; interrogative
INTERSTENO: International Federation of Short Hand and Typewriting Stenographers
Intertel: International Television
intertwangled: intertwined + wangled
inter/w: intersection with
intest: intestinal; intestine
INTEXT: International Textbook Company
intfc: interference
intg: interrogate; interrogator
inth: intrathecal
intip: integrated information processing
intl: international
intmed: intermediate
int med (Int Med): internal medicine
intmt: intermittent
int. noct.: *inter noctem* (Latin—during the night)
intns: intransit
INTO: Irish National Teachers' Organization
Intourist: Soviet Tourist Office
intox: intoxicant; intoxicate; intoxicated; intoxication
intpr: interpret; interpretation; interpreter
intr: intransitive; intruder; intrusion
intrans: intransitive
in trans: in transit
in trans.: *in transitu* (Latin—in transit)
intransit: intransitive
Int Rep: Intelligence Report
Int Rev: Internal Revenue
intrex: information transfer complex
intrmt: interment
intro: introduce; introduced; introducing; introduction; introductory; introversion; introvert
introd: introduction
introd: *introduzione* (Italian—introduction)
intropta.: *introscripta* (Latin—written within)
intro(s): introduction(s)
intrvlmtr: intervalometer
int std d: international standard depth
Int Sum: Intelligence Summary
INTUC: Indian National Trades Union Congress
intv: independent television
intvw: interview
I Nuc E: Institute of Nuclear Engineering
InUS: inside the United States
in ut.: *in utero* (Latin—within the uterus)
inv: invent; inventor; invert; inverter; invoice
inv.: *invenit* (Latin—he devised it)
Inv: Inverness
Inventor of Bifocals: Benjamin Franklin
Inventor of Calculus: Baron Gottfried Wilhelm von Leibniz and Sir Isaac Newton are both credited with this title
Inventor of the Stethoscope: René-Théophile-Hyacinthe Laennec
Inventor of the Telephone: Scottish-Canadian Alexander Graham Bell
invert.: invertebrate
inves: investigate; investigation; investigator
invest(s): investigation(s)
inv. et del.: *invenit et delineavit* (Latin—devised and drawn)
invic.: *invictus* (Latin—unconquerable)—title of a poem by William Ernest Henley—*Invictus*
invisible disease: dyslexia
in vit.: *in vitro* (Latin—within glass; within a test tube or other laboratory glass vessel)
in viv.: *in vivo* (Latin—within a living body)
invol: involuntary
invt: inventory
invtrx: inventrix
INWATS: Inward Wide Area Telephone Service
INWR: Imperial National Wildlife Refuge (Arizona); Iroquois National Wildlife Refuge (New York)
INX: Inexco Oil (stock-exchange symbol)
io: ion engine; intraocular
i/o: inboard-outboard (motorboat engine); input/output
i & o: input and output
Io: ionium
IO: India Office; Information Officer; Intelligence Office(r); Intercept Office(r); Irish Office; Issuing Office(r)
I/O: Inspection Order
IOAM: Institute of Appliance Manufacturers
IOAT: International Organization Against Trachoma
IOB: Institute of Brewing
IOBB: Independent Order of B'nai B'rith
IOBC: Indian Ocean Biological Center
IOBI: Institute of Bankers in Ireland
IOBS: Institute of Bankers in Scotland
ioc: initial operational capability; in our culture
IOC: Institute of Chemistry; Intergovernmental Oceanographic Commission; Inter national Olympic Committee; Interstate Oil Compact
IOCA: Interstate Oil Compounders Association
IOCC: Interstate Oil Compact Commission
IOCS: Input-Output Control System
IOCU: International Office of Consumers Unions; International Organization of Consumer Unions
IOCV: International Organization of Citrus Virologists
IOD: Imperial Order of the Dragon
IODE: Imperial Order of Daughters of the Empire
Iodine State: South Carolina
IOE: International Office of Epizootics; International Organization of Employers
IOEC: International Order for Ethics and Culture
IOF: Independent Order of Foresters; International Oceanographic Foundation
iofb: intraocular foreign body

IOFC: Indian Ocean Fishery Commission
IOFSI: Independent Order of the Free Sons of Israel
ioga: industry-organized government-approved
IOGP: Independent Oil and Gas Producers
IOGT: International Order of Good Templars
ioh: item(s) on hand
IOH: Institute of Heraldry
IOI: Israel Office of Information
I o J: Institute of Journalists
IOJ: International Organization of Journalists
IOJD: International Order of Job's Daughters
IO Ltd: Imperial Oil Limited
IOM: Institute of Metals; Institute of Metallurgists; Institute for Organization Management
IOME: Institute of Marine Engineers
IOMM & P: International Organization of Masters, Mates and Pilots
IOM SPC: Isle of Man Steam Packet Company
IOMTR: International Office for Motor Trades and Repairs
Ion: Ionic
ION: (pseudynymic initials—George Jacob Holyoake); Institute of Navigation
Ionians: Ionian Islands
IOO: Inspecting Ordnance Officer
IOC: International Olive Oil Council
IOOF: Independent Order of Odd Fellows
IOOTS: International Organization of Old Testament Scholars
iop: input-output processor; intraocular power
i & op: in-and-out processing
IOP: Institute of Petroleum
IOPAB: International Organization for Pure and Applied Biophysics
IOPC: Interagency Oil Policy Committee
IOP & LOA: Independent Oil Producers and Land Owners Association
IOQ: Institute of Quarrying
IOR: Independent Order of Rechabites (Quaker abstainers)
IORM: Improved Order of Red Men
IORS: International Orders' Research Society
IoS: Isles of Scilly; Isles of Shoals; Isles of the Sea
IOS: International Organization for Standardization; Investors Overseas Services
IOSA: Incorporated Oil Seed Association
IOSM: Independent Order of the Sons of Malta
iota.: information overload testing aid
IOTA: Institute of Traffic Administration
IOTC: International Originating Toll Center
iou: immediate operation use
I.O.U.: I owe you
I.O.U.s: (plural of I.O.U.)
IO UBC: Institute of Oceanography—University of British Columbia
IOUSP: Instituto Oceanográfico da Universidade de São Paulo (Oceanographic Institute of the University of São Paulo)
IOV: Instituto Oceanográfico de Valparaíso (Oceanographic Institute of Valparaíso)
IOVST: International Organization for Vacuum Science and Technology
iow: in other words
IOW: Institute of Welding
ip: incentive pay; identification point; industrial photographer; industrial photography; initial point; intermediate pressure; iron pipe; plate current (symbol)
i & p: indexed and paged
iP: *in Preussen* (German—in Prussia)
Ip: Ipanema
IP : Institut Pasteur; Instructor Pilot; Insular Police; Isla de Pinos (Isle of Pines); plate current (symbol)
IoP: Isle of Palms; Isle of Pines
I & P: *Izvestia* and *Pravda (Russian—News* and *Truth)*
I£: Israeli pound
ipa: including particular average; internal power amplifier; international phonetic alphabet (IPA)
IPA: Institute of Public Administration; Institute of Public Affairs; International Phonetic Association; International Police Archives (Manchester Central Library); International Police Academy; International Police Association; International Psychoanalytical Association; International Publishers Association
IPA: *Information Please Almanac*
IPAA: Independent Petroleum Association of America
IPAI: Information Processing Association of Israel
IPARS: International Programmed Airline Reservation System
IPAT: Institute for Personality and Ability Testing
ipb: illustrated parts breakdown
ipbm (IPBM): interplanetary ballistic missile
IPBMM: International Permanent Bureau of Motor Manufacturers
ipc: industrial process control; isopropyl carbanilate
IPC: Illinois Power Company; Industrial Process Control; Industrial Property Committee; Institute of Paper Chemistry; Institute of Pastoral Care; Institute of Printed Circuits; Inter-African Phytosanitary commission; International Packings Corporation; International Paper Chemists; International Petroleum Company; International Polar Commission; International Poplar Commission; Iraq Petroleum Company; Isopropyl Carbanilate
IPCA: Industrial Pest Control Association
IPCEA: Insulated Power Cable Engineers Association
IPCI: International Potato Chip Institute
IPCS: International Peace Corps Secretariat
ip cyl: intermediate-pressure cylinder
ipd: insertion phase delay
IPD: Institute for Professional Development
IPE: Institution of Plant Engineers; Institute of Production Engineers
IPE: International Petroleum Encyclopedia
IPEC: International Petroleum Exploration Company
ipecac: ipecacuanha
IPEU: International Photo Engravers' Union
IPF: Irish Printing Federation
IPFC: Indo-Pacific Fisheries Council
ipfm: integral pulse frequency modulation
IPG: Independent Publishers' Group
IPGH: *Instituto Panamericano de Geografía e Historia* (Spanish—Pan-American Institute

of Geography and History)

iph: impressions per hour; inches per hour; interphalangeal

IPHC: International Pacific Halibut Commission

IPHE: Institute of Public Health Engineers

i.p.i.: *in partibus infidelium* (Latin—in the region of unbelievers)

IPI: Institute of Poultry Industries; International Press Institute

IPIP: Information Processing Improvement Program

IPIR: Initial Photographic Interpretation Report (USAF); Institute for Public Interest Representation

ipl (IPL): information processing language

IPL: Italian Pacific Line

I Plant Eng: Institution of Plant Engineers

ipm: inches per minute; inches per month; interruptions per minute

IPM: Institute of Personnel Management; Institute for Police Management

ipmin: inches per minute

IPMP: Industrial Plant Modernization Program

IPMS: International Polar Motion Service

IPO: Israel Philharmonic Orchestra

IPOEE: Institution of Post Office Electrical Engineers

IPOT: Imperial Philharmonic Orchestra of Tokyo

ipp: imaging photopolarimeter; impact prediction point; india paper proof(s); intrapleural pressure

Ipp: Ippolito

IPP: Ivan Petrovich Pavlov

ippa: inspection, palpitation, percussion, auscultation

IPPA: International Planned Parenthood Association

IPPAU: International Printing Pressmen and Assistants' Union

ippb: intermittent positive-pressure breathing

ippb/i: intermittent positive pressure breathing/inspiratory

ippr: intermittent positive pressure respiration

IPPTT: *Internationale du Personnel des Postes, Télégraphes et Téléphones* (French—International Postal, Telegraph, and Telephone personnel)

ippv: intermittent positive pressure ventilation

ipq: intimacy potential quotient

ipr: inches per revolution

IPR: Individual Pay Record; Institute of Pacific Relations; Institute of Philosophical Research

IPR: *International Public Relations*

IPRA: International Public Relations Association

IPRC: Institute of Puerto Rican Culture

IPRO: International Patent Research Office

I Prod Eng: Institute of Production Engineers

ips: inches per second; interruptions per second; iron pipe size

Ips: Ipswich

IPS: Incremental Purchasing System; Industrial Planning Specification; Institute of Population Studies (Japan); Institute of Public Safety; International Phenomenological Society; International Pipe Standard; Interpretive Programming System

IPS: *Instituto Poligrafico dello Stato* (Italian—State Printing and Stationery office)

IPSA: Independent Passenger Steamship Association; Independent Postal System of America

IPSC: International Pacific Salmon Committee

IPSF: International Pharmacy Students Federation; International Piano Symphony Foundation

IPSFC: International Pacific Salmon Fisheries Commission

ipsp: inhibitory postsynaptic potential

IPSSB: International Processing Systems Standards Board

ipt: indexed, paged, titled; internal pipe thread

IPT: Initial Production Test (USA)

IPT: *Instituto Panameño de Turismo* (Spanish—Panamanian Institute of Tourism)

ipth (IPTH): immunoreactive parathyroid hormone

IPTPA: International Professional Tennis Players' Association

ipts: international practical temperature scale

IPTS: Improved Programmer Test Section; International Practical Temperature Scale

IPU: International Paleontological Union; Inter-Parliamentary Union

ipv: inactivated poliomyelitis vaccine; infectious pustular vaginitis; infectious pustular vulvovaginitis

ipv: *in plaats van* (Dutch—in place of)

IPW: interrogation prisoner of war

ipy: inches penetration per year; inches per year

IPY: International Polar Year

i.q.: *idem quod* (Latin—the same as)

Iq: Iraq

IQ: intelligence quotient

I.Q.: I Quit (smoking)

I of Q: Institute of Quarrying

IQA: Institute of Quality Assurance

IQCA: Irish Quality Control Association

IQCT: Institute for Quality Control Training

i.q.e.d.: *id quod erat demonstrandum* (Latin—that which was to be proved)

I Qk: interrupted quick (light)

I Qk: Fl: interrupted quick flashing (light)

iq & s: iron, quinine, and strychnine

IQS: Institute of Quality Surveyors; Institute of Quantity Surveyors

IQSY: International Quiet Sun Year (1964–1965)

Iqu: Iquique

ir: information retrieval; infrared; inland revenue; inside radius; inside right; instantaneous relay; instrument reading; insulation resistance; internal resistance; interrogator-responder

i-r: infra-red

i/r: interchangeability and replaceability

i & r: information and retrieval; intelligence and reconnaissance; interchangeability and replaceability

i R: *im Ruhestand* (German—in retirement)

Ir: Iran; Irania; Ireland; iridium; Irish

IR: Industrial Relations; Information Request; Inspection Rejection; Inspector's Report; Intelligence Report; Internal Revenue; Invention Report; Investigation Record

I-R: Ingersoll-Rand

I & R: Initiative and Referen-

dum; Intelligence and Reconnaissance
ira: independent retirement account (IRA)
Ira: Iraq
IRA: Indian Rights Association; Intercollegiate Rowing Association; International Reading Association; International Recreation Association; Iranian Airways; Irish Republican Army; Israel Railway Administration
IRAA: Independent Refiners Association of America
IRAB: Institute for Research in Animal Behavior
IRAC: Industrial Relations Advisory Committee; Interdepartmental Radio Advisory Committee; Interfraternity Research and Administrative Council
IRAD: Institute for Research on Animal Diseases
iran: inspect and repair as necessary
Iran: formerly Persia
Iran(ian): Persia(n)
IRANAIR: Iran National Airlines
IR/AR: Inspector's Report/Action Request
IRASA: International Radio Air Safety Association
iraser: infrared amplification by stimulated emission of radiation
IRB: Indiana Rating Bureau; Irish Republican Brotherhood
IRBDC: Insurance Rating Bureau of the District of Columbia
irbm (IRBM): intermediate range ballistic missile
irc: infrared countermeasures; item responsibility code
IRC: Industrial Recreation Council; Industrial Relations Committee; Industrial Relations Council; Institutional Research Council; Internal Revenue Code; International Railways of Central America (stock exchange symbol); International Rainwear Council; International Red Cross; International Rescue Committee; International Resistance Company; International Rice Commission
IRCA: International Railways of Central America
IRCO: Industrial Rustproof Company
IRCP: International Commission on Radiological Protection
ird (IRD): internal research and development
IRD: Instituto Rubén Darío
IR & D: International Research and Development
IRDA: Industrial Research and Development Authority
Ire: Ireland
IRE: Institute of Radio Engineers
IREC: Irrigation Research and Extension Commission
IREE: Institute of Radio and Electronic Engineers
IREF: International Real Estate Federation
Ireland the Great: Newfoundland's name given it by Irish explorers who found it in Viking times
irer: infrared extra rapid
IRF: International Road Federation
IRFAA: International Rescue and First Aid Association
IRFC: Ingersoll-Rand Finance Corporation
IRFM: *Industrias Reunidas Francisco Matarazzo* (Francisco Matarazzo's Reunited Industries)
IRFU: Iriah Rugby Football Union
IRG: Interdepartmental Regional Group
Ir Gael: Irish Gaelic
IRGDLP: International Research Group on Drug Legislation and Programs (Geneva, Switzerland)
irgl: immunoreactive glucagon
IRGRD: International Research Group on Refuse Disposal
IRH: *Internationalen Roten Hilfe* (German—International Red Aid)—Red Fighting Fund of international communists
irhd: international rubber hardness degrees
iri: immunoreactive insulin
IRI: Industrial Reconstruction Institute; Industrial Research Institute; Institute of the Rubber Industry
IRIA: Infrared Information and Analysis
IRICA: Industrial Research Institute for Central America
irid: iridescent
IRIG: Inter-Range Instrumentation Group
iris.: infrared interferometer spectrometer
Iris: Tennessee state flower and sobriquet
IRIS: Integrated Reconaissance Intelligence System
Irish Channel: New Orleans waterfront slum
Irish FP: Irish Fishing Port (registration symbols displayed on the bows of fishing vessels)
Irish Free State: Republic of Ireland
Irish VR: Irish Vehicle Registration (symbols on automotive vehicle licenses)
IRJC: Indian River Junior College
irl: information retrieval language
Irl: *Irlanda* (Italian, Portuguese, Spanish—Ireland)
IRLCS: International Red Locust Control Service
IRLS: Interrogation Recording Location System
irm: infrared measurement; innate release mechanism; intermediate range monitor
IRM: Improved Risk Mutuals; Islamic Republic of Mauritania
IRM (NYU): Institute of Rehabilitation Medicine (New York University)
irma: information revision and manuscript assembly
IRMP: Intermountain Regional Medical Program
IRMRA: Indian Rubber Manufacturers Research Association
IRN: Independent Radio News
IRNP: Isle Royale National Park (Michigan)
IRO: Industrial Relations Office(r); Inland Revenue Office(r); Internal Revenue Office(r); International Refugee Organization; International Relief Organization
IRO-ALA: International Relations Office—American Library Association
irod: instantaneous readout detector
iron.: ironic(al)
Iron Chancellor: Prince Otto Eduard Leopold von Bismarck-Schönhausen—first chancellor of German Empire
Iron City: place-name nickname shared by Bessemer, Alabama and Pittsburgh, Pennsylvania
Iron Curtain: barrier raised by Stalin at the end of World War II between eastern and western Europe—between communist-controlled Europe and free Europe

Iron Duke: Arthur Wellesley the Duke of Wellington
Iron Gate: narrow rapids in the Danube below Orsova in Romania
Iron Horse: baseball-fan nickname for Lou Gehrig; old nickname for a steam locomotive
iron pyrites: sulfide of iron
Ironquill: Eugene Fitch Ware
Ironsides: Oliver Cromwell
Iron Triangle: Cologne (Köln), Siegen, Solingen (all noted for their steel products including fine cutlery)
iros: ipsilateral routing of signal
IRP: Individualized Reading Program; Information Resources Press
IRPA: International Radiation Protection Association
IRPS: International Religious Press Service (Vatican City)
irr: infrared rays; infrared reflectance; irredeemable; irregular(ity)
IRR: Institute of Race Relations
IRRA: Industrial Relations Research Association
irrd: international road research documentation
IRRDB: International Rubber Research and Development Board
irreg: irregular
irrig: irrigation
IRs: Inspector's Reports
IRS: Ineligible Reserve Section; Internal Revenue Service; International Recruiting Service; International Rorschach Society
I & RS: Information and Research Services
IRSE: Institution of Railway Signal Engineers
IRSF: Inland Revenue Staff Federation
IRSG: International Rubber Study Group
IRSID: Institut des Recherches de la Sidérurgie Française (French Steel Research Institute)
IRSNB: Institut Royal des Sciences Naturelles de Belgique (Royal Belgian Institute of Natural Sciences)
IRSP: Irish Republican Socialist Party
IRSS: Instrumentation Range Safety System
irt: infrared tracker
IRT: Institute for Rapid Transit; Institute of Reprographic Technology; Interborough Rapid Transit (subway system)
IRTA: Illinois Retired Teachers Association
IRTE: Institute of Road Transport Engineers
IRTS: International Radio and Television Society
IRTU: International Railway Temperance Union
iru: international radium unit; international rat unit
IRU: International Road Transport Union
irv: inspiratory reserve volume
Irv: Irvin; Irving; Irwin
Irving Berlin: Irving Baline
Irving Stone: Irving Tannenbaum
IRW: Iowa Reformatory for Women
IRWC: International Registry of World Citizens
is.: ingot sheet; integrally stiffened; intercoastal space; internal shield; island; isle
is: his
i & s: inspection and security; inspection and survey
Is: Islam; Islamic; Island; Isle; Israel; Israeli
Is: *Isaías* (Spanish—Isiah)
IS: Igor Stravinsky; Indian Summer (freeboard marking); Irish Society
I of S: Institute of Sound; Isle of Skye
isa: international standard atmosphere
Isa: Isaiah, The Book of the Prophet
ISA: Independent Showmen of America; Instrument Society of America; Insulating Siding Association; International Schools Association; International Scientific Affairs; International Security Affairs; International Sign Association; International Silk Association; International Sociological Association; International Standards Association
Isab: Isabella
ISAB: Institute for the Study of Animal Behavior
ISAC: International Security Affairs Committee
ISACP: Italian Society of Authors, Composers, and Publishers
ISAD: Information Science and Automation Division (ALA)
ISAE: *Internacia Scienca Asocio Esperantista* (International Esperantist Scientific Association)
IsAF: Israeli Air Force
isaf black: intermediate superabrasive furnace black
Isak Dinesen: Baroness Karen Blixen-Finecke
ISALPA: Incorporated Society of Auctioneers and Landed Property Agents
ISAPC: Incorporated Society of Authors, Playwrights, and Composers
isar: information storage and retrieval
ISAS: Isotopic Source Assay System
ISAW: International Society of Aviation Writers
isb: independent sideband
ISB: International Society of Biometeorology
ISBA: Incorporated Society of British Advertisers
ISBB: International Society for Bioclimatology and Biometeorology
ISBN: International Standard Book Number
ISBS: Icelandic State Broadcasting Service
isc: interstate commerce
ISC: Icelandic Steamship Company; Idaho State College; Imperial Service College; Imperial Staff College; Indiana State College; Indian Staff Corps; Indoor Sports Club; Industrial Security Commission; Inter-American Society of Cardiology; International Science Center; International Sericultural Commission; International Society of Cardiology; International Softball Congress; International Statistical Classification; International Sugar Council; International Supreme Council (World Masons); Interseas Shipping Corporation; Interservice Sports Council; Interstate Sanitation Commission
ISCA: International Senior Citizens Association
iscan: inertialess steerable communication antenna
ISCB: International Society for Cell Biology
ISCC: Inter-Society Color Council
ISCE: International Society for Christian Endeavor
ISCEH: International Society for Clinical and Experimental Hypnosis
ISCERG: International Society

for Clinical Electroretinography
ISCET: International Society of Certified Electronics Technicians
ISCM: International Society for Contemporary Music
ISCOR: Iron and Steel Industrial Corporation (South Africa)
ISCP: International Society of Clinical Pathology
ISD: Internal Security Division (U.S. Dept of Justice)
ISDD: Institute for the Study of Drug Dependence (London, England)
ISDI: International Social Development Institute
ISDRA: International Sled Dog Racing Association
ISDS: Inadvertent Separation Destruct System
ise: integral square error
ISE: Institute for Sex Education; Institute of Social Ethics; Institution of Structural Engineers
ISEA: Industrial Safety Equipment Association
ISEEP: Infrared-Sensitive Element Evaluation Program
ISES: International Society of Explosives Specialists
ISEU: International Stereotypers' and Electrotypers' Union
isf: interstitial fluid
ISF: International Science Foundation; International Shipping Federation; International Society for Fat Research; International Softball Federation
ISFA: Intercoastal Steamship Freight Association; International Scientific Film Association
ISFR: Institute for the Study of Fatigue and Reliability
isg: imperial standard gallon
ISGE: International Society of Gastroenterology
ISGM: Isabella Stewart Gardner Museum
ISGS: International Society for General Semantics
ISGW: International Society of Girl Watchers
Ish: Isham; Ishbel; Ishmael
ISH: International Society of Hematology
ISHAM: International Society for Human and Animal Mycology
ISHL: Illinois Social Hygiene League
ISHS: International Society for Horticultural Science
ISI: Institute for Scientific Information; Intercollegiate Society of Individualists; Intercollegiate Studies Institute; International Statistical Institute; Iron and Steel Institute
ISIB: Inter-Services Ionospheric Bureau
ISIC: International Standard Industrial Classification
ISIM: International Society of Internal Medicine
isinglass: mica
ISIP: Iron and Steel Industry Profile Service
isis (ISIS): ionospheric studies
ISIS: Institute of Scrap Iron and Steel; International Science Information Service
ISK: Isambard Kingdom Brunel
ISKC: International Society for Krishna Consciousness
isl: island
Isl: *Islanda* (Italian—Iceland); *Islandia* (Spanish—Iceland); *Islândia* (Portuguese—Iceland)
ISL: Iceland Steamship Company; Interseas Shipping Lines; Iranian Shipping Lines; Irish Shipping Limited
I S-L: Instructor Sub-Lieutenant
isla: (Spanish—island, as in Isla de Cuba)
Islam: (Arabic—Submission) submission to the will of God
Islamic Century: the 600s—Mohammed flees from Mecca to Medina and dies in 632; Islam begins expanding throughout the Middle East and Africa—the 7th century
Island of Bearded Figs: Barbados
Island of Birds: Kusadasi
Island City: Manhattan, Montreal, Singapore, and Stockholm hold this title as all are built on islands
Island of Cloves: Zanzibar
Island Continent: Australia
Island of Death: Kahoolawe, Hawaii (used for target practice by Air Force and Navy)
Island of Dreams: Capri
Island at the End of the World: Madagascar as described by the Malagasy
Island of Flowers: Tobago in Panama Bay
Island Fortress: Malta
Island of Knights Hospitaliers: Malta
Island of Light: New Caledonia
Island-and-Mainland Province: Newfoundland
Island Ministate: Nauru in the Central Pacific
Island of the Moon: Madagascar
Island Nation: nickname shared by Australia, an island of continental magnitude, with the Bahamas, Bahrain, Barbados, the Cape Verde Islands, the Republic of China (offshore China or Taiwan), the Comoro Islands, Cuba, Cyprus, the Dominican Republic (sharing the island of Hispaniola with Haiti), Fiji, Grenada, Haiti, Iceland, Indonesia, Ireland, Jamaica, Japan, Madagascar, the Maldives, Malta, Mauritius, Nauru, New Zealand, Papua New Guinea, the Philippines, São Tomé and Principe, the Seychelles, Singapore, Sri Lanka (Ceylon), Tonga, Trinidad and Tobago, the United Kingdom consisting of Great Britain (England, Scotland, and Wales) plus Northern Ireland, Western Samoa
Island of Olives: Cyprus
Island of Roses: Rhodes in the Dodecanese
Island of Ruins and Roses: Gotland, Sweden
Island of Sages and Saints: Ireland
Islands of Eternal Spring: the Balearics (Ibiza, Formentera, Mallorca, Menorca)
Islands of the Maoris: New Zealand
Island State: Tasmania, Australia
Island of Venus: Tahiti
Isle of Fragrant Waters: Hong Kong
Isle of Roses: Rhodes
Isle of Saints: Ireland
Isles of the Blest: the Canary Islands
Isle of Sleep: Tasmania so nicknamed by other Australians
Isle of Springs: Jamaica
ISLFD: Incorporated Society of London Fashion Designers
ISLIC: Israel Society of Special Libraries and Information Centers
isl of Lan: islands of Langerhans
isln: isolation
ISLRS: Inactive Status List Reserve Section
isls L: islands of Langerhans
Islw: Indian spring low water
ISLWF: International Shoe and Leather Workers Federation
ism: industrial, scientific, medical wave length

ISM: International Society for Musicology
ISMA: International Superphosphate Manufacturers Association
ISME: International Society of Musical Education
ISMH: International Society of Medical Hydrology
ISMI: Institute for the Study of Mental Images
ism of the modern world: racism (according to anthropologist Ruth Benedict)
ISMRC: Inter-Services Metallurgical Research Council
ISMUN: International Student Movement for the United Nations
Is N: (Sir) Isaac Newton
ISN: International Society for Neurochemistry
ISNP: International Society of Naturopathic Physicians
isn't: is not
iso: isolate; isolation; isolator (Soviet penal colony specializing in solitary confinement of political prisoners); isotope; isotopic
ISO: Imperial Service Order; Indianapolis Symphony Orchestra; Information Services Office(r); International Standardization Organization
isobu: isobutyl
is/oc: individual system/organization cost
isochr: isochronal
Isol: Isolation; Isolator
Isolator of Dysentary: Kiyoshi Shiga
Isolator of Gangrene: Shibasaburo Kitazato
Isolde: Yseult
isoln: isolate; isolated; isolation
isom: isometric(s)
ISOMATA: Idyllwild School of Music and the Arts
isordil: isorbide dinitrate
ISOS: International Ship Operating Services
isot: isotropic
iso wd: isolation ward
isp: intraspinal
Isp: specific impulse (symbol)
ISP: Industrial Security Program; Institute of Social Psychiatry; Institute of Store Planners; Interamerican Society of Psychology
ISPA: International Screen Publicity Association; International Society for the Protection of Animals; International Sporting Press Association
Ispalis: (Latin—Sevilla)—Seville
ISPO: Instrumentation Ships' Project Office
ISPP: Inter-Services Plastic Panel
isr: information storage and retrieval
Isr: Israel; Israeli
isr: *Israel* (Portuguese or Spanish—Israel); *Israele* (Italian—Israel)
ISR: Indian State Railways; Institute for Sex Research; Institute for Social Research; International Society of Radiology
IS & R: Information Storage and Retrieval (system)
ISRAD: Institute for Social Research and Development
ISRB: Idaho Surveying and Rating Bureau; Inter-Services Research Bureau
ISRC: International Synthetic Rubber Company
ISRD: International Society for the Rehabilitation of the Disabled
ISRU: International Scientific Radio Union
iss: ideal solidus structures; issue
ISS: Industry Standard Specifications; Inspection suveillance Sheet; Institute of Space Sciences; Institute of Space Studies; Integrated Start System; International School Service; International Shoe Company (stock exchange symbol); International Social Service; International Students Society; International Sunshine Society
ISSA: International Social Security Association
ISSB: Inter-Services Security board
ISSC: International Social Science Council
ISSCB: International Society for Sandwich Construction and Bonding
ISSCT: International Society of Sugar Cane Technologists
issei: (Japanese—first generation)—Japanese immigrant to the U.S., (see *kibei, nisei, sansei*)
ISSLIC: Israel Societies of Special Libraries and Information Centers
ISSMFE: International Society of Soil Mechanics and Foundation Engineering
ISSN: International Standard Serial Number
issr: information storage, selection, and retrieval
ISSS: International Society of Soil Science; International Society for the Study of Symbols
ISST: International Society of Skilled Trades
IS Standards: International Safety Standards
ist: insulin shock therapy; interstellar travel
is't: is it
ist: *istituto* (Italian—institute)
Ist: Istanbul
IST: Indian Standard Time; International Society of Toxicology; Instanbul; Turkey (airport); Institute of Science and Technology (University of Michigan)
IST: *International Steam Table*
IS & T: *International Science and Technology*
ISTA: International Seed Testing Association
Istan: Istanbul
istar: information storage translation and reproduction
ISTC: Interdepartmental Screw Thread Committee; International Shade Tree Conference
ISTD: Institute for the Study and Treatment of Delinquency
ISTEA: Iron and Steel Trades Employers' Association
IS 201: Intermediate School 201 (for example)
Isthmian Nation: Panama
ISTI: Iowa State Technical Institute
ISTM: International Society for Testing Materials
ISTO: Italian State Tourist Office
I Struct E: Institute of Structural Engineers
istse: integral square time square error
ISU: Idaho State University; International Seamen's Union; International Skating Union; Iowa Southern Utilities; Iowa State University; Italian Service Unit; Southern Iowa Railway (railroad coding)
I-sub: inhibitor substance
ISUM: Intelligence Summary
ISUST: Iowa State University of Science and Technology
ISV: Institute for the Study of Violence (Brandeis U); International Scientific Vocabulary
ISVR: Institute of Sound and Vibration Research
ISVS: International Secretariat for Volunteer

isy: intrasynovial
isw: interstitial water
ISW: Institute for Solid Wastes
ISWG: Imperial Standard Wire Gauge
it: slang term for sex appeal
it.: inspection tag; internal thread; international tolerance; inventory transfer; item; itemization(s); itemize(d)
it: Intermediate Technology
it: *item* (Spanish—item)
i/t: *in transitu* (Latin—in transit)
i/t: intensity duration
it. (IT): intertuberous
It: Italy
IT: Immunity Test; Imperial Territory; Imperial Typewriter; Income Tax; Indian Territory; Inner Temple; Institute of Technology; International Telephone and Telegraph (Wall Street slang)
IoT: Isle of Thanet; Institute of Transport
ita: initial teaching alphabet
ITA: Independent Television Authority; Industrial Truck Association; Institut du Transport Aerien (Air Transport Institute); International Temperance Association; International Touring Alliance; International Twins Association
ITACS: Integrated Tactical Air Control System
ITAI: Institution of Technical Authors and Illustrators
ital: italic; italics
Ital: Italian
Italian: Mendelssohn's Symphony No. 4 in A major
Italian Riviera: resort area between La Spezia and Ventimiglia
itar: interstate and foreign travel (or transportation) in aid of racketeering enterprises
itax: italics
ITB: International Time Bureau; Irish Tourist Board; Integrated Tug Barge
itbh: internal broach
IT & BL: Island Tug & Barge, Ltd.
itc: installation time and cost
ITC: Illinois Terminal Company (railroad); Imperial Tobacco Company; Infantry Training Center; International Tin Council; International Toastmistress Clubs; International Traders Clubs; Island Trading Company
IT & C: Industry, Trade, and Commerce (Canada)
ITCA: International Typographic Composition Association
itcan: inspect, test, and correct as necessary
ITCP: Integrated Test and Check-out Procedures
ITCRM: Infantry Training Center—Royal Marines
ITCV: Inter-Tropical Convergence Zone
it'd: it had; it would
ITD: *International Telephone Directory*
itda: indirect target damage assessment
ITE: Institute of Traffic Engineers
itf: inland transit floater (insurance)
ITF: International Television Federation; International Trade Federation
ITFCS: Institute for Twenty-First Century Studies
itfs: instructional television fixed service
ITFS: International Television Fixed Service
itga: internal gage
ITGWF: International Textile and Garment Workers Federation
ithy: I'm only trying to help you
ITI: Inagua Transports Incorporated; Integrated Task Indices; International Technical Institute; International Theatre Institute; International Thrift Institute
ITIB: Iceland Tourist Information Bureau
ITIC: International Tsunami Information Center
itin: itinerary
itl: integrate-transfer-launch
Itl: Italian
it'll: it will
itlx: italics (used for items from Latin or other languages, titles of books and periodicals, physical symbols)
itm: inch trim moment
ITM: Institute of Travel Managers
ITMA: Institute of Trade Mark Agents
ITMA: *It's That Man Again* (Tommy Handley's most popular World-War-II BBC series)
ITMRC: International Travel Market Research Council
ITN: *Independent Television News*
ITO: Interim Technical Order; International Trade Organization (UN); Invitational Travel Orders
ITOA: Independent Taxi Owners Association
ITOFCA: Industrial Trailer-on-Flatcar Associates
itom: interstate transportation of obscene matter
itp (ITP): idiopathic thrombocytopenic purpura; immune thrombocytopenic purpura; inosine triphosphate
ITPP: Institute of Technical Publicity and Publications
ITPS: Income Tax Payers' Society
ITR: Indiana Toll Road
ITRC: International Tin Research Council
it's: it has; it is
its (ITS): invitation to send (data processing)
ITS: Idaho Test Station; Integrated Trajectory System; International Technogeographical Society; International Trade Secretariat; International Transportation Service
itsa: interstate transportation of stolen aircraft
ITSA: Institute for Telecommunication Sciences and Aeronomy
itsb: interstate transportation of strikebreakers
itsc: interstate transportation of stolen cattle
ITSC: International Telecommunications Satellite Consortium
itse: integral time square error
itsmv: interstate transportation of a stolen motor vehicle
itsp: interstate transportation of stolen property
itt: instant-touch tuning
ITT: Institute of Textile Technology; Insulin Tolerance Test
IT & T: International Telephone and Telegraph
ITTA: International Table Tennis Association
ITTCS: International Telephone and Telegraph Communications System
ITTE: Institute of Transportation and Traffic Engineering
ITTF: International Table Tennis Federation
ITTTA: International Technical Tropical Timber Association
ITU: Income Tax Unit; International Telecommunications

Union; International Typographical Union
ITUA: Industrial Trades Union of America
ITURM: International Typographical Union Ruling Machine
itv: instructional television
ITV: Independent Television
ITVA: Instructional Television Authority
ITW: Illinois Tool Works
ITWF: International Transport Workers Federation
Itz: Itzik
ITZEL: *Irgun Tzvai Le'umi* (Hebrew—National Military Organization)
iu: immunizing unit(s); international unit(s)
i of u: inevitability of the unpredictable
IU: Indiana University; Indianapolis Union (railroad); International Utilities
IÜ: Istanbul Üniversitesi (Universityo (University of Instanbul)
IUA: International Union of Architects
IUAA: International Union of Alpine Associations
IUAES: International Union of Anthropological and Ethnological Sciences
IUAI: International Union of Aviation Insurers
IUAJ: International Union of Agricultural Journalists
IUAO: International Union for Applied Ornithology
IUAPPA: International Union of Air Pollution Prevention Associations
IUAT: International Union Against Tuberculosis
IUB: International Union of Biochemistry; Interstate Underwriters Board
IUBS: International Union of Biological Sciences
IUC: International Union of Chemistry
IUCc: International Union of Crystallography
iucd: intrauterine contraceptive device
IUCN: International Union for Conservation of Nature and Natural Resources
IUCNNR: International Union for Conservation of Nature and Natural Resources
IUCr: International Union of Crystallography
IUCSTP: Inter-Union Commission on Solar-Terrestrial Physics
IUCW: International Union for Child Welfare
iud: intrauterine device; intrauterine diaphragm
Iud: *Iudicum* (Spanish—Epistle of St. Paul to the Hebrews)—Book of the Jews
IUD: Institute for Urban Development
iudr: idoxuridine
IUDZG: International Union of Directors of Zoological Gardens
IUE: International Ultraviolet Explorer (space vehicle); International Union of Electrical Workers; International Union for Electroheat
IUEC: International Union of Elevator Constructors
IUEF: International University Exchange Fund
IUER & MW: International Union of Electrical, Radio & Machine Workers
IUFA: International Union of Family Organizations
IUFRO: International Union of Forest Research Organizations
IUGG: International Union of Geodesy and Geophysics
IUGS: International Union of Geological Sciences
IUHA: Industrial Unit Heater Association
IUHPS: International Union of the History and Philosophy of Science
UHS: International Union of the History of Science
IUL: Indiana University Library
IULA: International Union of Local Authorities
IULIA: International Union of Life Insurance Agents
IUMC: Indiana University Medical Center
IUMI: International Union of Marine Insurance
IUMM & SW: International Union of Mine, Mill and Smelter Workers
IUMSWA: Industrial Union of Marine and Shipbuilding Workers of America
IUNS: International Union of Nutritional Sciences
IUOE: International Union of Operating Engineers
IUOPA: International Union of Practitioners in Advertising
IUOPAB: International Union of Pure and Applied Biophysics
IUOT: Indiana University Opera Theater
IUOTO: International Union of Official Travel Organizations
iup: intrauterine pregnancy
IUP: Irish Universities Press; Israel Universities Press
IUPAC: International Union of Pure and Applied Chemistry
IUPAP: International Union of Pure and Applied Physics
IUPLAW: International Union for the Protection of Literary and Artistic Works
IUPM: International Union for Protecting Public Morality
IUPN: International Union for the Protection of Nature
IUPS: International Union of Physiological Sciences
IUPW: International Union of Petroleum Workers
IUR: International Union of Railways
IUs: international units
IUS: International Union of Students
IUSP: International Union of Scientific Psychology
IUSSI: International Union for the Study of Social Insects
IUSSP: International Union for the Scientific Study of Population
IUT: Instituts Universitaires de Technologie (University Institutes of Technology)
IUTAM: International Union of Theoretical and Applied Mechanics
IUUCLGW: International Union, United Cement, Lime & Gypsum Workers
IUVDT: International Union against the Venereal Diseases and the Treponematoses
IUVSTA: International Union for Vacuum Science Techniques and Applications
IUWWML: International Union of Wood, Wire, and Metal Lathers
iv: initial velocity; intravenous(ly); intravertebral; inverted vertical (engine)
i/v: increased value
i.v.: *in verbo* (Latin—under the word)
i V: *in Vertretung* (German—as a substitute; by proxy)
IV: Ivan; Ivy
I-et-V: Ille-et-Vilaine
Iva: Godiva
IVA: Independent Voters Association
Ivan: (nickname for the typical

Russian)
Ivan-Kremlin disease: endemic antisemitism
Ivan the Terrible: Czar Ivan IV Vasilievich—ruler of Russia
IVBF: International Volley-Ball Federation
ivc: inferior vena cava
IVC: Imperial Valley College
ivcd: intraventricular conduction defect
Iv Cst: Ivory Coast
ivd: interpolated voice data
ivds: independent variable depth sonar
Ive: Ivan; Iven
I've: I have
IVECO: Industrial Vehicles Corporation
I've had it: I've had it: (popular American contraction—I have had enough of it)
IVF: Innocent Victims Fund
IVFZ: International Veterinary Federation of Zootechnics
IVGMMA: International Violin, Guitar Makers, and Musicians Association
IVI: Independent Voters of Illinois
IVIC: *Instituto Venezolano de Investigaciones Científicas* (Venezuelan Institute of Scientific Investigations)
IVIS: International Visitors Information Service
ivjc: intervertebral joint complex
IVK: Institutet för Vaxtforskning och Kyllagring (Institute for Foodstuff Research and Refrigeration—Sweden)
IVMB: *Internationale Vereinigung der Musikbibliotheken* (German—International Association of Music Libraries)
ivmu: inertial velocity measurement unit
Ivory Coast: Republique du Côte d'Ivoire
ivp: initial vapor pressure; inspected variety purity (certified seeds); intravenous pyelogram
IVP: *Instituto Venezolano de la Petroquimica* (Venezuelan Petrochemical Institute)
IVR: International Vehicle Registration (symbols displayed on automotive licence plates)
IVR: *Internationale Vereinigung des Rheinschiffsregisters* (German—International Association of Rhine Ships Registers)
IVS: International Voluntary Service
ivsd: interventricular septal defect
IVSU: International Veterinary Students Union
ivt: intravenous transfusion
IVU: International Vegetarian Union
Ivy League: college athletic conference consisting of Brown, Columbia, Cornell, Dartmouth, Harvard, Pennsylvania, Princeton, and Yale; students and graduates of the abovementioned schools as well as their "characteristic" style of dress, which was considered "quiet and neat." (The term was originally coined by Stanley Woodword, sports editor for *The Herald Tribune.*)
iw: indirect waste; inside width; isotopic weight; ivory woodpecker
i/w: in work
iW: *innere Weite* (German—inside diameter)
IW: Aero Trasporti Italiani (2-letter coding, Italian Air Transport)
IoW: Isle of Wight
IWA: Institute of World Affairs; Insurance Workers of America; International Woodworkers of America
IWAHMA: Industrial Warm Air Heater Manufacturers Association
IWC: Inland Waterways Corporation; International Whaling Commission; International Wheat Council
IWCA: International World Calender Association
IWCC: International Wrought Copper Council
IWCCA: Inland Waterways Common Carriers Association
IWCI: Industrial Wire Cloth Institute
IWCS: Integrated Wideband Communications System
IWCT: International War Crimes Tribunal
IWD: International Waterways and Docks
IWE: Institution of Water Engineers
IWG: Imperial Wire Gauge
IWGC: Imperial War Graves Commission
iwistk: issue while in stock
IWIU: Insurance Workers International Union
IWLA: Izaak Walton League of America
IWM: Imperial War Museum; Institute of Works Managers
IWMA: International Working Men's Association
IWML: Imperial War Museum Library
IWO: International Wine Office; International Workers Order
IWP: Indicative World Plan (FAO)
IWPC: Institute of Water Pollution Control
IWPS: Institute of War and Peace Studies (Columbia)
IWRI: International Wildfowl Research Institute
IWRMA: Independent Wire Rope Manufacturers Association
IWS: Inland Waterway Service; International Wool Secretariat
IWSA: International Water Supply Association
IWSB: Insect Wire Screening Bureau
IWSc: Institute of Wood Science
IWSG: International Wool Study Group
IWSP: Institute of Work Study Practitioners
IWST: Integrated Weapon System Training
IWT: Indus Water Treaty; Inland Water Transport
IWT: *Industriewerke Transportsystem* (cargo container system)
IWTA: Inland Water Transport Authority
IWTD: Inland Water Transport Department
IWTO: International Wool Textile Organization
iwu: illegal wearing of uniform
IWU: Illinois Wesleyan University
IWW: Industrial Workers of the World; Intracoastal Waterway
IWY: International Women's Year (1975-1984)
IWWP: *International Who's Who in Poetry*
IWVA: International War Veterans Alliance
IX: unclassified vessel (2-letter naval code)
I.X.: *Iesous Christos* (Greek—Jesus Christ)
Ixta: Ixtaccihuatl
iy: ionized yeast
IY: Imperial Yeomanry; International Petroleum (stock exchange symbol)
IYB: *International Year Book*

IYC: Inland Yacht Club
IYEO: Institute of Youth Employment Officers
IYHF: International Youth Hostel Federation
IYL: International Youth Library
IYRU: International Yacht Racing Union
iyswim: if you see what I mean
i y v: *ida y vuelta* (Spanish—round trip)
iz: izzard; zed
Iz: Izar: Izmir (Smyrna)
Izd: *izdatl'* (Russian—publisher)
izdat: *izdatel* (Russian—publisher)
IZL: *Irgun Z'vai Leumi* (Hebrew—National Army Organization)
izq^a^: *izquierda* (Spanish—left)
izq^o^: *izquierdo* (Spanish—left)
izs: insulin zinc suspension
Izv: *Izvestia* (Russian—news)—official newspaper of the Presidium of the Supreme Soviet—published in Moscow
Izzie: Isador; Isadora; Isadore; Isodoro; Isidro; Ysidro
Izzy: (*see* Izzie)

J

j: inner quantum number (symbol); jack; junior; square of minus 1 (symbol); unit vector in y direction (symbol)
j: *jour(nal)*](French—day; journal; newspaper)]
j.: *juris* (Latin—of law); *jus* (Latin—law)
J: action variable (symbol); advance ratio (symbol); electric current density (symbol); gram-equivalent weight (symbol); heat transfer factor (Symbol); Jacob; Jacobean; Jacobian; Jaen; January; jet; Jew; Jewish; joint; joule; Judaic; Judaism; Juliett—code for letter J; Julliard; July; June; North American Aviation (symbol); polar movement of inertia (symbol); radiant intensity (symbol)
J: *Jejunium* (Latin—fast; hunger); *Journal* (French—journal)
J-1: personnel section of joint military staff
J-2: intelligence section of joint military staff
J-3: operations and training section of joing military staff
J-4: logistics section of joint military staff
J-5: Plans and Policy (Joint Chiefs of Staff)
J-6: Communications, Electronics (Joint Chiefs of Staff)
ja: jack adapter; job analysis
j/a (J/A); joint account
j & a: junk and abandon; junked and abandoned
Ja: Jacob; Jacque(s); James; Japan; Japanese
JA: Japan Association; Jewish Agency; John Adams (2nd President U.S.); Judge Advocate; Junior Achievement
JAA: Japan Aeronautic Association
JAAF: Joint Army-Air Force
JAAFU: Joint Anglo-American Foulup
jaarg: *jaargang* (Dutch—annual volume)
JAARS: Jungle Aviation and Radio Service
JAAS: Jewish Academy of Arts and Sciences
Jab: Jabal; Jabalpur; Jabez; Jabneel
JAB: Joint Amphibious Board
jac: jet aircraft coating
Jac: Jacobean; Jacobite; Jacobus
Jac.: *Jacobus* (Latin—James)
JAC: Joint Advisory Committee; Joint Apprenticeship Council
JAC: *Journal of Applied Chemistry*
Jacaranda Capital: jacaranda-tree-lined avenues and streets comprising South Africa's capital city—Pretoria
JACC: Journalism Association of Community Colleges
Jace: Jason
jack: jackass
Jack: Jackson; Jacob; John
Jack Benny: Benjamin Kubelsky
Jack Frost: frosty weather personified
Jackie: Jacqueline Kennedy Onassis; Jack Roosevelt Robinson
JACKPOT: Joint Airborne Communications Center and Command Post
Jacksonopolis: Jackson, Michigan
Jacky: Jaqueline
JACL: Japanese-American Citizens League
JACOB: Junior Achievement Corporation of Business
Jacopo: Jacopo Tatti
Jacq: Jacques; Jacquin
Jacques Halévy: Jacques Francois Fromental Elias Levi
Jacques Offenbach: Jakob Eberst
JACS: *Journal of the American Chemical Society*
JACT: Joint Association of Classical Teachers
Jad: Jadavpur, India
JAD: Julian astronomical day
JADB: Joint Air Defense Board
JADE: Japanese Air Defense Environment
jadeite: sodium aluminum silicate
JADF: Japan Air Defense Force
jaditbhkycc: just a drop in the basket helps keep your city clean (anti-litter-civic-responsibility campaign)
Adv: Judge Advocate
J Adv Gen: Judge Advocate General
JAEC: Japan Atomic Energy Commission
JAERI: Japan Atomic Energy Research Institute
JAF: Jordanian Air Force; Judge Advocate of the Fleet
JAFC: Japan Atomic Fuel Corporation
Jaffna: Jaffnapatam
Jag: Jaguar
JAG: James Abram Garfield (20th President U.S.); Judge Advocate General
JAG-A: Judge Advocate General—Army
JAGC: Judge Advocate General's Corps
JAGD: Judge Advocate Gener-

al's Department
JAG-N: Judge Advocate General—Navy
JAGS: Judge Advocate General's School
JAH: John Adams House
Jahrb: *Jahrbuch* (German—yearbook)
Jahrg: *Jahrgang* (German—annual publication; year's growth; vintage of the year)
Jaksch's disease: infantile anemia
jai: juvenile amaurotic idiocy
JAIEG: Joint Atomic Information Exchange Group
JAIF: Japan Atomic Industrial Forum
Jak: Jakarta (Batavia)
Jake: Jacob; Jacobus
Jal: Jalisco
JAL: Japan Air Lines; Jet Approach and Landing Chart
Jam: Jamaica
JAM: James A. Michener; Joslyn Art Museum; Sir John Alexander Macdonald (Canada's first and third Prime Minister)
JAMA: *Journal of the American Medical Association*
JAMAG: Joint American Military Advisory Group
Jambalaya Capital: Gonzales, Louisiana
James O'Brien: James Bronterre
JaMi: Jacksonville-Miami (metropolitan area including Fort Lauderdale, Hollywood, Tampa, and St Petersburg)—also called Metro or Metro Area
Jamie: James
JAMMAT: Joint Military Mission for Aid to Turkey
jammies: pyjamas
jamocha: java & mocha (prison argot—coffee)
jams: pajamas
jamtrac: jammers tracked by azimuth crossings
JAMTS: Japan Association of Motor Trade and Service
jamwich: jam sandwich
jan: janitor; janitorial
Jan: Janice; Jansen; Janson; January; John
JAN: Jackson, Mississippi (airport); Joint Army-Navy
JANAF: Joint Army-Navy Air Force
JANAIR: Joint Army-Navy Aircraft Instrument Research
JANAP: Joint Army-Navy-Air Force Publication
JANAST: Joint Army-Navy-Air Force Sea Transport
JanFeb: January and February
Janie: Jane; Jean
Jan Peerce: Jacob Pincus Perelmuth
Jans: Janson
JANS: Jet Aircraft Noise Survey; Joint Army-Navy Specification
JANSRP: Jet Aircraft Noise Survey Research Program
janv: *janvier* (French—January)
Jan Valtin: Richard J. Krebs
jap: japanned
Jap: Japan; Japanese; Jasper
JAP: Joint Apprenticeship Program
J-AP: Jewish-American Prince(ss)
JA£: Jamaican pound
JAPAC: Japan Atomic Power Company; Joint Air Photo Center
Japanese Drama Painter: Torii Kyonobu—originator of this school of painting
Japanese Lacquer Artist: Korin (Ogata Korin)—regarded as Japan's greatest artist in lacquer decoration
Japanese Landscape Artist Supreme: Sesshu
Japanese Naturalist Artist: Korin
Japanese Riviera: Enoshima Island recreation area
Japan's Back Door: Sasebo
Japan's Front Gate: Yokohama
JAPC: Joint Air Photo Center
JAPCO: Japan Atomic Power Company
Jap Cur: Japan Current
Japdic: Japanese dictionary
Japex: Japan Petroleum Exploitation Company
JAPEX: Japan Express
JAPIA: Japan Auto Parts Industries Association
Japlish: Japanese & English
Jardines': Jardine, Matheson & Company
JARE: Japanese Antarctic Research Expedition
jarg: jargon; jargonese; jargonist; jargonistic; jargonize
Jas: James
JAS: Jamaica Agricultural Society; Jewish Agricultural Society
JASA: *Journal of the Acoustical Society of America*
Jascha: (Russian nickname—Jacob)—Jake
JASDF: Japan Air Self-Defense Force
JASG: Joint Advanced Study Group
jasp: jasper; jasperoid
Jasp: Jasper
Jaspr: Jasper
jastop: jet-assisted stop
jasu: jet aircraft starting unit
JAT: Jugoslovenski Aero-Transport (Yugoslav Airlines)
JATCC: Joint Aviation Telecommunications Coordination Committee
JATCRU: Joint Air Traffic Control Radar Unit
JATMA: Japan Automobile Tire Manufacturers Association
jato: jet-assisted takeoff
JATS: Joint Air Transportation Service
jaund: jaundice
Jav: Java; Javanese
JAVA: Jamaica Association of Villas and Apartments
javelle water: sodium hypochlorite solution (NaOCl)
JAVHS: Jane Addams Vocational High School
JAWA: *Jane's All the World Aircraft*
Jawbone Flats: Clarkston, Washington
Jax: Jacksonville, Florida
JAX: Jacksonville, Florida (airport)
jaycee (JC): Junior Chamber of Commerce
Jayhawker(s): Kansan(s)
jb: jet bomb (JB); junction box
Jb: Jacob
Jb: *Jahrbuch* (German—annual; yearbook)
JB: James Buchanan (15th President U.S.); Jodrell Bank; John Bull (British empire personified); Joint Board; Stetson hat (after its original maker—J.B. Stetson)
J.B.: *Jurum Baccalaureus* (Latin—Bachelor of Laws)
J-B: Jacques Barzun; Jean-Baptiste; Johannes Brahms
JBA: Japan Binoculars Association; Junior Bluejackets of America
JBAA: *Journal of the British Archeological Association*
J-bar: capital-J-shaped bar (as used in ski tow lifts)
JBC: Jamaica Broadcasting Corporation; Japan Broadcasting Corporation (*q.v.* NHK)
JB & C: John Brown and Company (shipbuilders)
JBCA: Jewish Book Council of America
JB & Co: John Brown and Company (shipbuilders)
JBCSA: Joint British Committee for Stress Analysis

JBe: Japanese B encephalitis
Jber: *Jahresbericht* (German—annual report)
JBES: Jodrell Bank Experimental Station (Cheshire, England)
JBG: Jewish Board of Guardians
JBHS: John Bartram High School
JBIA: Jewish Braille Institute of America
J-bird: jailbird (underground slang—convict)
JBL: *Journal of Business Law*
JBMA: John Burroughs Memorial Association
J-boat: large yacht, often 76 feet or longer; small racing boat sailed by youngsters
J-bolt: capital-J-shaped bolt
J-box: J-shaped bleaching box; junction box
JBPS: Jamaica Banana Producers Steamship
JBS: John Birch Society
JBSW: Joseph Bulova School of Watchmaking
JBT: Jewelers Board of Trade
JBUSDC: Joint Brazil-United States Defense Commission
JBUSMC: Joint Brazil-US Military Commission
JBYC: Jamaica Bay Yacht Club
jc: joint compound
Jc: Junction
JC: Jackson College; Jacksonville College; Jamestown College; Jefferson City; Jefferson College; Jersey City; Jet Club; Job Corps; Jockey Club; Johnstown College; Joliet College; Judson College; Juniata College; Junior Chamber (of Commerce; members called *Jaycees*)
J.C.: Jesus Christ; Julius Caesar
J.C.: *Juris Consultus* (Latin—Juris Consult)
J-C: *Jésus-Christ* (French—Jesus Christ)
JCA: Jewelry Crafts Association; Joint Commission on Accreditation (of colleges and universities); Joint Communication Activity; Joint Communications Agency; Joint Construction Agency; Junior College of Albany
JCAE: Joint Committee on Atomic Energy
JCAH: Joint Committee on Accreditation of Hospitals
JCAM: Joint Commission on Atomic Masses
JCAR: Joint Commission of Applied Radioactivity
J.C.B.: *Juris Canoni Baccalaureus* (Latin—Bachelor of Canon Law); *Juris Civilis Baccalaureus* (Latin—Bachelor of Civil Law)
JCBC: Junior College of Broward County
JCBL: John Carter Brown Library (of Americana)—Brown University, Providence, Rhode Island
JCC: Jamestown Community College; Jefferson Community College; Jewish Community Center; Job Corps Center; John C. Calhoun; Joint Communications Center; Junior Chamber of Commerce
JC of C: Junior Chamber of Commerce
JCCA: Joint Conex Control Agency
JCCRG: Joint Command Control Requirements Group
J.C.D.: *Juris Canonici Doctor* (Latin—Doctor of Canon Law); *Juris Civilis Doctor* (Latin—Doctor of Civil Law)
JCE: Johannesburg College of Education; Junior Certificate Examination
JCEC: Joint Communication Electronics Committee
JCED: Japan Committee for Economic Development
JCENS: Joint Communication Electronic Nomenclature System
JCFA: Japan Chemical Fibres Association
JCI: Junior Chamber International
JCIC: Johannesburg Consolidated Investment Company
JCIEABJ: Joint Commission for the Investigation of the Effects of the Atomic Bomb in Japan
JCII: Japan Camera Inspection Institute
JCJC: Jasper County Junior College; Jefferson County Junior College
Jck: Jacksonville
Jcl: Johnny come lately
JCL: Job Control Language; John Crerar Library
J.C.L.: *Juris Canonici Licentiatus* (Latin—Licentiate in Canon Law)
JCLA: Joint Council of Language Associations
JCLS: Junior College Libraries Section
JCM: Joint Committee on Microcards
JCNAFF: Joint Canadian Navy-Army-Air Force
JCNM: Jewel Cave National Monument
JCO: José Clemente Orozco
jcp: jungle canopy penetration
JCP: Japan Communist Party; J.C. Penney; Joint Committee on Printing (Congress); Junior Collegiate Players; Justice of the Common Pleas
JCPCI: Junior College of Packer Collegiate Institute
JCR: Junior Common Room
JCRFD: Joint Commission for Regulation of Fishing on the Danube
JCs: Job Corpsmen
JCS: Jewish Community Center(s); Joint Chiefs of Staff
JCSUK: Jersey Cattle Society of the United Kingdom
jct: junction
Jct: Junction (postal abbreviation)
JCTC: Japanese Cultural and Trade Center; Juneau County Teachers College
jct pt: junction point
JCU: John Carroll University
JCUS: Joint Center for Urban Studies (MIT and Harvard)
jd: joined; joint dictionary; junior debutante; jury duty; juvenile deliquent
jd: *jemand* (German—someone; somebody)
Jd: Jordanian dinar (monetary unit of Jordan)
JD: Julian day; Junior Deacon; Junior Dean; Justice Department
J.D.: Doctor of Jurisprudence; *Juris* or *Jurum Doctor* (Latin—Doctor of Law or Laws)
JDA: Japan Defense Agency; Japan Domestic Airline; Jefferson Davis Association
J-day: Judas Day (Wednesday before Good Friday when Judas is believed to have betrayed Jesus)
JDB: Japan Development Bank
JDC: Joint Distribution Committee; Juvenile Delinquency Control
JDCC: Juneau-Douglas Community College
J/deg: joule per degree
JDHS: Jefferson Davis High School
JDL: Jewish Defense League
JDP: John Dos Passos
jds: job data sheet
jd's: juvenile delinquents
JDS: John Dewey Society

JDSRF: Jim Dandy's Still and Refreshment Factory (Australian definition for the Joint Defense Space Research Facility near Alice Springs)
jé: *jésus* (French—paper of super-royal size)
jea: joint export agent
JEA: Jesuit Educational Association; Joint Engineering Agency
Jean Baptiste: French-Canadian's sobriquet
Jean Crapaud: (nickname for the typical Frenchman)
Jean-Jacques: Jean-Jacques Rousseau
Jean l'Oiseleur: (French—Jean the bird tamer)—pseudonym of Jean Cocteau
Jean Meslier: Voltaire's pseudonym concealing his authorship of an heretical tract whose title page reads— *Superstition In All Ages* by Jean Meslier, A Roman Catholic Priest, who after a pastoral service of thirty years at Entrepigny and But, in Champagne, France, wholly abjured religious dogmas, and left as his last will and testament the following pages entitled Common Sense (*Le Bon Sens*); Voltaire was an assumed name for François-Marie Arouet who without this double-cover pseudonym might have been burned at the stake along with his books and his tracts, his plays and his poems.
Jean Moreas: (pseudonym—Jannis Papadiamantopolous)
Jeanne d'Arc: Joan of Arc's original French name
Jeannie: Jane; Jean
Jean Paul: Johann Paul Friedrich Richter's pseudonym
jebm: jet engine base maintenance
Jeb Stuard: Major General J(ames) E(well) B(rown) Stuart, CSA
JEC: Joint Economic Committee (Congress)
JECC: Japan Eelctronic Computer Company
Jed: Jedediah
J Ed: *Journal of Education*
JEDEC: Joint Electron Device Engineering Committee
JEDS: Japanese Expeditions to the Deep Sea
JEE: Japan Electronics Engineering
jeep: (from GP meaning general purpose) 4-wheel-drive quarter-ton utility vehicle
JEEP: Joint Emergency Evacuation Plan
Jef(f): Geoffrey; Geoffroy; Jefferson; Jeffery; Jeffry
Jeff City: Jefferson City, Missouri
Jeff D: Jefferson Davis
Jefferson's Country: Charlottesville, Virginia
Jefferson Territory: old name of Colorado
jefm (JEFM): jet engine field maintenance
JEG: John Edward Gray
Jeho: Jehosaphat
JEI: Japan Electronics Industry
JEIA: Japanese Electronic Industries Association
JEIDA: Japan Electronic Industry Development Association
JEIPAC: Japan Electronic Information Processing Automatic Computer
JEJ: *Japan Economic Journal*
jejun: jejunectomy; jejunitis; jejunostomy
Jem: Jemima
JEMC: Joint Engineering Management Conference
JEN: Junta de la Energia Nuclear (Atomic Energy Board)
Jennie: Jane; Jean; Jennifer; Lady Randolph Churchill
Jen Jih: *Jen-min Jih-pao* (People's Daily)—published in Peking by Communist Party of China
Jenny: Jane; Jean; Jennifer
Jenny Lind: Johanna Maria Lind—the Swedish Nightingale
jentac.: *jentaculum* (Latin—breakfast)
JEOCN: Joint European Operations Communications Network
JEOL: Japan Electron Optics Laboratory
JEPIA: Japan Electronic Parts Industry Association
Jer: Jersey
Jer.: Jeremiah, The Book of the Prophet
Jer: *Jeroesjalaim* (Dutch—Jerusalem)
JER: *Japan Economic Review*
JERC: Japan Economic Research Center; Joint Electronic Research Committee
Jere: Jeremiah; Jerry
Jeremiah: Bernstein's Symphony No. 1 commemorating the prophet Jeremiah and his dire prophecies
JERI: Joint Economic Research Institute
jerky: beef jerky; buccan; charqui; jerked beef
jerob: jeroboam (4-bottle capacity)
Jeron°: Jerónimo (Spanish—Jerome)
Jerry: Gerald(ine); Governor Edmund G. Brown, Jr of California who shares this nickname with many others including President Gerald R. Ford; Jeremiah; Jeremy; Jerome
JERS: Japanese Ergonomics Research Society
Jersey Lily: Lily Langtry—English actress born on the island of Jersey where her original name was Emily Charlotte Le Breton
Jersey Shore: coastal New Jersey
Jerusalem of the West: Amsterdam
Jes: Jessica; Jesus
JES: James Ewing Society; John Ericsson Society
JESA: Japanese Engineering Standards Association
Jes Coll: Jesus College—Cambridge
Jessamine: South Carolina's state flower
Jessie: Jess; Jessica
jet: black lignite; jet-engine aircraft
jet.: jetsam
JETDS: Joint Electronics Type Designation System
JETEC: Joint Electron Tube Engineering Council
jet fag: jet flight fatigue
jetma: jet mechanic
jet-p: jet-propelled; jet propulsion
JETP: *Journal of Experimental and Theoretical Physics* (Academy of Sciences, USSR)
JETRO: Japan Exterior Trade Research Organization
JETS: Junior Engineers Technical Society
jett: jettison
jeu: *jeudi* (French—Thursday)
Jev: Japanese encephalitis virus
Jew.: Jewish
Jewel of Africa: Lake Kivu
Jewel of the East: Bali
Jewel of German Cities: Heidelberg
Jewel Island: Ceylon
jewelers' putty: stannous oxide
Jewels of the Caribbean: U.S. Virgin Islands

JEZ: Johannes Enschede en Zonen
jf: distant fog (meterological symbol)
j/f: journal folio
JFACT: Joint Flight-Acceptance Composite Test
jfb: jet flying belt
JFC: Japan Film Center
JFEA: Japan Federation of Employer's Associations
JFK: John Fitzgerald Kennedy—thirty-fifth President of the United States
JFKCAS: John F. Kennedy College of Arts and Sciences (Trinidad)
JFKCPA: John F. Kennedy Center for the Performing Arts
JFKMF: John F. Kennedy Memorial Forest (near Jerusalem, Israel)
JFKMH: John F. Kennedy Memorial Highway (Baltimore, Maryland to Wilmington, Delaware)
JFKML: John F. Kennedy Memorial Library
JFKSC: John F. Kennedy Space Center
JFKYCC: John F. Kennedy Youth Correctional Center
jfl: joint frequency list
JFMAMJJASOND: January, February, March, April, May, June, July, August, September, October, November, December (as abbreviated to conserve space on charts and graphs)
JFNP: John Forrest National Park (Western Australia)
JFO: San Francisco, California (heliport)
jfp: joint frequency panel
JFPS: Japan Fire Prevention Society
jfr: *jevnfr* (Dano-Norwegian—compare)
JFR: Joint Fiction Reserve
JFRC: James Forrestal Research Center
JFRCA: Japanese Fisheries Resources Conservation Association
JFRO: Joint Fire Research Organisation (UK)
JFS: Japan Fishery Society; Jewish Family Service
JFS: *Jane's Fighting Ships*
JFSOC: Junior Foreign Service Officers Club
JFTC: Joint Fur Trade Committee
JFU: Jersey Farmers' Union
JG: junior grade
jga: juxtaglomerular apparatus
JGC: Japan Gasoline Company
JGD: John George Diefenbaker (Canada's seventeenth Prime Minister)—also known as Dief the Chief
jg di: joggle die
JGE: *Journal of General Education*
J-girl: joy girl (prostitute)
jgn: junction gate number
JGNP: Japanese Gross National Product
JGR: Jaldapara Game Reserve (India)
JGSA: John G. Shedd Aquarium
jg sm: joggle shims
JGTC: Junior Girls Training Corps
JGW: Junior Grand Warden
JGWTC: Jungle and Guerrilla Warfare Training Center (USA)
jh: juvenile hormone
Jh: *Jahresheft* (German—yearly publication)
JH *Jugendherberge* (German—youth hostel)
J & H: Jack & Heintz
jha: job hazard analysis
JHAI: John Herron Art Institute
Jhb: Johannesburg
JHC: John Hancock Center
JHDA: Junior Hospital Doctors Association
JHH: Johns Hopkins Hospital
JHI: Jacob Hiatt Institute
JHMI: Johns Hopkins Medical Institutions
JHMO: Junior Hospital Medical Officer
JHO: Jam Handy Organization; Japan Hydrographic Office
JHOS: Johns Hopkins Oceanographic Studies
JHS: John Howard Society; Junior High School
J.H.S.: *Jesus Hominum Salvator* (Latin—Jesus Savior of Men)
JHU: Johns Hopkins University
JHUL: Johns Hopkins University Library
JHUSHPH: Johns Hopkins University School of Hygiene and Public Health
JHUSM: Johns Hopkins University School of Medicine
JHVH: Jehovah (transliteration of Hebrew tetragrammaton Yhwh, Yahwah, or Jahvah [he was, he is, he will be], used by Hebrew tribes in 3rd century BCE because they thought "Jehovah" was too sacred to pronounce); perhaps the world's oldest abbreviation
JI: Aerovias Sudamericanos (symbol)
JI: *Japan Interpreter*
JIB: Jack-in-the-Box; Japan International Bank
jíb(s): *jíbaro(s)* [(Spanish—peasant farmer(s)]—Puerto Rican(s)
JIC: Joint Industrial Council; Joint Industry Council; Joint Intelligence Center; Joint Intelligence Committee
JICA: Joint Intelligence Collecting Agency
JICST: Japan Information Center of Science and Technology
JICTAR: Joint Industry Committee for Television Advertising Research
JID: *Junta Interamericana de Defensa* (Spanish—Inter-American Defense Board)
JIDC: Jamaica Industrial Development Corporation
JIG: Joint Intelligence Group
JIE: Junior Institution of Engineers
JIIST: Japan Institute for International Studies and Training
JILA: Joint Institute for Laboratory Astrophysics
Jill: Jillian
Jim: James
JIM: Japan Institute of Metals
JIMA: Japan Industrial Management Association
Jimmu: Jimmu Tenno—first emperor of Japan who began his reign in 660 BCE
Jimmy: James; James Earl Carter—thirty-ninth President of the United States
Jimmy Higgins: Upton Sinclair's personification of the radical who does the work of running off the leaflets, setting up the speaker's platform, or sweeping out the meeting place of other comrades who feel themselves too superior for such menial tasks
Jimtown: Jamestown, North Dakota
JINR: Joint Institute for Nuclear Research
JIOA: Joint Intelligence Objectives Agency
JIR: Jewish Institute of Religion
JIS: Jail Inspection Service; Japan Industrial Standard; Jewish Information Society; Joint Intelligence Staff
JISA: Japan Industrial Safety Association

JISC: Japanese Industrial Standards Committee
JISP: Jack Island State Park (Florida)
jit: jitney bus
jj: jaw jerk
JJ: Judges, Justices
J-J: Jean-Jacques
J & J: Johnson & Johnson
J-J: *Jen-min Jih-pao* (Chinese—people's daily communist-controlled Peking newspaper
JJA: John James Audubon
JJC: Juvenile Justice Center (Los Angeles)
JJCA: Sir John Joseph Caldwell Abbott (Canada's fourth Prime Minister)
JJCCJ: John Jay College of Criminal Justice
JJHL: John Jay Hopkins Laboratory for Pure and Applied Science (General Atomic Division of General Dynamics Corporation)
JJHS: John Jay High School
JJS: James Joyce Society
JJSS: Jean-Jacques Servan-Schreiber
J-J S-S: Jean-Jacques Servan-Schreiber
jk: just kidding
JK: Jack Kerouac
J & K: Jammu and Kashmir (University)
J/°K: joule(s) per degree Kelvin (unit of entropy)
jkg: joules per kilogram
J/kg°K: joule(s) per kilogram degree Kelvin
JKP: James Knox Polk (11th President U.S.)
JKS: Julius Kayser (stock-exchange symbol)
jkt: jacket
JKT: Jakarta, Indonesia (airport); Job Knowledge Test
jl: just looking (pseudo customer)
Jl: Joel
JL: J. Lauritzen (steamship line); Johnson Line; Jones and Laughlin; Joseph Lewis
Jla: Julia
JLA: Jamaica Library Association; Japan Library Association; Jewish Librarians Association; Jordan Library Association
JLB: Jewish Lads' Brigade; John Logie Baird (tv's inventor)
JLC: Jewish Labor Committee
JLCU: Johnson Line container unit
Jlem: Jerusalem
JLMIC: Japan Light Machinery Information Center
JLP: Jamaica Labour Party
JLPPG: Joint Logistics and Personnel Policy Guidance
JLRSS: Joint Long-Range Strategic Study
JLS: Jail Library Service (California State Library)
Jlt: Juliet
JM: James Madison (4th President U.S.); James Monroe (5th President U.S.); Japan Mail; Jewish Museum; José Martí
J-M: Johns-Manville
J-M: *Jiyu-Minshuto* (Japanese—Liberal Democratic Party)
JMA: Japan Medical Association; Japan Meterological Agency; Jewish Music Alliance
JMB: J(ames) M(atthew) Barrie
JMBA: *Journal of the Marine Biological Association*
JMC: Jefferson Medical College
JMD: M(alaby) Dent
JMDC: Japan Machinery Design Center
jmed: jungle message encoder decoder
JMF: Jewish Music Forum; Juilliard Musical Foundation
JMHS: James Madison High School; James Monroe High School; John Muir High School
JMI: John Muir Institute
JMJ: Jesus, Mary, and Joseph
JMMC: James Madison Memorial Commission
JMMF: James Monroe Memorial Foundation
JMP: *Jen Men Piao* (Chinese—People's Bank Dollar)
JMPTC: Joint Military Packaging Training Center
JMRMA: John and Mable Ringling Museum of Art
JMS: Johannesburg Musical Society
JMSDF: Japanese Maritime Self-Defense Force
JMTBA: Japan Machine Tool Builders Association
JMUSDC: Joint Mexico-United States Defense Commission
jn: join; junction
j-n: jet navigation
Jn: John
Jn: *Juan* (Spanish—John)
JNA: *Jena Nomina Anatomica*
JNB: Johannesburg, South Africa (airport)
JNC: Joint Negotiating Committee
JNCA: Junior Naval Cadets of America
jnd: just noticeable difference
JND: Juvenile Narcotics Division
JNDC: Jamaica National Dance Company
JNDNWR: JnN. (Ding) Darling National Wildlife Refuge (Florida)
jne: *ja niin edespäin* (Finnish—and so on)
JNF: Jewish National Fund
Jnl: Journal
JNL: Japanese National Laboratory
jnls: journals
jnlst: journalist
Jno: John
JNODC: Japanese National Oceanographic Data Center
JNP: Jasper National Park (Alberta)
JNPGC: Japan Nuclear Power Generation Corporation
jnr: junior
Jnr: Jesurun
JNR: Japanese National Railways
jns: just noticeable shift
Jns: Johannes
JNS: Jet Noise Survey
JNSDA: Japan Nuclear Ship Development Agency
jnt: joint; junction; juncture
JNTA: Japan National Tourist Association
JNTO: Japan National Tourist Organization
jnt stk: joint stock
JNU: Juneau, Alaska (airport)
JNV: *Junta Nacional do Vinho* (Portuguese—National Wine Board)
jnwpu: joint numerical weather-prediction unit
jo: journalist
Jo: Joel; Joseph; Josephine
JO: Job Order
JO: *Justie Ombudsman* (Swedish—representative of justice)
Joa: Joachim
JOA: Joint Operating Agreement
Joaquin Miller: Cincinnatus Heine Miller's pen name
Jo Bapt: John the Baptist
jo block(s): johannson block(s)
jobman: job management
JOBS: Job Opportunities in the Business Sector
Jo'burg: Johannesburg
joc: jocose; jocular
JOC: Joint Operations Center
Jochanan: John
jock: jockey; jockstrap
Jock: John
jock(s): jock strap(s)—nickname

for physical education student(s)
joco: jocose
jod: joint occupancy date
JODC: Japanese Oceanographic Data Center
Jo Div: John the Divine
Joe: Joel; Joseph; Josephine
Jo Evang: John the Evangelist
Joe Zilch: the average American formerly called Joe Blow or Joe Doakes
J-off: jack off (underground slang—masturbate)
jog.: joggle
JOG: Joint Operations Group; Junior Ocean Group (*jay-oh-gees*—smallest sailing cruisers)
Jogja: Jogjakarta
Joh: *Johann(es)* (German—Hans; John)
Johan: Johannesburg
John: The Gospel According to John
John B: John B. Stetson (hat)
John Barleycorn: personification of beer or malt liquor
John Bull: Great Britain
John Calvin: Jean Chauvin
John D.: John D. Rockefeller, Sr.
John Gilbert: John Pringle's stage name
Johnny: John
Johnny Appleseed: John (Johnny) Chapman
Johnny Reb(s): Johnny Rebel(s)—Confederate soldier(s)
Johns H: Johns Hopkins University
John Sinjohn: John Galsworthy
John I: John the First (John Adams—second President of the United States)
John II: John the Second (John Quincy Adams—sixth President of the United States)
John XXIII: Angelo Giuseppe Roncalli
John Wayne: Marion Michael Morrison
Joh Seb Bach: Johann Sebastian Bach
JOIDES: Joint Oceanographic Institutions for Deep Earth Sampling
JOIDESP: Joint Oceanographic Institutions Deep Earth Sampling Program
join.: joinery
JOIN: Job Orientation in Neighborhoods; Jobs Or Income Now
JOK: Oakland, California (heliport)
Joke: Haydn's String Quartet in E flat (opus 33, no. 2)
Jolly Roger: black flag flown by pirates, sometimes emblazoned with a white hourglass or a white skull and crossbones
Jolyon: Joseph Lyons
JOMO: Junta of Militant Organizations (Black Nationalists)
Jon.: The Book of Jonah
Jona: Jonathan
Jonathan: Jonathan David
Jonathan Oldstyle: (pseudonym—Washington Irving)
JONS: Juntas de Ofensiva Nacional Sindicalista (Spanish fascist organization)
JOOD: Junior Officer of the Deck
JOR: Jet Operations Requirements
Jord: Jordan
Jord: *Jordania* (Spanish—Jordan); *Jordânia* (Portuguese—Jordan)
Jordan: (foermerly Transjordania)
Jordie: (Jordan(a)
Jordy: Jordan
Jos: Joseph; Joshua; Josiah; Jossie
Josa: Josepha; Josephine
Joseph: a Guarneri violin (short form of Giuseppe Guarneri)
Joseph Bentonelli: Joseph Horace Benton
Joseph Conrad: Teodor Josef Konrad Korzeniowski
Josephine: Josephine Baker
Josephus: Flavius Josephus—apostate Jew and recorder of the Roman conquests
Josh: Joshua; (pseudonym—Samuel L. Clemens)
Josh.: The Book of Joshua
Josh Billings: stage name of humorist Henry Wheeler Shaw
Josie: Josephina; Josephine
jot.: jump-oriented terminal
JOT: Joint Observer Team
JOTS: Job-Oriented Training Standards
Jotunheim: mountain range between Norway and Sweden—the land of the giants or jotuns
JOUAM: Junior Order of United American Mechanics
jour: journal; journalese; journalism; journalist; journalistic; journey
JOVE: Jupiter Orbiting Vehicle for Exploration
jp: jet penetration; jet pilot; jet power; jet propulsion; junior partner; precipitation in sight but not at weather station reporting (symbol)
j & p: joists and planks
Jp: Japan(ese)
JP: Japan Press (news agency); Jet Pilot; Justice of the Peace
J.P.: Jayaprakash Narayan; J. Pierpont Morgan
J : Jamaican pound (currency unit)
jpa: jack panel assembly
JPA: Japan Procurement Agency; Joint Passover Association
JPB: Joint Planning Board; Joint Production Board; Joint Purchasing Board
JPBHS: Judah P. Benjamin High School
jpbs: jettison pushbutton switch
JPC: Jan Pieterszoon Coen
JPCRSP: John Pennekamp Coral Reef State Park (Florida)
JPDC: Japan Petroleum Development Corporation
JPF: Jewish Peace Fellowship
JP-4: jet propellant 4
j-p fuel: jet-propulsion fuel
JPG: Job Proficiency Guide
JPGM: J.Paul Getty Museum
JPJ: John Paul Jones
JPL: Jacksonville Public Library; Java Pacific Line; Jet Propulsion Laboratory (California Institute of Technology)
Jpn: Japan(ese)
JPO: Joint Petroleum Office
jpp: *jälkeen puolenpäiven* (Finnish—afternoon; P.M.)
JPPS: Japan Pearl Promoting Society
J Prob: Judge of Probate
JPRS: Joint Publications Research Service
JPS: Jet Propulsion Systems; Jewish Publication Society; Johannesburg Philharmonic Society
JPSA: Jewish Publication Society of America
JPSO: Jamaica Philharmonic Symphony Orchestra
jpt: jet pipe temperature
JPTDS: Joint Photographic Type Designation System
jpto: jet-propelled take-off
JP-X: jet-propellant rocket fuel
jq: job questionnaire
JQ: *Japan Quarterly; Journalism Quarterly*
JQA: John Quincy Adams (6th President U.S.)
JQAH: John Quincy Adams House
Jr: Journal; Junior

JR: Joint Resolution
J.R.: *Jacobus Rex* (Latin—King James)
JRA: Japan Ryokan Association
JRAI: *Journal of the Royal Anthropological Institute*
JRATA: Joint Research and Test Activity
JRB: New York, New York (Wall Street Heliport)
JRC: Jamaica Railway Corporation
JRCA: Junior Ruritan Clubs of America
JRCS: Jet Reaction Control System
JRD: Riverside, California (heliport, 3-letter code)
JRDB: Joint Research and Development Board
JRDC: Japan Research and Development Corporation
JRF: Judicial Research Foundation
jrg: *jaargang* (Dutch—year)
jr gr: junior grade
Jr HS: Junior High School
JRHS: Julia Richman High School
jri: jail release information
JRIA: Japan Radioisotope Association
Jro: Jerome
JRS: Jerusalem, Jordan (airport)
JRTUR: *Jugoslovenska Radio-Televisija Udruzenja Radiostancia* (Yugoslav Association of Radio and Television Stations)
Jrw: Jarrow-on-Tyne
j/s: jamming-to-signal ration
Js: Jesuits
JS: Al-Jamhourya as-Souriya (Syria); Jan Sibelius; Japan Society; Johnson Society; Judeo-Spanish
JSA: Jewelers Security Alliance; Journeymen Stone Cutters Association
jsact: jetstream anti-countermeasure trainer
JSACT: Joint Strategic Air Control Team
JSB: Jewish Society for the Blind; Jewish Statistical Bureau; Johann Sebastian Bach
JSC: Jackson State College; Joint Standing Committee; Joint Stock Company
JS-C: Jesus College—Cambridge (also appears as JCC, J.C.C., and Jes Coll or Jes. Coll.)
JSCA: Journeyman Stone Cutters Association
J.Sc.D.: Doctor of Juristic Science
J-school: journalism school
JSCM: Joint Service Commendation Medal
JSCP: Joint Strategic Capabilities Plan
JSCR: Job Schedule Change Request
JS & CS: Jewish Family and Child Services
J.S.D.: *Jurum Scientiae Doctor* (Latin—Doctor of the Science of Laws)
JSDFA: Japan Self-Defense Forces Academy
JSDFs: Japan Self-Defense Forces
JSDT: Sir John Sparrow David Thompson (Canada's fifth Prime Minister)
JSDTI: John S. Donaldson Technical Institute (Trinidad)
JSE: Johannesburg Stock Exchange
JSEM: Japan Society for Electron Microscopy
JSESPO: Joint Surface Effect Ships Program
Jsey: Jersey
JSF: Japan Scholarship Foundation; Jewish Student Federation; Junior Statesman Foundation
JSGMF: John Simon Guggenheim Memorial Foundation
JSGMRAM: Joint Study Group for Material Resource Allocation Methodology
jsi: job satisfaction inventory
JSLB: Joint Stock Land Bank(s)
JSLS: Joint Services Liaison Staff
JSM: Juilliard School of Music
JSMA: Joint Sealers Manufacturers Association
JSME: Japan Society of Mechanical Engineers
J-smoke: (underground slang—marijuana cigarette)
JSO: Jackson Symphony Orchestra; Jacksonville Symphony Orchestra
JSOP: Joint Strategic Objectives Plan
JSP: Japan Socialist Party
JSPC: Joint Strategic Plans Committee
jspf: jet shots per foot
JSPG: Joint Strategic Plans Group
JSS: Joint Services Standard
JSSC: Joint Services Staff College; Joint Strategic Service Committee
JST: Japan Standard Time; Javanese Standard Time
J-stick: joystick (underground slang—marijuana cigarette)
JSTPB: Joint Strategic Target Planning Board
JSTPS: Joint Strategic Target Planning Staff
J-S unit: Junkerman-Schoeller unit (of thyrotrophin)
JSW: Japan Steel Works
JSWPB: Joint Special Weapons Publications Board
JSY: Jersey Airlines
jt: joint; joint tenancy; junction
JT: Jamaica Air Service (symbol); John Tyler (10th President U.S.); joint tenancy; Juvenile Templar
JT: *Japan Times* (Japan's oldest English newspaper); *John Thomas* (British slang—penis)
JTA: Jewish Telegraphic Agency (news service)
JTAC: Joint Technical Advisory Committee
jt agt: joint agent
jtb: joint bar
JTB: Jamaica Tourist Board; Japan Travel Bureau; Jute Trade Board
JTBI: Japan Travel Bureau International
JTC: Joint Telecommunications Committee; Junior Training Corps
J-teacher: journalism teacher
Jt Ed: Joint Editor
JTF: Joint Task Forces
Jth.: Apocryphal Book of Judith
JTI: *Jydsk Teknologisk Institut* (Danish—Jutland Technological Institute)
JTII: Japan Telescopes Inspection Institute
jtly: jointly
jtms: jamb-template machine screws
JTNM: Joshua Tree National Monument
jto: jump takeoff
JTO: Jordan Tourist Office
jt r: joint rate
JTR: Joint Termination Regulation; Joint Travel Regulation; Jordan Travel Research
JTRE: Joint Tsunami Research Effort
JTS: Job Training Standards
JTSA: Jewish Theological Seminary of America
jt ten.: joint tenant(s)
JTWC: Joint Typhoon Warning Center
ju: joint use
Ju: June; Junkers
JU: Jacksonville University; Jadavpore University

JU: *Jeunesse Universelle* (French—World Youth)
juana: marijuana
Juana la Loca: (Spanish—Crazy Jane)—Queen Juana who reigned in 1504 and whose lisp was imitated by her courtiers and called Castilian or *castellano*
Juan Bimba: the typical Venezuelan
Juan Carlos: Juan Carlos de Bourbon—chief of state and king of Spain succeeding Generalissimo Francisco Franco and supported by many democratic elements
Juan Gris: José Victoriano Gonzalez
Juanita: Juana (Jane; Joan)
juco: junior college
jucund.: *jucunde* (Latin—pleasantly)
jud: judgment; judicial; judo
Jud: Judah; Judaic; Judaism; Judean; Judson
J.U.D.: *Juris Utriusque Doctor* (Latin—Doctor of Civil and Canon Law)
JUDCLA: *Juventud Demócrata Cristiana Latino-Americana* (Spanish—Latin American Christian Democratic Youth)
Jude: The General Epistle of Jude
Judes: Judesmo (Ladino)
Judg.: The Book of Judges
Judge Adv Gen: Judge Advocate General
judgt: judgment
Judy: Judith
Juec: *Jueces* (Spanish—Judges)
juev: *jueves* (Spanish—Thursday)
JUG: Joint Users Group
Jugolinija: Yugoslav Line
Jugoslavija: Yugoslavia
juil: *juillet* (French—July)
jul: *julho* (Portuguese—July); *julio* (Spanish—July)
Jul: July
Jul Caes: *Julius Caesar*
Jules Romains: (pseudonym—Louis Farigoule)
Jules Verne: father of science fiction and grandson of Juliusz Olchewitz who left Poland to escape its pogroms but still found antisemitism strong enough in France to change the family name to Verne
Julia Marlowe: Sarah Frances Frost's stage name
Julians: Julian Alps (northwestern Yugoslavia)
Juliett: code for letter J
Jul^n: Julián (Spanish—Julius)
Julio Diniz: Joaquim Guilherme Coelho
Julust: July and August
JUMPS: Joint Uniform Military Pay System
jun: *junio* (Spanish—June); *juniore* (Italian—junior)
Jun: Juneau
Ju^n: *Julián* (Spanish—Julius)
Junc: Junction
Juno: (Latin—Hera)—goddess of the heavens
jun part.: junior partner
Junuly: June and July
Jup: Jupiter
Jupiter: (Latin—Zeus)—god of the heavens also called Jove; Mozart's Symphony No. 41 in C major—his last
Jupiter of Wall Street: J.P. Morgan
jur: juridical
jur: *juridisch* (Dutch—juridical)
Jur: Jurassic
Jur: *Juridisch* (German—juridical)
Juras: Jura Mountains between France and Switzerland
Jur.D.: *Juris Doctor* Latin—Doctor of Law)
juris: jurisdiction
JURIS: Juvenile Referral Information System; Justice Retrieval and Inquiry System (U.S. Department of Justice)
jurisd: jurisdiction
jurisp: jurisprudence
jus: justice(s)
jus': just
jusc.: *jusculum* (Latin—broth)
JUSE: Japanese Union of Scientists and Engineers
Jusepe: José de Ribera
JUSMAG: Joint United States Military Advisory Group; Joint United States Military Aid Group to Greece
JUSMAP: Joint United States Military Advisory and Planning Group
JUSMG: Joint United States Military Group
JUSMMAT: Joint United States Military Mission for Aid to Turkey
JUSPAO: Joint United States Public Affairs Office
juss: jussive
Juss: Jussieu
just.: justification
Just: Justinian
Justice Personified: Justitia (second goddess wife of the Roman god Jupiter or Themis who held the same post under the Greek god Zeus); she stands blindfolded, holding a balance in one hand and a palm frond in the other
Justin: Justin cowboy boots (made by Joe Justin in Fort Worth, Texas)
juv: juvenile
Juv: Juvenal
juve: juvenile
juvie: juvenile delinquent; juvenile hall; juvenile law-enforcement officer
JUWTFA: Joint Unconventional Warfare Task Force—Atlantic
JUWTFP: Joint Unconventional Warfare Task Force—Pacific
jux: juxtapose; juxtaposition
jv: japanese vellum
Jv: Java; Javanese
JV: Jules Verne; Junior Varsity
JVA: Jordan Valley Authority
JVC: Japan Victor Company
jvp: japanese vellum proofs
jvp (JPV): jugular venous pulse
JVS: Jewish Vocational Service; Joint Vocational School
jw: jacket water; jugwell (hydrocarbon storage well); junior wolf (a young philanderer)
JW: Jehovah's Witnesses
JWA: Japan Whaling Association
J-walk: jaywalk (cross streets against traffic lights, heedless of consequences, and at any part of the street except the pedestrian crossing)—some of the most expert jaywalkers may be found in hospital beds
J-walker: jaywalker
JWB: Jewish Welfare Board
jwc: junction wire connector
JWEF: Joinery and Woodwork Employers Federation
JWGA: Joint War Games Agency
JWJ: James Weldon Johnson
jwl: jewel; jeweler
JWL: Johnston Warren Lines
jwlr: jeweler
jwlry: jewelry
j & wo: jettison and washing overboard
JWO: Jardine Waugh Organisation
JWR: *Jane's World Railways*
JWR: Joint War Room
JWs: Jehovah's Witnesses
JWS: Japan Welding Society
JWT: J. Walter Thompson (advertising agency)
JWTC: Jungle Warfare Training Center
JWU: Jewelry Workers' Union

JWV: Jewish War Veterans (of the United States)
J.X.: Jesus Christ
Jy: Jenny; July; Jury
JY: British United Channel Islands Airways (2-letter coding)
JYL: Jugolinja-Yugoslav Line
Jyll: Jylland (Danish—Jutland)
***JZS:** Jugoslovenski Zavod za Standardizacija* (Jugoslavian Standards Institution)

K

k: Boltzman constant; carat (karat); cathode or vacuum tube; coefficient of alienation; compressibility factor; force constant; keel; kilo; knot(s); reaction velocity constant; reproduction factor; thermal conductivity; torsion constant; unit vector in Z-direction
K: capacity)symbol); centuple calorie (symbol); curvature (symbol); equilibrium constant (symbol); Fraunhofer line produced in part by calcium (symbol); Karman constant (symbol); Kelvin; Kerr constant; Kidde Fire Protection; Kilo—code word for letter K; hip; Kiwanis International; Knabe; Köchel, cataloger of Mozart's music; kopec(s); kosher; krone; kroner; luminous efficiency (symbol); modulus of cubic compressibility (symbol); pilotless aircraft (symbol); potassium (kalium); proportionality constant (symbol); radius of gyration (symbol); tanker (naval symbol)
***K:** kade (Dutch—embankment; quay); kald* (Norwegian—cold); *kall* (Swedish—cold); *kalt* (German—cold); *koel* (Dutch—cold); *köld* (Danish—cold); *Köln* (German—Cologne); *krinda* (Danish—women); *kvinne* (Norwegian—women); *kvinnor* (Swedish—women); *kylmä* (Finnish—cold)
^{0}K: degree Kelvin
K^2: Mount Godwin Austen, Kashmir (28,250-ft. mountain, second highest in the world)
K^5: Kunlun Mountain known on the Chinese-Kashmir border as Muztagh
K-9 Corps: Canine Corps (staffed by police dogs)
ka: cathode(s); kiloampere(s)
***Ka:** Komppania* (Finnish—company)
k/a: ketogenic to antiketogenic (diet ratio)
KA: Kapok Association; Karhumaki Airlines (Finland)
K of A: King(dom) of Aragon
kaa: keep-alive anode
kaad: kerosene, alcohol, acetic acid, dioxane (insect larva killer)
***Kaatsk:** Kaatskill* (Dutch—Catskill)—mountains beloved by New Yorkers and others such as the Hudson River school of painters
Kab: Kabel; Kabul
KAB: Keep America Beautiful
Kabul River City: Kabul, Afghanistan
KAC: Kuwait Airways Corporation
KACC: Kaiser Aluminum Chemical Corporation
KACF: Korean American Cultural Foundation
KACIA: Korean-American Commerce and Industry Association
Kaddish: Bernstein's Symphony No. 3 whose title indicates it is a prayer for the dead
Kae: Katherine
kaf: kaffir
KAF: Kenya Air Force
Kaffir King: Barney Barnato
KAH: Kahului Railroad
Kahlbaum's disease: dementia with muscular tension
Kahler's disease: bone-marrow destruction
KAIIN: third word of Sen Nihon Kaiin Kumiai—the All Japan Seamen's Union
Kaiser: (German—Caesar)—emperor's title
Kajiwara: Takuma Kajiwara
***KAK:** Kungliga Automobil Klubben* (Swedish—Royal Automobile Club)
kal: kalamein
***kal.:** kalendae* (Latin—calends, the first day of the month)
Kal: Kalgoorlie
***Kal:** Kalium* (Latin—potassium)
KAL: Korean Air Lines
kald: kalamein door
Kali: Kalimantan (Borneo)
Kali-yuga: (Sanskrit—Age of Quarrel)—modern times
KAM: Kimball Art Museum (Fort Worth)
Kamenev: Lev Borisovich Rosenfeld
Kamk: keyed alike and master keyed
Kan: Kansas; Kanpur
Kanakalanders: nickname for Queenslanders who hired so many South Sea Kanakas to work on their plantations
Kanawha River City: Charleston, West Virginia
Kanchen: Kanchenjunga
kangaroo: Australian symbol
Kangarooland: Australia
kang(s): kangaroo(s)
Kano: Eitoku Kano (late 16th-century Japanese painter)
Kans: Kansas; Kansan
k antigen: capsular antigen
KANU: Kenya African National Union (party)
kao: kaolin
Kao: Kaohsiung
kaocon: kaopectate concentrate
kaolin: aluminum silicate (Al_2O_3 $2SiO_2 \cdot 2H_2O$); kaolinite
kap: knowledge, attitude, practice
***kap:** kapitel* (Swedish—chapter)
Kap: (German—cape); *Kapital* [German—capital (money)]; *Kapitel* (Danish and German—chapter)
KAP: initials stand for Chinese Ministry of Public Security—external counterintelligence and internal secret police force of the People's Republic

of China
KAPL: Knolls Atomic Power Laboratory
Kar: Karachi; Karafuto
Kar: *Karabiner* (German—carbine)—short rifle
KAR: King's African Rifles
KARAI: Karhumaki Airways (Finland)
Karakorums: Karakorum Mountains of Kashmir
Karawankens: Karawanken Alps between Austria and Yugoslavia
Karel: Karelia; Karelian
Karl Johan: Jean Baptiste Jules Bernadotte
Kas: Kansas
KAS: Kentucky Academy of Science; Kroeber Anthropological Society
KASC: Knowledge Availability Systems Center
Kash: Kashmir
KASSR: Kalmyk Autonomous Soviet Socialist Republic; Karelian Autonomous Soviet Socialist Republic; Komi Autonomous Soviet Socialist Republic
Kat: Katowice
Kat: *Katar* (Spanish—Quatar)
KAT: Kenosha Auto Transport
Kate: Catherine; Katherine; Katherine Hepburn; Katrina
kath: *katholisch* (German—catholic)—as an adjective
Kath: Katherine
Kath: *Katholik* (German—Catholic)—as a noun
Katherine Mansfield: pseudonym—Kathleen Beauchamp Murry)
Kathy: Katharine; Kathleen; Kathryn
Katie: Catherine; Katherine
KATUSA: Korean (soldier) attached to (the) United States Army
Katy: Missouri-Kansas-Texas Railroad
Kauf: Kaufman
K-A units: King-Armstrong units
kay: knockout (*kayo*—spelled abbreviation of ko); okay (truncated slang)
Kay: Catherine
Kaz: Kazak(stan)
kb: kilobit(s); kitchen and bathroom; kite ballon; knee brace
k & b: kitchen and bathroom
Kb: *Kontrabass* (German—double bass)
KB: Koninkrijk Belgie (Flemish—Kingdom of Belgium)
K.B.: Knight of the Order of the Bath
K of B: King(dom) of Bavaria
kba: killed by air
K-band: 10,900–36,000 mc
kbar: kilobar(s); 1 kbar equals approx 14,500 lbs per square inch
KBART: Kings Bay Army Terminal
KBASSR: Kabardino-Balkar Autonomous Soviet Socialist Republic
KBC: King's Bench Court
KBD: King's Bench Division
kbe: keyboard encoder; keyboard entry
K.B.E.: Knight Commander of the Order of the British Empire
Kbhvn: Köbenhavn (Copenhagen)
KBI: Keyboard Immortals (record label)
KBL: Kabul, Afghanistan (airport)
KBNWR: Klamath Basin National Wildlife Refuges (California and Oregon)
K Bon: Klein Bonaire (Netherlands Antilles)
KBP: Koala Bear Park (Adelaide)
kbps: kilo bits per second
kbs: kilobits per second
KB & TS: Kuwait Broadcasting and Television Service
kbtu: kilo British thermal unit (1,000 btu's)
kc: kilocycle(s); koruna (Czechoslovakian monetary unit)
Kc: Kyle classification (social sciences)
KC: Kalamazoo College; Kansas City; Kendall College; Kenyon College; Keuka College; Keystone College; Keystone Shipping Company (flag code); Kilgore College; King College; King's College; Kirksville College (of osteopathy and surgery); Knox College; Knoxville College
K.C.: King's Counsel
K of C: Knights of Columbus
KC-50: tactical aerial tanker for refueling aircraft in flight
KC-97: Stratofreighter strategic tanker-freighter equipped for inflight refueling
KC-135: Stratotanker multipurpose aerial tanker-transport
KCA: *Keesings Contemporary Archives*
kcal: kilocalorie(s)
KCB: Kenya Commercial Bank
K.C.B.: Knight Commander of the Order of the Bath
kcc: kathodic closure contraction
KCC: Kellogg Community College; Kenai Community College; Kennedy Cultural Center; Ketchikan Community College; Kingsborough Community College; King's College, Cambridge
KCDMA: Kiln, Cooler, and Dryer Manufacturers Association
KCH: King's College Hospital
K.C.H.S.: Knight Commander of the Order of the Holy Sepulchre
kCi: kiloCurie(s)
KCI: Key Club International
KCIA: Korean Central Intelligence Agency
K.C.I.E.: Knight Commander of the Indian Empire
KCL: King's College, London
KCLY: Kent and County of London Yeomanry
KCM: Kansas City Museum
K.C.M.G.: Knight Commander of the Order of Saint Michael and Saint George
KCM & O: Kansas City, Mexico & Orient (railroad)
KCNP: Kings Canyon National Park (California); Ku-ring-gai Chase National Park (New South Wales)
KCNS: King's College, Nova Scotia
KCPA: Kaolin Clay Producers Association; Kennedy Center for the Performing Arts
KCPL: Kansas City Public Library
KCPO: Kansas City Philharmonic Orchestra
kcps: kilocycles per second
KCR: Kowloon-Canton Railway
kcs: Czechoslovakian KORUNA(s); kilocycles per second
kc/s: kilocycles per second
KCS: Kansas City Southern (railroad)
KCS: *Kansas City Star*
K.C.S.G.: Knight Commander of Saint Gregory the Great
KCSI: Knight Commander of the Star of India
KCSO: Kansas City Symphony Orchestra
KCT: Kansas City Terminal (railroad)
kcte: kathodic closure tetanus
K Cur: Klein Curaçao (Netherlands Antilles)
KCVO: Knight Commander of the Victorian Order
kd: killed; kiln dried; knocked down; pilotless aerial target

(code)
Kd: Konrad; Kuwait dinar(s)
KD: Kidderpore Docks (Calcutta); Kongeriget Danmark (Kingdom of Denmark)
KD: Kidderpore Docks (Calcutta); Kongeriget Danmark (Kingdom of Denmark)
K of D: King(dom) of Denmark
KDA: Kongelik Dansk Aeroklub (Royal Danish Aero Club)
K-day: basic date for introduction of convoy system or lane; carrier aircraft assault day
KDAK: *Kongelig Dansk Automobile Klub* (Royal Danish Automobile Club)
kdcl: knocked down in carload lots
KDD: Kokusai Denshin Denwa (Japan's Overseas Radio and Cable System)
kdf: knocked-down flat
K d F: *Kraft durch Freude* (German—Strength through Joy) —Nazi holiday association
KDG: King's Dragoon Guards
KDI: *Kwaliteitsdienst voor de Industrie Stichting* (Dutch—Industrial Quality Control Society)
KDs: Kadets
KDHNM: Kill Devil Hill National Memorial
kdlcl: knocked down in less than carload lots
kdm: kingdom
KDM: Kongelige Danske Marine (Royal Danish Navy)
Kdo: Kasado
K-do: *Kamarado* (Esperanto—comrade)
KDP: potassium dihydrogen phosphate
ke: kinetic energy
K_e: exchangeable body potassium
K-E: Krafft-Ebing
K + E: Keuffel & Esser
K of E: King(dom) of England; Knights of Equity
KEA: Kentucky Education Association
keas: knots estimated airspeed
Keb Coll: Keble College—Oxford
Kech: Kechua (Quechua)
KEF: Keflavik Airport, Iceland
KEHF: King Edward's Hospital Fund
Kelly Country: Australia's northern Victoria named after the nineteenth-century outlaw Ned Kelly
KEMA: Kitchen Equipment Manufacturers Association
KEMA: *Keuring van Electrotechnische Materialen* (Dutch—Testing Institute for Electrochemical Materials)
Ken: Kendall; Kenilworth; Kenneth; Kennit; Kent(on); Kentuckian; Kentucky; Kenya; Kenyan
Ken: *Kenia* (Spanish—Kenya)
Kens: Kensington
Kent: Kentucky
kep': kept
KEPZ: Kaohsiung Export Processing Zone
kerk: *kerkelijke term* (Dutch—ecclesiastical term)
Kermadecs: Kermadec Islands
kern: kernan
kero: kerosene
kerogen: oil shale's chief constituent
Kester: Christopher
keto: ketonaemia; ketogenic; ketone; ketonuria; ketoses; ketosis
ketol: ketone alcohol (compound)
kev: kilo electron volt; 1,000 electron volts
keV: kiloelectronvolt(s)
Kev: Kelvin; Kevin
Kew Gar: Kew Gardens
Kew Obs: Kew Observatory
Key of the Gulf: Cuba commanding the entrance to the Gulf of Mexico
Key of the Indian Ocean: Mauritius
Key of the Mediterranean: Gibraltar commanding the entrançe to the Mediterranean Sea
Key to Stockholm: offshore Aland Islands between Finland and Sweden
Keystone Province: Manitoba linking eastern and western Canada
Keystoner(s): Pennsylvanian(s)
Keystone State: Pennsylvania—central state of the original thirteen if they were arranged in an arch beginning with New Hampshire and ending with Georgia
kf: kitchen facilities; koff
KF: Kaiser-Frazer; Kellogg Foundation; Kent Foundation; Kooperative Forbunded (Federation of Cooperatives—Sweden); Kresge Foundation
K of F: King(dom) of France
KF: *Konservative Folkeparti* (Danish—Conservative Party)
KFA: Kenya Farmers Association; Krishnamurti Foundation of America
KFASSR: Karelo-Finnish Autonomous Soviet Socialist Republic (formerly the Karelia of Finland)
Kfc: Kentucky fried chicken
KFC: Kentucky Fried Chicken: Kropp Forge Company
KFEA: Korean Federation of Education Associations
KFH: Kaiser Foundation Hospitals
KFL: Kenya Federation of Labour
kfm: *kaufmännisch* (German—commercial)
Kfm: Kaufmann (German—merchant)
KFNP: Kaieteur Falls National Park (Guyana)
kfo: killing federal officer
KFP: *Kristelig Folkeparti* (Norwegian—Christian People's Party)
KFSR: Karakul Fur Sheep Registry
Kfz: *Kraftfahrzeug* (German—motor vehicle)
kg: keg; kilogram; known gambler
kG: kilogauss
Kg: Kirghiz(ian)
KG: Kelly Girl
K-G: Kanematsu-Gosho Ltd.
KG: *Kommanditgesellschaft* (German—limited partnership)
K.G.: Knight of the Order of the Garter
K of G: King(dom) of Granada
KGA: Kitchen Guild of America
KGB: Komitet Gossudarrstvennoi Bezopastnosti (Russian—Committee of State Security; Soviet Secret Police)
KGBW: Kewaunee, Green Bay, and Western (railroad)
KGC: Knights of the Golden Circle
K.G.C.: Knight of the Grand Cross
kg cal: kilogram calorie
kg-cal: kilogram calorie
K.G.C.B.: Knight of the Grand Cross of the Bath
kg cum: kilograms per cubic meter
kgf: kilogram-force
Kgf: *Kriegsgefangener* (German—prisoner of war)
KGFS: King George's Fund for Sailors
KGJT: King George's Jubilee Trust
KGK: Kabushiki Goshi Kaisha

(Japanese—joint stock limited partnership of members with unlimited liability and shareholders with limited liability)
kgl: *kongelig* (Danish—royal)
Kgl: *Königlich* (German—royal)
kgm: kilogram meter
kg/m²: kilograms per square meter
kg/m³: kilograms per cubic meter
Kgn: Kingston, Jamaica
KGNP: Kalahari Gemsbok National Park (South Africa); Katherine Gorge National Park (Australian Northern Territory)
kgps: kilograms per second
kgs: kegs
kg/s: kilograms per second
KGS: Kate Greenaway Society; Kigezi Gorilla Sanctuary (Uganda)
KGVDs: King George V Docks (London)
KGWS: Keoladeo Ghana Wildlife Sanctuary (India)
Kh: Khmer (Cambodia)
KH: King's Hussars; Knut Hamsun
KH: *Karen Hayesod* (Hebrew—United Israel Appeal); *Kjøbenhavns Handelsbank* (Danish—Copenhagen's Commercial Bank); *Kupat Holim* (Hebrew—Health Insurance Fund)
K-H: Kelsey-Hayes
K of H: King(dom) of Hungary
Khar: Kharkov
KHC: Karen Horney Clinic
KHDS: King's Honorary Dental Surgeon
KHI: Karachi, Pakistan (airport)
Khingans: Kinghan Mountains of northeast China
KHM: King's Harbour Master
Khmer: Cambodia
Khn: Knoop hardness number
KHNS: King's Honorary Nursing Sister
KHP: King's Honorary Physician
KHPC: Karen Horney Psychoanalytic Clinic
KHS: Kennedy High School
khz (kHz): kilohertz(es), formerly kilocycle(s) per second
kHz: kilohertz (kilocycles per second)
ki: kilo; kitchen
KI: Kiwanis International; Komministicheskii Internatsional (Russian—Communist International); Komunisticna Internacijonala (Yugoslav—Communist International)
KI: *Kol Israel* (Hebrew—Voice of Israel)—broadcasting service
K-I: Kaiser-Illin
K of I: King(dom) of Ireland; King(dom) of Italy
kia (KIA): killed in action
Kia: Kligler iron agar
kias: knots indicated airspeed
KIB: Kansas Inspection Bureau; Kentucky Inspection Bureau
Kick-'em-Jenny: Diamond Island's nickname (West Indian island near Grenada)
kid.: kidney
kidult: kid adult (older person who enjoys juvenile entertainment)
kidvid: children's television program
kieselguhr: silica (SiO_2)
Kifis: Kollsman integrated flight instrument system
K-i-H: *Kaiser-i-Hind* (Emperor of India medal)
KIICC: *Kommunisticheskaya Partiya Sovetskogo Soyuza* (Russian—Communist Party of the Soviet Union)
Kikdl: *Krokodil*
kiku: (Japanese-Chrysanthemum)—applications technology satellite made and launched in Japan
kild: kilderkin(s)
Kild: Kildare
Kili: Kilimanjaro
Kilk: Kilkenny
kilo: kilogram; 10^3
Kilo: code for K
kilobrick(s): kilo-weight brick(s) of marijuana measuring about 2½ x 5 x 12 inches(64 x 127 x 300 millimeters)
kilohm: kilo-ohm
Kilometer-high City: Boone, North Carolina
kilovar: kilovolt-ampere (reactive)
Kim: Kimball; Kimballton; Kimberley; Kimberly; Kimble; Kimbolton; Kimborough; Kimbrough; Kimiwan; Kimmell; Kimmins; Kimmswick; Kimsquit
K i M: Knudsen i Marken
Kin: Frank McKinney Hubbard; Kingston, Ontario (maritime contraction)
KIN: Kingston, Jamaica (airport); Kinross
Kinc: Kincardinel
kind.: kindergarten
kine: kinema (variation of cinema)
King: Kingston
kingd: kingdom
King of Bath: Richard (Beau) Nash
King of Beasts: the lion
King of Birds: the eagle
King of Courts: the forensic orator Quintus Hortensius of Rome
King of Filibusters: William Walker
King of the Gods: Jupiter (according to Roman mythology)
King of the Huns and Scourge of God: Attila
King of Jazz: Louis (Satchmo) Armstrong and Paul Whiteman share this sobriquet
King of Kings: Jehovah—God of the Christians and Jews; title of various presumptive rulers of African and Oriental lands
King of the Jews: Jesus, according to the *New Testament*
King of Laughter: Bert Williams (Egbert Austin Williams)
King of Metals: gold
King of the Octaves: Claudio José Domingo Brindis de Sala—German Baron and court violinist
King of Ornithological Painters: John James Audubon
King of the Pianists: Claudio Arrau
Kingdom of the Hellenes: Greece
Kingfish: Senator Huey P. Long of Louisiana
King of Rivers: sobriquet shared by North America's Colorado and South America's Amazon
King of Roads: John Loudon Macadam
King Cotton: personification of the cotton crop of the southern United States
King Crab Capital: Kodiak, Alaska
King of Snobs: Hudson, the otherwise faultless butler, in the tv play *Upstairs, Downstairs*
King of Steel: Andrew Carnegie
King of Swat: George Herman Ruth
King of Swing: Benny Goodman
King of Tasmanian Rivers: the Gordon
King of Terrors: personification of death
King of Trains and Train of Kings: Orient Express
King Tut: King Tutankhamen of Egypt
King of the Underworld: Osiris (Egyptian mythology)
King of Waters: the Amazon
Kings: either of two books in the

Old Testament of Jewish and Protestant bibles; either of four books in the Old Testament of Roman Catholic bibles

King's College: Columbia University in colonial times

king's English: correct English

king's evil: scrofula (lymph-gland tuberculosis)

King Who Lost America: Great Britian's George III

Kinr: Kinross-shire

KINTEL: K Laboratories (instruments and television)

Kintetsu: Kinki Nippon Railway Company, Ltd.

kip: thousand pounds (from contraction of kilo and pound)

KIP: Kennedy Institute of Politics (Harvard)

kip ft: thousand foot pounds

Kir: Kirghiz; Kirghizia; Kirghizian

Kircoobri: (Scottish contraction—Kircudbright)

Kircud Kircudbrightshire *(Kircoobrisheer)*

Kirk: Kirkudbright *(Kircoobri)*

Kirov: Sergei Mironovich Kostrikov

Kirsty: Kristina; Kristine

KISA: Korean International Steel Associates

kisc: knowledge industry system concept

kismif: keep it simple—make it fun

KI smog: potassium-iodide smog (automobile induced)

KISO: Kol Israel Symphony Orchestra

kiss: keep it simple, stupid

KIST: Korean Institute for Science and Technology

kit.: kitchen(ette)

Kit: Catherine; Christopher; Kitty

KIT: Kentucky and Indiana Terminal (railroad)

KIT: *Koninklijk Instituut voor de Tropen* (Dutch—Royal Institute for the Tropics)

kita: (Japanese—north)

Kit Carson: Christopher Carson nicknamed Monarch of the Prairies as well as Nestor of the Rocky Mountains

Kitchener of Khartum: General Horatio Herbert Kitchener

KITCO: Kwajalein Import and exporting Company

kiteoon: kite + balloon

kitsch: *kitschen* (German—thrown together)—commercial art or art objects cheapened by vulgarity; e.g., miniature reproduction of the Venus de Milo with an alarm clock set in her belly

Kitsi: Kathryn

Kittie: Katherine; Kitty Belairs

Kittsian(s): inhabitant(s) of St. Kitts

Kitty: Catherine

KIVI: *Koninklijk Instituut van Ingenieurs* (Dutch—Royal Institution of Engineers)

KIWA: *Keurings Instituut voor Waterleiding Artikelen* (Dutch—Inspection Institute for Waterwords Equipment)

kizil: (Turkish—red, as in Kizil Arvat, Kizil Kum, Kizil Uzen)

kj: kilojoule; kimberly joint (lumbing); knee jerk

k-j: knee-jerk(s)

kJ: kilojoule

KJ: Kahlil Jibran (Gibran)

KJC: Kaiser Jeep Corporation; Keystone Junior College

K John: *Life and Death of King John*

K.J.St.J.: Knight of Justice, Order of Saint John of Jerusalem

KJV: King James Version

kk: killer karate

k-k: knee-kicks (knee-jerks)

KK: *Kabushiki Kaisha* (Japanese—joint stock company of shareholders with limited liability) *Kaiserlich Königlich* (German—Imperial Royal)

K.K.: *Kahal Kadosh* (Hebrew—Holy Congregation)

K of K: Kitchener of Khartoum

KKASSR: Kara-Kalpak Autonomous Soviet Socialist Republic

KKI: *Keren Kayemeth le Israel* (Hebrew—National Fund of Israel)

KKK: Ku Klux Klan (secret organization antagonistic to certain racial & religious groups)

KKK: *Kinder, Kirche, Küche* (German—Children, Church, Kitchen)—traditional three K's of Teutonic womanhood

KKKK: Kansai Kisen Kabushiki Kaisha; Kawasaki Kisen Kabushiki Kaisha (steamship lies)

KKKK: *Koenhavns Kul og Koks Kompagne* (Copenhagen Coal and Coke Company)

KKKKs: Knights of the Ku Klux Klan

KKMKI: Kungliga Karolinska Mediko-Kirurgiska Institutet (Caroline Medico-Surgical Institute-Stockholm)

Kkr: Karlskrona

kl: kiloliter

kl: *klockan* (Swedish—o'clock); *klokken* (Dano-Norwegian—o'clock)

Kl: *Klasse* (German—class)

KL: Key Largo; Klebs-Loeffler; Knutsen Line; Kuala Lumpur; Kwik Lok

KL: *King Lear*

kla: klystron amplifier

KLA: Korean Library Association

Klamaths: Klamath Mountains bordering California and Oregon

Klan: Ku Klux Klan (*q.v.* KKK)

Klar: *Klarinette* (German—clarinet)

klax: klaxon

K-L bacillus: Klebs-Loeffler bacillus (diptheria)

Klebs: Klebsiella

klein: (Dutch or German—small)

Klem: Klemens; Klement; Klementi; Kliment

klepto: kleptomania (c; al)

kl Fl: *kleine Flöte* (German—piccolo)

Klg: Keelung

klh: keyhole limpet hemocyanin (KLH)

klim: (milk spelled backwards) dried milk

K Line: Kawasaki Kisen Kaisha

KLM: Koninklijke Luchtvaart Maatschappij (Royal Dutch Airlines)

Klmpb: Klampenborg

Kln: Köln (Cologne)

klo: klystron oscillator

k-lo: *kello* (Finnish—hour; o'clock)

Klondike Country: the Yukon

KLPA: Knuckeys Lagoon Protected Area (Australian Northern Territory)

kls: key lock switch

klt: kiloton (nuclear equivalent, 1,000 tons of high explosives)

klto: knurling tool

Kluxer: member of the Ku Klux Klan (*q.v.* KKK)

km: kilometer

km²: square kilometer

km³: cubic kilometer

Km: Kingdom

KM: Kaffrarian Museum; Kearny Mesa; Khedivial Mail (steamship line)

K.M.: Knight of Malta

K-M: Krauss-Maffei

K&M: King and Martyr (Charles Ist's sobriquet)

KMA: Kinematograph Manufac-

turers Association
KMAG: United States Military Advisory Group to the Republic of Korea
kmc: kilomegacycle
kmef: keratin, myosin, epidermin, fibrin (proteins)
KMF: Koussevitzky Music Foundation
km/h: kilometers per hour
KMH: Kleinhans Music Hall (Buffalo)
KMI: Kentucky Military Institute
KMMA: Korean Merchant Marine Academy
KMO: Kobe Marine Observatory
KMP: Kaiser Metal Products; Kearny Mesa Plant (Convair)
kmph: kilometers per hour
kmps: kilometers per second
Kmr: Khorramshahr
KMR: Kwajalein Missile Range
KMS: Keeve M. Siegel
KMT: Kuomintang
KMUL: Karl Marx Universität Leipzig (University of Leipzig)
kmw: kilomegawatt
KMW: Karlstads Mekaniska Werkstad (Swedish iron foundry)
kmwhr: kilomegawatt-hour
Kn: Knight
kn: kilonewton; knot; krone; kronen
KN: Koninkrijk der Nederlanden (Kingdom of the Netherlands); Kongeriket Norge (Kingdom of Norway)
K-N: Know-Nothing (political party)
K of N: King(dom) of Naples; King(dom) of Navarre; King (dom) of Norway
KNA: Kenya News Agency; Korean National Airlines
KNA: *Kongelig Norsk Automobilklub* (Royal Norwegian Automobile Club)
KNAC: *Koninklijke Nederlandsche Automobiel Club* (Dutch—Royal Netherlands Automobile Club)
KNAN: Koninklijke Nederlandse Akademie voor Naturwetenschappen (Royal Netherlands Academy of Sciences)
K'naw: Kanawha Rver
KNC: Kalamazoo Nature Center
KNGR: Kruger National Game Reserve
Knick: Knickerbocker
Knickerbocker(s): New Yorker(s)
knickers: knickerbockers
Knight of La Mancha: Don Quixote
Knight of the Rueful Countenance: Don Quixote
Knight of the Swan: Lohengrin
k9p: dog piss; urine produced by coyotes, dogs, foxes, hyenas, jackals, wolves, and other canines
K98k: German carbine (World War II)
KNK: Kita Nippon Koku (Northern Japan Airlines)
Knls: Knolls (postal abbreviation)
KNM: Katmai National Monument; Kongelige Norske Marine (Royal Norwegian Navy)
KNMI: Koninkliji Nederlands Meteorologisch Instituut (Royal Netherlands Meteorological Institute)
KNMR: Kenai National Moose Range (Alaska)
KNO: Kano, Nigeria (tracking station)
Knopf: Alfred A. Knopf
knork: knife + fork (combination utensil)
Knott's: Knott's Berry Farm
KNP: Kafue National Park (Zambia); Kalahari NP (South Africa); Kalbarri NP (Western Australia); Kanha NP (India); Kejimkujik NP (Nova Scotia); Kinabalu NP (Sabah); Kinchega NP (New South Wales); Kootenay NP (British Columbia); Kosciusko NP (New South Wales); Kruger NP (South Africa)
KNPC: Kuwait National Petroleum Company
KNR: Kinki Nippon Railway
KNSM: Koninklijke Nederlandsche Stoomboot Maatschappij (Royal Netherlands Steamship Company)
kn sw: knife switch
Knt: Knight
KNT: Knight-Knott Hotels (stock-exchange symbol)
KNT: *Koninklijke Nederlandsche Toeristenbond* (Dutch—Royal Netherlands Touring Club)
knu: knuckle
KNUST: Kwame Nkrumah University of Science and Technology
Knut Hamsun: Knut Pedersen
KNVL: Koninklijke Nederlandse Vereniging voor Luchtvaart (Royal Netherlands Aero Club)
KNWR: Kirwin National Wildlife Refuge (Kansas)
KNX: Kinney Company (stock-exchange symbol)
Knxv: Knoxville
ko: kilohm; knockout (KO)
k-o: knockout
Ko: Korea; Korean
KO: kickoff (football); knockout (boxing); Kodiak Airways (2-letter coding)
KOA: Kentucky Opera Association
Kob: Kobe (British Maritime contraction)
Køb: *København* (Dano-Norwegian—Copenhagen)
KOC: Kollmorgen Optical Corporation; Kuwait Oil Company
kod: kickoff drift
ko'd: knocked out
KODAK: trade name for Eastman Kodak photographic products
Kodak City: Rochester, New York
k-o drops: knockout drops (chloral hydrate sedative)
kOe: kiloOersted(s)
kog: kindly old gentleman
KOG: Kansas, Oklahoma & Gulf (railroad)
KOH: potassium hydroxide
kohm: kilohm
Ko-i-noor: (Persian—Mountain of Light)—Nadir Shah's name for the celebrated mountain-shaped diamond
Kok: Cochrane
KOKS: *Dul og Koks Selskab* (Danish—Coal and Coke Company)
Kol: Kolonia, Ponape (Trust Territory of the Pacific)
KOM: Knight of the Order of Malta
Komei: (Japanese—Komeito)—Buddhist party
Komp: *Kompanie* (German—company)
Komsomol: (Russian—Young Communist League)
Kon Dan: Kongeriget Danmark (Kingdom of Denmark)
Kon Nor: Kongeriket Norge (Kingdom of Norway)
Konr: Konrad
KONR: *Komitet Osvobozhdyeniya Narodov Rossii* (Committee for the Liberation of the Peoples of Russia)
Konst: Konstantin
Kon Sver: Konungariket Sverige (Kingdom of Sweden)
konz: *konzentriert* (German—concentrated)

kop: kopeck(s)
Kop: *Kopenhagen* (Dutch, Flemish, German—Copenhagen)
KOP: Koppers (company)
kops: keep off pounds sensibly
Kor: Korea; Korean; The Koran
Korin: Ogata Korin (early 18th-century Japanese decorative artist)
KORR: King's Own Royal Regiment
kos: kilos
KOSB: King's Own Scottish Borderers
KOTRA: Korea Trade Promotion Corporation
Koussi: Serge Koussevitzky
kov: key-operated valve
Kow: *Koweit* (Spanish Kuwait)
KOYLI: King's Own Yorkshire Light Infantry
kp: key personnel; kick plate; kill probability; kilopond; king post; kitchen police (KP); knotty pine
Kp: *Kochpunkt* (German—boiling point
KP: *Kommunistische Partei* (German—Communist Party); Komsomolskaya Pravda (Russian—Young Communist League Truth)—Moscow newspaper claiming circulation of three million; *Kuvendi Popullore* (Albanian People's Assembly)
K.P.: Knight of St Patrick
K of P: King(dom) of Poland; King(dom) of Portugal; King(dom) of Prussia; Knights of Pythias
KPA: Kraft Paper Association
kpc: keypunch cabinet
kp & d: kick plate and drip
KPD: Kommunistische Partei Deutschland (Communist Party of Germany)
KPDR: Korean People's Democratic Republic
KPFSM: King's Police and Fire Service Medal
kph: kilometers per hour; knots per hour
kpi: kips per inch
kpic: key phrase in context
KPL: Knoxville Public Library
kpm: kathode pulse modulation
KPM: King's Police Medal
Kpmtr: *Kapellmeister* (German—conductor)
KPNO: Kitt Peak National Observatory
KPNWR: Kern-Pixley National Wildlife Refuge (California)
kpo: keypunch operator
KPP: Keeper of the Privy Purse
kpps: kilopulses per second
kpr: keeper
Kpr: Kodak photo resist
KPR: Korean Presidential Ribbon
kps: kips (thousand pounds) per square foot
kpsi: kips (thousand pounds) per square inch
KPSS: *Kommunisticheskaya Partiya Sovetskovo Soyuza* (Russian—Communist Party of the Soviet Union)—CPSU
Kpt: Kaptajn (Danish—captain)
KPU: Kenya People's Union (party)
kq: line squall
kr: keel rider; kiloroentgen
Kr: krypton
KR: krona (Icelandic or Swedish monetary unit); krone (Danish or Norwegian monetary unit)
Krag: Krag-Jörgensen rifle
K-ration: Calorie ration (lightweight emergency meal)
KRC: Knight of the Red Cross
KREEP: K (potassium) REE (rare-earth elements) P (phosphate)—yellow brown glassy lunar material
Kreutzer: Beethoven's Sonata in A minor (opus 47) for violin and piano; dedicated to his friend the violinist Rudolphe Kreutzer
Kreuzb: Kreuzberg
KRF: Kentucky Research Foundation
Krh: Karachi
Kringleville: Racine, Wisconsin
Kripo: Kriminalpolizei (German—Criminal Investigation Department)
Krishaber's disease: dizzy-and-sleepy neurosis accompanied by fainting
Krist: Kristian; Kristijonas; Kristmann; Kristofer
Kristallnacht: (German—Night of Broken Glass)—nights of November 8th, 9th, and 10th in 1938 when Nazi mobs broke the windows and smashed the doors of German-Jewish stores and temples before looting them, burning them, and sending their inhabitants to concentration camps
Kronos: (Greek—Saturn)—god of time
KRR: King's Royal Rifles
krs: Korus (Turkish—piastre)
Krs: Kristiansand
KRs: (*see* CRs)
KRS: Kinematograph Renters Society
krt: cathode-ray tube
KRT: Khartoum, Sudan (airport)
KRU: Krueger Brewing (stock-exchange symbol)
Krungthep: Krungthep Mahanakhon Bovorn Ratanakosin Mahintharayutthaya Mahadilokpop Noparatratchanthani Burirom Udomratchanivetmahasathan Amornpiman Avatarnsathit Sakkathattiya-visnukarmprasit (full name of the capital city of Bangkok, Thailand formerly Siam)
Krupskaya: Nadezhda Konstantinovna Krupskaya Lenin
ks: drifting snowstorm (symbol); keep (type) standing
Ks: kyats (Burmese money)
K-s: King-size (doughnuts, frankfurters, hamburgers, steaks, etc.)
KS: King's Scholar; Kipling Society; Konungariket Sverige (Kingdom of Sweden)
K of S: King(dom) of Scotland; King(dom) of Siam (Thailand); King(dom) of Spain; King(dom) of Sweden
ksa: kite-supported antenna
KSAA: Keats-Shelley Association of America
KSB: Kypriakos Synthesmos Bibliothicarion (Modern Greek—Library Association of Cyprus)
KSC: Kansas State College; Kennedy Space Center; Kentucky State College; Korean Shipping Corporation; Kutztown State College
KSC: Komunisticka Strana Ceskoslovenska (Communist Party of Czechoslovakia)
ksf: kips (thousand pounds) per square foot
KSF: Kulkyne State Forest (Victoria, Australia)
KSFUS: Korean Student Federation of the United States
K.S.G.: Knight of Saint Gregory the Great
K sh: Kenya shilling(s)
ksi: kips (1000 pounds) per square inch
KSI: Keshvare Shahanshahiye Iran (Iran—Persia)
ksia: thousand square inches absolute
KSK: ethyl iodoacetate (tear gas)
ksl: kidney, spleen, liver
KSL: Kinsel Drug (stock-exchange symbol)
KSLI: King's Shropshire Light Infantry

KSM: Korean Service Medal; Kungliga Svenska Marinen (Royal Swedish Navy)
KSM: *Kommunisticheskii Soyuz Molodozhi* (Russian—All-Union League of Communist Youth)—Komsomol or Young Communist League—YCL
KSN: Kit Shortage Notice
KSNP: Khao Salob National Park (Thailand)
KSO: Kalamazoo Symphony Orchestra; Knoxville Symphony Orchestra
ksr: keyboard send-receive (set)
K.S.S.: Knight of Saint Sylvester
KSS: *Komunisticka Strana Slovenska* (Communist Party of Slovakia)
KSSR: Kazak Soviet Socialist Republic; Kirghizian Soviet Socialist Republic
KSSU: Kiev I.G. Shevchenko State University (University of Kiev)
kst: keyseat
KST: King-Seeley Thermos (company)
KSTC: Kansas State Teachers College
K.St.J.: Knight of the Order of Saint John of Jerusalem
ksu: key service unit
KSU: Kansas State University; Kent State University
KSUAAS: Kansas State University of Agriculture and Applied Science
KSY: King Seeley (stock-exchange symbol)
kt: karet (caret); kiloton (nuclear equivalent, 1000 tons of high explosives); knot
K_t: stress concentration factor
Kt: Knight
KT: Kentucky & Tennessee (railway); Knight of the Order of the Thistle; Knight Templar; Missouri-Kansas-Texas (Katy Route Railroad)
K.T.: Knight of the Thistle
K of T: Kingdom of Tonga
K-T: Kazin-Turkic
KTA: Knitted Textile Association
Ktb: *Kriegstagebuch* (German—war diary)
KTC: Keystone Tankship Corporation; Key Telephone System; Kodiak Tracking Station
KTH: Kungliga Tekniska Högskolan (Royal Institute of Technology, Stockholm)
ktl: *kai ta loipa* (Greek—et cetera)
KTN: Ketchikan, Alaska (Annette Island airport)
Kto: *Konto* (German—account)
K-truss: K-shaped truss
kts: knots
k through 12: kindergarten through high school
KTS: Key Telephone Systems; Kwajalein Test Site
KTTC: Kingston-upon-Thames Technical College
ktu: kill the umpire
KTX: Keith Railway Equipment (railway code)
KU: Kalmar Union; Kansas University; Keio University; Kuwait Airways (2-letter symbol)
KU: *Københavns Universitet* (Danish—Copenhagen University)
kub: kidney(s)-ureter(s)-bladder
ku'd: knocked up (made pregnant)
Ku'dam: Kurfürstendamm (Main street of West Berlin)
K u H: Kingston upon Hull (official name for Hull)
KUK: Kollege of Universal Knowledge
KUL: Kabul University Library (Kabul, Afghanistan)
Kung-fu-tse: (Chinese— Reverend Master King)—Confucius
K unit: Kimball unit
Kur: (British maritime contraction of Kure); Kurile Islands
kirchatovium: Russian name for element 104 named for A-bomb pioneer Igor Kurchatov
Kuria Murias: Kuria Muria Islands in the Arabian Sea
Kuril Cur: Kurile Current (Oyashio)
Kuriles: Kurile Islands in the North Pacific
KURRI: Kyoto University Research Reactor Institute
kutd: keep up to date
KUU: Kungliga Universitet i Uppsala (Royal University of Uppsala)
Kuw: Kuwait
Kuyb: Kuybyshev
kv: kilovolt
KV: *Köchel-Verzeichnis* (German—Kochel Catalog)— catalog of Mozart's compositions with a K number assigned to each one
kva: kilovolt ampere
KVA: Kungliga Vetenskaps Akademien (Royal Swedish Academy of Sciences)
kvah: kilovolt-ampere-hour
kvam: kilovolt ampere meter
kvar: kilovar; kilovolt ampere reactive
kvarh: kilovar hour
kvcp: kilovolt constant potential
K-Vets: Korean War Veterans of the United States
kvg: keyed video generator
KVHS: Kanawha Valley Historical Society
kvm: kilovolt meter
KVNP: Kidepo Valley National Park (Uganda)
kvp: kilovolt peak
KVP: *Katholieke Volkspartij* (Dutch—Catholic People's Party)
KVW: Kansas City Kaw Valley (railroad)
kw: kilowatt
kw: Zambian kwacha(s)—monetary unit(s)
KW: Key West
kwac: key word and context
K-W AG: Kitchener-Waterloo Art Gallery
Kwaj: Kwajalein
Kwan: Kwantung
kwat: key well allowable transfer
KWC: Kentucky Wesleyan College
kwe: kilowatts electrical
KWest: Key West
K-W findings: Keith-Wagener (opthalmoscopic findings)
kwh: kilowatt hour
kwhr: kilowatt hour
kwic: key word in context
kwit: key word in text: key word in title
kwm: kilowatt meter
KWMA: Kirtland's Warbler Management Areas (Michigan)
KWNWR: Key West National Wildlife Refuge (Florida)
kwoc: key word out of context
kwot: key word out of title
KWPL: Kitchener-Waterloo Public Library
kwr: kilowatts reactive
KWS: Kaziranga Wildlife Sanctuary (India)
KWSM: Korean War Service Medal
kwt: key word in title; kilowatts thermal
KWT: King William's Town
KWU: Kansas Wesleyan University
KWVZAB: *Ko-operative Wijnbouwers Vereeninging van Zuid Afrika Beperkt* (Dutch—Cooperative Wine Farmers Association of South Africa, Limited)

kwy: keyway
kxu: kilo-x-unit
ky: cocoa; keyer
Ky: Kentuckian; Kentucky
KY: Kentucky (zip code); (underground slang—federal hospital in Lexington, Kentucky where drug addicts are treated); Kol Yisrael (Israel Broadcasting Service)
kybd: keyboard
KYC: Knickerbocker Yacht Club
kyd: Kilo yard
kyeri: know your endorsers—require identification (advice to all who cash checks)
kymo: kymograph; kymography
KYNP: Khao Yai National Park (Thailand)
Kyo: Kyoto
Kyoto: (Japanese—Capital City)—capital of Japan for 1066 years and art shrine of the nation
Kyot Univ: Kyoto University
Kyr.: *Kyrie eleison* (Greek—Lord, have mercy upon us)
kytoon: kite balloon
kz: duststorm or sandstorm
Kz: Kazakh(stan)
KZ: *Konzentrationslager* (German—concentration camp)
K z S: *Käpitan zur See* (German— Sea Captain)—naval rating

L

l: azimuthal or orbital quantum number (symbol); elbow (plumbing); land; late; latent heat per unit mass (symbol); lateral; latitude; law; leaf; league; left or port (L or P); length; levorotatory; liaison; lignite; line; link; lire; liter; locus
l*: lumen
l/: *letra* (Spanish—letter)
l_1: first lumbar vertebra
l_2: second lumbar vertebra
l_3: third lumbar vertebra
l_4: l_5: fourth lumbar veterbra; fifth lumbar vetebra; etc.
l: *lectio* (Latin—reading)
L: Bell Aircraft (symbol); center line (symbol); elevated railroad (EL); inductance (symbol); kinetic potential (symbol); lactobacillus; lago; Lágrange function; lake; loch; lough; lake vessel; Lamar State College of Technology; lambert; Latin; launching; left (port side); lempira (Honduran currency unit); Leo; Leon; Liberal; lift (symbol); lift force; light; Lima—code for L; Linnaeus; Lions International; London; longitude; loran; Lorentz unit; Luckenbach Lines; Luxembourgh (auto plaque); Lykes Lines; rolling moment (symbol)
L: *lähteä* (Finnish—departure); *lämmin* (Finnish—warm); *länsi* (Finnish—wheat; *laudes* (Latin—praises); (Latin—Lucius); *levato* (Italian—raised); *Life Magazine; links* (German—left); *llegada* (Spanish—arrival)
1/3: lower third
L7: Hollywood slang for old-fashioned person or *square* as capital-letter L and figure 7 may be combined to form a square
L-1011: Lockheed's jumbo jetliner
la: lava; left angle; left atrium; left auricle; lighter than air; lightning arrestor; long-acting; low altitude; landing account
l/a: landing account; letter of advice; letter of authority; lighter than air
l & a: left and above; light and accommodation
la: (Italian—the); sixth tone in diatonic scale; A in fixed-do system
l.a.: *lege artis* (Latin—according to the art)—as directed
l/a: *lettre d'avis* (French—letter of advice)
La: Lane; lanthanum; Lao; Laos; Laotian; Louisiana; Louisianian
LA: Latin America(n); Legislative Assembly; Leschetizky Association; Letter of Activation; Library Association; Lieutenant-at-Arms; Local Authority; Los Angeles; Louisiana & Arkansas (railroad); Louvain Association
L-A: Loire-Atlantique (formerly Loire-Inférieure)
L & A: Louisiana & Arkansas (railroad)
LAA: League of Advertising Agencies; Library Association of Australia; Life Insurance Advertisers; Los Angeles Airways
LAADS: Los Angeles Air Defense Sector
laam (LAAM): levo-alpha acetylmethadol (alternative to methadone for treatment of drug addiction)
laar: liquid-air accumulator rocket
LAAS: Los Angeles Air Service
lab: label; labeling; labor; laboratory
Lab: Laboratory; Labour(ite); Labrador
LAB: Labor; Labour; Labour Party; Licquor [*sic.*] Administration Board; Liquor Administration Board; Lloyd Aereo Boliviano (Bolivian airline); low-altitude bombing
LABA: Laboratory Animal Breeders Association
La Belle Province: (French—the beautiful Province)—Québec
La Belle Rivierè: (French—The Beautiful River)— frontier nickname of the Ohio in the days of Audubon and Boone
Lab Cur: Labrador Current—cold Arctic current flowing southward along Atlantic coast of Canada and northern New England
LABEN: Laboratori Elettronici e Nucleari (Electronic and Nuclear Laboratories—Milan)
labe(s): label(s)
La Bonne Louise: Louise Michel remembered for her good works among the poor people of Paris
Labor: US Department of Labor
lab proc: laboratory procedure(s)
labs: laboratories

Lab(s): Labrador retriever(s)
LABS: Low-Altitude Bombing System
lac: lacquer; lacrimal; lactation; shellac
Lac: Lacerta; Lacertilia
LAC: Library Association of China; Leading Aircraftsman; Líneas Aéreas Chaqueñas (Aero Chaco); Lockheed Aircraft Corporation
LACAP: Latin American Cooperative Acquisitions Project
La Casa Grande: (Spanish—The Big House)—William Randolph Hearst's art museum, mansions, and wildlife gardens in San Simeon, California
LACATA: Laundry and Cleaners Allied Trades Association
lacc: lathe chuck
LACC: Los Angeles City College
Laccadives: Laccadive Islands
LACE: liquid-air cycle engine
LACES: London Airport Cargo Electronic Scheme; Los Angeles Council of Engineering Societies
La Chasse: Haydn's Quartet in B flat (opus 1, no. 1); Haydn's Symphony No. 73 in D major (The Hunt)
Lachie: Lachlan
LACJ: Los Angeles County Jail
LACM: Los Angeles County Museum
LACMA: Los Angeles Conservatory of Music and Arts; Los Angeles County Museum of Art
LACMedA: Los Angeles County Medical Association
laconiq: laboratory computer on-line inquiry
LACP: London Association of Correctors of the Press
lacr: low-altitude coverage radar
LACSA: Líneas Aéreas Costarricenses (Costa Rican Airlines)
LACW: Leading Aircraftswoman
lad.: ladder
Lad: Ladino
LAD: Library Administration Division (American Library Association); Light Air Detachment
ladar: laser detection and ranging
LADE: Líneas Aéreas del Estado (State Airlines, Argentina)
LADO: Latin American Defense Organization; Latin American Development Organization
ladp: ladyship
LADSIRLAC: Liverpool and District Scientific, Industrial, and Research Library Advisory Council
L Adv: Lord Advocate
LADWP: Los Angeles Department of Water and Power
Lady Bird: Mrs Claudia Alta Taylor Johnson—wife of President Lyndon Johnson
Lady Hamilton: Emma Lyon
Lady of 57th Street: New York City's Carnegie Hall
Lady of the Lamp: Nurse Florence Nightingale
Lady South: Charleston, South Carolina
Lady With Lamp: Statue of Liberty officially named Liberty Enlightening the World
Lady's Slipper: Minnesota state flower
laev.: *laevus* (Latin—left)
laf: laminar air flow
Laf: Lafayette
LaF: Louisiana French
LAF: L'Académie Française (The French Academy); Living Arts Foundation
LAFB: Lincoln Air Force Base
LAFC: Latin-American Forestry Commission
Lafe: Lafayette
LAFE: *Laboratorio de Fisica Espacial* (Portuguese—Space Physics Laboratory)
LA 400: 400 women of Los Angeles who raised 4 million dollars for its music center
La Font: La Fontaine
LAFS: Los Angeles Funeral Society
LAFTA: Latin American Free Trade Area; Latin American Free Trade Association
lag.: lagan
lag.: *lagena* (Latin—bottle; flask)
Lag: Lagoon; Laguna
La G: La Guaira
LAG: Layton Art Gallery
LAGB: Linguistics Association of Great Britain
LAGE: Los Angeles Grain Exchange
LAGEOS: Laser Geodetic Satellite
La Gioconda: (Italian—The Cheerful Woman)—another name for Leonardo da Vinci's portrait—the Mona Lisa
lags. (LAGS): laser-activated geodetic satellite
Lags: Lagunas
LAGS: Los Angeles Geographic Society
Lagunas: Laguna Mountains of California
Lah: Lahore
LAH: Licentiate Apothecaries Hall
LAHC: Los Angeles Harbor College; Los Angeles Harbor Commission
lahs: low-altitude high speed
lai: leaf are index
LAI: Library Association of Ireland
LAI: *Linee Aeree Italiane* (Italian Air Lines)
LAIC: Lithuanian-American Information Center
LAINS: Low-Altitude Inertial Navigation System
Laird of Skibo Castle: Andrew Carnegie
Laird of Woodchuck Lodge: John Burroughs
LAIS: Loan Accounting Information System (AID)
LAJ: Los Angeles Junction (railroad)
Lake State: Michigan bordering on Superior, Michigan, Huron, and Erie
laks: *lakrids* (Danish—licorice)
Laksha Divi: (Sanskrit—Hundred Thousand Isles)—the Laccadives
LAL: Langley Aeronautical Laboratory (Langley Research Center)
LA-LB: Los Angeles-Long Beach (ports)
lali: lonely aged of low income
Lalia: Eulalia
La Lollo: Gina Lollobrigida
lam: laminate
Lam: The Book of Lamentations; Lamarck; Lambretta
LAM: Lamarck; Lambert; Latin American Mission; London Academy of Music
L.A.M.: *Liberalium Artium Magister* (Latin—Master of Liberal Arts)
LAMA: Latin American Manufacturers Association; Lead Air Materiel Area
Lamb: Lambert; Lamberto; Lambertus; Lambeth
LAMBC: Los Angeles Motor Boat Club
lambwich: lamb sandwich
LAMC: Los Angeles Metropolitan College; Los Angeles Music Center
LAMCO: Liberian-American-Swedish Mineral Corporation
LAMDA: London Academy of Music and Dramatic Art
Lamia: P. L. Tyraud de Vosjoli

(French underground fighter and chief of intelligence)
LAMM: Los Angeles Master Morticians; Lutheran-American Melancthon Movement
Lamp: Lampeter
LAMP: Library Additions and Maintenance Program; Low-Altitude Manned Penetration; Lunar Analysis and Mapping Program
Lamp of Heaven: the Moon
LAMPP: Los Alamos Molten Plutonium Program (AEC)
LAMPS: Light Airborne Multipurpose System
LAMS: Launch Acoustic Measuring System
Lan: Lansing
L An: Los Angeles
LAN: Línea Aérea Nacional de Chile; Local Apparent Noon
lanac: laminair air navigation and anti-collision
Lanarks: Lanarkshire
Lan Bag: Lansing Bagnall
Lanc: Lancaster
Lance: Lancelot
Lancs: Lancashire
land.: landscaping
Land of Acadie: (*see* Land of Evangeline)
Land of Albert Schweitzer: Gabon
Land Between the Rivers: Mesopotamia better known as Iraq
Land of the Bible: Israel
Land of the Blacks: Guinea
Land of Bondage: Egypt in the time of Moses
Land of the Bulgars: Bulgaria
Land 'o Cakes: Land of Oatmeal Cakes—nickname Robert Burns gave his native land—Scotland
Land of the Cedars: Lebanon
LandCent: Allied Land Forces, Central Europe
Land of Cheese, Trees, and Ocean Breeze: Tillamook, Oregon
Land of the Cornstalk: Austraila
LandCraB: landing craft and bases
Land of the Croats: Croatian Yugoslavia
Land of the Czars and the Commisars: Russia—the USSR
Land of the Eagle: Albania
Land of Enchantment: New Mexico's official nickname
Land of Eternal Spring: Guatemala
Land of Evangeline: Maine east of the Kennebec River, New Brunswick, and Nova Scotia as well as Louisiana's coastal parishes
Land of Farmers and Fishermen: Denmark
Land of Five Peoples: Surinam, formerly Dutch or Netherlands Guiana, containing black, brown, red, white, and yellow people from Africa, Indonesia, South America, Europe, and the Orient, respectively
Land of the Fjords: Norway
Land of Flaming Waters: Malawi
Land of Flowers: Florida
Land of the Free: United States of America
Land of Freedom: Liberia
Land of Genghis Khan: Mongolia
Land God Gave Cain: Arctic Canada
Land of the Gaucho: Uruguay
Land of the Golden Lion: Iran
Land of Grass Roots: South Dakota
Land of the Heather: Scotland
Land of Heroes: Finland
Land of Hope and Glory: Great Britain
Land of Hope and Glory: Elgar's *Pomp and Circumstance,* March No. 1
Land of Hospitality and Charm: Thailand
Land of the Inland Sea: Chad surrounding the once-great inland sea—Lake Chad
Land of the Khmers: Cambodia
Land o' Lakes: Wisconsin
Land of Lakes and Fens: Finland
Land of Lakes and Forests: Sweden
Land of Lakes and Volcanos: El Salvador
Land of Leeks: Wales
Land of Legend: Canada's Yukon Territory
Land of Leopold: Belgium
Land of Lincoln: Illinois
Land of Liszt and Bartók: Hungary
Landlocked South American Nations: Bolivia and Paraguay
Land of the Long White Cloud: New Zealand—so called by the Maoris
Land of the Lotus Blossom: Ceylon, officially called Sri Lanka, where the lotus blossom symbolizes Buddha
Land of the Magyars: Hungary
Land of the Manchus: Manchuria
Land of the Maoris: New Zealand
Land of the Marsupials: Australia
Land of the Mayas: Honduras
Land of Mecca: Saudi Arabia
Land of the Midnight Sun: northern Alaska, Canada's Northwest Territories, Greenland, Iceland, Norway, Sweden, Finland, and Siberia share this sobriquet
Land of Milk and Honey: Israel's Jordan River Valley
Land of a Million Elephants: Laos
Land of the Moors: Algeria and Morocco
Land of the Mormons: Utah
Land of the Morning Calm: Korea
Land of Moses: Israel
Land of Mountains: the Austrian Tyrol; Norway; Sweden; Switzerland; Tibet
Land of My Fathers: Wales
Land of Nod: place where Cain was exiled after killing his brother Abel; the realm of sleep
Land of Opportunity: official nickname of Arkansas
Land of the Pentagram: Morocco whose flag and shield feature a five-pointed star of great complexity
Land of the Pharoahs: Egypt
Land of the Philistines: Palestine
Land of the Prophets: Israel
Land of the Quetzal: Guatemala
Land of the Red People: Oklahoma
Land of the Rising Sun: Japan
Land of the Rolling Prairie: Iowa
Land of the Rose: England
Lands: Landsmaal (Norwegian national language)
landsat: land satellite
Land of the Sea: The Netherlands—standing where the sea once stood
Land of Sea and Mountain: Norway
Land of the Shamrock: Ireland
Land of Six Peoples: Guyana, formerly British Guiana, containing Africans, Amerindians, Chinese, East Indians, Spaniards, and other Europeans including a few old British engineers
Land of Skillful Farmers: Lithuania
Land of the Sky: North Carolina
Landslide Lyndon: Senator Lyndon B. Johnson's nickname when elected by an 87-vote majority discovered by the Duke of Duval County—boss George Pharr
Land of Smiles: Thailand

Land South of the Clouds: Yunnan
Land of the Southern Cross: Brazil
Land of Spring: coastal southern California from San Diego to Santa Barbara
Land of Steady Habits: Connecticut
Land of Sunburned Faces: Ethiopia
Land of Sunshine: New Mexico, South Africa, and southern California vie for this descriptive title
Land of 10,000 Lakes: Minnesota's nickname
Land of the Thistle: Scotland
Land of the Thousand Lakes: Finland
Land of Togetherness: Kenya whose shield surmounts a riband reading *Harambee* (Swahili—Together)
Land of the Trade Winds: U.S. Virgin Islands
Land of the Vikings: Norway but particularly the Vestfold province on the western shore of Oslo Fjord where Viking remains are plentiful
Landw: *Landwirtschaft* (German—agriculture)
Land of Waterfalls: Norway
Land of the Wattle: Australia
Land of the White Ant: Australia's Northern Territory
Land of the White Eagle: Poland
Land of the White Elephant: Thailand
Land Where The Sun Never Sets: the Soviet Union
Lane's disease: chronic constipation
Lan Fus: Lancashire Fusiliers
lang: language
Lang: Langbridge; Langdon; Lange; Langer; Langford; Langhorne; Langlois; Langson; Langston; Languedoc
Lan Reg: Lancashire Regiment
LANSA: Líneas Aéreas Nacionales
Lant: Atlantic (naval short form)
LANWR: Laguna Atascosa National Wildlife Refuge (Texas); Lake Andes National Wildlife Refuge (South Dakota)
LANY: Linseed Association of New York
LAO: Licentiate of the Art of Obstetrics
LAOAR: Latin American Office of Aerospace Research
LAOD: Los Angeles Ordnance District (USA)
lap.: laparotomy; launch analyst's panel; left atrial pressure
Lap: Lapland
La P: La Paz
LAP: Laboratory of Aviation Psychology (Ohio State University); Líneas Aéreas Paraguayas (Paraguayan Air Lines)
La Pasionaria: Dolores Ibarruri famed for her impassioned speeches made during the Spanish civil war
LAPC: Los Angeles Pacific College; Los Angeles Pierce College
LAPD: Los Angeles Police Department
LAPDis: Los Angeles Procurement District (US Army)
La Perla: (Spanish—The Pearl)—San Juan
LAPES: Low-Altitude Parachute Extraction System
lapid.: *lapideum* (Latin—stony)
LAPL: Los Angeles Public Library
LAPO: Los Angeles Philharmonic Orchestra
LAPT: London Association for the Protection of Trade
La Pucelle: *La Pucelle d'Orléans* (French—The Maid of Orleans)—Joan of Arc
laq: lacquer
lar: left arm reclining; local-acquisition radar
LAR: Library Association of Rhodesia; Life Assurance Relief
lara (LARA): light armed reconnaissance aircraft
LARA: League of Americans Residing Abroad
La Raza: *La Raza Unida* (Spanish—The United Race)—Mexican-American political organization
larc: lighter, amphibious, resupply, cargo (vehicle)
LARC: Langley Research Center; League Against Religious Coercion; Library Automation and Consulting; Local Alcoholism Reception Center(s)
larg: *largamente* (Italian—broadly); *largeur* (French—width); *largo* (Italian—slow)
Large Print: Large Print Publications
Largest American City: New York
Largest Canadian City: Montreal
Largest Central American Republic: Nicaragua
Largest City in the Largest State: Anchorage, Alaska
Largest City in the South: Houston, Texas
Largest Latin American Republic: Brazil
Largest Province: Québec
Largest State: Alaska
largo.: *larghetto* (Italian—moderately slow)
Lark: Haydn's String Quartet in D (opus 64, no. 5)
LARO: Latin American Regional Office (FAO)
Larruping Lou: Henry Louis (Lou) Gehrig
Larry: Laura; Laurence; Lawrence
Lars: Lawrence
LART: Los Angeles Rapid Transit
larva (LARVA): low-altitude research vehicle
laryng: laryngological; laryngologist; laryngology
laryngol: laryngology
las: low-alloy steel; large astronomical satellite
las: *lassú* (Hungarian—slow intorductory passages leading to fast section, *friss*, of a csárdas or rhapsody)
LAS: Las Vegas, Nevada (airport); League of Arab States; Lebanese-American Society; Legal Aid Society; large astronomical satellite
LA & S: Liberal Arts and Sciences
LASAIL: Land-Sea Interaction Laboratory
LASC: Los Angeles State College
La Scala: Milan's opera house
LASCO: Latin American Unesco Science Cooperation Office
laser: light amplification by stimulated emission of radiation; lucrative approach to support expensive research
LASER: London and South Eastern Library Region
LASERS: London and South Eastern Regional Library SAystem
LASH: Legislative Action on Smoking and Health; Lighter Aboard Ship (cargo system)
LASL: Los Alamos Scientific Laboratory
LASMCO: Liberian American-Swedish Minerals Company
LASO: Los Angeles Society of Opthalmology
lasp: low-altitude space platform

LASRA: Leather and Shoe Research Association
lasrm (LASRM): low-altitude short-range missile
lass.: lighter-than-air submarine simulator (LASS)
LASSCO: Los Angeles Steamship Company
l'asses: molasses
Last Capital of the Confederacy: Danville, Virginia
Last Chance Gulch: gold miner's name for Helena, Montana
Last Cocked Hat: James Monroe—fifth President of the United States and last to wear the cocked hat of the American Revolution
Last Continent: Antarctica (last continent to be discovered)
Last Frontier: Alaska's old nickname and current nickname of Canada's Northwest Territories
Last of the Incas: Atahualpa
Last Lovely City: San Francisco
Last of the Prophets before Mohammed: Jesus, according to the Moslems
Last Remaining Polynesian Kingdom: Tonga—christened the Friendly Isles by Captain Cook
Last of the Romans: Rienzi
Last Stronghold of the Moors: Granada, Spain
last trump: the sound of the last trumpet believers expect to hear on Judgment Day
La Superba: (Italian—The Superb)—Genoa's proud appelation dating back to the time of Columbus—a Genoese Jew named Cristoforo Colombo
LASUSSR: Library of the Academy of Science of the USSR (Leningrad)
lasv (LASV): low-altitude surface vehicle; low-altitude supersonic vehicle
lat: lateral; latitude
lat.: *latus* (Latin—wide)
Lat: Latin; Latvia; Latvian
LAT: Local Apparent Time, Taxader (Bogotá)
LAT: *Los Angeles Times*
lat. admov.: *lateri admoveatum* (Latin—apply to the side)
LATCC: London Air Traffic Control Center
LATCRS: London Air Traffic Control Radar Station
lat. dol.: *lateri dolenti* (Latin—to the painful side)
LATH: Laos and Thailand Military Assistance
lat ht: latent heat
lats: long-acting thyroid stimulator
LATTC: Los Angeles Trade-Technical College
Latter-Day Saint: Joseph Smith—author of *The Book of Mormon*
Latter-Day Saints: the Mormons
Latv: Latvia; Latvian
LATWPNS: Los Angeles Times Washington Post News Service
lau: laundry
LAUA: Lloyd's Aviation Underwriters' Association
laughing gas: nitrous oxide (N_2O)
LAUK: Library Association of the United Kingdom
Lau Lib: Laurentian Library (Florence)
laun: launched
Launce: Lancelot
Launcelot Langstaff: pseudonym shared by Washington Irving, William Irving, and James K. Paulding when they published the *Salmagundi* essays
laund: launder; laundry
Laur: Laurence
Laura: World War II code name for Majuro, still in use by Americans and Marshallese islanders
Laurel: Pennsylvania's state flower is the Mountain Laurel
Laurence Templeton: Sir Walter Scott's pseudonym used in the publication of *Ivanhoe*
Laurie: Laurence
LAUSC: Linguistic Atlas of the United States and Canada
lav: lavatory
LAV: Linea Aeropostal Venezolana (Venezulean Airmail Line)
LAVC: Los Angeles Valley College
law.: lawyer; light assault weapon; low-altitude weapon
Law: Lawrence
LAW: League of American Wheelmen; League of American Writers; Legal Aid Warranty; Local Air Warning
Lawgiver of Ancient Greece: Solon of Athens
Law Lat: Law Latin
Lawr: Lawrence; Lawrencian
Lawrence of Arabia: Thomas Edward Lawrence
Law Rept: Law Report(s)
Lawrie: Lawrence
LAWRS: Limited Airport Weather Reporting System
LAWS: Leadership and World Society
Law West of the Pecos: Judge Roy Bean of Langtry, Texas, also known as the Hanging Judge because of the number of criminals he eliminated by hanging
lax.: laxative
LAX: Los Angeles, California (International Airport)
Laz: Lazarus
LAZ: Los Angeles Zoo
lb: landing barge; letter box; lifeboat; linoleum base; local battery; lumen band; pound
l-b: lemon-and-butter (sauce)
l & b: left and below
lb: *libra* (Latin—pound)
l.b.: *lectori benevolo* (Latin—to the kind reader)
LB: landing barge; Leonard Bernstein; Lloyd Brasileiro (Brazilian Steamship Line); Longview Bridge (Columbia River, Washington); Luther Burbank
L-B: Link-Belt
L v B: Ludwig van Beethoven
L.B.: *Baccalaureus Litterarum* (Latin—Bachelor of Letters)
LB & AL: Lever Brothers and Associates Limited
L-band: 390–1550 mc
lb ap: apothecaries' pound
L-bar: capital-L-shaped bar
lb av: avoirdupois pound
LBB: Lubbock, Texas (airport)
lbbsb: left bundle branch system block
Lbc: Lübeck
LBC: Liberian Broadcasting Corporation
lb cal: pound calorie
LBCC: Long Beach City College
LBCH: London Bankers' Clearing House
lbcd: left border of cardiac dullness
lb chu: pound centigrade heat unit
LBCM: Licentiate of Bandsmen's College of Music
lbd: left border of dullness; little black dress; lower-back disorder; lower bovine distemper
LBD: League of British Dramatists
L/Bdr: Lance Bombardier
L-beam: capital-L-shaped beam
lbf: pound-force
LBF: Louis Braille Foundation (for blind musicians)
lbf-ft: pound-force foot
lbf/in.²: pound-force per square inch
lb ft: pound foot

lb ft^2: pound per square foot
lb ft^3: pound per cubic foot
LBG: Paris, France (Le Bourget Airport)
lbh: length, breadth, height
LBHD: Long Beach Harbor Department
LBHS: Luther Burbank High School
LBI: Library Binding Institute; Licensed Beverage Industries; Lloyds Bank International
lb in.: pound inch
lb in.^{2}: pound per square inch
lb in.^{3}: pound per cubic inch
LBJ: Lyndon Baines Johnson—thirty-sixth President of the United States
LBJL: Lyndon Baines Johnson Library (Austin)
LBJSHP: Lyndon B. Johnson State Historic Park (Texas)
LBJTMC: Lyndon B. Johnson Tropical Medical Center (American Samoa)
LBK: landing barge, kitchen
lbm: lean body mass
lb m: pound mass
lb/m: pounds per minute
lb-mol: pound-mole (mass)
LBMS: London Boroughs Management Services
LBO: Lima, Peru, (Limatambo Airport)
lboe: lime-base oil emulsified
lbp: length between perpendiculars; low back pain; low blood pressure
LBP: Lester Bowles Pearson (Canada's eighteenth Prime Minister); London Borough Polytechnic
LBPL: Long Beach Public Library
lbr: labor; lumber
Lbr: Labrador; Librarian
lbs: pounds (from the Latin—*Librae)*
l.b.s.: *lectori benevolo salutem* (Latin—to the kind reader, greetings)
LBS: landing barge support; Libyan Broadcasting Service; Lifeboat Station; London Botanical Society
LBSC: Long Beach State College
LB & SCR: London, Brighton and South Coast Railway
LBSM: Licentiate of Birmingham and Midland Institute School of Music
lbs sq ft: pounds per square foot
lb t: pound(s) thrust; pound(s) troy
L v Bthvn: Ludwig van Beethoven
LBV: landing barge, vehicle
lbw: leg before wicket
lc: inductance-capacitance; laundry chute; lead-covered; left center; light case; line-carrying; load carrier; locked-closed; low carbon; lower case; single acetate single cotton
l-c: launch control; low calorie; low carbohydrate
l/c: letter of credit; lower center
l.c.: *loco citato* (Latin—in the place cited)
Lc: corrected middle latitude
LC: Lackawanna College; Ladycliff College; Lafayette College; Lake Central Airlines; Lakehead College; Lakeland College; Lambuth College; Lance Corporal; Lander College; landing craft; Lane College; Laredo College; Lassen College; L'Assumption College; Lawrence Colelge; Lee College; Legal Committee; Lesley College; Lewis College; Library of Congress; Limestone College; Lincoln College; Lindenwood College; line of communication; Linfield College; Livingstone College; Longwood College; Loras College; Louisburg College; Louisiana College; Loyola College; Luther College; Lycoming College; Lynchburg College
L-C: Liquid-Carbonic (Division of General Dynamics)
L of C: Library of Congress
L-et-C: Loir-et-Cher
LCA: Lake Carriers Association; Lake Central Airlines; landing craft—assault; Launcher Control Area; Library Club of America
lcal: lowercase alphabet length
lcat (LCAT): lecithin-cholesterol acyltransferase
L & C ATA: Laundry and Cleaners Allied Trades Association
lcb: longitudinal position of center of buoyancy
LCB: Liquor Control Board
LCBO: Liquor Control Board of Ontario
lcc: lateral center of gravity
LCC: landing craft, control (3-letter symbol); Lansing Community College; Launch Control Center; London County Council; Lower Columbia College
L & C C: Lewis and Clark College
LCcc: Library of Congress catalog card
LCCC: Lorain County Community College
lccs: low cervical caesarian section
lcd: liquid crystal display; lowest common denominator
LCD: Lord Chamberlain's Department; Lord Chancellor's Department
LCDHWIU: Laundry, Cleaning, and Dye House Workers International Union
lcdo: *licenciado* (Spanish—licensed)
Lcdo: *Licenciado* (Spanish—lawyer)
LCDs: Lower Court Decisions
lcdtl: load-compensated diode-transistor logic
lce: lance; left center entrance
LCE: Licentiate in Civil Engineering
lces: least-cost estimating and scheduling
lcf: least common factor; longitudinal position of center of flotation
LCF: landing craft, flak; launch control facility
LCFA: Lower California Fisheries Association
LCFTA: London Cattle Food Trade Association
lcg: liquid-cooled (under) garment; longitudinal position of center of gravity
LCGB: Locomotive Club of Great Britain
L Ch: Licentiate in Surgery
lchr: launcher
lci: locus of control interview
LCI: landing craft, infantry; Liquid Crystal Institute (Kent State University); Livestock Conservation Incorporated
LCJ: Lord Chief Justice
LCJ: *Louisville Courier-Journal*
LCJC: Lake City Junior College
Lcks: Locks (postal abbreviation)
lcl: less than carload lot; lifting condensation level; local(izer)
LCL: Licentiate in Common Law; Licentiate in Canon Law; Licentiate in Canonic Law
LCL: *La Casa del Libro* (Spanish—House of the Book)—Puerto Rico's typographic arts museum on San Juan's Calle del Cristo
LCLA: Lutheran Church Library Association

L-C-L bodies: Levinthal-Coles-Lillie bodies
LCLS: Livestock Commission Levy Scheme
lcm: lead-coated metal; least common multiple; left costal margin; limit-cycle monitor; lowest common multiple
lcm (LCM): lymphocytic choriomeningitis
LCM: landing craft, mechanized; London College of Music
LCMS: Launch Control and Monitoring System; Lutheran Church Missouri Synod
lcn: local civil noon
Lcn: Lincoln
LCN: *La Cosa Nostra* (Italian—Our Thing)—The Mafia
LCNM: Lehman Caves National Monument (Nevada)
LCNY: Linguistic Circle of New York
LCO: Launch Control Officer; London College of Osteopathy
lcoc: launch control officer's console
L Col: Lieutenant Colonel
lcp: last complete program; low-cost production
LCP: landing craft, personnel; Library Company of Philadelphia; Licentiate of the College of Preceptors; London College of Printing
LCPA: Lincoln Center for the Performing Arts
L Cpl: Lance Corporal
LCPS: Licentiate of the College of Physicians and Surgeons
LCP & SA: Licentiate of the College of Physicians and Surgeons of America
LCP & SO: Licentiate of the College of Physicians and Surgeons of Ontario
l/cr: letter of credit
l/cr: *lettre de crédit* (French—letter of credit)
LCR: landing craft, rubber
LCRA: Lower Colorado River Authority
LCRT: Lincoln Center Repertory Theater
lcs: launch-control simulator
LCS: landing craft, support
LCSA: Lewis and Clark Society of America
LCSH: *Library of Congress Subject Headings*
lct: less than truckload lot
LCT: ct: less than truckload lot
LCT: Laboratoire Central de Télécommunications (Central Télécommunications Laboratory); landing craft, tank; latest closing time; Local Civil Time; Loughsborough College of Technology
LCTC: Langlade County Teachers College; Leicester College of Technology and Commerce; Lewis and Clark Trail Commission
lcty: locality
lcu: launch-control unit; lower control unit
lcu: (LCU): large closeup
LCU: landing craft, utility
LCV: landing craft, vehicle
LCVP: landing craft, vehicle, personnel
lcx: launch complex
LCY: League of Communists of Yugoslavia
LCYC: Lemon Creek Yacht Club
LC zone: land conservation zone
ld: ladies day; land; lead; lethal dose; lid; lifeboat deck; light difference; line of departure; line of duty; load; load draft; low door; lower deck
l-d: low-density
l/d: length to diameter (ratio); life to drag (ratio)
l & d: loans and discounts; loss(es) and damage(s)
l.d.: *lepide dictum* (Latin—wittily related)
Ld: Leopold; Limited
LD: Labor (US department); line of departure; line of duty; Low Dutch; lower berth (double occupancy)
L/D: Letter of Deposit
L.D.: *Litterarum Doctor* (Latin—Doctor of Letters)
ld_{50}: median lethal dose
lda: left dorso-anterior
L^{da}: *Limitada* (Portuguese or Spanish—Limited); *Licenciada* (Spanish—lawyer)—feminine form of *L^{do}—Licenciado*
ldb: light distribution box
LDA: Lead Development Association
LDBHS: Louis D. Brandeis High School
ldc: long-distance call; lower dead center
LDC: Laundry and Dry Cleaning (union); Less Developed Countries; Light Direction Center; Local Defense Center
LD & C: Louis Dreyfus & Compagnie
LDCMMA: Laundry and Dry Cleaners Machinery Manufacturers Association
ldc's: less-developed countries
L Dent Sci: Licentiate in Dental Science
Lderry: Londonderry
LDF: Local Defense Force(s)
ldg: landing; loading; lodging
Ldg: Lodge (postal abbreviation)
ldg & dly: landing and delivery
Ldge: Lodge
ldgs: lodgings
ldh: lactic-acid dehydrogenase
Ld'H: *Légion* d'Honneur (French—Legion of Honor)
LDH: Ligue des Droits de l'Homme (League for the Rights of Man)
ldk: lower deck
ldl: low-density lipoprotein
ld lmt: load limit
LDMA: London Discount Market Association
Ld May: Lord Mayor
ld mk: landmark
Ldn: London; Londoner
L^{do}: *Licenciado* (Spanish—lawyer; licentiate holding master's degree)
LDO: Licensed Deck Officer
L-dopa: levodihydroxyphenylalanine (Parkinson's disease treatment drug)
LDOS: Lord's Day Observance Society
ldp: left dorso-posterior
Ldp: Ladyship; Lordship
LDP: Liberal Democratic Party (Japan)
ldr: launder; laundry; leader; ledger; lodger
l/d ratio: length to diameter ratio
LDRC: Lumber Dealers Research Council
L-drivers: learner-drivers
ldry: laundry
lds: loads
Lds: Leeds
LDS: Latter Day Saints (Church of Jesus Christ of); Licentiate in Dental Surgery
LDSc: Licentiate in Dental Science
LDSR: League of Distilled Spirits Rectifiers
LDV: Local Defense Volunteer
LDY: Leicestershire and Derbyshire Yeomanry
ldx: long-distance xerography
Ldy: Londonderry
le: leading edge; left eye; limit of error
l.e.: *lupus erythematosus* (skin disease)
Le: Lebanese; Lebanon
LE: light equipment; low explo-

sive
lea: leather
LEA: Local Education Authority; Loss Executives Association; Lutheran Education Association
LEAA: Lace and Embroidery Association of America; Law Enforcement Assistance Administration
LEAD: Law Students Exposing Advertising Deception
Leadbelly: Huddie Ledbetter
LEADER: Lehigh Automatic Device for Efficient Retrieval
LEADS: Law Enforcement Agencies Data System (Illinois)
Lead State: place-name nickname shared by Colorado and Missouri
Lea & F: Lea & Febiger
leaf(s): leaflet(s)
LEAJ: Law Enforcement and Administration of Justice (President's Commission on)
Leão do Mar: (Portuguese—Lion of the Sea)—the stormy Cape of Good Hope
leap.: liftoff elevation and azimuth programmer
LEAP: Loan and Educational Aid Program
LEAPS: Law Enforcement Agencies Processing System (Massachusetts); London Electronic Agency for Pay and Statistics
Lear: *The Tragedy of King Lear*
leaverats: leave rations
Leb: Lebanese; Lebanon
LEB: London Electricity Board
Leber's disease: congenital atrophy of the optic nerve
le bodies: lupus erythematosus bodies (LE bodies)
LEBS: London Emergency Bed Service
lec: lunar equipment conveyor
LEC: Livestock Equipment Council
LECE: *Ligue Européenne de Coopération Economique* (French—European League for Economic Cooperation)
le cells: lupus erythematosus cells (LE cells)
lech: lecher; lecherous; lechery
Le Corbu: Le Corbusiér
Le Corbusier: Charles Édouard Jeanneret-Gris
lect: lecture
lect.: *lectio* (Latin—lesson)
Lect: Lecturer
lectr: lecturer
'lectric: electric
led.: light-emitting dial; light-emitting diode(s)
Led: Ledbetter; Ledyard
L Ed: *Lawyer's Edition* (US Supreme Court Reports)
LED: Library Education Division (American Library Association)
LEDC: League for Emotionally Disturbed Children
Le Divin Poème: (French— The Divine Poem)—Scriabin's Symphony No. 3
Le Douainier: (French—The Custom House Officer)—nickname of Henri Rousseau the primitive painter
led's: light-emitting diodes
Lee: Leroy
Leedsloiner(s): native(s) of Leeds
Lee I: Leeward Islands
LEEP: Law Enforcement Education Program
Leewards: Leeward Islands
LEF: Life Extension Foundation; Lincoln Educational Foundation
LEF: *Liberté*, Egalité, Fraternité (Liberty, Equality, Fraternity—slogan of the French Revolution)
Lefty: Robert Grove
leg.: legal; legislative; legislature
leg.: *legato* (Italian—smoothly flowing)
Leg: Leghorn
Leg: *Legierung* (German—alloy)
LEG: Law Enforcement Group
legat: FBI agent or office working in an overseas legation of the United States; legation
leg com: legally committed
legg: *leggiero* (Italian—lightly and rapidly)
legis: legislative; legislature
legit: legitimate
Le Grand Siècle: (French—The Great Century)—the 1600s when France was founding her academies and Moliére was writing his comedies
legumes: *legumbres* (Spanish-American truncation—beans; greenstuff; vegetables)
LEG (UN): Legal Affairs department of United Nations)
leg. wt: legal weight
LEH: Licentiate in Ecclesiastical History
Leic: Leicester
leichtl: *leichtlöslich* (German—readily soluble)
Leics: Leicestershire
Leida: (Latin—Leiden)—Leyden
Leip: Lepzig
Le Is: Leeward Islands
Leit: Leitrim
LEIU: Law Enforcement Intelligence Unit
lej: longitudinal expansion joint
lel: lower explosive limit
LEL: Laureate in English Literature; Letitia Elizabeth Landon
LELDC: Law Enforcement Legal Defense Center
lem: lemon(ade)
lem (LEM): lunar excursion module
Lem: Lemuel
LeM: *Le Monde* (The World)—Paris
LEM: Lunar Excursion Module
LEMA: Lifting Equipment Manufacturers' Association
lemac: leading edge mean aerodynamic chord
lemo: lemonade
Lemonade Lucy: Mrs Lucy Ware Webb Hayes—wife of President Rutherford B. Hayes—who served only non-intoxicating fruit drinks while at the White House
LEMSIP: Laboratory for Experimental Medicine and Surgery in Primates
Len: Leningrad, formerly Petrograd, formerly St. Petersburg
Lena: Magdalen(a)
LENA: Lower Eastside Neighborhoods Association
Lena River City: Yukutsk, Siberia
Lenin: Vladimir Ilich Ulyanov
Leningrad: Shostakovich's Symphony No. 7
Leninpor: Lenin Port (Leningrad Harbor)
lenit.: *leniter* (Latin—gently)
Len Lib: Lenin Library (Moscow)
Lenny: Leonard
Lens-Grinder Philosopher: Benedictus de Spinoza
Lenson: Levensohn; Levenson; Levinson; Levinsky
lento: *lentando* (Italian—increasingly slow)
Leo: Leonard; Leonese; Leonidas; Leonine; Leopold; Leopoldville
LEO: Leopoldville, Congo (airport)
Leonard Q. Ross: (pseudonym—Leo Rosten)
leopon: leopard + lioness (hybrid offspring of male leopard and lioness)
lep: lepton (collective term embracing anti-neutrino, electron, neutrino, photon, posi-

tron); lowest effective power
LEP: Library of Exact Philosophy
lep. dict.: *lepide dictum* (Latin—well said)
LEPMA: Lithographic Engravers and Plate Makers Association
Lepmus: *Lepramuseet* (Norwegian—Leprosy Museum)—Bergen museum reflecting Dr Armanser Hansen's struggle against leprosy also known as Hansen's disease
LEPORE: Long-Term and Expanded Program of Oceanic Research and Exploration
LEPRA: Leprosy Relief Association (British)
lept (LEPT): long-endurance patrolling torpedo
Lepto: *Leptospira*
Ler: Lerida
LeRC: Lewis Research Center (NASA)
Le Roi Soleil: (French—The Sun King)—Louis XIV
les: lesbian; local excitatory state
Les: Lescombe; Lesley; Leslie; Lester
LES: Launch Escape System; Lincoln Experimental Satellite
LESA: Lunar Exploration System—Apollo
Les Adieux: Beethoven's Piano Sonata No. 23 in E flat (opus 81a) *Les Adieux, l'absence, et le retour*—the farewell, the absence, and the return
Le Sage: (French—The Wise)—Charles V
lesb: lesbian(ism)
Lesbian Poet: Sappho the poetess of Lesbos
lesbo: lesbian (Lesbos-type woman); lesbianism
Les L: *Licensie es Lettres:* (French—Licentiate in Letters)
Les Lip: Leslie Lipson (most articulate of commentators about overseas newspapers)
Leso: Lesotho (formerly Basutoland)
LESS: Least-cost Estimating and Scheduling Survey
Les Sc: *Licensie es Sciences:* (French—Licentiate in Science)
Lesser Antilles: Leeward and Windward Islands extending from the Netherlands Antilles (Aruba, Bonaire, Curaçao) to the Virgin Islands
Lesser Sundas: Lesser Sunda Islands east of Bali in Indonesia
Lester: Leicester
let.: letter; linear energy transfer
Let: Lettish (Latvian)
lett: *letteratura* (Italian—literature); *letterlijk* (Dutch—literally)
letch: slang shortcut—lecher: lecheress; lecherous; lecherous feeling for; lechery
let's: let us
letterk: *letterkunde* (Dutch—literature)
Letts: Lettish peoples (Latvians)
Letty: Leticia
Letz: Letzeburgesch (Flemish dialect of Luxembourg)
leu (LEU): leucine (amino acid)
lev: lever
lev: *levert* (Norwegian—delivered)
lev.: *levis* (Latin—light)
lev (LEV): lunar excursion vehicle
Lev: The Book of Leviticus; Leo; Leon
Leviathan of Literature: Dr Samuel Johnson
Le Vigan: Robert Coquillaud
levis: Levi Strauss' reinforced denim workclothes but particulary dungaree trousers with heavily-stitched-and-riveted pockets
Lew: Lewis; Llewellyn
le'ward: leeward
Lewis Carroll: Charles Lutwidge Dodgson
Lewis Grassic Gibbon: pseudonym of J(ames) L(eslie) Mitchell
lex: lexical; lexicographer; lexicography; lexicon
Lex: Lexington
LEX: Lexington, Kentucky (airport)
lexico: lexicographer
lexicog: lexicographer; lexicography
lexig(s): lexigram(s)—word symbol(s)
l/ext: lower extremity
Ley: Leyden
LEY: Liberal European Youth
Leyd: Leyden
lf: lawn faucet; life float; light face type; linoleum floor; low frequency (30–300 kc)
lf (LF): line feed character (data processing)
Lf: Loaf (postal abbreviation)
LF: Lindbergh Field
lfa: left fronto-anterior
LFB: London Fire Brigade
LFBC: London Federation of Boys' Clubs
lfc: laminar flow control
l-fc: low-frequency current
LFC: Lutheran Free Church
lfd: least fatal dose; low fat diet
lfd: *laufend* (German—current; consecutive)
Lfd: *Laufend* (German—current)
LFE: Laboratory For Electronics
Lfg (Lfrg): *Lieferung* (German—installment; party delivery)
lfl: lower flammable limit
lf/mf: low-frequency medium-frequency
lfo: low-frequency oscillator
LFO: Licentiate of the Faculty of Osteopathy
lfp: left fronto-posterior
LFP: Lindbergh Field Plant (Convair)
LFPP: Louisiana Family Planning Program
LFPS: Licentiate of the Faculty of Physicians and Surgeons
LFR: inshore fire-support ship (naval symbol)
LFRC: League for Fighting Religious Coercion
lfrd: low-friction reliability deviation
LFS: amphibious fire-support ship (naval symbol)
lft: left fronto-transverse
l/ft^2: lumens per square foot
LFTU: Landing Force Training Unit
LFU: Light Fighting Unit
lg: landing; landing gear; languages(s); length; long
l/g: locked gate
Lg: Landgrave; Landgraviate
LG: Leipzig Gewandhaus; Low German
L-et-G: Lot-et-Garonne
LGA: New York, New York (La Guardia Airport)
LGB: Long Beach, California (airport)
LGC: Laboratory of the Government Chemist
L-G C: Lockheed-Georgia Company
LGCC: Letchworth Garden City Corporation
lgd: leaderless group discussion
lge: large
LGEB: Local Government Examination Board
L-Gen: Lieutenant-General
L Ger: Low German
Lg of H-D: Landgrav(iate) of Hesse-Darmstadt
Lg of H-K: Landgrav(iate) of Hesse-Kassel
LGIO: Local Government Information Office

LGk: Late Greek
LGM: Lloyd's Gold Medal
LGM: *Laboratorium voor Grondmechanica* (Dutch—Soil Mechanics Laboratory)
LGMB: Lady Godiva Marching Band
Lgn: Leghorn
LGO: Lamont Geological Observatory (Columbia University)
LGOC: London General Omnibus Company
lgp: liquefied petroleum gas
lgr: ligroin
L Gr: Late Greek
LGRs: Local Government Reports
Lgs: Lagos
LGSM: Licentiate of the Guildhall School of Music
Lgt: Light (postal abbreviation)
LGTB: Local Government Training Board
lgth: length
lg tn: long ton
lg tpr: long taper
lg-type ed: large-type edition
lgv: lymphogranuloma venereum (venereal disease)
LGW: London, England (Gatwick Airport); Longines-Wittnauer (watches)
lh: left hand; lower half
lh (LH): left hand; luteinizing hormone
lH: *linke Hand:* (German—left hand)
LH: lighthouse; Lufthansa (airline)
L.H.: left hand
L + H: Lamport & Holt (Line)
lhb: left halfback
lhdc: lateral homing depth charge
L d'H: Légion d'Honneur—(French—Legion of Honor (decoration))
L o H: Library of Hawaii (Honolulu)
LH_2: liquid hydrogen
L-w-H: Lewis-with-Harris (Outer Hebrides)
lha: lower-half assembly
LHA: landing ship, helicopter, assault; local hour angle
LHAR: London-Hamburg- Antwerp- Rotterdam (range of ports)
LHAs: multipurpose amphibious-warfare ships (naval symbol)
LHC: Lord High Chancellor
LHCJEA: London and Home Counties Joint Electric Authority
L.H.D.: *Litterarum Humanorum Doctor* (Latin—Doctor of Human Letters); *In Litteris Humanioribus Doctor* (Latin—Doctor in Humane Letters)
lh dr: lefthand drive
LHe: liquid helium
L Heb: Late Hebrew
LHG: Library History Group
LHI: Ligue Homeopathique Internationale (International Homeopathic League)
L-hinge: capital-L-shaped hinge
lhm: letterhead memo(randum)
LHMC: London Hospital Medical College
LHO: Lovestock Husbandry Office(r)
lhr: lumen hour(s)
LHR: London, England (Heathrow Airport)
L & HR: Lehigh and Hudson River (railroad)
lhrf (LHRF): luteinizing hormone releasing factor
lhs: lefthand side
LHS: Lafayette High School
LHSC: Lock Haven State College
lhsv: liquid hourly space velocity
LHT: Lord High Treasurer
lh th: lefthand thread
LHW: League of Hispanic Women; lower high water
LHWI: lower high water interval
lhwnt: lowest high water neap tides
li: link; lithograph; lithographer; lithography
Li: lithium
LI: Leeward Islands; Liberia; Liberian; Lions International; Long Island (L.I.)
LI: *Lydveldid Island* (Icelandic—Republic of Iceland)
L-I: Loire-Inférieure
LIA: Lead Industries Association; Leather Industries of America; Lebanese International Airways; Ligue Internationale d' Arbitrage (International Arbitration League); Long Island Association
LIAA: Life Insurance Association of America
LIAMA: Life Insurance Agency Management Association
Liar of Biblical Antiquity: Ananias, struck dead for lying, according to *The Acts* in the New Testament
LIAT: Leeward Islands Air Transport
lib: liberal; liberalism; liberation(ist); libertarian(ism); liberty; librarian; library
lib.: *liber* (Latin—book); *libra* (Latin—pound)
Lib: Liberal; Liberal Party; Liberty Party; Libya; Libyan
Lib: *Libano* (Italian—Lebanon)
Líb: *Líbano* (Portuguese or Spanish—Lebanon)
LIB: Let's Ignite Bras
LIBBA: Long Island Beach Buggy Association
Libby: Elizabeth
lib cat.: library catalog
Lib Cong: Library of Congress
libe: librarian; library
lib ed: library edition
Libertador de Chile: (Spanish—Liberator of Chile)—Bernardo O'Higgins
Libertybellsville: Philadelphia
LIBGIS: Library General Information Survey
Lib-Lab: Liberal-Labour (Australian coalition)
libr: librarian; library
libr: *libretto* (Italian—opera or oratorio text)
Library Builder: Andrew Carnegie
Lib(s): Liberal(s)
libst: *librettist* (Italian—libretto author)
Lib UN: Library of the United Nations (New York headquarters)
Lic: Licentiate
LIC: Lands Improvement Company
Lic: *Licenciado* (Spanish—lawyer; licentiate holding master's degree)
Lic D: *Licenciado Don* (Spanish—Sir Lawyer)
LICeram: Licentiate of the Institute of Ceramics
licm: left intercostal margin
Lic Med: Licentiate in Medicine
Lic Phil: Licentiate in Philosophy
LICTBOSS: Life-Cycle Theory of Bureaucratic Ossfication
Lic Theol: Licentiate in Theology
LID: League for Industrial Democracy
L & ID: London and India Docks
lidar: laser-impulsed radar; light detection and ranging (laser-beam air pollution or smog measuring device)
LIDC: Lead Industries Development Council
lidoc: lidocaine (xylocain)
LIE: Liberal Intellectual Establishment (Philip Wylie's acronymic description of the befuddled and often nonsensical liberals of his time; the Old Left; the so-called New Left)
Liech: Liechtenstein

Lief: *Lieferung* (German—issue)
LIEMA: Long Island Electronics Manufacturers Association
Lieut: Lieutenant
Lieut Col: Lieutenant Colonel
Lieut Comdr: Lieutenant Commander
Lieut Gen: Lieutenant General
Lieut Gov: Lieutenant Governor
lif: left iliac fossa
LIF: Lone Indian Fellowship
LIFE: Ladies Involved For Education; League for International Food Education
Life Sta: Lifeboat Station (US Coast Guard)
LI Fire Eng: Licentiate of the Institution of Fire Engineers
lifmop: linearly frequency-modulated pulse
lifo: last in, first out
lig: ligament; ligature
Lig: Limoges
Lige: Elijah
liger: offspring of lion and tigress
light.: lighting; lightning
Light of the Ages: Moses ben Maimon of Cordoba also known as Maimonades
Light of Asia: Gautama Buddha
Lighthorse Harry: Major General Henry (Lighthorse Harry) Lee, USA—father of Robert E. Lee
lignite: brown coal
LIHDC: Low Income Housing Development Corporation
lil: lilliputian; little
li'l: little
Lil: Lilian; Lillian; Lily
LIL: Lunar International Laboratory (proposed in 1961 by Dr Theodore von Karman)
Lilac: New Hampshire state flower and nickname sometimes given New Hampshire girls recalling the Purple Lilac of this New England State
LILCO: Long Island Lighting Company
Lillian Nordica: Lilly Norton
Lillian Russell: Helen Louise Leonard
Lillibet: Elizabeth
Lilly: Lilian; Lillian
lilo: last in, last out
LILS: Lead-in-Light System (airport term)
Lily: Utah state flower the Sego Lily
Lily of France: symbolic *fleur de lis* or lily flower
Lily-Lilo: Rosalie Texier
lim: limber; limit(er); linear-induction motor(s)
Lim: Limerick
LIM: Lima, Peru (Callao International Airport)
Lima: code word for letter L
LIMAC: Linden Industrial Mutual Aid Council
lim dat: limiting date
lime: calcium oxide (CaO)
Limejuicer: British sailor
limestone: calcium carbonate ($CaCO_3$)
limewater: calcium-hydroxide solution—$Ca(OH)_2$; limejuice and water mixture
Limey(s): Limejuicer(s)—British sailor(s) or ship(s); nickname derived from their use of limejuice to ward off scurvy
limnol: limnology
limo: lemonade; limousine
limon: lime-and-lemon (hybrid citrus fruit)
limp: limp cloth binding; limp cloth bound
l'Impériale: Haydn's Symphony No. 53 in D major
LIMRA: Life Insurance Marketing and Research Association
limvr: linear-induction motor vehicle research
lin: lineal; linear
lín: *línea* (Spanish—line)
Lin: Lincoln; Linda; Lindenberg(er); Lindley; Limdolfo; Limdon; Lindsay; Linley; Linnaeus; Linsley, Linton; Linus
L i N: ***Lokalhistorisk institutt*** *Norge* (Norwegian Local History Institute)
LIN: Linjeflyg (Swedish airline); Milan, Italy (Linate Airport)
Lina: Angelina; Carolina; Caroline
linac: linear accelerator
Linc: Lincoln
LINC: Learning Institute of North Carolina
Linc Coll: Lincoln College—Oxford
Lincoln's State: Illinois
Lincs: Lincolnshire
LINCS: Language Information Network and Clearinghouse System
LINDE: Linde Air Products
Lindy: Colonel Charles A. Lindbergh
Line: The Line—the Equator
Lines: Line Islands (Caroline, Christmas, Fanning, Flint, Malden, Starbuck, Vostock, Washington)
L-Infre: Loire-Inférieure
lin ft: linear feet; linear foot
ling: linguist(ics)
linim: liniment
Linn: Linné; Linnaeus
Linnaeus: Carl von Linné
lino: linoleum; linotype; linotypist
linol: linoleum
LINOSCO: Libraries of North Staffordshire in Cooperation
L Inst Phys: Licentiate of the Institute of Physics
LINTAS: Lever's International Advertising Service
LINWR: Lake Ilo National Wildlife Refuge (North Dakota)
Linz: Mozart's Symphony No. 36 in C major named for the Austrian town of Linz
LIO: Lionel Corporation (stock exchange symbol); Lions International Organization
LIOB: Licentiate of the Institute of Building
Lion of the North: King Gustavus Adolphus of Sweden
Lion's Gate: harbor entrance of Vancouver, British Columbia
lip.: life insurance policy
Liparis: Lipari Islands
LIPM: Lister Institute of Preventive Medicine
lipo: lipogram(matic)
Lippy: Leo Ernest Durocher
lip sync: lip synchronization (in sound films)
liq: liquid; liquor
liq f rkt: liquid fuel rocket
liqn: *liquidación* (Spanish—liquidation)
liguid.: liguidation
LIR: Library of International Relations
lira.: loft-type infrared analysis
LIRA: Linen Industry Research Association
lirbm: liver, iron, red bone marrow
LIRI: Leather Industries Research Institute
LIRR: Long Island Railroad
lis: lobar in situ
Lis: Lisbon
LIS: Liberian Information Service; Lisbon, Portugal (airport); Long Island Sound
LISA: Library and Information Science Abstracts
Lisb: *Lisboa* (Portuguese or Spanish—Lisbon); *Lisbona* (Italian—Lisbon)
Lisbeth: Elisabeth; Eliza; Elizabeta; Elizabeth
LISM: Licentiate of the Incorporated Society of Musicians
lisp.: list processor (computer language)
LISPA: Long Island Sound Pilots Association

LISS: London Institute of Strategic Studies
LIST: Library and Information Services—Tees-side
LIST: *Library and Information Science Today*
lit.: liter; literal; literally; literary; literature; litter; little
l it: lire italiane (Italian lire)
lit.: *litterae* (Latin—letters)
Lit: *Litvak* (Yiddish—Lithuanian)—person of Judaic origin from Lithuania or nearby regions
LIT: Light Intratheater Transport (aircraft); Little Rock, Arkansas (airport)
lite: light
lith: lithograph; lithography; lithology
Lith: Lithuania; Lithuanian
litharge: lead oxide (PbO)
litho: lithograph
lithol: lithology
Litt.B.: *Litterarum Baccalaureus* (Latin—Bachelor of Letters)
Litt.D.: *Litterarum Doctor* (Latin—Doctor of Letters)
Little: Little, Brown
Little: Schubert's Symphony No. 6 in C
Little America: Antarctic camp at the edge of the Ross Ice Shelf and the Bay of Whales where Admiral Byrd headquartered; London's Grosvenor Square where John Adams lived at No. 9 when he was America's first ambassador to Great Britain; now site of the U.S. Embassy
Little Britain: Armorica or Brittany in northern France
Little Corporal: five-foot-high Napoleon Bonaparte (*Le Petit Caporal*)
Little Denmark: Solvang, California
Little Egypt: delta country of southern Illinois around Cairo and the confluence of the Ohio and Mississippi
Little England of the Caribbean: Barbados
Little Flower: Fiorello H. La Guardia
Little Giant: Knute Nelson—intellectually alive but physically small populist governor of Minnesota; oratorically gifted Senator Stephen Douglas of Illinois
Little Havana: Cuban-refugee-populated sections of Miami, Florida
Little Holland: Garibaldi, Oregon
Little Ida: Idaho—smallest of the western states
Little Italy: Italian section of any American or Canadian city
Little Joe: Apollo spacecraft booster designed and produced by General Dynamics, Convair
Little John: surface-to-surface rocket produced by Emerson Electric
Little Lad of Landau: American political cartoonist Thomas (Th) Nast born in Landau, Germany
Little Lunnon: Colorado Springs, Colorado (where so many Britishers abide)
Little Neddies: Economic Development Committees
Little Paradise: Queen Victoria's nickname for the Isle of Wight
Little Rhody: Rhode Island's official nickname
Little Russian: Tchaikovsky's Symphony No. 2 in C minor
Little's disease: congential spastic paralysis
Little Sure Shot: Annie Oakley (Mrs Frank Butler)
Little Tokyo: Japanese section of any American or Canadian city
Little Van: President Martin Van Buren
Little Van Dyke: Gonzales Cocx—Flemish portrait painter who imitated the style of Van Dyke but painted family groups on small canvases
Little Van's Lady: Hannah Van Buren—wife of President Martin Van Buren
Litt. M.: Master of Letters
Lits: Lithuanians; Litvaks
litur: liturgical; liturgy
liturg: liturgical; liturgistic; liturgy
litz: litzendraht (wire)
LIU: Long Island University
LIUNA: Laborers International Union of North America
liv: liver
liv: *le livre* (French—book) *la livre* (French—pound)
Liv: Liverpool
Liv: Titus Livius (Roman historian often referred to as Livy)
Live Oak State: Florida
Liver: Liverpool; Liverpudlian(s)
Living Declaration of Independence: Thomas Paine
livr: *livraison* (French—issue of a journal; part of a book or serial)
liv st: *livre sterling* (French—pound sterling)
Livy: Roman historian Titus Livius
lix: lixiviation
liz: Lizard; lizzie (as in *tin lizzie*, an old Ford Automobile)
Liz(a): Eliza(beth)
Lizbeth: Elizabeth
Lizzy: Elizabeth
lj: life jacket
LJ: Libby, McNeil & Libby (stock exchange symbol); Lord Justice; Sierra Leone Airways (2-letter coding)
LJ: *laufen Jahre* (German—current year)
LJ: *Library Journal*
LJC: Lackawanna Junior College; Laredo Junior College; Lincoln Junior College
LJMCA: La Jolla Museum of Contemporary Art
LJ/SLJ: *Library Journal/School Library Journal*
LJT: Lear jet airplane
lk: link
Lk: Lake (postal abbreviation); Luke
LK: Lockheed Aircraft Corporation (stock exchange symbol)
LKAB: Luossavaara-Kiirunavaara Aktiebolag (iron-ore mines in Luossa-Kiiruna range of northern Sweden)
LKB: Link-Belt Company (stock exchange symbol)
lkd: locked
lkg: locking
lkg & bkg: leakage and breakage
LKGR: Lake Kyle Game Reserve (Rhodesia)
LK & PRR: Lahaina-Kaanapali and Pacific Railroad
lkr: locker
Lkr: Landskrona
lks: liver, kidney, spleen
Lks: Lakes (postal abbreviation)
lkt: lookout
Lkw: *Lastkraftwagen* (German—lorry; truck)
lkwash: lockwasher
ll: light lock; live load; lower lid
'll: (contraction of till and will)
ll: *lectiones* (Latin—readings); *llegada* (Spanish—arrival)
l/l: library labels; line-by-line; lower left; lower limit
l & l: leave and liberty
LL: Lebanese pound; Lending Library; Loftleidir (Icelandic Airlines); Lord Lieutenant; Low Latin
L/L: *Lutlang* (Norwegian—limit-

ed company)

LLA: Lend-Lease Administration; Luther League of America

Llanfairp: Llanfairpwllgwyngll-gogershwyrrndro-bwllabtysil-iogogoch (Welsh place-name meaning the Church of St. Mary near the Raging Whirlpool and the Church of St. Tysilio by the Red Cave)—probably the longest word in any of the world's 2700 languages and well deserving of abbreviation

llano: (Spanish—plain; prairie, as in Llano Estacado)

L Lat: Late Latin; Low Latin

llb: long-leg brace

LLB: Little League Baseball

LL.B.: *Legum Baccalaureus* (Latin—Bachelor of Laws)

LLBA: *Language and Language Behavior Abstracts*

llbcd: left lower border of cardiac dullness

LLBO: Liquor License Board of Ontario

llc: lower left center

ll. cc.: *locis citatis* (Latin—in the places cited)

LLCM: Licentiate of the London College of Music

LLCO: Licentiate of the London College of Osteopathy

LLD factor: *Lactobacillus lactis* Dorner factor (vitamin B_{12})

LL.D.: *Legum Doctor* (Latin—Doctor of Laws)

lle: left lower extremity

lle: *llegada* (Spanish—arrival)

LLEI: *Lincoln Library of Essential Information*

L Lett: Licentiate of Letters

LLF: Laubach Literacy Fund

lli: latitude and longitude indicator

LLI: Lord Lieutenant of Ireland

LLJ: Leaf Library of Judaica

LLJJ: Lords Justices

lll: left lower limb; left lower lobe; light load line; loose-leaf ledger; low-level logic

l/ll: line-by-line libretto

LLL: Lutheran Laymen's League

LLL: *Love's Labour's Lost*

lllb: left long-leg brace

LLLI: La Leche League International

llll: left lower lung lobe

llltv: low light-level television

llm: localized leucocyte mobilization

LLI: Laubach Literacy International; Lord Lieutenant of Ireland

LL. M.: *Legum Magister* (Latin—Master of Laws)

LLN: League for Less Noise

LLNNR: Loch Leven National Nature Reserve (Scotland)

LLNWR: Long Lake National Wildlife Refuge (North Dakota)

Lloyd's: *Lloyd's Register of Shipping*

L L & P of H: Life, Liberty, and the Pursuit of Happiness (original draft of the *Declaration of Independence* read: "Life, Liberty, and the Pursuit of Profit")

LLPI: Linen and Lace Paper Institute

llq: left lower quadrant

llr: line of least resistance; load-limiting resistor

llrv (LLRV): lunar landing research vehicle

LLS: Lunar Logistics System

LLSS: Low-Level Sounding System

llsv (LLSV): lunar logistics system vehicle

llti: long lead time items

llltv: low-light-level television

llu: lending library unit

LLU: Loma Linda University

LLUU: Laymen's League—Unitarian Universalist

llv (LLV): lunar landing vehicle

llw: lower low water (LLW); low-level waste

LLWI: lower low water interval

llwl: light load water line

Lly: Llanelly

llyp: long-leaf yellow pine

lm: land mine; light metal(s); liquid metal(s); long meter; longitudinal muscle; lower motor; lumen(s)

l/m: lines per minute

lm: *livello del mare* (Italian—sea level)

l.m.: *locus monumenti* (Latin—place of the monument)

Lm: middle latitude

LM: Legion of Merit; Liggett Myers Tobacco (stock exchange symbol); Lincoln Memorial; Lord Mayor; Lunar Module

L.M.: Licentiate in Midwifery

L & M: Linotype and Machinery

lma: left mento-anterior

LMA: Last Manufacturers Association; League for Mutual Aid; Lingerie Manufacturers Association; London-Midlands Association

LMAC: Labor-Management Advisory Committee

LMAGB: Locomotive and Allied Manufacturers' Association of Great Britain

LMBA: London Master Builders' Association

LMBC: Liverpool Marine Biological Committee

LMBP: Lake Manyas Bird Paradise (Turkey)

lmc: liquid-metal cycle; low middling clause

LMC: Lake Michigan College; Liberia Mining Company; Lloyd's Machinery Certificate

LMCA: Lorry Mounted Crane Association

LMCC: Licentiate of the Medical Council of Canada

lmd: local medical doctor

LMDC: Lawyers Military Defense Committee

lme: liquid-metal embrittlement

LME: London Metal Exchange

LMEC: Liquid Metal Engineering Center (AEC)

L Med: Licentiate in Medicine

L Med Ch: Licentiate in Medicine and Surgery

LMEE: Light Military Electronic Equipment (department of General Electric)

lmfbr: liquid-metal fast-breeder reactor

lmfr: liquid metal fuel reactor

lm/ft²: lumen per square foot

Lmg: *Leichtesmachinengewehr* (German—light machine gun)

LMG: light machine gun

LMH: Lady Margaret Hall—Oxford

lm hormone: lipid mobilizing hormone

lm-hr: lumen-hour

LMI: Lawn Mower Institute; Logistics Management Institute

l/min: liters per minute

LMIS: Labor Market Information System

lml: left mediolateral

LML: Lerner Marine Laboratory

LMLA: Lizzadro Museum of Lapidary Arts

LMLI: Liberty Mutual Life Insurance

lm/lrv: lunar module/lunar roving vehicle (LM/LRV)

lmm: locator at middle marker (compass)

l/mm: lines per millimeter

lm/lm²: lumen per square meter

LMM: Library Microfilms and Materials

lmmi: like mamma made it

lmn: lineman; lower motor neu-

ron
LMNP: Lake Manyara National Park (Tanzania)
LMNRA: Lake Mead National Recreation Area (Arizona and Nevada)
lmo: lens-modulated oscillator; light machine oil
LMO: London Meteorological Office
lmp: last menstrual period; left mento-posterior
LMP: *Literary Market Place* (Directory of American Book Publishers)
LMPA: Library and Museum of the Performing Arts (Lincoln Center, New York City)
L Mq: Lourenço Marques
LMR: London Midland Region—British Railways
LMRC: London Medical Research Council
LMRCP: Licentiate in Midwifery of the Royal College of Physicians
LMRSH: Licentiate Member of the Royal Society for the Promotion of Health
lm's: lunar modules (LMs)
lm/s: lumen per second
LMS: Licentiate in Medicine and Surgery; London Mathematical Society
LMSA: Labor Management Services Administration
LMSC: Lockheed Missiles & Space Company
LMSD: Lockheed Missile and Space Division
LMSSA: Licentiate in Medicine and Surgery of the Society of Apothecaries
lmt: left mento-transverse
LMT: Local Mean Time
LMTA: London Master Typefounders' Association
lmtd: logarithmic mean temperature difference
LMUM: Ludwig-Maximilians-Universität München (University of Munich)
L Mus: Licentiate in Music
L Mus TCL: Licentiate in Music—Trinity College of Music
LMVUS: League of Men Voters of the United States
lm/w: lumen per watt
ln: liaison
Ln: Lane
LN: Air Liban (Lebanese Airlines); League of Nations; Napierian logarithm (symbol)
L & N: Leeds & Northrup; Louisville & Nashville (railroad)
L of N: League of Nations
LN_2: liquid nitrogen
LNA: Liberian National Airways; Libyan News Agency
LNC: Leith Nautical College
LNDC: Lesotho National Development Corporation
Lndg: Landing
lndrs: laundress
lndry: laundry
L & NE: Lehigh & New England (railroad)
LNER: London and North Eastern Railway
lng: lining; liquefied natural gas
LNG tanker: liquied-natural-gas tanker
LNHS: London Natural History Society
LNI: *Lega Navale Italiana* (Italian Naval League)
LNLA: Lithuanian National League of America
lnmp: last normal menstrual period
LNNP: Lake Nakuru National Park (Kenya)
LNNR: Lindisfarne National Nature Reserve (England)
LNOC: Libya National Oil Company
L-note: $50 bill
LNP: Lamington National Park (Queensland); Lincoln NP (South Australia); London Northern Polytechnic
lnpf: lymph node permeability factor
LNR: Loteni Nature Reserve (South Africa)
Lnrk: Lanark
LNS: Land Navigation System
LNT: Leo Nicholas Tolstoy
Lntl: lintel
lnu: last name unknown
LNU: League of Nations Union
LNWR: Lacassine National Wildlife Refuge (Louisiana); Lacreek NWR (South Dakota); London and North Western Railway; Lostwood NWR (North Dakota); Loxahatchee NWR (Florida)
lo: local; local oscillator; locked open; low; low(er) order; lubricating oil; lubrication order
'lo: hello
lo': look
Lo: low (gear)
Lo: *Lordag* (Danish—Lord's Day)—Saturday
LO: Launch Operator; Liaison Office(r); Lick Observatory (Mount Hamilton, California); Louisville Orchestra; Lowell Observatory (Flagstaff, Arizona); Lubrication Order
LO: *Landsorganisationen* (leading trade union in Norway and Sweden)
L/O: Letter of Offer
LO_2: liquid oxygen
loa: leave of absence; left occiput anterior; length overall
LOA: Light Observation Aircraft; Lithuanian Organists Alliance
loadg & dischg: loading and discharging
loadicator: computerized ship-loading indicator
loan/A: vessel(s) loaned to Army
loan/C: vessel(s) loaned to Coast Guard
loan/m: vessel(s) loaned to miscellaneous governmental activities (Maritime Academy)
loan/s: vessel(s) loaned to states
lob: line of balance
LOB: Launch Operations Building; Loyal Order of the Boar; Loyal Order of Boors; Loyal Order of Bores
lobal: long base-line buoy
lobar: long baseline radar
loboto: lobotomy
lob(s): lobster(s)
loc: locate; location
l-o-c: letter of credit
LOC: Lyric Opera of Chicago
lo-cal: low calorie
locat: location; low-altitude clear-air turbulence
LOCATE: Library of Congress Automation Techniques Exchange
loc.cit.: *loco citato* (Latin—in the place cited)
loc. dol.: *loco dolenti* (Latin—to the painful spot)
Lock City: Stamford, Connecticut
loc. laud.: *loco laudato* (Latin—cited in the approved place)
locn: location
loco: locomotion; locomotive
loc. primo cit.: *loco primo citato* (Latin—in the place first cited)
locpuro: local purchase order
LOCS: Librascope Operations Control System
loc. supra cit.: *loco supra citato* (Latin—in the place cited above)
locum tens.: *locum tenens* (Latin—temporary position)
locuz: *locuzione* (Latin—phrase)
lod: line of duty
lo-d: low-density
LOD: Launch Operations Directorate

lodestone: magnetic iron oxide; Fe_3O_4: magnetite
lodor: loaded (vessel) awaiting orders or assignment
LOEE: Loyal Order of Overtime Experts
lof: lecherous old fool; lowest operating frequency
L-O-F: Libbey-Owens-Ford
lo-fi: low fidelity (low-quality sound reproduction)
Lofotens: Lofoten Islands
loft.: low-frequency radio telescope
lofti: low-frequency trans-ionosphere (research satellite)
Loftleidir: Icelandic Airlines
log.: logarithm; logic; logical
LOG: Legion of Guardsmen
logair: logistics transport by air
logairnet: logistics air network
logan(s): loganberry; loganberries
Log Com: Logistical Command; Logistics Command
$log._e$: logarithm to the base e
logel: logic-generating language
logg: loggerhead; loggia; logging; log glass
logie: killogie
loglan: logical language
logland: logistics transport by land
logo: logogram [initial letter, number, or symbol used as an abbreviation or as part of an abbreviation as in Q & A (question and answer) 3M (Minnesota Mining and Manufacturing Company), ¢ (cents)]; logotype (two or more type characters cast as one piece of type, as in *and, on, re, the,* or as shown in many trademarks and trade names cast as one piece)
logol: logological; logologically; logologist; logology
logr: logistical ration; logistics ratio
Logr: Logroño
logsea: logistics transport by sea
logsup: logistical support; logistics support
$log._{10}$: logarithm to the base 10
loh (LOH): light observation helicopter
loi: loss on ignition
LOI: Lunar Orbit Insertion
loib: lunar orbit insertion burn
loid: celluloid (strip used by burglars to unlock doors)
lo-J: low inertia
loktal: locked octal tube
lol: length of lead (actual); little old lady
LOL: Lobitos Oilfields Limited
lola: lollapalooza (excellent or extraordinary person or thing)
Lola: Dolores
Lola Montez: stage name of Marie Dolores Eliza Rosanna Gilbert also known as the Comtesse de Lansfeld, Mrs Heald, Mrs Hull, and Mrs James
lolli: lollipop
lom: locater at outer marker (compass)
Lom: Columbus
LOM: Loyal Order of Moose
LOMA: Life Office Management Association
Lomb: Lombard; Lombardian; Lombardy
lo mi: low mileage
Lon: Alonso; London
LON: London, England (London-Central Airport)
Lond: London; Londonderry; Londoner(s)
Lond: *Londen* (Dutch—London); *Londra* (Italian—London); *Londres* French, Portuguese, Spanish—London)
London: Haydn's Trios No. 1 and 2 (for two flutes and cello); Haydn's Symphony No. 104 in D major; Symphony No. 2 by Vaughan Williams—A London Symphony
London Bach: Johann Christian Bach
London of the Scanians: King Canute the Great's name for Lund, Sweden; Scandic capital he founded to match his London of the English
London-super-Mare: Brighton
Lone Eagle: Charles A. Lindbergh
Lone Star State: Texas whose flag contains one lone star
long: longeron; longitude
Long: Longfellow; Longford; Long Island; Longjumeau; Long Key; Longmeadow; Longview
Longest Fjord: Sognefjord (extends 110 miles or 175 kilometers into the heart of Norway)
longl: longitudinal
'longside: alongside
Long Tom: Thomas Jefferson—third President of the United States
longv: longevity
long vac: long vacation
Lon'on Town: British nickname for London
LONRHO: London and Rhodesian Mining and Land Company Limited
loo: looker; looker-after; looker-on
looktr: lookout tower
LOOM: Loyal Order of Moose
Loop: The Loop—Chicago's business section
LOOS: League of Older Students
lop.: launch operator's panel; left occiput posterior
l-o-p: line-of-position
LOP: lunar orbiting photographic (vehicle)
lopar: low-power acquisition radar
L O P & G: Live Oak, Perry & Gulf (railroad)
loq: *loquitur* (Latin—he speaks)
lor: lunar orbital rendezvous
Lor: Lorenzo
LOR: *L'Osservatore Romano* (Papal Roman Observer)
lorac: long-range accuracy
lorad: long-range active detection
loran: long-range aid to navigation
LORAPHS: Long-Range Passive Homing System
lord.: lordosis
Lord Acton: 1st Baron John Emerich Edward Dalberg-Acton
Lord Baltimore: George Calvert
Lord Beaverbrook: William Maxwell Aitken
Lord Berners: Gerald Hugh Tyrwhitt-Wilson
Lord Byron: George Gordon Byron
Lord Chesterfield: Philip Stanhope
Lord De La Warr: Thomas West—Lord Delaware
Lord Dunsany: Edward John Moreton Drax Plunkett
Lord of the East: Vladivostok
Lord Kenneth: Kenneth Clark—Lord Clark of Saltwood
Lord Kinross: John Patrick Douglas Balfour
Lord North: Frederick North
Lord Palmerston: Henry John Temple nicknamed Pam
Lord Passfield: Sidney Webb
Lord Peter Death Brendon Wimsey: Ian Carmichael
Lord Russell: Bertrand A Russell
Lorenzo the Magnificent: Lorenzo de Medici
lorl (LORL): large orbital research laboratory
Lorrie: Laura; Lorraine
lorv (LORV): low orbital reentry vehicle

Lor[20]: Lorenzo
los: loss of signal
l-o-s: line-of-sight
LOS: Lagos, Nigeria (airport); Little Orchestra Society; Lockheed Ocean Systems
Losa: Los Angeles
Los Angeles' Sister City: Eilat—Israel's leading oil port at the head of the Gulf of Eilat off the Red Sea
lösl: **löslich** (German—soluble)
LOSS: Large Object Salvage System
los sys: landing observer's signal system
Lost City of the Incas: Machu Picchu, Peru
lot.: large orbiting telescope; lateral olfactory tract; left occipito-transverse; load on top
lot.: *lotio* (Latin—lotion)
LOT: Polish Air Lines (3-letter symbol)
LOTADS: Long-Term Air Defense Study (USA)
lo-temp: low temperature
Lot-et-Gar: Lot-et-Garonne
Lottie: Charlotte
lotw: loaded on trailers or wagons
Lou: Lewis; Louis; Louisa; Louisiana; Louisville
Louie: Louis; Louisa; Louise
Louis: Louisville
Louis Capet: King Louis XVI
Louis le Débonnaire: Louis I of France
Louis Graveure: Wilfred Douthitt
Louis Napoleon: Napoleon III—Emperor of France
Louisvillain(s): native(s) of Louisville
Lou Orc: Louisville Orchestra
Louv: Louvain
l'Ouverture: Toussaint l'Ouverture—founder and first president of Haiti after defeating Napoleon's troops numbering 25,000
love machine: bedroom-on-wheels type of recreation vehicle such as a camper, trailer, or van
lo wat: low water
Lower Austria: southern Austria bordering on Switzerland, Italy, Yugoslavia, and Hungary
Lower California: Baja California in Mexico
Lower Canada: French-speaking Québec and the lower St Lawrence region during the 19th century
Lower Egypt: Egypt from Cairo to the Nile delta leading to the Mediterranean
Lower Galilee: Israel south of the Sea of Galilee
Lower Lakes: southernmost Great Lakes—Erie and Ontario
Lower Peninsula: southern Michigan between Lake Michigan, Lake Huron, and Lake Erie
Lower Rhine: Rhine River between Bonn, Germany and the North Sea coast of the Netherlands
Low L: Low Latin
lox: liquid oxygen; also the name for smoked salmon
lox-sox: liquid oxygen, solid oxygen
loxygen: liquid oxygen
loy: loyalty
LOYA: League of Young Adventurers
Loyalist Province: New Brunswick
Loyola: Saint Ignatius de Loyola (Iñigo de Oñez y Loyola)
loz: liquid ozone
Loz: Lozère
Lozovsky: Solomon Abramovich Dridzo
lp: landplane; last paid; latent period; light perception; linear programming; liquid propellant; liquefied petroleum; litter patient; local procurement; long-play; long-playing; low pass; low point; low power; low pressure; lumbar puncture
l/p: lactate/pyruvate ratio; launch platform; listening post
Lp: Ladyship; Lordship
LP: Aeralpi (2-letter symbol); Labor Party; Labour Party; Liberal Party; Library of Parliament; litter patient; long-play (record); Lower Peninsula
LP: *lunga pausa* (Italian—long pause)
L-P: Lionel-Pacific
LPA: Labor Party Association; Labor Policy Association; Little People of America
LPAA: London Poster Advertising Association
L-pam: L-phenylalanine mustard (anti-cancer drug)
LPB: La Paz, Bolivia (airport)
lpc: low-pressure chamber
LPC: Lockheed Propulsion Company
LPCM: London Police Court Mission
lp cyl: low-pressure cylinder
lpd: least perceptible difference; local procurement direct
LPD: amphibious transport dock ship (naval symbol); Local Procurement District; low performance drone
LPE: London Press Exchange
L Ped: Licentiate in Pedagogy
lpf: leukocytosis-promoting factor; low-power field
lpg: liquefied petroleum gas
LPGA: Ladies Professional Golf Association; Liquefied Petroleum Gas Association
L Ph: Licentiate of Philosophy
lpi: lines per inch
LPI: Lightning Protection Institute; Louisiana Polytechnic Institute
ipicbm (LPICBM): liquid-propellant intercontinental ballistic missile
L-pills: cyanide L-pills (deadly poisonous)
LPIU: Lithographers and Photoengravers International Union
LPKS: Lone Pine Koala Sanctuary (Queensland)
LPKTF: London Printing and Kindred Trades' Federation
lpl: lightproof louver
LPL: Liverpool Public Libraries; London Public Library; Louisville Public Library; Lunar and Planetary Laboratory (University of Arizona)
LPL: *Lembaga Penelitian Laut* (Indonesian—Institute for Marine Research)—Jakarta
LP & L: Louisiana Power and Light
L-plane: US Army liaison aircraft
LP & LC: Louisiana Power Light Company
L Plms: Las Palmas
lplr: lock pillar
LPLs: Liverpool Public Libraries
lpm: lines per millimeter; lines per minute
LPN: Licensed Practical Nurse
LPNA: Lithographers and Printers National Association
LPNI: Langley Porter Neuropsychiatric Institute
lpo: local purchase order
LPO: London Philharmonic Orchestra; London Post Office
Lpool: Liverpool
LPPTFS: London and Provincial Printing Trades Friendly Society
lpr (LPR): liquid-propellant rocket
LPRC: Library Public Relations

Council
lps: lightproof shade; liters per second
lps (LPS): lipopolysaccharide
LPS: Lebanese Press Syndicate; Light Photo Squadron; London Philharmonic Society; Lord Privy Seal; Lyceum Performing Society
LPSA: Liberal Party of South Africa
LPSS: amphibious transport submarine (naval symbol)
LPT: Licensed Physical Therapist
lptv (LPTV): large payload test vehicle
Lpud: Liverpudlian (native to or inhabitant of Liverpool)
lpv: lightproof vent
lpw: lumens per watt
Lpz: Leipzig
LPZG: Lincoln Park Zoological Gardens
lq: last quarter; lowest quartile
l.q.: *lege quaeso* (Latin—please read)
lqdr: liquidator
lr: latency relaxation; leave rations; letter report; lire; long run; long range; lower
l/r: lower right
l-to-r: left-to-right (photo caption abbreviation)
l R: *laufen Rechnung* (German—current account)
Lr: lawrencium
LR: Laboratory Report; Lee Rubber (stock exchange symbol); Letter Report; Little Rock
LR: *Lloyd's Register*
lra: long-range aviation
LRA: Labor Research Association; Libertarian Republican Alliance; Lithuanian Regeneration Association
LRAD: Licentiate of the Royal Academy of Dancing
LRAFB: Little Rock Air Force Base
LRAM: Licentiate of the Royal Academy of Music
LRB: Laboratory of Radiation Biology (University of Washington); Loyalty Review Board
LRBA: Laboratoire de Recherches Balistiques et Aérodynamiques (Laboratory for Ballistic and Aerodynamic Research)
lrbm: long-range ballistic missile
lrc: lower right center
lrc (LRC): longitudinal redundancy check character (data processing)
LRC: Langley Research Center (NASA); Lewis Research Center (NASA)
LRCA: London Retail Credit Association
LRCE: Little Rock Cotton Exchange
LRCM: Licentiate of the Royal College of Music
LRCP: Licentiate of the Royal College of Physicians
LRCPE: Licentiate of the Royal College of Physicians of Edinburgh
LRCPI: Licentiate of the Royal College of Physicians of Ireland
LRCS: Licentiate of the Royal College of Surgeons
LRCSE: Licentiate of the Royal College of Surgeons of Edinburgh
LRCSI: Licentiate of the Royal College of Surgeons of Ireland
LRCVS: Licentiate of the Royal College of Veterinary Surgeons
L-rd: Lord (Hebraic contraction)
lrf: latex and resorcinol formaldehyde; liver residue factor
lrf (LRF): luteinizing hormone-releasing factor
LRFI: League for Religious Freedom in Israel
LRFPB: Louisiana Rating and Fire Prevention Bureau
LRFPS: Licentiate of the Royal Faculty of Physicians and Surgeons
LRFPSG: Licentiate of the Royal Faculty of Physicians and Surgeons of Glasgow
lrg: large
LRHL: *Law Reports—House of Lords*
lri: left-right indicator; long-range interceptor
LRI: Library Resources Incorporated
LRIBA: Licentiate of the Royal Institute of British Architects
LRIC: Licentiate of the Royal Institute of Chemistry
LRJC: Lake Region Junior College
LRKB: *Law Reports—King's Bench*
lrl's: living-room liberals
LRL: Lawrence Radiation laboratory; Lunar Receiving Laboratory
LRLS: London Regional Library System
LRN: *Landslaget for Reiselivet i Norge* (Norway Travel Association)
lrp: long-range planning
LR-P: La Rochelle-Pallice
LRPL: Liquid Rocket Propulsion Laboratory; Little Rock Public Library
LRQB: *Law Reports—Queen's Bench*
lrr: lower reduced rate
lrrp: lowest required radiated power
l/r/s: library rubber stamps (used-book trade abbreviation indicating book may belong or may have belonged to a public library)
Lrs: Lancers
LRS: Land Registry Stamp
LRS: *Lloyd's Register of Shipping*
LRSM: Licentiate of the Royal Schools of Music
LRSS: Long-Range Survey System
LRTgt: last resort target
LRTL: Light Railway Transport League
LRTS: *Library Resources and Technical Services*
lru: least recently used; line replacement unit
lrv (LRV): lunar roving vehicle
LRWES: Long-Range Weapon Experimental Station
LRY: Liberal Religious Youth
ls: landing ship; left side; lightship; light vessel; limestone; liminal sensitivity; limit switch; long shot; loudspeaker; low speed
l's: losers (gambling short form)
l-s: lumbo-sacral
l & s: launch(ing) and servicing
l/s: liters per second
l.s.: *locus sigilli* (Latin—place of the seal)
Ls: Lopes; Louis
LS: Lamson & Sessions; Linnaean Society
L-S: Lewis-Shepard
lsa: left sacro-anterior
lsa (LSA): lichen sclerosus et atrophicus
LSA: Labor Services Agency; Land Service Assistant; Land Settlement Association; Leukemia Society of America; Licentiate of the Society of Apothecaries; Linguistic Society of America; Lithuanian Society of America
LSA: *Library Science Abstracts*
LSAA: Linen Supply Association of America
LSAC: London Small Arms

Company
LSAT: Law School Admission Test
lsb: left sternal border; lower sideband
LSB: Launch Service Building; London School Board; Louisiana School Board
LSBA: Leading Sick-Bay Attendant
LSBR: Large Seed-Blanket Reactor (AEC)
l.s.c.: *loco supra citato* (Latin—in the foregoing place cited)
LSC: Laser Systems Center
lsca: left scapulo-anterior
LSCA: Library Services and Construction Act
LSCC: Library of the Supreme Court of Canada
lscp: left scapuloposterior
LSCT: Lamar State College of Technology
lsd: least significant difference
ls & d: liquor store and delicatessen
l s d: *librae, solidi, denarii* (Latin—pounds, shillings, pence)
LSD: landing ship, dock (naval symbol); League for Spiritual Discovery; lysergic acid diethylamide—dangerous psychedelic drug nicknamed *acid*
LSD: *Lyserginsaure Diathylamid* (German—lysergic acid diethylamide)
L.S.D.: Doctor of Library Science
lsd li: leased line (telephone)
LSDS: Low-Speed Digital System
lse: limited signed edition
LSE: London School of Economics; London Stock Exchange; Louisiana Sugar Exchange
LSECS: Life Support and Environmental Control System
l sect: longitudinal section
LSEL: London School of Economics Library
LSE & PS: London School of Economics and Political Science
LSEU: La Salle Extension University
LSF: Literary Society Foundation; Lock Security Force (Panama Canal)
Lsg: *Lösung* (German—solution)
L Sgt: Lance Sargeant
LSH: Latter-day Saints Hospital
LSHTM: London School of Hygiene and Tropical Medicine
lsi: large-scale integration
LSI: Lake Superior & Ishpeming (railroad); Law-Science Institute (University of Texas); Law of the Sea Institute; Lear Siegler Incorporated
LS & I: Lake Superior & Ishpeming (Railroad)
LSIA: Lamp and Shade Institute of America
lsk: liver, spleen, kidney
lsl: left sacrolateral
LSL: landing ship, logistic; Lucy Stone League
lslb: left short-leg brace
lsm: lysergic acid morpholide
l.s.m.: *litera scripta manet* (Latin—the written word remains)
lsm (LSM): lysergic acid morpholide
LSM: landing ship, medium
LS/mft: Leopold Stokowski/means fine tone; Lucky Strike/means fine tobacco
LSMI: Lake Superior Mining Institute
LSMR: rocket ship
LSMSC: Lake Superior Mines Safety Council
LSNR: League of Struggle for Negro Rights
LSNY: Linnean Society of New York
LSO: Landing Signal Officer; Leningrad Symphony Orchestra; London Symphony Orchestra
lsp: left sacro-posterior
LSPOJC: La Salle-Peru-Oglesby Junior College
LSPR: Library Society of Puerto Rico
L-square: capital-L-shaped square; carpenter's square
lsr: launch signal responder
Lsr: *Luftschutzraum* (German—air raid shelter)
Lsr Ant: Lesser Antilles (Leeward and Windward Islands)
LSS: Life Saving Service; Life Saving Station; Life Support System; Lockheed Space Systems; Logistic Support Squadron
L.S.S.: Licentiate of Sacred Scripture; Leopold-Sedar Senghor
LS Sc: Licentiate in Sanitary Science
lssm: local scientific surface module
LSSR: Latvian Soviet Socialist Republic (formerly Republic of Latvia); Lithuanian Soviet Socialist Republic (formerly Republic of Lithuania)
LSSS: London School of Slavonic Studies
L S St L: Louis Stephen St Laurent (Canada's sixteenth Prime Minister)
lst: large space telescope; left sacro-traverse; liquid-oxygen start tank; liquid storage tank; living structures tank
LST: landing ship, tank; Local Sidereal Time
LSU: landing ship, utility; Louisiana State University
LSUNO: Louisian State University (New Orleans)
LSV: landing ship, vehicle
lsw: least significant word
LSW: Licensed Shorthand Writer
lsw lt: landing signal wand light
LSWR: London and South Western Railway
lt: laundry tray; lid tank; light; light trap; long ton; low tension; low torque
l/t: loop test
l.t.: *locum tenens* (Latin—substitute)
lt: *laut* (German—according to)
lt (LT): lymphotoxin
Lt: Lieutenant
LT: landing team; large tug; London Transport; local time
lta: lighter-than-air
LTA: Lawn Tennis Association; lighter-than-air
LTAA: Lawn Tennis Association of Australia
LTAS: Lighter-Than-Air Society
ltb: laryngo-trachael bronchitis
Lt. B.: Bachelor of Literature
LTB: London Tourist Board; London Transport Board
LTBT: Limited Test Ban Treaty (prohibiting nuclear testing in certain environments)
ltc: long-term care
LTC: Le Tourneau College
LTCB: Long-Term Credit Bank (Japan)
Lt Cdr: Lieutenant Commander
LTCL: Licentiate of Trinity College of Music (London)
Lt Cmdr: Lieutenant Commander
Lt Col: Lieutenant Colonel
Ltd: Limited
Ltda: *Limitada* (Spanish—limited)
ltd ed: limited edition
lte: large table electroplotter; linear threshold element
Lte: (French—Limite)—limited
LTE: London Transport Executive
ltf (LTF): lipotrophic factor
LTF: Lithographic Technical

Foundation; tropical fresh water load line (Plimsoll mark)
ltfrd: lot tolerance fraction reliability deviation
ltg: lighting
ltgc: lithographic
ltge: lighterage
Lt Gen: Lieutenant General
ltgh: lightening hole
Lt Gov: Lieutenant Governor
lth: lath; lathing; luteotrophic hormone (LTH)
Lth: Leith
L Th: Licentiate in Theology
lthr: leather
lti (LTI): light transmission index
Lti: Laotian
LTI: Ladder Towers Incorporated; Lowell Technological Institute
LTIB: Lead Technical Information Bureau
Lt Inf: Light Infantry
Lt JG: Lieutenant Junior Grade
ltl (LTL): less than truckload
Ltl: Little (postal abbreviation)
ltm: long-term memory
LTM: Licentiate of Tropical Medicine
ltng: lightning
ltng arr: lightning arrester
lto: landing takeoff
Lto: *lento* (Italian—slowly)
LTO: Leading Torpedo Operator
ltof: low-temperature optical facility
LTon: long ton
ltp: limit on tax preferences
LTP: Library Technology Program
ltpp: lipothiamide-pyrophosphate
ltr: letter
LTR: Long Term Reserve
LTR: *Library Technology Reports*
Lt RN: Lieutenant—Royal Navy
LtrO: letter order
ltrs (LTRS): letters shift (data processing)
LTRS: Laser Target Recognition System
LTS: Landfall Technique School; London Transport System; London Typographical Society
LTSB: London Trustee Savings Bank
LT & SR: London, Tilbury and Southend Railway
LTT: Lymphocyte Transformation Test
ltta: long-tank thrust augmented
L-T Trade Agreement: Liao-Takasaki Trade Agreement
ltv: long tube vertical
L-T-V: Long-Temco-Vought (corporation)
lu: logic unit; lumen
lu.: *lues* (Latin—contagious disease)—plague or syphilis
lu. I: *lues I*—primary syphilis
lu. II: *lues II*—secondary syphilis
lu. III: *lues III*—tertiary syphilis
Lu: Lugano; Lugo; lutetium
LU: Langston University; Laurentian University; Laval University; Lehigh University; Lethbridge University; Ligue Universelle (Universal Esperantist League); Lincoln University; Liverpool University; London University; Loyola University
LUA: London Underwriters Association
lub: lubricant, lubricate; lubrication
lube: lubricate; lubrication
lub oil: lubricating oil
lubs: large undisturbed bottom sampler
Luc: Lucan; Lucifer; Lucretius; Lucullus
Lucan: Roman poet Marcus Annaeus Lucanus
Lucas: Luke
luchtv: *luchtvaart* (Dutch—aviation)
Luci: Lucifer
Lucifer: (Latin—light bearer)—Venus the pre-dawn morning star rising in the east as opposed to Venus the post-dusk evening star sometimes called Hesperus seen setting in the west
Lucil: Gaius Lucilius (Roman satiric writer)
Luck: Lucknow
Lucky: Lucky Luciano (Salvatore Lucania)—once America's foremost gangster controlling gambling, money lending, narcotics, prostitution, and related aspects of the so-called entertainment world
Lucky Black Swan: Western Australia's city of Perth where black swans swim about in Perth Water
Lucky Capital: Canberra, Australia
Lucky Country: Australia
lucom: lunar communication
Lucr: *The Rape of Lucrece*
Lucretius: Roman poet-philosopher Titus Lucretius
Lucy: Lucia; Lucilla; Lucille
Lucy Stone: maiden name of Mrs Henry Brown Blackwell who retained her maiden name so as not to lose her identity
lud: liftup door
Lud: Ludlow; Ludo; Ludolf; Ludolph; Ludovic; Ludovica; Ludovick; Ludovico; Ludovicus; Ludvig; Ludwell; Ludwig; Ludwik
Luddy: Ludlow (*see* Lud)
Ludwig van: Ludwig van Beethoven
lue: left upper entrance; left upper extremity
LUER: Land Use and Environmental Regulation
lues I: primary syphilis
lues II: secondary syphilis
lues III: tertiary syphilis
luf: lowest useful high frequency
LUFTHANSA: Deutsche Lufthansa (West German Airline)
lug: luggage; lugger; lugging; lugsail; lugworm
Lugd. Bat.: *Lugdunum Batavorum* (Latin—Leiden)—Leyden
lu h: lumen hour(s)
luhf: lowest usable high frequency
LUIP: London University Institute of Psychiatry
Lukas Foss: Lukas Fuchs
Luke: The Gospel according to St Luke
lul: left upper limb; left upper lobe
LUL: London University Library
LULA: Loyola University of Los Angeles
LULAC: League of United Latin-American Citizens
LULOP: *London Union List of Periodicals*
Lulu: Louise
lum: lumbago; lumbar; lumber; lumen; luminosity; luminous
lum (LUM): lunar excursion module
Lum: Columbus
LUMAS: Lunar Mapping System
lumb: lumber; lumbering
LUMC: Laval University Medical Center
Lumber State: Maine
Lumpen: *Lumpenproletariat* (German—unskilled city workers)
lun: lunar; lunette
lun: *lundi* (French—Monday); *lunedi* (Italian—Monday); *lunes* (Spanish—Monday)
Lunar: Lunar Society (Birmingham, England)

lunar caustic: silver nitrate ($AgNO_3$)
lunch: luncheon
Lunik: Soviet cosmic rocket landed on Moon September 14, 1959
lun int: lunitidal interval
LUP: Liverpool University Press; Loyola University Press
lupa: *lupanar* (Latin—brothel)
luq: left upper quadrant (abdomen)
LUS: Land Utilization Survey
LUSB: Land Utilization Survey of Britain
lusi: lunar surface inspection
Lusians: Portuguese
lusing: *lusingando* (Italian—coaxing)
Lusitania: (Latin—Portugal)—Roman name often used as the poetic equivalent of Portugal
lust.: lustrous
lut: launcher umbilical tower (LUT)
lut.: *luteum* (Latin—yellow)
LUT: Launcher Umbilical Tower; Ludwig Universe Tankships
Luth: Luther(an)
luv: let us vote (popular teenage plea); lightweight utility vehicle (pickup truck)
lux: luxurious; luxury
Lux: Luxembourg; Luxembourger
LUXAIR: Luxembourg Airlines
Lux Fr: Luxembourger franc
Lux: Luzon
lv: launch vehicle (LV); leave; low voltage
lv: *livre* (French—book)
Lv: Latvia; Latvian; lev (Bulgarian currency unit)
LV: Las Vegas; launch vehicle; Lehigh Valley (railroad); light vessel (light ship); Lindholmens Varv (Lindholmens Shipyard)
L da V: Leonardo da Vinci
LVA: Licensed Victuallers Association
LV-3: Atlas launch vehicle (Convair)
lvd: louvered door
lvda: launch vehicle data adapter
lvdc: launch vehicle digital computer
lved: left ventricular end diastolic
Lvfa: low-voltage fast activity
lvh: left ventricular hypertrophy
lvh (LVH): landing vehicle hydrofoil
lvhv: low volume high velocity
lvi: low viscosity index
LVI: Local Veterinary Inspector
lvl: level
LVL: La Verendrye Line (Hall Corporation)
LVN: Licensed Visiting Nurse; Licensed Vocational Nurse
LVNM: Lava Beds National Monument (California)
LVNP: Lassen Volcanic National Park (California); Luangwa Valley National Park (Zambia)
lvp: low-voltage protection
lvp (LVP): left ventricular pressure
LVP: Launch Vehicle Program(s)
lvp dr: leverpak drum
lvr: low-voltage release
LVRB: Launch Vehicle Reliability Board
Lvrpl: Liverpool
LVs: launch vehicles
LVS: Licentiate in Veterinary Science
LVT: landing vehicle, tracked
LVUSA: Legion of Valor of the USA
lw: low water
l & w: living and well
Lw: lawrencium (element 103)
l W: *lichte Weite:* (German—internal diameter)
LW: light warning; lower berth
lwb: long wheelbase
lwc: lightweight concrete
LWCA: London Wholesale Confectioners Association
lwd: larger word
lwest: low water equinoctial spring tide
LWF: Lutheran World Federation
LWFB: Lake Washington Floating Bridge
lwf & c: low water full and change
lwgr (LWGR): light-water-cooled graphite-moderated reactor
lwic: lightweight insulating concrete
lwl: length at waterline; load waterline; low-water line (tidal marking)
LWL: Limited War Laboratory (US Army)
lwm: low-water mark
LWM: Leonard Wood Memorial (American Leprosy Foundation)
LWMEL: Leonard Wood Memorial for the Eradication of Leprosy
LWNWR: Lake Woodruff National Wildlife Refuge (Florida)
lwont: low water ordinary neap tide
lwop: leave without pay
lwos: low-water ordinary spring
lwost: low-water ordinary spring tide
lwp: leave with pay; load water plane
lwr: lower
lwr (LWR): light water reactor
Lwr: Lower (postal abbreviation)
l'wrd: leeward
Lwt: Lowestoft
LWT: amphibious warping tug (naval symbol); London Weekend Television
LWU: Leather Workers Union
LWV: Lackawanna & Wyoming Valley (railroad); League of Women Voters
lww: launch window width
lwyr: lawyer
lx: lux
lx.: *lux* (Latin—light)
LX: Lox Angeles Airways (2-letter coding)
Lx^a: *Lisboa* (Portuguese—Lisbon)
Lxmbrg: Luxembourg
LXX: Septuagint (70)
lxxx: love and kisses
ly: langley (solar heat unit); last year; last year's model
Ly: Lyman; Lyon
LY: Love Year
LYC: Larchmont Yacht Club
Lyd: Lydia; Lydian
lye: potassium hydroxide (KOH) or sodium hydroxide (NaOH)
LYK: Lykes Brothers Steamship company (stock exchange symbol)
lym: last year's model(s); lymph; lymphatic(s)
lympho(s): lymphocyte(s)
lymphs: lymphocytes
lyn: lynch (named for Captain William Lynch, also called Judge Lynch, who advocated hanging on the basis of mob action rather than legal procedure; this type of violence is also called lynch law)
Lyn: Lynch; Lynde; Lyndon; Lyne; Lynn
Lynn Doyle: Leslie Alexander Montgomery
Lyo: Lyons (British maritime contraction)
lyr: lyric; lyrical; lyricism; lyricist; lyrics
L & YR: Lancashire and York-

shire Railway
lyric.: language for your remote instruction by computer
lys: lysine
Lyt: Lyttelton, New Zealand
Lz: Lopez
LZ: Landing Zone
lzm: lysozyme
LZOA: Labor Zionist Organization of America
LZSU: Leningrad A.A. Zhdanov State University (University of Leningrad)
LZT: Local Zone Time
L-Zug: *Luxus-Zug* (German—luxury railroad train)
lzy: lazy

M

m: difference of meriodional parts (symbol); magnetic dipole moment (symbol); main; male; malignant; manual; married; masculine; mass; mature; mean (arithmetical); measure; mediator (chemical); mega; megohm; member; memory; mentum; meridian; mesh; metabolite; meter; mile; mill; milli- (thousandth); minim; minute; minutes; modulus; molar; molecular weight; monkey; month; moon; morning; morphine; mother; motile; mucoid; murmur (heart); muscle; myopia
m: mass (symbol); *Mazda* (Japanese auto with German Wankel rotary engine)
m.: *macerare* (Latin—macerate)
'm: (contraction—am)—as in *I'm here*
m/: *med* (Norwegian—with)—as in *varm aplepai m/is* (hot apple pie with ice cream)
m_1: mitral first sound
m^2: square meter(s)
m^3: cubic meter(s)
m/3: middle third (long bones)
M: bending moment (symbol); Mach (Austrian physicist); mach number; mach speed; magnaflux; magnetic inspection; maintainability; Malay; Malaya; Malaysia; March; mark; Martin; materiel; Matson Navigation Company; median; medium; mega- (million); megacycle; metal; metropolitan; Mike—code for letter M; Min; missile; mixture; mobile; Mohammedan; Mohammedanism; molecular weight (symbol); moment; Monday; Monsieur (French—Mister); Montour (railroad); Moore-McCormack (steamship lines); Moslem; muscle; pitching moment (symbol); thousand (symbol)
M: *Marcus* (Latin); *Missa* (Latin—Mass); *mujeres* (Spanish—women)
M': *Mac* (Gaelic—son of)
M-1: U.S. semi-automatic service rifle used in Vietnam
M-14: U.S. fully-automatic or semi-automatic service rifle used in Vietnam
M-16: British Foreign Service Military Intelligence (secret intelligence service); U.S. fully-or semi-automatic lightweight small-bore service rifle used in Vietnam
M-20: Mystère 20 aircraft
ma: machine account; machine accountant; manufacturing assembly; map analysis; mechanical advantage; menstrual age; mental age mill annealed; milliampere
m/a: my account
mA: milliangstrom
Ma: Malayalam; Mama; Manchuria; Manchurian; María; masurium (symbol)
Ma: *Mandag* (Danish—Monday)
Ma: María
M^a: María
MA: Magma Arizona (railroad); Magnesium Association; Mahogany Association; Manpower Administration; Maritime Administration; Marshaling Area; May Department Stores (stock exchange symbol); Mediterranean Area; Menorah Association; Metric Association; Military Academy; Military Attaché
M.A.: *Magister Artium* (Latin—Master of Arts
M & A: Missouri & Arkansas (railroad)
Me es A: *Maitre es Arts* (French—Master of Arts)
maa: maximum authorized altitude
maa (MAA): macroaggregated albumin
Maa: *Maandag* (Dutch—Monday)
MAA: Manufacturers Aircraft Association; Master Army Aviator; Master-at-Arms; Master-of-Arms; Mathematical Association of America; Medieval Academy of America; Medical Assistance for the Aged; Mutual Aid Association; Mutual Assurance Association
MA of A: Motel Association of America
MAAC: Mutual Assistance Advisory Committee
MAAEE: *Ministero degli Affari Esteri* (Italian—Ministry of Foreign Affairs)
MAAF: Mediterranean Allied Air Force; Mediterranean Army Air Force
MAAG: Military Assistance Advisory Group
MAAGB: Medical Artists' Association of Great Britain
MAAH: Museum of African-American History
ma'am: madam
ma'amselle: mademoiselle
MAAN: Mutual Advertising Agency Network
MAAP: Minority Association for Animal Protection
M.A.Arch.: Master of Arts in Architecture
MAAS: Member of the American Academy of Arts and Sciences
MAATC: Mobile Antiaircraft Training Center
Mab: Mabel
MAB: Magazine Advertising Bureau; Maracaibo Oil Exploration (stock exchange symbol); Marine Air Base; Medical Advisory Board; Missile Assembly Building; Munitions

Assignment Board
MAB: *Manufacture d'Armes Automatiques Bayonne* (French—Bayonne Automatic Arms Factory)
Ma Bell: Mother Bell (Bell System telephone companies linked by AT & T)
MABO: Marianas-Bonin (islands)
mabp: mean arterial blood pressure
MABRON: Marine Air Base Squadron
MABYS: Metropolitan Association for Befriending Young Servants
mac: macerate; machine-aided cognition; maximum allowable concentration(s); mean aerodynamic chord; motion analysis camera; multiple-access computer
mac.: *macerare* (Latin—macerate)
Mac: Macao, Portuguese China; nickname of anyone whose surname begins with Mac
M.Ac.: Master of Accountancy
MAC: Maintenance Advisory Committee; Major Air Command; Marine Amphibious Corps; Maritime Advisory Committee; McDonnell Aircraft Corporation; Mediterranean Air Command; Miami Aviation Corporation; Middle Atlantic Conference; Military Airlift Command
MACAIR: Macao Air Transport
MACAP: Major Appliance Consumer Action Panel
Macc: Maccabees
MACC: Military Aid to the Civilian Community
m. accur.: *misce accuratissme* (Latin—mix very accurately)
MACD: Member of the Australian College of Dentistry
mace: billiard stick, ceremonial staff, medieval spike-headed club, tear gas containing chloroacetophenone and sold as MACE, tropical spice; not an acronym but a tear gas (MACE) used by the police to quell rioters and by postmen to control attacking dogs
Mace: (*see* CS-gas)
MACE: Machine-Aided Composition and Editing; Massachusetts Advisory Council on Education; Military Aircraft Capability Estimator(s); Missile and Control Equipment (North American Aviation); trade name for tear gas used by policemen and postmen
M.A.C.E.: Master of Air-Conditioning Education; Master of Air-Conditoning Engineering
Maced: Macedonia; Macedonian
MACG: Marine Air Control Group
mach: machine; machinery; machinist
Mach: *The Tragedy of Macbeth*
Mach: velocity unit equal to speed of sound at standard temperature and pressure (1115 fps); named in honor of Ernst Mach—Austrian physicist
mack: mackinaw; mackintosh; maststack (marine superstructure containing mast and smokestack)
mack(es): mackintosh(es)
MACR: Missing Air Crew Report
MacRobertson Land: Australian Antarctica
macrobio: macrobiologic(al); macrobiology; macrobiotic(s)
macrobop: macrobopper (underground slang—older teenager in sympathy with the modern scene
macrocephs: macrocephalics (large-headed people)
macroeco: macroeconomics
macrol: macrologic(al)(ly); macrologist(s); macrology
MACS: Marine Air Control Squadron
MACSS: Medium-Altitude Communication Satellite System
MACTU: Mines and Contermeasures Tactical Unit (USN)
MAC/V: Military Assitance Command, Vietnam
mad.: magnetic airborne detector; magnetic anomaly detector; midpoint air dose
Mad: Madeira; Madison; Madras
M. Ad.: Master of Administration
MAD: Madrid, Spain (airport); Manufacturing Assembly Drawing; Marine Air Detachment; Marine Aviation Detachment; Michigan alorithmetic decoder; Mine Assembly Depot; Mongolian Asiatic Development (plan)
MAD: *Militarischer Abschirmdienst* (German—Military Screening Service)—West German counterintelligence corps
MADAEC: Military Application Division of the Atomic Energy Commission
Madag: Madagascar
MADIAR: Societé Nationale Malgache des Transports Aériens (Madagascar Air Transport)
MADAM: Manchester Automatic Digital Machine
Madame Deficit: Marie Antoinette's nickname attributed to her wasteful use of public funds
Madame de Staël: Baronne Anne Louise Germaine
Mad Av: advertising and communications enterprises (many are located on Madison Avenue in New York City)
MADD: Manufactured of Artificial Dog Dung (probably the ultimate acronymic absurdity)
maddam: macromodule and digital differential analyzer
madevac: medical evacuation
Madge: Margaret; Margarita
Mad Genius of Sex and Psychiatry: Wilhem Reich—inventor of the orgone box
Mad Isl: Madeira Islands
Mad Meg: nickname of the Mayer van der Bergh Museum in Antwerp, Belgium
MAD Policy: Mutually-Assured Destruction Policy (nuclear warfare)
madr: minimum adult daily requirement
Madr: Madrid; Madrileño
madre: magnetic-drum receiving equipment
madrec: malfunction detection and recorder
mads: mind-altering drugs
MADs: Mothers Against Drugs
mae: mean absolute error
Mae: Mary
Ma.E.: Master of Engineering
MAE: Medical Air Evacuation; Museum of Atomic Energy
M.A.E.: Master of Aeronautical Engineering; Master of Art Education; Master of Arts in Education; Master of Arts in Elocution
M.A.Econ.: Master of Arts in Economics; Master of Arts in Economic and Social Studies
M.A.Ed.: Master of Arts in Education
MAEE: Marine Aircraft Experimental Establishment
MAEF: Master Asphalt Employers' Federation
MAELU: Mutual Atomic Energy Liability Underwriters

M.Aero.E.: Master of Aeronautical Engineering
maesto: *maestoso* (Italian—majestically)
Maestro of Abolition: Brazilian composer-conductor Carlos Gomes who fought for the abolition of slavery
Maestro Crescendo: Rossini's nickname
maf: major academic field; manpower authorization file; minimum audible field; multiplanar angular forces
MAF: Marine Air Facility; Middle Atlantic Fisheries
MA & F: Ministry of Agriculture and Fisheries
MAFA: Manchester Academy of Fine Arts
MAFB: Mitchell Air Force Base
MAFCA: Model-A Ford Club of America
MAFDAL: Miflaga Datit Le'umit (Hebrew—National Religious Party)
mafe: magnesium + iron (Ma + Fe)
MAFF: Minister of Agriculture, Fisheries and Food
MAFI: Medic-Alert Foundation International
MAFIA: *Morte Alla Francia Italia Anela* (Italian—Death to France Is Italy's Cry), acronym devised when the secret society was first organized in the 1860s, to combat French forces of intervention
mafr: merged accountability and fund reporting
MAFS: Mobilization Air Force Specialty
mag: magazine; magnesia; magnesium; magnet; magnetic; magnetism; magneto; magnetron; magnum
mag.: *magnus* (Latin—great)
Mag: Magallanes (Punta Arenas); Magallanic; Magyar; Margaret
Mag.: *Magnificat* (Latin—it magnifies)—song of the Virgin Mary
MAG: Magnavox (stock exchange symbol); magnesium (machine shop style); Marine Aircraft Group; Marine Aviation Group; Military Advisory Group
maga: magazine
Mag.Agg.: *Magister Aggregatus* (Latin—Master of Aggregation)—Head Master
mag ampl: magnetic amplifier
Magazinist: Edgar Allan Poe's self-invented title
mag cap: magazine capacity
MAGB: Microfilm Association of Great Britain
mag card: magnetic card
magcheck: magneto check
mag ci: magnetic cast iron
mag cs: magnetic cast steel
Magda: Magdalen(a)
Magdalens: Magdalen Islands (Iles de la Madeleine)
Magd Coll: Magdalen College—Oxford
M.Ag.Ec.: Master of Agricultural Economics
M.Ag.Ed.: Master of Agricultural Education
magg: *maggio* (Italian—May); *maggiore* (Italian—major)
Maggie: Margaret; stock market nickname for Magnavox
Magic City: any fast-growing city such as Billings, Montana or Birmingham, Alabama, or Miami, Florida, etc.
MAGIC: Madison Avenue General Ideas Committee
maglev: magnetic levitation
magloc: magnetic logic computer
mag mod: magnetic modulator
magn: magnetism
magn.: *magnus* (Latin—large)
magnalium: magnesium + aluminum (alloy)
magneform: magnetic forming (process)
magnesia: magnesium oxide (MgO)
MAG^ni^: *Magazini* (Italian—warehouse)
magno: manganese-nickel alloy
Magnolia: state flower of Louisiana and Mississippi
Magnolia City: Houston, Texas
Magnolia(s): Mississippian(s)
Magnolia State: Mississippi's official nickname
magnox: magnesium oxide
magnum: high-powered cartridge or weapon for firing magnum ammunition; $^2/_5$-gallon champagne bottle
mag. op.: *magnum opus* (Latin—major work)
M.Agr.: Master of Agriculture
mags: magazines; magnesium wheels
mag tape: magnetic tape
mah: mahogany
Mahatma: (Hindi—Great Souled) —sobriquet of India's greatest leader, Mohandas Karamchand Ghandi
MAHE: Michigan Association for Higher Education
mahog: mahogany
mai: marriage adjustment inventory; minimum annual income
MAI: Military Assistance Institute; Museum of the American Indian
MAI: *Moskovskiy Aviatsionny Institut* (Russian—Moscow Aviation Institute)
MA.I.: *Magister in Arte Ingeniaria* (Latin—Master of Engineering)
MAIBL: Midland and International Banks Limited
maid.: maintenance automatic integration detector
M-Aid: Marshall-Plan Aid (given European countries by the United States after World War II)
Maid of Orleans: Joan of Arc—*La Pucelle d'Orleans*
Maid of Zaragoza: Augustina de Aragón (Augustina Domenech Zaragoza—fighter for freedom during Spain's invasion by Napoleonic armies)
MAIG: Matsushita Atomic Industrial Group
Maimon: Maimonides
Maimonides: Moses ben Maimon
MAIN: Medical Automation Intelligence System
Main Drag: Main Street or the main street of any American city or town
Main Drag of Many Tears: 125th Street in New York City's Harlem
Maine Turn: Maine Turnpike
Mainichi: *Mainichi Shimbun* (Japanese—Everyday Newspaper)—modern Japan's oldest periodical
maint: maintenance
Maisie: Maria; Marie; Mary; Maryjane
maitre d': *maitre d'hotel* (French—head waiter)
maj: major; majority
Maj: Major
MAJ: Muhammad Ali Jinnah
majac: maintenance antijam console
Maj Com: Major Command
Maj Gen: Major General
Majocchi's disease: ringlike empurplement of the lower limbs
Major Prophets of the Old Testament: Isaiah, Jeremiah, Ezekiel, Daniel
Majulah Singapura: (Malay—Advance Singapore)—national motto of Singapore
Mak: Makdougall; Makoto; Maksim; Maksimovich
MAKN: *Mongol Ardyn Khuv's-*

galt Nam (Kalkha Mongol—Mongolian People's Revolutionary Party)
maksutsub: make suitable substitutions
Mal: The Book of Malachi; Malaga; Malagueña(o); Malay; Malayan; Malaysia; Malta; Maltese
Mal: *Maréchal* (French—Marshal)
MAL: Malaysian Airways Limited; Material Allowance List
Mala: Malaya; Malayan; Malaysia; Malaysian
malac: malacology
malachite: hydrated copper carbonate
Malagasy Republic: Madagascar
malaprop: *mal à propos* (French—out of place; unappropriate)
Malawi: formerly Nyasaland
Malayan Island Nation: Singapore
Malaysia: Federation of Malaya (Peninsular Malaysia) and the Colonies of North Borneo (Sabah and Sarawak)
Malbrook: (Louis XIVs mispronunciation of Marlborough—John Churchill—Duke of Marlborough—whose British soldiers drove the French from the field in battle after battle)—*see* Mambru
Malcolm X: Malcolm Little
Mald: Maldive Islands
Mal $: Malaya dollar
M.A.L.D.: Master of Arts in Law and Diplomacy
Maldives: Maldive Islands
MALEV: (Hungarian Airline)
Malg Rep: Malagasy Republic
Mali: formerly the French Sudan
MALI: Air Mali
malig: malignant
Mal Isl: Maldive Islands
mall: malleable
Mall: Mallorca
Mal-Port: Malay-Portuguese (East African patois)
malprac(s): malpractice(s); malpractitioner(s)
M.A.L.S.: Master of Arts in Liberal Studies; Master of Arts in Library Science; Master of Arts in Library Service
Mal St: Malay States
malt.: malted milkshake
Malt(s): Maltese sailor(s)
Malvenuto: nickname carping critics bestowed on the Berlioz opera *Benvenuto Cellini*
Malvinas: Malvinas Islands (Falklands)
mam: medium automotive maintenance; milliampere minute(s)
mam: *mot a mot* (French—word for word)
ma'm: madam
m + am: (compound) myopic astigmatism
MAM: Military Assistance Manual; Montclair Art Museum
MAMA: Mobile Air Materiel Area; Middletown Air Materiel Area
MAMB: Military Advisory Mission—Brazil
MAMBO: Mediterranean Association of Marine Biology and Oceanography
Mambru: (Spanish mispronunciation of Marlborough—John Churchill—Duke of Marlborough—whose military exploits were much admired by the Spaniards during the War of the Spanish Succession)—*see* Malbrook
MAMENIC: Marina Mercante Nicaraguense (Nicaraguan Merchant Marine—Mamenic Line)
mamie: minimum automatic machine for interpolation and extrapolation
Mamie: Margaret
mammal.: mammalogy
mamos: marine automatic meteorological observing station
MAMS: Missile Assembly and Maintenance Shop
Mamzel: Mademoiselle
man.: manhold; manifest; manifold; manual; manufacture; manure
man.: *manipulus* (Latin—handful)
m A n: *meiner Ansicht nach* (German—in my opinion)
Man: (La) Mancha; Manchester; Manhattan; Manila; Manitoba
MAN: Managua, Nicaragua (airport); Motorcyclists Against Noise
M-A-N: Maschinefabrik-Augsburg-Nurnberg
MANA: Manufacturers' Agents National Association
M.Anaes.: Master of Anaesthesiology
Manassa Mauler: Jack Dempsey born in Manassa, Colorado
Mana-Zucca: Augusta Zuckerman
Man of Blood and Iron: Prince Otto von Bismarck's nickname alluding to the speeches wherein he clamored for German blood and iron
Man Brdg: Manhattan Bridge (New York City)
manc: *mancando* (Italian—gradually softer)
Manc: Manchester; Mancunian—inhabitant of Manchester
Manch: Manchuria
mand: mandamus; mandate; mandatory; mandible; mandibular
Mand: Mandarin
Man of Destiny: Napoleon's self-named nickname; pre-Civil-War American filibuster William Walker; one-time dictator president of Nicaragua who planned for Central American unification and a Caribbean federation including Central America and Cuba
MANDFHAB: Male and Female Homosexual Association of Great Britain
Man Dir: Managing Director; Managing Directress
mandy: man day
Mandy: Amanda; Manda
Man Ed: Managing Editor
manf: manifold; manufacture; manufacturer; manufacturing
MANFORCE: Manpower for a Clean Environment
manganim: manganese-copper-nickel alloy
mang b: manganese bronze
Mangrove Coast: Florida's southernmost coast between the Everglades and the Keys
Man on Horseback: General Georges Boulanger
manhr: manhour
Man from Maine: James G. Blaine
Man of Monach Country: Fermanagh County in Ulster, Northern Ireland
MANI: Minister of Agriculture for Northern Ireland
mania (MANIAC): mathematical analyzer, numerical integrator, and computer
manif: manifest
Manil: Marcus Manilius (Roman poet)
manip.: *manipulus* (Latin—handful)
manit: man minute
Manit: Manitoba
Manitoulins: Manitoulin Islands in Lake Huron
Man[1]: Manuel (Spanish—Emanuel)
Man Med Dept: *Manual of the Medical Department (USN)*
manmo: man month

Manny: Emanuel; Manuel
mano: manograph; manometer
Manolete: Manuel Rodriguez
manop: manually operated; manual operation
man. p.: *mane primo* (Latin—early in the morning; first thing in the morning)
MANP: Masai Amboseli National Park (Kenya); Mount Apo NP (Mindanao, Philippines); Mount Arayat NP (Luzon, Philippines)
man(s) rep(s): manufacturer(s) representative(s)
Mans: Mansion
MANS: Map Analysis System
mansat: manned satellite
mansec: man second
Mansf Coll: Mansfield College-Oxford
Man's Oldest Disease: alcoholism
Man of a Thousand Faces: Lon Chaney
MANTIS: Manchester Technical Information Service
Manuel: Emmanuel
manuf: manufacture(r)
Manutius: Aldus Manutius—Latinized version of Aldo Manuzio—inventor of italic type
manuv: maneuvering
MANWEB: Merseyside and North Wales Electricity Board
Man You Loved To Hate: Erich von Stroheim
manwich: man-sized sandwich
manwk: man week
manyr: man year
Manzoni Mass: Verdi's *Requiem*
mao (MAO): monoamine oxidase
mao: *med andra ord* (Swedish—in other words); *med andre ord* (Danish—in other words)
Mao: Mao Tse-tung
MAO: Master of the Art of Obstetrics; Musica Aeterna Orchestra
MAO: *Magyar Allami Operhaz* (Hungarian State Opera)
maoi (MAOI): monamine oxidase inhibitor
MAOT: Member of the Association of Occupational Therapists; Military Assitance Observer Team
map.: manifold absolute pressure; manifold air pressure; mapping; minimum audible pressure; missed approach procedure
MAP: Maghreb-Arabe Presse (Maghreh Arab Press Agency); Medical Aid Post; Military Aid Program; Military Assitance Program; Military Association of Podiatrists; Ministry of Aircraft Production; Mutual African Press (agency)
M-A-P: Modified American Plan (breakfast and dinner included)
MAPA: Mexican-American Political Association
MAPAG: Military Assitance Program Advisory Group
MAPAI: *Miflaget Poaley Israel* (Hebrew—Israel Labor Party)—right-wing socialist
MAPAM: *Miflaget HaPaolim HaMe'uchedet* (Hebrew—United Workers Party)—left-wing socialist
mapche: mobile automatic programmed checkout equipment
MAPCO: Mid-America Pipeline Company
maph: manned ambient-pressure habitat
MAPHILINDO: Malaysia, Philippines, Indonesia (proposed unification of these Malayan countries)
MAPI: Machinery and Allied Products Institute
MAPL: Manufacturing Assembly Parts List
Maple City: Ogdensburg, New York
Maple Leaf: Canada's flag consisting of three vertical stripes—red, white, red—with a red maple leaf on the white center stripe
MAPNY: Maritime Association of the Port of New York
MAPOM: MAP-owned materiel
mapp: methylacetylenepropadiene
mapros: maintain production schedule(s)
MAPS: Major Assembly Perormance System; Management Analysis and Planning System; Middle Atlantic Planetarium Society; Military Products and Systems (RCA); Miniature Air Pilot System; Monetary and Payments System; Multiple Address Processing System
M.App.Sc.: Master of Applied Science
maq: monetary allowance in lieu of quarters
MAQ: Measures for Air Quality (NBS)
mar.: marine; maritime; married; marry; memory address register; minimal angle resolution; multiarray radar; multifunction array radar
mar.: *mardi* (French—Tuesday); *martedi* (Italian—Teusday); *martes* (Spanish—Tuesday)
Mar: Marathi; March; Marseilles; Marshall Islands
M.Ar.: Master of Architecture
MAR: Manistee and Repton (railroad); Maracaibo, Venezuela (airport); Maritime Central Airways; Mars Excursion Module
MARA: Mexican-American Research Association
MARAD: Maritime Administration (US Department of Commerce)
marb: marbling
Marb: Marblehead; Marbleheart; Marbury
marble: calcium carbonate ($CaCO_3$)
Marble Halls of Oregon: Oregon Caves National Monument
marc: monitoring and results computer
marc: *marcato* (Italian—marked)
Marc: Marcus
MARC: Machine-Readable Cataloging (Library of Congress magnetic-tape catalog system); Manpower Authorization Request for Change; Matador Automatic Radar Command; Metropolitan Applied Research Center; Model-A Restorers Club (Model-A Ford autos)
MarCad: Marine Cadet
Marcella Sembrich: Praxede Marcelline Kochanska
MARCEP: Maintainability and Cost-Effectiveness Program
March.: Marchioness
March: *Marchese* (Italian—Marquis)
M.Arch.: Master of Architecture
March King: John Philip Sousa
March^{sa}: *Marchesa* (Italian—Marchioness)
MARCOM: Maritime Command (Canadian)
MARCOR: US Marine Corps
Marcus: Mark
Mardi Gras Metropolis: New Orleans, Louisiana
marg: margarine; margin; marginal; marginalia
Marg: Margrave; Margravine
marge: margarine (oleomargarine); margin
Marge: Margaret; Margery
Margie: Margaret
Mar Gils Area: Marshalls-Gilberts (island) Area

Margot: Margaret
Marg^ta: Margarita (Spanish—Margaret)
marg trans: marginal translation
MARI: Middle America Research Institute
Maria Callas: Maria Calogeropoulos
Marianas: Mariana Islands
Marichu: (Spanish-American nickname—María de Jesús)—see *Chuey*
mariculture: marine culture (growing food in the sea)
Marie Brema: Minny Fehrman
Marie Corelli: Eva Mary Mackay
Marie's disease: chronic enlargement of the face, feet, and hands
marifarm: maritime farm
mariholic: marijuanaholic (addict)
Mariner: Venus-Mars fly-by space vehicle
Mario: Giovanni Matteo
Mariol: Mariolatry; Mariology
Marion: Mary; Maryjane
marit: maritime
Marit Admin: Maritime Administration
Marit Com: Maritime Commission
Maritime Alsp: *Alpes Maritimes* (French)—AM
Maritime Provinces: New Brunswick, Nova Scotia, and Prince Edward Island
Maritimes: Canada's Maritime Provinces; the Maritime Alps between France and Italy; the Soviet Union's Maritime Territory extending along the Sea of Japan
maritrain(s): maritime train(s)—articulated sea-going barges
Marj: Marja; Marjan; Marjorie; Marjory
mark.: market; marketing
Mark: The Gospel according to St Mark
Mark Aldanov: Mark Aleksandrovich Landau
Mark Antony: Anglicized name of the Roman general Marcus Antonius
Mark Twain: Samuel Langhorne Clemens
Mark Twain Town: Hannibal, Missouri
Marlag: *Marinenlager* (German—sailor's camp for prisoners of war)
Marlene: Mary + Helena
Marlene Dietrich: Magdalene von Losch
MARLF: Middle Atlantic Regional Library Federation
mar lic: marriage license
MARLIS: Multi-Aspect Relevance Linkage System
Marm: Marmaduke
Marmalade Capital: Dundee, Scotland
mar merc: *marina mercantile* (Italian—merchant marine)
mar mil: *marina militare* (Italian—navy)
Maro: *Marocco* (Italian—Morocco)
Marpril: March and April
Marq: Marquesas Islands
Marquesas: Marquesas Islands
Marquise de Pompadour: Jeanne Poisson
Marquis of Queensbury: Marquis of Queensbury boxing rules formulated by John Graham Chambers supervised by the 8th Marquis of Queensbury—Sir John Sholto Douglas father of Oscar Wilde's friend Lord Alfred Douglas
marr: marriage
Marr: Marranic; Marranism; Marranoism; Marrano(s)
Marr: *Marruecos* (Spanish—Morocco)
marr lic: marriage license
Marro: *Marrocos* (Portuguese—Morocco)
marr sett: marriage settlement
Marru: *Marruecos* (Spanish—Morocco)
mars: master attitude reference system; military affiliated radio system
Mars: Marseilles
Mars: Ares (Latin—god of war); *Marselha* (Portuguese—Marseilles); *Marsella* (Spanish—Marseilles); *Marsiglia* (Italian—Marseilles)
MARS: Manned Astronautical Research Station; Military Affiliate Radio System; Miniature Accurate Ranging System; Mobile Atlantic Range Station
MARSAP: Mutual Assistance Rescue and Salvage Plan
M.Ar.Sci.: Master of Arts and Sciences
Marse Robert: (southern American—Master Robert)—General Robert E. Lee
Marshalls: Marshall Islands in the western Pacific
marsh gas: methane (CH_4)
mart.: mean active repair time
mart: *martes* (Spanish—Tuesday)
Mart: Martinique
Mart.: Martyrology
Mart: Marcus Valerius Martialis (Roman poet)
MART: Metropolitan Area Rapid Transit
MARTA: Metropolitan Atlanta Rapid Transit Authority
Marth: Martha
Martial: Roman epigrammatist Marcus Valerius Martialis
Martov: Yuli Osipovich Tsederbaum
mart(s): market(s)
MARTS: Master Radar Tracking Station
Mart(y): Martin
Martyr Abolitionist: Elijah Parish Lovejoy
Marunouchi: Tokoyo's financial center
marv: maneuvering reentry vehicle (MaRV in Salt Talk reports; also MARV); marvel; marvelous
Marv: Marvin
Marylebone: St Marylebone
Mary Pickford: Gladys Mary Smith's stage name
Mary Queen of Scots: Mary Stuart
mas: masculine; masonry; metal angle slots; military assistance sales; milliampere second
MAS: Marine Acoustical Services; Maryland Academy of Sciences; Military Agency for Standardization
MAS: *Motoscafi Anti Sommergibli* (Italian—antisubmarine motor torpedo boat)
M.A.S.: Master of Applied Science
M & AS: Music and Art School
MASA: Member of the Acoustical Society of America; Military Automotive Supply Agency
Masaccio: Tommaso Guidi
Masaniello: contracted name of Tommaso Aniello
masc: masculine
masc.: *masculus* (Latin—male)
M.A. Sc.: Master of Applied Science
Mascarenes: Mascarene Islands
mascon: massive concentration
MASCOT: Meteorological Auxiliary Sea Current Observation Transmitter
maser: microwave amplification by stimulated emission of radiation
MASH: Medical Aid for Sick Hippies; Mobile Army Surgical Hospital; Multiple Ac-

celerated Summary Hearing (for alien deportation)

Masha: (Russian nickname—Mary)

MASHAE: Member of the American Society of Heating and Air Conditioning Engineers

mash(ed): mashed potatoes

MASHVE: Member of the Australian Society of Heating and Ventilating Engineers

MASIS: Management and Scientific Information Service

MASL: Military Assitance Articles and Services List

MASME: Member of the American Society of Mechanical Engineers; Member of the Australian Society of Mechanical Engineers

Mason and Dixon Line: boundary between Maryland and Pennsylvania used to describe former demarcation between southern slave and northern free states

mas. pil.: *massa piluarum* (Latin—pill mass)

mass.: masseter

Mas: Massachusetts; Massachusettsan

MASS: Marine Air Support Squadron; Michigan Automatic Scanning System

M.A.S.S.: Master of Arts in Social Science

masscult: mass culture (culture for the masses)

MASSR: Mari Autonomous Soviet Socialist Republic; Mordavian Autonomous Soviet Socialist Republic

Mass Turn: Massachusetts Turnpike

mast.: missile automatic supply technique

MAST: Military Assistance to Safety and Traffic

MAST: *Minimum Abbreviations of Serial Titles*

Ma State: New South Wales, Australia

Master of Color Contrasts: Bartolomé Esteban Murillo

Master of Guerrilla Warfare: Toussaint l'Ouverture

Master of Light and Shade: Rembrandt van Rijn and Leonardo da Vinci seem to vie for this pictorial accolade

Mastermind of Revolution: V.I. Lenin

Master of Neurological Anatomy: Santiago Ramón y Cajal

Master of Raphael: Il Perugino (Pietro Vannucci)

Master of Suspense: Alfred Hitchcock

MASTIF: Multiple Axes Space Test Inertia Facility

Mastodon of Literature: Emmanuel Swedenborg so nicknamed by Ralph Waldo Emerson

mat.: material; materiel; matins; microalloy transistor; molankothane (molybdenum disulfide urethane)

Mat: Matanzas; Matthew

MAT: Manual Arts Therapy; Mechanical Aptitude Test; Military Air Transport

M.A.T.: Master of Arts in Teaching

mata: multiple-answering teaching aid

MATA: Motorcycle and Allied Trades Association

Mata Hari: Gertrud Margarete Zelle

Mata Soc: Mattachine Society

MATCH: Manpower and Talent Clearinghouse

MATCOMTELNET: MATS Command Teletype Network

matcon: microwave aerospace terminal control

Mate: the Mate (Chief Officer)

Mat.E.: Materials Engineer

matern: maternal; maternity

math: mathematics

Math: Mathematics; Matthew; Matthews; Mathewson; Mathias; Mathieu; Mathilde; Mathurin; Mathys; Mattias

Math.D.: Doctor of Mathematics

mathn: mathematician

maths: mathematicians; mathematics; mathematics majors

Mat Lab: Material Laboratory

mat.med.: materia medica

matnav: mathematics for navigators

mato: (Portuguese—jungle, as in Mato Grosso)

MATP: Military Assitance Training Program

matr.: *matrimonium* (Latin—marriage)

Matriarch of Anthropology: Margaret Mead

matric: matriculate; matriculation

MATS: Military Air Transport Service

Matt: Matthew; Matthewtown, Great Inagua; The Gospel according to St. Matthew

MATTS: Multiple Airborne Target Trajectory System

Mattw: Matthew

Matty: Matthew

Matty the Great: Christy Mathewson

Matty Van: Martin Van Buren

matut.: *matutinus* (Latin—in the morning)

matv: master antenna television

MATVS: Master Antenna Television System

matw: metal awning-type window

Maud: Mathilda

Maude: Morse automatic decoder

Maude Adams: Maude Kiskadden

M. Au. E.: Master of Automotive Engineering

Maur: Mauritius

M.A. Urb. Plan.: Master of Arts in Urban Planning

Maureen Forrester: Katherine Stewart

Maurit: Mauritania (Islamic Republic of)

Mauritania: Algeria and Morocco where the Mauri or Moors reside

MAUS: Metric Association of the United States

mav: manpower authorization voucher

maw: medium assault weapon

maw: *met andere woorden* (Dutch—in other words)

Maw: Mama

MAW: Marine Aircraft Wing

MAWS: Marine Air Warning Squadron

max: maximal; maximum

m'ax: (American contraction—my ax)

Max: Maxim; Maximilian; Maxwell

maxi: maximum

maxibop: maxibopper (underground slang—fatter or older woman wearing miniskirts)

maxill: maxilla; maxillary

Maxim Gorki: Aleksei Maxsimovich Peshkov

maxis: maximum-length garments (coats, skirts, etc.)

Max Nordau: Max Simon Südfeld

Max Reinhardt: Max Goldmann

Max Stirner: Johann Kaspar Schmidt

May: Maybelle

MAYA: Maya Airways (British Honduras); Mexican-American Youth Association

mayday: international distress call (from the French *m'aidez*—help me)

May Day: Shostakovich's Symphony No. 3 also called *May*

First
Mayfair: London's residential district
Mayflower: Massachusetts state flower
Mayjun: May and June
May^{mo}: *Mayordomo* (Spanish—butler; estate manager; steward)
mayn't: may not
mayo: mayonnaise
MAYO: Mexican American Youth Organization
mayoralection: mayoral election
maz: mazda
Maz: Mazatlán
mazh: missile azimuth heading
mb: macrobiotic (MB); magnetic bearing; main battery; methyl bromide; methylene blue; midbody; millibar(s); motorboat
m.b.: *misce bene* (Latin—mix well)
m & b: matched and beaded; metes and bounds
m/B: male Black
Mb: myoglobin
MB: magnetic bearing; Sir Mackenzie Bowell (Canada's sixth Prime Minister) March-Bender (factor); Marine Barracks; Marine Base; Mechanized Battalion; Meridian & Bigbee (railroad); Munitions Board; Music for the Blind
M-B: Mercedes-Benz
M.B.: *Medicinae Baccalaureus* (Latin—Bachelor of Medicine)
M/B: Master Barber
M & B: metes and bounds
Mba: Mombasa
MBA: Make or Buy Authorization; Marine Biological Association; Military Benefit Association; Monument Builders of America; Mortgage Bankers of America
M.B.A.: Master of Business Administration
MBAA: Master Brewers Association of America
MBAC: Member of the British Association of Chemists
MBAL: Master Bookbinders' Alliance of London
m bale: 1000 bales
mbar: millibar
MBAUK: Marine Biological Association of the United Kingdom
MBAWS: Marine Base Warning System
m bbl: 1000 barrels
mbc: maximum breathing capacity
MBC: Malawi Broadcasting Corporation; Mauritius Broadcasting Corporation; Mercantile Bank of Canada
MBCA: Motor Boat Club of America
MBCC: Massachusetts Bay Community College; Migratory Bird Conservation Commission
MBCMC: Milk Bottle Crate Manufacturers Council
mbd: macro-block design; minimum brain damage
mbe: missile-borne equipment
M.B.E.: Member of the Order of the British Empire
M. B. Ed.: Master of Business Education
MBF: Military Banking Facility; Milk Bottlers Federation
M-B factor: Marsh-Bender factor
MBFR: Mutual Balanced-Forced Reduction
MBG: Midland Bank Group; Missouri Botanical Garden
mbge: missileborne guidance equipment
mbh: manual bomb hoist
mbH: *mit beschränkter Haftung* (German—limited liability)
mbi: may be issued
MBIA: Malting Barley Improvement Association
M. Bi. Chem.: Master of Biological Chemistry
M. Bi. Eng.: Master of Biological Engineering
M. Bi. Phy.: Master of Biological Physics
M. Bi. S.: Master of Biological Science
MBJ: Montego Bay, Jamaica (airport)
mbk: missing, believed killed
mbl: mobile; mobile branch library
Mbl: *Monatsblatt* German—monthly report)
MBL: Marine Biological Laboratory (Woods Hole, Massachusetts); Mobile, Alabama (airport)
MBLIC: Mutual Benefit Life Insurance Company
mbm: thousand feet board measure
MBM: Mac Bride Museum
M.B.M.: Master of Business Management
MBMA: Master Boiler Makers' Association; Metal Building Manufacturers Association
MBNA: Monument Builders of North America
MBNBR: Mount Bruce Native Bird Reserve (North Island, New Zealand)
mbo: management by objectives
MbO_2: oxymyoglobin
MBOU: Member British Ornithologists Union
mpb: mean blood pressure
MBPA: Military Blood Program Agency
mbp antigen: melitensis bovin porcine antigen
MB & PR: MacMillan, Bloedel & Powell River
mbps: megabits per second; million bits per second
MBPXL: Missouri Beef Packers Express Line
mbr: member
MBR: *Minerações* Brasileiras Reunidas (Brazilian Mining Reunited)
M Bret: Middle Breton
MBRF: Mission Bay Research Foundation
Mbro: Middlesbrough
mbrt: methylene-blue reduction time
mbruu: may be retained until unserviceable
mbrv: maneuverable ballistic reentry vehicle (MBRV)
mbs: magnetron beam switching; main bang suppressor
MBS: Miami Beach Symphony; Motor Bus Society; Mutual Broadcasting System
MBSA: Modular Building Standards Association; Munitions Board Standards Agency
M. B. Sc.: Master of Business Science
MBSI: Musical Box Society International
MBSJC: Metropolitan Boroughs Standing Joint Committee (of librarians)
MBSM: Mexican Border Service Medal
mbt: mean body temperature; mechanical bathythermograph; metal-base transistor
MBTA: Massachusetts Bay Transportation Authority; Metropolitan Boston Transit Authority; Midwest Book Travelers Association
MBTI: Manpower Business Training Institute
MBTS: Meteorological Balloon Tracking System
MBT-70: Main Battle Tank (designed for use in the 1970s)
MBUCV: Museo de Biología de la Universidad Central de

Venezuela (Biology Museum of the Central University of Venezuela)
M Build: Master of Building
M. Bus. Ed.: Master of Business Education
MBV: Mexican Border Veterans
MBW: Metropolitan Board of Works
MBYC: Manhasset Bay Yacht Club
mc: magnetic center (MC); magnetic course (MC); marginal check megacycle(s); message composer; metal case; metric carat; miles on course; military characteristics; millicurie(s); momentary contact; monkey cells; multiple contact
mc: *mois courant* (French—current month)
m-c: medico-chirugical (surgical); mineralo-corticoid (hormones)
m/c: middle center
m/c: *mi cargo* (Spanish—my debt; my responsibility); *mi casa* (Spanish—my home; my house); *mi cuenta* (Spanish—my account)
m & c: morphine and cocaine
Mc: Mac (Gaelic—son of)
MC: Macalester College; Machinery Certificate; Madison College; Madonna College; magnetic course; Mailet College; Maine Central (railroad); Malin College; Malone College; Manatee College; Manchester College; Manhattan College; Manhattanville College; Manpower Commission; Maria College; Marian College; Marietta College; Marine Corps; Marion College; Marist College; Maritime Commission; Marlboro College; Martin College; Mary College; Marycrest College; Maryglade College; Marygrove College; Marylhurst College; Marymount College; Maryville College; Marywood College; Master of Ceremonies; Materiel Center; Materiel Command; Maunaolu College; Medical Center; Medical College; Medical Corps; Member of Congress; Memorial Commission; Memphis College; Menlo College; Mesa College; Michigan Central (railroad); Microfilm Corporation; Microstat Corporation; Middlebury College; Midland College; Miles College; Military Committee; Military Cross; Milligan College; Mills College; Milsaps College; Milton College; Miseriocordia College; Mitchell College; Monmouth College; Monticello College; Moravian College; Morehouse College; Morris College; Morse College; Muhlenberg College; Multnomah College; Mundelein College; Munitions Command; Muskingum College; Muskogee College
MC: *Mercado Común* (Spanish—Common Market)
M.C.: Military Cross
M.C.: *Magister Chirurgiae* (Master of Surgery)
M de C: *Maître de Chapelle* (French—conductor)
mca: minimum crossing altitude
MCA: Malayan Chinese Association; Manufacturing Chemists Association; Maritime Central Airways; Maritime Control Area; Material Coordinating Agency; Maternity Center Association; Mechanical Contractors Association; Medical Correctional Association; Millinery Credit Association; Movers Conferences of America; Muscat Control Agency; Music Corporation of America; Music Critics Association; Musicians Club of America
MCAA: Mason Contractors Association of America; Mechanical Contractors Association of America; Military Civil Affairs Administration
MCAAA: Midland Counties Amateur Athletic Association
MCAB: Marine Corps Air Base
m car: 1000 carats
MCAD: Military Contracts Administration Department
MCADO: Micronesian Community Action Development Organization
MCAF: Marine Corps Air Facility; Marine Corps Air Field; Military Construction, Air Force
MCAIR: McDonnell Aircraft Company
MCAS: Marine Corps Air Station
MCAT: Medical College Admission Test; Midwest Council on Airborne Television
m. cau.: *misce caute* (Latin—mix cautiously)
MCAUSA: Military Chaplain's Association of the U.S.A.
mcb: membranes cytoplasmic bodies; miniature circuit breaker
McB: McBurney's (point)
MCB: Marine Corps Base; Mobile Construction Battalion
MCBA: Master Car Builders' Association
mcc: maintenance of close contact; modified close control
MCC: Maintenance Control Center; Marylebone Cricket Club; Manual Combat Center; Marine Corps Commandant; Mesta Machine Company (stock exchange symbol); Missile Control Center; Mission Control Center; Monroe Community College; Munitions Carriers Conference; Music Critics' Circle
MCCA: *Mercado Común Centro Americano* (Central American Common Market)
MCCC: Muskegon County Community College
MCCCA: Marine Corps Combat Correspondents Association
mcd: mean corpuscular diameter; median control death; metal-covered door
MCC-H: Mission Control Center—Houston (NASA)
McCL: McCabe Library (Swarthmore)
mcd: *minimo comune denomiatore* (Italian—least common denominator)
Mc D: Mc Donald; Mc Donald's
M.C.D.: Doctor of Comparative Medicine; Master of Civic Design
McDA: McDonnell Aircraft
MCDA: Motor Car Dealers Association
McDAC: McDonnell Aircraft Corporation
Mc D O: Mc Donald Observatory
MCDS: Management Control Data System
mcd/slv: minimum-cost-design/space launch vehicle (MCD/SLV)
mcdt: mean corrective down time
mce: military characteristics equipment
MCE: Memphis Cotton Exchange; Montgomery Cotton Exchange
MCE: *Mercado Común Europeo* (Spanish—European Common Market); *Mercato Comune Europeo* (Italian—

European Common Market)
M.C.E.: Master of Civil Engineering
MCEB: Military Communications Electronics Board
M.C.Eng: Master of Civil Engineering
M. Cer. E.: Master of Ceramic Engineering
MCET: Mississippi Center for Educational Television
mcf: medium corpuscular fragility; thousand cubic feet
mcfd: 1000 cubic feet of gas per day
mcfh: 1000 cubic feet of gas per hour
mcflm: microfilm; microfilming
mcfm: 1000 cubic feet of gas per month
mcg: microgram
MCG: Mandalay Coral Gardens (Queensland)
mc & g: mapping, charting, and geodesy
McG-H: McGraw-Hill
McGraw: McGraw-Hill
McG U: McGill University
McGUL: McGill University Library
mch: mail chute; mean corpuscular hemoglobin (MCH)
Mch: Manchester
M. Ch.: *Magister Chirurgiae* (Latin—Master of Surgery)
MCH: Maternal and Child Health
mchc: mean corpuscular hemoglobin concentration
M.Ch.D.: *Magister Chirugiae Dentalis* (Latin—Master of Dental Surgery)
M.Ch.E.: Master of Chemical Engineering
M. Chem. E.: Master of Chemical Engineering
M.Chir.: *Magister Chirugiae* (Latin—Master of Surgery)
M.Ch. Orth.: *Magister Chirurgiae Orthopaedicae* (Latin—Master of Orthopedic Surgery)
MCHP: Maternal and Child Health Program
mc hr: millicurie hour(s)
MCHRD: Mayor's Committee for Human Resources Development
M.Chrom.: Master of Chromatics
MCHS: Maternal and Child Health Service
M Ch S: Member of the Society of Chiropodists
mcht: merchant
Mchter: Manchester
mci: malleable cast iron; mottled cast iron
MCI: Marine Corps Institute; Massachusetts Correctional Institution (Framingham); Mexican Coffee Institute; Milk Can Institute
MCIE: Midland Counties Institution of Engineers
McINP: McIwaine National Park (Rhodesia)
M.C.J.: Master of Comparative Jurisprudence
MCJC: Mason City Junior College
McKay: David McKay
McKS: (Sir Colin) McKenzie Sanctuary (Victoria, Australia)
McKVHS: McKee Vocational High School
mcl: midclavicular line; midcostal line
MCL: Manchester Central Library; Marine Corps League; Master Control Log; Metal Control Laboratories; Metropolitan Central Library; Mid-Canada Line (radar warning fenceline); Moore-McCormack Lines; Mushroom Canners League
M.C.L.: Master of Civil Law
MCLA: Marine Corps League Auxiliary
M.Clin.Psychol.: Master of Clinical Psychology
MCLO: Medical Construction Liaison Office
M.Cl.Sc.: Master of Clinical Science
mcm: military characteristics motor vehicles; missile-carrying missile; thousand circular mils
mcm: *minimo comune multiple* (Italian—least common multiple; lowest common multiple)
MCM: Manual for Courts-Martial; Marine Corps Manual; Monte Carlo Method
MCMA: Machine Chain Manufacturers Association; Marine Corps Memorial Commission; Metal Cookware Manufacturers Association
MCMC: Marine Corps Memorial Commission
MCMS: Marin County Medical Society
MCM&T: Michigan College of Mining & Technology
McM U: McMaster University
McMUMC: McMaster University Medical Centre (Hamilton)
MCN: Management Control Number; Manual Control Number
MCNP: Mammoth Cave National Park (Kentucky); Mount Cook NP (South Island, New Zealand)
MCNY: Museum of the City of New York
mco: main civilian occupation; mills culls out
mço: *março* (Portuguese—March)
Mco: Morocco
MCOAG: Marine Corps Operations Analysis Group
MCODA: Motor Cab Owner-Drivers' Association
mcol: musicological; musicologist; musicology
M.Com.: Master of Commerce; Minister of Commerce
MCOM: Mobility Command (US Army)
M. Com. Adm.: Master of Commercial Administration
M. Comp. Law: Master of Comparative Law
M. Com. Sc.: Master of Commercial Science
MCON: Military Construction—Navy
mcos: *marcos* (Spanish—marks), German coins
MCOW: Medical College of Wisconsin
mcp: male chauvinist pig; manual control panel; mode control panel; multi-component plasma; multiple chip package
MCP: Management Control Plan; Maritime Company of Philadelphia; Maritime Company of the Philippines; Massachusetts College of Pharmacy; Master Control Program; Military Construction Program; Minerals and Chemicals Philipp; Model Cities Program
M.C.P.: Master of City Planning
MCPA: Member of the College of Pathologists of Australasia
mcph: metacarpal-phalangeal
MCPO: Master Chief Petty Officer
mcps: megacycles per second
MCPS: Member of the College of Physicians and Surgeons
McQ-E: McQuaid-Ehn (grain size)
mcr: metabolic clearance rate; military compact reactor; mother-child relationship
MCR: Marine Corps Reserve; Master Change Record; Manufacturing Change Request

M.C.R.: Master of Comparative Religion
MCRA: Member of the College of Radiologists of Australasia
MCRC: Mass Communications Research Center (University of Wisconsin)
MCRD: Marine Corps Recruit Depot
MCROA: Marine Corps Reserve Officers Association
mcrt: multichannel rotary transformer
mcs: meridian control signal; meter-candle second; motor circuit switch
mc/s: megacycles per second
MCs: Military Characteristics
MCS: coastal minesweeper (naval symbol); Maintenance Control Section; Marine Cooks and Stewards (union); Marine Corps School; Marine Corps Station; mine countermeasures support ship (naval symbol); Missile Commit Sequence; Mobile Checkout Station; Mobile Coastal Service
M.C.S.: Master of Commercial Science
MCSC: Medical College of South Carolina; Military College of South Carolina (The Citadel)
MCSH: Manhattan College of the Sacred Heart
MCSP: Member of the Chartered Society of Physiotherapy
mc spec: motorcycle specialist(s); motorcycle specification(s)
MC S & T: Manchester College of Science and Technology
mct: multiple-compressed tablet
MCT: Mechanical Comprehension Test
m/cta: *mi cuenta* (Spanish—my account)
MCTA: Metropolitan Commuter Transportation Authority
MCTI: Metal Cutting Tool Institute
MC & TS: Monotype Casters' and Typefounders' Society
mcu: median control unit; medium closeup
m & cu: monitor monitor and control unit
MCU: Modern Churchmen's Union
mcv: mean corpuscular volume
MCV: Medical College of Virginia
mcw: metal casement window; modulated continuous wave
MCW: Mallinckrodt Chemical Works
m cwt: 1000 hundredweight
mcx: maximum-cost expediting
MCZ: Museum of Comparative Zoology
md: maximum design; mean deviation; memorandum of deposit; mental(ly) defective; mentally deficient; message dropping; minute difference(s); mitral disease; month's date; movement directive; muscular dystrophy
md: *main droite* (French—right hand); *mano derecha* (Spanish—right hand) *mano destra* (Italian—right hand); *marchand* (French—good value; marketable); *milliard* (French—1000 million)
m-d: manic-depressive
m/d: memorandum of deposit(s); month(s) after date
m & d: medicine and duty
m d: *mano destra* (Italian—right hand)
Md: Maid; Maryland; Marylander; mendelevium
MD: Management Directive; Marine Detachment; Medical Department; Medical Discharge; Mess Deck; Middle Dutch; Mine Depot; Music Director; Musical Director
M$: Malaysia dollar (Singapore dollar)
M.D.: *Medicinae Doctor* (Latin—Doctor of Medicine)
M D: *mano destra* (Italian—right hand)
mda: maintenance depot assistance
Mda: Mérida (inhabitants—Meridanos)
MDA: Marking Device Association; Master Dyes Association; Material Disposal Authority; Multiple-Docking Adapter; Mural Decorators Association; Muscular Dystrophy Association; Mutual Defense Agency; Mutual Defense Assistance
MDAA: Mutual Defense Assistance Act
MDAC: McDonnell Douglas Astronautics Company; Mutual Defense Assistance—China area
MDAGT: Mutual Defense Assistance, Greece and Turkey
MDAIKP: Mutual Defense Assistance, Iran, Republic of Korea, and the Philippines
MDANAA: Mutual Defense Assistance, North Atlantic Area
MDAP: Mutual Defense Assistance Program
M-day: manufacturing day; mobilization day; moratorium day
M d B: *Mitglied des Bundestages* (German—member of the Bundestag)
MDB: *Movimento Democrático Brasileiro* (Portuguese—Brazilian Democratic Movement)—political party
MDBVHS: Mabel D. Bacon Vocational High School
mdc: maintenance data collection
MDC: McDonnell Douglas Corporation; Manhattan Drug Corporation; Metropolitan District Commission; Moncure Daniel Conway
MDCA: Master Diamond Cutters Association
MDC-W: McDonnell Douglas Corporation—West
mdd: milligrams per square decimeter per day
Mddx: Middlesex
MDE: *Modern Drug Encyclopedia*
M.D.E.: Master of Domestic Economy
m'dear: my dear
M.Dent.Sci.: Master of Dental Science
M.Des.: Master of Design
mdf (MDF): main distributing frame (data processing); manual direction finder
MDF: Modderfontein Dynamite Factory
MDFC: McDonnell Douglas Finance Corporation
MDG: Medical Director-General
mdh (MDH): malate dehydrogenase
MDHB: Mersey Docks and Harbour Board (Liverpool)
mdi: magnetic detection indicator
m. dict.: *more dictu* (Latin—in the manner directed)
M.Did.: Master of Didactics
M. Di. Eng.: Master of Diesel Engineering
M.Dip.: Master of Diplomacy
M.Div.: Master of Divinity
MDJC: Miami-Dade Junior College; Mississippi Delta Junior College
m dk: main deck
mdl: model
Mdl: Middle (postal abbreviation)
M d L: *Mitglied des Landtages*

(German—member of the Landtag)
MDL: Mine Defense Laboratory
Mdlle: *Mademoiselle* (French—Miss)
mdm (MDM): middiastolic murmur
Mdm: Madam
MDM: Movement (for a) Democratic Military (New Leftist device to destroy military morale)
Mdme: *Madame* (French—Missus)
m$n: *moneda (pesos) nacional* (Spanish—national monetary unit(s)—Argentinian peso(s))
mdn: median
MDNA: Machinery Dealers National Association
mdnb: metadinitrobenzene
MDNS: Modified Decimal Numbering System
mdnt: midnight
M-dog: mine dog (trained to find buried mines)
m.d.p.: *mento-dextra posterior* (Latin—right mento-posterior)
mdr: minimum daily requirement
Mdr: Madras
mds: minimum discernible signal; mission design and series
Mds: *Mesdames* (French—Ladies)
MDS: mail distribution schedule; mail distribution scheme; Main Dressing Station; Manufacturing Data Series; Medical-Dental Service; meteoroid detection satellite
M.D.S.: Master of Dental Surgery
M$S: **peso** (*moneda nacional*—Argentine letter symbol)
mdsa: multiple disc-sampling apparatus
M.D.Sc.: Master of Dental Science
mdse: merchandise
MDSF: Mission to Deep Sea Fishermen
mdsg: merchandising
MDST: Mountain Daylight Saving Time
mdt: mean down time; moderate
m.d.t.: *mento-dextra transversa* (Latin — right mento-transverse)
MDT: Mutual Defense Treaty
MDTA: Manpower Development and Training Act
MDTS: Modular Data Transmission System
MDU: Mine Disposal Unit; Mobile Development Unit
M du N: Magasin du Nord (Copenhagen's leading department store)
Mdv: Marek's disease virus
M.D.V.: Doctor of Veterinary Medicine
mdw: measured day work
MDW: Chicago, Illinois (Midway Airport); Military District of Washington; Minnesota, Dakota & Western (railroad)
Mdws: Meadows
Mdx: Middlesex
mdy: magnetic deflection yoke
MDY: Midland Oil (stock exchange symbol)
me.: marbled edges; marbled edging, maximum effect; maximum effort; metabolizable energy; methyl; milligram equivalent; miter end; most excellent; multi-engine; muzzle energy
me. (ME): measles encephalitis
m/e: mechanical/electrical; mobility equipment
m & e: music and (sound) effects
m E: *meines Erachtens* (German—in my opinion)
Me: Maine; Mainers; Mexican(s); Mexico
Me: *Maître* (French—Master)—advocate; attorney
ME: Managing Editor; Marine Engineer; Medical Examiner; Methodist Episcopal; Middle English; Military Engineer; Mining Engineer; Morristown and Erie (railroad); Mouvement Europeen (European Movement)
M.E.: Master of Education; Mechanical Engineer
mea: measure(s); measuring; minimum enroute altitude; monoethanolamine (MEA)
MEA: Medical Exhibitors Association; Michigan Education Association; Middle East Airlines; Minnesota Education Association; monoethanolamine; Montana Education Association; Music Educators Association; Musical Educators Association
M.E.A.: Master of Engineering Administration
Meadowlark: state bird of Montana, Nebraska, North Dakota, Oregon, and Wyoming
MEAF: Middle East Air Force
Meanie: nickname for a mean person
MEAR: Maintenance Engineering Analysis Record
meas: measure; measurement
Meas for M: *Measure for Measure*
M.E. Auto.: Master of Automobile Engineering; Master of Automotive Engineering
meb: military early bird
MEB: Marine Expeditionary Brigade; Master Electronics Board; Medical Board; Melbourne, Australia (airport); Midlands Electricity Board (UK)
MEBA: Marine Engineers' Beneficial Association
mec: main engine cutoff
M. Ec.: Master of Economics
MEC: Maine Central (railroad); Marine Expeditionary Corps; Master Executive Council; Methodist Episcopal Church
M.E.C.: Master of Engineering Chemistry; Member of the Executive Council
meca: maintainable electronics component assembly; malfunctioned equipment corrective action; mercury evaporation and condensation; multi-element component array
mecano: mechanotherapy
MECAS: Middle Eastern College for Arabic Studies (Beirut, Lebanon)
mecc: *meccanica* (Italian—mechanic)
MECCA: Minnesota Environmental Control Citizens Association
Mecca of Spain: Santiago de Compostela
mech: mechanic; mechanical; mechanism
ME Ch: Methodist Episcopal Church
MECHA: *Movimiento Estudiantil Chicano de Aztlán* (Mexico-Spanish—Chicano Student Movement of Aztlán)—in Spanish *chicano* partakes of chicanery and *Aztlán* is a mythical land northwest of Mexico to where the Aztecs departed and may be California where MECHA has many members
M.E. Chem.: Master of Chemical Engineering
Mech Eng: *Mechanical Engineering*
meco: main engine cutoff
M.Econ.: Master of Economics
MECU: Municipal Employees Credit Union
mecz: mechanized

med: medal; medalist; medallion; median; median erythrocyte diameter; medic; medical; medication; medicinal; medicine; medieval; medievalism; medievalist; medium; minimal effective dose; minimal erythema dose
Med: medieval; Mediterranean
Med: *Mediterraneo* (Italian—Mediterranean); *Mediterrâneo* (Portuguese—Mediterranean); *Mediterráneo* (Spanish—Mediterranean)
Méd: *Médico* (Italian, Portuguese, Spanish—Doctor); *Méditerranee* (French— Mediterranean)
M.Ed.: Master of Education
MED: Manhattan Engineer District (cover name used during World War II by the developers of the first atomic bomb); Metalworking Equipment Division (US Department of Commerce); Military Electronics Division (Motorola)
M.E.D.: Master of Elementary Didactics
medal.: micromechanized engineering data for automated logistics
Med C: Medical Corps
Med CAP: Medical Civil Action Program
medcat: medium clear-air turbulence
MEDCOM: Mediterranean Communications System
medda: mechanized defense decision anticipation
MED-DENT: Medical-Dental Division (USAF)
medevac: medical evacuation
medex: medical expert
medex: *medecin extension* (French— doctor's aides; medics)
Med Gr: Medieval Greek
Medi: (British seamen's short form—Mediterranean)
Media: Magnavox electronic data-image apparatus
MEDIA: Manufacturers Educational Drug Information Association; Missile Era Data Integration Analysis; Move to End Deception in Advertising
mediaese: cultivated English spoken by many entertainment, radio, and television personalities
medic: medical corpsman; medical doctor; medical student
medicaid: medicinal aid (free medicine for the needy)
Medical Exam: Medical Examination Publishing Company
Medical Essayist: Oliver Wendell Holmes
medicare: medical care
MEDICO: Medical International Corporation
Medit: Mediterranean
MEDIUM: Missile Era Data Integration Ultimate Method
medivac: medical evacuation
medix: medical students
med juris: medical jurisprudence
med lab(s): medical laboratories; medical laboratory
MEDLARS: Medical Literature Analysis and Retrieval System
Med Lat: Medieval Latin
MEDLINE: Medical On-Line (computer retrieval system)
M. Ed. L. Sc.: Master of Education in Library Science
med ray: medullary ray
med ray par: medullary ray parenchyma
med ray trac: medullary ray tracheids
MEDRC: Medical Reserve Corps
MEDRECO: Mediterranean Refining Company
MEDRESCO: Medical Research Council
MEDSAC: Medical Service Activity (USA)
Med. Sc. D.: Doctor of Medical Science
Med Sch: Medical School
med show: medicine show (carnival slang)
med tech: medical technology
Med Tech: Medical Technician; Medical Technologist
mee: methylethyl ether
M.E.E.: Master of Electrical Engineering
M.E. Eng.: Master of Electrical Engineering
meerschaum: hydrated magnesium silicate
mef: maximal expiratory flow
MEF: Marine Expeditionary Force; Mesopotamian Expeditionary Force; Middle East Forces; Musicians Emergency Fund
mef's: morality enhancing factors
mefv: maximum expiratory flow volume
meg: megacycle; megaton; megawatt; megohm
Meg: Margaret
MEG: Management Evaluation Group
mega: 10^6
megabuck: one million bucks (dollars)
megacorpses: one million corpses (atomic bomb unit)
megacurie: one million curies
megacycle: one million cycles
megadeaths: million deaths
megajoule: one million joules
megameter: one million meters
megamouse: one million mice (statistical unit—experimental biology)
megaton: one million tons
megawatt: one million watts
megger: megohmmeter
Meggie: Margaret
mego: megaphone; megohm(s)
megohm: one million ohms
megs: megacycles
megv: million volts
megw: megawatt
megwh: megawatt-hour
mei: mathematics in education and industry
MEI: Manual of Engineering Instructions; Metals Engineering Institute; Middle East Institute
MEIC: Member of The Engineering Institute of Canada
MEIS: Military Entomology Information Service
MEIU: Management Education Information Unit
Mej: *Mejuffrouw* (Dutch—Miss)
mek: methyl ethyl ketone
Mel: Melanesia; Melanesian; Melanesian Pidjin English (Bêche de Mer); Melanie; Melba; Melbourne; Melvil; Melville; Melvin; Melvina; Melvyn
MEL: Music Education League
M.E.L.: Master of English Literature
Melan: Melanesia; Melanesian
Melanchthon: Philipp Schwarzert
Melb: Melbourne
Meld: melt + weld
MELF: Middle East Land Forces
melg: most European languages
Mélisande: Melusina
melo: melodrama; melody
M. Elo.: Master of Elocution
melos: melodic lines
mem: member; memoirs; memorial
mem.: *memoria* (Latin—memory)
Mem: Memorial (postal abbreviation)
MEM: Mars Excursion Module; Member; memorial; Mem-

phis, Tennessee (airport)
MEMA: Marine Engine Manufacturers' Association
memb: membrane
'members: remembers
Member of the Unemployed: Scottish socialist leader Keir Hardie—founder of the Independent Labour Party (ILP)
MEMC: Marathon Electric Manufacturing Corporation
MEML: Master Equipment Management List
memo: memoranda; memorandum
MEMO: Medical Equipment Management Office
Memp: Memphis
men.: menses; menstruation; mensuration
men: *meno* (Italian—less)
M.En.: Master of English
MEN: Manasco (stock-exchange symbol)
MEN: *Middle East News*
MENC: Music Educators National Conference
Mencius: Meng-tse
Menckonaclast: Henry L. Mencken
MEND: Medical Education for National Defense
Mendl Lib: Mendelssohn Library
Mendy: Mendelssohn
Men of the East: Sherpas of northern India and Nepal
M.Eng.: Master of Engineering; Mining Engineer
M. Eng. P.A.: Master of Engineering and Public Administration
Ménière's disease: sudden dizziness, ear ringing, and vomiting due to disturbance of the labyrinth
Menn: Menninger
Mennon: Mennonite
meno: menopausal; menopause; menorrhoea
MENP: Mount Elgon National Park (Kenya)
menst: menstrual; menstruation
mensur: mensuration
ment: mental; mentalis
M. Ent.: Master of Entomology
mentd: mentioned
Mentor to Parisian Intellectuals: Théophile Gautier
Meo: Bartolomeo
mep: mean effective pressure
MEP: Management Engineering Program; Middle East Perspective
M.E.P.: Master of Engineering Physics
MEP: *Movimiento Electoral del Pueblo* (Spanish—People's Electoral Movement)—Venezuelan political party
MEPC: Metropolitan Estate and Property Corporation
M.E.P.H.: Master of Public Health Engineering
meq/l: millequivalents per liter
mer: meridian
mer (MER): methanol extraction residue
mer: *mercoledi* (Italian—Wednesday); *mercredi* (French—Wednesday)
m & er: mechanical and electrical room
Mer: Mercury
MERB: Mechanical Engineering Research Board
merc: mercury
Merc: Mercantile Exchange; Mercator; Mercedes; Mercedes-Benz; Mercury
MERC: Music Education Research Council
Mercator: Gerardus Mercator—real name of this 16th-century Flemish geographer is Gerhard Kremer
merch: merchantable
Merchants of Death: epithetic nickname sometimes applied to alcohol and tobacco vendors, armament makers, drug pushers, munitions makers, narcotics trafficers, and others whose business may result in the death of their customers
Merchants' Haven: Copenhagen, Denmark
Merch V: *Merchant of Venice*
'mercial: commercial
Mercury: (Latin—Hermes)—the messenger
MERDL: Medical Equipment Research and Development Laboratory (USA)
Meredith: Meredith Press
Meri: Merionethshire
'Merica(n): ((Cockney contraction—America(n))—in the Far East, the South Seas, and many other parts of the world this sometimes comes out as *'Mellica(n)*
merid: meridian
MERIT: Medical Relief International
MERL: Mechanical Engineering Research Laboratory
Merriam: G & C Merriam
Merritt Pkwy: Merritt Parkway
Merry Monarch: Charles II of Great Britain also nicknamed Patron of Bawdy Houses
Merry W: *Merry Wives of Windsor*
mersar: merchant ship search and rescue
MERT: Milwaukee Electric Railway and Transit
Mert Coll: Merton College—Oxford
MERU: Mechanical Engineering Research Unit
Merv: Mervin
mes: main engine start
Mes: Mesozoic
Mes: *Mesdames* (French—ladies)
MES: Michigan Engineering Society; Midwest Electronic Society
mesa.: modularized equipment storage assembly
MESA: Malarial Eradication Special Account; Mechanics Educational Society of America
mesbic (MESBIC): minority enterprise small business investment companies
mesc: mescaline
M. E. Sc.: Master of Engineering Science
MESCO: Middle East Science Cooperative Office (UNESCO)
MESF: Mobile Earth Station Facility
mesh.: medical headings
MeSH: Medical Subject Heading (National Library of Medicine's thesaurus)
Meslier: Jean Meslier—deceased and obscure parish priest whose name was used by Voltaire to escape persecution (*see* Jean Meslier); even the names of the parishes he served—Entrepigny and But—are not to be found in most atlases and gazetteers
meson: meso + electron: mesotron
Mesop: Mesopotamia (Iraq)
Mesopotamia: (Greek—Between Rivers)—land between the Euphrates and the Tigris; formerly Assyria, Babylonia, and Sumeria but presently Iraq
MESP: More Effective Schools Program
Mespot: Mesopotamia (Iraq)
Mess: *Messidor* (French—Harvest Month)—beginning June 19th—tenth month of the French Revolutionary Calendar
Messenger of the Gods: Hermes

(Greek); Mercury (Roman)
Messenger of Mercy: Swiss banker Jean Henri Dunant—founder of the Red Cross
Messner: Julian Messner
Messrs: *Messieurs* (French—Gentlemen)
mest: mestizo
met.: metal; metallic; metallize; metaphor; metaphysics; meteorology; methionine (amino acid) (MET); metronome; metropolitan
Met: Metropolitan Opera; Metropolitan Museum of Art
Meta: Margarita
META: Metropolitan Educational Television Association (Canadian)
metab: metabolism
metall: metallurgy
metallog: metallography
METALMA: Metalúrgica Matarazzo (Brazilian company)
metaph: metaphor(ical)(ly); metaphysical(ly); metaphysician; metaphysics
metaphys: metaphysics
metas: metastasis; metastasize
Metastasio: Pietro Antonio Domenico Bonaventura Trapassi
metath: metathesis
metb: metal base
met bor: metropolitan borough
metc: metal curb; mouse embryo tissue culture
Met Cen Lib: Metropolitan Central Library
METCO: Metropolitan Council for Educational Opportunity
metd: metal door
Met. E.: Metallurgical Engineer
METEI: Medical Expedition to Easter Island
meteor.: meteorology
meteorolo: meteorology
metf: metal flashing
metg: metal grille
meth: methadone; methamphetamine; methane; methedrine; methyl; methyprylon
Meth: Methodist
methanol: methyl alcohol or wood alcohol (CH_3OH)
Meth Epis: Methodist Episcopal
meth freak: methedrine freak (underground slang—habitual user of methedrine)
meth head: methedrine head (underground slang—methedrine addict)
metho: methodology; methyl alcohol
meths: methylated spirits (denatured alcohol)
methu: methuselah (8-bottle capacity)
meti: metal jalousie
M-et-L: Maine-et-Loire
metm: metal mold
M-et-M: Meurthe-et-Moselle
m. et n.: *mane et nocte* (Latin—morning and evening)
meto: maximum except takeoff
Met O: Meteorological Office(r)
METO: Middle East Treaty Organization
metol: methyl-p-aminophenol (photographic developer)
meton: metonomy
metp: metal partition
metr: metal roof
Met R: Metropolitan Railway
metro: metropolitan
métro: *chemin de fer métropolitain* (Paris subway system)
Metro: Metropolitan Life Insurance Company
METRO: New York Metropolitan Reference and Research Library Agency
metroc: meteorological rocket
metrocenter: metropolitan center
metrocomplex: metropolitan complex
metrocore: metropolitan core
metroframe: metropolitan framework
metrol: metrology
metrop: metropolis; metropolitan
metroplex: metropolitan complex
metropol: metropolis; metropolitan
Metropolis of America: New York City
Metropolis of the Magic Valley: Brownsville, Texas on the Rio Grande
Metropolis of the Missouri Valley: Kansas City
Metropolis of the South: Mark Twain's nickname for New Orleans
Metropolis of the State of Oregon: Portland
METRRA: Metropolitan Toronto Residents' and Rate Payers' Association
mets: metal strip
metsats: meteorological satellites
m. et sig.: *misce et signa* (Latin—mix and write a label)
metso: sodium metasilicate
Metternich: Prince Klemens Wenzel Nepomuk Lothar von Metternich-Winneburg—Austrian statesman convening Congress of Vienna at end of Napoleonic wars
METU: Middle East Technical University (Ankara)
Met- Vic: Metropolitan-Vickers (electrical company)
MEU: Marine Expeditionary Unit
MEU: *Modern English Usage*
mev: million electron volts
Mev: *Mevrouw* (Dutch—Missus)
MeV: megaelectronvolt; million electronvolt
Mevr: *Mevrouw* (Dutch—Missus)
MEW: Microwave Early Warning; Ministry of Economic Warfare
MEWA: Motor and Equipment Wholesalers Association
MEWS: Missile Early Warning Station
MEWTA: Missile Electronic Warfare Technical Area
Mex: Mexican; Mexico
MEX: Mexico City, Mexico (airport)
Mex C: Mexico City
Mex Cy: Mexican currency
Mex$: Mexican peso
MEXICANA: Compañía Mexicana de Aviación
Mexican National Composer: Carlos Chávez
MEXSM: Mexican Service Medal
Mex Sp: Mexican Spanish
Mexsur: Mexican (automobile) insurance
mez: mezcal(ine)
mez: *mezzo* (Italian—half)
MEZ: *mitteleuropäische Zeit* (German—Central European Time)
mezz: mezzanine; mezzotint
mezzo(s): mezzosoprano(s); mezzotint(s)
mf: machine finish; main feed; male-to-female (ratio); manufacture(d); manufacturing; mastic floor; medium frequency (300-3,000 kc); microfarad(s); mill finish; millifarad(s); motor field; motor freight; multiplying factor
m/f: marked for
mf: *mezzo-forte* (Italian—half loud; moderately loud)
m/f: *mi favor* (Spanish—my favor)
m & f: male and female
MF: Magazines for Friendship; Marshall Field (stock exchange symbol); Medal of Freedom; Middle Fork (railroad); Millard Fillmore (13th President U.S.)
M-F: Massey-Ferguson

M.F.: Master of Forestry
mfa: malicious false alarm
MFA: Military Flying Area
MFA: *Moviemento das Forças Armadas* (Portuguese—Armed Forces Movement)—military dictatorship
M.F.A.: Master of Fine Arts; Museum of Fine Arts
M Fac Hom: Member of the Faculty of Homeopathy
MFAH: Museum of Fine Arts of Houston
M.F.A. Mus.: Master of Fine Arts in Music
MFAR: Michigan Foundation for Advanced Research
mfb: message from base; metallic foreign object
MFB: MFB Mutual Insurance (Manufacturers, Firemen's and Blackstone combined)
mfc: microfilm frame card
m/fcha: *meses fecha* (Spanish—months dated)
mfco: manual fuel cutoff
mfd: manufactured; microfarad; minimum fatal dose (MFD)
MFE: *Movimento Federalista Europeo* (Italian—European Federalist Movement)
MFED: Manned Flight Engineering Division (NASA)
M. F. Eng.: Master of Forest Engineering
mfg: manufacturing; molded fiber glass
mfh: military family housing
MFH: Master of Fox Hounds; Mobile Field Hospital
mfi: melt-flow index
MFI: Musicians Foundation Incorporated
MFIANE: Mutual Fire Insurance Association of New England
MFIBNE: Mutual Fire Inspection Bureau of New England
MFIC: Military Flight Information Center
MFIT: Manual Fault Isolation Test
m fl: *med flere* (Dutch—and others)
MFL: Mobile Field Laboratory
M Flem: Middle Flemish
MFM: Miracle Food Mart
mf method: membrane or millipore filter method
mfn: most favored nation
mf(n): microfiche (negative)
MFNP: Mount Field National Park (Tasmania); Murchison Falls NP (Uganda)
MFOA: Municipal Finance Officers Association
M.For.: Master of Forestry
MFOWW: Marine Firemen, Oilers, Watertenders, and Wipers
mf(p): microfiche (positive)
mfp (MFP): monoflurophosphate
MFPB: Mineral Fiber Products Bureau
mfr: manufacture; manufactured; manufacturer; missile firing range (MFR)
M Fr: Mali franc(s); Moroccan franc(s)
MFRP: Midwest Fuel Recovery Plant (AEC)
mf & s: magazine flooding and sprinkling
MFS: Malleable Founders' Society; Manned Flying System; Medal Field Service; Military Flight Service; Missile Firing Station; Mountain Fuel Supply; steel-hulled fleet minesweeper (3-letter naval symbol)
M.F.S.: Master of Food Science; Master of Foreign Service; Master of Foreign Study
MFSA: Metal Finishing Suppliers' Association
mfso: main fuel shutoff
mfsov: main fuel shutoff valve
MFSS: Missile Flight Safety System(s)
mfst: manifest
mft: major fraction thereof; mechanized flamethrower
m. ft.: *mistura fiat* (Latin—make a mixture)
MFT: Muscle Function Test
M.F.T.: Master of Foreign Trade
MFTD: Mobile Field Training Detachment
m.ft.m.: *misce fiat mistura* (Latin—mix to make a mixture)
MFURB: Maryland Fire Underwriters Rating Bureau
mfv: magnetic field vector; microfilm viewer
MFV: Mars Flyby Vehicle
MfVB: Museum für Volkerkunde, Berlin
MFW: Maritime Federation of the World
mg: machine gun; marginal; milligram; motor generator; multigauge
m-g: machine glazed
m & g: mapping and geodesy
mg: *main gauche* (French—left hand)
m/g: *mi giro* (Spanish—my check; my draft)
mG: *méridien de Greenwich* (French—Greenwich meridian)
Mg: magnesium; Margrave; Margraviate
Mg: *Molekulargewicht* (German—molecular weight)
MG: machine gun; major general; Marine Gunner; Military Government; Minas Gerais; Morris Garage (M-G)
MG: *Maschinegewehr* (German—machine gun)
M-G: Morris-Garage (British sports car)
M & G: Mobile & Gulf
Mga: Malaga
MGA: Managua, Nicaragua (Las Mercedes airport); Military Government Association; Monongahela (railroad); Mushroom Growers Association
mgal: milligal
M-gauge: meter gauge (39.37-inch) railroad track
mgawd: make good all works disturbed
MGB: *Ministerstvo Gosurdastvennoi Bezopasnosti* (Russian—Ministry of State Security)—Soviet secret police
Mg of B: Margrave of Breslau; Margraviate of Breslau
mgc: manual gain control
MGC: Machinery of Government (committee); Marriage Guidance Council
mgcr: maritime gas-cooled reactor
mg/cu m: milligrams (dust, fume, or mist) per cubic meter of air
mgd: magnetogasdynamics; million gallons per day
Mgd: Magdeburg
MGD: Military Geographic Documentation
mge (MGE): maintenance ground equipment
M.G.E.: Master of Geological Engineering
M. Geol. Eng.: Master of Geological Engineering
MGF: Myasthenia Gravis Foundation
mgg: mouse gamma globulin
mgh: milligram hour(s)
MGH: Massachusetts General Hospital
MGI: Mining and Geological Institute of India
MGID: Military Geographic Information and Documentation
MGk: Medieval Greek
mgm (MGM): mobile guided missile
MGM: Metro-Goldwyn-Mayer
Mg of M: Margrave of Moravia; Margraviate of Moravia
MGMS: Manchester Geological

and Mining Society
mgmt: management
mgn: micrograin
MGP: Marcus Garvey Park (formerly Mount Morris Park)
mg %: milligrams percent
Mgr: Manager; Monseigneur (French—Monsignor); Monsignore (Italian—Monsignor)
M Gr: Middle Greek
MGR: Matusadona Game Reserve (Rhodesia)
mgs: missile guidance set (system)
m-g-s: meter-gram-second
MGSA: Military General Supply Agency
mgt: management
MGTB: Mexican Government Tourist Bureau
MGTD: Mexican Government Tourist Delegation
MGU: *Moskovskiy Gosudarstvenny Universitet* (Moscow State University)
M Gun Sgt: Master Gunnery Sergeant
mgw: maximum gross weight
MGW: *Manchester Guardian Weekly*
m'gwd: my gawd (my god)
mh: magentic heading; main hatch; manhole; marital history; materials handling; menstrual history; mental health; millihenries; millihenry; murine hepatitis
mH: millhenry
Mh: *Monatsheft* (German—monthly magazine)
MH: magnetic heading; Master Hosts; Medal of Honor; Ministry of Health; Mission Hills; Most Honorable; Most Honourable
MH: *Mo'etzet Hapo'alot* (Hebrew — Woman Workers Council)
M-H: Minneapolis-Honeywell (stock exchange symbol and trademark)
M & H: Mason and Hamlin
MHA: auxiliary minehunter (naval symbol); Marine Historical Association; Medal for Humane Action; Member of the House of Assembly; Mental Health Administration; Mental Health Association
M.H.A.: Master of Hospital Administration
M-H B: Mid-Hudson Bridge
MHC: coastal minehunter (naval symbol)
MHCOA: Motor Hearse and Car Owners Association
mh cp: mean horizontal candlepower
mhcv (MHCV): manned hypersonic cruise vehicle
mhd : magnetohydrodynamics
mhd lt: masthead light
mhe: materials handling equipment
M.H.E.: Master of Home Economics
MHEA: Mechanical Handling Engineers Association
M Heb: Middle Hebrew
MHEDA: Material Handling Equipment Distributors Association
M.H.E.E.: Master of Home Economics Education
M. H. E. Ed.: Master of Home Economics Education
mhf: medium high frequency
M-H-F: Massey-Harris-Ferguson
MHG: Middle High German
mhhw: mean nigher high water
MHI: Material Handling Institute; Metal Hydrides Incorporated; Mitsubishi Heavy Industry
M. Hi. E.: Master of Highway Engineering
M. Hi. Eng.: Master of Highway Engineering
MHII: Material Handling Institute Incorporated
MHJC: Mary Holmes Junior College
MHK: Member of the House of Keys (Isle of Man)
mhl: metal halide lamps
MHL: Manaus Harbour Limited
M.H.L.: Master of Hebrew Literature
MHLG: Ministry of Housing and Local Government
Mhm: Mannheim
MHM: Mill Hill Missionary
MHMA: Mobile Homes Manufacturers Association
MHMC: Mercy Hospital and Medical Center; Montefiore Hospital and Medical Center
MH,MH: *Mary Hartman, Mary Hatrman* (tv show)
mho: unit of conductance or reciprocal ohm
M. Hor.: Master of Horticulture
M. Ho. Sc.: Master of Household Science
MHR: Member of the House of Representatives
MHRA: Modern Humanities Research Association
MHRF: Mental Health Research Fund
MHRI: Mental Health Research Institute (University of Michigan)
mhs: medical history sheet
MHS: Massachusetts Historical Society: Morris High School; Musical Heritage Society
MHSc: Master (Mistress) of Household Science
MH strain: Mill Hill (viral) strain
mht: mean high tide; mild heat treatment; military hospital trainee
MHT: Museum of History and Technology (Smithsonian Institution)
mhtl: mean high tide line
M. Hu.: Master of Humanities
mhv: mean horizontal velocity; murine hepatitis virus
mhw: mean high water
mhwli: mean high water lunitidal interval
mhwn: mean high water neaps
mhws: mean high water springs
M. Hy.: Master of Hygiene
MH y C: Miguel Hidalgo y Costilla
M. Hyg.: Master of Hygiene
mhz (MHz): megahertz(es), formerly megacycle(s) per second
mi: malleable iron; manual input; metabolic index; middle initial; mile(s); mill; minor; minute(s); mitral; mitral insufficiency; mutual inductance
mi: (Italian—third tone in diatonic scale; *E* in fixed- *do* system)
mi ^{2}: square miles(s)
mi^3: cubic mile(s)
mi (MI): myocardial infarction
Mi: Mach indicated; Mach speed indicated; Miami; Mitte
MI: Mare Island; Marshall Islands; Match Institute; Mauritius Institute; Meat Inspection (US Department of Agriculture); Mellon Institute; Military Intelligence; Ministry of Information; Missouri-Illinois (railroad)
M-I: Missouri-Illinois (railroad)
M & I: Manpower and Immigration (Canada)
mia (MIA): missing in action
MIA: Marble Institute of America; Miami, Florida (airport); Mica Industry Association; Millinery Institute of America; missing in action
M.I.A.: Master of International Affairs
Miami Beach East: Tel Aviv, Israel's nickname
MIAPD: Mid-Central Air Procurement District

MIASI: Moore Institute of Art, Science, and Industry
MIB: Management Improvement Board; Maritime Index Bureau; Meat Inspection Branch; Mental Information Bureau; Michigan Inspection Bureau; Missouri Inspection Bureau; Sir Marc Isambard Brunel
mibk: methyl isobutyl ketone
mic: microphone; microwave integrated circuit; military-industrial complex
Mic: The Book of Micah
MIC: Malayan Indian Congress; Marshall Islands Congress; Monaco Information Centre; Motors Insurance Corporation; Music Industry Council
MICA: Moscow Institute for Complex Automation
micbm (MICBM); mobile intercontinental ballistic missile
micc: miniature integrated circuit computer
MICE: Member of the Institution of Civil Engineers
Mich: Michael; Michigan; Michiganite; Michoacan; Mitchell
Michael Angelo Titmarsh: Thackeray's pseudonym adorning some of his earlier works
Michael Curtiz: Mihály Kertész
Michael Tilson Thomas: Mike Thomashefsky
Michelangelo: Michael Angelo Buonarroti
MI Chem E: Member of the Institution of Chemical Engineers
Michl: Michael
Mick: Michael
Mickey Mouse: Walt Disney Productions (Wall Street nickname)
Micky: Micaela; Michael; Michelle
MICMD: Milwaukee Contract Management District
micpac: molecular integrated circuit package
mic. pan.: *mica panis* (Latin—bread crumb)
micr: magnetic ink character recognition; microscope; microscopic; microscopy
micro: 10^{-6}
Micro: Micronesia (Trust Territory of the Pacific); Micronesian
microbiol: microbiology
microbop: microbopper (underground slang—very young person attuned to the modern scene)— *see* macrobop
Microcard: Microcard Editions
microcephs: microcephalics (small-headed people)
microcom: microcomputer (pocket calculator)
Microcosm of Canadian Life: London, Ontario
Microg: Microgramma
micro-in.: micro-inch
micromation: microfilm + automation
micron: millionth of a meter
Micron: Micronesia; Micronesian
micropaleo: micropaleontology
micros: microscopy
microt: microtome
micr's: magnetic ink characters
MICRS: Magnetic Ink Character Recognition System
mic's: military-industrial complex executives; military-industrial complex salesmen
MICS: Museum of the International College of Surgeons
mid.: middle
mid. (MID): minimal inhibiting dose; minimum infective dose
Mid: Midshipman
MID: Merida, Yucatan (airport); Military Information Division
M.I.D.: Master of Industrial Design
Midac: Michigan digital automatic computer
MIDAS: Missile Defense Alarm System
midcult: middle-class culture
Middle America: Central America, Mexico, and the West Indies
Middle Atlantic States: Delaware, Maryland, New Jersey, New York, Pennsylvania, West Virginia
Middle Border: Hamlin Garlin's nickname for the American Middle West
Middle Colonies: New York, New Jersey, Pennsylvania, Delaware
Middle East: area extending from Afghanistan to Egypt and including India, Iran, Iraq, Saudi Arabia, Syria, Lebanon, Israel, Jordan, Kuwait, and the United Arab Emirates
Middle Kingdom: China—long believed by the Chinese to be the center of the inhabited world
Middle Passage: route of the slavers across the middle of the Atlantic between West Africa and the West Indies
Middle States: New York, New Jersey, Pennsylvania, Delaware, and Maryland—midway between New England and the Southern States
Middle West: United States from the Great Lakes to the northern border of the Gulf States and from the western slopes of the Appalachians to the eastern slopes of the Rockies, according to the author's *Worldwide What & Where*—geographic glossary published by Clio Books (ABC-Clio) in Santa Barbara
Middlx: Middlesex
Middy: Midshipman
Middys: Midshipmen
MIDEASTFOR: Middle East Air Force (USN)
MIDEC: Middle East Industrial Development Corporation
MIDELEC: Midlands Electricity Board
MIDFL: Malayan Industrial Development Finance Limited
midis: mid-length (below-the-knee) skirts
Midl: Midlands; Midlothian
Midland Capital: Birmingham, England
Mid Lat: Middle Latin
MIDLNET: Midwest Region Library Network
Mid Loth: Midlothian
Midn: Midshipman
mid. sag.: midsagittal
Mids N D: A Midsummer-Night's Dream
midw: midwestern
mie: military-industrial establishment
mie: *miércoles* (Spanish—Wednesday)
M.I.E.: Master of Industrial Engineering
MIECO: Marshall Islands Import-Export Company
MIEE: Member of the Institution of Electrical Engineers
mierc: *miércoles* (Spanish—Wednesday)
mif: merthiolate-iodine-formaldehyde (fecal examination technique)
mif (MIF): migratory inhibitory factor
MIF: Milk Industry Foundation
MI 5: (British) Military Intelligence Security Service (somewhat quivalent to American FBI)
MIFCT: Moscow Institute of Fine Chemical Technology
MIFI: *Moskovskiy Inzhenerno Fizicheskiy Institut* (Rus-

sian—Moscow Engineering Physics Institute)
mig: magnesium-inert gas
MIG: Mikhail Ivanovich Glinka; Soviet jet fighter aircraft named for designers Mikoyan and Gurevich
MIGB: Millinery Institute of Great Britain
mightn't: might not
Mighty Champion of Freedom: Frederick Douglass
Mig[l]: Miguel (Spanish—Michael)
mi/h: mile(s) per hour
Mihaly Munkacsy: Michael Lieb
MIHS: Marshall Islands High School
MIIA: Medical Information and Intelligence Agency
MIIS: Marshall Islands Intermediate School
mij: *maatschappij* (Dutch—company; society)
MIJ: Muhammad Ali Jinnah
mike: micrometer; microphone
Mike: code letter for M; Michael
Mikimotos: Mikimoto cultured pearls
Mikve Israel: (Hebrew—Ritual Bath of Israel)—oldest synagogue in the New World; in Willemstad on the island of Curaçao in the Netherlands Antilles near Venezuela
mil: mileage; military; militia; milieme; million; 1/1000 inch; 1/10 cent; 1/1000 Palestinian pound (currency formerly used in Israel)
m-i-l: mother-in-law
Mil: Milan
MIL: Malaya Indonesia Line; Microsystems International Limited; Milan, Italy (Malpensa Airport)
MILA: Merritt Island Launch Area
MilAdGru: Military Advisory Group
Mil Att: Military Attaché
MILC: Midwest Inter-Library Center
milcomsat: military communication satellite
mile: *mille passuum* (Latin—1000 paces), a pace being a double step
Mile-High City: Denver, Colorado
Mile-Square City: Hoboken, New Jersey
Mil-Hndbok: Military Handbook
Militaire: Paganini's Violin Caprice (opus 1, no. 14)
Military: Haydn's Symphony No. 100 in G major
Mil Jrn: *Milwaukee Journal*
Milk City: Carnation, Washington
milk of magnesia: magnesium hydroxide—$Mg(OH)_2$
mill.: millinery; milling
Mill: *Million(en)* (German—million(s))
milli: 10^{-3}
Millie: Mildred; Millicent
Million-Acre Farm: Prince Edward Island
milob: military observer
mil pers: military personnel
M.I.L.R.: Master of Industrial and Labor Relations
mils: missile impact locator system
milspec: military specification
Mil-Spec: Military Specification(s)
MILSTAMP: Military Standard Transportation and Movement Procedures
Mil-Std (MIL-STD): Military Standard
MILSTRAP: Military Standard Requisitioning and Accounting Procedures
MILSTRIP: Military Standard Requisitioning and Issue Procedures
Milt: Milton
Milw: Milwaukee
MILW: Milwaukee Route (Chicago, Milwaukee, St Paul & Pacific Railroad)
mim: micro-impulse mosaic; mimeograph(ing; y)
Mim: Mimi; Miriam; Miryam (niah)
MIM: Maintenance Instruction Manual (DoD); Mount Isa Mines (Queensland)
Mima: Jemima
MI Mar E: Member of the Institute of Marine Engineers
MIME: Midland Institute of Mining Engineers
MI Mech E: Member of the Institution of Mechanical Engineers
mimeo: mimeograph(ed)
mi/min: miles per minute
MIMR: May Institute of Medical Research
MIMS: *Monthly Index of Medical Specialties*
mimsy: miserable and flimsy
min: minim; minimum; minor; minority; minute
min: *minore* (Italian—minor)
Min: Minister; Ministry; Minoan
Mina: Wilhelmina
Min Agric: Ministry of Agriculture
minas: (Portuguese or Spanish—mines, as in Minas Gerais)
min b/l: minimum bill of lading
MINCEX: *Ministerio de Comercio Exterior* (Spanish—Ministry of Foreign Trade)
Mind: Mindanao
mindac: miniature inertial navigation digital automatic computer
mindd: minimum due date
Min Def: Ministry of Defence
Min. E.: Mining Engineer
Mineap: Minneapolis
minec: military necessity
minelco: miniature electronic component
mineola: orange + tangerine (hybrid citrus fruit)
mineral.: mineralogy
Mineral Soc: Minerological Society
Mineral Storehouse of the Nation: Canada's Hudson Bay area
Minerva: (Latin—Athene)—goddess of wisdom
MINFAR: *Ministerio de las Fuerzas Armadas Revolucionarias* (Spanish—Ministry of the Revolutionary Armed Forces)—Cuba
Min Fuel: Ministry of Fuel and Power
mingy: mean and stingy
Min Hous: Ministry of Housing
mini: minibop(per); minibra; minimum; miniskirt; mini-swimsuit
minibop: minibopper (underground slang—older child attuned to the modern scene)—*see* macrobop
minibra(s): miniature brassiere(s)—(less concealing—more revealing)
minibus: miniature autobus
minicam: miniature camera
minimax: (selecting move to) minimize maximum possible losses
Mining Baron: William A. Clark
MININT: *Ministerio del Interior* (Spanish—Ministry of the Interior)
minis: minimum-length skirts
miniskirt(s): miniature skirt(s)—(barely covering the upper thighs)
minisym: miniature symphony
minium: red lead (lead oxide)
Minkies: Minquier Islands (Rocks)
Minn: Minnesota; Minnesotan
Minne: Minnesota
Minnie: Minerva; Minneapolis; Minnesota

Minn Trib: *Minneapolis Tribune*
Min^o: *Ministro* (Spanish—Minister; Ministry)
Minor Prophets of the Old Testament: Hosea, Joel, Amos, Obadiah, Jonah, Micah, Nahum, Habakkuk, Zephaniah, Haggai, Zacharia, Malachi
Min P: Minister Plenipotentiary
MINP: Mallacoota Inlet National Park (Victoria, Australia) minpac; Mine Warfare Forces, Pacific (USN)
Min PBW: Ministry of Public Building and Works
Min Plenip: Minister Plenipotentiary
Min PW: Ministry of Public Works
Minquiers: Minquier Islands (Rocks)—also called the Minkies
Min Res: Minister Residentiary
MINREX: *Ministerio de Relaciones Exteriores* (Spanish—Ministry of Foreign Relations)
MINRON: Mine Squadron
mins: minutes
M Inst Met: Member of the Institute of Metals
Minstrel Composer: James Bland who composed *Carry Me Back to Old Virginny*
M Inst SP: Member of the Institution of Sewage Purification
MINTACTS: Mobile Integrated Telemetry and Tracking System
Min Tech: Ministry of Technology
M. Int. Med.: Master of Internal Medicine
Minute: Chopin's Waltz in D flat (opus 64, no. 1)
Minuteman: solid-fuel intercontinental ballistic missile produced by Boeing
MINWR: Merritt Island National Wildlife Refuge (Florida)
min wt: minimum weight
Minx of the Movies: Betty Compson
mio: meteoritic impact origin; minimum identifiable odor
MIO: Marine Inspection Office; Mobile Issuing Office; Movements Identification Order
Mioc: Miocene
MIOUDO: Museo del Instituto Oceanográfico de la Universidad de Oriente (Museum of the Oceanographic Institute of the University of Oriente)
mip: malleable iron pipe; marine insurance policy; mean indicated pressure; missile impact predictor; modulated interference plan; monthly investment plan; mortgage insurance premium(s)
MIP: Manufacturers of Illumination Products; Material Improvement Program; Methods Improvement Program; Military Improvement Program
mipir: missile precision instrumentation radar
MIPR: Military Interdepartmental Purchase Request
Mipu: *Mikropunkt* (German—microdot) — World-War-II masterpiece of espionage technique assuring transmission of microscopic messages no bigger than a dot
mir: mirror
M Ir: Middle Irish
MIR: *Movimiento de Izquierda Revolucionaria* (Spanish—Movement of the Revolutionary Left)—active in Bolivia, Chile, Ecuador, Peru, and Venezuela
MIRA: Motor Industry's Research Association
MIRA: *Monthly Index of Russian Accessions*
Miracle: Haydn's Symphony No. 96 in D major
Miracle of Nature: Queen Christina of Sweden
mirad: monostatic infrared intrusion detector
mird: medium internal radiation dose
MIRE: Member of the Institution of Radio Engineers
mirv: multiple independent reentry vehicle
mis: missing
Mis.: *Miserere* (Latin—have mercy)
MIS: Management Information System; Material Inspection Service; Military Intelligence Service; mine issuing ship (naval symbol); Minstrel Instruction Society
M.I.S.: Master of International Service
mis. accur.: *misce accuratissme* (Latin—mix very intimately)
misc: miscellaneous; miscible
miscend.: *miscendus* (Latin—to be mixed)
Mischa: (Russian nickname—Michael)—Mike
MI 6: (British) Military Intelligence Secret Service
mis. caute: *misce caute* (Latin—mix cautiously)
miscg: miscarriage
miscon: misconduct
mis doc: miscellaneous documents
MISE: Member of the Institution of Sanitary Engineers
miser.: microwave space relay
mis. et seg.: *misce et signa* (Latin—mix and write a label)
misg: missing
MISHAP: Missile High-Speed Assembly Program
MISI: Member of the Iron and Steel Institute
MISLIC: Mid-Staffordshire Libraries in Cooperation
mis. mei: *miserere mei* (Latin—have mercy on me)
misn: misnumbered
MISO: Military Intelligence Service Organization
MISP: Member of the Institution of Sewage Purification
mispo: mission summary printout
Misr: (Egyptian—Egypt)
M I Sr: *Muy Ilustre Señor* (Spanish—Very Illustrious Sir)
MISR: Macauley Institute for Soil Research; Major Item Status Report
miss.: mission; missionary
Miss.: Mississippi; Mississippian
Missie: Miss; Mississippi; Missus; Mrs.
missilese: engineering jargon of guided-missile experts
Missini: Mussolini's neo-fascist followers
Missionary to the Lepers: Father Damien
Mississippi River Painter: George Caleb Bingham
Miss New Orleans: Dorothy Lamour's title in 1931
Miss Tarbarrel: Ida M. Tarbell
mist.: *mistura* (Latin—mixture)
Mist: Mistress
MIST: Medical Information Service (via) Telephone
Mistletoe: Oklahoma state flower
MISTRAM: Missile Trajectory Measurement System
mistrans: mistranslation
mit: master instruction tape; milled in transit; minimum individual training; monoiodotyrosine
mit.: *mitte* (Latin—send)
M It: Middle Italian
Mit: *Mittwoch* (German—Wednesday)
MIT: Maritime Institute of Technology; Massachusetts Institute of Technology (M.I.T. preferred as periods set it

apart from all other MITs); Massachusetts Investors Trust; Military Intelligence Translator; Milwaukee Institute of Technology; Miracidial Immobilization Test

M.I.T.: Massachusetts Institute of Technology

MITAGS: Marine Institute of Technology and Graduate Studies

MITC: Magdalen Island Transportation Company

Mitch: Mitchell

MITGS: Marine Institute of Technology and Graduate Studies

MITI: Ministry of International Trade and Industry

mit insuf: mitral insufficiency

mito: minimum interval takeoff

mi tp: miniature template

Mitropa: Mitteleuropäische Schlafund Speisewagen Aktiengesellschaft (Middle- European Sleeping Car and Dining Car Company)

mit. sang.: *mitte sanguinem* (Latin—bleed)

Mitsubishi: Mitsubishi Bank; Mitsubishi Corporation; Mitsubishi International Corporation

mitt: *mittente* (Italian—sender)

Mitt: *Mitteilungen* (German—communications)

mit. tal.: *mitte tales* (Latin—send such)

Mitya: (Russian diminutive—Dmitri)

mitz: *mitzvah* (Yiddish from Hebrew *miswah*—a good deed)

Mitzi: Margaret

MIU: Maharishi International University

MIV: Moody's Investor Service (stock exchange symbol)

MIWE: Member of the Institution of Water Engineers

mix.: mixture

mixt: mixture

Mizrachi: *Merkaz Ruchani* (Hebrew—Spiritual Center)—orthodox organization

mizzle: mist + drizzle

Mizzou: Missouri

mj: marijuana

MJ: Mary Jane (underground slang)—marijuana

M.J.: Master of Journalism

MJA: Manuel José Arce

MJC: Manatee Junior College; Metropolitan Junior College; Moberly Junior College

mjd: management job description

mjg: management job guide

MJI: Member of the Journalists Institute

MJQ: Modern Jazz Quartet

MJS: Member of the Japan Society

MJV: Mojud Hosiery (stock exchange symbol)

mk: mark (British equivalent of type)

Mk: markka (Finnish monetary unit)

Mk: *Manualkoppler* (German—manual coupler)—organ

MK: Mackey Airlines; Member of Knesset

M-K: Morrison-Knudsen

M/K: Member of the Knesset

MKC: Kansas City, Missouri (airport)

mkd: marked

MKE: Milwaukee, Wisconsin (airport)

mkg: meter kilogram

MKH: Mackintosh-Hemphill (stock-exchange symbol)

MKK: Mitsubishi Kakoki Kaishi

mkm: marksman

MKNP: Malawi Kasungu National Park (Malawi); Mount Kenya National Park (Kenya)

MKO: Muskogee Company (stock exchange symbol)

mkr: *mikroskopisch* (German—microscopic)

MKR: Mkuzi Game Reserve (South Africa)

mks: meter, kilogram, solar second system of fundamental standards

mksa: meter, kilogram, second, ampere system

mkt: market

MKT: Missouri-Kansas-Texas (railroad)

mk tp: mark template

MKW: Military Knight of Windsor

MKY: McKee and Company (stock-exchange symbol)

ml: machine language; mean level; millilambert(s); milliliter(s); mine layer; mixed lengths; molder; mold line; money list; motor launch; muzzle-loading

ml: *moneda legal* (Spanish—legal tender)

m/l: middle left; missile lift

m/l: *mi letra* (Spanish—my letter)

m or l: more or less

mL: millilambert(s)

Ml: Malay; Malaya; Malayan; Malaysia; marl

ML: Manuel; Martin-Marietta (stock exchange symbol); Middle Latin; Military Liaison; Missile Launcher; motor launch; small minesweeper (naval symbol)

M/L: Maersk Line

M.L.: *Medicinae Licentiatus* (Latin—Licentiate in Medicine)

M de L: Metropolitano de Lisboa (Lisbon subway system)

M-et-L: Maine-et-Loire; Meurthe-et-Loire

mla: magnetic lens assembly; manpack loop antenna; microwave linear accelerator

MLA: Manitoba Library Association; Maryland Library Association; Medical Library Association; Member of the Legislative Assembly; Minnesota Library Association; Modern Language Association; Music Library Association

M-LA: Mont-Laurier Aviation

M.L.A.: Master of Landscape Architecture

MLAA: Modern Language Association of America

m'lady: my lady

ml ar: mill arbor

M. L. Arch. Master of Landscape Architecture

MLAT: Modern Language Aptitude Test

mlb: multilinear board

MLB: Maritime Labor Board

mlbm (MLBM): modern large ballistic missile

MLBPA: Major League Baseball Players Association

mlc: main lobe clutter; mesh level control; microelectric logic circuit; mixed leucocyte culture; motor load control; multilayer circuit; multilens camera; multiplanar chain link

MLC: Meat and Livestock Commission; Member of the Legislative Council; Military Liaison Committee; Mutual Life and Citizens (insurance company)

MLCAEC: Military Liaison Committee to the Atomic Energy Commission

ml cu: mill cutter

mld: middle landing; minimum lethal dose; minimum line of detection; molded

mld (MLD): metachromatic leukodystrophy

mld_{50}: minimum lethal (radioactive) dose

M. L. Des.: Master of Landscape

Design
mldg: moulding
mldr: molder
mle: maximum loss expectancy
mle: *modèle* (French—model; pattern)
Mle: Mile (postal abbreviation)
M. L. Eng.: Master of Landscape Engineering
MLEU: *Mouvement Libéral pour l'Europe Unie* (French—Liberal Movement for a United Europe)
MLF: Multi-Lateral Force
ml fx: mill fixture
mlg: main landing gear; most languages
MLG: Middle Low German
mlg(s): mailing(s)
Ml'H: Musée de l'Homme, Paris
mli: minimum line of interception
M-Li: Muller-Lyer (illusion)
M. Lib.: Master of Librarianship
M. Lib. Sci.: Master of Library Science
M. Lit.: Master of Letters; Master of Literature
MLL: Music Lovers League
Mlle: *Mademoiselle* (French—Miss)
Mlles: *Mesdemoiselles* (French—Misses)
mllw: mean lower low water
MLMA: Metal Lath Manufacturers Association
Mln: Milan
MLN: *Movimiento de Liberación Nacional* (Spanish—National Liberation Movement)—Uruguayan Tupamaros terrorists
MLNP: Malawi Lengwe National Park
mlnr: milliner
MLNR: Ministry of Land and Natural Resources
MLNS: Ministry of Labour and National Service
MLNWR: Medicine Lake National Wildlife Refuge (Montana)
MLO: Midland Light Orchestra; Military Liaison Office(r)
m'lord: my lord
Mloth: Midlothian
mlp: metal lath and plaster
m.l.p.: *mento-laeva posterior* (Latin—left mento-posterior)
MLQ: *Modern Language Quarterly*
mlr: main line of resistance
m-l r: muzzle-loading rifle
mlr (MLR): mixed lymphocyte response
MLR: Marine Life Resources (program)
MLR: *Modern Law Review*
MLRB: Mutual Loss Research Bureau
m-l rg: muzzle-loading rifled gun
MLRP: Marine Life Research Program
mls: machine literature search (ing); median longitudinal section; medium life span
Mls: Mills (postal abbreviation)
MLS: Moon Landing Site (attained by two men from spacecraft Apollo XI on July 20, 1969); Multiple Listing Service
M.L.S.: Master of Library Science
M & LS: Manistique & Lake Superior (railroad)
MLSU: Mowcow M.V. Lomonosov State University (University of Moscow)
mlt: mean low tide; median lethal (radioactive) time (MLT)
Mlt: Malta
mltl: mean low tide line
mltn: 1000 long tons
m'lud: my lord
mlv: murine leukemia virus
mlv(M): murine leukemia virus (Moloney)
mlv(R): murine leukemia virus (Rauscher)
ml vs: mill vise
mlw: mean low water; medium-level waste
MLW: Monrovia, Liberia (airport)
M.L.W.: Master of Labour Welfare
mlwli: mean low water lunitidal interval
mlwn: mean low water neaps
mlws: mean low water springs
mlx: millilux
MLYC: Moosehead Lake Yacht Club
mm: made merchantable; megameter(s); merchant marine; middle marker; millimeter(s); mismated; mucous membrane
m'm: madam
m/m: millimeter(s)—small-arms ammunition term meaning the diameter of a weapon's bore expressed in millimeters
mm: *med mera* (Swedish—and so forth; etc.)
m.m.: *mutatis mutandis* (Latin—with the necessary changes)
mm^2: square millimeter(s)
mm^3: cubic millimeter(s)
m & m: make and mend
mM: millimore
m/M: male Mexican
Mm: *Martyres* (Greek—witnesses; martyrs)
MM: Machinist's Mate; Maintenance Manual; Majesties; Marilyn Monroe; Marine Midland (stock exchange symbol); Martyres (martyrs); Master Mason; maximum misfit; Medal of Merit; mercantile marine; merchant marine; Messageries Maritimes; Messieurs (French—gentlemen); Metropolitan Museum; Military Medal; Minister of Munitions
MM: *Modern Medicine*
M.M.: Master of Music
M.M.: *Maelzel's Metronome*
M de M: Metropolitano de Madrid (Madrid subway system)
M-et-M: Meurthe-et-Moselle
M of M: Ministry of Munitions; Museum of Man
mma: major maladjustment
MMA: Maine Maritime Academy; Massachusetts Maritime Academy; Metropolitan Museum of Art; Monorail Manufacturers Association; Museum of Modern Art
MM of A: Minute Men of America
M. Math.: Master of Mathematics
MMB: Milk Marketing Board
mm bat: main missile battery
MMBC: Maryland Motor Boat Club
mmc: maximum metal condition
MMC: Marine Moisture Control; Materiel Management Code; Meharry Medical College
MMCNY: Marine Museum of the City of New York
MMcKNP: Mount McKinley National Park (Alaska)
MMCT: maritime mobile coastal telegraphy
MMD: minelayer, fast (naval ship symbol)
m mde: *marine marchande* (French—merchant marine)
mme: maximum maintenance effort
Mme: *Madame* (French—Missus)
MME: Manned Mars Expedition
M.M.E.: Master of Mechanical Engineering; Master of Music Education
M. Mech. Eng.: Master of Mechanical Engineering
M. Med.: Master of Medicine
MMEG: Meter Manufacturers' Export Group
Mmes: *Mesdames* (French—ladies)

M. Met: Master of Metallurgy
M. Met. E.: Master of Metallurgical Engineering
mmf: magnetomotive force
MMF: fleet mine layer (naval symbol); Maggio Musicale Fiorentino (Florence May Festival); Milbank Memorial Fund
MMFA: Montreal Museum of Fine Arts
mmfds: microfarads
MMFI: Moravian Music Foundation, Incorporated
MMFPI: Man-Made Fiber Producers Institute
mmg: medium machine gun
MMGR: Masai Mara Game Reserve (Kenya)
MMGS: Mount Muhavura Gorilla Sanctuary (Uganda)
M.Mgt.Eng.: Master of Management Engineering
mmHg: millimeter of mercury
MMI: Micro-Magnetic Industries; Moslem Mosque Incorporated (formerly American Mohammedan Society)
M. Mic.: Master of Microbiology
M. Mi. Eng.: Master of Mining Engineering
MMJC: Meridian Municipal Junior College
m mk: material mark
mmm: military medical mobilization; millimicron(s)
MMM: Modern Music Masters
MMM: *Membre de l'Ordre du Mérite Militaire* (French—Member of the Order of Military Merit)
MMMS: Modern Music Masters Society
MMN: Museum of Man and Nature (Winnipeg)
MMNP: Mount McKinley National Park (Alaska)
Mmo: Malmö
MMO: Music Minus One
mmp (MMP): maritime mobile phone
MMP: Masters, Mates and Pilots (union)
MM & P: Masters, Mates and Pilots
MMPA: Midland Master Printers' Alliance
MMPC: maritime mobile phone coastal
MMPDC: maritime mobile phone distress and calling
MMPI: Minnesota Multiphase Personality Inventory
MMPNC: Medical Materiel Program for Nuclear Casualties
mmpp: millimeters partial pressure
MMPP: Moose Mountain Provincial Park (Saskatchewan)
mmr: mass miniature radiography
MMRA: Maritime Marshland Rehabilitation Administration (Canada)
mmrbm (MMRBM): mobile medium-range ballistic missile
MMS: Manpower Management System; Mass Memory System; Metabolic Monitoring System; Mobile Monitoring System; Modulation Measuring System; Multiplex Modulation System
M.M.S.: Master of Management Studies; Master of Medical Science
MMSA: Mining and Metallurgical Society of America
M.M.S.A.: Master (Mistress) of Midwifery of the Society of Apothecaries
MMSC: Mediterranean Marine Sorting Center
mmscfd: million standard cubic feet per day
m&m session: morbidity and mortality session
MMSW: Mine, Mill and Smelter Workers (union)
mmt: maritime mobile telegraphy
MMT: Manual Muscle Test; maritime mobile telegraphy
MMTC: maritime mobile telegraphy calling
MMTDC: maritime mobile telegraphy distress and calling
mmtv: mouse mammary tumor virus; murine mammary tumor virus
mmu: millimass unit(s)
M.Mus.: Master of Music
MMWD: Marin Municipal Water District
MMY: *Mental Measurements Yearbook*
mn: million
m(n): microfilm negative
mn: *maison* (French—house)
m.n.: *mutato nomine* (Latin—the name being changed)
m. et n.: *mane et nocte* (Latin—morning and night)
m/n: *moneda nacional* (Spanish—national currency)
Mn: manganese
MN: Magnetic North; Merchant Navy
MN: *Magyar Nepkoztarsasag* (Hungarian People's Republic); *Musée Nationale* (French—National Museum)
M.N.: Master of Nursing
mna (MNA): multi-network area (tv)
MNA: Matematikmaskinnämnden (Swedish Computing Machinery Board)
M.N.A.: Master of Nursing Administration
MNAG: Museo Nacional de Antropología, Guatemala
MNAM: Museo Nacional de Antropología, Mexico
MNAOA: Merchant Navy and Airline Officers' Association
M. N. Arch.: Master of Naval Architecture
MNAS: Member of the National Academy of Sciences
Mnasi: Mnasidika
MNB: Moscow Narodny Bank
MNC: Major NATO Commanders; Multinational Corporation
MNCR: *Mouvement National Contre le Racisme* (French—National Movement Against Racism)
mnd: minimum necrosing dose
Mnd: Mound (postal abbreviation)
MND: Ministry of National Defence
M.N.E.: Master of Nuclear Engineering
MNEA: Merchant Navy Establishment Administration
mnem: mnemonic
M. N. Eng.: Master of Naval Engineering
MNF: Menagasha National Forest (Ethiopia); Multilateral Nuclear Force (NATO navy)
mnfrs: manufacturers
mng: managing
MNH: Museum of Natural History (Smithsonian)
mnl: marine navigating light
Mnl: Manuel
MNL: Manila, Philippines (airport)
MNLS: Marine Navigating Light System
MNM: Museum of New Mexico
MNNP: Malawi Nyika Pational Park
M-note: $1000 bill
MNP: Marsabit National Park (Kenya); Meru National Park (equatorial Kenya); Mikumi National Park (Tanzania); Mushandike National Park (Rhodesia)
MNPL: Machinist Non-Partisan Political League
mnr: massive nuclear retaliation; mean neap rise
Mnr: Manor

MNR: *Movimiento Nacionalista Revolucionario* (Spanish—National Revolutionary Movement)
MNRU: Medical Neuropsychiatric Research Unit
mns: metal-nitride-semiconductor (transistor)
Mns: Mines (postal abbreviation)
M.N.S.: Master of Nutritional Science
M. N. Sc.: Master of Nursing Science
m'ns'l: mainsail
MNT: Minnesota and Ontario Paper (stock exchange symbol)
MNTO: Moroccan National Tourist Office
MNU: Maniti Sugar (stock exchange symbol)
M.Nurs.: Master of Nursing
MNV: Marion Power Shovel (stock exchange symbol)
MNWEB: Merseyside and North Wales Electricity Board
MNWR: Malheur National Wildlife Refuge (Oregon); Mattamuskeet NWR (North Carolina); Merced NWR (California); Mingo NWR (Missouri); Minidoka NWR (Idaho); Missisquoi NWR (Vermont); Modoc NWR (California); Montezuma NWR (New York); Moosehorn NWR (Maine)
mnx: (short-order slang contraction—ham and eggs)
Mnzlo: Manzanillo
mo: mail order; manual operation; manually operated; mass observation; method of operation; moment; money order(s); month(s); monthlies; monthly; mustered out
m.o.: *modus operandi* (Latin—manner, method, or mode of operating; way of working)
m/o: *mi orden* (Spanish—my order)
m & o: management and organization
mo': more; morning
m/O: male Oriental
Mo: Missouri; Missourian; molybdenum; Morris; Moselle; Moses; Mozelle
Mo': Moses
Mo: *Maestro* (Italian—master; title given any great artist, composer, conductor, or teacher)
M^o: *Ministerio* (Spanish—Ministry)
MO: Mail Order; Medical Officer; Mobile Station; Mohawk Airlines (2-letter coding); Money Order; Monthly Order; Movement Order(s)
M-O: Morris-Oxford
M & O: Muscat and Oran
moa.: medium observation aircraft; minute of angle
MOA: Marine Office of America; Metropolitan Oakland Area; Metropolitan Opera Association; Ministry of Aviation; Music Operators of America
MOADS: Montgomery Air Defense Sector
MOAMA: Mobile Air Materiel Area
MOARS: Mobilization Assignment Reserve Section
mob.: mobilization; mobilize
mob.: *mobile vulgus* (Latin—disorderly group of people)
Mob: Mobile, Alabama (maritime abbreviation)
MOB: Mobile, Alabama (airport); Montreux-Oberland-Bernois (railway)
Mo' Bay: Mobile Bay, Alabama; Montego Bay, Jamaica
MOBCOM: Mobile Command (Canadian)
mobidic: mobile digital computer
mobil: mobility
mobilarian: mobile branch librarian
mobilary: mobile library
mobiles: motion sculptures (plastic forms in motion)
mobl: macro-oriented business language
möbl: *möbliert* (German—furnished)
mob lib: mobile librarian; mobile library
mob lt: man overboard and breakdown light
mobot(s): mobile robot(s)
MOBS: Multiple Orbit Bombardment System
mobula: model-building language
moc: mission operations computer; mocassin
MOC: Makapuu Oceanic Center (Hawaii); Mauna Olu College (Maui)
moca: minimum obstruction clearance altitude
mocamp: motor camp; motorists camp
Mo City: Motor City (Detroit)
Mockingbird: state bird of Arkansas; symbolic nickname given many of its citizens called Mockingbirds
MoCom: Mobile Command
MOCOM: Mobile Command (US Army)
mocp: missile out of commission for parts
mocr: mission operation control room
mocs: mocassins
mod: manned orbital development (MOD); mesial-occlusal-distal (dental cavities); model; moderate; modern; modernize(d); modification; modify
m-o-d: mesial-occlusal-distal (inlay)
MOD: Medical Officer of the Day; Ministry of Defense; Miscellaneous Obligation Document
modasm: modular air-to-surface missile
m-o-d-b: mesial-occlusal-distal-buccal (inlay)
modcom: modernity commercialized
ModE: Modern English
Model-A: worthy successor to the Model-T Ford
Model Republic: Orange Free State's nickname
Model-T: planetary-gear Model-T Ford automobile once the world's most popular vehicle despite its handcranking starter and its nickname—Tin Lizzie
moderm: modulator-demodulator
Modern Antigone: Maria Thérèse—daughter of Louis XVI
Modernizer of Navigation: Lieutenant Matthew Fontaine Maury, USN
Modern Lib: Modern Library
Modern Liberal Social Philosopher: José Ortega y Gasset
Modern Mother of Presidents: Ohio—birthplace of Presidents Grant, Hayes, Garfield, Benjamin Harrison, McKinley, Taft, Harding; (*see* Mother of Presidents)
ModGr: Modern Greek
ModHeb: Modern Hebrew
mod/iran: modification, inspection, and repair as necessary
modo.: *moderato* (Italian—moderately)
mod. pres.: *modo prescripto* (Latin—in the manner prescribed)
mods: mesial-occlusal-distal (dental cavities); models; moderates; moderators; moderns; modification; modifiers; modulators; modules
MODS: Manned Orbital Development Station (or System);

Manned Orbiting Development Station (or System)
Moe: Moses
mof: maximum observed frequency; member of (the police) force; metal oxide film
MOF: Ministry of Food
mo' fr: mother fucker
Mog: Margaret
MOG: Metropolitan Opera Guild
M.O.G.: Master of Obstetrics and Gynaecology
mogas: motor gasoline
MOH: Ministry of Health; Mohawk Airlines
Moham: Mohammedan
Mohammed Ali: Cassius Clay
MOHATS: Mobile Overland Hauling and Transport System (USAF)
mohms: milliohms
moho: Mohorovicic discontinuity
Mohole: a hole to the Mohorovicic discontinuity, the boundary between the earth's crust and mantle
moi: maximum obtainable irradiance; military occupational information; multiplicity of infection
MOI: Military Operations and Intelligence; Ministry of Information
MOIC: Medical Officer in Command
M.O.I.G.: Master of Occupational Information and Guidance
Moish: Moishe
MOK: Mohawk Carpet Mills (stock exchange symbol)
mol: machine-oriented language; molecular
mol.: *mollis* (Latin—soft)
Mol: Mollendo
M o L: Minister of Labour; Ministry of Labour
MOL: Manned Orbiting Laboratory
M.O.L.: Master (Mistress) of Oriental Languages
MOLAB: Mobile Lunar Laboratory
Moldv: Moldavia; Moldavian
mole.: molecular; molecule
Molière: Jean-Baptiste Poquelin
Molière of Music: André Grétry
Molink: Moscow link (teletype cable circuit linking Moscow's Kremlin with Washington, D.C.'s White House), The Hot Line
moll: metallo-organic liquid laser
mol/l: molecules per liter
Moll: Mary (slang); Molly
mollie: mollienisia (tropical fish)
Mollus: Mollusca
MOLLUSA: Military Order of the Loyal Legion of the U.S.A.
Molly: Maria; Marie; Mary
Molly Pitcher: Mrs John Hays also known as Captain Molly because she took her husband's place as cannoneer when he fell mortally wounded at the Battle of Monmouth—June 28, 1778
MOLNS: Ministry of Labour and National Service
MOLOC: Ministry of Labour Occupational Classification
Molotov: Vyacheslav Mikhailovich Skriabin
MOLS: Mirror Optical Landing System
Moluccas: Molucca Islands
mol wt: molecular weight
moly: molybdenum
mom: military ordinary mail
m-o-m: middle of month; milk of magnesia
m/ o m/: *más o menos* (Spanish—more or less)
Mom: Momma
MOM: Musée Océanographique Monaco
momar: modern mobile army
moms: *mervaerdiomsaetningsskat* (Danish—value-added tax); *mervardesomsattningsskatt* (Swedish—value-added tax)
MOMS: Mothers for Moral Stability
MOM/WOW: Men Our Masters/ Women Our Wonders (antifeminist acronym reading the same upside down as shown)
mon: monetary; monsoon; monument
mon: *maison* (French—house)
Mon: Monaco; Monday; Monegasque; Monmouthshire; Monsieur (French—Mister)
Mon: *Montag* (German—Monday)
Món: *Mónaco* (Spanish—Monaco)
Mona: Ramona
Mona: *Madonna* (Italian—Lady; Our Lady)
Monag: Monaghan
Monarchy of Mount Everest: Nepal
monbas: monobasic
MONC: Metropolitan Opera National Council
Mondrian: Pieter Cornelis Mondriaan
Mong: Mongol; Mongolia(n)
'mongst: amongst
mon-H: monohydrogen
Moni: Monica; Monika
Monitor: *Christian Science Monitor*
Monkey Trial: Scopes Trial (in 1925 when John Scopes, a Tennessee science teacher was on trial for having taught evolution; he was prosecuted by William Jennings Bryan and defended by Clarence Darrow)
Monkey Ward: Montgomery-Ward
Monk Lewis: pseudonum of Matthew Gregory Lewis
mono: mononucleosis; monophonic; monopropellant; monorail(road); monotype; monotyper
monob (MONOB): mobile noise barge
monic: monocular
monocl: monoclinic
monocot(s): monocotyledon(s)
monog: monogram; monograph
monokini: one-piece topless bikini (swimsuit)
Monod: Monon Railroad
monot: monotonous; monotony; monotype; monotypic
Mons: *Monsieur* (French—Mister)
Mons Cur: Monsoon Current
Monsieur de Paris: (French—Mr Paris)—guillotine operator
Monsig: *Monseigneur* (French—My Lord)
monsoons: seasonal storms of southern Asia
monstro(s): monstrosity; monstrosities
Mont: Montana; Montanan; Monterrey; Montevideo; Montgomery; Montpelier; Montreal
Monte: Montague; Monte Carlo; Montefiore
Montgom: Montgomeryshire
Monticello: (Italian—Little Mountain)— Thomas Jefferson's self-designed home near Charlottesville, Virginia
Montparno: Montparnasse
Montpelier: James Madison's home in Orange County, Virginia near Charlottesville
Montr: Montreal
montrg: monitoring
Mont S: *Montreal Star*
Monty: Montagu; Montague; Montmorency
Monumental Intellectual: John Locke
Monument City: Baltimore,

Maryland
Mony: monastery
MONY: Music Operators of New York; Mutual Life Insurance Company of New York
MOO: Money Order Office
Moody and Sankey: Dwight Lyman Moody and Ira David Sankey—an evangelist preacher and his organist partner
Moondog: Louis Thomas Hardin
Moon Goddess: Luna (Roman) whose Latin name means moon; Selene (Greek)
Moonlight: Beethoven's Piano Sonata No. 14 in C-sharp minor (opus 27, no. 2) *Sonata quasi una Fantasia*
MOOP: *Ministerstvo Okhranenia Obshehestvennogo Poriadka* (Russian—All-Union Ministry for the Preservation of Public Order)—secret police agency
Moore's Dig: *Moore's Digest* (of international law)
MOOSE: Move Out of Saigon Expeditiously (USA)
mop: mother-of-pearl; mustering-out pay
M o P: Member of Parliament; Minister of Pensions; Ministry of Pensions; Minister of Power; Ministry of Power; Minister of Production; Ministry of Production
MOP: *Ministerio de Obras Publicas* (Spanish—Ministry of Public Works)
mopa: master oscilator power amplifier
MoPac: Missouri Pacific—Texas & Pacific (railroad)
mopar: master oscillator-power amplifier radar
mopeds: motorized pedals (bicycles containing auxiliary motors saving riders much pedalling)
MOPH: Military Order of the Purple Heart
mopr: manner of performance rating; mop rack
MOPS: Missile Operations System
M. Opt.: Master of Optometry
mor: morocco; mortar
mor: *morendo* (Italian—dying away; gradual softening of tone and slowing of tempo)
mor (MOR): middle-of-the-road (tv program)
Mor: Morelia; Morelos; Morisco; Moroccan; Morocco
M of R: Minister of Reconstruction; Ministry of Reconstruction
Morand's disease: paresis affecting the feet
Morav: Moravia; Moravian
Morb: Morbihan
MORC: Medical Officers Reserve Corps; Midget Ocean Racing Club (*mor-sees*—smallest racing cruisers)
Mord: Mordehai
Mordhy: Mordehai
mor. dict.: *more dicto* (Latin—as directed)
Mordy: Mordehai
Moreton Bay Colony: Queensland's original name
mor fib: moral fiber
morg mar: morganatic marriage
MORL: Manned (or Medium) Orbital Research Laboratory
Morm: Mormon
Morm: *Mormon, Book of*
Mormon City: Salt Lake City
Mormon's Mecca: Salt Lake City, Utah
Mormon State: Utah
morn: morning
morph: morphine; morphology
morpha: hermaphrodite (mispronounced *morphadite*)
morpheme: smallest sound unit (linguistics)
Morrie: Maurice; Morris
morro: (Portuguese or Spanish—hill; promontory, as in Morro Castle
Morrow: William Morrow
mor. sol.: *more solito* (Latin—in the usual manner)
mort: mortal; mortality; mortar; mortgage; mortician; mortuary
mor t: Morse taper
Mort: Mortemart; Mortimer; Morton
mortal.: mortality
Morton's disease: metatarsal neuralgia
mos: metal-oxide semiconductor; metal-oxide-silicon (compound); missile on stand; mitout sound (silent film); months; mosaic
Mos: Moscow
Mos: *Mosca* (Italian—Moscow); *Moscou* (French or Portuguese—Moscow); *Moscu* (Spanish—Moscow); *Moskau* (German—Moscow); *Moskou* (Dutch—Moscow)
MOs: Military Observers (UN)
MOS: Management Operating System; Manned Orbital Station; Ministry of Supply
Mosby: C.V. Mosby
MOSC: Midland-Odessa Symphony and Chorale
Mose: Moisés; Mosè; Moseley; Mosen; Moses; Moshe
Moses: Moses in Egypt—Rossini's sacred melodrama in four acts (*Mosè in Egitto*)
MOSES: Manned Open Sea Experimentation Station
mosfet: metal-oxide semiconductor field-effect transistor
mosic: metal-oxide-semiconductor integrated circuit(s)
Moslem India: Bangladesh and Pakistan
Moslems: (Arabic—Those Who Submit)—also called Muslims
Moslem Sultanate: Oman—formerly Muscat and Oman
mosm: milliosmol(s)
Mosquitia: (Spanish—Mosquito Province)—Nicaragua's Caribbean coast formerly a British protectorate also called Mosquito
Mosquito Coast: Caribbean coast of much of Honduras and Nicaragua
MOSS: Manned Orbital Space Station
most.: metal-oxide semiconductor transistor
'most: almost
Most Beautiful College Town in America: Princeton, New Jersey
Most Gigantic Imbecility Since the Crusades: Hermann Sudermann's nickname for World War I
Most Glorious Hero of Norwegian Viking Times: Olav Tryggvasson
Most Northern Southern City: Tulsa, Oklahoma
mot: middle of target; motor; motorized
M o T: Minister of Transport; Ministry of Transport
MOT: Military Ocean Terminal
M o TCP: Ministry of Town and Country Planning
motel: hotel for motorists
Mother of American Kindergartens: Susan Blow
Mother of the American Legion: Ernestine Schumann-Heink
Mother of the American Red Cross: Clara Barton
Mother Ann: Shaker leader Ann Lee
Mother of Believers: Ayesha—Mohammed's favorite wife
Mother Bickerdyke: Mary Ann Bickerdyke
Mother Bloor: Ella Reeve Bloor

Mother Cabrini: Frances Xavier Cabrini
Mother Carey's chickens: stormy petrels
Mother Carey's geese: fulmars or great white petrels
Mother of Child Education: Doctor Maria Montessori
Mother Earth: the Greek Goddess Gaea or Ge, who according to mythology, arose out of chaos and in turn produced the sea, the sky, and the mountains; the Romans called her Tellus or Terra and sometimes called her Vesta Prisca
Mother of Exiles: Statue of Liberty overlooking New York's former immigration stations at Battery Park and Ellis Island
Mother of Feminine Psychology: Karen Horney
Mother of Ghosts: the Roman goddess of Death—Mania
Mother Goose: legendary authoress of children's rhymes and stories
Mother of the Japanese Novel: Baroness Murasaki Shikibu (*The Tale of the Genji*)
Mother Jones: Mary Harris Jones
Mother Lake: Leonora Marie Kearney Barry
Mother of Libraries: Alexandria, Egypt
Mother Maid: The Virgin Mary
Mother of Mountains: Nepal's Mount Everest
Mother of Muckrakers: Ida M. Tarbell (*see* Father of Muckrakers)
Mother of Presidents: Virginia—birthplace of Presidents Washington, Jefferson, Madison, Monroe, William Henry Harrison, Tyler, Taylor, Wilson
Mother of Prison Reform: Dorothea Lynde Dix
Mother of the Red Cross: Clara Barton
Mother of Rivers: Tibetan Highlands
Mother of Rivers and Waves: Tethys, wife of the god Oceanus, and mother of the rivers plus three thousand Oceanids—the waves
Mother of Russian Cities: Kiev
Mother of the Russians: Moscow
Mother of Trusts: Standard Oil
Mothers of Believers: the wives of Mohammed
Motion Picture Palace Potentate: Roxy (S.L. Rothafel)
motorcross: motorcycle cross (country race)
mot op: motor operated
Motor City: Detroit
MOTOREDE: Movement To Restore Decency
Motor Town: Detroit
Motown: Motor Town (Detroit founded by a French explorer named Cadillac)
mots: minitrack optical tracking system
MOTU: Mobile Technical Unit
Mound City: St Louis, Missouri
Mountain Devils: Tasmanians
Mountain Laurel: Connecticut state flower
Mountain of the Lion: Sierra Leone
Mountain State: West Virginia's official nickname
Mountain of Tarik: The Rock of Gibraltar named for the Moorish chief Jabal Tariq
mounties: mounted policemen (especially Royal Canadian Mounted Police)
Mount Vernon: George Washington's home on the banks of the Potomac below Washington, D.C.
MOUSE: minimum orbital unmanned satellite
mov: movement
mov: *movimento* (Italian—movement)
movi: movie; moving pictures
Movie Capital: Hollywood, California
movies: moving pictures
M o W: Minister of Works; Ministry of Works
MOW: Moscow, USSR (Vnukovo Airport)
M o WT: Minister of War Transport; Ministry of War Transport
MOWW: Military Order of the World Wars
mox: oxidized metal explosive
moy: money
Moz: Mozambique
Mozart Town: Salzburg, Austria—birthplace of Wolfgang Amadeus Mozart
Moz Cur: Mozambique Current (Natal)
mp: mail payment; manifold pressure; medium pressure; meeting point; melting point; milepost; motion picture; multipole
m(p): microfilm positive
mp: *mezzo-piano* (Italian—half soft; moderately soft)
m.p.: *mille pasuum* (Latin—thousand paces)—the Roman mile of 1000 paces
mP: polar maritime air
MP: Member of Parliament: Metropolitan Police: Military Police; Minister Plenipotentiary; Missouri Pacific (railroad); Mounted Police
MP: *Maschinenpistole* (German—submachine gun; tommy gun)
M & P: Maryland & Pennsylvania (railroad)
mpa: multiple-product (television) announcement
MPA: Magazine Publishers Association; Maryland & Pennsylvania (railroad); Mechanical Packing Association; Medical Procurement Agency; Metal Powder Association; Military Police Association; Mobile Press Association; Modern Poetry Association; Motion Picture Alliance; Music Publishers Association
M.P.A.: Master of Professional Accounting; Master of Public Administration; Master of Public Affairs
MPAA: Motion Picture Association of America; Musical Performing Arts Association
MPAGB: Modern Penthalon Association of Great Britain
m part: movable partition
MPAUS: Music Publishers Association of the United States
m payl: maximum payload
mpb: male pattern baldness
MPB: Miniature Precision Bearings; Missing Persons Bureau; Montpelier & Barre (railroad)
MPBC: Memphis Power Boat Club
mp br: multipunch bar
MPBW: Ministry of Public Buildings and Works
mpc: marine protein concentrate; material program code; maximum permissible concentration; military payment certificate; minimal planning chart
MPC: Manpower and Personnel Council; Manpower Priorities Committee; Manufacturing Plan Change; Member of Parliament of Canada; Military Payment Certificate; Military Pioneer Corps; Military Police Corps; Montana Power Company
MPCA: Magnetic Powder Core Association

mpc black: medium-processing channel black
MPCL: Movimiento Patriótico Cuba Libre (Free Cuba Patriotic Movement)
mpcp: missile power control panel
mpcur: maximum permissible concentration of unidentified radionuclides
mpd: magnetoplasmadynamics; missile purchase description
M. Pd.: Master of Pedagogy
MPD: Military Pay Division
M Pen: Minister of Pensions; Ministry of Pensions
MPDFA: Master Photo Dealers' and Finishers' Association
mpfg: 1000 proof gallons
mp di: multipunch die
MPDS: Message Processing Distribution System
mpe: maximum permissible exposure (to radiation)
M.P.E.: Master of Physical Education
MPEAUS: Master Printers and Engravers Association of the United States
M.Pe.Eng.: Master of Petroleum Engineering
MPers: Middle Persian
mpf: multipurpose food
MPF: Metropolitan Police Force (London)
mpg: miles per gallon
MPG: Magazine Promotion Group; Max Planck Gesellschaft
MPGA: Metropolitan Public Gardens Association
MPGR: Mana Pools Game Reserve (Rhodesia)
mph: miles per hour
M.Ph.: Master of Philosophy
MPH: Methodist Publishing House
M.P.H.: Master of Public Health
M. Phar.: Master of Pharmacy
M. Pharm.: Master of Pharmacy
M. Ph. Ed.: Master of Public Health Education
M. P.H. Eng.: Master of Public Health Engineering
M.Phil.: Master of Philosophy
M. Pho.: Master of Photography
mphps: miles per hour per second
M. Ph. Sc.: Master of Physical Science
M.P.H.T.M.: Master of Public Health and Tropical Medicine
M. Phy.: Master of Physics
mpi: magnetic particle inspection; maximum point of impulse; mean point of impact; multiphasic personality inventory
MPI: Max Planck Institute; Museum of the Plains Indians
M-pill: menstruation pill
mPk: polar maritime air colder than underlying surface
mpl: maximum payload; maximum permissible level
MPL: Maintenance Parts List; Memphis Public Library; Metropolitan Police Laboratory; Miami Public Library; Milwaukee Public Library; Minnesota Power and Light; Missouri Pacific Lines; Montreal Public Library
M.P.L.: Master (Mistress) of Patent Law
MPLA: Mountain Plains Library Association
MPLA: *Movimento Popular Libertação Angola* (Portuguese—Popular Movement for the Liberation of Angola)
MPLP: Marxist Progressive Labor Party
Mpls: Minneapolis
mpm: meters per minute; multipurpose meal
mpn: most probable number
MPNA: Midwest Professional Needlework Association
MPNI: Ministry of Pensions and National Insurance
MPO: Metropolitan Police Office (Scotland Yard); Miami Philharmonic Orchestra; Military Pay Order; Military Post Office; Mobile Printing Office
MPOIS: Military Police Operating Information System
M.Pol. Econ: Master (Mistress) of Political Economy
mpp: most probable position
MPP: Member Provincial Parliament (Canada)
M.P.P.: Master (Mistress) of Physical Planning
M & PP: Manitou & Pikes Peak (Railroad)
MPPA: Music Publishers Protective Association
mppcf: millions of particles per cubic foot of air
mp pl: multipunch plate
MPPWCOM: Military Police Prisoner of War Command
mpr: 1000 pair
MPR: Military Pay Record
MPRC: Military Personnel Records Center
M. Prof. Acc.: Master of Professional Accountancy
mps: marbled paper sides; megacycles per second; meters per second; motor parts stock
MPs: Members of Parliament
M.Ps.: Master of Psychology
MPS: Manufacturing Process Specification; Milwaukee Public Museum; Ministry of Public Security; Motor Products Corporation
M.P.S.: Member of the Pharmaceutical Society
mps (MPS): mucopolysaccharidosis
MPSA: Military Petroleum Supply Agency
MPSC: Military Provost Staff Corps
M.Ps.O.: Master (Mistress) of Psychology Orientation
MPSP: Military Personnel Security Program
M.P.S.W.: Master (Mistress) of Psychiatric Social Work
M.Psych.: Master (Mistress) of Psychology
mpt: male pipe thread; melting point; midpoint
MPT: Minister of Posts and Telecommunications
MPTA: Machine Power Transmission Association; Municipal Passenger Transport Association
MPU: Medical Practitioners Union
M. Pub. Adm.: Master of Public Administration
M-P v: Mason-Pfizer virus
mPw: polar maritime air warmer than underlying surface
MPW: Minneapolis-Moline (stock exchange symbol)
mpx: multiplex
Mpy: *Maatschappij* (Dutch—company)
MPZ: Mid-Continent Petroleum (stock exchange symbol)
mq: metol-quinol (MQ); multiple quotient (register); multiplier quotient
Mq: mosque
MQ: merit quotient
MQA: Manufacturing Quality Assurance
Mqe: Martinique
mqf: mobile quarantine facility
mqil: miniature quartz incandescent lamp
mql: miniature quartz lamp
MQO: Marksmanship Qualification Order
MQS: Mobile Quality Services
MQT: Model Qualification Test
mr: machine record(s); machine rifle; map reference; medium range; metabolic rate; methyl red; milliroentgen; mill run,

mineral rubber; mine run; motivational research (MR)
mr: *meester* (Dutch—master)—attorney-at-law; *mi remesa* (Spanish—my remittance)
m/r: middle right
m & r: maintainability and reliability; maintainability and repairs; maintenance and repair
Mr: Mister
MR: Machinery Repairman; Marketing Research (division, US Department of Agriculture); Master of the Rolls; Memorandum for Record; Memorandum Report; Military Railroad; Military Requirement; Minister Residentiary; Ministry of Reconstruction; Miscellaneous Report; Mobilization Regulation; Monon Railroad; Monthly Report; Morning Report; Municipal Reform
MR: *Motormannes Riksforbund* (Swedish—Motorists' Association)
M & R: maintenance and repairs
M/R: map reading
mra: medium-powered radio range (Adcock); minimum reception altitude
mra (MRA): metro rating area (tv)
MRA: Moral Rearmament
mrad: millirad
M. Rad.: Master of Radiology
M. Ra. Eng.: Master of Radio Engineering
MRAF: Marshal of the Royal Air Force
MRAM: Multimission Redeye Air-launched Missile
MRAP: Management Review and Analysis Program
MRAS: Manpower Resources Accounting System (USAF)
MRAUSCAN: Masonic Relief Association of the United States and Canada
mrb: marble base
MRB: Material Review Board; Mileage Rationing Board; Modification Review Board; Mutual Reinsurance Bureau
MRBA: Mississippi River Bridge Authority
mrbm: medium-range ballistic missile (MRBM)
MRBP: Missouri River Basin Project
MRC: Marine Research Committee; Market Research Council; Marlin-Rockwell Corporation; Material Redistribution Center; Material Review Crib; Medical Research Center (Council); Medical Reserve Corps; Men's Republican Club; Metals Reserve Company; Methods Research Corporation; Mississippi River Commission; Movement Report Center
mrca: multirole combat aircraft
MRCC: Medical Research Council of Canada
MRCGP: Member of the Royal College of General Practitioners
MRCI: Medical Registration Council of Ireland; Medical Research Council of Ireland
MRCO: Member of the Royal College of Organists
MRCOG: Member of the Royal College of Obstetricians and Gynaecologists
Mr Common Sense: Thomas Paine
MRCP: Member of the Royal College of Physicians
MRCPE: Member of the Royal College of Physicians of Edinburgh
MRCPI: Member of the Royal College of Physicians of Ireland
MRCS: Member of the Royal College of Surgeons
MRCSE: Member of the Royal College of Surgeons of Edinburgh
MRCSI: Member of the Royal College of Surgeons of Ireland
MRCVS: Member of the Royal College of Veterinary Surgeons
MRCWA: Midland Railway Company of Western Australia
mrd: metal rolling door; minimum reacting dose (MRD)
MRD: Microbiological Research Department
MRDC: Military Research and Development Center
MR & DC: Medical Research and Development Command (US Army)
MRDF: maritime radio direction finding
MR&DF: Malleable Research and Development Foundation
Mr Dooley: (pseudonym—Finley Peter Dunne)
MRDTI: Metal Roof Deck Technical Institute
mre: mean radial error
MRE: Microbiological Research Establishment (UK)
M.R.E.: Master of Religious Education
M. Ref. Eng.: Master of Refrigeration Engineering
mrem: milliroentgen equivalent man
mrep: milliroentgen equivalent physical
mrf: marble floor
MRF: Meteorological Rocket Facility; Music Research Foundation
MRFB: Malayan Rubber Fund Board
mr flight: meteorological research flight
mrg: magnetic radiation generator; margin; marginal; marginalia
MRG: Material Review Group; Minorities Research Group (aiding homosexuals)
MRGS: Member of the Royal Geographical Society
MRH: Member of the Royal Household
mrhm: milliroentgens per hour at one meter
MRHMC: Michael Reese Hospital and Medical Center
mr/hr: milliroentgens per hour
MRHS: Midwest Railway Historical Society
mri: mean rise interval; medium-range interceptor; milstrip routing identifier
MRI: Mental Research Institute: Meteorological Research Institute; Midwest Research Institute
mrir: medium resolution infrared
MRIS: Maritime Research Information System; Market Research Information System; Material Readiness Index System; Medical Research Information System; Mobile Range Instrumentation System
MRIW: Medical Research Institute of Worcester
Mr Klemps: Otto Klemperer
mrkr: marker
Mrkt-Deli: Market-Delicatessen
mrl: medium-powered radio range (loop radiators); multiple rocket launcher (MRL)
MRL: Materiel Requirements List; Medical Records Librarian
MRLA: Malayan Races Liberation Army (Chinese-communist guerrillas)
mrm: mail readership measurement; miles of relative movement

Mrn: Martin
MRN: Meteorological Rocket Network
mRNA: messenger RNA (ribonucleic acid)
mrng: morning
MRNP: Mount Rainier National Park (Washington); Mount Revelstoke National Park (British Columbia)
Mrnz: Martínez
Mro: Maestro
MRO: Maintenance, Repair, and Operation(s); Materiel Release Order
M-roof: M-shaped roof
mrp: manned reusable payload; maximum resolving power
M.R.P.: Master in Regional Planning
MRPP: Maoist Reorganization Movement of the Party of the Proletariat
M rps: Mauritius rupee(s)
Mr Q: Marquardt Corporation
MRQ: Marquardt Corporation (stock exchange symbol)
mrr: medical research reactor
MRR: Material Rejection Report
MRRC: Mechanical Reliability Research Center
Mr Republican: U.S. Senator Robert A. Taft
Mrs: Missus; Mistress
MRs: Maintenance Reports
MRS: Marseilles, France (airport); Military Railway Service
MR & S: Materials Research and Standards
M.R.Sc.: Master (Mistress) of Rural Science
Mrs Fletcher: Maria Jane Jewsbury's pseudonym
Mrs Grundy: nickname for the imaginary self-appointed arbiter of morality and taste; leader of the social set referred to as *they—they feel, they say, they think,* etc.
MRSH: Member of the Royal Society of Health
MRSL: Member of the Royal Society of Literature
MRSM: Member of the Royal Society of Medicine
MRSMGB: Member of the Royal Society of Musicians of Great Britain 4
MRSP: Myakka River State Park (Florida)
Mrs Patrick Campbell: stage name of Beatrice Stella Tanner
mrsss: manned revolving space systems simulator (MRSSS)
MRST: Member of the Royal Society of Teachers
mrt: mildew-resistant thread
Mrt: Martinique
Mrt: *Maart* (Dutch—March)
MR-13: *Movimiento Revolucionario de 13 de Noviembre* (Spanish—Revolutionary Movement of 13 November)—Guatemala
mrtm: maritime
Mrtnz: Martinez
MRTS: Master Radar Tracking Station
mru: minimal reproductive units; mobile radio unit (MRU)
MRU: mobile radio unit
MRUA: Mobile Radio Users' Association
Mr UN: Carlos P. Romulo
mrv: missile re-entry vehicle (MRV); mixed respiratory vaccine; multiple re-entry vehicle (MRV)
MRV: missile recovery vessel(s)
mrV-P: methyl red Voges-Proskauer
mrw: morale, recreation, and welfare
MRWA: Midland Railway of Western Australia
mrz: *marzo* (Spanish—March)
ms: machine screw; machine steel; main switch; maintenance and service; major subject; manuscript; margin of safety; master switch; maximum stress; mean square; medium shot; medium steel; meters per second; metric system; mild steel; minimum stress; mint state; mitral stenosis; months after sight; multiple sclerosis; muscle strength
ms.: manuscript
m s: *mano sinistra* (Italian—left hand)
m/s: marking and stenciling
m/s: *motorskib* (Norwegian—motorship)
ms (MS): multiple sclerosis
m & s: maintenance and supply
m^3/s: cubic meter per second
mS: millisiemens (millimho)
Ms: mature motion pictures (for adults); Mendes; mesothorium; (pronounced *Miz*)—feminine title replacing Miss and Mrs
MS: Machinery Survey; magnetic south; Mail Steamer; major subject; Manuscript Society; Master Sergeant; Material Specifications; Medical Survey; Metallurgical Society; Meteoritical Society; Michigan State University of Agriculture and Applied Science; Military Service; Military Standard; Ministry of Shipping; Ministry of Supply; Misair (Egyptian Airline); Motorship
MS: *Material Standard* (usually followed by a number)
M-S: Material Service (division of General Dynamics)
M-S: *Minshu-Shakaito* (Japanese—Democratic Socialist Party)
M.S.: Master of Science; Master of Surgery
M/S: Mannlicher-Schoenauer; motorship
M & S: Maintenance and Supply; Medicine and Surgery
M es Sc: *Maître es Sciences* (French—Master of Sciences)
MoS: Minister of Supply
msa: method of steepest ascent
m.s.a.: *misce secundum arten* (Latin—mix skillfully)
MSA: Malaysia Singapore Airlines; Medical Statistics Agency (US Army); Mineralogical Society of America; Mine Safety Appliances (company); Mutual Security Agency
M-S-A: Mine Safety Appliances
M.S.Agr.Eng.: Master of Science in Agricultural Engineering
MSA Inst MM: Member of the South African Institute of Mining and Metallurgy
MISAIT: Member of the South African Institute of Translators
m^s a^s: *muchos años* (Spanish—many years)
MSAUS: Masonic Service Association of the United States
MSB: Mackinac Straits Bridge (Michigan); Marine Safety Board; minesweeping boat (naval symbol)
M.S.B.A.: Master of Science in Business Administration
M.S.Bus.: Master (Mistress) of Science in Business
msc: millisecond; moved, seconded, and carried
m.s.c.: *mandatum sine clausula* (Latin—authority without restriction)
M. Sc.: Master of Science
MSC: coastal minesweeper (3-letter naval symbol); Maine Sardine Council; Manned Spacecraft Center (NASA);

Maple Syrup Council; Marine Safety Council; Marine Science Center (Lehigh University); Medical Service Corps; Medical Specialist Corps; Mediterranean Sub-Commission; Melbourne Steamship Company; Military Sealift Command; Missile and Space Council; Mississippi Central (railroad)

M & SC: Missile and Space Council

MSCA: Moore School of Automatic Computers; Mount Saint Agnes College; Murray State Agricultural College

M Scand: Middle Scandinavian

M.S.C.E.: Master of Science in Civil Engineering

M.S.Ch.E.: Master of Science in Chemical Engineering

Mschr: *Monatsschrift* (German—monthly magazine)

M. Sc. L.: Master of the Science of Law

MSCNY: Marine Society of the City of New York

MSC(O): old coastal minesweeper (naval symbol)

M.S. Conv.: Master of Science in Conservation

M. Sc. Ost.: Master of Science in Osteopathy

M Scot: Middle Scottish

mscp: mean spherical candlepower

MSCP: Master Shielding Computer Program

MSCRB: Margaret Sanger Clinical Research Bureau

mscrbl: manuscribble (handscribbled manuscript)

mscrg: miscarriage

MSCW: Mississippi State College for Women

msd: missile system development

MSD: Merck, Sharp & Dohme

M.S.D.: Master (Mistress) of Scientific Didactics; Master (Mistress) Surgeon Dentist; Medical Science Doctor

M & SD: Missile and Space Division (General Electric)

M.S. Dent.: Master of Science in Dentistry

M.S. Derm.: Master of Science in Dermatology

MSDF: Maritime Self-Defense Force (Japanese Navy)

M & SDI: Mayonnaise and Salad Dressing Institute

mse: mean square error; military stressful era(s)

MSE: Midwest Stock Exchange; Mississippi Export Railroad (stock exchange symbol); Montreal Stock Exchange

M.S.E.: Master of Sanitary Engineering; Master of Science in Education; Master of Science in Engineering

m sec: millisecond

M.S.Ed.: Master (Mistress) of Science in Education

M.S.E.E.: Master of Science in Electrical Engineering

M.S.E.M.: Master of Science in Engineering Mechanics

M.S. Eng.: Master of Science in Engineering

mses: *marchandises* (French—goods)

MSEUE: *Mouvement Socialiste pour les États Unis d'Europe* (French—Socialist Movement for the United States of Europe)

msf: muscle shock factor

MSF: fleet minesweeper (naval symbol); mobile striking force

MSF: *Médecins Sans Frontères* (French—doctors without borders)—international group of volunteer physicians

M.S.F.: Master of Science in Forestry

MSFC: Marshall Space Flight Center

ms fm: master form

msfn: manned space flight network

ms fx: master fixture

msg: message; monosodium flutamate

MSG: Madison Square Garden; Marine Systems Group (General Dynamics)

ms ga: master gauge

M.S.G.E.: Master of Science in Geological Engineering

msgfm: messageform

MSGp: Mobile Support Group

msgr: messenger

MSGR: Mobile Support Group

M Sgt: Master Sergeant

msh: melanocyte-stimulating hormone (MSH)

MSH: Music Society for the Handicapped

M.S.H.: Master of Science in Horticulture; Master of Science in Hygiene

M.S.H.A.: Master of Science in Hospital Administration

M.S.H.E.: Master of Science in Home Economics

Mshl: Marshal

M. S. Hort.: Master of Science in Horticulture

M. S. Hyg.: Master of Science in Hygiene

msi: medium-scale integration

MSI: minesweeper, inshore (naval symbol); Museum of Science and Industry

MSI: *Movimento Sociale Italiano* (Italian Social Movement)—neo-fascist followers of Mussolini known as Missini

MSIB: Mountain States Inspection Bureau

m'sieur: *monsieur* (French—mister; sir)

M.S.Ind.Eng.: Master of Science in Industrial Engineering

M.S.J.: Master of Science in Journalism

msk: mission support kit

MS-KCC: Memorial Sloan-Kettering Cancer Center

MSKK: Mitsui Sempaku Kabushiki Kaisha (Mitsui Line)

Mskr: *Manuskript* (German—manuscript)

msl: mean sea level; missile

msl: *mesela* (Turkish—for example)

Msl: Marseilles

MSL: Marine Science Laboratories; minesweeping launch (naval symbol)

M.S.L.: Master of Science in Linguistics

MSLC: Manufacturing Specification Liaison Change

ms lo: master layout

M.S.L.S.: Master (Mistress) of Science in Library Science

MSM: Manhattan School of Music; Montana School of Mines

M.S.M.: Master of Science in Music

MSMA: Master Sign Makers' Association

M.S.M.E.: Master of Science in Mechanical Engineering

M.S.Med.: Master (Mistress) of Medical Science

MSMM: Missouri School of Mines and Metallurgy

M.S. Mus.: Master of Science in Music

M.S. Mus. Ed.: Master of Science in Music Education

msn: mission

Msn: Mission (postal abbreviation)

MSN: Madison, Wisconsin (airport)

M.S.N.: Master of Science in Nursing

MSNB: Machine Screw Nut Bureau

M.S.N. Ed.: Master of Science in Nursing Education

M.S.Nucl.Eng.: Master of Science in Nuclear Engineering
MSNY: Mattachine Society of New York
mso (MSO): multiple-systems operator (tv)
MSO: Manila Symphony Orchestra; Melbourne Symphony Orchestra; Memphis Symphony Orchestra; Milwaukee Symphony Orchestra; Minneapolis Symphony Orchestra (former name of the Minnesota Symphony); Montreal Symphony Orchestra; ocean minesweeper (naval symbol)
M.Soc.Sci.: Master (Mistress) of Social Science
M. Soc. Wk.: Master of Social Work
m-sop: mezzo-soprano
M.S. Opthal: Master (Mistress) of Opthalmological Surgery
M.S.Ortho: Master (Mistress) of Orthopedic Surgery
msp: metal splash pan
MSP: Maximum Security Prison; Minneapolis, Minnesota (airport); Mutual Security Program
M.S.P.: Master (Mistress) of Science in Pharmacy
MSpC: Medical Specialist Corps
MSPE: Master of Science in Physical Education
M.S. Pet. Eng.: Master of Science in Petroleum Engineering
M.S.P.H.: Master of Science in Public Health
M.S.Pharm.: Master of Science in Pharmacy
M.S.P.H.E.: Master of Science in Public Health Engineering
M.S.P.H.Ed.: Master of Science in Public Health Education
ms pl: master plate
msr: main supply route; mineral-surface roof; missile site radar
m & sr: missile and surface radar
ms & r: merchant shipbuilding and repairs
MSR: Manufacturing Specification Request; mean spring tide
MSRA: Multiple Shoe Retailers' Association
M.S. Rad.: Master of Science in Radiology
MSRB: Mississippi State Rating Bureau
M.S. Rec.: Master of Science in Recreation
M.S. Ret.: Master of Science in Retailing
MSRG: Member of the Society for Remedial Gymnasts
MSRN: Manufacturing Specification Revision Notice
msrpp: multidimensional scale for rating psychiatric patients
MSRS: Missile Strike Reporting System
msry: masonry
mss.: manuscripts
Mss: Misses; Mizzes (plural of Miz written Ms)
MSS: Manufacturers Standardization Society of the Valve and Fittings Industry; Medical Service School (USAF)
M.S.S.: Master of Social Science
M.S.Sc.: Master of Sanitary Science; Master of Social Science
MSSCS: Manned Space Station Communications System
M & SSD: Missile & Space System Division (Douglas Aircraft)
M.S.S.E.: Master of Science in Sanitary Engineering
M.S. S. Eng.: Master of Science in Sanitary Engineering
MSSGB: Motion Study Society of Great Britain
MSSH: Massachusetts Society for Social Hygiene
MSSMS: Munition Section Strategic Missile Squadron
MSSR: Moldavian Soviet Socialist Republic
MSSRC: Mediterranean Social Science Research Council
M.S.S.S.: Master (Mistress) of Science in Social Service
M.S. St.Eng.: Master of Science in Structural Engineering
mssu: midstream specimen of urine
MSSVD: Medical Society for the Study of Venereal Diseases
MSSVFI: Manufacturers Standardization Society of the Valve and Fittings Industry
M.S.S.W.: Master (Mistress) of Science in Social Work
mst: mean survival time; measurement
MST: Marconi Telecommunications Systems; Maximum Service Telecasters; Military Science Training; Mountain Standard Time
M'st': Mister
M.S.T.: Master of Science in Teaching
MSTA: Michigan State Teachers Association
M.Stat.: Master (Mistress) of Statistics
mstb: 1000 stock tank barrels
mstc: mastic
MSTC: Maryland State Teachers College; Massachusetts State Teachers College
MSTD: Member of the Society of Typographic Designers
M.S. T.Ed.: Master of Science in Teacher Education
msth: mesothorium
M & ST L: Minneapolis & St Louis (railroad)
mstn: 1000 short tons
ms tp: master template
M ST P & SSM: Minneapolis, St Paul & Sault Ste Marie Railroad (Soo Line)
mstr: master
Mstr: Master
M.S.Trans: Master of Science in Transportation
M.S. in Trans.E.: Master of Science in Transportation Engineering
Mstr Mech: Master Mechanic
msts (MSTS): missile static test site
MSTS: Military Sea Transport Service; Missile Static Test Site
msu (MSU): maximum security unit
MSU: Memphis State University; Michigan State University; Mississippi State University; Montana State University
MSUC: Middle South Utilities Company
msud: maple-syrup urine disease
MSUL: Memphis State University Library; Michigan State University Library; Mississippi State University Library; Montana State University Library
MSU Lond: Medical Schools of the University of London
M. Surgery: Master of Surgery
M.Surv: Master of Surveying
msus: midstream urine specimen
msv (MSV): magnetically-supported vehicle; Martian surface vehicle; mean square velocity; miniature solenoid valve; molecular solution volume; murine sarcoma virus
MSVC: Mount Saint Vincent College
MSVD: Missile and Space-Vehicle Department (General Electric)
msv(M): murine sarcoma virus (Moloney)
M Sw: Middle Swedish
M.S.W.: Master of Social Work

MSX: Seaboard Oil (stock exchange symbol)
MSY: New Orleans, Louisiana (airport)
msyd: 1000 square yards
mt: empty; machine translation; mail transfer; maximum torque; mean tide; measurement ton; mechanical translation; mechanical transport; medical technology; megaton (MT); membrana tympani; metatarsal; metric ton; missile test; motor transport
m/t: mail transfer
mT: tropical maritime air
m & t: maintenance and test
Mt: Mount; tympanic membrane
MT: Machine Translation; Mandated Territory; Masoretic Text; Mechanical Translation; Medical Technologist; Meteorological Aids; Military Training; Military Transport; Ministry of Transport; Motor Transport; Mountain Time; Muscat Transport
M de T: *Mengano de Tal* (Spanish—so and so)
m^{ta}: *muita* (Portuguese—much)—feminine form
MTA: Maine Teachers Association; Manpower Training Association; Metropolitan Transit Authority; Mississippi Teachers Association; Mississippi Test Area
mtac: mathematical tables and other aids to computation
MTACCS: Marine Tactical Command and Control System
MTASCP: Medical Technologist of the American Society of Clinical Pathologists
mtb: maintenance of true bearing
MTB: Malayan Tin Bureau; Medium Tank Battalion; motor torpedo boat
MTBA: Machine Tool Builders' Association
mtbf: mean time before failure; mean time between failures
mtbff: mean time between first failure
mtbfl: mean time between function loss
mtbm: mean time between maintenance
MTBRON: Motor Torpedo Boat Squadron
mtbsf: mean time between system failure
MTC: Marine Technology Center (Electric Boat); Materiel Testing Command; Mechanical Transport Corps; Medical Training Center; Military Training Cadets; Missile Test Center; Montreal Trust Company; Monsanto Chemicals (stock exchange symbol); Morse Telegraph Club; Motor Transport Corps; Mystic Terminal (railroad)
M.T.C.: Master of Textile Chemistry
MTCA: Ministry of Transport and Civil Aviation
mtce: maintenance
MTCL: Metropolitan Toronto Central Library
MTCP: Minister of Town and Country Planning; Ministry of Town and Country Planning
mtd: midpoint tissue dose; mounted
m.t.d.: *mitte tales doses* (Latin—send such doses)
MTD: Mobile Training Detachment
M.T.D.: Master of Transport Design; Midwife Teachers' Diploma
MTDE: Maintenance Technique Development Establishment
MT$: Maria Theresa dollar (Yemeni currency unit)
MTDS: Marine Tactical Data System
mte: maximum temperature engine
MTE: Marine Technical Education
M. Tech.: Master (Mistress) in Technology
M.Tel.Eng.: Master (Mistress) of Telecommunication Engineering
M.Text.: Master (Mistress) of Textiles
mtf: mechanical time fuze
MTF: Mississippi Test Facility
mtg: main turbogenerator(s); meeting; mortgage; mounting
Mtg: Meeting (postal abbreviation)
mtgd: mortgaged
mtge: mortgage
mtgee: mortgagee
mtgor: mortgagor
mth: month
MTH: Master of Trinity House
M. Th.: Master of Theology
mti: moving target indicator; moving target information
MTI: Metal Treating Institute
MTI: *Magyar Távirati Iroda* (Hungarian Press Agency)
MTIRA: Machine Tool Industry Research Association
mTk: tropical maritime air colder than underlying surface
mtl: material; materiel; mean tide level
mtl: *monatlich* (German—monthly)
Mtl: Montreal
MTL: mean tide level
mtlp: metabolic toxemia of late pregnancy
mtm: methods time measurement(s)
MTM: Mary Tyler Moore
MTMC: Mother Teresa's Missionaries of Charity
Mt McK NP: Mount McKinley National Park
MTMTS: Military Traffic Management and Terminal Service
mtn: motion
Mtn: Mountain
MTNA: Music Teachers National Association
MTNWR: Mark Twain National Wildlife Refuge (Illinois)
m^{to}: *muito* (Portuguese—much)—masculine form
MTO: Mississippi Test Operations
Mton: Moncton
Mt P: Mount Palomar (observatory)
MTP: Mobilization Training Program
M.T.P.: Master (Mistress) of Town Planning
Mt P O: Mount Palomar Observatory
mtr: materials testing reactor; mean time to restore; missile-tracking radar; moving target reactor; multiple track radar
Mtr: Montrose
MTr: meridian transit
MTR: Materials Testing Report; Montour (railroad)
mtrcl: motorcycle
mtre: missile test and readiness equipment
Mt Rev: Most Reverend
MTRF: Mark Twain Research Foundation
mtrg: metering
mtri: missile test range instrumentation
mtrl: material
Mt R NP: Mount Rainier National Park
Mtro: *Maestro* (Spanish—Master)
M.T.R.P.: Master (Mistress) of Town and Regional Planning
mtr rdr: meter reader
mts: mountains
mt's: empties
MTS: Marine Technology Society; Mashinno-Traktornye

Stantsii (Russian—Machine Tractor Stations); Middlebare Technical School; Missile Test Stand; Missile Test Station
MTSC: Middle Tennessee State College
MT-6: mercaptomerin (diuretic)
MTSU: Middle Tennessee State University
mtt: mean transit time
MTTA: Machine Tools Trades' Association
MTTAGB: Machine Tool Trades Association of Great Britain
mttf: mean time to failure
mttff: mean time to first failure
mttr: mean time to repair
mtu: mobile tracking unit: mobile training unit
MTU: Michigan Technological University
MTU: *Motoren und Turbinen Union* (German—Motors and Turbines United)—corporation
M. tuberc.: *Mycobacterium tuberculosis*
MTUOP: mobile training unit out for parts
mtv: mammary tumor virus
MtV: Mount Vernon
M.Tv.: Master of Television
MTV: Motor Test Vehicle
MTVs: Motor Torpedo Vessels
mtw: main trawl winch
mTw: tropical maritime air warmer than underlying surface
Mt W O: Mount Wilson Observatory
mtx: methotrexate
MTX: Morrell Tank Line (railway symbol)
Mty: Monterrey (inhabitants—Regiomontanos)
MTY: Monterrey, Mexico (airport)
mtz: motorize
MTZS: Metropolitan Toronto Zoological Society
mu: marijuana user; mouse unit
mμ: millimicron
m/u: mockup
MU: Marquette University; Marshall University; Mercer University; Mercy University; Mercyhurst University; Meredith University; Merrimack University; Mesa University; Messiah University; Methodist University; Miami University; Midwestern University; Milliken University
MUA: Machinery Users' Association; Malayan Union Association; Monotype Users' Association
muap: motor unit action potential(s)
muc: mucilage
muc.: *mucilago* (Latin—mucilage)
MUC: Magee University College; Meritorious Unit Citation; Muchea, Australia (tracking station); Munich, Germany (Riem airport)
mu car: multiple-unit (railroad) car
MUCC: Michigan United Conservation Clubs
Much Ado: *Much Ado About Nothing*
Muckrakers: turn-of-our-century American crusader journalists David Graham Phillips, Charles Edward Russell, Lincoln Steffens, Upton Sinclair, Ida M. Tarbell
Mudcat(s): Mississippian(s)
Mudcat State: Mississippi
mudpie: Museum and University Data, Programs, and Information Exchange
muf: material unaccounted for; maximum usable frequency
MUFON: Mutual UFO Network
Muh: *Muharram* (Arabic—first month of the Mohammedan year)
Muhammad: (Arabic—The Praised)—Mahomet
Muhammad Ali: Cassius Clay
Mujib: Mujibur Rahman
Muk: Mukden
mulat: mulatto
Mulatas: Mulatas Islands
MULES: Missouri Uniform Law Enforcement System
mult: multiplication
multics: multiplexed information and computing service
multitran: multiple translation (translating one language into several target languages)
multr: multimeter
mulv: murine complex leukemia
mum: mumble(d); mumbling; mummed; mumbling; mummer(s); mummery
Mum: Mumford
MUMC: McMaster University Medical Center
Mum City, U.S.A.: Bristol, Connecticut famous for its chrysanthemums (mums)
MUMMS: Marine Corps Unified Management System
MUMPS: Multi-Programming System (Massachusetts General Hospital)
mums: chrysanthemums
mun: munition
Mün: Müngo; Munro; Munroe
Mun: Munster
MUN: Memorial University of Newfoundland; Model United Nations
Mund: Edmund
muni: municipal; municipality
munic: municipal; municipality
Munich Expressionist: Wassily Kandinsky
Municipal Muckraker: Lincoln Steffens—author of *The Shame of the Cities*
munit: munitions
Muñoz Marín: Luis Muñoz Marín—democratic leader and first governor of Puerto Rico
muo: myocardiopathy of unknown origin
MUO: Municipal University of Omaha
muon: mu meson (Siamese—town, as in Muong Boten, town on border of Laos and Thailand)
MUP: Manchester University Press
M.U.P.: Master of Urban Planning
MUR: *Mouvements Unis de la Résistance* (French—United Movements of the Resistance)
MURA: Midwestern Universities Research Association
Murasaki: Baroness Murasaki Shikibu *(The Tale of the Genji)*
muriatic acid: hydrochloric acid (HCI)
Murph: Murphy
Murrumbidgee: (Aboriginal Australian—Big Water)—affluent of the Murray River in New South Wales
Murrumbidgee River City: Canberra—Australia's capital
mus: musculoskeletal; museum; music; musical; musician
Mus: Muscat; museum; music; Muslim
MUS: Magnetic Unloading System; Manned Underwater Station
musa: multiple-unit steerable antenna
Mus. Bac.: Bachelor of Music
Mus Bks: Museum Books
musc: muscle; muscular
Mus. Doc.: Doctor of Music
Muse of Astronomy and Celestial Music: Urania
Muse of Comedy and Pastoral

Poetry: Thalia
Muse of Dancing and Choral Singing: Terpsichore
Mus.Ed.B.: Bachelor of Music Education
Mus.Ed.D.: Doctor of Music Education
Mus.Ed.M.: Master of Music Education
Muse of Epic and Heroic Poetry: Calliope, who according to Horace, could play any musical instrument
Muse of Erotic Poetry: Erato
Muse of History: Clio
Muse of Lyric Poetry and Music: Euterpe
Muse of Oratory, Rhetoric, and Sacred Song: Polyhymnia
Muse of Tragedy: Melpemone
museo: museography; museological; museologist; museololgy
Museum of Architecture: Leningrad (formerly Petrograd or Saint Petersburg)
Museum Cities: northern Italy's Padua, Venice, Verona, and Vicenza
Museum Metropolis: London, New York, and Paris compete for this title
MUSIC: Maryland University Sectored Isochronous Cyclotron
Musical Charlotte Russe: Tchaikovsky's Andante cantabile from his Symphony No. 5 in E minor
Music Capital of America: Los Angeles and New York claim this title
Music City, U.S.A.: Nashville, Tennessee
Music Man: Meredith Willson
musicol: musicological; musicologist; musicology
***MusiMus:** Musikkhistorisk Museum* (Norwegian—Music History Museum)
muskie: muskellunge
Mus.M.: Master of Music
Musso: Mussolini
must.: manned undersea station
MUST: Medical Unit, Self-contained, Transportable
mustargen: mustard-nitrogen (poison compound)
mustn't: must not
mut: mutation
mutil: mutilate; mutilated; mutilation
mutt: muttonhead
muttnik: second Soviet satellite launched in 1957, so nicknamed because its astronaut was a mongrel dog used to test the vehicle
mutu: mutual; mutualism
muw: music wire
MUWS: Manned Underwater Station
mux: multiplex
***muz:** muziek* (Dutch—music)
Muz: Muzio
mv: mean variation; millivolt; monochromatic vision; muzzle velocity
***mv:** meervoud* (Dutch—plural)
m & v: meat and vegetable
***m v:** mezzo voce* (Italian—middle voice)
Mv: megavolt; mendelevium
***MV:** Varia Vergine* (Italian—Virgin Mary)
***M.V.:** Medicus Veterinarius* (Veterinary Physician)
M/V: motor vessel
mva: mean vertical acceleration; megavolt ampere; motor vehicle accident
MVA: Machinists Vise Association; Mississippi Valley Association; Missouri Valley Authority
MVAS: Milwaukee Vocational and Adult School
MVB: Martin Van Buren (8th President U.S.)
MVBA: Mercado de Valores de Buenos Aires (Buenos Aires Stock Exchange)
mvbd: multiple V-belt drive
MVBL: Mississippi Valley Barge Line
mvc: manual volume control; manufacturing variation control
MVC: Military and Veterans Code
MVCC: Mount Vernon Community College
MVD: Montevideo, Uruguay (Carrasco Airport)
***MVD:** Ministerstvo Vnutrenniy Delo* (Russian—Ministry of Internal Affairs)—*(q.v.—VOT)*
MVDA: Motor Vehicle Dismantlers' Association
MVe: Murray Valley encephalitis
MVE: Metropolitan Vickers Electrical
M.V.E.: Master of Vocational Education
M.Vet.Med.: Master (Mistress) of Veterinary Medicine
M.Vet.Sci.: Master (Mistress) of Veterinary Science
mvg: most valuable girl
MVG: Medal for Victory over Germany
MVHS: Mergenthaler Vocational High School
mvi: multi-vitamin infusion
MVJC: Mount Vernon Junior College
mvm: million vehicle miles
MVM: Motor Vehicle Mechanic
MVMA; Motor Vehicle Manufacturers Association
mvmt: movement
MVNP: Mesa Verde National Park
MVNWR: Monte Vista National Wildlife Refuge (Colorado)
Mvo: Montevideo
MVO: Member of the Victorian Order
mvp: most valuable player (sports)
MVP: Manpower Validation Program
MVPBA: Mississippi Valley Power Boat Association
MVPCB: Motor Vehicle Pollution Control Board
mvri: mixed vaccine—respiratory infections
M.V.Sc.: Master of Veterinary Science
MVSS: Motor Vehicle Safety Standard
mvt: moisture-vapor transmission
MVT: Motor Vehicle Technician
MV & THS: Manhattan Vocational and Technical High School
MVTI: Mohawk Valley Technical Institute
mvv: maximum voluntary ventilation
mw: milliwatt; molecular weight
m/w: manufacturing week
m/W: male White
***mW:** meines Wissens* (German—as far as I know)
Mw: megawatt
MW: Montgomery Ward
M-W: Merriam-Webster
MWA: Modern Woodmen of America
MWAA: Movers' and Warehousemen's Association of America
MWB: Metropolitan Water Board; Minister of Works and Buildings; Ministry of Works and Buildings
MWAI: Mystery Writers of America, Incorporated
mwb: motor whale boat
MWC: Ministry of War Communications; Motorola Western Center
MWCG: Metropolitan Washington Council of Governments

MWD: Metropolitan Water District; Mutual Weapons Development
MWDP: Mutual Weapons Development Program
mwe: megawatts of electricity
MWF: Medical Women's Federation
mwg: music wire gauge
MWGCP: Most Worthy Grand Chief Patriarch
MWGM: Most Worshipful Grand Master; Most Worthy Grand Master
MWHS: Martha Washington High School
MWIA: Medical Women's International Association
MWJC: Marjorie Webster Junior College
MWLP: Meadowview Wild Life Preserve
MWMCA: Michigan Women for Medical Control of Abortion
MWN: *Medical World News*
MWNM: Muir Woods National Monument
mwnt: mean water neap tide
MWO: Marshallese Women's Organization; Midwest Oil; Modification Work Order; Mount Wilson Observatory
mwp: maximum working pressure; membrane waterproofing
MWP: Most Worthy Patriarch
MWPA: Married Women's Property Act
mwr: mean width ratio
MWR: Morton Wildlife Refuge (New York)
MWS: Manas Wildlife Sanctuary (India); Mudamalai Wildlife Sanctuary (India)
MWSC: Midwestern Simulation Council
M.W.T.: Master of Wood Technology
mwv: maximum working voltage
mww: manual wire wrap; municipal waste water
MWW: *Merry Wives of Windsor*
MWZ: Manischewitz (stock exchange symbol)
mx: maxwell; motocross (rough-terrain motorcycle race); multiplex
Mx: maxwell; Middlesex
MX: Mexicana de Aviación (2-letter code)
MXC: Minnesota Experimental City
mxd: mixed
Mxl: Mexicali (inhabitants—Cachanias)
maxm: maximum
MXP: Milan, Italy (Malpensa Airport)
mxr: mask index register
my.: myopia; myopic
My: Malayalam; Milo; Mylan
MY: Medinat Yisrael (State of Israel); motor yacht
Myc: Mycenaean
MYC: Manchester Yacht Club; Middletown Yacht Club; Milwaukee Yacht Club; Minnetonka Yacht Club; Mobile Yacht Club
myco: mycobacterium
mycol: mycology
myel(s): myelocyte(s)
myg: myriagram
myl: myrialiter
mylo: mylohyoid
mym: myriameter
myo: *mayo* (Spanish—May)
myob: mind your own business
myodyn: myodynamics
myo inf: myocardial infarction
myol: myology
myop: myopia
Myr: Myriopeda
Myrt: Myrtle
Mys: Mysore
myst: mystagogue; mystagogy; mysteries; mysterious; mystery; mystic; mystical; mysticism; mystics
Mysterious Billionaire: Howard Hughes
myth.: mythological; mythologist; mythology
mz: monozygotic
mz: *Mangelszahlung* (German—for non-payment)
Mz: Méndez
MZ: Mail Zone; Museum of Zoology; R.H. Macy and Company (stock exchange symbol)
M & Z: Mombasa and Zanzibar
MZA: Madrid, Zaragoza, Alicante
mzm: multiple-zone monitor
MZMA: (Russian—*Moskva Zavod Maloitrazhkaya Automobili*)—Moscow Small-Engine Car Factory producing the Moskvich auto
MZn: magnetic azimuth
MZNP: Mountain Zebra National Park (South Africa)
mzo: *marzo* (Spanish—March)
M-zone: manufacturing zone
mzs: mezzo-soprano
M.Z.Sc.: Master of Zoological Science
Mzt: Mazatlán (inhabitants—Mazatlecos)

N

n: nasal; national; nautical; naval; neap; negative; nerve; neuter; neutral; neutron; new; night; noon; norm; normal; noun; nuclear; number; refractive index (symbol); shear modulus of elasticity (symbol); transport number (code)
n: index of refraction (symbol); load factor (symbol); revolutions per second (symbol); rotative speed (symbol)
n': and
'n': and (*as in* fish 'n' chips, rock 'n' roll, strawberries 'n' cream, *etc.*)
n/: and
n.: haploid generation; *numerus* (Latin—number)
n/: *nuestro* (Spanish—our)
N: International Nickel (stock exchange symbol); national; nautical; naval; Navy; Negro; neon; neutral; night; nimbus; Nippon; nitrogen; noon; normal; Norse; north; Norway (auto plaque); November—code for letter N; nuclear-propelled vessel (naval symbol); nucleus
N: avogadro constant or number (symbol); *natus* (Latin—born); *neer* (Dutch—down); *noord* (Dutch—north); *nord* (Danish, French, Italian, Norwegian, Swedish—north);

Nord (German—north); *norre* (Danish—north); *norte* (Portuguese or Spanish—north); north; number of turns (symbol); rate of propeller rotation (symbol); revolutions per minute (symbol); revolutions per minute (symbol); yawing moment (symbol)

(N): nuclear-powered ship (naval symbol, as in CL[N]—nuclear-powered cruiser)

N1, N2, etc.: North One, North Two, etc. (London postal zones)

N^{14}; Radioactive Nitrogen

N_2: nitrogen

$n._2$: diploid generation

N_2O: nitric oxide

na: negative attitude; nicotinic acid; no account; not applicable; not appropriated; not authorized; not available; nucleic acid (NA); numerical aperture

na: *nestre ar* (Norwegian—next year)

n/a: next assembly; no account

Na: nadir; sodium (symbol)

Na^{24}: radioactive sodium

Na_2CO_3: sodium carbonate (sal soda)

NA: Narcotics Anonymous; National Academician; National Academy National Airlines; National Archives; National Association; Nautical Almanac; Naval Academy; Naval Architect; Naval Attaché; Naval Auxiliary; Naval Aviator; Netherlands Antilles (Aruba, Bonaire, Curaçao, Saba, Sint Eustatius, Sint Maarten); Neurotics Anonymous; North America; North American; Northrup Aircraft; Nurse's Aide

NA: *Nautical Almanac; Nederlandse Antillen* (Dutch—Netherlands Antilles)—Aruba, Bonaire, Curaçao, Saba, Sint Eustatius, Sint Maarten—the Dutch West Indies; *Nomina Anatomica* (Latin—Anatomical Names)—official nomenclature adopted by the International Congresses of Anatomists

naa: neutron activation analysis; not always afloat

NAA: National Academy of Arbitrators; National Aeronautic Association; National Alumni Association; National Apple Association; National Arborist Association; National Archery Association; National Association of Accountants; National Auctioneers Association ; Naval Attache for Air; North American Aviation

NAAA: National Alliance of Athletic Associations; National Association of American Academicians; National Auto Auction Association

NAAB: National Architectural Accrediting Board

NAABC: National Association of American Business Clubs

NAABI: National Association of Alcoholic Beverage Importers

naabsa: not always afloat but safe aground

NAAC: National Agricultural Advisory Commission

NAACC: National Association for American Composers and Conductors

NAACO: North American Arms Corporation of Canada

NAACP: National Association for the Advancement of Colored People

NAACP: (underworld jargon—Never Agitate Adam Clayton Powell)

NAADC: North American Area Defense Command

NAAF: North African Air Force (World War II)

NAAFA: National Association to Aid Fat Americans

NAAFI: Navy, Army, and Air Force Institutes

NAAG: National Association of Attorneys General

NAAMM: National Association of Architectural Metal Manufacturers

NAAN: National Advertising Agency Network

NAANACM: National Association for the Advancement of Native American Composers and Musicians

NAAO: National Association of Amateur Oarsmen; Navy Area Audit Office

NAAPPA: North American Association for the Protection of Predatory Animals

NAARI: National Aero- and Astronautical Research Institute

NAAS: National Agricultural Advisory Service; Naval Area Audit Service; Naval Auxiliary Air Station

NAASC: North American Aviation Science Center

NAA S & ID: North American Aviation Space and Information Division

NAATS: National Association of Air Traffic Specialists

NAAUS: National Archery Association of the United States

NAAW: National Association of Accordion Wholesalers

NAB: National Alliance of Businessmen; National Assistance Board; National Association of Businessmen; National Association of Broadcasters; Naval Advanced Base; Naval Air Base; Naval Amphibious Base; Newspaper Advertising Bureau

NABA: North American Benefit Association

NABACO: National Association for Bank Audit, Control, and Operation

NABBC: National Association of Brass Band Conductors

Nabby: Abigail

NABC: National Association of Boys' Clubs

NABD: North American Band Directors

NABDC: National Association of Blueprint and Diazotype Coaters

NABE: National Association of Book Editors

NABEO: National Association of Black Elected Officials

NABET: National Association of Broadcast Employees and Technicians

NABIM: National Association of Band Instrument Manufacturers

NABISCO: National Biscuit Company

NABMA: National Association of British Market Authorities

nabor: neighbor

NABP: National Association of Book Publishers

Nabrico: Nashville Bridge Company

NABRT: National Association for Better Radio and Television

NABS: National Association of Barber Schools; National Association of Black Students; nuclear-armed bombardment satellite

NABSP: National Association of Blue Shield Plans

NABT: National Association of Biology Teachers

NABTE: National Association for Business Teacher Education

nabu: non-adjusting ballup (unsolvable confusion)
nac: nacelle
NAC: National Achievement Clubs; National Agency Check; National Airways Corporation (New Zealand); National Americanism Commission (American Legion); National Arts Club; National Association of Cemeteries; National Association of Chiropodists; National Association of Coroners; National Association of Counties; National Aviation Club; National Aviation Corporation; National Can Corporation (stock exchange symbol); Naval Academy; Naval Air Center; Naval Aircraftman; Non-Airline Carrier; North Atlantic Council; Northeast Air Command; Norwegian-American Council
NACA: National Advisory Committee for National Aeronautics; National Agricultural Chemicals Association; National Air Carrier Association; National Armored Car Association; National Association of Cost Accountants; National Association of County Administrators
NACAC: National Ad Hoc Committee Against Censorship
NACAE: National Advisory Council for Art Education
NACAM: National Association of Corn and Agricultural Merchants
NACATTS: North American Clear-Air Turbulence-Tracking System
NACB: National Association of Convention Bureaus
NACCAM: National Coordinating Committee for Aviation Meteorology
NACCD: National Advisory Commission on Civil Disorders
NACCG: National Association of Crankshaft and Cylinder Grinders
NACDR: National Association of College Deans and Registrars
NACE: National Association of Corrosion Engineers
NACEL: Naval Air Crew Equipment Laboratory
NACF: National Art Collections Fund
NACFI: North American Council on Fishery Investigations
nach (nAch): need for achievement
Nach: Nachman
Nachf: *Nachfolger* (German—successor)
nachm: *nachmittags* (German—afternoon; p.m.)
NACHM: National Advisory Committee on Health Manpower
Nachr: *Nachrichten* (German—bulletin)
Nachtr: *Nachtrag* (German—appendix; supplement)
NACIMFP: National Advisory Council on International Monetary and Financial Problems
NaCl: sodium chloride (salt)
NACL: National Advisory Commission on Libraries
NACLIS: National Commission on Libraries and Information Science
NACM: National Association of Chain Manufacturers; National Association of Credit Management
naco: night-alarm cutoff
NACO: National Arts Centre Orchestra (Ottawa); National Association of Counties
NACOA: National Advisory Committee on Oceans and Atmosphere
NACOC: National Arts Centre Orchestra of Canada
NACODS: National Association of Colliery Overmen, Deputies, and Shotfirers
NACOM: National Communications
NACOR: National Advisory Committee on Radiation
NACRO: National Association for the Care and Resettlement of Offenders
NACS: National Association of College Stores; National Association of Cosmetology Schools
NACT: National Association of Careers Teachers; National Association of Craftsman Tailors; National Association of Cycle Traders; National Association of Cycle Trades
NACTA: National Association of Colleges and Teachers of Agriculture
NACTST: National Advisory Council on the Training and Supply of Teachers
NACUA: National Association of College and University Administrators; National Association of College and University Attorneys
NACUBO: National Association of College and University Business Office Associations
NACUFS: National Association of College and University Food Services
NACUSS National Association of College and University Summer Sessions
NACWC: National Association of Colored Women's Clubs
NACWPI: National Association of College Wind and Percussion Instruments
nad: nadir (lowest point); no appreciable difference; no appreciable disease; nothing abnormal discovered; not on active duty
nad (NAD^+): nicotinamide adenine dinucleotide; (same as DPN)
Nad: Nadine; Nedezhda
NAD: National Academy of Design; National Association of the Deaf; Naval Air Depot; Naval Air Division; Naval Ammunition Depot; North Atlantic Division
NADA: National Association of Dealers in Antiques; National Automobile Dealers Association
Nadar: Gaspard Félix Tournachon
NADAR: North American Data Airborn Recorder
NADB: National Aerometric Data Bank
NADC: National Anti-Dumping Committee; Naval Air Development Center
NADDIS: Narotics and Dangerous Drugs Intelligence File (computerized criminal file)
NADEE: National Association of Divisional Executives for Education
NaDefCol: Nato Defense College
NADEM: National Association of Dairy Equipment Manufacturers
NaDevCen: Naval Air Development Center
NADFS: National Association of Drop Forgers and Stampers
NADGE: NATO Air Defense Ground Environment Organization
NADGEMO: Nato Air Defense Ground Environment Management Office
nadh (NADH): dihydronicotina-

mide adenine dinucleotide; (same as dpnh or DPNH)

nadi: (Indian—creek; river; stream, as in Mahanadi, southwest of Calcutta)

NADL: National Association of Dental Laboratories; Navy Authorized Data List

NAD/NADH$_2$: nicotinamide adenine dinucleotide (coenzyme system affecting hydrogen transfer in biological oxidation-reduction reactions)

NADO: Navy Accounts Disbursing Office

NADOP: North American Defense Operational Plan

nadp (NADP$^+$): nicotinamide adenine dinucleotide phosphate; (same as tpn or TPN)

NADPAS: National Association of Discharged Prisoners' Aid Societies

nadph (NADPH): dihydronicotinamide adenine dinucleotide phosphate

NADSA: National Association of Dramatic and Speech Arts

NADWARN: National Disaster Warning System

nAe: no American equivalent

Na$_e$: exchangeable body sodium

NAE: National Academy of Education; National Academy of Engineering; National Association of Evangelicals

NAEA: National Art Education Association; National Association of Estate Agents

NAEB: National Association of Educational Broadcasters

NAEBM: National Association of Engine and Boat Manufacturers

NAEC: National Aviation Education Council

NAEd: National Academy of Education

NAEDS: National Association of Engravers and Die Stampers

NAEF: Naval Air Engineering Facility

NAEFTA: National Association ofEnrolled Federal Tax Accountants

NAEP: National Assessment of Educational Progress

NAES: National Association of Educational Secretaries; National Association of Episcopal Schools

NAESU: Naval Aviation Engineering Service Unit

NAEYC: National Association for the Education of Young Children

naf: nonappropriated funds

NAF: National Amputation Foundation; National Arts Foundation; Naval Aircraft Factory; Naval Air Facility; Netherland-America Foundation; Northern Attack Force

NAF: *Norges Automobil Forbund* (Norway's Automobile Association)

NAFA: National Academy of Foreign Affairs; National Association of Fleet Administrators

NAFAG: NATO Air Force Armaments Group

NAFAS: National Association of Flower Arrangement Societies

NAFB: National Association of Franchised Businessmen

NAFBRAT: National Association for Better Radio and Television

NAFC: National Association of Food Chains

NAFCA: North American Family Campers Association

NAFD: National Association of Funeral Directors

NAFEC: National Aviation Facilities Experimental Center

naff (nAff): need for affiliation

NAFFBIA: National Association of Former FBI Agents

NAFFP: National Association of Frozen Food Producters

NAFI: Naval Avionics Facility

NAFM: National Armed Forces Museum; National Association of Furniture Manufacturers

NAFMB: National Association of FM Broadcasters

NAFO: National Association of Fire Officers

N Afr: North Africa

NAFRLG: National Alliance of Financially-Responsible Local Governments

NAFS: National Association of Foot Specialists

NAFSA: National Association of Foreign Sudent Advisers; National Association of Foreign Student Affairs

NAFTA: North Atlantic Free Trade Area (Canada, United Kingdom, United States)

NAFWR: National Association of Furniture Warehousemen and Removers

nag.: net annual gain

Nag: Nagasaki; Nagoya

NAG: National Action Group; National Association of Gag Writers; National Association of Gardeners; Naval Advisory Group; Naval Applications Group (USN); Negro Actors Guild

NA & G: Norgulf Lines (North Atlantic & Gulf)

NAGARD: NATO Advisory Group for Aeronautical Research and Development

NAGC: National Association for Gifted Children

NAGE: National Association of Government Employees

NAGM: National Association of Glove Manufacturers; National Association of Glue Manufacturers

Nagp: Nagpur

NAGS: National Allotments and Gardens Society

NAGT: National Association of Geology Teachers

nagy: (Hungarian—big; great; large, as in Nagykörös)

Nah: The Book of Nahum

NAHA: National Association of Handwriting Analysts

Nahal: *Na'or Halutsi Lohem* (Hebrew—Fighting Pioneer Youth)—youngest section of the Israeli army

NAHB: National Association of Home Builders

NAHC: National Advisory Health Council

NAHCAC: National Ad Hoc Committee Against Censorship (sometimes abbreviated NACAC)

NAHSA: National Association of Hearing and Speech Agencies

NAHT: National Association of Head Teachers

nai: no action indicated; no address instruction

NAI: National Agricultural Institute

NAIA: National Association of Insurance Agents; National Association of Intercollegiate Athletics

NAIC: National Association of Insurance Commissioners; National Association of Investment Clubs; Naval Aircraft Investigation Center

NAIEC: National Association for Industry-Education Cooperation

NAIG: Nippon Atomic Industry Group

NAIL: Neurotics Anonymous International Liaison

Nail City: Wheeling, West Virginia where so many nails are

made
NAILSC: Naval Air Integrated Logistics Support Center
naiop: navigational aids inoperative for parts
NAIRE: National Association of Internal Revenue Employees
Nairns: Nairnshire
NAIS: National Association of Independent Schools
NAISS: National Association of Iron and Steel Stockholders
NAIT: Northern Alberta Institute of Technology
naivnik: naive person or politician
NAJC: Northwest Alabama Junior College
NAJE: National Association of Jazz Education
nak: negative knowledge
nak (NAK): negative acknowledge character (data processing)
nakl: *naklad* (Polish—edition; publisher); *nakladatel* (Czech—edition; publisher)
NAL: National Agricultural Library (US Department of Agriculture); National Airlines; Norwegian America Line
NALC: National Association of Letter Carriers; National Association of Litho Clubs
NALCC: National Automatic Laundry and Cleaning Council
NALCO: Newfoundland and Labrador Corporation
NALDEF: Native American Legal Defense and Education Foundation
NALGO: National and Local Government Officers Association
NALM: National Association of Lift Makers
NALS: National Association of Legal Secretaries
NALSAT: National Association of Land Settlement Association Tenants
NALU: National Association of Life Underwriters
Nam: (military slang—Vietnam); Namibia (South-West Africa)
N Am: North America
NAM: National Air Museum (Smithsonian Institution); National Association of Manufacturers; Naval Aircraft Modification; Newspaper Association Managers; North America(n)
NAM: *Nederlandsche Aluminium Maatschappij* (Netherlands Aluminum Company)
NAMA: New Amsterdam Musical Association; North American Maritime Agencies
NAMB: National Association of Master Bakers
NAMBO: National Association of Motor Bus Operators
Namby-Pamby: 18th-century English dramatist-poet Ambrose Philips
NAMC: Naval Air Materiel Center; Naval Air Materiel Command
NAMCC: National Association of Mutual Casualty Companies
NAMCO: Naval and Mechanical Company
NAMDI: National Marine Data Inventory
NAME: National Association of Marine Engine Builders; National Association of Marine Engineers
NAMESU: National Association of Music Executives in State Universities
NAMF: National Association of Metal Finishers
NAMFI: NATO Missile Firing Installation
NAMH: National Association for Mental Health; Norwegian-American Historical Museum
NAMIA; National Association of Mutual Insurance Agents
Namib: Namibia or South-West Africa
Namibia: South-West Africa
NAMIC: National Association of Mutual Insurance Companies
NAMilCom: North Atlantic Military Committee
naml: *namligen* (Swedish—namely)—viz.
NAMM: National Association of Music Merchants
NAMMC: Natural Asphalt Mineowners' and Manufacturers' Council
NAMMO: NATO Multi-Role Combat Aircraft Development and Production Management Oganization
NAMMW: National Association of Musical Merchandise Wholesalers
NAMOA: National Association of Miscellaneous Ornamental and Architectural Products Contractors
NAMOS: National Art Museum of Sport
NAMP: National Association of Magazine Publishers; National Association of Married Priests
namppf: nautical air miles per pound of fuel
NAMS: National Association of Marine Surveyors
NAMSB: National Association of Mutual Savings Banks
NAMSO: NATO Maintenance and Supply Organization
NAMT: National Association for Music Therapy
NAMTC: Naval Air Missile Test Center
NAMTRADET: Naval Air Maintenance Detachment
NAMTRAGRU: Naval Air Maintenance Training Group
n.a.n.: *nisi aliter notetur* (Latin—unless it is otherwise noted)
Nan: Anna; Nancy; Nanette; Nanking
NAN: Nandi, Fiji Islands (airport)
nana (NANA): N-acetylneuraminic acid
NANA: National Advertising News Association; North American Newspaper Alliance
NANAC: National Aviation Noise Abatement Council
Nancy: Agnes; Ann; Anna; Annabelle; Anne
NAND: NOT AND (data-processing logic operator)
NANE: National Association for Nursery Education
Nannerl: Maria Anna
nano: 10^{-9}
NANTIS: Nottingham and Nottinghamshire Technical Information Service
Nanty: Anthony
NANWEP: Navy Numerical Weather Problems (USN)
NAO: Noise Abatement Office
NAOA: Navy Officers Accounts Office
NAOC: Nigerian Agip Oil Company
NaOH: sodium hydroxide (caustic soda)
NAOP: National Association of Operative Plasterers
NAOT: National Association of Organ Teachers
NAOTS: Naval Aviation Ordnance Test Station
nap.: knapsack; napalm (naphthalene and coconut oil—jellied gasoline incendiary mixture); naphtha; naval aviation pilot (NAP); non-agency purchase; not at present

Nap: Naples; Napoleon; Napoleonic
NAP: Naples, Italy (airport); Narragansett Pier (railroad); National Association of Parliamentarians; National Association of Postmasters; National Association of Publishers; Naval Aviation Pilot
NAP: *Nomina Anatomica, Paris*
NAPA: National Asphalt Paving Association; National Association of Performing Artists; National Association of Purchasing Agents
NAPAC: National Program for Acquisitions and Cataloging
napalm: naphthene palmitate (napththalene plus coconut oil—jellied gasoline used in flame-throwers)
NAPAN: National Association for the Prevention of Addiction to Narcotics
NAPBL: National Association of Professional Baseball Leagues
NAPC: National Association of Precancel Collectors
NAPCA: National Air Polution Control Administration
NAPE: National Alliance of Postal Employees; National Association of Port Employees; National Association of Power Engineers
NAPECW: National Association for Physical Education of College Women
NAPF: National Association of Pension Funds
NAPFE: National Alliance of Postal and Federal Employees
naph: naphtha; naphthyl
NAPH: National Association of Professors of Hebrew
NAPL: National Association of Photo Lithographers
NAPM: National Association of Punch Manufacturers; National Association of Purchasing Management
NAPNES: National Association for Practical Nurse Education and Service
NAPO: National Association of Performing Artists; National Association of Probation Officers; National Association of Property Owners; National Association of Purchasing Agents
Napoleon: Napoleon Bonaparte
Napoleon Bonaparte: Napoleon I—Emperor of the French
Napoleon of Peace: Louis Philippe
nap(py): napkin
na pr: *na priklad* (Czech—for example)
NAPR: National Association for Pastoral Renewal
NAPS: National Alliance of Postal Supervisors
NAPSAE: National Association for Public School Adult Education
NAPT: National Association of Physical Therapists; National Association for the Prevention of Tuberculosis
NAPTC: Naval Air Propulsion Test Center
NAPUS: National Association of Postmasters of the United States; Nuclear Auxiliary Power Unit System
NAPV: National Association of Prison Visitors
NAPVD: National Association for the Prevention of Venereal Disease
nar: narrow
Nar: Narragansett
NAR: National Association of Realtors; National Association of Rocketry; Nelson Aldrich Rockefeller; North American Rockwell; North American Royalties; Northern Alberta Railway
NARAD: Navy Research and Development
NARAL: National Association for the Repeal of Abortion Laws
NARAS: National Academy of Recording Arts and Sciences
NARB: National Advertising Review Board
narc: narcotic; narcotics agent; narcotics; narcotics officer
NARC: National Agricultural Research Center; National Archives and Records Service; National Association for Retarded Children
narco: narcotic; narcotics hospital; narcotics officer; narcotics treatment center
Narconon: Narcotics Anonymous
narcos: narcotics; narcotics police officers
nard: spikenard
NARD: National Association of Regimental Drummers; National Association of Retail Druggists
NARDIC: Naval Research and Development Information Center
NAREB: National Association of Real Estate Boards; National Association of Real Estate Brokers
NAREIF: National Association of Real Estate Investment Funds
NARF: Naval Air Rework Facility; Nuclear Aircraft Research Facility
NARFE: National Association of Retired Federal Employees
NARI: National Atmospheric Research Institute
Nar Inv: Narcotics Investigation
NARL: National Aero Research Laboratory; Naval Arctic Research Laboratory
NARM: National Association of Relay Manufacturers; National Association of Retail Merchants
NARMCO: National Research and Manufacturing Company
NARO: North American Regional Office
NAROCTESTSTA: Naval Air Rocket Test Station
NARP: National Association of Railroad Passengers
Narrow-Gauge Capital of the World: Durango, Colorado
Narrow Seas: English Channel and the Irish Sea
NARS: National Archives and Records Service; Non-Affiliated Reserve Section
NARSIS: National Association for Road Safety Instruction in Schools
NARST: National Association for Research in Science Teaching
NARTB: National Association of Radio and Television Broadcasters
NARTEL: North Atlantic Radio Telephone Committee
NARTM: National Association of Rope and Twine Merchants
NARTS: Naval Air Rocket Test Station
NARTU: Naval Air Reserve Training Unit
NARUC: National Association of Regulatory Utility Commissioners
NARVRE: National Association of Retired and Veteran Railroad Employees
nas: nasal; nasalis; nasology
n-a-s: no added salt
NAS: Nassau, Bahamas (airport); National Academy of Sciences; National Advocates

Society; National Aerospace Standard(s); National Aircraft Standard(s); National Airspace System; National Association of Sanitarians; National Association of Stevedores; National Association of Supervisors; National Audubon Society; Naval Air Station; Nursing Auxiliary Service

N A S: Noise Abatement Society

N^{a}S^{a}: Nuestra Señora (Spanish—Our Lady)

NASA: National Acoustical Suppliers Association; National Aeronautics and Space Administration; National Appliance Service Association; National Association of Securities Administrators; National Association of Schools of Art; National Automobile Salesmen's Association

NASAA: National Aeronautics and Space Administration Act

NASA-CF: NASA—Cocoa Beach, Florida

NASA-CO: NASA—Cleveland, Ohio

NASA-EC: NASA—Edwards, California

NASAEN: National Association for State-Enrolled Assistant Nurses

NASA-GM: NASA—Greenbelt, Maryland

NASA-HA: NASA—Huntsville, Alabama

NASA-HT: NASA—Houston, Texas

Nasakom: Nationalist-Communist

NASA LST: NASA Large Space Telescope

NASA-LV: NASA—Langley Field, Virginia

NASA-MC: NASA—Moffett Field, California

NASAO: National Association of State Aviation Officials

NASCO: National Academy of Sciences Committee on Oceanography

NASA-SC: NASA—Santa Monica, California

NASBE: National Association of State Boards of Education

NASC: National Aeronautics and Space Council; National Aircraft Standards Committee; National Association of Student Councils; NATO Supply Center; North American Supply Council

NASCAR: National Association of Sports Car Racing; National Association for Stock Car Advancement and Research

NASCom: Naval Air Systems Command

NASCOM: NASA's tracking network, also performing command and control functions

NASD: Naval Aviation Supply Depot

NASDAQS: National Association of Security Dealers Automated Quotation System

nase: neutral atom space engine (sputtering engine)

NASE: National Academy of Stationary Engineers; National Association of Stationary Engineers; National Association of Steel Exporters

NASEES: National Association for Soviet and East European Studies

NASF: National Association of State Foresters

NASFAA: National Association of Student Financial Aid Administrators

NAS & FCA: National Automatic Sprinkler and Fire Control Association

NAS-GB: Noise Abatement Society of Great Britain

Nash: Nashville

NASH: National Association of Specimen Hunters

NASIS: National Association for State Information Systems

NASL: North American Soccer League

NASM: National Air and Space Museum (Smithsonian); National Association of Schools of Music; Naval Aviation School of Medicine

NASM: *Nederlandsche-Amerikaansche Stoomvaart Maatschappij* (Holland-American Line)

NASML: National Air and Space Museum Library (Smithsonian Institution)

NASN: National Air Sampling Network

NASNI: Naval Air Station, North Island (Halsey Field, San Diego, California)

NAS-NRC: National Academy of Science—National Research Council

NASP: National Airport Sytems Plan; Negro Anglo-Saxon Protestant

NASPM: National Association of Seed Potato Merchants

Nas Par: *Nasionale Party* (Afrikaans—National Party)—South Africa's Apartheid party

Nas Pers: *Nasionale Pers* (Afrikaans—National Press)—publisher of apartheid books and periodicals

N^{a}Sr^{a}: *Nossa Senhora* (Portuguese—Our Lady); *Nuestra Senora* (Spanish—Our Lady)

NASRC: National Association of State Racing Commissioners

NASRP: National Association of Special and Reserve Police

Nass: Nassau

NASS: National Association of School Superintendents; National Association of Summer Sessions

NASSC: National Alliance on Shaping Safer Cities

NASSCO: National Steel and Shipbuilding Company

NASSO: National Association of Socialist Students' Organizations

NASSP: National Association of Secondary-School Principals

NASSR: Nahichevan Autonomous Soviet Socialist Republic

NASTBD: National Association of State Text Book Directors

NASTI: Naval Air Station, Terminal Island

NASTL: National Anti-Steel-Trap League

NASU: National Adult School Union

NASULGC: National Association of State Universities and Land-Grant Colleges

NASW: National Association of Science Writers; National Association of Social Workers

nat: nation; national; nationalist; native; natural; naturalist; naturalization; naturalize(d); nature

nat: *natuurkunde* (Dutch—natural science)

Nat: Natalia; Natalie; Nathalie; Nathan; Nathaniel; Nathaniel; Natasha; Nation; National; Nationalist; naturalized

Nat: *Naturkunde* (German—natural science)

NAT: National Air Transport; National Arbitration Tribunal

NATA: National Association of Tax Accountants; National Association of Tax Administrators; National Association of Transportation Advertisers; National Athletic Trainers Association; National Automated Transportation

Association; National Aviation Trades Association; North Atlantic Treaty Alliance
Nat Absten: National Abstentionalist
Natalie Wood: Natasha Gurdin
NATAPROUBU: National Association of Professional Bureaucrats
Nat Arc: National Archives
NATAS: National Academy of Television Arts and Sciences
Nat Assn: National Association
natat: natation
NATB: National Automobile Theft Bureau; Naval Air Training Base
Nat Bur Econ Res: National Bureau of Economic Research (Columbia and Princeton)
NATC: National Air Transportation Conferences; Naval Air Training Command
NATCG: National Association of Training Corps for Girls
natch: naturally
Natch: Natchez
NATCO: National Automatic Tool Company; National Tank Company
natcom: national communications
Nat Con: Nature Conservancy
NATCS: National Air Traffic Control Service
NATD: National Association of Teachers of Dancing
Nat Dem: National Democrats
Nate: Nathan(iel)
Nat Fed: National Federation
Nat Gal: National Gallery
Nath: Nathan(iel)
Nath B: Nathaniel Bowditch
nat hist: natural history
Nathl: Nathaniel
nation.: nationality
NATIONAL: National Cash Register
National Anthem City: Baltimore, Maryland
National Pastime: baseball in America; cricket in Britain
Nation of Big Cities: China with at least fourteen cities each with a million people
Nation of Cities: the United States with more than 150 cities containing 100,000 or more and 6 with a million or more people
Nation of Gentlemen: Scotland so named by King George IV
Nation's Capital: District of Columbia
Nation of Shopkeepers: England, according to Samuel Adams as well as Napoleon
Nation's Hottest Town: Quartzsite, Arizona where July temperatures average 108°F (42°C)
Nativ: Nativity
NATKE: National Association of Theatrical and Kine Employees
natl: national
N Atl: North Atlantic
N Atl Cur: North Atlantic Current
Nat Lib: National Liberal; National Library of Canada (Ottawa)
Nat Mon: National Monument
Nat Mus: Natal Museum; National Museum
nato: no action—talk only
NATO: National Association of Taxicab Owners; National Association of Trailer Owners; National Association of Travel Organizations; North Atlantic Treaty Organization (Belgium, Canada, Denmark, France, Greece, Iceland, Italy, Luxembourg, Netherlands, Norway, Portugal, Turkey, United Kingdom, United States, West Germany)
NATO-AGARD: North Atlantic Treaty Organization—Advisory Group for Aeronautical Research and Development
Nat Obs: *National Observer*
NATO Council: Belgium, Canada, Denmark, France, Federal Republic of Germany, Greece, Iceland, Italy, Luxembourg, Netherlands, Norway, Portugal, Turkey, United Kingdom, United States
NATO-ELLA: North Atlantic Treaty Organization—European Long Lines Agency
NATO-LRSS: North Atlantic Treaty Organization—Long-Range Scientific Studies
Nat Ord: Natural Order
NATO-RDPP: North Atlantic Treaty Organization—Research and Development Production Program
NATOs: National Association of Theatre Owners
NATPE: National Association of Television Program Executives
nat phil: natural philosophy
Nat Pk: National Park
natr.: *natrium* (Latin—sodium)
Nat Rev: National Review
Nats: Nationalists; naturalized citizens
NATS: National Association of Teachers of Singing; Naval Air Test Station; Naval Air Transport Service
Nat. Sc.D.: Doctor of Natural Science
Nat Sci: Natural Science(s)
NATSOPA: National Society of Operative Printers and Assistants
NATSPG: North Atlantic Systems Planning Group
N Att: Naval Attaché
NATTC: National Tank Truck Carriers; Naval Air Technical Training Center
NATTKE: National Association of Theatrical, Television, and Kine Employees
NATTS: Naval Air Turbine Test Station
Nat U: Nations Unies (French—United Nations)
NAT Uni: National University
natur: naturalist
NATUSA: North African Theater of Operations
Nat West: National Westminster (British bank)
Nau: Nauruan(s); Nauru Island
NAU: Naval Administrative Unit
NAUA: National Aircraft Underwriters' Association
Naughty: MacNaughton; McNaughton
NAUS: National Association for Uniformed Services
naut: nautical
nav: naval; navigable; navigate; navigatiation; navigational; navigator
n/a/v: net asset value
Nav: Navaho; naval; Navarra; Navarre
NAVA: National Audio-Visual Association; North American Vexillological Association
NAVAERORECOVF: Naval Aerospace Recovery Facility
navaid(s): navigation aid(s)
NAVAIR: Naval Air (Systems Command)
NAVAIRLANT: Naval Air Forces, Atlantic
NAVAIRPAC: Naval Air Forces, Pacific
NAVAIRREWORKF: Naval Air Rework Facility
NAVAIRSYSCOM: Naval Air Systems Command
Nav. Arch.: Naval Architect
NavAus: navigation in Australian waters
NAVBASE: Naval Base
nav brz: naval bronze

NavCad: Naval Cadet
NAVCENT: Allied Naval Forces, Central Europe
NavCm: navigation countermeasures and deception
Nav.Const.: Naval Constructor
navdac: navigation data assimilation computer
NAVDAC: Navigation Data Assimilation Center
Nav.E.: Naval Engineer
NavEams: navigation in the eastern Atlantic and the Mediterranean
NavEast: navigation along the east coast of Asia
Navel of the Nation: Butte County, South Dakota (geographic center of the United States including Alaska and Hawaii); Smith County, Kansas (geographic center of the forty-eight conterminous states)
NAVELEX: Naval Electronic (Systems Command)
NAVEOFAC: Naval Explosive Ordnance Disposal Facility
NAVFE: Naval Forces Far East
NAVFEC: Naval Facilities
NAVFECENGCOM: Naval Facilities Engineering Command
NAVFOR: Naval Forces
NAVFORJAP: Naval Air Forces, Japan
NAVFORKOR: Naval Air Forces, Korea
NAVH: National Aid to Visually Handicapped
NAVIC: Navy Information Center
navicert(s): navigation certificate(s)
Navidad: *Natividad* (Spanish—Nativity)—Christmas
navig: navigation
Navigator's Nightmare: the Bermuda Islands—scene of so many shipwrecks
NavInd: navigation in the Indian Ocean
NAVLIS: Navy Logistics Information System
NAVMAR: Naval Forces, Marianas
NAVMEDIS: Naval Medical Information System
NavMisCen: Naval Missile Center
NavNoPac: navigation in the North Pacific
NavNorlant: navigation in the North Atlantic
NAVNORTH: Allied Naval Forces, Northern Europe
NavOceanO: Naval Oceanographic Office (USN)
NAVOCS: Naval Officer Candidate School
NAVORDSYSCOM: Naval Ordnance Systems Command
NAVPERSRANDLAB: Naval Personnel Research and Development Laboratory
NAVPHIL: Naval Forces—Philippines
NAVPORCO: Naval Port Control Officer
NAVPRO: Naval Plant Representative Office(r)
NAVROM: Romanian merchant marine
NAVS: National Anti-Vivisection Society
navsat: navigational satellite
NavSat: navigation in the South Atlantic
NAVSEACENTLANT: Naval Sea Support Center—Atlantic
NAVSEACENTPAC: Naval Sea Support Center—Pacific
NAVSEC: Naval Ship Engineering Center
NavShipyd: Naval Shipyard
NAVSMO: Navigation Satellite Management Office
NavSoPac: navigation in the South Pacific
NAVSPASUR: Naval Space Surveillance (USN)
NAVSTA: Naval Station
NAVSUPORANT: Naval Support Forces, Antarctica
NAVTRACEN: Naval Training Center
NAVTRADEVCEN: Naval Training Device Center
NAVUWSEC: Naval Underwater Weapons Systems Engineering Center
navvies: navigators (unskilled canal builders; unskilled laborers)
NAVWAG: Naval Warfare Analysis Group
NAW: National Association of Wholesalers; National Association for Women; North African Waters
NAWA: National Association of Women Artists
NAWAPA: North American Water and Power Alliance
NAWAS: National Air Warning Service
NAWB: National Association of Workshops for the Blind
NAWCC: National Association of Watch and Clock Collectors
NAWCH: National Association for the Welfare of Children in Hospitals
NAWDC: National Association of Women Deans and Counselors
NAWF: North American Wildlife Foundation
NAWM: National Association of Wool Manufacturers
NAWND: National Association of Wholesale Newspaper Distributors
NAWPA: North American Water and Power Alliance
NAWS: National Aviation Weather System
Naxas: Naxalites (Maoist extremists active in India)
Nay: Nayarit
NAYC: National Association of Youth Clubs
NAYRU: North American Yacht Racing Union
naz: *nazionale* (Italian—national)
Naz: Nazaire
Nazi: adherent of the former National Socialist German Workers' Party *(Nationalsozialistische Partei)*
nb: narrow band; no bias (relay)
n/b: no ball(s)
n.b.: *nota bene* (Latin—note well)
Nb: nimbus; niobium (formerly columbium)
Nb^{94}: radioactive niobium
NB: Navy Band; New Brunswick; North Borneo
NB: *Norsk Bibliotekforening* (Norwegian Library Association)
NBA: National Band Association; National Bankers Association; National Banking Association; National Bar Association; National Basketball Association; National Boat Association; National Bowling Association; National Boxing Association; National Button Association
NBAA: National Business Aircraft Association
N balance: nitrogen balance
NBBB: National Better Business Bureau
NBBC: National Brass Band Club
NBBS: New British Broadcasting Station
NBBU: New Brunswick Board of Underwriters
NBC: National Ballet of Canada; National Baseball Congress; National Beagle Club; National Beef Council; National Book Committee; National Bowling Council; National

Braille Club; National Broadcasting Corporation; Navy Beach Commando; Nigerian Broadcasting Corporation

NB & C: Norfolk, Baltimore and Carolina Line

NBCA: National Baseball Congress of America; National Beagle Club of America

NBD: National Bank of Detroit

NBDA: National Bicycle Dealers Association

NB & DA: National Barrel & Drum Association

NBE: National Bank Examiner(s)

NBEA: National Business Education Association

NBER: National Bureau of Economic Research; National Bureau of Engineering Registration

NBET: National Business Entrance Test(s)

NBF: National Boating Federation

NB & FAA: National Burglar and Fire Alarm Association

NBF Life: National Ben Franklin Life Insurance

nbfm: narrow-band frequency modulation

NBFU: National Board of Fire Underwriters; Newfoundland Board of Fire Underwriters

nbg: no bloody good

NBGC: National Ballet Guild of Canada

NBH: National Bellas Hess

NBHA: National Builders Hardware Association

NBHC: New Broken Hill Consolidated

nbi: no bone(y) injury

NBI: Nathaniel Branden Institute; National Benevolent Institution

NBI: *Norges Byggforskninginstitutt* (Norwegian Building Institute)

NBIT: New Bedford Institute of Technology

nbl: not bloody likely

NBL: National Basketball League; National Book League

NBLC: *Nederlands Bibliotheek en Lektuur Centrum* (Dutch—Netherlands Center for Public Libraries and Literature)

NBL & P: National Bureau for Lathing and Plastering

nbm: nothing by mouth

NBM: New Brunswick Museum

NBME: National Board of Medical Examiners

NBMG: Navigation Bombing and Missile Guidance System

NBMV & NSL: New Bedford, Martha's Vineyard, and Nantucket Steamship Line

nbn (NBN): national book number

NBNZ: National Bank of New Zealand

NBO: Nairobi, Kenya (airport); Navy Bureau of Ordnance

n-bomb: neutron bomb

nbp: normal boiling point

NBP: National Business Publications

NBPC: National Border Patrol Council

NBPI: National Board for Prices and Income

NBPRP: National Board for the Promotion of Rifle Practice

n br: naval brass; naval bronze

n Br: *nördliche Breite* (German—north latitude)

NBR: National Bison Range (Montana

nbre: *noviembre* (Spanish—November)

NBRF: National Biomedical Research Foundation

NBRI: National Building Research Institute

NBRMP: National Board of Review of Motion Pictures

NBRPC: New Brunswick Research and Productivity Council

NBS: National Bureau of Standards; New British Standard

NBSA: National Bank of South Africa; Netherlands Bank of South Africa

NBSBL: National Bureau of Standards Boulder Laboratory

nb st: nimbo-stratus

NBT: National Book Trust (India)

NBTA: National Baton Twirlers Association; National Business Teachers Association

NBTC: New Brunswick Teachers College

NBTS: National Blood Transfusion Service

n butt: national buttress (thread)

nbv: net book value

nbw: noise bandwidth

NBW: National Book Week

Nby: Newbury

nc: national coarse (thread); nitrocellulose; no charge; no connection; noise criteria; normally closed; not cataloged; not catalogued; nuclear capability; numerical control(s)

nc: *non chiffre* (French—unnumbered)

n-c: numerical control (automation)

n/c: numerical control (automation)

nC: *na Christus* (Dutch—after Christ)

NC: Napa College; Nashville, Chatanooga & St. Louis (railroad; Nasson College; Natchez College; National Coarse (screw threads); National Cash Register (stock exchange symbol); Newark College; Newberry College; New Caledonia; Newcomb College; Nicholls College; Nichols College; Norfolk College; Norman College; North Carolina; North Carolinian; Northland College; Northwestern College; Nuclear Congress; Nurse Corps

N.C.: N.C. Wyeth

nca: neurocirculatory asthenia; no copies available

NCA: National Camping Association; National Canners Association; National Capital Award; National Cashmere Association; National Charcoal Association; National Cheerleaders Association; National Chiropractic Association; National Civic Association; National Club Association; National Coal Association; National Coffee Association; National Commission on Accrediting; National Confectioners Association; National Constructors Association; National Contesters Association; National Costumers Association; National Council on Alcoholism; National Council on the Arts; National Coursing Association; National Cranberry Association; National Creameries Association; National Credit Association; Naval Communications Annex; Navy Contract Administrator; Ngorongoro Conservation Area (Tanzania); North Central Airlines; Northern Consolidated Airlines

N C A: National Cricket Association

NCAA: National Collegiate Athletic Association

NCAAA: National Center of Afro-American Artists

NCAB: National Cancer Advisory Board
NCAB: *National Cyclopedia of American Biography*
NCAE: National Center for Audio Experimentation; National College of Agricultural Engineering
NCAI: National Congress of American Indians
NCANH: National Council for the Accreditation of Nursing Homes
N-CAP: Nurses Coalition for Action in Politics
NCAPC: National Center for Air Pollution Control
NCAR: National Center for Atmospheric Research
NCARB: National Council of Architectural Registration Boards
NCASF: National Council of American-Soviet Friendship
NCAT: Northampton College of Advanced Technology
NCVAE: National Council for Audio-Visual Aids in Education
NCAW: National Council for Animal Welfare
ncb: new crime buffer; nickel-cadmium battery
Ncb: Norrlands Skogsägaves Cellulosa AB
NCB: National Cargo Bureau; National Coal Board; National Conservation Bureau
NCBA: National Cattle Breeders' Association; Northern California Booksellers Association
NCBFAA: National Customs Brokers and Forwarders Association of America
NCBMP: National Council of Building Material Producers
NCBR: National Council of Black Republicans
NCC: Nassau Community College; National Carloading Corporation; National Castings Council; National Computer Center; National Conference on Citizenship; National Container Committee; National Cotton Council; National Council of Churches of Christ in the USA; National Cultural Center; Newhouse Communications Center (University of Syracuse); Newspaper Comics Council; Noise Control Committee; NORAD Control Center; Northwest Community College
NCC: *Nederlands Cultureel Contact* (Netherlands Cultural Contact)
NCCA: National Coil Coaters Association
NCCAS: National Center of Communication Arts and Sciences
NCCAT: National Committee for Clear Air Turbulence
NCCC: Niagara County Community College
NCCCC: Navy Command, Control, and Communications Center
NCCCLC: Naval Command Control Communications Laboratory Center (formerly NEL—Navy Electronics Laboratory)
NCCCUSA: National Council of the Churches of Christ in the U.S.A.
NCCD: National Council on Crime and Delinquency
NCCF: National Committee to Combat Fascism (Black Panther front); National Commission on Consumer Finance
NCCH: National Council to Control Handguns
NCCI: National Committee for Commonwealth Immigrants
NCCJ: National Conference of Christians and Jews
NCCL: National Council for Civil Liberties; National Council of Canadian Labor
NCCPA: National Council of College Publications Advisers
NCCPV: National Commission on the Causes and Prevention of Violence
NCCR: National Council for Civic Responsibility
NCCS: National Command and Control System; National Council for Civic Responsibility
NCCVD: National Council for Combating Venereal Diseases
NCCW: National Council of Catholic Women
NCCY: National Council of Catholic Youth
ncd: no can do
NCD: Naval Construction Department
NCD: *New Collegiate Dictionary*
NCDA: National Center for Drug Analysis
NCDAD: National Council for Diplomas in Art and Design
NCDAI: National Clearinghouse for Drug Abuse Information
NCDC: National Center for Disease Control; National Communicable Disease Center
NCDS: National Center for Dispute Settlement (American Arbitration Association)
NCE: Newark College of Engineering; Nice, France (Côte d'Azur airport)
NCEA: National Catholic Educational Association; North Carolina Education Association
NCEC: National Committee for an Effective Congress
5 **NCEI:** National Commission on Emerging Institutions
NCEL: Naval Civil Engineering Laboratory
NCER: National Center for Earthquake Research
NCERT: National Council for Educational Research and Training
NCES: National Center for Educational Statistics
NCET: National Council for Educational Technology
ncf: nerve cell food
NCF: National Consumer Federation
NCFA: National Commission of Fine Arts; National Consumer Finance Association; Navy Campus for Achievement
NCFC: National Council of Farmer Cooperatives
NCFDA: National Council on Federal Disaster Assistance
NCFIRB: North Carolina Fire Insurance Rating Bureau
NCFM: National Commission on Food Marketing
NCFPC: National Center for Fish Protein Concentrate
NCFR: National Council on Family Relations
NCFT: National College of Food Technology
NCG: National Council for the Gifted; National Cylinder Gas (division of Chemotron)
NCGE: National Council for Geographic Education
NCGG: National Council for Geodesy and Geophysics
NCH: National Children's Home
NCHA: National Campers and Hikers Association; National Capital Housing Authority
N Chem L: National Chemical Laboratory
n chg: normal charge
NCHMT: National Capitol Historical Museum of Transportation
NCHP: Nouvelle Compagnie

Havraise Peninsulaire (de Navigation) (Havre Peninsula Navigation Line)

NCIC: National Cancer Institute of Canada; National Crime Information Center

n Chr: *nach Christus* (German—after Christ; A.D.)

NCHS: National Center for Health Statistics

NCHSR & D: National Center for Health Services Research and Development (HEW)

NCHVRFE: National College for Heating, Ventilating, Refrigeration, and Fan Engineering

nci: napthalene-creosote-iodiform (lice-control powder); no-cost item

NCI: National Cancer Institute; National Casing Institute; National Cheese Institute; Naval Cost Inspection; Naval Cost Inspector

NCIC: National Crime Information Center

NCIO: National Council on Indian Opportunity

nci powder: naphthalene ceosote iodoform powder (for killing lice)

NCISC: Naval Counterintelligence Support Center

NCIT: National Council on Inland Transport

NCJSC: National Criminal Justice Statistics Center

NCJW: National Council of Jewish Women

Nck: Neck (postal abbreviation)

NCL: National Central Library; National Chemical Laboratory; National Consumers League; National Culture League

NCLC: National Council of Labour Colleges

NCLIS: National Commission on Libraries and Information Science

ncm: non-corrosive metal; non-crew member

NCMC: NORAD Cheyenne Mountain Complex

NCMDA: National Commission on Marijuana and Drug Abuse

NCME: National Council on Measurements in Education

NCMEA: National Catholic Music Educators Association

NCMH: National Committee on Maternal Health; National Committee for Mental Hygiene

NCMHE: National Clearinghouse for Mental Health Education

NCMLB: National Council of Mailing List Brokers

NCN: National Council of Nurses; New Caledonian Nickel

NCNA: National Council on Noise Abatement; New China News Agency (mainland China)

NCNC: National Council of Nigeria and the Cameroons

NCNE: National Campaign for Nursery Education

NCNP: National Conference for New Politics (coalition of communist, left socialist, and militant revolutionary elements comprising the New Left); North Cascades National Park (Washington)

NCNW: National Council of Negro Women

NCO: Noncommissioned Officer

NCOA: National Council on the Aging

NCOAUSA: Non-Commissioned Officers Association of the U.S.A.

NCOIC: Noncommissioned Officer in Charge

N/COM: Navy/Chief of Naval Operations

NCOMP: National Catholic Office for Motion Pictures

NCOR: National Committee on Oceanographic Research

ncos: non-commissioned officers

ncp: nitrogen charge panel; normal circular pitch

NCP: National Capital Parks; Naviera Chilena del Pacífico (Chilean Pacific Line)

NCPC: National Capital Planning Commission; Northern Canada Power Commission

NCPI: National Clay Pipe Institute; Navy Civilian Personnel Instructions

NCPL: National Center for Programmed Learning

NCPPL: National Committee on Prisons and Prison Labor

NCPRV: National Council of Puerto Rican Volunteers

NCPS: National Cat Protection Society; National Commission on Product Safety

NCPT: National Congress of Parents and Teachers

NCPTWA: National Clearinghouse for Periodical Title Word Abbreviations

NCQR: National Council for Quality and Reliability

ncr: natural circulation reactor; no calibration required; no carbon required

n Cr: *novo Cruzeiro* (Portuguese—new cruzeiro)—Brazilian monetary jnit

NCR: National Cash Register; National Council of Reconciliation (in Vietnam)

NCRA: National Correctional Recreation Association

NCRD: National Council for Research and Development

NCRE: Naval Construction Research Establishment

NCRFCL: National Commission on Reform of Federal Criminal Laws

NCRFP: National Council for a Responsible Firearms Policy

NCRL: National Chemical Research Laboratory

NCRLC: National Committee on Regional Library Cooperation

NCRP: National Committee on Radiation Protection

ncr paper: no-carbon-required paper

NCRPM: National Committee on Radiation Protection and Measurements

NCRS: National Committee for Rural Schools

NCRT: National College of Rubber Technology

NCS: National Cartoonists Society; National Cemetery System; National Chrysanthemum Society; National Communications System, Naval Communication Station; Net Control Station; Numerical Control Society

NCSA: National Carl Schurz Association; National Council of Seamen's Agencies; National Crushed Stone Association; National Customs Service Association; North Coast of South America

NCSAW: National Catholic Society for Animal Welfare

NCSBEE: National Council of State Boards of Engineering Examiners

NCSC: National Council of Senior Citizens

NCSE: National Commission on Safety Education

NCSF: National College Student Foundation

NCSGC: National Council of State Garden Clubs

NCSH: National Clearinghouse for Smoking and Health

NCSI: National Council for Stream Improvement

NCSL: National Civil Service League; National Conference of Standards Laboratories; Naval Code and Signal Laboratory
NCSO: Naval Control of Shipping Office(r); North Carolina Symphony Orchestra
NCSP: National Conference on State Parks
NCSPA: North Carolina State Ports Authority
NCSPS: National Committee for the Support of Public Schools
NCSRC: National Centre for Social Research and Criminology (Cairo)
NCSS: National Center for Social Statistics; National Council for Social Studies
NCSSA: Naval Command Systems Support Activity
NCSSC: Naval Command Systems Support Center
NCSSFL: National Council of State Supervisors of Foreign Languages
NCSTAS: National Council of Scientific and Technical Art Societies
NC & ST L: Nashville, Chattanooga & St. Louis (railroad)
NCSW: National Conference on Social Welfare
NCSWCL: National Commission on State Workmen's Compensation Laws
NCSWD: National Center for Solid Waste Disposal
NCSWR: National Conference on Solid Waste Research
NCT: National Chamber of Trade; National Culture Trust
n/cta: *nuestra cuenta* (Spanish—our account)
NCTA: National Cable Television Association; National Capital Transport Agency; National Community Television Association; National Committee for Technological Awards; National Council for Technological Awards
NCTAEP: National Committee on Technology, Automation, and Economic Progress
NCTC: National Collection of Type Cultures
NCTE: National Council of Teachers of English
NCTEC: Northern Counties Technical Examinations Council
NCTJ: National Council for the Training of Journalists
NCTM: National Council of Teachers of Mathematics
NCTR: National Center for Toxicological Research
NCTS: National Council of Technical Schools
ncu: nitrogen control unit
NCU: National Cyclists' Union
NCUA: National Credit Union Administration; National Credit Union Association
NCUMC: National Council for the Unmarried Mother and her child
ncup: no commission until paid
NCUPUFUB: National Clean-up, Paint-Up, Fix-Up Bureau
NCUSA: Navy Club of the U.S.A.
NCUSIF: National Credit Union Share Insurance Fund
NCUTLO: National Committee on Uniform Traffic Laws and Ordinances
ncv: no commercial value
NCVA: National Center(s) for Volunteer Action
NCW: National Council of Women
NCWC: National Catholic Welfare Conference
NCWSA: National Council of Women of South Africa
NCWUS: National Council of Women of the U.S.
NCY: National Cylinder Gas (stock-exchange symbol)
NCYC: National Council of Yacht Clubs
NCYMCA: National Council of Young Men's Christian Association
nd: national debt; next day; no date; no decision; no deed; no delay; no drawing; not dated; not deeded; not drawn; nothing doing; nuclear detonation
nd: *niederdruck* (German—low pressure)
n-d: non-drying
n/d: neutral density
Nd: neodymium; refractive index (symbol)
ND: National Dairy Products (stock exchange symbol); Naval District; Navy Department; New Drugs; North Dakota; Notre Dame
N.D.: Doctor of Naturopathy
nda: new drug application
N d A: *Nota dell 'Autore* (Italian—Author's Note)
NDA: National Dairymens' Association; National Dental Association; National Diploma in Agriculture
ndaa: not dated at all
NDAA: National District Attorneys Association
NDAC: National Defense Advisory Commission; Nuclear Defense Affairs Committee (NATO)
N Dak: North Dakota; North Dakotan
n da r: *nota da redação* (Portuguese—author'snote)
ndb: non-directional beacon
NDB: Navy Department Bulletin
NDBC: National Duckpin Bowling Congress
NDBI: National Dairymen's Benevolent Institution
NDBS: National Data Buoy System
NDC: National Dairy Council; National Defense Contribution; National Defense Corps; National Democratic Club; National Development Corporation; NATO Defence College; Naval Dental Clinic; Nuclear Development Corporation
NDCS: National Deaf Children's Society
N d D: *Nota della Direzione* (Italian—Director's Note)
NDD: National Diploma in Dairying
NDDT: National Diploma in Dairy Technology
NDEA: National Defense Education Act
NDEI: National Defense Education Institute
n del a: *nota del autor* (Spanish—author's note)
n del e: *nota del editor* (Spanish—editor's note)
n del t: *nota del traductor* (Spanish—translator's note)
N de M: Ferrocarriles Nacionales de México (Spanish—National Railways of Mexico)
NDER: National Defense Executive Reserve
ndf: nacelle drag efficiency factor
NDF: National Diploma in Forestry
NDG: National Dance Guild
NDH: Delhi, India (airport); National Diploma in Health; National Diploma in Horticulture
NDHA: National District Heating Association
NDHS: New Drop High School
ndi: numerical designation index
Ndl: *Nederland* (Dutch—The Netherlands)
NDL: Nuclear Defense Labora-

tory
NDLB: National Dock Labour Board
NDMB: National Defense Mediation Board
ndp: normal diametric pitch
NDP: National Dairy Products; New Democratic Party (Canada)
NDP: *Nationaldemokratische Partei Deutschlands* (Germany's National-Democratic Party)—neo-Nazi oriented
NDPA: National Democratic Party of Alabama
NDPBC: National Duck Pin Bowling Congress
NDPH: National Diploma in Poultry Husbandry
NDPP: National Drug Prevention Program
NDPS: National Data Processing Service
N d R: *Nota della Redazione* (Italian—Editor's Note)
NDR: *Norddeutscher Rundfunk* (North German Radio)
NDRC: National Defense Research Committee
NDRI: Naval Dental Research Institute
ndro: nondestructive readout
nds (NDS): nuclear detection satellite
NDSB: Narcotic Drugs Supervisory Body
NDSF: North Dakota School of Forestry
NDSK: *Nippon Dendo Sharyo Kyokai* (Japan Electric-Powered Vehicle Association)
NDSL: National Direct Student Loan
NDSM: National Defense Security Medal
NDSSS: North Dakota State School of Science
ndt: nondestructive testing
ndt: *nota del traductor* (Spanish—translator's note); *nota del traduttore* (Italian—translator's note); *note du traducteur* (French—translator's note)
NDT: Ferrocarril Nacional de Tehuantepec (National Railroad of Tehuantepec—symbol); National Driver's Test; Newfoundland Daylight Time
NDTA: National Defense Transportation Association
NDTC: Nottingham and District Technical College
NDU: Notre Dame University
Ndv: Newcastle disease virus
ne: new edition; not enlarged
ne: *non ebarbe* (French—untrimmed)
n/e: no effects
Ne: neon; Nepal; Nepalese; Netherlander; Netherlands
NE: National Emergency; Naval Engineer(ing); new edition; New England(er); northeast; Northeast Airlines (2-letter coding); Nuclear Engineer(ing)
N.E.: Nuclear Engineer
ne/6m: new edition in preparation, expected in 6 months (for example)
NEA: National Education Association; National Endowment for the Arts; New England Aquarium (Boston); Newspaper Enterprise Association; Northeast Airlines; Nuclear Energy Agency (UN)
N.E.A.: Newspaper Enterprise Association
NEAC: New English Art Club
NEACSS: New England Association of Colleges and Secondary Schools
NEAF: Near East Air Force
NEAFC: Northeast Atlantic Fisheries Commission
NEAHI: Near East Animal Health Institute
NEAP: National Assessment of Educational Progress
Neapolitan Painter and Poet: Salvator Rosa
Neapolitans: islands off Naples; natives of Naples
NEAR: National Emergency Alarm Repeater
NEARA: New England Antiquities Research Association
Near East: the Middle East as opposed to the Far East
Nears: Near Islands (Agattu, Attu, Shemya, etc.)
NEATE: New England Association of Teachers of English
'neath: beneath; underneath
neb: *nebbisch* (Yiddish—colorless; plain, retiring; socially ill at ease)
NEB: National Energy Board (Canada)
NEB: *New English Bible*
nebbie: (underground slang—nembutal)
NEBHE: New England Board of Higher Education
Nebr: Nebraska; Nebraskan
NEBSS: National Examinations Board for Supervisory Studies
nebuchad: nebuchadnessar (16-quart-capacity champagne bottle)
nebul.: *nebula* (Latin—spray)—nebulizer
nec: necessary; not elsewhere classified
NEC: National Economic Council; National Egg Council; National Electrical Code; National Exchange Club; New England Conservatory of Music; New England Council; Nippon Electric Company
NECA: National Electrical Contractors' Association; Near East College Association
NECCO: New England Confectionary Company
NECM: New England Conservatory of Music
NECMD: Newark Contract Management District
NECP: New England College of Pharmacy
necr: necrosis
necrol: necrology
NECS: National Electrical Code Standards
necy: necessary
ned: normal equivalent deviation
Ned: Edmund; Edward; Edwin
NED: *New English Dictionary (Oxford English Dictionary)*
NEDA: National Economic Development Association
Ned Buntline: Edward Zane Carroll Judson
NEDC: National Economic Development Council (of Great Britain where it is nicknamed Neddy); Near East Development Council
Neddy: Edgar; Edmund; Edward; Edwin; Edwina; National Economic Development Council's nickname
NEDICO: Netherlands Engineering Consultants
NEDL: New England Deposit Library
Nedlloyd: Netherlands Line
NEDO: National Economic Development Office
NEDT: National Educational Development Tests
NEDU: Navy Experimental Diving Unit
NEEB: North Eastern Electricity Board (UK)
NEEC: National Export Expansion Council
need.: needlework
needn't: (contraction—need not)
ne'er: never (contraction)
NEES: Naval Engineering Experiment Station; New England Electric Service

nef: national extra fine (screw thread); net energy for fattening; noise exposure forecast; nuclear energy factor(s)
NEF: Naval Emergency Fund; Near East Foundation; New Education Fellowship
nefa: nonesterified fatty acid
NEFA: Northeast Frontier Agency
NEFC: Near East Forestry Commission
NEFEN: Near and Far East News
NEFIRA: New England Fire Insurance Rating Association
Nefos: New Emerging Forces
NEFSA: National Education Field Service Association
neg: negation; negative; negotiate; negritude
nég: *négation* (French—negation)
Neg: Negro; Negroid
negatron: negative electron
Negrasian(s): person(s) of African and Asian parents such as Afro-Chinese, Afro-Indian, Afro-Japanese, etc.
negro: (Portuguese, Spanish—black as in Rio Negro)
NEGRO: National Economic Growth and Reconstruction Organization
Negro Explorer: Matthew Henson who pushed Peary to the North Pole after accompanying him on all his Arctic expeditions
négt: *négociant* (French—merchant)—wholesaler
negtax: negative (income) tax
Neh: The Book of Nehemiah
NEH: National Endowment for the Humanities
NEHA: National Executives Housekeepers Association
nehi: knee-high
nei: not elsewhere indicated
n.e.i.: *non est inventus* (Latin—it is not found)
NEI: National Eye Institute; Netherlands East Indies
NEIC: National Earthquake Information Center
nek: nekton
NEK: *Norsk Electrotecnisk Komite* (Norwegian Electrotechnical Committee)
nekolim: neocolonialist-colonialist-imperialist (Indonesian acronym)
Nel: Eleanor(a); Ellen; Helen(a); Nelly
NEL: National Engineering Laboratory (Great Britain); Navy Electronics Laboratory (USN)
NELA: National Electric Light Association; New England Library Association
NELC: Naval Electronics Laboratory Center (formerly NEL)
NELIA: Nuclear Energy Liability Insurance Association
NELINT: New England Library Information Network
Nell: Eleanor(e)
NELL: North East Lancashire Libraries
Nellie: Nellie McClung (pronounced *Mc Clue*)—Canadian novelist and women's rights champion in the early 1900s
Nellie Melba: Helen Porter Mitchell
Nello: Emmanuel
Nelly: Eleanor(a); Ellen; Helen
Nelly Bly: Elizabeth Cochrane Seaman
NELMA: Northeastern Lumber Manufacturers Association
Nel-Mar: Nelson-Marlborough (NZ)
Nels: Nelson
NELS: National Environmental Laboratories
NELTAS: North East Lancashire Technical Advisory Services
NEly: north-easterly
nem: not elsewhere mentioned
nema: nematode
NEMA: National Ecletic Medical Association; National Electrical Manufacturers Association
nemat: nematology
Nemat: Nemathelminthes
NEMC: New England Medical Center
nem. con.: *nemine contradicente* (Latin—no one contradicting)
nem. dis.: *nemine dissentiente* (Latin—no one dissenting)
NEMI: National Elevator Manufacturing Industry
NEMLA: New England Modern Language Association
nemmies: nembutal capsules (dangerous sedative)
Nemo: Guillaume; Guillermo
NEMO: Naval Edreobenthic Manned Observatory (for sedentary sea bottom research); Naval Experimental Manned Observatory
NEMPA: North-Eastern Master Printers' Alliance
NEMPS: National Environmental Monitoring and Prediction System
NEN: New England Nuclear (corporation)
ne/nd: new edition in preparation—no date can be given
N Eng: Naval Engineer(ing); New England; North England
NENP: New England National Park (New South Wales)
neo: near earth orbit
NEOB: New Executive Office Building (D.C.)
Neo-Cath: Neo-Catholic(ism)
Neo-Christ: Neo-Christian(ity)
neoclas: neoclassical; neoclassicism
neocol: neocolonial(ism)
neocolim: neocolonial-colonial-imperalist
Neo-Conf: Neo-Confucian(ist)
Neo-Dar: Neo-Darwinian; Neo-Darwinist(ic)
NEODTC: Naval Explosive Ordinance Disposal Technical Center
Neo-Goth: Neo-Gothic
Neo-Heg: Neo-Hegelian
neo-imp: neo-impressionism; neo-impressionistic
Neo-Kant: Neo-Kantian(ism)
neol: neologism
Neo-Lam: Neo-Lamarckian; Neo-Lamarckism; Neo-Lamarckist
Neo-Lat: Neo-Latin(ism)
Neo-Luth: Neo-Lutheran(ism)
Neo-Mel: Neo-Melanesian (pidgin English of Melanesia, New Guinea, and North-East Australian islanders)
Neo-Nor: Neo-Norwegian
Neopagan Eclectic: Miguel de Unamuno
Neo-Plas: Neo-Plastic(ism)
Neo-Plat: Neo-Platonic; Neo-Platonism
Neo-Pyth: Neo-Pythagorean(ism)
Neo-Real: Neo-Realism; Neo-Realistic
Neo-Rom: Neo-Romantic(ism)
Neo-Schol: Neo-Scholastic(ism)
neotrop: neotropical
neotwy: (last-letter mnemonic—when, where, who, what, how, why)
Nep: Nepal; Nepomucene; Nepomuceno; Nepomuk; Neptune
Nep: Cornelius Nepos (Roman biographer)
NEP: New Economic Policy; New England Power (company); Nixon Economic Policy
nepa (NEPA): nuclear energy for the propulsion of aircraft
NEPA: National Environmental Policy Act

NEPAL: National Egg Packers' Association, Ltd
NEPCO: New England Provision Company
NEPE: National Emergency Planning Establishment (Canada)
NEPLEX: New England Power Exchange
neph: nephew
nepho: nephograph; nephological; nephologist; nephology
Nep Rs: Nepalese rupees
Nept: Neptune
Neptune: (Latin—Poseiden)—god of the sea
Nequam: Alexander Necham
N Equ Cur: North Equatorial Current
ner: nervous system
NER: National Educational Radio; National Elk Refuge (Wyoming); North Eastern Railway (England)
NERA: National Emergency Relief Administration
NERC: National Electronic Reliability Council; National Environmental Research Center; Natural Environment Research Council
ne rep.: *ne repetatur* (Latin—do not repeat)
NERO: Near East Regional Office (FAO); Nutrition Education Research Organization
nerv: nervous; nuclear emulsion recovery vehicle (NERV)
nerva: nuclear engine for rocket vehicle application
nes: not elsewhere specified
Nes: Nesta; Nestor
NES: National Extension Service; Naval Education Service; News Election Service
NESA: Near East and South Asia; New England School of Art
NESBIC: Netherlands Student's Bureau for International Cooperation
NESC: National Electric Safety Code; National Environmental Satellite Center
NESO: Naval Electronics Supply Office
Ness: Agnes
NESS: National Environmental Satellite Service
Nessa: Agnes
Nessie: Agnes
nest.: node execution selection table
NEST: Naval Experimental Satellite Terminal
Nesta: Agnes
nestor: neutron source thermal reactor
Nestor of American Botany: William Darlington
Nestor of American Pediatrics: Abraham Jacobi
Nestor of Congregationalism: Leonard Bacon
Nestor of the Rockies: Kit Carson
net.: network; not earlier than; nuclear electronic transitor
Net: Antoinette; Nettie; Netty
NET: National Educational Television
NETA: Northwest Electronic Technical Association
NETF: Nuclear Engineering Test Facility
Neth: Netherlands
Neth Ant: Netherlands Antilles
Netherlands Antilles: Dutch West Indies ABC Islands—Aruba, Bonaire, Curaçao and the 3 Ss—Saba, Sint Eustatius, Sint Maarten)
Netherlands East Indies: former name of Indonesia
Netherlands Guiana: Dutch Guiana or Surinam
Netherlands Indies: old name of Indonesia
Netherlands New Guinea: former name of West Irian now part of Indonesia
netic: nonretentive nonshocksensitive (alloy made for high-level attenuation)
n. et m.: *nocte et mane* (Latin—night and morning)
netma: nobody ever tells me anything
NETRC: National Educational Television and Radio Center
nets.: network techniques
Nettie: Henrietta
Net(ty): Antonia
Netty: Henrietta
Netza: *Netzahualcoyotl* (Aztec—Hungry Coyote)—Mexico's second largest city
neu: neuter; neutral; neutrality
NEU: Northeastern University
neubarb: *neubearbeitet* (German—revised)
Neuk: Neuköln
neur: neuralgia; neurasthenia; neuritis; neurology
neuro: neurotic
neurol: neurological; neurologist; neurology
neuropath: neuropathology
neurophys: neurophysiological
neuropsychiat: neuropsychiatry
neurosurg: neurosurgeon; neurosurgery; neurosurgical
neurs: neurosis
NEUS: Northeastern United States
neut: neuter; neutral; neutralize; neutralizer
neutron: neutral ion
Nev: Nevada; Nevadan
Nevil Shute: Nevil Shute Norway
new: newton
New Albion: Sir Francis Drake's name for what is now British Columbia, plus the states of Washington, Oregon, and California
New Am Lib: New American Library
New Amsterdam: former name of New York City called Nieuw Amsterdam by the original Dutch settlers
Newc: Newcastle-upon-Tyne
New Cal: New Caldonia
New Colossus: Statue of Liberty's sobriquet derived from the poem by Emma Lazarus—*The New Colossus*—proclaiming: "Give me your tired, your poor, Your huddled masses yearning to breathe free, The wretched refuse of your teeming shore. Send these, the homeless, tempest-tossed to me, I lift my lamp beside the golden door!"
New Deal: (administration of Franklin Delano Roosevelt—thirty-second President of the United States)
New England: Maine, New Hampshire, Vermont, Massachusetts, Rhode Island, and Connecticut
New England Colonies: Massachusetts, New Hampshire, Rhode Island, Connecticut
Newf: Newfoundland
Newfie(s): Newfoundlander(s)
New France: old name for French Canada
New Freedom: (administration of Woodrow Wilson—twenty-eighth President of the United States)
New Frontier: (administration of John F. Kennedy—thirty-fifth President of the United States)
New Granada: Colombia's original Spanish name—*Nueva Granada*
New Heb: New Hebrides (Anglo-French island condominium in the South Pacific)
New Heb Con: New Hebrides Condominium
New Hebrides: New Hebrides Is-

lands
New Holland: old name for Australia discovered by Dutch navigators
New Lib: Newberry Library
New Majority: (administration of Richard M. Nixon—thirty-seventh President of the United States)
New Mex: New Mexico
New Netherlands: old name for what is now New York together with parts of Connecticut and New Jersey
New Orl: New Orleans
new par: new paragraph
NEWRADS: Nuclear Explosion Warning and Radiological Data System
news.: naval electronic warfare simulator; news agency; news agent; new standards
newscast(er): news broadcast(er)
New Sib: New Siberian Islands
New Siberians: New Siberian Islands (Novosibirskiye Ostrova)
Newt: Newton
New Test.: New Testament
NEWWA: New England Water Works Association
New World: North and South America
New World: Dvőrák's Symphony No. 9 in E minor (formerly No. 5)
New Yorican: New York Puerto Rican
nf: national fine; near face; no fool; no funds; noise factor; non-ferrous; non-fundable; nose fuze; not fordable
n-f: nonfordable
n.f.: *ny foljd* (Swedish—new series)
n/f: no funds
n/f: *nuestro favor* (Spanish—our favor)
n & f: near and far
n.F.: *neue Folge* (German—new series)
NF: National Fine (threads); National Formulary; National Foundation; Newfoundland; Norfolk, Virginia (airport); Norman French; nouveau franc (French—new franc, issued in 1960); Nutrition Foundation
NF: *Neue Folge* (German—new series); *Nuestra Familia* (Spanish—Our Family)—prison racketeers also called *La Nuestra Familia*
N-F: Norman-French
nfa: no further action
NFA: National Federation of Anglers; National Food Administration; National Foundry Association; Nature Friends of America; Naval Fuel Annex; New Farmers of America; Night Fighters Association; Northwest Fisheries Association
NFAA: National Field Archery Association
NFAH: National Foundation for the Arts and the Humanities
NFAL: National Foundation of Arts and Letters
nfb: no feedback
NFB: National Federation of the Blind; National Film Board (Canada)
NFB: *Nippon Fudosan Bank* (Japan Real Property Bank)
NFBC: National Film Board of Canada; Newfoundland Base Command
NFBF: National Farm Bureau Federation
NFBPM: National Federation of Builders' and Plumbers' Merchants
NFBTE: National Federation of Building Trades' Employers
NFBTO: National Federation of Building Trades' Operatives
NFBPWC: National Federation of Business and Professional Women's Clubs
nfc: not favorably considered
NFC: National Foundry College; National Freight Corporation; Navy Finance Center
NFCA: National Federation of Community Associations
NFCC: National Foundation for Consumer Credit
nfcs: night fire-control sight
NFCSA: National Finance Corporation of South Africa
NFCTA: National Federation of Corn Trade Associations; National Fibre Can and Tube Association
NFCU: Navy Federal Credit Union
Nfd: Newfoundland
NFD: National Federation of Doctors; Naval Fuel Depot
NFD: National Faculty Directory
nfd(m): non-fat dry (milk)
NFDA: National Food Distributors Association
nfe: nose-fairing exit; not fully equipped
NFEA: National Federated Electrical Association
NFEMC: National Federation of Export Management Companies
NFER: National Foundation for Education Research
NFF: National Froebel Foundation; Naval Fuel Facility
NFFC: National Film Finance Corporation
NFFE: National Federation of Federal Employees
NFFF: National Federation of Fish Friers
NFFPT: National Federation of Fruit and Potato Trades
NFFS: National Foundation for Funeral Services; Non-Ferrous Founders' Society
NFFTR: National Federation of Fishing Tackle Retailers
NFGCA: National Federation of Grandmother Clubs of America
NFHS: National Federation of Housing Societies
NFI: National Fisheries Institute; Nature Friends of Israel
NFIB: National Federation of Independent Business
NFIC: National Foundation for Ileitis and Colitis
NFIP: National Foundation for Infantile Paralysis
NFIU: National Federation of Independent Unions
Nfl: *Nachfolger* (German—successor)
NFL: National Football League; National Forensic League; National Foresters League
Nfld: Newfoundland
NFLPN: National Federation of Licensed Practical Nurses
NFLSV: National Front for the Liberation of South Vietnam
NFLTA: National Federation of Language Teachers Associations
nfm: next full moon
NFMC: National Federation of Music Clubs; National Food Marketing Commission
NFMD: National Foundation for the March of Dimes
NFME: National Fund for Medical Education
NFMLTA: National Federation of Modern Language Teachers Association
NFMPS: National Federation of Master Printers in Scotland
NFMTA: National Federation of Meat Traders' Associations
NFND: National Foundation for Neuromuscular Diseases
NFO: National Farmers Organization; Naval Flight Officer
NFOO: Naval Forward Observ-

ing Officer
NFPA: National Fire Protection Association; National Flaxseed Processors Association; National Flexible Packaging Association; National Fluid Power Association; National Forest Products Association; Niagara Frontier Port Authority
NFPC: Niagra Falls Power Company
NFPCA: National Fire Prevention and Control Administration
NFPW: National Federation of Press Women
nfr: no further requirement
NFRC: National Forest Reservation Commission
NFRN: National Federation of Retail Newsagents, Booksellers, and Stationers
nfs: not for sale
NFS: National Fire Service; National Forest Service
NFSA: National Fertilizer Solutions Associations
NFSA & IS: National Federation of Science Abstracting and Indexing Services
NFSG: National Federation of Students of German
NFSHSA: National Federation of State High School Associations
NFSNC: National Federation of Settlements and Neighborhood Centers
NFSO: Navy Fuel Supply Office
NFT: National Film Theatre
NFTB: Nuclear Flight Test Base
NFTC: National Foreign Trade Council
nfu: not for us
NFU: National Farmers Union
n-fuel: nuclear fuel
NFWA: National Farm Workers Association; National Furniture Warehousemen's Association
NFWI: National Federation of Women's Institutes
NFYFC: National Federation of Young Farmers' Clubs
ng: narrow gauge; nasogastric; new genus; nitroglycerine; no go; no good; not good; not ground; nut grounds
n/g: *nuestro giro* (Spanish—our draft)
Ng: Norwegian
NG: National Gallery; National Guard; National Gypsum; New Guinea
Nga: Nagoya
NGA: National Gallery of Art; National Glider Association; National Guard Association; Needlework Guild of America; Never Go Away (travel club dedicated to seeing America first)
NGAA: National Gift and Art Association; Natural Gasoline Association of America
NGAC: National Guard Air Corps
N-gauge: narrow gauge (railroad track less than standard gauge: gauge: 4 feet 8-1/2 inches)
NGAUS: National Guard Association of the United States
NGB: National Garden Bureau; National Guard Bureau
NGC: National Gallery of Canada; National Gypsum Company
NGC: *New Galactic Catalog; New General Catalog* (astronomical)
NGCM: Navy Good Conduct Medal
NGCMS: National Guild of Community Music Schools
NGDA: National Glass Dealers Association
NGDC: National Geophysical Data Center
NGE: New York State Electric & Gas (stock exchange symbol)
n gen: new genus
ngf: naval gunfire
NGF: National Genetics Foundation; National Golf Foundation; Naval Gun Factory; Nordic Gunners Federation
NGFLO: Naval Gunfire Liaison Officer
NGFLT: Naval Gunfire Liaison Team
NGI: National Garden Institute
NGI: *Navigazione Generale Italiana* (Italian General Navigation Line)
NGJC: North Greenville Junior College
N Gk: New Greek
NGK: Nihon Gakujutsu Kaigi (Japan Research Council)
ngl: natural gas liquids
NGL: North German Lloyd Line
N Gmc: North Germanic
ngo: national gas outlet (thread); nongovernmental organization
NGOs: Nongovernmental Organizations (UN)
NGPA: Natural Gas Processors Association
NGPT: National Guild of Piano Teachers
ngr: narrow gauze roll
NGr: New Greek
NGR: Ndumu Game Reserve (Zululand)
NGRI: National Geophysical Institute
NGRS: Narrow Gauge Railway Society
NGS: National Geographic Society
NGSA: National Gallery of South Africa
NGSR: Nizam's Guaranteed State Railway
ngt: *negociant* (French—merchant)—wholesaler
NGT: National Guild of Telephonists; North German Traders
NGTE: National Gas Turbine Establishment
ngu: nongonococcal urethritis
NGUS: National Guard of the United States
ngv: nongonococcal vulvovaginitis
NGV: *Nederlands Genootschap van Vertalers* (Dutch—Netherlands Translators Association)
nh: no hurry (hospitalese); nonhygroscopic
NH: Naval Home; Naval Hospital; New Hampshire; New Hampshirite; New Haven, Connecticut; New York, New Haven & Hartford (railroad); New Hebrides
NH: *Norges Hjemmenfrontmuseum* (Norwegian Home-Front Museum)—Oslo exhibit recalling anti-German resistance from 1940 to 1945
N & H: Nedlloyd & Hoegh (steamship lines)
nha: never has anything; next higher assembly; next higher authority
NHA: National Hay Association; National Health Association; National Hide Association; National Hockey Association; National Housing Act; National Housing Administration; National Housing Agency; New Homemakers of America; Nigerian Housing Administration
NHAGB: National Horse Association of Great Britain
NHAIAC: National Highway Accident and Injury Analysis Center
NHAL: National Hellenic Ameri-

can Line
NHAS: National Hearing Aid Society
NHB: National Harbours Board (Canada)
NHBRC: National House Builders' Registration Council
NHBU: New Hampshire Board of Underwriters
NHC: National Health Council; National Hurricane Center
NHCA: National Hairdressers and Cosmetologists Association
N.H.D.: Doctor of Natural History
NHDC: Naval Historical Display Center
nh di: notch die
nhe: nitrogen heat exchange
NHEA: National Higher Education Association; New Hampshire Education Association
N Heb: New Hebrew
NHEF: National Health Education Foundation
NHESA: National Higher Education Staff Association
NHF: National Heart Fund; National Hemophilia Foundation; Naval Historical Foundation
NHF Bull: *National Health Federation Bulletin*
NH_4: ammonium radical
NH_4CL: ammonium chloride; sal ammoniac
NH_4OH: ammonium hydroxide (ammonia)
NHFPL: New Haven Free Public Library
NHG: New High German
nhn: neither help nor hinder
NHHS: New Hampshire Historical Society
NHI: National Health Insurance; National Heart Institutes
NHIC: National Home Improvement Council
NHK: *Nippon Hoso Kyokai* (Japanese—Japan Broadcasting Corporation)
NHL: National Hockey League
NHLA: National Hardwood Lumber Association
NHLI: National Heart and Lung Institute
NHMRCA: National Health and Medical Research Council of Australia
NHMS: New Hampshire Medical Society
NHO: Navy Hydrographic Office
NHOS: National Hellenic Oceanographic Society
nhp: nominal horsepower
NHP: Natural History Park (Calgary, Alberta); Natural History Press; New Haven Police; New Hebrides Protectorate
NHPA: National Horseshoe Pitchers Association
NHPC: Natjional Historical Publications Commission
NHPL: New Haven Public Library
NHPLO: NATO Hawk Production and Logistics Organization
NHPMA: Northern Hardwood and Pine Manufacturers Association
NHR: National Housewives Register; National Hunt Rules; National Hurricane Research
NHRA: National Hot Rod Association
NHRL: National Hurricane Research Laboratory
NHRP: National Hurricane Research Project
NHRR: New Haven Railroad
NHRU: National Home Reading Union
NHS: National Health Service; National Historical Society; National Honor Society; Newport Historical Society
NHSA: Negro Historical Society of America
NHSB: National Highway Safety Bureau
NHSC: National Home Study Council
NHSO: New Haven Symphony Orchestra
NHSR: National Hospital Service Reserve
NHTI: New Hampshire Technical Institute
NHTPC: National Housing and Town Planning Council
NHTSA: National Highway Traffic Safety Administration
NH Turn: New Hampshire Turnpike
NHUC: National Highway Users Conference
Nhv: Newhaven
NHV: New Haven Clock and Watch (stock exchange symbol)
NHYC: New Haven Yacht Club
ni: night
Ni: Nica; Nicaragua; Nicaraguan; Nicaragüense; Nicas; nickel
NI: Naval Intelligence; Netherlands Indies; Northern Ireland
NI: ampere turns (symbol)
NIA: National Intelligence Authority; Neighborhood Improvement Association
NIAA: National Institute of Animal Agriculture
NIAAA: National Institute of Alcohol Abuse and Alcoholism
NIAB: National Institute of Agricultural Botany
NIABC: Northern Ireland Association of Boys' Clubs
NIAE: National Institute of Agricultural Engineering (UK); National Institute for Architectural Education
Niagara Frontier: Buffalo-Niagara Falls area
Niagara Fruit Belt: Canadian fruit-growing region on the Niagara Peninsula between lakes Erie and Ontario
NIAID: National Institute of Allergies and Infectious Diseases
NIAL: National Institute of Arts and Letters
NIAMD: National Institute of Arthritis and Metabolic Diseases
NIASA: National Insurance Actuarial and Statistical Association
nib: noninterference basis
NIB: National Information Bureau; Nebraska Inspection Bureau
nibo: *nibonitschjo (ni boga ni tschjorta)* (Russian—neither in god nor the devil)—materialist sceptics unaffected by Marxism—Leninism
nic: negative impedance converter; not in contact
Nic: Nicaragua; Nicolayev; Nicosia
NIC: Natick Industrial Centre; National Indications Center; National Industrial Council; National Institute of Credit; National Interfraternity Conference; National Inventors Council; National Investors Council; Niagara International Centre; Nicosia, Cyprus (airport)
Nica: Nicaragua(n)
nicad: nickel cadmium
NiCad battery: nickel-cadmium (rechargeable) battery
Nicaea: (Latin—Nice)
NICAP: National Investigations Committee on Aerial Phenomena
Nicas: Nicaraguans
NICB: National Industrial Conference Board
Nice: Eunice

NICE: National Institute of Ceramic Engineers
NICEIC: National Inspection Council for Electrical Installation Contracting
NICF: Northern Ireland Cycling Federation
Nich: Nicholas
NICHA: Northern Ireland Chest and Heart Association
NICHHD: National Institute of Child Health and Human Development
Nicholas Blake: C(ecil) Day-Lewis' pseudonym
nichrome: nickel-chromium alloy
NICIA: Northern Ireland Coal Importers' Association
NICJ: National Institute of Consumer Justice
Nick: Nicholas
Nick Carter: J. Russell Coryell
Nickel Plate Road: New York, Chicago and St Louis Railroad Company
Nicky and Alicky: Czar Nicholas II and Czarina Alexandra Feodorovna of Russia—the last of the Romanov Czars
NICM: Nuffield Institute of Comparative Medicine
MICMA: National Ice Cream Mix Association
Nico: Nicobar Islands
NICO: Navy Inventory Control Office(r)
Nicobars: Nicobar Islands in the Indian Ocean
Nicolas-Favre disease: lymphogranuloma venerea involving inguinal lymph glands and characterized by an exuding lesion
NICOP: Navy Industry Cooperation Plan
NICP: National Inventory Control Point
NICRA: Northern Ireland Civil Rights Association
NICSO: NATO Integrated Communications System Organization
NICSS: Northern Ireland Council of Social Science
NICUFO: National Investigations Committee on Unidentified Flying Objects
NID: National Institute of Drycleaning; Naval Intelligence Department
NID: *New International Dictionary (Webster's Third New International Dictionary of the English Language Unabridged)*
NIDA: National Institute of Drug Abuse
NIDC: National Institute of Dry Cleaning
NIDER: *Nederlands Instituut voor Documentatie en Registratuur* (Dutch—Netherlands Institute of Documentation and Filing)
NIDFA: National Independent Drama Festivals Association
NIDH: National Institute of Dental Health
NIDM: National Institute for Disaster Mobilization
NIDR: National Institute of Dental Research
nie: not included elsewhere
NIE: National Institute of Education; National Intelligence Estimate
niedr: *niedrig* (German—low)
NIEHS: National Institute of Environmental Health Sciences
niels bohrium: Russian name for element 105 named for Danish physicist Niels Bohr
NIER: National Industrial Equipment Reserve
NIESR: National Institute for Economic and Social Research
NIEU: Negro Industrial Economic Union
nif: nickel-iron film
nife: nickel + iron (Ni + Fe)
NIFES: National Industrial Fuel Efficiency Service
nig(s): renege(s); revoke(s)
Nig: Nigeria
nig.: *niger* (Latin—black)
Nig: *Niger* (Spanish—Niger)
NIGC: National Iranian Gas Company
Nigger: non-pejorative nickname for Dvőrák's *American* Quartet filled with Negro spiritual themes
nightie(s): nightdress(es); nightgown(s)
NIGP: National Institute of Governmental Purchasing
nigyysob: now I've got you, you SOB
nih: not invented here
NIH: National Institutes of Health
NIH 204: antimalarial drug
NIHE: Northern Ireland Housing Executive
nihil: *nihil obstat quominus imprimatur* (Latin—nothing hinders it from being printed)—*nihil obstat* usually suffices for censors of the Roman Catholic Church
nihil obs.: *nihil obstat* (Latin—nothing stands in the way)—official Catholic publications must obtain this before their publication
NIHT: Northern Ireland Housing Trust
NII: Netherlands Industrial Institute
NIIP: National Institute of Industrial Psychology
NIIS: Niagara Institute for International Studies
NIJC: North Idaho Junior College
NIJFCM: National Institute of Jig and Fixture Component-Manufacturers
Niko: (Russian nickname—Nikolai)—Nicholas; Nick; Nicky
Nikolaus Lenau: (pseudonym—Nikolaus Franz Niembsch von Strehlenau)
NIL: National Instrument Laboratories; National Investment Library
NILA: National Industrial Leather Association
NI Lab: Northern Ireland Labour (party)
NILE & CJ: National Institute of Law Enforcement and Criminal Justice
Nile River Cities: Cairo, Egypt and Khartoum, Sudan
NILI: *Netzach Israel Lo Ishakare* (Hebrew—The eternity of Israel will not die)—acronymic password of the Nili spies who aided Britain by facilitating Turkish defeat in an effort to establish a homeland for Jews in Palestine
'nilla: vanilla
NILOJ: National Institute for Law/Order/Justice
NILP: Northern Ireland Labour Party
NIMA: National Insulation Manufacturers Association
NIMAC: National Interscholastic Music Activities Commission
NIMH: National Institute of Mental Health
nimm: nuclear-induced missile malfunction
n imp: new impression
nimphe: nuclear isotope monopropellant hydrazine engine
NIMR: National Institute for Medical Research
NIN: National Information Network
Nina: Ann; Anna; Anne; Annette

NINB: National Institute of Neurology and Blindness
NINDB: National Institute of Neurological Diseases and Blindness
nine old men: nine justices of the United States Supreme Court
Ninon de Lenclos: court name of courtesan Anne Lenclos
NIO: National Institute of Oceanography; National Iranian Oil; Naval Institute of Oceanology
NIOC: National Iranian Oil Company
NIOSH: National Institute of Occupational Safety and Health
nip.: nipple
Nip: Nipponese
NIP: Northern Ireland Parliament
NIPA: National Institute of Public Affairs
NIPCC: National Industrial Pollution Control Council
NIPH: National Institute of Public Health
Nippon: Japan
NIPR: National Institute for Personnel Research
ni pri: nisis prius (Latin—unless before)
NIPS: National Information Processing System
NIPSSA: Naval Intelligence Processing Systems Support Activity
nipts: noise-induced permanent threshold shifts
N Ir: Northern Ireland
NIR: Northern Ireland Railways
NIRA: National Industrial Recovery Administration
NIRC: National Industrial Relations Court
NIRD: National Institute of Research in Dairying
N Ire: Northern Ireland
NIRI: National Investor Relations Institute
NIRMP: National Intern and Resident Matching Program
NIRNS: National Institute for Research in Nuclear Science
NIROP: Naval Industrial Reserve Ordnance Plant (USN)
NIRR: National Institute for Road Research
NIRRA: Northern Ireland Radio Retailers' Association
n i s: not in stock
NIS: National Institute of Science; National Insurance Scheme; National Intelligence Survey
NISBS: National Institute of Social and Behavioral Science
NISC: National Industrial Safety Committee
NISP: National Information System for Psychology
NISS: National Institute of Social Sciences
NIST: National Institute of Science and Technology
NISUCO: Nigerian Sugar Company
nit.: negative income tax
nit: unit of luminance (symbol)
NIT: National Intelligence Test; National Invitation Tournament; Northrop Institute of Technology
Nita: Juanita
NITA: National Industrial Television Association
NITC : National Iranian Tanker Company
NiteDevRon: Night Development Squadron
NITHC: Northern Ireland Transport Holding Company
NITL: National Industrial Traffic League
ni tp: nibbling template
NITR: National Institute for Telecommunications Research
nitrate of soda: sodium nitrate ($NaNO_3$)
nitre: potassium nitrate (KNO_3)
nitric acid: HNO_3
nitro: nitrocellulose; nitroglycerine
nitros: nitrostarch
nitts: noise-induced temporary threshold shift
NITV: National Iranian Television
NIU: Northern Illinois University; Northern Interparliamentary Union
Niv: *Nivose* (French—Snowy Month)—beginning December 21st—fourth month of the French Revolutionary Calendar
NIVE: Nederland Instituut voor Efficiency (Netherlands Institute for Efficiency)
NIW: National Industrial Workers Union
NIWAAA: Northern Ireland Women's Amateur Athletic Association
NIWR: National Institute for Water Research
nix: (from the German *nichts*) to ban; to cancel; to forbid; no one; nothing; to prohibit; to reject; to veto
NIYC: National Indian Youth Council
n J: *nächstes Jahr* (German—next year)
NJ: New Jersey; New Jerseyite
NJA: National Jail Association; National Jogging Association
NJAC: National Joint Advisory Council
NJCAA: National Junior College Athletic Association
njb: nice Jewish boy
NJC: Natchez Junior College; Navarro Junior College; Newton Junior College; Norfolk Junior College
NJCC: Northeastern Junior College of Colorado
NJDA: National Juvenile Detention Association
NJEA: New Jersey Education Association
NJF: *Nordiske Jordburgsforskeres Forening* (Nordic Agricultural Research Workers' Association)
NJFR: National Joint Fiction Reserve
njg: nice Jewish girl
NJH: National Jewish Hospital
NJ Hist Soc: New Jersey Historical Society
NJHS: New Jersey Historical Society
njk: not just kidding
NJLA: New Jersey Library Association
NJPBA: New Jersey Public Broadcasting Authority
NJPC: National Joint Practices Commission
NJROTC: Naval Junior Reserve Officers Training Corps
NJRW: New Jersey Reformatory for Women (Clinton)
NJSO: New Jersey Symphony Orchestra
NJ Turn: New Jersey Turnpike
NJWB: National Jewish Welfare Board
NJZ: New Jersey Zinc
nk: neck; not known; not ours (publishing)
NK: Nippon Gakushiin (the Japanese Academy); Nomenklatur Kommission (Anatomical Nomenclature Commission); Nordiska Kompaniet (the Norse Company, Stockholm's leading department store); North Korea(n)
NK: *Nihon Kyosanto* (Japanese Communist Party)
NKA: National Kindergarten Association
NKDR: National Key Deer Refuge (Florida)

NKF: National Kidney Foundation
NKG: *Nordiska Kommissionen for Geodesi* (Nordic Commission for Geodesy)
NKGB: People's Commissariat for State Security *(q.v. VOT)*
NKK: Nippon Kokan Steel (Japan)
NKL: *Norges Kooperative Landsforening* (Norwegian Consumer Cooperative)
NKM: New Park Mining (stock exchange symbol)
N.K. Naomi: code for chemical and biological warfare
NKOA: National Knitted Outerwear Association
NKP: Nickel Plate Railroad (stock exchange symbol for New York, Chicago & St Louis Railroad)—locomotives on this line gleamed with nickel-plated ornaments
NIP: *Norges Kommunistiske Parti* (Norwegian Communist Party)
NKPA: National Kraut Packers Association
NKr: Norwegian krone(r)
NKS: *Norge Kjemisk Selskap* (Norwegian Chemical Society)
NKSO: *Narodniy Kommissariat Sotsialnogo Obespecheniya* (Russian—People's Commissariat of Social Security)
NKVD: *Narodnyi Kommissariat Vnutrennikh Del* (Russian—People's Commissariat for Internal Affairs, Soviet secret police; *q.v.* VOT)
NKZ: *Narodniy Kommissariat Zdravokhranenia* (Russian—People's Commissariat of Health)—contains a special section to combat prostitution
nl: new line; non-lubricant; not listed
nl: *nicht löslich* (German—not soluble); *non longue* (French—not so far)
n/l: *nuestra letra* (Spanish—our letter)
n.l.: *non licet* (Latin—not permitted)
nl (NL): new line character (data processing)
NL: National League (of Professional Baseball Clubs); National Liberal; naval lighter (naval symbol); Navy League; Navy (US department) Library; Netherlands (auto plaque); New Latin; New London, Connecticut; Night Letter; North Latitude; Nuevo León
NL: Norddeutscher Lloyd (North German Lloyd Line)
N.L.: *non liquet* (Latin—unclear)
NLA: National Libraries Authority; National Lumbermen's Association
NL-A: Nationaal Luchtvaartlaboratorium-Amsterdam
NLAA: National Legal Aid Association
NLA & DA: National Legal Aid and Defender Association
NLAPW: National League of American Pen Women
N Lat: north latitude
NLB: National Library for the Blind
NLC: National Lead Chemicals; National League for Cities; National Leathersellers College; National Legislative Conference; National Legislative Council; National Liberal Club; National Library of Canada; New Location Code; New Orleans & Lower Coast (railroad)
NLCA: Norwegian Lutheran Church of America
NLCIF: National Light Castings Ironfounders' Federation
NLD: National Legion of Decency
NLEC: National Lutheran Educational Council
NLETS: National Law Enforcement Telecommunications System
nlf: nearest landing field
NLF: National Liberation Front; National Liberal Federation; nearest landing field
nlg: nose landing gear
NLGI: National Lubricating Grease Institute
NLHE: National Laboratory for Higher Education
NLI: National Library of Ireland
NLL: National Lending Library; Nedlloyd Lines
NLL cards: National Lucht-en-ruimtevaart Laboratorium (international card catalog devised in Amsterdam)
NLLST: National Lending Library for Science and Technology (UK)
nl lt: net-laying light
NLM: National Liberation Movement; National Library of Medicine
NLMA: National Lumber Manufacturers Association
NLMC: National Labor Management Council
NLN: National League for Nursing
NLNE: National League of Nursing Education
NLNP: Naujan Lake National Park (Philippines)
NLO: Naval Liaison Office(r)
NLOGF: National Lubricating Oil and Grease Federation
NLP: National League of Postmasters
NLPI: National Loss Prevention Institute
NLR: Nationaal Lucht- en Ruimtevaartlaboratorium (National Aero- and Astronautical Research Institute), Amsterdam
NLRB: National Labor Relations Board
NLs: New Leftists
NLS: National Library of Scotland (Edinburgh); National Library Service (New Zealand and elsewhere); Non-Linear Systems
NLSB: National League Service Bureau
NLSCS: National League for Separation of Church and State
nlt: not later than; not less than
NLT: *Navigazione Libera Triestina* (Italian Line)
NLTA: National Lawn Tennis Association; National League of Teachers Associations
NLUS: Navy League of the United States
NLW: National Library of Wales (Aberystwyth); National Library Week
Nly: northerly
NLYL: National League of Young Liberals
nm: nanometer; nautical mile(s); neuromuscular; nitrogen mustards; nomenclature; nonmetallic; non-motile (bacteria)
nm: *nachmittags* (German—afternoon; P.M.); *namiddag* (Dutch—afternoon; P.M.); nanometer; nautical mile(s); nomenclature; nonmetallic
n/m: no mark
n/m^3: newton per square meter
n. et m.: *nocte et mane* (Latin—night and early morning)
n M: *nächster Monat* (German—next month)
Nm: newtonmeter
NM: Nigeria Museum
N de M: Nacional de México (railroad)
nma: negative mental attitude
NMA: National Management As-

sociation; National Medical Association; National Microfilm Association; Navy Mutual Aid (Association); Northwest Mining Association

NMAA: National Machine Accountants Association; Navy Mutual Aid Association

nmac: near mid-air collision

NMAF: National Medical Association Foundation

NMB: National Maritime Board; National Mediation Board

NMC: National Meteorological Center; National Museum of Canada; National Museums of Ceylon; National Music Council; Naval Material Command; Naval Medical Center; Naval Missile Center

NMCA: Navy Mother's Clubs of America

NMCB: National Metric Conversion Board

NMCC: National Military Command Center

NMCDA: National Model Cities Directors Association

NMCO: Naval Material Catalog Office

NMCP: National Memorial Cemetery of the Pacific

NMCS: National Military Command System

NMCSSC: National Military Command System Support Center

NMDA: National Metal Decorators Association

NMDL: Navy Mine Defense Laboratory

NME: National Military Establishment

NMERI: National Mechanical Engineering Research Institute

N Mex: New Mexico; New Mexican

NMF: National Marine Fisheries

NMFMA: National Mutual Fund Managers Association

NMFRL: Naval Medical Field Research Laboratory

NMFS: National Marine Fisheries Service

NMFSL: National Marine Fisheries Service Laboratories

nmh: nautical miles per hour

NMH: Northwestern Memorial Hospital

NMHA: National Mental Health Association

nmi: no middle initial

n mi: nautical miles

NMI: New Mexico Military Institute

NMIM & T: New Mexico Institute of Mining and Technology

NMJ: Northern Masonic Jurisdiction

NML: National Municipal League; National Music League; Northwestern Mutual Life (insurance)

NMLRA: National Muzzle-Loading Rifle Association

NMM: National Maritime Museum (Greenwich)

NMMA: National Macaroni Manufacturers Association

NMN$^+$: nicotinamide mononucleotide

nmnc: nonmercuric noncorrosive

NMNH: National Museum of Natural History (D.C.)

NMO: Navy Management Office

nmoc: new man on campus

nmp: navigational microfilm projector

NMPA: National Music Publishers Association

NMPC: National Maintenance Publications Center (USA)

nmr: nuclear magnetic resonance

NMR: Natal Mounted Rifles

NMRA: National Model Railroad Association

NMRI: Naval Medical Research Institute

NMRL: Naval Medical Research Laboratory

NMRP: New Mexico Research Park

NMRTC: New Mexico Research and Treatment Center

nms: nuclear materials safeguards

NMS: National Medal of Science; National Meteorological Service; Nobles of the Mystic Shrine

NMSE: Naval Material Support Establishment

NMSM: New Mexico School of Mines

NMSQT: National Merit Scholarships Qualifying Test

NMSS: National Multiple Sclerosis Society

NMSSA: NATO Maintenance Supply Service Agency

NMSU: New Mexico State University

NMSWF: National Manufacturers of Soda Water Flavors

nmt: not more than

NMT: National Museum of Transport

NMTA: National Metal Trades Association

NMTBA: National Machine Tool Builders' Association

NMTF: National Market Traders' Federation

NMTFA: National Master Tile Fixers' Association

NMTS: National Milk Testing Service

NMU: National Maritime Union

NMW: National Museum of Wales

NMWA: National Mineral Wool Association

nn: nouns

nn: *non numerato* (Italian—unnumbered)

n.n.: *nemini notus* (Latin—known to no one); *nescio nomen* (Latin—I do not know the name)

n/n: not to be noted

NN: Newport News; Northwestern National

N/N: Northrop/Nortronics

NNA: National Neckwear Association; National Newspaper Association; National Notary Association

NNBPWC: National Negro Business and Professional Women's Clubs

NNC: Naval Nuclear Club (rival members include France, the United Kingdom, the United States, and the USSR); Navy Nurse Corps

NNCR: North Norfolk Coast Reserves (England)

nnd: neonatal death

NND: New and Non-Official Drugs

NNE: north northeast

NNEB: National Nursery Examination Board

NN & EB: National Newark & Essex Bank

NNF: Northern Nurses Federation

NNG: Netherlands New Guinea; Northern Natural Gas (company)

nni: noise and number index (sound pollution)

NNI: Norwegian Nobel Institute

NNI: *Nederlands Normalisatie Instituut* (Dutch—Netherlands Standards Institute)

nnk (NNK): notify next of kin

NNL: Nigerian National Line

nnm: next new moon

NNMC: National Naval Medical Center

NNN: Novy-Nicolle-McNeal (bacteriological culture)

NNO: *noord noordoost* (Dutch—north northeast)
NNOC: Nigerian National Oil Company
n. nov.: *nomen novum* (Latin—new name)
nnp: net national product
NNP: Nairobi National Park (Kenya); Ngezi National Park (Rhodesia); Nimule National Park (Sudan)
NNPA: National Negro Press Association; National Newspaper Promotion Association; National Newspaper Publishers Association
NNR: New and Nonofficial Remedies
NNRC: Neutral Nations Repatriation Commission
NNRI: National Nutrition Research Institute
N Ns: Newport News
NNS: National Newspaper Syndicate
NNSC: Neutral Nations Supervisory Commission
NNS & DDC: Newport News Shipbuilding and Dry Dock Company
NNSL: Nigerian National Shipping Line
NNSS: Navy Navigational Satellite System
NNTO: Netherlands National Tourist Office; Norwegian National Travel Office
NNW: north northwest
NNW: *noord noorwest* (Dutch—north northwest)
NNWR: Necedah National Wildlife Refuge (Wisconsin); Noxubee National Wildlife Refuge (Mississippi)
no.: normally open; number
no. (NO): neuromyelitis optica
n°: *número* Spanish—number)
No: nobelium; Norskie (Norwegian-American); Norway; Norwegian
No.: *Numero* (Latin—number)
NO: Naval Observatory; Naval Officer; New Orleans; North Central Airlines; Nuffield Observatory (Jordrell Bank, England)
NO: *noordoost* (Dutch—northeast); *Nordosten* (German—northeast)
No. 1: first; first quality; first rate; first person; most important; most important person; number one
No. 2: next in line; next in rank; number two; second; second person; second quality; second rate
noa: new obligational authority (NOA); not otherwise authorized
NOA: National Onion Association; National Opera Association; National Optical Association; National Orchestral Association
NOAA: National Oceanic and Atmospheric Administration
NOAB: National Outdoor Advertising Bureau
NO-AB: New Orleans-Algiers Bridge
NOAL: National Order of Arts and Letters
noala: noise-operated automatic level adjustment
NOASSR: North Ossetian Autonomous Soviet Socialist Republic
nob.: noble; nobility; no open burning
nob.: *nobis* (Latin—to us)
NOB: Naval Operating Base
NOB: *Nationaal Orkest van Belgie* (Flemish—National Orchestra of Belgium)
Nobelst: *Nobelstiftelsen* (The Nobel Foundation)
noc: not otherwise classified
NOC: National Oceanographic Council
NOCHA: National Off-Campus Housing Association
NOCIL: National Organic Chemical Industries
NOCM: Nuclear Ordnance Commodity Manager
No Co: Northern Counties
noct.: *nocte* (Latin—by night; nocturnal)
noct. maneq.: *nocte maneque* (Latin—night and morning)
nod.: night observation device
NOD: Navigation and Ocean Development
NODA: Night Operatic and Dramatic Association
NODAC: Naval Ordnance Data Automation Center
Nodaks: North Dakotans
NODC: National Oceanographic Data Center
Noddy: Nicodemus
NODL: National Organization for Decent Literature (Catholic)
no do a: *nota do autor* (Portuguese—author's note)
no do e: *nota do editor* (Portuguese—editor's note)
no do t: *nota do tradutor* (Portuguese—translator's note)
noe: not otherwise enumerated
NOE: Notice of Exception Oceanographic Foundation; National Osteopathic Foundation
NOFI: National Oil Fuel Institute
noforn: no foreign nationals; special handling—not to be released to foreign nationals
noft: notification of foreign travel
NOGC: *Nationaal Overleg voor Gewestelijke Cultuur* (Dutch—National Council for Regional Culture)
nohp: not otherwise herein provided
noibn: not otherwise identified by name; not otherwise indexed by name
NOIC: National Oceanographic Instrumentation Center; Naval Officer in Charge
NOISE: National Organization to Insure Sound-controlled Environment
NOJC: National Oil Jobbers Council
nok: next of kin
NOK: Norsk Aero Klub
NOL: Naval Ordnance Laboratory
NOLA: New Orleans, Louisiana
NOLC: Naval Ordnance Laboratory, Corona
nol. con.: *nolo contendere* (Latin—I do not wish to contend)
Noll: Oliver; Olivera; Oliver Cromwell—Lord Protector of England
Nolly: Oliver; Olivera
nolo: *nolo contendere*
nol. pros.: *nolle prosequi* (Latin—to be unwilling to prosecute)
NOLS: National Oceanographic Laboratory System
nol. vol.: *nolens volens* (Latin—unwilling or willing); willy-nilly
nom: nominal; nominate; nominated; nomination
NOMA: National Office Management Association
NOMAD: Navy Oceanographic and Meteorological Device (world's first nuclear-powered weather station)
nom cap: nominal capital
nom. con.: *nomen conservandum* (Latin—generic or specific name to be preserved by special sanction)
nom dam: nominal damages
nom. dub.: *nomen dubium* (Latin—doubtful name)

nomen: nomenclature
nomin: nominative
nom. nov.: *nomen novum* (Latin—new name)
nom. nud.: *nomen nudem* (Latin—naked name); mere name for an animal or plant but lacking further description
NOMSS: National Operational Meteorological Satellite System
NOMTF: Naval Ordnance Missile Test Facilities
NON: National Organization of Non-Parenthood
non-coll: non-collegiate
noncom(s): nonconformist(s)
Non-Com: noncommissioned officer
noncon(s): nonconformist(s)
non cul.: *non culpabilis* (Latin—not culpable; not guilty)
non-cum: non-cumulative
none: no one; not one
None: Nonesuch
non est: *non est inventus* (Latin—he was not found; it is wanting)
non flam: non-flammable
non-flam: non-flammable film (slow-burning acetate-base film)
N/ONI: Navy/Office of Naval Intelligence
non obs.: *non obstante* (Latin—notwithstanding)
n-on-p: negative on positive
non perf: non-perforated
nonporno: not pornographic
non pos.: *non possumus* (Latin—we cannot)
non pros.: *non prosequitur* (Latin—does not prosecute)
N/ONR: Navy/Office of Naval Research
non repetat.: *non repetatur* (Latin—do not repeat)
non-res: nonresident
non seq.: *non sequitor* (Latin—it does not follow)
non-sked: non-scheduled (airplane, bus, train, etc.)
non std: nonstandard
non-U: not upper class
NOO: Navy Oceanographic Office (formerly Hydrographic Office, USN)
NOOA: New Orleans Opera Association
noodle-noodle-noodle-noodle: tremolo passages played by the strings and called noodling by many musicians
no op: no opinion
no op (NO OP): no operation (data processing)
nop: not open (to the) public; not our publication
NOP: National Oceanographic Program; National Opinion Poll
NOPA: National Office Products Association
no par.: no paragraph (matter runs on)
NOPE: New Orleans Port of Embarkation
NOPHN: National Organization for Public Health Nursing
NOPL: New Orleans Public Library
NOPO: New Orleans Philharmonic Orchestra
NOPS: New Orleans Public Service
NOPWC: National Old People's Welfare Council
NOQUIS: Nucleonic Oil Quantity Indication System
nor.: normal
nor': norther (Middle English contraction); north
nør: *nørre* (Danish—north)
Nor: Norway; Norwegian
Nor: Norr (Swedish—north)
NOR: North Central Airlines; NOT OR (data-processing logic-operator equivalent)
Nora: Eleanora
NORAD: North American Air Defense
Nor Ant: Norwegian Antarctica (Bouvet Island, Peter I Island, Queen Maud Land)
Nor Arc: Norwegian Arctic (Bear, Edge, and Hope islands in Barents Sea; Jan Mayen Island in Norwegian Sea; Svalbard or Spitsbergen in Arctic Ocean)
nor'ard: northward
norc: national ordnance research computer
NORC: National Opinion Research Center (University of Chicago); Naval Ordnance Research Computer
Nor-Cor: Northland-Coromandel (NZ)
Nor Cur: Norwegian Current
nor'd: northward
NORD: Naval Ordnance
NORDEK: Nordic Economic Community (Denmark, Finland, Norway, Sweden)
NORDSFORSK: *Nordiska Samarbetsorganisationen för Teknisk -Naturventenskaplig -Forening* (Nordic Council for Applied Research)
Nordic: Hanson's Symphony No. 1
Nordic Council: Scandinavian union including Denmark, Finland, Iceland, Norway, and Sweden
NORDITA: Nordic Institute for Theoretical Atomic Physics
nor'easter: northeaster (storm from the northeast)
Norelco: North American Philips Company
Norf: Norfolk
Norlina: North Carolina
NORK: New Orleans Rhythm Kings
norm.: normal; normalize; normalizing; not operationally ready (because of) maintenance; nuclear operational readiness maneuvers
Norm: Norman
Normands: Norman Islands (Channel Islands)
NORML: National Organization for the Repeal of Marijuana Laws (funded by the Playboy Foundation)
Noroil: Norwegian Oil
Nor Pac: Northern Pacific
Nor Pol: Norsk Polarinstitutt (Norwegian Polar Institute)
nors: not operationally ready, supplies (supply)
Norse God of Thunder: Thor, whose Roman counterpart is Jove or Jupiter
Norsker(s): Norwegian sailor(s)
Norskie: Norwegian-American
north.: northerly; northern
NORTHAG: North European Army Group
Northants: Northamptonshire
North Baltic Nation: Estonia
North Borneo: called Sabah since 1963
North Britain: Scotland
North Central States: Michigan, Indiana, Illinois, Wisconsin
Northcliffe: Viscount Northcliffe (Alfred Charles William Harmsworth)
Northern Bear: political cartoonist's symbol for Russia or the Soviet Union
northern lights: aurora borealis
Northernmost American Town: Point Barrow, Alaska
Northernmost Canadian Town: Inuvik, Northwest Territories
Northernmost Point of the European Mainland: Nordkyn, Norway (nearby North Cape)
Northernmost Province: Québec
Northernmost State: Alaska
Northernmost Territories: Northwest Territories
Northerns: Burlington, Great

Northern, and Northern Pacific railroads
Northern Way: Norway
North Jersey Coast: Atlantic City to the Atlantic Highlands
Northland Riviera: Sweden's summer beach on the Gulf of Bothnia and the Polar Route
Northld: Northumberland
North Star: Minnesota's nickname
North Star State: Minnesota's official nickname
Northum: Northumberland
North Western Line: Chicago and North Western Railway
NORTLANT: North Atlantic
Nortown: W.W. Norton
Nortraship: Norwegian Trade and Shipping Mission
Norumbega: historian John Fiske's name for what is now New York City (see *Norvegia*)
Norvegia: (Latin—Norway)—also appears on some of the earliest maps of the east coast of North America as Norbega or Norumbega over an area extending from the Bay of Fundy to Florida and known for its Norse viking explorations and settlements in pre-Columbian times; sometimes spelled Norvega or Norbegia as well as Norumbega
Norvic.: *Norvicensis* (Latin—of Norwich)
Norw: Norwegian
Norway's Most Popular Sculptor: Adolf Gustav Vigeland
NORWEB: North Western Electricity Board
Norwegian Expressionist: Edvard Munch
Norwegian National Composer: Edvard Grieg
NORWESTLANT: Northwest Atlantic (project)
nos: not otherwise specified; numbers
NOS: National Ocean Survey; Night Observation Sight
N OS: New Orleans
NOS: *Nederlandse Omroep Stichting* (Dutch—Netherlands Broadcasting Foundation)
NOSA: National Occupational Safety Association
NOSC: Naval Ordnance Systems Command (USN)
NOSCAF: New Orleans Sickle Cell Anemia Foundation
NOSE: Neighbors Opposing Smelly Emissions
NOSG: Naval Operations Support Group
no sig: no signature
Nosodak: North Dakota + South Dakota—the Dakotas
NOSOPEX: Northern Sumatra Offshore Petroleum Exploration
NOSSOLANT: Naval Ordnance System Support Atlantic
NOSSOPAC: Naval Ordnance System Support Pacific
NOSTA: National Ocean Science and Technology Agency
Not: Notary
Nostradamus: Michel de Nostradame also called Michel de Notredame
notal: not to, nor needed by, all addressees
NOTAM: Notice to Airmen
NOTB: National Ophthalmic Treatment Board
No. 10: Number 10 Downing Street (London residence of the British prime minister)
noto: numbering tool
NOTP: *New Orleans Times-Picayune*
NOTS: Naval Ordnance Test Station
Not(t): Nottingham
Notts: Nottinghamshire
notwg: notwithstanding
NOU: Noumea, New Caledonia (airport)
Nou Heb: *Nouvelles Hébrides* (French—New Hebrides)
nov: novels; novelist; novels
nov.: *novum* (Latin—new)
Nov: November
Novalis: Friedrich Leopold von Hardenberg
Novdec: November and December
nov^{e}: noviembre (Spanish—November)
November: code for letter N
nov. n.: *novum nomen* (Latin—new name)
Novo: Novosibirsk
NOVS: National Office of Vital Statistics
nov. sp.: *novum species* (Latin—new species)
Novy(s): Nova Scotian(s)
NoW: *News of the World*
NOW: National Organization for Women; Negotiable Order of Withdrawal (interest-earning checking account)
NOWAPA: North American Water and Power Alliance
NOWC: National Association of Women's Clubs
NOx: nitrous oxide (smog component)
noxema: knocks eczema
noy: (unit of noisiness)
Noy: *Noybr* (Russian—November)
noz: nozzle
np: napalm (incendiary gasoline mixture); national pipe; neap; neap range; near point; net proceeds; neuropsychiatric; neuropsychiatry; new paragraph; nickel-plated; nonparticipating; nonpropelled; no paging; no place; no place of publication; no protest; normal pressure; nose plug; nursing procedure
n.p.: *nedsat pris* (Dano-Norwegian—reduced price)
n/p: net proceeds; new pence
Np: neap; neap range; neap tide; neper; neptunium (symbol)
N_p: neper
NP: Narragansett Pier; National Park; National Pipe; Naval Prison; Newport, Rhode Island; New Providence, Bahama Islands; no parking; Northern Pacific (railroad); Notary Public
NP: not published
N-P: Non-Partisan
N/P: nitrogen phosphorus ratio
NPA: National Paperboard Association; National Parenthood Association; National Parking Association; National Parks Association; National Particleboard Association; National Personnel Associates; National Pet Association; National Petroleum Association; National Pharmaceutical Association; National Pigeon Association; National Pilots Association; National Planning Association; National Preservers Association; National Proctologic Association; National Production Authority; Naval Procurement Account; Navy Postal Affairs; Nigerian Ports Authority
NPABC: National Public Affairs Broadcast Center
NPAC: National Program for Acquisitions and Cataloging (Library of Congress)
N Pac Cur: North Pacific Current
NPACI: National Production Advisory Council on Industry
NPACT: National Public Affairs Center for Television
NPAP: National Psychological Association for Psychoanal-

ysis
NPB: National Parole Board (Canada)
NPBA: National Paper Box Association; National Pig Breeders' Association
NPBI: National Pretzel Bakers Institute
npc: near point of convergence
NPC: National Patent Council; National Peach Council; National Peanut Council; National Personnel Consultants; National Petroleum Council; National Pharmaceutical Council; National Potato Council; National Press Club; Naval Photographic Center; Nigerian Population Commission
NPCA: National Parks and Conservation Association; National Pest Control Association
NPCI: National Potato Chip Institute
NPCP: National Press Club of the Philippines
npcr: no periodic calibration required
npd: north polar distance
N-P d: Neimann-Pick's disease
NPD: *Nationaldemokratische Partei Deutschlands* (National Democratic Party of Germany)
NPDC: National Patent Development Corporation
NPDEA: National Professional Driver Education Association
NPE: Navy Preliminary Evaluation
npf: not provided for
NPF: National Piano Foundation
NPFA: National Playing Fields Association
NPFC: Naval Publications and Forms Center
NPFI: National Plant Food Institute
NPFSC: North Pacific Fur Seal Commission
NPG: National Portrait Gallery
NP en G: Nederlandse Postcheque en Girondienst (Netherlands Postal Check and Transfer Service)
NPGS: Naval Postgraduate School
n ph: nuclear physics
npH: neutral protamine Hegedorn (isoophane insulin)
NPI: Neuro-Psychiatric Institute
NPIA: Norfolk Port and Industrial Authority
NPIC: Naval Photographic Interpretation Center
NPIPF: Newspaper and Printing Industries Printing Fund
NPIS: National Physics Information System
npl: new program language; nipple
NPL: Nashville Public Library: National Physical Laboratory; Newark Public Library; Norfolk Public Library
nplu: not people like us
NPMAA: National Piano Manufacturers Association of America
npn (NPN): nonprotein nitrogen
NPN: negative positive negative
npna: no protest for nonacceptance
N & PNWR: Ninepipe and Pablo National Wildlife Refuge (Montana)
npo: nothing by mouth
n.p.o.: *ne per oris* (Latin—not by mouth)
NPO: National Philharmonic Orchestra (Manila); Navy Post Office Navy Purchasing Office(r); New Philharmonia Orchestra (London)
NPOAA: National Police Officers Association of America
np or d: no place or date (of publication)
NP & OSR: Naval Petroleum and Oil Shale Reserve
npp: no passed proof
NPP: Naval Propellant Plant
NPPA: National Press Photographers Association
NPPF: National Planned Parenthood Federation
NPPO: Navy Publications and Printing Office
NPPR: Nationalist Party of Puerto Rico
NPPS: Navy Publication Printing Service
N-P Pubns: National Press Publications
NPQ: Naviera de Productos Quimicos (Chemical Products Shipping Line)
npr: night press rate
n/p/r: noise/power/ratio
NPR: National Public Radio; Nickel Plate Road (railroad)
NPRA: National Petroleum Refiners Association; Naval Personnel Research Activity
NPRL: National Physical Research Laboratory
NPRO: Navy Plant Representative Office(r)
NPROA: National Police Reserve Officers Association
npr's: nuclear-power reactors
nps: normal pipe size; no prior service
NPS: National Park Service
npsh: net positive suction head
npt: normal pressure and temperature
Npt: Newport
NPT: national (taper) pipe thread; Non-Proliferation Treaty
NPTA: National Passenger Traffic Association; National Piano Travelers Association
NPTC: National Postal and Travelers Censorship
NPTRL: Naval Personnel Training Research Laboratory
n.p.u.: *ne plus ultra* (Latin—nothing beyond (it); the summit; the ultimate)
NPU: National People's Union; National Police Union; National Postal Union
npv: net present value
NPVLA: National Paint, Varnish, and Lacquer Association
NPW: *Naturpark Pfalszer Wald* (German—Falls Forest Nature Park)—in western Germany near France
NPWS: National Parks and Wildlife Service (Australia)
NPX: National Phoenix Industries (stock-exchange symbol)
NPY: National Productivity Year
nq: notes and queries
N & Q: *Notes and Queries*
nqa: net quick assets
NQD: Notice of Quality Discrepancy
nqokd: not quite our kind, dear
nqos: not quite our sort
nr: near; nonreactive (relay); number
nr: *non rogne* (French—untrimmed); *nummer* (Polish—issue; number); *nummer* (Dano-Norwegian or Swedish—number)
n.r.: *non repetatur* (Latin—not to be repeated)
n/r: no record; not required; not responsible (for)
nR: *neue Reihe* (German—new series)
Nr: *Nummer* (German—number)
NR: Norks Rikskringkasting (Norwegian Broadcasting)
NR: *National Review*
nra: never refuse anything; no repair action
nra: *nuestra* (Spanish—our)
NRA: National Reclamation Association; National Recovery

Act; National Recovery Administration; National Recreation Association; National Reform Association; National Rehabilitation Association; National Research Associates; National Restaurant Association; National Rifle Association (of America); Naval Reserve Association
NRAA: National Rifle Association of America
NRAC: National Resources Analysis Center
NRACCO: Navy Regional Air Cargo Control Office(r)
nrad: no risk after discharge
NRAF: Navy Recruiting Aids Facility
NRAO: National Radio Astronomy Observatory
NRAS: Navy Readiness Analysis Section; Navy Readiness Analysis System
Nra Sra: *Nuestra Señora* (Spanish—Our Lady)
NRB: National Roads Board; National Rubber Bureau
NRB: *Narodna Republika Blgariya* (Bulgarian Peoples' Republic)
Nrbi: Nairobi
NRC: Nacorazi Railroad Company; National Referral Center (Library of Congress); National Republican Club; National Research Corporation; National Research Council ; National Resources Committee; National Resources Council; National Roofing Contractors; Naval Retraining Command; Netherlands Red Cross; Nuclear Regulatory Commission; Nuclear Research Council
NRC: *Nieuwe Rotterdamse Courant* (New Rotterdam Courrant)
NRCA: National Retail Credit Association
NRCC: National Research Council of Canada
NRCD: National Reprographic Center for Documentation
NCRI: National Red Cherry Institute
NRC-NAS: National Research Council—National Academy of Sciences
ncrp: nonreinforced concrete pipe
NRCR: Northern Railway of Costa Rica (Ferrocarril del Norte de Costa Rica)
NR Crit: Nuclear Rocket—Critical
NRD: National Range Division
NRDA: National Research and Development Authority (Israel)
NRDB: Natural Rubber Development Board
NRDC: National Research Development Corporation
NRDC: Natural Resources Defense Council
NRDL: Naval Radiological Defense Laboratory
NRDO: National Research and Development Organization
NRDS: Nuclear Rocket Development Station
NREB: Navy Reserve Evaluation Board
NREC: National Resource Evaluation Center
NRECA: National Rural Electric Cooperative Association
nrem (NREM): non-rapid eye movement
nrems (NREMS): non-rapid eye-movement sleep
nrem sleep: non-rapid eye-movement (spindle) sleep
NRF: Naval Reactor Facility; Naval Repair Facility
NRF: *Nouvelle Revue Française*
NRFA: National Retail Furniture Association
NRFC: Navy Regional Finance Center
NRFL: National Rugby Football League
NRG: Naval Research Group
NRGA: National Rice Growers Association
NRh: Northern Rhodesia
NRHA: National Roller Hockey Association
NRHC: National Rural Housing Coalition
NRHS: National Railway Historical Society
NRIAD: National Register of Industrial Art Designers
NRIMS: National Research Institute for Mathematical Sciences
Nrk: Newark
NRK: Nikolai Rimsky-Korsakov
NRK: *Norsky Rikskringkasting* (Royal Norwegian Broadcasting)
nrl: normal rated load
NRL: National Research Library; Naval Research Laboratory
NRLCA: National Rural Letter Carriers' Association
NRLDA: National Retail Lumber Dealers Association
NRLSI: National Reference Library of Science and Invention
nrm: next to reading matter; normal rabbit serum
NRM: Naval Reserve Medal
NRMA: National Retail Merchants Association
NRMC: National Records Management Council; Naval Records Management Center
NRMCA: National Ready-Mixed Concrete Association
nrml: normal
nro: *nuestro* (Spanish—our, m.)
NRO: Narcotic Rehabilitation Officer; Naval Research Objectives
NROO: Naval Reactors Operations Office
NROTC: Naval Reserve Officers Training Corps
nrp: net rating points
NRPA: National Recreation and Park Association
NR & PA: National Recreation and Park Association
NRPB: National Research Planning Board
NRPC: National Railroad Passenger Corporation
NRPRA: Natural Rubber Producers' Research Association
NRR: Northern Rhodesia Regiment
NRRE: Netherlands Radar Research Establishment
nrs: normal rabbit serum
N rs: Nepalese rupee(s)
NRS: National Runaway Switchboard; Navy Relief Society
NRSA: National Rural Studies Association
nrt: net register(ed) tonnage (tons)
NRTA: National Retired Teachers Association
NRTC: Naval Reserve Training Center
nrts: not reparable this station
NRTS: National Reactor Testing Station
nru: nuclear reactor—universal
Nru: Nauru
NR-U: Nederlandsche Radio-Unie (Netherlands Union of Radio Broadcasters)
nrv: non-return value
NRVC: National Railway Utilization Corporation
Nrvkg: *Nervenkrieg* (German—nerve warfare)
NRVN: Navy of the Republic of Viet Nam
Nrw: Norwegian
NRWC: National Right to Work

Committee
nrx: nuclear reactor—experimental
NRYC: New Rochelle Yacht Club
NR Yorks: North Riding, Yorkshire
nrz c (NRZ C): non-return-to-zero change (data processing)
nrz m (NRZ M): non-return-to-zero mark recording (data processing)
ns: nanosecond; near side; neuro-psychiatric; new series; nickel steel; nonstandard; not specified
ns: *nouvelle serie* (French—new series)
n/s: not sufficient
nS: *neue Serie* (German—new series)
ns (NS): neurosurgery
Ns: nimbostratus; Nunes; Nuñez
NS: National Society; National Special (screw threads); Naval Shipyard; Naval Station; New Style; Norfolk Southern (railroad); North Sea; Nova Scotia; Nuclear Ship; Nuclear Submarine; Numismatic Society
NS: *Nachschrift* (German—postscript); *Nasjonal Samling* (Norwegian—National Unification)—fascist collaborationists headed by Vidkun Quisling during World War II (*see* quis); *Notre Seigneur* (French—Our Lord); *Nuestro Señor* (Spanish—Our Lord)
N.S.: New Style; Norfolk Southern (railroad)
N.S.: *Nuestro Señor* (Spanish—Our Lord)
nsa (NSA): nonenyl succinic acid
NSA: National Secretaries Association; National Security Agency; National Service Acts; National Shellfisheries Association; National Sheriff's Association; National Shipping Authority; National Showmen's Association; National Silo Association; National Ski Association; National Slag Association; National Slate Association; National Society of Auctioneers; National Standards Association; National Students Association; Naval Stock Account; Naval Supply Account; Neurological Society of America; Norwegian Seamen's Association
NSA: *Nuclear Science Abstracts*
NSAA: Norwegian Singers' Association of America
NSAC: Nova Scotia Agricultural College
NSACS: National Society for the Abolition of Cruel Sports
NSAD: National Society of Art Directors
NSAE: National Society of Art Education
NSAM: Naval School of Aviation Medicine
NSAS: National Smoke Abatement Society
NSASAB: National Security Agency Scientific Advisory Board
NSB: National Science Board; Norske Stasbaner (Norwegian State Railways)
NSB: *Norges Statsbaner* (Norwegian State Railway)
NSBA: National School Boards Association; National Small Business Association; National Sugar Brokers Association
NSBC: National Student Book Club
NSIBU: Nova Scotia Board of Insurance Underwriters
NSBMA: National Small Business Men's Association
nsc: non-service connected
NSC: National Safety Council; National Security Council; National Steel Corporation; Naval Supply Center; Newark State College
NSCA: National Society for Clean Air; Nova Scotia College of Art
NSCAR: National Society of Children of the American Revolution
NSCBS: National Society for the Conservation of Bighorn Sheep
NSCC: National Society for Crippled Children
NSCCA: National Society for Crippled Children and Adults
NSCD: National Society of Colonial Dames
NSCDRF: National Sickle Cell Disease Research Foundation
NSCID: National Security Council Intelligence Directive
NSCR: National Society for Cancer Relief
NSCT: North Staffordshire College of Technology
nsd: noise-suppression device
NSD: Naval Supply Depot
NSDA: National Soft Drink Association
NSDAP: Nationalsozialistische Deutsche Arbeiterpartei (German National Socialist [Nazi] Workers Party)
NSDF: National Sex and Drug Forum
NSDP: National Society of Dental Prosthetists
NSDS: National Shut-in Day Society
nsec: nanosecond
NSEC: National Service Entertainments Council
NSES: National Society of Electrotypers and Stereotypers
nsf: not sufficient funds
NSF: National Science Foundation
NSF: *Norges Standardiserings Forbund* (Norwegian Standards Institute)
NSFGB: National Ski Federation of Great Britain
nsftd: normal spontaneous full-term delivery
nsg: neurosecretory granules
NSG: Naval Security Group
NSGA: National Sporting Goods Association
NSGT: Non-Self-Governing Territories; Non-Self-Governing Territory
nsh: not so hot
NSHA: National Steeplechase and Hunt Association
NSHEB: North of Scotland Hydro-Electric Board
nsi: nonstandard item
NSI: National Stock Exchange
NSIA: National Security Industrial Association
NSID: National Society of Interior Designers
NSIO: Nova Scotia Information Office
NSJC: *Nuestro Señor Jesucristo* (Spanish—Our Lord Jesus Christ)
nsk: not specified by kind
NSKK: Nito Shosen Kabushiki Kaisha (Japanese steamship line)
NSL: Northrop Space Laboratory
NSLF: National Socialist Liberation Front (American-Nazi student organization)
NSLI: National Service Life Insurance
NSLL: National Savings and Loan League
NSLS: National Science Library System
nsm: noise source meter; number of similar negative (matches)
ns/m²: newton second per square

meter
NSM: National Security Medal; National Selected Morticians; Naval School of Music; Nevada State Museum
NSMA: National Scale Men's Association
NSMC: Naval Submarine Medical Center
NSMHC: National Society for Mentally Handicapped Children
NSMM: National Society of Metal Mechanics
NSMP: National Society of Master Patternmakers; National Society of Mural Painters
NSMPA: National Screw Machine Products Association
NSMR: National Society for Medical Research
NSMS: National Sheet Music Society
NSMSES: Naval Ship Missile Systems Engineering Station
NSNA: National Student Nurses' Association
NSNC: Nova Scotia Normal College
NSO: Nashville Symphony Orchestra; National Symphony Orchestra; Navy Subsistence Office(r); Norfolk Symphony Orchestra; Northern Sinfonia Orchestra
NSOA: National School Orchestra Association
n sp: new species
NSP: Navy Standard part; Northern States Power
NSPA: National Scholastic Press Association; National Society of Public Accountants; National Soybean Processors Association; National Split Pea Association; National Standard Part Association; Naval Shore Patrol Administration
NSPB: National Society for the Prevention of Blindness
NSPC: National Security Planning Commission; National Society of Painters in Casein; Northern States Power Company
NSPCA: National Society for the Prevention of Cruelty to Animals
NSPCC: National Society for the Prevention of Cruelty to Children
NSPD: Naval Shore Patrol Detachment
NSPE: National Society of Professional Engineers
nspf: not specifically provided for
NSPI: National Society for Programmed Instruction; National Swimming Pool Institute
NSPO: Navy Special Projects Office; Nuclear Systems Project Office
NSPS: National Sweet Pea Society
NSPSE: National Society of Painters, Sculptors, and Engravers
NSPWA: National Society of Patriotic Women of America
nsq: neuroticism scale questionnaire
nsr: natural sinus rhythm; normal sinus rhythm
NSR: National Scientific Register; Norfolk Southern Railway
NSRA: National Shoe Retailers Association; National Shorthand Reporters Association; National Street Rod Association; North-South Reconstruction advisors
NSRB: National Security Resources Board
NSRDC: National Standards Reference Data System
NSRDF: Naval Supply Research and Development Facility
NSRDL: Naval Supply Research and Development Facility
NSRDL: Naval Ship Research and Development Laboratory
NSRDS: National Standard Reference Data System
NSRF: Nova Scotia Research Foundation
NSRP: National States Rights Party
nsrt: near-surface reference temperature
nss (NSS): normal saline solution
NSS: National Sculpture Society; National Serigraph Society; National Slovak Society; National Speleological Society; National Stockpile Site; Newburgh and South Shore (railroad)
NSSA: National Sanitary Supply Association; National Skeet Shooting Association
NSSAR: National Society of the Sons of the American Revolution
NSSC: National Society for the Study of Communication
NSSCC: National Space Surveillance Control Center
NSS Co: Northern Steam Ship Company (New Zealand)
NSSE: National Society for the Study of Education
NSSF: National Shooting Sports Foundation
NSSFC: National Severe Storm Forecast Center; National Society of Student Film Critics
NSSFNS: National Scholarship Service and Fund for Negro Students
NSSGA: Nicherin Shoshu Soka-Gakkai Academy (international peace society)
NSSL: National Severe Storms Laboratory
NSSMA: National Spanish-Speaking Management Association
NSSP: National Severe Storms Project
NSSR: New School for Social Research
NSSU: National Sunday School Union
nst: nonslip thread
NST: Newfoundland Standard Time
NSTA: National Science Teachers Association
NSTAP: National Strategic Targeting and Attack Policy
NSTC: Nebraska State Teachers College
NSTI: Norwalk State Technical Institute
NSTIC: Naval Scientific and Technical Information
NSTL: National Strategic Target Line
NSTP: Nuffield Science Teaching Project
NS Tripos: Natural Science Tripos
NSTS: National Sea Training Schools
nsu: non-specific urethritis
NSU: Neckarsulmer Fahrzeugwerke (NSU Motorenwerke)
NSUC: North Staffordshire University College
nsurg: neurosurgeon; neurosurgery; neurosurgical
NSVP: National Student Volunteer Program
NSW: New South Wales
NSWC: New South Wales Centre
NSWGR: New South Wales Government Railways
NSWPP: National Socialist White People's Party (formerly American Nazi Party)
NSY: New Scotland Yard
NSYF: Natural Science for Youth Foundation
nt: nit (unit of luminous intensi-

ty); nontight; no trace
nt: Northern Telecom
n.t.: *nel testo* (Italian—in the text)
n't: not
n/t: net tonnage
n & t: nose and throat
Nt: nitron
NT: New Testament; Northern Territory
N.T.: *Novum Testamentum* (Latin—New Testament)
NT$: New Taiwan dollar
nta: nitrilotriacetic (phosphate substitute for detergents); nuclear test aircraft (NTA)
NTA: National Tax Association; National Technical Association; National Tourist Association; National Travel Association; National Tuberculosis Association; Northern Textile Association; Northern Trade Association
NTAA: National Travelers Aid Association
NTAC: *Nederlandse Touring en Auto Club* (Netherlands Touring and Auto Club)
NTAs: Nielsen Television Areas
NTB: Norsk Telegrambyra (Norwegian news service)
NTBL: Nuffield Talking Book Library (for the blind)
NtBuStnds: National Bureau of Standards
ntc: negative temperature coefficient
NTC: National Teacher Corps; National Theatre Conference; National Travel Club; Naval Training Center
NTCC: Nimbus Technical Control Center
ntd: non-tight door
NTDA: National Tire Distributors Association; National Trade Development Association; National Tyre Distributors Association
NTDC: Naval Tactical Data System; Naval Technical Data System; Naval Training Device Center
NTDPMA: National Tool, Die, and Precision Machining Association
NTDS: Naval-Tactical Data System; Naval Technical Data Sytem
nte: *norte* (Spanish—north)
NTE: National Teacher Examination
N-terror(ism)(ist): nuclear terrorism; nuclear terrorist
N-test: nuclear test(ing)
NTETA: National Traction Engine and Traction Association
NTF: Navy Technological Forecast
ntfy: notify
NTGB: North Thames Gas Board
NT Gk: New Testament Greek
Nth: Netherlands
NTH: Norges Tekniske Hogskole (Norwegian Technical University, Trondheim)
Nth country: next country of a series acquiring nuclear power
n/30: net (payment) in 30 days
nthn: northern
NTHP: National Trust for Historic Preservation
NTI: Nielsen Television Index (tv rating)
NTIAC: Nondestructive Testing Information Analysis Center
NTIATA: National Tax Institute of America Tax Association
NTID: National Technical Institute for the Deaf
NTIS: National Technical Information Service
NTK: *Nippon Toshokan Kyokai* (Japan Library Association)
ntl: no time lost
NTL: National Tennis League; National Training Laboratories
NTLS: National Truck Leasing System
ntm: net ton mile
Ntm: Nottingham
NTNP: Natchez Trace National Parkway
nto: not tried on
nto: *neto* (Spanish—net)
NTO: National Tenants Organization; National Theatre Organisation (South Africa)
ntp: normal temperature and pressure; no title page
NTPC: National Technical Processing Center; Navy Training Publications Center
ntpl: nut plate
ntr: noise temperature ratio
NTR: National Tape Repository; Northern Test Range
Ntra Sra: *Nuestra Señora* (Spanish—Our Lady)
NTRB: Northern Territory Reserve Board (Australia)
NTRL: Naval Training Research Laboratory
nts: not to scale
Nts: Nantes
NTS: National Traffic System; Naval Transportation System; Nederlandse Televisie Stichting (Netherlands Television Foundation); Nevada Test Site
NTS: *Narodnyi Trudovoy Soyuz:* (Russian—National Labor Union)—anti-communist Russian exiles
NTSA: National Traffic Safety Agency
NT & SA: National Trust and Savings Association
NTSB: National Transportation Safety Board
NTSC: National Television Standards Committee; North Texas State College
NTSWG: National Training School for Women and Girls
NTTC: National Tank Truck Carriers
NTT & TTI: National Truck Tank and Trailer Tank Institute
NTU: National Taiwan University; Navy Toxicology Unit
NTUC: National Trades Union Congress
ntv: nerve tissue vaccine
NTV: Nippon Television
nt wt: net weight
NTX: Navy Teletype Exchange
Ntzrm: *Nutzraum* (German—cubic capacity)
nu: name unknown; new
Nu: Nusselt number
NU: Naciones Unidas (Spanish—United Nations); Nations Unies (French—United Nations); Niagara University; Northeastern University; Northwestern University; Norwich University
NUAAW: National Union of Agricultural and Allied Workers
NUAW: National Union of Agricultural Workers
NUB: National Union of Blastfurnacemen
nube(s): nubile(s)
NUBE: National Union of Bank Employees
NUBSO: National Union of Boot and Shoe Operatives
nuc: nuclear; nucleated; nucleus
NUC: National Urban Coalition; Naval Undersea Center
NUC: *National Union Catalog*
Nuc.E.: Nuclear Engineer
nuc(l): nuclear; nucleus
NUCMC: *National Union Catalog of Manuscript Collections*
NUCO: National Union of Cooperative Officials
nuc phy: nuclear physics
Nuc Reg Com: Nuclear Regulato-

ry Commission
NUCS: National Union of Christian Schools
NUCUS: National Union of Conservative and Unionist Associations
nud: nudism; nudist
nud: *nudnick* (Yiddish—nuisance; pest)
NUDBTW: National Union of Dyers, Bleachers, and Textile Workers
NUDET: Nuclear Detonation Report
NUDETS: Nuclear Detonation, Detection, and Reporting System
NUE: Nuremberg, Germany (airport)
NUEA: National University Extension Association
NUF: National Urban Fellows
NUFCOR: Nuclear Fuels Corporation
NUFCW: National Union of Funeral and Cemetery Workers
NUFLAT: National Union of Footwear, Leather, and Allied Trades
NUFTO: National Union of Furniture Trade Operatives
nug: nuggar (cargo boat used on the Nile)
NUGMW: National Union of General and Municipal Workers
NUHS: New Utrecht High School
NUHW: National Union of Hosiery Workers
NUI: National University of Ireland (Ollscoil na h-Éireann)
NUIW: National Union of Insurance Workers
NUJ: National Union of Journalists
nuke: nuclear (slang)
nukes: nuclear explosives; nuclear power plants
nul: no upper limit
nul (NUL): null character (data processing)
NUL: National Urban League; Northwestern University Library
nullies: nullifiers
NULWAT: National Union of Leather Workers and Allied Trades
num: number; numbered; numbering; numeral(s); numeration(s); numerical; numerologist; numerology
num: *numero(s)* (Portuguese or Spanish—number(s))
Num: The Fourth Book of Moses, called Numbers
NUM: National Union of Mineworkers; New Ulster Movement
numb.: numbered
Number-One Host of the Jersey Coast: Atlantic City, New Jersey
NUMEC: Nuclear Materials and Equipment Corporation
numer: numeral; numerative
numis: numismatics
numism: numismatic(s); numismatist
nuna: not used on next assembly
NUOS: Naval Underwater Ordnance Station
NUP: Negro Universities Press
NUPBPW: National Union of Printing, Bookbinding, and Paper Workers
NUPE: National Union of Public Employees
NUPI: *Norsk Utenrikspolitisk Institutt* (Norwegian Foreign Policy Institute)
nuplex: nuclear-powered complex (of manufacturers)
NUPT: National Union of Press Telegraphists
NUR: National Union of Railwaymen
NURA: National Union of Ratepayers' Associations
NURC: National Union of Retail Confectioners
NURT: National Union of Retail Tobacconists
NUS: National Union of Students; Nuclear Utility Service(s)
nusar: nuclear sweep and radar
NUSAS: National Union of South African Students
NUSC: Naval Underwater Systems Center
NUSEC: National Union of Societies for Equal Citizenship
NUSL: Navy Underwater Sound Laboratory
NUSMWCHDE: National Union of Sheet Metal Workers, Coppersmiths, Heating and Domestic Engineers
NUSRL: Navy Underwater Sound Reference Laboratory
NUSS: National Union of Small Shopkeepers
nusum: numerical summary
Nu T: Newcastle-upon-Tyne
NUT: National Union of Teachers (Great Britain)
NUTAT: *Nordisk Union for Alkoholfri Trafic* (Nordic Union for Alcohol-free Traffic)
NUTAW: National Union of Textile and Allied Workers
nu-tec: nuclear detection (radiation monitoring device)
NUTGW: National Union of Tailors and Garment Workers
Nutmegs: Connecticuters
Nutmeg State: Connecticut's nickname
NUTN: National Union of Trained Nurses
nutr: nutrition
NUVB: National Union of Vehicle Builders
NUWA: National Unemployed Workers' Association
NUWC: Naval Undersea Warfare Center
NUWT: National Union of Women Teachers
NUWW: National Union of Women Workers
nv: naked vision; needle valve; new version
nv.: *novicius* (Latin—new; recent)
n-v: non-vaccinated; non-veteran; non-voting
n & v: nausea and vomiting
NV: Nord-Viscount
NV: *Naamloze Vernootschap* (Dutch—corporation); *Naviera Vascongada* (Basque Navigation Company); *Norske Veritas* (Norwegian Register of Shipping)
nva: *nueva* (Spanish—new)
NVA: North Vietnamese Army
NVAiO: Norske Videnskaps-Akademi i Oslo (Norwegian Academy of Science and Letters in Oslo)
NVB: National Volunteer Brigade
NVB: *Nederlandse Vereniging van Bedrijfsarchivarissen* (Dutch—Netherlands Association of Business Archivists); *Nederlandse Vereniging van Bibliothekarissen* (Dutch—Netherlands Library Association)
NVBF: *Nordisk Viedenskabeligt Bibliotekarieforbund* (Nordic Federation of Research Librarians)
NVC: National Violence Commission
NVF: National Volunteer Force
NVFC: National Vulcanized Fibre Company
nvg: null voltage generator
NVGA: National Vocabulary Guidance Association
NVL: Night Vision Laboratory
nvm: non-volatile matter
NVMA: National Veterinary

Medical Association
NVNS: Naamloze Vernootschap Nederlandsche Spoorwagen (Netherlands Railway Corporation)
NVO: Northern Variety Orchestra
nvp: natural vegetable powder (powdered psyllium seed and dextrose laxative)
NVPA: National Visual Presentation Association
NVPO: Nuclear Vehicle Projects Office (NASA)
nvr: no voltage release
NVRS: National Vegetable Research Station
nvs: neutron velocity selector
NVS: Night Vision System
NVT: National Veld Trust
NVTS: National Vocational Training Service
NVV: *Nederlands Verbond van Vakverenigingen* (Dutch—Netherlands Trade Union Federation)
nw: nanowatt; no wind
Nw: New (postal abbreviation sometimes confused with NW—Northwest)—when in doubt, spell it out
NW: Chicago & North Western Railway; Noah Webster; Norfolk & Western (railroad); Northern Wings Ltd; North Wales; Northwest; Northwest Airlines
NW: *noordwest* (Dutch—northwest); *Nordwesten* (German—northwest)
NW1, NW2, etc.: Northwest One, Northwest 2, etc. (London postal zones)
N & W: Norfolk & Western (railroad)
NWA: Northwest Airlines
NWAA: National Wheelchair Athletic Association
NWAH & ACA: National Warm Air Heating and Air Conditioning Association
nwb: non-weight bearing
NWB: National Westminster Bank
NWBA: National Wheelchair Basketball Association
nwc: nuclear war capability
Nwc: Newcastle-upon-Tyne
NWC: National War College; National Water Commission; National Writers Club
NWCC: Northern Wyoming Community College
NWCCL: Naval Weapons Center—Corona Laboratories
NWCTU: National Woman's Christian Temperance Union
NWD: *New World Dictionary*
NWDR: Nordwestdeutscher Rundfunk (North-West German Broadcasting System)
NWEB: Northwestern Electricity Board (UK)
NWES: New World Exploration Society
NWF: National Welfare Fund; National Wildlife Federation
NWF: *National War Formulary*
Nwfld: Newfoundland
NWFP: North-West Frontier Province
nwg: national wire gauge
NWGA: National Wheat Growers Association; National Wool Growers Association
nwh: normal working hours
NWI: Netherlands West Indies
NWIDA: North West Industrial Development Association
NWIP: Naval Warfare Instruction Publication
NWIRP: Naval Weapons Industrial Reserve Plant
NWIJA: National Wholesale Jewelers Association
NWL: Naval Weapons Laboratory
NWLB: National War Labor Board
NWLF: New World Liberation Front (terrorists)
NWly: northwesterly
NWMC: Northwest Michigan College
NWMPA: North Wales Master Printers' Alliance
Nw Ned: Nieuw Nederland (Dutch—New Netherlands)
NWNT: North Wales Naturalists' Trust
NWO: Nuclear Weapons Office(r)
nwoc: new woman on campus
n-word: nonce word (word coined for the nonce or the occasion)
NWP: Naval Weapons Plant; North West Provinces
NWPC: National Women's Political Caucus
NWPFC: Northwest Pacific Fisheries Commission
NWPSC: Northwestern Public Service Company
NWQAO: Naval Weapons Quality Assurance Office
nwr: next word request
NWR: National Welfare Rights; National Wildlife Refuge; National Wildlife Reserve; Nuclear Weapon Report
NWRC: National Weather Records Center
NWRF: Naval Weather Research Facility
NWRLF: New World Radical Liberation Front
NWRO: National Welfare Rights Organization
NWRS: National Wildlife Refuge System
nws: normal water surface
NWS: National Weather Service; Naval Weapons Station; Nimbus Weather Satellite
NWSA: National Welding Supply Association
NWSC: National Weather Satellite Center; Naval Weather Service Command
NWSF: Nuclear Weapons Storage Facility (USA)
NWSO: Naval Weapons Services Office
NWSS: Nuclear Weapons Support Section (USA)
NWSY: Naval Weapons Station—Yorktown, Va
nwt: nonwatertight
NWT: Northwest Territories
nwtd: nonwatertight door
NWTEC: National Wool Textile Export Corporation
nwu: nosewheel up
NWU: Nebraska Wesleyan University
NWUS: Northwestern United States
NWWA: National Water Well Association
nx: nonexpendable
NXDO: Nike-X Development Office (USA)
NXMIS: Nike-X Management Information Office
NXPM: Nike-X Project Manager
NXPO: Nike-X Project Office
nxr: non-crossing rule
NXSO: Nike-X Support Office
ny: no year
Ny: Niles; Nylan
NY: New York; New York Airways (2-letter code); New Yorker
NY: *Neu York* (German—New York); *New Yorker* (magazine); *Nieuw York* (Dutch—New York); *Nova Iorque* or *Nova York* (Portuguese—New York); *Nueva York* (Spanish—New York)
Nya: Nyasaland
NYA: National Youth Administration; Neighborhood Youth Association; New York Aquarium
NYAC: New York Athletic Club
NYADS: New York Air Defense

Sector
NYAM: New York Academy of Medicine
NYANA: New York Association for New Americans
NYAO: New York Assay Office
Nyas: Nyasaland
NYAS: New York Academy of Science
NYATI: New York Agricultural and Technical Institute
NYBFU: New York Board of Fire Underwriters
NYBG: New York Botanical Garden
NYBSBC: New York Bureau of State Building Codes
NYC: National Yacht Club; Neighborhood Youth Corps; Newburgh Yacht Club; New York Central (railroad); New York City; New York Coliseum
NYCC: New York Cultural Center
NYCCC: New York City Community College
NYCCIW: New York City Correctional Institution for Women
NYCE: New York Cocoa Exchange; New York College of Education; New York Cotton Exchange
NYCERS: New York City Employees Retirement System
NYCHA: New York City Housing Authority
NYCJG: Nikka Yuko Centennial Japanese Garden (Lethbridge, Alberta)
NYCMA: New York City Metropolitan Area
NYCMD: New York Contract Management District
NYCMSL: New York County Medical Society Library
NYCNHA: New York City Nursing Home Association
NYCOC: New York City Opera Company
NY Col: New York Coliseum
NYCPM: New York City Police Museum
NYCS: New York Choral Society
NYCSE: New York Coffee and Sugar Exchange
NYC & ST L: New York, Chicago & St Louis (Nickel Plate Line)
NYCT: New York Community Trust
NYCTA: New York City Transit Authority
NYCWRU: New York Cooperative Wildlife Research Unit
nyd: not yet diagnosed
NYDMC: New York Downstate Medical Center
NYDR: New York Dock Railway
Nye: Aneurin
NYF: New York Foundation
NYFDM: New York Fire Department Museum
NYFIRO: New York Fire Insurance Rating Organization
NYGC: New York Governor's Conference
NYH–CMC: New York Hospital—Cornell Medical Center
NYHD: New York House of Detention
NYHS: New York Historical Society
NY Hist Soc: New York Historical Society
NYIAS: New York Institute of the Aerospace Sciences
NYIT: New York Institute of Technology
N Yk: New York
NYK: Nippon Yusen Kaisha Line
nyl: nylon
NYLA: New York Library Association
NY & LB: New York & Long Branch (railroad)
NYLS: New York Law School
nym: *nymon* (Greek—name) —as in antonym, homonym, pseudonym, synonym, etc.
NYMC: New York Maritime College
NYME: New York Mercantile Exchange
nympho: nymphomania; nymphomaniac; nymphomaniacal
N Y N H & H: New York, New Haven and Hartford (railroad)
nyo: not yet out
NYOGB: National Youth Orchestra of Great Britain
NYOL: New York Opera Library
NYOSL: New York Oceans Science Laboratory
NYOTBC: New York Off-Track Betting Corporation
NYOW: National Youth Orchestra of Wales
NYO & W: New York, Ontario and Western (railroad)
nyp: not yet published
NYP: New York Philharmonic (orchestra)
NYPA: New York Port Authority
NYPD: New York Police Department
NYPDis: New York Procurement District (US Army)
NYPE: New York Port of Embarkation; New York Produce Exchange
NYPFO: New York Procurement Field Office (USAF)
NYPL: New York Public Library
NYPM: New York Pro Musica
NYPs: Neighborhood Youth Programs
NYPS: New York Psychiatric Society; New York Publishing Society
NYPSS: New York Philharmonic-Symphony Society
Nyq: Nyquist (data-processing time or rate)
nyr: not yet returned
NYRA: New York Racing Association
NYRB: *New York Review of Books*
NYRM: New York Reformatory for Men
NYRW: New York Reformatory for Women (Westfield Farm)
NYS: New York State
NYSA: New York Shipping Association
NYSAA: New York State Aviation Association
NYSAC: New York State Athletic Commission
NYSASDA: New York State Atomic and Space Development Authority
NYSAVC: New York State Audio-Visual Council
NYSBB: New York State Banking Board
NYSBC: New York State Barge Canal (modern extension of Erie Canal)
NYSC: New York Shipbuilding Corporation
NYSCC: New York State Crime Commission
NY Sch Indus Rel: New York State School of Industrial Relations (Cornell University)
NYSE: New York Stock Exchange
NYSES: New York State Employment Service
NYSF: New York Shakespeare Festival
NYSL: New York Society Library
NYSM: New York State Museum
NYSMM: New York State Maritime Museum (New York City)
NYSP: New York School of Printing; New York State Police

NYSPA: New York State Power Authority
NYSSMA: New York State School Music Association
NYSTA: New York State Teachers Association; New York State Thruway Authority
NYS & W: New York, Susquehanna and Western (railroad)
NYT: *The New York Times*
NY Thru: New York Thruway
NYTNS: New York Times News Service
NYU: New York underworld (used in law-enforcement circles); New York University
NYUL: New York University Library
NYUMC: New York University Medical Center; New York Upstate Medical Center
NYUSM: New York University School of Medicine
NYWASH: Navy Yard, Washington
NYYP: New York Yacht Club
NYZP: New York Zoological Park
NYZS: New York Zoological Society
Nz: Nuñez
NZ: New Zealand; New Zealand National Airways (2-letter coding); Novaya Zemlya
N-Z: Nike-Zeus
NZ : New Zealand pound
NZAB: New Zealand Associaion of Bacteriologists
NZAS: New Zealand Association of Scientists
NZb: New Zealand black (mice hybrids)
NZB: New Zealand Ballet
NZBC: New Zealand Broadcasting Corporation
NZBS: New Zealand Broadcasting Service
NZCER: New Zealand Council for Educational Research
NZD: New Zealand Division
NZDA: New Zealand Department of Agriculture
NZDCS: New Zealand Department of Census and Statistics
NZDE: New Zealand Department of Education
NZDLS: New Zealand Department of Lands and Survey
NZDSIR: New Zealand Department of Scientific and Industrial Research
NZED: New Zealand Electricity Department
NZedder(s): [En-zed-der(s)]—New Zealander(s)
NZEF: New Zealand Expeditionary Force
NZEI: New Zealand Electronics Institute
nzf: near zero field
NZFL: New Zealand Federation of Labor
NZFRI: New Zealand Forest Research Institute
NZFS: New Zealand Forest Service
nzg: near zero gravity
NZGR: New Zealand Government Railways
NZGS: New Zealand Geographical Society
NZGTC: New Zealand Government Travel Commissioner
NZHC: New Zealand High Commission
NZIC: New Zealand Institute of Chemistry
NZIE: New Zealand Institution of Engineers
NZIM: New Zealand Institute of Management
NZIS: New Zealand Information Service
NZLA: New Zealand Library Association
NZLR: *New Zealand Law Reports*
NZLS: New Zealand Library Service
NZMS: New Zealand Meteorological Service
NZNAC: New Zealand National Airways Corporation
NZOC: New Zealand Opera Company
NZOI: New Zealand Oceanographic Institute
NZP: National Zoological Park; New Zealand Players
NZPA: New Zealand Press Association
NZPBA: New Zealand Publishers' Association
NZR: New Zealand Railways
NZS: New Zealand Standards Institute
NZSA: New Zealand Statistical Association
NZS Co: New Zealand Shipping Company
NZ Sea Fron: New Zealand Sea Frontier (NZSEAFRON)
NZTC: New Zealand Trade Commission
NZVA: New Zealand Veterinary Association
NZw: New Zealand white (mice hybrids)
NZZ: *Neue Züricher Zeitung* (New Zurich Newspaper)

O

o: observer; occasional; occidental; octavo; ohm; oil; oiliness; Olivetti; opium; orange; oriental; overcast
o: (Japanese—big; great; large)
o.: *oculus* (Latin—eye); *oeste* (Portuguese or Spanish—west); *oost* (Dutch—east); *op* (Dano-Norwegian or Dutch—up); *os* (Latin—bone); *ouest* (French—west); *ovest* (Italian—west)
ö: (Dano-Norwegian or Swedish—island); *öster* (Swedish—east)
ø: *øst* (Dano-Norwegian—east)
o/: *order* (Spanish—order)
'o: (Gaelic contraction—also)
o': (Gaelic contraction—of; on)
O: absence of perception of sound (symbol); New Orleans Mint (coin symbol); observation; ocean; Oceanic Steamship Company; October; office; officer; Ohio; Olsen Line; Omaha; Ontario; order; Oregon; ortho; Oscar—code for letter O; oxygen; unofficial abbreviation for Ohio
O': (Gaelic prefix meaning of)
O: center of the earth (symbol); observer (symbol); *oeste* (Portuguese or Spanish—west); *oost* (Dutch—east); *optimus* (Latin—best possible); *Ost* (German—east); *ouest*

(French—west); *ovest* (Italian—west)
Ö: Österreich (German—Eastern Empire)—Austria
ϕ: shortage (symbol)
O1: organized seagoing naval reserve
O2: organized naval reserve aviation
O_2: oxygen
O_2cap: oxygen capacity
O_2sat: oxygen saturation
O_3: ozone
oa: occiput anterior; old age; on account; on or about; osteoarthritis; overall
o/a: on account; on or about
oa: och andra (Swedish—and others)
o/A: oro Americano (Spanish—American gold; American money)
OA: Obligation Authority; Office of Applications; Olympic Airways; Operations Analysis; Osborne Association; overall noise level (symbol)
oaa (OAA): oxalo-acetic acid
OaA: Office of Aging
OAA: Old Age Assistance; Organisation des Nations Unies pour l'Alimentation et l'Agriculture (United Nations Organization for Food and Agriculture)
OAAA: Outdoor Advertising Association of America
oaad: ovarian ascorbic acid depletion
OAAU: Organization of Afro-American Unity
oac: on approved credit
OAC: Operating Agency Code; Ordnance Ammunition Command; Oregon Agriculture College
OACI: Organisation de l'Aviation Civile Internationale (French—International Civil Aviation Organization); *Organización de Aviación Civil Internacional* (Spanish—International Civil Aviation Organization)
OACT: Ohio Association of Classroom Teachers
oad: overall depth
OAD: ordered, adjudged, and decreed
oadc: oleic acid, albumin, dextrose, catalase
oaf: open-air factor
OAFIE: Office of Armed Forces Information and Education
OAG: Office of the Adjutant General; Office of the Attorney General
OAG: Official Airline Guide
OAGB: Osteopathic Association of Great Britain
oah: overall height
OAH: Organization of American Historians
OAHE: Ohio Association for Higher Education
OAI: Office of Aeronautical Intelligence; Osborne Association, Incorporated
oais: opinion, attitude, and interest survey
oak.: oakum
Oak: Oakland
Oak City: Raleigh, North Carolina
OAK: Oakland, California (Metropolitan International Airport)
Oak Sym: Oakland Symphony
oal: overall length
OAL: Ordnance Aerophysics Laboratory
o. alt. hor.: omnibus alternis horis (Latin—every other hour)
OALMA: Orthopedic Appliance and Limb Manufacturers Association
OAM: Office of Aviation Medicine
OAMA: Ogden Air Material Area
oame: orbital attitude and maneuvering electronics
OAMS: Orbital Attitude and Maneuvering System
ÖAMTC: Österreichischer Automobil-Motorrad und Touring Club (German—Austrian Automobile Motoring and Touring Club)
OANA: Organization of Asian News Agencies
oao: off and on
OAO: Orbiting Astronomical Observatory
oap: opthalmic artery pressure
OAP: Office of Aircraft Production; Old-Age Pension
OAPC: Office of the Alien Property Custodian
OAPs: Old-Age Pensioners
O Ar: Old Arabic
OAR: Office of Aerospace Research; Organized Air Reserve
OARP: Old Age Revolving Pensions (Townsend Plan)
OART: Office of Advanced Research and Technology (NASA)
oas: old-age security; on active service
OAS: Office of Appalachian Studies; Old Age Security; Organization of American States
OAS: Organisation de l'Armée Secrete (French—Organization of the Secret Army)—General Salan's secret counter-revolutionary group attempting to crush Algerian independence
OASD-AE: Office Assistant Secretary of Defense, Application Engineering
OASDHI: Old-Age, Survivors, Disability, and Health Insurance Social Security
OASDI: Old Age, Survivors, and Disability Insurance
OASD-R & D: Office Assistant Secretary of Defense, Research and Development
OASD-S & L: Office Assistant Secretary of Defense, Supply and Logistics
OASI: Old-Age and Survivor's Insurance
Oasis City: Roswell, New Mexico
oasp: organic acid-soluble phosphorus
oat.: outside air temperature
OAT: Office of Advanced Technology (USAF)
OATC: Oceanic Air Traffic Control
OATS: Office of Air Transportation Security; Old-Age Theatre Society (Great Britain)
OAU: Organization for African Unity
oaw: old abandoned well; overall width
Oax: Oaxaca
OAYR: Outstanding Airman of the Year Ribbon
ob: oboe; oboes; obsolete; obstetric; obstetrical; obstetrician; obstetrics; old boy; on board; operational base (OB); ordered back; outboard buffer; output buffer; overboard (vent line)
ob.: obit (Latin—died)
o/b: opening of books
ob (OB): outside broadcast (TV from a remote location)
o B: off Broadway
o B: ohne Befund (German—without findings)
Ob: object art (art accented with real objects, *e.g.*, a real watch chain dangling between two pockets of a man's vest in a painting)
OB: Old Bailey; Operating Base;

Operational Base; Order of Battle; Ordnance Battalion; Ordnance Board; Ox Box (corporation)
OB: *Oranjeboom* (Dutch—orange tree)—Amsterdam-brewed beer
O.B.: obstetrical; obstetrician; obstetrics
O'B: O'Brien
oba: optical bleaching agent
OBAA: Oil-Burning Apparatus Association
OBAR: Ohio Bar Automated Research
OBAWS: On-Board Aircraft Weighing System
Obad: The Book of Obadiah
obb: obbligato
OBB: battleship, old (3-letter naval symbol)
ÖBB: Österreichische Bundesbahnen (Austrian Federal Railways)
obc: on-board checkout
OBC: Outboard Boating Club
obce: on-board checkout equipment
obd: omnibearing distance
ob d'am: oboe d'amore
ob dk: observation deck
obdt: obedient
OBE: Office of Business Economics; Officer of the British Empire; Order of the British Empire
Obediah Skinflint: (pseudonym—Joel Chandler Harris)
OBEV: *Oxford Book of English Verse*
obfusc: obfuscated
Ob-G: Obstetrician-Gynaecologist
ob^{go}: *obrigado* (Portuguese—thank you)
ob-gyn: obstetrical-gynecological; obstetrician-gynecologist
obi: omnibearing indicator
obit: obituary
obj: object; objective
object.: objective(ly)
objn: objection
obl: obligation; oblique; oblong; obloquy
ob/l: ocean bill of lading
OBL: Ohio Barge Line; Order of the Brave Librarian
oblg: obligate; obligation
OBLI: Oxford and Birmingham Light Infantry
oblig: obligation(s); obligatory
obln: obligation
obo: oil/bulk freight/ore (multipurpose seagoing carrier)
ob ph: oblique photograph(y)
OBRA: Overseas Broadcasting Representatives' Association
obre: *octubre* (Spanish—October)
Ob River City: Novosibirsk, Siberia
obro: *outubro* (Portuguese—October)
obs: observation; observe; observer; obsolete; obstacle; obstetrical; obstetrics; obstetrician
obs: *oboes*
obs (OBS): organic brain syndrome
Obs: *The Observer*
obsc: obscure(d)
obsd: observed
obsn: observation
obsol: obsolescent
ob. s.p.: *obiit sine prole* (Latin—died without issue)
obss: ocean bottom scanning sonar
obs spot: observation spot
obst: obstacle; obstruction
obstet: obstetrical; obstetrician; obstetrics
obstr: obstruction
obsv: observation; observatory; observer
obt: obedient
obt.: *obiit* (Latin—he died)
OBTA: Oak Bark Tanners' Association
obtd: obtained
OBU: One Big Union
O Bul: Old Bulgarian
obv: obverse, ocean boarding vessel
obw: observation window
oc: ocean; odor control; on camera; on center; oral contraceptive
o'c: o'clock (of the clock)
o.c.: *opere citato* (Latin—in the work cited)
o-c: open-curcuit
o/c: overcharge
o & c: onset and course (disease)
oc (OC): obstetrical conjugate; on camera (tv performer heard and seen)
Oc: Ocean
OC: Oakland City; Oakwood College; Oberlin College; Oblate College; Occidental College; Odessa College; Office of Censorship; Officer Candidate; Ohio College; Okolona College; Olivet College; Olympic College; Orlando College; Otero College; Overseas Chinese; Overseas Commands
O.C.: Officer Commanding
O.C.: *Organo Corale* (Latin—choir organ)
O-in-C: Officer-in-Charge
O of C: Order of the Coif
oca: ocarina (flutelike clay instrument nicknamed "sweet potato")
OCA: Office of Consumer Affairs (ombudsman function of the U.S. Postal Service); Ontario College of Art
OCAA: Oklahoma City-Ada-Atoka (railroad)
OCAC: Office of Chief of Air Corps
OCADS: Oklahoma City Air Defense Sector
OCAFF: Office Chief of Army Field Forces
OCAM: Organisation Commune Africaine et Malgache [Organization of the African and Malagasy Community (of former French colonies)]
OCAMA: Oklahoma City Air Materiel Area
OCAS: Organization of Central American States
O Cat: Old Catalan
OCAW: Oil, Chemical and Atomic Workers (union)
ocb: oil circuit breaker
OCB: Officer Career Brief (DoD résumé)
oc b/l: ocean bill of lading
occ: occupation
Occ: occulting (light)
OCC: Olney Community College; Onondaga Community College; Orange Coast College
OCCA: Oil and Colour Chemists Association
occas: occasional(ly)
OCCC: Orange County Community College
OCCL: Ontario Community College Librarians
Oc C Cm O: Office of the Chief Chemical Officer
OCC-E: Office of the Chief of Communications—Electronics (USA)
occip: occipital; occiput
OCCIS: Operational Command and Control Intelligence System (USA)
OCCM: Office of Commercial Communications Management
OCCO: Office of the Chief Chemical Officer
occ th: occupational therapy
occup: occupation(al)
ocd: on-line communications driver; ovarian cholesterol depletion

OCD: Office of Civil Defense
OCDA: Ordnance Corps Detroit Arsenal
OCDE: *Organización Común Africana, Malgache y Mauriciana* (Spanish—African Common Organization including Madagascar and Mauritius); *Organización de Cooperacion y Desarrollo Económico* (Spanish—Organization of Cooperation and Economic Development)
OCDM: Office of Civil and Defense Mobilization
OCDR: Office of Collateral Development Responsibility
O/Cdt: Officer-Cadet
OCE: Office of the Chief of Engineers; Ontario College of Education
OC & E: Oregon, California, and Eastern (railroad)
OCEAN: Oceanographic Coordination Evaluation Analysis Network
OCEANAV: Oceanographer of the U.S. Navy
oceaneer(ing): ocean engineer (ing)
Ocean Inst: Oceanografiska Institute (Oceanographic Institute in Göteborg, Sweden)
oceanog: oceanography
Ocean Personified: Oceanus (Roman); Okeanos (Greek)
Ocean State: Rhode Island
OCEE: Organisation de Coopération Économique Européene (European Economic Cooperation Organization)
OCEL: *Oxford Companion to English Literature*
O Celt: Old Celtic
ocf: originally cultured formulation
OCF: Officiating Chaplain to the Forces
OC of F: Office of the Chief of Finance
ocg: omnicardiogram
och: ochre
OCHAMPUS: Office for the Civilian Health and Medical Program of the Uniformed Services
OCI: Office of the Coordinator of Information
OCL: Ocean Cargo Line; Overseas Containers Limited
OCLAE: *Organización Continental Latino-Americana de Estudiantes* (Spanish—Continental Organization of Latin American Students)
OCLC. Ohio College Library Center
o'clock: of the clock
OCM: *Oxford Companion to Music*
OCMA: Oil Companies' Material Association
OCMH: Office of the Chief of Military History
OCMS: Optional Calling Measured Service (telephone)
OCNM: Oregon Caves National Monument (limestone caverns near Medford, Oregon)
oco: open-close-open
OCO: Office of the Chief of Ordnance; Ontario College of Opthalmology; San José, Costa Rica (El Coco Airport)
o'coat: overcoat
OComS: Office of Community Services
OConUS: outside continental limits of the United States
OCORA: *Office de Coopération Radiophonique* (French—Office of Radiophonic Cooperation)—French overseas radio help for former colonies
O Corn: Old Cornish
ocp: overland common points
OCP: Office of Consumer Protection; Office of Cultural Presentations
OCPL: Oklahoma City Public Library
ocr: optical character recognition
OCR: Office of Civilian Requirements; Office of Coal Research; Office of Coordinating Responsibility; Office of the County Recorder; Organization Change Request; Organization for the Collaboration of Railways
OCRA: *Organisation Clandestine de la Révolution Algerienne* (French—Secret Organization of the Algerian Revolution)
OCRD: Office of the Chief of Research and Development
ocs: outer continental shelf
oc's: obscene (telephone) callers; obscene (telephone) calls
OCS: Office of Civilian Supply; Office of Commercial Services; Office of Contact Settlement; Officer Candidate School; Officers' Chief Steward; Outer Continental Shelf
OCS: *Organe de Controle des Stupéfiants* (French—Narcotic Drug Control Organization)
OCS': Overseas Civil Servants (members of the British Overseas Civil Service)
OC of SA: Office, Chief of Staff, Army
OCSIGO: Office of the Chief Signal Officer
ocst: overcast
oct: octagon; octane; octave; octet
Oct: October
OCT: Office of the Chief of Transportation
oct^e^: *octubre* (Spanish—October)
Octember: October and November
October: October Railway (Leningrad-Moscow); October Revolution (Bolshevik insurrection of October 1917)
October Revolution: Shostakovich's Symphony No. 2
oct. pars: *octava pars* (Latin—eighth part)
OCTU: Officer-Cadet Training Unit
octup.: *octuplus* (Latin—eightfold)
octv: open-circuit television
OCUC: Oxford and Cambridge Universities' Club
ocul.: *oculis* (Latin—to the eyes)
ocv: open-circuit voltage
OCZM: Office of Coastal Zone Management (NOAA)
od: olive-drab; optical density; outside diameter; overdose; overdrive
od: *och dylika* (Swedish—and the like)
o/d: on demand; overdraft
o & d: origin and destination
o.d.: *oculus dexter* (Latin—right eye)
Od: *Odyssey*
OD: Aerocondor (Aerovias Condor de Columbia); external grinding; officer of the day; olive drab; Ordnance Department; original design; outside dimension
O.D.: Doctor of Optometry
oda: occipito-dextra anterior
Oda: Odessa
ODa: Old Danish
ODA: Office of Debt Analysis; Office of the District Administrator; Overseas Development Administration
ODALE: Office of Drug Abuse Law Enforcement
odb: opiate-directed behavior
ODC: Old Dominion College
ODCTI: Old Dominion College Technical Institute
od'd: overdosed
odde: (Dano-Norwegian—cape; point)

ODDRE: Office of the Director of Defense Research and Engineering
ODEC: Ocean Design Engineering Corporation
ODECA: Organización de Estados Centroamericanos (Organization of Central American States)
ODECO: Ocean Drilling and Exploration Company
ODEE: *Oxford Dictionary of English Etymology*
ODESSA: *Organisation Der Ehemaligen SS Angehörigen* (German—Organization of Former Members of the SS)—device for simulating suicides and arranging new names, occupations, and countries for war criminals who served Hitler
Ode to Heavenly Joy: Mahler's Symphony No. 4 in G major
Ode to Joy: Beethoven's Symphony No. 9 in D minor—the symphony whose closing movement is based on the text of Schiller's *Ode to Joy*
Oder-Neisse Line: rivers forming boundaries between East Germany and Poland
ODF: Old Dominion Foundation
ODFI: Open Die Forging Institute
O d G: *Ordine del Giorno* (Italian—Order of the Day)
ODGSO: Office of Domestic Gold and Silver Operations
ODH: Ontario Department of Health
ODI: Open-Door International (championing economic emancipation of women workers)
o-d-ing: overdosing
O Div: Ontario Division (RCMP)
ODJB: Original Dixieland Jazz Band
o dk: orlop deck
ODL: Office of Defense Lending
ODM: Office of Defense Mobilization; Order of De Molay; Overseas Development Ministry
odn: own doppler nullifier
Odn: Odense; Odin; Odinist (member of Nordic-supremacy sect)
ODO: Outdoor Office(r)
odom: odometer
odont: odontology
odop: offset doppler
odoram.: *odoramentum* (Latin—perfume)
odorat.: *odoratus* (Latin—odorous; perfuming)
odorl: odorless
odp: occipito-dextra posterior
ODP: Orbit Determination Program
ODR: Office of Defense Resources
o'drive: overdrive
o d's: other denominations
ODS: Ocean Data Station
odsd: overseas duty selection date
ODSI: Ocean Data Systems Inc.
odt: occipito-dextra transverse
od units: optical-density units
ODWIN: Opening Doors Wider in Nursing
ODWSA: Office of the Directorate of Weapon Systems Analysis (USA)
Odysseus: (Greek—*Ulysses*)
oe: oersted; omissions expected
öe: *öesterreichisch* (German—Austrian)
Oe: oersted
OE: Office of Education; Old English; Oregon Electric (railroad)
OEA: Organización de los Estados Americanos (Organization of American States); Outdoor Education Association; Overseas Education Association
OEB: Oregon Educational Broadcasting
OEC: Österreichischer Aero-Club; Ohio Edison Company
OECD: Organization for Economic Cooperation and Development
OECE: Organisation Européenne de Cooperation Économique (Organization for European Economic Cooperation)
OECF: Overseas Economic Cooperation Fund
oeco: outboard engine cutoff
OECQ: Organisation Européene pour la Contrôle de la Qualité (European Quality-Control Organization)
OED: *Oxford English Dictionary*
OEDP: Office of Employment Development Programs
oee: outer enamel epithelium
OEEC: Organization for European Economic Cooperation
OEEO: Office of Equal Educational Opportunities
OEF: Osteopathic Educational Foundation
OEG: Operations Evaluation Group
oegt: observable evidence of good teaching
OEI: *Oficina de Educación Ibero-americana* (Spanish—Office of Ibero-American Education)
OEIU: Office Employees International Union
OEL: Organization Equipment List
oem: original equipment manufacturer
OEM: Office of Executive Management
oen: oenanthic; oenanthyl; oenolyn; oenology; oenological; oenologist; oenomancy; oenomel (wine and honey); oenometer; oenophilist; oenophobist; oenopoetic
OEO: Office of Economic Opportunity
OEOB: Old Executive Office Building (D.C.)
OEP: Office of Emergency Planning; Office of Emergency Preparedness
OEPP: Organisation Européenne et Méditerranéenne pour la Protection des Plants (European and Mediterranean Organization for the Protection of Plants)
oer: oersted (unit of magnetic force); original equipment replacement
o'er: over
OER: Office of Aerospace Research (USAF); Officer Effectiveness Report; Officer Efficiency Report; Officers Emergency Reserve; Officer Engineering Reserve; Organization for European Research
oerc: optimum earth-reentry corridor
OERPA: Office of Exploratory Research and Problem Assessment (National Science Foundation)
OERS: *Organisation Européenne de Recherches Spatiales* (French—European Space Research Organization)
OES: Office of Economic Stabilization; Official Experimental Station; Order of the Eastern Star; Organization of European States
oesbr: oil-extended styrene-butadiene rubber
oesoph: oesophagus
OESP: *O Estado de São Paulo* (State of Sao Paulo)—Brazil's leading newspaper
OESS: Office of Engineering Standards Services

OET: Office of Education and Training
OEW: Office of Economic Warfare
OEX: Office of Educational Exchange
OEZ: *osteuropäische Zeit* (German—East European Time)
of.: old face (type); optional form; outside face; oxidizing flame
o/f: oxidation/fermentation
OF: Oceanographic Facility; Odd Fellows; Old French; Operating Forces; Ophthalmological Foundation; Osteopathic Foundation; Oxbow Falls; Oxenstierna Foundation; Oxford Foundation
OFA: Office of Financial Analysis
OFAC: Owens Fine Arts Center (Dallas)
O-factor: oscillation factor
ofc: office
OFC: Overseas Food Corporation
OFCA: Ontario Federation of Construction Associations
OFCC: Office of Federal Contract Compliance
ofcl: official
OFDI: Office of Foreign Direct Investments
OFEMA: *Office Français d'Exportation de Matériel Aéronautique* (French Office for the Exportation of Aeronautical Materiel)
off.: office(r); official
offen: offensive (ammunition)
offer.: offertories; offertory
offg: offering
offic: official(ly)
OFHA: Oil Field Haulers Association
ofhc: oxygen-free high-carbon (copper)
Oflag: *Offizierlager* (German—officer's prison camp)
OFlem: Old Flemish
OFM: Office of Flight Missions (NASA)
OFPA: Order of the Founders and Patriots of America
OFPM: Office of Fiscal Plans and Management
O of R: Office for Research (ALA)
O Fr: Old French
OFR: Office of the Federal Register
OFR-ALA: Office of Recruitment—American Library Association
OFris: Old Frisian
O Frk: Old Frankish
OFS: Orange Free State
OFST: Office of the Secretary of the Air Force
OFT: Ohio Federation of Teachers
OFY: Opportunities for Youth (Canada)
og: oh gee; old girl; on ground; on guard; original gum
o-g: orange-green
OG: Old Gaelic; Olympic Games
OG: *O Globo* (Rio de Janeiro's Globe)
ÖG: Österreichische Galerie (Austrian Gallery)
O/G: Opto/Graphic
O Gael: Old Gaelic
OGAMA: Ogden Air Materiel Area
Ogasawaras: Ogasawara Islands (Bonins)
O-gauge: 1-1/4-inch track gauge (model railroads)
OGB: *Österreichischer Gewerkschaftsbund* (German—Austrian Trade Union Federation)
OGCMD: Ogden Contract Management District
Ogd: Ogdensburg
oge (OGE): operational ground equipment
OGEM: *Overzees Gas en Elektriciteit Maatschappij* (Dutch—Overseas Gas and Electric Company)
O Ger: Old German
ogg: *oggetto* (Italian—object)
OGJ: *Oil and Gas Journal*
ogl: obscure glass
OGMC: Ordnance Guided Missile Center
OGNR: Oribi Gorge Nature Reserve (South Africa)
OGO: Orbiting Geophysical Observatory
OGPU: *Obiedinennoye Gosudarstvennoye Politicheskoye Upravlenie* (Russian—United State Political Administration)—*q.v.m.*—VOT
OGR: Ontario Government Railway (Ontario Northland)
ogse: operational ground-support equipment
OGSEL: Operational Ground-Support Equipment List
o-g stain: orange-green stain
OGU: Occupational Guidance Unit
OGR: *Official Guide of the Railways*
oh.: office hours; on hand; open hearth; out home; oval head; overhead; over-the-horizon (communication)
o.h.: *omni hora* (Latin—hourly)
o-H: on-Hudson
OH: hydroxyl radical (symbol); San Francisco and Oakland Helicopter Airlines (2-letter code)
O/H: *Overzuche Handelsmaatschappij* (Dutch—Overseas Trading Company)
oha: outside helix angle
OHBMS: On Her (His) Britannic Majesty's Service
ohc: outer hair cells; overhead cam
OHC: Ottumwa Heights College; Overseas Hotel Corporation
ohd: organic hearing disease; organic heart disease; overhead drive
OHDETS: Over-Horizon Detection System
OHD & W: Outer Harbor Dock and Wharf
OHE: Office of Health Economics
O Henry: William Sydney Porter
Ohf: Omsk hemorrhagic fever
OHG: Old High German
OHG: *Offene Handelsgesellschaft* (German—ordinary partnership)
ohi: ocular hypertension indicator
OHI: Oil Heat Institute
OHIA: Oil Heat Institute of America
Ohio's Beautiful Capital: Columbus
Ohio Turn: Ohio Turnpike
Ohio Valley: Ohio, West Virginia, Kentucky, Indiana, and Illinois—all along the Ohio River starting in Pennsylvania
OHIP: Ontario Hospital Insurance Plan
ohm.: ohmmeter
ohm-cm: ohm-centimeter
OHMS: On Her (His) Majesty's Service
oho: out-of-house operation
ohp: oxygen at high pressure
OHRG: *Official Hotel and Resort Guide*
ohs: open-hearth steel
OHS: Office of Highway Safety; Ontario Humane Society; Oregon Historical Society; Overland Highway Society
OHSGT: Office of High-Speed Ground Transportation
OHSIP: Ontario Health Services Insurance Plan
ohv: overhead valve; overhead vent
ohv's: off-highway vehicles
oi: oil-immersed; oil-immersion

o-i: orgasmic impairment
o/i: opsonic index
OI: Office Instruction; Operating Instruction; Optimist International; Oriental Institute
O-I: Owens-Illinois
OIA: Ocean Industries Association; Office of Industrial Associates; Office of International Administration; Oil Import Administration; Oil Insurance Association; Outboard Industry Associations
OIAA: Office of International Aviation Affairs
OIAB: Oil Import Appeals Board
OIB: Ohio Inspection Bureau; Oklahoma Inspection Bureau
oic: oil cooler
O-i-C: Officer-in-Charge
OIC: Oceanographic Instrumentation Center; Officer in Charge; Ohio Improved Chester (white swine); Opportunities Industrialization Centers
OIC: *Organisation Internationale du Commerce* (French—International Trade Organization)
OIcel: Old Icelandic
OICS: Office of Interoceanic Canal Studies
OIE: Office of International Epizootics
OIEA: *Organismo Internacional de Energia Atómica* (Spanish—International Atomic Energy Agency)—IAEA
OIF: Office for Intellectual Freedom (ALA)
OIG: Office of the Inspector General
oih (OIH): ovulation-producing hormone
OIHP: *Office International d'Hygiene Publique* (French—International Office of Public Health)—UN
OII: Office of Invention and Innovation
OIJ: *Organisation Internationale des Journalistes* (French—International Organization of Journalists)
OIL: Operation Inspection Log
OIL: *Organizzazione Internazionale del Lavoro* (Italian—International Labor Organization)
Oil Baron: John D. Rockefeller
oil of ben: fine lubricant extracted from seeds of Arabian tree called *Moringa oleifera*
oil of cade: juniper oil
oil cake: cottonseed, linseed, or soybean mass used for cattle feed after oil is extracted
Oil Capital of Canada: Edmonton, Alberta
Oil Capital of the Rockies: Casper, Wyoming
Oil Capital of the World: Tulsa, Oklahoma
Oil Dorado: northwestern Pennsylvania in the Oil City—Titusville area
oilies: oilskin coats; oilskin garments
oil of mirbrane: nitrobenzene
Oil Province: Alberta
OILSR: Office of Interstate Land Sales Registration
oil of wintergreen: methyl salicylate
oil of vitriol: concentrated sulfuric acid (H_2SO_4)
OIM: Oriental Institute Museum (University of Chicago)
OINA: Oyster Institute of North America
OINC: Officer in Charge
oint: ointment
OIP: Operations Improvement Program
OIPC: *Organisation Internationale de Police Criminelle* (French—International Criminal Police Organization)—also known as Interpol
OIPH: Office of International Public Health
OIr: Old Irish
OIR: Office of Inter-American Radio
OIRB: Oregon Insurance Rating Bureau
OIRT: Organisation Internationale de Radiodiffusion et Télévision (International Radio and Television Organization)
OIS: Overseas Investors Services
OISA: Office of International Scientific Affairs
OISE: Ontario Institute for Studies in Education
OISTV: *Organisation Internationale pour la Science et la Technique du Vide* (French—International Organization for Vacuum Science and Technology)
OIt: Old Italian
OIT: Organic Integrity Test
OIT: *Organisation Internationale du Travail* (French); *Organización* Internacional del *Trabajo* (Spanish)—International Labor Organization also known as ILO
OITF: Office of International Trade Fairs
OIUC: Oriental Institute of the University of Chicago
OIVV: Office International de la Vigne et du Vin (International Office of Vines and Wines)
OIW: Oceanographic Institute, Wellington (New Zealand)
OIWR: Office of Indian Water Rights
oj: open-joint; open-joist(ed) orange juice
oJ: *ohne Jahr* (German—without year)—no date
OJC: *Organisation Juive de Combat* (French—Jewish Combat Organization)
OJD: Office de Justification de la Diffusion
oJr: old Jamaica rum
ojt: on-the-job-training
ok: all correct; okay; outer keel
ok: *ohne kosten* (German—without cost)
OK: all correct; okay; Old Kinderhook (birthplace and home of President Martin Van Buren; Democratic O.K. Club believed to have started practice of putting "O.K." on deals and documents they approved of); Old Kingdom (Egypt)
Ø K: *Østasiatiske Kompagni* (East Asiatic Company—Danish)
oka: otherwise known as
OKA: Okinawa, Ryukyu Islands (airport)
OKC: Oklahoma City, Oklahoma (airport)
OKd: okayed
OKH: *Oberkommando des Heeres* (German—Army High Command)
Okie: Oklahoman
Okin: Okinawa(n)
OKL: *Oberkommando der Luftwaffe* (German—Air Force High Command)
Okla: Oklahoma; Oklahoman
OklaC: Oklahoma City
OKM: *Oberkommando der Marine* (German—Naval High Command)
Okt: *Oktober* (German—October); *Oktyabr* (Russian—October)
OKT: Oslo Kommune Tunnelbanekontoret (Oslo subway system)
Oktronics: Oklahoma Electronics (corporation)
OKW: *Oberkommando der Wehrmacht (German—Armed Forces High Command)*
ol: oil level; operating license; or

less
ol.: *oleum* (Latin—oil)
o.l.: *oculus laevus* (Latin—left eye)
o/l: operations/logistics
ö L: *östlich Längengrad* (German—east longitude)
Ol: olive
OL: Olsen Line; Oranje Line (Orange Line)
ola: occipito-laeva anterior
OLA: Ontario Library Association; Osteopathic Libraries Association
OLAS: Organization of Latin American Students
OLAS: *Organización Latinoamericana de Solidaridad* (Latin American Solidarity Organization)
Olav Hunger: King Olav I of Denmark
Olav Tryggvesson: King Olav I of Norway, Sweden, and Denmark
olbm (OLBM): orbital-launched ballistic missile
OlBr: olive brown
olc: on-line computer
OLC: Oak Leaf Cluster
OLD: Office of Legislative Development
Old Abe: Abraham Lincoln
Old Ace of Spades: Lieutenant General Robert E. Lee, CSA
Old Andy: Andrew Jackson—seventh President of the United States
Old Beeswax: Captain Raphael Semmes, CSN
Old Billie: Brigadier General William Tecumseh Sherman, USA
Old Blighty: nickname for blighted London before the era of air-pollution control
Old Blood and Guts: General George S. Patton, USA
Old Buena Vista: General Zachary Taylor who attacked Mexicans at Buena Vista in February 1847; later was twelfth President of the United States
Old Cape Stiff: Cape Horn
Old Castile: old Spanish province of Castilla la Vieja
Old Chapultepec: General Winfield Scott whose victory at Chapultepec ended Mexican War in September 1847
Old Colony: Massachusetts—founded in 1620
Old Denmark: General Christian Febiger, USA
Old Dirigo: Maine whose state motto is *Dirigo* (Latin—I direct)
Old Dominion: Virginia—oldest English colony in America—founded in 1607
Oldest City in North America: Mexico City built by the Aztecs in 1325
Oldest and Quaintest City in the United States: Santa Fé, New Mexico
old-fash: old-fashioned
Oldfos: Old Established Forces
Old French Town: New Orleans
Old Fuss and Feathers: General Winfield Scott, USA
Old Glory: the American Flag
Old Greasy: West Virginian nickname for the Kanawha River or K'naw
Old Guard: conservatives; Napoleon's imperial guard who made the last charge at Waterloo; the establishment
Old Harry: (the devil)—Satan
Old Hickory: General Andrew Jackson—seventh President of the United States
Old Ironsides: USS *Constitution*
Old Jeb: Major General J(ames) E(well) B(rown) Stuart, CSA
Old Kinderhook: Martin Van Buren—eighth President of the United States
Old Lady: the boss; mother; wife
Old Lady of the Thames: London
Old Lady of Threadneedle Street: Bank of England
Old Legal Lion: Clarence Darrow
Old Line State: Maryland
Old Man: the boss; the captain; father; the skipper
Old Man Eloquent: Isocrates in the opinion of Milton, John Quincy Adams in the opinion of the Congress he served after being sixth President of the U.S.
Old Man of Ferney: Voltaire who lived in Ferney, France
Old Man of the Mountain: New Hampshire's Profile Mountain—the Great Stone Face
Old Man River: the Mississippi
Old Nick: (the devil)—Satan
Old Noll: Old Oliver Cromwell
Old North State: North Carolina's official nickname
Old Ossawatomie: John Brown
Old Pam: Lord Palmerston (Henry John Temple)
Old Party: W(illiam) Somerset Maugham
Old Peg Leg: Petrus Stuyvesant—director-general of New Amsterdam and the New Netherlands
Old Point: Old Point Comfort, Virginia
old pro(s): old professional(s)
old rep: old repertory; old reprobate
Old Rough-and-Ready: General Zachary Taylor—twelfth President of the United States
Olds: Oldsmobile
OLDS: On-Line Display System
Old Sarum: Salisbury, England
Old Scratch: Satan
Old Sol: the sun (*see* Sun God)
Old South: southern United States before 1865
Old Swamp Fox: Brigadier General Francis Marion, USA
Old Tecumseh: General William Tecumseh Sherman, USA
Old Test.: Old Testament
Old Three Stars: General U.S. Grant, USA
Old Tippecanoe: General William Henry Harrison—ninth President of the United States
Old Vic: repertory theater in London
Old Viking: Norwegian-American able seaman and labor leader Andrew Furuseth
Old World: Africa, Asia, and Europe
Old Zach: Zachary Taylor—12th President of the United States
Ole: Olaf(sen); Olav(sen)
OLE: Office of Library Education (American Library Association)
OLEA: Office of Law Enforcement Assistance
Oleander City by the Sea: Galveston, Texas
Ole Miss: Old Mississippi (The University of Mississippi)
oleo: oleomargarine; oleoresins; oleum
OLEP: Office of Law Enforcement and Planning
olericult: olericulture
'oleum: petroleum
O-levels: ordinary levels (of educational tests)
olf: olfactory
OLF: Orbital Launch Facility
OlG: olive green
OLG: Old Low German
O-license: operator's license
Olig: Oligocene
Oliver Optic: pseudonym of William Taylor Adams
OLL: Office of Legislative Liaison
Ollie: Olive(r)
olmr (OLMR): organic liquid-moderated reactor
olp: occipito-laeva posterior

OLPR: Office for Library Personnel Resources (ALA)
OLPS: On-Line Programming System
olq: officer-like qualities
olr: overload relay
OLRB: Ontario Labor Relations Board
ol res: oleoresin
olrt: on-line real time
ol's: office ladies (divorces and spinsters); old girls
OLS: Optical Landing System
OLSD: Office for Library Service to the Disadvantaged (ALA)
olt: occipito-laeva transverse
ol & t: owners, landlords, and tenants
olv: olivaceous; olive
Oly: Olympia; Olympic
Olym: Olympia
Olympics: Olympic Games; Olympic Mountains, Washington
om: old measurement; old man; old men; outer marker
o.m.: *omni mane* (Latin—every morning)
o & m (O & M): operation and maintenance
Om: Omaha; Oman
OM: Old Man (colloquial)
OM: *Ostmark* (East German mark)
O.M.: Order of Merit
O & M: Organization and Methods
OMA: Office of Maritime Affairs; Oklahoma Military Academy; Omaha, Nebraska (airport); Ontario Medical Association
OMAI: *Organisation Mondiale Agudas Israel* (French—Agudas Israel International Organization)
omarb: *omarbetad* (Swedish—revised)
OMARS: Outstanding Media Advertising by Restaurants
Omar Sharif: Omar Cherif
OMAT: Office of Manpower, Automation, and Training
Omb: Ombudsman
OMB: Office of Management and Budget: Ontario Municipal Board
OMBE: Office of Minority Business Enterprise
OMC: Office of Munitions Control; Outboard Marine Corporation
'ome: (Cockney contraction—home)
OME: Office of Minerals Exploration
OMEL: Orient Mid-East Lines
O-Mess: Officer's Mess
omfp: obtaining money by false pretenses
OMGE: Organisation Mondiale de Gastro-Entérologie (World Gastro-Enterological Organization)
OMGUS: Office of Military Government, United States
OMI: Operation Move-In
O.M.I.: Oblate of Mary Immaculate
OMII: Oxy Metal Industries International
omiom: original meaning is the only meaning
omkr: *omdring* (Norwegian—about)
oml: outside mold line
OML: Ontario Motor League; Orbiting Military Laboratory
OMM: Office of Minerals Mobilization, Organisation Météorologique Mondiale; Organisation Mondiale de la Santé (World Health Organization)
OMM: *Organización Meteorológica Mundial* (Spanish—World Meteorological Organization)—WMO
OMMA: Outboard Motor Manufacturers Association
OMMS: Office of Merchant Marine Safety (USCG)
omn. bih.: *omni bihora* (Latin—every two hours)
omn. hor.: *omni hora* (L atin—every hour)
omni: omnidirectional; omnirange; omnivisual
omn. man.: *omni mane* (Latin—every morning)
omn. noct.: *omni nocte* (Latin—every night)
omn. quad. hor.: *omni quadrante hora* (Latin—every quarter of an hour)
OMPER: Office of Manpower Policy Evaluation and Research
ompf: omphaloskepsis
OMR: Officer Master Record
oms: output per man shift
OMS: *Organisation Mondiale de la Santé* (French); *Organización Mundial de la Salud* (Spanish)—World Health Organization—WHO
OMSA: Orders and Medals Society of America
OMSF: Office of Manned Space Flight (NASA)
OMSIP: Ontario Medical Surgical Insurance Plan
OMT: Old Merchant Taylors
OMTS: Organizational Maintenance Test Station
on.: octane number
on.: *onomastikon* (Greek—lexicon)
o.n.: *omni nocte* (Latin—every night)
On: *Onorevole* (Italian—Honorable); *Onsdag* (Danish—Wednesday)
ON: Ogden Nash; Old Norse
ÖN: Österreichische Nationalbibliotek (Austrian National Library)
O.N.: Orthopedic Nurse
O & N: Oregon & Northeastern (railroad)
ona: optical navigation attachment
ONA: Office of Noise Abatement; Overseas National Airways; Overseas News Agency
ONAC: Office of Noise Abatement and Control
ONAP: Orbit Navigation Analysis Program
on approv: on approval
onbep: *onbepaald* (Dutch—indefinite)
onc: operational navigational chart(s)
ONC: Oficina Nacional del Café (National Coffee Administration—Honduras); Oregon-Nevada-California (fast freight truck line)
oncol: oncology
OND: Opthalmic Nursing Diploma
ONEO: Office of Navajo Economic Opportunity
ONERA: Office National des Etudes et des Recherches *Aérospatiales (French space research agency)*
ONF: Old Norman-French
onfm: on nearest full moon
ong: *ongaku* (Japanese—music); *ongeveer* (Dutch—about; approximately; roughly)
ONG: *Organisation Non-Gouvernementale* (French—Non-Governmental Organization)
ONI: Office of Naval Intelligence
Only Town in the U.S. with an Apostrophe in Its Name: Coeur d'Alene, Idaho
ONM: Ocmulgee National Monument; Office of Naval Materiel
ONNI: Office of National Narcotics Intelligence
onnm: on nearest new moon

ono: or near offer
ONO: *Oesnoroeste* (Spanish—west northwest); *oost noord oost* (Dutch—east northeast)
onomast: onomastic(al)(ly); onomastics; onomatologist; onomatology
onomat: onomatopoeia
O Nor: Old Norwegian
O North: Old Northumbrian
o noz: oil nozzle
onp: operating nursing procedure
ONP: Olympic National Park (Washington)
ONR: Office of Naval Research
ONRL: Office of Naval Records and Library
ONRRR: Office of Naval Research Resident Representative
ON Rwy: Ontario Northland Railway
ONSR: Ozark National Scenic Riverways (Missouri)
ont: ontology
Ont: Ontario
ONT: Our New Thread (Clark's trademark)
ONTC: Ontario Northland Transportation Commission
Ont Pen: Ontario Penitentiary
Ont Sci Cen: Ontario Science Center
ONU: Organisation Nations Unies (French—United Nations Organization); Organización de las Naciones Unidas (Spanish—United Nations Organization)—UNO; Organizzazione Nazioni Unite (Italian—United Nations Organization)
ONUC: Operation des Nations Unies, Congo (United Nations Operation in the Congo)
ONUESC: Organisation des Nations Unies pour l'Education, la Science et la Culture Intellectuelle (UNESCO)
ONULP: Ontario New Universities Library Project
on w: *onovergankelijk werkwoord* (Dutch—intransitive verb)
ONWR: Okefinokee National Wildlife Refuge (Florida and Georgia); Ottawa National Wildlife Refuge (Ohio); Ouray National Wildlife Refuge (Utah)
ony: onymous (opposite of anonymous)
onyx marble: alabaster
o-and-o: one-and-only
o/o: on order
oo (OO): office of origin
OO: Oceanic Operators; Oceanographic Office
O/O: Office of Oceanogrphy (UNESCO)
O of O: Order of Owls
OOA: Office of Ocean Affairs
OOAA: Olive Oil Association of America
OOAMA: Ogden Air Materiel Area
oob: out of bed
o-o B: off-off Broadway
oobe: out of body experience
OoC: Office of Censorship
OOD: Officer of the Day; Officer of the Deck
Oody: Eunice
OO/Eng: out of stock but on order from England (for example)
OOG: Office of Oil and Gas; Officer of the Guard
OOHA: Operation Oil Heat Associates
ooj: obstruction of justice
ool: oology; operator-oriented language
OOL: Orient Overseas Line
oolr: opthalmology, otology, laryngology, rhinology
OOM: Officers Open Mess
Oom Paul: (Afrikaans—Uncle Paul)—sobriquet of Stephanus Johannes Paulus Kruger—leader of Boer rebellion and president of Transvaal
o/o/o: out of order
OOO-gauge: + -inch track gauge (model railroads)
oop: out of pocket (expenses); out of print (book)
OOP: Oceanographic Observations of the Pacific
oops: offshore oil-pollution sleeve
OOQ: Officer of the Quarters
OOR: Office of Ordnance Research
oos: orbit-to-orbit shuttle
o & o's: owned and operated (tv broadcast) stations (controlled by a network)
OOSC: Olfactronics and Odor Sciences Center (IITRI)
oost: (Dutch—east)
oot: out of town
oote: out-of-town executive
ootg: one of the greats
Ooty: Ootacamund, Madras
OOW: Officer On Watch
op: open policy; opera; operation; operational; operation plan(s); operational priority; operetta; opposite prompt (stage left); opus; other people's (possessions); outer panel; out of print; outside production; overproof; overprune; overpuff
Op: optical art (art accented with or based on optical illusions); Oregon pine
OP: Observation Post; Office of Protocol (US Department of State); Oregon pine
O.P.: *Optimus Maximus* (Latin—supreme and best)—Jupiter's title as he was believed to be the king of the gods and the ruler of all rulers
O-P: Oppenheimer-Phillips (process)
opa: optical plotting attachment
OPA: Office of Population Affairs; Office of Price Administration; Office of Public Affairs
opal: hydrous silica ($SiO_2 .nH_2O$)
opal.: optical platform alignment linkage
op amp: operational amplifier
OPANAL: *Organismo para la Proscripción de las Armas Nucleares en la América Latina* (Spanish—Organization for the Prohibition of Nuclear Weapons in Latin America)
op art: optical art (art involving optical illusion)
OPBMA: Ocean Pearl Button Manufacturers Association
opc: office percentage
OPC: Ohio Power Company; Out-Patient Clinic; Overseas Press Club
OPCA: Overseas Press Club of America
op. cit.: *opere citato* (Latin—in the work cited); *opus citato* (Latin—in the work cited)
OPCNM: Organ Pipe Cactus National Monument
op code: operation code (data processing)
OPCS: Office of Population Censuses and Surveys
opd: optical path difference
OPD: Officer Personnel Directorate; Out Patient Department
opdar: optical direction and ranging
OPDD: Operational Plan Data Document
op dent: operative dentistry
OPDR: Oldenburg - Portugiesische - Dampfschifs - Reiderei (steamship company)
ope: open-point expanding
OPE: Office of Planning and Evaluation (FBI)
O P & E: Oregon, Pacific & East-

ern (railroad)
OPEC: Organization of Petroleum Exporting Countries
op ed: opposite the editorials (newspaper page usually reserved for readers' letters and syndicated columns)
open.: open circuit; opening
Opener of Japan: Commodore Matthew Calbraith Perry, USN
opens.: open circuits (electrical parlance); openings
opep (OPEP): orbital plane experiment package
OPEP: *Organisations des Pays Exportateurs de Pétrole* (French—Organization of Petroleum Exporting Countries)
oper: operational
O Per: Old Persian
Opéra-Com: Opéra-Comique (Paris)
Operation Keelhaul: Allied policy of forcing escaping anti-communists to return to their communist masters
OPers: Old Persian
opex: operational (and) executive (personnel)
OPEX: Operational, Executive (and Administrative Personnel Program of the United Nations)
opg: opening
OPG: Overseas Project Group
oph: ophicleide; ophthalmologist; ophthalmology; ophthalmoscope; ophthalmoscopic
Oph.D.: Doctor of Ophthalmology
ophth: opthalmologist; opthalmology
OPIC: Overseas Private Investment Corporation
opis: opisometer
Opium Eater: Thomas De Quincey
Opium's Golden Triangle: opium-growing fields between borders of Cambodia, Laos, and Vietnam
opl: operational
opl: *oplag* (Danish—edition)
OPL: Omaha Public Library; Orlando Public Library; Ottawa Public Library
OPLP: Office of Program and Legislative Planning
opm: operations per minute; operator programming method; optically-projected map; other people's money
OPM: Office of Production Management
OPMAC: Operation for Military Aid to the Community
opn: operation
o.p.n.: *ora pro nobis* (Latin—pray for us)
OpNav: Office of the Chief of Naval Operations
opng: opening
Op. no.: opus number
opo: one price only
Opo: Oporto
OPO: Office of Personnel Operations (US Army)
O Pol: Old Polish
OPOR: Office of Public Opinion Research
opord: operation(s) order
O por O: *Ojo por Ojo* (Spanish—Eye for an Eye)—Guatemalan right-wing terrorists
O Port: Old Portuguese
opp: opportunity; opposed; opposite; opposition; out of print at present
OPP: Ontario Provincial Police
Oppenheim's disease: congenital lack of muscular development of the ankles and feet
opplan: operating plan
oppor: opportunity
oppy: opportunity
Oppy: Oppenheimer(er)
opr: operate; operator
OPr: Old Provençal
OPR: Office of Population Research (Princeton); Office of Primary Responsibility
opr's: old prices riots
OPruss: Old Prussian
ops: operations; opposite prompter's side (of stage)
op's: other people's (cigarettes or money)
OPS: Office of Price Stabilization; Oxygen Purge System
OPS: *Organisation Panaméricaine de la Santé* (French—Pan-American Health Organization) *Organización Panamericana de la Salud* (Spanish—Pan-American Health Organization)
ops analysis: operations analysis
opt: optic; optical; optician; optics; optimal; optimum; option; optional
OPTA: Organ and Piano Teachers Association
Opt.D.: Doctor of Optometry
OPTEVFOR: Operational Test and Evaluation Force
opthal: opthalmic; opthalmologist; opthalmology
opti: optimist(ic); optimize; optimum
opticon: optical tactical converter
optmrst: optometrist
optn: optician
optoel: optoelectronics
optom: optometrist; optometry
optr: optryk (Dano-Norwegian—reprint)
opur: objective program utility routines
OPUS: Older People United for Service
opv: oral polio virus
oq: oil quench; overmation quotient
OQ: Officers Quarters
oqe: objective quality evidence
OQMG: Office of the Quartermaster General
OQR: Officer's Qualification Record
or.: operationally ready; other ranks; out of range; outside radius; outside right; overseas replacement; owner's risk; oxidation-reduction
or.: *oratio* (Latin—speech; discourse)
o & r: ocean and rail; overhaul and repair
or. (OR): orienting reflex
OR: Officer Records; omnidirectional radio range (symbol); Operating Room; Operational Requirement; Operations Requirement; Operations Research; Operations Room; Ordnance Report; Owasco River (railroad); Oyster River
OR: *Operations Research*
O.R.: Operating Room (hospital abbreviation)
ÖR: Österreichischer Rundfunk (Austrian Radio and Television)
ORA: Oil Refiners Association; Operations Research Analyst
ORACLE: Optimum Record Automation for Courts and Law Enforcement (Los Angeles, CA.)
ORAD: Office of Rural Areas Development
orang: orangutan
Orange Blossom: Florida's state flower
orange flag: potential danger signal
orange light: change approaching; potential danger
Orange State: California, Florida, and Texas claim this title
orat: oration; orator; oratorio; oratory
ORAU: Oak Ridge Associated Universities
o-r-b: owner's risk of breakage
orb. (ORB): oceanographic re-

search buoy
orbic: orbicular; orbicularis
Orbis: Polish Travel Office
ORBIT: On-line Retrieval of Bibliographic Information
ORBS: Orbital Rendezvous Base System
Orc: Orcadian (inhabitant of or pertaining to Orkney Islands)
ORC: Officers Reserve Corps; Opinion Research Corporation; Ozarks Regional Commission
ORCA: Ocean Resources Conservation Association
ORCB: Order of Railway Conductors and Brakemen
orch: orchestra; orchestral; orchestration
Orch: Orchard (postal abbreviation easily confused with Orchestra)—when in doubt, spell it out
Orchard City: Burlington, Iowa also called Porkopolis of Iowa
Orch Consv: *Orchestre de la Société des Concerts du Conservatoire de Paris*
orches: orchestration
Orch H: Orchestra Hall
Orchid Capital of Hawaii: Hilo
Orch Nat: *Orchestre National de la Radiodiffusion Française*
Orch de l'Opera de Paris: *Orchestre du Théâtre National de l'Opera de Paris*
Orch Suisse Rom: *Orchestré de la Suisse Romande*
ORCMD: Orlando Contract Management District
orcon: organic control
ord: order(s); ordinal; ordnance
o-r-d: owner's risk of damage
Ord: Order; Orderly; Ordinary Seaman
ORD: Chicago, Illinois (O'Hare Airport); Office of Research and Development
ORDA: Oceanographic Research for Defense Application
ORD-ALA: Office of Research and Development—American Library Association
Ord Bd: Ordnance Board
OrdC: Ordnance Corps
Ord Dept: Ordnance Department
ordn: ordnance
Ord Sgt: Ordnance Sergeant
Ordo: Ordovician
ORE: Ocean Research Equipment; Operational Research Establishment
OR & E: Office of Research and Engineering
Oreg: Oregon; Oregonian
Oregon Grape: state flower of Oregon
Ore-Ida pots: Oregon-Idaho potatoes
o/r enema: oil-retention enema
ORESCO: Overseas Research Council
orf: orifice
o-r-f: owner's risk of fire
ORF: Norfolk, Virginia (airport)
ÖRF: *Österreichischer Rundfunk* (Austrian radio and TV network)
Or F S: Orange Free State
org: organ; organic; organization; organize; organizer
ORG: Operations Research Group
organ.: organic; organization
Organ: Saint-Saëns Symphony No. 3 for orchestra and organ
org art: organic art(ist)
Orgburo: Organizational Bureau of the Central Committee (of the Communist Party)
orgl: organizational
org-man: organization man
orgn: organization
orgst: organist
ori: orientation inventory
Ori: Oriente
ORI: Ocean Research Institute; Ocean Resources Institute; Operation Readiness Inspection
orient.: oriental; orientation
Orient(al): Asia(tic)
ORIENT: Orient Airways
oriental amethyst: purple corundum
oriental emerald: green corundum
Oriental Republic: Eastern Republic of Uruguay *(República Oriental del Uruguay)*
oriental topaz: yellow corundum
orif: open reduction with internal fixation
orig: origin; original; originator
Original Glamour Girl: Theda Bara (Theodosia Goodman) also called Queen of the Vampires in the early days of American motion pictures
O-ring: O-shaped ring
Orinoco River City: Ciudad Bolivar, Venezuela
Oriole: Maryland's state bird and symbolic nickname of Marylanders—Orioles
ORINS: Oak Ridge Institute of Nuclear Studies
oris: orismological; orismologist; orismology
ORIT: Operational Readiness Inspection Test
or j: orange juice
Ork: Orkney Islands
Orkneys: Orkney Islands
orl: orlon (synthetic fiber)
o-e-l: owner's risk of leakage
ORL: Orbital Research Laboratory; Ordnance Research Laboratory; Orlando, Florida (Harndon Airport)
ORM: Ohio Reformatory for Men
orn: orange; ornament
Orn: Oran (British maritime contraction)
orn: *orne* (French—decorated; ornamented)
ORN: Operating Room Nurse
ornith: ornithology
ORNL: Oak Ridge National Laboratory
ORO: Operations Research Office (Johns Hopkins University)
or. obliq.: *oratio obliqua* (Latin—indirect speech; oblique speech)
orog: orographer; orographic; orographical; orography
ORP: *Okret Rzecypospolitej Polskiej* (Polish—Ship of the Polish Republic)
orph: orphan; orphanage; orphaned; orphans
orpiment: arsenic sulfide
o-r pot.: oxidation-reduction potential
orr: operations research research (ORR)
o-r-r: owner's risk rates
o-r release: own-recognizance release (legal device freeing responsible citizens from need for going to jail or posting bail bond until case comes to court for hearing)
ORRRC: Outdoor Recreation Resources Review Commission
ors: owner's risk of shifting
ors.: *orationes* (Latin — speeches)
ors (ORS): orthopaedic surgery
ORS: Old Red Sandstone; Operational Research Society
ORSA: Operations Research Society of America
ORSANCO: Ohio River Valley Water Sanitation Commission
ORSTOM: Office de la Recherche Scientifique et Technique d'Outre Mer (Overseas Office of Scientific and Technical Research)
ort: operational readiness training
ORT: Operational Readiness Test; Order of Railroad Tele-

graphers; Organization for Rehabilitation through Training; Overage Retirement Training (program)
ORTF: *Office de Radiodiffusion Telévision Française* (French Office of Television Broadcasting)
ortho: orthochromatic; orthographic; orthography; orthopedic(s)
Ortho: Greek Orthodox
orthog: orthography
orthop: orthopedics
orthor: orthorhombic
ORTO: Occupational Rehabilitation Training for Overseas
ORTPA: Oven-Ready Turkey Producers' Association
ORTU: Other Ranks Training Unit
ORU: Oral Roberts University
ORuss: Old Russian
ORV: Ocean Range Vessel (naval symbol)
orw: owner's risk of wetting
ORW: Ohio Reformatory for Women
ORY: Paris, France (Orly Airport)
os: oil switch; old series; old style; on station; out of stock; output secondary; outside; outsize; overseas; oversize
os (OS): operating system (data recording)
o/s: out of service
os: (Latin—bone; mouth)
o.s.: *oculus sinister* (Latin—left eye)
Os: osmium
03 OS: Ocean Station; Old Saxon; Old Series; Operation Sandstone; Operation Snapper; Ordinary Seaman; Ordnance Specifications; Optical Society
O.S.: Old Style
Osa: Osaka
OSA: Office of the Secretary of the Army; Official Secrets Act; Omnibus Society of America; Optical Society of America; Osaka, Japan (airport); Overseas Supply Agency; Oyster Shell Association
OSAF: Office of the Secretary of the Air Force
OSAP: Ontario Student Awards Program
OSAS: Overseas Service Aid Scheme
O Sax: Old Saxon
O.S.B.: Order of St Benedict
OSBA: Ohio School Boards Association
OSBM: Office of Space Biology and Medicine
osc: oscillator
Osc: Oscan
OSC: On-Scene Commander; Ontario Securities Commission; Ordnance Systems Command (formerly Bureau of Weapons); Overseas Shipping Company
O.S.C.: Oblate of Saint Charles
O of SC: Order of Scottish Clans
OSCA: Office of Senior Citizens Affairs
OSCA: *Officine Specializzate Costruzione Automobili* (Italian—Special Office of Automobile Construction)
O Scan: Old Scandinavian
oscar: orbital-satellite-carrying amateur radio; oxygen steelmaking computer and recorder
Oscar: code for letter O
oscp: oscilloscope
osd: on-line systems driver
o s & d: over, short, and damaged
OSD: Office of the Secretary of Defense; Operational Support Directive; Ordnance Supply Depot
osdp: on-site data processing
ose: operational support equipment
OS & E: Ocean Science and Engineering
o'seas: overseas
OSerb: Old Serbian
OSFI: Open Steel Flooring Institute
O.S.F.S.: Oblate of Saint Francis of Sales
OSG: Office of Sea Grant (NOAA): Office of the Secretary General (UN)
OSG: *Official Steamship Guide*
Osh: Ossian
o.s.h.: *omni singula hora* (Latin—every hour)
OSHA: Occupational Safety and Health Act: Occupational Safety and Health Administration
OSHRC: Occupational Safety and Health Review Commission
OSHS: Occupational Safety and Health Scheme
OSI: Office of Special Investigation (USAF)
OSIA: Order of the Sons of Italy in America
OSIS: Office of Science Information Service
Osk: Oskarshamm
OSK: Osaka Syosen Kaisha (Osaka Mercantile Steamship Company)
Osl: Oslo
OSl: Old Slavonic
OSL: Oslo, Norway (airport)
OSLat: Old-Style Latin
Osloenser: native of Oslo
osm: osmosis; osmotic
Osm: osmol(s)
OSM: One of the Swinish Multitude (Philip Freneau, poet of the American Revolution, used this three-letter device after his name, thereby deriding similar-looking British titles)
OSM: *Overzees Scheepvaart Maatschappii* (Overseas Shipping Company)
OSMM: Office of Safeguards and Materials Management (AEC)
OSN: Office of the Secretary of the Navy
OSN: *Orquesta Sinfónica Nacional* (Spanish—National Symphonic Orchestra)
OSNC: Orient Steam Navigation Company
OSNY: Oratorio Society of New York
oso (OSO): orbiting solar observatory
OSO: Omaha Symphony Orchestra; Oregon Symphony Orchestra
OSO: *Oessudoeste* (Spanish—west southwest); Orbiting Solar Observatory; Ordnance Supply Office
OSODS: Office of Strategic Offensive and Defensive Systems (USN)
osp: outside purchased
o.s.p.: *obiit sine prole* (Latin—died without issue)
OSp: Old Spanish
OSP: *Oficina Sanitaria Panamericana* (Pan-American Sanitation Office)
OSPA: Overseas Pensioners' Association
OSPA: *Organisation de la Santé Panaméricaine* (French—Pan-American Health Organization)
OSPAAL: *Organización de Solidaridad de los Pueblos de Asia, Africa, y Latino-América* (Spanish—Organization of Solidarity of the Peoples of Asia, Africa, and Latin America)—communist directed and inspired
OSPIC: Overseas Private Investment Corporation

OSQ: *Orchestre Symphonique de Québec* (French—Quebec Symphonic Orchestra)
OSR: Office of Scientific Research; Office of Security Review; Operational Support Requirement(s); Orchestre de la Suisse Romande (Orchestra of French Switzerland); Oversea Returnee
OSRB: Overseas Service Resettlement Bureau
OSRD: Office of Scientific Research and Development; Office of Standard Reference Data
OSRO: Office of Scientific Research and Development
OSRTN: Office of the Special Representative for Trade Negotiations
oss(OSS): orbiting space station
OSS: Orbital Space Station; Office of Strategic Services; old submarine (3-letter code)
OSSA: Office of Space Sciences and Applications (NASA)
Ossie: Oswaldtwistle, England
OSSS: Orbital Space Station Studies
OSSTF: Ontario Secondary School Teachers Federation
ost: oldest; ordinary spring tides
OST: Office of Science and Technology; Old Spanish Trail (US 90); Operational Suitability Test
OS & T: Office of Science and Technology
osteo: osteopath(ic)
osteoart: osteoarthritic; osteoarthritis
osteol: osteology
osteomy: osteomyelitis
osteop: osteopath(ic); osteopathy
OSTF: Operational System Test Facility
OSTI: Office for Scientific and Technical Information
OSTIV: *Organisation Scientifique et Technique Internationale du Vol à Voile* (French—International Scientific and Technical Organization for Soaring Flight)
O.St.J.: Officer of the Order of Saint John of Jerusalem
Ostpr: *Ostpreussen* (German—East Prussia)
OSTS: Office of State Technical Services; Official Seed Testing Station
OSU: Ohio State University; Oklahoma State University; Oregon State University
OSUK: Ophthalmological Society of the United Kingdom
OSUL: Ohio State University Library; Oklahoma State University Library; Oregon State University Library
osv: *och sa vida* (Swedish—and so forth); *og sa videre* (Dano-Norwegian—and so forth)—etc.
Osv: Osvald; Osvaldo
OSV: Ocean Station Vessel
Osv Rom: *Osservatore Romano* (Vatican newspaper)
Osw: Oswald
OSw: Old Swedish
OSW: Office of Saline Water
os & y: outside screw and yolk
ot: observer target; oiltight; old terms; old tuberculin; on time; on track; otitis; otology
ot (OT): occupational therapy; otolaryngology; overtime
o't: (Gaelic contraction—of it)
o/t: overtime
o-T: on-Thames
OT: Occupational Therapist; Occupational Therapy; Ocean Transportation; Office of Territories; Old Testament; Operational Training; Oregon Trunk (railroad); Organization Table; Otis Elevator (stock exchange symbol); Overseas Tankship (Caltex Line)
OT: *Organisation Todt* (German—Death Organization)—Hitler's extermination corps
OTAC: Ordnance Tank and Automotive Command
OTAG: Office of the Adjutant General (USA)
OTAN: *Organisation du Traite del l'Atlantique Nord* (French—NATO); *Organizacion del Tratado del Atlántico Norte* (Spanish—NATO)—North Atlantic Treaty Organization
OTAS: *Organización del Atlántico Septentrional* (Spanish—North Atlantic Treaty Organization)—NATO
OTASE: Organisation du Traite de l'Asie du Sud-Est (SEATO)
OTAT: Orthotoluidine Arsenite Test
OTATO: One-Trip Air Travel Orders
otb: off-track betting
otbd: outboard
otc: over the counter
OTC: Officer in Tactical Command; Organization for Trade Cooperation; Ottawa Transit Commission
OTC: *Office de Tourisme du Canada* (French—Canadian Government Office of Tourism)
otd: organ tolerance dose
OTD & SP: Office of Technical Data and Standardization Policy
ote: *oriente* (Spanish—east)
OTeut: Old Teutonic
OTF: Ontario Teachers Federation
Oth: *Othello, The Moor of Venice*
oti: official test insecticide
OTI: Oregon Technical Institute
OTIA: Ordnance Technical Intelligence Agency
OTIS: Occupational Training Information System; Oregon Total Information System
otj: on the job
otK: old tuberculin Koch
otl: output transformerless; out to lunch
OTM: Office of Telecommunications Management
oto: one time only (tv)
o-to-o: out-to-out
otol: otology
otolaryngol: otolaryngology
Ottoman Empire: Turkish Empire
OTO/Neth: only to order from Netherlands (for example)
otorhinol: otorhinolaryngology
otp: obstacle to progress; oxygen tanking panel
OTP: Office of Telecommunications Policy
otr: on the rag (underground slang—on the menstrual cycle)
OTR: Registered Occupational Therapist
OTRACO: *Office de l'Exploitation des Transports Coloniaux* (Congolese railway and river transportation administration)
otran: ocean test range and instrumentation
OTS: Office of Technical Services; Officers Training School
OTSG: Office of the Surgeon General
ott: one-time tape; otter; outgoing teletype
ott: *ottobre* (Italian—October)
Ott: Ottawa
otu (OTU): operational training unit
OTU: Office of Technology Utilization (NASA)
O Turk: Old Turkish
OTUS: Office of the Treasurer of the United States

ou: oat unit; official use
'ou: thou
o.u.: *oculus uterque* (Latin—either eye)
o & u: over and under
OU: Oglethorpe University; Ohio University; Ottawa University; Otterbein University; Owen University; Owosso University; Oxford University
OUA: Order of United Americans
OUA: *Organisation de l'Unité Africaine* (French—OAU); *Organización de Unidad Africana* (Spanish—OAU)—Organization of African Unity
OUAC: Oxford University Appointments Committee; Oxford University Athletic Club
OUAFC: Oxford University Association Football Club
OUAM: Order of United American Mechanics
OUAS: Oxford University Air Squadron
OUBC: Oxford University Boat Club
OUCC: Oxford University Cricket Club
OUDS: Oxford University Dramatic Society
OUCC: Oxford University Cricket Club
Ouga: Ougadougou, Upper Volta
OUGC: Oxford University Golf Club
oughtn't: ought not
OUHC: Oxford University Hockey Club
OUHS: Oxford University Historical Society
Ouida: pseudonym of Marie Louise de la Ramée who as a child pronounced Louise as Ouida
OULC: Oxford University Lacrosse Club
OULCS: Ontario Universities Library Cooperative System
OULTC: Oxford University Lawn Tennis Club
OUM: Oxford University Mission
OUN: *Organizatsia Ukrainiskikh Nationalistiv* (Russian—Ukrainian Nationalist Organization)—anti-communist
OUP: Oxford University Press
oupt: output
OURC: Oxford University Rifle Club
OURFC: Oxford University Rugby Football Club
Our Lady of the Snows: Kipling's nickname for Canada
OUSC: Oxford University Swimming Club
OUSF: Oxford University School of Forestry
o/US: *oro US* (Spanish—American gold; American money)
out.: outlet
outbd: outboard
Outer China: Mongolia, Sinkiang, Tibet
Outer Ring: sections of counties surrounding London, England
out of sync: out of synchronization
Outpost of the West: the Philippines
ouv: *ouvrage* (French—work)
ov: orbiting vehicle (OV); over
ov: *oi vay* (Yiddish—alas)
ov.: *ovum* (Latin—egg)
Ov: Ovid; Oviedo
OV: *Oranje Vrystaat* (Afrikaans—Orange Free State); Orbital Vehicle
Österreichische Volkspartei (German—Austrian People's Party)
o^{va}***:*** *ottava* (Italian—octave)
OVA: Office of Veterans' Affairs
OVAC: Overseas Visual Aids Center
ovbd: overboard
ovc: other valuable consideration(s); overcast
ovcst: overcast
ove: on vehicle equipment
over.: overture
overmation: over instrumentation
overs: overshoes
ovfl: overflow
ovh: overhead
ovhd: oval head; overhead
ovhl: overhaul
ovh p: overhead projector
ovh: overheat
Ovid: Roman poet Publius Ovidus Naso
ovk: overkill
OVKOT: *On Various Kinds of Thinking* (essay by James Harvey Robinson)
ovld: overload
ovm: on-vehicle material
ovm: *oi vayz mir* (Yiddish—woe unto me)
ovpd: overpaid
OVR: Office of Vocational Rehabilitation
OVRA: Opera Voluntaria per la Repressione dell' Anti-fascismo (Italian—Voluntary Work for the Repression of Anti-Fascism)—Facist secret police
ovrd: override
ovsp: overspeed
OVSVA: *Oranje Vrystaatse Veld Artillerie* (Afrikaans—Orange Free State Field Artillery)
ov w: *overgankelijk werkwoord* (Dutch—transitive verb)
ow: old woman (slang for wife); one way; ordinary warfare (OW); outer wing; out of wedlock (born of unmarried parents)
o-w: oil-in-water
oW: *ohne Wert* (German—without value)
öW: *österreichische Währung* (German—Austrian currency)
OW: Observation Ward; Old Welsh
OWAA: Outdoors Writers' Association of America
OWAEC: Organization for West African Economic Cooperation
OWC: Outline of World Cultures
Owen Meredith: Edward Robert Bulwer-Lytton's pseudonym
Owen Stanleys: Owen Stanley Mountains of New Guinea
owf: optimum working frequency
owgl: obscure wire glass
OWH: Office of the War on Hunger
OWHA: Oliver Wendell Holmes Association
OWI: Office of War Information
OWL: Older Women's Liberation; Other Woman, Limited
OWM: Office of Weights and Measures
OWMA: Oscar Wells Museum of Art (Birmingham, Alabama)
owp: outer wing panel
OWPP: Office of Welfare and Pension Plans
owpr: ocean wave profile recorder
OWR: Ouse Washes Reserve (England)
OWRR: Office of Water Resources Research
ows (OWS): operational weapon satellite
OWS: Ocean Weather Station
OWSS: Ocean Weather Ship Service
OWU: Ohio Wesleyan University
OWWS: Office of World Weather Systems
ow/ym: older woman/younger man
ox.: oxalic; oxide; oxygen
Ox.: Oxford
OX: oxygen (commercial sym-

bol)
oxa: oxalic acid
oxalic acid: $(COOH)_2$
Oxbridge: Oxford + Cambridge (the ultimate in British formal education)
Oxf: Oxfordshire
OXFAM: Oxford Committee for Famine Relief
Oxf & Bucks: Oxfordshire and Buckinghamshire (light infantry)
Oxford: Haydn's Symphony No. 92 in G major
Oxford UP: Oxford University Press
Oxm: Oxmantown
OXOCO: Offshore Exploration Oil Company
Oxon: Oxfordshire
Oxon.: *Oxonia* (Latin—Oxford); *Oxoniensis* (Latin—Oxonian)
oxr: oxidizer
oxwld: oxyacetylene weld
oxy: oxygen
Oxy: Occidental Petroleum Corporation; Oxy Metal Industries International
oxycephs: oxycephalics (pointed skulled people)
oxym: oxymel (honey-water-vinegar solution)
OY: orange yellow
O/Y: *Osakeytiö* (Finnish—limited company)
OYA: Oy Yleisradio Ab (Finnish Broadcasting Company)
Oya Cur: Oyashio Current (Kurile or Okhotsk or Oyasiwo)
OYD: Office of Youth Development
oys: oysters
Oyster(s): Marylander(s)
Oyster State: Maryland
oz: ounce
Oz: ooze
OZ: Ozark Airlines (two-letter-designation)
OZA: Ozark Airlines
oz ap: apothecaries' ounce(s)
ozarc: ozone-atmosphere rocket
Ozarks: Ozark Mountains
oz avd: avoirdupois ounce(s)
ozd: observed zenith distance
oz-in.: ounce-inch
OZO: *oost zuidoost* (Dutch—east southeast)
ozone: O_3
ozs: ounces
oz t: ounce troy
Ozy: Ozzie
Ozzie: Osborn; Oscar; Oswald; Oswaldo

P

p: page; pamphlet; park; parking; part; participle; past; paste; pawn; pebbles; pectoral; pence; pengü (Hungarian monetary unit); penny; percentile; perceptual (speed); percussion; perforate; perforated; perforation; perimeter; period; perishable; peseta; peso; peyote; piaster; piastre; picot; pie; pilaster; pink; pint; pipe; pitch; pitcher; plasma; plaster; plate; plus; point; polar; pole; pond; population; porcelain; port, or left side of an airplane or vessel when looking forward (P or L); position; positive; post; postage; posterior; postpartum; power; predicate; predict(ion); premolar; presbyopia; present; pressure; primary; primitive; principal; principle; probability (ratio); product; proprionate; proton; publication; pulse; pupil
p: fluid density (symbol); *piano* (Italian—softly); pitch; *per* (Latin—by)
p.: *pagina* (Italian, Latin, Portuguese, Spanish—page)—*pagina* in Portuguese; *parte* (Latin—part); *pater* (Latin—father); *per* (Latin—by); *pondere* (Latin—by weight); *proximum* (Latin—near); *pugillus* (Latin—fistful)—handful
p %: *por ciento* (Spanish—per hundred; percent)
P: Pacific; pamphlet; Panama Line; Papa—code letter for P; Paris; Parisian; passenger vessel (symbol); patrol; Pennzoil; Philadelphia Mint (symbol); phosphorus; Piasecki; plate; Pleyel; polar; polarization; pole; police; poor; Pope; port; Portugal (auto plaque); power; present value; President; Prince Line; principal; priority; project; propulsion; Protestant; protozoa; pulse
P: (Latin—Publius); pilot (white *P* on a blue flag flown on a pilot boat); *Pilot* (German); *pilota* (Italian); *pilote* (French); *piloto* or *practico* (Spanish)
P.: protein(s) (dietary symbol)
P_1: first parental generation
P_2: pulmonic second sound
P 1/C: Private First Class
P 1/C M: Private First Class Marine
P-2: Neptune twin-jet all-weather long-range land-based antisubmarine aircraft
P-3: Orion four-engine turboprop all-weather long-range land-based antisubmarine aircraft
P-5: Marlin twin-engine all-weather seaplane for long-range antisubmarine patrol and electronic reconnaissance
P2: *Panzer* (German—armor; armor plated; tank)
P.38: German 9mm service pistol (World War II)
P-38: U.S. pursuit aircraft
P^{33}: radioactive phosphorus
P_{55}: partial pressure of O_2 wherein hemoglobin is half saturated with O_2
P-60: 60-minute parking
pa: intensity of atmospheric pressure (symbol); paper; paralysis agitans; participial adjective; particular average; patient; pattern analysis; pending availability; performance analysis; permanent appointment; pernicious anemia; personal appearance; piaster; piastre; point of aim; position approximate; power amplifier; power approach; power of attorney; press agent; pressure altitude; private account; provisional allowance; psychoanalyst; public address (system); public assistance; publication announcement; purchasing agent
p/a: power of attorney
p-a: psychogenic aspermia

p & a: percussion and auscultation; price and availability
pa (PA): posteroanterior
p.a.: *per abdomen* (Latin—by the abdomen); *per annum* (Latin—by the year)
p A: *por autorización* (Spanish—in care of)
Pa: Panama; Panameña; Panamanian; Panameño; Papa; Para; Pennsylvania; Pennsylvanian; protactinium
Pa: Pará (Belem do Pará)
PA: Passenger Agent; Pennsylvanian Railroad (stock exchange symbol); Philippine Army; Philippine Association; Piedmont Airlines; Port Agency; Post Adjutant; Prefect Apostolic; Press Agent; Press Association; Prince Albert (coal); Proprietary Association; Prosecuting Attorney; Prothonotary Apostolic; psychological age; Public Act; Puppeteers of America; Purchasing Agent
PA: *Psychological Abstracts*
P-A: Pacific-Atlantic Line; Pan-Atlantic Line
P/A: Picatinny Arsenal
P & A: Professional and Administrative
P of A: Port of Anchorage
p.a.a.: *parti affectae applicetur* (Latin—apply to the affected parts or region)
PAA: Pacific Alaska Airways; Pan American World Airways System (3-letter designation); Potato Association of America; Purchasing Agents Association
PAAA: Premium Advertising Association of America
PAAC: Program Analysis Adaptable Control
PAADC: Principal Air Aide-de-Camp
PAAE: Pennsylvania Association for Adult Education
PAAO: Pan-American Association of Opthalmology
pab: per acre bonus
pab (PAB): p-aminobenzoic acid
PAB: Panair do Brasil (airline); Petroleum Administrative Board; Price Adjustment Board
paba: para-amino benzoic acid
PAB (CIA): Problems Analysis Branch of the CIA
pabla: problem analysis by logical approach
Pablo Picasso: Pablo Diego José Francisco de Paula Juan Nepomuceno Crispin Crispiano de da Santísima Trinidad Ruiz y Picasso
Pablo Neruda: Neftali Ricardo Reyes
pabx: private automatic branch telephone exchange
pac: phenacetin-aspirin-caffeine (all-purpose capsule); prearrival confirmation; production acceleration capacity; pursuant to authority contained (in); put and call (stock exchange jargon)
pac (PAC): premature atrial contraction
Pac: Pacific
PAC: Pacific Air Command; Pacific Automotive Corporation; Pacific Telephone & Telegraph (stock exchange symbol); Palo Alto Clinic; Pan-Africanist Congress; Pan-American Congress; Pharmaceutical Advertising Club; Philbrook Art Center; Political Action Committee; Public Affairs Committee; Public Assistance Cooperative
Pac: *Pacifico* (Italian—Pacifico); *Pacífico* (Portuguese or Spanish—Pacific); *Pacifique* (French—Pacific)
Paca: Francesca
PACAF: Pacific Air Force
PACB: Pan-American Coffee Bureau
PACCS: Post Attack Command and Control System
PacD: Pacific Division
pace (PACE): package-crammed executive; performance and cost evaluation; precision analog computing equipment; pre-launch automatic checkout equipment; program to advance creativity in education; programmed automatic communications equipment; projects to advance creativity in education
PACE: Professional Association of Consulting Engineers
PACECO: Pacific Coast Engineering Company
PACED: Program for Advanced Concepts in Electronic Design
PACFLT: Pacific Fleet
'pache: Apache
Pacif: Pacific
Pacific Coast Province: British Columbia
Pacific Northwest: Alaska to California, including the Yukon, British Columbia, Washington, and Oregon
Pacific Province: British Columbia
Pacific States: Alaska, Washington, Oregon, California, Hawaii
pack.: packing
pacm: pulse amplification code modulation
PACMD: Philadelphia Contract Management District
Paco: Pancho (Francisco)
PacO: Pacific Ocean
PACOM: Pacific Command
pacor: passive correlation and ranging
Pa_{CO_2}: arterial carbon dioxide pressure
PACRNB: President's Advisory Commission on Recreation and Natural Beauty
PACS: Pacific Area Communications System
PACT: Production Analysis Control Technique; Project for the Advancement of Coding Techniques
Pac T & T: Pacific Telephone and Telegraph
pacv (PACV): personnel air-cushion vehicle
PACV: Patrol Air-Cushioned Vehicle (naval)
pad.: padding; padlock
pad: padding; padlock; para-aminobenzoic acid
PAD: Port of Aerial Debarkation; Public Administration Division
padal: pattern for analysis, decision, action and learning
padar: passive detection and ranging
Paddy: an Irishman; Patrick
PADL: Pilotless Aircraft Development Laboratory
padloc: passive detection and location of countermeasures
p Adr: *per Adresse* (German—in care of)
padre.: portable automatic data-recording equipment
Padre de Independencia: (Spanish—Father of Independence)—José Martí—Cuban patriot, poet, and soldier
p. ae.: *partes aequales* (Latin—equal parts)
PAE: Peoria and Eastern (railroad); Port of Aerial Embarkation
PAEC: Pakistan Atomic Energy Commission; Philippine Atomic Energy Commission
paf: peripheral airfield; pulmo-

nary arteriovenous fistula; punishment and fine
pa & f: percussion, auscultation, and fermitus
paf: *puissance au frein* (French—brake horsepower)
PAF: Pacific Air Force(s); Pet Assistance Foundation; Philippine Air Force
PAFA: Pennsylvania Academy of Fine Arts
PAFB: Patrick Air Force Base
PAFMECA: Pan-African Freedom Movement of East and Central Africa
PAFS: Primary Air Force Specialty
PAFSC: Primary Air Force Specialty Code
pag: *pagaré* (Spanish—I will pay); *pagina* (Italian—page)
pág(s): *página(s)* [Spanish—page(s)]
Pag: pagoda
PaG: Pennsylvania-German
PAG: Prince Albert's Guard
pageos (PAGEOS): passive geodetic satellite
Pa Ger Soc: Pennsylvania German Society
PAGB: Proprietary Association of Great Britain
Paget's disease: bone distortion or cancer of the nipples of women
pagg segg: *pagine seguenti* (Italian—following pages)
PAGT: Port Authority Grain Terminal
pah: polynuclear aromatic hydrocarbon(s)—(photochemical smog ingredient)
pah (PAH): para-aminohippuric acid
Pah: Pahlavi
PAH: Pan-American Highway (also called Inter-American Highway)
PAHC: Pan American Highway Congress
PAHO: Pan-American Health Organization
PAI: Panama Airways Incorporated; Piedmont Airlines (3-letter coding)
PAIGCV: *Partido Africano da Independencia da Guine e Cabo Verde* (Portuguese—African Party for an Independent Guinea and Cape Verde)
PAIGH: Pan-American Institute of Geography and History
PAIN: Pan-American Institute of Neurology
paint.: painter; painting
PAIRC: Pacific Air Command
PAIS: Project Analysis Information System (AID); Public Affairs Information Service
PAIT: Program for the Advancement of Industrial Technology
PAJU: Pan-African Journalists Union
Pak: Pakistan
PAK: Pëtr Alekseevich Kropotkin
Paki(s): Pakistani(s)
PAKISTAN: *Pak* (Persian—holy) plus *tan* (Urdu—land)—hence Pakistan means Holy Land; it is also an acronym made up of Punjab, Afghan Border states, Kashmir, Sind, and *tan* from Baluchistan
pal.: paleontology; permissive action link; phase-alteration line (color tv system); prescribed action link
pal. (PAL): phase alternate line
Pal: Palace; Palencia; Paleozoic; Palestine
PAL: Pacific Aeronautical Library; phase-alternating (television) line; Philippine Air Lines; Police Athletic League; prisoner-at-large; Public Archives Library
Palat: Palatinate
PALC: Point Arguello Launch Complex
paleo: paleography
paleob: paleobotany
paleon: paleontology
Palestinian Salt Sea: the Dead Sea
Palestrina: Giovanni Pierluigi da Palestrina
Palgrave: Francis Meyer Cohen
PALI: Pacific and Asian Linguistics Institute (University of Hawaii)
palin: palindrome; palindromic
PALINET: Pennsylvania Area Library Network
palm.: palmist(ry)
Palmach: *Plugot Machatz* (Hebrew—Spearhead Units)—commando units active in the establishment of Israel when still called Palestine
Palm Coast: Florida's east coast from Daytona to Jacksonville
Palmetto City: Charleston, South Carolina
Palmetto(s): South Carolinian(s)
Palmetto State: South Carolina's official nickname
palp: palpable; palpitation
palpi: palpitation
PALs: Parcel Air Lifts (U.S. Post Office parcel-post service for servicemen)
PALS: Permissive Action Link Systems
pam: pamphlet; pulse amplified modulation; pulse amplitude modulation
Pam: Lord Palmerston; Pamela
PAM: Palestine Archeological Museum; Pasadena Art Museum; Portland Art Museum
PAMA: Pan-American Medical Association
PAMC: Pakistan Army Medical Corps
PAMETRADA: Parsons Marine Experimental Turbine Research and Development Association
PAMIPAC: Personnel Accounting Machine Installation Pacific Fleet
Pamirs: Pamir Mountains of Soviet Central Asia
PAML: Pan American Mail Line
PAMO: Port Air Materiel Office
PAMPA: Pacific Area Movement Piority Agency (DoD)
pamph: pamphlet
Pamphleteer for American Independence: Thomas Paine
PAMT: Port Authority Marine Terminal
pan (PAN): peroxyacetyl nitrate (smog ingredient)
pan.: panchromatic; panorama; panoramic; pantomime; pantry
Pan: Panama; Panamanian; Panameño
PAN: Pan American Navigation; Parents Against Narcotics; peroxyacetylnitrate (air-pollutant poison)
PAN: *Partido Acción Nacional* (Spanish—National Action Party)—Mexican; *Polska Akademia Nauk* (Polish Academy of Sciences)
PANAGRA: Pan American-Grace Airways
PANAIR: *Panair do Brasil* (Brazilian airline)
Pan-Am: Pan-American World Airways
PANANEWS: Pan-Asia Newspape Alliance (Hong Kong)
pan b: panic bolt
panc: pancreas
Pan Can: Panama Canal
Pan Canal: Panama Canal
Pancho: Francisco
Pancho Villa: Doroteo Arango
pandex: *pan* (Greek—all) + *dex* (from index)—all-inclusive index
Pango: (naval argot—Pago Pago,

American Samoa)
Panhandle State: West Virginia
Pank: Pankow
panol: panology
panorams: panoramas
PANS: Procedures for Air Navigation Services
PANSDOC: Pakistan National Scientific and Technical Documentation Center
Pan Sea Fron (PANSEAFRON): Panama Sea Frontier
panth: pantheism; pantheist; pantheistic(al) (ly)
panto: pantograph(ic); pantomime; pantomimic
pants: pantaloons
PANY: Power Authority of the State of New York
PAO: Public Affairs Officer
PAOA: Pan-American Odontological Association
PAODAP: President's Action Office for Drug Abuse Prevention
Pa_{O_2}: arterial oxygen pressure
PA_{O_2}: alveolar oxygen pressure
pap.: papa; papacy; papal; paper; papyrus
pap: *prét à porter* (French—ready to wear)
Pap: Papa; Papist; Pappie; Papua; Papuan
PAP: Port-au-Prince, Haiti (airport); Polska Agencja Prasowa (Polish News Agency)
Papa: code for letter P
Papa Bach: Johann Sebastian Bach
Papa Doc: Haiti's former dictator François Duvalier
Papa Haydn; Franz Joseph Haydn
Pap diag: Papanicolaou diagnosis
Papermac: paperback book published by Macmillan
PAPI: Pacific Automation Products Incorporated
papil: papilla; papillae
Pap Inf: Papal Infallability
Pap Lib: Paperback Library
Pap NG: Papua New Guinea
p app: *puissance apparente* (French—apparent power)
Pappies: Papists
Pap(s): [(Irish-Protestant English-Papist(s)—*see* Prod(s)]
Pap smear: Papanicolaou smear
Pap Sta: Papal States
Pap Ter: Papua Territory
Pap Test: Papanicolaou Test (for cervical cancer)
Paquita: Francisca (Frances)
par.: paragraph; parallax; parallel; per acre rental; precision approach radar
par (PAR): perimeter acquistion radar
Par: Parish
Par: *Parigi* (Italian—Paris); *Parijs* (Dutch—Paris)
PAR: Paris, France (Orly airport); Program Appraisal and Review
para: parachute; paragraph; parallel; perceiving and recognition automation
Para: Paraguay(an)
para I; para II; para III; etc.: unipara; bipara; tripara; etc.—having given birth to one child, to two children, to three children, etc.
parab: parabola
Paracelsus: Theophrastus Bombastus von Hohenheim
paracent: paracentesis
parad: paradicholorobenzene; paradigm(atic)(al)(ly); paradisiac(al)(ly); paradisal; paradise; paradisiacal(ly); paradox(ical)(ly); paradoxicalness
Paradise of the Pacific: Hawaii
paradrop: parachute airdrop
par. aff.: *pars affecta* (Latin—to the part affected)
Parg: Paraguay; Paraguayan
Paraguay River City: Asunción
paral: parallax; paralysis
Parami: Parsons active ring around miss indicator
paramp: parametric amplifier
parapsych: parapsychologist; parapsychology
paras: parasite(s); parasitic; parasitism; paratroopers
parasail: parachute sail (steerable parachute)
parasitol: parasitology
parasym div: parasympathetic division
Parbo: Paramaribo
parc: progressive aircraft repair cycle
PARC: Public Archives Records Centre
PARCA: Pan American Railway Congress Association
parch.: parchment
pard: partner
pardop: passive-ranging doppler
paren: parenthesis
parens: parentheses
parent.: parental(ly)
Parents: *Parents Magazine*
par for: par for the course (golfer's term meaning average, typical, usual)
pari: parietal
Paris: Mozart's Symphony No. 31 in D major
Paris Expressionist: Henri Matisse
paris green: copper acetoarsenite
parkade: parking arcade
Park City: Bridgeport, Connecticut
Parkinson's disease: nervous tremors accompanied by muscular weakness and rigidness; also called palsy, paralysis agitans, or the shakes
Parl: Parliament
PARL: Palo Alto Research Laboratory (Lockheed)
Parl Agt: Parliamentary Agent
Parl Const: Parliamentary Constituency
Parlour Panther: *New York Review of Books*
Parl Sec: Parliamentary Secretary
PARM: *Partido Autentico de la Revolución Mexicano* (Authentic Party of the Mexican Revolution)
Parmigianino: Francisco Massuoli
parochiaid: parochial-school aid (provided by tax monies)
paros: passive ranging on submarines
parot: parotid
parox: paroxysm(al)
Parrot's disease: syphilitic infantile paralysis (disease named not for a bird but for a French physician—Jules Marie Parrot—its discoverer)
Parry's disease: exopthalmic goiter
pars: paragraphs
PARS: Passenger Airlines Reservation System; Programmed Airlines Reservation System
parsec: parallax second (3.26 lightyears or 19.2 trillion miles)
parsq: pararescue
parsyn: parametric synthesis
part.: partial; participate; particle; partition; partner; partnership
part.: *partim* (Latin—part)
part. aeq.: *partes aequales* (Latin—equal parts)
partan: parallel tangents
Partas: Partagas cigars
parth: parthenogenesis
partic: participle; particular
partit: partitive
part. vic.: *partibus vicibus* (Latin—in divided doses)
paru: postanesthetic recovery unit
par uni: party unity (political utopia)
parv: paravane

parv: *parvus (Latin—small)*
pas: passive; power-assisted steering; public-address system
paS: periodic acid Schiff
Pas: Pasadena; Pascagoula; Pashto; Passaic; Passau
Pas.: *Paschae* (Latin—Easter)
PAs: Police Agents
PA's: purchasing agents
PAS: Percussive Arts Society; Pregnancy Advisory Service; Primary Alerting System; Professor of Air Science
pasa (PASA): para-aminosalicylic acid
pasar: psychological abstracts search and retrieval
PASB: Pan-American Sanitary Bureau
PASC: Palestine Armed Struggle Command (controlled by El Fatah); Pan-American Standards Committee
PASCO: Pan American Sulfur Corporation
p'ase: alkaline phosphatase
pasim: pasimological; pasimologically; pasimologist; pasimology (study of gestures as means of communication)
PASL: Pakistan Association of Special Libraries
PASLIB: Pakistan Association of Special Libraries
PASO: Pan-American Sanitary Organization
Pasque: South Dakota state flower
pass.: passage; passenger; passivate
pass.: *passim* (Latin—far and wide; here and there; up and down)
Pass: Passover
PASSIM: President's Advisory Staff on Scientific Information Management
Passionate Pilgrim: John Bunyan
Past: *Pasteurella*
Pastoral: Beethoven's Piano Sonata No. 15 in D (opus 28); Beethoven's Symphony No. 6 in F major (opus 68); Symphony No. 3 by Vaughan Williams
Pastoral God: Pan
p-a system: public-address sytem
pat.: patent(s); patrol(s): points after touchdown
pat. (PAT): paroxysmal atrial tachycardia
Pat: Patricia; Patrick
Pat: *Patrone* (German—cartridge; round of ammunition)
PAT: Pacific Air Transport; Philippine Aerial Taxi
PATA: Pacific Area Travel Association
Patag: Patagonia(n)
PATCA: Panama Air Traffic Control Area
PATCO: Port Authority Transit Corporation; Professional Air Traffic Controllers Association
patd: patented
path.: pathological; pathologist; pathology; pituitary adrenotrophic hormone (PATH)
PATH: Port Authority Trans-Hudson (Hudson Tubes)
Pathétique: Beethoven's Piano Sonata No. 8 in C minor (opus 13); Tchaikovsky's Symphony No. 6 in B minor
Pathfinder: Major General John C. Frémont, USA
Pathfinder of the Seas: Matthew Fontaine Maury
Path of Gold: Market Street, San Francisco
Pathmaker of the West: John C. Frémont
patho: pathological
pathogen: pathogenic
pathol: pathological; pathologist; pathology
Patience and Fortitude: Mayor La Guardia's nickname for the couchant lions flanking the steps of the New York Public Library
Patk: Patrick
pat. med: patent medicine
Pat Off: Patent Office
pat pend: patent pending
PATRA: Printing, Packaging, and Allied Trades Research Association (also appears as PPATRA)
Patriarch of Ferney: Voltaire
Patriarch of New England: John Cotton
Patriarch of Philosophy: Bertrand Russell
Patriarch of the West: the Pope
Patriot Financier: Robert Morris
patron.: patronym(ic)(al)(ly)
Patronat: (French equivalent of National Association of Manufacturers in United States)
Patroness Saint of Spain: Santa Teresa of Ávila
Patron Saint of American Orchards: John (Johnny Appleseed) Chapman
Patron Saint of England: St George
Patron Saint of Ireland: St Patrick
Patron Saint of Scotland: St Andrew
Patron Saint of Wales: St David
Patroon: Stephen Van Rensselaer's nickname
pats.: patents
patt: pattern
Patty: Martha; Patience; Patricia
PATWAS: Pilot's Automatic Telephone Weather Answering Service
Pau: Pablo
PAU: Pan American Union
Paul Muni: Muni Neisenfreund
Paul VI: Giovanni Batista Montini
P-au-P: Port-au-Prince
pav: paving
p/av: particular average
Pav: pavilion
PAV: Personnel Allotment Voucher
PAV: *Poste Avion* (French—airmail)
PAVAA: Polish Army Veterans Association of America
pave.: position and velocity extraction
PAVE: Professional Audiovisual Education (study)
PAVN: Peoples Army of Viet Nam
pav. noc.: *pavor nocturnus* (Latin—nightmares; night terrors)
paw.: portable auxiliary workroom
Paw: Papa
PAWA: Pan American World Airways
PAWO: Pan-African Women's Organization
pax.: passenger(s); private automatic exchange
Pax: Paxon; Paxton
pax vob.: *pax vobiscum* (Latin—peace be with you)
Pay: Paymaster; Paymistres
Pay Cmdr: Paymaster Commander
paye (PAYE): pay as you earn (United Kingdom scheme of income tax paying while earning); pay as you enter
Paymr: Paymaster; Paymistress
PAYS: Patriotic American Youth Society
payt: payment
pb: painted base; patrol bombing; pull box; push button
p/b: pass book; poor bastard
pB: purplish blue
Pb: *plumbum* (Latin—lead)
PB: Packard Bell; patrol bomber; patrol bombing; Publication Bulletin
P-B: Pitney-Bowes
PB: *Planta Baja* (Spanish—

ground floor), elevator pushbutton designation
***P.B.**: Pharmacopeia Britannica*
pba: poor bloody assistant; pressure-breathing assister
PBA: Patrolmen's Benevolent Association; Port of Bristol Authority; Professional Bookmen of America; Public Buildings Administration
***pbai**: proyectil balístico de alcance intermedio (PBAI)*—(Spanish—intermediate range ballistic missile)
P-band: 225–390 mc
PBBH: Peter Bent Brigham Hospital (Boston)
pbb's (PBBs): polybrominated biphenyls
pbc: point of basal convergence
PBC: Palisade Boat Club; Philadelphia Blood Clinic; Provincial Bank of Canada
pbdndb: perceived barking dog noise decibels
Pbe: Perlsucht bacillen emulsion
PBEC: Pacific Basin Economic Council; Public Broadcasting Environment Center
P. B. Ed.: Bachelor of Philosophy in Education
***PBF**: Prins Bernhard Fonds* (Prince Bernhard Fund)
PBGC: Pension Benefit Guaranty Corporation
pbhp: pounds per brake horsepower
pbi: poor bloody infantry; protein-bound iodine
***pbi**: proyectil balístico intercontinental (PBI)* (Spanish—intercontinental ballistic missile)
PBI: Paper bag Institute; Paving Block Institute; Pitney-Bowes Incorporated; Plumbing Brass Institute; Projected Books Incorporated; West Palm Beach, Florida (airport)
***PBiB**: Paperback Books in Print*
PBJC: Palm Beach Junior College
PBK: Phi Beta Kappa
PBKTOA: Printing, Bookbinding, and Kindred Trades Overseers' Association
PBL: Public Broadcast Laboratory
pbm (PBM): permanent bench mark
PBM: Mariner twin-engine Navy bomber built by Martin; Paramaribo, Surinam (airport)
PBMA: Peanut Butter Manufacturers Association
pbo: polite brushoff
P-boat: Patrol Boat
***P. Bor.**: Pharmacopoeia Borussica* (Latin—Prussian Pharmacopoeia)
PBOS: Planning Board for Ocean Shipping (USA)
pbp: pushbutton panel
PBPS: Program Budgeting and Planning System
pbr (PBR): power breeder reactor; precision bombing range
pb's: paperback books; petrol bombs (Irish-style Molotov-cocktail-type incendiary bombs)
p-bs: phosphate-buffered saline (solution)
PBS: Public Broadcasting Service; Public Buildings Service
PB & SC: Power Boat and Ski Club
PBSCMA: Peanut Butter Sandwich and Cookie Manufacturers Association
PBSE: Philadelphia-Baltimore Stock Exchange
pbt: performance-based teaching
PBT: President of the Board of Trade
PBTB: Paper Bag Trade Board; Paper Box Trade Board
pbte: performance-based teacher education
Pburg: Pittsburgh
pbw: parts by weight; posterior bite wing
PBWSE: Philadelphia-Baltimore-Washington Stock Exchange
pbx: private branch exchange
pbz: phosphor bronze
pbz (PBZ): pyribenzamine (antihistamine)
pc: parent cells; paycheck; pay clerk; percent; percentage; percentile; personal correction; petty cash; pica(s); piece(s); pitch circle; point of curve; port of call; postcard; prices current; printed circuit; privileged character; pull chain; pulsating current; purchasing and contracting purified concentrate
p-c: phophlogistic-corticoid
p/c: percent; percentage; programmer-comparator
p & c: put and call
***pc**: point de congélation* (French—freezing point)
***p.c.**: post cebum* (Latin—after a meal; after meals)
PC: Pace College; Pacific Airlines; Pacific Coast (railroad); Pacific College; Paine College; Palmer College; Palomar College; Panama Canal; Panola College; Paris College; Park College; Parsons College; Pasadena College; Peace Corps; Pembroke Collge; Pepperdine College; personnel carrier; Pfeiffer College; Pharmacy Corps; Philadelphia College; Philippine Constabulary; Phoenix College; Piedmont College; Pikeville College; Pilotage Chart(s); Pineland College; Plane Commander; Pomona College; Porterville College; Presbyterian College; Principia College; Privy Council; Privy Councillor(s); Procurement Command; Producers Council; Providence College; submarine chaser patrol vessel (naval symbol)
P-C: Penn-Central (railroad)
***PC**: Partido Colorado* (Spanish—Colorado Party)—the reds; *Partido Comunista* (Spanish—Communist Party); *Partido Conservador* (Spanish—Conservative Party); *Poder Chicano* (Spanish—Chicano Power)
P.C.: Penal Code; Plaid Cymru (party)
pca: permanent change of assignment
pca (PCA): p-chloraphenylalanine
Pca: Pensacola
PCA: Parachute Club of America; Permanent Court of Arbitration (The Hague); Pollution Control Agency; Portland Cement Association; Production Credit Association
***PCA**: Partido Comunista Argentina* (Spanish—Argentine Communist Party)
PCAC: Professional Classes Aid Council
pcam: punchcard accounting machine
PCAPA: Pacific Coast Association of Port Authorities
PCAPK: President's Commission on the Assassination of President Kennedy
PCAs: Progressive Citizens of America
pcb: petty cash book; printed circuit board
PCB: Pest Control Bureau; Program Control Board
***PCB**: Partido Comunista Boliviano* (Spanish—Bolivian Communist Party); *Partido Comunista Brasileiro* (Portuguese—Brazilian Communist Party)
pcb's: polychlorinated biphenyls

(industrial pollutants of lakes, reservoirs, and streams)
pcb's (PCBs): polychlorinated biphenyls
pcc: phosphate carrier compound
PCC: Pacific Coast Conference; Palmer Community College; Panama Canal Company; Port of Corpus Christi; Portland Community College
PCC: *Partido Comunista Cubano* (Spanish—Cuban Communist Party)
PCCC: Pakistan Central Cotton Committee
PCCEMRSP: Permanent Commission for the Conservation and Exploitation of the Maritime Resources of the South Pacific
PCCI: President's Committee on Consumer Interests
pccu: progressive coronary care unit
PCCU: President's Commission on Campus Unrest
pcd: pounds per capita per day
PCD: Planned Community Development
PCDG: Prestressed Concrete Development Group
pc di: pierce die
P Cdr: Paymaster Commander
pce: pyrometric cone equivlent
PCE: patrol craft escort (3-letter coding)
PCE: *Partido Comunista Española* (Spanish Communist Party)
PCEA: Pacific Coast Electrical Association
PCEH: The President's Committee on Employment of the Handicapped
PCEM: Parliamentary Council of the European Movement
PCEQ: President's Council on Environmental Quality
PCER: rescue escort (naval symbol)
pcf: pounds per cubic foot; power per cubic foot
Pcf: *Pacifico* (Italian—Pacific); *Pacífico* (Portuguese or Spanish—Pacific); *Pacifique* (French—Pacific)
PCF: *Parti Communiste Français* (French Communist Party)
PCFAP: The President's Committee on the Foreign Aid Program
pcg: phonocardiogram
PCGN: Permanent Committee on Geographical Names
pch: paroxysmal cold hemoglobinuria
P Ch: Parish Church
PCH: hydrofoil submarine chaser (3-letter coding)
pci: peripheral command indicator; perpetual cost index
PCI: Packer Collegiate Institute; Planning Card Index; Prestressed Concrete Institute
PCI: *Partito Comunista Italiano* (Italian Communist Party)
PCIB: Pacific Cargo Inspection Bureau
PCIFC: Permanent Commission of the International Fisheries Convention
PCII: Potato Chip Institute International
PCIM: Presidential Commission on Income Maintenance
Pck: conditional probability of kill (armament)
pckt: printed circuit
pcl: printed-circuit lamp
PCL: Pacific Coast Line
PCLEAJ: President's Commission on Law Enforcement and the Administration of Justice
pclk: pay clerk
pcm: phase-change material(s); pulse-code modulation; pulse-count modulation; punchcard machine(s)
PCM: Peabody Conservatory of Music; President's Certificate of Merit
PCM: *Partido Comunista Mexicano* (Mexican Communist Party)
PCMA: Professional Convention Management Association
pcmi: photographic microimage(s)—microdot photos
PCMO: Principal Colonial Medical Officer
pcm/pl: pulse-code modulated/ polarized light
PCMR: President's Committee on Mental Retardation
PCMSER: President's Commission on Marine Science, Engineering, and Resources
PCN: Part Control Number; Procurement Control Number
PCN: *Partido de Conciliación Nacional* (Spanish—National Conciliation Party)
PCNB: Permanent Control Narcotics Board
PCNG: President's Commission on National Goals
PCNR: Part Control Number Request
PCN's: Planning Change Notices
PCNV: Provisional Committee on Nomenclature of Viruses
pc/o: *por ciento* (Spanish—percent)
PCO: Printing Control Office(r); Procuring Contracting Office(r); Public Carriage Office(r)
PCOB: Permanent Central Opium Board (UN)
PCOOS: Pacific Coast Oto-Opthalmological Society
PCOP: President's Commission on Obscenity and Pornography
P_{CO_2}: carbon dioxide pressure (or tension)
pcp: production change point
pcp (PCP): phencyclidine
PCP: Postgraduate Center of Psychotherapy; Program Change Proposal; Progressive Conservative Party
PCP: *Partido Comunista Panameño* (Spanish—Panamanian Communist Party); *Partido Comunista Paraguayo* (Spanish—Paraguayan Communist Party); *Partido Comunista Peruviano* (Spanish—Peruvian Communist Party); *Partido Communista Portugues* (Portuguese Communist Party)
PCPA: Panama Canal Pilots Association; parachlorophenylalanine
PCPD: Portland Commission of Public Docks
PCPF: President's Council on Physical Fitness
PCPS: Philadelphia College of Pharmacy and Science
PC & PS: Professional Credentials and Personnel Service (nursing)
pcpt: perception
pcpv: prestressed concrete pressure vessel
PCR: Program Change Request; Publication Contract Requirement
pcr: photoconductive relay
PCR: *Partidul Comunist Roman* (Roman Communist Party)
PC R & D C: Pomona Colleges Research and Development Center
PCRC: Paraffined Carton Research Council
PCRI: Papanicolaou Cancer Research Institute
PCRS: Poor Clergy Relief Society
pcrv: prestressed concrete reactor vessel
pcs: permanent change of station; picas; pieces
PCs: Police Constables

PCS: 136-foot submarine chaser (3-letter coding)
PCSA: Polish Cultural Society of America
PCSE: Pacific Coast Stock Exchange; President's Council on Scientists and Engineers
pc sh: pierce shell
PCSIR: Pakistan Council of Scientific and Industrial Research
PCSP: Permanent Commission for the South Pacific
PCSW: President's Commission on the Status of Women
pct: percent
pct: *procent* (Norwegian—percent)
Pct: Precinct
PCT: Patent Cooperation Treaty; Portsmouth College of Technology
PCT: *Partido Conservador Tradicional* (Spanish—Traditional Conservative Party)—Nicaragua
pctfe: polychlorotrifluoroethylene
pc tp: pierce template
PCTS: President's Committee for Traffic Safety
pcu: photocopy unit; power-control unit; pressurization-control unit
PCUS: Propeller Club of the United States
PCU-USA: Portuguese Continental Union of the U.S.A.
pcv: packed-cell volume; pollution-control valve; positive crankcase ventilation
PCV: Peace Corps Volunteer(s); Pestalozzi Children's Village
PCV: *Partido Comunista Venezolana* (Spanish—Venezuelan Communist Party)
PCVC: Public Citizen Visitor's Center
PC virus: Port Chalmers (New Zealand) type of influenza virus
PCVs: Peace Corps Volunteers
pcx: periscope convex
PCY: coastal yacht (3-letter naval symbol); Pittsburgh, Chartiers & Youghiogheny (railroad)
PCYC: Port Credit Yacht Club
PCZ: Panama Canal Zone
PCZST: Panama Canal Zone Standard Time
pd: interpupillary distance; paid; paralysing dose; passed; period; pitch diameter; point detonating; poop deck; port dues; position doubtful; postage due; post date; post dated; potential difference; pound; pour depressant; preliminary design; prism diopter; procurement directive; property damage; public domain; pulse duration; purchase description
p-d: prism diopter
p& d: pickup and delivery
p.d.: *per diem* (Latin—by the day)
Pd: palladium
PD: Pharmacopoeia Dublin; Phelps-Dodge; Physics Department; Police Department; Port of Debarkation; Port Director; Port Dues; position doubtful (chart marking); Preliminary Design; Production Department
P-D: Parke-Davis
PD: *Partido Democrático* (Spanish—Democratic Party); *(Cleveland) Plain Dealer*
P.D.: *Pharmacopoeia Dublinensis* (Latin—Dublin Pharmacopoeia)
P-D: *St Louis Post-Dispatch* (a leading daily newspaper)
P-de-D: Puy-de-Dome
P of D: Port of Duluth
pda: patient distress alarm; predicted drift angle; public display of affection
pda: *pour dire adieu* (French—to say goodbye)
PDA: Photographic Dealers' Association
PDAD: Probate, Divorce, and Admiralty Division
PDAS: Police Department American Samoa
P-day: day when rate of production of an item for military consumption equals rate required by armed forces
pdb: paradichlorobenzine
Pd.B.: *Pedagogiae Baccalaureus* (Latin—Bachelor of Pedagogy)
pdc: preliminary diagnostic clinic; private diagnostic clinic
Pdc: probability of detection and conversion
PDC: Petroleum Development Corporation; Prevention of Deterioration Center (National Academy of Sciences)
PDC: *Partido Democrático Cristiano* (Spanish—Christian Democratic Party)
Pd.D.: *Pedagogiae Doctor* (Latin—Doctor of Pedagogy)
PDD: Public Documents Department (GPO)
pdda: power-driven decontaminating apparatus
pde: paroxysmal dyspnea on exertion
PDE: Post-test Disassembly Examination
P de C: *Pas de Calais* (French—Strait of Calais)—Dover Strait
P-de-D: Puy-de-Dôme
pdf: point detonating fuse
PDF: Parkinsons' Disease Foundation
PDFLP: Popular Democratic Front for the Liberation of Palestine
PDG: Paymaster Director-General
pdga (PDGA): pteroyldiglutamic acid
PDGW: Principal Director of Guided Weapons
pdh: past dental history
pdi: powered-descent initiation
PDI: Printing Developments Incorporated
pdic: periodic
p dk: poop deck
pdl: poundal
pdm: pulse-delta modulation; pulse-duration modulation
Pd.M.: Master of Pedagogy
pdn: production
pdo: *pasado* (Spanish—past)
PDO: Publication Distribution Office(r); Property Disposal Office(r)
p/doz: per dozen
pdp: project definition phase
PDP: Program Definition Phase; Program Development Plans
pd pt: production pattern
p d q: pretty damn (or darn) quick
pdr: pounder; powder; precision depth recorder (PDR)
PDR: People's Democratic Republic; Philippine Defense Ribbon
PDR: *Physicians' Desk Reference*
PDRK: People's Democratic Republic of Korea (North Korea)
PDRL: Permanent Disability Retirement List
PDRP: Power Distribution Reactor Program
PDRY: People's Democratic Republic of Yemen (capitals—Aden and Medina as-Shaab)
pds: point detonating self-destroying
pd's: public defenders
PDS: Priority Distribution System
PDSA: People's Dispensary for

Sick Animals
PDSC: Performers and Teachers Diploma—Sydney Conservatorium
PDSR: Principal Director of Scientific Research
PDST: Pacific Daylight Saving Time
pdt: power distribution trailer
PDT: Pacific Daylight Saving Time
PDTC: Plymouth and Devonport Technical College
PDTLO: Pierre Dominique Toussaint l'Ouverture
pdu: power distribution unit
pd work: public domain work (of art, history, literature, publication, etc.)
PDX: Portland, Oregon (airport)
pe: personnel equipment; probable error; program element; printer's error
p/e: porcelain enamel; price earning
pe: *par exemple* (French—for example); *per esempio* (Italian—for example); *por ejemplo* (Spanish—for example)
pe (PE): physical examination
Pe: Pecltet number; Pernambuco
P^e: *Padre* (Spanish—father)
PE: Pacific Electric (railroad); patrol vessel (naval symbol); Petroleum Engineer(ing); Philadelphia Electric; Pistol Expert; Plant Engineer(ing); Port of Embarkation; Port Everglades, Florida; Post Exchange; probable error; Production Engineer(ing); Professional Engineer; Protestant Episcopal
P & E: Peoria & Eastern (railroad)
P.E.: *Pharmacopoeia Edinburgensis* (Latin—Edinburgh Pharmacopoeia)
pea. (PEA): primary expense account
PEA: Plastics Engineers Association; Potash Export Association; Publication Effectiveness Audit; Public Education Association
PEAB: Professional Engineer's Appointments Bureau
PEACE: People Emerging Against Corrupt Establishments; Project Evaluation and Assistance in Civil Engineering (USAF)
Peace Garden State: North Dakota
Peacemaker: William Penn
Peach Blossom: Delaware's state flower
Peach Capital of British Columbia: Penticton
Peach State: Georgia's official nickname
Peacracker(s): native(s) of Lowestoft
PEAL: Professional Engineers Association Limited
Pea Mus: Peabody Museum
Peanut Capital of Alabama: Dothan
Peanut City: Suffolk, Virginia
Peanut King: Amadeo Obici who organized the Planters Peanut Company in 1906
PEAQ: Personal Experience and Attitude Questionnaire
Pear City: Medford, Oregon
Pearl: Pearl Harbor—Oahu, Hawaii
PEARL: (Committee for) Public Education and Religious Liberty
Pearl of the Adriatic: Dubrovnik, Yugoslavia
Pearl of the Antilles: Cuba
Pearl of the Baltic: Bornholm Island, Denmark
Pearl King: Mikimoto Kokichi (Japanese who discovered the secret of creating cultured pearls)
Pearl of the Orient: Sri Lanka (Ceylon)
Pearl of the Pacific: Honolulu, Pago Pago, Papeete, and other Pacific Ocean ports share this sobriquet
Pearl and Petroleum Sheikdom: El Qatar on the Persian Gulf
Pearls: Pearl Islands (Las Perlas)
Pearl of the Sharon: Netanya, Isreal
Pearl of the South Seas: sobriquet shared by Tahiti, Tonga, Samoa, and other South Sea islands
PEAS: Production Engineering Advisory Service
Peasant Breughel: Pieter Breughel the Elder
Pe. B.: *Pediatriae Baccalaureus* (Latin—Bachelor of Pediatrics)
PEB: Physical Evaluation Board
pebd: pay entry base date
pec: photoelectric cell; program element code
PEC: Production Equipment Code; Protestant Episcopal Church
pecan.: pulse envelope correlation air navigator
PECE: President's Emergency Committee for Employment
'pecker: woodpecker
Peck's Bad Boy: (pseudonym—George W. Peck)
pecto: pectoral
Peculiar Institution: Mount Holyoke College founded by Mary Lyon and described by her as a peculiar institution as it was for women
ped: pedagogue; pedagogy; pedal; pedestal; pedestrian
Ped: pedal (music); Pediatrics
P Ed: Physical Education
pedag: pedagogue; pedaguese (patois of pedants)
pedageese: pedagogue jargon
Ped.B.: Bachelor of Pedagogy
Ped.D.: Doctor of Pedagogy
pediat: pediatrics
PE Dir: Physical Education Director
Ped.M.: Master of Pedagogy
pedol: pedologic(al); pedologist; pedology
Pedrarias: Pedro Arias
PED XING: Pedestrian crossing (America's most perplexing highway abbreviation)
P & EE: Proving and Experimental Establishment
Peeb: Peebles
Peebl: Peebleshire
peep.: positive and expiratory pressure
peep. (PEEP): pilot's electronic eye-level presentation
pees: South Vietnamese piasters
pef: peak expiatory flow
PEF: Palestine Exploration Fund
peg.: polyethylene glycol
Peg: Peggy
PEGE: Program for Evaluation of Ground Environment
Peggy: Margaret
PEI: Porcelain Enamel Institute; Preliminary Engineering Inspection; Prince Edward Island
pej: premolded expansion joint
p ej: *por ejemplo* (Spanish—for example)
pejor: perojative(ly)
Pek: Peking; Pekinese
peke: pekinese dog
pel: pelagic; pellet; pelvis
P EL: Port Elizabeth
Pelagies: Pelagian Islands in the Mediterranean between Sicily and Tunisia
Pelican: Louisiana's state bird and symbolic nickname often given Louisianians—Pelicans
Pelican State: Louisiana's official nickname
Pelikaanstraat: (Flemish—Pelican Street)—Antwerp's dia-

mond-dealer's center
Pellews: Pellew Islands in the Gulf of Carpentaria
PELNI: Pelajaran Nasional Indonesia (National Shipping Company of Indonesia)
pem: program element monitor
Pem: Pembrokeshire
PEM: Production Engineering Measures
Pemb: Pembrokeshire
Pemb Coll: Pembroke College—Cambridge
Pemex: Petróleos Mexicanos
PE Mus: Port Elizabeth Museum
Pem Yeo: Pembroke Yeomanry
pen.: penal; penetrate; penology; peninsula; penitentiary; penmanship
Pen: Penitentiary
PEN: Poets, Playwrights, Editors, Essayists, and Novelists (international organization often referred to as the P.E.N. Club)
pen. aids: penetration aids
Penamite(s): Pennsylvanian(s)
PEN Club: (*see* PEN)
Pene: Penelope
Penguin: Penguin Books
peni: penicillin
penic: penicillin
penic.: *penicillum* (Latin—brush)
penic. cam.: *penicillum camelinum* (Latin—camel's-hair brush)
Peninsular Malaysia: States of the Federation of Malaysia (Federated Malay States also known as Malaya)
Peninsular State: Florida
Penit: Penitentiary
Penman of the Revolution: John Dickinson of Delaware
Penn: Pennsylvania; Pennsylvanian
Penna: Pennsylvania
Penn Central: Pennsylvania New York Central Transportation Company (merger of Pennsylvania, New York Central, New Haven, and Lehigh Valley railroads)
Pennines: Pennine Alps between Italy and Switzerland; Pennine Hills ranging from southern Scotland to central England—the Pennine Chain
Pennsy: Pennsylvania; Pennsylvania Railroad
Penn Turn: Pennsylvania Turnpike
Penny: Penelope
Pen of the American Revolution: Thomas Paine
Penobscot River City: Bangor, Maine
Pennsylvania Farmer: John Dickinson's pseudonym
Pennsylvania's Capital City: Harrisburg
penol: penological; penologist; penology
penrad: penetration radar
Pensy: (naval argot—Pensacola, Florida)
pent.: penetrate; penetration; pentode
Pent: Pentagon; Pentecost
Pent: *Pentateuch*
pento: (sodium) pentothal
PEO: Protect Each Other (secret women's organization)
PEOC: Publishing Employees Organizing Committee
Peony: Indiana state flower; Indiana girl's nickname
People's Daily: communist government gazette published in Peking
People of the Lion: Singhalese of Ceylon
People's Lawyer: Associate Justice Louis Dembitz Brandeis of the Supreme Court of the United States
Peory: nickname of Peoria, Illinois
pep.: pepper; peppermint; peppy
pep. (PEP): phosphoenolypyruvate; polyestradiol phosphate; Public Employment Program
P e P: *Partija e Punes:* (Albanian—Workers Party)
PEP: P.E.P. Deraniyagala; Pepsi-Cola (stock-exchange symbol); Personalized Engineering Program; Petroleum Electric Power; Political and Economic Planning; Program Evaluation Procedure
PEPA: Petroleum Electric Power Association
Pepco: Potomac Electric Power Comapny
Pepe: José (Joseph)
pepg: piezo-electric power generator
Pepita: Josefa; Josefina
PEPP: Professional Engineers in Private Practice
pepr: precision encoder and pattern recognizer
peps.: pepsin
PEPs: Public Employment Programs
PEPSU: Patiala and East Punjab States Union
PEQC: President's Environmental Quality Council
per: period; periodic; perodicity; person; personal; personate
per: *perito* (Italian—expert)
Per: Persia; Persian
Per: *Perciles, Prince of Tyre*
PER: Perth, Australia (airport)
PERA: Production Engineering Research Association
per agrim: *perito agrimensore* (Italian—surveyor)
per an.: *per annum* (Latin—by the year); *per anum* (Latin—by the anus)
per art: *perito artistico* (Italian—art expert)
perc: percolate; percussion
PERC: Peace on Earth Research Center
per call: *perito calligrafo* (Italian—handwriting expert)
Perce: Persival; Percy
per cent.: *per centum* (Latin—by the hundred)—percent
perco: percobarg (barbiturate synthetic morphine derivative); percodan (synthetic morphine derivative—both addictive and dangerous
per con.: *per contra* (Italian—on the other side)
PERCOS: Performance Coding System
Percy: Percival
perden.: *perdendosi* (Italian—dying away)
perf: perfection; perforate; performance; perfume
Perfect Butler: The Perfect Butler—nickname shared by Sir James M. Barrie's *The Admirable Crichton* and Hudson as played by Gordon Jackson in *Upstairs, Downstairs*
Perfector of Opalescent Glass: Louis Comfort Tiffany
perg: *pergamino* (Spanish—parchment)
Pergamon: Pergamon Press
perh: perhaps
peri: perigee; perimeter
PERI: Platemakers Educational and Research Institute
periap: periapical
Peric: Periclean
Perico: Pedro
peridot: yellog-green tourmaline
PERINTREP: Periodic Intelligence Report
period.: periodical
periodontol: periodontology
peris: periscope
perjy: perjury
perk.: payroll earnings record keeping
perk(s): perquisite(s)
perla: pupils equal—react to light and accommodation

perm: permanent
Perm: Permian
permaflowers: permanent (plastic) flowers
permafrost: permanent frost
permafruit: permanent (plastic) fruit
permed: permanently waved
perms: permanents; permanent waves
per nav: per navale (Italian—ship expert)
Pero: (Russian—Pen)—one of Trotsky's pseudonyms
PERO: President's Emergency Relief Organization
per. op. emet.: *peracta operatione emetici* (Latin—when the emetic action is over)
peroxide: hydrogen peroxide (H_2O_2)
perp: perpendicular
per pro.: *per procurationem* (Latin—by proxy)
perq(s): perquisite(s)
per rec: *per rectum* (Latin—through the rectum)
perrla: pupils equal, round, react to light and accommodation
pers: person; personal; personality; personnel; persons
Pers: Persia(n)
Pers: Aulus Persius Flaccus (Roman satiric poet)
PERS: Public Employees' Retirement System
Per.Sac.Lit.: Peritus in Sacred Liturgy
Perse: Percival; Percy
Persian Gulf States: Bahrain, Qatar, and the Trucial States
personi: personification; personified; personifier; personifying
pers n: personal noun
Personification of Death: Thanatos (Greek)—whose brother was Hypnos or sleep
Personification of the Destroying Principle: Siva
Personification of Justice: (*see* Justice Personified)
Personification of the Preserving Principle: Vishnu
Personification of Sleep: Hypnos (Greek)—whose brother was Thanatos or death
Personification of the Soul: Psyche in the Greek mythology where the word meant breath or soul
persp: perspective
pers pron: personal pronoun
Persymfans: *Pervyi Symfonitchesky Ansamble* (Russian—First Symphonic Ensemble)—conductorless orchestra organized in 1922 in Moscow
pert.: pertaining
pert.: *pertussis* (Latin—whooping cough)
PERT: Program Evluation Review Technique
per tecn comm: *perito tecnico-commerciale* (Italian—estimator)
Perths: Perthshire
Peru Cur: Peruvian Current
Perugino: Piero Vannucci
Peruv: Peruvian
perv: perversion; pervert; perverted
pes: photoelectric scanner
P es: *per esempio* (Italian—for example)—e.g.
PEs: Professional Engineers
PES: Philosophy of Education Society
PESA: Petroleum Equipment Suppliers Association
PESC: Public Expenditure Survey Commission
Pesh: Peshawar
PEST: Pressure for Economic and Social Toryism (leftwing conservatives)
pet.: petroleum; petrological; petrologist; petrology; point of equal time
Pet: Petronius
PET: Pierre Elliott Trudeau (Canada's nineteenth Prime Minister); Pet Milk Company (stock-exchange symbol); Production Environmental Test(ing,s); Production Evaluation Test(ing,s)
Pete: Peter; St Petersburg
Peter Arno: Curtis Arnoux Peters
Peterhouse: Saint Peter's College, Cambridge
Peter Martyr: Pietro Martin d'Anghierra's pseudonym
Peter McGill: (American slang—Pedro Miguel)—Panama Canal Locks near Balboa
Peter Mennin: Peter Mennini
Peter Pindar: Dr. John Wolcot
Peter Porcupine: William Cobbett's pseudonym
Peter Warlock: Philip Arnold Heseltine
peth: petroleum ether
petn: petition
petr: petrifaction; petrified
Petr: Petronius Arbiter (Roman satirist)
PETR: Preliminary Flight Test Report
Petrarch: Francesco Petracco
petri: petroleum
Petriburg.: *Petriburgensis* (Latin—Peterborough)
petro: petrochemical; petroleum; petrology
Petro: *Petrograd* (Russian—City of Peter)—Leningrad's name in the early days of the Russian Revolution
PETROBAS: *Petróleo Brasileiro* (Portuguese—Brazilian Petroleum Corporation)
petro-chem: petroleum-chemical
petrodollars: petroleum-controlled dollars
Petrofina: *Compagnie Financiere Belges des Pétroles* (Belgian Financed Petroleum Company)
petrog: petrography
petrol.: petroleum; petrological; petrologist; petrology
Petroleum Emirate: Kuwait
Petroleum V. Nasby: David Ross Locke's pseudonym
Petropolis: (Latin—City of Peter)—St Petersburg, Petrograd, Leningrad
pets.: prior to expiration of term of service
PETS: Posting and Enquiry Terminal System
Petya: (Russian nickname—Pyotr)—Peter
peua: pelvic examination under anesthesia
PEVE: Prensa Venezolana (Venezuelan press service)
pewter: lead-tin alloy containing some antimony
p ex: *par exemple* (French—for example
Peyronies's disease: (*see* bent-nail syndrome)
pf: perfect; performance factor; pfennig; picofarad; penumatic float; power factor; preferred; preflight; profile; profiled; proximity fuse; public funding; public funds; pulse frequency
p/f: portfolio
pf: *pro forma* (Latin—for the sake of the form), an advance declaration for a financial statement or overseas invoice
pf.: *piano e forte* (Italian—soft and then loud)
Pf: Pfennig (German—penny)
PF: frigate—patrol escort vessel (naval symbol); Physician's Forum; Pioneer & Fayette (railroad); Procurator Fiscal
P/F: Peace and Freedom (political party)
pfa: psychologic-flight avoidance; pulverized fuel ash
PFA: Private Fliers Association

P factor: hypothetical pain-producing substance produced in ischemic muscle; preservation factor
PFAS: President of the Faculty of Architects and Surveyors
pfb: preformed beam(s)
PFBMF: Polaris Fleet Ballistic Missile Force
PFBrg: pneumatic float bridge
pfc: passed flying college
Pfc: Private first class
PFC: Pusan Fisheries College
pfce: performance
pfd: preferred, present for duty; primary flash distillate
Pfd: *Pfund* (German—pound)
pf di: progressive die
pfd s: preferred spelling
PFEFES: Pacific and Far East Federation of Engineering Societies
PFEL: Pacific Far East Line
pff: pie-fed farmer
pffb: pie-fed farm boy
PFFBI: Pacific Fire Fighters Burn Institute (Sacramento)
pffg: pie-fed farm girl
PFF Inc: Police-FBI Fencing Incognito (Washington, D.C. traffickers in stolen goods)
pf fx: profiling fixture
PFGX: Pacific Fruit Growers Express
pfi: physical fitness index (PFI)
PFI: Pacific Forest Industries; Pet Food Institute; Photo Finishing Institute; Picture and Frame Institute; Pie Filling Institute; Pipe Fibrication Institute
pfk (PFK): phosphofructokinase
pfl: pressed-for-life (dress materials)
PFL: Pacific Freight Lines
PFLO: Popular Front for the Liberation of Oman
PFLP: Popular Front for the Liberation of Palestine
pfm: power factor meter; pulse frequency modulation
PFMA: Plumbing Fixture Manufacturers Association
PFNM: Petrified Forest National Monument
PFNP: Petrified Forest National Park
pfo: patent foramen ovale
pfr: peak flow rate; peak flow reading; programmable film reader; prototype fast reactor (PFR)
PFRB: Pacific Fire Rating Bureau
PFRS: Programmed Film Reader System
PFRT: Performance Flight-Rating Test; Preliminary Flight-Rating Test
pfsa: *pour faire ses adieux* (French—to say goodbye)
pfst: pianofortist (pianist)
pft: portable flame thrower
pft acct: pianoforte accompaniment
PFTC: Pestalozzi Froebel Teachers College
pfte: pianoforte (piano)
pfu: pock-forming units
pfv: physiological full value
pfv: *pour faire visite* (French—to make a call)
PFV: *Pestalozzi-Froebel Verband* (Pestalozzi-Froebel Association)
pfx: prefix
PFX: Pacific Fruit Express
pg: page; paregoric; paris granite; pay group; paying guest; permanent grade; pistol grip; postgraduate; pregnant (pronounced *pee-gee*); program guidance; proving ground; public gaol
pg: *pago* (Portuguese—paid)
p.g.: *persona grata* (Latin—an acceptable person)
pg (PG): prostaglandin
Pg: Paraguay; Paraguayan
P.G.: Preacher General
PG: gunboat patrol vessel (naval symbol); Pan American-Grace Airways; Pennsylvania-German; Post Graduate; Proctor & Gamble
PG: *Prisonnier de Guerre* (French—prisoner of war)
P.G.: *Pharmacopoeia Germanica* (Latin—German pharmacopoeia)
P & G: Procter & Gamble
P of G: Port of Galveston
pga: pressure garment assembly
pga (PGA): pteroylglutamic acid (folic acid)
PGA: Professional Golfers Association
PGAH: Pineapple Growers Association of Hawaii
p-gal(s): proof gallon(s)
pgc: per gyro compass
PGC: Peoples Gas Company
PGCE: Post-Graduate Certificate of Education
PGCOA: Pennsylvania Grade Crude Oil Association
pgd: paged; paradigm
PGD: Past Grand Deacon
PGDF: Pilot Guide Dog Foundation
pgdo: *pagado* (Spanish—paid)
pge: phenyl glycidyl ether
PGE: Pacific Great Eastern (railroad); Portland Grain Exchange
PG & E: Pacific Gas and Electric
PGEC: Professional Group on Electronic Computers
PGER: Pacific Great Eastern Railway
pgh (PGH): pituitary growth hormone
PGH: patrol gunboat—hydrofoil (naval); Philadelphia General Hospital
P-girls: pub girls (waitresses in British barrooms)
PGIT: Professional Group on Information Theory (IEEE)
PGJD: Past Grand Junior Deacon
pgl: puppy beagle (pronounced *pee-gul*)
P Gl: Port Glasgow
PGL: Provincial Grand Lodge
pgm: program
pgm (PGM): phosphoglucomutase
PGM: motor gunboat (3-letter naval symbol); Past Grand Master
PGMA: Private Grocers' Merchandising Association
pgn: pigeon
pgn (PGN): proliferative glomerulonephritis
PGNP: Pagsanjan Gorge National Park (Philippines)
PGNS: Primary Guidance and Navigation System
PGOC: Philadelphia Grand Opera Company
PGPR: Provincial Guild of Printers' Readers
pgr: population growth rate; psychogalvanic reaction; psychogalvanic response
PGRO: Pea Growing Research Association
pgs: predicted ground speed
pg's (PGs): prostaglandins
PGS: Pennsylvania-German Society; Pidaung Game Sanctuary (Burma); Power Generation System; Primary Guidance System
PGSD: Past Grand Senior Deacon
PGSW: Past Grand Senior Warden
pgt: per gross ton
PGT: Pacific Gas Transmission (company)
PGTB: General Pierre Gustave Toutant de Beauregard, CSA
PGU: Pontifical Gregorian University
pgut (PGUT): phosphogalactose

uridyl transferase
PGWA: Pottery and Glass Wholesalers' Association
ph: pharmacopoeia; phase; phone; phosphor; phot; photon; power house; precipitation hardening; previous hardening
p/h: per hour
p & h: postage and handling
ph (PH): past history
pH: hydrogen-ion concentration
Ph: Pahari; phenyl
PH: Pearl Harbor; Parachute Handler; Philharmonic Hall; Plane Handler; Power House; Public Health; Purple Heart (military decoration awarded Americans wounded in action)
pha (PHA): phytohemagglutinin
PHA: Public Housing Administration
PHADS: Phoenix Air Defense Sector
Phaedr: Phaedrus (Roman fabulist-poet)
phal: phalange; phalanx
phar: pharmacy
Phar. B.: Bachelor of Pharmacy
Phar. C: Pharmaceutical Chemist
Phar. D.: Doctor of Pharmacy
pharm: pharmaceutical; pharmacist; pharmacology; pharmacopoeia(s); pharmacy
Phar. M.: *Pharmaciae Magister* (Master of Pharmacy)
Pharmaceutical: Pharmaceutical Press
pharmacol: pharmacology
pharm chem: pharmaceutical chemistry
Pharm.D.: *Pharmaciae Doctor* (Latin—Doctor of Pharmacy)
Ph.B.: *Philosophiae Baccalaureus* (Latin—Bachelor of Philosphy)
Ph. B.J.: Bachelor of Philosophy in Journalism
ph brz: phosphor bronze
Ph. B. Sp.: Bachelor of Philosophy in Speech
Ph. C.: Pharmaceutical Chemist
PHC: Patrick Henry College
PHCC: Plumbing, Heating, Cooling Contracters
PHCIB: Plumbing-Heating-Cooling Information Bureau
ph const: phase Constant
phd: piled higher and deeper
Ph. D.: *Philosophiae Doctor* (Latin—Doctor of Philosophy)
PHD: Port Huron and Detroit (railroad)
P.H.D.: Public Health Doctor
Ph. D. Ed.: Doctor of Philosophy in Education
PHE: phenylalanine (amino acid)
P.H.E.: Public Health Engineer
PHEAA: Pennsylvania Higher Education Assistance Agency
P-head: pinhead (underground slang—small-minded person; user of amphetamine)
pheno: phenobarbital; (underground slang—user of phenobarbital)—hypnotic drug
phenolp: phenolphthlein
phenom: phenomena; phenomenal; phenomenon
Ph. G.: Graduate in Pharmacy
Ph. G.: *Pharmacopoeia Germanica* (Latin—German Pharmacopoeia)
PHG: Postman Higher Grade
PHHS: Patrick Henry High School
phi: philosophy
Phi: Philips
Ph I: *Pharmacopoeia Internationalis*
phial.: *phiala* (Latin—bottle)
PHIBLANT: Amphibious Forces —Atlantic (USN)
PHIBPAC: Amphibious Forces—Pacific (USN)
phil: philosophy
Phil: Philadelphia; Philadelphian; Philbert; Philharmonia; Philharmonic; Philip; Philippa; Philippine; Philippines; Phillip; Phillipa; The Epistle of Paul to the Philippians
Phila: Philadelphia; Philadelphian
Philada: Philadelphia (old-style abbrevation)
Philadelphia Painter: Thomas Eakins
philat: philately
PHILDis: Philadelphia Procurement District (US Army)
Philem: The Epistle of Paul to Philemon
Philidor: François Andre Danican
Philippines: Philippine Islands
Philipp Melanchthon: Philipp Schwarzerd
Philips': *Philips' Gloeilampenfabrieken* (Dutch—Philips' Electric Lamp Factory)—fifth largest corporation worldwide
Phil Is: Philippine Islands
Phil Lip: Philosophical Library
Phillies: Philadelphians
PHILLIPS: Phillips Petroleum Company
Philly: Philadelphia
Phil Mag: *Philosophical Magazine*
philol: philology
Philomela: Mercy Otis Warren whose writings under this pen name embraced drama, history, and political satire; she has been called the First Lady of the American Revolution
Phil Orch: Philadelphia Orchestra
philos: philosophy
philos educ: philosophy of education
Philosopher of the Absolute: Georg Wilhelm Friedrich Hegel
Philosopher Freethinker: Elbert Hubbard
Philosopher of Malmesbury: Thomas Hobbes
Philosopher Physician: Averroes
Philosopher of Sans Souci: Voltaire's nickname for Frederick the Great
Philosopher of the Superman: Friedrich Wilhelm Nietzche
Phil Soc: Philharmonic Society
Phil Sp: Philippine Spanish
Phil Trans: *Philosophical Transactions* (Royal Society of London)
phiz: physiognomy
Phiz: Hablot K. Browne—illustrator of the *Pickwick Papers* of Dickens—Boz
phk cells: postmortem human kidney cells
Phl: (Port of) Philadelphia
Ph. L.: Licentiate in Philosphy
PHL: Philadelphia, Pennsylvania (airport)
phl h: phillips head
PHLS: Public Health Laboratory Service
phm: phase meter
Ph. M.: *Philosophiae Magister* (Latin—Master of Philosophy)
Phm. B.: Bachelor of Pharmacy
Phm. G.: Graduate in Pharmacy
PHMS: Patrol Hydrofoil Missile Ship(s)
PHN: Public Health Nurse; Public Health Nursing
PHO: Public Hazards Office
PhOD: Philadelphia Ordnance Depot
Phoen: Phoenix
PHOENIX: Plasma Heating Obtained by Energetic Neutral Injection Experiment
Phoenixes: Phoenix Islands (Canton, Enderbury, Birnie, McKean, Phoenix, Hull, Sydney, Gardner)
Phoenix of Spain: Lope de Vega

phofl: photoflash
phon: phonetics; phonology
phone: telephone
phoneme: smallest sound unit (linguistics)
phonet: phonetic(s)
phono: phonograph
phonovision: telephone television
Phor: Phoronida
phos: phosphate; phosphorescent
phot. photograph; photographer; photographic; photography; photon; photostat; photostatic
phot: *photographie* (French—photography)—plus all derivatives such as *photocopie* (photostat), *photographe* (photographer), *photogravure, phototype,* etc.
Phot: *Photographie* (German—photography)—plus all derivatives
photac: photographic typesetting and composing (AT & T)
photint: photographic intelligence
photo: photograph; photographer; photography
photocomp: photocomposed; photocomposition
photog: photograph; photographer; photographic; photography
photogeog: photogeography
photogeol: photographic geology
Photographic Purist: Ansel Adams and Edward Weston vie for this enviable title sometimes used by others of their school
photograv: photogravure
photog(s): photographer(s)
photom: photometry
Photo Reportress: Margaret Bourke-White
phot r: photographic reconnaissance
p'house steak: porterhouse steak
php: pounds per horsepower; propeller horsepower
PHP: Public Health Plan
phr: phrase; pounds per hour; preheater
PHRA: *Poverty and Human Resources Abstracts*
Phrasemaker of Versailles: Woodrow Wilson—28th President of the United States
phraseo: phraseogram; phraseograph; phraseological (ly); phraseologist; phraseology
phren: phrenic; phrenology
PHRI: Public Health Research Institute
Phronie: Sophronia
Ph S: Philosophical Society of England
PHS: Pennsylvania Historical Society; Printing House Square; Public Health Service; Pubic Hair Society
pht: pitch, hit, and throw
Ph T: putting husband through (college or university)
PHTS: Psychiatric Home Treatment Service
phv: phase velocity
phw: pressurized heavy water
phwr (PHWR): pressurized heavy-water-moderated reactor
PHX: Phoenix, Arizona (airport)
phy: physical; physics
phyce: photocopy-control electronics unit
phylo: phylogeny
phys: physic; physical; physician; physics
phy s: physiological saline
phys dis: physical disability
phys ed: physical education
physexam: physical examination
physiat: physiatric(s); physiatrical; physiatrist
Physician Extraordinary: Sir William Osler
Physician's Physician: Jacob Mendez Da Costa
physiog: physiognomy
physiogr: physiography
physiol: physiology
physl: physiological
phys med: physical medicine
physocean: physical oceanography
Phys S: Physical Society
phys sci: physical science
phys ther: physical therapy
pi: personal income; photo interpreter; photo interpretation; pigeon trainer; pig iron; pilotless interceptor; pimp; point initiating; point insulating; point of interception; point interception; poison ivy; position indicating; position indicator; present illness; private investigator; production interval; programmed instruction; protamine insulin; protocol international (international protocol); public investigation
pi: Greek-letter symbol (π) indicating ratio of circumference of a circle to its diameter; the ratio itself; expressed as a number, *pi* is approximately 3.14159
p & i: principal and interest; protection and indemnity
Pi: piaster
P_i: inorganic orthophosphate
PI: Packaging Institute; Paducah and Illinois (railroad); Paul Isnard (Mana River settlement, French Guiana); Perlite Institute; Philippine Islands; Piedmont Airlines; Plastics Institute; Popcorn Institute; Pratt Institute; Public Information
PI: *Printer's Ink*
P.I.: *Pharmacopoeia Internationalis*
P-I: *Seattle Post-Intelligencer*
PIA: Pakistan International Airlines; Plastics Institute of America; Printing Industries of America
PIAI: Printing Industry of America, Incorporated
PIANC: Permanent International Association of Navigation Congresses
piang: *piangendo* (Italian—mournful; plaintive)
pianiss: *pianissimo* (Italian—very softly)
Pianist's Pianist: Richard Buhlig
PIARC: Permanent International Association of Road Congresses
pias: piaster
piat: projector infantry antitank (weapon)
pib: power ionosphere beacon
PIB: Polytechnic Institute of Brooklyn; Prices and Incomes Board
PIBAC: Permanent International Bureau of Analytical Chemistry of Human and Animal Food
pibal: pilot balloon
pic: piccolo; picture
pic: (French—peak)
PIC: Physics International Company; Poison Information Center (Cleveland Academy of Medicine)
PICA: Palestine Israel Colonization Association; Printing Industry Computer Associates
picar: picaresque
Piccy: Piccadilly
PICGC: Permanent International Committee on Genetic Congresses
Pickle Works: nickname of building occupied by Central Intelligence Agency in Langley, Virginia
PICIC: Pakistan Industrial Credit and Investment Corporation
Pickpocket Heroine: Defoe's *Moll Flanders*

Pick's disease: brain disorder characterized by loss of speech
PICM: Permanent International Committee of Mothers
pico: 10^{-12}
PICOE: Programmed Initiations, Commitments, Obligations, and Expenditures
PICOP: Philippine Industries Corporation of the Philippines
pics: pictures
PICS: Pacific Islands Central School
pict: pictorial; picture
Pictorial Satirist Supreme: William Hogarth
Picture Island: Enoshima, Yokahama
Picture Province: Canada's New Brunswick
pid: pelvic inflammatory disease; prolapsed intervertebral disk
PID: Procurement Information Digest
PIDA: Pet Industry Distributors Association
PIDC: Pakistan Industrial Development Corporation
PIDE: *Policia Internacional e de Defesa do Estado* (Portuguese—International Police and Defense of the State)—security police
Pid Eng: Pidgin English (hybrid dialect spoken throughout Far East)
pie.: pulmonary infiltration (with) eosinophilia
PIE: Pacific Intermountain Express (fast freight); St. Petersburg, Florida (airport)
PIEA: Petroleum Industry Electrical Association
Piedmont Plateau: Appalachian Mountain region extending from Alabama to New York, including Georgia, the Carolinas, Virginia, West Virginia, western Maryland, and Pennsylvania
Pierre Loti: (pseudonym—Louis-Marie Julien Viaud
Pierre Louÿs: (pseudonym—Pierre Louis)
Pierre-Paul Prud'hon: Pierre Prudon
Pieter Timmerman: (Dutch—Peter Carpenter)—pseudonym used by Peter the Great of Russia while working as a shipwright in Dutch shipyards
pif (PIF): prolactin inhibiting factor
PIF: Pilot Information File
pig.: pigment; pigmentation
PIG: Pride, Integrity, Guts (acronym adopted by the Chicago police)
Pig Alley: Place Pigalle
Pig Islander: New Zealander (Australian slang)
pigmt: pigment(ation)
PIGS: Poles, Italians, Greeks, Slavs—(some of America's most talented minorities)
pig's ear: (Cockney English—beer)
pik: payment in kind
pil: percentage increase in loss
pil.: *pilula* (Latin—pill)
PIL: Pest Infestation Laboratory
pilc: paper-insulated lead covered
pill: the pill (birth-control pill)
Pillars of Hercules: promontories flanking the Straits of Gibraltar—Abyla in Africa facing Gibraltar in Europe
pilnav: piloting navigation
PILO: Public Information Liaison Officer
pilot.: printing industry language for operations of typesetting
PILOT: Piloted Low-speed Test
pilot-on-board flag: signal flag consisting of a white and a red vertical band; letter H or Hotel in the international code
pilot-wanted flag: yellow-and-blue vertically-striped signal flag flown to indicate a pilot is wanted; letter G or Golf in the international code
Pilsner Country: Czechoslovakia
Pil Sta: Pilot Station
pim: penalties in minutes; pulse-interval modulation
PIMA: Paper Industry Management Association
pimola: pimento olive (pimento-stuffed olive)
pimpmobile: pimp's automobile (often custom-made with bedroom facilities)
pin.: position indicator
p in the a: pain in the ass
p/in.^{2}: parts per square inch
p/in.^{3}: parts per cubic inch
PIN: Police Information Network
PINAC: Permanent International Association of Navigation Congresses
Pind: Pindar
Pineapple Island: Lanai, Hawaii
Pine Tree State: Maine's official nickname
pin.: *pinguis* (Latin—fat; grease)
pins.: person in need of supervision
PINS: Padre Island National Seashore (Texas)
Pinturicchio: Barnardino Betti
PINWR: Pungo National Wildlife Refuge (North Carolina)
pinx.: *pinxit* (Latin—he painted it)
PINZ: Plastics Institute of New Zealand
PIO: Public Information Office(r)
pi-on: pi-meson; pioneer
Pioneer: deep-space probes designed for interplanetary investigation
Pioneer American Composer: William Billings
Pioneer of Antisepsis: Ignaz Philipp Semmelweis
Pioneer Bacteriologist: Robert Koch
Pioneer Heart Surgeon: Daniel Hale Williams
Pioneer of University Surgery: William Halsted
Pioneer of Visceral Surgery: Theodor Billroth
Pioneer Liturgical Dancer: Carla De Sola, Ruth St Denis, and Ted Shawn may all claim the name
PIOSA: Pan Indian Ocean Science Association
Piotr: (Russian—Peter)—nickname for Petersburg or St. Petersburg now Leningrad and formerly Petrograd—City of Peter
pip.: proximal interphalangeal
Pip.: Philip
PIP: Product Improvement Program
PIPA: Pacific Industrial Property Association
piper.: pulsed intense plasma for exploratory research (PIPER)
Pippa: Philipa; Philippa
PIPR: Polytechnic Institute of Puerto Rico
pips.: pulsed integrating pendulums
piq: property in question
Pir: Piraeus
PIR: Phillip Island Reserve (Victoria, Australia); Philippine Independence Ribbon
PIRA: Paper Industries Research Association; Printing Industry Research Association
Pirate City: Tampa, Florida where the pirate chief Gasparilla once ruled
PIRG: Public Interest Research Group (Ralph Nader's)
PIRGs: Public Interest Groups
pi rm: pilot reamer
Pis: Pisces
PISC: Phoenix International

Science Center
Pish: Parish
pit.: pitot static; progressive inspection tag
Pit: Pitanga; Pitcairn; Pitkin; Pitman; Piton; Pittsboro; Pittsburg; Pittsburgh; Pittsfield; Pittsford; Pittston; Pittsylvania
PIT: Pasadena Institute of Technology; Petr Ilich Tchaikovsky; Pittsburgh, Pennsylvania (airport)
PITAC: Pakistan Industrial Technical Assistance Center
Pitcher Plant Province: Newfoundland
Piter: (Russian nickname for Petrograd or St. Petersburg)
piti: principal, interest, taxes, insurance
pit. log: pitot-static log
PITO: Portuguese Information and Tourist Office
Pitons: Piton Mountains (St. Lucia)
pitr: plasma iron turnover rate
PITS: Pacific Islands Training School
Pius XII: Eugenio Pacelli
piv: peak inverse voltage; post indicator valve
PIV: Positive Infinity Variable
pix: photographs; pictures
pix/sec: pictures per second
PIYA: Pacific International Yachting Association
pizz.: *pizzicato* (Italian—plucked)
Pizza (PIE): Pacific Intermountain Express (stock exchange nickname)
pj: prune juice
PJ: Police Judge; Presiding Judge; Probate Judge
PJ: *Police Judiciare* (French—criminal investigators; detective division)
P of J: Port of Jacksonville
PJBD: Permanent Joint Board on Defense (Canada-US)
PJC: Paducah Junior College; Paris Junior College
pjm: postjunctional membrane
pj's: physical jerks
Pjs: Pasajes
pk: pack; peak; peck; psychokinesis
pK: negative logarithm of the dissociation constant (symbol)
Pk: Park; Peak; pink
Pk: *Pauken* (German—kettledrums)
PK: probability of kill (symbol)
PK: *Posta Kutusu* (Turkish—post office box)
P-K antibodies: Prausnitz-Küstner antibodies
pkb: photoelectric keyboard
PKbanken: *Post- och Kreditbanken* (Swedish—Post and Credit Bank)
pkdom: pack(ed) for domestic use
pkg: package; packing
PKL: Possum Kingdom Lake
pkmr: packmaster
PKN: *Polski Kometet Normalizacyny* (Polish Standards Committee)
PKNP: Pu Kradeung National Park (Thailand)
pkp: pre-knock pulse
PKP: *Partido Komunista Pilipinas* (Pilipino—Communist Party of the Philippines)
pkr: packer
PKR: Parker Pen (stock exchange symbol)
Pk Rdg: Park Ridge
P-K reaction: Prausnitz-Küstner reaction
pks: packs; pecks
PKS: Photo-Kit System (criminal identification)
pksea: pack(ed) for overseas use
PKSRP: Possum Kingdom State Recreation Park (Texas)
pkt: packet
PKTF: Printing and Kindred Trades Federation (UK)
pkts: packets
pku: phenylketonuria
Pkw: *Personenkraftwagen* (German—automobile; passenger vehicle)
Pkwy: Parkway
pky: pecky
Pky: Parkway (postal abbreviation)
pl: parting line; party line; perception of light; phase line; pipeline; place; plastic; plate; plural
p/l: plain language
p & l: profit and loss
pl. *plenarius* (Latin—complete; fully attended)
pl (PL): party line
Pl: Place
Pl: *Place* (French—place; plaza); *plantage* (Dutch—plantation); *plass* (Scandinavian—place; plaza); *Platz* (German—place; plaza); *plaza* (Spanish—place; plaza); *plein* (Dutch—place; plaza); Titus Maccius Plautus (Roman writer of comedies)
PL: perception of light (symbol); Place; Pluto (usually not abbreviated but sometimes as shown in honor of Percival Lowell); Point Loma; Poland (auto plaque); Port Line; Public Law; Public Library
P.L.: Poet Laureate
PL: *Partido Liberal* (Spanish—Liberal Party)
P des L: Parc des Laurentides (Quebec)—Laurentian Mountains Park
£L: pound Lebanese
PL/l: Programming Language 1
pla: plasma resin activity; probation and rehabilitation of airmen
Pla: Plaza; Pula (Pola)
PLA: Pedestrian's League of America; People's Liberation Army (Chinese communist); Philadelphia Library Association; Philatelic Literature Association; Port of London Authority; Port of Los Angeles; Private Libraries Association; Public Library Association; Pulverized Limestone Association
P of LA: Port of Los Angeles
place.: programming language for automatic checkout equipment
Place of Plenty: Indian name for what is now Toronto, Ontario
PLADS: Parachute Low-Altitude Delivery System
plame (PLAME): propulsive lift aerodynamic maneuvering entry
plan.: planet; planetarium
PLAN: Paterson Looks Ahead Now
Plan A: North Atlantic Treaty Reginal Planning Group
plane(s): airplane(s)
Planner of the New York Public Library: John Shaw Billings
PLANNET: Planning Network
Plantation State: Rhode Island whose official title is the State of Rhode Island and Providence Plantations
plantflex: plantar flexion
plantk: *plantkunde* (Dutch—botany)
Plant Wizard: Luther Burbank
plas: plaster
plaster of paris: calcium sulfate $(CaSO_4)_2 \cdot H_2O$
plat.: plateau; platinum; platoon
Plateglasses: ultra-modern style in universities
Plate River Ports: Buenos Aires, Argentina and Montevideo, Uruguay
platf: platform

Platine States: Argentina and Uruguay so named because they border on the La Plata River estuary
PLATO: Port Lincoln Advancement Trust Organization; Programmed Logic for Automatic Teaching Operations
Plato's School: the Grove of Academe near Athens where it was later referred to by the Romans as the Academia
platy: *platypoecilus* (genus of tropical fishes); platysma
Platy: Platyhelminthes
Plaut: Plautus
PLAV: Polish Legion of American Veterans
plb: plumber; plumbing; pull button
PLB: Poor Law Board
plc: power-line carrier
PLC: Probe Launch Complex; Products List Circular
P.L.C.: *Poeta Laureatus Caesareus* (Latin—Imperial Poet Laureate)
P of L C: Port of Lake Charles
PLCA: Pipe Line Contractor's Association
plcs: propellant-loading control system
plcu: propellant-level control unit
plcy: policy
pld: payload
Pld: Portland, Oregon
PLD: Paul Lawrence Dunbar
PLDG: Portuguese Language Development Group
PLDTC: Philippine Long Distance Telephone Company
P & LE: Pittsburgh & Lake Erie (railroad)
PLEA: Poverty Lawyers for Effective Advocacy
plebe: plebeian
PLEI: Public Law Education Institute
Plein-Air Painter: Manet—advocate of painting in the open air instead of in the stinking studio
Pleis: Pleistocene
Plen: Plenary; Plenipotentiary
plenipo: plenipotentiary
pleon: pleonastical(ly)
plf: polyforming
PLF: Pacific Legal Foundation
plff: plaintiff
plg: piling
PLG: Poor Law Guardian
plgl: plateglass
p-lgv: psittacosis-lymphogranuloma venereum
plh (PLH): palaemontes-lightening hormone
PLI: Plant Location International
pli: preload indicating
PLI: *Partido Liberal Independiente* (Spanish—Independent Liberal Party); *Partito Liberale Italiano* (Italian Liberal Party); *Photo-Lab-Index*
PLIDCO: Pipe Line Development Company
Plim 1: Plimsoll line
Plin C: Gaius Plinius Secundus major (Roman naturalist often referred to as Pliny the Elder)
Plin L: Plinius Caecilius Secundus minor (Roman writer often referred to as Pliny the Younger)
Plioc: Pliocene
plis: propellant-level indicating system
plk: plank
PLK: Phi Lambda Kappa; Poincare-Lighthill-Kuo (mathematical method)
p lkr: peacoat locker
PLL: Prince Line Limited
plm: pulse-length modulation
P-L-M: Paris-Lyon-Méditerranée (famous French railway)
plmb: plumber; plumbing
Plms: Palms (postal abbreviation)
pln: posterior lymph node
pl-n: place-name
Pln: Plain (postal abbreviation)
PLN: *Partido Liberación Nacional* (Spanish—National Liberation Party); *Partido Liberal Nacionalista* (Spanish—National Liberal Party)
plng: planning
PLNP: Port Lincoln National Park (South Australia)
Plns: Plains (postal abbreviation)
PLO: Palestine Liberation Organization; Presidential Libraries Office (Library of Congress)
PLO: *Pairti Lucht Oibre* (Irish—Labour Party); *Polskie Linie Oceaniezne* (Polish Ocean Lines)
plot.: plotting
PLP: Parliamentary Labour Party; Progressive Labor Party
pl & pd: personal loss and personal damage
PLPP: Pennsylvania League for Planned Parenthood
plr: pillar
Plr: Pillar (postal abbreviation)
PLR: Philippine Liberation Ribbon
PLR: *Partido Liberal Radical* (Spanish—Radical Liberal Party)
P L & R: Postal Laws & Regulations
PLRA: Photo Litho Reproducers' Association
plry: poultry
pls: plates; please
PLS: Purnell Library Service
plsd: promotion list service date
Pl Sgt: Platoon Sergeant
plshr: polisher
PLSS: Portable Life-Support System
plstc: plastic
plstr: plasterer
plt: pilot: psittacosis-lymphogranuloma trachoma
pltc: political
pltf: plaintff
pltry: poultry
PLTS: Point Loma Test Site (Convair)
plu: plural; plurality
PLU: Patrice Lumumba University (Moscow)
Plucky: Pierre Salinger
Plum: Sir Pelham Warner; Sir P.G. Wodehouse
plumb.: plumber; plumbing
plumb.: *plumbum* (Latin—lead)
plumcot: plum plus apricot (hybrd)
Plumed Knight: Robert G. Ingersoll's name for James G. Blaine when nominating him for President
PLUNA: Primeras Líneas Uruguayas de Navegación Aérea (First Uruguayan Aerial Navigation Lines)
pluperf: pluperfect
Plus Brave des Braves: (French—Bravest of the Brave)—Napoleon's nickname for Marshal Ney
Plus Ultra: (Spanish—Better than Best; More Beyond)—official motto of Spain
plute(s): plutocrat(s)
pluto (PLUTO): pipeline under the ocean
Pluto: (Latin—Hades or Pluton)—god of the dead and the underworld
Pluv: *Pluviôse* (French—Rainy Month)—beginning January 20th—fifth month of the French Revolutionary Calendar
plx: plexus; propellant-loading transfer
Ply: Plymouth
plywd: plywood

Plz: Plaza
pm: post mortem; premium; premolar; presystolic murmur; preventive maintenance (PM); publicity man; pulse modulation; pumice
P.M.: *post meridiem* (Latin—after noon)
p-m: permanent magnet; phase modulation
p/m: pounds per minute
pm: *poids molículaire* (French—molecular weight)
Pm: promethium
PM: Past Master; Pattern Maker; Pay Master; Peabody Museum; Pére Marquette (railroad); Petróleos Mexicanos; Physical Medicine; Police Magistrate; Pontifex Maximum; Postmaster; Prime Minister; Provost Marshal (pronounced *provo marshal*); publicity man
P.M.: Prime Minister
P.M.: *Piae Memoriae* (Latin—of pious memory)
P/M: Pacific Molasses
P de M: Principaute de Monaco (Monte Carlo)
pma: positive mental attitude
PMA: Pacific Maritime Association; Parts Manufacturing Associates; Peat Moss Association; Pencil Makers Association; Pharmaceutical Manufacturers Association; Philadelphia Museum of Art; Philippine Mahogany Association; Phonograph Manufacturers Association; Precision Measurements Association; Primary Mental Abilities (test); Production and Marketing Administration
PMAE: Peabody Museum of Archeology and Ethnology
PMAF: Pharmaceutical Manufacturers' Association Foundation
PMATA: Paint Manufacturers' and Allied Trades Association
pmb: post-menopausal bleeding
PMB: Potato Marketing Board
PMBC: Pacific Motor Boat Club; Portland Motor Boat Club (Oregon)
pmbx: private manual branch exchange
PMC: Pacific Medical Center; Pennsylvania Military Academy; Princeton Microfilm Corporation
PMDS: Property Management and Disposal Service
P Me: Portland, Maine
PMEA: Powder Metallurgy Equipment Association
PMEL: Precision Measuring Equipment Laboratory
pmest: personality, matter, energy, space, time (Raganathan's fundamental categories)
pmet: painted metal
pmf: progressive massive fibrosis
PMF: Presidential Medal of Freedom
PmG: Paymaster General; Postmaster General
PMG: Provost Marshal General
PMG: *Pall Mall Gazette*
pmh: past medical history
pmi: photographic micro-image
PMI: Palma de Mallorca, Balearic Islands, Spain (airport)
PMIS: Personnel Management Information System
PMJC: Pine Manor Junior College
pmk: pitch mark; postmark(ed)
PML: Pacific Micronesian Line; Pierpont Morgan Library
PMLA: Publications of the Modern Language Association of America
PMLO: Principal Military Landing Officer
pmm: pulse mode multiplex
PMMI: Packaging Machinery Manufacturing Institute
pmn: polymorphonuclear neutrophil
PMNA: Parkers Marsh Natural Area (Virginia)
PMNH: Peabody Museum of Natural History
pmnr: periadenitis mucosa necrotica recurrens
PMO: Palomar Mountain Observatory; Principal Medical Officer
PM & OA: Printers' Managers and Overseers Association
pmp: precious metal plating; previous menstrual period
pm & r: physical medicine and rehabilitation
Pmr: Paymaster
PMR: Pacific Missile Range
PMRAFNS: Princess Mary's Royal Air Force Nursing Service
PMRL: Pulp Manufacturer's Research League
PMRM: Periodic Maintenance Requirements Manual
PMRS: Physical Medicine and Rehabilitation Service
pms: poor miserable soul; postmenopausal syndrome; pregnant mare's serum
pm's: push monies
pms (PMS): phenazine methosulphate
PMS: Public Message Service
pmsg: pregnant mare's serum gonadotrophin
PMST: Professor of Military Science and Tactics
pmt: payment; premenstrual tension
PMTS: Predetermined Motion Time System
PMU: Pattern Makers Union
PMVB: Pocono Mountain Vacation Bureau
pmvi: periodic motor vehicle inspection
p mvr: prime mover
pmx: private manual exchange (telephone)
pmyob: please mind your own business
pn: partition; part number; percussion note; percussive note; please note; position; promissory note; psychiatry-neurology; psychoneurotic
p-n: positive-negative
p/n: part number; promissory note
p & n: psychiatry and neurology
Pn: North Pole; North Celestial Pole; perigean range
PN: Pacific Northern (airline); Pan-American World Airways (stock exchange symbol); part number; plasticity number; point of no return; Practical Nurse
P/N: Part Number
P & N: Piedmont and Northern (railroad)
PN: *Partido Nacional* (Spanish—National Party); *Partido Nacionalista* (Spanish—Nationalist Party)
pna (PNA): pentosenucleic acid
Pna: Panama
PNA: Pacific Northern Arilines
PNAI: Provincial Newspapers Association of Ireland
pnavq: positive-negative ambivalent quotient
PNB: Philippine National Bank
PNB: *Produto National Bruto* (Portuguese—Gross National Product)
PNBA: Pacific Northwest Booksellers Association
PNBB: *Parc National de la Boucle du Baoule* (French—Baoule River Bend National Park)—in the highlands of Mali
PNBC: Pacific Northwest Bibliographic Center (American and

Canadian libraries)
PNBP: *Parc National de la Boucle de la Pendjari* (French—Pendjari River Bend National Park)—in northwestern Dahomey
pnbt: paranitroblue tetrazoleum
pnc: penicillin
P 'n C: Picnic 'n Chicken
PNC: Prohibition National Committee
PNC: *Parque Nacional Canaima* (Spanish—Canaima National Park)—encloses Venezuela's Angel Falls—world's tallest waterfall
Pncla: Pensacola
pnd: paroxysmal nocturnal dyspnoea; postnasal drip
pndb: perceived noise decibels
pndg: pending
P-N-D-L-R: parking-neutral-driving-low-gear-reverse (positions on automatic automotive transmission dial)
Pndo: Pinedo
pne: practical nurse's education
PNE: Pacific National Exhibition (Vancouver)
PNEA: *Parque Nacional El Ávila* (Spanish—El Avila National Park)—between Caracas and the Caribbean where it encloses the Humboldt National Monument of Venezuela
P Ned: *Pharmacopee Nederlandsche* (Dutch—Netherlands' Pharmacopeia)
Pnes: Pines (postal abbreviation)
pneu: pneumatic(s)
PNEU: Parents' National Education Union
pneumonoultra: pneumonoultramicroscopicsilicovolcanoconiosis (miner's lung disease)
pnf: propriceptive neuromuscular facilitation
pnfd: present not for duty
p.n.g.: *persona non grata* (Latin—an unacceptable person)
Png: Penang
PNG: Papua New Guinea; Professional Numismatists Guild
PNG: *Parque Nacional Guatopo* (Spanish—Guatopo National Park)—near Caracas, Venezuela
pnh (PNH): paroxysmal nocturnal hemoglobinuria
PNH: Phnom-Penh, Cambodia (airport)
PNHA: Physicians National Housestaff Association
PNHP: *Parque Nacional Henri Pittier* (Spanish—Henri Pittier National Park)—near Maracay, Venezuela
PNI: *Parque Nacional Iguazu* (Spanish—Iguazu National Park)—international park surrounding the Iguazu Falls shared by Argentina, Brazil, and Paraguay
pnl: panel
PNL: Pacific Naval Laboratories; Pacific Northwest Laboratories; Philippine National Line
PNLA: Pacific Northwest Library Association; Pacific Northwest Loggers Association
PNM: Pinnacles National Monument (California)
pno: *pergamino* (Spanish—parchment)
P 'n' O: P and O (Peninsular and Occidental Steamship Company; Peninsular and Oriental Line)—P & O
PNO: Port of New Orleans
PNO: *Parque Nacional Ordesa* (Spanish—Ordesa National Park)—near Spain's French frontier
pnp: positive negative positive
PNP: People's National Party; Platt National Park (Oklahoma)
pnpn: positive-negative positive-negative
pnpr: positive-negative pressure respiration
pnr: prior notice required
Pnr: Pioneer
PNR: Passenger Name Record (airlines); Pulletop Nature Reserve (New South Wales)
pns: parasympathetic nervous system; peripheral nervous system
PNS: Pacific Navigation Systems; Pakistan Naval Ship; Philadelphia Naval Shipyard; Philippine News Service; Professor of Naval Science
PNSN: *Parque Nacional Sierra Nevada* (Spanish—Sierra Nevada National Park)—encloses Venezuela's Mount Bolívar—highest peak in the republic
PNSTDC: Pakistan National Scientific and Technical Documentation Center
PNSY: Portsmouth Naval Shipyard
Pnt: Pentagon
PNT: *Parque Nacional Tijuca* (Portuguese—Tijuca National Park)—on the slopes of Mount Tijuca in the ring of mountains enclosing Rio de Janeiro, Brazil
Pnt Anx: Pentagon Annex
PNTBT: Partial Nuclear Test Ban Treaty
pntd: painted
PNTO: Principal Naval Transport Officer
pntr: painter
PNU: Pneumatic Scale Corporation (stock-exchange symbol)
p-nut butter: peanut butter
PNW: Parc National du W (W-shaped national park on the borders of Dahomey, Niger, and Upper Volta)
PNWL: Pacific Northwest Laboratory (AEC)
PNWR: Piedmont National Wildlife Refuge (Georgia); Presquile National Wildlife Refuge (Virginia); Pungo National Wildlife Refuge (North Carolina)
pnx: pneumothorax
PNYA: Port of New York Authority
PNYCTC: Pennsylvania New York Central Transportation Company (merger of Pennsylvania and New York Central railroads)
Pnz: Penzance
po: poetry; polarity; power-operated; power oscillator; previous orders
po': poor
p-o: postoperative
p/o: part of
p & o: paints and oil; pickled and oiled
p.o.: *per os* (Latin—by mouth)
Po: polonium; Portugal; Portuguese
P°: Pedro
pO_2: oxygen pressure
PO: Passport Office; Patent Office; Personnel Office(r); Petty Officer; Philadelphia Orchestra; Port Office(r); Post Office; Project Office; Province of Ontario; purchase order
P-O: Pyrénées-Orientales
P/O: Parole Officer; Pilot Officer; Probation Officer
P & O: Peninsular & Occidental Steamship Company; Peninsular & Oriental Line
PO: *Portland Oregonian*
PO 1/C: Petty Office First Class
PO 2/C: Petty Office Second Class
PO 3/C: Petty Officer Third Class
poa: primary optical area; pri-

mary optic atrophy
POA: Police Officers Association; Portland Opera Association
POAC: Peace Officers Association of California
POADS: Portland Air Defense Sector
POAU: Protestants and Other Americans United for Separation of Church and State
pob: point of beginning
POB: post office box
po'-boy: poor-boy (sandwich)
pobra: pony + zebra (hybrid)
poc: privately-owned conveyance
POC: Pittsburgh Opera Company; port of call
Pocahontas: (Algonquin—Tomboy)—nickname of Matoka the daughter of Chief Powhatan; her married name was Rebecca Rolfe
Poca(loo): Pocatello, Idaho
po'ch: porch
pocill.: *pocillum* (Latin—small cup)
pock: pocket
Pocket Bks: Pocket Books
Poconos: Pocono Mountains of eastern Pennsylvania
poc's: ports of call
POCS: Patent Office Classification System
pocul.: *poculum* (Latin—cup)
pod.: payable on (or upon) death; point-of-origin device; port of debarkation; port of departure
POD: Port of Debarkation; Post Office Department
POD: *Pocket Oxford Dictionary*
POE: Pacific Orient Express; port of embarkation; port of entry
poe buoy: plank-on-edge buoy
p o'ed: put out
POED: Post Office Engineering Department
P.08: German marking denoting the so-called luger service pistol
poet.: poetical(ly); poetry
Poet of the American Revolution: Philip Freneau
Poet of the Body—Poet of the Soul: Walt Whitman's self-imposed nickname
Poet of Childhood: Eugene Field
Poet of Democracy: Walt Whitman
Poet of Imperialism: Rudyard Kipling
Poet King: Ossian of Ireland
Poet Laureate of England: Sir John Betjeman
Poet Laureate of New England: John Greenleaf Whittier
Poet Laureatess of Venezuela: Irma De Sola Ricardo
Poet Naturalist: Henry David Thoreau
Poet of the Piano: Frédéric Chopin
Poet of Poets: Shelley
POETS: Phooey On Everything—Tomorrow's Saturday
POEU: Post Office Engineering Union
P of E: Port of Entry
pof: please omit flowers
pof (POF): pyruvate oxidation factor
POFI: Pacific Oceanographic Fisheries Investigation
POG: Pacific Oceanographic Group (British Columbia)
POGO: Pennzoil Offshore Gas Operators; Polar Orbiting Geophysical Observatory
pOH: alkalinity factor
poi: poison; poisonous (on labels should be spelled out and symbolized with skull and crossbones)
POI: Personal Orientation Inventory; Program of Instruction
pois: poison
Poison Ivy: Upton Sinclair's nickname for Ivy Lee
Poke: slang shortcut—Poughkeepsie
pol: petroleum-oil-and-lubricants (POL); polar; polarize(d); police; political; politician; problem-oriented language
Pol: Poland; Polish
Pol: *Polonia* (Italian, Latin, Spanish—Poland); *Polonia* (Portuguese—Poland)
POL: Pacific Oceanography Laboratories; petroleum-oil-and-lubricants; Polish Ocean Lines
p-ola: payola (remuneration for touting a so-called hit tune)—device of disreputable disc jockeys and record reviewers
Pola: Appolina; Policarpa Salabarrieta
POLA: Prostitutes of Los Angeles (protective association)
Pol Ad: Political Adviser
polad(s): political adviser(a)
Pola Negri: Appolina Chapulez
polar.: polarity; polarization; polarize(d)
pol com: political committee
pol econ: political economy
POLEX: Polar Experiment (weather)
POLFER: *Polizia Ferroviaria* (Italian—Railroad Police)
pol ind: pollen index
polio: poliomyelitis
poli sci: political science
Polish: Tchaikovsky's Symphony No. 3 in D major
Polish City: Hamtramck, Michigan
Polish National Composer: Frédéric Chopin
Polish Story Teller: Isaac Bashevis Singer
Polish Town: Panna Maria, Texas—settled in 1853 and America's oldest Polish settlement
polit: political; politician; politics
Politburo: Politicheskoe Byuro (Russian—Political Bureau of the Central Committee)
poll.: pollution
Polly: Mary; Pauline; Pollyanna
pols: political prisoners; politicians
pol(s): politician(s)
POLs: Problem-Oriented Languages (computer)
pol sci: political science
POLSTRADA: *Polizia Stradale* (Italian—Highway Police)
polwar: political warfare
poly: polyethylene; polymer; polytechnic; polytechnical; polyvinyl
po'ly: poorly
Poly: Polynesia; Polynesian; Polytechnic (institute or school)
Polyb: Polybius
poly bot: polyethylene bottle
polymorph: polymorphous
poly sci: political science
polysex: polysexual(ity)
polytech: polytechnic(al)
polywater: polymerized water
pom: pomeranian; pomological; pomology; pom-pom; preparation for overseas movement
pom: *pomeridiano* (Italian—afternoon; p.m.)
POM: Port Moresby, New Guinea (airport)
POME: Prisoners of Mother England—Pommies; early convict immigrants (Australian slang)
POMFLANT: Polaris Missile Facility, Atlantic
POMPAC: Polaris Missile Facility, Pacific
Pompey: Cneius Pompeius; nickname of Portsmouth, England
pom-pom: antiaircraft gun
POMR: Problem-Oriented Medical Record
POMS: Panel on Operational

Meteorological Satellites
pomsee: preparation, operation, maintenance, shipboard electronics equipment
POMSIP: Post Office Management Service Improvement Program
pon: pontoon
Pon: Ponce
pona: paraffin, olefin, napthene, aromatic (test for petroleum octane rating)
PonBrg: pontoon bridge
pond.: *pondere* (Latin—by weight)
p-on-n: positive on negative
Pont: Pontevedra
pont b: pontoon bridge
Ponti: Pontiac
Pontines: Pontine Islands off Anzio, Italy or the Pontine Marshes of Italy
Pont. Max.: *Pontifex Maximus* (Latin—Supreme Pontiff—the Pope
PONY: Prostitutes of New York (protective association)
POO: Post Office Order
pood: poodle dog; (Russian—36-lb. weight)
POOD: Provisioning Order Obligation Document
poof.: peripheral on-line-oriented function
poop.: nincompoop
Poor Richard: Richard Saunders (pseudonym used by Benjamin Franklin in writing *Poor Richard's Almanack*)
pop: carbonated beverage; poppet; popular; population
pop.: carbonated beverage; perpendicular ocean platform (POP); persistent occipito-posterior; plasma osmotic pressure; plaster of paris; popliteal; poppet; popular; population
p-o-p: plaster of paris; printing-out-paper
p-op: post-operative
Pop: Poppa
POPA: Property Owners Protection Association
pop art: popular art (advertising displays, comic strips, posters)
Popcorn Capital of the World: Shaller, Iowa
Pope of Geneva: Calvin's nickname
Pope John XXIII: Angelo Giuseppe Roncalli
Pope Paul VI: Giovanni Battista Montini
Pope Pius XI: Achille Ratti
Pope Pius XII: Eugenio Pacelli
popex: population explosion
popf: prepared-on-premises flavor
popi: post office position indicator (navigation system developed by British post office)
poplit: popliteal
Popo: Popocatepetl
pops: popular concerts; popular tunes
Pop Sci: *Popular Science*
POQ: *Public Opinion Quarterly*
por: porosity; porous; public opinion research
p-o-r: pay-on-receipt; payable-on-receipt
Por: Porifera
POR: *Policy, Organisation, and Rules* (of the Girl Guides and Scouts)
PORAC: Peace Officers Research Association of California
porc: porcelain
PORC: Peralta Oaks Research Center
PORIS: Post Office Radio Interference Station
Pork Packer: Philip D. Armour
porn: pornographic; pornography (see *porno*)
Porn Capital of America: San Francisco
porno: pornofilm; pornographer; pornographic; pornographically; pornographic bookshop; pornography (defined by Irvin S. Cobb as when the depth of the dirt exceeds the width of the wit)
pornobio: pornographic biography
pornofilm: pornographic motion picture
pornos: pornographic books, moving pictures, photographs, recordings, etc.
pornovel: pornographic + novel (usually what it sounds like—a poor novel)
porp(s); porpoise(s)
PORS: Post Office Research Station
port.: portable; portrait; portraiture
Port: Portland; Portugal; Portuguese
Port Chi: Port Chicago; Portuguese China
Porter of Heaven: Janus the Two-Faced (so named because the door he guards, like all doors, faces two ways)
Portia: pen name of Abigail Smith Adams—wife of President John Adams and America's First Suffragist
Port Ind: Portuguese India
Port Jeff: Port Jefferson
Port of the Pilgrims: Provincetown, Massachusetts
Portrait Painter of Presidents: Gilbert Stuart
port side: *lefthand* side of an airplane, ship, or other craft when looking forward, symbolized by a fixed *red* light—on the *lefthand* wingtip of an airplane or set against a red background on the *lefthand* side of a ship's bridge or pilothouse
Port Tim: Portuguese Timor
Portuguese America: Brazil—formerly Portugal's largest possession
Portuguese China: Macao (near Hong Kong)
Portuguese East Africa: Mozambique—formerly a colony of Portugal
Portuguese Mars: Affonso d'Alboquerque also called Affonso o Grande (Alphonse the Great)—Portuguese empire builder and viceroy of Portuguese India
Portuguese Paradise: Sintra near Lisbon
Portuguese-speaking Places: Angola, Azores Islands, Brazil, Cape Verde Islands, Guinea-Bissa, Macao, Madeira Islands, Mozambique, Portugal, São Tomé and Principe Islands, plus a few other former Portuguese port possessions in India and Indonesia such as Goa and Timor, respectively
Portuguese Timor: former Portuguese outpost of empire on Timor Island in Indonesia
Portuguese West Africa: Angola—formerly a colony of Portugal
Port Wine Port: Oporto, Portugal
pos: position; positive
PoS: Point of Sale; Point of Service; Port of Spain
POs: Police Officers; Postal Orders
POS: Port-of-Spain, Trinidad (airport)
POSB: Post Office Savings Bank
POSD: Post Office Savings Department
posdcorb: planning-organization-staffing-directing-coordinating-reporting-budgeting (mnemonic device for remember-

ing the functions of management)
Poseidon: (Greek—Neptune)—god of the sea
posh: port side out, starboard side home (British slang)
positron: positive electron
posm: patient-operated selected mechanisms
posn: position
POSNY: People of the State of New York
pos pron: possessive pronoun
poss: possession; possessive
POSS: Passive Optical Satellite Surveillance (System)
P-O-S S: Point-of-Sale System; Point-of-Service System
post.: postage; postal; posterior; post mortem
POST: Frederick Post Drafting Equipment; Police Officer Student Training
post-Aug: post-Augustan
post. d: posterior diameter
poster.: posterior
postgangl: postganglionic
postgrad(s): postgraduate(s)
posth: posthumous
postl: postlude
post-mort: post mortem (autopsy)
post-op: post-operative
post-sync: post-synchronization of a sound track made after a motion-picture film has been shot
pot.: point of tangency; potash; potassa (potassium hydroxide); potassium; potential; potentiometer; (slang— marijuana)
pot.: *potaguaya* (Mexican Indian—marijuana); *potio* (Latin—dose; draft; potion)
Potain's disease: pleural and pulmonary edema
'potamus: hippopotamus
potash: potassium carbonate (K_2CO_3)
potash alum: potassium aluminum sulfate
Potash City: Saskatoon, Saskatchewan
potass: potassium
potats: potatoes
POTC: PERT *(q.v.)* Orientation and Training Program
Potomac River City: Washington, D.C.
pots.: potentiometers
pott: pottery
Pott's disease: vertebral inflammation
PotUS: Lyndon Johnson's acronym meaning President of the United States
pot w: potable water
poul: poultry
POUM: *Partido Obrero de Unificación Marxista* (Spanish—Workers Party of Marxist Unification)
POUNC: Post Office Users' National Council
POUR: President's Organization for Unemployment Relief
pov: privately owned vehicle
pow: power; prisoner of war (POW)
P o W: Prince of Wales
POW Country: Potash, Oil, and Wheat Country around Saskatoon, Saskatchewan
powd: powder; powdered
Powder Keg of Europe: the Balkans
POWER: Professionals Organized for Women's Equal Rights
pows (POWS): prisoners of war
POWS: Pyrotechnic Outside Warning System
Poz: Poznan
pozn: *poznamka (Czech-footnote)*
pp: pages; panel point; parcel post; part paid; partial pay; partially paid; past participle; passive participle; pellagra preventive (factor); permanent party; petticoat peeping; physical profile; physical properties; pickpocket; postpaid; postage paid; present position; pressure-proof; privatel printed; private property; professional paper; purchased part(s); push-pull
p-p: peak-to-peak; push-pull
p-to-p: peak-to-peak; point-to-point
pp: *pianissimo* (Italian—very softly)
p.p.: *piena pelle* (Italian—full leather)
Pp.: *Papa* (Latin—father or Pope)
PP: Pacific Petroleum; Parcel Post; Parish Priest; Past President; Power Plant; Proletarian Party (Communist)
PP: *Polizei Pistole* (German—police pistol)
P-P: pellegra-preventive factor
P-au-P: Port-au-Prince
PP: *Patres* (Latin—Fathers)
P.P.: *Pater Patriae* (Latin—Father of his Country)
ppa: palpitation, percussion, auscultation; photo-peak analysis
p. pa.: *per procura* (Latin—by proxy)
p.p.a.: *phiala prius agitate* (Latin—bottle having first been shaken)—shake well before using
pp & a: palpitation, percussion, and auscultation
PPA: Pakistan Press Association; Paper Pail Association; Paper Plate Association; Parcel Post Association; Periodical Publishers Association; Popcorn Processors Association; Poultry Publishers Association; President's Professional Association; Produce Packaging Association; Professional Photographers of America; Proletarian Party of America; Public Personnel Association; Purple Plum Association
PPATRA: Printing, Packaging, and Allied Trades Research Association (also appears as PATRA)
ppb: parts per billion
Ppb: *Pappband* (German—boards; hard cover)
ppb (PPB): polybrominated biphenyl (cattle poison)
PPBAS: Planning-Programming-Budgeting-Accounting System
PPBES: Planning-Programming-Budgeting-Evaluation System
PPBS: Planning-Programming-Budgeting System
ppc: picture postcard; progressive patient care
p p c: *pour prendre congé* (French—to take leave)
PPC: Pet Population Control; Policy Planning Council (U.S. Department of State); Purchase Price Control
ppca: plasma prothrombin conversion accelerator
PPCD: Plant Pest Control Division
ppcf: plasma prothrombin conversion factor
PPCLI: Princess Patricia's Canadian Light Infantry
PPCS: Primary Producers' Cooperative Society
ppd: prepaid; purified protein derivative (tuberculin)
PPD: Portland Public Docks
PPD: *Partido Popular Democrático* (Spanish—Popular Democratic Party)
PPDA: Produce Packaging Development Association
p p^{do}: *próximo pasado (Span-*

ish—last month)
PPDP: Preprogram Definition Phase
PPDS: Publishers' Parcels Delivery Service
PPDSE: Plate Printers, Die Stampers, and Engravers (union)
ppe: philosophy, politics, and economics
(PPF): Plumbers and Pipefitters (union)
PPFA: Planned Parenthood Federation of America
p-p factor: pellagra-preventive factor
PPG: Pago Pago, Samoan Islands (airport); Pittsburgh Plate Glass
ppga: post-pill galactorrhea-amenorrhea
pph: post-partum hemorrhage; pounds per hour; pulses per hour
pphpm: parts per hundred parts of mix; pints per hundred parts of mix
pphr: parts per hundred parts of rubber
PP[1]: inorganic pyrophosphate
ppi: pages per inch; parcel post insured; plan position indicator
PPI: Plastic Pipe Institute; Project Public Information
pp/in.: pages per inch
pPk: purplish pink
ppl: pipeline
PPL: Philadelphia Public Library; Phoenix Public Library; Pittsburgh Public Library; Portland Public Library; Providence Public Library; Provisioning Parts List
PP&L: Pennsylvania Power and Light (company)
P-plane: pilotless airplane (explosive carrying and reaction propelled)
pple: past participle
pplo: pleuropneumonia-like organism(s)
ppm: parts per million; pounds per minute; pulse position modulation
***PPM:** Persutuan Perpustakaan Malaysia* (Malay—Library Association of the Federation of Malaya)
PPMS: Plastic Pipe manufacturers' Society
ppn: proportion(al)
PPNP: Point Pelee National Park (Ontario)
ppo: polyphenylene oxide; prior permission only
p-p-ola: political plugola (media plugging or touting of a candidate or an ideological issue)—propaganda device in disrepute
ppp: petty political pismire
p & pp: pull and push plate
***ppp:** piu pianissimo* (Italian—very very softly)
PPP: Peoples Party of Pakistan; Petroleum Production Pioneers; Population Policy Panel (Hugh Moore Fund)
ppr: present particple; prior permission required
PPR: Permanent Pay Record; Permanent Personal Registration; Procurement Problem Report
PPRA: Past President of the Royal Academy
PPRICA: Pulp and Paper Research Institute of Canada
pps: pictures per second; pounds per second; pulses per second
PPS: Paper Publications Society, Pennsylvania Prison Society
***PPS:** Partido Popular Salvadoreño* (Spanish—Salvadoran Popular Party)—of El Salvador, Central America; *Partido Popular Socialista* (Spanish—Popular Socialist Party), *Persatuan Perpustakaan Singapura* (Malay—Library Association of Singapore)
***P.P.S.:** post postscriptum* (Latin—additional postscript)
PPSA: Pan-Pacific Surgical Association
PPSAWA: Pan Pacific and Southeast Asia Women's Association
PPSB: Periodical Publishers' service Bureau
PPSEAWA: Pan-Pacific and South-East Asia Women's Association
ppt: precipitate
PPT: Papeete, Society Islands (airport); Pre-Production Test(ing)
pptd: precipitated
pptn: precipitation
ppty: property
PPU: Peace Pledge Union
P & PU: Peoria and Pekin Union (railroad)
ppv: people-powered vehicle(s)
PPVT: Peabody Picture Vocabulary Test
PPWC: Pines to Palms Wildlife Committee; Pulp, Paper, and Woodcutters of Canada
PPWP: Planned Parenthood-World Population
pq: peculiar; permeability quotient; personality quotient (PQ); previous question; punishment quarters
p & q: peace and quiet (solitary confinement)
PQ: personality quotient; Province of Quebéc; South Pacific Airlines of New Zealand (2-letter code)
***PQ:** Parti Quebecois* (French—Québec Party)
pqa: procurement quality assurance
PQAP: Procurement Quality Assurance Program
PQC: Production Quality Control
PQD: Plant Quarantine Division
***PQD:** Partido Quisqueyano Demócrata* (Spanish—Democratic Quisqueyan Party)—Dominican Republic's people called Quisqueyanos
PQIH: Plant Quarantine Inspection House
pr: pair; payroll; percentile rank; peripheral resistance; public relations
***p.r.:** per rectum* (Latin—by the rectum); *punctum remotum* (Latin—remote point)—far point of vision
p/r: per rectum
p & r: parallax and refraction
pR: purplish red
Pr: Parana; Prairie (postal abbreviation) prandtl number; praseodymium; presbyopia; Press; Prince; propyl
***Pr:** Praca* (Portuguese—plaza; square); *Presbyter* (Latin—elder or priest)
PR: Parachute Rigger; Performance Report; Photoreconnaissance; Pinar del Rio; Plant Report; Problem Report; Progress Report; Public Relations; Puerto Rican(s); Puerto Rico; river gunboat (2-letter naval symbol)
P-R: Pennsylvania-Reading (Seashore Lines)
P/R: payroll
***PR:** Partido Republicano* (Spanish—Republican Party); *Peking Review; Polskie Radio* (Polish Radio); *Puerto Rico*
P.R.: (Latin—Populus Romanus)—Roman people
pra: plasma renin activity; probation and rehabilitation of airmen
***Pra:** Prachtausgabe* (German—de luxe edition)
PRA: Pay Readjustment Act;

Personnel Research Activity; Popular Rotocraft Association; Psoriasis Research Association; Psychological Research Association; Public roads Administration; Puerto Rico Association
P.R.A.: President of the Royal Academy
prac: practice; practitioner
pract: practical; practice; practitioner
Praeger: Frederick A. Praeger
praen: praenomen
prag: pragmatic; pragmatism
Pragmatist Philosopher: William James
Prague: Mozart's Symphony No. 38 in D major he named for Bohemia's capital containing his favorite audiences
PRAICO: Puerto Rican American Insurance Company
Prair: *Prairial* (French—Meadowy Month)—beginning May 20th—ninth month of the French Revolutionary Calendar
Prairie City: Bloomington, Illinois
Prairie Provinces: Alberta, Manitoba, Saskatchewan
Prairie State: official nickname of Illinois
Prairie States: North and South Dakota, Nebraska, Kansas, Minnesota, Iowa, and Illinois
pral: *principal* (Spanish—principal)
pram: perambulator
Pr of An: Principality of Ansbach
prand.: *prandium* (Latin—dinner)
PRANG: Puerto Rico Air National Guard
PRAT: Prattsburgh (railroad)
p. rat. aet.: *pro ratione aetatis* (Latin—in proportion to age)
Prater: Vienna's park along the Danube
PRATRA: Philippines Relief and Trade Rebilitation Administration
Pravda: (Russian—truth)—seven-days-a-week newspaper published in Moscow by the Central Committee of the Communist Party of the Soviet Union
PRAY: Paul Revere Associated Yeoman
PRB: Personnel Review Board; Population Reference Bureau; Pre-Raphaelite Brotherhood
prc: procedure
PRC: Pension Research Council; People's Republic of China (Red China); Picatinny Research Center (Picatinny Arsenal); Planning Research Corporation; Postal Rate Commission; Public Relations Club
P.R.C.: *Post Roman Conditam* (Latin—after the founding of Rome)—753 Before the Christian Era
PRCA: Professional Rodeo Cowboys Association; Puerto Rico Communications Authority
Pr Ch: Parish Church
prchst: parachutist
prcht: parachute
PRCP: President of the Royal College of Physicians
prcs: process; processing
PRCS: President of the Royal College of Surgeons
prcst: precast
prd: partial reaction of degeneration
PRD: Pesticides Regulation Division (USDA); Planned Residential Development; Program Requirement Document
PRD: *Partido Revolucionario Dominicano* (Spanish—Dominican Revolutionary Party)
PRDC: Power Reactor Development Corporation
PRDL: Personnel Research and Development Laboratory (USN)
pre: progressive resistance exercise
preamp(s): preamplifier(s)
preb: prebend
prec: precedence; precision
Prec: Precentor
Precious Province; Kueichow
precip: precipitate; precipitation
PRECIS: Preserved Context Index System
Precursor of Dutch Painting: Lucas van Leyden
Precursor of Expressionism: Edvard Munch
Precursor of Japanese Art: Kose no Kanaoka
Precursor of Pharmacology: Paracelsus
Precursor of Pictorial Realism: Mathias Grünewald (Mathis der Mahler)
Precursor of Sociology: Charles de Secondat Baron de la Brède et de Montesquieu
Precursor of Surrealism: Hieronymus Bosch (Hieronymus van Aken)
PREDA: Puerto Rico Economic Development Administration
pre-design: preliminary design
predic: predicate; predicative; prediction
pre-em: preeminence; preeminent; preempt; preemptible; preemption; preemptive; preemptor; preemptory
preemies: premature babies
preemy: premature baby
pref: preface; prefatory; prefecture; preference; prefix
Pref: Prefect
prefab: prefabricated
Pref-Ap: Prefect-Apostolic
prefaz: *prefazione* (Italian—foreword)
prefd: *preferred*
preg: pregnancy; pregnant
pregang: preganglionic
prehis: *prehistoric*
Preiser's disease: porosity of the wristbone
prej: prejudice
prel: prelude
prelim: preliminary
prelim diag: preliminary diagnosis
prelims: preliminaries; preliminary pages (frontmatter)
prem: premature; premium
pre-med: premedical
Premier Primitive: Henri Rousseau
Prensa: *La Prensa* (Buenos Aires' Press)
'prentice: apprentice
Prenzl Bg: Prenzlauer Berg
pr enzyme: prosthetic-group removing enzyme
pre-op: preoperation; preoperational
prep: preparation; preparatory; prepare; preposition
PREP: Personal Radio-Equipped Police; Preparation Rehabilitation Education Program; Pupil Record of Educational Progress
prepd: prepared
prep'ed: prepared
prepn: preparation
prepr: *prepracovane* (Czech—rewritten)
Pre-Raphaelite Founders: Holman Hunt, Sir John Everett Millais, Daniel Gabriel Rossetti
pres: present
Pres: President
PRES: Puerto Rico Employment Service
presby: presbyopia; presbyopic
Presby: Presbyterian

presc: prescription
***Presdte*:** *Presidente* (Spanish—President)
preserv: preservation
Presidents' conference: conference of presidents of major Jewish organizations (in America)
President ships: American President Line vessels named after such statesmen as *President Lincoln, President Roosevelt, President Taft*
presilection: presidential election Pennsylvania)
press.: pressure
PRESS: Pacific Range Electromagnetic Signature Studies
***Presse*:** *Die Presse* (Neue Freie Presse)—Vienna's Press
presstitute: poison-pen prostitute of the press (columnist skilled in writing personally or politically defamatory articles)
***prestmo.*:** *prestissimo* (Italian—very quickly)
PRESTO: Program Reporting and Evaluation System for Total Operations
Preston K. Swinehart: (nickname—movie actor Alan Dinehart in villain roles)
presv: preservation; preserve
pret: preterit
Pret: Pretoria
pre-Teut: pre-Teutonic
PRETTYBLUEBATCH: Philadelphia Regular Exchange Tea Total Young Belles Lettres Universal Experimental Bibliographical Association To Civilize Humanity (initialism contrived by Edgar Allan Poe to satirize all such pseudo-intellectual devices)—appears in his essay on *How to Write a Blackwood Article*
pretz: pretzel
Pretzel City: nickname shared by Lancaster and Reading, Pennsylvania
prev: previous
preven: preventive
prevoc: prevocational
prex(y): president (usually college or university)
prf: proof; pulse recurrence frequency; pulse repetition frequency
***prf.*:** *praefatio* (Latin—introduction; preface)
prf (PRF): prolactin-releasing factor
PRF: Petroleum Research Fund; Plywood Research Foundation; Public Relations Foundation; Puerto Rican Forum
prfnl: professional
prfr: proofreader
PRG: Prague, Czechoslovakia (airport); Provisional Revolutionary Government (of South Vietnam)
PRHS: Port Richmond High School
pri: primary; primer; primitive; priority; private
PRI: Paleontological Research Institute
***PRI*:** *Partido Revolucionario Institucional* (Spanish—Institutional Revolutionary Party); *Partito Repubblicano Italiano* (Italian Republican Party)
***PRIA*:** *Proceedings of the Royal Irish Academy*
Pribilovs: Pribilov Islands in the Bering Sea off Alaska
PRIDCO: Puerto Rico Industrial Development Company
PRIDE: Personal Responsibility in Defect Elimination
Pride of the Yankees: Lou Gehrig
prim.: primary
Primate of Italy: the Pope
prime.: precision recovery including maneuvering entry
Prime Minister of the Underworld: Frank Costello
prin: principal
Prin: Principal; Principality
PRINAIR: Puerto Rico International Airlines
PRINCE: Parts, Reliability, and Information Center (NASA)
Prince of American Letters: Washington Irving
Prince of the Apostles: the Pope, according to the Roman Catholics
Prince of Artists: Albrecht Dürer
Prince of Gossips: Samuel Pepys
Prince of Humbugs: P(hineas) T(aylor) Barnum
Prince of Humorists: Mark Twain (Samuel Langhorne Clemens)
Prince of Journalists: Horace Greeley
Princely Province: Prince Edward Island
Prince of Losers: Dr Frederick A. Cook who claimed he reached the North Pole nearly a year before Commander Robert E. Peary, who was credited with the discovery by his supporters who discredited Cook despite support he got from Amundsen and other Arctic experts and explorers
Prince of the Meistersingers: Hans Sachs of Nuremberg also known as the Cobbler Poet
Prince of Men: Robert Louis Stevenson's nickname for Henry James
Prince of Music: Palestrina
Prince of Orators: Demosthenes
Prince of the Oyster Pirates: Jack London
Prince of Philosophers: Plato
Prince of Physicians: Avicenna (Abu ibn Sina)
Prince of Pistoleers: James Butler (Wild Bill) Hickok
Prince of Poets: Alexander Pushkin, according to Russian literary critics; Edmund Spenser
Prince of Prose Writers: John Bunyan
Prince of Scoffers: Voltaire
Prince of Showmen: P.T. Barnum
Prince Siddhartha: Gautama Buddha
Prince of Skeptics: Voltaire
Princess of Fruits: (Linnaeus' sobriquet for the pineapple)
Prince of Trees: (Linnaeus' nickname for the palm)
Principality of the Grimaldi: Monaco
***Principe de la Paz*:** (Spanish—Prince of the Peace)—Manuel Godoy y Alvarez de Faria
print.: printed; printing
PRINUL: Puerto Rico International Undersea Laboratory
PRIO: Peace Research Institute, Oslo (Norway)
prior.: priority
PRI & RB: Puerto Rico Inspection and Rating Bureau
pris: prison(er)
PRISE: Pennsylvania's Regional Instruction System for education (intercollegiate network)
***pris g*:** *prisonnier de guerre* (French—prisoner of war)
prism.: prismatic
PRISM: Personnel Record Information System; Program Reliability Information System for Management
Prisoner of Chillon: François de Bonnivard
Pris(sy): Priscilla
pritac: primary tactical radio circuit
prithee: I pray thee
priv: private
Privatdozent: (German) university professor not belonging to a professorial staff
priv pr: privately printed
priv pub: privately published
PRJC: Puerto Rico Junior Col-

lege

pr kassa: *per kassa* (Norwegian—for cash)

Pr of L: Prince of Liechtenstein; Principality of Liechtenstein

PRL: Personnel Research Laboratory; Polska Rzeczpospolita Ludowa (Polish Republic); Precision Reduction Laboratory

prm: prime

PRMA: Puerto Rican Maritime Authority

p-r man: public-relations man

prmld: premolded

p.r.n.: *pro re nata* (Latin—as needed; for an emergency)

PRNC: Potomac River Naval Command

PRNL: Pictured Rocks National Lakeshore (Michigan)

PRNS: Point Reyes National Seashore

prntr: printer

PRNWR: Parker River National Wildlife Refuge (Massachusetts)

pro: procedure; proceed; procure; procurement; profession; professional; professionally; prophylactic

pro (PRO): proline (amino acid)

Pro: Provost

PRO: Personnel Relations Office(r); Plant Representative's Office; Public Relations Office(r)

PROA: Public record Office Archives

pro-am: professional-amateur

prob: probability; probable; probably; problem; problematic; problematical

Prob: Probate

probcost: probabilistic budgeting and costing; probable cost

Prob Off: Probation Officer

proc: procedure; proceeding(s); procure; procurement

Proc: Procedure; Proceedings; Proctor

Procd: procedure

Procoll: Proletarian Collective of Soviet Musicians

procomm: program communication

Procop: Procopius

Proc Roy Soc: *Proceedings of the Royal Society*

procto: proctocolitis; proctocolonoscopy; proctologist; proctology; proctosigmoidoscopy; proctosigmoidectomy; proctoplegia

prod: product; production

Prod(s): (Irish-Catholic English—Protestant)—[(*see* Pap(s)]

PRODAC: Production Advisers Consortium

Prodigy of Learning: Dr Samuel Hahnemann

prof: profession; professional; professor

Prof: Professor

PROF: Peace Research Organization Fund

profac: propulsive fluid accumulator

Prof D: *Profesor Don* (Spanish—Sir Professor)

Prof D^{na}: *Profesora Doña* (Spanish—Madam Professor)

Prof Eng: Professional Engineer

Professor Julius Caesar Hannibal: (pseudonym—W.H. Levinson)

Professor Seagull: Joe Gould

Proff: *Professori* (italian—Professors)

Profintern: Red international of Trade Unions

Prof Lib Pr: Professional Library Press

prog: progenitor; progeny; prognose; prognosis; prognostic; prognostication; prognosticator; program; programmer

progr: program(mer); programme

Prog(s): Progressive(s)

prohib: prohibit(ion)

proj: project; projectile; projection; projector

prole(s): proletarian(s)

PROLLAP: Professional Library Literature Acquisition Program

prolong.: *prolongatus* (Latin—prolonged)

ProLt: procurement lead time

prom: promenade (concert or dance); prominent; promontory; promote; promoter; promotion; promotional; prompter

Prom: The Prom—Wilson's Promontory—national park at the southernmost tip of Australia

PROMIS: Prosecution Management Information System (U.S. Attorney's Office—Washington, D.C.)

Promised Land: Israel, promised to the Israelites by Moses and to the Israelis by Balfour

proml: promulgate

promo: promotional

pron: pronoun; pronounced; pronunciation; pronunciator(y)

prond: pronounced

pronom: pronominal

pro note: promissory note

pronunc: pronunciation

PROOF: Parole Resource Office and Orientation Facility (Jersey City, New Jersey)

prop: propaganda; propeller; property; proportion(al); proposed; proprietary

Prop: Sextus Propertius (Roman poet)

PROP: Portland Regional Opportunities Program

propay: proficiency pay

proph: prophetic; prophylactic; prophylaxis

Prophet of Allah: Mohammed

Prophet of Christianity: John the Baptist

Prophet of Democracy: William Penn

Prophet of Israel: Moses

Prophet of Mythology: Teiresias

Prophet Outcast: Leon Trotsky

Prophets of Israel: Moses, Samuel, Nathan, Elijah, Elisha

Prophet of the Strenuous Life: Jack London

propjet: propeller turned by jet engine (same as turboprop)

propn: proportion(al)

props: (theatrical) properties

prop wash: propeller wash

pro rect.: *pro recto* (Latin—by rectum)

PRORM: Pay and Records Office—Royal Marines

pros: prosody; prostitute

Pros Atty: Prosecuting Attorney

prosc: proscenium

prosig: procedure signal

prosine: procedure sign

prosp: prospecting

prost: prostate; prothetics; prostitution

prosth: prosthesis

prostie(s): prostitute(s)

prot: protective; protectorate; protein; protestant; protozoa; protractor

prot (PROT): protein anion

Prot: Protectorate; Protestant; Protozoa

protag: protagonist

Prot-Ap: Protonotary-Apostolic

Protec: Protectorate

Protector of the Indians: Rodrigo de Bastidas—Spanish navigator who explored the coasts from Panama to Venezuela and founded Santa Marta; Las Casas and Eliot share the title—Protector of the Indians

Protectress from Fever: Febris (Roman goddess whose Latin name means fever)

Protectress from Poison Gases: Mephitis—Roman goddess venerated in volcanic lands where poisonous gases abounded
Protectress of the Protestants: Marguerite de Navarre
Protectress of Seafarers: the Greek goddess Brizo
pro tem.: *pro tempore* (Latin—for the time being)
Protestant Hero: Frederick the Great of Prussia
prothrom: prothrombin
pro time: prothrombin time
Protoch: Protochorda
prov; provide; provision; provisional; proviso
Prov: Provençal; Provence; Proverbs, The (book of the Bible); Providence; Province
Prov: *Provinz* (German—province)
Prov Eng: Provincial English
prover: procurement - value - economy - realiability
Prov GM: Provincial Grand Master
Providence Plantations: Rhode Island
Provisional President of Africa: Marcus Garvey
Provision State: Connecticut in Revolutionary times when it furnished so much for the Continental Army
provn: provision
Provo: Provisional (member of the IRA)
provos: *provokers* (Dutch—street people engaged in militant tactics to provoke the police)
Provos: Provisionals (Provisional Sinn Fein party members of Northern Ireland)
PROVOST: Priority Research and Development Objectives for Vietnam Operations Support
proword: procedure word
prox: proximal; proximity
prox.: *proximo* (Latin—next, *adv.*)
prox. luc.: *proxima luce* (Latin—the day before)
prp: pulse repetition period
Prp: Principality
PRP: Production Requirements Plan; Production Reserve Policy; Public Relations Personnel
PRPA: Puerto Rico Ports Authority
prpln: propulsion
prpp (PRPP): 5-phosphoribosyl 1-pyrophosphate
pr. pr.: *praeter propter* (Latin—about; nearly)
PRPUC: Philippine Republic Presidential Unit Citation
prr: pulse repetition rate
PRR: Pennsylvania Railroad
PRRI: Puerto Rico Rum Institute
PRRWO: Puerto Rican Revolutionary Workers Organization (communist)
prs: pairs; printers
Prs: Preston
PRs: Pakistani rupees; Problem Reports; Puerto Ricans
PRS: Pennsylvania-Reading Seashore (railroad); Precision Ranging System
PRSA: Public Relations Society of America
prsd: pressed
prsd met: pressed metal
prsfdr: pressfeeder
prsmn: pressman
PRSO: Puerto Rico Symphony Orchestra
PRSS: Pennsylvania-Reading Seashore Lines
PRST: Puerto Rican Standard Time
Pr strain: Prague (viral) strain
PRSY: People's Republic of Southern Yemen
prt: parachute radio transmitter; personnel research test; publication requirement table(s); pulse repetition time
p & rt: physical and recreational training
Prt: Port (postal abbreviation)
PRT: Personnel Research Test; Philadelphia Rapid Transit; Production Re-evaluation Testing
prtg: printing
PRTS: Personal Rapid Transit System
pru: peripheral resistance unit; prude; prudence; prudent
Pru: Prudence; Prudential Life Insurance Company
PRU: Polish-Russian Union (South African Jews who joined this were called Peruvians because of their abbreviation of their society seemingly alien to their Christian neighbors)
Prue: Prudence
Prunepicker(s): Californian(s)
Prus: Prussia; Prussian
prussic acid: hydrocyanic acid
prv: pressure-reducing valve
prv: *pour rendre visite* (French—to return a call)
Prv: *Pravda* (Russian—truth)—daily newspaper published in Moscow by Central Committee of the Communist Party
prx: pressure regulator exhaust
PRY: Pittsburgh Railways Corporation (stock exchange symbol)
PRZ: People's Republic of Zanzibar
ps: parlor snake; parts shipped; parts shipper; passenger service; passing scuttle; patient's serum; penal servitude; picosecond; pieces; plastic surgery; point of switch; point of symmetry; proof shot; pseudo; pseudonym(s); pull switch; pulmonary stenosis
p's: pennies
p-s: pressure-sensitive
p & s: paracentesis and suction; port and starboard
Ps: Psalms, The (book of the Bible); South Pole; South Celestial Pole; static pressure
Ps: *Posaunen* (German—trombones)
PS: Paleontological Society; Palm Society; Paymaster Sergeant; Pennsylvania State University; Pharmaceutical Society; Philippine Scouts; Photo(graphic) Service; picket ship(s); Pistol Sharpshooter; Pittsburg & Shawmut (railroad); Plastic Surgery; Privy Seal; Public Safety; Public School; Puget Sound
P.S.: paddle steamer; public school
P-S: Pullman-Standard
P & S: Physicians and Surgeons; Pittsburg & Shawmut (railroad)
P of S: Port of Spain
PS: *Pferdestärke* (German—horsepower)
P.S.: *post scriptum* (Latin—written after)
psa: passed staff college; psychoanalytic(al)
psa (PSA): public service announcement (radio or television)
PSA: Pacific Science Association; Pacific Southwest Airlines; Photographic Society of America; Poetry Society of America; Port of Singapore Authority; Poultry Science Association; Program Study Authorization
PSA: *Proceedings of the Society of Antiquaries*
PSAB: Public Schools Appointments Bureau
p sac: pericardial cavity

PSAC: President's Science Advisory Committee; Public Service Alliance of Canada
PSACPOO: President's Scientific Advisory Committee Panel On Oceanography
psad: prediction-stimulation-adaptation-decision (data processing)
PSAL: Public School Athletic League
Psalt.: *Psalterium* (Latin—Book of Psalms)
ps an: psychoanalysis; psychoanalyst; psychoanalytic(al)(ly); psychoanalyze
PSAODAP: Presidential Special Action Office for Drug Abuse Prevention
PSAT: Palm Springs Aerial Tramway; Preliminary Scholastic Aptitude Test(ing)
psb: public service band (radio)
PSB: Psychological Strategy Board
P & SB: Portland & South Bend (railroad)
PSBA: Public Schools Bursars' Association
PSBLS: Permanent Space-Based Logistics System
PSBO: Public Savings Bond Office
psc: passed staff college; per standard compass
PSC: Pacific Sea Council; Peralta Shipping Corporation; Pittsburgh Steel Company; Point Shipping Company; Porcelain-on-Steel Council; Potomac State College; Product Safety Commission(er); Program Structure Code; Public Service Commission
PSC: *Partido Social Cristiano* (Spanish—Social Christian Party)—Catholic actionists
PSCC: Public Service Commission of Canada
PSCD: Patrol Service Central Depot
PSCNI: Public Service Company of Northern Illinois
psd: power spectral density; promotion service date
P Sd: Port Said
PSD: Pittsburgh Steamship Division (United States Steel); Port of San Diego
ps detn: particle size determination
PSDI: *Partito Socialista Democratico Italiano* (Italian Social Democratic Party)
ps distn: particle size distribution
psdo: pseudo; pseudonym
PSDUPD: Port of San Diego Unified Port District
pse: please; point of subjective equality
pse (PSE): psychological stress evaluator (voice-analysis lie detector)
PSEA: Pennsylvania State Education Association; Physical Security Equipment Agency
PSE & GC: Public Service Electric and Gas
PSE & G: Public Service Electric and Gas Company
pset: permanent service on earth tides
pseud: pseudandry (women using male names as pseudonyms); pseudepigraphy (attributing false names to artists, authors, or composers); pseudograph (falsely attributing a work to an artist, author, or composer); pseudojyn (men using female names as pseudonyms); pseudonym (false name, nom de plume, pen name; pseudonyma (pseudonymous works)
psf: payload-structure-fuel (ratio); pounds per square foot
PSF: Phelps-Stokes Fund
P & SF: Panhandle and Santa Fe (railroad)
P of SF: Port of San Francisco
PSFC: Pacific Salmon Fisheries Commission
PSFL: Puget Sound Freight Lines
PSFS: Philadelphia Savings Fund Society
PSGBI: Pathological Society of Great Britain and Ireland
psgi: permanent service on geomagnetic indices
psgr: passenger
PSHFA: Public Servants Housing and Finance Association
psi: posterior saggital index; pounds per square inch; public school(s) investigation
PSI: Pacific Semiconductors Incorporated; Physician's Services Incorporated; Population Services Incorporated
PSI: *Partito Socialista Italiano* (Italian Socialist Party); *Pollution Standards Index*
psia: pounds per square inch absolute
PSIC: Pacific Scientific Information Center (Bernice Pauahi Bishop Museum, Honolulu)
psig: pounds per square inch gage
psil: preferred-frequency speech interference level
PSIP: Poultry Stock Improvement Plan
PSIUP: *Partito Socialista Italiano di Unita Proletaria* (Italian Socialist Party of Proletarian Unity)
psk: phase shift keying
p sl: pipe sleeve
PSL: Pacific Star Line; Peruvian State Line; Philharmonic Society of London
p-slips: old-fashioned postcard-size (3- × 5-inch) slips of paper used for filing
psl sol: potassium, sodium chloride, sodium lactate solution
ps lt: port side light
psm: passed school of music
psm (PSM): presystolic murmur
PSM: Product Sales Manager
psma: progressive spinal muscular atrophy
PSMA: Power Saw Manufacturers Association
PSMFC: Pacific States Marine Fisheries Commission
psmsl: permanent service for mean sea level
psn: position
PSN: *Partido Socialista de Nicaragua* (Spanish—Socialist Party of Nicaragua)—Moscow-oriented group
PSNA: Phytochemical Society of North America
PSNC: Pacific Steam Navigation Company
PSNS: Puget Sound Naval Shipyard
PSO: Pad Safety Officer; Pasadena Symphony Orchestra; Phoenix Symphony Orchestra; Pilot Systems Operator; Pittsburgh Symphony Orchestra; Portland Symphony Orchestra; Prague Symphony Orchestra
p sol: partially soluble; partly soluble
pson: person
PS 166: Public School 166 (for example)
psp: phenolsulfonphthalein (test); pierced-steel plank; positive screened print
PSP: Pocahontas State Park (Virginia); Programs Support Plan
PSP: *Pacifistisch Socialistische Partij* (Dutch—Pacifist-Socialist Party)
PSPCD: Puget Sound Pollution-Control District
PSP & L: Puget Sound Power and Light (company)

PSPMW: Pulp, Sulphite and Paper Mill Workers
PSPP: Proposed System Package Plan
PSPS: Paddle Steamer Preservation Society
PSQC: Philippine Society for Quality Control
p's & q's: expression about minding your p's & q's originated when printers instructed apprentices about similarity of lowercase p's and q's when handsetting type; also used in saloons to keep count of the number of pints and quarts of beer consumed
psr: plow-steel rope
PSR: Physicians for Social Responsibility
PSRF: Profit Sharing Research Foundation
PSRI: Public Systems Research Institute (UCLA)
PSRO: Professional Services (Standards) Review Organization
pss: physiological saline solution
Pss: Princess
PSS: Pad Safety Supervisor
P.S.S.: Professor of Sacred Scripture
P.S.S.: *postcripta* (Latin—postscripts)
PSSC: Physical Science Study Committee (National Science Foundation)
P.S.S.C.: Pious Society of Saint Charles
PSSNY: Philharmonic Symphony Society of New York
psso: passed slip stitch over (knitting)
pst: polished surface technique
pst (PST): prefrontal sonic treatment
PST: Pacific Standard Time
PSTBC: Puget Sound Tug and Boat Company
PSTC: Pressure Sensitive Tape Council
PSTD: Prison Service Training Depot (Pretoria)
p stg c: per steering compass
pstl: postal
PSTMA: Paper Stationery and Tablet Manufacturers Association
PSTO: Principal Sea Transport Officer
P-strip: P-shaped strip
PSU: Pennsylvania State University
PSU: *Partito Socialista Unitario* (Italian—Unitary Socialist Party)
p-substance: protein substance
PSUC: Pennsylvania State University Center(s)
PSUC: *Partido Socialista Unificado de Cataluña* (Spanish—Unified Socialist Party of Catalonia)
p surg: plastic surgeon; plastic surgery
psv: public service vehicle
PSW : Psychiatric Social Worker
PSWB: Plateau State Water Board
psy: psychological
Psy: Paisley
psych: psychiatry; psychology; psychopathology
psychedeli: psychedelicatessen (store selling the paraphernalia of drug addicts)
Psychedelphia: San Francisco's Haight-Ashbury district inhabited by so many drug addicts
psychiat: psychiatric; psychiatry
psycho: dangerous lunatic; a psychiatric hospital or ward; a psychoneurotic personality; a psychotic individual (pseudoscientific slang)
psychoan: psychoanalytic; psychoanalysis; psychoanalyst
psychol: psychological; psychologist; psychology
psychomet: psychometric
psychopathol: psychopathological; psychopathologist; psychopathology
psychophys: psychophysical; psychophysics; psychophysicist
psychophysiol: psychophysiology (and derivatives)
psychot: psychotic
psychother: psychotherapist; psychotherapeutic(al, s); psychotherapy
psych test.: psychological testing
psyop: psychological operation
psypath: psychopath(ic)
psysom: psychosomatic
psywar: psychological warfare
pt: part; personal trade; physical therapy; physical training; pint(s); plenty tough; plenty trouble; pneumatic tube; point; point of tangency; point of turn; point of turning; primary target; private terms; prothrombin time
p & t: personnel and training; posts and timbers
pt: *partie* (French—part)
pt.: *perstetur* (Latin—let it be continued)
p.t.: *protempore* (Latin—temporarily)
Pt: platinum; Point; Port; Porto; Puerto
PT: motor torpedo boat (naval symbol); Pacific Time; Peninsula Terminal (railroad); Philadelphia Transportation; Physical Therapist; physical therapy; physical training; Postal Telegraph; primary trainer; Provincetown-Boston Airline (2-letter coding)
£T: pound Turkish
P & T: Pope & Talbot (steamship line)
pta: plasma thromboplastin antecedent; posttraumatic amnesia; primary target area; prior to admission; proposed technical approach; peseta (Spanish monetary unit, diminutive of peso)
Pta: *Punta* (Spanish—Point)
Pt A: Port Arthur, Ontario
PTA: Paper and Twine Association; Parent-Teacher Association; Pope and Talbot; Postal Transportation Association; Protestant Teachers Association
Pt Ant: Port Antonio
PTAR: Prime Time Access Rule
Ptarmigan: Alaska state bird; symbolic nickname given some Alaskans in preference to Sourdough recalling frontier times
Pt Art: Port Arthur
ptas: pesetas
pta's: part-time alcoholics
PTAs: Passenger Transport Authorities
PTAS: Productivity and Technical Assistance Secretariat
ptb: patellar-tendon bearing
PTB: *Partido Trabalhista Brasileiro* (Portuguese—Brazilian Workers Party)
ptbl: portable
PT-boat: patrol torpedo boat
PTBM: P.T. Barnum Museum (Bridgeport, Connecticut)
ptbr: punched-tape block reader
PTBT: Partial Test Ban Treaty
ptc: personnel transfer capsule; positive temperature coefficient
ptc (PTC): phenylthiocarbamide; plasma thromboplastin component (clotting factor IX)
PTC: Pacific Tin Consolidated; Paisley Technical College; patrol vessel (naval symbol); Peoria Terminal (railroad); Philadelphia Transportation Company; Pine Tree Camp;

Pipe and Tobacco Council; Power Transmission Council; Press Trust of Ceylon; Private Truck Council
PTCA: Private Truck Council of America
ptd: painted
P o TD: Port of The Dalles
PTDA: Power Transmission Distributors Association
PTDP: Preliminary Technical Development Plan
PTDR: Post- Test Disassembly Report
PTDS: Photo Target Detection System
pte; parathyroid extract
p^te^: *parte* (Spanish—part)
pte (PTE): pulmonary thromboembolism
Pte: *Pointe* (French—Point)
pte: *poriente* (Spanish—west)
PTE: Passenger Transport Executive
pt ed: patient education
pt ex: part exchange
ptf: plasma thromboplastin factor
PTF: fast patrol boat (naval symbol); Propulsion Test Facilities
ptfe: polytetrafluorethylene
ptfp: prime-time family programming
ptg: printing
Ptg: Portugal; Portuguese
PTG: Piano Technician's Guild
ptgt: primary target
pth: parathormone
pti: persistent tolerant infection; physical training instructor (PTI)
PTI: Philips Telecommunicatie Industrie; Press Trust of India
PTIDG: Presentation of Technical Information Discussion Group
PTIS: Piano Teachers Information Service
ptl: pintle; primary target line
PTL: Photographic Technology Laboratory
ptm: proof test model; pulse-time modulation
Ptm: Pietermaai
ptma: phosphotungstomolybdic acid
ptn: partition
Ptnr: Partner
pto: please turn over; power takeoff
Pto: Porto; Puerto; Punto
PTO: Public Trustee Office
Pto Cab: Puerto Cabello
Ptol: Ptolemaic; Ptolemy
Ptolemy: Alexandrian astronomer Claudius Ptolemaeus
ptp: paper-tape printer
PTP: Pointe à Pitre, Guadeloupe (airport)
ptpg: participating
pt/pt: point-to-point
ptr: printer
PTR: pool test reactor
pts: *pesetas* (Spanish—plural of peseta); pints
Pts: Portsmouth
PTS: Postal Transportation Service; Princeton Theological Seminary
pts/hr: parts per hour; pieces per hour
Ptsmth: Portsmouth
Pt Sp: Port of Spain
ptt: push to talk
ptt (PTT): partial thromboplastin time
PTT: Posta, Telgraf ve Telefon (Turkish—Post, Telegraph, and Telephone); Postes, **Télégraphes, Téléphone** (French—national postal, telegraph, and telephone system)
PTTA: Philippine Tourist and Travel Association
PTTI: Postal, Telegraph, and Telephone International
pt-tm: part-time
pttnmkr: patternmaker
ptu: propylthiouracil
PTU: Plumbers' Trade Union; Plumbing Trade Union; Psychiatric Treatment Unit
PTUC: Philippine Trade Unions Council
ptv: public television
ptv (PTV): propulsion test vehicle
ptw: per thousand words
Pt W: Port Weller
Pty: Party; Proprietary
pu: pickup; plant unit; pregnancy urine; propellant utilization; propulsion unit; pump unit
p-u (pee-you): phew (what a stench)
p.u.: *plus ultra* (Latin—beyond the pinnacle; beyond the ultimate)
Pu: plutonium
PU: Pacific University; Phillips University; Princeton University; Purdue University
PUAS: Postal Union of the Americas and Spain
pub: public; publican; publication; public house; publicity; publish; published; publisher; publishing
Pub: Publican; Public House; Publisher's Announcement
PUB: Public Utilities Board
pub aide: publication aide
pubbl: *pubblicità* (Italian—advertising; publicity)
Pub Doc: Public Document
pub ed: publication editor
pubinfo: public information
publ: publication; publicity, publisher; publishing
Publius: allonymic name used by Alexander Hamilton, John Jay, and James Madison in writing *The Federalist*
pub(s): public house(s) (British short form)
Pub Wks: Public Works
puc: papers under consideration; pickup car
PUC: Peoples University of China; Presidential Unit Citation; Public Utilities Code; Public Utilities Commission; Public Utilities and Corporations
PUC: *Post Urbem Conditam* (Latin—after the foundation of the city)—city usually means Rome
pud: puddle; pudding
PUD: Planned Unit Development
Pue: Puebla
PUF: Presses Universitaires de France (University Presses of France)
pufa: polyunsaturated fatty acid
pug.: puggy; pugilism; pugilist
Puggy Booth: Joseph Mallord William Turner's nickname given him in his last years by East Kent's seaside neighbors who believed he was a retired sea captain named Booth—a name he used to gain anonymity
PUHS: Phoenix Union High School
PUK: Pechiney Ugine Kuhlmann
pul: pulley
PUL: Princeton University Library
Pula: (Setswana—Rain)—official motto of the arid republic of Botswana
pulheems: physical capacity, upper and lower limbs, hearing, eyesight, emotional capacity, mental stability
pul ins: pulmonary insufficiency
pulm: pulmonary
pulm.: *pulmentum* (Latin—gruel)
pulmo: pulmonary
pulmotor: (pulmonary + motor)
pulsar: pulse + star (pulsed radio-wave-emitting star); pulsing astronomical signal (received from outer space)
pul sten: pulmonary stenosis

pulv: pulverize(r)
pulv.: *pulvis* (Latin—powder)
pulv. gros.: *pulvis grossus* (Latin—coarse powder)
pulv. subtil.: *pulvis subtilis* (Latin—smooth powder)
pulv. tenu: *pulvis tenuis* (Latin—very fine)
PUM: Postal Union Mail
Pumfret: Pontefract
pump.: pumping
PUMP: Protesting Unfair Marketing Practices
pums: permanently unfit for military service
pun.: puncheon
PUN: *Partido Union Nacional* (Spanish—National Union Party)
punc: punctuation
pundonor: *punta de honor* (Spanish—point of honor)
Punj: Punjabi
Punkie Town: Punxsutawney, Pennsylvania
Punks' Paradise: nickname given any gambling center and sometimes to the State of Nevada and the casino cities of Reno and Las Vegas
Punxey: Punxsutawney
puo: pyrexia of unknown origin
pup: puppy
PUP: Princeton University Press
pups: puppies
pur: purchase; purchaser; purchasing; purifier; purification; purify; purple; purplish; pursuant; pursuit
purch: purchasing
purg.: *purgativus* (Latin—purgative)
Puritan City: Boston, Massachusetts
Puritan State: Massachusetts
purp: purple
Purple Islands; the Madeiras
Purple Land: W.H.Hudson's sobriquet for Uruguay
Purple Violet: New Jersey state flower
purpurite: iron magnesium phosphate
purv: powered underwater research vehicle
pus.: permanently unfit for service
Pus: Pusan
PUs: Public Utilities
PUS: Parliamentary Under-Secretary; Permanent Under-Secretary
Push: Pushtu
PUSH: People United to Save Humanity
puta(s): *prostituta(s)*—(Spanish—prostitute(s))
Putnam: G.P. Putnam
putty: linseed oil and powdered chalk mixture
puva: psoralen (drug) + ultraviolet-A (light)
PUVAS: Plutonium Value Analysis System
puvep: propellant-utilization vehicle-borne electronic package
Puy-de-D: Puy-de-Dôme
pv: paravane; par value; plasma value; position value; prime vertical; public voucher
pv: *prossimo venturo* (Italian—next month)
p/v: peak-to-valley
p v: *petite vitesse* (French—slow train); *piccola velocity* (Italian—slow train)
Pv: Peru; Peruvian
PV: Eastern Provincial Airways (2-letter coding); patrol vessel; Post Village; Priest Vicar; Puerto Vallarta
P.V.: *Procès verbaux* (French—official report); *Processi verbali* (Italian—official report)
pva: polyvinyl acetate
PVA: Paralyzed Veterans of America
pval: polyvinyl alcohol
pvb: potentiometer voltmeter bridge
PVB: Prison Visitors' Board
pvc: polyvinyl chloride (thermoplastic)
pvc (PVC): premature ventricular contractions
PVC: Precision Valve Corporation
pvd: peripheral vascular disease; pulmonary vascular disease
PVD: Providence, Rhode Island (airport)
PvdA: *Partij van de Arbeid* (Dutch—Labor Party)
pvdc: plyyvinyl dichloride
pvem: pulse-vector emittance meter
pvf: polyvinyl fluoride
pvm: polyvinyl methyl
PVMNM: Perry's Victory Memorial National Monument
pvnt: prevent; preventive
PVO: Principal Veterinary Officer
pvp: polyvinylpyrrolidone (plasma extender)
PVPMPC: Perpetual Vice President and Member of the Pickwick Club
pvpp: polyvinyl-polypyrrolidone
PVS: Pecos Valley Southern (railroad)
pvt: pressure volume temperature; private
pvt: *par voie télégraphique* (French—by telegraph)
Pvt: Private
Pvt 1/C: Private First Class
PVU: Prairie View University
pw: packed weight; passing window; pivoted window; postwar; prisoner of war; projected window; psychological warfare; public works; pulse width
p/w; parallel with
p & w: pension and welfare (retirement benefits)
PW: Philadelphia & Western (railroad); Pittsburgh & West Virginia (railroad); prisoner of war; Public Works
PW: *Publishers' Weekly*
P & W: Pratt and Whitney Aircraft Division, United Aircraft Corporation
PWA: Pacific Western Airlines; Public Works Administration
PWA: *Papierwerke Waldhof-Ashaffenburg* (German—Waldhof-Ashaffenburg Paper Works)
p-wave: pressure wave
p waves: primary (earthquake) waves
pwc: physical working capacity
PWC: Public Works Canada: Public Works Center (USN)
pwd: powered
PWD: Public Works Department
PWE: Political Warfare Executive; Prisoner of War Enclosure
pwf: pregnancy without fear (pillow-simulated pregnancy); present-worth factor
PWFP: Prince William Forest Park (Virginia)
PWI: Physiological Workload Index
PWIF: Plantation Workers' International Federation
PWJC: Piney Woods Junior College
PWLB: Public Works Loan Board
pwm: pokeweed mitogen (PWM); pulse width modulation
PWMS: Public Works Management System (USN)
PWNDA: Provincial Wholesale Newspaper Distributors' Association
PWNP: Parra Wirra National Park (South Australia)
PWO: Public Works Office(r)
PWP: Parents Without Partners

pwr: power; pressurized water reactor (PWR)
PWR: Police War Reserve
PWRS: Pacific War Research Society
pwr sup: power supply
pws: paddlewheel steamer
pw's: prisoners of war
PWS: Periyar Wildlife Sanctuary (India); Private Wire System
pwt: pennyweight; propulsion wind tunnel
pwtr: pewter
P & WV: Pittsburgh & West Virginia (railroad)
px: past history; physical examination; please exchange; pneumothorax; prognosis
PX: Aspen Airways (2-letter code); Post Exchange
PXCMD: Phoenix Contract Management District
pxe (PXE): pseudoxanthoma elasticum
px in: time of arrival
px me: report my arrival and departure
pxo: *próximo* (Spanish—next)
px out: takeoff time
pxt.: *pinxit* (Latin—he painted it)
py: pitch and yaw
PY: commissioned and armed yacht (2-letter naval symbol); Surinam Airways (2-letter symbol); program year
PYA: plan, year, age (insurance)
Pya: *Pyatnitsa* (Russian—Friday)
pyc: proteose-yeast castione
PYC: Philadelphia Yacht Club; Portland Yacht Club (Maine); Poughkeepsie Yacht Club
PYE: Protect Your Environment
pyg broth: proteose-yeast-glucose broth
pyph: polyphase
pyr; pyridine
p-y-r: pitch-yaw-roll
Pyrenees: Pyrenees Mountains between France and Spain
pyrite: fool's gold; iron disulfide; iron pyrites
pyrites: copper, iron, tin pyrite; also known as fool's gold
pyro: pyromaniac; pyrotechnic(s); pyroxylin
pyroglu: pyroglutamic acid
pyrolag: pyrolagnia(c)
pyrom: pyrometer; pyrometry
Pyr-Or: Pyreneés-Orientales
pyrot: pyrotechnics
pyx.: *pyxis* (Latin—box; vessel)
pz: pancreozymin
PZ: Paolei Zion(ist); Pickup Zone; Police Zone
pza: pyrazinamide
pza: *pieza* (Spanish—piece)
p^za^: *Piazza* (Italian—Square)
pzi: protamine zinc insulin
PZM: Polska Zegluga Morska (Polish Merchant Marine)
PZPR: *Polska Zjednoczona Partia Robotnicza* (Polish United Workers Party)
PZS: President of the Zoological Society
pzt: photographic zenith tube
p^zza^: *Piazza* (Italian—Square)

Q

q: coefficient of association (statistical symbol ; cue (gesture or signal to cease or commence); dynamic pressure (symbol); electric charge (symbol); quality factor; quart; quarter; quartile; quarterly; quarto; quench; quenching; queries; query; question(s); quick; quintal; quire; semi-interquartile range (symbol); stagnation pressure (symbol)
q: *quaque (Latin—each; every)*
q^2h^: *quaque secunda hora* (Latin—every two hours)
q^3h^: *quaque tertia hora* (Latin—every three hours)
q^4h^: *quaque quarta hora* (Latin—every four hours)
Q: bankruptcy or receivership (stock exchange symbol); electric quadruple moment of atomic nucleus (symbol); Fairchild (symbol); Polaris correction (symbol); quadrillion; Quaker Line; quarantine; Quartermaster; quartile variation (symbol); Quebec—code for letter Q; Queen; Queensland; quetzal (Guatemalan monetary unit named after this plume-tailed bird); radio inductive reactance to resistance (symbol); semi-interquartile range (symbol); target or drone (symbol); thermoelectric power (symbol)
Q_1, Q_2, Q_3, Q_4: first quartile, second quartile, third quartile, fourth quartile
Q: pseudonym for Sir Arthur Quiller-Couch; *Quai* (French — embankment or quay); *quetzal* (Guatemalan monetary unit); (Latin—Quintus) torque (symbol)
Ql: *quintal* (Spanish—hundredweight)
qa: quality assurance; quick-acting; quiescent aerial
QA: Quality Assurance; Quarters Allowance
Q-A: Quint-A
Q & A: question and answer
QAA: Quality Assurance Assistant
QAB: Queen Anne's Bounty (for indigent clergymen)
qac: quaternary ammonium compound
QAC: Quality Assurance; Quarters Allowance
qad: quick-attach-detach
QAD: Quality Assurance Directive; Quality Assurance Division
QADC: Queen's Aide-de-Camp
qadk: quick attach-detach kit
QADS: Quality Assurance Data System
QAE: Quality Assurance Engineer(ing)
qaf: quality-assurance firing
qafo: quality-assurance field operation(s)
QAG: Quaker Action Group
qagc: quiet automatic gain control
QAI: Quality Assurance Instruction; Queen's Award to Industry
QAIMNS: Queen Alexandra's Imperial Military Nursing Service
QAIP: Quality Assurance Inspection Procedure
qak: quick-attach kit
qal: quartz aircraft lamp
qal: *quintal* (French—hundred-

weight)
QAL: Quality Assurance Laboratory; Quarterly Accession List; Quebec Airways Limited
QALAS: Qualified Associate of the Land Agents' Society
qall: quartz aircraft landing lamp
QALTR: Quality Assurance Laboratory Test Request
qam: quadrature amplitude modulation
QAM: Quality Assurance Manager
QAM: Quality Assurance Manual
QANTAS: Queensland And Northern Territories Aerial Services
qao: quality assurance operation
QAO: Quality Assurance Office (USN)
QAOP: Quality Assurance Operating Procedure
qap: quinine, atebrin, plasmoquine (malaria treatment)
QAP: Quality Assurance Procedure(s); Quality Assurance Program
QA & P: Quanah, Acme & Pacific (railroad)
QAPL: Queensland Airlines Proprietary Limited
qar: quick-access recording
QAR: Quality Assurance Representative
QAR: *Quality Assurance Report*
QARAFNS: Queen Alexandra's Royal Air Force Nursing Service
QARANC: Queen Alexandra's Royal Army Nursing Service
QARNNS: Queen Alexandra's Royal Naval Nursing Service
qas: quick-acting scuttle
QAs: Queen Alexandra's
QAS: Quality Assurance Service
QASP: Quality Assurance Standard Practice
QAST: Quality Assurance Service Test(s)
Qat: Qatar
QATP: Quality Assurance Technical Publication(s); Quality Assurance Test Procedure(s)
qavc: quiet automatic volume control
qb: qualified bidders; quarterback; quick break
QB: Queensboro Bridge (New York City); Quiet Birdmen (glider enthusiasts)
Q.B.: Queen's Bench
QBA: Quebecair
QBAA: Quality Brands Associates of America
QBAC: Quality Bakers of America Cooperative
Q-band: 36,000-46,000 mc
Qbc: Quebec
QBD: Queen's Bench Division
qbi: quite bloody impossible
QBL: Qualified Bidder's List
Q-boats: mystery ships used in antisubmarine warfare by the British in World War I
QBSM: *que besa su mano* (Spanish—who kisses your hand)—used in closing personal letters
QBSP: *que besa sus pies* (Spanish—who kisses your feet)—used in closing personal letters
qc: qualification course; quality control; quantitative command; quantum counter; quartz crystal; quick connect; quit claim
qc: *qualcosa* (Italian—something)
QC: Quality Control; Quartermaster Corps; Québec Central (railroad); Queens College; Queen's College; Quezon City; Quincy College; Quinnipiac College; Quit Claim
Q.C.: Queen's Counsel
QCA: Queen Charlotte Airlines; Queensland Coal Associates
Q-card: qualification card
qcb (QCB): queue control block (data processing)
qcc: qualification correlation certification; quick-connect coupling(s)
QCC: Queensborough Community College; Quinsigamond Community College
QCCARS: Quality Control Collection Analysis and Reporting System
qcd: quality-control data; quitclaim deed
QCD: quit claim deed
QCDR: Quality Control Deficiency Report
QCE: Quality Control Engineering
qcf: quartz-crystal filter
qcfo: quartz-crystal frequency oscillator
qch: quick-connect handle
QCH: Queen Charlotte's Hospital
qci: quality-control information
QCI: Quota Club International
Q Cic: Quintus Tullius Cicero (the brother of the Roman orator Marcus Tullius Cicero)
QCIM: *Quarterly Cumulative Index Medicus*
QC Isl: Queen Charlotte Islands
qck: quick-connect kit
qcl: quality-control level
QCM: Quality Control Manager
QCM: *Quality Control Manual*
qco: quartz-crystal oscillator
Q Co: Queens County
QCO: Quality Control Officer
QCOP: Quality Control Operating Procedure
QCP: Quality Control Procedure
QCPE: Quantum Chemistry Program Exchange
qcr: quick-change response
QCR: Quality Control Representative
QC & R: Quality Control and Reliability
QCRC: Québec Central Railway Company
QC Rep: Quality-Control Representative
QC Rept: Quality-Control Report
QC Ry: Québec Central Railway
QCS: Quality Control System; Quality Cost System
QCSR: Quaker Committee on Social Rehabilitation
QC Stand: Quality-Control Standard
qct: quiescent carrier telephony; questionable corrective task
QCT: Quality Control Technology
QC & T: Quality Control and Test
QCTR: Quality Control Test Report
qcu: quartz crystal unit; quick-change unit
qcus: quartz crystal unit set
qcvc: quick-connect valve coupler
qcw: quadrant continuous wave
QCWA: Quarter-Century Wireless Association
Qcy: Quincy
QCYC: Queen City Yacht Club
qd: quarterdeck
q-d: quick-disconnect
q & d: quick and dirty
q.d.: *quater in die* (Latin—four times a day)
QD: Sadios Transportes Aéreos
qda: quantity discount agreement
qdc: quick dependable communications; quick-disconnect cap; quick-disconnect connector; quick-disconnect coupling
qdcc: quick-disconnect circular connection
qdc's: quick, dependable, communications

qdd: qualified for deep diving; quantized decision detection
QD/GD: Quincy Division/General Dynamics
qdh: quick-disconnect handle
qdk: quick-disconnect kit
qdn: quick-disconnect nipple
q^{do}: *quando* (Portuguese or Spanish—when)
Qd'O: Quai d'Orsay
qdp: quick-disconnect pivot
QDRI: Qualitative Development Requirements Information (program)
qds: quick-disconnect series; quick-disconnect swivel
qdta: quantitative differential thermal analysis
qdv: quick disconnect valve
qe: quadrant elevation
q.e.: *quod est* (Latin—which is)
QE: Quality Engineer(ing)
QEA: Qantas Empire Airways
qeav: quick—exhaust air valve
qec: quick engine change
qecu: quick engine-change unit
qed: quantitative evaluative device; quantum electrodynamics; quick-reaction dome
q.e.d.: *quod erat demonstrandum* (Latin—that which was to be proved)
qee: quadruple expansion engine
q.e.f.: *quod erat faciendum* (Latin—that which was to be done)
QEFD: Queen Elizabeth's Foundation for the Disabled
QEH: Queen Elizabeth Hall
q.e.i.: *quod erat inveniendum* (Latin—that which was to be discovered)
qel: quiet extended life
QEL: Quality Evaluation Laboratory
qem: quadrant electrometer
QEM: Qualified Export Manager
QENP: Queen Elizabeth National Park (Uganda)
qeo: quality engineering operations
QEONS: Queen Elizabeth's Overseas Nursing Service
QEOP: Quartermaster Emergency Operation Plan
QEP: Quality Examination Program; Queen Elizabeth Park; Queen Elizabeth Planetarium; Queensland Environmental Program
qer: qualitative equipment requirements
QER: *Quarterly Economic Review*
qescp: quality engineering significant control points
QESP: Queen Emma Summer Palace
QEST: Quality Evaluation System Test(s)
QE2: *Queen Elizabeth 2* (passenger vessel)
QET: Queen Elizabeth Theatre (Vancouver)
qev: quick exhaust valve
QEW: Queen Elizabeth Way (Canadian highway linking Buffalo with Toronto)
qf: quality factor; quick freeze
QF: quick-firing
Q-factor: quality rating
q-fastener(s): quick-fastener(s)
qfc: quantitative flight characteristics
qfcc: quantitative flight characteristics criteria
Q fever: query fever (of uncertain cause); Balkan grippe or nine-mile fever (viral disease with pneumonial symptoms caused by rickettsia)
qff: quadruple flip-flop
QFI: Qualified Flight Instructor
qfirc: quick-fix interference-reduction capability
qfl: quasi-fermi level
qfm: quantized frequency modulation
qfo: quartz frequency oscillator
qfp: quartz fiber product
QFP: Quick-Fix Program
Q-fract: quick fraction (membrane potentials)
QFRI: Queensland Fisheries Research Institute
qft: quantized field theory
qg: quadrature grid
QG: Quartermaster General
QG: *Quartier Général* (French—Headquarters); *Quartier Generale* (Italian—Headquarters)
qgb: searchlight sonar (symbol)
qgv: quantized gate video
qh: quartz helix
q.h.: *quaque hora* (Latin—every hour)
QH: Queen's Hall
QHC: Queen's Honorary Chaplain
QHDS: Queen's Honorary Dental Surgeon
QHM: Queen's Harbour Master
QHNS: Queen's Honorary Nursing Sister
QHP: Queen's Honorary Physician
QHS: Queen's Honorary Surgeon
QHV: Queen's Honorary Veterinarian
qi: quality indices
QI: Quota International
QI: *Quality Index; Quarterly Index*
qic: quality inspection criteria; quartz-iodine crystal
QIC: Quality Information Center
q.i.d.: *quater in die* (Latin—four times a day)
QIDN: Queen's Institute of District Nursing
QIE: Qualified International Executive
qil: quartz incandescent lamp; quartz iodine lamp
qip: quartz insulation part
Q.I.P.: *Quiescat in Pace* (Latin—Rest in Peace)
qit: qualification information and test (system)
QJC: Quincy Junior College
qk: quick
Qk Fl: quick flashing (light)
qkm: *Quadratkilometer* (German—square kilometers)
ql: quick look
ql: *quilate* (Portuguese—carat)
q.l.: *quantum libet* (Latin—as much as you like)
QL: Queen's Lancers
QLAP: Quick Look Analysis Program
QLCS: Quick Look and Checkout System
Qld: Queensland
qli: quality of life index
qlit: quick-look intermediate tape
qll: quartz landing lamp
qlm: quasi-laser machine
QLR: *Québec Law Reports*
qlsm: quasi-laser sequential machine
qlt: quantitative leak test
qlty: quality
qm: *Quadratmeter* (German—square meter); *quintal métrico* (Spanish—metric quintal; 220 pounds)
q.m.: *quaque mane* (Latin—every morning); *quo modo* (Latin—in what manner)
QM: Decca navigation system; Quartermaster; Queen's Messenger
qma: quality material approach
QMA: Quartermasters Association
QMAAC: Queen Mary's Army Auxiliary Corps
qmao: qualified for mobilization ashore only
Q-max: quarantine maximum
QMC: Quartermaster Corps
QMC & SO: Quartermaster Cataloging and Standardization Office

QMDEP: Quartermaster Depot
qmdk: quick mechanical disconnect kit
QMDO: Qualitative Materiel Development Objective
QMDPC: Quartermaster Data Processing Center
QMEPCC: Quartermaster Equipment and Parts Commodity Center
QMFCI: Quartermaster Food and Container Institute
QMFCIAF: Quartermaster Food and Container Institute for the Armed Forces
QMG: Quartermaster General
QMGF: Quartermaster-General to the Forces
QMGMC: Quartermaster General—Marine Corps
QMI: Qualification Maintainability Inspection
QMIMSO: Quartermaster Industrial Mobilization Services Offices
qmo: qualitative material objective
QMORC: Quartermaster Officers Reserve Corps
QMP: Quezon Memorial Park (Philippines)
QMPA: Quartermaster Purchasing Agency
QMPCUSA: Quartermaster Petroleum Center US Army
qmqb: quick-make quick-break (connection)
qmr: qualitative materiel requirement
QMRC: Quartermaster Reserve Corps
QMR & E: Quartermaster Research and Engineering
QMRL: Quartermaster Radiation Laboratory
QMs: quartermasters
QMS: Quartermaster School (US Army)
Qm Sgt: Quartermaster Sergeant
QMSO: Quartermaster Supply Office(r)
qmsw: quartz metal sealed window
QMT: Queens-Midtown Tunnel
QMTOE: Quartermaster Table of Organization and Equipment
qmw: quartz metal window
qn: question; quotation
q.n.: *quaque nocte* (Latin—every night); *quid nunc* (Latin—what now?)—person eternally interested in getting the latest news
Qn: Queen
QNP: Quezon National Park (Philippines)
qns: quantity not sufficient
Qns: Queens
Qns Coll: Queen's College
Qnsd: Queensland
Qnsk: Quensk (language of the Quains)
QNS & L: Québec North Shore and Labrador Railway
Qnsld: Queensland
qnty: quantity
QNWR: Quivira National Wildlife Refuge (Kansas)
qo: quick opening; quick outlet
qO_2: oxygen quotient
QO: Quaker Oats; Qualified in Ordnance; Quartermaster Operation; Queen's Own (regiment)
Q & O: Quebéc and Ontario (transportation company)
QO_2: oxygen consumption (or quota)
QOA: Quasi-Official Agencies
QOCH: Queen's Own Cameron Highlanders
qod: quick-opening device
QOD: Quebéc Order of Dentists
QOF: Quaker Oats Foundation
QOIC: Quarantine Officer in Charge
qon: quarter ocean net
qor: qualitative operational requirement
Qor: Qoran (Koran)
QOR: Queen's Own Royal (regiment)
QORC: Queen's Own Rifles of Canada
qp: queen post; quick process(ing)
q.p.: *quantum placet* (Latin—at discretion)
q-P: quanti-Pirquet (reaction)
QP: Qualification Proposal; Queen's Printer
QPA: Queensland Police Academy
QPC: Quatar Petroleum Company
QPF: Québec Police Force
QPFC: Queen's Park Football Club
qpi: quadratic performance index
QPIS: Quality Performance Instruction Sheet
QPL: Qualified Parts List; Queens Public Library
QPM: Queen's Police Medal
QPP: Québec Provincial Police; Quetico Provincial Park (Ontario)
QPR: Quality Progress Report; Quantity Progress Report: Quarterly Progress Report; Queen's Park Rangers
QPRI: Qualitative Personnel Requirements Information
qpsk: quad-phase shift key
qq: quartos; questionable questionnaires
qq: *quelques* (French—some); *quintales* (Spanish—quintals)
qq.: *quaque* (Latin—each); *quoque* (Latin—every)
QQ: Celestial Equator
q.q.d.: *quantum quatra die* (Latin—every fourth day)
qqf: *quelquefois* (French—sometimes)
q.q.h.: *quantum quatra hora* (Latin—every four hours)
qq. hor.: *quaque hora* (Latin—every hour)
qqpr: quantitative and qualitative personnel requirements
q.q.v.: *quae vide* (Latin—which see)
qr: qualifications record; quick reaction; quire
qr.: *quadrans* (Latin—farthing)
q.r.: *quantum rectus* (Latin—quantity is correct)
QR: Queensland Railways; Quintana Roo
QR: *Quarterly Review*
Q & R: Quality and Reliability
qra: quality reliability assurance; quick reaction alert
qrbm: quasi-random band model
qrc: quick reaction capability
QRDC: Quartermaster Research and Development Command
QRDEA: Quartermaster Research and Development Evaluation Agency
qrga: quadrupole residual gas analyzer
qri: qualitative requirements information
QRICC: Quick Reaction Inventory Control Center
Qrmr: Quartermaster
qro: quick reaction operation
Qro: Queretaro
QRO: Quick Reaction Operation; Quick Reaction Organization
Q Roo: Quintana Roo
Q-room: cue room (billiard room)
QRPA: Quartermaster Radiation Planning Agency
QRPS: Quick Reaction Procurement System
QRR: Queen's Royal Rifles
QRRR: extreme emergency amateur radio call signal
QR's: Quality Reports
qrtg: quartering
qrtly: quarterly

qrtmstr: quartermaster
qrv: quick-release valve
QRV: Qualified Real-estate Valuer
qry: quality and reliability year
QRZ: *Quaddel Reaktion Zeit* (German—lump reaction time; rash reaction time; wheal reaction time)
qs: quarter section; quarter sessions
q.s.: *quantum satis* (Latin—as much as is sufficient); *quantum sufficit* (Latin—as much as suffices)
Qs: Conquistadores; Conquistadors; questions
QS: Quarantine Station; Quarter Section; Quarter Sessions; Quartermaster Sergeant; Queensland Society; Queen's Scholar
QS: *Quecksilbersäule* (German—mercury column)
QSAL: Quadripartite Standardization Agreements List
qsbg: quasi-stellar blue galaxies
QSC: Quebec Securities Commission
QSD: Quality Surveillance Division (USN); Quincy Shipbuilding Division—General Dynamics
qse: qualified scientists and engineers
qsf: quasi-static field; quasi-stationary front
qsg: quasi-stellar galaxy
Q-ship: disguised man-of-war used to decoy enemy vessels
qsi: quality salary increase
qsic: quality standard inspection criteria
qs & l: quarters, subsistence, and laundry
Q & SL: Qualifications and Standards Laboratory
qsm: quadruple-screw motorship; quarter-square multipliers
QSMO: Quaker State Motor Oils
qso: quasibiennial stratospheric oscillation: quasistellar object
QSO: Québec Symphony Orchestra
QSOP: Quadripartite Standing Operating Procedure(s)
qsp: quality search procedure
QSPP: Québec Society for the Protection of Plants
QSR: Quarterly Status Report; Quarterly Summary Report
qsrs: quasi-stellar radio sources
qss: quasi-stellar source
QSS: quadruple-screw ship; Quota Sample Survey
qssa: quasi-stationary-state approximation
qssp: quasi-solid-state panel
QSSR: Quarterly Stock Status Report
QST: Québec Standard Test
QSTAG: Quadripartite Standardization Agreement
Q-star: quiet observation aircraft
qstnr: questionnaire
qstol: quiet-and-short takeoff and landing
qsts: quadruple-screw turbine steamship
q. suff.: *quantum sufficit* (Latin—as much as needed; as much as will suffice)
qsy: quiet sun year
qt: quantity; quart; quick test; quiet (*see* q.t.)
q.t.: quiet (as "on the q.t.")
q & t: quenched and tempered
QT: Quick's Test (pregnancy or prothrombin)
qta: quadrant transformer assembly
q^{ta}: *quanta* (Portuguese or Spanish—how much)—feminine form
qtam: queued telecommunication access method
qtaux: *quintaux* (French—quintals)
qtb: quarry-tile base
QTC: Queensland Turf Club
qtd: quartered
QTDGs: Quaker Theological Discussion Groups
qtf: quarry-tile floor
QTIB: Québec Tourist Information Bureau
qtly: quarterly
QTM: Quechon Tribal Museum (Yuma, Arizona)
qto: quarto
q^{to}: *quanto* (Portuguese or Spanish—how much)—masculine form
qtp: quantum theory of paramagnetism
QTP: Qualification Test Procedure
qtr: quarry-tile roof; quarter; quarterly
QTR: Quarterly Technical Report
qtrs: quarters
qts: quarts
qtte: quartette
qty: quantity
qtydesreq: quantity desired or requested
qtz: quartz
qtze: quartzose
qtzic: quartzitic
qtzt: quartzite
qu: quart; quarter; quarterly; query; question
qu.: *quasi* (Latin—as it were; like)
Qu: Queen
QU: Queen's University
qua: quadrate; quadratus
quack: quacksalver (person pretending to be a doctor)
quad: quadrangle; quadrangular; quadrant; quadrat; quadruplet(s); quadruplicate(s); quadruplication
quad c: quadripod cane
Quad Cities: adjacent and across-the-river cities of Davenport, East Moline, and Moline, Illinois, plus Davenport in Iowa across the Mississippi River—cities so named because they form a quadrangle
quad .50's: quadruple .50-caliber machine guns
quadradar: four-way radar (surveillance)
Quadrangle: New York Times Book Company; Quadrangle Books
quadrip: quadriplegia
quadrivium: the four liberal arts—arithmetic, astronomy, geography, and music
quadrup: quadruped(s); quadruple
quadrupl.: *quadruplicato* (Latin—four times as much)
quads: quadraphonic records; quadruplets
Quail: California's state bird—the Golden Valley Quail; Californians are sometimes nicknamed Quail
Quaker: Quaker Oats; Quaker Press
Quaker City: Quaker-founded-and-settled Philadelphia
Quaker Dolley: Mrs Doreathea (Dolley) Madison—wife of President James Madison
Quaker Founder: George Fox—founder of the Society of Friends who were nicknamed Quakers by an English judge who persecuted them
Quaker Liberal: Elias Hicks
Quaker Poet: John Greenleaf Whittier
Quaker Preacher: Elias Hicks—founder of the Hicksite Friends championing the abolition of slavery and opposing any set creeds approved by the elders
Quaker Reformer: Elizabeth Fry—noted for her campaign to better the life of inmates in

insane asylums and prisons; also worked for the betterment of education
Quakers: members of the Society of Friends
Quaker State: Pennsylvania
Quakertown: Philadelphia
quake(s): earthquake(s)
qual: qualification; qualify; quality
qual anal.: qualitative analysis
quals: qualifying examinations; qualifying tests
quam: quadrature-amplitude modulation
quant: quantity; quantum
quant anal.: quantitative analysis
quantras: question analysis transformation and search (data processing technique)
quant. suff.: *quantum sufficit* (Latin—sufficient quantity)
quar: quarantine
quarantine flag: yellow flag flown when a vessel requests pratique; letter Q or Québec in the international signal code
quar. pars: *quarta pars* (Latin—one-fourth part)
quarpel: quartermaster water-repellent (cloth or clothing)
quarr: quarries; quarry; quarrying
quart: quarter gallon; quarterly
quart.: quartet; quartette; quartile
Quart: Quarterly
QUART: Quality Assurance and Reliability Team
quartz: crystalline silica (SiO_2)
quartzite: granular quartz rock
quasar: quasi-stellar radio (object)
quaser: quantum-amplification-by-stimulated-emission-of-radiation (acronym covering irasers, lasers, and masers varying only in operational frequency)
quat: quaternary; quaternary era
quat.: *quattuor* (Latin—four)
Quat: Quaternary
QUB: Queen's University of Belfast
Que: Québec (inhabitants—Québecois); Quechua; Quechuan
Que: *Quênia* (Portuguese—Kenya)
QUE: Quebecair
Quebec: code for letter Q
Queen: *The Queen* (La Reine)—Haydn's Symphony No. 85 in B-flat major
Queen of the Adriatic: Venice
Queen Alice: Alice Lee (Roosevelt) Longworth
Queen of the Amazons: Hippolyta
Queen of the Angels: the Virgin Mary
Queen of the Antilles: Cuba
Queen of Belgian Beaches: Ostend
Queen of the Caribbees: Nevis
Queen Charlottes: Queen Charlotte Islands off British Columbia
Queen City of Alabama: Gadsden
Queen City of Canada: Toronto
Queen City of the Hudson: Yonkers, New York
Queen City of the Lakes: Buffalo, New York and Toronto, Ontario complete for this title
Queen City of the Lehigh Valley: Allentown, Pennsylvania
Queen City of the Merrimack Valley: Manchester, New Hampshire
Queen City of the Mississippi: St Louis, Missouri
Queen City of the Mountains: Knoxville, Tennessee
Queen City of the Ohio: Cincinnati, Ohio
Queen City of the Pacific: place-name nickname shared by San Francisco, California and Seattle, Washington
Queen City of the Rio Grande: Del Rio, Texas
Queen City of the Sea: Charleston, South Carolina where loyal Charlestonians agree the Ashley and the Cooper rivers join to form the Atlantic Ocean
Queen City of the Sound: Seattle, Washington on Puget Sound
Queen City of the South: Sydney, New South Wales
Queen City of the Trails: Independence, Missouri where so many homesteaders and pioneers began their westward march to California
Queen City of Vermont: Burlington
Queen of the Comstock Lode: Virginia City, Nevada
Queen of the Cowtowns: Fort Dodge, Iowa
Queen of the Danube: Budapest
Queen Elizabeths: Queen Elizabeth Islands in the Canadian Arctic
Queen Emma: Curaçao's floating bridge across Willemstad's harbor
Queen of Heaven: Ashtoreth (Semitic); Astarte (Phoenician); Hera (Greek); Inanna (Sumerian); Ishtar (Assyrian and Babylonian); Isis (Egyptian); Juno (Roman); Virgin Mary (Christian)
Queenie: Regina
Queen of Lake Mälaren: Stockholm
Queen of Lake Michigan: Chicago
Queen of Long-Distance Roads: the Appian Way extending from Brindisi to Rome and begun in 312 B.C.
Queen of Love and Lust: Aphrodite or Venus
Queen Maud Land: Norwegian Antarctica
Queen of the Missions: Mission San José in San Antonio, Texas and Mission Santa Barbara in Santa Barbara, California
Queen of the Mississippi: St Louis
Queen of the Mountains: Helena, Montana
Queen of the North: Edinburgh
Queen of the Ohio: Cincinnati
Queen of the Plains: Regina, Saskatchewan
Queen of the Prairies: Canada's Province of Saskatchewan
Queen of Queens: Brutus' nickname for Cleopatra
Queen Sarah: Sarah, the Duchess of Marlborough
Queen's College: Rutgers University in colonial times
queen's English: correct English
Queen's House: Buckingham Palace
Queensl: Queensland
Queen of the South: New Orleans
Queen of the Spas: Saratoga Springs, New York
Queen of Summer Resorts: Newport, Rhode Island
Queen of Watering Places: Brighton, England
Queen of the West: Longfellow's nickname for Cincinnati
Quen: Quentin
ques: question
quest.: quality electrical system test; questioned
QUEST: Quality Electrical Systems Test; Queens Educational and Social Team
questal: quiet, experimental, short-takeoff-and-landing (program of NASA)
quester: quick and efficient system to enhance retrieval
questn: questionnaire
QUI: Queen's University of Ireland: Quincy (railroad)
Quich: Quichua
quicha: quantitative inhalation

challenge apparatus
quicklime: calcium oxide—CaO
quicksilver: mercury (Hg)
quico: quality improvement through cost optimization
Quiet Americans: soft-voiced well-mannered Canadians
Quiet River: Russia's quiet-flowing Don
quiktran: quick fortran (programming language)
quím: *química* (Portuguese or Spanish—chemistry)
quin: quintet; quintette; quintuplet; quintuplicate; quintuplication
Quin: Quincy; Quinten; Quintilianus; Quintilius; Quintillian; Quintin; Quintino; Quintius; Quintus
Quincke's disease: edema of the skin; giant hives
quinq: *quinque* (Latin—five)
Quinquad's disease: inflammation of the scalp resulting in bald patches
quins: quintuplets
quint: quintuplicate
quint.: *quintus* (Latin—fifth)
Quint.: Quintilian—Roman critic and rhetorician Marcus Fabius Quintilianus
Quinten: Haydn's String Quartet in D (opus 76, no. 2)—nickname refers to the fifth form or grade in Austrian schools
Quintilian: Marcus Fabius Quintilianus
quint(s): quintet(s); quintuplet(s); quintuplicate(s)
quintupl: quintuplicate
Quintuplets: Herbert Morrison so nicknamed because he did the work of five
quip.: questionnaire interpreter program
quis: quisling (term for traitor derived from Vidkun Quisling who during World War II headed Norway's puppet government set up by the German invaders)
Quisquellano(s): Santo Domingan(s)
Quisqueya: Hispaniola's native name
QUJ: true course to station
QUL: Queen's University Library
quo': quoth
quod.: *quodlibet* (Latin—as you please)
Quoddy: Passamaquoddy Bay between Maine and New Brunswick
Quoins: Gunners Quoin and Quoin Channel north of Mauritius in the Indian Ocean; other Quoins in Australia, Burma, and South Africa
Quon Pt: Quonset Point, Rhode Island
quor: quorum
quor.: *quorum* (Latin—of which)
quot: quotation
quot.: *quotidie* (Latin—daily)
quotes: quotation marks
quote-unquote: quotation marks (slang shortcut—some phrase or word set between quotation marks)
quotid.: *quotidie* (Latin—every day)
qup: quantity per unit pack
QUSA: "Q" Airways
q.v.: *quantum vis* (Latin—as much as is desired); *quod vide* (Latin—which see)
QVM: Queen Victoria Museum (Launceston, Tasmania)
QVR: Queen Victoria's Rifles
qvt: quality verification test
qw: quarter wave
qwa: quarter-wave antenna
qwd: quarterly world day
q-wedge: quartz wedge
QWG: Quadripartite Working Group
qwl: quick weight loss
QWMP: Quadruped Walking Machine Program (US Army)
qwp: quarter-wave plate
qx: *quintaux* (French—hundredweights)
qy: quantum yield; query
QYC: Quincy Yacht Club
qz: quartz
Qz: quartz
QZ: Zambia Airways (2-letter coding)
QZS: Quebec Zoological Society

R

r: angle of reflection (symbol); position vector (symbol); race-mic; radius; rain; range; rare; rate of interest; received; recipe; reconnaissance; recto; red; redetermination; refraction; registered; relative; relative humidity; report; reprint; research; reserve; resistance; restricted; retard; retarded; right or starboard side of an airplane or vessel looking forward (R or S); ring; ringer; riser; rod; rook; rough; rule; rules; runs; rupee (Indian monetary unit); rupees; solubilizing agent (symbol)
r: angular yaw velocity (symbol); front of the sheet (recto)
r: *remotum* (Latin—far; remote)
R: acoustic resistance (symbol); annual rent; electrical resistance; gas constant; ohmic resistance; product moment coefficient of statistical correlation; Rabbi; radioactive range; radiolocation; Rankine; rare; ratio; Réaumur; received solid; reconnaissance; Regina (Queen); registered; Reiz; report(s); Representative; reprint; Republic; Republican; research; reserve; resistance; respiration; restricted; Rex (King); rial (Iranian monetary unit); Richfield Oil; right; ring; river; Road; Robin Line; rocket; Rocketdyne Division of North American Aviation; Roentgen; Roger—radio slang meaning all right or okay; Roma; Roman; Rome; Romeo—code for letter R; Rotary Internation; ruble (Russian monetary unit); rupee (Indian monetary unit); Rwanda; Rydberg; US Rubber Company
R: *rechts* (German—right); resultant force (symbol); *rett (Danish—right); río* (Portuguese—river); *río* (Spanish—river); rogue (designated by the capital letter R branded on British convicts transported overseas in the early

1800s); *rua* (Portuguese—street); *rubeus* (Latin—red); *rue* (French—street); symbolic letter on the flag of Rwanda where it stands for Rwanda, a Republic born of Revolution and confirmed by Referendum; The Book of Ruth
R.: rand (South African monetary unit)
R: (Latin—Romanus; Rufus)
R_1: primary roots
R_2: secondary roots
ra: radio; radioactive; radioactivity; reduced area; right angle; right angulation; right ascension; right atrium; right auricle; robbery committed while armed (RA); rubber-activated; ruling action
r/a: radioactive; return to author
r & a: right and above
Ra: radium
RA: Argentina (auto plaque); Coast Radar Station (symbol); high-powered radio range (Adcock symbol); Rabbinical Assembly; Rdeca Armada (Yugloslav—Red Army); Rear Admiral; Reduction of Area; Regular Army; Remington Arms; Rental Agreement; República Argentina; Republic Aviation; Resident Auditor; Right Arch; right ascension; Rotogravure Association; Royal Academician; Royal Academy; Royal Arcanum; Royal Artillery
R.A.: right ascension
R/A: Redstone Arsenal
r.a.a.: *reductio ad absurdum* (Latin—reduction to an absurdity)—in mathematics sometimes appears as raa or RAA
RAA: Rabbinical Alliance of America; Royal Academic Association; Royal Academy of Arts
RA (A): Rear Admiral (Aircraft Carriers)
RAAA: Red Angus Association of America
RAAC: Regional Affirmative Action Clearinghouse
RAAF: Royal Afghan Air Force; Royal Australian Air Force
RAAFNS: Royal Australian Air Force Nursing Service
RAAMC: Royal Australian Army Medical Corps
RAANC: Royal Australian Army Nursing Corps
RAANS; Royal Australian Army Nursing Service
RAAS: Royal Amateur Art Society
Rab: Rabat; Rabbi; Rabbinic Hebrew
RAB: Radio Advertising Bureau
rabar: Raytheon advanced battery acquisition radar
rabb: rabbinate; rabbinic; rabbinical
Rab(bie): Robert
RABDF: Royal Association of British Dairy Farmers
RABFM: Research Association of British Flour Millers
RABI: Royal Agricultural Benevolent Institution
RABPCVM: Research Association of British Paint Colour and Varnish Manufacturers
RABT: Rederiaktiebolaget Transatlantic **(Swedish Transatlantic Line)**
rac: racemic
rac: *raccommadage(s)* (French—repair(s))
RAC: Railway Association of Canada; Rear Admiral Commanding; Reliability Action Center; Republic Aviation Corporation; Research Advisory Council; Research Analysis Corporation; Royal Air Cambodge; Royal Arch Chapter; Royal Armoured Corps; Royal Automobile Club; Rubber Allocation Committee
RACA: Royal Automobile Club of Australia
RACB: Royal Automobile Club of Belgium
racc: radiation and contamination control
racc: *raccomandata* (Italian—registered letter)
race.: rapid automatic checkout equipment
RACE: Research on Automatic Computation Electronics
RACE: *Real Automóvil Club de España* (Royal Automobile Club of Spain)
racep: random access and correlation for extended performance
races. (RACES): radio amateur civil emergency service
RACI: Royal Australian Chemical Institute
RACIC: Remote Area Conflict Information Center
racine: (French—root)
racon: radar beacon
RACP: Royal Australasian College of Physicians
RACS: Remote Access Computing System; Royal Australasian College of Surgeons
RACV: Royal Automobile Club of Victoria
rad: radar; radian; radiation; radiation-absorbed dose; radiator; radical; radicalism; radio; radioactive; radius; radix; released from active duty; return to active duty; roentgen-administered dosage; roentgen-administered dose
rad.: *radix* (Latin—root)
Rad: Radnor; Radnorshire **RAD:** Royal Academy of Dancing; Royal Albert Docks; Rural Area Development
RA (D): Rear Admiral (Destroyers)
rada: radioactive
RADA: Royal Academy of Dramatic Arts
radac: rapid digital automatic computing
radal: radio detection and location (system)
radan: radar doppler automatic navigator
radar: radio detection and ranging
RADAS: Random Access Discrete Address System (battlefield communications system)
radat: radar data transmission and ranging; radiosonde observation data
radata: radar automatic data transmission assembly
RADC: Rome Air Development Center; Royal Army Dental Corps
RADCC: Rear Area Damage Control Center
rad-ch: radical-changing
RADCM: radar countermeasures and deception
radcon: radar data converter
RADD: Royal Association in Aid of the Deaf and Dumb
raddef: radiological defense
raddol: *raddolcendo* (Italian—growing calmer)
radem (RADEM): random access data modulation
rad encl: radiator enclosure
radep: radar departure
radex: radiation exclusion plot (actual or predicted fallout)
radfac: radiating facility
radhaz: radiation hazard(s)
radi: radiological inspection
radiac: radioactivity-detection-indication-and-computation
RADIC: Research and Development Information Center
radic-lib: radical liberationist

radiclib(s): radical liberal(s)
radint: radar intelligence
Radio City: Radio City Book Store
radiog: radiography
radiol: radiology
radir: random access document indexing and retrieval
radist: radar distance indicator
RA Dks: Royal Albert Docks
radl: radiological
rad lab: radiation laboratory
radlfo: radiological fallout
radlic: radio link
radlop: radiological operations
RADLO: Radiological Defense Officer
radlsafe: radiological safety
radlwar: radiological warfare
R Adm: Rear Admiral
radmon: radiological monitor (ing)
radn: radiation
radnote: ratio note
radome: radar dome
rad op: radio operator
radose: radiation dosimeter satellite
radot: real-time automatic digital-optical tracker
RadPropCast: radio propagation forecast
rad rec: radiator recess
RADRON: Radar Squadron (USAF)
rad/s: radians per second
Rad(s): Radical(s)
RADS: Ryukyu Air Defense System
RadSo: Radiological Survey Officer
radsta: radio station
radu: radar analysis and detection unit
radvs: radar altimeter and doppler velocity sensor
radwar: radiological warfare
rae (RAE): radio astronomy explorer
Rae: Rachel; Raquelle
RAE: Royal Aircraft Establishment
RAE: *Real Academia Española* (Royal Spanish Academy)
R Ae C: Royal Aero Club
RAEC: Royal Army Educational Corps
Raedwulf: (Early English—Ralph)—this redwolf alleged to be the imp of mischief in a printing house
RAEL: Real Academia Española de la Lengua (Royal Spanish Academy of Language)
RAeS: Royal Aeronautical Society
raet: range-azimuth-elevation-time
Raf: Rafael; Rafe; Rafelsz; Raffaele; Raffaello
RAF: Regular Air Force; Royal Aircraft Factory; Royal Air Force
RAFA: Royal Air Force Association; Royal Australian Field Artillery
rafar: radio-automated facsimile and reproduction
rafar: radar-automated facsimile reproduction
rafax: radar facsimile transmission
RAFB: Randolph Air Force Base
RAFBF: Royal Air Force Benevolent Fund
Rafe: Ralph
RAFES: Royal Air Force Educational Service
Raffaello: Raphael
RAFGSA: Royal Air Force Gliding and Soaring Association
Raf[l]: Rafael
RAFMS: Royal Air Force Medical Services
RAFO: Reserve of Air Force Officers
rafos: long-range navigation system (sofar reversed)
RAFR: Royal Air Force Regiment
RAFRO: Royal Air Force Reserve of Officers
RAFS: Royal Air Force Station
RAFSAA: Royal Air Force Small Arms Association
RAFSC: Royal Air Force Staff College
RAFT: Regional Accounting and Finance Test
RAFTC: Royal Air Force Technical College
RAFVR: Royal Air Force Volunteer Reserve
rag.: ragtime
rag: *ragioniere* (Italian—accountant)
RAG: Red Army Group (see *B-M B*); River Assault Group; Royal and Ancient Game (of golf)
RAGA: Royal Australian Garrison Artillery
RAGB: Refractories Association of Great Britain
RAGC: Royal and Ancient Golf Club (St Andrews, Scotland)
RAGE: Radio Amplification of Gamma Emissions
RAH: Royal Albert Hall
ragheads: turbaned Arabs
RAHS: Royal Australian Historical Society
rai: radioactive interference; random access and inquiry
RAI: *Radiotelevisione Italiana; Réseau Aérien Interinsulaire (Tahiti);* Royal Albert Institution; Royal Anthropological Institute
RAI: *Radiotelevisione Italiana* (Italian Radio-Television)—broadcasting system
RAIA: Royal Australian Institute of Architects
RAIC: Royal Architectural Institute of Canada
rail.: railroad; railway
Railroad City: nickname given by railroaders to cities such as Atlanta, Boston, Buffalo, Chicago, Cincinnati, Cleveland, Detroit, Edmonton, Houston, Indianapolis, Kansas City, Los Angeles, Milwaukee, Minneapolis, Montreal, New Orleans, New York, Omaha, Philadelphia, St Louis, San Antonio, San Francisco, Seattle, Toronto, Washington, D.C., Winnipeg; (*see* Railway City)
rails.: runway alignment indicator lights
Railsplitter: Abraham Lincoln
railwayac: railway + maniac (railway fan)
Railway King: George Hudson
Rain: Violin and Piano Sonata in G (opus 78) by Brahms who uses the theme of his *Regenlied* or Rain Song
Raindrop: Chopin's Piano Prelude No. 15 in D-flat major
RAIRS: Recordak Automated Information Retrieval System
RAI-TV: *Radio Audizioni Italiane—TV* (Italian Radio Audition—TV)
raiu: radioactive iodine uptake
Raj; Rajasthan
Rajah: Rogers Hornsby
ra k: raised keel
RAK: *Rikets Allmanna Kartverk* (Swedish—Geographical Survey Office)
Rakóczy: **traditional Hungarian** march used by Berlioz in his *Damnation of Faust* and by Liszt in his Hungarian Rhapsody No. 15 in A minor
ral: resorcyclic acid lactone
Ral: Raleigh
RAL: Resort Airlines; Royal Air Laos
Ralegh: Sir Walter Raleigh (who spelled his name *Ralegh*)
rallo.: *rallentando* (Italian—slower by degrees)

Ralph Iron: Olive Schreiner's pseudonym
ralv: rat leukemia virus
ram.: radio attenuation measurement; random access memory; rapid area maintenance; right ascension of the meridian
ram. (RAM): research and applications module
Ram: Raman effect in spectrum analysis; Ramona
RAM: Revolutionary Action Movement; Royal Academy of Music; Royal Air Maroc; Royal Arch Masons
RAMA: Rome Air Materiel Area
ramac: random access memory accounting
Ramapos: Ramapo Mountains of New Jersey and New York
ramb(s): rambler(s)
RAMC: Royal Army Medical College; Royal Army Medical Corps
RAMIS: Rapid Automatic Malfunction Isolation System
ramont: radiological monitoring
ramp.: rate-acceleration measuring pendulum
RAMP: Radar Mapping of Panama; Radiation Airborne Measurement Program
rampallion: ramp + rapscallion
rampant lion: symbol of Great Britain and the British people
RAMPC: Raritan Arsenal Maintenance Publication Center
RAMPS: Resources Allocation and Multiproject Scheduling
rams.: right ascension of mean sun
Rams: Ramsgate
RAMS: right ascension mean sun
RAMSA: Radio Aeronáutica Mexicana S.A.
RAMSS: Royal Alfred Merchant Seamen's Society
ran.: reconnaissance-attack navigator; request for authority to negotiate
Ran: Rangoon
RAN: Royal Australian Navy
Ranally: Rand McNally
RANC: Royal Australian Naval College
Rance: Ransom(e)
rancom: random communication satellite
Rand: Witwatersrand (Johannesburg)
randam: random-access nondestructive advanced memory
RAND Corporation: Research and Development Corporation (corporate style insists on use of capital letters as shown)
randid: rapid alphanumeric digital indicating device
Random: Random House
Randy: Randolph
Ranger: American program for investigation of the Moon and region between the Moon and the Earth; Texas state policeman
Ranier: Ranier Bancorporation (National Bank of Commerce of Seattle)
RANN: Research Applied to National Needs
RANR: Royal Australian Naval Reserve
RANSA: Rutas Aéreas Nacionales
RANVR: Royal Australian Naval Volunteer Reserve
rao: radio astronomical observatory
RAO: Rudolf A. Oetker (steamship line)
RaOb: radiosonde observation
RAOC: Royal Army Ordnance Corps
raomp: report of accrued obligations—military pay
RAOU: Royal Australasian Ornithologists' Union
rap.: rapid; rapport; rupees, annas, pies
rap: *rapido* (Spanish—rapid)—fast train
Rap: H. Rap Brown
RAP: Radiological Assistance Plan (AEC): Regimental Aid Post; Royal Army Post
RAPC: Royal Army Pay Corps
rapcoe: random access programming and checkout equipment
rapcon: radar approach control
rapec: rocket-assisted personnel ejection catapult
Raph: Raphael
Raphael: Raffaello Sanzio
RAPM: Russian Association of Proletarian Musicians
rapp: rapport; rapporteur; raprochement
RAPP: radiologists, anesthesiologists, pathologists, and psychiatrists
RAPRA: Rubber and Plastics Research Association
rap's: rocket-assisted projectiles
RAPS: Risk Appraisal of Programs System
rap. & sup.: rapport and support
raptap: random access parallel tape
raptus.: rapid thorium-uranium-sodium (reactor)
rar: radio acoustic ranging; rapid-access recording; right arm reclining
RAR: Reliability Action Report; Rhodesian African Rifles; Royal Australian Regiment(s)
rarad: radar advisory
RARDE: Royal Armament Research and Development Establishment
rare.: ram air rocket engine
RARE: Rehabilitation of Addicts by Relatives and Employers
rarep: radar report
RARO: Regular Army Reserve of Officers
ras: radome antenna structure; radula sinus; rapid audit summary; rectified air speed; requirements allocation sheet; rheumatoid arthritis serum
ras.: *rasurae* (Latin—shavings)
ras (RAS): reticular activating system
Ras: Desiderius Erasmus
RAs: Resident Agencies; Resident Agents
RAS: Report Audit Summary; Royal Aeronautical Society; Royal Asiatic Society; Royal Astronomical Society
RASA: Railway and Airline Supervisors Association
RASB: Royal Asiatic Society of Bengal
RASC: Royal Army Service Corps; Royal Astronomical Society of Canada
RASC/DC: Rear Area Security and Damage Control
RASE: Royal Agricultural Society of England
raser: range and sensitivity extending resonator
RASK: Royal Agricultural Society of Kenya
Rasmus: Erasmus
RASPB: Royal and Ancient Society of Polar Bears (Hammerfest, Norway's town-hall club)
Rasputin: (Russian—Dissolute)—nickname of the Siberian monk Gregory Efimovitch long associated with the last of the Romanovs
rastac: random access storage and control
rastad: random access storage and display
RASTAS: Radiating Site Target Acquisition System
Rastus: Erastus; Theophrastus
Rasumovsky: Beethoven's Quar-

tets in F major, E minor, and C major for two violins, viola, and cello (opus 59, nos. 1, 2, 3); dedicated to Count Rasumovsky
rat.: ram air turbine; ratchet; rate; rating; ration(s); rocket-assisted torpedo (RAT)
rat. (RAT): repeat-action tablet
RAT: Remote Associates Test
ratac: radar analog target acquisition computer
ratan: radio television aid to navigation
ratc: radar-aided tracking computer
RATCC: Radar Air Traffc Control Center
ratcon: radar terminal control
rate.: remote automatic telemetry equipment
ratel: radiotelephone
ratelo: radio telephone operator
ratepayer(s): (Canadian English—taxpayer(s))
rat/epr: ram air temperature/engine pressure ratio
ratg: radiotelegraph
Ratipole: nickname of Napoleon III
rato: rocket-assisted takeoff
RATP: Régie Autonome des Transports Parisiens (Le métro—Paris subway system)
***RATR:** Reliability abstracts and Technical Reviews*
rats.: repeat-action tablets
Rats: Rat Islands (Amchitka, Kiska, Rat, etc.)
RATS: Ram Air Turbine Systems
ratscat: radar target scatter site
RATSEC: Robert A. Taft Sanitary Engineering Center
ratt: radioteletypewriter
***RAU:** Repubblica Araba Unita* (Italian—United Arab Republic)— Egypt
RAUS: Retired Association for the Uniformed Services
'raus mit i'm: *heraus mit ihm* (German—out with him)
R Aux AF: Royal Auxiliary Air Force
Rav: Roux-associated virus
RAVA: Rochester Audiovisual Association
RAVC: Royal Army Veterinary Corps
rave.: radar acquisition vocal-tracking equipment
raven.: ranging and velocity navigation
rawarc: radar and warning coordination
RAWI: Radio American West Indies (Virgin Islands)
rawin: radar wind sounding
raws: radar altimeter warning set
rawx: returned account of weather (aviation)
rax: random access (computing system)
'ray: hurray
Ray: Rachel; Raymond
Raynaud's disease: circulatory disorder of the extremities
razel: range, azimuth, elevation
razon: range and azimuth only
Razor: The Razor—General Hideki Tojo's nickname
Razorback(s): Arkansan(s)
Razor Clam Capital: Cordova, Alaska
razz: razzberry (slang for raspberry)
rb: relative bearing; rigid boat; road bend; rubber-base(d)
r & b: rhythm and blues; right and below
Rb: rubidium
RB: reconnaissance bomber; Regiment Botha; Renegotiation Board; Republica Boliviana (Bolivian Republic); Republic of Burma; Rifle Brigade; Ritzaus Bureau (Danish news agency); Royaume de Belgique (Kingdom of Belgium)
R.B.: Robert Browning
R_B: Rockwell hardness (B-scale)
RBA: Rabat, Morocco (airport); Roadside Business Association
RBAF: Royal Belgian Air Force
RBB: Richard Bedford Bennett (Canada's fourteenth Prime Minister)
rbbsb: right-bundle-branch system block
rbc: red blood cell; rd blood cell (count); red blood corpuscle
RBC: Richard Bland College; Roller Bearing Company; Royal Bank of Canada
rbcd: right border of cardiac dullness
rbd: rapid beam deflector; right border of dullness (heart response to percussion)
rbde: radar bright-display equipment
rbe: relative biological effectiveness
RBEC: Roller Bearing Engineering Committee
rbelet: relative biological effectiveness linear energy transfer
rbf: renal blood flow
RBF: Rockefeller Brothers Fund
RBG: Royal Botanic Gardens (Kew Gardens)
RBH: Rutherford Birchhard Hayes (19th President U.S.)
rbí: reply by indorsement; request better information
***rbí:** recibí* (Spanish—I received)
RBI: Reserve Bank of India; Rochester Business Institute
rb imp: rubber-base impression
RBK: Royal Borough of Kensington
rbl: ruble
R Bn: radio beacon
RBN: Registry of Business Names
RBNA: Royal British Nurses' Association
RBNM: Rainbow Bridge National Monument (Utah)
rbo: right back outside
RBO: Russian Brotherhood Organization
RBP: Raffinerie Belge de Petroles
rbr: risk-to-benefit ratio; rubber
rBr: reddish brown
RBR: Renegotiation Board Regulation
RBRF: Reproductive Biological Research Foundation
rbs: radar bomb scoring
RBS: Ranganthittoo Bird Sanctuary (India); Research for Better Schools; Royal Botanical Society
rbt: rabbet; roundabout
RBU: Rabindra Bharati University
rc: radio code; radio coding; rate of change; ready calendar; red cell; red corpuscle; reinforced concrete; resistance capacitance; resistor-capacitor; respiratory center; reverse course; right center; rigid center; rock-crushed; rubber-cushioned
r/c: recredited
***r/c:** rés-do-chão* (Portuguese—ground floor)
RC: Radcliffe College; Radio City; Radio Code; Reception Center; Reconstruction Commission; Red China; Red Cross; Regina College; Regis College; Reinhardt College; Renison College; República de Chile; República de Colombia; República de Cuba; Ricker College; Ricks College; Rider College; Río Colorado; Ripon College; Rivier College; Roanoke College; Rockefeller Center; Rockford College; Rockhurst College; Rockmount College; Rollins College; Roman Catholic, Ro-

sary College; Rosemount College; Rosenwal College; Rust College

R, C: Cauchy constant

R_c: Rockwell hardness (C-scale)

R.C.: *Rendiconti* Italian—proceedings or reports)

R de C: *Radiodiffusion du Cameroun* (French—Radio Network of Cameroon)

R of C: Republic of China (nationalist offshore China)

RCA: Rabbinical Council of America; Radio Club of America; Radio Corporation of America; Rocket Cruising Association; Rodeo Cowboys Association; Roofing Contractors Association; Royal Canadian Academician; Royal Canadian Academy; Royal Canadian Artillery

RCA: *République Centrafricaine* (French—Central African Republic)

RCAA: Royal Cambrian Academy of Art; Royal Canadian Academy of Arts

RCAC: Radio Corporation of America Communications

RCAF: Royal Canadian Air Force

RCAM: Royal Canadian Artillery Museum

R Cam A: Royal Cambrian Academy of Art

RCAMC: Royal Canadian Army Medical Corps

R Can: Rio Canario

RCAT: Royal College of Arts and Technology

RCA Vic: RCA Victor

RCB: Regiment Christiaan Beyers; Retail(ers) Credit Bureau

RCAS: Royal Central Asian Society

RCASC: Royal Canadian Army Service Corps

RCBB: Royal Commission on Bilingualism and Biculturalism (Canada)

rcc: rough combustion cutoff

r & cc: riot and civil commotion

RCC: Radio-Chemical Center; Radiological Control Center; Rag Chewers Club; Reply Coupon Collector(s); Rescue Control Center; Rescue Coordination Center; Rockland Community College; Roman Catholic Church; Royal Crown Cola

RCCC: Republican County Central Committee

RCCE: Regional Congress of Construction Employers

RC Ch: Roman Catholic Church

rcd: received; relative cardiac dullness

RCD: Regional Cooperation for Development (Pakistan, Iran, Turkey)

RCDA: Retail Coin Dealers Association

RCDC: Royal Canadian Dental Corps

RCDEP: Rural Civil Defense Education Program

RCDI: Reliability Control Departmental Instruction

rce: right center entrance

RCE: Reliability Control Engineering

RCEEA: Radio Communications and Electronic Engineers Association

RCEME: Royal Canadian Electrical and Mechanical Engineers

RCEP: Royal Commission on Environmental Pollution

RCET: Royal College of Engineering Technology; Rugby College of Engineering Technology

rcf: relative centrifugal force

RCFA: Reliability Control Failure Analysis

RCFCA: Royal Canadian Flying Clubs Association

RCG: Reception Guidance Center

RCGA: Royal Canadian Golf Association

RCGP: Royal College of General Practitioners

RCGS: Royal Canadian Geographical Society

Rch: Rochester

RCH: Railway Clearing House

RCHM: Royal Commission on Historical Monuments (England)

rci: radar coverage indicator

RCI: Range Communications Instructions, Reichold Chemicals Incorporated; Research Council of Israel; Resident Cost Inspection; Resident Cost Inspector; Royal Canadian Institute

RCIA: Retail Clerks International Association; Retail Credit Institute of America

RCIC: Rumor Control and Information Center

rcirc: recirculate

RCIs: Recontres Culturelles Internationales (International Cultural Meetings)

rcj: reaction-control jet

RCJ: Royal Courts of Justice

RCK: *Research Centrum Kalkzandsteen Industrie* (Dutch—Research Center for the Calcium Silicate Industry)

RCL: ramped cargo lighter (naval designation); Royal Canadian Legion

rclm: reclaim; reclamation

rcm: radar countermeasure(s); radio-controlled mine; radio countermeasure(s); right costal margin

RCM: Reliability Control Manual; Royal College of Music

RCMP: Royal Canadian Mounted Police

RCN: Reactor Centrum Nederland; Record Control Number; Republic of China Navy; Royal Canadian Navy; Royal College of Nursing

RCN: *Radio Cadena Nacional* (Spanish—National Radio Chain)—Mexican broadcasting system

RCNC: Royal Corps of Naval Constructors

RCNM: Russell Cave National Monument

RCNR: Royal Canadian Naval Reserve

RCNT: Registered Clinical Nurse Teacher

RCNVR: Royal Canadian Naval Volunteer Reserve

rco: rendezvous compatible orbit

RCO: Radio Control Office; Royal College of Organists

RCOA: Radio Club of America; Record Club of America

RCOC: Royal Canadian Ordnance Corps

RCOG: Royal College of Obstetricians and Gynecologists

RCP: Royal College of Physicians

RCPL: Realtors Co-op Photo Listing

RCPS: Royal College of Physicians and Surgeons

rcpt: receipt

rcr: reverse contactor

RCR: República de Costa Rica

RCRBSJ: Research Council on Riveted and Bolted Structural Joints

rcrd: record

RCs: Roman Catholics

RCS: Reaction Control System; Rearward Communications System; Reentry Control System; Reliability Control Standard; Report Control Symbol; Royal College of Science; Royal College of Surgeons; Royal Common-

wealth Society (formerly Royal Empire Society)
RCSE: Royal College of Surgeons—Edinburgh
RCSI: Royal College of Surgeons—Ireland
RCSS: Random Communication Satellite System
RCST: Royal College of Science and Technology
Rct: Recruit
RCT: Regimental Combat Team(s); Rorschach Content Test; Royal Corps of Transport
rctl: resistor capacitor transistor logic
rcu: remote control unit
RCU: Road Construction Unit
RCUEP: Research Center for Urban and Environmental Planning (Princeton U)
rcv: receive
rcvr: receiver
RCVS: Royal College of Veterinary Surgeons
RCYC: Royal Canadian Yacht Club
R Cy N: Royal Ceylon Navy
RCZ: Radiation Control Zone
rd: reaction of degeneration; readiness date; renal disease; required date; research and development (R & D); restricted data; retinal detachment; round; rutherford
r & d: reamed and drifted; research and development
Rd: Road
RD: Air Lift International; Radio Denmark; República Dominicana; Restricted Data; Royal Dragoons; Royal Dutch Petroleum (stock exchange symbol); Rural Delivery
R.D.: Royal (Naval Reserve) Decoration
R/D: Research/Development
RD$: República Dominicana peso (Dominican currency)
R & D: research and development (should be in lowercase letters but scientists, engineers, and other recognize it as shown)
R of D: Report of Debate
rda: recommended dietary allowance; right dorso-anterior
rd a (Rd A): reading age
RDA: Reliability Design Analysis; Respiratory Diseases Association; Royal Docks Association
***RDA:** Reader's Digest Almanac*
R & D A: Research and Development Association
RDAF: Royal Danish Air Force
Rdam: Rotterdam
RDAR: Reliability Design Analysis Report
rdb (RDB): radar decoy balloon
RDB: Ramped Dump Barge; Research and Development Board; Royal Danish Ballet
rd bot: rubber diaphragm (stoppered) bottle
rdc: rail diesel car; running down clause
RDC: Rand Development Corporation; Rural District Council
RDCA: Rural District Councils' Association
RDCO: Reliability Data Control Office
rdd: required delivery date
rde: receptor-destroying enzyme
r d & e: research, development, and engineering (usually R D & E)
RDE: Research and Development Establishment
R de T: Ralph de Toledano
rdf: radio direction finder
RDF: Royal Dublin Fusiliers
Rdg: Reading; Ridge (postal abbreviation)
RDG: Reading Railroad
rd hd: round head
RDI: Royal Designer for Industry
RDL: Radiocarbon Dating Laboratory (Florida State University); Ritter Dental Laboratories
RDLI: Royal Durban Light Infantry
RdlR: Regiment de la Rey
rdm: root drum
***RDM:** Rand Daily Mail* (Johannesburg)
Rdm3c: Radarman, third class
rdmu: range-drift measuring unit
RDN: Royal Danish Navy
rdo: research and development objectives
RDO: Radiological Defense Office(r)
rdp: right dorso-posterior
RDPC: Research Data Publication Center
rdpe: radar data-processing equipment
rd/q: reading quotient
rdr: radar
RDR: Reliability Diagnostic Report
rdr rel: radar relay
rdrsmtr: radar transmitter
rds: respiratory distress syndrome
Rds: Rixdllar; Roads; Roadstead
RDs: Revolutionary Development teams
RDS: Royal Dublin Society
RD/S: Royal Dutch/Shell
RD & S: Research, Development, and Studies (USMC)
RD/SG: Royal Dutch/Shell Group (world's largest industrial corporation)
rdt: reserve duty training
RDT: Regiment Danie Theron; Reliability Demonstration Test
***RDT:** Repubblica Democratica Tedesca* (Italian—German Democratic Republic)—East Germany
R.D.T.: Registered Dental Technician
rdt & e (RDT & E): research, development, test, and evaluation
***R du Z:** République du Zaïre* (French—Republic of Zaire)
rdvu: rendezvous
RDW: Regiment De Wet
rdx: cyclonite (research department explosive)
rdy: ready
RDY: Royal Dock Yard
RDZ: Radiation Danger Zone
***RDZ:** République Démocratique du Zaïre* (French—Democratic Republic of Zaire)—formerly the Belgian Congo
rdz(s) (RDZ or RDZs): radiation danger zone(s)
re: radium emanation; real estate; research and engineering (R & E); reticulo-endothelium; right eye
re: (Italian—second tone; *B* in diatonic scale, *D* in fixed-do system)
r/e: rate of exchange
Re: Reno; Reynold's Number; rhenium; rupee (Ceylon, India, Pakistan currency)
***R_e:** récipe* **(Spanish—recipe; prescription)**
RE: Radio Eireann (Radio Ireland); Reformed Episcopal (church); Reliability Engineering; República de Ecuador; Rifle Expert; Right Excellent; Royal Engineers; Royal Exchange
r & e (R & E): research and engineering
REA: Railway Express Agency; Request for Engineering authorization; Rice Export Association; Rubber Export Association; Rural Electrification Administration (US Department of Agriculture)

reac: reactor
REAC: Reeves electronic analog computer; Reliability Engineering Action Center
react: reactance; reaction; reactor; register-enforced automated-control technique
REACT: Radio Emergency Associated Citizens Team; Register-Enforced Automated Control Technique; Resource Allocation and Control Techniques
READ: Real-Time Electronic Access and Display
readi: rocket-engine-analyzer-and-decision-instrumentation
readm: readmission
READS: Reno Air Defense Sector
REAL: Rape Emergency Assistance League; Real-Aerovias do Brasil
realcom: real-time communication(s)
real est: real estate
realgar: arsenic sulfide
Realistic Recorder of Spanish Life: Goya (Francisco José de Goya y Lucientes)
Realm of Exotic Flavors: Thailand
REAP: Rural Environmental Assistance Program
reapt: reappoint; reappointment
REAR: Reliability Engineering Analysis Report
Rear Adm: Rear Admiral
reasm: reassemble
REAT: Radiological Emergency Assistance Team
Réau(m): Réaumur
Reb: Reba; Rebecca; Rebekah
REB: Regional Examining Body
Reba: Rebecca
Rebecca West: Cecily Isabel Fairfield
Rebel of Salem: Roger Williams
Rebel of Walden: Henry David Thoreau
reb(s): rebel(s)
rec: receipt; receive; record; recreation
rec.: *recens* (Latin—fresh)
Rec: Recife
REC: Recife, Brazil (airport)
R & EC: Research and Engineering Coucil
Recafellow: Andrew Carnegie's nickname for John D. Rockefeller Sr
recap: recapitulate; recapitulation
RECAP: Reliability Evaluation Continuous Analysis Program
rec chg: record change(r)
recco: reconnaissance
recd: received
recep: reception
recg: radioelectrocardiograph
rec hall: recreational hall
recid: recidivism; recidivist(ic); recidivous
recids: recidivists
recip: reciprocating
recip & lp turb: reciprocating steam engine and low-pressure turbine
recirc: recirculate; recirculation
reci: recitation
recit.: *recitativo* (Italian—recitative)
reclam: reclamation
Reclus' disease: cystic growths in the breasts
recm: recommend
RECMF: Radio and Electronic Component Manufacturers Federation
recog: recognition; recognize
recom: recommendation; recommend(ed)
recon: reconcentration; reconciliation; recondite; recondition; reconduction; reconnaissance; reconnoiter; reconsign; reconsigned; reconsignment; reconstruct; reconstructed; reconstruction; reconversion; reconvert; reconverted; reconvey; reconveyance; reconveyed
RECON: Retrospective Conversion of Bibliographic Records (Library of Congress)
recond: recondition
R Econ S: Royal Economic Society
RECONS: Reliability and Configurational Accountability System
reconst: reconstruct
recov: recover; recovery
recp: receptacle; reciprocal; reciprocating
RECP: Rural Environmental Conservation Program
recpt: receptionist
recr: receiver
rec room: receiving room; reception room; record room; recreation room
Rec S; Record of Survey
recryst: recrystallize
Rec S: Record of Survey
Rec Sec: Recording Secretary
RECSTA: Receiving Station
recsys: recreational systems analysis
rect: rectified; rectifier; rectify
rect.: *rectificatus* (Latin—rectified)
Rect: Rector(y)
recto: obverse; right-hand page (opposite of verso)
recur.: recurrence; recurrent; recurring
rec vehicle(s): recreation vehicle(s)—campers, dune buggies, snowmobiles, trailers, vans, etc.
red.: reduce; reduction
red: *redaktör* (Swedish—editor); *rédigé* (French—compiled; edited)
Red: Sinclair Lewis
Red: *Rederi* (Scandinavian—shipowners)
REDAR: R. E. Darling (Company)
Redbricks: red-brick universities
red burgee: burgee-shaped red signal flag flown when explosives or flammable fuel is being loaded aboard a vessel; letter B or Bravo in the international code
redcape: readiness capability
redcat: readiness requirement
Red Chamber: Canadian Senate
Red China: People's Republic of China
Red Clover: Vermont state flower
redcon: readiness condition
Redcraft: Red aircraft (communist-controlled aircraft)
Red Crescent: equivalent of the Red Cross in the Moslem world (symbolized by a red crescent on a white field)
Red Cross: red cross on a white field; used on ambulances, hospitals, and hospital ships to denote their neutrality; also called the Cross of Geneva or the Geneva Cross as its function in war is accepted by the Geneva Convention and its design is the reverse of the Swiss flag
Red Cross and Crescent: Soviet equivalent of the Red Cross (symbolized by a red cross and a red crescent on a white field)
Redd Foxx: John Elroy Sanford
Red Duster: Red Ensign flown from British merchant vessels
red flag: danger; stop sign
redig: *redigerat* (Swedish—edited)
Red Indians: North America's copper-colored Indians
redig. in pulv.: *redigatur in pulverem* (Latin—reduce to powder)
red. in pulv.: *reductus in pul-*

verem (Latin—reduced to a powder)
redisc: rediscount
red lead: lead oxide (minium)
REDLARS: Reading Literature Analysis and Retrieval Service
red lead: lead oxide—Pb_3O_4; minium
red light: danger signal; port side of aircraft, ships, or other vessels; stop signal; warning signal
redlight district: whorehouse neighborhood; zone of prostitution
Red Lion and Sun: Iran's equivalent of the Red Cross (symbolized by a red lion beneath a red sun on a white field)
red ochre: reddle (hematite red)
redox: reduction oxidation
Red Planet: Mars
Red Priest: red-headed Antonio Vivaldi
Red Rosa: Rosa Luxemburg—co-founder with Karl Liebnecht of the Spartacus League, later to become the Communist Party of Germany
redsg: redesign; redesigned; redesigning
redsh: reddish
Red Skelton: Richard Bernard Skelton
red star: symbol of the Soviet Union and many communist-controlled lands
redup(l): reduplicate; reduplication
ree: rare-earth elements
REE: Regional Economic Expansion (Canada)
REECO: Reynolds Electrical and Engineering Compay
Reed: *Reederei* (German—shipowners)
reef: The Reef—Australia's Great Barrier Reef off the coast of Queensland
reefer(s): marijuana cigarette(s); refrigerated compartment(s) or hold(s) in a ship; refrigerator(s)
Reefer(s): inhabitant(s) of the Great Barrier Reef
reeg: radioelectroencephalograph
reenl: reennlist
reep: range estimating and evaluation procedure
ref: refer; referee; reference; refraction; refresher
ref: *refondue* (French—reorganized)
ref (REF): renal erythropoietic factor
Ref: *Referate* (German—abstract; compedium)
refash: refashion(ed)
Ref Ch: Reformed Church
refd: refund
ref dent: referring dentist
ref doct: referring doctor
refl: reflection; reflective; reflector; reflex; reflexive
ref l: reference line
refl pron: reflexive pronoun
Reform: Reformatory
Reforma: National Association of Spanish-Speaking Librarians in the United States
Reformation: Mendelssohn's Symphony No. 5 in D major
reforst: reforestation
ref phys: referring physician
ref press: reference pressure
refr: refraction; refractory; refrigerate; refrigerator
refrg: refrigerate; refrigeration; refrigerator
refrig: refrigeration; refrigerator
Refrig Eng: *Refrigerating Engineering*
ref temp: referece temperature
Ref Zhu: *Referativnyi Zhurnal* (Russian—Abstract Journal)
reg: region; regular; regulate; regulation
Reg: Registered
RegAF: Regular Air Force
regal.: range and elevation guidance for approach and landing
Reg Bez: *Regierungsbezirk* (German—administrative district)
reg bot: regular bottle (3/4-liter of wine)
regd: registered
regen: regenerate; regeneration
Regg: *Reggimento* (Italian—Regiment)
Reg Gen: Registrar General
Reggie: Regina(ld)
Reg(gie)(y): Reginald
Region of Four Streams: Szechwan Province, China
regis: register; rgistered; registration; registry
Regnery: Henry Regnery
Reg Prof: Regius Professor
Regr: Registrar
regs: regions; regulars; regulations
regt: regiment
Reg TM: Registered Trade Mark
reh: rehearsal
rehab: rehabilitate
rehob: rehoboam (6-bottle capacity)
REI: Régie Aérienne Interinsulaire
REIC: Radiation Effects Information Center; Rare Earth Information Center (Atomic Energy Commission, Ames Laboratory, Iowa State University)
Reichmann's disease: continuous and excessive gastric secretion
reig: rare-earth iron garnets
reils: runway end identification lights
reimb: reimburse; reimbursement
reincorp: reincorporate(d)
reinf: reinforce(d); reinforcing
reinfmt: reinforcement
reins.: radio-equipped inertial navigation system
reit: reiteration
REIT: Real Estate Investment Trusts
rej: reject; rejected; rejection
rejase: re-using junk as something else (old bathtub as setee; ouija board as coffee table; radio cabinet as bookcase, etc.)
rejn: rejoin
REK: Reykjavik, Iceland (airport)
rekenk: *rekenkunde* (Dutch—arithmetic)
rel: rate of energy loss; relation; relative; relay; release; relief; relieve; religion; religionist
rel: *relie; reliure* (French—bound; binding)
REL: Radio Engineering Laboratories
RELACS: Radar Emission Location Attack Control System
rel adv: relative adverb
RELCV: Regional Educational Laboratory for the Carolinas and Virginia
RELHS: Robert E. Lee High School
rel hum: relative humidity
relig: religion; religious
reliq.: *reliquus* (Latin—remainder)
reloc: relocate; relocated; relocation
rel pron: relative pronoun
Rel R: Reliability Report
rem: rapid eye movements; remission; remit; remittance; removable; remove; removed; roentgen equivalent, man
Rem: Remington; roentgen equivalent, man
REM: Registered Equipment Management
REMA: Refrigeration Equipment Manufacturers Associa-

tion
remab: radiation equivalent manikin absorption
remad: remote magnetic anomaly detection
Rembrandt: Rembrandt Harmenszoon van Rijn—RvR
remc: resin-encapsulated mica capacitor
remcal: radiation equivalent manikin absorption
remd: rapid eye movement (sleep) deprivation
REME: Royal Electrical and Mechanical Engineers
REML: Radiation Effects Mobile Laboratory
rems (REMS): rapid-eye-movement sleep
REMS: Registered Equipment Management System
REMSA: Railway Engineering Maintenance Suppliers Association
rem sleep: rapid-eye-movement (paradoxical) sleep
REMT: Radiological Emergency Medical Teams
ren. *renovetur* (Latin—renew)
Ren: Renaissance
rene: rocket-engine nozzle ejector
Rene: Irene
Renegade Irishman: James Joyce
Renf: Renfrew
RENFE: Red Nacional de los Ferrocarriles Españoles (National Network of Spanish Railroads)
ren. sem.: *renovetum semel* (Latin—renew only once)
rent.: reentry nose tip
renv: renovate; renovation
reo: rare-earth oxide; regenerated electrical output
Reo: (early American automobile named after initials of its maker, Ransom E. Olds of Oldsmobile fame)
REO: Regional Education Officer
reoc: report when established on course (aviation)
REORG: reorganization; reorganize; reorganized
reorgn: reorganization
REOS: Reflective Electron Optical System
reo viruses: respiratory-enteric-orphan viruses
rep: repair; repertory; represent; reputation
r-ep: rational-emotive psychotherapy
rep.: *repetatur (Latin—let it be repeated)*
Rep: Representative; Republic; Republican; Republican Party; roentgen equivalent, physical
REP: Radical Education Project; Recovery and Evacuation program; Republic Corporation (stock exchange symbol); Research Expenditure Proposal; Reserve Enlisted Program; River Engineering Program
REPA: Research and Engineers Professional Employees Association
REPC: Regional Economic Planning Council
rept.: *repetatur* (Latin—let it be repeated)
repl: replace(d); replacement; replacing
REPM: Representatives of Electronic Products Manufacturers
repo: repossess; repossessed; repossession
reppac: repetitively-pulsed plasma accelerator
repr: repairman; representative; reprint; reprinted; reprinting
repro: reproduce; reproducing; reproduction
reprosex: reproductive sex
repro typ: reproduction typist; reproduction typing
reps: representatives
REPS: Rail(way) Express Parcel Service
rep. sem.: *repetatur semel* (Latin—let it be repeated once)
rept: report; reprint; reptile; reptilia(n)
Rept: Reptilia
repub: republication; republish(ed)
REPUBLIC: Republic Aviation Corporation
Republocrat: Republican Democrat
Repubs: Republicans
req: request; require
reqafa: request advise as to further action
reqd: required
reqdi: request disposition instructions
reqfolinfo: request following information
reqid: request if desired
requint: request interim (reply)
reqmad: request mailing address
reqn: requisition
reqs: requires
reqssd: request supply status (and expected delivery) date
reqsupstafol: request supply status of following
reqt: requirement
reqtat: requested that
rer (RER): radar effects reactor
REREI: Redwood Empire Research and Education Institute
RERF: Radiation Effects Research Foundation
rerl: residual equivalent return loss
RERO: Royal Engineers Reserve of Officers
res: research; researcher; rescue; reservation; reserve; reservoir; resistant; respiratory; reticuloendothelial system (RES)
Res: Reservation
RES: República de El Salvador; Royal Economic Society; Royal Entomological Society
RESA: Research Society of America
ResAF: Reserve of the Air Force
Res Aud: Resident Auditor
resc: rescue
rescan: reflecting satellite communication antenna
rescu: rocket-ejection seat catapult upward
RESCU: Radio Emergency Search Communications Unit
rescue.: remote emergency salvage and cleanup equipment
reser: reentry system evaluation radar
resgnd: resigned
resig: resignation
RESIG: Research and Engineering System Integration Group
resist.: resistance; resistor
resojet: resonant pulse jet
resp: responsibility; responsible
Res Phys: Resident Physician
respir: respiration; respiratory
RESPO: Responsible Property Officer
Resrt: Resort (postal abbreviation)
RESS: Radar Echo-Simulation Study; Radar Echo-Simulation System
Res Sec: Resident Secretary
rest: restrict; restricted; restriction
rest. (REST): regressive electric shock therapy
REST: Radar Electronic-Scan Technique; Reentry Environment and Systems Technology; Reentry System Test Program
resta: reconnaissance, surveillance, and target acquisition
restr: restaurant

ResTraCen: Reserve Training Center
resup: resupply
Resurrection: Mahler's Symphony No. 2 in C minor
resvr: reservoir
RE system: reticuloendothelial system
ret: retainer; retire; retirement
r-et: rational-emotive psychotherapy
RET: Rotterdamse Elektrische Tram (Rotterdam electric tramway and subway system)
reta: retrieval of enriched textual abstracts
RETA: Refrigerating Engineers and Technicians Association
retain.: remote technical assistance and information network
retard.: retardation; retarded
RETC: Regional Employment and Training Consortium
retd: retired
retics: reticulocytes
retic count: reticulocyte count
retl: retail
RETL: Rocket Engine Test Laboratory
RETMA: Radio-Electronics-Television Manufacturers Association
retng: retraining
retnr: retainer
retr: retractable
retro: retroactive; retrofit; retrograde; retrorocket
retros: retrogrades; retrorockets
RETS: Renaissance English Text Society
Retto: (Japanese—archipelago)
Reun: Reunion Island
rev: reverse; reversed; review; revise; revised; revision; revolute; revolution
rev: *revisado* (Spanish—revised)
rev (REV): reentry vehicle
Rev: Reverend; The Revelation of St John the Divine
rev a/c: revenue account
rev ed: revised edition
revel.: reverberation elimination
Revel: Fleming H. Revell
revid: *reviderad* (Swedish—revised)
Revilla Gigedos: Revilla Gigedo Islands
rev/min: revolutions per minute
revocon: remote volume control
Revolutionary: Chopin's Piano Etude No. 12 in C minor
revs: revolutions
REVS: Rotor-Entry Vehicle System
Rev Stat: Revised Statutes
rev of sym: review of symptoms
rew: reward
rewrc: report when established well to right of course
REWSON: Reconnaissnce Electronic Warfare Special Operations and Naval Intelligence Processing System(s)
rex: real-time executive routine; reduced exoatmospheric cross- section
Rex: Reginald
REX: Rexall Drug and Chemical (stock exchange symbol)
Reykjvk: Reykjavik
rf: radiofrequency; range finder; reception fair; reflight; relative flow; replacement factor; representative fraction; rheumatic fever; rheumatoid factor; right fullback; rim fire; rubber-free
rf: *rinforzando* (Italian—reinforcing)
r-f: radiofrequency
r_f: rate of flow
Rf: Reef; rutherfordium (element 104)
rfa: radiofrequency attenuator; request further airways; right fronto-anterior
RF: République Française; Reserve Force; Rockefeller Foundation; Rodeo Foundation; Royal Fusiliers
R de F: Repûblica de Filipinas
rfa: radiofrequency authorization(s)
RFA: République Fédérale Allemande (Federal Republic of Germany) West Germany; Royal Field Artillery; Royal Fleet Auxiliary
RFAC: Royal Federation of Aero Clubs; Royal Fine Arts Commission
R factor: resistance factor
rfad: release for active duty
rfa's: return(ed) for alterations (tailoring)
rfb: request for bid
RFB: Recording for the Blind
RFB: *Républica Federativa do Brasil* (Portuguese Federal Republic of Brazil)
rf black: reinforcing furnace black
rfc: radiofrequency choke
RFC: Reconstruction Finance Corporation; Royal Flying Corps
RFCWA: Regional Fisheries Commission for Western Africa
rfd: raised foredeck; reentry flight demonstration; reporting for duty
RFD: Radio Frequency Devices; Rural Free Delivery
rfdr: rangefinder
RFDS: Royal Flying Doctor Service
RFE: Radio Free Europe
RFED: Research Facilities and Equipment Division (NASA)
RFFS: River and Flood Forecasting Service
rfg: roofing
RFH: Royal Festival Hall
rfi: radiofrequency interference; ready for issue
R Fix: running fix
rfl: refuel(ing); right frontolateral
RFL: Rugby Football League
rfls: rheumatoid factor-like substance
RFMA: Reliability Figure of Merit Analysis
Rfn: Rifleman
RFN: Registered Fever Nurse
rfna: red-fuming nitric acid
rfo: request for factory order
rfp: right frontoposterior
RFP: Request for Proposal
RF & P: Richmond, Fredericksburg and Potomac (railroad)
RFPS(G): Royal Faculty of Physicians and Surgeons of Glasgow
RFQ: Request for Quotation
rfr: refraction; reject failure rate; required freight rate
R fr: Ruanda franc(s)
RFR: Royal Fleet Reserve
FRRC: Reliability Flight Readiness Center
rfrd: referred
rfs: regardless of future size
Rfs: Reefs (as in Minerva Reefs supposed location of the Republic of Minerva created by minters of commemorative coins)
RFS: Registry of Friendly Societies; Royal Forestry Service
rf scale: representative fraction scale
RFSU: Rugby Football Schools' Union
rft: right frontotransverse
RFT: *Repubblica Federale Tedesca* (Italian—German Federal Republic)—West Germany
rfts: radiofrequency test set
RFU: Rugby Football Union
R-F unit: Reitland-Franklin unit
rfw: rapid-filling wave
rfz: *rinforzando* (Italian—with extra emphasis)
rg: real girl (not a birl)
RG: República de Guatemala; Reserve Grade

R te G: ***Rijksuniversiteit te Groningen*** **(State University at Groningen) Netherlands**
Rga: Riga
RGA: Republican Governors Association; Royal Garrison Artillery; Rubber Growers' Association
RGAHS: Royal Guernsey Agricultural and Horticultural Society
R-gauge: Russian gauge (5-foot) railroad track
rgb: red-orange, green, blue-violet (television's triad of primary colors)
RGC: Reception and Guidance Center
rgd: reigned
R Gd: Rio Grande
RGDATA: Retail Grocery, Dairy, and Allied Trades Association
rge: relative gas expansion
Rge: range
RGE: *República de Guinea Ecuatorial* (Spanish—Republic of Equatorial Guinea)
RGEB: Rockefeller General Education Board
rgf: range-gated filter
RGG: Royal Grenadier Guards
RGH: Royal Gloucestershire Hussars
RGI: Robert G. Ingersoll
rgn: region
Rgn: (Port of) Rangoon
RGN: Rangoon, Burma (airport); Registered General Nurse
RGNR: Rugged Glen Nature Reserve (South Africa)
RGO: Royal Greenwich Observatory
RGP: Riegel Paper Company (stock-exchange symbol)
rgs: radar ground stabilization
RGS: Rio Grande do Sul; Royal Geographical Society
RG do S: Rio Grande do Sul
RGSA: Royal Geographical Society of Australasia
Rgt: Regiment
RGTC: Robert Gordon's Technical College
Rgtl: Regimental
rg tp: rough template
RGV: Rio Grande Valley Gas Company (stock exchange symbol)
rgz: recommended ground zero
RGZ: Rio Grande Zoo (Albuquerque)
rh: righthand (RH); roundhead
rh.: *rhonchi* (Latin—rales)
r/h: relative humidity; roentgens per hour
Rh: Rhesus factor (symbol); rhodium
Rh−: Rhesus negative
Rh+: Rhesus positive
Rh: *Rhein* (German—Rhine)
RH: Air Rhodesia; Random House; República de Honduras; Round House; Royal Highlanders; Royal Highness
R d'H: République d'Haiti
RH^{106}: radioactive rhodium
RHA: Road Haulage Association; Royal Hibernian Academy; Royal Humane Association; Rural Housing Alliance
RHAF: Royal Hellenic Air Force
R Hamps: Royal Hampshire (regiment)
rhap: rhapsody
RHAWS: Radar Homing and Warning System
RHB: Regional Hospital Board
rhbdr: rhombohedral
rhc: respirations have ceased; rubber hydrocarbon
RHC: Rosary Hill College
RHC: *Radio Habana Cuba* (Spanish—Havana, Cuba Radio)
RHCSA: Regional Hospitals Consultants' and Specialists' Association
rhd: radioactive health data; relative hepatic dullness; rheumatic heart disease
RHD: Robin Hood Dell (Philadelphia)
RHD: *Random House Dictionary*
RHDO: Robin Hood Dell Orchestra
rhe: reversible hydrogen electrode
RHE: Reliability Human Engineering
RHEL: Rutherford High-Energy Laboratory
Rhenish: Schumann's Symphony No. 3 in E-flat major
rheo: rheostat
rheol: rheological; rheology
rhet: rhetoric; rhetorical; rhetorician
rheu: rheumatic; rheumatism; rheumatoid
rheu fev: rheumatic fever
rheu ht dis: rheumatic heart disease
rheum: rheumatic; rheumatism
rhf: right heart failure
RHF: Royal Highland Fusiliers
Rh factor: Rhesus group of red cell agglutinogens
RHG: Royal Horse Guards
RHGPS: Rhodesian Hunters and Game Preservation Society
RHHI: Royal Hospital and Home for Incurables
rhi: range height indicator
rhino: range height indicator not operating
rhinol: rhinological; rhinologist; rhinology
rhino(s): rhinoceros(es)
rhip: rank has its privileges
rhir: rank has its responsibilities
R Hist S: Royal Historical Society
RHK: Radio Hong Kong
RHL: Radiological Health Laboratory
rhm: roentgen per hour per meter
RHMS: Royal Hibernian Military School
RHN: Royal Hellenic Navy
Rho: Rhoda
RHO: Regional Hospital Office(r)
RHOB: Rayburn House Office Building
Rhod: Rhodesia
Rhode Island Red: Rhode Island's state bird and symbolic nickname of a Rhode Islander
Rhode Island Reds: Rhode Islanders
Rhodesia: (formerly Southern Rhodesia)
Rhodesias: Northern and Southern Rhodesia (Zambia and Rhodesia, respectively)
Rhododendron: state flower of Washington and West Virginia; in Washington the flower is the Western Rhododendron and in West Virginia it is the Big Rhododendron
rhodo(s): rhododendron(s)
RHOFLIGHT: Rhodesian Air Services
rhom: rhombic; rhomboid; rhombus
rhp: rated horsepower
RHQ: Regimental Headquarters
rhr: roughness height reading
r/hr: roentgens per hour
RHR: Royal Highland Regiment (Black Watch)
rhs: righthand side; roundheaded screw
RHS: Radio Ham Shack (amateur radio operator's station); Royal Historical Society; Royal Horticultural Society
RHSI: Royal Horticultural Society of Ireland
Rhumba: (stock exchange short form for Royal McBee Company whose symbol is RMB)
RHV: *République de Haute-Volta* (French-Republic of Upper Volta)

ri: random interval; reflective insulation; refractive index; reliability index; require identification; respiratory illness; retroactive inhibition; rubber-insulated; rubber insulation
RI: Recruit Instruction; Refractories Institute; Republic of India; Republik Indonesia; Rhode Island (R.I.); Rhode Islanders; Rice Institute; Rock Island (Chicago, Rock Island & Pacific Railroad); Rotary International; Royal Institute
RI: *Repubblica Italiana* (Italian Republic); *Républicains Independants* (French — Independent Republicans); *Ring Index*
R. et I.: *Regina et Imperatrix* (Latin—Queen and Empress)—title of Victoria—Queen of England and Empress of India—The Queen
ria: (Spanish—river mouth)
RIA: Research Institute of America; Rock Island Arsenal; Royal Irish Academy
RIAA: Record Industry Association of America
RIAC: Research Information Analysis Corporation
RIAEC: Rhode Island Atomic Energy Commission
RIAF: Royal Indian Air Force; Royal Iranian Air Force; Royal Iraqui Air Force
RIAI: Royal Institute of Architects of Ireland
RIAL: Rock Island Arsenal Laboratory
RIAM: Royal Irish Academy of Music
RIAS: Rundfunk im amerikanischen Sektor (Radio in the American Sector), Berlin
RIASLP: Rattlesnake Island Air Service Local Post
rib.: ribbon
RIB: Railway Information Bureau; Referee in Bankruptcy; Rural Industries Bureau
RIBA: Royal Institute of British Architects
ric: radar intercept calculator
ric: *ricevuta* (Italian—receipt)
Ric: Ricardo; Richard
RIC: Republic Industrial Corporation; Republic of the Ivory Coast; Richmond, Virginia (airport); Royal Institute of Chemistry
RICA: Research Institute on Communist Affairs (Columbia University)
RICASIP: Research Information Center and Advisory Service on Information Processing
RICE: Rhode Island College of Education
Rich: Richard; Richards; Richardson; Richford; Richmal; Richmond
Rich II: *King Richard II*
Rich III: *King Richard III*
Richard Burton: Richard Jenkins
Richard Coeur de Lion: Richard I of England
Richard Tauber: Ernst Seiffert
Rich Coast: Costa Rica's name translated from Spanish
Richd: Richard; Richmond
Richest Hill on Earth: Butte, Montana
Rich-Pete Turn: Richmond-Petersburg Turnpike (Virginia)
Rick: Richard
ricksha(w): *jinrikisha* (Japanese—man-drawn two-wheeled carriage)
Ricky: Richard
ricm: right intercostal margin
RICM: *Registre International des Citoyens du Monde* (French—International Registry of World Citizens)
RICMD: Richmond Contract Management District
RICMO: Radar Input Countermeasures Officer
RICS: Royal Institute of Chartered Surveyors
RICU: Russian Institute, Columbia University
RID: Riddle Aviation
RIDA: Rural and Industrial Development Authority
RIDE: Research Institute for Diagnostic Engineering
Riders: *Riders of the Purple Sage*
ridp: radar-iff (if friend or foe) data processor
RIE: Royal Institute of Engineers
RIEC: Royal Indian Engineering College
RIEI: Republic Industrial Education Institute (Republic Steel)
RIEM: Research Institute for Environmental Medicine
Rienzi: Niccolo Gabrini
rif: reduction in force; right iliac fossa
rif: *rifatto* (Italian—restored; repaired)
rif (RIF): resistance-inducing factor
RIF: Reading Is Fundamental; Royal Irish Fusiliers
Rif Brig: Rifle Brigade
rifc: rat intrinsic factor concentrate
rifi: radio interference field intensity
Rifle City: Springfield, Massachusetts
rifma: roentgen-isotope-fluorescent method of analysis
rift. (RIFT): reactor-in-flight test
Rig: Riga
Riga's disease: ulceration of the tongue
RIGB: Royal Institution of Great Britain
Rigg's disease: inflammation of the gums with pus deposits in the tooth sockets; also called alveolar pyorrhea
RIGHT: Rhodesian Independence Gung-Ho Troops
RIH: Royal Institute of Horticulture
RIHS: Rhode Island Historical Society
rihsa: radioactive iodinated human serum albumin
RIIA: Royal Institute of International Affairs
RIISOM: Research Institute for Iron, Steel, and Other Metals
RIL: Royal Interocean Lines
rim.: radar input mapper; receiving, inspection, and maintenance; rubber insulation material
RIM: Resident Industrial Manager
RIMB: Roche Institute of Molecular Biology
RIMR: Rockefeller Institute for Medical Research
Rin: Rintintin
RIN: Registro Italiano Navale (Italian ship-classification agency)
rina: reinitiation
RINA: Royal Institution of Naval Architects
RINA: *Registro Italiano Navale e Aeronautico* (Italian Air and Shipping Registry)
RIND: Research Institute of National Defense
rinf: *rinforzando* (Italian—with additional emphasis)
Ring Cycle: The Ring of the Nibelungen *(q.v.)*
Ring of the Nibelungen: Wagner's Ring Cycle consisting of *Das Rheingold* (Rhinegold), *Die Walküre* (Valkyries), *Siegfried*, and *Götterdämmerung* (Twilight of the Gods)
RINM: Resident Inspector of Naval Material

RINS: Research Institute for the Natural Sciences
RINSMAT: Resident Inspector of Naval Stores and Materiel
Rio: Rio de Janeiro
RIO: Reporting In and Out; Rhodesian Information Office; Rio de Janeiro (Galeao Airport)
Rio Branco: José Mariá de Silva Paranhos—Baron of Rio Branco—Brazil's great statesman
Rioj: La Rioja
riometer: relative ionospheric opacity meter
RIOP: Royal Institute of Oil Painters
RIOPR: Rhode Island Open-Pool Reactor
riot.: real-time input-output transducer (translator)
rip.: radar identification point
rip: *ripieno* (Italian—filling up)
Rip: Rip Van Winkle; Robert; Rupert
RIP: Reduction in Implementation Panel; Reduction in Personnel (layoffs); Reliability Improvement Program; Reserve Intelligence Program; Rockefeller Institute Press
R.I.P.: *requiesca[n]t in pace* (Latin—may he [they] rest in peace)
RIPH: Royal Institute of Public Health
RIPHH: Royal Institute of Public Health and Hygiene
RIPO: Rhode Island Philharmonic Orchestra
ripple.: radioactive isotope-powered pulsed-light equipment (RIPPLE)
RIPPR: Reliability Improvement Program Progress Report
ripr viet: *riproduzione vietata* (Italian—reproduction forbidden)
RIPS: Range-Instrumentation Planning Study; Range-Instrumentation Planning System
rip viet: *riproduzione vietata* (Italian—reproduction forbidden)
RIPWC: Royal Institute of Painters in Water Colours
rir: reduction in requirement
rirb: radio-iodinated rose bengal
RIS: Range Instrumentation Ship; Regulatory Information System; Royal Infantry Society
risa: radioactive iodinated serum albumen
RISCO: Rhodesian Iron and Steel Company
RISCOM: Rhodesian Iron and Steel Commission
RISD: Rhode Island School of Design
rise.: reusable inflatable salvage equipment
RISE: Research Information Services for Education
rising sun: symbol of Japan and the Japanese
RISM: Research Institute for the Study of Man (USA)
risp: *rispettivamente* (Italian—respectively)
RISS: Range Instrumentation and Support System
RISW: Royal Institution of South Wales
rit: ritard; ritardando; ritornello; ritual; ritualism; ritualistic; ritualization; ritualize
rit: *ritardando* (Italian—holding back; retarding)
RIT: Radio Information Test; Radio Network for Inter-American Telecommunication; Rochester Institute of Technology; Rorschach Inkblot Test; Royal Institute of Technology
RIT: *Red Interamericana de Telecomunicaciones* (Inter-American Telecommunication Network)
Rita: Margaret; Margarita
RITA: Rural Industrial Technical Assistance
ritard: *ritardando* (Italian—holding back; retarding)
RITE: Rapid Information Technique for Evaluation
riten: *ritenuto* (Italian—retaining the tempo)
Ritter's disease: skin scaling sometimes fatal when it attacks infants
RITU (Profintern): Red International of Trade Unions
ritz: ritzier; ritziest; ritziness; ritzy
riv: radio influence voltage; river; rivet(ed)
riv: *riveduto* (Italian—revised)
Riv: River; Riviera; Rivington; Rivke
Rivalta's disease: lumpy jaw
River of Grass: Florida's Everglades
River of Hades or Hell: the Styx, according to mythology it encircles the underworld nine times and the dead are ferried over its waters by Charon
River of the North: the Yukon
Riviera of South America: Uruguay
RIZ: Radio Industry Zagreb
rj (RJ): ramjet
RJ: Rio de Janeiro; Royal Jordanian (airlines)
R de J: Rio de Janeiro
RJA: Reform Jewish Appeal; Retail Jewelers of America
RJAF: Royal Jordanian Air Force
RJAS: Royal Jersey Agricultural Society
RJC: Rochester Junior College; Rosenwald Junior College; Roswell Junior College
Rjk: Reykjavik
RJM: Royal Jersey Militia
RJJ: R.J. Reynolds
rk: rock; run of kiln
r-k: *rooms-katholiek* (Dutch—Roman Catholic)
Rk: Rock (postal abbreviation)
RK: Air Afrique (2-letter coding); Radio Kabul
RK: *Rdeci Kriz* (Yugoslavian—Red Cross)
rkg: radiocardiogram
RKN: Republic of Korea Navy
RKO: Radio-Keith-Orpheum (theater circuit)
rkt: rocket
Rkt Sta: Rocket Station
RKU: Ruprecht-Karl-Universität (Heidelberg)
RKV: Rose Knot (tracking station vessel)
rkva: reactive volt-ampere
rky: rocky; roentgen kymography
rl: coarse rales; rail; reduction level; rocket launcher
r/l: radio location
r & l: rail and lake
rl_1: few line rales
rl_2: moderate number of rales
rl_3: many coarse rales
Rl: Raphael
RL: high-powered radio range loop radiator(s); Radiation Laboratory; Reading List; Regent's Line; Republic of Liberia; Research Laboratory; Richfield Oil (stock exchange symbol); River Lines (railroad); Roland Line
R te L: Rijksuniversiteit te Leiden (State University at Leyden)
rla: restricted landing area
RLA: Religious Liberty Association
rladd: radar low-angle drogue delivery
RLAF: Royal Laotian Air Force
RLB: Sir Robert Laird Borden (Canada's ninth Prime Minis-

ter)
rlbcd: right lower border of cardiac dullness
rlbm (RLBM): rearward-launched ballistic missile(s)
RLC: Radio Liberty Committee
RLCA: Rural Letter Carriers' Association
RLCS: Radio-Launch Control System
rld: radar laydown delivery; rolled
RLD: Raymond L. Ditmars
RLDPAS: Royal London Discharged Prisoners' Aid Society
rld: radar laydown delivery; rolled
rld's: retail liquor dealers
rle: right lower extremity
rl est: real estate
rletfl: report leaving each thousand-foot level
rlf: relief; retrolental fibroplasia
RLF: Royal Literary Fund
rlg: railing
rlg: *rilegato* (Italian—bound)
RLG: Research Library Group; Royal Laos Government
RLHTE: Research Laboratory of Heat Transfer in Electronics (MIT)
RLI: Rhodes-Livingstone Institute
rll: right lower limb; right lower lobe (lung)
rllb: right long-leg brace
RLM: Regional Library of Medicine (PAHO)
rlmd: rat-liver mitochondria
RLNWR: Rice Lake National Wildlife Refuge (Minnesota); Ruby Lake National Wildlife Refuge (Nevada)
RLO: Regional Liaison Office(r)
RLPAS: Royal London Prisoners' Aid Society
RLPO: Royal Liverpool Philharmonic Orchestra
rlq: right lower quadrant (abdomen)
rlr: right lateral rectus (eye muscle)
Rls: rial (Iranian currency unit)
RLS: Robert Louis Stevenson; Royal Lancastrian Society
RLSS: Royal Life Saving Society
rltr: realtor
RLTS: Radio-Linked Telemetry System
rltv: relative
rlty: realty
rlv: relieve
rly: relay
rm: range mark(s); raw material; ream; receiving memorandum; respiratory movement; ring micrometer; room; rubber marker(s)
r/m: revolutions per minute
r & m: redistribution and marketing; reliability and maintainability; reports and memoranda
Rm: Romania (Rumania); Romanian (Rumanian)
RM: Radioman; Raybestos-Manhattan; Registered Mail; Reichsmark (German currency); Research Memorandum; Ringling Museum; Royal Mail; Royal Marine; Royal Marines
R & M: Robbins & Myers
R/M: Raybestos/Manhattan
rma: right mento-anterior
RMA: Radio Manufacturers Association; Rice Millers Association; Ringling Museum of Art; Robert Morris Associates (Bank Loan Officers and Credit Men's Association); Royal Marine Artillery; Royal Military Academy; Rubber Manufacturers Association
RMADB: Reactor Maintenance and Disassembly Building
RMAF: Royal Moroccan Air Force
RMAG: Rocky Mountain Association of Geologists
RMAI: Radio Manufacturers' Association of India
rm ar: reaming arbor
RMAS: Rochester Museum of Arts and Sciences
r mast: radio mast
RMB: Royal McBee
RMBAA: Rocky Mountain Business Aircraft Association
rmc: rod memory computer
RMC: Radio Monte Carlo; Reynolds Metal Company; Rochester Manufacturing Company; Royal Military College
RMCC: Royal Military College of Canada
RMCM: Royal Manchester College of Music
RMCPA: Rocky Mountain College Placement Association
RMCS: Royal Military College of Science
rmd: ready money down; retromanubrial dullness
RMD: Reaction Motors Division (Thiokol Chemical Corporation)
RMEA: Rubber Manufacturing Employers' Association
R-meter: radiation meter
R Met S: Royal Meteorological Society
RMFVR: Royal Marine Forces Volunteer Reserves
rmi: reliability maturity index
RMI: Rack Manufacturers Institute; Reaction Motors Incorporated; Reactive Metals Incorporated; Roll Manufacturers Institute
rmicbm (RMICBM): roadmobile intercontinental ballistic missile
r/min: revolutions per minute
RMJC: Robert Morris Junior College
rml: right mediolateral; right middle lobe
RML: Rand Mines Limited; Royal Mail Lines
RMLF: Robert M. La Folette
RMLI: Royal Marine Light Infantry
RMM & EA: Rolling Mill Machinery and Equipment Association
RMMNH: Regar Memorial Museum of Natural History (Anniston, Alabama)
RMN: Registered Mental Nurse; Richard Milhaus Nixon (37th President of the United States and first to resign the presidential office); Royal Malaysian Navy
RMNP: Rhodes Matopos National Park (Rhodesia); Riding Mountain National Park (Manitoba); Rocky Mountain National Park (Colorado)
RMNS: Royal Merchant Navy School
RMO: Regional Medical Officer
RMOGA: Rocky Mountain Oil and Gas Association
rmp: right mento-posterior
RMP: Reentry Measurement Program; Regional Medical Program; Research Management Plan; Research and Microfilm Publications; Royal Marine Police; Royal Mounted Police
RMPA: Royal Medico-Psychological Association
rmpc: rubber-mold plaster casting
RMQ: *Records Management Quarterly*
RMRA: Royal Marines Rifle Association
Rmrs: Ramirez
rms: root mean square
RMS: Royal Mail Service; Royal Mail Ship; Royal Microscopical Society
RMSA: Rural Music Schools As-

sociation
rmse: root mean square error
RMSM: Royal Marines School of Music; Royal Military School of Music
RMSP: Royal Mail Steam Packet (company)
rmt: right mento-transverse
rmte: remote
rmu: remote maneuvering unit
rmv: respiratory minute volume
RMWC: Randolph-Macon Woman's College
rn: reception nil; research note; running noose; running nose
Rn: radon; Rangoon
RN: radionavigation; Registered Nurse; República de Nicaragua; Reynold's number; Royal Navy
rna (RNA): ribonucleic acid
RNA: Romantic Novelists' Association
R/NAA: Rocketdyne/North American Aviation
RNAC: Royal Nepal Airline Corporation
RNADC: Royal Netherlands Air Defense Command
RNAF: Royal Naval Air Force
RNAFF: Royal Netherlands Aircraft Factories Fokker
RNAO: Registered Nurses Association of Ontario
RNAS: Royal Naval Air Station
rnase: ribonuclease
RNAV: Royal Naval Artillery Volunteers
RNAW: Royal Naval Aircraft Workshop
RNAY: Royal Naval Aircraft Yard
rnb: received—not billed
RNB: Royal Naval Barracks
RNBT: Royal Naval Benevolent Trust
RNC: Republican National Committee
Rnch: Ranch (postal abbreviation)
Rnchs: Ranches (postal abbreviation)
RN & CR: Ryde, Newport, and Cowes Railway
RNCSRL: Ralph Nader Center for the Study of Responsive Law
rnd: round
RND: Royal Naval Division
RND: *Rijksnijverheidstdienst* (Dutch—Government Industrial Advisory Service)
RNE: Radio Nacional de España (Spanish— National Radio Broadcasting System)
RNEC: Royal Naval Engineering College
RNES: *Radiodifusora Nacional de El Salvador* (Spanish—National Radio Network of El Salvador)—in Central America
rnf: receiver noise figure
Rnf: Renfrew
RNF: Royal Northumberland Fusiliers
rnfp: radar not functioning properly
RNFU: Rhodesia National Farmers' Union
rng: range
R ng P: *Republika ng Pilipinas* (Pilipino—Republic of the Philippines)
rngt: renegotiate
RNIB: Royal National Institute for the Blind
RNID: Royal National Institute for the Deaf
rnit: radio noise interference test
RNL: Raffles National Library (Singapore); Royal Netherlands Line
RNLAF: Royal Netherlands Air Force
RNLI: Royal National Lifeboat Institution
RNLO: Royal Naval Liaison Office(r)
rnm (RNM): radionavigation mobile
RNMD: Registered Nurse for Mental Defectives
RNMDSF: Royal National Mission to Deep-Sea Fishermen
RNMS: Royal Naval Medical School
RNMWS: Royal Naval Minewatching Service
RNN: Royal Nigerian Navy
RNNP: Royal Natal National Park (South Africa)
RNoAF: Royal Norwegian Air Force
RNOC: Royal Naval Officers Club
R No N: Royal Norwegian Navy
RNP: Redwood National Park (California); Rondane National Park (Norway); Ruaha National Park (Tanzania); Ruhana National Park (Ceylon)
RNP: *Radio Nacional de Peru* (Spanish—National Radio of Peru)
RNPFN: Royal National Pension Fund for Nurses
RNPL: Royal Naval Physiological Laboratory
RNPS: Royal Naval Patrol Service
r-'n-r: rock-'n-roll
RNR: Royal Naval Reserves
RNRA: Royal Naval Rifle Association
RNRRA: Royal Naval Reserve Rifle Association
rns: radar netting station
RNS: Royal Naval School; Royal Numismatic Society
RNSA: Royal Naval Sailing Association
RNSC: Royal Netherlands Steamship Company
RNSR: Royal Naval Special Reserve
RNSS: Royal Naval Scientific Service
rnt: roentgenologist; roentgenology
RNT: Registered Nurse Tutor
RNTE: Royal Naval Training Establishment
rnth: raised non-tight hatch
RNTU: Royal Naval Training Unit
rnu: radar netting unit; radio noise voltage
RNVR: Royal Naval Volunteer Reserve
RNW: Radio Navigational Warning
RNWMP: Royal Northwest Mounted Police
RNWR: Ravalli National Wildlife Refuge (Montana)
rnwy: runway
RNYC: Royal Northern Yacht Club; Royal Norwegian Yacht Club
RNZ: Radio New Zealand
RNZAC: Royal New Zealand Aero Club
RNZAF: Royal New Zealand Air Force
RNZAS: Royal New Zealand Astronomical Society
RNZN: Royal New Zealand Navy
ro: receive only; right opening; right orifice; road oil; rough opening; runover
ro: recto (frontside of page)
ro.: *recto* (Latin—front of the page; right-hand page)
r^o: *recto* (Portuguese—face of page; right-hand page; this side)
r/o: roll out (final turn of an interceptor); rule out
r & o: rail and ocean
ro: reddish orange
RO: Radar Observer; Radar Operator; Radio Observer; Radio Operator; Recorder's Office; Recruiting Officer; Reserve Order
RÖ: Republik Österreich (Re-

public of Austria)
***R-O:** Residentie-Orkest* (Dutch—Residency Orchestra)—at The Hague where the Netherlands government resides
R de O: Rio de Oro (Spanish Sahara
roa: received on account; right occiput anterior
ROA: Reserve Officers Association; Retired Officers Association; Royal Order of Altruists
***ROA:** Russkaya Osvoboditelnaya Armiya* (Russian Liberation Army)
ROAD: Reorganization Objective Army Division; Re-Organize Army Division
Roadrunner: New Mexico state bird and nickname applied to many New Mexicans
roads.: roadstead
roam.: return of assets managed (banking)
ROAMA: Rome Air Materiel Area
roar.: right of admission reserved
Roaring Forties: storm-tossed seas between 40 and 50 degrees south latitude
ROAUS: Reserve Officers Association of the United States
rob.: remaining on board (aircraft or ship cargo)
Rob: Robert
Robber Barons: (*see* American Railroad Barons, Banker Barons, Mining Baron, Oil Baron, Pork Packer, Steel Baron)
robeps: radar operating below prescribed standards
Robert Taylor: Spangler Arlington Brugh
robin. (ROBIN): rocket-balloon instrument
Robin: state bird of Connecticut, Michigan, and Wisconsin
Robinson's Island: Niihau, Hawaii
robo: rocket orbital bomber
Rob Roy: (Gaelic—Red Rob)—Robert Macgregor the Scottish freebooter
Robt: Robert
roc: receiver operating characteristic (curve); required operational capabilities
R o C: Republic of Congo
ROC: Rochester, New York (airport); Royal Observer Corps
R o Cam: Republic of Cameroons
ROCAPPI: Research on Computer Applications in the Printing and Publishing Industries
roce: return on capital employed
Roch: Rochester
R o Ch: Republic of Chad
Rochambeau: Count Jean Baptiste Donatien de Vimeur de Rochambeau
rochelle salts: sodium potassium tartrate
Rochester: actor Eddie Anderson
Roch Phil: Rochester Philharmonic
rocid: reorganization of combat infantry divisions
Rock: Knute Kenneth Rockne; Mount Desert Island's nickname used by generations of seafarers; Rockaway; Rock of Gibraltar
rock-a-billy: rock-'n-roll + hillbilly (music)
Rock City: Nashville, Tennessee
Rockie: Nelson A. Rockefeller
Rockies: Rocky Mountains
Rock Lizards: Gibraltarians
Rock of Notre Dame: Knute K(enneth) Rockne
rockoon(s): balloon-supported rocket(s)
rock salt: halite (sodium chloride)
Rock of Uluru: Ayers Rock near Mount Olga, Australia
Rocky Mountain Columbine: Colorado state flower
Rocky Mountain States: Alaska, Idaho, Montana, Wyoming, Colorado, Utah, New Mexico, and Arizona
ROCMD: Rochester Contract Management District
rocp: radar (or radio) out of commission for parts
rod.: required operational data; required operational date
Rod: Roderick; Rodney; Rodrigues; Rodriguez
***ROD:** Rosskoye Osvoboditelnoye Dvizheniye* (Russian Liberation Movement)
Rodale: Rodale Books
Roddy: Roderick; Rodney
rodiac: rotary dual input for analog computation
roe. (ROE): reflector orbital equipment
ROE: Royal Observatory—Edinburgh
roentgen: roentgenology
rof: reporting organizational-file
ROF: Royal Ordnance Factory
ROFA: Radio of Free Asia
rofor: route forecast
roft: radar off target
rog: rise-off-ground
R o G: Republic of Guinea
roger: your message received and understood
Roger Williams City: Providence, Rhode Island
roi: return on investment
ROI: Range Operating Instructions
Roi Citoyen: (French—Citizen King)—Louis Philippe
Roi Soleil: (French—Sun King)—Louis XIV
Rois: Rodrigues
Roiz: Rodriguez
roj: range on jamming
Rok: a South Korean
ROK: Republic of Korea
ROKA: Republic of Korea Army
ROKAF: Republic of Korea Air Force
ROKN: Republic of Korea Navy
ROKPUC: Republic of Korea Presidential Unit Citation
roksonde: rocket sounding
rol: right occipitolateral
Rolf: Rudolf; Rudolph
rol k: rolling keel
Rolls: Rolls-Royce
ROLS: Recoverable Orbital Launch System
rom: radar operator mechanic; range of motion; range of movement; roman (type)
rom (ROM): read-on memory
Rom: The Letter of Paul to the Romans; Roman; Romance language
R O M: Republic of Malagasy
ROM: Rome, Italy (Fiumicino airport); Royal Ontario Museum
Romanian National Composer: Georges Enesco
Rom Ant: Roman Antiquities
Romantic: Bruckner's Symphony No. 4; Hanson's Symphony No. 2
Rom Cath: Roman Catholic
romemo: refer to our memorandum
Romeo: code for letter R
Rom Hist: Roman History
***Rom & Jul:** Romeo and Juliet*
romom: receiving-only monitor
ROMT: Range-of-Motion Test
romv: return on market value
ron: remain overnight; research octane number
Ron: Ronald
rond: rondeau; rondeaux; rondel; rondels
RONDA: Royal Oriental Nut Date Association
Ronnie: Ronald; Ronda; Veronica
Ronny: Ronald
ROO: Range Operations Of-

fice(r)
Roof Garden of Texas: Alpine
Roof of the World: Pamir Plateau of central Asia
roo(s): kangaroo(s)
Roosevelt I: Theodore Roosevelt—26th President of the United States
Roosevelt II: Franklin D. Roosevelt—32nd President of the United States
root.: relaxation oscillator optically tuned
rop: right occiput posterior; run of press
ROP: Regional Occupational Program
ropp: receive-only page printer
Roques: Los Roques Islands
ror: rocket-on-rotor (device for assisting helicopter takeoffs)
Ror: Rorschach (inkblot test)
RORA: Reserve Officer Recording Activity
RORC: Royal Ocean Racing Club
ro/ro: roll on/roll off
ros: reduced operational status
ros (ROS): run of schedule (radio or television)
Ros: Roscommon; Rostock
R o S: Republic of Senegal
ROS: Royal Order of Scotland
Rosa Bonheur: Rosalie Mazeltov
roscoe: (underworld slang—handgun, rifle, shotgun)
rose.: rosewood
Rose: New York state flower
Rose of Venice: Haydn's Quartet in D for Strings (opus 20, no. 4)
rosie (ROSIE): reconnaissance by orbiting ship-identification equipment
Rosie: Rosa; Rosamund; Rose; Rosemarie; Rosemary
rosla: raising of school-leaving age
ROSPA: Royal Society for the Prevention of Accidents
Ross: Ross and Cromarty
Rossbach's disease: gastric juice secreted excessively
rot.: remedial occupational therapy; right occipito-transverse; rotary; rotate; rotation; rotor
Rot: Rotterdam
ROTC: Reserve Officers Training Corps
rotcc: receiver-off-hook-tone connecting circuit
Rothermere: Viscount Rothermere (Harold Sidney Harmsworth)
roti: recording optical tracking instrument
rotn: rotation
roto: rotary press; rotogravure
rotr (ROTR): receive-only typing reperforator (data processing)
ROTS: Reusable Orbital Transport System
Rou: Rouen
ROU: República Oriental del Uruguay
Rough Rider: Theodore Roosevelt—26th President of the United States
roul: roulette
Roum: Roumanian
'round: around
Roundheads: Cromwell's followers in the Puritan Party noted for the close-cropped hair of its members
Roundup City: Pendleton, Oregon
rout: routine
Rov: Rover(s)
Rover(s): Coloradan(s)
row.: reverse-osmosis water; risk of war
RoW (ROW): Right of Way
R-O-W disease: Rendu-Osler-Weber disease
Rox: Roxburgh; Roxburghshire; Roxbury
Roxy: Roxana; S.L. Rothafel
Roy: Royal
Royal Brute of Great Britain: King George III of Hanover (in the opinion of Thomas Paine and many other Americans and Britons)
Royal Martyr: Charles I of England
Roy Com Soc: Royal Commonwealth Society (formerly Royal Empire Society; formerly Royal Colonial Institute)
ROY G. BIV: (acronymic mnemonic for recalling spectral colors—red, orange, yellow, green, blue, indigo, violet)—*see* vibgyor
Roy Liv Phil Orch: Royal Liverpool Philharmonic Orchestra
Roy Opera: Royal Opera House Orchestra (Covent Garden)
Roy Phil: Royal Philharmonic Orchestra
Roy Rogers: Leonard Slye
Roz: Rodriguez; Rosalind(a); Rozhdestvensky
rp: plate resistance (symbol); raid plotter; rally point; received pronunciation (RP); reception poor; release point; relay paid; reporting post; reprint; retained personnel; rhodium-plated; rhodium plating; rocket projectile (RP); rocket propellant; rust preventive
r-p: reprint; reprinting
rP : reddish purple
Rp: *Rappen* (Swiss—centime); rupiah (Indonesian currency unit)
RP: remote pickup (broadcast); República de Panamá; República del Paraguay; República del Peru; República Portuguesa (Portugal); rocket projectile; Rules of Procedure
RP: *Radiotelevisão* Portugesa (Portuguese—Radio-Television)
R/P: Royal Provincial (Tory American troops)
R-P: Rhône-Poulenc
R de P: República de Panamá; República del Paraguay; República Portuguesa
RP-1: rocket-propellant type-1 fuel (kerosene)
rpa: radar performance analyzer
RPA: Rationalist Press Association; Regional Planning Association
RPB: Regional Preparedness Board; Research to Prevent Blindness (fund)
rpc: radar planning chart; remote position control; reply postcard; request (the) pleasure (of your) company; reversed phase column
RPC: Reliability Policy Committee; Republican Party Conference; Royal Pay Corps; Royal Pioneer Corps
RPC: *République* Populaire du Congo (French—Popular Republic of the Congo)—formerly the French Congo
RPCC: Reactor Physics Constants Center
RPCFT: Reiter Protein Complement Fixation Test
rpd: radar planning device
RPD: Regional Port Director; Regius Professor of Divinity; Rocket Propulsion Department; Rocket Propulsion Division
R.P.D.: *Rerum Politicarum Doctor* (Latin—Doctor of Political Science)
RPDL: Radioisotope Process Development Laboratory
Rpds: Rapids (postal abbreviation)
rpe: related payroll expense
RPE: Radio Propagation Engineering; Rocket Propulsion Establishment
RPEA: Regional Planning and

Evaluation Agency
rpf: radiometer performance factor; relaxed pelvic floor; renal plasma flow
RPF: *Rassemblement du Peuple Français* (Rally of the French People)—de Gaulle's party; Gaullists
RPFMA: Rubber and Plastics Footwear Manufacturers' Association
rpfod: reported for duty
rpg: radiation protection guide; report program generator; rocket-propelled grenade; rounds per gun
rph: revolutions per hour
RPH: Royal Perth Hospital
RPHST: Research Participation for High School Teachers
rpi: radar precipitation integrator
RPI: Railway Progress Institute; Rensselaer Polytechnic Institute; Rose Polytechnic Institute; Royal Pakistan Institute; Ryerson Polytechnical Institute
RPIA: Rocket Propellant Information Agency
rpie (RPIE): real property installed equipment
rp index: respiratory rate index; respiratory pulse index
RPK: Regiment President Kruger
rpl: running program language
RPL: Radiation Physics Laboratory (NBS); Regina Public Library; Repair Parts List; Richmond Public Library; Roanoke Public Library; Rochester Public Library; Rocket Propulsion Laboratory; Rockhampton Public Library
rplca: replica
rpm: reliability performance measure; repairman; revolutions per minute; rotations per minute
RPM: Rustenburg Platinum Mines
RPMF: Radiation Pattern Measurement Facility
rpmi: revolutions-per-minute indicator
RPMI: Roswell Park Memorial Institute
rpo: revolutions per orbit
RPO: Rochester Philharmonic Orchestra; Rotterdam Philharmonic Orchestra; Royal Philharmonic Orchestra
RPO: *Rotterdams Philharmonisch Orkest* (Dutch—Rotterdam Philharmonic Orchestra)
rpoc: report proceeding on course
rpp: radar power programmer; reply paid postcard; request present position; return paid postal
RPP: Radio Propagation Physics
rppe: research, program, planning, evaluation
RPQ: Request for Price Quotation
rpr: read printer
rpr (RPR): rapid plasma reagin
RPR: Republica Populara Romana (Romania)
RPRAGB: Rubber and Plastics Research Association of Great Britain
rprt: report
RPRT: Rapid Plasma Reagin Test
rps: revolutions per second
RPS: Railway Progress Society; Rapid Processing System; Registered Publication Section; Reliability Problem Summary; Republika Popullore e Shqiperise (Albania); Royal Philharmonic Society; Royal Photographic Society
RPSM: Resources Planning and Scheduling Method
RPSs: Reliability Problem Summary Cards; Republic of the Philippines Ships
rpt: repeat
RPT: Registered Physical Therapist
RPU: Radio Propagation Unit (USA)
rpv: remotely-piloted vehicle
rq (RQ): respiratory quotient
R/Q: Request for Quotation
R & QA: reliability and Quality Assurance
rqdcz: request clearance to depart control zone
rqecz: request clearance to enter control zone
rql: reference quality level
RQMS: Regimental Quartermaster Sergeant
rqmt: requirement
rqr: require; requirement
rqs: ready qualified for standby
rqtao: request time and altitude over
rr: radiation response; radio range; radio ranging; railroad; rapid rectilinear; rear; rearward; respiratory rate; rifle range; rural route; rush release; rush and run
r & r: rate and rhythm (pulse); rest and recreation; rest and rotation (of military personnel); rock and roll; rock and rye (whiskey); rush and run
RR: Railroad; Raritan River (railroad); Recovery Room; Recruit Roll; Reliability Requirements; Remington Rand; Renegotiation Regulations; Research Report; Rifle Range; Right Reverend; Rolls-Royce; Rural Route
R-R: Rolls-Royce
R v R: Rembrandt van Rijn
rRA: specific acoustic resistance
RRA: Radiation Research Associates
R/RA: Repair/Rework Analysis
RRAF: Royal Rhodesian Air Force
RRB: Railroad Retirement Board
RRBC: R.R. Bowker Company
RRBS: Rapid-Response Bibliographic Service
rr & c: records, reports, and control
RRC: Recruit Reception Center; Requirements Review Committee; Rocket Research Corporation; Royal Red Cross; Rubber Reserve Committee; Rubber Reserve Company; Rubber Reserve Corporation
R.R.C.: Lady of the Royal Red Cross
RRCC: Redwood Region Conservation Council
rr cells: radiation reaction cells
rrd: receive, record, display
rr & d: reparations, removal, and demolition
RRD: Reliability Requirements Directive
rrda: rendezvous retrieval, docking, and assembly (of orbital station or space vehicle)
rr & e: round, regular, and equal (eye pupils)
RRE: Railroad Enthusiasts; Royal Radar Establishment
R Rep: Records Repository (USAF)
RRF: Refrigeration Research Foundation
rri: range rate indicator
RRI: Radio Republik Indonesia; Rocket Research Institute; Rubber Research Institute
RRIC: Rubber Research Institute of Ceylon
RRIM: Rubber Research Institute of Malaya
RRIS: Remote Radar Integration Station
RRL: Regimental Reserve Line; Registered Record Librarian; Reserve Retired List; Road Reserve Laboratory

R.R.L.: Registered Record Librarian (hospital)
RRLNWR: Red Rock Lakes National Wildlife Refuge (Montana)
RRLs: Registered Record Librarians
rrna (RRNA): ribosomal ribonucleic acid
rRNA: ribosomal RNA (ribonucleic acid)
rrp: recommended retail price
RRP: Rotterdam-Rhine Pipeline
RRPS: Ready Reinforcement Personnel Section (USAF)
rrr: rebel, resist, riot (New Left student-activist program in abbreviated form)
RRRA: Regional Rail Reorganization Act
RRS: Radiation Research Society; Reaction Research Society; Retired Reserve Section; Royal Research Ship
rrt: rendezvous radar transponder
RRU: Radio Research Unit (USA)
rrv: rate of rise of voltage
rs: radio station; reading of standard; ready service; rear spar; receiver station; receiving ship; receiving station; reception station; regulating station; reinforcing stimulus; response stimulus; right side; road space; rubble stone
r/s: range safety; revolutions per second
r & s: rapport and support; reenlistment and separation
rs (RS): report separator character (data processing)
Rs: restricted motion pictures (adults only); rupees
RS: Radio Station; Receiving Ship; Receiving Station; Reception Station; Reconnaissance Squadron; Reconnaissance Strike; Recording Secretary; Recruiting Station; Regular Station; Regulating Station; Regulation Station; Republic Steel; Research Summary; Revised Statutes; Ringer's Solution; Rio Grande do Sul; Roberval & Saguenay (railroad); Royal Scots; Royal Society
RS: *Rengo Sekigun* (Japanese—United Red Army)—urban guerrila group active in the Middle East
RS-70: reconnaissance-strike bomber (formerly B-70)
rsa: radar signature analysis; remote station alarm; right sacro-anterior
RSA: Railway Supervisors Association; Railway Supply Association; Redstone Arsenal; Regional Science Association; Renaissance Society of America; Rental Service Association; Republiek van Suid-Afrika; Royal Scottish Academy; Royal Society of Arts
RSA (AFL-CIO): Railway and Airline Supervisors Association
RSAF: Royal Swedish Air Force
RSAI: Royal Society of Antiquaries of Ireland
rsalt: running, signal, and anchor lights
RSAM: Royal Scottish Academy of Music
RSAS: Royal Sanitary Association of Scotland; Royal Surgical Aid Society
RSASA: Royal South Australian Society of Arts
rsb: range safety beacon
RSB: Regimental Stretcher Bearer
RSBA: Rail Steel Bar Association; Royal Society of British Artists
RSBS: Radar Safety Beacon System
rsbt: rhythmic sensory bombardment therapy (RSBT)
rsc: range-safety command; range-safety control
RSC: Range Safety Command; Records Service Center; Richard Strauss Conservatory (Munich); Royal Society of Canada
rsca: right scapuloanterior
RSCDS: Royal Scottish Country Dance Society
rsch: research
RSCM: Royal School of Church Music
RSCN: Registered Sick Children's Nurse
rscp: right scapuloposterior
RSCS: Rate Stabilization and Control System
RSCT: Rhode Sentence Completion Test
rsd: rolling steel door
RSD: Riverside Drive; Royal Society of Dublin
RSD-ALA: Reference Services Division—American Library Association
rsdp: remote-site data processor
RSDS: Range Safety Destruct System
RSE: Royal Society of Edinburgh
rseu: remote scanner-encoder unit
RSF: Religious Society of Friends; Royal Scots Fusiliers; Russell Sage Foundation; Russian Socialist Forces; Russian Soviet Forces
RSFPP: Retired Serviceman's Family Protection Plan
RSFS: Royal Scottish Forestry Society
RSFSR: *Rossiskaya Sovietskaya Federatvnaya Sotsialisticheskaya Respublika* (Russian Soviet Federal Socialist Republic)
rsg: reassign; receiver of stolen goods; receiving stolen goods; regional seat of government
RSG: Royal Scots Greys
RSGB: Radio Society of Great Britain
RSGS: Royal Scottish Geographical Society
rsh: radar status history
Rsh: Rosyth
RSH: Royal Society for the Promotion of Health
RSHA: Reichssicherheitshauptampt (Nazi German Secret Police headed by Heinrich Himmler)
RSHWC: Royal Society for the Health of Women and Children (New Zealand's Plunkett Society)
rsi: radarscope interpretation; reflected signal indication; replacement stream input
rs & i: rules, standards, and instructions
RSI: Research Studies Institute
RSIC: Radiation Standards Information Center; Redstone Scientific Information Center
R Sigs: Royal Signals
RSIS: Reference, Special, and Information Section (Library Association)
rsivp: rapid sequence intravenous pyelogram
rsj: rolled-steel joist
rsl: right sacrolateral
RSL: Radio Standards Laboratory; Red Star Line; Royal Society of London
rsla: range safety launch approval
rslb: right short-leg brace
rsm (RSM): reconnaissance strategic missile
RSM: Regimental Sergeant Major; Royal Society of Medi-

cine; Royal Society of Musicians
RSM: *Repubblica di San Marino* (Italian—Republic of San Marino)
RSMA: Railway Systems and Management Association; Republica di San Marino (San Marino—world's smallest republic); Royal School of Mines; Royal Society of Medicine
rsn: reason
RSN: Radiation Surveillance Network (USPHS)
RSNA: Radiological Society of North America
RSNP: Registered Student Nurse Program
RSNZ: Royal Society of New Zealand
rso: railway sorting office; railway suboffice; research ship of opportunity
RSO: Range Safety Officer; Research Ships of Opportunity; Richmond Symphony Orchestra
rsp: rear-screen projection; right sacro-posterior
RSPA: Royal Society for the Prevention of Accidents
RSPB: Royal Society for the Protection of Birds
RSPCA: Royal Society for the Prevention of Cruelty to Animals
RSPCC: Royal Society for the Prevention of Cruelty to Children
RSPE: Royal Society of Painter-Etchers and Engravers
RSPH: Royal Society for the Promotion of Health
RSPP: Royal Society of Portrait Painters
RSPWC: Royal Society of Painters in Water Colours
rsq: rescue
rsr: regular sinus rhythm; required supply rate
RSR: Range Safety Report; Request for Scientific Research; Research Study Requests
r-s ratio: response-stimulus ratio
R-SR B: Richmond-San Rafael Bridge
RSRC: Remote Sensing Research Center (UCB)
RSROAA: Roller Skating Rink Operators Association of America
RSRS: Radio and Space Research Station
rss: root-sum square
R s-s: Russian spring-summer (encephalitis)
RSS: Range Safety System; Reactant Service System; Rehabilitation Support Schedule; Royal Security Service; Royal Statistical Society; Rural Sociological Society
RSSA: Royal Society of South Africa
RSSAILA: Returned Sailors, Soldiers, and Airmen's Imperial League of Australia
RSSC: Rand School of Social Sciences
RSSPCC: Royal Scottish Society for the Prevention of Cruelty to Children
RSSS: *Regiae Societatis Socius Sodalis* (Latin—Fellow of the Royal Society)
RSST: Recruiter-Salesman Selection Test
rst: radius of safety trace; reinforcing steel; right sacro-transverse
r-s-t: readability—signal strength — tone (amateur radio signal)
Rst: Rest (postal abbreviation)
RST: Royal Society of Teachers
RST: *Republica Socialista Romania* (Romanian Socialist Republic)
R Sta: radio station
RSTMH: Royal Society of Tropical Medicine and Hygiene
rstr: restricted
rsu: road safety unit
RSU: Radical Student Union
rsv: respiratory syncytial virus
Rsv: Rous sarcoma virus
RSV: Revised Standard Version (Bible)
rs virus: respiratory synctial virus
rsvp: research-selected vote profile; restartable solid variable pulse
RSVP: Retired Senior Volunteer Persons; Retired Senior Volunteer Program
R.S.V.P.: *répondez s'il vous plaît* (French—please reply)
rsvr: reservoir
rswc (RSWC): right side up with care
R Sw N: Royal Swedish Navy
RSWS: Royal Scottish Water-Colour Society
rt: radio telephone; radio telephony; rate; reaction time; receive-transmit; reduction table(s); right; rocket target; room temperature; round table; round trip; runup & taxi
r/t: radiotelephone
r & t (R & T): research and technology
RT: Radio Technician; Ranger Tab; Reading Test; Recreational Therapy; Registered Technician; Registered X-ray Technician; République Togolaise (Togo Republic); River Terminal (railroad); Rubber Technician
RT: *République Togolaise* (French—Togolese Republic)—Togo
R/T: Record of Trial
R de T: Ralph de Toledano
rta: road traffic accident
RTA: Rail Travel Authorization; Railway Tie Association; Refrigeration Trade Association; Royal Thai Army; Rubber Trade Association
RTA: *Radiodiffusion et Télévision Algérienne* (French—Algerian Radio and Television Network)
RTAC: Regional Technical Aids Center
rt ad: router adapter
RTAF: Royal Thai Air Force
rtb: return to base
RTB: Radiodiffusion Télévision Belge (Belgian Radio-Television Broadcasting)
RTB: *Radiodiffusion-*Télévision Belge (French—Belgian Radio-Television Network)
RTB/BRT: *Radifussion-Télévi*sion Belge/Belgische Radio den Televisie (French and Dutch—Belgian Radio and Television Network)
RTBL: Richard Thomas and Baldwins Limited
rtc: ratchet
RTC: Rail Travel Card; Real Time Command; Replacement Training Center; Reserve Training Corps; Revenue and Taxation Code; Rochester Telephone Corporation; Royal Trust Company
RTCA: Radio Technical Commission for Aeronautics
rtcc: real-time computer complex
RTCEG: Rubber and Thermoplastic Cables Export Group
rtcu: real-time control unit
rt cu: router cutter
rtd: returned
RTD: Rapid Transit District (Southern California); Research and Technology Division
rtdd: real-time data distribution
RTDHS: Real-Time Data Handling System

rtd ht: retired hurt
rt dr: returnable-trip drum
RTDS: Real-Time Data System
rte: route
r-t-e: ready-to-eat (breakfast foods and cereals)
RTE: *Radio Telefis Eireann* (Irish Radio Television)
RTEB: Radio Trades Examination Board
R te G: *Rijksuniversiteit te Groningen* (Dutch—State University of Groningen)
rtem: radar tracking error measurement
RTES: Radio and Television Executives Society
RTESO: Radio Telefis Eireann Symphony Orchestra (Irish Radio Television Symphony Orchestra)
R test: reductase test
rtf: resistance-transfer factor; rubber-tile floor; rubber-tile foundation
RTF: *Radiodiffusion-Télévision Française* (French tv network)
rt fm: router form
RTFR: Reliability Trouble and Failure Report
rtfv: radar target folder viewer
rtg: radioactive thermal generator; rare tube gas; reusable training grenade
RTG: Royal Thai Government
RTG: *Radiodiffusion Télévision Gabonaise* (French—Gabonese Radio- Television Network)
rtgd: room temperature gamma detector
rt gu: router guide
rtgv: real time generation of video
Rt Hon: Right Honourable
RTHPL: Radio Times Hulton Picture Library
rti: rise time indicator; rotor temperature indicator
RTI: Reliability Trend Indicator; Research Triangle Institute; Roanoke Technical Institute
RTI: *Radiodiffusion Télévision Ivoirienne* (French—Ivorian Radio-Television Network)—Ivory Coast
rtip: radar target identification point
RTIR: Reliability Trend Indicator Report
RTITB: Road Transport Industry Training Board
RTK: Ras Tafari Makonnea (Haile Selassie)
R Tks: Royal Tank Regiment; Royal Tanks
rtl: reinforced tile lintel; resistor transistor logic
RTLA: Road Transport Lighting Act
RTLO: Regional Training Liaison Office(r)
rtm: running time meter
RTM: Rotterdam, Netherlands (airport)
RTM: *Radiodiffusion Télévision Marocaine* (French—Moroccan Radio-Television Network)
RTMA: Radio and Television Manufacturers Association
RTMS: Radar Target Measuring System
rtn: retain; return
RTN: registered trade name; Royal Thai Navy
rto: radio-telephone operator
RTO: Railway Transport Office
rtol: restricted takeoff and landing
rtp: reinforced thermoplastic
R Tp: radio telephone
RTP: Request for Technical Proposal (DoD)
RTP: *Radiotelevisão Portuguesa* (Portuguese Radio Television)
rtqc: real-time quality control
rtr: returning to ramp
R Tr: radio tower
RTR: Reliability Test Requirement(s); Royal Tank Regiment
RTR: *Radiodifuziunea Televisiunea Romana* (Romanian Radio-Television Network)
RTRA: Radio and Television Retailers' Association; Road Traffic Regulation Act
rtrc: radio telemetry and remote control
RTRC: Regional Technical Report Centers
Rt.Rev.: Right Reverend
rts: radar target simulation; radar tracking station
RTS: Repair Technical Service (tractor stations—USSR)
RTSA: Retail Trading Standards Association
RTSD: Resources and Technical Services Division (American Library Association)
RTSRS: Real-Time Simulation Research System
rtt: radiation tracking transducer
RTT: *Radiodiffusion Télévision Tunisienne* (French—Tunisian Broadcasting—radio and tv)
RTTC: Road-Time Trials Council
RTTDS: Real-Time Telemetry Data System
rt tp: router template
rttv: research target and test vehicle
r-ttv: real-time television
rtty (RTTY): radio-teletypewriter communication(s)
rtu: remote terminal unit; returned to unit
RTU: Railroad Telegraphers Union; Reinforcement Training Unit; Reserve Training Unit
rtv: reentry test vehicle (RTV); room-temperature vulcanizing
RTVS: Royal Television Society
rtw: ready to wear
rtx: rapid-transit experimental (bus); report time crossing
rty: rarity; realty
rtz: return to zero
RTZ: Rio Tinto Zinc
ru: radium unit; rat unit; roentgen unit
Ru: Rumania (Romania); Rumanian (Romanian); Russia; Russian; ruthenium
RU: Rhodes University; Roosevelt University; Rugby Union; Rutgers University; Rumanian Union
RU: **Regno Unito (Italian—United Kingdom)**
R te U: Rijksuniversiteit te Utrecht (State University at Utrecht)
RUA: Royal Ulster Academy
RUAS: Royal Ulster Agricultural Society
rub.: rubber
rub: *rubato* (Italian—with varying tempo); *ruber* (Latin—red)
RUB: Radio Ulan Bator
Rubber Capital of the U.S.: Akron, Ohio
Rubber City: Akron, Ohio
rubd: rubberized
Rube: Ruben
rubel: rubella (german measles)
Rube Waddell: George Edward Waddell
Rubén Darío: Félix Rubén García Sarmiento
Rubg: Rummelsburg
ruby: red corundum
ruby copper: cuprite (cuprous oxide)
ruby spinel: red spinel gemstone
RUC: Royal Ulster Constabulary
RUC: *République Unie du Cameroun* (French—United Republic of Cameroon)
Ruch: Ruchel
Rucos: Russian Communists

RUCR: Royal Ulster Constabulary Reserve
rud: rudder
Rud: Rudd; Rüdiger; Rudolf; Rudolph; Rudulph; Rudyard
Rud Kip: Rudyard Kipling
Rudy: Rudolf; Rudolph
Rud(dy): Rudyard
Rudolf Valentino: Rodolpho d'Antongnolla
rue.: right upper entrance; right upper extremity
RUE: Regional Urban Environment
RUFAS: Remote Underwater Fisheries Assessment System
Rufe: Rufus
rug: red under gold
rugger: rugby football
RUI: Royal University of Ireland
RUKBA: Royal United Kingdom Beneficent Association
rul: right upper limb; right upper lobe (lung)
RUL: Rutgers University Library
Ruler of the East: Vladivostok
rum (RUM): remote underwater manipulator
Rum: Rumania (Romania); Rumanian (Romanian)
RUM: Royal University of Malta
rumnog: rum-flavored eggnog
RUN: Revolutionary United Nations
R unit: millimeter of mercury divided by milliliters per second; unit of resistance in the cardiovascular system
RUP: Rockefeller University Press
rupp: road used as public path
rupt: rupture(d)
ruq: right upper quadrant (abdomen)
***RUR:** Rossum's Universal Robots* (acronym-titled play by Karel Capek)
Rus: Russ; Russia; Russian
Rusdic: Russian dictionary
rush.: remote use of shared hardware
Rush: Rushdi; Rushmore; Rushton; Rushworth
RUSI: Royal United Service Institution
RUSM: Royal United Service Museum
russ: russet; russian (leather)
Russ: Russia(n)
Russian-American Capital: Sitka, Alaska
Russian National Composer: Mikhail Ivanovich Glinka
Russian Physiologist Extraordinary: Ivan Petrovich Pavlov
Russian Symphonist: Peter Ilyitch Tchaikovsky
Russki(s): Russian(s)
***rúst:** rústico, à la* (Spanish—paperback; paperbound)
Rustic Wedding: Karl Goldmark's Symphony in E flat (opus 26)
Rust's disease: tuberculosis of the upper cervical vertebrae
Rut: Rutland Railroad; Rutlandshire
rutile: titanium dioxide
rv: rear view; reentry vehicle (RV); relief valve; residual volume; retroversion; right ventricle
r/v: reentry vehicle
RV: Rahway Valley (railroad); Reading and Vocabulary Test; República de Venezuela; Revised Version; Rifle Volunteer(s)
***RV:** Radkikale Venstre* (Danish—Radical Left)—Radical Liberal Party
R/V: rendezvous; research vessel
rva: reactive volt-ampere (meter)
***RvA:** Rouva* (Finnish—Madam)
RVA: Regular Veterans' Association
R & VA: Rating and Valuation Association
rvb: radar video buffer
rvbr: riveting bar
rvc: random vibration control; relative velocity computer
RVC: Rifle Volunteer Corps; Royal Veterinary College
RVCI: Royal Veterinary College of Ireland
rvd: radar video digitizer; right vertebral density
RVDA: Recreational Vehicle Dealers of America
rvdp: radar video data processor
rve: radar video extractor
RVFN: Report of Visit of Foreign Nationals
rv fx: riveting fixture
rvh: right ventricular hypertrophy
RV(H)R: Road Vehicles (Headlamps) Regulations
RVI: Recreational Vehicle Institute
RVIA: Royal Victoria Institute of Architects
RVLP: Rift Valley Lakes Park (Ethiopia)
RVLR: Road Vehicles Lighting Regulations
rvm: reactive voltmeter
Rvn: Ravenna
RVN: Republic of Vietnam
RVNAF: Republic of Vietnam Air Force; Republic of Vietnam Armed Forces
rvo: relaxed vaginal outlet; runway visibility observer
***R v O:** Rijksinstituut voor Oorlogsdocumentatie* (Netherlands State Institute for War Documentation)
RVO: Regional Veterinary Officer; Royal Victorian Order
rpv: remote pilotless vehicle
Rvp: Reid vapor pressure
rvpa: rivet pattern
rvr: runway visual range
***R & VR:** Rating and Valuation Reports*
rvs: reported visual sensation
rv's: recreation vehicles
rvsc: reverse self check
***R.V.S.V.P.:** répondez vite, s'il vous plaît* (French—please reply at once)
rvsz: riveting squeezer
rvtol: rolling vertical takeoff and landing
rvu: relief valve unit
rvx: reentry vehicle—experimental
RVYC: Royal Vancouver Yacht Club; Royal Victoria Yacht Club
rw: radiological warfare; railwater (transport); random widths; raw water; recreation and welfare; recruiting warrant; rotary wing; runway
r/w: right-of-way
r & w: rail and water
Rw: Rwanda
RW: radiological war; radiological warfare; Recruiting Warrant; redwood; Richard Wagner; Right Worshipful; Right Worthy; Royal Welsh
rwa (RWA): rotary-wing aircraft
RWA: Railway Wheel Association
RWAFF: Royal West African Frontier Force
R War R: Royal Warwick Regiment
RWAS: Royal Welsh Agricultural Society
rwb: rear wheel brake
RWB: Rand Water Board; Royal Winnipeg Ballet
rwbh: records will be handcarried
rwc: rainwater conductor; read, write, compute; read, write, continue; receive with code
RWC: Roberts Wesleyan College
RWDGM: Right Worshipful Deputy Grand Master

RWEMA: Ralph Waldo Emerson Memorial Association
RWF: Royal Wholesalers' Federation; Royal Welch Fusiliers
rwg: rigid waveguide
RWG: Radio Writers' Guild; Reliability Working Group; Roebling Wire Gage
rwgl: rough wire glass
RWGM: Right Worshipful Grand Master
RWGR: Right Worthy Grand Representative
RWGT: Right Worthy Grand Templar; Right Worthy Grand Treasurer
RWGW: Right Worthy Grand Warden
rwh: radar warning and homing
rwi: read, write, initial; real world interval; remote weight indicator
R Wilts Yeo: Royal Wiltshire Yeomanry
RWJC: Roger Williams Junior College
RWJF: Robert Wood Johnson Foundation
RWJGW: Right Worthy Junior Grand Warden
rwk: rework
RWK: Royal West Kent (regiment)
rwl: relative water level
rwlr: relative water-level recorder
rwm: rectangular wave modulation; resistance welding machine; roll wrapping machine
RWMA: Resistance Welding Manufacturers' Association
rwp: radio wave propagation
RWQCB: Regional Water Quality-Control Board(s)
RWR: rail-water-rail
rwrc: remain well to right of course
rws: range while search; reaction wheel scanner; reaction wheel system
RWS: Royal Water Colour Society
RWSGW: Right Worshipful Senior Grand Warden
rwt: read-write-tape
R-W Test: Rideal-Walker Test
rwth: raised watertight hatch
rwv: read-write-versify
rwy: railway; runway
rx: reverse; rix dollar; tens of rupees
Rx: recipe; prescription
rxb: roxburgh (binding)
rxp: radix point
rxs: radar cross-section
ry: railway; rydberg
Ry: railway; Ryukyu (islands)
RY: Royal Air Lao (coding)
RYA: Railroad Yardmasters of America; Royal Yachting Association
Ry Age: *Railway Age*
ryal: relay alarm
Ryan: Ryan Aeronautical Company (coding)
RYC: Rochester Yacht Club
Ry I: Ryukyu Islands
rym: refer to your message
RYM: Revolutionary Youth Movement
Rys: Railways
RYS: Royal Yacht Squadron
Ryu: Ryukyu; Ryukyuan
Ryukyus: Ryukyu Islands between Japan and Taiwan
R y'u R: *Republika y'u Rwanda* (Kinyarwanda—Rwanda)
rz: return to zero
Rz: Rodriguez
RZ: République du Zaire (formerly Belgian Congo)
R of Z: Republic of Zambia
RZA: Religious Zionists of America
RZMA: Rolled Zinc Manufacturers Association
RZn: relative azimuth
RZS: Royal Zoological Society
RZ S: Royal Zoological Society of Scotland
RZSI: Royal Zoological Society of Ireland
RZSS: Royal Zoological Society of Scotland
rzl: return to zero level
rzm: return to zero mark

S

s: displacement (symbol); sacral; saline; sand; schilling (Austrian currency); scuttle; sea-air temperature difference correction (symbol); second; secret; section; sections; sedimentation (coefficient); sen (Japanese currency unit); sensation; sensitive; separate; separation; share(s); shilling (British monetary unit); ship; sign; silicate; silver; simultaneous transmission of range signals and voice (symbol); slope; slow; small; smooth; snow; soft; sol (Peruvian monetary unit); soluble; son; sou (French monetary unit); space; spar; specific; specific factor; speed; spherical; spherical lens; steel; stere; stimulus; stock; string; subject; substrate; succeeded; sucre (Ecuadorian monetary unit); sum; summary; summer; supravergence; surface; symbol surface; surgeon; symbol; syphilis (sometimes indicated in reports by a Greek sigma)
s.: *sinister* (Latin—left)
s: *signa* (Latin—write;) signetur (Latin—label; let it be written); *sinister* (Latin—left)
's: (contraction—does; has; is)
s_1: first heart sound
s_2: second heart sound
S1, S2, S3, etc.: first sacral nerve, second sacral nerve, third sacral nerve, etc.
s 1 s 1 e: surfaced on one side and one edge (lumber)
s 4 s: surfaced on four sides (lumber)
S: antisubmarine (symbol); sailing vessel (symbol); San; San Francisco (coin symbol denoting San Francisco mint); Santa; Santo; satisfactory; Saturday; Saturn; Saxon; Schilling (Austrian currency); school; Schweitzer; Schweizer Aircraft; Scotland; Seaman; seaplane; search and rescue; Sears, Roebuck (stock exchange symbol); Seatrain Lines; secondary winding (symbol); secret; Section; See; sen (Japanese currency); Senate; Senate

Bill; Senator; Shinto; Shintoism; Shintoist; ship; siemens (mho); Sierra—code for letter S; sign; Signor (Italian—mister); Sigma; Sikorsky; silver; Silver Lines; Sinclair; Sister; Socialist; sol (Peruvian monetary unit); solo; solubility; son; soprano; south; southern; spar buoy; specific factor; specification(s); Sperry; Staff; Statute; steamer; steamship; Steinway; stop; subject; sucre (Ecuadorian monetary unit); sune; sunur; summer; sun; Sunday; Sweden (auto plaque); Sylvania; total entropy (symbol); wing plan area (symbol)

S: general area (symbol); *Sábado* (Spanish—Saturday); Sacrum (Latin); *San* or *Santo* (Italian, Spanish—saint, *m*); *Santa* (Italian, Portuguese, Spanish—saint, *f*); *São* (Portuguese—saint, *m*); *semis* (Latin—half); *sinister* (Latin—left); *sisälle* (Finnish—in); *söder* (Swedish—south); *sør* (Norwegian—south); south; *strada* (Italian—street); *subir* (Spanish—to go up; mount); *sud* (French or Italian—south); *Süd* (German—south); *sul* (Portuguese—south); *sur* (Spanish—south); *syd* (Danish—south)

S/: sol (Peru); sucre (Ecuador)

S-1: military personnel; personnel officer

S1c: Seaman, first class

S-2: military intelligence; intelligence officer

S2F: Tracker twin-engine antisubmarine aircraft flown from carriers

S-3: military operations and training; military operations and training officer

S^3: Systems, Science, and Software

S-4: military logistics; military logistics officer

S^{35}: radioactive sulfur

:/S/: sign (music)

sa: sail area; semiannual(ly); semiautomatic; sex appeal; shaft alley; sinoatrial; small arms; soluble in alkaline; special activities; spectrum analyzer; stone arch; subject to approval; subsistence allowance; sun-affected; superabnormal; supra-abdominal; sustained action

sa: *siehe auch* (German—see also)

s.a.: *secundum artem* (Latin—according to the art)

s-a: sinoatrial

s/a: storage area

s & a: safety and arming (mechanism)

Sa: samarium; Sara; Sarah; Sarita; Serra; Sierra

Sa: *Summa* (German—total)

s^a: *Señora* (Spanish—Madam)

SA: Safeway Stores (stock exchange symbol); Salvation Army; Saudi Arabia; Saudia Arabian; Savannah & Atlanta (railroad); Seaman Apprentice; second attack (lacrosse); search amphibian; Secretary of the Army; sex appeal; Shipping Authority; Society of Actuaries; South Africa; South African; South African Airways (2-letter coding); South America; South American; South Australia; South Australian; Southern Association; Special Agent; Special Artificer; Springfield Armory; State's Attorney; Sugar Association; Supplemental Agreement; Supplementary Agreement

SA: *Société Anonyme* (French—limited company)

S.A.: *Sociedad Anónima* (Spanish—corporation); *Sturmabteilung* (German—Stormtroopers, Adolf Hitler's brown-shirted Nazis); *Sucursales Asociados* (Spanish—associated branches)

S/A: *Societa Anonima* (Italian—limited company)

SA£: South African pound

S of A: Society of Actuaries

S por A: *Sociedad por Acciones* (Spanish—limited liability company)

saa: small arms ammunition

SAA: Saudi Arabian Airlines; Shakespeare Association of America; Signal Appliance Association; Society for Academic Achievement; Society for American Archeology; Society of American Archivists; Society for Applied Anthropology; Society for Asian Art; South African Airways; Southern Ash Association; Speech Association of America; Surety Association of America; Swedish-American Association

SAAA: Salvation Army Association of America

SAAARNG: Senior Army Advisor, Army National Guard

SAAAS: South African Association for the Advancement of Science

SAAASE: South African Association for the Administration and Settlement of Estates

SAAB: Svenska Aeroplan Aktiebolaget (Swedish Airplane Company)

SAAC: Sciences and Arts Camps; Seismic Array Analysis Center (IBM); Special Assistant for Arms Control (DoD)

SAAD: Sacramento Army Depot; Small-Arms Ammunition Depot; Society for the Advancement of Anesthesia in Dentistry

SAAEB: South African Atomic Energy Board

SAAF: Saudi Arabian Air Force; South African Air Force

SAAL: Syrian Arab Airlines

SAALIC: Swindon Area Association of Libraries for Industry and Commerce

SAAMA: San Antonio Air Materiel Area

SAAMI: Sporting Arms and Ammunition Manufacturers Institute

SAAP: Saturn-Apollo Applications Program; South Atlantic Anomaly Probe (NASA)

sa ar: saw arbor

Saar River City: Saarbrücken, Germany

SAAS: Science Achievement Awards for Students; Society of African and Afro-American Students

SAAT: Society of Architects and Allied Technicians

SAAU: South African Agricultural Union

SAAVS: Submarine Acceleration and Velocity System

SAAWK: *Suid Afrikaanse Akademie vir Wetnenskap en Kuns* (Afrikaans—South African Academy for Science and Art)

sab: sabbath; sabbatical; soprano, alto, baritone (SAB)

sáb: *sábado* (Portuguese or Spanish—Saturday); *sabato* (Italian—Saturday)

s-a b: steel-arch bridge

Sab: Sabah; Sabbatarian; Sabbatarianism; Sabbath; Sabelian; Sabine; Sabra(s)

SAB: Sabena; Scientific Advisory Board; Society of American Bacteriologists

***SAB:** Sveriges Allmänna Biblioteksforening* (Swedish Library Association)

SABA: Scottish Amateur Boxing Association

Sabah: (formerly British North Borneo)

sabbat: sabbatical

SABC: South African Broadcasting Corporation

SABCO: Society for the Area of Biological and Chemical Overlap

SABCOA: Screw and Bolt Corporation of America

SABE: Society for Automation in Business Education

SABENA: Société Anonyme Belge d'Exploitation de la Navigation Aérienne (Belgian World Airlines)

saber (SABER): semiautomatic business environment research

sabh: simultaneous automatic-broadcast homer

Sabine River City: Orange, Texas

sabir: semi-automatic bibliographic information retrieval

SABMIS: Seaborne Anti-Ballistic Missile Intercept System (USN)

SABMS: Safeguard Anti-Ballistic Missile System

sabo: sabotage

SABRA: South African Bureau of Racial Affairs

sabre: self-aligning boost and reentry

SABS: South African Bureau of Standards

SABW: Society of American Business Writers

sac: sacral; sacrament; sacramental; sacred

Sac: Sacramento, California (nickname)

SAC: Sacramento, California (airport); San Angelo College; San Antonio College; Society of Analytical Chemistry; Southwest Automotive Company; Special Agent in Charge (FBI); Strategic Air Command; Suburban Authorization Committee

***SAC:** Sveriges Arbetares Centralorganisation* (Swedish—Swedish Workers Central Organization)

SACA: Steam Automobile Club of America

sacad: stress analysis and computer-aided design

SACANGO: Southern Africa Committee on Air Navigation and Ground Operation

SACB: Subversive Activities Control Board

***S Acc:** Società in Accomandita* (Italian—limited partnership)

SACC: Supplemental Air Carrier Conference; Supporting Arms Coordination Center

SACCS: Strategic Air Command Control System

SACEM: Société des Auteurs, Compositeurs et Éditeurs de la Musique (Society of Authors, Composers, and Editors of Music)

SACEUR: Supreme Allied Command, Europe

sach: solid ankle cushion heel (prosthetic foot)

SACH: Small Animal Care Hospital

Sacha: Alexander

Sacha Guitry: (pseudonym—Alexandre Pierre Georges)

SACI: South Atlantic Cooperative Investigations

SA & CL: South Atlantic & Caribbean Line

SACLant: Supreme Allied Commander, Atlantic

SACLANTCEN: SACLANT Anti-Submarine Warfare Research Centre (NATO)

SACM: South African College of Music; South African Corps of Marines; South Arabian Common Market

SACMP: South African Corps of Military Policy

SACO: Sveriges Akademikers Centralorganisation (Swedish Professional Central Organization)

Sacr: Sacramento

SACS: South African College System; South African Corps of Signals; Southern Association of Colleges and Schools

SACSEA: Supreme Allied Command South-East Asia

SACSIR: South African Council for Scientific and Industrial Research

Sacto: Sacramento

SACTU: South African Congress of Trade Unions

SACU: Service for Admission to College and University

SACUBO: Southern Association of College and University Business Officers

SACVT: Society of Air Cushion Vehicle Technicians

sad.: safety, arming, destruct; safety and arming device; situation attention display

SAD: simple, average, or difficult; Social Affairs Department (Communist China's espionage agency)

***SAD:** South African Digest*

S & AD: Science and Applications Directorate (NASA)

sadap: simplified automatic data plotter

***SADE:** Sociedad Argentina de Escritores* (Argentine Writers' Society)

SADF: South African Defence Forces

sadic: solid-state analog-to-digital computer

sadie: scanning analog-to-digital input equipment; semiautomatic decentralized intercept environment

Sadie: Sara; Sarah; Sarita

sado-sex: sado-sexual(ity)

SADS: Swiss Air Defense System

sadsac: sampled data simulator and computer

sadsact: self-aligned descriptors from self and cited titles (automatic index)

sad sam (SAD SAM): sentence appraiser and diagrammer—semantic analyzer machine

SADTC: Shape Air Defense Technology Center

s-a-d test: sugar-acetone-diacetic acid test

sae: San Diego Aircraft Engineering (corporate symbol); self-addressed envelope; standard average European

SAE: Society of American Etchers; Society of Automotive Engineers

S.A.E.: Société Anonyme Egyptienne (Egyptian limited company)

SAEA: Southeastern Adult Education Association

saeb: self-adjusting electric brake

***saec.:** saeculum* (Latin—century)

SAEC: South African Engineer Corps; Sumitomo Atomic Energy Commission (Japan)

SAEH: Society for Automation in English and the Humanities

SAEI: Sumitomo Atomic Energy Industries (Japan)

SAEL: South African Emergency League

SAEMR: Small Arms Expert Marksmanship Ribbon

SAET: Spiral Aftereffect Test

saf: safety
SAF: Secretary of the Air Force; See America First; Society of American Florists; Society of American Foresters; Strategic Air Force
SAF: *Svenska Arbetsgivareforeningen* (Swedish Employers' Confederation)
SAF£: South African Pound
safa: solar-array failure analysis; soluble-antigen fluorescent antibody
SAFA: School Assistance in Federally Affected Areas; Society for Automation in the Fine Arts
SAFAA: South African Fine Arts Association
SAFB: Scott Air Force Base; Shaw Air Force Base
saf black: super-abrasion furnace black
SAFC: South African Flying Corps
SAFCB: Secretary of the Air Force Correction Board
SAFCO: Standing Advisory Committee on Fisheries in the Caribbean Organization
safe.: satellite alert force employment; system, area, function, equipment
SAFE: Braathens South American & Far East Air Transport; Survival and Flight Equipment Association
S.A.F.E.: Society of Aeronautic Flight Engineers
SAFE TRIP: Students Against Faulty Tires Ripping in Pieces
SAFI: Senior Air Force Instructor
SAFMARINE: South African Marine (corporation)
SAFO: Senior Air Force Officer (present)
SAFOH: Society of American Florists and Ornamental Horticulturists
S Afr: South Africa(n)
SAFR: Senior Air Force Representative
S-Afr Du: South-African Dutch (Afrikaans)
SAFS: Secondary Air Force Specialty
SAFSL: Secretary of Air Force Space Liaison
SAFSO: Safeguard System Office(r)
SAFSR: Society for the Advancement of Food Service Research
SAFTI: Singapore Armed Forces Training Institute
SAFU: Scottish Amateur Fencing Union
sa fx: saw fixture
Sag: Sagittarius
SAG: Scientific Advisory Group; Screen Actors Guild; Society of Arthritic Gardeners; Systems Analysis Group
SAGA: Sand and Gravel Association; Scout and Guide Activity; Society of American Graphic Artists
Saga City: Stavanger, Norway
Sagamore Hill: Theodore Roosevelt's home on Long Island at Oyster Bay, New York
SAGB: Spiritualist Association of Great Britan
sag. d: saggital diameter
SAGE: semi-automatic ground environment (for continental defense against air attack)
Sage of America: Benjamin Franklin
Sage of Anacostia: Frederick Douglass
Sage of Ashland: Henry Clay
Sage of Auburn: Secretary of State William H. Seward
Sage of Baltimore: H(enry) L(ouis) Mencken
Sagebrush: Nevada state flower; state bird—the Mountain Bluebird
Sagebrush Princess: Sarah Winnemucca
Sagebrush State: Nevada's official nickname
SAGE/BUIC: Semi-Automatic Ground Environment and Back-Up Interceptor Control (systems)
Sage-hen(s): Nevadan(s)
Sage of Chappaqua: Horace Greeley
Sage of Chelsea: Thomas Carlyle
Sage of Concord: Ralph Waldo Emerson—American philosopher-poet
Sage of East Aurora: Elbert Hubbard
Sage of Ebury Street: George Moore
Sage of Emporia: William Allen White
Sage of Ferney: Voltaire
Sage of Grammercy Park: Samuel H. Tilden—benefactor of the New York Public Library and governor of New York
Sage of Jena: Ernst Haeckel
Sage of Kinderhook: Martin Van Buren—eighth President of the United States
Sage of Monticello: Thomas Jefferson editor of the *Declaration of Independence*, founder of the University of Virginia, third President of the United States
Sage of Montpelier: James Madison—Father of the *Constitution*, fourth President of the United States
Sage of Mount Vernon: George Washington—first President of the United States
Sage of Nininger: Ignatius Donnelly
Sage of Philadelphia: Benjamin Franklin
Sage of Princeton: Grover Cleveland
Sage of Roanoke: John Randolph
Sage of Samos: Pythagorus
Sage of Walden Pond: Henry David Thoreau
Sage of Wheatland: James Buchanan—15th President of the United States
SAGGA: Scout and Guide Graduate Association
SAGP: Society for Ancient Greek Philosophy
SAGS: Semiactive Gravity Gradient System (NASA)
SAG & U: San Antonio, Gulf & Uvalde (railroad)
Saguaro Cactus Blossom: Arizona's state flower
sah: subarachnoid hemorrhage
SAH: Society of American Historians
Sah Esp: *Sahara Español* (Spanish Sahara)
sahf: semiautomatic height finder
SAHR: Society for Army Historical Research
sahyb: simulation of analog and hybrid computers
sai: sell (sold) as is
Sai: Saigon
SAI: Schizophrenics Anonymous International; South African Irish (regiment)
SAI: *Società Anonima Italiana* (Italian Incorporated Company); *Son Altesse Impériale* (French—Her or His Imperial Highness); *Su Alteza Imperial* (Spanish — Your Imperial Highness)
SAIA: South Australian Institute of Architects
SAIC: Special Agent in Charge (Secret Service)
said.: speech auto-instructional device
SAIF: South African Industrial Federation
SAIL: Sea-Air Interaction Laboratory

Sailor City: San Diego, California where the Navy is always welcome
Sailor King: William IV of England
Sailors's Friend: Samuel Plimsoll
Sailor Town: Norfolk, Virginia
SAIMR: South African Institute for Medical Research
SAIMS: Selected Acquisition Information and Management System
St Dymphna's disease: insanity
Saint Gotthard's disease: intestinal hookworms
St Hel: St Helena; St Helens; St Helier
St John's evil: epilepsy
St Kitts: West Indian islands of Anguilla, Nevis, and St Christopher (also often shortened to St Kitts)
St Martin's: St Martin's Press
St Martin's evil: dipsomania
Saint-Simon: Claude-Henri de Rouvroy, Compte de Saint-Simon
Saint Vitus' dance: chorea; involuntary muscular twitching
SAIRR: South African Institute of Race Relations
SAIS: School of Advanced International Studies (Johns Hopkins University)
SAIT: Southern Alberta Institute of Technology
SAJ: Society for the Advancement of Judaism
SAJ: *Suomen Ammattijärjestö* (Finnish Federation of Trade Unions)
SAJC: Southern Association of Junior Colleges
sa ji: saw jig
SAK: *Suomen Ammattilittojen Keskulitto* (Finnish—Finnish Trade Union Confederation)
Saki: Hector Hugh Munro
sal: salt; salicylate; saloon
s.a.l.: *secundum artis leges* (Latin—according to the rules of art)
Sal: Salamanca; Salaverry; Salem; Salomon
Sal: *salida* (Spanish—departure; exit); *Salmonella*
SAL: San Salvador, El Salvador (airport); Seaboard Airline Railroad; Svenska-Amerika Linien (Swedish-America Line)
SALA: Scientific Assistant Land Agent; South African Library Association; Southwest Alliance for Latin American(s)
Salad Bowl of California: Salinas in lettuce-productive Monterey County
SALALM: Seminars on the Acquisition of Latin American Library Materials
salam: salamanzar (12-bottle capacity)
sal ammoniac: ammonium chloride (NH_4Cl)
sale.: simple algebraic language for engineers
sal gal: saloon girl
salicyl: salicylate
SALJ: *South African Law Journal*
Sall: Gaius Sallustius Crispus (Roman historian often referred to as Sallust)
Sallie: Sarah
Sallust: Roman historian Gaius Sallustius
Sally: Sara(h); South Atlantic (baseball) League (nickname)
Sally Ann: Salvation Army (hobo abbreviation)
Salm: Salamon
Salm: *Salmonella*
SALM: Society of Airline Meteorologists
salmiak: sal ammoniac (ammonium chloride)
Salmon City: Astoria, Oregon
Salomon Symphonies: Haydn's last twelve symphonies written for his London impresario—the violinist Johann Peter Salomon
Salop(ian): Shrewsbury; Shropshire
SALP: South African Labour Party
SALR: *South African Law Reports*
SALRC: Society for the Assistance of Ladies in Reduced Circumstances
salt: sodium chloride (NaCl)
SALT: Strategic Arms Limitation Talks (begun in Helsinki between US and USSR on November 17, 1969)
Salt City: Syracuse, New York
saltpeter: potassium nitrate
salts of lemon: oxalic acid
salt of tartar: potassium carbonate
salut: salutation; sea-air-land-and-underwater targets (SALUT)
salv: salvage
Salv: Salvador
Salv Army: Salvation Army
Salvatoriello: Salvator Rosa
Salzburg Philospher: Balduin V. Schwarz
sam: served available market; space-available mail (SAM); surface-to-air missile (SAM); synchronous amplitude modulation
sam: *samedi* (French—Saturday)
Sam: Samoa; Samoan; Samson; Samoyed; Samuel; Samuelito
Sam: *Samstag* (German—Saturday)
S Am(er): South America(n)
SAM: School of Aerospace Medicine; Society for the Advancement of Management; Society of American Magicians; Special Air Mission
SAMA: Sacramento Air Materiel Area; Scientific Apparatus Makers Association; Student American Medical Association
SAMB: School of Aviation Medicine—Brooks AFB
SAMBA: Special Agents Mutual Benefit Association (FBI); Systems Approach to Managing Bureau of Ships Acquisitions (USN)
SAMC: South African Marine Corporation; South African Medical Corps
SAM/CAR: South America/Caribbean
SAME: Society of American Military Engineers
SAMH: Scottish Association for Mental Health
sami: socially-acceptable monitoring instrument
Samian Sage: Pythagoras of Samos
Sam J: Dr Samuel Johnson
Saml: Samiel; Samuel
SAMLA: South Atlantic Modern Language Association
Samml: *Sammlung* (German—collection)
Sammy: American soldier (British slang); Samuel
SAMNS: South African Military Nursing Service
Samoa i Sisifo: (Samoan Polynesian—Western Samoa)— formerly British Samoa
Samoas: Samoa Islands
samos (SAMOS): satellite and missile observation system
SAMPE: Society of Aerospace Material and Process Engineers
SAMS: South American Missionary Society
SAMSA: Silica and Moulding Sands Association
SAM-SAC: Special Aircraft Modification for Strategic Air

Command
SAM/SAT: South America/ South Atlantic
Sam Slick: Thomas Chandler Haliburton's nickname
SAMSO: Space and Missile System Organization (USAF)
Samson: *Samson et Dalila* (three-act opera by Saint-Saëns based on the biblical legend of Samson and Delilah)
SAM/SPAC: South America/ South Pacific
SAMTEC: Space and Missile Test Center
SA Mus: South African Museum (Cape Town)
san: sanitary; styrene-acrylonitrile copolymer
SAN: San Diego, California (Lindbergh Field); South African Navy
SAN: *Space Age News*
SANA: State (Department), Army, Navy, Air (Force)
San Antone: (Southwestern slang—San Antonio, Texas)
sanat: sanatoria; sanatorium
SANB: *South African National Bibliography*
San Berdoo: San Bernardino, California
Sanc.: *Sanctus* (Latin—holy)
SANCAD: Scottish Association for National Certificates and Diplomas
SANCAR: South African National Council for Antarctic Research
San Carlo: Teatro di San Carlo—Naples' opera house
SANCOB: South African Foundation for the Conservation of Birds
SANCOR: South African National Committee for Oceanographic Research
sand: silicon dioxide—SiO_2
Sand: *Sandford's New York Reports*
San. D.: Doctor of Sanitation
SAND: Sampling Aerospace Nuclear Debris
SANDA: Supplies and Accounts
Sandcutters: Arizonans
Sand Eng: Sandalwood English (Polynesian Pidgin English)
Sanders: Alexander
Sandhurst: Royal Military Academy at Sandhurst on the Blackwater River in southeast Berkshire, England
Sandra: Alessandra
Sandro: Alessandro
sand(s): sandwich(es)—invented by a gambler, the Earl of Sandwich, who disliked leaving the gaming table just to eat, and had thin slices of cheese or meat brought to him between two pieces of bread; his culinary invention is called a sandwich and was devised by him around 1776 when he was First Lord of the Admiralty
SANDT: School of Applied Non-Destructive Testing
Sandy: (nickname—San Diego, California; Sandra; Sandro; Saundra; a Scotsman)
sane.: severe acoustic noise environment
SANE: National Committee for a Sane Nuclear Policy
Sa Nev: Sierra Nevada(s)
San Fran: San Francisco
sanit: sanitar; sanitation; sanitize
San Jac: San Jacinto
San Juans: San Juan Islands (Washington); San Juan Mountains (Colorado and New Mexico)
sanka: sans kaffeine (coffee without caffeine)
San Le: San Leandro, California
San Martin: José de San Martín—patriot-soldier who fought to liberate Argentina, Chile, and Peru from the Spanish rule
s-a node: sino-atrial node
sanr: subject to approval—no risks
sans: sans serif
SANS: South African Naval Service
San Salvador: (Spanish—Holy Savior)—capital of the Central American republic of El Salvador; first landfall of Columbus on the outer fringe of the Bahamas where it was called Guanahani by the Lucayan Indians and Watlings Island by the British
Sansan: San Diego to San Francisco (city complex)
sansei: (Japanese—third generation)—grandchild of Japanese immigrants to the United States; (see *issei, kibei, nisei*)
Sansk: Sanskrit
Sansovino: Andrea Contucci
Sant: Santander; Santiago
SANTA: South African National Tuberculosis Association; Souvenir and Novelty Trade Association
Santa Barbaras: Santa Barbara Islands off Santa Barbara, California
SANTAS: Send A Note To A Serviceman
Santa ships: Grace Line vessels—all names begin with Santa: *Santa Clara, Santa Magdalena, Santa Teresa,* etc.
Santiagos: Santiago Mountains in the Big Bend National Park in Texas
SANU: Sudanese African National Union
SANWR: Santa Ana National Wildlife Refuge (Texas)
SANZ: Standards Association of New Zealand
SAO: São Paulo, Brazil (airport); Secret Army Organization; Smithsonian Astrophysical Observatory
SAORC: Supreme Assembly of the Order of the Rainbow for Girls
SAOS: Scottish Agricultural Organization Society
Sa_{O_2}: arterial oxygen saturation
sap: saphead
sap.: soon as possible
sap: scruple, apothecaries
SAP: San Pedro Sula, Honduras (airport); Scottish Academic Press; South African Police
SAPA: South African Press Association
SAPAT: South African Picture Analysis Test
SAPE: Society for Automation in Professional Education
SAPF: South African Police Force
SAPL: San Antonio Public Library; South African Public Library
SAPM: Scottish Association of Paint Manufacturers; Society for the Aid of Psychological Minorities
sap. no.: saponification number
sapon: saponification; saponify
saponite: soapstone (hydrous magnesium aluminum silicate)
Sapper: pseudonym of Lt Col Cyril McNeile—creator of Bulldog Drummond
sapphire: blue corundum gemstone
SAPRI: South African Plain Research Institute
SAPS: South African Price Schedule
sar: search and rescue; semiautomatic rifle; submarine advanced reactor
Sar: Saracen; Saracenic; Sardinia; Sardinian
SAR: Society of Authors' Repre-

sentatives; Solar Aircraft (company); Sons of the American Revolution; South African Railways; South African Republic; South Australian Railways
SARAH: Search and Rescue and Homing (radio lifesaving beacon)
Sarah Bernhardt: Rosine Bernard's stage name
Saraw: Sarawak
SARB: South African Reserve Bank
SARBE: Search and Rescue Beacon Equipment
SARCCUS: South African Regional Committee for the Conservation and Utilisation of the Soil
sarcol: sarcological; sarcologist; sarcology
SARD: Special Airlift Requirement Directive
Sardine Capital of the United States: Eastport, Maine
Sardine Capital of Norway: Stavanger
sardonyx: chalcedony consisting of alternate layers of onyx and sard
sare: self-addressed return envelope
sarge: sergeant
SAR & H: South African Railways and Harbours
SARHA: South African Railways, Harbours, and Airways
SARL: Sociedade Anónima de Responsabilidade Limitada (Portuguese—Limited Liability Corporation)
SARLANT: Search-and-Rescue, Atlantic
Sarmiento: Domingo Faustino Sarmiento—Argentinian educator and early president hostile to dictatorship
Sarong Girl: Dorothy Lamour
SARPAC: Search-and-Rescue, Pacific
SART: St Alban's Repertory Theater
sartac: search radar device
sartel: search and rescue telephone
sas: so and so
sas (SAS): supersonic attack seaplane
SAs: Special Agents (FBI)
SAS: Scandinavian Airlines System
SAS: Societa in Accomandita Semplice (Italian—Limited Partnership Company)
SASBO: Southeastern Association of School Business Officials
SASC: South African Staff Corps
SASCOM: Special Ammunition Support Command (USA)
sase: self-addressed stamped envelope
Sasha: (Russian nickname—Aleksandra)—Alexandra; Sandra
Sask: Saskatchewan
SASI: Society of Air Safety Investigators
SASIDS: Stochastic Adaptive Sequential Information Dissemination System
SASL: South American Saint Line
SALSO: South African Scientific Liaison Office
SASMIRA: Silk and Artificial Silk Mills Research Association
SASO: San Antonio Symphony Orchestra; South Australia Symphony Orchestra
SASOL: South African Coal, Oil, and Gas Corporation
SASR: Special Air Service Regiment
SASS: San Antonio Symphony Society
SASSO: Senior Air Staff Officer
SASSY: Supported Activity Supply System
SAST: Society for the Advancement of Space Travel
sat.: satisfactory; saturate
Sat: Satan; Satanic; Saturday; Saturn
S At: South Atlantic
SAT: San Antonio, Texas (airport); Scholastic Aptitude Test; School of Applied Tactics; Specific Aptitude Test
SATA: Sociedade Açoriana de Transportes Aéreos (Azores Air Transport Line)
SATAF: Site Activation Task Force
satan: satellite automatic tracking antenna; sensor for airborne terrain analysis
satanas: semi-automatic analog setting
Satanic City: Devils Lake, North Dakota
satar (SATAR): satellite for aerospace research
satb (SATB): soprano, alto, tenor, bass
SATC: South African Tourist Corporation
Satchel: Leroy Paige
Satchmo: Satchel-Mouth—Louis Armstrong's truncated nickname
satco: signal automatic air traffic control
satcom: satellite communication
SATCOM: Satellite Communications Agency (US Army)
satd: saturated
satel: satellite
SATENA: Servicio Aeronavegación a Territorios Nacionales (Bogotá)
SatEvePost: Saturday Evening Post
satex: semi-automatic telegraphic exchange
satfy: satisfactory
SATGA: Société Aérinne des Transports Guyane Antilles
SATIF: Scientific and Technical Information Facility (NASA)
Satirist of the Mexican Revolution: José Clemente Orozco
SAtk: strike attack
S Atl Cur: South Atlantic Current
satn: saturation
SATO: South American Travel Organization; Southern Africa Treaty Organization
SATOUR: South African Tourist Corporation
SATRA: Shoe and Allied Trade's Research Association
Sat Rev: Saturday Review
sats (SATS): short airfield for tactical support
SATs: Scholastic Aptitude Tests
sat sol: saturated solution
SATU: South African Typographical Union
Saturn: (Latin—Kronos)—god of time
SATW: Society of American Travel Writers
saty: satyagraha; satyriasis; satyr(ic)(al)(ly); satyrid
Sau: Saudi Arabia
SAUCERS: Saucer and Unexplained Celestial Events Research Society
Saudia: Saudi Arabia
SAUS: Statistical Abstract of the United States
S Austral: South Australia(n)
sav: savings; stock at valuation
Sav: Savannah
SAV: Savannah, Georgia (airport)
Savannahians: native of Savannah, Georgia
SAVE: Service Activities of Volunteer Engineers; Society of American Value Engineers; Stop Addiction through Voluntary Effort; Student Action Voters for Ecology

Savior of Babies: Nathan Straus
Savior of England: Oliver Cromwell
Savior of the Nations: sobriquet earned by the Duke of Wellington at Waterloo
savor: single-actuated voice recorder
Savoyards: performers in the Savoy Operas of W.S. Gilbert and Arthur Sullivan
SAVS: Scottish Anti-Vivisection Society
Savus: Savu Islands of Indonesia
saw.: space at will
SAW: Special Air Warfare
SAWA: Screen Advertising World Association
SAWAS: South African Women's Auxiliary Services
Sawbuck: Sears-Roebuck
Sawdust City: Oshkosh, Wisconsin's nickname based on its many sawmills
SAWE: Society of Aeronautical Weight Engineers
SAWF: Special Air Warfare Force
SAWG: Special Air Warfare Center
Sawney: (nickname—a Scotsman)
SAWS: Small Arms Weapons Study
SAWTRI: South African Wool Textile Research Institute
sax: saxophone
Sax: Saxon
Sax Duc: Saxon Duchies; Saxon Dukes
saxist: saxophonist
Saxon Shore: English coastline including Norfolk, Suffolk, Essex, Kent, Sussex, and Hampshire
SAY: Salisbury, Rhodesia (airport)
Saybolt: viscosity number
saye: save as you earn
Say Hey Kid: Willie Mays
SA y P: *San Andrés y Providencia* (Spanish—San Andres and Providence)—Caribbean island possessions of Colombia
SAZF: South African Zionist Federation
sb: simultaneous broadcast(ing); single-bayonet (lamp base); single-breasted (coat or jacket); small business; smooth bore; solid body; southbound; special bibliography; stove bolt; stretcher bearer; subbituminous; submarine (fog) bell; switchboard
sb: *styrbord* (Swedish—starboard; right side of an airplane or vessel looking forward, from Viking steering board or steering oar on right side of their long boats)
s/b: should be; surface based
Sb: *stibium* (Latin—antimony)
SB: Savings Bank; scouting-bombing (aircraft); Seaboard World Airlines (2-letter coding); Secondary Battery; Section Base; Selection Board; Senate Bill; Service Bulletin; shipbuilding; Signal Battalion; Signal Boatswain; South Buffalo (railroad); Standard Brands (stock exchange symbol); Stanford-Binet (intelligence test); Submarine Base
S.B.: *Scientiae Baccalaureus* (Latin—Bachelor of Science)
SB: *Sitzungbericht* (German—report of a proceeding)
S & B: sterilization and bath
SBA: School of Business Administration; Sick Bay Attendant; Small Business Administration
SBAC: Society of British Aerospace Companies
sbae: stabilized bombing approach equipment
S-bahn: *Stadt-Schnellbahn* (German—State Rapid Transit)—Berlin's electric railway system
SBAMA: San Bernardino Air Materiel Area
S-band: 1550–5200 megahertz radio-frequency band
SBAW: Santa Barbara Academy of the West
SBAs: Sick Bay Attendants
Sbb.: *Sabbatum* (Latin—Sunday)
SBB: Schweizerische Bundesbahnen (Swiss Federal Railways)
SBBNF: Ship and Boat Builders' National Federation
SBC: Service Bureau Corporation; Surinam Bauxite Company
SBCC: Santa Barbara City College
SBCPO: Sick-Bay Chief Petty Officer
SBCR: Stock Balance Consumption Report
sbdt: surface-barrier diffused transistor
sbe: soft-boiled egg(s); subacute bacterial endocarditis
s-b-e: standby engine(s)
SBE: State Board of Equalization
SBEA: Southern Business Education Association
S-bend: S-shaped bend
sbfc: standby for further clearance
sbg: selenite brilliant green
Sbg: Solvesborg
SBGI: Society of British Gas Industries
SBH: Scottish Board of Health
SBI: Southern Burn Institute (Baton Rouge)
sbic's: small business investment companies
SBII: *Serikat Buruh Islam Indonesia* (Central Islamic Labor Union of Indonesia)
sbis (SBIS): satellite-based interceptor systems
SBIW: Sybil Brand Institute for Women (Los Angeles correctional facility)
SBL: Stephen B(utler) Leacock
sbm: submission; submit
SBM: Société Anonymes des Bains de Mer et du Cercle des Etrangers à Monaco (company managing gambling casino of Monte Carlo)
SBMA: Santa Barbara Museum of Art
SBME: Society of Business Magazine Editors; State Board of Medical Examiners
SBMI: School Bus Manufacturers Institute
sbn: standard book number(ing)
Sb^{n}: Sebastian (Spanish—Sebastian
SBN: South Bend, Indiana (airport)
SBNO: Senior British Naval Officer
SBNS: Society of British Neurological Surgeons
sbo: secure base of operations
Sbo: Sasebo
s'board: starboard
sbom: soy bean oil meal
sbp: slotted-blade propeller; systolic blood pressure
SBP: Society of Biological Psychiatry
SBMPIM: Society of British Printing Ink Manufacturers
sbr: styrene-butadiene rubber
s Br: *südliche Breite* (German—south latitude)
SBR: Society of Biological Rhythm
SBRC: Santa Barbara Research Center
sbre: *septiembre* (Spanish—September)
SBRI: Simon Baruch Research

Institute
sbs: surveyed before shipment
sb's: sonic booms
SBS: Swiss Broadcasting Society
SBSA: Standard Bank of South Africa
SBSUSA: Sport Balloon Society of the United States
sbtg: sabotage
sbti: soy bean trypsin inhibitor
sbv: sea-bed vehicle
SBW: Seaboard & Western (Airlines); single-engine scout bomber (3-letter naval symbol)
SBWR: Seal Beach Wildlife Refuge (near Long Beach, California); South Bay Wildlife Refuge (south end of San Francisco Bay)
sbx: S-band transponder
SBX: Student Book Exchange
sby: standby
sc: sad case (slang—unpopular person); same case; separate cover; shaped charge; single circuit; single contact; sized and calendered; slow cool; small caps (small capital letters); smooth contour; statistical control; supercycle; superimposed current
s & c: shipper and carrier; sized and calendered
s/c: short circuit (electrical); single-column (bookkeeping)
sc.: *scilicet* (Latin—mainly)
s/c: *su cuenta* (Spanish—your account)
sc (SC): systolic click
Sc: scandium; stratocumulus
SC: Sacra Congregatio (Sacred Congregation); Sacramento City; Salem College; Sandia Corporation; Sanitary Corps; Scripps College; Seamen's Center; Security Council (United Nations); Service Club; Service Command; Shasta College; Shaw College; Shell Transport; Shelton College; Shenandoah College; Shepherd College; Sheridan College; Shimer College; Ship's Cook; Shorter College; Siena College; Sierra College; Signal Corps; Simmons College; Simpson College; Sinclair College; Skidmore College; Smith College; South Carolina; South Carolinian; Southern California; Southern Californian; Southern Conference; Southwestern College; Spelman College; Springfield College; Staff College; Staff Corps; Stephens College; Sterling College; Stockton College; Stonehill College; Stratford College; Strike Command; submarine chaser; Sullins College; Summary Court; Sumter & Choctaw (railroad); Suomi College; Supply Corps; Support Command; Supreme Court; Swarthmore College; Systems Command
S-C: Serbian-Croatian (people); Serbo-Croat (language); Stromberg-Carlson
S en C: *Sociedad en Comandita* (Spanish—limited partnership)—silent partnership
S-in-C: Surgeon-in-Chief
S/C: Star & Crescent (excursion steamer, ferry, towing, water-taxi service)
SCA: Schipperke Club of America; School and College Ability (test); Science Clubs of America; Screen Composers Association; Senior Citizens of America; Shipbuilders Council of America; Soybean Council of America; Stock Company Association; Sub-Contract Authorization; Suez Canal Authority; Svenska Cellulose AB; Switzerland Cheese Association; Synagogue Council of America
SCAA: State Communities Aid Association
SCAAP: Special Commonwealth African Assistance Plan
SCAC: Sunrise Cultural and Art Center (Charleston, West Virginia)
SCACOP: Southern California Area Construction Opportunity Program
scad: schedule, capability, availability, dependability
SCAD: State Commission Against Discrimination (New York)
scadar: scatter detection and ranging
SCADS: Sioux City Air Defense Sector
SCAF: Supreme Commander of Allied Forces
SCAG: Southern California Association of Governments; Supplier Corrective Action Group
sc al: steel-cored aluminum
scama (SCAMA): switching, conferencing, and monitoring arrangement
scan.: self-correcting automatic navigation; suspected child abuse and neglect; switched-circuit automatic network
Scan: Scandinavia; Scandinavian
SCAN: Scheduling and Control by Automated Network; Selected Current Aerospace Notices (NASA-computerized dissemination of information); Self-Correcting Automatic Navigator; Switched-Circuit Automatic Network
SCANCAP: System for Comparative Analysis of Community Action Programs
Scand: Scandinavia; Scandinavian
Scandinavia: Denmark, Iceland, Norway, and Sweden (the Faeroe Islands, Finland, and Greenland are sometimes included)
Scandinavian Fun Capital: Copenhagen, Denmark
ScanDoc: Scandinavian Documentation Center
scan. mag.: *scandalum magnatum* (Latin—defamation of high-placed persons)
SCANPED: System for Comparative Analysis of Programs of Educational Development
SCANs: Southern California Answering Networks (cooperative library information-retrieval system)
SCAO: Senior Civil Affairs Officer
scap: scapula; scapular; scapuloid
SCAP: Supreme Commander, Allied Powers
Scapa: (British naval contraction—Scapa Flow)
SCAPA: Society for Checking the Abuses of Public Advertising
'scape: escape(ment); landscape; seascape; skyscape
scaphocephs: scaphocephalics (narrow-skulled people)
s caps: small capital letters
scar.: subcaliber aircraft rocket; submarine celestial altitude recorder
SCAR: Scandinavian Council for Applied Research; Scientific Committee for Antarctic Research
Scarmouche: Tiberio Firoella
scard: signal conditioning and recording device
SCARF: Special Committee on the Adequacy of Range Facilities
Scarface: Mafia mobster Al Ca-

pone
Scarface Al: Alphonse Capone
Scarlet Carnation: Ohio state flower
scarp: escarpment
scat. (SCAT): speed-control attitude range; supersonic commercial air transport
scat.: *scatula* (Latin—box)
SCAT: School and College Ability Test; Service Command Air Transportation (USN)
scata: survival sited casualty treatment assemblage
SCATANA: Security Control of Air Traffic and Air Navigational Aids
SCATE: Stromberg-Carlson automatic test equipment
scat. orig.: *scatula originalis* (Latin—original box or package)
scats (SCATS): sequentially-controlled automatic transmitter start (data processing)
scat's: supersonic commercial air transports
SCATs: Southern California Acrobatic Teams
SCATS; Simulation, Checkout, and Training System
scav: scavenge
scb: strictly confined to bed (*q.v.* fob)
sc b: screw base (lamp)
Sc.B.: *Scientia Baccalaureus* (Latin—Bachelor of Science)
SCB: Sawyer College of Business
SCBA: Southern California Booksellers Association
SCBC: Somerset Cattle Breeding Centre
Sc C: Scottish Command
SCC: Shoreline Community College; Sitka Community College; Society of Cosmetic Chemists; Spokane Community College; Standard Commodity Classification; Stromberg-Carlson Corporation
SCCA: Southeastern Cottonseed Crushers Association; Sports Car Club of America
SCCAPE: Scottish Council for Commercial, Administrative, and Professional Education
SCCC: Suffolk County Community College; Sullivan County Community College
sccrt: sub-zero cooled, cold-rolled, and tempered
scd: screen door; screwed; service computation date; standard change dispenser
Sc.D.: *Scientiae Doctor* (Latin—Doctor of Science)
SCD: Specification Control Drawing
SCD: *Standard College Dictionary*
scda: scapula-dextra anterior
SCDA: Scottish Community Drama Association
SCDL: Scientific Crime Detection Laboratory
scdp: scapula-dextra posterior
sce: situationally caused error; standard calomel electrode
SCE: Schedule Compliance Evaluation; Southern California Edison
S.C.E.: Scottish Certificate of Education
SCEI: Safe Car Educational Institute
SCEL: Signal Corps Engineering Laboratories
scen: scenario(s); scenarist(s); scenographic(al)(ly)
Scenic Center of the South: Chattanooga, Tennessee's self-created sobriquet
Sceptered Isle: England; Great Britain
SCF: Save the Children Federation; Stephen Collins Foster
SCFA: Southern California Fishermen's Association
sc f & a: screw forward and aft
scfh: standard cubic feet per hour
scfm: standard cubic feet per minute
scfs: standard cubic feet per second
scg: scoring
SCG: Society of the Classic Guitar
Sc Gael: Scottish Gaelic
SCGB: Ski Club of Great Britain
SCGC: Southern California Gas Company; Southern Counties Gas Company
SCGR: Sale Common Game Refuge (Victoria, Australia)
SCGRL: Signal Corps General Research Laboratory
SCGSA: Signal Corps Ground Signal Agency
SCGSS: Signal Corps Ground Signal Service
sch: school
Sch: Schiedam; School (postal abbreviation)
SCHAVMED: School of Aviation Medicine (USN)
Schbg: Schönberg
sched: schedule
scheepv: *scheepvaart* (Dutch—navigation; shipping)
scheik: *scheikunde* (Dutch—chemistry)
schem: schematic
Schen: Schenectady
scherz: *scherzando* (Italian—jesting; in a sportive manner)
Schirmer: E.C. Schirmer (Boston); G. Schirmer (New York)
Sc Hist: Scottish History
schizo: schizoid; schizophasia; schizophrenia; schizophrenic
SCHLA: School of Latin America
Schlags: *Schlagobers* (Austrian German—whipped cream)
schlem: *schlemiel* (Yiddish—person afflicted with bad luck)
schlemazl: (victim of a *schlemiel*)
Sch Lib Sci: School of Library Science
schm: schematic
Sch M: School Master
Schmarg: Schmargendorf
Sch Mist: School Mistress
schmoo: space cargo handler and manipulator for orbital operations
Schnozzola: Jimmy Durante
schol: schola cantorum; scholar(ly); scholarship; scholastic(ally); scholasticate; scholasticism; scholiast(ic); scholium
Schoolmaster in Politics: Woodrow Wilson—twenty-eighth President of the United States
Schoolmaster of the Republic: Noah Webster
schr: schooner
Schr: *Schriften* (German—publication; script; text; writing)
Schupo: *Schutzpolizei* (German—defense police used as a paramilitary force by Hitler)
sci: science; scientific; scientist
SCI: Seamen's Church Institute; Shipping Container Institute; Shipping Corporation of India; Simulation Councils Incorporated; Society of the Chemical Industry; Sponge and Chamois Institute; Supervisory Cost Inspector
SCI: *Science Citation Index*
SCIA: Signal Corps Intelligence Agency
SCI/ARC: Southern California Institute of Architecture
Sci D: Doctor of Science
Sci D Com: Doctor of Science in Commerce
Scidgie: Sicilian-Italian (dialect)
Sci D Met: Doctor of Science in Metallurgy
sci-fi: science-fiction
scil.: *scilicet* (Latin—namely)
Scillies: Scilly Islands better re-

ferred to as the Isles of Scilly or the Sorlings
Scillonian(s): inhabitant(s) of the Isles of Scilly
scim: standard cubic inches per minute
Sci M: Science Master
Sci Mist: Science Mistress
scinti: scintillate; scintillation
scioneer: scientist + engineer
SCIPA: Servicio Cooperativo Interamericano de Producción de Alimentos (Interamerican Cooperative Service for the Production of Food)
scipp: sacrococcygeal-to-inferior pubic point
SCI & RB: South Carolina Inspection and Rating Bureau
Sci Res Assoc: Science Research Associates
Sci-Tec: Science-Technology Division (American Libraries Association)
SCI(s): Success Motivation Institutes
SCISP: ***Servicio Cooperativo Interamericano de Salud Pública*** **(Interamerican Cooperative Public Health Service)**
SCITEC: Association of the Scientific, Engineering, and Technological Community of Canada
SCI-TECH-SLA: Science-Technology Division of the Special Libraries Association
scl: scleroderma; space charge limited
SCL: Santiago, Chile (airport); Scottish Central Library; Seaboard Coast Line; Society of County Librarians; Southeastern Composers' League; Springfield City Library
scla: scapula-laeva anterior
SCLC: Southern Christian Leadership Conference
SCLH: Standing Committee for Local History; Standing Conference for Local History
SCLI: Seaboard Coast Line Industries; Somerset and Cornwall Light Infantry
sclp: scapulo-laeva posterior
Sc.M.: *Scientiae Magister* (Latin—Master of Science)
SCM: Section Communication Manager; Smith-Corona-Marchant; Special Court-Martial; Summary Court-Martial
S.C.M.: State Certified Midwife
SCMA: Southern Cypress Manufacturers Association
SCMAI: Staff Committee on Meditation, Arbitration, and Inquiry (ALA)
SCMES: Society of Consulting Marine Engineers and Ship Surveyors
Scn: Scunthorpe
SCNAWAF: Special Category Navy with Air Force
SCNM: Sunset Crater National Monument (Arizona)
SCNO: Senior Canadian Naval Officer
SCNR: Scientific Committee of National Representatives (NATO)
scns: self-contained navigation system
SCNUL: Standing Conference of National and University Libraries (UK)
SCNVYO: Standing Conference of National Voluntary Youth Organisations (UK)
SCNWR: Squaw Creek National Wildlife Refuge (Missouri)
sco: subcarrier oscillator; sustainer cutoff
ScO: Scientific Officer
SCO: Statistical Control Office(r)
scoda; scan coherent doppler attachment
SCOFF: Society for the Conquest of Flight Fear
S Coll: Staff College
SCOLLUL: Standing Conference of Librarians of Libraries of the University of London
SCOLMA: Standing Conference on Library Materials on Africa
scon: self-contained
scond: semiconductor
SCONUL: Standing Conference of National and University Libraries
scoop.: scientific computation of optimum procurement
Scoop: Senator Henry Martin (Scoop) Jackson
scop (SCOP): single copy order plan
scope: microscope; oscilloscope; telescope
SCOPE: Selected Contents of Periodicals for Educators; School-to-College Opportunity for Post high-school Education; Simple Checkout-Oriented Program Language; Special Committee on Problems of the Environment (ICSU); Student Council on Pollution and Environment
Scor: Scorpio
SCOR: Scientific Committee on Oceanographic Research
score.: signal communications by orbiting relay equipment
SCORE: Service Corps of Retired Executives
scot: steel car of tomorrow
SCORE: Service Corps of Retired Executives
Scot: Scotch; Scotland; Scotsman; Scotswoman; Scottish
SCOTAPLL: Standing Conference of Theological and Philosophical Libraries in London
Scotch: Mendelssohn's Symphony No. 3 in A minor
Scotch Bard: Robert Burns
ScotGael: Scots Gaelic
Scotland Yard: old London police headquarters near Trafalgar Square; replaced by New Scotland Yard along the Thames River Embankment
ScotNats: Scottish Nationalists
Scott: Scott, Foresman; Scott Publications; William R. Scott
Scott Fredericks: Carl Shapiro
SCOTUS: Supreme Court of the United States
Scot virus: Scottish type of influenza virus sometimes called Scotland virus
Scourge of God: Attila's nickname
Scourge of Princes: Pietro Aretino
scp: single-cell protein; spherical candlepower
SCP: Social Credit Party; Survey Control Point
SCP (AFL-CIO): Sleeping Car Porters
SCPA: South Carolina Ports Authority
SCPCU: Society of Chartered Property and Casualty Underwriters
SCPE: State Committee on Public Education
SCPI: Structural Clay Products Institute
SCPL: Social Credit Political League (New Zealand Party)
SCPN: Society of Certified Professional Numismatists
SCPO: Senior Chief Petty Officer
SCPR: Scottish Council of Physical Recreation
SCPt: security control point
SCQ: Coastal Sentry (tracking station vessel—naval symbol)
scr: screw; scruple; silicon-controlled rectifier
SCR: Signal Corps Radio; Standardized Casualty Rate
SCRA: Southern California Restaurant Association; Stanford Center for Radar Astronomy

scram: self-contained radiation monitor
scrap.: simple-complex reaction-time apparatus
SCRAP: Society for Completely Removing All Parking (Meters); Students Challenging Regulatory Agency Proceedings
Scrap Iron: baseball catcher Clint Courtney's nickname
Scrapple City: Allentown, Pennsylvania
SCRATA: Steel Castings Research and Trade Association
scr bh: screen bulkhead
SCR brick: Structural Clay Research brick
SCRC: Southern California Research Council
SCRCC: Soil Conservation and Rivers Control Council
SCRE: Scottish Council for Research in Education
SCREAM: Society for the Control and Registration of Estate Agents and Mortgage Brokers
SCREAMS: Society to Create Rapprochement among Electrical, Aeronautical, and Mechanical Engineers
SCRF: Scripps Clinic and Research Foundation
Scribner: Charles Scribner's Sons
scrim: scrimmage
scrip: scriptural; scripture
script: manuscript; prescription
Script: Scriptural; Scripture
SCRIS: Southern California Regional Information Study (Bureau of the Census)
SCRL: Signal Corps Radar Laboratory
scr's: silicon-controlled rectifiers
Scrt: Sanskrit
SCRTD: Southern California Rapid Transit District
Scrtrt: the Secretariat (UN)
Scrubs: Wormwood Scrubs
scrum: scrummage
scs: satellite control system; secret cover sheet; space command station; stabilization control system
sc & s: strapped, corded, and sealed
SCS: Society of Civil Servants; Society of Clinical Surgery; Soil Conservation Service
SCSA: Soil Conservation Society of America; Southern California Symphony Association
SCSBM: Society for Computer Science in Biology and Medicine
SCSC: South Carolina State College
SCSEA: Southern California Solar Energy Association
SCSS: Scottish Council of Social Service
sct: structural clay tile; sub-zero cooled and tempered
SCT: Society of Commercial Teachers
s/cta: *su cuenta* (Spanish—your account)
SCTE: Society of Cable Television Engineers
sctl: short-circuited transmission line
sct's: sugar-coated tablets
SCTS: Sycamore Canyon Test Site (Convair)
Sctsmn: *The Scotsman* (Edinburgh)
scty: security
SCU: Special Care Unit
SCUA: Suez Canal Users' Association
scuba: self-contained underwater breathing apparatus
scubasub: scuba-diver's submarine; scuba-diver's submersible
SCUK: South Coast of the United Kingdom
sculp: sculptor; sculpture
sculp.: *sculpsit* (Latin—he carved or engraved it)
Sculptor of the Colossal: Frédéric Auguste Bartholdi (*Liberty Enlightening the World*)
Sculptor of Great American and French Scientists and Statesmen: Jean Antoine Houdon
SCUM: Society (for) Cutting Up Men
scup: scupper
S-curve: S-shaped curve
SCUS: Supreme Court of the United States
'scutcheon: escutcheon
scv: single concave
s-c-v: single-capsulated-virulent (bacteria)
SCV: Sons of Confederate Veterans
SCV: *Santa Città Vaticana* (Italian—Holy Vatican City)—but Roman wiseacres insist SCV means *Se Cristo Vedesse* (If Christ could see!)
S.C.V.: *Stato della Città del Vaticano* (Italian—Vatican City State)
s & cv: stop and check valve
scvtr: scan-converting video tape recorder
SCW: State College of Washington
SCWC: Special Commission on Weather Modification
scwr (SCWR): supercritical water reactor
SCWS: Scottish Co-operative Wholesale Society
scx: single convex
SCYC: South Coast Yacht Club
S Cz: Salina Cruz
sd: second defense (lacrosse); self-destroying; semidiameter; shell-destroying; sight draft; single deck; sound; special duty; stage door; standard deviation; storm detection; system demonstration; systolic discharge
sd: *siehe dies* (German—see this)
s.d.: *sine die* (Latin—without date)
s-d: slow-drying
s/d: sea-damaged
s & d: search and destroy; song and dance
sD: *samme Dato* (Danish—same date)
Sd: Sound
Sd£: Sudanese pound (currency unit)
SD: San Diegan; San Diego; Secretary of Defense; Senior Deacon; snare drum; Specification for Design; Spectacle Dispenser (oculist); Standard Oil Company of California (stock exchange symbol); State Department; Superintendent of Documents; Supply Depot
SD: Social(ist) Democrat(ic) (party); *Stronnictwo Demokratyczne* (Polish—Democratic Party)
sda: sacro-dextra anterior; source data automation; specific dynamic action; succinic dehydrogenase activity
SDA: Seventh Day Adventist; Soap and Detergent Association; Source Data Automation; Students for Democratic Action
Sdad: *Sociedad* (Spanish—Society
SD & AE RR: San Diego & Arizona Eastern Railroad
S Dak: South Dakota; South Dakotan
SDAM: San Diego Aerospace Museum
SDB: Salesian of Don Bosco
sdbl: sight draft bill of lading
sd bl: sandblast
SDBRI: San Diego Biomedical Research Institute
sdc: shipment detail card; single

drift connection; submersible decompression chamber
SDC: Southern Defense Command; Special Devices Center; State Defense Council; Strategic Defense Command; Support Design Change
SDCA: Society of Dyers and Colourists of Australia
SDCC: San Diego City College
SDCCD: San Diego Community College District
SDCCs: San Diego Community Colleges
SDCE: Society of Die Casting Engineers
SD Class.: Superintendent of Documents Classification
SDCMD: San Diego Contract Management District
SD Co: San Diego County
SDCS: San Diego City Schools
s-d curve: strength-duration curve
sdd: store-door delivery
SDD: System Definition Directive
sde: self-disinfecting elastomer; simple designational expression
SDEA: South Dakota Education Association
's' death: god's death
SDEC: San Diego Ecology Center; San Diego Engineering Council; San Diego Evening College
SDECE: Service de la Documentation Extérieure et du Contre-Espionage (French equivalent of American CIA)
SDEE: Société de la Diffusion d'Equipements Electroniques
S de M: Salvador de Madariaga
sdf: single-degree-of-freedom (gyroscope)
SDF: Louisville, Kentucky (airport); Self-Defense Forces (Japan)
SDFD: San Diego Fire Department
sdg: siding
Sdg: Siding (postal abbreviation)
SDG: Self-Development Group
S.D.G.: *Solo Deo Gloria* (Latin—Glory to God Alone)
SDG & E: San Diego Gas & Electric
sdh (SDH): sorbitol dehydrogenase
sdhe: spacecraft data-handling equipment
SDHRC: San Diego Human Relations Commission
sdi: selective dissemination of information
SDI: Saudi Arabian Airlines
SDIBM: San Diego Institute for Burn Medicine
S Diego: San Diego
SDJC: San Diego Junior Colleges
sdk: shelter deck
sdl: saddle
SDL: Special Duties List(ing); Systems Dimensions Limited
SDLP: Social Democratic and Labour Party
SDMA: Surgical Dressing Manufacturers' Association
SDMC: San Diego Mesa College
SDMICC: State Defense Military Information Control Committee
sdml: seaward defense motor launch
SDMM: San Diego Museum of Man
SDMS: San Diego Memorial Society
S d N: *Sociedad de Naciones* (Spanish—League of Nations); *Sociedade de Nações* (Portuguese—League of Nations); *Società delle Nazioni* (Italian—League of Nations); *Société des Nations* (French—League of Nations)
SDN: System Designation Number
SDNHM: San Diego Natural History Museum
SDNS: Scottish Daily Newspaper Society
SDO: Santo Domingo
S Doc: Senate Document
SDOG: San Diego Opera Guild
sdp: sacro-dextra posterior; social, domestic, and pleasure
SDPD: San Diego Police Department
SDP: *Sozialdemokratische Partei Deutschlands* (Germany's Social-Democratic Party)
SDPL: San Diego Public Library
S Dpo: Station Depot
SDQ: Santo Domingo, Dominican Republic (airport)
sdr: scientific data recorder; self decoding readout; simple detection response; sodium deuterium reactor; sonar data recorder; splash-detection radar; strip domain resonance; successive discrimination reversal
SDR: Special Despatch Rider; Special Dispatch Rider; Special Drawing Rights; Special Drilling Rights
SdRng: sound ranging
SDRs: Special Drawing Rights; Special Drilling Rights
sds: speech discrimination score; sudden death syndrome
SDS: Scientific Data Systems; Samuel De Sola; Solomon De Sola; Sons and Daughters of the Soddies; Special District Services; Students for a Democratic Society (united front of communists and leftist socialists)
SDSC: San Diego State College; San Diego Steamship Company
SDSMT: South Dakota School of Mines and Technology
SDSNH: San Diego Society of Natural History
SDSO: San Diego Symphony Orchestra
SDSS: Self-Deploying Space Station
SDSU: San Diego State University
sdt: sacro-dextra transversa; scientific distribution technique; sea depth transducer; serial data transmission; serial data transmission; source distribution technique; surveillance data transmission
SDT: Society of Dairy Technology
SDTD: San Diego Transit District
sdtdl: saturating drift transistor diode logic
SDTU: Sign and Display Trades Union
sdu: shelter decontamination unit; signal display unit; spectrum display unit; subcarrier display unit
SDU: Rio de Janeiro, Brazil (Santos Dumont Airport)
SDU: *San Diego Union*
SDUK: Society for the Diffusion of Useful Knowledge; Spoiled Duck (according to Edgar Allan Poe in his essay on *How to Write a Blackwood Article*)
SDUPD: San Diego Unified Port District
SDUSD: San Diego Unified School District
sdv: slowed-down video; swimmer delivery vehicle
sdw: swept delta wing
SDX: Stromberg DatagraphiX; Sunray Mid-Continent Oil Company
SDYC: San Diego Yacht Club
SDZ: San Diego Zoo
se: second entrance; semiannual; single end; single-ended; single engine; single entry; spe-

cial equipment; spherical equivalent; standard error; straight edge
s/e: standardization/evaluation
sE: standard English
Se: selenium
SE: Sanford & Eastern (railroad); Sanitary Engineer(ing); Servel (stock exchange symbol); Southeast; Stock Exchange; Student Engineer
SE: *Son Eminence* (French—His Eminence)
sea.: sheep erythrocyte agglutination; spontaneous electrical activity
Sea: (Port of) Seattle
Sea: Symphony No. 1 by Vaughan Williams
SEA: Safety Equipment Association; Seattle, Washington (Seattle-Tacoma Airport); Ships Editorial Association; Society for Education through Art; Southeast Airlines; Southeast Asia; Southern Economic Association; Special Equipment Authorization; Students for Ecological Action; Subterranean Exploration Agency
SEA: *Sociedad Española de Automoviles* (Automobile Society of Spain)
SEAAC: South-East Asia Air Command
Seabees: Construction Battalion (USN)
Sea-born City: Venice
seac: standards electronic automatic computer
seacel: silver-chloride/magnesium cell (battery)
SEACOM: South East Asia Commonwealth Cable
seacon: seafloor construction
SEADAG: Southeast Asia Development Advisory Group
Sea Devil: Count Felix von Luckner
Sea Dogs: originally the nickname of British pirates and privateers but more recentiy applied to British seamen and other seamen
SEADS: Seattle Air Defense Sector
Sea-girt Isle: Great Britain
Sea-girt Province: Nova Scotia
Sea-green Incorruptible: Carlyle's nickname for Robespierre
Seagull: Utah's state bird and symbolic nickname sometimes given its citizens—Seagulls
Sea H: Seaforth Highlanders
seal.: sea-air-land
SEAL: South-East Area Libraries
sealab: sea laboratory (underwater research vessel)
SEALF: South-East Asia Land Forces
Sea of Lot: Dead Sea
SEALS: Sea-Air-Land Forces (counterinsurgents)
Seamen's Bible: Nathaniel Bowditch's *New American Practical Navigator*
SEAMEO: South East Asian Ministers of Education Organisation
seamount: sea mountain
Sea of the Plains: Dead Sea along the Jordan River Plain of Israel
searam: semi-active radar missile
SEARCH: System for Electronic Analysis and Retrieval of Criminal Histories; Systematized Excerpts, Abstracts, and Reviews of Chemical Headlines
Sea of Reeds: the Red Sea
SEARS: Sears, Roebuck
seasat: sea satellite
seascarp: undersea escarpment
Seashell Capital: Sanibel Island, Florida
S-E Asia: Southeast Asia (Burma, Cambodia, Hong Kong, Indonesia, Laos, Malaysia, Philippines, Singapore, Thailand, Vietnam)
sea story teller: (*see* Story Teller of the Sea)
Sea of Straw: Tagus River estuary
SEAT: *Sociedad Español de Automoviles de Turismo* (Spanish—Spanish Society of Touring Automobiles)—manufacturer's name
Seatac: Seattle-Tacoma (area)
seatainer(s): seagoing container(s)—theftproof steel containers for overseas cargo
Seatl: Seattle
SEATO: Southeast Asia Treaty Organization
sea water: 96.4% water plus 2.8% sodium chloride (common salt) and smaller quantities of magnesium chloride, magnesium sulfate, calcium sulfate, and potassium chloride; in inland seas such as the Dead Sea and the Salton Sea these percentages vary
seb: static error band
Seb: Sebastian(o)
SEB: Southern Electricity Board
SEB: *Skandinaviska Enskilda Banken* (Swedish—Scandinavian Loan Bank)
Sebastian Melmoth: name assumed by Oscar Wilde after he was released from Reading Gaol and lived in Paris until his death three years later
S & EBC: Ship and Engine Building Company
sebkha: (Arabic—marsh)
SEBM: Society of Experimental Biology and Medicine
SEBT: South-Eastern Brick and Tile (federation)
sec: secant; second; secondary; secret; section; security
sec.: *secundum* (Latin—according to)
Sec: Secretary
SEC: Section Emergency Coordinator; Securities and Exchange Commission; State Electricity Commission; Supreme Economic Council (USSR)
S.E.C.: Springfield Equipment Company
SecA: Secretary of the Army
SECA: Southern Educational Communications Association
secam: *séquential couleur à mémoire* (French—sequential color memory)—Franco-Soviet television color transmission standard sometimes translated as the system contrary to the American method (SE-CAM)
SECAM: *Séquential à Mémoire* (French—sequence and memory color television system)
secar: secondary radar
sec. art.: *secundum artem* (Latin—according to the art)
secd: second
SECDA: Southeastern Community Development Association
SECDEF: Secretary of Defense
secesh: secessionist
Sec-Gen: Secretary-General
sec. leg.: *secundum legem* (Latin—according to law)
Sec Leg: Secretary of the Legation
sec. nat.: *secundum naturam* (Latin—according to nature)
SECNAV: Secretary of the Navy
seco: second-stage engine cutoff; sustainer engine cutoff
Second Estate: The Nobility
Second International: Second International Workingmen's As-

sociation (of socialists convening in Paris in 1889 and rejecting anarchist and communist extremists)
secor (SECOR): sequential collation of range
secr: secret
sec. reg.: *secundum regulam* (Latin—according to regulations; according to rule)
secret^a: *secretaria* (Spanish—secretariat)
secs: secants; seconds
sec's: soft elastic capsules
sect: section; sector
Section 8: mental case (military code)
Secty: Secretary
SECUS: Sex Education Council of the United States
Sec'y: Secretary
sed: sedative; sediment; sedimentation; skin erythema dose
sed.: *sedes* (Latin—a chair; a stool)
SED: Scientific Equipment Division (Westinghouse)
SED: *Sozialistische Einheitspartei Deutschlands* (Germany's Socialist Unity Party)—Soviet-oriented East German Party
sedar: submerged electrode detection and ranging
SEDEIS: Société d'Etudes et de Documentation Economiques, Industrielles et Sociales (Paris)
sedi: sediment(ation)
sedi time: sedimentation time
sed rate: sedimentation rate
sedtn: sedimentation
see.: secondary electron emission; survival, evasion, and escape; systems efficiency expert(ise)
SEE: Society of Environmental Engineers
SEEA: *Société Européenne d'Energie Atomique* (French—European Atomic Energy Society)
SEEB: Southeastern Electricity Board (UK)
Seec: Saburo exhaust-emission control
SEECTS: Subaru Exhaust Emission-Control Thermal System
SEED: Skills Escalation and Employment Development; Special Elementary Education (for the underdeveloped)
SEEJ: *Slavic and East European Journal*
SEEK: Search for Elevation and Educational Knowledge (NY State dropout program); Systems Evaluation and Exchange of Knowledge
Seekers: truth-seeking Quakers
seeo: *sauf erreur et omission* (French—excepting errors and omissions)
s.e.e.o.: *salvis erroribus et omissis* (Latin—excepting errors and omissions)
seep: seagoing jeep (amphibious vehicle)
seer.: submarine explosive echo ranging
SEER: System for Electronic Evaluation and Retrieval
seex: systems evaluation experiment
sef: small end first
SEF: Space Education Foundation
SEFA: Scottish Educational Film Association
SEFT: Society for Education in Film and Television
seg: segment; segmentation; segmented; segments; segregate; segrated; segregation; segregationist
seg: *segno* (Italian—sign); *segue* (Italian—comes after; follows)
Seg: Segovia
seg (SEG): sonoencephalogram
SEG: Screen Extras Guild; Society of Economic Geologists; Society of Exploration Geophysicists; Systems Engineering Group
SEGB: South Eastern Gas Board
segm: segmented
Segr: *Segretario* (Italian—Secretary)
Segr^{to}: *Segretariato* (Italian—Secretariat)
segs: segmented neutrophils; segments
SEH: St. Elizabeth's Hospital
SEH: *Société Européenne d'Hématologie* (French— European Society of Haematology)
seha: specific emotional hazards of adulthood
sehc: specific emotional hazards of childhood
SEHMF: South of England Hat Manufacturers' Federation
SEI: Scientific Engineering Institute
SEIA: Solar Energy Industries Association
SEIC: Solar Energy Information Center; System Effectiveness Information Center
SEIF: *Secretaria de Estado da Informação e Turismo* (Portuguese—Secretariat of Information and Tourism)
SEIFSA: Steel and Engineering Industries' Federation of South Africa
Seiji: Seiji Ozawa
seis: seismograph; seismography; seismology; submarine emergency identification signal (SEIS)
SEISA: South Eastern Intercollegiate Sailing Association
Seiscor: Seismograph Service Corporation
seismo: seismograph(er); seismographic(al)(ly); seismologist; seismology
seismol: seismology
sel: selectee; selector
sel (SEL): socio-economic level
SEL: Seoul, Korea (airport); Signal Engineering Laboratories; Stanford Electronics Laboratories
SELA: Southeastern Library Association
SELA: *Sistema Económica Latino Americana* (Spanish—Latin American Economic System)
SELC: South Eastern Louisiana College
sel-cl: self-closing
selectric: single-element electric typewriter
selen: selenography; selenology
self-prop: self-propelled
Selk: Selkirk
Selkirks: Selkirk Mountains of British Columbia
SELMA: S.E.L. Maduro
Selma Lagerlöfland: Sweden's province of Värmland where the Nobel prize-winning authoress was born
SELNEC: South-East Lancashire North-East Cheshire
sels: selsyn
selsyn: self-synchronous
Selvagens: Selvagen Islands between the Canaries and Madeira
Selw: Selwyn College—Cambridge
Sely: southeasterly
sem: scanning electron microscope; semi; semicolon; seminal; slow eye movements; standard error of mean; systolic ejection murmur
sem.: *semen* (Latin—seed); *semper* (Latin—always; ever)
sem (SEM): systolic ejection murmur

Sem: Seminary; Semitic
SEM: Society for Ethno-Musicology
SEMA: Spray Equipment Manufacturers' Association
seman: semantic(s)
semcor: semantic correlation
SEMFA: Scottish Electrical Manufacturers' and Factors' Association
semi: semicolon
semicol: semicolon
semidr.: *semidrachma* (Latin—half drachma)
semidur: semiduration
semih.: *semihora* (Latin—half hour)
Seminex: Seminary in Exile
semiot: semiotic(al)(ly); semiotician; semiotics
semp: *sempre* (Italian—always)
semipro: semiprofessional(ly)
semis: semifinished; semitrailers
sems: screw and washer assemblies
SEMT: Société d'Etudes des Machines Thermiques (Society for the Study of Thermal Machines)
sem ves: seminal vesicle
sen: *seno* (Italian—sine); *senza* (Italian—without)
Sen: Senate; Senator
Sen: Marcus (or Lucius) Seneca (Roman rhetorician) or his second son Lucius Annaeus Seneca (Roman author); *Senatore* (Italian—senator)
SEN: State-Enrolled Nurse
Senator Sam: U.S. Senator Sam Ervin, Jr., of North Carolina
S en C: *Société en Commandite* (French—limited partnership)
Sen Clk: Senior Clerk
Sen Doc: Senate Document
Seneg: Senegal; Senegalese
Senegambia: Senegal + Gambia
S Eng O: Senior Engineering Office(r)
senior(s): senior citizen(s)
Sen M: Senior Master
Sen Mist: Senior Mistress
S en NC: *Société et Nom Collectif* (French—joint stock company)
senr: senior
Sen Rept: Senate Report
Senr Tech Weld I: Senior Technician of the Welding Institute
sens: sensitivities (test)
sensistor: semiconductor resistor
sent.: sentence
Sent: *Sentyabr* (Russian—September)
Sen Wt O: Senior Warrant Officer
seo: *salvo errori e omissioni* (Italian—excepting errors and omissions)
Seo: Seoul
SEO: Senior Experimental Officer
SEODSE: Special Explosive Ordnance Disposal Supplies and Equipment (USA)
SEOG: Supplemental Educational Opportunity Grant
SE1, SE2, etc.: Southeast One, Southeast Two, etc. (London postal zones)
seoo: *sauf erreurs ou omissions* (French—excepting errors and omissions)
seou: *salve error u omisión* (Spanish—except for error or omission)
sep: separate; separation
sep (SEP): somatosensory-evoked potential
Sep: September
SEP: Selective Employment Payments (UK); Society of Engineering Psychologists; Society of Experimental Psychologists; Student Expense Program
SEP: *Saturday Evening Post*
SEPA: Southeastern Power Association
separ.: *separatum* (Latin—separately)
SEPE: Seattle Port of Embarkation
Seph: *Sephardim* (Hebrew—Jews from Portugal and Spain)
SEPO: Space Electric Power Office (AEC)
SEPR: Société pour l'Etude de la Propulsion par Réaction
SepRos: separation processing
SEPSA: Society of Educational Programmers and Systems Analysts
sept.: *septem* (Latin—seven)
Sept: September
SEPTA: Southeastern Pennsylvania Transportation Authority
sept^e: *septiembre* (Spanish—September)
septel: separate telegram
Septober: September and October
seq: sequence
seq.: *sequens* (Latin—the following); *sequente* (Latin—what follows); *sequitur* (Latin—it follows)
seq. luce: *sequenti luce* (Latin—the following day)
Seq NP: Sequoia National Park
S Equ Cur: South Equatorial Current
ser: serial; series
ser: *série* (French—series)
ser (SER): serine (amino acid)
SER: Soil Erosion Service
SER: *Sociedad Española Radiodifusión* (Spanish Broadcasting Society)
Sera: Seraphim
SERA: Services, Education, Rehabilitation for Addiction
Serb: Serbia; Serbian
SEREB: Société pour l'Etude et la Réalisation d'Engins Balistiques
serendip: serendipitous(ly); serendipity
SERI: Solar Energy Research Institute
Serg: *Sergente* (Italian—Sergeant)
Serg Magg: *Sergente Maggiore* (Italian -Sergeant Major)
Serg(t): Sergeant
SERL: Services Electronics Research Laboratory
SERLANT: Service Forces, Atlantic (USN)
serm: sermon
SERM: Society of Early Recorded Music
serol: serology
SERPAC: Service Forces, Pacific (USN)
serpentine: hydrous magnesium silicate
Serpentine Suicide: Harriet Shelley—sad first wife of the poet. She drowned herself in the Serpentine of London's Hyde Park.
SERPLANT: Service Forces, Atlantic (USN)
serr: serrate
serra: (Italian—mountain range)
serran^ia: *(Spanish—mountainous region)*
ser sect: serial sections
sert: space electronic rocket test
serv: service
serv.: *serva* (Latin—keep; preserve)
Serv: Servia(n)
serv chge: service charge
serv clg: service ceiling
SERVE: Serve and Enrich Retirement by Volunteer Experience
Servetus: Michael Servetus whose real name was Miguel Servet although neither name saved him for once he escaped the Spanish Inquisition he was burned at the stake in Switzerland by order of Cal-

vin

servo: anything using a servomechanism; servoamplifier, servocontrol, servodyne, servomotor, servosystem

serv^o: *servicio* (Spanish—service)

serv^or: *servidor* (Spanish—servant)

servos: servomechanisms

Seryozha: (Russian nickname—Sergei)—Serge

ses: secondary engine start; single-ended scotch (boilers); socioeconomic strata; solar environment stimulator; surface-effect ship

SES: Society of Engineering Science; Solar Energy Society; Standards Engineers Society; State Employment Service; Steam Engine Systems

SESA: Social and Economic Statistics Administration; Society for Experimental Stress Analysis; Solar Energy Society of America

SESAC: Society of European Stage Authors and Composers

SESAME: Search for Excellence in Science and Mathematics Education

sesco: secure submarine communications

se (sem): standard error of the mean

SESL: Space Environment Simulation Laboratory

SESO: Senior Equipment Staff Officer

sesoc: surface-effects ship for ocean commerce

sesquih: *sesquihora* (Latin—an hour and a half)

sess: session

SESS: Space Environmental Support System; Summer Employment for Science Students

set.: settlement

set: *setembro* (Portuguese—September)

SET: Scientists, Engineers, Technicians; Security Escort Team; Senior Electronic Technician; Simplified Engineering Technique; Synchro Error Tester

S.E.T.: Selective Employment Tax

SETAF: Southern European Task Force

SETCO: Summit and Elizabeth Trust Company

set^e: *septiembre* (Spanish—September)

SETIL: Société de l'Equipement de Tahiti et des Iles (Equipment Company of Tahiti and the Islands)

S-et L: Saône-et-Loire

S-et-M: Seine-et-Marne

S-et-O: Seine-et-Oise

SETP: Society of Experimental Test Pilots

SETS: Solar Energy Thermionic Conversion System

sett: settling

sett: *settembre* (Italian—September)

SEU: Southeastern University

SEUA: South Eastern Underwriters Association

seuo: *salvo error u omision* (Spanish—errors and omissions excepted)

SEUS: Southeastern United States

sev: sever

sev: *sever* (Russian—north)

Sev: Sevilla; Seville

SEV: *Soviet Ekonomischeskoy Vzaimopomoschchi* (Russian—Soviet Council for Mutual Economic Aid)—the COMECON

Seven Deadly Sins: Anger, Covetousness, Envy, Gluttony, Lust, Pride, Sloth

Seven Provinces: (*see* United Provinces)

Seven Sages of Greece: Bias, Chilon, Cleobulus, Periander, Pittacus, Solon, Thales

Seven Seas: Antarctic, Arctic, Indian, North Atlantic, South Atlantic, North Pacific, South Pacific oceans; term also applied to the Andaman, Baltic, Bering, Caribbean, Mediterranean, South China, and Yellow seas

Seven Sisters: Barnard, Bryn Mawr, Mount Holyoke, Radcliffe, Smith, Vassar, and Wellesley—all colleges for women when first organized

Seven Sisters: BP (British Petroleum), Exxon (Esso—Standard Oil), Gulf, Mobil, Shell, SOCAL (Standard Oil of California — Chevron), Texaco—world's leading oil companies

Seven Wonders of the Ancient World: Pyramids of Egypt, Lighthouse of Pharos of Alexandria, Hanging Gardens and Walls of Babylon, Temple of Artemis or Diana at Ephesus, Statue of Zeus by Phidias at Olympia, Mausoleum at Halicarnassus, Colossus of Rhodes

Seven Wonders of the Modern World: Fort Peck Dam across the Missouri in Montana; Pecos, Texas oilwell; Royal Gorge Bridge in Colorado; Simplon Tunnel between Italy and Switzerland; TV Tower at Blanchard, North Dakota; Verrazano-Narrows Bridge over New York Harbor; World Trade Center in downtown New York—each represents an engineering superlative—the biggest dam, the deepest well, the highest bridge, the longest tunnel, the tallest structure, the longest single-span bridge, the tallest buildings

SEVFLT: Seventh Fleet, Pacific (USN)

sevocom: secure voice communications

sew.: sewage; sewer; sewerage

Seward's Folly: nickname given Alaska in 1867 when Secretary of State William H. Seward purchased the area from Russia for $7,200,000 and it was said he bought a collection of icebergs and polar bears; it was also called Seward's Polar Bear Garden

SEWT: Simulator for Electronic Warfare Training

sex.: sextet; sexual

Sexag: Sexagesima

sexcite: excite sexually

SExO: Senior Experimental Officer

sexcitement: sexual excitement

sexorgies: sexual orgies

sexpert: sex expert; sexual expert; sexpertise

sexploitation: sex(ual) exploitation

sexplosion: sexual explosion

sexslanguage: sexual slang language

sexploiter: sex exploiter

sexploit(s): sexual exploit(s)

s. expr.: *sine expressione* (Latin—without expressing; without pressing)

sext: sextant

Seychelles: Seychelles Islands

sf: safety factor; salt free; science fiction; semifinished; single-feed; single feeder; sinking fund; sound and flash; special facilities; spinal fluid; spotface; standard form;

stress formula; sulphation factor; sunkface
sf: *sans frais* (French—without expense); *sforzando* (Italian—accented strongly; forced; reinforced)
s.f.: *sub finem* (Latin—near the end)
SF: San Franciscan; San Francisco; Santa Fe, New Mexico; Santa Fe (Atchison, Topeka & Santa Fe Railway); Scouting Force; Security Force; Security Forces; Shipfitter; Special Facilities; Special Forces; Standard Frequency; Swedenborg Foundation; Swiss Federation (auto plate); Syrian Forces
SF: *Slovenska Filharmonica* (Serbo-Croat—Slovene Philharmonic—in Ljubljana, Yugoslavia;) *Socialistisk Folkeparti* (Dano-Norwegian—Socialist People's Party); *Système français* (French system, of screw threads)
S/F: *Sinn Fein* (Irish Gaelic—Ourselves Alone)
sfa: simulated flight automatic; slow flying aircraft; spatial frequency analyzer
s & fa: shipping and forwarding agent
SFA: Saks Fifth Avenue; Scandinavian Fraternity of America; Scientific Film Association; Show Folks of America; Slide Fastener Association, ***Société Française d'Astronautique (French Astronautical Society); Solid Fuels Administration; Soroptimist Federation of the Americas; Southeastern Fisheries Association; Symphony Foundation of America***
SFAAW: Stove, Furnace, and Allied Appliance Workers (International Union of North America)
SFAC: Société des Forges et Ateliers du Creusot (Schneider-Creusot Forges and Factories)
SFAD: Society of Federal Artists and Designers
SFAO: San Francisco Assay Office
sfar: sound fixing and ranging
SFAR: System Failure Analysis Report
SFB: Sender Freies Berlin (Free Berlin Broadcasting Station); Spencer Fullerton Baird
SFBARTD: San Francisco Bay Area Rapid Transit District
sf bh: surface broach
SFBMS: Small Farm Business Management Scheme
SFBNS: San Francisco Bay Naval Shipyard
sfc: S-bank frequency converter; sight fire control; specific fuel consumption; supercritical fluid chromatography; switching filter connector; synchronized framing camera
sfc (SFC): spinal fluid count
Sfc: Sergeant First Class
SFC: Saint Francis College; Sioux Falls College; Space Flight Center
SFC: *San Francisco Chronicle*
SFCC: San Francisco City College
SFCM: San Francisco Conservatory of Music
SFCMD: San Francisco Contract Management District
SFCP: Shore Fire Control Party
SFCTA: San Francisco Classroom Teachers Association
sfcw: search for critical weakness
SFCW: San Francisco College for Women
sfe: stacking fault energy; surface-energy
SFE: Society of Fire Engineers
SFEA: Survival and Flight Equipment Association
SFEL: Standard Facility Equipment List
sff: *se faz favor* (Portuguese—please)
SFF: Solar Forecast Facility
sfff: salt-free fat-free (diet)
SFG: *Studien und Förderungsgesellschaft* (German—Studies and Advancement Society)
sfgd: safeguard
SFGGB: San Francisco Golden Gate Bridge
SFGH: San Francisco General Hospital
SFHS: Stephen Foster High School
SFI: Sport Fishing Institute
SFI: *Société* Financière *Internationale* (French—International Finance Corporation)
SFIO: *Section Française de l'Internationale Ouvriere* (French section of the Worker's International)—former name of the French Socialist Party
SFIT: Standard Family Interaction Test
sfl: sequenced flashing lights (airport runways)
s fl: Surinam florin
SFL: Society of Federal Linguists
sfm: surface feed per minute; surface feet per minute
SFMA: San Francisco Museum of Art
SFMC: San Francisco Medical Center (University of California
SFMR: San Francisco Municipal Railway (operates the cable cars)
SFMS: Shipwrecked Fishermen and Mariners (Royal Benevolent Society
SF & NV: San Francisco & Napa Valley (railroad)
sfo: simulated flame out; submarine fog oscillator
S Fo: (Port of) San Francisco
SFO: San Francisco, California (airport); San Francisco-Oakland Airlines; San Francisco Opera; Service Fuel Oil; Space Flight Operations
SF-OBB: San Francisco-Oakland Bay Bridge (Transbay Bridge)
SFOD: San Francisco Ordnance District; Special Forces Operational Detachment
SFOF: Space Flight Operations Facility
SFP: Sherbrooke Forest Park (Victoria, Australia)
SFPDis: San Francisco Procurement District (US Army)
sf pe: surface plate
SFPE: San Francisco Port of Embarkation; Society of Fire Protection Engineers
SFPL: San Francisco Public Library
sfpm: surface feet per minute
SFPR: Society of Friends of Puerto Rico
sfprf: semifireproof
sfqa (SFQA): structurally fixed question-answering system
sfr (SFR): submarine fleet reactor
SFR: Safety of Flight Requirement
SFRA: Science Fiction Research Association
S Fran: San Francisco
SFRJ: Socijalisticka Federativna Republika Jugoslavija (Socialist Federated Republic of Yugoslavia)
sfrr: sinking fund rate of return
SFRS: Sea Fisheries Research Station (Haifa)
sfs: strictly for suckers; surfaced four sides
SFs: Special Forces (Green Ber-

ets)

SFS: San Francisco Symphony

s 4 s: smooth 4 sides

SFSA: Steel Founders' Society of America

SFSAFBI: Society of Former Special Agents of the Federal Bureau of Investigation

SFSC: San Francisco State College

SF & SC: Standard Fruit & Steamship Company

SFSE: San Francisco Stock Exchange

SFSO: San Francisco Symphony Orchestra

SFSSP: Society of the Friendly Sons of St Patrick

sft: soft; specified financial transactions; stop for tea; superfast train

SFTA: Scientific Film Television Award; Society of Film and Television Arts

SFTI: San Fernando Technical Institute (Trinidad)

SFU: Simon Fraser University

S_f units: Svedberg flotation units

sfv: sight feed valve

SFVAH: San Francisco Veterans Administration Hospital

SFVSC: San Fernando Valley State College

SFWA: Science Fiction Writers of America

sftwd: softwood

sftwr: software (officialese for paperwork as opposed to hardware)

SFWR: Stewardesses for Women's Rights

sfx: sound effects (radio or television)

sfxd: semifixed

sfxr: superflash X-ray

sfy: standard facility year(s)

SFYC: San Francisco Yacht Club

sfz: *sforzando* (Italian—accented strongly; forced; reinforced)

sg: screen grid; single groove; singular; smoke generator; soluble gelatin; specific gravity; steel girder; structural glass; swamp glider

s-g: sub-generic; sub-genus

sg: *selon grandeur* (French—according to size); on menus, sg or SG indicates an item is priced according to the size of the serving

Sg: spring range of tide

SG: Aerotransporte Litoral Argentino (Argentine Coastal Air Transport); Scots Guards; Solicitor General; South Georgia (railroad); Standing Group; Sunset Gun; Surgeon General

S-G: Saint-Gobain; Space-General (Corporation)

SGA: Saskatchewan Government Airways; Society of the Graphic Arts; Southern Gas Association; Standards of Grade Authorization; Student Government Association

SGAE: *Sociedad General de Autores de España* (General Society of Authors of Spain)

S-gauge: standard gauge (4-foot 8 1/2-inch) railroad track

SGB: Société Générale de Belgique

SGBIP: *Subject Guide to Books in Print*

sgc: screen grid current; simulated generation control; spartan guidance computer (SGC); spherical gear coupling; stabilizer gyro circuit

Sg C: Surgeon Captain

SGC: Saint Gregory College; South Georgia College

S-G C: Space-General Corporation

SGCA: *Secrétariat Général à l'Aviation Civil* (French—Secretariat General of Civil Aviation)

Sg Cr: Surgeon Commander

sgd: signed

SGD: Senior Grand Deacon

sgdg: *sans garantie du gouvernement* (French—patent issued without government guarantee)

sg di: swaging die

S Ge: South Georgia

SGF: Scottish Grocers' Federation

sgg: sustainer gas generator

sghwr: steam-generating heavy-water reactor

SGI: Spring Garden Institute

SGINDEX: System Generation Cross-Reference Index (NASA)

SGIO: State Government Insurance Office

sgl: signal; single

Sg L Cr: Surgeon Lieutenant Commander

SGLS: Space-Ground Link Subsystem

SGM: Sea Gallantry Medal

sg md: swaging mandrel

SGMT: Société Générale des Transports Maritimes

Sgn: (Port of) Saigon

SGN: Saigon, Vietnam (airport); Surgeon General of the Navy

sgnr: signature

SGO: Surgeon General's Office

sgot: serum glutamic oxaloacetic transaminase

sgp: starch graft polymers

SGP: Shell Gasification Process; Society of General Physiologists

SGP: *Staatkundig Gereformeerde Partij* (Dutch—Political Reformed Party)

sgpt: serum glutamic pyruvic transaminase

sgr: steam gas recirculation (oil-from-shale removal process)

SGR: Sumbu Game Reserve (Zambia)

Sg RA: Surgeon Rear Admiral

SGS: Sunderbans Game Sanctuary (Bangladesh)

SGSB: Stanford Graduate School of Business

SGSR: Society for General Systems Research

Sgt: Sergeant

SGT: Society of Glass Technology

S-G Test: Sachs-Georgi Test

Sgt 1/C: Sergeant First Class

Sgt Maj: Sergeant Major

SGU: Scottish Gliding Union; Scottish Golf Union; Singapore Golfers Union

Sg VA: Surgeon Vice Admiral

SGVHS: Samuel Gompers Vocational High School

SGW: Senior Grand Warden

SGX: Seeger Refrigerator Express (stock exchange symbol)

sh: scleroscope hardness; serum hepatitis; ship's heading; shop; shopping; sick in hospital; social history; somatotrophic hormone; surgical hernia

s/h: shorthand

Sh: shells; shilling (British East Africa)

SH: Schenley Industries (stock exchange symbol); Soldier's Home; Station Hospital; Symphony Hall

S-H: Scripps-Howard

S & H: Sperry & Hutchinson (green stamps); Sundays and Holidays

sha (SHA): sidereal hour angle

SHA: Safety and Health Administration; Southern Historical Association

SHAA: Society of Hearing Aid Audiologists

shab: soft and hard acids and bases

sh abs: shock absorber

SHAC: Seale-Hayne Agricultural College
shaco: shorthand coding
SHAEF: Supreme Headquarters, Allied Expeditionary Forces
shags: shaggy carpets or rugs
Shah: *Shahanshah* (Persian—King of Kings)
Shak(e): Shakespeare
Shakes: Shakespeare
Shalom Aleichem: Solomon Rabinowitz' pseudonym
Sham: Shamrock
shamateur(s): sham amateur(s)
shamburger: sham hamburger (containing more additives and adulterants than meat)
SHAME: Save, Help Animals Man Exploits
shamrock: symbol of Ireland and the Irish
shandy: shandygaff (beer-and-ginger-ale mixture)
Shang: Shanghai
Shank End: Cape Peninsula below Cape Town, South Africa
shan't: shall not (colloquial)
SHAPE: Supreme Headquarters, Allied Powers, Europe
SHARP: Ships Analysis and Retrieval Project
SHAS: Shared Hospital Accounting System
Shaston: Shaftesbury, England
SHAWCO: Students Health and Welfare Centers Organization
SHB: Svenska Handelsbanken (Swedish Bank of Commerce)
shbd: serum X-hydroxy-butyrate dehydrogenase
shbg: sex-hormone-binding globulin
SHC: Sacred Heart College; Seton Hall College; Siena Heights College; Spring Hill College; Streets and Highways Code; Surveillance Helicopter Company
SHCJ: Society of the Holy Child of Jesus
shco: sulfonated hydrogenated castor oil
sh con: shore connection
shd: should
SHD: Scottish Home Department; State Hydroelectric Department
she.: signal handling equipment; standard hydrogen electrode
Shearith Israel: (Hebrew—Remnant of Israel)—oldest American congregation of Jews whose first synagogue was on Mill Street in New York City and now is at Central Park West and Seventieth Street
she'd: she had; she would
Sheed: Sheed & Ward
Sheff: Sheffield
Sheila: Cecilia
she'll: she will
SHELL: Shell Oil Company
SHELREP: Shelling Report
Shelty: Shetland pony
Shen NP: Shenandoah National Park
Sher: Sherbrooke
Sheridan: Sheridan House
Sherlock: nickname for a supersleuth detective; Sherlock Holmes; Sherlockian(s); (*see* Dr Watson)
she's: she has; she is
Shet: Shetland
Shetlands: Shetland Islands
Shevvie(s): native(s) of Sheffield, Yorkshire
Shex: Sundays and holidays excepted
shf: super high-frequency—300-30,000 mc
Shf: Sheffield
SHFF: Scottish House Furnishers' Federation
S-H-G diet: Sauerbruch-Herrmannsdorfer-Gerson (tubercular) diet
SHH: Sociedad Honoraria Hispánica
Shi: Shanghai
Shick - Shocks: Shick-Shock Mountains of Québec
Shig: *Shigella*
Shillelagh: anti-tank surface-to-surface guided missile produced by Aeronutronic
Shim: Shimonoseki
shinerium: shoe-shine stand
ship.: shipment; shipping
SHIP: Self-Help Improvement Program
Ship of the Desert: the camel
ShipDTO: ship on depot transfer order
shipmt: shipment
SHJC: Sacred Heart Junior College
shk: shank
Shl: Shields; shoal
Sh L: Shipwright Lieutenant
SHL: Society for Humane Legislation
shld: shoulder
shl dk: shelter deck
SHLM: Society of Hospital Laundry Managers
shlp: shiplap
Shls: Shoals (postal abbreviation)
shm: simple harmonic motion
Shm: Shoreham
SHM: Service Hydrographique de la Marine (Naval Hydrographic Service)
SHMO: Senior Hospital Medical Officer
shnoz: shnozzle; shnozzola
shmt: shock mount
SHNHS: Sagamore Hill National Historic Site
SHNNR: Studland Heath National Nature Reserve (England)
ShNP: Shenandoah National Park
SHO: Senior House Officer; Student Health Organization
SHOC: Self-Help Opportunity Center
SHOCK: Students Hot on Conserving Kilowatts
shocks.: shock absorbers
S. Holmes, Esq: Sherlock Holmes
shoran: short-range navigation
shorlans: armored cars built on the shores of Northern Ireland
shortg: shortage
short(s): short circuit(s)
shorted: short circuited (electrical parlance)
SHOT: Society for the History of Technology
shouldn't: should not
show biz: show business
Show-Me State: Missouri's official nickname
shp: shaft horsepower
SHPBG: Small Horticultural Production Business Grant
SHPC: Scenic Hudson Preservation Conference
shpt: shipment
SHP Test: Strongin-Hinsie-Peck (salivary secretion) Test
SHQ: Station Headquarters
shr: share(s)
Shr: Shore (postal abbreviation)
shram (SHRAM): short-range air-to-surface missile
shrap: shrapnel
SHRMA: South Hampton Roads Metropolitan Area (Norfolk, Portsmouth, Chesapeake, and Virginia Beach)
Shrops: Shropshire
Shrs: Shores (postal abbreviation)
shrtg: shortage
shs: ship's heading servo
SHS: Sacred Heart Seminary; Senior High School; Stuyvesant High School
SHS: *Srba, Hrvata, i Slovenaca* (Serbo-Croatian — Serbs, Croats, and Slovenes)—Yugoslavia
SHSA: Steamship Historical So-

ciety of America
SHSL: Sherlock Holmes Society of London
SHSLB: Street and Highway Safety Lighting Bureau
SHSN: Sod House Society of Nebraska
SHSP: Sam Houston State Park (Louisiana)
SHSS: Sanford Hypnotic Susceptibility Scale
SHSSI: Steamship Historical Society of Staten Island
sht: sheet
SHT: Society for the History of Technology
shtg: shortage
sht mtl: sheet metal
sh tn: short ton
SHU: Seton Hall University
Shula: Shulamite; Shulamith
shv: solenoid hydraulic valve
s.h.v.: *sub hoc voce* (Latin—under this work)
shw: safety, health, and welfare
SHW: Sherwin-Williams (stock exchange symbol)
S & H x: Sundays and Holidays excepted
SHYC: Sachem's Head Yacht Club
si: salinity indicator; short interest; slight imperfection; sçark ignition; straight-in (aircraft landing approach); subicteric; subindex; subinguinal
s-i: semiconductor-integrated (circuits)
s/i: signal/intermodulation; subject issue
s & i: stocked and issued
si (SI): shift-in character (data processing)
Si: Silas; silicon (symbol); Simon; Simone
SI: Sandwich Islands; Saturday Inspection; Serra International; Sertoma International; Service Instruction; Shipping Instruction(s); Smithsonian Institution; Society of Illustrators; Spokane International (railroad); Staff Inspector; Staten Island; Stevens Institute; Sulfur Institute; Survey Instruction(s)
SI: *Système International des Unités* (French—International System of units)
S-I: Spokane International (railroad)
sia: subminiature integrated antenna
sia (SIA): storage instantaneous audimeter
SIA: Sanitary Institute of America; School of International Affairs (Columbia University); Self-Insurers Institute; Ski Industries of America; Society of Insurance Accountants; Soroptimist International Association; Sprinkler Irrigation Association; Standard Instrument Approach; Strategic Industries Association
SIA: *Schweizerischer Ingenieur und Architekten Verein* (German—Swiss Institute of Engineers and Architects)
SIAD: Society of Industrial Artists and Designers
SIAE: *Società Italiano degli Autori ed Editori* (Italian Society of Authors and Editors)
sial: silicon + aluminum (Si + Al)
siam: signal information and monitoring
SIAM: Society for Industrial and Applied Mathematics
SIAO: Smithsonian Institution Astrophysical Observatory
SIAP: *Sociedad Interamericana de Planificación* (Spanish—Interamerican Planning Society)
sib: satellite ionospheric beacon(s); sibilant; sibling; sibship
Sib: Siberia; Siberian
SIB: Shipbuilding Industry Board; Society of Insurance Brokers; Soviet Information Bureau
SIBC: *Socété Internationale de Biologie Clinique* (French—International Society of Clinical Biology)
Sib Or: *Sibylline Oracles*
Sibr: Siberia
sibs: siblings
SIBS: Salk Institute for Biological Studies
sic: specific inductance capacity
sic: (Latin—so written)
sic.: *siccus* (Latin—dry)
Sic: Sicilian; Siciliana; Siciliano; Sicily
SIC: Scientific Information Center; Security Intelligence Corps; Société International de Cardiologie; Société Internationale de Chirurgie; Société Intercontinentale des Containers; Standard Industrial Classification; Survey Information Center
SICA: Society of Industrial and Cost Accountants
sicbm (SICBM): super-intercontinental ballistic missile
SICC: Staten Island Community College
Sick Man of Europe: Turkey in the last years of the Ottoman Empire and the reign of the sultans during most of the nineteenth century and up to 1922 when the sultanate was abolished
SICOT: *Société Internationale de Chirurgie Orthopédique et de Traumatologie* (French— International Society of Orthopedic Surgery and Traumatology)
SICR: Specific Intelligence Collection Requirement
sicsva: sequential-impaction cascade-seive volumetric air (sampler)
sic transit: *sic transit gloria mundi* (Latin—so passes away the glory of the world)
sid: sidereal; standard instrument departure; sudden infant death; sudden ionospheric disturbance
Sid: Sidney; Sydney
S.i.D.: *Spiritus in Deo* (Latin—His Spirit is with God)—he's dead
SID: Security and Intelligence Department; Society for Information Display; Society for International Development; Society for Investigative Dermatology; Standard Instrument Departure; Sudden Ionospheric Disturbance Division
SIDA: Swedish International Development Agency
sidase: significant data selection
Siddhartha: Gautama Buddha
SIDEC: Stanford International Development Education Center
sids: sudden infant-death syndrome
SIDs: Sports Information Directors
SIDS: *Société Internationale de Défense Sociale* (French—International Society of Social Defense)
SIE: Scientific information Exchange; Society of Industrial Engineers; Southwestern Industrial Electronics
SIEC: Scottish Industrial Estates Corporation
SIECUS: Sex Information and Educational Council of the United States
SIEE: Student of the Institution

of Electrical Engineers
Siem: Siemensstadt
Sierra: code for letter S
Sierras: Sierra Nevada Mountains; Sierra Mountains
SIES: Soils and Irrigation Extension Service
sif: selective identification feature
SIFE: Society of Industrial Furnace Engineers
SIFF: Suomen Illmailuliitto Finlands Flygforbund (Finnish Aeronautical Association)
sif/iff: selective identification feature/identification friend or foe
SIFS: Special Instructors Flying School
sig: signal; signaling; signature
sig.: *signetur* (Latin—mark with directions)
Sig: Siegfried; Sieglinde; Sigdrifa; Sigmund; Sigmunt; Sigsbee; Sigurd; Sigyn
Sig: *Signor* (Italian—Mister; Sir); *Signore* (Italian—Gentlemen; Our Lord; Sir); *Signori* (Italian—Gentlemen; Lords)
SIG: Snowy Irrigation Scheme (Snowy Mountains Authority—Australia)
siga: sigatoka (banana leaf spot disease)
Sig^a: *Signora* (Italian—Missus)—Mrs
SigC: Signal Corps
Sigg: *Signori* (Italian—Messrs)
sigill.: *sigillum* (Latin—seal)
sigint: signals intelligence
Sig L: Signal Lieutenant
Siglo de Oro: (Spanish—Golden Age)—the Spanish Century before and after 1600 when discovery and colonization were matched by great artistic and literary productions
SIGMA: Science in General Management
Sigmn: Signalman
sigmoido: sigmoidoscopy
Sigmund Fraud: nickname of anyone practicing psychiatry without a license
sign.: signature
Sig^{na}: *Signorina* (Italian—Miss)
sig. nom. pro.: *signa nomine proprio* (Latin—label with the proper name)
Sig O: Signal Officer
Sig Sam Lib: Sigmund Samuel Library (Toronto)
Sig Und: Sigrid Undset
SIH: Samuel Ichiye Hayakawa
SIH: *Société Internationale d'Hématologie* (French—International Hematology Society)
SIHS: Society for Italian Historical Studies
SII: Standards Institution of Israel
SIIA: Stevenson Institute of International Affairs
Sik: Sikkim
Sig Sta: signal station
SIIAS: Staten Island Institute of Arts and Sciences
SIIP: Systems Integration Implementation Plan
sil: silver; speech interference level
s-i-l: sister-in-law
Sil: Silesia; Silesian; Silurian
SIL: *Société International de la Lèpre* (French—International Leprosy Society)
Silas: Silvanus
silcads: silver-cadmium batteries
Sile: Cecilia
Silence Dogwood: Benjamin Franklin's pseudonym used by him at age 15 when he wrote articles for the *New England Courant*
Silent: The Silent (William I—Prince of Orange)
Silent Cal: taciturn President Calvin Coolidge
silent service: the silent service (submarine service)
silic: silicate; siliceous
silica: silicon dioxide (SiO_2)
Silk City: Paterson, New Jersey, and Soochow, China share this nickname
Silk Country: China
silkool: silk + wool (Japanese synthetic textile combining qualities of silk and wool)
Silly Billy: nickname of William IV
sils: silver solder
sil(s): speech interference level(s)
silv: silver; silvery
silvercel: silver-zinc cell (battery)
Silver City: Taxco, México
Silver Gate: entrance to San Diego Bay on the coast of California
Silverines: Coloradans
Silver Republic: Argentina
Silver State: official nickname of Nevada but one also applied to silver-rich Colorado
Silver Streak: the English Channel
silvicult: silviculture
sim: similar; simile; simple; simulate; simulated approach
Sim: Simm(s); Simon(d); Sims: Syme(s); Symme; Syms; etc.
SIM: Society for Industrial Microbiology
SIM: *Servizio Informazioni Militari* (Italian—Military Intelligence Service); *Société Internationale de Musicologie* (French—International Musicological Society)
SIMA: Scientific Instrument Manufacturers' Association; Steel Industry Management Association; Suburban Insurance Managers' Association
SIMC: *Société Internationale pour la Musique Contemporaine* (French—International Society for Contemporary Music)
SIMCA: Société Industrielle de Mécanique et Carosserie Automobile
simch: single mach change
simcon: simulated control
Simmond's disease: premature senility caused by atrophy of the pituitary
Simons: Simonstown
simp: simpleton
simp.: *simplex* (Latin—simple)
SIMPL: Scientific, Industrial, and Medical Photographic Laboratories
simula: simulation language
simulcast: simultaneous broadcast (am & fm)
Simyens: Simyen Mountains of Ethiopia
sin.: sine; single
sin.: *sinister* (Latin—left)
sin': *sino* (Italian—as far as; until)
Sin: Sinaloa (inhabitants—Sinaloens)
SIN: Singapore (airport); Société Industrielle et Navale; Stop Inflation Now
SIN: *Scientific Information Notes* (National Science Foundation)
SINB: Southern Interstate Nuclear Board
Sind: Sindhi
S Ind Cur: South Indian Current
sinema: sin-filled cinema
sinf: *sinfonia* (Italian—symphony)
Sinfonia Antarctica: Symphony No. 7 by Vaughan Williams
Sinfonia Espansiva: Nielsen's Symphony No. 3
Sinfonia Semplice: Nielsen's Symphony No. 6
sing.: singer; single; singing; singular
sing.: *singulorum* (Latin—of

each)
Sing: Singapore
Singa: Singapore
Singing Satellite: Red China's first satellite, launched in spring of 1970, broadcast rhymed song about Communist Party chairman Mao Tse-tung
Sing Sing: nickname of the New York State Penitentiary at Ossining formerly named Sing Sing
Sing U: Singapore University
Sinn Fein: (Gaelic—Ourselves Alone)
sinh: hyperbolic sine
Sinh: Sinhalese
Sinjent: St John
Sink: Sinkiang
sins.: ship-inertial-navigation systems
Sin Sin: Singapore
SINTO: Sheffield Interchange Organisation
si n. val.: *si non valet* (Latin—if of no value)
sio: satellite in orbit; staged in orbit
SIO: Scripps Institution of Oceanography; Ship's Information Office(r)
sioh: supervision, inspection, and overhead
SIOP: Single Integrated Operations Plan
si op. sit: *si opus sit* (Latin—if necessary)
Sioux State: North Dakota's official nickname
sip.: standard inspection procedure; step in place
SIP: Sociedad Interamericana de la Prensa (Inter-American Press Association—IAPA); Standard Inspection Procedure
SIP: *Société Interaméricaine de Psychologie* (French—Inter-american Society of Psychology)
SIPC: Securities Investor Protection Corporation
SIPI: Southwestern Indian Polytechnic Institute
Sipo: security police (Nazi)
Sipo: *Sicherheitspolizei* (German—State Security Police)—Nazi controlled
SIPRC: Society of Independent Public Relations Consultants
SIPRE: Snow, Ice, and Permafrost Research Establishment
SIPRI: Stockholm International Peace Research Institute
siq: superior internal quality
sir. (SIR): submarine intermediate reactor
Sir: Siria (Italian, Latin, Spanish—Syria); *Síria* (Portuguese—Syria)
SIR: Society for Individual Responsibility; Society of Industrial Realtors; Staten Island Rapid Transit (railroad code)
SIR: *Società Italiana Resine* (Italian Resin Association)
SIRA: Scientific Instrument Research Association
Sir Dan Supreme: Sir Dan Godfrey
SIRE: Small investors Real Estate (plan); Society for the Investigation of Recurring Events
Sirens: three nymphs named Leucosia, Ligeia, and Parthenope; their seductive singing lured sailors to their death on rockbound coasts but when they failed to lure Odysseus (Ulysses) they flung themselves into the waves and perished
Sir Guatteral: (Hobson-Jobson—Sir Walter Raleigh)—as known to many Spaniards in colonial times
Sir John Mandeville: Jehan de Bourgogne
SIRR: Spokane International Railroad
SIRS: Student Information Record System
SIRT: Staten Island Rapid Transit
SIRTF: Spacelab Infrared Telescope Facility
sis: sterile injectable suspension
Sis: Cecilia; sister
SIS: Secret Intelligence Service; Shut-In Society; Strategic Intelligence School; Submarine-Integrated Sonar (system)
S & IS: Space and Information System(s)
SISAL: *Società Italiana Sistemi a Lotto* (Italian Lotteries)
sisi: short-increment sensitivity index
Sisister: (British contraction—Cirencester)
sisp: sudden increase of solar particles
siss: single-item single-source
SISS: Semiconductor-Insulation Semiconductor System; Submarine Improved Sonar System; System Integration Support Service
SISS: *Société Internationale de la Science du Sol* (French—International Society of Soil Science)
Sissy: Cecilia; sister
SISTER: Special Institution for Scientific and Technological Education and Research
Sister Cities: San Diego and Yokohama
SISUSA: Scotch-Irish Society of the United States of America
sit.: situation; statement of inventory transaction; stopping in transit
SIT: Society of Industrial Technology; Stevens Institute of Technology; Sugar Industry Technicians
SITA: *Société Internationale de Télécommunications Aeronautiques*
SITA: Students International Travel Association
SITC: Standard International Trade Classification
sitcom: situation comedy (tv)
SITE: Satellite Instructional Television Experiment
SITES: Smithsonian Institution Traveling Exhibition Service
sitol: sitological; sitologist; sitology
sitpro: simplification of international trade procedures
sitr: silent treatment
SITRA: South India Textile Research Association
sitrag: situation tragedy
sitrep: situation report
SITS: Securities Instruction Transmission System; Société Internationale de Transfusion Sanguine (International Organization for Blood Transfusion)
sitt: sitting room
Sitting Bull: Tatanka Iyotanka also known as Sitting Buffalo Bill
SITU: Society for the Investigation of the Unexplained
SIU: Seafarers International Union; Southern Illinois University; Special Investigating Unit (NY Police Bureau of Narcotics)
SIU: *Société Internationale d'Urologie* (International Urological Society)
SIUL: Southern Illinois University Library
SIUM: Southern Illinois University Museum
SI unit: *Système International unit* (French—International System of Units)
SIUP: Southern Illinois Universi-

ty Press
siv: survey of interpersonal values
si vir. perm.: *si vires permitant* (Latin—if the strength will permit)
siw (SIW): self-inflicted wounds
Six Counties: Northern Ireland or Ulster's counties of Antrim, Armagh, Derry, Down, Fermanagh, and Tyrone
Six Nations: Five Nations plus the Tuscaroras (*see* Five Nations)
SIXFLT: Sixth Fleet (USN)
SIXPAC: System for Inertial Experiment Pointing to Attitude Control
Six-Shooter Junction: old name of Harlingen, Texas
SIYC: Shelter Island Yacht Club; Staten Island Yacht Club
SIZ: Security Identification Zone
SIZS: Staten Island Zoological Society
sj: slip joint; subject(s)
s.j.: *sub judice* (Latin—under judicial consideration)
SJ: San Juan; Society of Jesus (S.J.—Jesuits), Statens Järnvägar (Swedish State Railways)
SJ: *Solicitors' Journal*
SJAA: St John Ambulance Association
SJAC: Society of Japanese Aircraft Constructors
SJC: San Juan Carriers (ore and tankships); Snead Junior College; Spartanburg Junior College
S.J.D.: *Scientiae Juridicae Doctor* (Latin—Doctor of Juridical Science)
sje: swivelling jet engine
SJI: Steel Joist Institute
SJIs: San Juan Islands
SJJC: Sheldon Jackson Junior College
sk (SK): streptokinase
SJO: San José, Costa Rica (La Sabana Airport)
SJPC: South Jersey Port Commission
SJPL: San Jose Public Library
SJSC: San Jose State College
SJSO: San Jose Symphony Orchestra
SJU: San Juan, Puerto Rico (airport); St. John's University
sk: sick; sketch
Sk: *Skizze* (German—sketch)
SK: end of transmission (telegraphic symbol); South Korea(n)
SK: *Stuttgarter Kammerorchester* (German—Stuttgart Chamber Orchestra); *Suomen Kansallisoopera* (Finnish National Opera)
s-ka: *spolka* (Polish—association; company)
SKA: Switchblade Knife Act
skamp: station keeping and mobile platform
Skate City: Northbrook, Illinois
skb: *skindbind* (Dano-Norwegian—leatherbound)
skc: sky clear
SKC: Scottish Kennel Club
skd: skilled
sked: schedule
skel: skeletal; skeleton
S Ken: South Kensington
skep: skeptic(al)(ly); skepticism
SKF: Svenska Kullagerfabriken (Swedish ball-bearing factory)
SK & F: Smith Kline & French
SKI: Sloan-Kettering Institute
Skidrow on the Sound: (street people's nickname—Seattle, Washington, on Puget Sound)—the original skidrow
skill.: satellite kill
SKIP: Skimmer Investigation Platform
Skipper: the Captain; the Commander
skiv: skiver
SKJ: *Savez Komunista Jugoslavije* (Yugoslavian Communist League)—political party
SKKCA: Supreme Knight of the Knights of Columbus of America
skl: spleen, kidney, liver
Skm: Stockholm
skmr (SKMR): hydroskimmer
skort: short skirt
Skowse: Liverpool seaman
skp: station-keeping position
skpo: slip one, knit one, pass slipped-stitch over (knitting)
skr: standardized kill rate; station-keeping radar
Skr: Sanskrit
Skr: *Skrifter* (Swedish—publication)
SKr: Swedish krona (kronor)
SKR: South Korea Republic
sks: sacks
SKS: Søren Kierkegaard Society; station-keeping ship
SKS: *Savvezna Komisija za Standardizacija* (Serbo-Croatian—Federal Commission for Standardization)
Skt: Sanskrit
Skt: *Sankt* (German—saint)
SKY: Skyways Limited (aviation symbol)
Skybright Axe: Paul Bunyan
Sky City: Pueblo Acoma near Albuquerque, New Mexico
skyjack: skyjacked; skyjacker; skyjacking (all indicate aircraft hijacking)
skys'l: skysail
sl: sales letter; sand-loaded; sea level; searchlight; shipowner's; liability; slightly; sound locator; stock length; support line
s-l: short-long (flashlight or whistle signals); sound-locator sublease
s/l: self-loading
s & l: savings and loan; supply and logistics
s.l.: *secundum legem* (Latin—according to law); *sensu lato* (Latin—in the broad sense); *sine loco* (Latin—no place of publication)
s/l: *sobreloja* (Portuguese—mezzanine floor); *su letra* (Spanish—your letter)
Sl: Slovak; Slovakian; small diurnal range
SL: San Luis Obispo; Savings and Loan (association or bank); Sea-Land (America's seagoing motor carrier); Sierra Leone; Solicitor-at-Law; Squadron Leader; Sub-Lieutenant; Support Line; Sydney & Louisburg (railroad)
S-L: short-long
S & L: Supply and Logistics
S-et-L: Saône-et-Loire
sla: sacro-laeva anterior; single-line approach
SLA: School Library Association; Scottish Library Association; Showmen's League of America; Southeastern Library Association; Southwestern Library Association; Special Libraries Association; Standard Life Association; State Liquor Authority; Supply Loading Airfield; Supply Loading Airport; Symbionese Liberation Army
SLAA: Surf Lifesaving Association of Australia
SLAB: Students for Labelling Alcoholic Beverages
Slabsides: rustic cabin built by John Burroughs near Esopus, New York
SLAC: Stanford Linear Accelerator Center
SLADE: Society of Lithographic Artists, Designers, Engravers, and Process Workers
slaked lime: calcium hydroxide

($Ca[OH]_2$)
slam. (SLAM): supersonic low-altitude (nuclear-powered) missile
s.l.a.m.: *sine loco, anno, nomine* (Latin—without place, year, or name)
SLANG: Systems Language
slanguage: slang (slum language)
S Lan R: South Lancashire Regiment
SLANT: Student League Against Narcotic Traffic
slar: side-looking airborne radar
S Lat: south latitude
slate.: small lightweight altitude-transmission equipment
SLATE: Structured Learning and Teaching Environment; Systems for Learning by Applications of Technology to Education
Slav: Slavic; Slavonic
Slave States: former slave-holding states comprising the Confederacy (Virginia, North and South Carolina, Georgia, Florida, Alabama, Mississippi, Louisiana, Texas, Arkansas, Tennessee) plus slave states not seceding—Delaware, Maryland, Kentucky, Missouri
slb: short-leg brace
slbm (SLBM): submarine-launched ballistic missile
slc: searchlight control
sl & c: shipper's load and count
SLC: Salt Lake City, Utah (airport); Scout Launch Complex; Space Launch Complex
SLCL: Sierra Leone Council of Labour
slcm (SLCM): sea-launched cruise missile
SLCMD: St Louis Contract Management District
SLCPL: Salt Lake City Public Library
SLCR: *Scottish Land Court Reports*
sld: sailed; solid; specific learning disability
sld (SLD): serum lactate dehydrogenase
Sld: Sunderland
sldf: solidification
sl di: slot die
S Ldr: Squadron Leader
sld's: specific learning disabilities
sle (SLE): systemic lupus erythematosus
S le: Sierra Leone leone(s)—monetary unit(s)
SLe: St Louis encephalitis
SLE: Society of Logistics Engineers
SLEAT: Society of Laundry Engineers and Allied Trades
Sledge and Hoe: official symbol of Zaire
Sleep Personified: Hypnos (Greek—sleep) whose brother was Thanatos or death
s.l. et a.: *sine loco et anno* (Latin—without place and year)
S level: scholarship level
slf: straight-line frequency
SLF: Scottish Landowners' Federation; Silcock and Lever Feeds
S-L Fl: short-long flashing (light)
SLGB: Society of Local Government Barristers
SLHC: St Luke's Hospital Center
Sli: Sligo
SLI: Slick Airways
slic: selective listing in combination
SLIC: Supreme Life Insurance Company
SLICE: Southwestern Library Interstate Cooperative Endeavor
SLID: Student League for Industrial Democracy
slim. (SLIM): submarine-launched inertial missile
SLIM: South London Industrial Mission
Slim Jannie: Jan Christian Smuts
Slinging Sammy: Sam(uel) (Adrian) Baugh of baseball and football fame
SLIP: Skills Level Improvement Plan
slithy: lithe and slimy (Lewis Carroll's portmanteau word from *Through the Looking Glass*)
SLJ: *School Library Journal*
SLLA: Scottish Ladies Lacrosse Association
slm: *sul livello del mare* (Italian—at sea level)
slm (SLM): ship-launched missile
SLMC: Scottish Ladies' Mountaineering Club
SLMSU: Scientific Library of Moscow State University
SLMTA: St Louis Municipal Theatre Association
sln: standard library number
slnd: *sans lieu ne date* (French—without place or date of publication)
SLNM: Statue of Liberty National Monument
SLNWR: Sand Lake National Wildlife Refuge (South Dakota); San Luis NWR (California); Swan Lake NWR (Missouri)
Slo: Saltillo (inhabitants—Saltilleños or Saltilleros); Slovak; Slovakia; Slovene(s)
SLO: San Luis Obispo; Senior Liaison Officer
SLOBB: Stop Littering Our Bays and Beaches
SLOE: Special List of Equipment
slomar: space logistics, maintenance, and rescue
slooow seller(s): slow-selling book(s)
s/loss: salvage loss
Slot: The Slot—San Francisco's downtown Mission Street off Market Street
Slov: Slovene; Slovenian
SLOWPOKE: Safe Low-Power Critical Experiment (AEC)
slp: sacro-laeva posterior
s.l.p.: *sine legitima prole* (Latin—without legitimate issue)
SLP: San Luís Potosí; Socialist Labor Party
Slphr: Sulphur (postal abbreviation)
SLPL: St Louis Public Library
slr: side-looking radar; single-lens reflex (camera)
s-l r: sea-level resident(s)
S & LR: Sydney and Louisburg Railway
SLR: Scottish Land Reports
SLRB: State Labor Relations Board
SLRC: San Luis Rey College
sl rd: searchlight radar
SL Rev: Scottish Law Review
SLRP: St Lawrence River Pilot
sls: sequential light switch
SLS: Sea-Land Service; St Lawrence Seaway; St Louis Symphony
sl sa: slotting saw
SLSA: Saint Lawrence Seaway Authority; Surf Life Saving Association
SLSC: Swedish Lloyd Steamship Company
SLSDC: Saint Lawrence Seaway Development Corporation
S L S F: St Louis-San Francisco (railroad)
SLSFC: Severe Local Storm Forecast Center
slsmgr: salesmanager
slsmn: salesman; salesmen
SLST: Sierra Leone Selection Trust
SLS-UBC: School of Library Science—University of Brit-

ish Columbia
slt: sacro-laeva transversa; searchlight
SLT: Solid-Logic Technology; Stress Limit Test(ing)
***SLT:** Scots Law Times*
SLTA: Scottish Licensed Trade Association
SLTAN: Società Lloyd Triestino per Azioni di Navigazione (Lloyd Triestino)
SLTC: Society of Leather Trades Chemists
slto: sea-level takeoff
sl tr: silent treatment
Slu: slough
SLU: Saint Lawrence University; Saint Louis University, Southern Labor Union
Slumbering Giant of Capitol Hill: The Library of Congress
slumlord: slum landlord
slurb: slum suburb
slurp.: self-levelling unit to remove pollution
SLUSSR: State Library of the USSR (Lenin Library, Moscow)
Slut of the North: Empress Elizabeth of Russia so nicknamed by Frederick the Great of Prussia who called her *la Catin du Nord*
slv: satellite launching vehicle; space launch vehicle; standard launch vehicle (SLV)
SLV-3: Atlas standard launch vehicle (Convair)
sly: slowly
Sly: southerly
slyp: short-leaf yellow pine
SLZG: St Louis Zoological Gardens
sm: service module; servomechanism; sheet metal; small; statute mile; strategic missile (SM); streptomycin; sustained medication; systolic murmur; syzygy mathematical
s-m: sadist-masochist; sadomasochism
s/m: sensory-to-motor (ratio)
s & m: sadism and masochism; sausages and mashed potatoes; surface and matched
Sm: samarium
***Sm:** Seemeile* (German—nautical mile)
***s/M:** sur mer* (French—by the sea)
SM: mine-laying submarine; Salvage Mechanic; San Marino; Scientific Memorandum; Senior Magistrate; Sergeant-Major; Service Module; Shipment Memorandum; Signalman; Society of Mary; Society of Medalists; Soldier's Medal; Special Memorandum; Spiritual Mobilization; Staff Memorandum; State Militia; States Marine (steamship lines); Structures Memorandum; submarine; Summary Memorandum; Suomi Merivorma (Finnish Seapower); Supply Manual; Svenska Metallverken (Swedish Metal Works)
***S.M.:** Scientiae Magister* (Latin—Master of Science)
***S-M:** Seine-Maritime* (formerly *Seine-Inférieure*)
***S.M.:** Sanctae Memoriae* (Latin—of sacred memory); *Su Majestad* (Spanish—Her/His Majesty)
S-et-M: Seine-et-Marne
SM-65: Atlas intercontinental ballistic missile (Convair)
SM-68: Titan intercontinental ballistic missile (Martin)
SM-75: Thor intermediate-range ballistic missile (Douglas)
SM-78: Jupiter intermediate-range ballistic missile (Chrysler)
SM-80: Minuteman intercontinental ballistic missile (Boeing)
sma: subject matter area
SMA: Safe Manufacturers Association; San Miguel Arizona (railroad); Santa María, Azores (airport); Scale Manufacturers Association; Screen Manufacturers Association; Senior Military Attaché; Service Merchandisers of America; Sheffield Metallurgical Association; Society of Makeup Artists; Solder Makers Association; Squadron Maintenance Area; Steatite Manufacturers Association; Steel Manufacturers Association; Stoker Manufacturers Association
SMAB: Solid Motor Assembly Building
SMAC: Scientific Machine Automation Corporation
SM & ACCNA: Sheet Metal and Air Conditioning Contractors National Association
s mach: sounding machine
SMAE: Society of Model Aeronautical Engineers
SMAJ: Sugar Manufacturers' Association of Jamaica
smalgol: small computer algorithmic language
Smallest Capital in America: Carson City, Nevada
Smallest Latin American Republic: El Salvador
Smallest Province: Prince Edward Island
Smallest State: Rhode Island
SMAMA: Sacramento Air Materiel Area
S Mar: San Marino
smarea (SMAREA): squadron maintenance area
SMART: Silent Majority Against Revolutionary Tactics; Supersonic Military Air Research Track; Supersonic Missile and Rocket Track
smartie: simple-minded artificial intelligence
SMASH: Students Mobilizing on Auto Safety Hazards
s-m-a showing: suggested-for-mature-adult showing (motion picture producers code)
smat: see me about this
smaze: smoke + haze (*see* smog)
SMB: Straits of Mackinac Bridge
***SMB:** Sa Majesté Britanique* (French—Her/His Britannic Majesty)
SMBA: Scottish Marine Biological Association
smbl: semimobile
smc: sperm (spore) mother cell; standard mean chord
Smc: Samic (Lapp)
SMC: Saugus Marine Corporation; Scientific Manpower Commission
S & MC: Supply and Maintenance Command (US Army)
sm caps: small capital letters
SMCC: Saint Mary's College of California; Santa Monica City College
SMCCL: Society of Municipal and County Chief Librarians
SMCD: Saint Mary's Dominican College
smcln: semicolon
smd: submanubrial dullness
SMD: Submarine Mine Depot
SMDA: Sewing Machine Dealers' Association
SME: School of Military Engineering; Society of Manufacturing Engineers; Standard Medical Examination
***S.M.E.:** Sancta Mater Ecclesia* (Latin—Holy Mother Church)
SMEC: Strategic Missile Evaluation Committee
SMEG: Spring Makers' Export Group
smel: single and multiengine li-

cense
smelt.: smelter; smelting
SMERSH: *Smert Shpionam* (Russian—Death to Spies)—Soviet organization for murdering political enemies
S Met O: Senior Meteorological Officer
SMfVL: *Stuttgart Museum för Volker und Landerkunde*
smg: speed made good; submachine gun
Smg: Samarang
SMG: *Stato Maggior Generale* (Italian—General Staff)
SMH: *Sydney Morning Herald*
s mi: statute mile(s)
SMI: Scale Manufacturers Institute; School Management Institute; Secondary Metal Institute; Spring Manufacturers Institute; Success Motivation Institute; Super Market Institute
SMI: *Sa Majesté Imperiale* (French—Her/His Imperial Majesty)
SMIA: Sheet Metal Industries Association
SMIC: Study of Man's Impact on Climate
smicbm (SMICBM): semi-mobile intercontinental ballistic missile
SMIG: Sergeant-Major Instructor of Gunnery
SMILE: Something Meaningful In Local Effort (predelinquency file kept in Orange County, California)
S-mine: shrapnel-filled mine
SMIS: Society for Management Information Systems
smit: spin-motor interruption technique
Smithsonian: Smithsonian Institution (United States National Museum)
SMJ: Southern Masonic Jurisdiction
SMJC: Saint Mary's Junior College
smk: smoke
smk gen: smoke generator
smkls: smokeless
sml: simulate; simulation; simulator; small; symbolic machine language
sml: *sammenlign* (Danish—compare)
Sml: Samuel
SML: States Marine Lines
SML: Science Museum Library; States Marine Lines
SMLA: *Samoa Muamua Le Atua* (Samoan—In Samoa God Is First)
SMLE: short-model Lee Enfield (British service rifle used in both world wars)
smlm: simple-minded learning machine
smls: seamless
SMLS: Saint Mary of the Lake Seminary
smm: standard method of measurement
S.M.M.: *Sancta Mater Maria* (Latin—Holy Mother Mary)
SMMB: Scottish Milk Marketing Board
smmp: screw machine metal part
SMMT: Society of Motor Manufacturers and Traders
SMN: Société Maritime Nationale
SMNA: Safe Manufacturers National Association
SMNH: Saskatchewan Museum of Natural History
SMNO: Singapore Malays National Organization
SMNP: Simien Mountains National Park (Ethiopia)
SMNRA: Shadow Mountain National Recreation Area (Colorado)
Smnry: Seminary
SMNWR: Saint Marks National Wildlife Refuge (Florida)
SMO: Senior Medical Officer
SMO: *Servicio Militar Obligatorio* (Spanish—Compulsory Military Service)
smog: smoke + fog (*see* smaze); smoky air (with or without fog)
smogway: smog-polluted automobile freeway
SMOH: Society of Medical Officers of Health
smoker: smoking car
smokies: smoked haddocks
Smokies: Smoky Mountains between North Carolina and Tennessee
Smoking Moses: Shishaldin Volcano on South Umiak Island off southwestern Alaska
Smokeless City: Reykjavik, Iceland—heated by natural hot springs
Smoke that Thunders: Victoria Falls (Zambia)
Smoky City: nickname of Pittsburgh, Pennsylvania before its Renaissance Plan cleared the skies above it
smon: subacute myelo-optic neuropathy
smor: standard mean ocean water
smörgas: *smörgåsbord* (Swedish appetizers or delicatessen-style meal)
smorz: *smorzando* (Italian—dying away)
smp: scanning measuring projector; social marginal productivity; sound motion picture(s)
s.m.p.: *sine mascula prole* (Latin—without male issue)
SMP: St Martin's Press
SMPC: Saint Mary of the Plains College
SMPS: Society of Master printers of Scotland
SMPTE: Society of Motion Picture and Television Engineers
smpx: smallpox
smr: somnolent metabolic rate; standard mortality rate; submucous resection
SMR: Student Master Record; South Manchurian Railway
SMR: *Sa Majesté Royale* (French—Her/His Royal Majesty)
SMRA: Spring Manufacturers' Research Association
SMRC: South Manchurian Railway Company
smrd: spin-motor rotation-detector
SMRE: Safety in Mines Research Establishment
SMRI: Sugar Milling Research Institute
SMRL: Submarine Medical Research Laboratory
sms: silico-manganese steel; subject matter specialist; synchronous meteorological satellite (SMS)
SMS: Sacramento Medical Society; Sequence Milestone System
SMS: *Seine Majistäts Schiffe* (German — His Majesty's Ship)
smsa: standard metropolitan statistical area
SMSB: Strategic Missile Support Base
SMSG: School Mathematics Study Group
SMSgt: Senior Master Sergeant
SMSO: Senior Maintenance Staff Officer
SMSP: Spring Mill State Park (Indiana)
SMSSS: Sheet Metal Screw Statistical Society
smstrs: seamstress
smt: ship's mean time
Smt: Summit (postal abbreviation)
SMT: Scottish Motor Traction

SMTA: Scottish Motor Trade Association
SMTF: Scottish Milk Trade Federation
smti: selective moving target indicator
SMTO: Senior Mechanical Transport Officer
SMTS: Scottish Machinery Testing Station
SMU: Southern Methodist University
SMUN: Soviet Mission to the United States
SMUSE: Socialist Movement for the United States of Europe
smw: standard metal window
SMW: Society of Magazine Writers
s m w d sep: single; married; widowed; divorced; separated (vital statistic headings)
smx: submultiplexer unit
sn: sanitation; sanitary; service number; solid neutral; stock number
s-n: *sin número* (Spanish—unnumbered; without number)
s/n: serial number; service number; signal-to-noise ratio
s.n.: *secundum naturam* (Latin—according to nature); *sine nomine* (Latin — without name)
Sn: (postal abbreviation—San; Santa; Santo); stannum (Latin—tin)
S^n San (Spanish—saint)
SN: Sacramento Northern (railroad); Scientific Note; Secretary of the Navy; Serial Number; Service Number; Standard Oil (stock exchange symbol)
S-N: stress versus number of cycles
S/N: Serial Number; Service Number
S/N: stress versus number of cycles (to failure); successes versus total number of trials
S of N: Sons of Norway
SNA: Society of Naval architects
SNAC: *Syndicat National des Auteurs et Compositeurs* (National Union of Authors and Composers)
snafu: situation normal, all fouled up
SNAM: *Società Nazionale Metanodotti*
SNAME: Society of Naval Architects and Marine Engineers
SNAP: Society of National Association Publishers; Student Naval Aviation Pilot; Systems for Nuclear Auxiliary Power
Snapp: *Servicos de Navegacão da Amazonia e de Administração do Porto do Pará*
snap(s): snapshot(s)
snark: snake and shark (Lewis Carroll)
snc: severe noise environment; standard navigation computer
SNC: *Socĕté Navale Caennaise (Lamy et Cie)*
SNCASCO: *Société Nationale de Constructions Aéronautique de l'Ouest*
SNCC: Student Nonviolent Coordinating Committee (also called SNIC)
SNCFB: *Société Nationale des Chemins de Fer Belges* (Belgian State Railways)
SNCFF: *Société Nationale des Chemins de Fer Français* (French—State Railways)
snd: sound
SNDA: Sunday Newspaper Distributing Association
SNDO: Standard Nomenclature of Diseases and Operations
sndp: *sin nota de precio* (Spanish—without indication of price)
sndv (SNDV): strategic nuclear delivery vehicle
SNEA: Student National Education Association
sneaks.: sneakers (tennis shoes)
SNECMA: *Société Nationale d'Etude et de Construction de Moteurs d'Aviation*
SNEMSA: Southern New England Marine Sciences Association
snf: solids-non-fat
SNF: Serbian National Federation
SNFA: Standing Naval Force, Atlantic
SNFU: Scottish National Farmers' Union
sng: synthetic natural gas
sng: *sans notre garantie* (French—without our guarantee)
Sng: Singapore
SNHM: Stanford Natural History Museum
sni: sequence-number indicator
SNI: San Nicolas Island; Sports Network Incorporated
SNI: *Secretariado Nacional da Informção* (Portuguese — State Tourist Bureau); *Syndicat National des Instituteurs* (French—National Union of Teachers)
SNIC: Student Non-Violent Coordinating Committee (SNCC)
snirt: snort of laughter
SNL: Standard Nomenclature List
SNL: *Science News Letter*
snlr: services no longer required
snm: signal-to-noise merit
SNM: Saguaro National Monument (Arizona); Senior Naval Member; Sitka National Monument (Alaska); Society of Nuclear Medicine
SNMT: Society of Nuclear Medical Technologists
SNN: Shannon, Eire (airport)
sno: snow (used in combinations such as snocat, snomobile)
s no: serial number
SNO: Scottish National Orchestra; Singapore National Orchestra
snob: *sine nobilitate* (Latin—without nobility)—anyone trying to outdo the manners and style of the nobility; person putting on airs in an attempt to outpeer the peers
snok: secondary next of kin
SNOOP: Students Naturally Opposed to Outrageous Prying
snoopervise: snoop and supervise
snop: standardized nomenclature of pathology
SNORT: Supersonic Naval Ordnance Research Track
Snow King: Gustavus Adolphus of Sweden
Snow Queen: Christina—Queen of Sweden
Snowys: Snowy Mountains of New South Wales
Snowy Scheme: Snowy Mountains Scheme (Australian hydroelectric and irrigation system)
snp: soluble nucleoprotein
SNP: Salorp National Park (Thailand); Scottish Nationalist Party; Sebakwe NP (Rhodesia); Sequoia NP (California); Serengeti NP (Tanzania); Shenandoah NP (Virginia); Sivpuri NP (India); Sitka NP (Alaska); Snowdonia NP (Wales); Swiss NP (Switzerland)
SNPA: Scottish Newspaper Proprietors' Association; Southern Newspaper Publishers Association
SNPO: Space Nuclear Propulsion Office
snr: signal-to-noise ratio

Snr: *Senhor* (Portuguese—Mister)
Sñr: *Señor* (Spanish—Mister)
SNR: Society for Nautical Research
Snra: *Senhora* (Portuguese—Missus)
Sñra: *Señora* (Spanish—Missus)
SNRA: Sanford National Recreation Area (Texas)
Snrta: *Senhorita* (Portuguese—Miss)
Sñrta: *Señorita* (Spanish—Miss)
Sñrto: *Señorito* (Spanish—Master)
sns: sympathetic nervous system
SNSC: Scottish National Ski Council
SNSN: Standard Navy Stock Number
SNSO: Superintending Naval Stores Officer
snt: *so nota* (Japanese—and so forth)—etc.
SNT: Society for Nondestructive Testing
snto: spinning tool
SNTO: Spanish National Tourist Office; Swedish National Tourist Office; Swiss National Tourist Office
SNTPC: Scottish National Town Planning Council
SNW: Symphony of the New World
SNWMA: Stillwater National Wildlife Management Area (Nevada)
SNWR: Sabine National Wildlife Refuge (Louisiana); Sacramento NWR (California; Santee NWR (South Carolina); Savannah NWR (South Carolina); Seedskadee NWR (Wyoming; Seney NWR (Michigan); Sherburne NWR (Minnesota); Shiawasse NWR (Michigan); Slade NWR (North Dakota)
so.: seller's option; senior officer; sex offender; shipping order; ship's option; shop order; show off; south(ern); special order; staff officer; standing order; strikeout; suboffice; supply office(r)
so.: *siehe oben* (German—see above)
s-o: shutoff
s/o: shipping order
so (SO): shift-out character (data processing)
s/o: *su orden* (Spanish—your order)
So.: Somali(a)
So: *Sondag* (Danish—Sunday)
SO: Scottish Office; Scouting-Observation (naval aircraft); Secretary's Office; Senior Officer; Shipment Order; Shipping Order; Shop Order; somalo (Somalian currency unit); Southern Airways (letter coding); Southern Company (stock exchange symbol); Special Order(s); Staff Officer; Standard Oil; Standing Order(s); Stationery Office; Supply Office(r)
SO: *sudoeste* (Spanish—southwest); *Südosten* (German—southeast)
S-et-O: *Seine-et-Oise*
SO_2: sulfur dioxide
SO_4: sulfate
soa: speed of advance; speed of approach
SOA: Seattle Opera Association; Shoe Corporation of America (stock exchange symbol)
soap.: symbolic optimum assembly programming
SOAP: Society of Airway Pioneers
Soap Box Derby Center: Akron, Ohio
SOAPD: Southern Air Procurement District
soapstone: saponite (hydrous magnesium aluminum silicate)
Soapy: G. Mennen Williams
SOAR: Save Our American Resources; Society of Authors' Representatives
SOAS: School of Oriental and African Studies (University of London)
sob.: see order blank; shortness of breath; still on board; suboccipitobregmatic
s-o-b: son of a bitch (a dog; a no-good person)
SOB: Senate Office Building; State Office Building; Society of Bookmen; son of a bitch
sobe: sober; sobriety
SOBHD: Scottish Official Board of Highland Dancing
soblin: self-organizing binary-logic network
sob's: silly old buggers; sons of bitches; souls on board (aircraft, ship, or other vehicle)
SOBs: Sons of Bosses
soc: social; society; sociology; socket; state of consciousness (SoC)
Soc: Socialist; Society
Soc: *Sociedad* (Spanish—society); *Sociedade* (Portuguese—society); *Società* (Italian—society); *Société* (French—society)
S o C: Society of Cyprus
SOC: Southwestern Oregon College
So Ca: South Carolina's old abbreviation
SOCAL: Standard Oil of California (Chevron)
Soc An: *Société Anonyme* (French—corporation)
Soc. Chr.: *Societas Christi* (Latin—Christian Society)
Soc-Dem: Social-Democrat(ic) (Party)
SOCEM: Society of Objectors to Compulsory Egg Marketing
SOCGPA: Seed, Oil Cake, and General Produce Association
Soc I: Society Islands
Societies: Society Islands of Polynesia in the South Pacific
Society of Friends: the Quakers
Socinus: Faustus Socinus (Fausto Sozzini)—nephew of Lelius Socinus and founder of the Polish Brethren of Unitarians; Laelius Socinus (Lelio Sozzini)—Italian anti-trinitarian religious reformer and ideologist of unitarianism
sociol: sociological; sociologist; sociology
SOCMA: Synthetic Organic Chemical Manufacturers Association
Soc NC: *sociedad en nombre colectivo* (Spanish—general partnership under a collective name)
So Co: Southern Counties
SOCO: Standard Oil Company of California
socom: solar communication
SOCONY: Standard Oil Corporation of New York
SOCRATES: System for Organizing Content to Review and Teach Educational Subjects
socs: survey of clerical skills
soc sci: social science; social scientist
Soc Sec: Social Security
sod.: sodium; sodomite; sodomy
soda (SODA): source-oriented data acquisition
soda ash: sodium carbonate (Na_2CO_3)
SODAC: Society of Dyers and Colourists
Sodaks: South Dakotans
sodar: sound-detecting and ranging
soda water: water charged with carbon dioxide (CO_2)
SODOMEI: *Nihon Rodo Kumiai Sodomei* (Japanese Trade

Union Federation)
SODRE: Servicio Oficial de Difusión Radio Eléctrica (Uruguayan radio and tv network)
SOE: Special Operations Executive (World War II British intelligence operation for rescuing scientists and other useful citizens from Hitler)
SOED: *Shorter Oxford English Dictionary*
SOE/F: SOE in France
soep (SOEP): solar-oriented experiment package
sof: sound on film
Sof: Sofia
S o F: Society of Friends
SOFA: Student Overseas Flights for Americans
sofar: sound fixing and ranging
SOFCS: Self-Organizing Flight-Control System
SOFINA: *Société Financière de Transports et d'Entreprises Industrielles* (Belgian investment syndicate)
sofnet: solar observing and forecasting network
SOFT: Status of Forces Treaty; Swedish Orienteering Federation
softlenses: soft contact lenses
software: design documents instructing computers
sog: speed over (the) ground
sog: *sogenannt* (German—so called)
SOG: Seat of Government (Washington, D.C.)
SOGAT: Society of Graphical and Allied Trades
SOGC: Society of Gynecologists and Obstetricians of Canada
SO & GC: Signal Oil and Gas Company
sogg: *soggettivo* (Italian—subjective); *soggetto* (Italian—subject)
soh (SOH): start of heading character (data processing)
soha: soft hard
SOHIO: Standard Oil of Ohio
SoHo: South of Houston Street (New York City artist's colony in lower Manhattan)
SOHO: Save Our Heritage Organization
SOHYO: *Nihon Rodo Kumiai Sohygikai* (Japanese General Council of Trade Unions)
soi: space object identification
SOI: Signal Operation Instruction(s); Southern Indiana (railroad); Specific Operating Instruction(s)
SO (I): Staff Officer (Intelligence)
soit: *soitenly* (New Yorkese—certainly)
Sojourner Truth: Isabella Baumfree
sok: *sokak* (Turkish—lane; street)
sol: solar; soldier; solenoid; soluble; solubility; solution; solvent(s)
sol: (Italian—fifth tone, *E* in diatonic scale, *G* in fixed-do system)
sol.: *solutio* (Latin—solution)
s-o-l: short of luck
Sol: Solomon; Solomon Islands
SOL: *Svenska Orient Line* (Swedish Orient Line)
Solar Energy Capital: Los Angeles
Solar Energy State: Arizona
SoLaS: Safety of Life at Sea (international conference)
sold.: solder; soldering
solder: 50% lead, 50% tin (common solder)
soldier's heart: Da Costa's syndrome
sol hgt: solid height
solidif: solidification
Solina: South Carolina
SOLINET: Southeastern Library Network
Sol J: *Solicitors' Journal*
Sol(ly): Solomon
soln: solution
solion: solution of ions
SOLog: standardization of certain aspects of operations and logistics
sologs: standardization of operations and logistics
solomon: simultaneous-operation linked-ordinal modular network
Solomons: Solomon Islands in the Coral Sea sector of the South Pacific
Solomon seal: six-pointed star consisting of two interlocking triangles; sometimes called the shield of David and not to be confused with the Suliman seal of Islam and Morocco (*see* Suliman seal)
Solovetskis: Solovetski Islands (penal colonies in the Archangelsk Region of the USSR—part of the Gulag Archipelago populated by political prisoners)
Solovki: Solovetski Islands
soly: solubility
solr: solicitor
solrad: solar radiation
solut: solution
SOM: Society of Occupational Medicine
s l s l e: smooth 1 side 1 edge
solv: solvent
solv.: *solve* (Latin—dissolve)
som: somatology; start of message
Som: Somali(a); Somaliland(er); Somerset
SOM: Society of Occupational Medicine
SOMA: Society of Mental Awareness
somat: somatic
SOME: Senior Ordnance Mechanical Engineer
Somers' Islands: Bermuda
SOMEX: *Sociedad Mexicana de Credito Industrial* (Spanish—Mexican Industrial Credit Society)
Som LI: Somerset Light Infantry
Somnolent City of the Sahara: Timbuktu
Som sh: Somali shilling
Son: Sonora
SON: Snijders-Oomen Non-verbal (intelligence scale)
Son: *Sonntag* (German—Sunday)
sonac: sonacelle (sonar nacelle)
SONAP: *Sociedade Nacional de Petroleos* (Portuguese—National Petroleum Company)
sonar: sound navigation and ranging
Sonbrit: *Simfonischen orkestur na bulgarskoto radio i televiziya* (Bulgarian Radio and Television Symphony Orchestra)
Song of the Night: Mahler's Symphony No. 7 in E minor
Song Sol: The Song of Solomon
Song of Songs: The Song of Solomon
Sonia: Sophia
sonmc: sonar countermeasures and deception
Sonn: *Sonnets* of Shakespeare
Son of Nature: Henry David Thoreau
sono: sonobuoy
sonoan: sonic noise analyzer
Son of the Ocean: Yangtse River
Son of the Star: Bar Kochba—military leader of the Jews who revolted against the Romans in the year 132 A.D.
Son of Valladolid: José Zorilla
Sonya: Sophia
Sonya: (Russian nickname—Sophia)
Soo: Sault Ste Marie (canal and locks)
SOO: Staff Officer Operations
SO (O): Staff Officer (Operations)

Soo Bridge: Sault Ste Marie International Bridge
Soo Canals: Sault Ste Marie Canals
Soo Line: Minneapolis, St Paul & Sault Ste Marie (railroad)
Sooner State: Oklahoma's official nickname recalling many of its first settlers entered the territory sooner than others who waited for the signal gun
SOOP: Submarine Oceanographic Observation Program
s-o-p: standard operating procedure
sop.: soprano
SOP: Senior Officer Present; Standard Operating Procedure
SOPA: Senior Officer Present Afloat
Sopac: Southern Pacific Railroad (stock exchange nickname)
Soph: Sophocles
SOPHE: Society of Public Health Educators
Sophia Loren: Sofia Scicolone
soph(s): sophomore(s)
SOPLASCO: Southern Plastics Company
Soppnata: Sociedade Portuguese de Navios Tanques (Portuguese Tankers)
sor: sorority; specific operating requirement
s-o-r: stimulus-organism-response
Sor: *Señor* (Spanish—Mister)
S^{or}: *Sênior* (Portuguese —Mister)
SOR: Special Order Request; Specific Operational Requirement
Sorbonne: University of Paris
sord: submerged object recovery device
Sores: *Señores* (Spanish—gentlemen)
Sorghum Capital of the World: Hawesville, Kentucky
SORI: Southern Research Institute
Sorlings: Sorling Islands (Isles of Scilly)
SORO: Special Operations Research Office
SORT: Slosson Oral Reading Test; Structured-Objective Rorschach Test
sorti: satellite orbital track and intercept
sos: same old stew; same only softer (musical direction); slag on a shingle (military description of creamed chicken or beef served on a slice of toast)
s.o.s.: *si opus sit* (Latin—if necessary)
SOS: (international distress signal—three dots, three dashes, three dots); Save Our Schools; Share our Spectacles; *Sources of Supply;* Squadron Officer School; Stamp Out Smog; etc
SOSC: Smithsonian Oceanographic Sorting Center
So sh: somali shilling(s)
SOSS: Shipboard Oceanographic Survey System
sost: *sostenuto* (Italian—sustained)
Sost: *Sostavitel* (Russian—compiler)
SOSUS: Sound and Surveillance System
sot.: shower over tub
sota: state of the art
SOTAA: State-of-the-Art Association
sotd: stabilized optical tracking device
sotim: sonic observation of the trajectory and impact of missiles
Soton: Southampton
sotus (SOTUS): sequentially-operated teletypewriter universal selector (data processing)
Sou: Southampton
SOU: Southern Airways
Soul City: Harlem district of New York City
soundamp: sound amplification; sound amplifier
SOUP: Students Opposed to Unfair Practices
Sou Pac: Southern Pacific
Source of the Sun: Japan (called Nihon by the Japanese as it means Source of the Sun and is emblazoned on their flag)
South-African Dutch: Afrikaans
South Arabia: Southern Yemen
South Britain: England and Wales
South Carolina's Capital City: Columbia
South Central States: Arkansas, Kansas, Missouri, Oklahoma
South End: Boston, Massachusetts slum
souther: storm from the south
Southern: Southern Railway
Southern Alplands: Albania, France, Italy, Yugoslavia
Southern California: California south of the Tehachapis
Southern Colonies: Virginia, Maryland, North Carolina, South Carolina, Georgia
Southern Cross: constellation visible in the southern hemisphere where it adorns the flags of Australia and New Zealand as well as the coat of arms of Brazil
Southern Ireland: Republic of Ireland
southern lights: *aurora australis*
Southernmost American Town: Naalehu, Island of Hawaii
Southernmost Canadian Town: Kingsville, Ontario
Southernmost Province: Ontario
Southernmost State: Hawaii
Southern Ocean: Antarctic sections of the Atlantic, Indian, and Pacific oceans
Southern Rhodesia: Rhodesia's name when it was still a British colony
Southern States: former slave-holding states of the Confederacy such as Virginia, North and South Carolina, Georgia, Florida, Alabama, Mississippi, Tennessee, Arkansas, Louisiana, and Texas—all part of the Confederate States of America plus temporary government in Kentucky and Missouri
South Holland: Dutch province containing Dodrecht, The Hague, Leiden, and Rotterdam
South Jersey Coast: Atlantic City to Cape May
South Ken: South Kensington Imperial Institute (London's museum of science and industry)
South Orkneys: South Orkney Islands in British Antarctica
South Pacific: South Pacific Ocean
South Providence: Rhode Island's largest slum
South Sandwiches: South Sandwich Islands
South Seas: South Pacific Ocean
South Shetlands: South Shetland Islands off British Antarctica
South Side: Chicago slum area
Southwest: southern California and Nevada, Arizona, New Mexico, and western Texas
sov: shutoff valve; special orientation visit
Sov: Soviet; Sovietic; Soviets
Soviet Central Asia: Kazakh, Kirghiz, Tadzhik, Turkmen, and Uzbek Soviet Socialist Republics
Soviet Film Pioneer: Sergei Ei-

senstein
Soviet Symphonist: Serge Prokofiev and Dmitri Shostakovich share this title
Sovinformburo: Soviet Information Bureau
s-o vlv: shutoff valve
Sov strike: attack by the Soviet Union
SOW: Sunflower Ordnance Works
SOWETO: Southwestern Townships (South Africa)
sox: socks; solid oxygen; stockings
sp: self-propelled; selling price; shear plate; single-phase, single-pole; single-purpose; small paper; smokeless powder; solid-propellant; space; spare; spare part; special; special paper; special propellant(s); special-purpose; specie; species; specific; speed; starting point; starting price; static pressure; stop payment; summary plotter; summary programmed
sp: *sans prix* (French—without price)
sp.: *species* (Latin—species)
s & p: systems and procedures
s/p: soft-point (bullet with lead core exposed to increase expansion)
sp (SP): space character (data processing)
s.p.: *sine prole* (Latin—without issue)
Sp: Spain; Spanish
Sp: *Spalten* (German—column; division); *Spitz* (German—point)—pointed high-velocity bullet
SP: San Pedro, California; São Paulo, Brazil; Scientific Paper; Section Control; Security Publication; Shore Party; Shore Patrol; Shore Police; Socialist Party; Society of Protozoologists; Southern Pacific (railroad); Special Publication; Standard Practice(s); Strategic Plan(ning); subliminal perception; Submarine Patrol; sub-professional (civil service rating)
S-P: Studebaker-Packard
SP: *Senterpartiet* (Norwegian—Centrist party); *Socialdemokratiet Parti* (Danish—Social Democratic Party); *Sozialistische Partei* (German—Socialist Party)
S.P.: *Sanctissimus Pater* (Latin—Most Holy Father); *Summus Pontifex (Latin—Supreme Pontiff; the Pope)*
S & P: Standard & Poor's Corporation
S of P: Society of Philaticians
Sp/1: Specialist, 1st class
spa.: subject to particular average; sudden phase anomaly
S p A: *Società per Azioni* (Italian—joint stock company)
SPA: Salt Producers Association; School of Performing Arts; Società per Azioni (Italian—joint stock company); Société Protectrice des Animaux (Society for the Protection of Animals); Society of Participating Artists; Society for Personnel Administration; Society of Philatelic Americans; Songwriters Protective Association; Southern Pine Association; South Pacific Area; Southwestern Power Administration; Standard Practice Amendment(s); Systems and Procedures Association
SPAAMFAA: Society for the Preservation and Appreciation of Antique Motor Fire Apparatus in America
SPAB: Society for the Protection of Ancient Buildings
spac: spatial computer
SPAC: Saratoga Performing Arts Center
S Pac Cur: South Pacific Current
Space City: Houston, Texas (NASA headquarters)
spad (SPAD): space patrol air defense
SPAD: Space Patrol Air Defense; Support Planning and Design
SPADETS: Space Detection and Tracking System
spam: spiced pork and meat (canned meat introduced during World War II when meat byproducts fed people as well as their pets)
SPAM: Society for the Publication of American Music
SPAMS: Ship Position and Altitude Measurement System
span.: space navigation
Span: Spanish
SPAN: Solar Particle Alert Network
SPANA: Society for the Protection of Animals in North Africa
spandar: space-and-range radar
Spanglish: Spanish + English (Latin American mixture of the two tongues; common along the Mexican Border and in many port cities)
Spanish Africa: Ifni, Spanish Sahara, and formerly Spanish Guinea and Spanish Morocco
Spanish America: Spanish-speaking countries of Latin America
Spanish Artist and Sculptor: Pablo Picasso
Spanish Etcher-Lithographer-Painter: Francisco José de Goya y Lucientes
Spanish Film Pioneer: Luís Bunuel
Spanish Impressionist: Joaquín Sorolla y Bastida
Spanish Lithographer: Francisco José de Goya y Lucientes
Spanish Main: Spanish-speaking mainland of Central America and northern South America bordering the Caribbean from Mexico to Venezuela, including Belize, Guatemala, Honduras, Nicaragua, Costa Rica, Panama, and Columbia
Spanish Monastic Painter: Francisco de Zurbarán
Spanish National Composer: Manuel de Falla
Spanish Naturalist Painter: Diego Rodriguez de Silva y Velázquez
Spanish Netherlands: all the Lowland Countries (Belgium, Luxembourg, and the Netherlands) when they were under Spanish rule
Spanish Riviera: Spain's Mediterranean resorts
Spanish Sahara: Rio de Oro
Spanish-speaking Places: Andorra, Argentina, Balearic Islands, Bolivia, Canary Islands, Ceuta and Melilla, Chile, Colombia, Costa Rica, Cuba, Dominican Republic, Ecuador, El Salvador, Equatorial Guinea, Guam, Guatemala, Honduras, Mexico, Morocco, Nicaragua, Panama, Paraguay, Peru, Philippines, Puerto Rico, Spain, Spanish Sahara, United States (especially in many large cities such as New York as well as in the South, the Southwest, and southern California) Uruguay, Venezuela, etc.
Spanish Town: Tampa, Florida, where so many expatriate Spaniards reside
Spanish West Africa: Sidi Ifni

Span Neth: Spanish Netherlands
span(s): spaniel(s)
Spansule: span + capsule (prepared so different drugs encapsulated are released at various times)
SPAR: Seagoing Platform for Acoustics Research; Selection Program for ADMIRAL Runs (*see* ADMIRAL)
sparc: steam power automation and results computer
SPARC: Space Program Analysis and Review Council
sparr: steerable paraboloid altazimuth radio reflector (Jordrell Bank Radio-Telescope, Cheshire, England)
SPARS: Women's Coast Guard Reserve (from the Coast Guard motto, *Semper Paratus*—Always Ready)
SPARTAN: Special Proficiency at Rugged Training and National Building (Green Beret training program); System for Personnel Automated Reports, Transactions, and Notices (NASA)
SPAS: *Societatis Philosophicae Americanae Socius* (Latin—Fellow of the American Philosophical Society)
SPASM: Society for the Prevention of Asinine Student Movements
spasur: space surveillance
spat.: self-protective antitank (weapon); silicon precision alloy transistor
SPAT: Submarine Processing Action Team
SPATC: South Pacific Air Transport Council
spats: spatterdashes
S Pau: São Paulo
Spauld Turn: Spaulding Turnpike
spb: special boiling point
SPB: Special Branch Policeman (British English—detective)
spc: salicylamide-phenacetin-caffeine; special fuel consumption; suspended plaster ceiling
SPC: Society for the Prevention of Crime; South Pacific Commission; Space Projects Center; Standard Products Committee; Subcontract Plans Committee
SPCA: Society for the Prevention of Cruelty to Animals
SPCC: Ships Parts Control Center; Society for the Prevention of Cruelty to Children
sp cd: spinal cord
SPCH: Society for the Prevention of Cruelty to Homosexuals
SPCK: Society for Promoting Christian Knowledge
SPCM: Special Court-Martial
SPCMO: Special Court-Martial Order
SPCO: St Paul Civic Opera
spcr: spacer
SPCs: Suicide Prevention Centers; Suicide Prevention Clinics
Sp Cttee 24: Special Committee of 24 (United Nations' 24-member Special Committee concerning Granting Independence to Colonial Countries and Peoples)
spd: ship pays dues
Spd: Spandau
SPD: Sales Promotion Department; Sozialdemokratische Partei Deutschlands (Social Democratic Party of Germany); System Program Director
SPDC: Spare Parts Distributing Center
sp del: special delivery
spdl: spindle
spdltr: speedletter
sp dt: single pole, double throw
spe: special purpose equipment
SPE: Society of Petroleum Engineers; Society of Plastics Engineers; Society for Pure English
SPEARS: Satellite Photo-Electronic Analog Rectification System
SPEBSQSA: Society for the Preservation and Encouragement of Barber Shop Quartet Singing in America
spec: specification; specimen; speculation
's'pec': suspect
Spec: Speculative Society (of debaters)
SPEC: Society for Pollution and Environmental Control; Systems and Procedures Exchange Center
spec appt: special appointment
specat: special category
special.: specialization; specialized
specif: specific; specifically
specl: specialist; specialize
specs: specifications; spectacles
SPECTRE: Special Executive for Counterintelligence, Terrorism, Revenge, and Extortion (fictional organization created by Ian Fleming for his James Bond books)
spectrog: spectrography
spectrophotom: spectrophotometry
spectros: spectroscopy
SPEDE: System for Processing Educational Data Electronically
S Pedro: San Pedro
speed: speed kills (nickname for killer-type psychedelic drugs of methamphetamine type)—nickname derived from automotive safety slogan—"speed kills"
SPEED: Systematic Plotting and Evaluation of Enumerated Data
speedo: speedometer
Spel Soc Am: Speleological Society of America
Spen: Spencer; Spencerian
Spence: Spencer
Sperm: Strom (Sperm) Thurmond—potent South Carolina politician—father at 73
Sperry: Sperry Rand Corporation
SPERT: simplified program evaluation and review task (technique)
S Pete: St Petersburg
Spett: *Spettabile* (Italian—Dear Sir)
Spett ditta: *Spettabile ditta* (Italian—Messrs)
SPF: Society for the Propagation of the Faith
sp fl: spinal fluid
spg: spring
spg: sponge
Spg: Spring (postal abbreviation)
SPG: Society for the Propagation of the Gospel
SPGA: Scottish Professional Golfers' Association
SPGB: Socialist Party of Great Britain
Spgfld: Springfield
spgg: solid-propellant gas generator
sp gr: specific gravity
Spgs: Springs (postal abbreviation)
sph: sphenoidal
sphd: special pay for hostile duty
sp hdlg: special handling
SPHE: Society of Packaging and Handling Engineers
SP & HE: Society of Packaging & Handling Engineers
sphen: sphenodon (tuatara lizard); sphenoid; sphenoidal
spher: spherical; spheroid
sp—hl: sun present—horizon lost

SPHS: Seward Park High School; Swedish Pioneer Historical Society
sp ht: specific heat
spi: scientific performance index
spi (SPI): serum precipitable iodine
SPI: *Secrétariats Professionnels Internationaux* (International Professional Secretariats); *Service Pédagogique Interafricain* (Inter-African Teaching Service)
SPI: Society of Photographic Illustrators; Society of the Plastics Industry; Spanish Paprika Institute
SPIC: Society of the Plastics Industry of Canada; Society for the Promotion of Identity on Campus
spicbm (SPICBM): solid-propellant intercontinental ballistic missile
Spice Islands: Indonesia's islands
spid: submerged portable inflatable dwelling
Spider of Florence: Machiavelli
spids: sensor personnel intrusion devices
spie: self-programmed individualized education
SPIE: Society of Photographic Instrumentation Engineers
SPIL: Society for the Promotion and Improvement of Libraries
Spinach Capital of the World: Crystal City, Texas (replete with a statue of Popeye)
sp. indet.: *species indeterminata* (Latin—species indeterminate)
SPIndex: Subject Profile Index (ABC-Clio's innovative new indexing system)
spinel: magnesium aluminum oxide
sp. inquir.: *species inquirendae* (Latin—species of doubtful status)
s'pipe: standpipe
spir: spiral
spir.: *spiritus* (Latin—spirits)
SPIRES: Standard Personnel Information Retrieval System
SPIRGs: Student Public Interest Groups
spirit: *spiritoso* (Italian—spirited)
Spirit: Spiritualism
spirits of hartshorn: ammonia water (NH_4OH)
spirits of salts: hydrochloric acid
spis: service packaging instruction sheet
spis: *spissus* (Latin—dried)
spit.: selective printing of items from tape
spital: (Early English contraction—hospital)
Spits: Spitsbergen Islands
spiw: special-purpose infantry weapon
ŠPJČ: Saint Petersburg Junior College
spk: speckled
Spk: Spokane
spkr: speaker
spl: simplex; sound pressure level; special
s.p.l.: *sine prole legitima* (Latin—without legitimate offspring)
Spl: Sevastopol
SPL: Sacramento Public Library; Saskatoon Public Library; Seattle Public Library; Space Programming Language; Spokane Public Library; Springfield Public Library; Syracuse Public Library
SPLAN: School Organization Budget-Planning System
SPLC: Standard Point Location Code
Splendid Sprinter: Ted Williams
splf: simplification
splsm: single-position letter-sorting machine
spm: self-propelled mount; strokes per minute
s.p.m.: *sine prole mascula* (Latin—without male issue)
SPM: Saint-Pierre et Miquelon
SPM: *Scuola Professionale Marittima* (Italian—Professional Maritime School)
SPMA: Sewage Plant Manufacturers' Association
Sp Mor: Spanish Morocco
SPMRL: Sulfite Pulp Manufacturers' Research League
SPMS: System Program Management Surveys
SPMU: Society of Professional Musicians in Ulster
spn: sponsor
sp. n.: *species nova* (Latin—new species)
Spn: Spain; Spaniard; Spanish
SPN: Separation Program Number
SPNI: Society for the Protection of Nature in Israel
SPNM: Society for the Promotion of New Music
sp. nov.: *species novum* (Latin—new species)
SPNR: Society for the Promotion of Nature Reserves
SPNWR: Salt Plains National Wildlife Refuge (Oklahoma)
spo: sausages, potatoes, and onions
S Po: São Paulo
SPO: Sea Post Office; Special Project(s) Office; System Program Office
SPÖ: *Socialistische Partei Österreichs* (German—Austrian Socialist Party)
spoc: single-point orbit calculator
SPOE: Society of Post Office Engineers
SPOIE: Society of Photo-Optical Instrumentation Engineers
Spoke: Spokane, Washington
Spokesman for the Negro: Booker T. Washington
spont: spontaneous
Spoon River Poet: Edgar Lee Masters
spoorw: *spoorwegen* (Dutch—railway car)
Sporades: Sporades Islands
Spore: Singapore
spork: spoon + fork (combination utensil)
sport.: sporting; sportsman; sportsmanship; sportswoman
Sport of Kings: (horseracing—a ruinous sport only kings can afford)
sportscast(er): sports broadcast(er)
spot.: spotlight
spots: spotlights
spp: species
spp.: *species* (Latin—two or more species) singular is *sp.*: species
SPP: System Package Program
SPPL: St Paul Public Library; St Petersburg Public Library
spps: stable plasma protein solution (SPPS)
Sp Pt: Sparrows Point
spqr: small profits and quick returns
S.P.Q.R.: *Senatus Populusque Romanus* (Latin—the Senate and People of Rome)
spr: solid-propellant rocket (SPR); spring
Spr: Springfield
SPR: Simplified Practice Recommendation(s); Society for Pediatric Research; Society for Psychical Research; solid-propellant rocket; Special Project Report; Supplementary Progress Report
SPRC: Society for the Prevention and Relief of Cancer
SPRDO: Service Parts Repairable Disposition Order
spre: *siempre* (Spanish—always)

SPRE: Society of Park and Recreation Educators
Spree River City: Berlin
SPRI: Scott Polar Research Institute
Spring: Beethoven's Sonata No. 5 for Violin and Piano (opus 24); Schumann's Symphony No. 1 in B-flat major
sprint (SPRINT): solid-propellant rocket-intercept missile
SPRL: *Société de Personnes à Responsabilité Limitée* (French—limited company)
spr's: small parcels and rolls
Sprs: Springs
sps (SPS): service propulsion system
s.p.s.: *sine prole supersite* (Latin—without surviving issue)
SpS: Special Services
SPS: Society of Pelvic Surgeons; Society of Plastic Surgeons; Society of Saint Patrick; Southwestern Public Service; Spokane, Portland & Seattle (railroad); Standard Pressed Steel; Steam Power Systems; Submerged Production System; Symbolic Programming System; System of Procedure Specifications
SP & S: Spokane, Portland & Seattle (railroad)
SPSA: Senate Press Secretaries Association
SPSE: Society of Photographic Scientists and Engineers
SPSL: Society for the Protection of Science and Learning
SPSO: Senior Principal Scientific Officer
sp st: single pole, single throw
spt: seaport; support
spt.: *spiritus* (Latin—alcohol; spirits)
Spt: Split (Yugoslavia)
sptc: specified period of time contract
Sp3c: Specialist, third class
sptg: sporting
SptL: support line
SPTL: Society of Public Teachers of Law
sptr: spectrum
spu: swimmer propulsion unit
SPUC: Society for the Protection of Unborn Children
spud.: solar power unit demonstrator
SPUD: St Paul Union Depot
SPUR: Space Power Unit Reactor
SPURT: Short Public Responsibility Theory
spurv: self-propelled underwater research vehicle
sputnik: *iskustvennyi sputnik zemli* (Russian—artificial fellow-traveler around the earth, Soviet satellite launched October 4, 1957)
SPV: Society for the Prevention of Vice (prurient book burners in search of the putrid)
SPVD: Society for the Prevention of Venereal Disease
SPW: Sillonian Plant Watchers; Society for the Protection of Whitey; Society of Protestant Wardens
SpWAfr: Spanish West Africa
SPWLA: Society of Professional Well Log Analysts
spx circuit: simplex circuit (data processing)
sq: squadron; square; stereo-quadraphonic; superquick
sq.: *sequens, sequentia* (Latin—what follows; result; sequel)
Sq: Square
SQ: stereo-quadraphonic (discs and recordings)
SQ: *Secondo Quantità* (Italian—according to the quantity consumed)—menu abbreviation
sqa: stereo-quadraphonic amplifier
sqc: self-quenching control; statistical quality control
sq cell ca: squamous cell carcinoma
sq cm: square centimeter(s)
SQCP: Statistical Quality Control Procedure
sqd: squad
sqdc: special quick-disconnect coupling
Sqdn Ldr: Squadron Leader
sq ft: square foot (feet)
sq hd: square head
sq in.: square inch (inches)
sq m: square meter; square mile
SQMS: Staff Quartermaster Sergeant
Sqn Ldr: Squadron Leader
SqNP: Sequoia National Park
Sq O: Squadron Office(r)
SQP: San Quentin Prison (California)
sq rd: square rod
sq's: stereo-quadraphonic recordings; stereo-quadraphonic records
SQS: Stochastic Queuing System; Supplier Quality Services
Sqs SM: Squadron Sergeant-Major
sq3r: survey, question, read, review, recite (psychological sequence)
sqt: square rooter
SQT: Ship Qualification Test (USN)
squa: squamoid; squamous
squak: squall and squeal
square: symbol of four corners of the earth; four points of the compass; male symbol; quadrature; symbol of rigid uprightness as in, "Always honest, always fair, doing business on the square"; slang term for someone with unsophisticated tastes, "a square"
Squaresville: area, city, or neighborhood inhabited mainly by square-type citizens who frown on all types of criminal activity and even cooperate with the police
squarson: squire + parson
'squitoes: mosquitoes
sq yd: square yard
sr: scientific research; sedimentation rate; selective ringing, sensitization response; separate rations; sex ratio; shipment request; short range; sigma reaction; single-reduction (geared turbine); sinus rhythm; slow release; sound ranging; spares requirement; split ring; standard range (aviation landing); steradian; stimulus response
sr: *srovnej* (Czech—compare)
sr (SR): saturable reactor; surveillance radar
Sr: Saudi Arabia; Saudi Arabian; Senior; strontium
Sr. *Señor* (Spanish—Mister)
Sr^{85}; radioactive strontium
SR: saturable reactor; Scientific Report; Scottish Rifles; Seaman Recruit; seaplane reconnaissance (naval aircraft); Section Report; Senate Resolution; Senior Registrar; Service Record; Service Report; Shipping Receipt; Simulation Report; Society of Radiologists; Society of Rheology; Sons of the Revolution; Sound Report; Southern Railway; Special Regulation(s); Special Report; Specification Requirement(s); Staff Report; Standardization Report; Star Route (rural postal delivery); Statsjanstemannens Riksforbund (National Association of Salaried Government Employees, Sweden); Status Report; Study Requirement; Summary Report; Supporting Research; surveillance radar;

Sveriges Radio (Swedish radio broadcast network); Swissair
SR: Saudi Arabian riyal (currency unit)
S-R: Saunders-Roe; stimulus-response
sra: sulforicinocleic acid
Sra: *Señora* (Spanish—Missus; Mistress)
SRA: Science Research Associates; Screw Research Association; Society of Residential Appraisers; Special Refractories Association; Station Representatives Association
SRAB: Sveriges Radio AB (Swedish Broadcasting Corporation)
Sra Dña: *Señora Doña* (Spanish—Lady Madam)
s'raight: straight
sram (SRAM): short-range attack missile
Sras: *Señoras* (Spanish—ladies)
SRAs: Senior Resident Agents
SRBC: Susquehanna River Basin Compact
Srb-Crt: Serbo-Croat (Yugoslavian)
srbm (SRMB): short-range ballistic missile
srbp: synthetic resin-bonded paper
src: sample return container; solvent-refined coal
SRC: Science Research Council; Signal Reserve Corps; Southern Regional Council; Southwest Research Corporation; Standard Requirements Code; Sul Ross State College; Swiss Red Cross
SRC: *Santa Romana Chiesa* (Italian—Holy Roman Church)
srcc: strikes, riots, and civil commotions
s-r cells: sensitization-response cells
srch: search (computer)
Sr D: *Señor Don* (Spanish—Sir Mister)
SRD: Secret Restricted Data
SRD: *Standard Rate and Data*
SRDA: Scottish Retail Drapers Association
SRDC: Standard Reference Data Center
SRDE: Signals Research and Development Establishment
Sre: *Sreda* (Russian—Wednesday)
SRE: Society of Reproduction Engineers
S.R.E.: *Sancta Romana Ecclesia* (Latin—Holy Roman Church)
SR EB: Southern Regional Education Board
SRED: Scientific Research and Experiments Department
srem: sleep with rapid eye movements
Sres: *Señores* (Spanish—Messrs)
srf: self-resonant frequency; semi-reinforced furnace; solar radiation flux; stable radio frequency; submarine range finder; supported ring frame; system recovery factor
srf black: semireinforcing furnace black
srg: sound ranging
SRGM: Solomon R. Guggenheim Museum
SRHE: Society for Research into Higher Education
SRHL: Southwestern Radiological Health Laboratory
Sr HS: Senior High School
sri: servo repeater indicator; silicone rubber insulation; spectrum resolver integrator; surface roughness indicator
SRI: Scientific Research Institute; Southern Research Institute; Southwestern Research Institute; Space Research Institute; Stanford Research Institute
SRI: *Sacro Romano Impero* (Italian—Holy Roman Empire)
Sria; *Secretaria* (Spanish—secretariat)
srif: somatotropin release-inhibiting factor
Sri Lan: *Sri Lanka* (Singhalese—Resplendent Land)—Ceylon
SRILTA: Stanford Research Institute Lead Time Analysis
Srio: *Secretario* (Spanish—Secretary)
SRIS: Safety Research Information Service; School Research Information Service
srj: self-restraint joint; static round jet
SRJC: Santa Rosa Junior College
SRL: Save-the-Redwoods League; Scientific Research Laboratory; Study Reference List
SRL: *Saturday Review of Literature; sociedad de responsabilidad limitada* (Spanish—limited liability company)
Srls: Saudi Arabian riyal(s)
srm: speed of relative movement
srm (SRM): short-range missile
SRM: Society for Range Management
SRME: Society for Research in Music Education
Sr M Sgt: Senior Master Sergeant
SRMU: Space Research Management Unit
SRN: State Registered Nurse
srna (SRNA): soluble ribonucleic acid
sRNA: soluble or transfer RNA (same as tRNA)
SRNA: Shipbuilders and Repairers National Association
SR NC: Severn River Naval Command
SRNP: Stirling Range National Park (Western Australia)
SRO: standing room only; Superintendent of Range Operations
s rod: stove rod
srp: supply refuelling point
SRP: Scientific Research Proposal
s-r psychology: stimulus-response psychology
srr: survival, recovery, and reconstitution
SRR: Supplementary Reserve Regulations
SRRA: Scottish Radio Retailers' Association
SRRC: Sperry Rand Research Center
srs: slow reacting substance
SRs: Socialist Revolutionaries (moderates in czarist Russia)
SRS: Sight Restoration Society; Sperry Rail Service; Statistical Reporting Service; Structural Research Series
S.R.S.: *Societatis Regiae Sodalis* (Latin—Fellow of the Royal Society)
SRSA: Scientific Research Society of America
SRSC: Sul Ross State College
SRSM: *Serenissima Repubblica di San Marino* (Italian—Most Serene Republic of San Marino)—official name of San Marino
SRSNY: Sons of the Revolution in the State of New York
S-R strain: Schmidt-Ruppin (viral) strain
srt: speech reception threshold
SRT: Standard Radio och Telefon (Swedish Radio and Telephone)
Srta: *Señorita* (Spanish—Miss)
SRTC: Salford Royal Technical College
SRTN: Solar Radio Telescope Network
Srto: *Señorito* (Spanish—master; young gentleman)

sru: shop-replaceable unit
SRU: Scottish Rugby Union
SRUBLUK: Society for the Reinvigoration of Unremunerative Branch Lines in the United Kingdom
srv (SRV): submarine research vehicle
srvlv: servovalve
SRW: Sherwin-Williams Company of Canada (stock exchange symbol)
SRY: Sherwood Rangers Yeomanry
ss: saline soak; semisteel; setscrew; single-seated; single signal; single strength; sparingly soluble; spin-stabilized; stainless steel; sterile solution; straight shank; superspeed; sword stick; sworn statement
ss.: *scilicet* (Latin—namely); *semis* (Latin—one-half); *supra scriptum* (Latin—written above; ss. usually printed to left of signature line in sworn statements)
s.s.: *sensu stricto* (Latin—in the strict sense)
s-s.: solid-state
s/s: same size; suspended sentence
s & s: signs and symptoms
s of s: source of sex (also appears as sos)
s to s: ship-to-shore; station-to-station
sS: *siehe Seite* (German—see page)
s/S: *sur Seine* (French—on the Seine)
Ss: students; subjects
SS: Science Service; Secret Service; Secretary for Scotland; Secretary of State; Selective Service; Sharpshooter; Ship Service; Ship's Stores; Silver Star; Social Security; Special Service; Special Staff; Specification(s) for Structure; Standard Score; steamship; Straits Settlements; diesel-powered attack submarine (naval symbol); Submarine Studies; Sunday School; supersonic; Support System; Surveillance Station; sworn statement
SS: *Saints; Schutzstaffel* (German—Nazi blackshirt elite corps)
SS.: *Sanctissimus* (Latin—most holy)
S-S: Sans-Serif
S & S: Simon & Schuster; Steen & Strom
S of S: Society of Separationists
ssa: smoke-suppressant additive
ssa (SSA): skin-sensitizing antibodies
SSA: Scottish Schoolmasters' Association; Secretary of State for Air; Seismological Society of America; Soaring Society of America; Social Security Administration; Society for the Study of Addiction (to alcohol and other dangerous drugs); Society of Scottish Artists; Southern Surgical Association
SSAC: Soldier's, Sailor's, and Airmen's Club
SSAFA: Soldiers', Sailors', and Airmen's Families Association
***SS* agar:** *Shigella* and *Salmonella* agar
SSAGO: Student Scout and Guide Organisation
ss ar: spotface arbor
SSAR: Society for the Study of Amphibians and Reptiles
SSASA: Social Services Association of South Africa
ssb: single side band
SSB: fleet ballistic missile submarine (3-letter naval symbol); Security Screening Board; Selective Service Board; Society for the Study of Blood
SSBN: nuclear-powered fleet ballistic missile submarine (4-letter naval symbol)
s & sc: sized and supercalendered
ssc (SSC): station-selection code (data processing)
SSC: Sacramento State College; Sarawak Shipping Company; Sculptors' Society of Canada; Ships Systems Command (formerly Bureau of Ships); Straits Steamship Company; Supply Systems Command (formerly Bureau of Supplies and Accounts)
S.S.C.: *Societas Sanctae Crucis* (Latin—Society of the Holy Cross)
sscc: spin-scan cloud camera
SSCC: Space Surveillance Control Center
S.Sc.D.: Doctor of Social Science
SSCDS: Small Ship Combat Data System
SSCI: Steel Service Center Institute
SSCNS: Ship's Self-Contained Navigation System
SSCQT: Selective Service College Qualification Test
ss cr: stainless-steel crown
SSCS: Shipboard Satellite Communications System
ssd: source skin distance
ssd (SSD): sentence-structure determination
SSD: Space Systems Division (USAF)
SSD: *Staatssicherheitsdienst* (German—State Security Service)—East German political police
SS.D.: *Sanctissimus Dominus* (Latin—Most Holy Lord)—the Pope
S.S.D.: *Sacrae Scripturae Doctor* (Latin—Doctor of Sacred Scripture)
SSDA: Self-Service Development Association
ssdr: subsystem development requirement
SSE: south southeast
S.S.E.: Society of Saint Edmund
SSEB: South of Scotland Electricity Board
SSEC: Secondary School Examination Council
SSEES: School of Slavonic and East European Studies
ss enema: soap-suds enema
ssf: saybolt seconds furol; single-seated fighter; standard saybolt furol (viscosity)
SSF: Service Storage Facility; Ship's Service Force; Social Science Foundation (University of Denver); Special Service Force
SSFA: Scottish Schools' Football Association; Scottish Steel Founders' Association
SSFF: Solid Smokeless Fuels Federation
ss fx: spotface fixture
SSG: guided missile submarine (3-letter naval symbol)
SSGN: nuclear-powered guided-missile submarine (4-letter naval symbol)
SSgt: Staff Sergeant
SSH: Sailor's Snug Harbor
S Sh A: *Soyedinennye Shaty Ameriki* (Russian—United States of America)
SSHA: Scottish Special Housing Association
ssi: sites of scientific importance
Ssi: *Sũrekasi* (Turkish—company)
SSI: Society of Scribes and Illuminators
SSI: *Service Social International*

(French—International Social Service)
SSIB: Seaway Skyway International Bridge
SSIC: Southern States Industrial Council
SSIE: Smithsonian Science Information Exchange
SSIH: *Société Suisse pour l'Industrie Horlogère* (French—Swiss Society of the Horological Industry)
SSISI: Statistical and Social Inquiry Society of Ireland
ssk: soil stack
SSL: Saguenay Shipping Limited; Sapphire Steamship Lines; Seven Stars Line; Space Science Laboratory (Convair); Space Sciences Laboratory (GE)
S.S.L.: *Sacrae Scripturae Licentiatus* (Latin—Licentiate of Sacred Scripture)
SS loran: sky-wave synchronized loran
SSLS: Solid-State Laser System
ss lt: starboard side light
sslv (SSLV): standard space-launched vehicle
ssm (SSM): surface-to-surface missile
SSM: Singer Sewing Machine; System Support Management; System Support Manager
ssma: solid-state microwave amplifier
SSMA: Stainless Steel Manufacturers' Association
ssmm: space station mathematical model
SS MM: *Sus Majestades* (Spanish—Their Majesties; Your Majesties)
SSMS: Submarine Safety Monitoring System
ssmt: supersonic magnetic (railroad) train
SSN: Space Surveillance Network
SS(N): nuclear-powered submarine (3-letter naval symbol)
SSNC: Scindia Steam Navigation Company
ssnd: solid-state neutral dosimeter
ssnf: source spot noise figure
SS^{no}: *escribano* (Spanish—court clerk; notary; scribe)
SSO: Sacramento Symphony Orchestra; Savannah Symphony Orchestra; Seattle Symphony Orchestra; Shreveport Symphony Orchestra; Spokane Symphony Orchestra; Springfield Symphony Orchestra; Sydney Symphony Orchestra; Syracuse Symphony Orchestra; System Staff Office(r)
SSO: *sudsudoeste* (Spanish—south southwest)
SSOFS: Smiling Sons of the Friendly Shillelaghs
s sord: *senza sordini* (Italian—without mutes)
SSOs: Student Services Organization members
ssp: seismic section profiler; ship's stores profit; single-shot probability; standby-status panel; steam service pressure; subspecies; sustained superior performance
SSP: scouting seaplane (3-letter naval symbol); Seashore State Park (Virginia); S.S. Pierce; Sunshine State Parkway
S.S.P.: Society of Saint Paul
sspc: solid-state power controller
SSPC: Steel Structures Painting Council
SSPCA: Scottish Society for the Prevention of Cruelty to Animals
sspe: subacute sclerosing panencephalitis
SSPFC: Stainless Steel Plumbing Fixture Council
SSPHS: Society for Spanish and Portuguese Historical Studies
SSPN: Satellite System for Precise Navigation
SSPP: Society for the Study of Process Philosophies
S-spring: S-shaped spring
SSPV: Scottish Society for the Prevention of Vivisection
ssq: simple sinusoidal quantity
SSQ: Station Sick Quarters
SSQT: Selective Service Qualification Test
ssr: secondary surveillance radar
SSR: Soviet Socialist Republic(s)
SSRA: Scottish Squash Rackets Association
SSRB: Soil Survey Research Board
SSRC: Social Science Research Council
SSRI: Social Science Research Institute
SSRL: Systems Simulation Research Laboratory
sss: single-screw ship; specific soluble substance; sterile saline soak
sss (SSS): *su seguro servidor* (Spanish—your sure servant; yours truly)
s.s.s.: *stratum super stratum* (Latin—layer upon layer)
SSS: Secretary of State for Scotland; Selective Service System; System Safety Society
S.S.S.: *Societas Sanctissimi Sacramenti* (Latin—Congregation of the Most Blessed Sacrament)
S-S-S: *Schweiz-Suisse-Svizzera* (Switzerland in the three languages of the country)
SSSA: Soil Science Society of America
S-S SA: Singapore-Soviet Shipping Agency
SSSB: System Source Selection Board
sssc: soft-sized super-calendered (paper)
SSSC: Space Science Steering Committee (NASA)
sssd: second-stage separation device; solid-state solenoid driver
sssi: sites of special scientific importance
SSSJ: Student Struggle for Soviet Jewry
SSSL: Solid State Sciences Laboratory (USAF)
sssm: site space surveillance monitor
SSSM: South Street Seaport Museum (New York City)
SSSP: Space Shuttle Synthesis Program
SSSR: *Soyuz Sovietskikh Sotsialisticheskikh Respublik* (Russian—Union of Soviet Socialist Republics)
SSSS: Society for the Scientific Study of the Sea
ssst: (not an abbreviation but the symbol for the sound of an aerosol spray)—see ***ffft***
sst: stainless steel; supersonic transport (airplane)
SST: Samoan Standard Time; Society of Silver Collectors; Space Systems Center (Douglas); Submarine Supply Center; supersonic transport (airplane); target and training submarine (naval symbol)
SSTA: Scottish Secondary Teachers; Association
SSTO: Superintending Sea Transport Office(r)
sstu: seamless steel tubing
ssu: saybolt seconds universal; self-serving unit
s.s.v.: *sub signa veneni* (Latin—under a poison label)
SSV: ship-to-surface vessel
S.S. Van Dine: Willard Huntington Wright's pen name and one he used in writing detec-

tive stories
SSvd: Selective Service
SSV/GC & N: Space Shuttle Vehicle/Guidance, Control and Navigation
ssvs: slow-scan video simulator
ssw: safety switch
SSW: south southwest
SSWA: Scottish Society of Women Artists
SSWS: Seismic Sea Wave Warning System
SSX: South Coast Corporation (stock exchange symbol)
ssz: specified strike zone
SSZ: Society of Systematic Zoology
st: sedimentation time; service test; short ton; single-throw; single tire; slight trace; sounding tube; special text; special translation; statement(s); steel truss; stock transfer; stone; strata; surface tension; survival time; syncopated time
st.: *stet* (Latin—let it stand, usually referring to what has been mistakenly crossed out)
s & t: sink and laundry tray
St: Saint; Sainte; Stanton number; State; status; Street; strontium
ST: Seaman Torpedoman; Service Test(ing); Shipping Ticket; Sons of Temperance; Speech Therapist; speech therapy; Standardized Test; Summer Time; Suomen Tsavalta (Finnish—Finland); Syrian Territory
S.T.: sidereal time
S & T: Supply and Transport
S of T: Sons of Temperance
sta: station; stationary; stationery; stator
Sta: *Santa* (Italian, Portuguese, Spanish—Saint) —feminine; *Señorita* (Spanish—Miss)
STA: Scottish Typographical Association; Society of Typographic Arts; Southern Textile Association; Supersonic Tunnel Association
STAA: Survey Test of Algebraic Aptitude
STAAS: Surveillance and Target Acquisition Aircraft System
stab.: stabilizer
STAB: *Svenska Tandsticks Aktiebolaget* (Swedish—Match (stick) Company)
Sta'b'd: starboard
stabiles: static abstract sculptures
stac: *staccato* (Italian—separately and with great distinction)
STAC: Science and Technology Advisory Committee (NASA)
STACO: Society of Telecommunications Administrative and Controlling Officers
stadan: space tracking and data acquisition network
sta eng: stationary engineer
STAFF: Stellar Acquisition Flight Feasibility (guidance system)
Staffs: Staffordshire
staflo: stable-flow (free-boundary electrophoresis apparatus)
stag.: stagger; staggered
STAG: Special Task Air Group; Standards Technical Advisory Group; Strategy and Tactics Analysis Group
Stagecoach Town: Fort Worth, Texas
stagflation: stagnant (consumer demand) (price-wage) inflation; stagnant economy marked by rising unemployment and spiralling inflation
Stagirite: Aristotle the Stagirite—so named as he was born in Stagira, Macedonia
Stalag: *Stammlager* (German—base camp, for military prisoners)
Stalin: (Russian—steel)—Iosif Vissarionovich Dzhugashvili
stam: sequential thermal anhysteric magnetization; stammer(er); stammering
sta mi: statute miles
STAMP: Systems Tape Addition and Maintenance Program
Stampa: *La Stampa* (Turin's Press—one of Italy's leading newspapers)
STAMPS: Structural Thermal and Meteorite Protection System
stan: stanchion; standard; standing
Stan: Standard; Stanford; Stanley; Stanleyville; Stanton
STANAG: Standardization Agreement (NATO)
STANAVFORCHAN: Standing Naval Force Channel (NATO)
STANAVFORLANT: Standing Naval Force Atlantic (NATO)
St And: St. Andrews
standard.: standardization
Standard Oil King: John D(avison) Rockefeller, Sr
STANDINAIR: Standing Instructions for Air Attachés
stanine score: standard-nine score (USAF standard psychological score)
Stanley: Sir Henry Morton Stanley whose original name was John Rowlands
Stan Psychiat Nomen: Standard Psychiatric Nomenclature
Stan the Man: Stan Musial
STANVAC: Standard Vacuum (oil company)
staph: staphylococcus
star: symbol of perfection
STAR: Serial Titles Automated Record (National Agricultural Library); Ship-Tended Acoustic Relay; Space Thermionic Auxiliary Reactor; submersible test and research (Electric Boat)
STAR: *Scientific and Technical Aerospace Reports*
starboard side: *righthand* side of an airplane, ship, or other craft when looking forward, symbolized by a fixed *green* light—on the *righthand* wingtip of an airplane or set against a *green* background on the *righthand* side of a ship's bridge or pilothouse
Star City of the South: Roanoke, Virginia
Star and Crescent: Moslem symbol appearing on arms and flags of Algeria, Libya, Malaysia, Mauritania, Pakistan, Singapore, Tunisia, Turkey
Star of David: Judaic symbol consisting of two superimposed equilateral triangles forming a six-pointed star; device also called the Seal of Solomon or the Shield of David
Star of the East: Vladivostok
Star of the Indian Ocean: Mauritius
STARLAB: Space Technology Applications and Research Laboratory (NASA)
starquake: star + earthquake
stars.: specialized training and reassignment students; stationary automotive road stimulator (Toyota)
STARS: Satellite Telemetry Automatic Reduction System
Stars and Bars: flag of the Confederate States of America
Stars and Stripes: flag of the United States of America
Star Spangled Banner: anthem of the United States of America and nickname of its flag
START: Spacecraft Technology and Advance Reentry Test; Space Technology and Reen-

try Test(s); Space Transport and Reentry Test(s)
stas: staff-to-arm signal
Stash: Stanislas; Stanislaus
STASH: Student Association for the Study of Hallucinogens
Stasia: Anastasia
stat: electrostat; electrostatic; microstat; photostat; static; stationary; statistic(al); statuary; statue; statute
stat.: *statim* (Latin—immediately; right now)
Stat: Publius Papinius Statius (Roman poet)
state.: simplified tactical approach and terminal equipment (STATE)
States: in the States, the States, Stateside—all such expressions refer to the United States of America
State of the Thousand Islands: Maldive Islands
Statesman's: *Statesman's Year Book*
Stat Hall: Stationers' Hall
Statia: Sint Eustatius (Netherlands Antilles)
STATIC: Student Taskforce Against Telecommunication Concealment
STATLIB: Statistical Computing Library (Bell System)
Stats: statutes
Stat Off: Her (His) Majesty's Stationery Office
St AU: University of St. Andrew
STAUK: Seed Trade Association of the United Kingdom
St A YC: St Augustine Yacht Club
s-t b: steel-truss bridge
STB: Surinam Tourist Bureau
S.T.B.: *Sacrae Theologiae Baccalaureus* (Latin—Bachelor of Sacred Theology)
stbd: starboard
st brz: statuary bronze
stbt: steamboat
stc: security time control; sensitivity time control; short time constant; sound transmission class; stepchild
STC: Satellite Test Center; Satellite Tracking Committee; Scandinavian Travel Commission; Short Title Catalog; Society for Technical Communication; Southwestern Technical College; Standard Telephone and Cables; Standard Transmission Code; Sunderland Technical College
STC: *Short Title Catalogue*
S.T.C.: Samuel Taylor Coleridge
STCA: Stereo Tape Club of America
STCCM: Sistema de Transporte Colectivo Ciudad de México (Mexico City Collective Transportation System)
Stckhlm: Stockholm
st cl: storage closet
STCS: Society of Technical Civil Servants
std: salinity, temperature, depth; sexually-transmitted disease; skin test dose; standard; standard test dose; state-of-the-technology design; subscriber trunk dialing
St D: Stage Director
STD: Society for Theological Discussion; Subscriber Trunk Dialing
S.T.D.: *Sacrae Theologiae Doctor* (Latin—Doctor of Sacred Theology)
std by: stand by
St DC: St David's College
STDC: Society of Typographic Designers of Canada
stder: social introversion, thinking introversion, depression, cycloid tendencies, rhathymia (personality traits)
Stde: *Stunde* (German—hour)
st diap: stopped diapason (organ)
stdn: standardization
std p: stand pipe
st dr: single-trip drum
Stdy: Saturday
Ste.: *Sainte* (French—saint, *f.*)
Sté.: *Société* (French—Society)
St E: St. Etienne
STE: Society of Telecommunications Engineers; Society of Tractor Engineers
steakwich: steak sandwich
steamers: (slang nickname—steaming clams)
STECC: Scottish Technical Education Consultative Council
Steel Baron: Andrew Carnegie
steelie: steel ball-bearing playing marble
Steelmaker: Joe Magarac
Steel-Master Philanthropist: Andrew Carnegie
STEFER: *Società della Tranvia e Ferrovia Elettrica di Roma* (Rome transportation system)
STEG: Supersonic Transport Evaluation Group
St E H: St Elizabeth's Hospital
Steinbeck: Grosssteinbeck (original name of author John Steinbeck's family spelled with three s's as shown)
STEL: *Studenta Tutmonda Esperantista Liga* (Esperanto—Worldwide Esperanto Students League)
Stella: Estella; Estelle
STELO: *Studenta Tutmonda Esperantista Ligo* (World League of Esperanto Students)
stem.: storable tubular extendible member
STEM: stay time excursion module
sten: stencil
Stendhal: (pseudonym—Marie-Henri Beyle)
Sten gun: Sheppard and Turpin Bren gun (submachine gun)
steno: stenographer; stenography; stenotype; stenotypy
stent: *stentando* (Italian—delaying)
STEP: Safety Test Engineering Program; Scientific and Technical Exploitation Program; Secondary Teachers Education Program; Sequential Tests of Educational Progress; Solutions to Employment Problems
Steph: Stephen
STEPS: Solar Thermionic Electric Power System; Specialized Training and Employment Placement Service
ster: stereoscope; stereotype; sterilization; sterilize; sterilizer; sterling
stereo: stereophonic; stereoprojection; stereoprojector; stereoscope; stereoscopic
STERILE: System of Terminology for Retrieval of Information through Language Engineering
sterling silver: 92% silver, 8% copper
stet: let stand what has been crossed out
Stetson: Stetson hat (broad-brim high-crown hat made by John B. Stetson of Philadelphia, Pa)
stev: stevedore; stevedoring
Steve: Stephan; Stephen; Steven
stewbum: man sexually attracted to flight stewardesses
stew(s): steward(esses)
stewzoo: hotel or motel catering to flight attendants resting between flights
St Ex: Stock Exchange
stf: staff
STF: Sycamore Test Facility
STF: *Svenska Turisforeningen* (Swedish Tourist Information)
st fm: stretcher form

stg: stage; staging; sterling
stg ar: staging area
stge: storage
St George: (patron saint of England)
stgg: staging
Stgo: Santiago
Stgo de C: Santiago de Chile (Compostela, Cuba)
stgr: stringer
stge: strings
STgt: secondary target
STGWU: Scottish Transport and General Workers' Union
sth (STH): somatotrophic hormone
Sth: Stockholm
Sthlm: Stockholm
sti: service and taxes included
s & ti: scientific and technical information
St I: St. Ives
STI: Service Tools Institute; Space Technology Institute; Steel Tank Institute
STIC: Scientific and Technical Intelligence Center
stiction: static friction
STID: Scientific and Technical Information Division (NASA)
STIF: Scientific and Technical Information Facility (NASA)
stiff.: stiffener; stiffened corpse
stillat.: *stillatim* (Latin—by drops; in small amounts)
stilli: stillicide; stillicidium; stilliform
stim: stimulant
stimn: stimulation
STIMS: Scientific and Technical Modular System
stinfo: scientific and technical information
STING: Stellar Inertial Guidance (System)
STINGS: Stellar Inertial Guidance System (USAF)
Stinkstein: (German—stinkstone) —coal-black limestone or marble giving off a fetid odor when rubbed because of its bituminous or carbonaceous inclusions; also called anthraconite
stip: stipend(iary); stipulation
STIP: Science Teaching Improvement Program
STIPIS: Scientific, Technical, Intelligence, and Program Information Service (HEW)
Stir: Stirling
Stirner: Max Stirner whose original name was Kaspar Schmidt
St J: St John (New Brunswick)
STJC: South Texas Junior College; Southwest Texas Junior College
St-John Perse: Alexis Saint-Leger's pen name
StJU: St John's University
stjw: stretcher jaws
stk: sticky; stock
Stk: Stockton
St K-N-A: St Kitts-Nevis-Anguilla (Caribbean island federation)
stl: steel; studio transmitter link
St L: St Louis
STL: Seatrain Lines; Space Technology Laboratories (Thompson-Ramo-Wooldridge;) Speech Transmission Laboratory; Standard Telecommunication Laboratories; St. Louis, Missouri (airport); studio transmitter link (FM); (Swedish Transatlantic Line)
StLGR: Saint Lucia Game Reserve (South Africa)
St Lo: St Louis
STLO: Scientific and Technical Liaison Office(r)
STLOs: Scientific/Technical Liaison Offices
STLOUISPDis: St Louis Procurement District (US Army)
St L P-D: *St Louis Post-Dispatch*
stlr: semi-trailer
ST L SW: St Louis Southwestern (railroad)
STLT: studio transmitter link-TV
St LU: St Lucia; St Louis University
St L YC: St Louis Yacht Club
St L ZG: St Louis Zoological Garden
STM: scientific, technical, and medical; shielded tunable magnatron; short-term memory; special test missile; surface-to-target missile; synthetic timing mode
St M: St Malo
STM: Science Teaching Museum (Franklin Institute); System Training Mission
S.T.M.: *Sacrae Theologiae Magister* (Latin—Master of Sacred Theology)
stmftr: steamfitter
stmn: stimulation
Stmn: *The Statesman* (Calcutta)
STMSA: Scottish Timber Merchants' and Sawmillers' Association
stmt: statement
stn: stain
Stn: Station
St N: St Nazaire
stnd: stained
sto: standing order; stoker
Sto: *Santo* (Spanish—saint); *Señorito* (Spanish—master; young gentleman)
St^{o}: *Santo* (Portuguese or Spanish—Saint)
STO: Stockholm, Sweden (Arlanda Airport)
Stock: Stockholm
stol: short takeoff and landing
stolport: short-takeoff-and-landing airport
stol/ved: short takeoff and landing/vertical climb and descent
stom: stomach
stomat: stomatology
S'ton: Southampton
STon: short ton
Stonehenge: prehistoric monument on Salisbury Plain near Amesbury, England
Stonewall: General Thomas Jonathan Jackson, CSA
Stonewall Jackson: General Thomas Jonathan Jackson of the Confederate Army
stop.: slight touch on pedal; spin tires on pavement
STOP: Strategic Orbit Point
STOPP: Society of Teachers Opposed to Physical Punishment
stor: storage; stored
STOR: Scripps Tuna Oceanographic Research
storet: storage and retrieval
Stormalong: Arthur Bulltop
Stormont: Stormont Castle—official Belfast resident of Northern Ireland's prime minister; Northern Ireland's capital district near Belfast where it contains the home and office of the governor general as well as the House of Commons and the Senate of Northern Ireland
Story Teller of the Sea: sobriquet shared by Conrad, Cooper, de Hartog, Forester, Innes, London, McFee, Marryat, Masefiield, Melville, Nordhoff and Hall, Verne, and your favorite writer of sea stories
stow.: stowage
sto: standard temperature and pressure; stop; stoppage
St P: St. Paul
STO: nickname of dangerous psychedelic drug—methylmethoxyamphetamine; Scientifically Treated Petroleum (gasoline additive); sodium tripolyphosphate (water softener); stop the police (dirty street people's slogan)
S.T.P.: *Sacrae Theologae Professor* (Latin—Professor of Sa-

cred Theology)
St & P: São Tome and Principe
st part: steel partition
stpd: standard temperature and pressure—dry (0°C, 760mm Hg)
St Pete: St Petersburg
STPL: Space Tracking Pty Ltd
St P & M: St Pierre and Miquelon Islands
s tpr: short taper
stps: specific thalamic projection system
str: steamer; straight; strainer; strait; strength; structural; structure; submarine test reactor (STR)
str: *strana(y)* (Czech—page(s))
str (STR): synchronous transmitter receiver (data processing)
Str: *Strasse* (German—street); *Streptococcus*
STR: section, township, range; Society for Theatre Research; Southern Test Range; Stuttgart, Germany (airport); submarine test reactor
STRA: State Teacher's Retirement System
STRAC: Strategic Army Corps
strad: stradivarius (violin made by Antonio Stradivari or his sons Francesco and Omobono)
strad (STRAD): signal transmitting—receiving and distributing
stradap: storm radar data processor
STRAF: Strategic Army Forces
strag: straggler
StragL: straggler line
Strangler: wrestler Ed (Strangler) Lewis originally named Robert H. Friedrich
Stras: Strasbourg
strag: strategic; strategist; strategy
STRATAD: Strategic Aerospace Division (USAF)
stratig: stratigraphy
strato: stratosphere
straw: strawberry
STRAYS: Society To Rescue Animals You've Surrendered
STRC: Science and Technology Research Center; Scientific, Technical, and Research Commission
Stream of Pleasure: Thames River above London
Street: The Street—London's Fleet Street (center of periodical publishing); New York's Wall Street (financial center)
Street of Ink: Fleet Street, London with its many newspaper offices
Street of Sorrows: New York City's Wall Street; old-fashioned nickname for any thorofare frequented by streetwalkers
strep: streptococcus
stress. (STRESS): structural engineering system solver
STRESS: Stop the Robberies, Enjoy Safe Streets (program of the Detroit Police Department)
stret: *stretto* (Italian—squeezed together; more rapid [as musical notes]; strait)
STRICOM: Strike Command (US Army)
STRIKFORSOUTH: Striking and Forces Support, Southern Europe (USN)
string: *stringendo* (Italian—accelerate)
strip.: standard taped routines for image processing
Strip: The Strip—main street of Las Vegas, Nevada
Strix: Peter Fleming
S-t-R L: Save-the-Redwoods League
Strm: Stream (postal abbreviation)
strobe: satellite tracking of balloons and emergencies
strobed: stroboscopically illuminated; stroboscopically measured
strobo: stroboscope
strobotron: stroboscope + electron (tube)
struc: structure
struct: structural
's' truth: god's truth
sts: ship-to-shore (radio or radio telephone); special treatment steel; surfaced two sides
STS: Serological Test for Syphilis; Standard Test for Syphilis; Stockpile-toTarget Sequence
STSA: State Technical Services Act
STSC: Southwest Texas State College
STSD: Society of Teachers of Speech and drama
STSO: Senior Technical Staff Officer
st st: stocking stitch (knitting)
St T: (Port of) St Thomas
STT: Medical Stenographer (USN); St Thomas, Virgin Islands (airport); Sensitization Test
S-T T: Skin-Temperature Test
STTA: Scottish Table Tennis Association
ST T NHS: St Thomas National Historic Site
stu: service trials unit; skin test unit; student; submersible test unit
Stu: Stewart; Stuart
STU: *Styrelsen foer Teknisk Utveckling* (Swedish—Board for Technical Development)
STUC: Scottish Trades Union Congress
stud.: student
Stud: Studebaker
stude(s): student(s)
Studioland: Hollywood, California
stud(s).: student(s)
stuff.: system to uncover facts fast
Stuka: *Sturzkampfflugzeug* (German—dive bomber)
stuns'l: studdingsail
stupidental(ly): stupidly accidental(ly)
stuvs: standard unit variance scale
stv: subscription television
stv (STV): subscription television
St V: St Vincent
STV: Scottish Television; Separation Test Vehicle
STV: *Solidaridad de Trabajadores Vascos* (Spanish—Solidarity of Basque Workers)
stvd r: stevedore
st w: storm water
STW: Society of Technical Writers
ST WAPNIACLE: (abbreviation mnemonic for U.S. departments in order of their creation before new ones were added and some were consolidated: State Treasury, War, Attorney General (Justice), Post Office, Navy, Interior, Agriculture, Commerce, Labor, Education
STWE: Society of Technical Writers and Editors
STWP: Society of Technical Writers and Publishers
stwy: stairway
stx: start of test (data processing)
STX: St Croix, Virgin Islands (airport)
Sty: Stymie
STZ: Sterling Drugs (stock exchange symbol)
su: sensation unit(s); service unit(s); setup; strontium unit(s); sulfur unit(s)

s u: *siehe unten* (German—see below)
Su: Sudan; Sudanese
SU: Saybolt Universal; Seattle University; Shaw University; Skinner Union; Southeastern University; Southwestern University; Soviet Union; Stanford University; Stetson University; Student Union; Suffolk University; Syracuse University
su.: *sumat* (Latin—let him take)
SU: *Stati Uniti* (Italian—United States)
sua: shipped unassembled
sua (SUA): serum uric acid
SUA: Silver Users Association; State Universities Association
SUA: *Stati Uniti d'America* (Italian—United States of America)
SUAB: *Svenska Utvecklinasaktiebolaget* (Swedish Development Corporation)
SUADPS: Shipboard Uniform Automatic Data Processing System (USN)
sub: submarine; submerse; subordinate; substitute; suburb; subway
sub (SUB): substitute character (data processing)
SUB: *Subbota* (Russian—Saturday)
subac: subacute
SUBAN: Scottish Union of Bakers and Allied Workers
Sub Base: Submarine Base
sub-bell: submarine fog bell
sub chap: subchapter
Subcontinent of Asia: India
subcontr: subcontract(or)
subcrep: subcrepitant
subcut: subcutaneous(ly)
subd: subdivide; subdivision
subdeb: subdebutante
SUBDIZ: Submarine Defense Identification Zone
sub-ed: sub-editor
sub. fin. coct.: *sub finem coctionis* (Latin—at the end of boiling)
subgen.: *subgenus* (Latin)
subic (SUBIC): submarine integrated control program
subing: substituting
subj: subject; subjunctive
subl: sublimes
SUBLANT: Submarine Forces, Atlantic (USN)
subling: sublingual
Sub Lt: Sub-Lieutenant
subm: submission; submit
submand: submandibular
submtl: submittal
subn: substitution
subor: subordinate
sub-osc: submarine oscillator
subot: submarine bottom
SUBPAC: Submarine Forces, Pacific (USN)
sub para: sub paragraph
subplane: submersible seaplane
sub-pro: subprofessional
subq: subsequent
subroc (SUBROC): submarine rocket
subrog: subrogation
subs: submarines; subscription(s); subsistence; substitutes
subsan: submarine sandwich (also called sub)
sub sec: subsection
subseq: subsequent(ly)
subsis: subsistence
subsp.: *subspecies* (Latin)
subst: substantive
substa: substation
substance P: polypeptide found in the brain
substand.: substandard
substd: substandard
subsys: subsystem
subtopia: suburban utopia
subtr: subtraction
sub u: substitute unit
subtr: subtraction
suc: succeed; success; successor
suburb: suburban; suburbanite; suburbia; suburbian
suc: succeed; success; successor
suc.: *succus* (Latin—juice)
SUC: Sussex University College
Succ: *Successori* (Italian—Successors); *Succursale* (Italian—Branch)
Successor of Saint Peter: the Pope
Sucker State: Illinois nickname dating from pioneer days when settlers sucked water from underground springs with long hollow tubes called suckers
Sucr: *Sucursal* (Spanish—subsidiary; branch)
Sucre: Antonio José de Sucre—South American liberator fighting with Bolivar for freedom of Venezuela, Colombia, Ecuador, Peru, and Bolivia from Spanish rule
Sud: Sudan; Sudanese
SUD: Aerovias Sud Americanas (3-letter airline coding)
Sudáf: *Sudáfrica* (Spanish—South Africa)
SUDAM: *Superintêndencia do Desenvolvimento da Amazonia* (Portuguese—Superintendency for the Development of Amazonia)
Sudan: formerly the Anglo-Egyptian Sudan
SUDAN: Sudan Airways
SUDENE: *Superintêndencia do Desenvolvimento do Nordeste* (Portuguese—Superintendency for the Development of North-East (Brazil))
SUDS: Silhouetting Underwater Detecting System; Submarine Detecting System
Suds City: Milwaukee, Wisconsin—famous for beer
Sue: Susan; Susannah; Suzanne
suec: *suéco* (Spanish—Swedish); *sueco* (Portuguese—Swedish)
Suec: *Suecia* (Spanish—Sweden); *Suécia* (Portuguese—Sweden)
SUEL: Sperry Utah Engineering Laboratory
Suet: *Gaius Suetonius Tranquillus* (Roman biographer)
suf: sufficient; suffix
Suff: Suffolk
suffoc: suffocating
sug: suggest(ion)
SUG: Southern California Gas Company (stock exchange symbol)
SUGAR: Services, (to diabetics through) Understanding, Grants, Assistance, Recreation
Sugar Country: tropical Queensland, Australia
Sugar Islands: sugarcane-producing Leeward Islands of the West Indies
sugar of lead: lead acetate
Sugar State: Louisiana famous for its sugar beets
SUI: State University of Iowa
Suicide: European nickname for Tchaikovsky's Symphony No. 6 in B major—the Pathétique
suid: sudden unexplained infant death (crib death)
Suidwes-Afrika: (Afrikaans—South West Africa)—formerly German Southwest Africa and often called Namibia
SUIT: Scottish and Universal Investment Trust
suiv: *suivant* (French—following)
Suiz: *Suiza* (Spanish—Switzerland)
Suky: Susan; Suzanne
Sul: *Suleiman* (Arabic—Solomon)
SUL: Stanford University Libraries

Sula: Sulawesi (Celebes)
sulcl: set up in less than carloads
sulf: sulfate; sulfur
sulfa: sulfanilamide
sulfd: sulfide(s)
sulfuric acid: H_2SO_4
Suliman seal: five-pointed pentagrammic star of perplexing aspect as it seems to consist of two interlocking triangles but is not; symbol of Morocco and other Islamic lands
Sulli: Sullivan
Sulphur King: Herman Frasch
Sult: Sultan(a)
Sultan of Swat: George Herman (Babe) Ruth
Sulus: Sulu Islands in the Sulu Sea between Indonesia and the Philippines
sum.: summary; surface-to-underwater missile (SUM)
sum.: *sume* (Latin—take)
sum (SUM): surface-to-underwater missile
Sum: Sumatra; Sumatran; Sumer; Sumeria; Sumerian
SUMCMO: Summary Court-Martial Order
Sumi: Sumitomo Bank
Sumitomo: Sumitomo Shoji America; Sumitomo Shoji
SUMOC: *Superintendencia da Moeda e do Crédito* (Portuguese—Superintendency of Money and Credit)
sumr: summer
sums.: summons
sum. tal.: *sumat talem* (Latin—take one like this)
sun.: symbolic unit number (SUN)
Sun: Sunday
Sun: *The Baltimore Sun*
SUN: Solar Usage Now; Symbols, Units, and Nomenclature Commission
Sun City: St Petersburg, Florida; Yuma, Arizona; and a few other sunny places vie for this name
sund: (Danish, Norwegian, Swedish—sound, as in Haugesund)
Sund: Sunda Islands; Sundanese
Sundas: Sunda Islands of Indonesia
SUNFED: Special United Nations Fund for Economic Development
Sunflower: Kansas state flower
Sunflower(s): Kansan(s)
Sunflower State: official nickname of Kansas
Sun God: Adonis (Syrian); Apollo (Roman); Apollon (Greek); Baal (Chaldean); Helios Hyperion (Greek in Homer's time); Horus (symbolized in Upper Egypt by a hawk); Mithras (Persian); Moloch (Canaanite); Osiris (Egyptian); Ra or Re (symbolized in Egypt's Old Kingdom by an obelisk); Sol Invictus (Latin—Sun Invincible)—Romans shortened this to Sol and to this day Old Sol is the sun's nickname; Surya (Hindu)
Sun King: Louis XIV (*Le Roi Soleil*)
Sun of May: *El Sol de Mayo*—revolutionary symbol on the great seals of Argentina, Ecuador, and Uruguay; standing for national emergence in the fight for freedom
sunnie(s): sunfish(es)
Sunny Alberta: Canada's Province of Alberta
Sunnyside: Washington Irving's home near Tarrytown, New York
Sunny South: southern United States
SUNOCO: Sun Oil Company
Sunrise: Haydn's String Quartet in B flat (opus 76, no. 4)
Sunrise Poet: Sidney Lanier
SUNS: Sonic Underwater Navigation System
Sunshine Capital of the United States: Yuma, Arizona
Sunshine City: Saint Petersburg-Tampa, San Diego, Tucson, and Yuma are among many places in the South and the Southwest claiming this nickname also coveted by Durban, South Africa—City of Sunshine
Sunshine Coast: British Columbia's coast from Lund to Vancouver; Queensland's coast from Brisbane to Noosa
Sunshine Continent: Australia
Sunshine Province: Alberta, Canada
Sunshine State: Florida, New Mexico, and South Dakota contest this title with each other and with subtropical Queensland in Australia; official nickname of Florida
SUNY: State University of New York
SUNYAB: State University of New York at Buffalo
sup: superfine; superior; superlative; supersede(s); supplement(ary)); supplies; supply; support; supposition; supreme
sup: *supérieure* (French—higher; superior; upper)
sup.: *supra* (Latin—above)
SUP: Sailors Union of the Pacific; Socialist Unity Party; Sussex University Press
supchg: supercharger
Sup Ct: Superior Court; Supreme Court
supdel: superdelicious
Sup Dpo: Supply Depot
supe (slang): superintendent; supernumerary
super: superficial; superfine; superheterodyne; superintendent; superior; supermarket; supernumerary; supersede; supersession
super: *supermercado* (Spanish—supermarket)
superaero: superaerodynamics
Supercop: Philadelphia's mayor Frank Rizzo—a former policeman
superf: *superficie* (Italian—area; surface; surface area)
superhet: superheterodyne
superl: superlative
Superman of the Prize Ring: Joe Louis
Superpowers: U.S.A. and the USSR (materially and militaristically); Israel and North Vietnam (morally and patriotically)
super(s): supercargo(s); supercharger(s); superheater(s); superheterodyne(s); superhighway(s); superhuman(s); superintendent(s); superior(s); superior court(s); superior planet(s); superlative(s); superliner(s); supermarket(s); superorganism(s); superpatriot(s); superpower(s); superscript(s); supersonic(s); superstition(s); superstructure(s); supervisor(s)
Superstition Personified: Abessa who sought sanctuary behind convent walls shielding her from truth, according to Spenser's *Faerie Queene*
superstr: superstructure
Super^te: *Superintendente* (Spanish—superintendent)
superv: supervisor
SUPIR: Supplementary Photographic Interpretation Report
sup. lint.: *super linteum* (Latin—on lint)
Sup O: Supply Office(r)
supp: supplement; suppuration
Sup P: Supply Point
suppl: *supplement* (French—sup-

plement)
Supporter of the Universe: Atlas, in the Roman mythology; the ash tree Ygdrasil in Norse mythology
suppos: suppository
supps: supplements
SupPt: supply point
suppy: supplementary
supr: superior; supreme
supra cit.: *supra citato* (Latin—cited above)
Supreme Genius of Spanish Painting: Diego Rodríguez de Silva y Velázquez
Supreme God of the Hindus: Brahma
Supreme Governor of the Church of England: the King or Queen
Supreme Pontiff of the Universal Church: the Pope
supsd: supersede(d)
supt: superintend; superintendent
supv: supervise; supervisor
supvr: supervisor
supvry: supervisory
sur: surface; surfacing
Sur: Surinam (Netherlands Guiana)
Suralco: Surinam Aluminum Company
surano: surface radar and navigation operation
sur art: surrealistic art
surcal: surveillance calibration (satellite)
Sur Cdr: Surgeon Commander
Sur f: Surinam florin (guilder)
surf. a: surface area
Surfburgia: California seaside suburban communities such as Malibu, Santa Monica, Seal Beach, Pacific Beach, Imperial Beach
surg: surgeon; surgery; surgical
Surg Cdr: Surgeon Commander
Sur Gen: Surgeon General
Surg Gen: Surgeon General
Surgeon of the Rusty Knife: Dr José Pedro de Freitas Arigo of Congonhas do Campo, Brazil
Surg Lt Cdr: Surgeon Lieutenant Commander
Surg Maj: Surgeon Major
Suri: Surinam (formerly Dutch Guiana)
suric: surface ship integrated control
surpic: surface picture
Surprise: Haydn's Symphony No. 94 in G major
surr: surrender
Surr: Surrogate
SURSAN: *Superintendência de Urbanismo e Saneamento* (Portuguese—Superintendency of Urbanism and Sanitation)
surv: survey; surveying; surveyor
Surveyor: American program for lunar surface and subsurface exploration
Surv Gen: Surveyor General
survll: surveillance
sus: supressor sensitive
Sus: Saybolt universal second; Susanna, The (Apocryphal) History of Sussex
SUS: Scottish Union of Students; Society of University Surgeons
Susie: Susan; Susannah; Suzanne
susp: suspend
susp b: suspension bridge
sus. per coll.: *suspensio per collum* (Latin—hanging by the neck)
suspn: suspension
sust: sustainer
Susx: Sussex
SUT: Society for Underwater Technology
Suth: Sutherland
s'uth'ard: southward
SUV: Saybolt Universal Viscosity; Suva, Fiji Islands (Nandi Airport)
SUVCW: Sons of Union Veterans of the Civil War
SUX: Sioux City, Iowa (airport)
Suz: Suez
sv: sailing vessel (SV); selectavision (SV); (RCA patent); simian virus; single vibrations; sinus venosus; stroke volume; survey; surveyor
sv: *sotto voce* (Italian—in an undertone; in a whisper); *svacek* (Czech—volume)
s.v.: *spiritus vini* (Latin—alcohol); *sub verbo* or *sub voce* (Latin—under the word; under the voice)
s/v: surrender value; survivability/vulnerability
SV: sailing vessel; Selective Volunteer; Sons of Veterans
S & V: Sinclair and Valentine
Sva: Suva
Sval: Svalbard (Spitsbergen)
SVB: Stephen Vincent Benét
svc: service; superior vena cava
SVC: Skagit Valley College; Society of Vacuum Coaters
SVCP: Special Virus Cancer Program
svcs: superior vena cava syndrome
svd: swine vesicular disease
SVD: *Schweizerische Vereinigung für Dokumentation* (German—Swiss Documentation Association)
SVE: Society for Visual Education
Sven Akad: *Svenska Akademien* (Swedish Academy)
Svensker(s): Swedish sailor(s)
Sver: *Sverdlovsk; Sverige* (Swedish Academy)
svg: saving
s.v. gal.: *spiritus vini gallici* (Latin—brandy)
s.v.i.: *spiritus vini industrialis* (Latin—industrial alcohol)
svib: strong vocational interest blank
SVIOC: South Varanger Iron Ore Company
SVN: Student Vocational Nurse
Svn Dag: *Svenska Dagbladet* (Swedish Daily Blade)
SVNV: *Societa Veneziana di Navigazione a Vapore* (Venetian Steamship Company)
SVO: Moscow, USSR (Sheremetyevo Airport)
SVP: Society of Vertebrate Paleontology
S V P: *s'il vous plaît* (French—if you please)
s.v.r.: *spiritus vini rectificatus* (Latin—rectified spirit of wine)
SVR: Suomen Valtion Rautatiet (Finnish State Railways)
sv's: security violators
SVS: Society for Visiting Scientists
SVS: *Sveriges Standardiseringkommission* (Swedish Standards Commission)
s.v.t.: *spiritus vini tenuis* (Latin—proof alcohol; proof spirit)
SVTL: Services Valve Testing Laboratory
svtp: sound, velocity, temperature, pressure
s.v.v.: *sit venia verbo* (Latin—forgive the expression)
svy: survey
sw: salt water; sea water; sent wrong; shipper's weights; short wave; shotgun wedding; single weight; special weapon; spotweld; spotwelding; steelworker; stock width; switch; switchband wound
s-w: shortwave
s/w: salt water; sea water; seaworthy; standard weight
Sw: Sweden; Swedish
SW: Secretary of War; Security Watch; Senior Warden; Shelter Warden; Ship's Warrant;

South Wales; southwest; Southwest Airways (2-letter coding); Stone & Webster (stock exchange symbol)
S-W: Sherwin-Williams
S & W: Seaboard & Western (airlines); Smith & Wesson
swa: single-wire armored; super-wide angle
Swa: Swahili
SWA: Seaboard World Airlines; South-West Africa; Southwest Airways
swabk: sealed with a big kiss
swac: special warhead arming control
SWAC: South-West Africa Company
SWACS: Space Warning and Control System
SWAFAC: Southwest Atlantic Fisheries Advisory Commission
swag(s): scientific wild-assed guess(es)
SWAI: South-West African Infantry
swak: sealed with a kiss
swalk: sealed with a loving kiss
Swamp Fox: sobriquet shared by Revolutionary War general Francis Marion as well as by Confederate generals Nathan Bedford Forrest and Philip Dale Roddey
Swan of Avon: Ben Jonson's name for Shakespeare
Swan City: Perth, Western Australia
Swanland: southwestern Australia
Swan of Mantua: Virgil
Swan of Meander: Homer
Swans: Swan Islands off Honduras
Swanside: Perth, Western Australia
Swansider(s): inhabitant(s) of Perth on the Swan River estuary of Western Australia
SWANU: South-West Africa National Union
SWANUF: South-West Africa National United Front
SWAPO: South-West Africa People's Organization
swash: sea wash (scouring surf running up a beach after a wave breaks)
SWAT: Special Weapons and Tactics (team of law-enforcement officers trained to combat guerrillas and terrorists)
swatson: so what's on?
s waves: secondary (earthquake) waves
Swaz: Swaziland
swb: short wheelbase; single with bath; swing bridge
SWB: South Wales Borderers
swbd: switchboard
swc: specific water content
SWC: Soil and Water Conservation (US Department of Agriculture); Special Weapons Command; Supreme War Council
Swch: Switch (postal abbreviation)
SWCLR: Southwest Council of La Raza
swd: sewed
SWD: South Wales Docks
SWDA: Scottish Wholesale Druggists' Association
SWE: Society of Women Engineers
sweatl: student work experience and training
SWEB: South Wales Electricity Board; South West Electricity Board
Swed: Swede; Sweden; Swedish
Sweden's Most Popular Sculptor: Vilhelm Carl Emil Milles (originally surnamed Anderson)
Swedish Film Pioneer: Ingmar Bergman
Swedish Nightingale: Jenny Lind
SWETM: Society of West End Theatre Managers
Sweyn Forkbeard: King Svend of Denmark
Sw Fr: Swiss franc
sw fx: spotweld fixture
SWG: Society of Women Geographers; Standard Wire Gauge
Sw-Ger: Swiss-German (derived from Alemannic)
SWI: Spring Washer Institute
SWIE: South Wales Institute of Engineers
swife: sexual wife
swift.: selected words in full title
SWINE: Students Wildly Indignant (about) Nearly Everything (cartoonist Al Capp's contribution to contemporary acronyms)
Swinglish: Swedish-English
SWIRL: South Western Industrial Research Limited
SWIRS: Solid Waste Information Retrieval System
SWISSAIR: Swiss Air Transport
Swiss Cheese Capital of the U.S.A.: Monroe, Wisconsin
Swiss Family of Mathematicians and Scientists: the Bernoullis
Swiss Family of Painters: the Fuesslis
switch: switchblade knife
Switz: Switzerland
swives: sexual wives
Sw kr: Swedish krona (monetary unit)
swl: shor twave listener
SWL: safe working load (for cargo booms and derricks; SWL 5T 15 deg means the safe working load is 5 tons at 15 degrees off the horizontal); Swedish American Line
SWLA: Southwestern Library Association
SWLI: Southwestern Louisiana Institute
swlolak's: sealed with lots of love and kisses
SWly: south-westerly
SWM: Southwest Museum
SWMA: Steel Wool Manufacturers's Association
SWMF: South Wales Miners' Federation
SW1, SW2, etc.: Southwest One, Southwest Two, etc. (London postal zones)
SWO: Solid Waste Office (Environmental Protection Agency)
SWOA: Scottish Woodland Owners' Association
swoc: subject word out of context
swog: special weapons overflight guide
SWOPSI: Stanford Workshops on Political and Social Issues
's' word: god's word
SWORDS: Shallow-Water Oceanographic Research Data System
's' wounds: god's wounds
swp: safe working pressure; sweep; sweeper; sweeping
SWP: Saskatoon Wheat Pool; Sherwin-Williams Paints; Socialist Workers Party; South Wales Ports; Southwest Pacific; Special Weapons Project
SWPA: Southwest Pacific Area; Southwestern Power Administration; Surplus War Property Auministration
swr: serum wassermann reaction; standing-wave ratio; switch rails
S-W RI: Sterling-Winthrop Research Institute
swrj: split wing ramjet
sws: seam-welding system; service-wide supply; slow-wave sleep; solar-wind spectrometer; still water surface
Sws: Swansea

SWS: Sariska Wildlife Sanctuary (India); Space Weapons System; Special Weapons System
SWSC: Schlumberger Well Surveying Corporation
swt: short-wave transmitter; spiral-wrap tubing
SWT: School of Welding Technology; Scottish Wildlife Trust
SWTC: Scottish Woolen Technical College
swtchmn: switchman
SWTEA: Scottish Woolen Trade Employers' Association
swtg: switching
SWTMA: Scottish Woolen Trade Mark Association
SWUS: Southwestern United States
swv: swivel
SWWJ: Society of Women Writers and Journalists
swymmd: see what you made me do
sx: section
Sx: (medical) signs and symptoms
SX: Southern Pacific (stock exchange symbol)
sxa: stored index to address
SXC: Saint Xavier College
sxl: short-arc xenon lamp
SXM: St Maarten, Netherlands Antilles (airport)
sxn: section
SXO: Senior Experimental Officer
sxr: soft X-ray region
sxrm: straight reamer
sxs: stellary X-ray spectra
SXS: Sigma Xi Society
sxt: sextant; stable X-ray transmitter
sy: shipyard; square yard; sticky; supply; sustainer yaw
Sy: Syria; Syrian
SY: (U.S. State Department) Security Office; steam yacht (naval symbol)
***SYB:** Statesman's Year-Book*
SYC: Sanduskey Yacht Club; Savannah Yacht Club; Seattle Yacht Club; Springfield Yacht Club; Stamford Yacht Club
Sycamore City: Terre Haute, Indiana
SYCATE: Symptom-Cause Test
sycom: synchronous communication(s)
sy crs: sundry creditors
syd: see your doctor; sum of the year's digits
Syd: Sydney
***Syd:** sydlig* (Danish—southerly)
SYD: Scotland Yard; Sydney, Australia (airport)
S Yem: South Yemen
syh: see you home
SYHA: Scottish Youth Hostels Association
syl: syllogism
syll: syllabication (syllabification)
SYLP: Support Your Local Police
Sylvia-Ducalis: (Latin—Bois le Duc or 's Hertogenbosch)—also known as Sylvia Ducis
sym: symbol; symbolic; symbolism; symmetric; symmetrical; symmetry; symphonic; symphony
***sym.:** symbolus* (Latin—token; sign)
symb: symbol; symbolic; symbolism
symp: symposia; symposium
sympath: sympathetic; sympathy
Symphonia domestica: (German—Domestic Symphony)—autobiographical tone poem by Richard Strauss
Symphonie fantastique: (French—Fantastic Symphony)—major orchestral work of Berlioz
Symphony of Heavenly Length: Schumann's name for Schubert's Great Symphony in C major—the ninth
Symphony of a Thousand: Mahler's Symphony No. 8 in E-flat major
sympt : symptom(s)
syn: synagogue; synesthesia; synonym; synonymous; synonymy; syntax; synthetic
syn (SYN): synchronous idle character (data processing)
Syn: Synagogue
Synanon: anti-drug addiction group
sync: synchronize; synchronous
synchro: synchronize; synchronous
synchros: synchronous devices
synco: syncopate(d); syncopation; syncopative; syncopator
syncom: synchronous communication (satellite)
syncop: syncopate(d); syncope
synd: syndicalism; syndicate
syndet(s): synthetic detergent(s)
syndro: syndrome
synec: synecdoche
SYNMAS: Synchronous Missile Alarm System
synon: synonomous; synonym
synonym.: synonymous
synop: synopsis; synoptic
syns: synopsis
synscp: synchroscope
synt: syntax
syntan: synthetic tanning
synth: synthesis; synthetic
Synthesizer of Adrenalin: Jokichi Takamine
syntol: syntagmatic organization of language
SYP: Society of Young Publishers
syph: syphilis; syphilitic
syphil: syphilology
Sy PO: Supply Petty Officer
SYPR: Southern Yemen People's Republic
syr: syrup
***syr.:** syrupus* (Latin—syrup)
Syr: Syracusan; Syracuse; Syria; Syriac; Syrian
SYR: Syracuse, New York (airport)
Syrac: Syracusan; Syracuse
syrg: syringe
Syringa: Idaho state flower
sys: system; systematic; systematization; systematize; systemic; systems
SYS: Sun Yat-sen
sysgen: systems generation
SYSP: Sixth-Year Specialist Program (library science)
syst: system; systematic; systemic; systems
System ABC: System of Automation of Bibliography through Computerization
systol: systolic
systran: systems analysis translator
syt: sweet young thing
syz: syzgetic; syzygial; syzygium; syzygy
sz: seizure; size
***s Z:** seinerzeit* (German—at that time)
Sz: Swiss; Switzerland
SZA: Student Zionist Association
SZG: Salzburg, Austria (airport)
***Szle:** Szemle* (Hungarian—journal; review)
SZO: Student Zionist Organization
szvr: silicon zener voltage regulator

T

t: airfoil temperature thickness (symbol); hour angle (symbol); meridian angle (symbol); table; tabulated (loran); tackle; tardy; tare; teaspoon; teeth; telephone; temperature; temporary; tenor; tense; tensor; tentative; tentative target; thunder; thunderstorm; tide; tide rips; time; title; ton; tonnage; tons; toward; town; trace of precipitation; transferred; transit; transitive; translation; tread; tropical; troy; true; tug; tugline

't: it

$t_{1/2}$: radioactive half life

t: *tome* (French—volume); *tomo* (Spanish—volume)

t.: *ter* (Latin—three times; thrice)

't: *het* (Dutch—the)

T: Northrup Aircraft (symbol); Pacific Transport Lines (1-letter symbol); propeller thrust (symbol); tablespoon; tactical; Tango—code for letter T; tanker; Taoism; Taoist; T-bar; tee; teletype; temperature; temple; temporary magnitude; tension of eyeball; Testla; Texaco; Texas; Texas Company; Thursday; torpedo; trainer; training; transport number; triangle; triple bond; true; truss; Tuesday; turboprop; Turk; Turkey; Turkish

T: (Latin—Titus); tea (underground slang—marijuana or Texas tea as some users nickname this hallucinogen drug); *Teil* (German—division; part); thrust (symbol); *Time* (magazine); transformer (symbol); *tulo* (Finnish—arrival)

T_1,T_2,T_3, etc.: first thoracic vertebra, second thoracic vertebra, third thoracic vertebra, etc.

T - 1, T - 2, T - 3, etc.: decreasing stages of interocular tension

T + 1, T + 2, T + 3, etc.: increasing stages of interocular tension

T-04: Tupolev 104 aircraft

T$: Taiwan dollar(s)

T2: stabilized

T2g: Technician (second grade)

T_3: triiodothyronine

T4: heat treated

T_4: thyroxine

T6: heat treated and aged

T7: heat treated and stabilized

T51: specially aged

T-144: Tupelov 144 (Soviet supersonic transport)

T-1824: Evans blue

ta: target area; temperature, axillary; test accessory; third attack (lacrosse); time and attendance; toxin-antitoxin; travel allowance; true altitude; tuberculin, alkaline

ta: transit authority (New York City Transit Authority—lower-case italic emblem on rolling stock)

t.a.: *testantibus actis* (Latin—as the records show)

t-a: toxin-antitoxin

t & a: taken and accepted; time and attendance; tonsillectomy and adenoidectomy; tonsils and adenoids

Ta: tantalum; Tasmania; Tasmanian

TA: Table of Allowances; Tax Amortization; Technical Assistance; Territorial Army; Trade Agreement(s); Trans-Air; Trans-america Corporation (stock exchange symbol)

T/A: Temporary Assistant

taa: turbine-alternator assembly

TAA: Technical Assistance Administration; Trade Agreements Act; Trans-Australia Airlines; Transit Advertising Association; Transportation Association of America

TAAF: Terres Australes et Antarctiques Française (French Southern and Antarctic Territories)

taalk: *taalkunde* (Dutch-linguistics)

TAALS: The American Association of Language Specialists

TAAP: Total Action Against Poverty

TAARS: The Army Ammunition Reporting Service

taas: three-axis attitude sensor

TAAS: Telfair Academy of Arts and Sciences (Savannah)

tab.: table; tablet; tabulate; tabulated; tabulation; tabulator

tab.: *tabella* (Latin—small board; tablet)

Tab: Tabascan; Tabasco

Tab: *Tabelle* (German—table; index)

TAB: Technical Assistance Board (UN); Tobago (airport)

TAB: *Technical Abstract Bulletin*

TABA: *Transportes Aéreos Buenos Aires*

tabc: typhoid-paratyphoid A, B, and C vaccine (TABC)

tabel: *tabella* (Latin—tablet)

TABL: Tropical Atlantic Biological Laboratory

tabl(s): tablet(s)

tab run: tabulator run

Tabs: Cantabrigians or Cantabs—Cambridge University undergraduates

TABS: Transatlantic Book Service

TABSO: Transport Aerien Civil Bulgare (Bulgarian Civil Air Transport)

tabsol: tabular systems-oriented language

tabt: tab vaccine plus tetanus toxoid (TABT)

tabtd: combined tab vaccine plus tetanus and diptheria toxoid

TAB vaccine: typhoid plus paratyphoid A and B vaccine (triple vaccine)

tac: tactic; tactical; tactician; tactics; total automatic color (tv); try and collect

Tac: Tacitus; Tacoma

TAC: Tactical Air Command; Thai Airways Company; Trade Agreements Committee

TACA: Texas and Central American Airlines

tacan: tactical air navigation

Tac Brdg: Tacoma Bridge

TACC: Tactical Air Control Center

taccar: time-averaged clutter-coherent airborne radar

tacco: tactical coordinator

tacden: tactical data-entry device

TACG: Tactical Air Control Group

tach: tachometer

Tacho: Anastasio

tachy: tachygraphy (shorthand)

tacit.: *tacitus* (Latin—unmen-

tioned)
taclan: tactical landing system
tacmar: tactical malfunction-array radar
tacnav: tactical navigation
tacnuc: tactical nuclear (weapon)—also written *taknuk*
TACO: Tactical Coordinator
tacoda: target coordinate date
tacol: thinned-aperture computed lens
Taconics: Taconic Mountains ranging from New York to Vermont but called the Berkshires in Connecticut and Massachusetts
TACP: Tactical Air Control Party
TACRON: Tactical Air Control Squadron
TACs: Technical Assistance Committees (UN)
TACS: Tactical Air Control System
tacsatcom: tactical satellite communications
tact.: technological aids to creative thought
TACT: Truth About Civil Turmoil
TACTIC: Technical Advisory Committee to Influence Congress (Federation of American Scientists)
tacv: tracked air-cushion vehicle
Tad: Thaddeus; Theodore
TAD: Thrust-Augmented Delta
TADA: Teletypewriter Automatic-Dispatch System
TADARS: Tropo Automated Data Analysis Recorder System
TADC: Tactical Air Direction Center; Training and Distribution Center
tadic: telemetry analog-to-digital information computer
tad(s): tadpole(s)
Tadz: Tadzhik; Tadzhikistan; Tadzhikistanian
Tadzhik SSR: Tadzhik Soviet Socialist Republic (Tadzhikistan)
TAE: National Greek Airlines
TAEA: Texas Art Educators Association
TAEC: Turkish Atomic Energy Commission
TAEHS: Thomas A. Edison High School
ta'en: taken
TAERF: Texas Atomic Energy Research Foundation
taf: terminal aerodrome forecast
taf (TAF): toxoid-antitoxin floccules
Taf: *Bildtafel* (German—list of illustrations)
TAf: *Tuberculin Albumose frei* (German—albumose-free tuberculin)
TAF: Tactical Air Force
TAFA: Territorial and Auxiliary Forces Association
tafcsd: total active federal commissioned service date
Taffy: (nickname for a Welshman)
tafg: two-axis free gyro
TAFI: Technical Association of the Fur Industry
tafmsd: total active federal military service date
tafor: terminal aerodrome forecast
TAFSEA: Technical Applications for Southeast Asia
tafubar: things are fouled up beyond all recognition
ta fx: tapping fixture
tag.: the acronym generator (RCA device)
Tag: Tagalog
TAG: The Adjutant General; Timken Art Gallery
T A & G: Tennessee, Alabama & Georgia (railroad)
TAGA: Technical Association of the Graphic Arts
tagawi: try and get away with it
tägl: *täglich* (German—daily; per day)
TAGP: Transportes Aéreos do Guine Portuguesa (Air Transport of Portuguese Guinea)
tagw: takeoff gross weight
tah: temperature, altitude, humidity; total abdominal hysterectomy
Tah Pac: Tahitian Pacific (area around Tahiti)
TAHq: Theater Army Headquarters
TAHRI: Tobacco and Health Research Institute
tai: taiga (coniferous evergreen forests of subarctic America, Asia, and Europe)
Tai: Taipei; Taiwan (Formosa)
Tai: *Tailandia* (Spanish—Thailand)—Siam
Taig: Terence
TAI: Thai Airways International; Transports Aériens Intercontinentaux
TA & IC: Texas Arts and Industries College
TAICH: Technical Assistance Information Clearinghouse
taid (TAID): thrust-augmented improved delta
TA-ISSA: Travelers Aid—International Social Service of America
Taiwan: (Chinese—Terraced Bay) —Formosa—the offshore nationalist Republic of China
TAJAG: The Assistant Judge Advocate General (USA)
Taju: Tajumulco
take 5: take 5 minutes' rest
tako: terms and conditions of employment
take 10: take 10 minutes' rest
tal: traffic and accident loss
Tal: *Talmud* (Hebrew canon and civil lawbook)
TAL: Transair Limited
tal.: *talis* (Latin—such)
talar: tactical landing-approach radar
talbe: talk and listen beacon
talc: hydrous magnesium silicate (agalmatolite); take a look see
TALC: Texas Association for the Advancement of Local Culture
Talco: Talcahuano
Tales: *The Tales of Hoffmann*—Offenbach's three-act opera *Les Contes d'Hoffmann*
TALIC: Tyneside Association of Libraries for Industry and Commerce
Talla: Tallahassee
Talleyrand: Charles Maurice de Talleyrand-Périgord
'talpa(s): catalpa(s)
TALOA: Transocean Airlines
Talos: ship-to-air missile produced by Bendix and fired from destroyers and cruisers
tal. qual.: *talis qualis* (Latin—as they come; average quality)
TALUS: Transportation and Land Use Study
tam: tambourine; tam-o'-shanter; tam-tam; total available market
t-a m: toxoid-antitoxin mixture
Tam: Tamil; Tamualipas (inhabitants—Tamualipecos); Tampa; Tampan; Tampico (inhabitants—Tampiqueños)
TAM: Tel Aviv Museum; Transporte Aéreo Militar (Paraguayan Military Air Transport)
tambo: tambourine
TAMC: Tripler Army Medical Center
TAME: Television Accessory Manufacturers Institute
TAMIS: Technical Meetings Information Service
Tammany Boss: William M. Tweed
Tam(my): Thomas; Tom(my)

Tamp: Tampico
Tamps: Tamaulipas
TAMS: Token and Medal Society
Tam Shrew: *Taming of the Shrew*
tan.: tangent; tangential; tannery; tanning; total ammonia nitrogen; twilight all night
Tan: Tanganyika; Tangier
TAN: Transportes Aéreos Nacionales
Tanan: Tananarive
Tanana River City: Fairbanks, Alaska
tan. bkt: tangency bracket
tandel: tandem + parallel
TANESCO: Tanzania Electric Supply Company
Tang: Tanganyika; Tangier
tangelo: tangerine + pomelo (tangerine-grapefruit hybrid citrus fruit)
tanglo(s): tangelo(s)
Tango: code for letter T
tanh: hyperbolic tangent
Tania: Tatiana
Tanimbars: Tanimbar Islands of Indonesia
tan's: tax anticipation notes (TANs)
TANS: Territorial Army Nursing Service
tanstaafl: there aint no such thing as a free lunch (abbreviated slogan of Young Americans for Freedom)
TANU: Tanganyika African National Union
TANY: Typographers Association of New York
Tanya: (Russian nickname—Tatiana; Tatyana)
Tanyu: Morinobu Kano (*see* Kano)
Tanz: Tanzania (Tanganyika + Zanzibar)
Tanzam: Tanzania-Zambia (railway)
Tanzania: Tanganyika (formerly German East Africa) together with Zanzibar and Pemba
tao: thromboangiitis obliterans
TAO: Taxi Aéreo Opita (Bogotá); The Athenaeum of Ohio
TAOC: Tactical Air Operations Center
TAP: Total Action Against Poverty; Transportes Aéreos Portugueses (Portuguese Air Transport)
TAPE: Target Profile Examination (USAF); Transactional Analysis of Personality and Environment; Trust for Agricultural Political Education
TAPLINE: Trans-Arabian Pipeline
TAPPI: Technical Association of the Pulp and Paper Industry
taps: tapaderos (Mexican Border Spanish—leather hoods covering stirrups to protect the feet while riding through thorny cactus or mezquite); the last bugle call, the *taptoo*, meaning *lights out* or sounding the last honors at a military funeral
TAPS: Trajectory Accuracy Prediction System (USAF); Trans-Alaska Pipeline System
TAPSC: Trans-Atlantic Passenger Steamship Conference
tapvc: total anomalous pulmonary venous connection
tar.: tariff(s); terrain-avoidance radar
TAR: Technical Action Request (USA); Trans-Australian Railways
TARA: Technical Assistant—Royal Artillery; Territorial Army Rifle Association
Taraco: (Latin—Tarragona)—also called Tarrazona or Tirasso or Turiaso
taran: test and replace as necessary
TARC: Tactical Air Reconnaisance Center
tarfu: things are really fouled up
targ: target
TARGET: Team to Advance Research for Gas Energy Transformation
Target Island: Kahoolawe, Hawaii
Tarheeler(s): North Carolinian(s)
Tar Heel State: North Carolina's official nickname
tarmac: tar plus macadam (tarred road or runway)
Tar-Man: Taranaki-Manawatu (NZ)
tarn.: tarnish; tarnishes; tarnishing
TARO: Territorial Army Reserve Office(r)(s)
TAROM: Transporturile Aeriene Romine (Romanian Air Transport)
TARP: Test and Repair Processor
tarp(s): tarpaulin(s)
Tarr: Tarragona
TARS: Technical Assistance Recruitment Service
tart.: tartaric
TART: Test Analysis Reduction Technique (USN)
tart. a: tartaric acid
Tartar: shipborne surface-to-air guided missile (General Dynamics)
tartar emetic: potassium antimony tartrate
Tartu: Dorpat
tas: true airspeed
Tas: Tasmania
TAs: teaching assistants
TAS: Texas Academy of Science; Traveler's Aid Society; Turk Anonim Sirketi (Turkish Joint Stock Company)
TASAMS: The Army Supply and Maintenance System
tasc: terminal area sequence and control; treatment alternatives to street crimes
TASC: Test Anxiety Scale for Children
tascon: television automatic sequence control
TASES: Tactical Airborne Signal Exploitation System
TASF: Teachers Association of San Francisco
Tash: Tashkent
Tasha: (Russian nickname—Natasha)
TASHAL: *Tseva Hagana LeIsrael* (Hebrew—Defense Army of Israel)
tasi: time-assignment speech interpolation
TASKFLOT: task flotilla
Tasm: Tasman; Tasmania; Tasmanian
TASO: Television Allocations Study Organization
tasr: terminal area surveillance radar
TASS: Telegrafnoie Agenstvo Sovietskavo Soyuza (Soviet News Agency)
Tassie(s): Tasmanian(s)
TASSO: Tactical Special Security Office(r)
TASSq: Tactical Air Support Squadron (USAF)
TASSR: Tartar Autonomous Soviet Socialist Republic; Tuva Autonomous Soviet Socialist Republic
Tassy: Tasmania (in Australian slang)
Tassyland: Tasmania (in Australian slang)
TAST: Tactical Assault Supply Transport
tat. (TAT): tetanus antitoxin
Tat: Tatar (Turkestan)
TAT: tetanus antitoxin; Thematic Appreciation Test; Thrust-Augmented Thor; Transportes Aéreos de Timor

Tat Aut Sov Soc Rep: Tatar Autonomous Soviet Socialist Republic
TATC: Trans-Atlantic Telephone Cable
TATCO: Tactical Automatic Telephone Central Office
'tater(s): potato(es)
Tatertown: Gleason, Tennessee—shipping point for potatoes grown in the region
Tatras: Tatra Mountains of Czechoslovakia
TATSA: Transportation Aircraft Test and Support Activity
Tatts: Tattersalls
TATU: Tanganyika African Traders Union
Tau: Taurus
TAU: Tel Aviv University
TAUN: Technical Assistance of the United Nations
taurom: tauromachia
TAUSA: Tea Association of the U.S.A.
taut.: tautology
T-à-v: *Tout-à-vous* (French—Yours truly)
Tave: Octave; Octavius
Tavia: Octavia
Tavita: Octavita
T & AVR: Territorial and Army Volunteer Reserve
tav(s): tavern(s)
TAVSS: Toward, Away, Versus Selection System
Tavy: Octavius
taw: twice a week
TAW: *Times Atlas of the World*
T A & W: Toledo, Angola & Western (railroad)
TAWC: Tactical Air Warfare Center
tax.: taxation; taxes; taxonomic; taxonomy
taxi: taxicab; taxiing
taxid: taxidermy
taxon: taxonomy
Tay Pay: Irish journalist Thomas Power O'Connor
tb: temporary buoy; terminal board; thymol blue; tile base; total bouts; tractor biplane; trial balance; true bearing; tubercle bacillus; tuberculosis; turbine; turret-base; turret-based
t/b: title block
t & b: top and bottom; turned and bored
Tb: terbium
TB: Tank Battalion; temporary buoy; Troop Basis; Twin Branch (railroad); Tyburn (reports)
TB: *Technical Bulletin*
tba: tires-batteries-accessories; to be announced; to be assigned
TBA: Tables of Basic Allowance; Television Bureau of Advertising; Torrey Botanical Association
tban: to be announced
T-bar: T-shaped bar
tbawrba: travel by aircraft, military and/or naval water carrier, commercial rail and/or bus is authorized (USA)
TBB: tenor, baritone, bass
TBB: *Television Blue Book*
TBC: The British Council; Trinidad Broadcasting Company
tbd: to be determined
TBD: torpedo-boat destroyer
TBDS: Test Base Dispatch Service
tbe: to be expended
tbe (TBE): tuberculin bacillen emulsion
TBE: Toronto Board of Education
T-beam: T-shaped beam
tb ex: tube expander
TBF: single-engine torpedo bomber (3-letter naval symbol)
tbfx: tube fixture
tbg: testosterone-binding globulin; thyroxine-binding globulin
t & bg: top and bottom grille
tbi: tooth-brushing instruction
TBI: Texas Board of Insurance; The Business Institute
T-bird: Thunderbird
t-bk: talking-book
tbl: table; tablet; through back of loops (knitting); through bill of lading
tb lc: term birth, living child
tbm (TBM): tired businessman
TBM: Ten Broeck Mansion (Albany)
TBMA: Timber Building Manufacturers' Association
tb md: tube mandrel
TBMD: Terminal Ballistic Missile Defense (USA)
tbo: time between overhaul(s)
TBO: Test Base Office
T-bolt: bolt with T-shaped square head
T-bone: T-bone steak; T-shaped bone; trombone
T-bowl: toilet bowl
tbp: true boiling point
tbpa: thyroxine-binding prealbumin
tbr: to-be-remembered (word)
TBRI: *Technical Book Review Index*
tbs: tablespoon; talk-between-ships (radiotelephone)
tb & s: top, bottom, and sides
TBs: Torpedo Boats (World War I)
TBS: Tokyo Broadcasting System
tb sa: tube saw
TBSI: The Baker Street Irregulars
tbsn: tablespoon
tbsp: tablespoon
TBT: Terminal Ballistic Track
TB & TA: Triborough Bridge & Tunnel Authority
tbv: tubercle bacillus vaccine
TB & VD C: Tuberculosis and Venereal Diseases Clinic
tbw: total body washout; total body water
tc: temperature controlled; terra cotta; tetracycline; thermocouple; thermocoupled; thermocoupling; thrust chamber; tierce(s); time check; time closing; top chord; trip coil; true course (TC); type certification
tc: *tre corde* (Italian—three strings)
t/c: tabulating card; temperature coefficient; thermocouple; transformer rectifier; trim coil; type certificate
t & c: threads and couplings; turn and cough
Tc: technetium; tropic tides
TC: Air Canada (formerly TCA); Tabor College; Taft College; Talladega College; Tariff Commission; Tarkio College; Tax Court; Teachers College; Tea Council; Technical Circular; Technical Communication; Tennessee Central (railroad); Texarkana College; Texas College; The Citadel; Thiel College; Tift College; Training Center; Training Circular; Transaction Code; Transportation Corps; Transylvania College; Trial Counsel; Tri-State College; troop carrier; Trucial Coast (Arabian sheikdoms); True Course; Trusteeship Council; Turret Captain; Tusculum College
TC: *Technical Communications*
T & C: Turks and Caicos Islands
TC 1: Traffic Conference 1—North and South America, Greenland, Bermuda, West Indies, Hawaiian Islands
TC 2: Traffic Conference 2—Europe, adjacent islands, Ascension Island, Africa, and

Asia west of and including Iran

TC 3: Traffic Conference 3—Asia, adjacent islands, East Indies, Australia, New Zealand, Pacific Islands except Hawaiian

tca: telemetering control assembly; track crossing angle; trichloro-acetate

TCA: Tanners Council of America; Technical Cooperation Administration; Temporary Change Authorization; Terminal Control Area; Textile Converters Association; Theater Commander's Approval; Thoroughbred Club of America; Tile Council of America; Tissue Culture Association; Trailer Coach Association; Trans-Canada Airlines

TCAA: Technical Communication Association of Australia

tcam: telecommunications access method

TCAS: The College of Advanced Science

tcb: take care of business

TCB: Thames Conservancy Board

TCBI: Television Center for Business and Industry

tcbs (TCBS): thiosulfate-citrate-bile salt sucrose

tcc: tatical control computer; television control center; test conductor console

TCC: Telecommunications Coordinating Committee; Transcontinental Corps; Transport Control Center; Transportation Control Committee; Troop Carrier Command

T-C C: Tri-Continental Corporation

TCCB: Test and County Cricket Board

tcd: task completion date; tungsten carbide depositing

TCD: Trinity College, Dublin

tcd's: time certificates of deposit (TCDs)

tce: total composite error

TCF: 20th-Century Fox; Twentieth Century Fund

TCF: *Touring Club de France* (Touring Club of France)

TCFB: Transcontinental Freight Bureau

TCG: Theatre Communications Group

T C & G B: Tucson, Cornelia & Gila Bend (railroad)

tch: travel counselor's handbook

TCH: Trans-Canada Highway

tchg: teaching

TcHHW: tropic higher high water

TcHHWI: tropic higher high water interval

TcHLW: tropic higher low water

tchr: teacher

TCI: The Combustion Institute; Theoretical Chemistry Institute

TCI: *Touring Club Italiano* (Italian Touring Club)

T & CI: Turks and Caicos Islands

tcj: terminal coaxial junction

tcl: transistor-coupled logic

TCL: Transatlantic Carriers Limited; Turkish Cargo Lines

TcLHW: tropic lower high water

TcLLW: tropic lower low water

TcLLWI: tropic lower low water interval

TCM: Texas Citrus Mutual; Trinity College of Music

TCMA: Telephone Cable Makers' Association

TCN: Transportation Control Number

TCNCO: Test Control Noncommissioned Officer

TCNM: Timpanagos Cave National Monument (Utah)

TCO: Termination Contracting Office(r); Test Control Office(r); Trinity College—Oxford

TCO: *Tjänstemännens Centralorganisation* (Swedish—Salaried Employees' Central Organization)

TCOC: Tri-Cities Opera Company (Binghamton)

TCOM: Tethered Communications

T-conn: T-shaped connection

tcp: traffic control post

TCP: Task Change Proposal; Task Control Proposal; Technical Cooperation Program (between Australia, Canada, the United Kingdom, and the United States); Temporary Change Proposal; Traffic Control Post

TCPA: Town and Country Planning Association

TCPL: Trans-Canada Pipe Lines

tcr: temperature coefficient of resistance

TCR: Tennessee Central Railway

TCRB: *Touring Club Royal de Belgique* (French—Royal Belgian Touring Club)—automobile club

TCRMG: Tripartite Commission for the Restitution of Monetary Gold (American-British-French commission, headquartered in Brussels)

TCS: Twin City Securists

TCS: *Touring Club Suisse* (French—Swiss Touring Club)

T & CS: Transportation and Communication Service

TCSO: Tri-City Symphony Orchestra

tct: total-controlled tabulation

tctl: tactical

TCTO: Time Compliance Technical Order(s)

TCU: Texas Christian University; Tokyo Commercial University

TCUS: Tax Court of the United States

T-cushion: T-shaped cushion

tcv: temperature-control valve

TCV: Terminal-Configured Vehicle (NASA)

tcw: time code work

TCWH: Teamsters, Chauffeurs, Warehousemen and Helpers (union)

TCWP: Texas Committee for Wildlife Protection

td: tank destroyer; technical data; test data; third defense (lacrosse); tile drain; time delay; time of departure; time disintegration; tod (28 pounds of wool); tool design; tool disposition; touchdown (football); transmitter distributor; trust deed; turbine drive; 'tween deck

t/d: time deposit

t.d.: *ter die* (Latin—thrice daily)

t & d: taps and dies

td (TD): technical director

TD: Table of Distribution; Tactical Division; tank destroyer; Teachers Diploma; Territorial Decoration; Testing and Development (USCG); Topographic Draftsman; Training Detachment; Treasury Decision; Treasury Department; Treasury Division; Trinidad and Tobago; Typographic Draftsman

TD: *Teachta Dala* (Gaelic—Member of the House of Commons)

tda: tunnel-diode amplifier

TDA: Timber Development Association; Toa Domestic Airlines; Train Dispatchers Association

T-day: day for time schedule testing

tdb: total disability benefit (TDB)
TDB: Toronto-Dominion Bank
tdc: top dead center
TDC: Telemetry Data Center
td cu: tinned copper
TDD: Diploma in Tubercular Diseases
tddl: time-division data link
tddlpo: time division data link printout
tdf: two-degree-of-freedom (gyroscope)
tdg: twist drill gauge
TDG: Transport Development Group
tdh: total dynamic head
Tdh: Trondheim
tdi: toluene di-isocyanate
TDI: Target Data Inventory; Tool and Die Institute; Transportation Displays Incorporated
TDK: *Turk Dil Kurumu* (Turkish Language Association)
t dk(s): 'tween deck(s)
tdl: total damn loss
tdm: tandem; time division multiplexing
tdm/pcm: time-division multiplex (using) pulse-code modulation
tdn: totally digestible nutrients
TDO: Technical Development Objective
TDOT: Thorndike Dimensions of Temperament
tdp: target director post; technical data package; technical development plans; thermal death point
TDP: Technical Development Plan
tdpfo: temporary duty pending further orders
tdr: time-delay; time domain reflectometry
tdr: *tous droits réservés* (French—all rights reserved)
TDR: Technical Documentary Report
TDRL: Temporary Disability Retired List
t/d rly: time-delay relay
tds: telemetering decommutation system
t.d.s.: *ter die sumendum* (Latin—to be taken three times daily)
tds (TSS): temperature, depth, salinity
TDS: Tanami Desert Sanctuary (Northern Territory, Australia)
TDS: *Toronto Daily Star*
TDSTS: Tidbinbilla Deep-Space Tracking Station
TDT: Transport Department Tasmania
tdu: target detection unit
tdw: tons deadweight (tare of a ship)
tdwy: treadway
tdy: temporary duty; toady
te: table of equipment; task element; technical exchange; tenants; tenants by the entirety; thermal efficiency; tinted edge; trailing edge; transverse electric; transverse wave (symbol); trial and error; turbine electric; turboelectric; twin engine
t & e: testing and evaluation; trial and error
Te: tellurium
TE: Table of Equipment; Task Element; Technical Exchange; Telefis Eireann (Television Ireland); Topographical Engineer
T & E: Toledo & Eastern (railroad)
TEA: Tennessee Education Association; Tucson Education Association
teach.: teacher; teaching
Teacher of Doctors: Sir William Osler
Teacher President: James Abram Garfield—twentieth President of the United States
Teague: (nickname for an Irishman); Terence
TEAL: Tasman Empire Airways, Limited
TEAM: Technique for Evaluation and Analysis of Maintainability
tear gas: chloroacetophenone; irritant gas also known as mace (MACE); used to quell riots as it causes temporary blindness as well as irritation of the mucous membranes and the skin
Tear-Jerker Composer: Giacomo Puccini—opposite of Gioacchino Rossini who wrote music productive of smiles, chuckles, and laughter
TEAS: Threat Evaluation and Action Selection (program)
tease: tracking errors and simulation evaluation (radar)
teatr: *teatrale* (Italian—theatrical)
Teatro Colón: (Spanish—Columbus Theater)—Buenos Aires opera house
TEB: Tax Exemption Board; Textile Economics Bureau
tec: technic; technical; technician; technics; technological; technology
TEC: Technical Education Council; Technician Education Council
tech: technic; technical; technician; technics; technique(s); technological; technology
Tech CEI: Technician of the Council of Engineering Institutions
tech ed: technical editing; technical editor
tech memo: technical memorandum
techn: technician
technol: technological; technologist; technology
tech rep: technical representative
tech rept: technical report
Tech Weld Inst: Technician of the Welding Institute
tech writer: technical writer
TECOM: Test and Evaluation Command (US Army)
tecquinol: hydroquinone
TECS: Treasury Enforcement Computer File
Tec Sgt: Technical Sergeant
ted: *tedesco* (Italian—German)
Ted(dy): Edward; Theodore; Theodosia
TEE: Trans Europe Express
Teenie: Christina
teenybop: teenybopper (underground slang—young child attuned to the modern scene)—*see* macrobop
TEFL: teaching English as a foreign language
teflon: tetrafluoroethylene (polymerized synthetic plastic resin)
teg: top edge gilt
Teg: Tegel
te ga: taper gauge
TEGMA: Terminal Elevator Grain Merchants Association
Tegoose: Tegucigalpa (Honduras)
teg(s): thermoelectric generator(s)
Tegusi: Tegucigalpa's nickname
Teh: Teheran
TEI: Texaco Experiment Incorporated
TEJA: *Tutmonda Esperantista Jurnalista Asocio* (International Association of Esperantist Journalists)
TEJO: *Tutmonda Esperantista Junulara Organizo* (International Organization of Esperantist Youth)
tel: telegraph; telegraphic; telegraphy; telephone; telephonic; telephony; teletype; teletype-

writer; television; tetraethyl lead
tel (TEL): transporter-erector launcher
Tel: Telefunken; Telugu
TELAM: Telenoticiosa Americana (Argentine press service)
telaut: telautograph; telautography
telco: telephone company
telcos: telephone companies
tele: television
telecast(er): television broadcast(er)
telecom: telecommunication
telecon: telephone communication
telecopy: telephonic copying process (developed by Xerox)
telecourse: television-constructed course
teledrama: televised drama; television drama
telef: *telefon* (Norwegian—telephone)
telefac: television facsimile
telefilm: television film
teleg: telegrapher; telegraphy
telegr: *telegrafie* (Dutch—telegraphy)
Tel Eir: *Telefis Eireann* (Gaelic—Irish Television)
Télémaque: Denmark Vesey
teleol: teleology
teleosts: teleostomist fishes (bony fishes)
telep: telephathic(ally); telepathy
telepak: telemetering package
teleph: telephony
teleplay: televised play; television play
teleran: televised radar aerial navigation
telesurance: television insurance
telethon: television marathon
teletrial: television trial
telev (TV): television
Television City: Hollywood, California
telex (tex): teletype exchange
Teller of Tall Tales: folklorist, religious, and secularist authors share this sobriquet; among the latter are Nathaniel Hawthorne, E.T.A. Hoffmann, Washington Irving, Baron von Munchausen, Edgar Allan Poe, Aleksander Sergeevich Pushkin, and Mark Twain
tellie(s): television (sets)
telly: television
tel no.: telephone number
telsat: telecommunications satellite
telsim: teletypewriter simulator
tel sur: telephone survey
telw: *telwoord* (Dutch—word count)
tem: temporal
tem.: *tempus* (Latin—time); *tempo* (Italian—time)
Tem: temple
TEM: Territorial Efficiency Medal
TEMA: Telecommunications Engineering and Manufacturing Association
temar: thermoelectric marine application
temp: temper; temperature; tempered; tempering; template; temporary; temporize
temp.: *tempore* (Latin—in the time of); *tempo* (Italian—time)—musical time
Temp: *Tempest, The*
temp. dext.: *tempori dextro* (Latin—to the right temple)
Tempest: Beethoven's Piano Sonata No. 17 in D (opus 31, no. 2); Tchaikovsky's Symphonic Fantasy—*Tempest*
temping: (office girl's jargon—temporary substituting)
Temple Mount: Jerusalem's sobriquet
TEMPO: Technical Military Planning Operation
tempos: temporary buildings, houses, offices, officials, workers, et cetera
temp prim: *tempo primo* (Italian—tempo or time in the musical sense as at the start)
temp sec: temporary secretary
temp. sin.: *tempori sinistro* (Latin—to the left temple)
tempy: temporary
ten.: tenant; tender; tenderize(d); tenement; tenor
ten.: *tenuto* (Italian—to hold, a chord or tone)
Ten: *Tenente* (Italian or Portuguese), *Teniente* (Spanish)—Lieutenant
T(en) Col: *Tenente Colonnello* (Italian), *Tenente Coronel* (Portuguese), *Teniente Coronel* (Spanish)—Lieutenant Colonel
ten. com: tenant(s) in common
tency: tenancy
tend.: tendon
ten. ent: tenant(s) by the entireties
Teng: Teng Hsiao-ping
Ten Gen: *Tenente General* (Portuguese), *Tenente Generale* (Italian), *Teniente General* (Spanish)—Lieutenant General
Tenn: Tennessee; Tennessean
tenna(s): antenna(s)
Tenneco: Tennessee Gas Companies
Tennessee Williams: Thomas Lanier Williams
TENOC: ten years of oceanography (1961-1970)
tenot: tenotomy
Ten Provinces: Ten Canadian Provinces (Alberta, British Columbia, Manitoba, New Brunswick, Newfoundland, Nova Scotia, Ontario, Prince Edward Island, Québec, Saskatchewan)
tens: tensile; tension
tens str: tensile strength
tent.: tentative
Ten^te: *Teniente* (Spanish—Lieutenant)
Tenth Muse: Sappho, according to Plato, who esteemed the lyric poetess of Mytilene on the island of Lesbos
Ten Vasc: *Tenente di Vascello* (Italian—Lieutenant of the Vessel)—Navy Lieutenant
Teol: *Teología* (Portuguese—Spanish—Theology)
TEOO: Territorial Economic Opportunity Office(r)
tepi: training equipment planning information
TEPS: Teacher Education and Professional Standards
ter: terminal; terminate; termination; terrace; terrazzo; territory; teritary
ter.: *tere* (Latin—rub)
Ter: Terrace; Territory; Teruel
Ter: *Terence* (Publius Terentius Afer)—Roman writer of comedies
tera: 10^{12}
TERA: The Electrical Research Association
Te Rangi Hiroa: Sir Peter Buck
terat: teratology
tercom: terrain contour matching
t & e rec: time and events recorder
Teri: Theresa; Therese
TERL: Transit Expressway Revenue Line (mass transportation)
Term: Terminal (postal abbreviation)
therm.: terminal; terminate; terminology
te rm: taper reamer
TERPACIS: Trust Territory of the Pacific Islands
terps: (drug user's slang—elixir of terpin hydrate and codeine)—cough mixture and

codeine combination
terr: terrace; territory
Terr: Terrace
TERRA: Terricide Escape by Rethinking, Research, Action
Terrapin State: Maryland
Terry: Terence; Teresa; Terrell; Terrill; Theresa; Therese
ter. sim.: *tere simul* (Latin—rub together)
Tert. Tertiary
Tertullian: Quintus Septimus Florens Tertullianus
TES: Telemetering Evaluation Station
TES: *Times Educational Supplement*
tesl: teaching English as a second language
TESO: *Texel's Eigen Stoomboot Onderneming* (Dutch—Texel's Own Steamship Society)
TESOL: Teachers of English to Speakers of Other Languages
tess: *tessili* (Italian—textiles)
Tess(ie); Theresa
TEST: *Thesaurus of Engineering and Scientific Terms*
test^{mto}: *testamento* (Spanish—testament)
test^{o}: *testigo* (Spanish—witness)
testran: test translator (data processing)
tet: test equipment tool; tetanus; tetrachloride
TET: Teacher of Electrotherapy; Teacher Evaluation Testing
T-et-G: *Tarn-et-Garonne*
TETOC: Technical Education and Training for Overseas Countries
tetr: tetragonal
tetrac: tetraiodothyroacetic acid
tetrah: tetrahedral
tet tox: tetanus toxin
TEU: Test of Economic Understanding
Teut: Teuton; Teutonic
tew (TEW): tactical early warning
tex: telex (teletype exchange)
t ex: *till exempel* (Swedish—for example)
Tex: Texan; Texas
Texhoma: Texas + Oklahoma
TEX: Corpus Christi, Texas (tracking station)
TEXACO: The Texas Company
TEXAS: Trained Experienced Area Specialist
Texas RRC: Texas Railroad Commission
Texico: Texas + New Mexico
Tex Instr: Texas Instruments (Corporation)
Texola: Texas + Oklahoma
text.: textile
Textel: Trinidad and Tobago External Telecommunications Company
textir: text indexing and retrieval
text. rec.: *textus receptus* (Latin—received text)
tf: tabulating form; tactile fremitus; temporary fix; thin film; tile floor; till forbidden (run ad until stopped by advertising client); transfer function; tuberculin filtrate
TF: Tallulah Falls (railroad); Task Force; Tax Foundation; Test Flight; Tolstoy Foundation; torpedo-fighter (airplane); trainer-fighter (airplane); training film; tropical freshwater (vessel loadline marking); Twentieth Century-Fox Films (stock exchange symbol)
T del F: Tierra del Fuego
tfa: total fatty acids; transfer function analyzer
TFA: Textile Fabrics Association; Tie Fabrics Association; Trout Farmers Association
TFAA: Track and Field Athletes of America
TFAI: *Territoire Français des Afars et des Issas* (French Territory of Afars and Issas)—**formerly French Somaliland**
TFB: Thatcher Ferry Bridge (over Panama Canal)
tfc: traffic
TFCRI: Tropical Fish Culture Research Institute
tfcsd: total federal commissioned service date
tfd: target-to-film distance
tfe: tetrafluoroethylene (halon or teflon plastic)
TFF: Tropical Fish Farm
tfg: typefounding
TFI: Table Fashion Institute; Tax Foundation Incorporated; Textile Foundation Incorporated
tfis: theft from an interstate shipment
TFLA: Texas Foreign Language Association
TFNS: Territorial Force Nursing Service
tf/p: tubular fluid divided by plasma concentration (concentration of a substance in renal tubular fluid divided by its concentration in plasma)
TFP: Trees for People
tfr: terrain-following radar
TFr: Tunisian franc
TFR: Territorial Force Reserve
tft: thin-film technology; thin-film transistor
TFTA: Textile Finishing Trades Association
tfu: telecommunications flying unit
TFX: variable geometry supersonic fighter-bomber
tg: tail gear; telegram; telegraph; tollgate; type genus; tongue and groove
tg: *tangente* (Italian—tangent)
t/g: tracking and guidance
t & g: tongue and groove
Tg: *Tanjong* (Malayan—cape)
TG: Task Group; Texas Gulf Sulphur (stock exchange symbol); Torpedo Group; Traffic Guidance
T & G: Traveres & Gulf (Florida railroad); Tremont & Gulf (Louisiana railroad)
T-et-G: Tarn-et-Garonne
tga: thermogravimetric analysis
TGA: Toilet Goods Association
t'gal'n't: topgallant (sail)
tgb: tongued, grooved, and beaded
TGC: Travel Group Charter(s)
tgca: transportable ground-control approach
tge: transmissible gastroenteritis
TGG: temporary geographic grid
TGH: Toronto General Hospital
tGiF: thank God it's Friday (TGIF)
tgl: toggle
TG loran: traffic guidance loran
TGM: Thomas G. Masaryk
tgn : tangent
TGO: Timber Growers' Organization
TGP: Terminal Guidance Program
TGPLC: Transcontinental Gas Pipe Line Corporation
TGR: Tiger International
T-Group: Training Group
tgt: target
TGT: Tennessee Gas Transmission
TGU: Tegucigalpa, Honduras (airport)
TGV: *Two Gentlemen of Verona*
TGWU: Transport and General Workers' Union
th: tee handle
t & h: transportation and handling
Th: Thai (Siamese); Thailand (Siam); Thomas; thorium
Th: *Theil* (German—part)
TH: Toynbee Hall; Transport House; Trinity House; true heading

T H: *Technische Hochschule* (German—technical college)
T & H: Thames and Hudson
Th A: Theological Association
THA: Transvaal Horse Artillery
Thad: Thaddeus
Thai: language or people of Thailand (formerly called Siamese)
THAI: Thai Airways International
Thaler: (German abbreviation—Joachimsthaler)—Joachim's dollar—Bohemian coin struck in 16th century at Czech town of Jachymov (Joachimsthal)—its name has become *dollar*
thanat: thanatology
That Man: Franklin Delano Roosevelt
that's: that is
Th.B.: *Theologiae Baccalaureus* (Latin—Bachelor of Theology)
TH & B: Toronto, Hamilton and Buffalo (railroad)
TH & BA: Toll, Highways and Bridge Authority
thc: tetrahydrocannabinol (active ingredient in psychedelic drugs such as hashish, indian hemp. and marijuana)
THC: Toronto Harbour Commission; Toronto Harbour Commissioners
thd: thread; threaded; threads; total harmonic distortion
Th.D.: *Theologiae Doctor* (Latin—Doctor of Theology)
THD: Technisch Hogeschool te Delft (Technological University of Delft)
th di: thread die
the. (THE): tetrahydrocortisone
The.: Theodora; Theodore
THE: Technical Help to Exporters
thea: theater
Thea: Theadora; Theodeline; Theodosia; Theresa
T-head: Texas-tea head (underground slang—marijuana user)
theat: theater; theatrical
The Bank: The Bank of England
The Bay: Hudson's Bay Company
The Brothers: Rockefeller brothers—John D. III, Nelson, Laurance, David
The Carthaginian Lion: General Hannibal
Theda Bara: Theodosia Goodman
The Enlightenment: Europe's 18th century when encyclopedias appeared in France and England, when Voltaire and Lavoisier were matched across the Channel by Paine and Priestley
The Fed: The Federal Reserve Board
The Fuzz: [American underworld slang—detective(s); law-enforcement officer(s); police; etc.]
The Immortals: (jocular nickname—forty members of the French Academy)
The Invincible: Spanish Armada defeated by English vessels commanded by Sir Francis Drake
The Just Society: (nickname—Prime Minister Pierre Trudeau's administration of Canada)
The Lady: nickname of The Statue of Liberty in New York Harbor
The Maestro: Arturo Toscanini
Thiefrow: nickname for London's Heathrow Airport where security has been so lax and thievery so prevalent
THEN: Those Hags Encourage Neuterism
The Navigator: Prince Henrique of Portugal (1394 to 1460)
Theo: Theobald; Theobold; Theocritus; Theodoor; Theodor; Theodora; Theodore; Theodorus; Theodosia; Theodosius; Theodoric; Theodric; Theodule; Theophil; Theophile; Theophilus; Theophraste; Theophrastus
THEO: They Help Each Other
Theoc: Theocritus
theod: theodolite
theol: theologian; theological; theologist; theology
The Old: King Grom of Denmark (860-935)
The Old Party: W(illiam) Somerset Maugham
Theoph: Theophrastus
theor: theorem; theoretical
theos: theosophical; theosophist; theosophy
Theo Soc: Theosophical Society
The President: the President of the United States
ther: therapy
therap: therapeutic; therapeutics; therapy
there's: there is
therm: thermometer; thermostat(ic)
Therm: *Thermidor* (French—Hot Month)—beginning July 19th—eleventh month of the French Revolutionary Calendar also called the *Fervidor*
thermistor: thermal resistor
thermoc: thermocouple
thermochem: thermochemical; thermochemistry
thermodyn: thermodynamics
thermonuc: thermonuclear
THES: *Times Higher Education Supplement*
Thespian Maids: another name for the Nine Muses *(see entry)*
thesp(s): thespian(s)
the States: the United States of America
The Sun King: Louis XVI
The Terrible: Ivan IV—Czar of Russia 1547 to 1584
The Tower: The Tower of London
The Tragic Queen: Marie Antoinette
The Tribune Man: (pseudonym—Henry Ten Eyck White)
they'd: they had; they would
they'll: they will
they're: they are
they've: they have
t_hf: Trust Houses Forte (British motel chain)
thf (THF): tetrahydrocortisol
THF: West Berlin, Germany (Tempelhof Airport)
THG: Technische Hochschule Graz (Technical University of Graz)
th ga: thread gauge
THHS: Townsend Harris High School
THhwm: Trinity House high-water mark
thi: temperature-humidity index
Third Estate: The Commons—the legislature
Third International: Lenin's organization of seemingly ultraradical communists meeting in Moscow in 1919 and rejecting social-democratic forces
Thirstland: waterless country north of Bechuanaland
Thirty Rock: nickname of the National Broadcasting Company (NBC) at Thirty Rockefeller Center in New York City
This Is The Place: Salt Lake City, Utah's sobriquet repeating the words of its founder—Brigham Young
thistle: symbol of Scotland and the Scots

THIWRP: The Hoover Institution on War, Revolution, and Peace
thixo: thixotropic
Th:J: Thomas Jefferson (initials written by him as shown)
thk: thick(ness)
THK: *Turk Hava Kurumu* (Turkish Air Association)
Th. L.: Theological Licentiate
THlwm: Trinity House low-water mark
Th.M.: *Theologiae Magister* (Latin—Master of Theology)
tho': th though
Tho: Thomas
Thomas Jefferson Snodgrass: (pseudonym—Samuel L. Clemens)
THOMIS: Total Hospital Operating and Medical Information System
thor: thorax; thoracic
Thor: medium-range ballistic missile
thoro: thorough
thoro': thorough
Thoro: thoroughfare
Thos: Thomas
Thos Jeff: Thomas Jefferson
thou.: thousand
thp: thrust horsepower; track history printout
THq: theater headquarters
thr: their; threonine (amino acid) (THR); through; thrust
THR: Teheran, Iran (airport)
Three Baltic Duchies: Estonia, Latvia, Lithuania
three-R's: reading, writing, arithmetic (colloquially: readin', 'ritin', 'rithmetic)
thro': through
thro' b/l: through bill of lading
thrombo: thrombosis
Throne of Solomon: Ethiopia
throt: throttle
thru: through
Thru: Thruway
thruppence: threepence
THS: Technical High School; Tiwi Hot Springs (Philippines); Tottenville High School
THT: Teacher of Hydrotherapy
th ta: thread tap
thtr: theater
THTRA: Thorium High-Temperature Reactor Association
Thu: Thursday
THU: The Hebrew University (Jerusalem)
Thuc: Thucydides
THUMS: Texaco, Humble, Union, Mobil, Shell (oil-drilling complex dominating Long Beach, California)
Thur: Thuringia(n); Thursday
Thurs: Thursday
Thus: (nickname—Calcutta Steam Tug); Thursday
Thv: Thorvald(sen)
THW: Technische Hochschule Wien (Technical University of Vienna)
THwm: Trinity House water mark
THY: Turk Hava Yollari (Turkish airline)
thz (tHz): tetraherz
ti: target identification; temperature indication; temperature indicator; termination instruction; tricuspid insufficiency
ti: Texas Instruments (trademark); *tudni illik* (Hungarian—that is)
t/i: target identification; target indicator
Ti: titanium
Ti: *Tirsdag* (Danish—Tuesday); (Latin—Tiberius)
TI: Technical Inspection; Technical Institute; Technical Intelligence; Terminal Island; Termination Instruction; Texas Instruments; Textile Institute; Thread Institute; Title Insurance (and Trust Company); Toastmasters International; Tobacco Institute; Tonga Islands; Training Instruction; Treasure Island; Tungsten Institute; Tuskegee Institute
T of I: *Times of India*
tia: transient ischemic attack
TIA: Tax Institute of America; Trans International Airlines; Tricot Institute of America; Trouser Institute of America
TIAA: Teachers Insurance and Annuity Association of America
TIAS: Treaties and Other International Acts Series (U.S. Department of State)
tib: tibia(l); trimmed in bunkers
Tib: Isabel; Tibet; Tibetan
Tib: Albius Tibullus (Roman poet)
TIB: Technical Information Bulletin; Tennessee Inspection Bureau; Thousand Islands Bridge; Tourist Information Bureau
Tib(by): Isabel(la); Ishbel(le)
tibc: total iron-binding capacity
Tiber River City: Rome
tic.: target intercept computer
TIC: Technical Information Center; Technical Institute Council; Technical Intelligence Center; Texas Industrial Commission
TICA: Technical Information Center Administration
TICCI: Technical Information Center for the Chemical Industry
tick.: tickler
Tico: Costa Rican; Ticonderoga; USS *Ticonderoga* (attack aircraft carrier)
Ticos: Costa Ricans (nickname given them by other Central Americans because of their frequent use of the Spanish diminutive *ico*)
tictac: time compression tactical communications
TICUS: Tidal Current Survey System
tid: task initiation date
t.i.d.: *tres in die* (Latin—thrice a day)
tidskr: *tidskrift* (Swedish—periodical)
TIDU: Technical Information and Documents Unit
tie.: technical integration and evaluation
TIE: Truck Insurance Exchange
Tiempo: *El Tiempo* (Time—Bogota's leading newspaper)
Tien: Tientsin
tier.: tierce
tier: *tierce* (French—third)
Tierg: Tiergarten
tif: telephone influence factor; telephone interference factor; tumor inducing factor
Tif: Tiflis
Tiff: Tiffany
Tiff: *Tiffany's Reports*
TIFR: Tata Institute of Fundamental Research
tig: time in grade; tungsten-inert gas
TIG: The Inspector General
Tiger of France: Georges Clémenceau
Tigers of the Sun: Sherpas of northern India and Nepal
Tight Little Island: Great Britain
Tightrope Walker Extraordinaire: Charles Blondin who crossed Niagara Falls in 1855 on an 1100-foot (336-meter) tightrope suspended 160 feet (48 meters) above the falls and five years later carried his agent across piggyback; in 1974 Philippe Petit crossed between the twin towers of the World Trade Center in New York on a tightwire 1350 feet (412 meters) above the

city sidewalk
tigon: offspring of tiger and lioness
Tigres River City: Baghdad
TIH: Their Imperial Highnesses
TII: Texas Instruments Incorporated; Toastmasters International Incorporated
TIIAL: The International Institute of Applied Linguistics
TIJ: Tijuana, Mexico (airport)
'til: until
TIL: Tube Investments Limited
Till: *Till Eulenspiegels lustige Streiche* (German—Till Eulenspiegel's Merry Pranks)—symphonic poem by Richard Strauss
Tilda: Mathilda
Tilly: Mathilda
TILS: Technical Information and Library Service
tim: time is money
Tim: Timor; Timothy
Tim: *Timon of Athens*
timation: time navigation
timb: *timbales* (French—kettledrums)
TIMC: The Industrial Management Center
time imm: time immemorial (time beyond memory; time out of mind)
Time-Life: Time-Life Books
Time Personified: the aged Chronos of the Greeks and Romans—Father Time
Times: *The New York Times* (leading American newspaper, published in New York City); *The Times* (leading British newspaper, published in London); local designation for all other newspapers containing *Times* in their title
Times Roman: Times Roman type (sometimes abbreviated T-R)
timet: titanium metal(s)
timm: thermionic integrated micromodules
Timmy: Timothy
timp: *timpani* (Italian—kettledrums)
TIMS: The Institute of Management Sciences
Tim-Tim: (Portuguese—Timor, Timur)—former colony in the Lesser Sunda islands of Indonesia
TIN: Transaction Identification Number
Tina: Albertina; Christina; Clementina; Valentina
Tin City : Jamaica slum named after its tin-can huts; sometimes called River Tin City as much of it is inundated during rains
tinc: tincture
tinct: tincture
tinct.: *tinctura* (Latin—tincture)
Tin Lizzie: Model-T Ford's nickname
TINs: Temporary Instruction Notices
Tinseltown: Hollywood, California
t_{int}: international practical temperature
Tintoretto: Jacopo Robusti
tio: time in office (TIO); time interval optimization
TIO: Target Indication Office(r); Television Information Office(r); Test Integration Office(r); Troop Information Office(r)
tip: tax information plan; theory in practice; to insure promptness (a gratuity given to insure promptness); translation-inhibiting protein (TIP)
tip: *tipografia; tipografico* (Italian—printing firm; typographic); truly important person (TIP)
Tip: Thomas Phillip O'Neill, Jr
TIP: The Institute of Physics; Tripoli, Libya (airport); Troop Information Program(s); truly important person
TIPAC: Texas Instruments Programming and Control
tip.bkt: tipping bracket
Tipp: Tipperary
TIPRO Texas Independent Producers and Royalty Onwers
tips.: to insure prompt service (gratuities); truly important persons (TIPS)
TIPS: Technical Information Processing Sytem; Total Integrated Pneumatic System; truly important persons
tiptop: tape input—tape output
TIP & TPS: The Institute of Physics and The Physical Society
tir: total indicator reading
TIR: *Transport International des Marchandises par la Rout*ᵉ (French—International Transport of Merchandise by Road)—twenty-six nation custom agreement permitting trucks marked TIR to avoid customs until reaching their final destination
Tiradentes: (Portuguese—Tooth Puller)—nickname of José Joaquim da Silva Xavier—first Brazilian fighter for independence from Portuguese rule—a dentist
TIRB: Transportation Insurance Rating Bureau
TIRC: Tobacco Industry Research Committee
T-iron: T-shaped iron or steel section
Tiros: American meteorological satellite designed to observe cloud coverage and infrared heat radiation of the earth; television and infrared observation satellite
TIRR: Texas Institute of Rehabilitation and Research
Tirso de Molina: (pseudonym—Gabriel Tellez)
tis: tissue(s)
'tis: it is
TIs: Thousand Islanders; Thursday Islanders; Tonga Islanders
TIS: Technical Informations Service; Total Information System
Tish: Letitia
TISPM: Territorie des Îles St Pierre et Miquelon (French territory offshore Canada)
tit.: title; titular; titulary
tít: *tître* (French—title)
tit: *título* (Spanish—title)
Tit: Titus, The Epistle of Paul to
TIT: Tokyo Institute of Technology; Tustin Institute of Technology
Tit A: *Titus Andronicus*
Titan: Mahler's Symphony No. 1 in D major—he preferred to call it his *Werther* symphony comparing it with Goethe's first novel
Titan: intercontinental ballistic missile (Martin)
titanox: titanium dioxide
Titian: Tiziano Vecellio
tit°: *título* (Spanish—title)
Tito: Josip Broz(ovich)
TIU: Tokyo Imperial University
tiv: total indicator variation
Tiv: Tivoli
tix: ticket(s)
TIYC: Thousand Island Yacht Club
tj: tomato juice; triceps jerk; turbojet (TJ)
tj: *to jest* (Polish—that is)
TJ: Thomas Jefferson—third President of the United States
TJAG: The Judge Advocate General
tjc: trajectory
TjC: trajectory chart
TJC: The Jockey Club; Trenton

Junior College; Tyler Junior College
TjD: trajectory diagram
TJHS: Thomas Jefferson High School
TJM: The Jewish Museum; Thomas Jefferson Memorial
tjp (TJP): turbojet propulsion
TJPOI: Twisted Jute Packing and Oakum Institute
TJSUSA: Thomas Jefferson Society of the United States of America
tk: track; truck; trunk
tk: *to kum* (printer's expression meaning material is *to come*)
tk (TK): transkelotase
Tk: Turkmenian; Turkmenistan
tkd: tokodynamometer
tkg: tanking; tokodynagraph(y)
TKK: Teikoku Kaiji Kyokai (Imperial Japanese Marine Corporation, ship classifiers)
tko: technical knockout
TKP: Türkiye Komünist Partisi (Turkish Communist Party)
tkr: tanker
tks: thanks
tkt: ticket
tl: terminal limen; test link; thrust line; time length; time limit; total load; transmission level; transmission line; truckload; truck loading
t-l: trade last (slang, a compliment)
t/l: total loss
t.l.: *tukus lecker* (Yiddish—ass licker)—flatterer; sycophant
Tl: thallium
TL: Technical Letter; Technical Library; Texas League; The Leprosarium (U.S. Public Health Service, Carville, Louisiana); Townland (UK); Turk lirasi (Turkish pound)
T/L: Telegraphist/Lieutenant; Torpedo Lieutenant
T-L: *Time-Life* (books, magazines, recordings)
tla: translumbar aortogram
TLA: Texas Library Association; Theatre Library Association; The Library Association (of the United Kingdom); Trinidad Lake Asphalt
Tlax: Tlaxcala (inhabitants—Tlaxcaltecas)
TLB: temporary lighted buoy
tlc: tender loving care; thin-layer chromatography; total lung capacity
TLCPA: Toledo-Lucas County Port Authority
tld: tooled
tle: theoretical line of escape
tlf: *telefon* (Norwegian—telephone)
tlg: tail landing gear; telegraph
TLG: Theatrical Ladies' Guild; Tiger Leasing Group
TLH: Tallahassee, Florida (airport)
tili: translunar injection
tlm: telemeter; telemetry
Tln: Tallinn
tlo: total loss only
TLO: Technical Liaison Officer
tlp: term-limit pricing; threshold learning process
TLP: Telefones de Lisboa de Pôrto **(Lisbon and Oporto Telephone Company)**
tlr: trailer
TLR: Tool Liaison Request
tls: testing the limits for sex
TLS: Terminal Landing System; The Law Society; Trinity Lighthouse Service
TLS: Times Literary Supplement
tlt: transportable link terminal
tltr: translator
tlu: table look up
tlv: threshold limit value(s)
TLV: Tel Aviv, Israel (airport)
tlvsn: television
tlz: titanium, lead, zinc
tm: standard mean temperature; tactical missile (TM); team; temperature meter; time modulation; tractor monoplane (TM); trademark; transport mechanism; transverse magnetic; true mean; twisting moment
tm: *tonelada métrica* (Spanish—metric ton, 2,200 pounds)
t/m: test and maintenance
t & m: time and material
Tm: thulium
TM: tactical missile; Technical Manual; Technical Memoranda; Technical Memorandum; Technical Minutes; Technical Monograph; Telemetering; Test Manual; Texas Mexican (railroad); The Maccabees; Toledo Museum; tractor monoplane; trademark; Training Manual; Training Mission(s); Trainmaster; Transcendental Meditation; Tropical Medicine
TM: *Technical Manual; Turk Mali* (Turkish—Made in Turkey)
T/M (t/m): trailmobile (automobile trailer)
T de M: Teléfonos de México (Telephone System of Mexico)
tma: total material assets; total military assets
TMA: Texas Maritime Academy; Theatrical Mutual Association; Tile Manufacturers Association; Tobacco Merchants Association; Toiletery Merchandisers Association; Toy Manufacturers Association
TMAMA: Textile Machinery and Accessory Manufacturers' Association
tmar: trial marriage
TMB: Travelling Medical Board
TMBC: Toronto Motor Boat Club
tmbr: timber
TMC: Technical Measurement Corporation; Texas Medical Center (Houston); Trans Mar de Cortés (Mexican airline)
TMCA: Titanium Metals Corporation of America
tmcd: tetramethylcyclobutanediol
tmcp: trimethylenecyclopropane
TME: Teacher of Medical Electricity
T-men: Treasury Department law-enforcement officers
t'ment: tournament
TMF: The Menninger Foundation
tmh: tons per manhour
tmi: technical market index (TMI)
TMI: Telemeter Magnetics Incorporated; Tool Manufacturing Instruction; Tube Methods Incorporated
TMIS: Technical Meetings Information Service
tmj: temporo-mandibular joint
TMJ: Trade Marks Journal
tmkpr: timekeeper
tml (TML): three-mile limit
TML: Transport Managers License
TMMG: Teacher of Massage and Medical Gymnastics
TMNP: Tamborine Mountain National Parks (Queensland)
tmo (TMO): telegraph money order
TMO: telegraph money order; Traffic Management Officer
TMORN: Texaco Metropolitan Opera Radio Network
tmp: temperature; trimethyl phosphate (male contraceptive)
Tmp: Tampico
tmpry: temporary
tmp's: transcedental meditation practitioners
tmr: timer; total materiel re-

quirement; trainable mentally retarded (semi-artistic children)
TMRB: Tropical Medicine Research Board
tmrbm (TMRBM): transportable midrange ballistic missile
tms: type, model, and series
tms: *tai muuta semmoista* (Finnish—and so on)
TMS: Tactical Missile Squadron; Technical Museum, Stockholm
TMS: *Tribunal Maritime Special* (French—Special Maritime Court)—disciplinary prison court functioning in French Guiana
tmsd: total military service date
tmt: turbine-motored train
TMT: transonic model tunnel
TMTB: The Malayan Tin Bureau
TMU: Tokyo Metropolitan University
TMUS: Toy Manufacturers of the United States
tmv: true mean value
tmv (TMV): tobacco-mosaic virus
TMV: Transportadora Maritima Venezolana (Venezuelan Line)
tmw: thermal megawatts; tomorrow
TMW: Textile Machine Works
TMWC: *Trial of the Major War Criminals*
tn: tariff number; telephone number; thermonuclear; train; true north
Tn: thoron (chemical symbol); Ton (postal abbreviation)
TN; Technical Note
TN: *Twelfth Night*
T & N: Turner and Newhall
TNA: The National Archives
tnc: total numerical control
TNC: Thai Navigation Company
TNDC: Thai National Documentation Center
t^{nes}: *tonnes* (French—tons)
tng: training
TNG: Tangier, Morocco (airport); The National Grange
tnge: tonnage
TNI: *Tentara Nasional Indonesia* (Indonesian National Army)
Tn IOB: Technician of the Institute of Building
tnm: tumor, node, metastasis
tnm (TNM): tactical nuclear missile
TNM: *Telégrafos Nacionales de México*
TNM: Texas-New Mexican; Texas-New Mexico; Tokyo National Museum; Tumacacori National Monument
TNNP: Taman Negara National Park (Malaysia); Terra Nova National Park (Newfoundland)
T & NO: Texas and New Orleans (railroad)
t no c: threads no couplings
TNP: Tarangire National Park (Tanzania); Taroba NP (India); Tonariro NP (North Island, New Zealand); Tsavo NP (Kenya)
TNP: *Théâtre National Populaire* (French—Popular National Theater)
tnpg: trinitrophloroglucinol
TNPG: The Nuclear Power Group
Tnpk: Turnpike
tnr: trainer
TNR: Tananarive, Malagasy (airport); Tucki Nature Reserve (New South Wales)
Tnry: Tannery
tns: transcutaneous nerve stimulator
Tns: Tunis
TNS: Transit Navigation System
t'n't: tequila and tonic (mixed drink)
tnt (TNT): trinitrotoluene
tntc: too numerous to count
TNTC: Thames Nautical Training College
tntv: tentative
tn wep(s): thermonuclear weapon(s)
TNWR: Tamarac National Wildlife Refuge (Minnesota); Tewaukon NWR (North Dakota); Tishomingo NWR (Oklahoma)
tnx: thanks
to.: telephone order (TO); time off time opening; tool order (TO); turn off; turn over
t.o: *tinctura opii* (Latin—tincture of opium)
t^{o}: *tomo* Spanish—volume)
t/o (TO): takeoff
t & o: taken and offered; technical and office (workers)
To: Togo; Toronto
TO: Table of Organization; takeoff; Technical Observer; Technical Order(s); Theater of Operations; Tool Order; Transportation Office(r); Travel Order
To: *Torsdag* (Danish—Thursday)
TO: *Technical Order*
toa: total obligational authority
TOA: Theater Owners of America; Toledo Opera Association
toac: tool accessory
tob: tobacco
Tob: Tobago; The (Apocryphal) Book of Tobit
T o B: Tour of Britain (bicycle)
tobac: tobacco; tobacconist
Tobacco City: Winston-Salem, North Carolina
TOBE: Test of Basic Education
TOBWE: Tactical Observing Weather Element (USAF)
Toby: Tobyhanna; Tobias
toc: table of contents; top-blown oxygen converter
TOC: Tactical Operations Center; Technical Order Compliance; Television Operating Center
TOCCWE: Tactical Operations Control Center Weather Element (USAF)
tod: time of delivery
TOD: Technical Objective Document
to'ds: toads; towards
Tod und Verklärung: (German—Death and Transfiguration)—symphonic poems by Richard Strauss
toe.: term of enlistment; total operating expense
TOE: Table of Equipment
T O & E: Texas, Oklahoma & Eastern (railroad)
TOEFL: Test of English as a Foreign Language
TOES: Tradeoff Evaluation System
TOET: Test of Elementary Training
tof: time of flight
T of A: *Timon of Athens*
tofc: trailer on flatcar (or piggyback)
tog.: together
TOGA: Tests of General Ability
to'gal'nt: topgallant (mast or sail)
Togo: Admiral Togo Heihachiro (victor of the Battle of Tsushima where his forces annihilated the Russian fleet in 1905)
togr: together
togw: takeoff gross weight
tog/wi: together with
tohp: takeoff horsepower
Toinette: Antoinette
toj: track on jamming
Tojo: Premier Tojo Hideki (Japanese general and premier during World War II)
Tok: Tokyo
Tokaido Corridor: urban strip between Kyoto and Tokyo

(Kyoto, Kobe, Osaka, Nara, Nagoya, Hamamatsu, Shizuoka, Yokohama, Tokyo)
Tokelaus: Tokelau Islands
Tok Uni: Tokyo University
tol: tolerance; toluene
Tol: Toledo; Toledan
T o L: Tower of London
TOL: Toledo, Ohio (airport)
tol'able: tolerable
Tolliver: Tagliafiero
Tol Orc: Toledo Orchestra
to lt: towing light
tom: *tomo* (Spanish—volume)
t-o-m: the old man (the boss; the captain; the chief; the father)
Tom: Thomas
TOM: *Territoire d'Outre-Mer* (Overseas Territory)
tom(at): tomato
tomats: tomatoes
tomcat (TOMCAT): theater-of-operations missile continuous-wave anti-tank (weapon)
Tom, Dick, and Harry: the crowd; ordinary people; the mob; no one in particular
Tommie: Thomas
Tommy: nickname for a British soldier; Thomas
Tommy Atkins: (nickname for a British Army private)
Tommy the Cork: Thomas Corcoran
Tommy gun: Thompson submachine gun
toms: tired old movies
tom thumb: (Cockney—rum)
ton: *toneel* (Dutch—scene, set; stage); *tyurma osobogo naznacheniya* (Russian—special-purpose prison)
Ton: Tonga or Firendly Islands
TONACS: Technical Order Notification and Completion System
Tongas: Tonga Islands in the South Pacific
Toni: Antonia
Ton Isl: Tonga Islands
tonk: honky tonk
tonn: tonnage
Tono: Tomuelo (Tony derived from Anthony)
Tony: Anthony; Antoinette Perry Awards (American Theatre Wing)
Tony Curtis: Bernie Schwartz
too.: time of origin
Toothpicks: nickname given early settlers of Arkansas who were believed to pick their teeth with bowie knives
top.: temporarily out of print; topographica (three-dimensional) art; torque oil pressure
t-o-p: temporal-occipital-parietal (lobes of the brain)
Top: Topeka
topa: tooling pattern
topaz: hydrous aluminum fluosilicate
TOPICS: Tables of Periodical Indices Concerning Schools
to po: topographic; topography
TopoCom: Topographic Command (USA)
topog: topography
topol: topology
topony: toponym(ic)(al); toponomist; toponomy
tops. (TOPS): take off pounds sensibly
TOPS: Teen-age Opportunity Programs in Summer
Top Sec: Top Secret
Top of the World: Point Barrow, Alaska
tops'l: topsail
tor: time of receipt; torque; torquing; torquing up
Tor: Toronto
Toray: Tokyo Ranyon Company (tradename)
TORCH: Toronto Orthopaedic Recreational Center's Headquarters
Tor Dep: Torpedo Depot
Tor Dom: Toronto Dominion (bank)
Tor Int Air: Toronto International Airport
torn.: tornado
torp: torpedo; torpedoman
torr: 1mm of mercury
Tortugas: Tortuga Islands (Dry Tortugas and Wet Tortugas)
tos: term of service
TOS: Tape Operating System; The Orton Society; Tiros Operational Satellite
Tosa: Tsunetaka
tosc: *toscano* (Italian—Tuscan)
TOSCA: Toxic Substances Control Act
tose: tooling samples
Toshiba: Tokyo Shibaura Electric
TOSS: Tiros Operation Satellite System
tot: time on (over) target; total; totalize; totalizer
t o t: *tukus om tisch* (Yiddish—put your cards on the table)
TOT: Tourist Occupancy Tax; Tourist Organization of Thailand; Transient Occupancy Tax
TOTCO: Technical Oil Tool Corporation
tote.: totalizator
TOTES: Test-Operate-Test-Exit System
t'other: the other
TOTO: Tongue of the Ocean (deep-water channel in Great Bahama Bank)
totp: tooling template
Tou: Toulon
Tough Guy: (stock exchange nickname for Texas Gulf Sulphur company)
tour.: tourism, tourist
Tourette's disease: convulsive facial tic
tourn: tournament
TOUS: Test on Understanding Science
tov: *ten opzichte van* (Dutch—with regard to)
TOVALOP: Tanker Owner's Voluntary Agreement concerning Liability for Oil Pollution
tow.: tug of war
Towel Town: Kannapolis, North Carolina where Cannon towels are made
TOWER: Testing, Orientation, and Work Evaluation in Rehabilitation
Towers: Charters Towers
townet: towing net
Town of Fools: Chelm (*see* Chelmer)
Town of Merchants: Shanghai
Town of Roses: Molde, Norway
Town Too Tough To Die: Tombstone, Arizona
Town on the Water: Stockholm
tox: toxemia; toxic; toxicant; toxicologist; toxicology
toxicol: toxicology
TOXLINE: Toxicology On-Line (computer retrieval system)
Toy: *Toy* Symphony usually ascribed to Haydn but now believed to be part of a larger work by Leopold Mozart
Toy Bulldog: Mickey Walker
tp: target practice; teaching practice; technical paper; telephone; teleprinter; title page; total points; total protein; transport pilot; treaty port; turning point
tp: *tempo primo* (Italian—speed as at the outset)
t/p: test panel
t & p: theft and pilferage
Tp: Township; Troop
TP: Technical Pamphlet; Technical Paper; Technical Problem; Technical Publication; Technographic Publication; Texas & Pacific (railroad); Thompson Products; Torrey Pines (Institute); True Position

***T.P.**: Tempore Pachale* (Latin—Easter time)
T & P: Texas and Pacific (railroad)
tpa: travel by privately owned conveyance authorized
TPA: Tampa, Florida (Tampa International Airport); Tampa Port Authority; Trans-Pacific Airlines (Aloha Airline); Travelers' Protective Association
TPAC: Thomas Performing Arts Center (Akron)
tpb: tryptone phosphate broth
TPBC: Toledo Power Boat Club
TPC: The Peace Corps (US Department of State)
tpd: tons per day
tp'd: toilet papered (some teenager's idea of house-and-garden decoration)
TPDC: Tanjong Pagar Dock Company (Singapore)
TPE: Taipei, Formosa (airport)
TPEQ: Task of Public Education Questionnaire
TPF: Tactical Police Force; Thomas Paine Foundation
tpgh: tons per gang hour
tph: tons per hour
TPH: Theosophical Publishing House
TPH & PCA: Toy Pistol, Holster, and Paper Cap Association
TPHS: Thomas Paine High School
tpi: teeth (threads, tons, or turns), per inch; treponema pallidum immobilization (test)
t-p i: title-page, index
Tpi test: *Treponema pallidum* immobilization (for the detection of syphilis)
TPI: Tennessee Polytechnic Institute; Torrey Pines Institute; Truss Plate Institute
Tpk: Turnpike
Tpke: Turnpike (postal abbreviation)
TPL: Tallahasee Public Library; Tampa Public Library; Toledo Public Library; Toronto Public Libraries; Tucson Public Library; Tulsa Public Library
TPLA: Turkish People's Liberation Army
tpm: tape preventive maintenance; tons per minute
tpn (TPN): triphosphopyridine nucleotide; (same as nadp or $NADP^{+}$)
***TPN**: Tatrzanskiego Parku Narodowego* (Polish—High Tatra National Park)—in the Tatra Mountains of Poland
tpnh (TPNH): reduced triphosphopyridine nucleotide
TPNHA: Thomas Paine National Historical Association (New Rochelle, NY)
tyng: topping
TPNHS: Thomas Paine National Historical Society
tpnl: test panel
tpo: transmitter (signal) power output
***tpo**: tiempo* (Spanish—time)
TPO: Tulsa Philharmonic Orchestra
tpob: true point of beginning
tpp (TPP): thiamine pyrophosphate
TPP: Total Package Procurement
TPPC: Total Package Procurement Concept; Trans-Pacific Passenger Conference
tpqi: teacher-pupil question inventory
tpr: telescopic photographic recorder; temperature profile recorder; thermoplastic recording
tpr (TPR): temperature, pulse, respiration
Tpr: Trooper
TPRC: Thermophysical Properties Research Center
tpri: teacher-pupil relationship inventory
TPRI: Tropical Pesticides Research Institute
T & P Ry: Texas and Pacific Railway
tps: technical problem summary
tp's: taxpayers
TPS: Technical Publishing Society; The Physical Society
tpt: tetraphenyl tetrazolium; total protein tuberculin; transport; trumpet
TPT: Toy Preference Test; Transonic Pressure Tunnel (NASA)
tptg: turned plate turned grid
tptr: trumpeter
tpw: title page wanting
TP & W: Toledo, Peoria & Western (railroad)
***t.q.**: tale quale* (Latin—as is)
TQCA: Textile Quality Control Association
TQE: Technical Quality Evaluation
tr: temperature, rectal; test run; tons registered; toothed ring; trace; tracking radar; translation; transmit-receive; transmitter-receiver; tuberculin R
***tr**: trillo* (Italian—rolled or shaken, as in drumming or when shaking a tambourine); *traduit* French—translated); *trykkeri* (Dano-Norwegian—printing office); *tryckt* (Swedish—printed); *trykt* (Dano-Norwegian—printed)
t-r: transmit-receive
t/r: transmit(ter)/receive(r)
Tr: Transcript; Trieste
TR: Tasmanian Railway; Technical Regulation; Technical Report; Test Report; Texas Gulf Production Company (stock-exchange symbol); Theodore (Teddy) Roosevelt (26th President U.S.); therapeutic radiology; torpedo reconnaissance (naval aircraft); Training Regulation(s); Transportation Request; Travel Request; Trieste; Trip Report; Triumph (British auto or motorcycle); Turkey (auto plaque)
T-R: Times-Roman
tra: transformer-reactor assembly
TRA: Technical Report Authorization; Textile Refinishers Association; Theodore Roosevelt Association; Thoroughbred Racing Associations; Tire and Rim Association; Trade Relations Association; Travel Research Association
traac: transit-research and altitude-control (satellite)
trac: tracer; tractor
TRACALS: Traffic Control and Landing System
tracdr: tractor-drawn
TRACE: Trane Air Conditioning Economics
trach: trachea; trachael; tracheate; tracheation; tracheoscopy; tracheostomy; tracheotomy
TRACIS: Traffic Records and Criminal Justice Information System (Iowa)
tracon: terminal radar control
TRACS; Telescoping Rotor Aircraft System
Tracy: Theresa
trad: tradition(al)
***trad**: traducido* (Spanish—translated)
TRADA: Timber Research and Development Association
tradex: target resolution and discrimination experiment
Trader Horn: nickname of Alfred Aloysius Smith
tradic: transistor digital computer

traf: traffic
trag: tragedy
Tragic: overture by Brahms; Symphony No. 6 by Mahler; Symphony No. 4 by Schubert
Tragic Patriot: Thomas Paine
Tragus: Heironymus Bock
T-rail: T-shaped rail
train.: trainee; trainer; training
TRAIN: Telerail Automated Information Network
TRAIN: To Restore American Independence Now
TRAIS: Transportation Research Activity Information Service (Department of Transportation)
tram.: tracking radar automatic monitoring; tramcar; trammel; tramway
tramps.: temperature regulator and missile power supply
tran: transient
tran (TRAN): transmit (data processing)
trans: transactions; transfer; transit; transport; transportation; transpose; transposition
Trans: Transactions
transac: transaction(s)
Transan: Transandean Railway
transatl: transatlantic
Transbai: Transbaikal Railway
transc: transcription
Trans-Carib: Trans-Caribbean Airways
Transcau: Transcaucasian Railway
trans d: transverse diameter
TRANSDEC: Transducer Electronic Center
transec: transmission security
transf: transfer; transference; transformer
transfax: facsimile transmission
transie(s): transvestite(s)
transistor: transfer resistor
transit.: transitive
Transj: Transjordan; Transjordanian
Transjordania: Jordan
Transk: Transkei
Trans-Ky Exp: Trans-Kyusho Expressway
transl: translation; translator
translit: transliteration
translu: translucent
translun: translunar; translunarian; translunarite
transm: transmission
Transmark: Transportation Systems and Market Research (British rails)
transmog: transmogrification; transmogrify(ing)
Transnistria: Trans-Dniestria
transp: transparent
transpac: transpacific
transpl: transplant(ation); transplanted
transport.: transportation
Transron: Transport Squadron
trans sect: transverse section
Trans-Sib: Trans-Siberian (railroad)
transv: transverse
Transv: Transvaal
transv sect: transverse section
trany: transparency
trap.: trapdoor; trap drums; trapeze; trapezoid(al); trapezium
TRAP: Tracker Analysis Program
traps.: trap drums; trap drummer(s)
tratel: trailer motel
trau: traumatic
TRAUS: Thoroughbred Racing Association of the US
trav.: travel
Trav: Travancore; Travis
Trav: *Travessa* (Portuguese—Lane)
Traven: B. Traven (pseudonym used by Berick Traven Torsvan)
trb: tribunal; tribune; trombone
trc: total response to crisis
TRC: Trans-Caribbean Airways; Transportation Research Command
Tr & C: *Troilus and Cressida*
trccc: tracking radar central control console
Tr Co: Trust Company
tr coil: tripping coil
Tr Coll: Training College
TRCS: Trade Relations Council of the United States
Trd: Trinidad
TRD: Test Requirements Document
TRDA: Timber Research and Development Association
TRDCOM: Transportation Research and Development command
trdto: tracking radar data takeoff
TRE: Telecommunications Research Establishment
treas: treasure; treasurer; treasury
Treas: Treasurer
Treasure State: Montana's official nickname
trec: tracking radar electronic components
TRECOM: Transportation Research and Engineering command
tree: trustee
trem: *tremolando* (Italian—trembling)
trem card: transport or truck emergency card
Tren: Trenton
trend.: tropical environment data
treph: trephining (trepanning)
Tres Marías: *Tres Marías Islands* (Mexican penal settlement)—prisoners kept on Maria Madre
très sec: (French—extra-dry, almost tart champagne or wine)
trf: transfer: tuned radio frequency
trf (TRF): thyrotropin-releasing factor
TRF: Transportation Research Foundation; Turf Research Foundation
trg training
trgt: target
trh (TRH): thyrotrophin-releasing hormone
TRH: Their Royal Highnesses
TRHS: Theodore Roosevelt High School
tri: total response index (TRI); triangle; triangulation; tricolor; tricycle; triode
Tri: Trieste
Tri: *Tohtori* (Finnish—doctor)
TRI: Technical Report Instruction; Textile Research Institute; The Rockefeller Institute; Tin Research Institute; Tire Retreading Institute; total response index
TRIAL: Technique for Retrieving Information from Abstracts of Literature
trian: triangle; triangulation
Trias: Triassic
trib: tribade; tribadism; tribal; tribalism; tribalist; tribasic; tribunal; tribune; tributary
Trib: *Tribune*
Tri B: Triborough Bridge
tribas: tribasic
TRIBE: Teaching and Research in Bicultural Education
trib^l: *tribunal* (Spanish—tribunal; court of justice)
Tribune of the People: John Bright
tric: trachoma inclusion conjunctivitis; trichloroethylene
tricaphos: tricalcium phosphate
Tricia: Patricia
trick: (slang—trichomoniasis)
Tricky Dick: politician Richard M. Nixon's nickname
tricl: triclinic
trico: trichomoniasis
tricolor: flag divided into three horizontal or vertical stripes; the Tricolor, initially capital-

ized, refers to the Tricolor of France consisting of red, white, and blue vertical stripes
trid.: *triduum* (Latin—three days)
tridundant: triple redundant
TRIEA: Tea Research Institute of East Africa
trig: trigonal; trigonometric; trigonometry
triga: trigger reactor
trihem: trihemeral; trihemirer
tri ins: tricuspid insufficiency
trik: trichloroethylene
trike: tricycle
trim.: trimetric
trim.: *trimestre* (Latin—quarter; three months)
TRIM: Targets, Receivers, Impacts, and Methods; Technical Requirements Identification Matrices; Tax Reform Immediately
trimaran: three-hulled catamaran
Trin: Trinidad; Trinity
Trin Col: Trinity College
Trin H: Trinity Hall
Trinity of Science: Experience, Observation, and Reason
triol: triolism; triolist
triols: triolists (also called troilists)
trip.: triple; triplicate; triplication; tripos
TRIP: The Road Improvement Program
triphib: triphibian; triphibious (land, sea, air)
tripl: triplication; triplicate
triple-A S: AAAS (American Association for the Advancement of Science)
Triple Cities: Binghampton, Endicott, Johnson City (also called Tri-cities)
Tripsville: Haight-Ashbury district of San Francisco where drug addicts take so many so-called trips
tris: tris (hydroxymethyl) aminomethane
trishaw: tricycle rickshaw
trisk: triskelion
Tristan da Cunha: Tristan da Cunha Islands (Gough, Inaccessible, Nightingale, Tristan da Cunha)
tri sten: tricuspid stenosis
trisyll: trisyllable
trit.: *tritura* (Latin—triturate)
Trix(ie)(y): Beatrice; Beatrix
trk: track; truck; trunk
Trk: Turk; Turkey; Turkic; Turkish
trkdr: truck-drawn
trkg: tracking
trkhd: truckhead
trl: trailer
Trl: Trail
TRLB: temporarily replaced by lighted buoy
trlfsw: tactical-range landing-force support weapon
trlr: trailer
Trlr: Trailer (postal abbreviation)
trm: task response module (engineer's desk area)
trmn: trainman
trmr: trimmer
trmt: treatment
tRNA: transfer RNA (same as sRNA)
trnbkl: turnbuckle
trng: training
TRNMP: Theodore Roosevelt National Memorial Park
trnsp: transport; transportation
TRO: Technical Reviewing Office
troch: troche
troch: *trochiscus* (Latin—cough drop; lozenge; troche)
Troch: Trochelminthes
troil: troilism; troilist
Troj: Trojan
Troldhaugen: (Norwegian—Troll's Hill)—Edvard Grieg's home near Bergen
Trollstigen: (Norwegian—Troll's Path)—steep zigzag road linking Andalsnes with Valldal
trom: tromba; trombone
T Rom: Times Roman
trombst: trombonist
tromp: *trompette* (French—trumpet)
T-room: (American slang—toilet) not a tea room
Trooper Turned Physician: Thomas Sydenham

trop: tropic; tropical; tropics
troparium: tropical aquarium
Trop Can: Tropic of Cancer—$23^1/_2$°N Lat
Trop Cap: Tropic of Capricorn—$23^1/_2$° S Lat
tropec: tropical experiment
Tropical North: northern Queensland, Australia
Tropic Metropolis: Miami, Florida
TROPICS: Tour Operators Integrated Computer System
trop med: tropical medicine
troposcatter: beyond-the-horizon communication
Trots: Trotskyite(s)
Trotsky: Lev Davydovich Bronstein
Trout: Schubert's Quintet in A major for violin, viola, cello, double bass, and piano
trp: troop
trp (TRP): tryptophan
tr pl: treatment plan
trr: teaching and research reactor
TRRA: Terminal Railroad Association (of St. Louis)
TRRB: Test Readiness Review Board (NASA)
TRRG: Tax Reform Research Group
trs: transfer; transpose; trustees
trs (TRS): tetrahedral research satellite
TRs: Technical Reports; Temporary Reserves
TRS: Ticket Reservation System; Transair Limited
trsd: total rated service date
tr sh: trim shell
TrSMS: triple-screw motor ship
trsp: transport
TRSP: Turtle River State Park (North Dakota)
trsr: taxi and runway surveillance radar
TrSS: triple-screw steamer
trssgm: tactical range surface-to-surface guided missile
trsv (TRSV): tobacco-ringspot virus
trt: total response to trauma; treatment; turret
TRTA: Traders' Road Transport Association
TRTC: Tropical Radio Telegraph Company
Tru: Trucial Sheikdoms; Truman
Tru: *Truman's Railway Reports*
TRU: The Rockefeller University
TRUB: temporarily replaced by unlighted buoy
Trucial States: (*see* United Arab Emirates)
Tru Cst 1: Trucial Coast Number 1
Tru Cst 2: Trucial Coast Number 2
trud: time remaining until dive (of satellite into Earth's atmosphere)
Trudy: Gertrude
TRUE: Teachers Resources for Urban Education
tru-fi: tru fidelity (sound reproduction)
trump.: trumpet
TRUMP: Target Radiation Measurement Program
trun: trunnion
trunch: truncheon

tr unit: turbidity reducing unit
Truron: (Church Latin—Truro)
tru(s): trustee(s)
trust.: trusteeship
Trust Buster: Theodore Roosevelt—26th President of the United States
Trust Territory: Micronesian islands of the Pacific (Carolines, Marianas, Marshalls, Ponape, Truk, Yap, etc.) under American administration
truth serum: sodium pentathol
trw: trawler
TRW: the corporation whose advertising states: "formerly Thompson-Ramo-Wooldridge'
trwov: transit without visa
TRW SL: *TRW Space Log*
trxrx: transmitter-receiver
try.: truly
try. (TRY): tryptophan
TRY: Teens for Retarded Youth (juvenile correctional program)
Tryg: Trygve Lie
tryp (TRYP): tryptophan
ts: taper shank; temperature switch; tensile strength; terminal sensation; test solution; time shack; too short; tool steel; tough situation; transit storage; transmitter station; triple strength; tubular sound; typescript; type specification(s)
t's: twins
t/s: test stand; third stage; transship(ed)(ment)
t/s: transship(ed)(ment)
t/s (T/S): thyroid serum
t & s: toilet and shower
TS: Tasmanian Steamers; Tentative Specification; Terminal Service; Test Summary; Theosophical Society; Thoreau Society; Tidewater Southern (railroad); top secret; Training Ship; Transmittal Sheet; Type Specification
T S: *tasto solo* (Italian—play without accompaniment)
T de S: Teatro della Scala (La Scala)
tsa: tax-sheltered annuity; total survey area; two-step antenna
tsa (TSA): total survey area (radio and tv)
TSA: Transportation Standardization Agency; Tourist Savings Association; Track Supply Association; Transportation Service, Army
tsac: title, subtitle, and caption
TSAC: Target Signature Analysis Center
TSB: Trustee Savings Bank
TSBA: Trustee Savings Banks Association
TSBR: Thomas Stamford Bingley Raffles
tsc (TSC): transmitter start code (data processing)
TSC: Texas Southmost College; Transamerican Steamship Corporation
TSCA: Top Secret Control Agency
tscf: top secret cover folder
TSCO: Thomas Scherman's Concert Opera; Top Secret Control Officer
t-s curve: temperature-salinity curve
tsd: tactical simulator display; target skin distance
Tsd: *Tausend* (German—thousand)
TSd: Tay-Sachs disease (TSD)
TSD: Tay-Sachs Disease; Technical Services Division (CIA); towed submersible drydock (naval symbol)
TSD-CIA: Technical Services Division—Central **Intelligence Agency**
tsdd: temperature-salinity-density-depth
tsds: two-speed destroyer sweeper
tse (TSE): test support equipment
TSE: Texas South-Eastern (railroad); T(homas) S(tearns) Eliot; Toronto Stock Exchange
T-sect: cross-section; transverse section
TSES: Thumb-Signature Endorsement System
tsf: tower shield facility
tsf: *telegrafia sem fios* (Portuguese), *telegrafo senza fili* (Italian), *télégraphie sans fil* (French)—radio or wireless telegraphy
tsfr: transfer
TSG: Television and Screen Writers' Guild
TSgt: Technical Sergeant
tsh: *telegrafía sin hilos* (Spanish—wireless telegraphy)—radio
tsh (TSH): thyroid stimulating hormone
T sh: Tanzanian shilling(s)
TSH: Their Serene Highnesses
tsi agar: triple sugar (glucose, lactose, sucrose) iron agar
T-shirt: T-shaped shirt; T-shaped undershirt
tsi: tons per square inch
tsi: The Socialist International
tsiaj: this scherzo is a joke (abbreviation devised and used by composer Charles Ives)
TSID: Technical Service Intelligence Detachments
TSJC: Trinidad State Junior College
TSKK: *Tsentralnya Kontrolnaya Komissiya* (Russian—Central Control Commmission)
TSL: Terrestrial Sciences Laboratory; Texas Short Line (railroad)
TSLNP: Tung Slang Luang National Park (Thailand)
tsms: twin-screw motor ship
Tsn: Tientsin
TSNHS: Touro Synagogue National Historic Site
tso: time-sharing option
TSO: Taiwan Symphony Orchestra; Teheran Symphony Orchestra; Toronto Symphony Orchestra; Tucson Symphony Orchestra
TSOR: Tentative Specific Operational Requirements
tsp: teaspoon; tracking station position
TSP: thyroid-stimulating (hormone of) prepituitary; trisodium phosphate (Na_3PO_4)
tspn: teaspoon
T-square: T-shaped ruler for making right angles
TSR: Sir Thomas Stamford Raffles (founder of Singapore as well as the London Zoo)
T & SRC: Tubular and Split Rivet Council
tss: time-sharing system
TSS: Trident Submarine System; turbine steamship; twinscrew ship
tssm: total ship simulation model
TSSR: Tadzhikistan Soviet Socialist Republic; Turkmenistan Soviet Socialist Republic
tsta: tumor specific transplantable antigen (TSTA)
TSTA: Texas State Teachers Association
tstr: tester
tsu: this side up
tsu (TSU): triple sugar urea (agar)
TSU: Texas Southern University; Tulsa-Sapulpa Union(railway)
TSUS: *Tariff Schedule of the United States*
tsvp: *tournez s'il vous plaît* (French—please turn over)
TSW: tropical summer winter (load line mark)
TSX: Telecommunications Satellite Experiment

tt: tablet triturate; technical test(ing); teetotaler; telegraphic transfer; teletype; teletypewriter; tetanus toxoid; torpedo tube(s); transit time; tree top(s); tuberculin tested
tt.: *tantum* (Latin—fixed allowance; so much)
t.t.: *totus tuus* (Latin—all yours)
t-t: tube-in-tube
t/t: time to turn
TT: tam-tam (Chinese gong); target-towing (naval aircraft); technical test(ing); Tidningarnas Telegrambyra (Swedish News Agency); Toledo Terminal (railroad); Trans-Texas (Airways); Troop Test
T/T: twin turbine (steamship)
T & T: Trinidad and Tobago
tta: test target array
TTA: Taiwan Telecommunication Administration; Trans-Texas Airways; Travel Time Authorization
ttab; Trademark Trial and Appeal Board (US Patent Office)
TTAF: Technical Training Air Force
ttc: temperature test chamber; tetrazolium chloride; tight tape contact; tin telluride crystal; tow target cable; transient temperature control; tube temperature control
TTC: Technical Training Command; Teletypewriter Center; Texas Technological College; Tobacco Tax Council; Tokyo Tanker Company; Toronto Transit Commission
ttce: tooth-to-tooth composite error
ttci: transient temperature-control instrument
TTCS: Truck Transportable Communications Station
ttd: transponder transmitter detector
TTE: Tropical Testing Establishment
ttdr: tracking telemetry data receiver
tte: temporary test equipment; trailer test equipment
Tte: *Teniente* (Spanish—Lieutenant)
Tte Cnel: *teniente coronel* (Spanish—Lieutenant Colonel)
ttf: time to failure; tone telegraph filter; transistor text fixture
TTF: Timber Trade Federation
ttfn: ta-ta for now
ttg: time to go
TT-gauge: Tiny Tim Gauge—$^1/_4$-inch track gauge (model railroads)
ttgd: time-to-go engine dial
tth: thyrotropic hormone
tti: time-temperature indicator
TTI: The Technological Institute
T-time: takeoff time
TTIO: Turkish Tourism and Information Office
TTJC: Tyne Trade Joint Committee
ttk: two-tone keying
ttl: to take leave; transitor-transistor logic
TTL: Tokaido Trunk Line (Japanese railroad running trains at 125 miles per hour)
ttm: two-tone modulation
TTMA: Truck-Trailer Manufacturers Association
TTPI: Trust Territory of the Pacific Islands
tto: this transaction only
Tto: Toronto
TTO: Tanzania Tourist Office
T-town: Tijuana
ttp: total taxable pay
ttr: type token ratio
ttr (TTR): target-tracking radar; thermal test reactor
T & T RR: Tijuana and Tecate Railroad
tts: teletypesetter (TTS); teletypesetting; temporary threshold shift
ttt: telemetry time transposition; time to target; time to think; time to turn
TTT: Transamerica Trailer Transport; Tyne Tees Television
TT & T: Texas Transport and Terminal
t't'ta: triple-note trumpet flourish
TTTB: Trinidad and Tobago Tourist Board
TTTC: Technical Teachers Training College
T & T TS: trinidad and Tobago Television Service
ttu: timing terminal unit
TTV: Taiwan Television (offshore China)
ttvm: thermal transfer voltmeter
ttw: total temperature and weight
ttwl: twintandem wheel loading
tty: teletypewriter
tu: thermal unit; toxic unit; trade union (TU); traffic unit; transfer unit; transmission unit; turbidity unit
Tu: Turkey; Turkish
TU: Taylor University; Temple University; Tiffin University; Trade Union; transmission unit; Trinity University; Tufts University; Tulane University; Tunis Air; Typographical Union
TU: *Technische Universität* (German—technical university); *temps universel* (French—universal time)
T.U.: tuberculin unit(s)
TU-144: Tupolev supersonic transport
TU-154: Tupolev 154 supersonic aircraft
TUAC: Trade Union Advisory Committee
Tuamotus: Tuamotu Islands
tu ar: turning arbor
tub.: tubing
TUB: temporary unlighted buoy
TUBA: Tubists Universal Brotherhood Association
Tubais: Tubai Islands
tube: the tube (television tube)
TUBE: Terminating Unfair Broadcasting Excesses
tuberc: tuberculosis
tuc: transportation, utilities, communications
Tuc: Tucson
TUC: Trades-Union Congress (British)
tu ca: turning cam
TUCC: Temple University Community College; Triangle Universities S Computation Center
TUCGC: Trades Union Congress General Council
TUCSA: Trade Union Council of South Africa
tudor: two-door
Tue: Tuesday
Tues: Tuesday
TUF: Tokyo University of Fisheries; Trade Union Federation (British)
TUFEC: Thailand-Unesco Fundamental Education Center
tu fx: turning fixture
TUH: Taiwan University Hospital
TUI: Trade Union International
TUIAFW: Trade Unions International of Agricultural and Forestry Workers
Tul: Tulsa
TUL: Tokyo University Library; Tulane University of Louisiana; Tulsa; Oklahoma (airport)
Tully: Marcus Tullius Cicero
tum: tummy (stomach); tumor
TUM: Panama City, Panama (Tocumen Airport)
Tum-Tum: portly Albert Edward, HRH the Prince of

Wales who later became King Edward the Seventh
tun: tuning
Tun: Tunis; Tunisia; Tunisian
Tun: *Túnez* (Spanish—Tunisia)
tung: tungsten
Tung Tree Capital: Picayune, Mississippi
Tunic: Tunicata
Tunl: Tunnel (postal abbreviation)
tuppenny: twopenny
Tupun: Tupungato
tur: transurethral resection (TUR); turbine; turret
Tur: Turin
turb: transurethral resection of the bladder (TURB); turbine
turbid.: turbidity
turboalt: turboalternator
turbo-elec: steam turbine connected to electric motor
turbogen: turbogenerator
turbojet: turbine-driven jet (airplane engine)
turboprop: turbine-driven jet engine (moving the) propeller
turbosuch: trubosupercharter
turbotrain: turbine-driven railroad train
turbpmp: turbopump
Turch: *Turchia* (Italian—Turkey)
Turk.: Turkey; Turkish
Turkey Capital of the World: nickname shared by Berryville, Arkansas and Worthington, Minnesota
Türk-Is: *Tükiye Isçi Sendikalari Konfederasyonu* (Turkish Confederation of Trade Unions)
Turkish: Mozart's Violin Concerto in A major (K 219)
Türkiye: Turkey
Turks: Turkish people; Turks Islands
Turkmen: Turkmenia; Turkmenian
Turkmen SSR: Turkmen Soviet Socialist Republic (Turkmenistan)
Turk-Sib: Turkestan-Siberian (railroad)
Turk-Tat: Turko-Tataric
turn.: turning
Turn: Turnpike
Turner's syndrome: genetic abnormality in females inheriting only forty-five chromosomes as this causes retarded sexual development
Turner Turn: Turner Turnpike
turp: turpentine
turp: transurethral resection of the prostate (TURP); turpentine
Turpentine State: North Carolina
turps: turpentine
TURPS: Terrestrial Unattended Reactor Power System
Turq: *Turquía* (Spanish—Turkey)
turquoise: hydrargillite (basic hydrated copper aluminum phosphate)
Turtles: Turtle Islands of Indonesia; Turtle Mountains of southern California
tuss.: *tussis* (Latin—cough)
TUs: Tenant's Unions
TUS: Tuscon, Arizona (airport)
TUSAFG: The United States Air Force Group (American Mission for Aid to Turkey)
TUSC: Technology Use Studies Center
Tuscans: Tuscan people; Tuscan Islands
Tusitala: (Samoan—Teller of Tales)—Robert Louis Stevenson's nickname
TUSLOG: The United States Logistic Group
TUSM: Tufts University School of Medicine
tut: tutor; tutorial
Tut: Tutankahmen
TUT: The University of Tokyo
TUTI: Temple University Technical Institute
tuwr: turning wrench
tux: tuxedo (dinner jacket)
tv (TV): television; terminal velocity; test vehicle; tetrazolium violet; total volume; transverse; trichomonas vaginalis; true view; tuberculin volution
t/v: thrust-to-weight
TV: television; test vehicle; Tidewater Oil (stock exchange symbol); transport vehicle
tva: thrust vector alignment
tva: *taxe à la valeur ajoutée* (French—value added tax)
TVA: Temporary Variation Authorization; Tennessee Valley Authority
tvac: time-varying adaptive correlation
TVAs: Temporary Variation Authorizations
TVB: Television (Advertising) Bureau
TVBS: Television Broadcast Satellite
tvc: temperature valve control; thermal voltage converter; throttle valve control; thrust vector control; time-varying coefficient; timed vital capacity; torsional vibration characteristics
TVC: Technical Valve Committee
TVCC: Treasure Valley Community College
tvd: toxic vapor damper; toxic vapor detector; tuned viscoelastic damper
tvdc: test volts—direct current
TVDC: Tidewater Virginia Development Council
tvdp: thrust-vector display (unit)
tvdy: television deflection yoke
tve: test vehicle engine; thermal vacuum environment
TVE: Televisión Española (Spanish TV network)
tvel: track velocity
TVERS: Television Evaluation and Renewal Standards
tvft: television flyback transformer
tvg: threshold voltage generator; triggered vacuum gap
TVG: *T V Guide*
tvhh (TVHH): television households
TV household: television-equipped home
tvi: television interference
TVIC: Television Interference Committee
tvig: television and inertial guidance
tvist: television information-storage tube
tvk: terminal volume kill
T v K: Theodore von Karman
tvl: tenth value layer; travel
Tvl: Transvall
tvm: tachometer voltmeter; track via missile; trailer van mount; transistorized voltmeter
TVN: *Television News*
tvor: terminal visual omnirange; very high frequency terminal omnirange station
tvp: television poor (audio-visual addicts who have never learned how to read or who have lost the faculty during the course of their addiction); textured vegetable protein; time-varying parameter
tvq: top visual quality
tvr: textured vegetable protein
TV-RI: *TV-Republik Indonesia* (Bahasa Indonesia—Republic Indonesia Television)
Tvrn: Tavern
tvs: tactical vocoder system; telemetry video spectrum; television viewing system
tv's: television dinners; transvestites

tvsd: time-varying spectral display
tvsg: television signal generator
tvsm: time-varying sequential measuring (apparatus)
tvso: television space observatory
tvr's: television recordings
TVSTI: Thames Valley State Technical Institute
tvu: total volume urine
tw: tail water; tail wheel; tail wind; taxiway; tempered water; tile wainscot; traveling wave; twin(s)
tw: tussenwerpsel (Dutch—interjection)
Tw: Twaddell
TW: Trans World Airlines (2-letter coding)
twa: time-weighted average; trailing-wire antenna
TWA: Textile Waste Association; Thames Water Authority; Tooling Work Authorization; Toy Wholesalers Association; Trans World Airlines
TWAD: Twadell
'twas: it was
twb: twin with bath
twbp: transcribed weather broadcast program
TWC: Tail Waggers' Club
***TWC:** Trials of War Criminals*
twcrt: travelling-wave cathode ray tube
twd: tail wags dog
twds: tradewinds
twe: tap-water enema
TWE: Textile Waste Exchange
TWEA: Trading With the Enemy Act
'tween: between
***Twel N:** Twelfth Night*
Twelve Apostles: twelve Apostle Islands in Lake Superior off northern Wisconsin
Twelve-Tone Technician: Arnold Schönberg
Twentieth-Century Romantic: Rachmaninoff, Sibelius, and Richard Strauss share this musical nickname
'twere: it were
twerl: tropical wind, energy conversion, and reference level
TW & FS: The Wine and Food Society
twh: typically wavy hair
twi: training within industry
TWI: The West Indies
Twiggy: Leslie Hornby
Twilight of the Gods: Gotterdämmerung (German mythology); Ragnarok (Norse mythology)
'twill: it will
twimc (TWIMC): to whom it may concern
Twin Cities: place-name nickname share by Bristol on the Tennessee-Virginia border; Central Falls and Pawtucket, Rhode Island; Champaign and Urbana, Illinois; Minneapolis and St Paul, Minnesota; Texarkana on the Arkansas-Texas border; Winston-Salem, North Carolina, etc.
Twin Sisters: North and South Dakota
Twin States: New Hampshire and Vermont
twister: dustwhirl, sandspout, tornado, or waterspout wherein ascending and rotating movement of air column is especially apparent
'twixt: betwixt
twi zn: twilight zone
twk: typewriter keyboard
twl: top water level
twm: traveling-wave maser
Twn: Town (postal abbreviation)
two.: this week only
Two Eyes of Greece: Athens and Sparta
***Two Gent:** Two Gentlemen of Verona*
Two-headed Eagle: popular symbol of the Austro-Hungarian Empire, Imperial Russia, and the Holy Roman Empire
twot: travel without troops
'twould: it would
Twp: Township
TWP: True Whig Party (Liberia)
TWPD: Tactical and Weapons Policy Division
twr: tower
Twr: Tower (postal abbreviation)
TWR: Trans-World Radio
tws: timed wire service; track while scan
tw/s: twin-screw (ship)
twsr: track-while-scan radar
twsrs: track-while-scan radar simulator
twt: travelling-wave tube; travel with troops
t/wt: tare weight
TWT: Transonic Wind Tunnel
twta: travelling-wave-tube amplifier
TWU: Tata Workers Union; Transport Workers Union
TWUA: Textile Workers Union of America
T WW: Thick Weater Watch (Coast Guard)
twx: time-wire transmission
TWX: teletypewriter exchange (message)
twy: taxiway; twenty
twzo: trade-wind-zone oceanography (term of derision by experts or about armchair oceanographers)
tx: torque transmitter; traction
txe: telephone exchange electronic
txh: transfer on index high
txi: transfer on index incremented
txl: transfer on index low
txn: taxation
ty: territory; thank you; truly; type
Ty: Territory; Tyrone; Tyrus Raymond Cobb
Tybalt: Theobald
tyc: tycoon
TYC: Thames Yacht Club; Toledo Yacht Club
Ty Cobb: Tyrus Raymond Cobb—idol of baseball fans
tydac: typical digital automatic computer
tylenol: acetaminophen (trade name for an analgesic found safer than aspirin)
tymp: tympanic(ity); tympany
tymp memb: tympanic membrane
tyo: two-year-old (horse)
TYO: Tokyo, Japan (airport)
typ: typical; typing; typist; typographer; typography; typewriter
TYP: Ten-Year Plan; Twenty-Year Plan; etc.
type.: typewriter; typewriting
type metal: antimony-copper-lead-tin alloy
typh: typhoon
typo: typographical (error)
TYPOE: Ten-Year Plan for Ocean Exploration
typog: typographer; typographical; typography
typol: typological(ly); typologist; typology
typr: typewritten
typw: typewriter
tyr (TYR): tyrosine (amino acid)
Tyr: Tyrol; Tyrolean; Tyrolese; Tyrone
Tyrol: Tyrol(ean); Tyrolese
tys: tensile yield strength
TYS: Knoxville, Tennessee (airport)
tysd: total years service date
Tyskl: Tyskland (Danish—Germany)
***tyurzak:** tyuremnoye zakyucheniye* (Russian—prison con-

finement)

tz: tidal zone; time zero

Tz: tuberculin zymoplastiche (symbol)

TZ: Tactical Zone; Transair Limited, Canada (2-letter code)

tzd: true zenith distance

tze: transfer on zero

tzg: thermofit zap gun

TZIK: Tzentralny Ispolnitelny Kommitet (Russian—Central Executive Committee)

tzj: tubular zippered jacket

TZm: true azimuth

TZM: titanium-zirconium-molybdenum (alloy)

tzp: time zero pulse

tzt: *te zijner tijd* (Dutch—in due time)

tzv: tetrazolium violet

U

u: density of radiant energy (symbol); ugly threatening weather (symbol); unified atomic mass (symbol); unit(s); unknown; unoccupied; unsymmetrical; unwatched; upper; velocity (symbol); you (as in iou, IOU)

u: *und* (German—and); viscosity (svmbol)

μ: micron (symbol); micro

μ^2: square micron

μ^3: cubic micron

u/3: upper third

U: Chance Vought Aircraft (symbol); kilourane (1000 uranium units—symbol); overall co-efficient of heat transfer (symbol); potential energy (symbol); total internal energy (symbol); unclassified; Uniform—code for letter U; University; up; uranium; Utah; Utahans; U Thant; utility; you

U: *ud* (Danish—out); *uit* (Dutch—out); *ulos* (Finnish—out); *unter* (German—down); up; *upp* (Swedish—up); *ute* (Swedish—arrival); *violaceus* (Latin—violet-color)

U-2: high-altitude high-performance photo-reconnaissance airplane

U^{234}: trace component of natural uranium

U^{235}: 0.7 percent of natural uranium (atomic energy source)

U^{238}: 99.3 percent of natural uranium (atomic energy source)

U^3O^8: uranium oxide

ua: unauthorized absence; unauthorized absentee; uniform allowance; upper arm; urine aliquot

u a: *und andere(s)* (German—among other things; and others; inter alia)

ua: *uden ar* (Dano-Norwegian—without date)

u.a.: *usque ad* (Latin—as far as; up to)

u a: *und ähnliche(s)* (German—and the like)

μa: microampere

u/a: unit of account

ua (UA): urinalysis

uA: *und* ändere (German—and others)

UA: United Aircraft; United Air Lines (2-letter coding); United Artists; Universidad de las Americas

U-A: Universal-American

U de A: Universidad de Alcala; Universidad de Antioquia

U di A: Università di Arezzo

U of A: University of Aberdeen; University of Akron; University of Alabama; University of Alaska; University of Alberta; University of the Americans; University of Arizona; University of Arkansas

U van A: Universiteit van Amsterdam

UAA: United Arab Airlines; University Aviation Association

UAAGM: University of Alberta Art Gallery and Museum

UAASUS: Ukrainian Academy of Arts and Sciences in the United States

UAB: Unemployment Assistance Board

UABS: Union of American Biological Societies

UAC: United Aircraft Corporation; Urban Affairs Council; Utility Aircraft Council

UACC: Upper Area Control Center

UACL: United Aircraft of Canada, Limited

uacte: universal automatic control and test equipment

UADPS: Uniform Automatic Data Processing System

UADW: Universal Alliance of Diamond Workers

UAE: United Arab Emirates (Trucial Sheikdoms of Trucial States)

UAEMS: University Association for Emergency Medical Services

uaf: unit authorization file

uafs/t: universal aircraft flight simulator/trainer

UAG: Universidad Autónoma de Guadalajara (University of Guadalajara)

UAHC: Union of American Hebrew Congregations

uai: universal azimuth indicator

UAI: Urban America Incorporated (Action Council for Better Cities)

UAI: *União Astronomica Internacional* (Portuguese—International Astronomical Union); *Union Académique Internationale* (French—International Academic Union); *Union des Associations Internationales* (French—Union of International Associations); *Union Astrónomica Internacional* (Spanish—International Astronomical Union); *Unione Astronomica Internazionale* (Italian—International Astronomical Union)

uaide: uses of automatic information display equipment

ual: upper acceptance limit

UAL: United Air Lines; University of Aberdeen Library; University of Akron Library; University of Alabama Library; University of Alaska Library; University of Alberta Library; University of the

Americas Library; University of Arizona Library; University of Arkansas Library
UALL: University of Arizona Lunar Laboratory
U of Alla: University of Allahabad
uam (UAM): underwater-to-air missile
UAM: Union Africaine et Malgache (African and Malagasy Union); United American Mechanics
UAMC: United Arab Maritime Company
***UAMPT:** Union Africaine et Malagactie des Postes et Telecommunications* (French—Union of African and Malagasy Postal Service and Telecommunication)
uan: uric-acid nitrogen
***UANA:** Unión Amateur de Natación de las Americas* (Spanish—Amateur Swimming Alliance of the Americas)
uao: unexplained aerial object
UAOD: United Ancient Order of Druids
UAOS: Ulster Agricultural Organisation Society
uap: unexplained atmospheric phenomenon
UAP: Union of American Physicians; Union of Associated Professors; United Australia Party
uar: underwater acoustic resistance; underwater angle receptacle, upper air route; upper atmosphere research
UAR: Uniform Airman Record; United Arab Republic
UARAEE: United Arab Republic Atomic Energy Establishment
UARL: United Aircraft Research Laboratories
UARTO: United Arab Republic Tourist Office
uas: unmanned aerial surveillance; upper air space
UAS: Unit Approval System
UASCS: United States Army Signal Center and School
UASM: University of Arkansas School of Medicine
UASS: Unmanned Aerial Surveillance System
UASSR: Udmurt Autonomous Soviet Socialist Republic
uat: ultraviolet acquisition technique
***UAT:** Union Aéromaritime de Transport*
***UATI:** Union des Associations Techniques Internationales* (French—Union of International Technical Organizations)
UATO: United Airlines Tour Order
UATP: Universal Air Travel Plan
UAU: Universities Athletic Union
UAW: United Automobile Workers
***uAwg:** um Antwort wird gebieten* (German—reply requested)
uax (UAX): unit automatic exchange
Ub: Universiteitsbibliotheek (University Library, Amsterdam)
UB: Union of Burma; United Biscuit; Universität *Basel, Universität Berne*
***U de B:** Universidad de Barcelona; Université de Bâle* (University of Basel)
U di B: Università di Bologna
***U do B:** Universidade do Brasil* (Portuguese—University of Brasil)—in Brasilia
U i B: Universitet i Bergen
U of B: University of Baltimore; University of Birmingham; University of Bombay; University of Bridgeport; University of Bristol; University of Buffalo
***U zu B:** Universität zu Berlin*
uba: undenatured bacterial antigen
UBA: Union of Burmah Airways; United Business Associates
U de BA: Universidad de Buenos Aires
***UBAF:** Union de Banques Arabes et Françaises* (Union of Arab and French Banks)
***U-bahn:** Untergrundbahn* (German—underground road)—subway system
Ubangi Republic: Central African Republic
UBAV: United Buddhist Association of Vietnam
UBBA: United Boys' Brigades of America
ubc: universal buffer controller
UBC: United Baltic Corporation; Universal Bibliographic Control; University of British Colombia
***UBC:** Uniform Building Code* (legal)
U of BC: University of British Columbia
UBC & J: United Brotherhood of Carpenters and Joiners
UBCL: University of British Columbia Library
UBCP: Union Bag-Camp Paper
ubd: utility binary dump
UBEA: United Business Education Association
U-beam: U-shaped beam
UBEM: Union Belge d'Enterprises Maritimes
***übers:** übersetzt* (German—translated)
ubf: universal boss fitting
UBF: Union of British Fascists
ubfc: underwater battery fire control
ubi: ultraviolet blood irradiation; universal battlefield identification
UBI: United Business Investments
***UBI:** Unione Bocciofila Italiana* (Italian Bocce-Ball (Bowling) Association); *Unione Bibliografica Italiana* (Italian Bibliographical Society)
ubitron: undulating beam interaction electron tube
UBL: Union Barge Line; United Benefit Life
UBLS: University of Botswana, Lesotho, and Swaziland
ubm: ultrasonic bonding machine; unit bill of material
***U-boat:** Unterseeboot* (German—submarine)
U-bolt: capital-U-shaped bolt
U-bomb: uranium-cased atomic or hydrogen bomb
U Books: University Books
UBP: United Business Publications
UBR: University Boat Race
UBS: United Bank of Switzerland; United Business Service
UBSA: United Business Schools Association (formerly American Association of Commercial Colleges)
UBSO: Uinta Basin Seismological Observatory
ubt: universal book tester
ubv: ultraviolet
uc: universal coarse (screw thread); upper case (capital letters)
u/c: upper center
UC: Umpqua College; Union Carbide; Union College; University of California; University of Ceylon; University of Colorado; University of Connecticut; Upland College; Upsala College; Ursinus College; Ursuline College; Utica College
***UC:** una corda* (Italian—one string)—soft pedal

U de C: *Universidad de Cartagena; Universidad de Cauca; Universidad de Chile; Universidad de Córdoba; Universidad de Cuzco; Universidade de Coimbra*
U of C: University of Calcutta; University of California; University of Chattanooga; University of Chicago; University of Cincinnati; University of Colorado; University of Connecticut; University of Corpus Christi
UCA: United Chemists' Association
UCAE: Universities Council for Adult Education
UCAF: You See America First
UCAR: Union of Central African Republics; University Corporation for Atmospheric Research
UCAS: Uniform Cost Accounting Standards; Union of Central African States
UCATT: Union of Construction, Allied Trades, and Technicians
ucb: unless caused by
UCB: United California Bank; University of California at Berkeley
ucc: unadjusted contractual changes; universal copyright convention
UCC: Uniform Commercial Code; Union Carbide and Carbon; Union de la Critique Cinématographique (Society of Cinema Criticism); United Cancer Council; United Community Campaign; United Electric Coal Companies (stock exchange symbol); University College (Cork)
U-CC: Upper Canada College
UCCA: United Citizens Concerned with America; Universities Central Council on Admissions
UCCC: Ulster County Community College; Uniform Consumer Credit Code
UCCD: United Christian Council for Democracy
UCCELLO: Paolo di Dono
UCCS: Universal Camera Control System
ucd: usual childhood diseases
UCD: University of California at Davis; University College, Dublin
ucdp: uncorrect data processor
UCEA: University College of East Africa (Makerere College); University Council for Educational Administration
UCEMT: University Consortium in Education Media and Technology
U of Cey: University of Ceylon
UCF: United Community Funds
UCFE: Unemployment Compensation for Federal Employees
UCFGB: University Catholic Federation of Great Britain
UCFH: University College of Fort Hare
UCG: University College, Galway; University College of Ghana
UCH: University College Hospital
U-channel: U-shaped channel
uchd: usual childhood diseases
U Chi: University of Chicago
U Chi Lib: University of Chicago Library
uci: unit construction index
UCI: *Union Cycliste Internationale* (Cyclists International Union)
UCIrv: University of California at Irvine
UCIW: Union of Commercial and Industrial Workers
ucj: unsatisfied claim and judgement
ucl: upper control limit; urea clearance test
UCL: Union Castle Line; Union Central Life; Union Oil Company of California (symbol); University of California Library; University College, London
U c de L: *Université catholique de Louvain*
UCLA: University of California at Los Angeles
U-class: upperclass
UCM: University Christian Movement
UCMC: University of Colorado Medical Center
UCMEA: *Ufficio Centrale di Meteorologia e di Ecologia Agraria* (Italian—Central Office of Meteorology and Agrarian Ecology)
UCMJ: Uniform Code of Military Justice
U-C M S: Union-Castle Mail Steamship
UCN: University College of Nigeria
UCNW: University College of North Wales
UCP: Unified Command Plan; United Cerebral Palsy; United Country Party; Universal Citizen Plan
UCPA: United Cerebral Palsy Associations
ucr: unconditioned response
UCR: Uniform Crime Reports; University of California at Riverside; Utah Coal Route (railroad)
U de CR: Universidad de Costa Rica
UCRA: University Centers for Rational Alternatives
UCRI: Union Carbide Research Institute
UCRL: University of California Radiation Laboratory
UCR & N: University College of Rhodesia and Nyasaland
UCRS: Uniform Crime Reporting Section (FBI); University, College, and Research Section (Library Association)—also appears as UCR
ucs: unconditioned stimulus; unconscious
UCs: Urban Coalitionists
UCS: United Community Service; Universal Classification System; Universal-Cyclops Steel; University Computer Systems (computerized real estate listings); Upper Clyde Shipbuilders
UCSB: University of California at Santa Barbara
UCSC: University of California at Santa Cruz; University City Science Center
UCSD: University of California at San Diego
UCSF: University of California at San Francisco
UCSL: University College of Sierra Leone
UCSW: University College of South Wales
UCT: United Commercial Travelers; University of Cape Town
UCTA: United Commercial Travellers' Association
UC & U: Union College and University
UCUC: University College of the University of Cincinnati
ucv: uncontrolled variable
UCV: Universidad Central de Venezuela
UCVs: United Confederate Veterans
UCW: University College of Wales
UCWC: University College of the Western Cape
UCWI: University College of the

West Indies
UCWP: University College of the Western Province
ucwr: upon completion will return
UCWRE: Underwater Countermeasures and Weapons Research Establishment
UCX: Unemployment Compensation for Ex-Servicemen
UCY: United Caribbean Youth
UCZ: University College of Zululand
ud: upper berth, double occupancy ; upper deck
u.d.: *ut dictum* (Latin—as directed)
Ud: *Udjung* (Malay—point); *usted* (Spanish—you)
UD: Undesirable Discharge; United Dairies; University of Denver; University of Detroit; Urban District
UD: *Unlisted Drugs*
U of D: University of Dallas; University of Dayton; University of Delaware; University of Delhi; University of Denver; University of Detroit; University of Dublin; University of Dubuque; University of Durham
UDA: Ulster Defence Association (Protestant counterpart of the IRA)
udaa: unlawfully driving away auto
udarg: *udarbeidet* (Danish—prepared)
udc: universal decimal classification (UDC); upper dead center; usual diseases of childhood
UDC: United Daughters of the Confederacy; United Dye & Chemical; universal decimal classification; Urban District Council
UDCA: Urban District Councils' Association
'Uddersfield: (Cockney contraction—Huddersfield)
UDE: Union Douanière Equatoriale (Equatorial Customs Union)
UDEAO: *Union Douanière des États de l'Afrique de l'Ouest* (French—Customs Union of West African States)—former French colonies
UDEL: *Union des Editeurs de Littérature* (French—Literature Editors Union)
udf: *und die folgende* (German—and the following)
UDF: Ulster Defence Force; Union Defence Force
udg: *udgave* (Danish—edition)
u dgl (m): *und dergleichen (mehr)* (German—and the like)
Ud'H: Université d'Haiti (University of Haiti)
UDI: Unilateral Declaration of Independence
UDI: *Unione Donne Italiane* (Italian Women's Alliance)
u dk: upper deck
udk: *udkom* (Dano-Norwegian—published)
udl: up-data link
udm: upright drilling machine
udM: *unter dem Meeresspiegel* (German—below sea level)
udM: *über dem Meersspiegel* (German—above sea level)
UDM: United Merchants and Manufacturers (stock exchange symbol); Universal Drafting Machine (corporation)
Udm Aut Sov Soc Rep: Udmurt Autonomous Soviet Socialist Republic
udn: ulcerated dermal necrosis
UDN: Underwater Doppler Navigation
UDN: *União Democrática Brasileira* (Portuguese—Brazilian Democratic Union)
udo: unwilling drop-out
udom: udometer; udometric; udometrical
UDP: United Democratic Party
udpg (UPDG): uridine diphosphoglucose
UDP-gal: uridine diphosphate galactose
UDP-glu: uridine diphosphate glucose
udr: universal data report(er); universal digital readout; usage data report; utility data reduction
UDR: Ulster Defence Regiment
UDR: *Union des Democrates pour la cinquième Republique* (French—Union of Democrats for the Fifth Republic)
udrc: utility data retrieval control
UDRI: University of Denver Research Institute
udro: utility data retrieval output
Uds: *ustedes* (Spanish—you, *pl.*)
UDS: Ultraviolet Detection System; Underwater Demolition School
udt: underdeck tonnage
UDT: Underwater Demolition Team; Union for a Democratic Timor
UDTC: University of Dublin Trinity College
UDU: Underwater Demolition Unit
udw: ultra-deep water
UDY: United Dye and Chemical Corporation (stock exchange symbol)
ue: unit equipment
u E: *unseres Erachtens* (German—in our opinion)
UE: United Electrical Workers; University Extension
U of E: University of the East (Manila); University of Edinburgh; University of Exeter
UEA: Universal Esperanto Association; University of East Africa; Utah Education Association
ueac: unit equipment aircraft
ueb: ultrasonic epoxy bonder
UEB: *Union Économique Benelux*
UEC: United Engineering Center
UECC: United Electric Coal Companies
UECM: Union Electric Company of Missouri
uee: unit essential equipment
UEE: *Unione Economica Europea* (Italian—European Economic Union)
uef: universal extra fine (screw thread)
UEFA: Union of European Football Associations
UEI: Union of Educational Institutions
uel: upper explosive limit
UEL: Unilever Export Limited; United Empire Loyalists
u enr: uranium enrichment
UEO: *Union de l'Europe Occidentale* (Western European Union)
uep: underwater electrical potential; uniform external pressure
UEP: Union Electric Power Company; Union Européenne des Payements (European Payments Union—EPU)
UEPA: Utility Electric Power Association
UER: University Entrance Requirements
UER: *Unione Europea di Radiodiffusione* (Italian), *Union Européenne de Radiodiffusion* (French)—European Broadcasting Union
UERD: Underwater Explosives Research Division (USN)
UES: United Engineering Societies
uesk: unit essential spares kit

UET: United Engineering Trustees
u/ext: upper extremity
uf: urea-formadehyde
μf: microfarad
UF: United Fruit
U-F: Ugro-Finnic
U de F: *Université de Fribourg*
U di F: Università di Firenze (University of Florence)
U of F: University of Florida
UF_6: uranium hexafluoride
ufa: until further advised
ufa (UFA): unesterified free fatty acid
UFA: Universum-Film-Aktiengesellschaft (German—Universe Film Company)
ufac: unlawful flight to avoid custody
UFACCC: United Faculty Associations of California Community Colleges
ufaed: unit forecast authorization equipment data
ufap: unlawful flight to avoid prosecution
ufat: unlawful flight to avoid testimony
UFAW: Universities Federation for Animal Welfare
ufc: uniform freight classification
UFC: United Fruit Company
UFCc: United Free Churches
UFCE: Union Fédéraliste des Communautés Ethniques Européennes (French—Federal Union of European Nationalities)
UFCS: Underwater Fire-Control System
UFCT: United Federation of College Teachers
UFCU: Uniflex Container Unit
uff: ufficiale (Italian—officer; official); *ufficio* (Italian—bureau; office); *und folgende* (German—and the following)
UFF: Ulster Freedom Fighters; University Film Foundation
UFI: University Foundation International
UFI: Union des Foires Internationales (French—Union of International Fairs)
ufl: upper flammable limit
UfM: University for Man
ufn: until further notice
ufo: unidentified flying object
UFOD: Union Française des Organismes de Documentation (French Union of Documentary Organizations)
ufol: ufological; ufologist; ufology
UFORA: Unidentified Flying Objects Research Association
ufo's: unidentified flying objects
uf p: unemployed full pay
UFP: United Federal Party
UFPA: University Film Producers Association
UFPC: United Federation of Postal Clerks
U-frame: U-shaped frame
UFT: United Federation of Teachers
UFU: Ulster Farmers' Union
UFW: United Farm Workers; United Furniture Workers
ug: underground
μg: microgram
Ug: Uganda; Ugandan; Ugric; Ugus
UG: Underground Railroad—secret system set up before and during Civil War to aid Negro slaves seeking freedom in the northern United States and Canada; United Gas
UG: Universität Graz
U de G: Universidad de Granada; Universidad de Guadalajara; Universidad de Guanajuato; Université de Genève; Université de Grenoble
U di G: Università di Genova
U i G: Universitet i Göteborg
U of G: University of Georgia; University of Glasgow; University of Guelph; University of Guyana
U zu G: Universität zu Göttingen
uga: unity gain amplifier
ugb: unity gain bandwidth
ugc: ultrasonic grating constant; unity grain crossover
UGC: United Gas Corporation; University Grants Committee
UG & CW: United Glass and Ceramic Workers
UGDP: University Group Diabetes Program
ugf: unidentified growth factor
UGGI: Union Géodésique et Géophysique Internationale (French—International Geodesic and Geophysical Union)
UGI: Unione Geografica Internazionale (Italian), *Unión Geografica Internacional* (Spanish), *Union Géographique Internationale* (French)—International Geographical Union
UGLE: United Grand Lodge of England
Ugly Frontier: barbed-wired-and-guarded Iron Curtain stretching between East and West Germany from the Baltic to Czechoslovakia's border
UGM: Union of Graduates in Music
ugmit: you got me into this
UGPL: United Gas Pipe Line
ugr: ultrasonic grain refinement; universal graphic recorder
UGR: Umfolozi Game Reserve (South Africa)
UGS: United Girls' School
ugt: urgent
UGT: Union General de Trabajadores (Spanish—General Union of Workers)—Socialist trade union
UGW: United Garment Workers
uh: upper half
μh: microhenry
UH: Universidad de la Habana; Universität Hamburg
U d'H: Université d'Haiti
U de H: Universidad de la Habana
U of H: University of Hartford; University of Hawaii; University of Houston; University of Hull
uha: upper-half assembly
UHA: Union House of Assembly
UHAA: United Horological Association of America
uhc: under honorable conditions
UHCBCN: United Hebrew Congregations of the British Commonwealth of Nations
UHCC: Upper House of the Convocation of Canterbury
uhcs: ultra-high-capacity storage
UHCY: Upper House of the Convocation of York
uhf: ultra-high frequency—300-3000 mc
UHF: United Health Foundation
uhfdf: ultra-high-frequency direction finder
uhff: ultra-high-frequency filter
uhfg: ultra-high- frequency generator
uhfj: ultra-high-frequency jammer
uhfo: ultra-high-frequency oscillator
uhfr: ultra-high-frequency receiver
UHK: University of Hong Kong
U of HK: University of Hard Knocks
uhmw: ultra-high molecular weight
uhp: ultra-high purity
UHP: University of Hawaii Press
uhr: ultra-high resistance; ultra-high resolution
uhs: ultra-high speed
UHS: Union High School
UHU: Unhappy Hookers United (prostitues protesting professional discrimination)

uht: ultrasonic hardness tester
uhv: ultra-high vacuum
uhtv: unmanned hypersonic test vehicle
uhvc: ultra-high vacuum chamber
UHVS: Ultra-High Vacuum System
ui: ultrasonic industries
u/i: unit of issue
u.i.: *ut infra* (Latin—as below)
UI: Ube Industries; Unemployment Insurance; Universität Innsbruck
U of I: University of Idaho; University of Illinois; University of Iowa; University of Israel; University of Istanbul
UIA: Union of International Associations; United Israel Appeal
UIA: *Union Internationale des Architects* (French—International Alliance of Architects); *Union Internationale des Avocats* (French—International Alliance of Attorneys)
UIAA: *Union Internationale des Associations d'Alpinisme* (French—International Union of Alpinism Associations)
UIAS: Union of Independent African States
UIB: Unemployment Insurance Benefits; United International Bank
uibc: unsaturated iron-binding capacity
uic: ultraviolet image converter
UIC: Unemployment Insurance Code
UIC: *Unio Internationlis Contra Cancrum* (International Union Against Cancer)
UICC: *Unione Internazionale Contro il Cancro* (Italian—International Union for the Control of Cancer)
UICN: *Union Internationale pour la Conservation de la Nature* (International Union for the Conservation of Nature)
UI Comm: Unemployment Insurance Commission
UICPA: *Union Internationale de Chimie Pure et Appliquéee* (French—International Union of Pure and Applied Chemistry)
UICPS: Uniform Inventory Control Points System
UICT: *Union Internationale Contre la Tuberculose* (French—International Union Against Tuberculosis)
UIE: UNESCO Institute for Education
UIEIS: *Union Internationale pour l'Étude des Insectes Sociaux* (French—International Union for the Study of Social Insects)
UIES: *Union Internationale pour l'Education Sanitaire* (French— International Union for Health Education)
UIEO: Union of International Engineering Organizations
uif: ultraviolet interference filter; unfavorable information file; universal intermolecular force
UIF: Unemployment Insurance Fund
UIHL: *Union Internationale de l'Humanisme Laïque* (French — International Union for Ethical Humanism)
UIHPS: *Union Internationale d'Histoire et de Philosophie des Sciences* (French—International Union of the History and Philosophy of Science)
UIL: University of Idaho Library; University of Illinois Library; University of Indiana Library; University of Iowa Library
UIM: *Union Industrielle & Maritime (Société Française de l'Armement)*
UIMNH: University of Illinois Museum of Natural History
UIN: United States and International Securities (stock exchange symbol)
UINF: *Union Internationale de la Navigation Fluviale* (French—International Union for River Navigation)
UIO: *Union Internationale des Orientalistes* (French—International Union of Orientalists)
UIOOT: *Union Internationale des Organismes Officiels de Tourisme* (French—International Union of Official Travel Organizations)
UIP: United Irish Party
UIP: *Union Internationale de Patinage* (French—International Skating Union); *Union Internationale de Physique* (French—International Union of Physics)
UIPC: *Union Internationale de la Presse Catholique*
UIPC: Utah Industrial Promotion Commission
UIPD: *Ulrich's International Periodicals Directory*
UIPVT: *Union Internationale contre le Péril Vénérien et les Tréponématoses* (French—International Union against the Peril of Venereal Diseases and Syphilis)
UIR: University Industrial Research
UIS: Unemployment Insurance Service; Unit Identification System
UISAE: *Union Internationale des Sciences Anthropologiques et Ethnologiques* (French—International Union of Anthropological and Ethnological Sciences)
UISB: *Union Internationale des Sciences Biologiques* (French — International Union of the Biological Sciences)
uisc: unreported interstate shipment of cigarettes
UISE: *Union Internationale de Secours aux Enfants* (French —International Child Welfare Union)
UISN: *Union Internationale des Sciences de le Nutrition* (French—International of Nutritional Sciences)
uit: unit impulse train
uit: *uitgaaf* (Dutch—publication)
UIT: *Unión Internacional de Telecomunicaciones* (Spanish), *Union Internationale des Télécommunications* (French), *Unione Internazionale Telecomunicazione* (Italian)—International Telecommunications Union)—ITU
uitg: *uitgegeven* (Dutch—published)
UITS: *Unione Italiana Tiro e Segno* (Italian Rifle Association)
UIU: Quito, Ecuador (airport)
UJ: *Universidad Javeriana (Bogotá and Sucre)*
UJA: United Jewish Appeal
UJC: Union Jack Club
U.J.D.: *Utriusque Juris Doctor* (Latin—Doctor of Civil and Canon Law)
U-joint(s): U-shaped joint(s)
uk (UK): urokinase
UK: United Kingdom; Universita Karlova (Karl University—University of Prague)
U of K: University of Kansas; University of Keele (formerly University College of North Staffordshire); University of Kentucky
UKA: United Kingdom Alliance

UK(A): United Kingdom All-comers (athletics)
UKAC: United Kingdom Automation Council
UKAEA: United Kingdom Atomic Energy Authority
UKAPE: United Kingdom Association of Professional Engineers
ukb: universal keyboard
U of KC: University of Kansas City; University of King's College
UKCA: United Kingdom Citizens Association
UKCBDA: United Kingdom Carbon Block Distributors' Association
UKDA: United Kingdom Dairy Association
UKBG: United Kingdom Bartenders' Guild
UKCSBS: United Kingdom Civil Service Benefit Society
UKCTA: United Kingdom Commercial Travellers' Association
UKDA: United Kingdom Dairy Association
uke: ukulele
UK fo: United Kingdom for orders
UKGBNE: United Kingdom of Great Britain and Northern Ireland
UKGPA: United Kingdom Glycerine Producers' Association
UKHH: United Kingdom-Havre-Hamburg (range of ports)
UKJGA: United Kingdom Jute Goods Association
UKL: University of Kansas Library
U K£: United Kingdom pound
UKM: University of Kansas Museums
UKMC: University of Kansas Medical Center
UK(N): United Kingdom National (athletics)
UKOP: United Kingdom Oil Pipelines
UKPA: United Kingdom Pilots' Association
Ukr: Ukraine; Ukrainian
Ukraine: Ukrainian Soviet Socialist Republic
Ukrainian SSR: Ukrainian Soviet Socialist Republic (Ukraine)
UKRAS: United Kingdom Railway Advisory Service
UKSATA: United Kingdom South Africa Trade Association
UKSM: United Kingdom Scientific Mission; University of Kansas School of Medicine
UKSMA: United Kingdom Sugar Merchants' Association
Ukulele (UK): stock exchange slang for Union Carbide
UKW: *Ultra-Kurzwellen* (German—ultra-short wave)
ul: up link; upper left; upper leg; upper lid
u⅃: upper left; upper limit
UL: Underwriters Laboratories; Universal League; University Libraries; University Library
UL: *Union List*
U de L: *Universidad de Lérida; Universidad de Lima; Universidade de Lisboa (Lisbon); Université de Lausanne*
U i L: *Universitet i Lund*
U of L: University of Laval; University of Leeds; University of Leicester; University of Liverpool; University of London; University of Louisville
U de LA: Universidad de Los Andes
ULA: Ulster Launderers' Association
ULAD: Unilever Limited Accounts Department
ulan: (Mongolian—red)
ULAP: Universitywide Library Automation Program (University of California)
ulb: universal logic bloc
ULB: *Université Libre de Bruxelles* (Free University of Brussels)
ulc: unsafe lane change (vehicular code); upper left center
u & lc: upper and lower case
ULC: Ulster Loyalist Council; Underwriters' Laboratories of Canada
ULCA: United Lutheran Church of America
ULCC: Ultra Large Cargo Carrier (bulk freighter or tanker of 400,000 or more tons)—superfreighter or supertanker
ULCI: Union of Lancashire and Cheshire Institutes
uldest: ultimate destination
ulf: ultra-low frequency; unfair labor practice
ULI: Urban Land Institute
ULII: *Union pour la Langue Internationale Ido* (French—Union for the International Language Ido)
ULICS: University of London Institute of Computer Science
ull: ullage
'Ull: (Cockney contraction—Hull)
ULL: Unitarian Laymen's League; University of Liverpool Library
ullv (ULLV): unmanned lunar logistics vehicle(s)
ulm: ultrasonic light modulator; universal logic module
Ulma: (Latin—Ulm)
ULMS: Underwater Long-range Missile System
ULO: United Licensed Officers (union); Unmanned Launch Operations
ULP: University of London Press
ulpr: ultra low-pressure rocket
uls: unsecured loan stock
ULS: Universities Libraries Section (Association of College and Research Libraries)
ULS: *Union List of Serials*
ult: ultimate; ultimo
ult.: *ultimo* (Latin—at last)
ULT: United Lodge of Theosophists
Ult Bod: Ultra Bodoni
ulto: ultimo
ult^{o}: *último* (Spanish—last)
ult. praes.: *ultimum praescriptus* (Latin—last prescribed)
ultracom: ultraviolet communications system
ultra hi-fi: ultra-high fidelity
ultrason: ultrasonic(s)
ultra-x: universal language for typographic reproduction applications
ult ts: ultimate tensile strength
ulv: ultra-low volume
U of Luck: University of Lucknow
Ulysses': fifty-dollar bills bearing the portrait of President Ulysses S. Grant
um: umpire; unmarried
u/m: unit of measure
üM: *über dem Meeresspiegel* (German—above sea level)
UM: Universal Match; Universal Mill; University of Malaysia (University of Malaya—Raffles Institute); University of Manitoba; University Museum(s)
U de M: Universidad de Madrid; Universidad de México; Université de Montreal
U di M: Universitá di Milano
U of M: University of Maine; University of Malaysia; University of Manchester; University of Manitoba; University of Maryland; University of Massachusetts; University of Miami; University of Michigan; University of Minnesota

University of Mississippi; University of Missouri; University of Montreal
U Ma: Ursa Major (Big Bear)
UMA: Ultrasonic Manufacturers Association; Union de Mujeres Americanas (United Women of the Americas)
U-magnet: U-shaped magnet
U of Mand: University of Mandalay
UMAS: United Mexican-American Students
umb: umber; umbilical; umbilicus
Umb: Umbrian
***UMB:** Union Mondiale de Billard* (French—World Billiards Union)
UMBIR: University of Michigan Bureau of Industrial Relations
umbl: umbilical
UMBR: Umbria(n)
Umbrian Historical Painter: Pinturicchio (Bernardino di Betto)
UMC: Universal Match Corporation; Upstate Medical Center
UMCA: Urabá, Medellín and Central Airways
UMD: Unit Manning Document
U of Mdrs: University of Madras
umf: ultramicrofiche
UMFC: United Methodist Free Churches
***umgearb:** umgearbeitete* (German—revised)
***UMHK:** Union Minière du Haut-Katanga* (United Mines of Upper Katanga)
umi: (Japanese—gulf; sea)
U Mi: Ursa Minor (Little Bear)
UMI: University Microfilms Incorporated
***U/min:** Umdrehungen in der Minute* (German—revolutions per minute)
UMIST: University of Manchester Institute of Science and Technology
UML: University of Michigan Library; University of Minnesota Library; University of Missouri Library
umler: universal machine language
UMLS: University Microfilm Library Service
UM & M: United Merchants and Manufacturers
UMMS: University of (Maine, Manchester, Manitoba, Maryland, Massachusetts, Michigan, Minnesota, Mississippi, Missouri, Montana, etc.) Medical School
UMMZ: University of Michigan Museum of Zoology
umn: upper motor neuron
UMNO: United Malay National Organization
umoc: ugly man on campus
U of Monc: University of Moncton
ump: umpire
UMP: Upper Mantle Project; Upper Merion and Plymouth (railroad); University of Massachusetts Press
'Umphrey: (Cockney contraction—Humphrey)
UMPO: Upper Manhattan Planning Office
U MR: Umvoti Mounted Rifles
UMREL: Upper Midwest Regional Educational Laboratory
UMRWFR: Upper Mississippi River Wildlife and Fish Refuge (Minnesota)
ums: unmanned machinery space
UMS: Undersea Medical Society; Universal Military Service
UMT: Universal Military Training
***UMT:** Union Marocaine du Travail* (French—Moroccan Labor Union)
UMTA: Urban Mass Transportation Administration
umtd: using mails to defraud
UMTS: Universal Military Training and Service
UMW: United Mine Workers
UMWA: United Mine Workers of America
U of Mys: University of Mysore
un (UN): unsatisfactory
Un: Union (postal abbreviation)
UN: Union Twist Drill (trademark); United Nations; unsatisfactory
***UN:** União Nacional* (Portuguese—National Union)
***U di N:** Università di Napoli*
U of N: University of Natal; University of Nebraska; University of Nevada; University of Nottingham
UNA: United Nations Association; United Natives Association
UNAA: United Nations Association of Australia
UNAAF: Unified Action Armed Forces
unab: unabridged
unabr: unabridged
UNAC: United Nations Appeal for Children
UNACC: United Nations Administrative Committee on Coordination
unaccomp: unaccompanied
UNACIL: United Africa Commercial and Industrial Limited
UNACOMS: Universal Army Communications System
unalot: unallotted
***UNAM:** Universidad Nacional Autónoma de México* (National University of Mexico)
***UNAM:** Universidad Nacional Autónoma de México* (Spanish—National University of Mexico)
unamace: universal automatic map compilation equipment
un-Amer: un-American (something contrary to democratic tradition and the principles of American government and way of life)
unan: unanimous
UNAPO: United National Association of Post Office (Craftsmen)
UNARCO: United Nations Narcotics Commission
unasgd: unassigned
unatt: unattached
UNAUS: United Nations Association of the United States
unauthd: unauthorized
unb: unbound; universal navigation beacon
UNB: United Nations Bookshop
U of NB: University of New Brunswick
UN Bank: International Bank for Reconstru ction and Development
unbd: unbound
unc: unconscious; undercurrent; unified coarse (thread)
Unc: Uncle
UNC: United Nations Command; Universidad Nacional de Colombia; University of Northern Colorado
***UNC:** Union Nationale Camerounaise* (French—Cameroon National Union)—party
U of NC: University of North Carolina
UNCAST: United Nations Conference on the Applications of Science and Technology
UNCC: United Nations Cartographic Commission
UNCF: United Nations Children's Fund (formerly UNICEF); United Negro College Fund
unch: unchanged
UNCIO: United Nations Conference on International Organi-

zation
UNCIP: United Nations Commission on India and Pakistan
uncir: uncirculated
UNCL: University of North Carolina Library
unclas: unclassified
U.N.C.L.E.: United Network Command for Law Enforcement (fictional organization created for television)
Uncle Billie: General William Tecumseh Sherman, USA
Uncle Gene: Eugene Ormandy
Uncle George: George Geist
Uncle Ho: Ho Chi Minh
Uncle Horace: Horace Greeley
Uncle Joe: U.S. Representative Joseph Gurney Cannon also known as the Watchdog of the Treasury
Uncle Remus: (pseudonym—Joel Chandler Harris)
Uncle Robert: Robert E. Lee; Robert L. Sheppard
Uncle Sam: cartoon symbol and nickname for an American citizen or the United States of America
Uncle Sam's Crib: Treasury of the United States
Uncle Sam's Pocket Handkerchief: Delaware—second smallest state in the U.S.
Uncle Sap: (derisive nickname—Uncle Sam)—self-bankrupting giveaway programs extended to even the most unfriendly nations account for this well-known nickname of recent years
UNCMAC: United Nations Command Military Armistice Commission
unco: uncouth
UNCO: United Nations Civilian Operations Mission (to the Congo)
UNCOK: United Nations Commission on Korea
uncol: universal computer-oriented language
uncomp: uncompensated
uncond: unconditioned
Unconditional Abolitionist: William Lloyd Garrison
Unconditional Surrender Grant: General Ulysses Simpson Grant, USA
UNCOPUOS: United Nations Committee on the Peaceful Uses of Outer Space
uncor: uncorrected
uncov: uncover; uncovered; uncovers
Uncrowned King of Ireland: Charles Stewart Parnell
un cs: unconditioned stimulus
unct.: *unctus* (Latin—smeared)
UNCTAD: United Nations Conference on Trade and Development
UNCURK: United Nations Commission for the Unification and Rehabilitation of Korea
und: under
U of ND: University of North Dakota; University of Notre Dame
unded: underdeduction
undercover narc: undercover narcotics agent
undergrad: undergraduate
Under Sec Nav: Under Secretary of the Navy
Undex: *United Nations Index*
UNDI: *United Nations Document Index*
undies: underthings (underwear)
UNDP: United Nations Development Program
undsgd: undersigned
UNDSM: University of North Dakota School of Medicine
undtkr: undertaker
undw: underwater
undwrtr: underwriter
UNE: University of New England (New South Wales)
UNEC: United Nations Education Conference
UNECA: United Nations Economic Commission for Asia
UNECOLAIT: *Union Européenne du Commerce Laitier* (French—European Milk Trade Union)
UNEDA: United Nations Economic Development Association
unef: unified national extra fine (screw thread)
UNEF: United Nations Emergency Forces
UNESCO: United Nations Educational, Scientific, and Cultural Organization
UNESEM: *Union Européenne des Sources d'Eaux Minérales du Marché Commun* (French — European Union of Natural Mineral Water Sources of the Common Market)
UNETAS: United Nations Emergency Technical Aid Service
unex: unexecuted
unexpl: unexplained; unexploded; unexplored
unexpur: unexpurgated
UNEXSO: Underwater Explorers Society
unf: unified fin thread; unfuzed
UNF: United National Front
U of NF: University of North Florida
UNFAO: United Nations Food and Agricultural Organization
unfav: unfavorable
UNFB: United Nations Film Board
UNFC: United Nations Food Conference
unfd: unfurnished
UNFDAC: United Nations Fund for Drug Abuse Control
UNFICYP: United Nations (Peace-Keeping) Force in Cyprus
unfin: unfinished
Unfinished: Schubert's Symphony No. 8 in B minor
UN Fund: International Monetary Fund
ung: unguent
ung: *ungarische* (German—Hungarian)
ung.: *unguentum* (Latin—ointment)
Ung: Ungava; Ungavan
UNGA: United Nations General Assembly
Ungar: Frederick Ungar Publishing company
U of NH: University of New Hampshire
UNHCR: United Nations High Commissioner for Refugees
UNHQ: United Nations Headquarters
UNI: United News of India
UNI: *Unione Naturista Italiana* (Italian Naturist Association)
UNIA: Universal Negro Improvement Association (Garveyites)
UNIC: United Nations Information center
UNICCAP: Universal Cable Circuit Analysis Program
UNICE: *Union des Industries de la Communauté Européenne (Industrial Union of the European Community)*
UNICEF: United Nations International Children's Emergency Fund
unicike: unicycle
unicom: universal communication
UNICOM: aeronautical advisory station operating on 122.8 mc
UNIDO: United Nations Industrial Development Organization
unif: uniform; uniformity
unif coef: uniformity coefficient
Unif Gift Min Act: Uniform Gifts to Minors Act

Uniform: code for letter U
unilat: unilateral
UNIMA: *Union Internationale de grands Magasins* (French—International Union of Department Stores)
UNINCO: *Union Internationale des Corps Consulaires* (International Consular Corps Union)
unincorp: unincorporated
UNIO: United Nations Information Organization
Union Jack: United Kingdom's national flag also called the Union Flag as it combines the Cross of St. Andrew (Scotland), the Cross of St. George (England), and the Cross of St. Patrick (Ireland)
UNIP: United Independence Party
UNIPEDE: *Union Internationale des Producteurs et Distributeurs d'Energie Électrique* (French—International Union of Producers and Distributors of Electric Energy)
unipol: universal procedure-oriented language
uni(s): unisexual(s)
unis: *unisoni* (Italian—unison)
UNIS: United Nations International School
UNISIST: Universal System for Information in Science and Technology
UNISOMI: Universal Symphony Orchestra and Music Institute
Unit: Unitarian
UNIT: *Union Nationale des Ingénieurs Techniciens*
UNITAR: United Nations Institute for Training and Research
Unitarian Quaker: Elias Hicks
United Arab Emirates: (formerly Trucial States—Abu Dhabi, Ajman, Dubai, Ras el Khaimah, Sharjah, Umm al Qaiwain)
United Kingdom: United Kingdom of Great Britain and Northern Ireland (Great Britain comprising England, Scotland, and Wales)—UK
United Nations Capital: New York City
United Provinces: United Provinces of the Netherlands (Friesland, Gelderland, Groningen, Holland, Oberyssel, Utrecht, Zeeland)—the Seven Provinces
United Provinces colors: blue and white displayed in flags of El Salvador, Guatemala, Honduras, and Nicaragua—formerly federated after their liberation from Spain
UNITS: United Nations Information for Teachers
univ: universal
Univ: Universal; Universalist; University
univac: universal automatic computer
Univ-Buchdr: *Universitats-Buchdrukerei* (German—university press)
Univ C: University College (Oxford)
Univ. D.: Doctor of the University (degree)
unk: unknown
Unk: Uncle
unkn: unknown
UNLA: *Unione Nazionale per la Lotta contro l'Analfabetismo* (Italian—National Association for the Fight Against Illiteracy)
UNLC: United Nations Liaison Committee
UNKRA: United Nations Korean Reconstruction Agency
UNLL: United Nations League of Lawyers
unldh: underloading
unliq: unliquidated
unlk: unlock
UNM: Ukrainian National Museum (Chicago)
U of NM: University of New Mexico
UNMC: University of Nebraska Medical Center
UNMEM: United Nations Middle East Mission
UNMSC: United Nations Military Staff Committee
UNMSM de L: *Universidad Nacional de San Marcos de Lima* (University of Lima)
UNO: United Nations Organization; University of New Orleans
UNO: *Union Nacional Odría* (Spanish—Odria National Union)— Peruvian-general's party
UNOC: United Nations Operations in the Congo
unodir: unless otherwise directed
unof: unofficial
UNOID: United Nations Organization for Industrial Development
unoindc: unless otherwise indicated
UNOLS: University-National Oceanographic Laboratory System
unop: unopposed
unp: unpaged
UNP: University of Nebraska Press; Urewara National Park (North Island, New Zealand)
UNPA: United Nations Postal Administration
unpd: unpaid
unpleas: unpleasant
UNPOC: United Nations Peace Observation Commission
UNPP: United Nations Partition Plan
unpub: unpublished
unqual: unqualified
UNR & EC: United Nuclear Research and Engineering Center
Unreconstructed Rebel: Senator George Carter Glass so nicknamed by President Franklin D. Roosevelt
UNREF: United Nations Refugee Emergency Fund
unrep: unreported; unrepresented
UNRISD: United Nations Research Institute for Social Development
UNRRA: United Nations Relief and Rehabilitation Administration
UNRWA: United Nations Relief and Works Agency
uns: unified special (thread); unsymmetrical
UNSA: United Nations Specialized Agencies; University of Nottingham School of Agriculture
unsat: unsatisfactory
unsatfy: unsatisfactory
unsatis: unsatisfactory
UNSC: United Nations Security Council
UNSCC: United Nations Standards Coordinating Committee
UNSCCUR: United Nations Scientific Conference on the Conservation and Utilization of Resources
UNSCEAR: United Nations Scientific Committee on the Effects of Atomic Radiation
UNSCOB: United Nations Special Commission on the Balkans
UNSCOP: United Nations Special Commission on Palestine
Unser Fritz: (German—Our Fritz)—Frederick William III of Prussia
unscv: unserviceable
UNSDRI: United Nations Social Defense Research Institute

UNSG: United Nations Secretary General
unsgd: unsigned
unskd: unskilled
UNSM: United Nations Service Medal; University of Nebraska State Museum
UNSR: United Nations Space Registry
unst: unstable
un stim: unconditioned stimulus
unsvc: unserviceable
UNSvM: United Nations Service Medal
UNSW: University of New South Wales
UNSY: *United Nations Statistical Yearbook*
unsym: unsymmetrical
UNTA: United Nations Technical Assistance
UNTAA: United Nations Technical Assistance Administration
UNTC: United Nations Trusteeship Council
unthd: unthreaded
UNTSO: United Nations Truce Supervision Organization
UNTT: United Nations Trust Territory
UNTTA: United Nations Trust Territory Administration
UNWCC: United Nations War Crimes Commission
unwmk: unwatermarked
u & o: use and occupancy
uo: *und öfters* (German—and often)
UO: Ulster Orchestra (Belfast)
U de O: *Universidad de Oviedo*
U i O: *Universitet i Oslo*
U of O: University of Ohio; University of Oklahoma; University of Omaha; University of Oregon; University of Ottawa; University of Oxford
uoc: ultimate operational capability
UOCO: Union Oil Company
uod: ultimate oxygen demand
UOFS: University of the Orange Free State
uohc: under other than honorable conditions
μohm: microhm
uol: underwater object locator
uoo: undelivered orders outstanding
UOP: Universal Oil Products
UOPWA: United Office and Professional Workers of America
UOR: Uniform Officer Record; Unusual Occurrences Report
UORI: University of Oklahoma Research Institute
U or non-U: upperclass or not upperclass
uo's: undelivered orders
uos: Underwater Ordnance Station (USN)
uot: uncontrolled overtime
UOT: United Ocean Transport (Daido Line)
UOTS: United Order of True Sisters
uov: unit of variance
up.: underproof; underproofed; underproofing; unpaged; upper
u/p: urine-plasma concentration
u & p: uttering and publishing
UP: Union Pacific (railroad); Union Postale (Postal Union); United Press; United Province; University of Paris; University of Pennsylvania; University of Pittsburgh; Uttar Pradesh
UP: *Unidad Popular* (Spanish—Popular U Unity)—political party; *Unión Panamericana* (Spanish—Pan-American Union); *Union Postale* (French—Postal Union)—international mail organization
U di P: *Università di Padova; Università di Perugia; Università di Piacenza; Università di Pisa*
U do P: *Universidade do pôrto* (University of Oporto)
U of P: University of the Pacific; University of Pennsylvania; University of Pittsburgh; University of Portland; University of Pretoria; University of Puget Sound
UPA: *Union Postale Arabe* (Arab Postal Union); *Unions Professionnelles Agricoles* (Professional Agricultural Unions)
UPA: United Productions of America; University Photographers Association
UPADI: *Unión Panamericana de Asociaciones de Ingenieros* (Pan-American Union of Engineers Associations)
UPAE: *Union Postale des Amériques et de l'Espagne* (French—Postal Union of the Americas and Spain)
U de Pan: *Universidad de Panamá*
UPC: Unesco Publications Center; United Power Company; Universal Product Code
upd: unpaid
UPD: Unified Port District
UPDW: United Piece Dye Works
UPE: *Union Parlementaire Européenne* (European Parliamentary Union)
U of PE: University of Port Elizabeth
uphd: uphold
uphol: upholsterer; upholstery
UPI: United Press International (merger of United Press and International News Service)
UPIGO: *Union Professionnelle Internationale des Gynéocologistes et Obstétriciens* (French—International Professional Union of Gynecologists and Obstetricians)
UPIN: United Press International Newsfeatures
UPL: United Philippine Line; University of Pensylvania Library; University of Pittsburgh Library; University of Portland Library
UPNE: Unversity Press of New England
UPNG: University of Papua and New Guinea
upo: undistorted power output
UPO: Unit Personnel Office(r)
UPO: United Partisans' Organization; Unit Personnel Office(r)
UPOW: Union of Post Office Workers
upp: *upplaga* (Swedish—edition)
UPPC: Union Pacific Petroleum Corporation
Upper Austria: northern Austria bordering Bavaria and Czechoslovakia
Upper California: southern California called Alta California when under Spanish and Mexican rule
Upper Canada: English-speaking Ontario and the upper St Lawrence region during the 19th century
Upper Egypt: Egypt from Cairo south to the Sudan
Upper Galilee: Israel north of the Sea of Galilee
Upper Lakes: northernmost Great Lakes—Huron, Michigan, Superior
Upper Peninsula; northern Michigan between Lake Michigan and Lake Superior
Upper Peru: an old name for Bolivia
Upper Rhine: Rhine River between Basel in Switzerland and Mainz in Germany
UPPPP: Underprivileged Peoples' Public Pool
upr: upper
Upr: Upper (postal abbreviation)
U Pr: University Press (Wash-

ington, D.C.)
UPR: Union Pacific Railroad; University of Puerto Rico
UPREAL: Unit Property Record and Equipment Authorization List
ups: uninterrupted power supply; United Parcel Service (trademark in lowercase)
UPS: Underground Press Syndicate; Underground Publication Society; Underwater Production System(s)
UPSG: universal polar stereographic grid
UPSM: University of Pennsylvania School of Medicine
up tor: upper torso
up tr: up train
UPU: United Prisoners Union; Universal Postal Union
UPU: Unión Postal Universal (Spanish—Universal Postal Union)
UPV: Ulster Protestant Volunteers (paramilitary counterpart of the IRA)
UPW: Union of Postal Service Workers
UPWA: United Public Workers of America
uq: upper quartile
U de Q: Universidad de Quito (Universidad Central)
ur: unconditioned response; up right (stage direction); upper right; urinal; urinary; urine; utility rectifier
u/r; upper right
Ur: Urania; Uranus; Urdu; Uruguay; Uruguayan
UR: Uniform Regulations; Unsatisfactory Report; Urban Renewal
UR: Universidad de la República (University of Uruguay)
U di R: Università di Roma
U of R: University of Reading; University of Redlands; University of Richmond; University of Rochester
URA: United Republicans of America; Urban Renewal Administration
u-rail: U-shaped rail
Urals: Ural Mountains
Uran: Uranus
U of Rang: University of Rangoon
ur anal.: urine analysis
uranog: uranographer; uranographic; uranography
urb: urban; urbanism; urbanist; urbanistic; urbanite; urbanization; urbanize; urbicultural; urbiculture
urbanol: urbanologic(al); urbanologist; urbanology
urb guer(s): urban guerilla(s)
urbol: urbanologist; urbanology
urbm (URBM): ultimate-range ballistic missile
urc: upper right center
URC: Universal Resources Corporation; Urban Renewal Commission
urd: upper disease (head cold)
Urd: Urdu (literary language of pakistan)
Ur$: Uruguayan peso
URD: Unión Republicana Democrática (Spanish—Democratic Republican Union)—political party active in Venezuela
URESA: Uniform Reciprocal Enforcement of the Support Act (for the collection and enforcement of child support)
uret: urethra(l)
urf (URF): uterine-relaxing factor
urg: urgent
uri: upper respiratory illness (head cold)
URI: Union Research Institute (Hong Kong)
U of RI: University of Rhode Island
URISA: Urban and Regional Information System Association
Urista: Uriel da Costa
URL: Unilever Research Laboratory
urltr: your letter
urmsg: your message
uro: urological; urology
urogen: urogenital
urol: urological; urology
U-room: U-boat room (petty officer's quarters)
URP: United Revolutionary Party
URR: Union for the Resurrection of Russia
URs: Unsatisfactory Reports; University Rationalists
UR's: Unsatisfactory Reports
URS: Universal Reporting System; Universal Reference System
URSI: Union Radio Scientifique Internationale (International Scientific Radio Union)
urspr: ursprünglich (German—originally)
URSS: União das Repúblicas Socialistas Soviéticas (Portuguese—Union of Socialist Soviet Republics)—the USSR; *Union des Républiques Socialistes Soviétiques* (French—Union of Socialist Soviet Republics) — the USSR
Ursula Bloom: Mrs A.C.G. Robinson's pen name
urt: upper respiratory tract; utility radio transmitter
URT: United Republic of Tanzania (Tanganyika and Zanzibar)
urtel: your telegram
urti: upper respiratory tract infection (common cold; influenza)
URTU: United Road Transport Union
Uru: Uruguay; Uruguayan
urv: underseas research vehicle
URWA: United Rubber Workers of America
us.: under seal; undersize; uniform sales
u-s: upper-stage
u/s: unserviceable
u.s.: ubi supra (Latin—where mentioned above); *ut supra* (Latin— as above)
ultimo scorso (Italian—last month)
us. (US): unconditioned stimulus
US: United States (to many Americans US or U.S. means us—you and I)
U.S.: United States
U.S.: Ufficio Stampa (Italian—Press Agency)
U de S: Universidad de Salamanca; Universidad de San Andrés (La Paz); Universidad de San Augustín (Arequipa); Universidad de San Javier (Panama); Universidad de San Marcos (Lima); Universidad de Santiago; Universidad de Santo Tomás (Bogotá or Santo Domingo)
U di S: Universitá di Siena
U i S: Universitet i Stockholm
U of S: University of Saskatchewan; University of Scranton; University of Sheffield; University of the South (Sewanee, Tennessee); University of Southampton; University of Sudbury
USA: Underwriters Service Association; Union of South Africa; United States of America (more correctly U.S.A., to distinguish the country from USA, United States Army); United States Army
U.S.A.: United States of America

U of SA: University of South Africa
U.S. of A.: United States of America (as abbreviated a century ago); United Secularists of America
USAAA: US Army Audit Agency
USAABMDA: United States Army Advance Ballistic Missile Defense Agency
USAAC: United States Army Air Corps (now USAF)
USAACDA: United States Army Aviation Combat Development Agency
USAAD: US Army Airmobile Division
USAADC: United States Army Air Defense Center
USAADEA: US Army Air Defense Engineering Agency
USAAF: United States Army Air Forces
USAAFINO: United States Army Aviation Flight Information and Navigation Aids Office
USAAFO: US Army Avionics Field Office
USAAMR & DL : United States Army Air Mobility Research and Development Laboratory
USAASO: United States Army Aeronautical Services Office
USAAVNC: United States Army Aviation Center
USAAVNS: United States Army Aviation School
USAAVSCOM: United States Army Aviation Systems Command
USABAAR: United States Army Board for Aviation Accident Research
USABRL: US Army Ballistic Research Laboratories
USAC: United States Aircraft Carriers (air cargo line); United States Auto Club; US Air Conditioning Corporation
USA CAC: United States Army continental Army Command
USACC: U.S.-Arab Chamber of Commerce
USACDA: United States Arms Control and Disarmament Agency
USACDC: US Army Combat Developments Command
USACDCCA: United States Army Combat Development Command Combined Arms Agency
USACDCEC: United States Army Combat Development Command Experimentation Command
USACDCFAA: United States Army Combat Developments Command Field Artillery Agency
USACDCNG: United States Army Combat Developments Command Nuclear Group
USACDCOA: United States Army Combat Developments Command Ordnance Agency
USACDCQA: United States Army Combat Developments Command Quartermaster Agency
USACDCSWCAG: United States Army Combat Developments Command Special Warfare and Civil Affairs Group
USACE: US Ar my Corps of Engineers
USACENDCDSA: United States Army Corps of Engineers National Civil Defense Computer Support Agency
USACPEB: United States Army Central Physical Evaluation Board
USACSA: US Army Combat Surveillance Agency
USAD: US Army Dispensary
USADSC: US Army Data Services and Administrative Systems Command
USAE: United States Army Engineer
USAEC: US Army Electronics Command; United States Atomic Energy Commission
USAECBDE: United States Army Engineer Center Brigade
USAECLRA: United States Army Electronics Command Logistics Research Agency
USAED: United States Army Engineer Division
USAEDC: United States Army Engineer Division—Caribbean
USAEDH: United States Army Engineer Division—Huntsville, Alabama
USAEDLMV: United States Army Engineer Division—Lower Mississippi Valley
USAEDM: United States Army Engineer Division—Mediterranean
USAEDMR: United States Army Engineer Division—Missouri River
USAEDNA: United States Army Engineer Division—North Atlantic
USAEDNC: United States Army Engineer Division—North Central
USAEDNE: United States Army Engineer Division—New England
USAEDNP: United States Army Engineer Division—North Pacific
USAEDOR: United States Army Engineer Division—Ohio River
USAEDPO: United States Army Engineer Division—Pacific Ocean
USAEDSA: United States Army Engineer Division—South Atlantic
USAEDSP: United States Army Engineer Division—South Pacific
USAEDSW: United States Army Engineer Division—Southwest
USAEEA: United States Army Enlistment Eligibility Activity
USAEL: US Army Electronic Laboratories
USAEMA: US Army Electronics Materiel Support Agency
USAEMCA: United States Army Engineer Mathematical Computation Agency
USAEMSA: United States Army Electronics Materiel Support Agency
USAENGCOM: United States Army Engineer Command
USAEPG: US Army Electronic Proving Ground
USAERA: United States Army Electronic Command Research Agency
USAERDAA: United States Army Electronics Research and Development Activity (Fort Huachuca, Arizona)
USAERDL: US Army Electronics Research and Development Laboratory
USAERG: United States Army Engineer Reactor Group
USAES: United States Association of Evening Students
USAETDC: U.S. Army Engineer Topographic Data Center (D.C.)
USAEUR: United States Army Europe
U S A f: Union of South Africa
USAF: United States Air Force
USofAF: Under Secretary of the Air Force
USAFA: US Air Force Academy
USAFABD: United States Army Field Artillery Board
USAFACS: US Air Force Air-

crew School
USAFAGOS: US Air Force Air Ground Operations School
USAFAPS: US Air Force Air Police School
USAFAS: United States Army Field Artillery School
USAFB: United States Army Field Bank
USAFBMS: US Air Force Basic Military School
USAFBS: US Air Force Bandsman School
***USAFD:** United States Air Force Dictionary*
USAFE: US Air Forces in Europe
USAFECI: United States Air Force Extension Course Institute
USAFEURPCR: United States Air Force European Postal and Courier Region
USAFFGS: US Air Force Flexible Gunnery School
USAFFSR: US Air Force Flight Safety Research
USAFI: United States Armed Forces Institute
USAFIGED: United States Armed Forces Institute Tests of General Educational Development
USAFIT: US Air Force Institute of Technology
US AFLANT: US Air Force, Atlantic
USAFMPCR: United States Air Force Mideast Postal and Courier Region
USAFNS: US Air Force Navigation School
USAFOCS: US Air Force Officer Candidate School
USAFOF: United States Army Flight Operations Facility
USAFPACPCR: United States Air Force Pacific Postal and Courier Region
USAFPS: US Air Force Pilot School
USAFSAB: US Air Force Scientific Advisory Board
USAFSAM: US Air Force School of Aerospace Medicine
USAFSAWC: US Air Force Special Air Warfare Center
USAFSC: US Air Force Systems Command; United States Army Food Service Center
USAFSE: US Air Force Supervisory Examination
USAFSG: United States Air Field Support Group
USAFSO: US Air Forces, Southern Command
USAFSOC: United States Air Force Special Operations Center
USAFSOF: United States Air Force Special Operations Force
USAFSOS: United States Air Force Special Operations School
USAFSS: US Air Force Security Service
USAFSTDS: US Army-Air Force Standards
USAFSTRIKE: US Air Force Strike Command
USAFTS: US Air Force Technical School
USAGETA: United States Army General Equipment Test Activity
USAH: United States Army Hospital
USAIC: US Army Infantry Center; US Army Intelligence Corps
USAICA: US Army Interagency Communications Agency
USAID: United States Aid for International Development
USAIG: United States Aircraft Insurance Group
USAIIG: United States Army Imagery Interpretation Group
USAILG: United States Army International Logistics Group
USAIMS: United States Army Institute for Military Systems
USAINTS: US Army Intelligence School
USAIPSG: US Army Industrial and Personnel Security Group
USAirA: United States Air Attaché
USAIRE: United States of America Aerospace Industries Representatives in Europe
USAir MilComUN: US Air Force Representative, UN Military Staff Committee
USAPDC: United States Army Petroleum Distribution Command
USAPEB: United States Army Physical Evaluation Board
USAPHC: United States Army Primary Helicopter Center
USAPO: United States Antarctic Projects Office
USAPRO: US Army Personnel Research Office
USAR: US Army Reserve
USARA: United States Army Reserve Affairs
USARADCEN: US Army Air Defense Center
USARADCOM: US Army Air Defense Center
USARADCOM: US Army Air Defense Command
USARAE: United States Army Reserve Affairs—Europe
USARAL: US Army, Alaska
USARSC: U.S.A. Roller Skating Confederation
USAREUR: US Army, Europe
USARIEM: US Army Research Institute of environmental Medicine
USARJ: US Army, Japan
USARP: United States Antarctic Research Program
USARPA: US Army Radio Propagation Agency
USARPAC: US Army, Pacific
USARPACINTS: United States Army Pacific Intelligence School
USARSA: United States Amateur Roller Skating Association
USARSO: US Army, Southern Command
USARV: US Army, Vietnam
USAS: United States of America Standard
US ASA: US Army School of the Americas; US Army Security Agency
USASADEA: United States Army Signal Air Defense Engineering a Agency
USASAE: United States Army Security Agency—Europe
USASAFO: United States Army Signal Avionics Field Office
USASC: US Army, Southern Command—Caribbean; United States Army Support Center
USASCAF: US Army Service Center for Army Forces
USASCC: US Army Strategic Communications Command
USASCII: USA Standard Code for Information Interchange (data processing)
USASCSA: US Army Signal Communications Security Agency
USASG: United States Army Standardization Group
USASI: United States of America Standards Institute
USA Sig C: United States Army Signal Corps
USASMC: US Army Supply and Maintenance Command
USASMSA: United States Army Signal Corps Material Support Agency
USASRDL: United States Army

Signal Research and Development Laboratory
USASSA: United States Army Signal Supply Agency
USASSG: United States Army Special Security Group
USAT: United States Army Transport
USATA: US Army Transportation Aviation
USATC: United States Army Traffic Command
USATEA: US Army Transportation Engineering Agency
USATEC: United States Army Test and Evaluation Command
USATECOM: US Army Test and Evaluation Command
USATIA: US Army Transportation Intelligence Agency
USATISU: US Army Troop Information Support Unit
USATMACE: United States Army Traffic Management Agency—Central Europe
USATopoCom: United States Army Topographic Command
USATRATCOM: United States Army Strategic Communications Command
USATSC: United States Army Terrestrial Sciences Center
USATTC: US Army Tropic Test Center
USATTU: United States Army Transportation Terminal Unit
USAU: United States Aviation Underwriters
usaw (USAW): underwater security advance warning
USAWC: United States Army Weapons Command
USAWES: United States Army Waterways Experiment Station
USAWF: U.S. Amateur Wrestling Society
usb: unified S-band
USB: United States Borax (company)
USBA: United States Brewers Association
USBC: United States Bureau of the Census; United States Bureau of Customs
USB & C: United States Borax and Chemical (company)
USBCSC: United Society of Believers in Christ's Second Coming (Shakers)
USBE: Universal Serials and Book Exchange (formerly United States Book Exchange)
USBG: United States Botanic Garden
USBGN: United States Board on Geographical Names
USBH: United States Bureau Highways
USBLS: United States Bureau of Labor Statistics
USBM: United States Bureau of M ines
USBP: United States Board of Paroles; United States Border Patrol; United States Bureau of Prisons
USBPA: United States Bicycle Polo Association
USBPR: United States Bureau of public Roads
USBS: United States Border Station; United States Bureau of Standards
USBTA: United States Board of Tax Appeals
USBuStand: United States Bureau of Standards
usc: under separate cover
USC: United Shipping Company; United States Congress; United Steamship Company; Uni versity of South Carolina; University of Southern California
USC: United States Code (legal)
USCA: Ulster Special Constabulary Association; United States Copper Association
USCA: United States Code Annotated
USCAC: US Continental Army Command
USCANS: Unified S-band Communication and Navigation System
USCB: United States Customs Bonded
USCC: United States Chamber of Commerce; United States Circuit Court; United States Commercial Company; United States Customs Court
USCCA: United States Circuit Court of Appeals
USCCPA: United States Court of Customs and Patent Appeals
USCF: United States Chess Federation; United States Churchill Foundation
USCG: United States Coast Guard
U de SC de G: Universidad de San Carlos de Guatemala
USCGA: US Coast Guard Academy
USCGAD: United States Coast Guard Air Detachment
USCGAS: United States Coast Guard Air Station
USCG Aux: United States Coast Guard Auxiliary
USCGC: United States Coast Guard Cutter
USCGI: United States Coast Guard Institute
USCE: US Coast Guard Reserve
USC & GS: United States Coast and Geodetic Survey
USCHS: United States Capitol Historical Society; United States Catholic Historical Society
USCIIC: United States Civilian Internee Information Center (USA)
USCINCEUR: United States Commander-in-Chief, Europe
USCINSO: United States Commander-in-Chief, Southern Command
USCM: United States Conference of Mayors
USCMA: United States Coal Mines Administration; United States Court of Military Appeals
USCO: Union Steel Corporaton (South Africa)
USCONARC: US Continental Army Command
US Const: *Constitution of the United States*
USCP: United States Coast Pilot
USCRS: United States Cotton Research Station
USCS: United States Civil Service; United States Claims Service; United States Conciliation Service; Universal Ship Cancellation Society
USCSC: United States Civil Service Commission
USCSup: United States Code Supolement
USCT: United States Colored Troops (1862–1865)
USCUN: United States Committee for the United Nations
USCUNICEF: U.S. Committee for UNICEF
USCWHO: U.S.Committee for the World Health Organization
US Cy: United States currency
usd: ultimate strength design
USD: Unified School District; University of San Diego; University of South Dakota
USD: United States Dispensatory
US$: United States dollar
U de SD: Universidad de Santo Domingo
USDA: United States Department of Agriculture
USDARS: United States Depart-

ment of Agriculture Research Service
USDB: United States Disciplinary Barracks
USDC: United States Department of Commerce; United States District of Columbia; United States District Court
USDEA: United States Drug Enforcement Agency
USDHEW: United States Department of Health, Education, and Welfare (HEW)
USDHUD: United States Department of Housing and Urban Development
USDJ: United States District Judge
USDL: United States Department of Labor
USDLGI: United States Defense Liaison Group—Indonesia
USDOCO: United States Document Officer
USDoD: United States Department of Defense
USDR: United States Divorce Reform
USDSA: United States Deaf Skiers Association
USDSEA: United States Dependent School European Area
USDT: United States Department of Transportation
USE: United States Envelope (corporation)
usea: undersea
μsec: microsecond
U/Sec: Under Secretary
USELMCENTO: United States Element Central Treaty Organization
USEP: United States Escapee Program
USES: United States Employment Service
USEUCOM: United States European Command
usf: *und so fort* (German—et cetera)—and so forth
USF: United States Forces
USFA: United States Food Administration (World War I)
U of SF: University of South Florida
USFAA: United States Fronton Athletic Association
USFC: United States Foil Company
USFET: United States Forces—European Theater
USFF: United States Flag Foundation
USF & G: United States Fidelity — Guaranty (insurance underwriters)
USFIS: United States Foundation for International Scouting
USFJ: United States Forces Japan
USForAz: US Forces in the Azores
USFPL: United States Forest Products Laborattory
USfs: United States frequency standard
USFS: United States Forest Service
USFSA: United States Figure S Skating Association
USFWS: United States Fish and Wildlife Service
USG: Ulysses Simpson Grant (18th President U.S.); United States Gypsum (company)
U.S.G.: United States Government (railroad)
USGA: United States Golf Association
US gal: United States gallon
USGLI: United States Government Life Insurance
USGOM: *United States Government Organization Manual*
USGPO: United States Government Printing Office
USGRS: United States Graves Registration Service
USGS: United States Geological Survey
ush: usher
Ush: Ugandan shilling(s)
USHA: United States Handball Association
USHDA: United States Highland Dancing Association
U of Sherb: University of Sherbrooke
USHGA: U.S. Hang Gliding Association
USHL: United States Hygienic Laboratory
USHR: United States Highway Research
USHS: United States Hospital Ship
USI: United States of Indonesia; United States Industries
USIA: United States Information Agency
USian: United Statesian
USIAS: Union Syndicale des Industries Aéeronautiques et Spatiales
USIB: United States Intelligence Board
USIBR: United States Institute of Behavioral Research
USIC: United States Industrial Chemicals; United States Instrument Corporation
USIF: United States Investment Fund
USIH: United States Indian Health Service
USILA: United States Intercollegiate Lacrosse Association
USI & NS: United States Immigration and Naturalization Service
USIOSLCC: United States Inter-Oceanic Sea-Level Canal Commission
USIP: University of Stockholm Institute of Physics
USIS: United States Information Service
USISL: United States Information Service Library
USITC: United States International Trade Commission
USITA: United States Independent Telephone Association
USITT: United States Institute for Theater Technology
USIU: United States International University
USJ: United States Jaycees
USJC: United States Job Corps
USJCC: United States Junior Chamber of Commerce
USJF: United States Judo Federation
USJPRS: United States Joint Publications Research Service
USL: United States Legation; United States Lines; Union Steamships Limited
U-slag: upperclass slang
USLant: United States Atlantic Subarea
USLANTCOM: United States Atlantic Command
USLO: United States Liaison Office(r); University Students for Law and Order
USLSA: United States Livestock Sanitary Association
USLTA: United States Lawn Tennis Association
usm (USM): underwater-to-surface missile
USM: United Shoe Machinery; United States Mail (U.S.M.); United States Mint
U de SM: *Universidad de San Marcos* (Lima, Peru)
USMA: United States Military Academy
USMACTHAI: United States Military Assistance Command Thailand
USMACV: United States Military Assistance Command Vietnam
US MAIL: (not an abbreviation

although some juvenile New Yorkers used to insist the letters stood for Uncle Sam Married An Irish Lady)

USMBPHA: United States-Mexico Border Public Health Association (of American and Mexican Public health officials)

USMC: United States Marine Corps; United States Microfilm Corporation (company)

USMCR: United States Marine Corps Reserves

USMD: United States Medical Doctor

USMeMilComUN: United States Military Members, UN Military Staff Committee

USMH: United States Marine Hospital

USMICC: United States Military Information Control Committee

USMilComUN: United States Delegation, UN Military Staff Committee

USMilLias: United States Military Liaison Office

USMILTAG: United States Military Technical Advisory Group

USMM: United States Merchant Marine

USMMA: United States Merchant Marine academy

USMMCC: United States Merchant Marine Cadet Corps

USMO: United States Marshal's Office

USMS: United States Maritime Service

USMSMI: United States Military Supply Mission to India

USMUN: United States Mission to the United Na tions

USN: United States Navy

USNA: United States Naval Academy; United States Naval Archives

USNAM: US Naval Academy Museum

USNAS: US Naval Amphibious School

USNB: United States National Bank

USNC: United States Navigation Company (North German Lloyd—Hamburg-American Line); United States Nuclear Corporation

USNCB: US Naval Construction battalion (Seabees)

USND: United States Navy Department

USNEL: US Naval Electronics Laboratory

USNFEC: United States National Fruit Export Council

USNG: United States National Guard

USNH: United States Naval Harbor; United States Naval Hospital

USNHO: US Naval Hydrographic Office

USNI: United States Naval Institute

USNII: United States National Indian Institute

USNLM: United States National Library of Medicine

usnm: United States National Museum (Smithsonian Institution)

USNMR: United States National Military Representative

USNO: US Naval Observatory

USNOO: US Naval Oceanographic Office

USNPC: US Naval Photographic Center

USNPS: US Naval Postgraduate School

USNR: US Naval Reserve

USNRDL: US Naval Radiological Defense Laboratory

USNS: US Naval Ship (Military Sea Transport Service); United States Nuclear Ship

USNSA: United States National Student Association

USNSMC: United States Naval Submarine Medical Center

USNTAF: US Navy Training Aids Facility

USNTS: United States Naval Torpedo Station

USNUSL: United States Navy Underwater Sound Laboratory

USNWD: United States Naval War College

USNWR: Union Slough National Wildlife Refuge (Iowa); Upper Souris NWR (North Dakota)

USN & WR: *U.S. News & World Report*

uso: unmanned seismological observatory

USO: United Service Organizations; Utah Symphony Orchestra

U-soc: upperclass society

USOC: United States Olympic Committee

USOE: United States Office of Education

USOEO: United States Office of Economic Opportunity

USOICP: United States Oil import Control Program

USOID: United States Oversea Internal Defense (USA)

USOM: United States Operations Mission

usp: unique selling proposition

USP: U.S. Penitentiary (Atlanta, Georgia; Leavenworth, Kansas; Lewisburg, Pennsylvania; Marion, Illinois; McNeil Island, Washington; Terre Haute, Indiana); United States Plywood (company); University of the South Pacific (Fiji)

USP: *United States Pharmacopeia*

U de SP: *Universidade de São Paulo*

USPA: United States Philatelic Agency; United States Polo Association

USPACAF: United States Pacific Air Forces

US Pat: United States Patent

USPB: United States Parole Board

USPC: United States Peace Corps

USPDO: United States Property and Disbursing Office(r)

U-speech: upperclass speech

USP & F: United States Pipe and Foundry (company)

USPFO: United States Property and Fiscal Officer

US Phar: *United States Pharmacopeia*

USPHS: United States Public Health Service

USPHSH: United States Public Health Service Hospital

USPO (U.S.P.O.): United States Post Office

USPS: United States Postal Service; United States Power Squadron

USPUN: U.S. People for the United Nations

USPWIC: United States Prisoner of War Information Center

usr: unheated serum reagin

USR: United States Reserves; United States Rubber

USR: *United States Supreme Court Reports*

USRA: United States Railway Association; United States Revolver Association; Universities Space Research Association

USRB: United States Renegotiation Board

USRD: Underwater Sound Reference Division (USN)

USRepMilComUN: United States Representative, UN Military Staff Committee
USRL: Underwater Sound Reference Laboratory
USRS: United States Rocket Society
USRS: *United States Revised Statutes*
USS: Under-Secretary of State; Union Switch and Signal; United States Senate; United States Ship (U.S.S.); United States Shoe (company); United States Standard; United States Steel (company)
USS: *Union Syndicale Suisse* (French—Swiss Trade Union Syndicate)
US & S: Union Switch and Signal
U of SS: University of the Seven Seas (Chapman College's classes held aboard motorship *Seven Seas)*
USSA: United States Salvage Association; United States Ski Association
USSAF: United States Strategic Air Force
USSB: United States Savings Bond(s); United States Shipping Board (World War I)
USSBD: United States Savings Bonds Division
USSC: United States Strike Command; United States Supreme Court
USS Co: Ulster Steam Ship Company; Union Steam Ship Company (New Zealand)
USSDP: Uniformed Services Savings Deposit Program
USSEI: United States Society of Esperanto Instructors
USSF: US Special Forces (Green Berets); United States Steel Foundation
USSFA: United States Soccer Football Association
USSG: United States Standard Gauge
USSIC: United States Sex Information Council
USS & LL: United States Savings & Loan League
US Soc Fed: United States Soccer Federation
USSOUTHCOM: United States Southern Command
USSPA United States Student Press Association
USSR: Union of Soviet Socialist Republics
USSRA: United States Squash Rackets Association
USSS: United States Secret Service; United States Steamship
USSSA: United States Social Security Administration
USSTRICOM: United States Strike Command
UST: undersea technology
ust.: *ustus* (Latin— burnt)
UST: United States Treaties
UST: *UnderSea Technology: The Magazine of Oceanography, Marine Sciences, and Underwater Defense*
U de ST: *Universidad de Santo Tomás (Manila)*
USTA: United States Trademark Association; United States Trotting Association
U of St A: University of St Andrews
USTC: United States Tariff Commission
USTDC: United States Taiwan Defense Command
USTEMC: United States Territorial Expansion Memorial Commission
USTES: United States Training and Employment Service
USTFF: United States Track and Field Federation
USTMA: United States Trade Mark Association
ustol: ultra short takeoff and landing
USTS: United States Travel Service
USTTA: United States Table Tennis Association
USTTA: United States Table Tennis Association
usu: usual; usually
USU: Utah State University
USUN: United States Mission to the United Nations
usurp.: *usurpandus* (Latin—to be used)
USV: US Volunteers
USVA: United States Veterans Administration; United States Volleyball Association
USVB: United States Veterans Bureau (former name of the Veterans Administration)
USVH: United States Veterans Hospital
USVI: United States Virgin Islands (St Croix, St John, St Thomas)
USVMS: Urine Sample Volume Measurement System
usw: ultra short wave: underwater submarine warfare
usw: *und so weiter* (German—and so forth)
USW: United Show Workers
USWA: United Steel Workers of America
USWAC: United States Women's Army Corps
USWACC: United States Women's Army Corps Center
USWACS: United States Women's Army Corps School
USWB: United States Weather Bureau
USWD: Undersurface Warfare Division
USWGA: United States Wholesale Grocers' Associ at ion
USWI: United States West Indies (Virgin Islands—St Thomas, St John, St Croix, and smaller islands in that group)
USWLS: United States Wild Life Service
USWV: United Spanish War Veterans
USY; United Synagogue Youth
usysf; United States Youth Symphony Federation
ut: universal trainer; urinary tract; user test; utilitarian; utility
u/t: untrained
UT: Union Terminal (railroad); United Territories; United Territory; United Utilities (stock-exchange symbol); Universal Time (Greenwich Mean Time); Universal Tubes; Utilities Man
U.T.: U Thant
U de T: *Universidad de Toledó; Universidad de Trujillo (Peru)*
U di T: *Università di Torino*
U of T: University of Tampa; University of Tennessee; University of Texas; University of Toledo; University of Toronto; University of Tulsa
UTA: Ulster Transport Authority; Union des Transports Aeriens; United Typothetae of America; Urban Transportation Administration
UTAD: Utah Army Depot
Utagawa: Utagawa Toyokuni
Utamaro: Kitagawa Utamaro
utarb: *utarb eidet* (Norwegian—prepared)
U of T (Austin): University of Texas in Austin
UTB: Universal Technological Bureau
UTC: United Tank Car; United Technology Center (United Aircraft); United Transformer Corporation Universe Tankships Corporation (National Bulk Carriers)

utd: united
UTDA: Ulster Tourist Development Association
ut dict.: *ut dictum* (Latin— as ordered)
UTE: underwater tracking equipment
U of T (El Paso): University of Texas in El Paso (also UTEP)
uten: utensil(s)
utend.: *utendus* (Latin—to be used)
utdne. mor. sol.: *utendus more solito* (Latin—use in the usual way)
utg: *utgave* (Norwegian—edition)
uti: urinary tract infection
UTI: Union Title Insurance
UTIAS: University of Toronto Institute for Aerospace Studies
util: utility; utilization
utilit: utilitarian(ism); utilities
Utilitarian Philosopher: Jeremy Bentham
ut inf.: *ut infra* (Latin—as below)
utl: universal transpor(er) loader
UTL: University of Tampa Library; University of Tennessee Library; University of Texas Library; University of Toronto Library; University of Tulsa Library
utm: universal transverse mercator
UTO: United Town Organisation
U of Tok: University of Tokyo
utop: utopian (from the Greek *utopia*—no place)—pertaining to an imaginary republic created by the dreamers of democracy
Utopian Author: title bestowed by readers on authors such as Bacon, Bellamy, Butler, Cabot, Campanella, Fourier, Huxley, More, Morris, Owen, Plato, Proudhon, Rabelais, Rousseau, Saint-Simon, Wells, and other visionaries
upt (UTP): uridine triphosphate
UTP: Unified Test Plan; University of Toronto Press
utr (UTR): university training reactor
UTR: United Tire and Rubber
uts: ultimate tensile strength; unit training standard
UTS : Underwater Telephone System; Uniform Thread Standard; Union Theological Seminary; University of Toronto Schools
UTSSM: University of Texas-Southwestern School of Medicine
ut sup.: *ut supra* (Latin—as above)
uttc; universal tape-to-tape converter
UTU: United Transportation Union
U-tube: U-shaped tube
U-turn: U-shaped turn
utv (UTV): underwater television
UTV: Universal Test Vehicle
UTWA: United Textile Workers of America
UTX: 4-engine jet utility transport
uu: micromicron
uu (UU): urine urobilinogen
u U: *unter Umständen* (German—circumstances permitting)
UU: Ulster Unionist; Union University
UU: *ustedes* (Spanish—you, *pl.*)
U & U: Underwood and Underwood
U i U: Universitet i Uppsala
U of U: University of Uppsala; University of Utah
UUA: Unitarian Universalist Association
UUCM: University of Utah College of Medicine
uue: use until exhausted
***uu*f:** micromicrofarad
UUI: United Utilities Incorporated
UUIP: Uppsala University Institute of Physics
uum (UUM): underwater-to-underwater missile
UUP: Ulster Unionist Party
uut: unit under test
UUUC: United Ulster Unionist Coalition
uuv: *unter üblichen vorbehalt* (German—errors and omissions escepted)
UUWF: Unitarian Universalist Women's Federation
uv: ultraviolet; under voltage
***u*v:** microvolt
u-v: ultraviolet
UV: Ulster Vanguard; Unadilla Valley (railroad); Upper Volta
U de V: Universidad de Valencia; Universidad d e Valladolid
U di V: Università di Venezia; Universersità de Vicenza
U OF V: University of Vermont; University of Virginia
uvas: ultraviolet astronomical satel lite (UVAS)
uvaser: ultraviolet amplification by stimulated emission of radiation
UVCM; University of Vermont College of Medicine
UVCT: University of Vermont College of Technology
uvd: undervoltage device
UVDC: Urban Vehicle Design Competition
UVE: *Unión Velocipédica Española* (Spanish Bicycle Union)
UVF: Ulster Volunteer Force
UVH: University of Virginia Hospital
UVI: *Unione Velocipedistica Italiana*)Italian Cycling Association)
uviol: ultraviolet
UVL: University of Virginia Library
U-vocab: upperclass vocabulary
UVSA: Unie van Suid Afrika (Union of South Africa)
uvsc: ultraviolet solar constant
UVSM: University of Virginia School of Medicine
uw: unconventional warfare; underwater; underwing; underwriter; unwound
***u* w:** microwatt
u/w: underwriter; used with
UW: Universität Wien (University of Vienna)
U o f W: University of Wales; University of Washington; University of Wichita; University of Wisconsin; University of Witwatersrand; University of Wyoming
UWA: University of Western Australia
UWTU: Underwater Training Unit
UWCE: Underwater Weapons and Countermeasures Establishment
U-wear: underwear
U-weld: U-shaped weld
UWF: United World Federalists
UWFL: University of Washington Fisheries Laboratory
UWGB: University of Wisconsin at Green Bay
UWH: University of Washington Hospital
UWI: University of the West Indies (Jamaica)
UWIST: University of Wales Institute of Science and Technology
UWL: University of Wales Library; University of Washington Library; University of Wichita Library; University of Wisconsin Library; University of Witwatersand Library; University of Wyoming Library

UWM: United World Mission; University of Wisconsin at Milwaukee
UWMI: University of Wisconsin Management Institute
UWO: University of Western Ontario
uwoa: unclassified without attachments
UWP: University of Wales Press;
UWP: University of Wales Press; Up With People
UWSM: University of Washington School of Medicine
uwtr: underwater
UWW: University Without Walls (Antioch College)
ux.: *uuxor* (Latin—wife)
uxb (UXB): unexploded bomb
uxgb: unexploded gas bomb
uxib: unexploded incendiary bomb
'UXLEY: ((Cockney contraction—Huxley)
uxor: uxoricide
UY: Universal Youth
UYA: University Year for Action
UYL: United Yugoslav Lines
Uz: Uzbek; Uzbekistan; Uzbekistanian
Uz: *Uhrzuender* (German—clockwork fuze)
UZ: *Universität Zürich*
U de Z: *Universidad de Zaragoza*
Uzbekistan: *Uzbekistan, Soviet Socialist Republic*
Uzbek SSR: Uzbek Soviet Socialist Republic (Uzbekistan)
Uzi: Uziel Gal
UZM: *Universitet Zoologiske Museum* (Copenhagen)
UZRA: United Zionist Revisionists of America

V

v: vacuum; vacuum tube; vagabond; vagrant; value; valve; van; vapor; variable; variation; vector; vein; velocity; vent; ventilator; ventral; verb; verbal; verse; version; vertex; vertical; very; vice; vincinal; violet; violin; virus; viscosity; vise; visibility; vision; visual acuity; voice; volt; voltage; voltmeter; volume; volunteer; vowel
v: *van* (Dutch—of)
v: *verso* (Latin—back of page or sheet; lefthand page); *versus* (Latin—against); vibrational quantum number; *voltare* (Italian—turn; turn the page); *von* (German—of; from; used in titles)
v/: *vostra* (Italian—your)
v-1 p: vernier engine 1 pitch
v-1 y: vernier engine 1 yaw
v 26 d M: *von 26 dieses Monats* (German—of the 26th instant; of the 26th of this month)
V: coefficient of vibration (symbol); five-dollar bill; Lockheed (symbol); potential (symbol); relative wind velocity (symbol); stalling velocity (symbol); Standard Fruit & Steamship Company (Vaccaro Line); vanadium; Venerable; Ventzke; Venus; Verdet constant; Vicar; Vice (as in Vice-President); Victor—code for letter V; Victory—Winston Churchill's symbol in World War II; Village; volume (symbol)
V: airspeed, forward velocity (symbol); speed (symbol); vacuum tube (symbol); *varm* (Dano-Norwegian or Swedish—hot); *väst* (Swedish—west); *vertrek* (Dutch—departure); *vest* (Dano-Norwegian—west); *Via* (Italian—highway road; way); *Villa* (Spanish—village); *violaceus* (Latin—violet color); *viridis* (Latin—green); *vrouw* (Dutch—woman)
V: *Venstre* (Danish or Norwegian—Left)—Liberal Party
V^1: *violino primo* (Italian—first violin)
V^2: *violino secondo* (Italian—second violin)
V-1, V-2: rockets launched by the Germans in World War II
V_1: decision speed (go-no-go) for aircraft to continue takeoff run or abort flight; valve-current voltage
V_2: aircraft takeoff speed or position where nose is lifted so plane becomes airborne
V-4: four-cylinder engine with two cylinders in each side of V-shaped engine block
V-6: six-cylinder engine with three cylinders in each side of V-shaped engine block
V-8: eight-cylinder engine with four cylinders in each side of V-shaped engine block
V-10: Viscount 10 jet airplane
va: variable; variance; verb active; verbal adjective; viola; voltampere(s)
v-a: volt-ampere(s)
v/a: verbal auxiliary; voucher attached
v.a.: *vixit—annas* (Latin—he lived—years)
Va: Virginia; Virginian
V^a: *Viuda* (Spanish—widow)
Va: *Vila* (Portuguese—Villa; Village); *Villa* (Italian or Spanish—Villa; Village)
VA: Veterans Administration (United States); Veterans' Affairs (Canada); Voice of America; voltaic alternative (symbol); Volunteers of America
V-A: Vickers-Armstrong Limited
V & A: Victoria and Albert (Museum)
V of A: Volunteers of America
V.A.: Order of Victoria and Albert; Vicar Apostolic
VAA: Vaccination Assistance Act; Vietnamese-American Association
V-AA: Vietnamese-American Association
VAACR: Vietnamese Association for Asian Cultural Relations
vab: voice answer back
VAb: Van Allen belt (zone of high-intensity radiation surrounding the earth at altitudes of about 500 miles)
VAB: Vandenberg Air Force Base; Vertical Assembly Building (world's largest all-steel structure of its type; used for assembling missiles

and space exploration vehicles on Merritt Island at Cape Kennedy, Florida)
Va Bk: Virginia Book Company
VABM: vertical angle bench mark (capitalized on topographic maps)
vac: vacant; vacate; vacation; vacuum; volts alternating current (*volts AC* preferable)
VAC: Volunteer Advisor Corps
Vacation City on Casco Bay: Portland, Maine
Vacationland: Maine's self-created sobriquet supported by miles of islands, lakes, and mountains
Vacationland of Opportunity: Alaska
vacc: vaccination; vaccine
Vaccaro: Standard Fruit & Steamship Company
vacci: vaccinate; vaccination; vaccine
vac-dist: vacuum-distilled
vac pmp: vacuum pump
vacs: vacuum cleaners
v/act.: verb active
VAd: Veterans Administration
VAD: Voluntary Aid Detachment
vada: versatile automatic data exchange
V Adm: Vice Admiral
vad. mec.: *vade mecum* (Latin—go with me)—companion volume; handbook; manual; ready reference
VAEA: Virginia Adult Education Association
VAF: Vendor Approval Form; Vincent Astor Foundation
VAFB: Vandenberg Air Force Base
vag: vagabond; vagina; vaginal; vaginitis; vagrant; vagrancy
VAG: Vancouver Art Gallery
Vagen: (Norwegian—Bay)—old Bergen and its waterfront along the bay
vagonzak: *vagon zaklyuchennykh* (Russian—railroad prisoner car)
vags: vagabonds; vagrants
VAH: Veterans Administration Hospital
va & i: verb active and intransitive
vakt: visual-auditory-kinesthetic-and tactual (imagery applied to teaching reading)
val: valance; valence; valenciennes (lace); valentine; valise; valley; valuation; value; valued; valve; valvular
val (VAL): valine (amino acid)
Val: Valencia; Valentina; Valentine; Velentino; Valerie
VAL: Vehicle Authorization List; Veterans Administration Library
VALA: Viewers and Listeners Association
VALB: Veterans of the Abraham Lincoln brigade
Vald: Valdivia
Valentine State: Arizona so nicknamed as it was admitted on St Valentine's Day—February 14, 1912
Val Fl: Gaius Valerius Flaccus (Roman epic poet)
valid.: validate; validation
valium: diazepam
Valka: Valentin
Vall: Valladolid
Valley Between Two Worlds: Rio Grande Valley (between Mexico and the United States)
Valley of God's Pleasure: Cleveland, Ohio's suburban section around Shaker Heights
Valley Isle: Maui, Hawaii
Valley of Opportunity: New York State's Triple Cities area including Binghampton, Endicott, and Johnson City
Valley of the Sun: Arizona's central valley
Valley of Wonders: Yellowstone National Park (in Idaho, Montana, and Wyoming)
Valpo: Valparaiso
valsas: variable-length word symbolic assembly system
VALUE: Visible Achievement Liberates Unemployment (Air Force program for disadvantaged youth)
vam: volt ammeter
VAMCO: Village and Marketing Corporation
vamp: vampire; vampirism
van.: caravan; vanguard; vanilla; vanillin
VAN: *Vereniging van Archivarissen in Nederland* (Dutch—Association of Archivists in the Netherlands)
Vanc: Vancouver
Van Cliburn: Harvey Lavan Cliburn
Vancoo: Vancouver, British Columbia
Vancoram: Vanadium Corporation of America
Van Diemen's Land: Tasmania's old name
Vanechka: (Russian nickname—Ivan)
Vang: Vickers-Armstrong Vanguard (aircraft)
Vang Esp: *Vanguardia Española* (Barcelona's Spanish Vanguard)
van. pub.: vanity publisher; vanity publishing
Van Sun: *Vancouver Sun*
VAP: Victims Assistance Program; Victims Assistance Project
vapi: visual approach path indicator
vapor.: vaporization
Vapor City: Hot Springs, Arkansas
vap prf: vaporproof
var: variable; variant; variation; variety; variometer; visualaural range; volt-ampere reactive
var: *variazione* (Italian—variation)
VAR: Volunteer Air Reserve
varactor: variable capacitor
varad: varying radiation
var con: variable condenser
var dial.: various dialects
var ed & trans: various editions and translations
vari: VariType(r)
VARIG: Empresa de Viação Aérea Rio Grandense (airline in southern Brazil)
varistors: variable resistors
varizistor: variable resistor
var. lect.: *varia lectio* (Latin—variant reading)
varn: varnish
varr: variable-range reflector
Varr: Marcus Terentius Varro (Roman writer on agriculture and natural history)
vars: varieties
Vars: *Varsavia* (Italian or Latin—Warsaw); *Varsovia* (Spanish—Warsaw); *Varsóvia* (Portuguese—Warsaw)
varsity: university
vas: vasectomy
VAs: Voluntary Aids
VAS: Virginia Academy of Science; Vocational Advisory Service
VASA: Virginia Association of School Administrators
vas bund: vascular bundle
vasc: vascular
VASCA: (electronic) Valve and Semi-Conductor (manufacturers') Association
vascar: visual average-speed computer recorder
VASCO: Vanadium-Alloys Steel Company
VASEC: vasectomy
vasi: visual approach slope indicator

VASP: Viação São Paulo (São Paulo airline)
VASSS: Van Allen Symplified Scoring System
vas vit.: *vas vitrium* (Latin—glass vessel)
vat.: value-added taxes (VAT); ventricular activation time
Vat: Vatican
VAT: Vertical Assembly Tower; Visual Apperception Test
vate: versatile automatic test equipment
VATI: Vermont Agricultural and Technical Institute
Vatic: Vatican
Vat Lib: Vatican Library (Rome)
VATLS: Visual Airborne Target Location System
Vat Sta: Vatican State
vaud: vaudeville
v aux: verb auxiliary
vav: variable air volume
vavbd: *vavband* (Swedish—clothing)
v/a v/e: value-analyst value-engineer
vb: verb; verbal; vertical bomb (VB); vibration
v/b: vehicle-borne
VB: Navy bomber (2-letter naval symbol); very bad
VBFNPVGFPMTF: *Véndemaire, Brumaire, Frimaire, Nivôse, Pluviôse, Ventôse, Germinal, Floréal, Prairial, Messidor, Thermidor, Fructidor* (as abbreviated on the French Revolutionary Calendar—*see Vend, Brum, Frim, Niv, Pluv, Vent, Germ, Flor, Prair, Mess, Therm, Fruc*
V^o^ B^o^: *visto bueno* (Spanish—okay)
vba: verbal adjective
VBA: Veterans Benevolent Assoiation
V-band: 46,000–56,000 mc
VBEC: Venezuelan Basic Economy Corporation
V-belt: V-shaped belt (cross-section of belt is V-shaped)
VBI: Venetian Blind Institute
vbl: verbal
V-block: V-shaped block
vbn: verbal noun
V-bomb: German long-range missile-type bomb used during World War II; designated as V-1 and V-2
vbos: veronal-buffered oxalated saline
V-bottom: V-shaped bottom
V B R: Virginia Blue Ridge (highway)
VBRA: Vehicle Builders' and Repairers' Association
VBS: Vedanthangal Bird Sanctuary (India); Vocabulary Building System
vc: valuation clause; venereal case, violoncello; visual communication
vc: *vuelta de correo* (Spanish—by return mail)
v/c: *vuelta de correo* (Spanish—return mail)
vc (VC): vital capacity
vC: *voor Christus* (Dutch—Before Christ)
Vc: Vietcong
VC: acuity of color vision (symbol); Vassar College; Vatican City; Vehicle Code; Vennard College; Ventura College; Vermont College; Veterinary Corps; Vice Consul; Victoria College; Victoria Cross; Viterbo College; Volusia College
VCA: Volunteer Civic Association
VCAR: Vendor Corrective Action Request
VCAS: Vice-Chief of Air Staff
vcc: vasoconstrictor center
Vcc: supply voltage
VCC: Value Control Coordinator
vc card index (or reader): visual coincidence index (or reader)
vccs: voltage-controlled current source
Vce: Venice
VCE: Venice, Italy (airport)
vcg: vertical line through center of gravity
VCG: Vice-Consul General
vch: vehicle; vinyl cyclohexane (VCH)
VCH: Victoria County History
v Chr: *vor Christis* (German—before Christ)
vci: visual communication instructor; volatile corrosion inhibitor
VCI: Variety Clubs International; Vision Conservation Institute
VCIGS: Vice-Chief of the Imperial General Staff
vcl: vertical center line; visual comfort light(ing)
VCL: Vancouver Public Library
vcllo: violincello
VCLU: Virginia Civil Liberties Union
vcm: vacuum; vinyl chloride monomer
VCN: Vendor Contact Notice
VCNS: Vice-Chief of Naval Staff
vcnty: vicinity
vco: voltage-controlled oscillator
v coul: volt coulomb
VCP: Vendor Change Proposal; São Paulo, Brazil (Viracopas Airport)
vcr: variable compression ratio
Vcr: Vancouver
VCR: Victor Comptometer (stock exchange symbol)
vcs: vasoconstrictor substances; voices
VCs: Viet Congs; Vigilance Committeemen; Vigilant Committeemen; Vigilante Committeemen
VCS: Vice Chief of Staff
V & C S: Virginia & Carolina Southern (railroad)
vctv: vocative
VCU: Virginia Commonwealth University
vcxo: voltage-controlled crystal oscillator
V Cz: Vera Cruz
vd: vapor density; various dates; venereal disease (VD); void
v/d: vandyke reproduction
Vd: vanadium
Vd: *usted* (Spanish—you; derived from *vuestra merced*—your grace)
V.D.: Volunteer Officer's Decoration
vda: venereal disease awareness; visual discriminatory acuity
Vda: *Viuda* (Spanish—widow)
VDA: Vermont Department of Agriculture
V-day: day of victory
VDB: Venereal Disease Branch (US Public Health Service); Verband Deutscher Biologen (Association of German Biologists)
VDBC: Vertol Division, Boeing Company (helicopter design and manufacturing)
vdc: volts direct current (*volts DC* proferable)
VDE: *Verband Deutscher Elektrotechniker* (Association of German Electrical Engineers)
v def: verb defective
VDEH: *Verein Deutscher Eisenhüttenleute* (German Foundry Society)
VDEL: Venereal Disease Experimental Laboratory
vdem: vasodepressor material
v dep: verb deponent
VdF: *Vigili del Fuoco* (Italian—Fire Brigade)
vdfg: variable diode function
vd-g: venereal disease—gonorrhea

vdh (VDH): valvular disease of the heart
vdi: vegetation draught index
VDI: *Verein Deutscher Ingenieure* (Association of German Engineers)
V-dies: V-shaped dies
VdK: *Verband der Kriegsbeschädigten* (German—League of War Invalids)
vdl: ventilation deadlight
VDL: Van Dieman's Land (Tasmania)
vdm: vector-drawn map
vdm (VDM): vasodepressor material
Vdm: Veendam
VDMA: *Verein Deutscher Maschinenbau Anstalten* (German—Mechanical Engineering Association)
VDN: *Varudeklarationsnamnden* (Swedish—Institute for Informative Labelling); *Vin Doux Naturel* (French—fortified wine; natural sweet wine)
vdp: vehicle deadlined for parts
vdr: variable-diameter rotor
VDRL: Veneral Disease Research Laboratory
VDRT: Venereal Disease Reference Test
vds: variable depth sonar
vd-s: venereal disease—syphilis
Vds: *ustedes* (Spanish—you all)—third person plural form of you
VDSI: *Verein Deutscher Sicherheits Ingenieure* (German—Association of Safety Engineers)
vdt: variable density wind tunnel
vdt (VDT): video display terminal
VDT: Visual Distortion Test
vdu: visual display unit
ve: vernier engine
've: have
ve: *veuve* (French—widow)
Ve: Venezuela; Venezuelan
VE: Value Engineer(ing); Vasileion tis Ellados (Kingdom of Hellas—Greece)
ve/a: value engineering/analysis (program)
VEA: Valve Engineering Association; Virginia Education Association; Vocational Education Act
veb: variable elevation beam
VEB: *Volks Eigener Betriebe* (German—Peoples-Owned Companies)
vec: vector
veco: vernier engine cutoff
VECP: Value Engineering Change Proposal
VECR: Vendor's Engineering Change Request
vecto: vectograph; vectographic; vectographical
ved: *vedova* (Italian—widow)
Ved: Vedic
VED: Vickers Electric Division
VEDA: Victorian Eastern Development Association
V-E Day: May 8, 1945, German surrender in World War II
VEDC: Vitreous Enamel Development Council
vedr: *vedrorende* (Danish—concerning)
Vee: Venezuelan equine encephalomyelitis
Veecees: Vietcongs
vee dee: venereal disease; visiting dignitary
VEENAF: (South) Vietnamese Air Force
Veenees: Vietnamese
Veep: Vice-President
veg: vegetable; vegetarian; vegetarianism; vegetation
vegans: vegetarians
Vegas: Las Vegas
Veg Soc: Vegetarian Society
vegtan: vegetable tanning
veh: vehicle; vehicular
vehic.: *vehiculum* (Latin—vehicle)
Vehicle City: Flint, Michigan
VEIS: Vocational Education Information System
vel: vellum; velocity; velvet
Vell: Gaius Velleius Paterculus (Roman historian)
veloc: velocity
Velvet Breughel: Jan Breughel the Elder
vem: vasoexciter material
ven: veneer; veneering; venerable; venereal; venery; venetian; venetian blind(s); venison; venom; venomous; ventral; ventricle
ven: *vendredi* (French—Friday); *venerdi* (Italian—Friday)
Ven: Venetian; Venice; Venus
vend: vending; vending machine; vendor(s)
Vend: *Vendémaire* (French—Vintage Month)—beginning September 22nd—first month of the French Revolutionary Calendar
vend. mach: vending machine
Venerable Nestor of Massachusetts: John Quincy Adams—sixth President of the United States who served it from his 14th to his 80th year when he dropped dead during a debate on the floor of the House of Representatives in Washington, D.C.
Venereal Disease of the New Morality: Herpes Virus type 1—above the waist; Herpes Virus type 2—below the waist
Venetian Family of Painters: term applies to the Bellinis and the Tintorettos
venetian red: ferric oxide (FE_2O_3)
Venez: Venezuela; Venezuelan
V-engine: V-shaped engine
VENISS: Visual Education National Information Service for Schools
vent.: ventilate; ventilating; ventilation; ventilator; venting; ventral; ventricle; venture
Vent: *Ventôse* (French—Windy Month)—beginning February 19th—sixth month of the French Revolutionary Calendar
vent. fib.: ventricular fibrillation
ventric: ventricular
Venus: (Latin—Aphrodite)—goddess of beauty and love
vep: visual-evoked potential
VEP: Voter Education Project
VEPCO: Virginia Electric and Power Company
ver: verification; verify; verse(s); versine; vertex (Ver)
Ver: Vera Cruz
Ver: *Verband; Verein* (German—association)
VERA: Vision Electronic Recording Apparatus (videotape)
verand: *verandert* (German—revised)
verb: *verbesserte* (Dutch or German—improved)
verb. et lit.: *verbatim et literatim* (Latin—exact copy; word for word)
verb. sap.: *verbum satis sapienti* (Latin—a word to the wise is sufficient)
Vercors: (pseudonym—Jean Bruller)
verdigris: copper acetate
Verds: Cape Verde Islands
verdt: verdict
Verf: *Verfasser* (German—author)
Verg: Publius Vergilius Maro (Roman poet often referred to as Virgil)
Vergl: *Vergleische* (German—compare)
Verh: *Verhandlungen* (German—proceedings)
verisim: verisimilar; verisimili-

tude; verisimilitudinous
verkhnyaya: (Russian—higher; upper)
Verl: *Verlag* (German—publisher)
Verlagshdlg: *Verlagshandlung* (German—book-publishing house)
verlort: very-long-range tracking (radar)
verm: vermiculite
verm: *vermehrte* (German—enlarged)
Verm: Vermont
Vermeer: Jan van der Meer van Delft
Vermilionville: Lafayette, Louisiana's old name
vern: vernacular
Vern: *Vernon's Law Reports*
vernac: vernacular(ism); vernacularly
Vernon Castle: Vernon Blythe
Veronica: Berenice
Vernon Lee: Violet Paget's pseudonym
Veronese: Paolo Cagliari
Verrocchio: Andrea di Michele Cione
vers: versed sine; verses; versification; versine (versed sine)
versine: versed sine
verso: reverso (left-hand page; reverse side of a page)—opposite of recto
Ver St: *Vereinigte Staaten* (German—United States)
vert: vertebra; vertebrate; vertical; vertigo
verticam: vertical camera
ves: vessel
ves.: *vesica* (Latin—bladder)
Ves: Sylvester
VESC: Vehicle Equipment Safety Commission
vesca(s): vessel(s) and cargo
VESIAC: Vela Seismic Information Analysis Center
vesic.: *vesicula* (Latin—blister)
VESO: Value Engineering Services Office
vesp.: *vesper* (Latin—evening)
VESPER: Voluntary Enterprises and Services and Part-time Employment for the Retired
vest: vestibule
VEST: Volunteer Engineers, Scientists, and Technicians (organization)
Vesta: (Latin—Hestia)—goddess of hearth and home
Vesters: Vester Islands
ves. ur.: *vesica urinaria* (Latin—urinary bladder)
vet: veteran; veterinarian; veterinary
v. et.: *vide etiam* (Latin—also see)
VET: Verbal Test
Vet Admin: Veterans' Administration
Vet M. B.: Bachelor of Veterinary Medicine
vet med: veterinary medicine
vet reg: veterans' regulations
vet rep: veteran's representative
vets: veterans; veterinaries
vet sci: veterinary science
Vet Surg: Veterinary Surgeon
vev: voice-excited vocoder
V Ex^{a}: *Vossa Excelência* (Portuguese—Your Excellency)
vexdex: vexation index
vexil: vexillogical; vexillologist; vexillology
vf: vertical file; very fair; very fine; video frequency; visual field; voice frequency, vulcanized fiber
Vf: *Verfasser* (German—author)
VF: fixed-wing fighter airplane (2-letter naval symbol); Valley Forge
V.F.: Vicar Forane
VF: *Vigili del Fuoco* (Italian—Fire Brigade)
V f A: Voice for America (Alistair Cooke)
VFA: Video Free America; Voluntary Foreign Aid
V-FA: Vietnamese-France Association
V-factor: verbal (comprehension) factor
v-f band: voice-frequency band
vfc: voice frequency carrier
vff black: very-fine furnace black (rubber filler)
VFHS: Valley Forge Historical Society
VFI: Vocational Foundation Incorporated
vfl: variable focal length
VFMJC: Valley Forge Military Junior College
vfn: very-flowery no
VFNP: Victoria Falls National Park (Rhodesia)
vfo: variable-frequency oscillator
VFOAR: Vandenberg Field Office of Aerospace Research (USAF)
vfp: variable-factor programming
VfR: *Verein für Raumschiffahrt* (German—Space Travel Society)
VFR: Visual Flight Rules
VFSTC: Valley Forge Space Technology Center (General Electric)
vftg: voice frequency telegraph
vfu: vertical format unit
VFW: Vereinigte Flugtechnische Werke; Veterans of Foreign Wars
vfy: verify
vg: velocity gravity; very good (VG)
vg: *verbigracia* (Spanish—for example); *virgen* (Spanish—virgin)
v.g.: *verbi gratia* (Latin—for example)
Vg.: *Virgo* (Latin—virgin)
VG: *Vaisseau de Guerre* (French—warship)
V.G.: Vicar General
vga: variable gain amplifier
VGA: Victor Gruen Associates
VGAA: Vegetable Growers Association of America
VGB: Vandenberg Air Force Base
vgc: viscosity gravity constant
vge: visual gross error
VGH: Vancouver General Hospital
V-girl: vice girl (equivalent to B-girl or C-girl)
vgl: *vergelijken* (Dutch—compare); *vergleiche* (German—compare)
Vgm: Vizagapatam
vgo: vacuum gas oil
VGP: Volunteer Grandparent Program
vgpi: visual glide path indicator(s)
V gr: *verbigracia* (Spanish—for example)
V-groove: V-shaped groove
VGSA: Viola da Gamba Society of America
vgu: *vorgelesen-genehmigt-unterschrieben* (German—read, confirmed, signed)
vgw: *voegwoord* (Dutch—conjunction)
vh: very high
v/h: vulnerability/hardness
v/h: *vorheen* (Dutch—formerly)
v H: *vom Hundert* (German—percent; per hundred)
VH: Veterans Hospital
vhb: very heavy bombardment
vhc: very highly commended
vhf : very high frequency (30,000 kc-300 mc)
vhf/df: very high frequency direction finding
vhf/uhf: very high and ultra high frequency
VHIS: Vaal-Hartz Irrigation Scheme
VHMCP: Voluntary Home Mort-

gage Credit Program
Vhn: Vickers hardness number
vho: very high output
vhocm: very-heavy oil-cut mud
vhp: very high performance
VHS: Vocational High School
V-hut: inverted V-shaped hut (sometimes called A-hut)
vi: variable interval; verb intransitive; viscosity index; volume index
v/i: verb intransitive
v.i.: *vide infra* (Latin—see below)
Vi: Viola; Violet; Virginia; Vivian
VI: Vancouver Island; Vermiculite Institute; Virgin Islander(s); Virgin Islands (V.I.)
VI: *Veiligheids Institut* (Dutch—Safety Institute)
via: virus inactivating agent
Via: Viaduct
VIA: Vancouver, British Columbia (Vancouver International Airport)
viad: viaduct
vi antigen: virulence antigen
VIAR: Volcani Institute of Agricultural Research (Israel)
VIAs: Vocational Information Agencies
VIAS: Voice Interference Analysis System
VIASA: Venezolana Internacional de Aviación SA
vib: vibrate; vibration; vibratory
VIB: Vertical Integration Building
vibes: vibraphones; vibrations
vibgyor: (mnemonic for remembering the spectral colors—violet, indigo, blue, green, yellow, orange, red)—*see* ROY G. BIV
vibra: vibraphone
vibs: vocabulary-information-block-design similarities
VIBS: Virgin Islands Broadcasting System
vic: vicinal; vicinity; victor; vic-
vic: *vices* (Latin—times)
Victor; Vicar; Victor;
Vic: RCA Victor; Vicar; Victor; Victoria; Victorine
VIC: Virginia Intermont College; Virgin Islands Corporation
VICA: Vocational Industrial Clubs of America
Vic Adm: Vice Admiral
Vicar of Christ: the Pope
Vic Hist: *Victoria History of the Counties of England*
Vicki: Victoria
vicoed: visual communication education
vicom: visual communication management
VICORP: Virgin Islands Corporation
vic(s): convict(s)
Vict: Victor(ia)
Vic^{ta}: Victoria (Spanish)
Vic^{te}: Vincente (Spanish—Vincent)
Victim of Religion and Revolt: Northern Ireland also called Captive of History
Victor: code for letter V
Victor Borge: Borge Rosenbaum
Victor-Charlie: VC; Vietcong
Victoria de los Angeles: Victoria Gomez Cima
Victor Seastrom: Viktor Sjöström
Victor Serge: Victor Lvovich Kibalchich
Victory: popular nickname for Beethoven's Symphony No. 5 in C minor as its opening chords reminded World-War-II audiences of the V for Victor(y) in the international radio code . . . —; Nelson's flagship at the Battle of Trafalgar
Victory Personified: Nike the Greek goddess or her Roman counterpart Victoria
vid.: *vide* (Latin—see); *Viuda* (Spanish—widow)
VID: Volunteers for International Development
vidat: visual data acquisition
VIDC: Virgin Islands Department of Commerce
VIDD: Virgin Islands Development Department
video: (Latin—I see)—picture portion of a tv broadcast
videocomp: videocomposition (highspeed phototypesetting controlled by programmed digital-control unit)
videot(s): video (television) idiot(s)
vie: *viernes* (Spanish—Friday)
VIE: Vienna, Austria (airport)
Vien: Vienna
vier: *viernes* (Spanish—Friday)
Viet: Vietnam
Viet Cong: *Vietnam Congsan* (Vietnamese—Vietnamese Communists)
Vietminh: Vietnam Doc Lap Dong Ming (League for the Independence of Vietnam)
Vietnam congsam: Vietnamese communist (see *congsam*)
Vieux Carre: (French—Old Square)—French Quarter of New Orleans
VIEW: Vital Information for Education and Work (education-on-microfilm program)
vig: video image generator
vig (VIG): vaccine-immune globulin
VIG: Virgin Islands Government
Vig Com: Vigilance Committee (men); Vigilant(e) Committee (men)
VIGIC: Virgin Islands Government Information Center
vign: vignette
VIGOPRI: Virgin Islands Government Office of Public Relations and Information
vii: viscosity index improver
VIJ: Vera Institute of Justice
vik: (Dano-Norwegian or Swedish—bay; cove; creek; inlet)—hence the Vikings were from the bays, coves, creeks, and inlets of Scandinavia where many place-names end in *vik*
Vik: Vickers; Vikelas; Vikenti; Vikentievich; Viki; Vikie; Viking; Viktor; Viktoria; Vikramaditya; Viktorovich
Viki: Victoria; Victorine
Viking Capital: Oslo, Norway
Viking Genius: John Ericsson
Viking Land: Norway
Viking Program: systematic investigation of Mars from orbit and from the surface with emphasis on the search for life on this planet
vil: village
Vil: Las Villas (Santa Clara)
vill: village
Villa Acuña: former name of Ciudad Acuña
VIM: Vertical Improved Mail (conveyorized mail handling in tall buildings); Virgin Islands Museum; Visible Impact Management
v imp: verb impersonal
v imper: verb imperative
VIMS: Vertical Improved Mail Service; Virginia Institute of Marine Science
vin: vehicle identification number; vinegar
vin.: *vinum* (Latin—wine)
Vin: Vincent
VIN: Vehicle Identification Number
VINB: Virgin Islands National Bank
Vince: Vincent
vind: vindicate; vindication
vinegar: acetic acid (CH^3COOH)
Vinegar Joe: General Joseph Warren Stilwell, USA
VINHS: Virgin Islands National

Historic Site
vini: viniculture
VINITI: *Vsesoyuznyi Institut Nauchnoi Tekhnicheskoi Informatsii* (Russian—All-Union Institute of Scientific and Technical Information)
Vinny: Vincent
VINP: Virgin Islands National Park (West Indies)
VIO: Veterinary Investigation Office(r)
viol: *violino* (Italian—violin)
Violet: state flower of Illinois, New Jersey, Rhode Island, and Wisconsin
vip: value improving product(s); variable information processing; variable input phototypesetting (VIP); very important passenger; very important people; very important person; visual identification point
vip: Virgil I. Partch
VIP: Value Improvement Project(s); Variable Information Processing; Very Important Person; Very Important Program; Vías Internacionales de Panamá (Panamanian airline); Virgin Islands Police
VIPAC: Virgin Islands Public Affairs Council
VIPI: Volunteers in Probation, Incorporated
vipre: visual precision
vips: voice interruption priority system
VIP-VIP: Value in Performance through Very Important People (motivational program)
vir.: *viridis* (Latin—green)
Vir: Virgil; Virgo
VIR: Vendor Information Request
V.I.R.: *Victoria Imperatrix Regina* (Latin—Victoria Empress and Queen)
VIRB: Virginia Insurance Rating Bureau
Virg: Virgil; Virgin; Virginia
Virgil: Roman poet Publius Virgilius Maro
Virgin Goddesses: Artemis, Athena also known as Parthenia (*parthenos*—Greek for virgin), and Hestia
Virgin Queen: Elizabeth I
Virgins: American and British Virgin Islands in the West Indies
virol: virology
virr: verb irregular
v/irr: verb irregular
vis: viscera; visible; visibility; visual
Vis: Visayan; Vista (postal abbreviation)
VIS: Veterinary Investigation Service; Visual Instrumentation Subsystem
visc: viscosity
Visc: Viscount(ess)
vissr: visible infrared spin-scan radiometer
VISTA: Volunteers in Service to America
Vistula River Cities: Cracow and Warsaw
vit: vital; vitamin; vitreous
vit A: carotene vitamin
VITA: Volunteers for International Technical Assistance
vit A_1: nutritive vitamin found in egg yolk, milk, and milk products such as butter
vit A_2: freshwater fish-liver-oil vitamin
VITAL: Variably-Initialized Translator for Algorithmic Languages
Vitalis: Erik Sjöberg
vit B: nutritive vitamin essential to digestive and nervous systems; found in breads, egg yolk, lean meats, fruits, nuts, green vegetables
vit Bc: folic-acid vitamin
vit B cx: vitamin B complex (water-soluble vitamins B_1, B_2, etc.)
vit B_1: thiamine vitamin
vit B_2: riblflavin vitamin
vit B_3: nicotinamide vitamin
vit B_6: pyridoxine vitamin
vit B_{12}: cobalmine-cyancobalmine vitamin
vit B_{12}b: hydroxycobalmine vitamin
vit C: ascorbic acid vitamin
vit cap.: vital capacity
vit D: antirachitic vitamin
vit D_1: calciferol and lumisterol vitamin
vit D_2: calciferol vitamin
vit D_3: cholecalciferol (natural vitamin D)
vit E: antisterility vitamin; tocopherol vitamin
vitel.: *vitellus* (Latin—egg yolk)
vit G: riboflavin vitamin
vit H: biotin vitamin
viti: viticulture
vit K: coagulant vitamin
vit K_1: blood-clotting vitamin
vit M: folic-acid vitamin
vit. ov. sol.: *vitello ovi solutus* (Latin—dissolved in egg yolk)
vit P: permeability vitamin (bioflavonoid found in paprika)
vit PP: pellagra-preventive vitamin (nicotinamide nicotinic acid)
vitr: vitreous
vtr.: *vitreum* (Latin—glass)
Vitr: Vitruvius Pollio (Roman writer on architecture)
vit rec: vital records
vitriol: concentrated sulfuric acid (oil of vitriol); copper sulfate (blue vitriol); ferrous sulfate (green vitriol); zinc sulfate (white vitriol)
vit stat: vital statistics
vit U: cabagin (anti-ulcer) vitamin
VIUS: Virgin Islands of the United States
viv: vivace
Viv: Vivian; Vivien; Vivienne; Vivyan; Vivyanne
VIV: *Virgin Islands View*
VIVA: Virgin Islands Visitors Association; Voices in Vital America (organization)
Vivazza: (Italian—Vivacity)—Gioacchino Antonio Rossini's nickname
VIVB: Virgin Islands Visitors Bureau
vivi: vivisection
vix.: *vixit* (Latin—he/she lived)
viz.: *videlicet* (Latin—namely)
Viz: Vizcaya (Biscay); Vizcayan (Biscayan)
Vizc: Vizcaya
vj: jet velocity
v J: *vorigen Jahres* (German—last year)
V-J agar: Vogel-Johnson agar
VJC: Vallejo Junior College
V-J Day: August 15, 1945, Japanese surrender in World War II
V-joint: angular V-shaped masonry joint
Vjschr: *Vierteljahrschrift* (German—quarterly)
vk: vertical keel; volume kill
V of K: Voice of Kenya (radio-television network)
VKC: Von Karman Center
VKIFD: Von Karman Institute for Fluid Dynamics
VKO: Moscow, USSR (Vnukovo Airport)
VKR: *Vodennaya Kontr Rozvedka* (Russian—Counter-Infiltration Organization)
vl: vision, left
v-1: vernier engine 1
v/l: vapor-to-liquid
Vl: Ville
V/l: vapor-liquid ratio
Vl: *Violino* (Italian—violin)
VL: Vaasa Line; Vaasan Laiva; Venezuelan Line; Viking Line; Volcano Line; Vulgar

Latin
vla: very low altitude
vla: *viola* (Italian—viola)
VLA: Veterans' Land Administration (Canada)
Vlad: Vladimir; Vladivostok
vladd: visual low-angle drogue delivery
Vladimir Nabokov: Vladimir Sirin
Vladimir Sirin: Vladimir Nabokov's pseudonym
v-l b: vertical-lift bridge
VLCC: very large cargo carrier (bulk freighter or tanker)
vld: visual laydown delivery
vldl (VLDL): very-low-density lipoproteins
V^{le}: *Viale* (Italian—Avenue; Boulevard)
vlf: very low frequency (to 30 kc)
Vlg: Village (postal abbreviation)
vllo: *violoncello* (Italian—cello)
vln: very low nitrogen; violin
vlnt: *van links naar rechts* (Dutch—from left to right)
vlr: very long range
vlrc: very long range commuter
vlt: violet
vltg: voltage
vlv: valve; valvular
Vly: Valley (postal abbreviation)
vm: voltmeter
vm: *voormiddag* Dutch—forenoon; A.M.); *vormittags* (German—forenoon; A.M.)
v/m: various marks; volts per meter
v M: *vorigen Monats* (German—last month)
VM: Viet Minh; Vulcan Materials
V.M.: *Votre Majesté* (French—Your Majesty); *Vuestra Majestad* (Spanish—Your Majesty); *Vuestra Merced* (Spanish—Your Worship)
V & M: Virgin and Martyr
vma: vanillymandelic acid
VMA: Valve Manufacturers Association
VMAG: Vanderpoel Memorial Art Gallery
V-Mann: *Vertrauensmann* (German—Trusted Man)—idealistically motivated and especially trustworthy intelligence agent
vmap: video map equipment
V max: maximum flight velocity
vmc: visual meteorological conditions
VMCCA: Veteran Motor Car Club of America
vmd: vertical magnetic dipole
V.M.D.: *Veterinariae Medicinae Doctor* (Latin—Doctor of Veterinary Medicine)
VMH: Victoria Medal of Honour
VMI: Virginia Military Institute
v/mil: volts per mil
V min: minimum flight velocity
v & mm: vandalism and malicious mischief
vm & p: varnish makers and painters
vmt: vehicle miles travelled; very many thanks
vn: *vellón* (Spanish—copper-silver alloy)
v/n: verb neuter
VN: Vietnam; Vietnamese
Vna: Vienna
VNA: Air Vietnam; Visiting Nurses Association
VNAF: Vietnamese Air Force
VNB: Valley National Bank
V-N B: Verrazano-Narrows Bridge
VN$: Vietnamese dollar
V-neck: V-shaped neck (line)
Vni: Violini (Italian—violins)
VNM: Victoria National Museum (Ottawa)
VNMC: Vietnam Marine Corps
VNN: Vietnam Navy
VNNBS: Vietnamese National Broadcasting Service
Vno: *Violino* (Italian—violin)
VNO: Vital National Objective
V-note: $5 bill
VNP: Vietnamese piastre; Voyageurs National Park (Minnesota)
VNR: Van Nostrand Reinhold
VNRC: Vegetarian Nutritional Research Center
VNs: Vietnamese
VNS: Vereenigde Nederlands Scheepvaartmaatschappij (United Netherlands Navigation Company)
vnw: *voornaamwoord* (Dutch—pronoun)
VNWR: Valentine National Wildlife Refuge (Nebraska)
vo: voluntary opening
vo.: *verso* (Latin—back of the page; lefthand page); *violino* (Italian—violin)
v^{o}: *verso* (Portuguese—lefthand page; other side; over; reverse)
v/o: *vossa ordem* (Portuguese—your order)
VO: Valuation Office(r); verbal order(s); very old; Veterinary Office(r); Victorian Order; voice over
VOA: Vancouver Opera Association; Vasa Order of America; Voice of America
VOA: *Vereeniging Ontwikkeling Arbeidstechniek* (Dutch—Work Study Association)
vo-ag: vocational agriculture (educators' jargon)
vob: vacuum optical bench
$V^{o}B^{o}$: *vista bueno* (Spanish—approved; okay)
voc: vocal; vocalist; vocation; vocational
VOC: Very Old Company (Dutch East India Company)
VOC: *Vereenigde Oostindische Compagnie* (Dutch—United East India Company)—often called the Very Old Company as that it was
vocab: vocabulary
vocat: vocation(al); vocative
voc ed: vocational education
vocg: verbal orders—commanding general
voco: verbal order—commanding officer
vocoder: voice coder
VOCOSS: Voluntary Organisations Cooperating in Overseas Social Service
vocs: verbal orders—chief of staff
voctl: vocational
vod: vision of right eye (d standing for *dexter*—Latin for right)
vodacom: voice data communication(s)
vodactor: voice data compactor
vodat: voice-operated device for automatic transmission
vodaro: vertical ozone distribution (from) absorption and radiation of ozone
voder: voice-operated demonstrator
VÖEST: Vereinigte Österreichische Eisen and Stahlwerke (United Austrian Iron and Steel Works)
Vog: Vogue
VoG: Voice of Germany
VOG: Vanguard Operations Group
vogad: voice-operated gain-adjusting device (data processing)
VOICE: Voice of Informed Community Expression
Voice of the American Revolution: Patrick Henry
Voice of the Century: Marian Anderson
Voice from the Fo'c's'le: Richard Henry Dana in *Two Years Before the Mast;* Herman Melville in *Whitejacket*
Voice of Polish Nationalism:

Adam Mickiewicz

Voice of the Revolution: Patrick Henry

VOIS: Visual Observation Instrumentation Subsystem

voit: *voiture* (French—railroad coach, truck, wagon, etc.)

vol: volume; volunteer

vol.: *volatilis* (Latin—volatile)

Vol: Volcán; Volcano

vol ash: volcanic ash

volat: volatile; volatizes

volc: volcanic; volcano; volcanology

Vol Isl: Volcano Islands (south of Japan and Bonin Islands)

Volks: Volkswagen

vollst: *vollstandige* (German—complete)

Volodya: (Russian nickname—Vladimir)

volatile alkali: ammonia

Volcano Land: Iceland

volkst: *volkstaal* (Dutch—slang; vernacular)

vol %: volume percent

vols: volumes

VOLS: Voluntary Overseas Libraries Service

Voltaire: assumed name of François-Marie Arouet (*see* Jean Meslier)

volts AC: volts alternating current

volts DC: volts direct current

volum: volumetric

Volunteer(s): Tennessean(a)

Volunteer State: Tennessee's official nickname honoring its many volunteers for the Mexican War

volvend.: volvendus (Latin—to be rolled)

Volvo: (Latin—I roll)—Swedish automobile

voly: voluntary

vom: volt milliammeter; volt-ohm microammeter; vomer; vomerine; vomit; vomitory; vomitus

vom.: *vomitus* (Latin—vomit)

vom neg: *vomito negro* (Spanish—black vomit)—last stage of yellow fever

VON: Victorian Order of Nurses (public health)

vona: vehicle of the new age (computer-controlled rapid-transit shuttle)

Von Economo's disease: encephalitis lethargica

V.O.N.O.: Vendor of Oysters in New Orleans (Walt Whitman's invention used in his story about Timothy Goujon, V.O.N.O.)

von Reuter: Israel Beer Josphat (founder of Reuter's news agency)

vop: valued as in original policy

VOP: very oldest procurable

Vo-Po: *Volks Polizei* (East German Police)

VOQ: Visiting Officer's Quarters

vor: very high frequency omnidirectional range (VOR); visual omnirange

vorm: *vormals* (German—formerly); *vormittags* (Germans—forenoon; A.M.)

Vor Mus: Voortrekker Museum (Pietermaritzburg)

Vors: *Vorsitzender* (German—chairman)

vort: vortex; vortices

vortac: visual omnirange and tacan

vos: vision of left eye (s standing for *sinister*—Latin for left)

vo('s): verbal order(s)

vos: *vostok* (Russian—east, as in Vladivostok)

v.o.s.: *vitello ovi solutus* (Latin—dissolved in egg yolk)

Vos: *Voskresene (Russian—Sunday)*

VOS: Victims of Superstition; visual observation airplane (naval symbol)

vot: voice on set time; voluntary overtime

vot.: *votivus* (Latin—promissory or votive)

VOT: Foreign Operational Center of Soviet Intelligence forces (formerly called MGB, MVD, NKGB, NKVD, OGPU, GPU, VECHEKA, and originally CHEKA—founded in December 1917, six weeks after Bolshevik seizure of power in October Revolution)

VOTE: Voters Organized to Think Environment

votem: voice-operated typewriter employing morse

vou: voucher

VOW: Voice of Women

VOWS: Vilas-Oneida Wilderness Society

vox: voice-operated transmission

vox pop.: *vox populi* (Latin—voice of the people)

voy: voyage

Voyager: American spacecraft destined for landings on Mars and Venus

vp: vanishing point; variable pitch; vertically polarized; vistaphone

v/p: verb passive

V_p: valve-position voltage

VP: British United Air Ferries (2-letter code); fixed-wing fighter airplane (2-letter naval symbol); Ville de Paris; Vice-President

VP: *Vigilancia de la Pesca* (Spanish—Fishery Patrol)

VPA: Vancouver Public Aquarium; Videotape Production Association

v pag: various paging

vpc: volume-packed cells

vpd: vapor-phase degrease; variation per day; vehicles per day

vpg: very pregnant guppy (NASA); voltage pressure gradient

vph: variation per hour; vehicles per hour; vertical photography

VPI: Virginia Polytechnic Institute

VPL: Van Pelt Library (University of Pennsylvania)

vpm: vehicles per mile; versatile packaging machine; vertical panel mount; vibrations per minute; volts per meter; volts per mile

VPM: Vendor Part Modification

Vpn: Vickers pyramid number

V P/N: vendor('s) part number

VP (NSC): Verification Panel (National Security Council)

Vpo: Valparaiso

VPO: Vienna Philharmonic Orchestra

vpp: viral porcine pneumonia

V Pres: Vice President

vps: vibrations per second; volume pressure setting

VPS: Visual Programme Systems

VPSA: Vertebrate Paleontological Society of America

V-P test: Voges-Proskauer test

vq: virtual quantum; visual quotient

vqa: vendor quality assurance

vqc: vendor quality certification

vqd: vendor quality defect

VQMG: Vice Quartermaster General

vqzd: vendor quality zero defects

vr: variable ratio; variable response; vision, right; voltage regulator; vulcanized rubber

v/r: verb reflexive

vr: *vedi retro* (Italian—please turn over)

VR: fixed-wing transport airplane (2-letter naval symbol); Victoria Railways (Australia)

V-R: Veeder-Root

VR: *Valtionrautatiet* (Finnish—State Railways)
V.R.: Victoria Regina
V.R.: *Victoria Regina* (Latin—Queen Victoria)
V f R: Verein für Raumschiffahrt (German—Society for Space Travel)
vra: *vuestra* (Spanish—your, *f.*)
VRA: Vocational Rehabilitation Administration
vras: *vuestras* (Spanish—your, pl.)
vrb: voice rotating beacon
vrbl: variable
VRC: Vehicle Research Corporation
VRD: (Royal Naval) Volunteer Reserve Decoration
vre: voltage-regulator exciter
v refl: verb reflexive
V Rev: Very Reverend
VRF: Vehicular Research Foundation
vrg: veering
Vrg: Varig (Brazilian Airlines)
vri: virus respiratory infection
vri (VRI): visual rule instrument landing
Vri: *Vrijdag* (Dutch—Friday)
VRI: Vehicle Research Institute
VR et I: Victoria Regina et Imperatrix (Victoria, Queen and Empress)
V-ring: V-shaped ring
VRIS: Vietnam Refugee and Information Services
vrm: variable-rate mortgage(s)
v rms: volt(s) root mean square
Vroni: Veronica
vros: *vuestros* (Spanish—your, *pl*)
vrp: very reliable product
VRP: Volta River Project
vrps: voltage-regulated power supply
vrr: visual radio range
VRR: Veterans Reemployment Rights
VRS: Vanguard Recording Society; Van Riebeeck Society
V & RS: Vocational and Rehabilitation Service
vrt: visual recognition threshold
vru: voltage readout unit
vr vnw: *vragend voornaamwoord* (Dutch—interrogative pronoun)
Vry: Viceroy
vs: venesection; ventricles; volumetric solution
V.S.: verysoluable metricsolution
vs.: *ve soire* (Turkish—and so forth); *versus* (Latin—against)
v.s.: *vide supra (Latin—see above)*
VS: scouting airplane (2-letter symbol); Vancouver Symphony; Victoria Symphony
VS: *Vereinigte Staaten* (German—United States); *Vostra Signoría* (Italian—Your Honor)
V S: *volti subito* [Italian—turn (music page) swiftly]
V.S.: Veterinary Surgeon
V & S: Valley & Siletz (railroad)
VSA: Volunteer Services to Animals
vs (VS): vital signs
VSA: Victorian Society of America
vsb: vestigial sideband
vs. b.: *venesectio brachii* (Latin—bleeding in the arm)
VSBA: Virginia School Boards Association
vsby: visibility
v.s.c.: *vidi siccam cultam* (Latin—I have seen a dried cultivated specimen)—botanic term
VSC: Virginia State College; Vocations for Social Change
VSCC: Vintage Sports Car Club
vscf: variable-speed constant-frequency
vsd: ventricular septal defect
VSD: Vancouver School of Design; Vendor's Shipping Document(s)
vsff: *volte, se faz favor* (Portuguese—please turn over)
VSGLS: Vehicle Space Ground Link Subsystem
V-shape: V-shaped
vshps: vernier solo hydraulic power supply
vsi: variable-speed indicator; very seriously ill; very slight imperfection; very slight inclusion
V-sign: victory sign (raised index and middle fingers)
VSL: Venture Scout Leader
vs jw: vise jaws
vsm: vibrating-sample magnetometer
vsmf: visual search microfilm file
VSMF: *Vendor Spec Microfilm File*
VSMS: Vermont State Medical Society
vsn: vision
V S/N: vendor('s) serial number
vso: very special old; very superior old
VSO: Vancouver Symphony Orchestra; Victoria Symphony Orchestra
vsop: very superior old pale (cognac)
Vsp.: *Vespertina* (Latin—Vespers)
VSPA: Virginia State Port Authority
V-spot: $5 bill
vsq: very special quality (VSQ)
vsr: very short range
vss: versions
v.s.s.: *vidi siccam spontaneam* (Latin—I have seen a dried wild specimen)—botanic term
VSS: Vermont State Symphony
vst: violinest
V St A: *Vereinigte Staaten von Amerika* (German—United States of America)
vstol: vertical and/or short takeoff and landing
vsv: vesicular stomatitis virus
vsw: vitrified stoneware
vswr: voltage standing wave ratio
VSX: heavier-than-air antisubmarine warfare carrier-based aircraft (naval symbol)
vt: vacuum technology; vacuum tube; variable time; velocity; verb transitive; voice tube
vt: *vaart* (Dutch—canal); *viz tez* (Czech—see also)
v-t: vacuum technology; variabletime (fuze); velocity-time (diagram)
v/t: verb transitive
v & t: volume and tension (of the pulse)
vt (VT): vertical tabulation character (data processing)
v T: *vom Tausend* (German—per thousand)
Vt: Vermont; Vermonter
VT: fixed-wing trainer-type airplane (2-letter naval symbol); Reseau Aérien Interinsulaire (Tahiti)
V.T.: *Vetus Testamentum* (Latin—Old Testament)
v^{ta}: *vuelta* (Spanish—turn)
VTA: Virginia Teachers Association
VTB: *Vereniging voor het Theologisch Bibliothecariaat* (Dutch—Association of Theological Librarians)
vtc: voting trust certificate
VTC: Vermont Technical College
vte: vertical-tube evaporator (for producing freshwater from the sea); vicarious trial and error
Vte: Vicomte
Vtesse: Vicomtesse
V-test: Voluter test
vtf: vertical test fixture
vt fuse: variable-time fuse

vtg: voting
vti: volume thickness index
VTI: Valparaiso Technical Institute
vtl: variable threshold logic; vertical turret lathe
VTM: Victorian Tourist Ministry (Australia)
vto: vertical takeoff
v^{to}: *vuelto* [Spanish—change (money)]
Vto: *Vtornik* (Russian—Tuesday)
vtoc: volume table of contents (data processing)
vtohl: vertical takeoff and horizontal landing
vtol: vertical takeoff and landing
vtolport: vertical-takeoff-and-landing airport
vtovl: vertical takeoff vertical landing
vtpr: vertical temperature profile radiometer
vtr: video tape recorder; video tape recording
VTRS: Video Tape Recorder System
VTTA: Veteran's Time Trial Association
VTU: Volunteer Training Unit
vtvm: vacuum-tube voltmeter
vu: voice unit; volume unit; volumetric unit
vu: *von untem* (German—from the bottom)
VU: Air Ivoire (2-letter code); fixed-wing utility airplane (2-letter naval symbol); Valparaiso University; Vanderbilt University; Victoria University; Villanova University; Vincennes University
VU: *Vigile Urbano* (Italian—Traffic Policeman)
VUA: Valorous Unit Award
VUH: Vanderbilt University Hospital
vu indicator: volume-unit indicator (data processing)
Vul: Vulgate
vulc: vulcanize(d; r)
vulcan: vulcanization; vulcanize; vulcanizer; vulcanizing
Vulcan: (Latin—Hephaistos)—the blacksmith
vulg: vulgar; vulgar fraction; vulgarian; vulgarism; vulgarist; vulgrization
Vulg: Vulgar Era (Christian Era); Vulgar Latin; Vulgate
v-u meter: volume-unit meter
VUNC: Voice of United Nations Command
v u p (VUP): very unimportant person
VUSM: Vanderbilt University School of Medicine
vuv: vacuum ultraviolet
vv: vagina and vulva; verbs; verses; vice versa
v/v: volume for volume:
v.v.: *vice versa* (Latin—conversely); *violini* (Italian—violins)
Vv.: *Virgines* (Latin—Virgins)
VV: Villa Viscaya (Dade County Art Museum, Miami, Florida); Voice of Vietnam (Hanoi)
VV: *ustedes* (Spanish— you, *pl.*)
VVAW: Vietnam Veterans Against the War
v.v.c.: *vidi vivam cultam* (Latin—I have seen a living cultivated specimen)—botanic term
VVD: *Volkspartij voor Vrijheid en Democratie* (Dutch—People's Party for Freedom and Democracy)—Liberal Party
Vve: *Veuve* (French—widow)
vv hr: vibration velocity per hour
vv. ll.: *variae lectiones* (Latin—variant readings)
VVN: Verein der Verfolgten des Naziregimes (League of Victims of Naziism)
VVO: very, very old
vvr: variable-voltage rectifier
vvrm: vortex valve rocket motor
vvs: very, very superior
v.v.s.: *vidi vivam spontaneam* (Latin—I have seen a living wild specimen)—botanic term
vvsi: very very slight imperfection; very very slight inclusion
VVT: Visual-Verbal Test
VV UU: *Vigili Urbani* (Italian—Traffic Police)
v.v.v.: *veni, vidi, vici* (Latin—I came, I saw, I conquered)
VVV: Vasili Vasilievich Vereschagin
vw: vessel wall
vw: *voegwoord* (Dutch—conjunction)
Vw: View (postal abbreviation)
VW: Very Worshipful; Volkswagen (People's Car)
VWD: *Vereinigte Wirtschafte Dienst* (German News Agency)
vwg: vibrating wire gage
vwl: variable word length
vwp: variable width pulse
VWPI: Vacuum Wood Preservers Institute
VWWI: Veterans of World War I
vx: vertex
VX: Experimental Squadron (symbol)
vxo: variable crystal oscillator
Vxtmps: Vieuxtemps
vy: various years; very
VY: Air Cameroun; Victualling Yard
vyd: *vydani* (Czech—edition)
Vy Rev: Very Reverend
vyt: *vytah* (Czech—abstract)
vz: virtual zero
v-z: varicella-zoster
vzd: vendor zero defect(s)
VZP: Venezuelan Petroleum Company (stock exchange symbol)

W

w: transverse acoustical displacement (symbol); wall; war; warm; waste; water; water vapor constant; watt; weather; week; weight; wet; white; wide; widow; widowed; width; wife; win; wind; wine; with; won; wood; word; work; wrong
w: loading (symbol); work (symbol)
W: Canadian Car & Foundry (naval designator symbol); College of Wooster; gross weight (symbol); irradiance (symbol); tungsten (Wolfram); very wide (symbol); Wales; Ward Line; warning; Washington; water; Waterman Steamship Line; weather reconnaissance; Wednesday;

Welsh; west; Westinghouse; Weyerhaeuser; Whiskey—code for letter W; Willys-Overland; Woolworth; Wu

W: warm (Dutch or German—hot); west; *west* (Dutch—west; *West* (German—west); Wilhelmsen (steamship line); women

W1, W2, etc.: West One, West Two, etc. (London postal zones)

wa: warm air; wire armored; with average; work energy

Wa: *Waffenamt* (German—**Ordnance Department)—Third Reich marking followed by a code number and stamped on all military equipment**

WA: Wabash Railroad (stock exchange symbol); Watchmen's Association; Welfare Administration; West Africa; West African; Western Airlines; Western Approaches (to British Isles); Western Australia; Wheeler Airlines; Wire Association; Workshop Assembly

W A: *World Almanac and Book of Facts*

W of A: Western of Alabama (railroad)

waa: wartime aircraft activity; welded aluminum alloy

WAA: War Assets Administration; Warden's Association of America; Western Amateur Astronomers; Women's Auxiliary Association

WAAC: West African Airways Corporation

WAACs: Women's Auxiliary Army Corps

WAADS: Washington Air Defense Sector

WAAF: Women's Auxiliary Air Force

WAAFB: Walker Air Force Base

waaj: water-augmented air jet

waapm: wide-area anti-personnel mine

WAAS: Women's Auxiliary Army Service; World Academy of Art and Science

wab: water-activated battery; when authorized by

WAB: Wabash (railroad); Wage Adjustment Board; Western Actuarial Bureau; Westinghouse Air Brake; Wine Advisory Board

WABCO: Westinghouse Air Brake Company

wac: wage analysis and control; weapon assignment console; write address counter

WAC: Women's Army Corps (USA); Worked All Continents; World Aeronautical Chart

WACB: Women's Army Classification Battery

WACM: Western Association of Circuit Manufacturers

waco: written advice of contracting officer

WACRI: West African Cocoa Research Institute

WACSM: Women's Army Corps Service Medal

WACVA: Women's Army Corps Veterans Association

Wad: Wadham College, Oxford

WAD: Wright Aeronautical Division (Curtiss-Wright Corporation)

WADC: Western Air Defense Command; Wright Air Development Center

WADD: Westinghouse Air Arm Division; Wright Air Development Division (USAF)

wadex: word and author index

WADF: Western Air Defense Force

WADS: Wide Area Data Service

Wadsworth: Wadsworth Atheneum (Hartford)

wae: when actually employed

WAED: Westinghouse Aerospace Electrical Division

waf: with all faults

WAF: Women in the Air Force

WAFB: Warren Air Force Base

WAFC: West African Fisheries Commission

WAFF: West African Frontier Force

waffle.: wide-angle fixed-field locating equipment

waf(s): waffle(s)

WAG: Walters Art Gallery; Winnipeg Art Gallery

W A & G: Wellsville, Addison & Galeton (railroad)

WAGBI: Wildfowlers' Association of Great Britain and Ireland

WAGGGS: World Association of Girl Guides and Girl Scouts

wagr: windscale advanced gas-cooled reactor

WAGR: Western Australian Government Railways

WAGRO: Warsaw Ghetto Resistance Organization

wags.: weighted agreement scores

wai: walk-round inspection

WAIF: World Adoption International Fund

WAIS: Wechsler Adult Intelligence Scale

Waistline of the Western Hemisphere: Isthmus of Panama

WAITR: West African Institute for Trypanosomiasis Research

waj: water-augmented jet

WAJ: World Association of Judges

wak: water analyzer kit

wal: walnut; wide-angle lens

Wal: Wallace; Wallach; Wallachian; Wallsend-on-Tyne

WA : West African pound

WAL: Western Airlines; Westinghouse Astronuclear Laboratory; Westland Aircraft Limited

W-AL: Westinghouse-Astronuclear Laboratory

WALA: West African Library Association

Waldstein: Beethoven's Piano Sonata No. 21 in C (opus 53); dedicated to Count von Waldstein

Wal I: Wallops Island

WALIC: Wiltshire Association of Libraries of Industry and Commerce

Wall: Walloon

Wall: Wallace (US Supreme Court Reports)

Wally: Wallace; Walter

walopt: weapons allocation optimizer

Walrussia: nickname for Alaska in 1867 when it was purchased from Russia and believed by some critics to have nothing but walruses

WALST: Western Alaska Standard Time

Wal Sta: Wallops Station

Walt: Walter; Walton

Walter Hampden: Walter H. Dougherty

Waltz King: musical nickname shared by Lanner, Lehar, Lumbye, Kalman, and others as well as by Johann Strauss Sr and Jr, Josef Strauss, Oskar Straus, and similar composers

wam: walk-around money; wife and mother; words a minute

wAm: white American male

WAM: Wolfgang Amadeus Mozart; Women Against Men; Worcester Art Museum

WAMI: Washington, Alaska, Montana, Idaho

WAML: Watertown Arsenal Medical Laboratory

wamoscope: wave-modulated os-

cilloscope
wampum.: wage and manpower process utilizing machines
WAMRU: West African Maize Research Unit
WAN: West Africa Navigation (steamship line)
WANA: We Are Not Alone
WANAP: Washington National Airport
Wand: Wanderers
Wanderer: Schubert's Piano Fantasie in C (opus 15)
WANDPETLS: Wandsworth Public Educational and Technical Library Services
WANL: Westinghouse Astronuclear Laboratories
WANR: Wadi Amud Nature Reserve (Israel)
WANS: Women's Australian Nursing Society
WAO: Weapons Assignment Office(r)
WAOS: Wide-Angle Optical System
wap: wide-angle panorama
WAP: Work Assignment Plan; Work Assignment Procedure
WAPC: Women's Auxiliary Police Corps
WAPD: Westinghouse Atomic Power Division
WAPET: Western Australia Petroleum Pty Ltd
WAPOR: World Association for Public Opinion Research
WAP's: Work Assignment Plans
WAPS: World Association of Pathology Societies
WAPT: Wild Animal Propagation Trust
WAPV: gunboat (4-letter USCG symbol)
war.: warrant; with all risks
War: War Department; Warsaw; Warwickshire
War Between the States: Civil War; War of the Secession
WARC: Western Air Rescue Center
WARES: Workload and Resources Evaluation System
Warf: Warfarin (rodenticide)
WARF: Wisconsin Alumni Research Foundation
WARFI: Western Alumni Research Foundation Institute; Wisconsin Alumni Research Foundation Institute
War Fury: Bellona—Roman goddess of war whose Greek counterpart is Enyo
wargasm: war + orgasm (sudden outbreak of war)
warhd: warhead
Warhorse of the Confederacy: Lieutenant General James Longstreet, CSA
WARI: Waite Agricultural Research Institute
Warks: Warwickshire
warla: wide-aperture radio location array
warn.: warning
War of the Pacific: Chile vs. Bolivia and Peru (1879–1883)
warr: warranty
WARRS: West African Rice Research Station
was.: wide-angle sensor; wideband antenna system
WAS: Worked All States
WASAL: Wisconsin Academy of Sciences, Arts, and Letters
WASC: Western Association of Schools and Colleges
WASCO: War Safety Council
Wash: Washington; Washingtonian
WASH: White Anglo-Saxon Hebrew
Wash Corr Cen: Washington Correctional Center
Wash DC: Washington, D.C.
Washoe Giant: Mark Twain
washing soda: sodium carbonate crystals ($Na_2CO_3 + 10H_2O$)
Washmic: Washington, (D.C.) military-industrial complex
WASHO: Western Association of State Highway Officials
Wash Post: *The Washington Post*
wasn't: was not
wasp.: weightless analysis sounding probe; window atmosphere sounding projectile
WASP: White Anglo-Saxon Protestant; Women Against Soaring Prices
WASP(S): White Anglo-Saxon Protestant(s)
Wass: Wasserman
Wassermann: Wassermann test to determine presence of syphilis
WAST: Western Australian Standard Time
WASU: West African Student's Union
wat: weight, altitude, temperature
Wat: Waterford
WAT: Word Association Test
WATA: World Association of Travel Agencies
watashi: *watakushi* (Japanese—I; me; myself)
Watch City: old nickname of Waltham, Massachusetts
Watchdog of Central Park: *New York Times* publisher Adolph S. Ochs
Watchungs: Watchung Mountains of northern New Jersey
WATDA: Western Australia Tourist Development Authority
water: H_2O
Watergab: Watergate English (Nixon-era federalese exemplified by the substitution of *at this point in time* for *now*, *in point of fact* for *in fact*, *utilization* for *use*, and similar circumlocutions)
Water Gap: Delaware Water Gap between New Jersey and Pennsylvania
Watergate: Potomac River waterfront of Washington, D.C., including Kennedy Center for the Performing Arts, Watergate Amphitheater for outdoor concerts, Watergate apartment-hotel-office-shopping center; synonym for a national scandal first detected here at the Watergate office building
waterglass: sodium silicate (Na_2SiO_3)
Waterland: the Netherlands
wats: wide-area telephone service
WATS: Wide Area Telephone Service
watt's: wide-area telephone transmission lines
Watts: Black section of Los Angeles
Wat(ty): Walter
W Aust: Western Australia
W Aust Cur: West Australian Current
WAVES: Women Accepted for Volunteer Emergency Service (USN)
WAVFH: World Association of Veterinary Food Hygienists
WAW: Warsaw, Poland (airport)
WAwa: West Africa wins again
WAWF: World Association of World Federalists
wax.: weapon assignment and target extermination
WAY: World Assembly of Youth
WAYC: Welsh Association of Youth Clubs
'ways: always
wb: warehouse book; water ballast; waybill; weber; wheelbase
w/b: will be
Wb: weber
WB: Wage Board; Weather Bureau; World Bank for Reconstruction and Development

(UN)
W-B: Wilkes-Barre
wba: wideband amplifier
WBA: Washington Booksellers Association; Wisconsin Booksellers Association; World Boxing Association
WBAFC: Weather Bureau Area Forecast Center
WBAN: Weather Bureau, Air Force-Navy
wbat: wideband adapter transformer
WBAWS: Weather, Briefing, advisory, and Warning Service
wbc: white blood cell; white blood cell (count); white blood corpuscle
WBC: World Boxing Commission
wbco: waveguide below cutoff
wbct: wideband circuit transformer
wbd: wideband data
WBD: *Webster's Biographical Dictionary*
wbdl: wideband data link
WBEA: Western Business Education Association
WBF: World Bridge Federation
wbgt: wet-bulb globe temperature; wet-bulb globe thermometer
WBH: Welsh Board of Health
wbi: will be issued
WBI: Wooden Box Institute
WBINA: Wreck and Bone Islands Natural Area (Virginia)
WBIT: Wechsler-Bellevue Intelligence Test
wbl: wideband laser; wood blocking
Wbl: *Wochenblatt* (German—weekly publication)
WBL: Western Biological Laboratories
wblc: waterborne logistics craft
WBMA: Wirebound Box Manufacturers Association
WBMC: William Beaumont Medical Center (El Paso)
wbn: well-behaved net
wbnl: wideband noise limiting
WBNM: Wright Brothers National Monument
WBNP: Wood Buffalo National Park (northwest Territories, Canada)
WBNR: Wadi Bezet Nature Reserve (Israel)
wbns: water boiler neutron source
wbnv: wideband noise voltage
wbo: wideband oscilloscope; wideband overlap; wide bridge oscillator
wbp: weather and boilproof
WBP: Wartime Basic Plan
WBPA: Western Book Publishers Association
wbr: water boiler reactor; whole body radiation; wideband receiver
W Branch: Wireless Branch (British intelligence)
wbrbn: will be reported by notam (Notice to Airmen)
wbs: without benefit of salvage
WBSI: Western Behavioral Sciences Institute
WB Sig Sta: Weather Bureau Signal Station
wbt: wet-bulb temperature; wet-bulb thermometer; wideband transformer; wideband transmitter
WBT: World Board of Trade
WBTA: Webb-Pomerene Trade Association
W B T & S: Waco, Beaumont, Trinity & Sabine (railroad)
wbtv: weather briefing television
wbv: wideband voltage
wbvco: wideband voltage-controlled oscillator
W By: Walvis Bay
wc: wadcutter; wage change; water closet (English euphemism for *lavatory*); weapon carrier; wheelchair; will call; without charge; wood casing; working capital; working circle; workmen's compensation
w/c: wave change; with corrections (correct proof before printing)
WC: Wabash College; Wagner College; Waldorf College; Walker College; Walsh College; Wartburg College; Washington College; Waynesburg College; Weatherford College; Webber College; Weber College; Webster College; Wellesley College; Wells College; Wesley College; West African Airlines (2-letter code); (West Coast Airlines (2-letter code); Westmar College; Westminster College; Westmont College; Wheaton College; Wheeling College; Wheelock College; Whitman College; Whittier College; Whitworth College; Wiley College; Wilkes College; Williams College; Wilmington College; Wilson College; Windham College; Winthrop College; Wofford College; Woodbury College; Woodstock College; World Court; Wycliffe College
W/C: Wing Commander
WC1, WC2, etc.: West Central One, West Central Two, etc. (London postal zones)
wca: wideband cassegrain antenna; worst case analysis
WCA: Washingtonian Center for Addiction; Women's Correctional Association; World Calendar Association
WCAA: West Coast Athletic Association
w cab: wall cabinet
WCAFS: Wideband Cassegrain Antenna Feed System
WCAP: Westinghouse Commercial Atomic Power
WCAT: Welsh College of Advanced Technology
WCB: Workmen's Compensation Board
WCBA: West Coast Bookmen's Association
WCBHS: William Cullen Bryant High School
wcc: water-cooled copper; wilson cloud chamber
WCC: Wayne County Community College; Westchester Community College; White Citizens Council (southern segregationist organization); World Council of Churches
wcca: worst-case circuit analysis
WCCE: West Coast Commodity Exchange
WCCU: World Council of Credit Unions
wcdb: wing control during boost
wcdo: war consumable distribution objective
wce: weapon control equipment
WCEMA: West Coast Electronic Manufacturers' Association
WCEU: World's Christian Endeavor Union
wcf: white cathode follower
WCF: Winchester Center Fire (rifle shell designation)
W.C. Fields: Claude William Dukenfeld
WCFPR: Washington Center of Foreign Policy Research
WCFST: Weigl Color-Form Sorting Test
wci: white cast iron; wind chill index
WCJE: World Council on Jewish Education
WCK: West Virginia Coal and Coke (stock exchange symbol)
wcl: watercooler
WCL: West Coast Line; World

Confederation of Labor
wcld: watercooled
WCLIB: West Coast Lumber Inspection Bureau
wcm: welded cordwood module; wired-core matrix; wired-core memory; word combine and multiplexer
WCMA: Wisconsin Cheese Makers' Association
WCMR: Western Contract Management Region
WCNM: Walnut Canyon National Monument
WCNP: Wind Cave National Park (South Dakota)
WCOTP: World Confederation of Organizations of the Teaching Profession
wcp: welder control panel; white combination potentiometer
WCP: Weapon Control Plan; Work Control Panel; Work Control Plan
WCPA: Western College Placement Association; World Constitution and Parliament Association
WCPT: World Confederation for Physical Therapy
wcr: water-cooled reactor; water-cooled rod; water cooler; wire contact relay; word-control register
WCR: Western Communication Region (USAF)
WCRA: Weather Control Research Association
wcs: wing center section
WCS: Wisconsin Correctional Service
WCSA: West Coast of South America
WCSI: World Center for Scientific Information
WC & S's S & EBC: William Cramp & Son's Ship and Engine Building Company
WCT: World Championship Tennis
WCTL: Western Center Telecommunications Laboratory
WCTU: Women's Christian Temperance Union
WCU: West Coast University
WCUK: West Coast of United Kingdom
wcv: water check valve
WCW: William Carlos Williams
WCWB: World Council for the Welfare of the Blind
wd: weed; well deck; whole depth; wind; window; withdrawn; wood; word; would; wound
w/d: weight-displacement ratio; wind direction
Wd: weeds
WD: War Department; Water Department; Waterworks Department; Western Division
wda: wheeldrive assembly; withdrawal of availability
WDC: Women's Detention Center
WDC-A: World Data Center-A (Washington, D.C.)
WDC-B: World Data Center-B (Moscow, USSR)
wdd: Western Development Division (USAF Air Research and Development Command)
wdf: wood door and frame
wdg: winding; wording
wdk: wives don't know
WDL: Western Defense Laboratories (Philco subsidiary of Ford Motor Company)
WDM: Western Development Museum (Saskatoon)
wdmf: wall-defective microbial forms
WDNR: Wadi Dishon Nature Reserve (Israel)
wdo: willing dropout
wdp: wood door panel
WDPC: Western Data Processing Center
wdr: white drum
Wdr: Wardmaster
Wdr L: Wardmaster Lieutenant
wds: wood-dye stain; word discrimination score; words; wounds
wd sc: wood screw
wdt: width
wdtahtm (wahm, for short): why does this always happen to me?
WDTC: Western Defense Tactical Command
wdu: window de-icing unit
wdv: written-down value (tax)
wdwn: well developed, well nourished
W$W: *Wall Street Week* (educational tv program)
we.: watch error; weekend
w/e: weekend
w & e: windage and elevation
We: Welsh
WE: Western Electric
W E: *Wärmeeinheit* (German—thermal unit)
wea: weapon(s); weather
WEA: Washington Education Association; Wisconsin Education Association; Workers Educational Association
WEAAC: Western European Airports Association Conference
WEAL: Women's Equity Action League
Wealth Personified: Ploutus (Greek); Plutus (Roman)
WeAPD: Western Air Procurement District
WEARCONS: Weather Observation and Forecasting Control System
weat: weathertight
Web: *Webster's Third New International Dictionary of the English Language Unabridged*
WEBDEC: W.E.B. Du Bois Club(s)
Webelos: We'll be loyal scouts.
Webfeet: Oregonians so nicknamed because of the high average annual rainfall of Oregon
webrock: weather buoy rocket
WEBS: Weapons Effectiveness Buoy System
WEC: Westinghouse Electric Corporation
WeCen: Weather Center (USAF)
WECO: Western Electric Company
WECOM: Weapons Command (USA)
we'd: we had; we would
Wed: Wednesday
Wed: *Weduwe* (Dutch—widow)
WED: Walter Elias Disney
WEDA: Wholesale Engineering Distributors' Association
Wedd: Wedding (Berlin borough)
Wedy: Wednesday
Wee: Western equine encephalitis
Wee Willie: William Keeler
wef: with effect from
WEF: World Education Fellowship
WE & FA: Welsh Engineers' and Founders' Association
wefax: weather facsimile
WEFC: West European Fisheries Conference
weft: wings, engine, fuselage, tail
weg: war emergency grant
weg(s): wild-eyed guess(es)
WEH: William Ernest Henley
WEHS: Wadleigh Evening High School
WEI: World Education Incorporated
weia: wife's earned income allowance (tax)
Weil's disease: jaundice
weir: wife's earned income relief (tax)
Weiss: Weissensee
WEIU: Women's Educational and Industrial Union
Wel: Welsh

Wel Adm: Welfare Administration
Wel Can: Welland Canal
Welcher(s): person(s) of Welsh origin
weld: welding
Wel Dept: Welfare Department
we'll: we shall; we will
Well: Wellington
wellies: wellington boots
Welsh Landscape Painter: Richard Wilson
Welt: *Die Welt* (Hamburg's World)
Welts: *Weltschmerz* (German—world pain)—universal misery
WEMA: Western Electronic Manufacturers Association
WEMTA: Wisconsin Emergency Technician's Association
Wen: Wendel; Wendell; Wendy
WEN: Western Educational Network; Wien-Alaska Airlines
Wend: *Wendell's Reports*
WENOA: *Weekly Notice to Airmen* (CAA)
wep: water-extended polyester
WEP: Wisconsin Electric Power Company
WEPA: Welded Electronic Packaging Association
WEPCO: Weather-Proof Company
we're: we are
weren't: were not
Wes: Wesley; Weston
WES: Water Electrolysis System; Waterways Experiment Station; Weather Editing Section (FAA); Women's Engineering Society
WESCON: Western Electronics Show and Convention
wesentl: *wesentlich* (German—essential; main)
WESO: Weapons Engineering Service Office
Wes Pac: Western Pacific
WESRAC: Western Research Application Center
Wes Sam: Western Samoa (formerly British Samoa)
WEST: Western Energy Supply and Transmission (Association); Women's Enlistment Screening Test
WESTAF: Western Transport, Air Force
WESTCOMMRGN: Western Communications Region
West Country: southwestern England—Cornwall, Devonshire, Dorset, Somerset
West End: fashionable London
wester: storm from the west
Westernmost American Town: Adak, Aleutian Islands, Alaska
Westernmost American Territory: Guam
Westernmost Canadian Territory: Yukon
Westernmost Canadian Town: Dawson, Yukon
Westernmost Prairie Province: Alberta
Westernmost Province: British Columbia
Westernmost State: Alaska
Western Prairie Province: Alberta
Western Samoa: Samoa i Sisifo (formerly German Samoa)
Western Tip of Florida: Pensacola
Western Tip of Texas: El Paso
West Indies: Greater and Lesser Antilles in the Caribbean Sea
West Jersey: southern and western New Jersey
WestLant: Western Atlantic Area
West LB: *Westdeutsche Landesbank* (West German Land Bank)
Westm: Westminister; Westmorland
Westmld: Westmorland
Westo: West Countryman
West Pac: Western Pacific (ocean or railroad)
WESTPAC: Western Pacific
West Point of Law Enforcement: FBI National Academy at Quantico, Virginia
Westport Landing: pioneer name for Kansas City
Westralia: Western Australia
Westralia(n): Western Australia(n)
West's: *West's Annotated Education Code*
West Sam: Western Samoa
Westy: Westmoreland
Wes Univ: Wesleyan University
WET: Weapon(s) Effectiveness Test(ing)
WETA: Washington Educational Television Association
wetensch: *wetenschap* (Dutch—knowledge; science)
WeTip: We Turn in Pushers (of narcotics)
Wet Mary: Western Maryland Railway (stock exchange slang)
Wet Tortugas: rainswept Florida Keys
WETUC: Workers' Educational Trade Union Committee
WEU: Western European Union (Belgium, France, Italy, Luxembourg, Netherlands, United Kingdom, West Germany)
we've: we have
Wex: Wexford
WEX: Westinghouse Electric Company (stock exchange nickname)
Wexf: Wexford
Wey: Weymouth
WEZ: *westeuropäische Zeit* (German—West European Time); Greenwich Mean Time
wf: wrong font
w/f: white female
w & f: water and feed
WF: Wake Forest; Wake Forest College; Wells Fargo & Company
W.F.: White Father
W & F: Wallis and Futuna Islands
WFA: War Food Administration (World War II); White Fish Authority; World Friendship Association
w factor: will factor
WFALW: *Weltbund Freiheitlicher Arbeitnehmerverbände auf Liberaler Wirtschafsgrundlage* (German—World Union of Liberal Trade Union Organizations)
WFB: Wells Fargo Bank
WFBI: Wood Fiber Blanket Institute
WFBMA: Woven Fabric Belting Manufacturers Association
WFC: Wake Forest College
wfd: wool forward (knitting)
WFD: World Federation of the Deaf
WFDY: World Federation of Democratic Youth (communist)
wfe: with food element
WFEA: World Federation of Educational Associations
WFEB: Worcester Foundation for Experimental Biology
WFEO: World Federation of Engineering Organizations
WFEX: Western Fruit Express
WFF: World Friendship Federation
wfg: waveform generator
WFGA: Women's Farm and Garden Association
WFI: Wheat Flour Institute
WFJCC: World Federation of Jewish Community Centers
wfl: worshipful
WFL: Women's Freedom League; World Football League
W Flem: West Flemish

WFM: Walter F. Mondale; Western Federation of Miners
WFMH: World Federation for Mental Health
WFMW: World Federation of Methodist Women
wfn: well-formed net
WFN: World Federation of Neurology
wfna: white-fuming nitric acid
WFNS: World Federation of Neurosurgical Societies
wfo: wide-field optics
wfof: wide-field optical filter
WFOT: World Federation of Occupational Therapists
wfp: warm frontal passage
WFP: World Food Program (UN)
WFP: *Winnipeg Free Press*
WFPA: World Federation for the Protection of Animals
WFPT: World Federation for Physical Therapy
W Fris: West Frisian
WFS: World Future Society
WFSA: World Federation of Societies of Anaesthesiologists
WFSPL: Wright Field Special Projects Laboratory
WFSW: World Federation of Scientific Workers
WFTU: World Federation of Trade Unions
WFUNA: World Federation of United Nations Associations
WFW: *Woltföderation der Wissenschaftler* (German—World Federation of Scientific Workers)
WFY: World Federalist Youth
wg: water gauge; wing; wire gauge
Wg: Wolfgang
WG: Western Gear (company)
WG: Welsh Guards; Western Gear (company); West German; W.G. Grace (cricketer and physician)
WG: *Westminster Gazette*
wga: wheat-germ agglutinin
WGA: Writers' Guild of America
w-gal(s): wine gallon(s)
W-gauge: wide-gauge railroad track (exceeding the standard gauge of 4 feet $8^1/_2$ inches)
WGB: *Weltgewerkschaftsbund* (German—World Federation of Trade Unions)
wgbc: waveguide operating below cutoff
WGC: West Georgia College
Wg-Comdr: Wing-Commander
WGD: *Webster's Geographical Dictionary*
WGDS: Warm Gas Distribution System
W Ger: West Germany
WGER: Working Group on Extraterrestrial Resources
wgf: waveguide filter; wound glass filter
WGGB: Writers' Guild of Great Britain
WGH: William Gamaliel Harding (29th President U.S.)
WGI: Work Glove Institute
WGIPP: Waterton-Glacier International Peace Park (Alberta, Canada, and Montana, U.S.A.)
wgj: wormgear jack
w gl: wireglass
WGL: Weapons Guidance Laboratory
WGM: Worthy Grand Master
WGMA: Wet Ground Mica Association
WGmc: West Germanic
WGP: Western Gas Processors
WGPMS: Warehousing Gross Performance Measurement System
wgr: wide gauze roll
WGR: War Guidance Requirements
Wg & Rgn Comdr: Wing and Regional Commander
W Grnld Cur: West Greenland Current
wgs: waveguide glide slope; web guide system
WGs: Welsh Guards
wgsj: wormgear screw jack
WGU: Welsh Golfing Union
WGVN: Willard Gibbs Van Name
wgw: waveguide window
wh: water heater; watt hour; white; withholding
w/h: withholding
Wh: Whig Party
WH: White House
WHA: Welsh Hockey Association; Western History Association; World Health Assembly; World Hockey Association
wha': what
W'hampton: Wolverhampton
whap: when or where applicable
Wharf of North America: Nova Scotia's nickname celebrating its many excellent ports
WHASA: White House Army Signal Agency
whate'er: whatever
what's: what has; what is
whatso'er: whatsoever
WHCA: White House Communications Agency
WHCOA: White House Conference on Aging
WHCT: West Ham College of Technology
whd: warehead
WHD: Women's House of Detention (NYC)
whdm: watt-hour demand meter
whe: water hammer eliminator
Wheat: *Wheaton's* (US Supreme Court Reports)
Wheat Provinces: Alberta, Manitoba, Saskatchewan
wheats: wheatcakes
Wheat State: South Australia
whecon: wheel control
whene'er: whenever
where'er: wherever
wheresoe'er: wheresoever
whf: wharf
WHFAM: William Hayes Fogg Art Museum
whfg: wharfage
whfr: wharfinger
WHH: William Henry Harrison (9th President U.S.)
WHHA: White House Historical Association
Whi: Whitehall
WHI: Western Highway Institute
whis: whistle (fog)
Whiskey: code for letter W; Western Kentucky (coal company; stock exchange slang)
Whit: Whitaker; Whitbread; Whitcomb; Whitman
Whitaker's: *Whitaker's Almanac*
White Carpathians: White Carpathian Mountains of Czechoslovakia
White City of the North: Helsinki
White Ensign: flag of the Royal Navy and the Royal Yacht Club—St George cross on a white ground with the Union Jack in the upper canton corner
white flag: symbol of surrender or truce
White House: executive office and residence of the President of the United States in Washington, D.C.
white lead: lead carbonate
white light: signal indicating apparatus, craft, or vehicle has power and is illuminated
White Man's Grave: equatorial West Africa
White Metropolis: Helsinki
White Mountain State: New Hampshire
white plague: pulmonary tuberculosis
White Russia: Byelorussia
whites: the whites—thick whitish

vaginal discharge; synonym for leukorrhea
White Town of Lake Mjosa: Gjøvik, Norway
whitewings: white-uniformed street cleaners
white vitriol: zinc sulfate
Whitman: Albert Whitman (Chicago); Whitman Publishing Company (Racine)
WHL: Western Hockey League
wh lt: white light
WHMA: Women's Home Missionary Association
WHML: Wellcome Historical Medical Library
whmstr: weighmaster
WHMV & NSA: Woods Hole, Martha's Vineyard and Nantucket Steamship Authority
Whn: Whitehaven
WHO: White House Office; World Health Organization (UN)
who'd: who had
WHODAP: White House Office of Drug Abuse Prevention
WHOI: Woods Hole Oceanographic Institution
whol: wholesale(r)
who'll: who shall; who will
whoretel: whore hotel
who's: who is
who've: who have
whp: water horsepower; whirlpool
W & H & PC: Wage and Hour and Public Contracts
wh pl: whole plate (silver)
whr: watt hour
WHRA: Welwyn Hall Research Association; Western Historical Research Associates; Western Housing Research Association
WHRC: World Health Research Center
whrlp: whirlpool
whs: warehouse
WHS: Walton High School; White Sands, New Mexico (tracking station)
whse: warehouse
whsl: wholesale
whsmn: warehouseman
whsng: warehousing
whs rec: warehouse receipt
Wht: White (postal abbreviation)
WHT: William Howard Taft (27th President of the U.S.)
WHTHS: William Howard Taft High School
whvs: wharves
why.: what have you?
why'd: why did
Why Not Town: Minot, North Dakota, nicknamed Why Not Minot?
wi: wrought iron
wi': (Gaelic contraction—with)
w & i: weighing and inspection
WI: Wake Island; West India; West Indian; West Indies; Windward Islands; Wine Institute; Wire Institute
wia (WIA): wounded in action
WIAB: Wistar Institute of Anatomy and Biology
Wib: Wibbert; Wilbert
WIBC: Women's International Bowling Congress
WIC: Welfare and Institutions Code; Women in Construction
WICHE: Western Interstate Commission for Higher Education
Wick: Wicklow
WICS: Women's Institute for Continuing Study
wid: widow; widower
WID: West India Docks
WIDF: Women's International Democratic Federation
Widm: *Widmung* (German—dedication)
Widow at Windsor: Queen Victoria who was a widow for the last 39 years of her life
WIF: West India Fruit and Steamship Company; West Indies Federation
wig: periwig
Wig: Wigtown(shire)
wigo: what is going on?
Wigorn.: *Wigorniensis* (Latin—of Worcester)
Wigwam: Tammany Hall
wih: went in hole
WIHM: Wellcome Institute of the History of Medicine
WIHS: Washington Irving High School
Wil: Wilber; Wilbert; Wilbur; Wilburn; Wiley; Wilford; Wilfred; Wylie
WIL: West India Lines
Wil Blvd: Wilshire Boulevard
wilco: will comply
Wild Bill: William Joseph (Wild Bill) Donovan; James Butler (Wild Bill) Hickok
Wilderness of Judah: western shores of the Dead Sea in Israel
Wilderness Trail Blazer: Daniel Boone
Wildflower State: Western Australia
Wild Prairie Rose: North Dakota state flower
Wild Rose: Iowa state flower; Iowa girl's nickname
Wilkes Land: Australian Antarctica
Will: Willard; William; Willis
Willa: Welhelmina
William Ashenden: W. Somerset Maugham
William Bolitho: William Bolitho Ryall
William the Conqueror: William I of Normandy and England
William B. Goodrich: Roscoe (Fatty) Arbuckle's pseudonym
William of Nassau: William I—Prince of Orange and Count of Nassau—founder of the Dutch Republic; also called William the Silent
Will Rogers Turn: Will Rogers Turnpike
William the Silent: William—Prince of Orange
William Tell's Town: Altdorf in Switzerland's Uri Canton
Willie: William
Willie Mays: Willie Howard Mays
Willies: Good Will Industries
Willy: William
Wilm: Wilmersdorf; Wilmington
Wilma: Wilhelmina
WILPF: Women's International League for Peace and Freedom
Wilts: Wiltshire
Wilts R: Wiltshire Regiment
W I & M: Washington, Idaho & Montana (railroad)
WIMA: Western Industrial Medical Association; Writing Instrument Manufacturers Association
Wimb: Wimborne
w i m c: whom it may concern
Win: Winchester Arms
WIN: Whip Inflation Now; Work Incentive Program
WINA: Webb Institute of Naval Architecture
win'ard: windward
WINBAN(GA): Windward Islands Banana Growers Association
Winch: Winchester
wind.: windlass
W Ind: West Indies
Wind I: Windward Islands
Windwards: Windward Islands
Windy City: Chicago
WINE: Webb Institute of Naval Engineering
Winesburg: dramatist Sherwood Anderson's place-name nickname for his hometown—Clyde, Ohio

Wing Cdr: Wing Commander
winkle(s): periwinkle(s)
Winn: Winnipeg; Winnipegger
Winnie: Sir Winston Churchill—British Prime Minister
Win(nie): Winslow; Winston
wino: alcoholic a ddicted to wine
win'rd: windward (pronounced *win-urd* by sailors)
WINS: Western Integrated Navigation System
wint: winter; wintry
Wintergarden of the East: frost-free southern Florida
Wintergarden of the Gulf: lower Rio Grande Valley
Wintergarden of the West: the Imperial Valley
Winter Reveries: Tchaikovsky's Symphony No. 1 in G minor *(Rêverie d'Hiver)*
Winter Wind: Chopin's Piano Etude No. 11 in A minor
Wint Gard: Winter Garden
Wint T: *The Winter's Tale*
Winton.: *Wintoniensis* (Latin—of Winchester)
wip: work in process; work in progress
WIP: West Indian Process (for sorting ripe from unripe coffee berries); Work Incentive Program
WIPO: World Intellectual Property Organization
WIR: *Weekly Intelligence Report*
WIRA: Wool Industry Research Association
WIRDS: Weather Information Reporting and Display System
Wis: Wisconsin; Wisconsinite
WIS: Weizmann Institute of Science; West Indies Shipping
WISA: West Indian Sugar Association; West Indies Students Association
Wisc: Wisconsin
WISC: Wechsler's Intelligence Scale for Children
WISCo: West Indies Sugar Company
Wisd of Sol: Wisdom of Solomon (apocryphal book of the Bible)
Wisest Man of Greece: Socrates who declared it was only because he knew he knew nothing
wisk: *wiskunde* (Dutch—mathematics)
wisp.: wide-range-imaging spectrometer
Wiss: *Wissenschaft* (German—science)
wit.: witness
wit: *witcar* (Dutch—white car)—golf-cart size high-dome electric vehicle rented to members of the witcar cooperative union to cut down traffic congestion by renting these witcars
WIT: West India Tankers; World International Tennis
WITCH: Women's International Terrorist Conspiracy (from) Hell
Witch of Wall Street: Hetty Green
withdrl: withdrawal
witht: without
witned: witnessed
witneth: witnesseth
WITS: Westinghouse Interactive Time-Sharing System
Wits U: Witwatersrand University
WIVAB: Womens' Inter-Varsity Athletic Board
wiz: wizard
Wizard of American Drama: David Belasco
Wizard of Kinderhook: Martin Van Buren—eighth President of the United States
Wizard of Menlo Park: Thomas Alva Edison whose research laboratory was in Menlo Park, New Jersey
Wizard of the Saddle: Lieutenant General Nathan Bedford Forrest, CSA
Wizard of Tuskegee: George Washington Carver
Wizard from Vienna: Franz Anton Mesmer
Wizard of Word Music: Edgar Allan Poe
WIZO: Women's International Zionist Organization
wjc: wife's judicial separation
WJC: Westbrook Junior College
W & JC: Washington and Jefferson College
WJCB: World Jersey Cattle Bureau
WJCC: Western Joint Computer Conference
WJFITB: Wool, Jute, and Flax Industry Training Board
wk: walk; warehouse keeper; weak; week; well-known; work; wreck
Wk: Walk; wreck
WK: Western Alaska Airlines
wkd: worked
W-K disease: Wilson-Kimmelstiel disease
wkds: weekdays
wkg: working
wkly: weekly
WKNR: Wadi Kziv Nature Reserve (Israel)
wkr: workers; wrecker
wks: weeks; works; workshop(s)
Wks: Works (postal abbreviation); wreckage (navigational abbreviation)
WKSC: Western Kentucky State College
wkt: wicket
wk vb: weak verb
WKY: Western Kentucky (coal company); Wall Street slang for this company is *Whiskey*
W Ky Pkwy: Western Kentucky Parkway
wl: wall lavatory; waterline; waterplane coefficient; wavelength
w L: *westlichst Längengrad* (German—west longitude)
WL: Sir Wilfred Laurier (Canada's eighth Prime Minister); Waiting List; West Lothian; Women's Liberation
WL: *Wagon Lits* (French—sleeping cars)
W-L: Westfal-Larsen Line
W & L: Washington and Lee University
WLA: Washington Library Association; Welsh Library Association; Western Literature Association; Wisconsin Library Association
wlb: wallboard
WLB: War Labor Board; Women's Liberation Party
WLB: *Werkgroep Instrument Beoordeling* (Dutch—Working Group on Instrument Behavior); *Wissenschaftliche Internationale Bibliographie* (German—International Scientific Bibliography)
WLC: World Liberty Corporation (Niarchos)
WL & Co: Westfal-Larsen & Company (steamship line)
wl coef: waterline coefficient
wld: west longitude date; would
wld ch: world championship
wldr: welder
WLF: Women's Liberation Front; World Law Fund
WLFNWR: William L. Finley National Wildlife Refuge (Oregon)
wl fwd: wool forward
WLG: Wellington, New Zealand (airport)
WLGS: Women's Local Government Society
WLHB: Women's League of Health and Beauty

W-L LL: Washington-Lincoln Laurels for Leaders
WLM: Women's Liberation Movement
WLMK: William Lyon Mackenzie King (Canada's eleventh, thirteenth, and fifteenth Prime Minister)
Wlmsbrg Brdg: Williamsburgh Bridge
Wln: Wellington
W Long: west longitude
W'loo: Waterloo
W Loth: West Lothian
WLP: Wallops Island, Virginia (tracking station)
WLPS: Wild Life Protection Society
WLPSA: Wild Life Preservation Society of Australia
Wlr: Walter
***WLR:** Weekly Law Reports*
WLRI: World Life Research Institute
Wls: Wells (postal abbreviation)
WLS: Wild Life Sanctuary
WLSC: West Liberty State College
WLSR: Wild Life Society of Rhodesia
WLTBU: Watermen, Lightermen, Tugmen, and Bargemen's Union
WLU: World Liberal Union
W & LU: Washington and Lee University
WLUS: World Land Use Survey
Wly: westerly
wlz: waltz
wm: wattmeter; wavemeter; white metal; wire mesh
w/m: weight or measure; white male
Wm: William
WM: Western Maryland (railroad); White Motors; William McKinley (25th President of the U.S.); Women Marines; Worshipful Master
W & M: College of William and Mary; Washburn & Moen (wire gauge)
WMA: Wildlife Management Area; Women Marines Association; World Medical Association
WMAA: Whitney Museum of American Art
WMATA: Washington Metropolitan Area Transit Authority
WMATC: Washington Metropolitan Area Transit Commission
WMB: War Mobilization Board
WMBL: Wrightsville Marine Biomedical Laboratory
WMC: Ways and Means Committee; Western Maryland College
WMCCA: Washington Metropolitan Coalition for Clean Air
WMCE: Western Montana College of Education
WMCIU: Working Men's Club and Institute Union
WMcK: William McKinley (25th President of the U.S.)
WMCL: William Mitchell College of Law
WMCP: Women's Medical College of Pennsylvania
wmd: wind measuring device
Wmd: Willemstad
WMD: Weights and Measures Division
WMECO: Western Massachusetts Electric Company
Wmg Cal: Wilmington, California
Wmg, Del: Wilmington, Delaware
WMI: Webbing Manufacturers Institute; Wildlife Management Institute
wmk: watermark
w/m^{o}k: watt per meter degree kelvin (thermal conductivity unit)
WMM: World Movement of Mothers
WMMA: Woodworking Machinery Manufacturers' Association
Wmn: Wilmington, North Carolina
WMNF: White Mountain National Forest
WMO: World Meteorological Organization
WMOAS: Women's Migration and Overseas Appointments Society
wmp: with much pleasure (the invitation is accepted)
WMR: Wasatch Mountain Railway
WMS: Webster Memory Scale; Women in Medical Service; Women's Medical Specialist; Work Measurement System; World Magnetic Survey
***WMS:** Willem Mengelberg Stichting* (Dutch—Willem Mengelberg Foundation)
W & MS: Wisconsin & Michigan Steamship (company)
WMSC: Women's Medical Specialist Corps
W & M SS Co: Wisconsin & Michigan Steamship Company
wmt: weighing more than
WMT: Wilson Marine Transit
WMTC: Women's Mechanized Transport Corps
WMU: Western Michigan University
W M W & NW: Weatherford, Mineral Wells & Northwestern (railroad)
WMWR: Wichita Mountains Wildlife Refuge (Oklahoma)
w/n: well-nourished
WN: Worlds of Nature (Amarillo botanical and zoological gardens)
***WN:** Weekly Notes*
WNA: Washington, D.C., National Airport; winter North Atlantic (loadline marking for ships voyaging across the North Atlantic in winter)
WNAP: Washington National Airport
wnb: will not be
WNBA: Women's National Book Association
WnBanc: Western Bancorporation
wndml: windmill
WNE: Welsh National Eisteddfod
wndp: with no down payment
wng: warning
wnl: within normal limits
WNLF: Women's National Liberal Federation
wnm: white noise making
WNM: Washington National Monument
WNNP: Walpole-Nornalup National Park (Western Australia)
WNP: Wankie National Park (Rhodesia); Warrumbungle NP (New South Wales); Welsh National Party; Westland NP (South Island, New Zealand); Wilpattu NP (Ceylon); Wyperfeld NP (Victoria, Australia)
WNRE: Whiteshell Nuclear Research Establishment
WNS: Washington National Symphony (District of Columbia); Women's News Service
WNSB: White Nile Scheme Board (Sudanese cotton production)
wintr: winter
WNW: west northwest
***WNW:** west noordwest* (Dutch—west northwest)
WNWR: Wapanocca National Wildlife Refuge (Arkansas);

Washita NWR (Oklahoma); Wheeler NWR (Alabama); Willapa NWR (Washington)
WNYNRC: Western New York Nuclear Research Center
WNYNSC: Western New York Nuclear Service Center
wo: wait order; work order; write out; written order
wo': war; wore
w-o: water-in-oil (emulsion); without
w/o: without
wo: *wie oben* (German—as previously mentioned)
WO: Warrant Officer; Welsh Office
WOA: Wharf Owners' Association
wob: washed overboard
Wobblies: International Workers of the World (so named because Chinese members pronounced IWW as *I Wobbly Wobbly*)
Wobs: Wobblies
woc: without compensation
WOCCI: War Office Central Card Index
wocg: weather outline contour generator
WOCL: War Office Casualty List
W & O D: Washington & Old Dominion (railroad)
WODA: World Dredging Association
WODECO: Western Offshore Drilling and Exploration Company
woe.: without equipment
Woe: *Woensdag* (Dutch—Wednesday)
wog: golliwog; polliwog; water or gas (valve); with other goods
'wog: golliwog; polliwog
WOG: Wily Oriental Gentleman (nickname applied to Farouk I of Egypt and similar monarchs of the area)
WOGA: Western Oil and Gas Association
wogs: (British slang—wily oriental gentlemen; wily oriental peoples)
WOHC: Warrant Officer, Hospital Corps
WOJG: Warrant Officer, Junior Grade
wol: wharf owners' liability
WOL: War Office Letter
wolfram: iron manganese tungstate
Wolfs: Wolfson College (Oxford)
Wolverine: fierce Michigan mammal often serving as a symbolic nickname for a Michiganite
Wolverine State: Michigan's official nickname
wom: wireless operator mechanic
WOM: Woomera, Australia (tracking station)
WOMAN: World Organization of Mothers of All Nations
Women's Lib: Women's Liberation Movement
womlib: women's liberation
won.: wool on needle (knitting)
Wonder City of the World: New York
Wonder State: Arkansas
won't: will not
WOO: Western Operations Office (NASA); World Oceanographic Organization
Wood: Woodbine; Woodbridge; Woodburn; Woodbury; Woodfield; Woodfin; Woodhill; Woodley; Woodrow; Woodruff; Woodson; Woodville; Woodward; Woodworth
wood alcohol: methyl alcohol (CH_3OH)
Wooden Leg: Governor Peter Stuyvesant of Nieuw Amsterdam
Woodie: Woodmansee; Woodrow
Woody: Woodrow
Woody Allen: Allen Stewart Konigsberg
woof: (cartoonist's language—dog's bark)
woof(s): woofer(s)
Wool: *Woolworth's* (Circuit Court Reports)
woool: words out of ordinary language
Wooster(sheer): (British contraction—Worcestershire)
wop.: with other property; without (immigration papers; without personnel
wope: without personnel or equipment
WOQT: Warrant Officer Qualification Test
wor: without our responsibility
Wor: Worshipful
Worc: Worcester (*Wooster*)
WORC: Washington Operations Research Council
Worc Coll: Worcester College—Oxford
Worc Reg: Worcester Regiment
Worcs: Worcestershire (*Woostersheer*)
Words: Wordsworth
WORK: Wanted Older Residents (with) Knowhow
Workers' Paradise: derisive nickname applied to the communist-controlled USSR whose propaganda led many people to believe it was the workers' paradise
workh: workhouse
Work. Comp: Workmen's Compensation
Workmen's: Workmen's Circle; Workmen's Compensation
Workshop of the Orient: Japan
World: *World Almanac*
World's Biggest Bookend: nickname of the Secretariat building of the United Nations overlooking New York's East River
World's Largest Art Gallery: Hermitage and Winter Palace in Leningrad
World's Largest Dictionary: 13-volume *Oxford English Dictionary*
World's Largest Library: Library of Congress, Washington, D.C.
World's Largest Lumber Shipping Port: Coos Bay, Oregon
World's Largest Museum: New York City's American Museum of Natural History
World's Largest Newspaper: *The New York Times*
World's Largest Opera House: Metropolitan Opera House, Lincoln Center, New York City
World's Largest Public Library: New York Public Library at Fifth Avenue and 42nd Street plus its more than 80 branches
World's Largest Publisher: U.S. Government Printing Office
World's Longest-Lived People: the Japanese and the Scandinavians share this epithet
World's Lowest City: Brawley, California (184 feet or 56 meters below sea level)
World's Most Exciting City: Hong Kong, London, New York, Tokyo, and San Francisco vie for this title
World's Northernmost City: Hammerfest, Norway
World's Oldest Constitutional Democracy: the United States of America
World's Shortest Poem: Eli Siegel's two-line two-word poem—*I? Why?*
World's Workshop: productive nations such as Germany, Great Britain, Japan, and the United States often bear this title
World War Photographer: Ed-

ward Steichen
worse: word selection
WOS: Washington Opera Society; Wilson Ornithological Society
wosac: worldwide synchronization of atomic clocks
WOSB: War Operations Selection Board
WOSD: Weapon Operational Systems Development
WOSL: Women's Overseas Service League
wot: wide-open throttle
WOTAG: Women's Taxation Action Group
wouldn't: would not
W & O V: Washington & Ouachita Valley (railroad)
wow: waiting on weather
WOW: Woodmen of the World
w/o wn:without winch
wp: waste pipe; water repellency; water repellent; way point; weather permitting; white phosphorus; will proceed; working paper; working party; working point; working pressure
w-p: waterproofed
w/p: without prejudice
Wp: Worship(ful)
WP: War Plan(s); Warsaw Pact; Western Pacific (railroad); West Point; West Virginia Pulp and Paper (stock exchange symbol); Worthington Pump; Worthy Patriarch
WP: *Wiener Philharmoniker* (German—Vienna Philharmonic Orchestra); *Winkler Prins Encyclopedieen* (Dutch—Winkler Prins Encyclopedia)
wpa: with particular average
WPA: Western Pine Association; William Penn Association; Works Progress Administration; World Parliament Association; World Psychiatric Association
WPAFB: Wright-Patterson Air Force Base
wpb: wastepaper basket
WPB: War Plan Basic; War Production Board (World War II)
WPBA: Western Power Boat Association
WPBS: Welsh Plant Breeding Station
wpc: water pollution control; watts per candle; wood plastic combination; world planning chart
WPC: Washington Press Club; William Penn College; Women's Press Club
WPCA: Water Pollution Control Act
WPCC: Western Pharmaceutical and Chemical Corporation
WPCF: Water Pollution Control Federation
wpe: white porcelain enamel
WPF: World Peace Foundation
WPFC: Western Pacific Fisheries Commission
Wpfl: Worshipful
wpg: waterproofing
WPg: West Point graduate
WPG: gunboat (3-letter USCG symbol)
WPGR: Willem Pretorius Game Reserve (South Africa)
WPHC: Western Pacific High Commissioner
WPHI: Western Pennsylvania Horological Institute
wpi: wholesale price index
WPI: Wall Paper Institute; Waxed Paper Institute; Worcester Polytechnic Institute; World Press Institute
WPI: *World Port Index*
W pk: Ward's (mechanical tissue) pack
wpl: warning point level
WPL: Weapons Propulsion Laboratory; Wichita Public Library; Winnipeg Public Library; Worcester Public Library
WPLO: Water Port Liaison Office(r)
wpm: words per minute
WPMSF: World Professional Marathon Swimming Federation
wpn: weapon
WPN: West Penn Traction (stock exchange symbol)
WPN: *World Press News*
WPO: Water Programs Office (Environmental Protection Agency); Wiener Philharmonic Orchester (Vienna Philharmonic Orchestra); World Ploughing Organization
WPOD: Water Port of Debarkation
WPOE: Water Port of Embarkation
wpp: waterproof paper packing
WPP: West Penn Power Company
WPPC: West Penn Power Company
WPPSS: Washington Public Power Supply System
wp & r: work-planning-and-review (discussions)
WPRA: Wallpower and Paint Retailers' Association; Waste Paper Recovery Association
WPRL: Water Pollution Research Laboratory
wps: with prior service; words per second
WPs: Warsaw Pact members; Warsaw Pact nations
WPS: Wildlife Preserve Society
WPSA: World's Poultry Science Association
WPSL: Western Primary Standard Laboratory
wpu: write punch
W-P-W syndrome: Wolff-Parkinson-White syndrome
wpwod: will proceed without delay
WPY: World Population Year (1974)
WP & Y: White Pass & Yukon (railroad)
WP & YR: White Pass & Yukon Route
WPZ: Woodland Park Zoo (Seattle)
wq: water quench
WQF: Wider Quaker Fellowship
wr: war risk
w/r: water and rail; water resistant
w & r: water and rail; welfare and recreation
Wr: Walter
WR: Ward Room; War Reserve; Wassermann Reaction; Western (railway) Region; West Riding
W.R.: *Wilhelmus Rex* (Latin—King Wilhelm; King William)
WRA: Water Research Association; Western Railway of Alabama
WRAAC: Women's Royal Australian Army Corps
WRAAF: Women's Royal Australian Air Force
WRAC: Women's Royal Army Corps
wraceld: wounds received in action combat with enemy or in line of duty
WRAF: Women's Royal Air Force
WRAIN: Walter Reed Army Institute of Nursing
WRAIR: Walter Reed Army Institute of Research
WRAMA: Warner-Robins Air Material Area
WRAMC: Walter Reed Army Medical Center
WRANS: Women's Royal Australian Naval Service
WRAP: Weapons Readiness Analysis Program

WRAT: Wide-Range Achievement Test
WRB: War Refugee Board; Water Resources Board
WRBC: Weather Relay Broadcast System
wrc: water-retention coefficient
WRC: Weather Relay Center; Welding Research Council
wrcr: wife's restitution of conjugal rights
WRDC: Westinghouse Research and Development Center
WRE: Weapons Research Establishment (Woomera, Australia)
w ref: with reference
w reg: with regard (to)
WREN: Women's Royal Naval Service
wresat: weapons research establishment satellite
W-response: whole response
WRF: World Rehabilitation Fund
wrfg: wharfage
WRGH: Walter Reed General Hospital
WRH: Walter Reed Hospital
WRHS: Western Reserve Historical Society
wri: war risk insurance
WRI: War Resisters' International; Weatherstrip Research Institute; Wellcome Research Institute; Wire Reinforcement Institute; Wire Rope Institute
WRIR: Walter Reed Institute of Research
W.R. Knottman: (abbreviated signature—we are not man and wife)—appears on the pages of many hotel and motel registers
wrl: wing reference line
WRL: Wantage Research Laboratory; War Readiness Materiel; War Resisters League; Westinghouse Research Laboratories; Willow Run Laboratories (University of Michigan)
WRLC: World Role of Law Center (Duke University)
wrm: war readiness materiel
WRM: Wasatch Railway Museum
wrn: wool round needle (knitting)
WRNGA: William Rockhill Nelson Gallery of Art (Kansas City)
WRNR: Women's Royal Naval Reserve
WRNS: Women's Royal Naval Service
wrnt: warrant
WRNWR: White River National Wildlife Refuge (Arkansas)
wro: war risk only
WRO: Weed Research Organization
WRP: Workers' Revolutionary Party (British Trotskyite communists)
WRPA: Water Resources Planning Act
WRPC: Weather Records Processing Center(s)
WRRA: Women's Road Records Association (cycling)
WRRC: Willow Run Research Center
WRRR: Walter Reed Research Reactor
WRRS: Wire Relay Radio System
WRSA: Western Regional Science Association
WRSIC: Water Resources Scientific Information Center
wrsk: war-readiness spares kit
WRSP: *World Register of Scientific Periodicals*
wrt: wrought
wrtd: warranted
wrtr: writer
wru: who are you?
WRU: Western Reserve University
wrv: water relief valve
WRVS: Women's Royal Voluntary Service
wr(w): war reserve (weapon)
WRX: Western Refrigerator Express (railroad code)
WRY: World Refugee Year
WR Yorks: West Riding, Yorkshire
W Ry A: Western Railway of Alabama
ws: water supply; weather station
w & s: whiskey and soda
WS: Wallops Station (NASA); Ware Shoals; Warner & Swasey; weapon system; Western Samoa; West Saxon(y); Wilderness Society; Wildlife Society; windspeed; Writer to the Signet (Scottish lawyer)
W S: *Washington Star*
wsa: weapons system analysis
WSA: Weed Society of America; Worker-Student Alliance
WSAC: West of Scotland Agricultural College
WSAD: Weapon System Analysis Division (USN)
WSAG: Washington Special Action Group (personnel in Situation Room in White House basement)
W Sam: Western Samoa
WSAO: Weapons System Analysis Office
wsb: will send boat
WSB: Wharton School of Business
wsc: weapon system contractor
WSC: Western Simulation Council; Winona State College; Wisconsin State College; Writing Services Center
WSCC: Western State College of Colorado
WSCF: World Student Christian Federation
Wschr: *Wochenschrift* (German—weekly magazine)
WSCS: Woman's Society for Christian Service
wsd: working stress design
WSDL: Weapons System Development Laboratory
WSEC: Washington State Electronics Council
WSECL: Weapon System Equipment Component List
WSED: Weapon Systems Evaluation Division
WSEG: Weapons Systems Evaluation Group
WSEL: Weapons System Engineering Laboratory
WSEP: Waste Solidification Engineering Prototype Plant (AEC); Weapon System Evaluation Program
WSF: Washington State Ferries; Western Sea Frontier; Women's Strike for Peace; World Sephardic Federation
WSFI: Water Softener and Filter Institute
wsg: worthiest soldier in the group
WSG: Wesleyan Service Guild
WSGE: Western Society of Gear Engineers
WSHS: Wisconsin State Historical Society
WSI: Writers and Scholars International
WSJ: *Wall Street Journal*
WSL: Warren Spring Laboratory; Washington State Library
WSLO: Weapon System Logistics Office(r)
WSM: Weapon System Manager; W. Somerset Maugham
WSMAC: Weapon System Maintenance Action Center
WSMO: Weapon System Materiel Office(r)
WSMR: White Sands Missile Range

WSNM: White Sands National Monument
WSO: Western Support Office (NASA); Wichita Symphony Orchestra
WSO: *Wiener Symphonisches Orchester* (German—Vienna Symphony Orchestra)
WSOC: Wider Share Ownership Council
wsp: water supply point
WSP: Women Strike for Peace; Wyoming State Parks
WSPACS: Weapon System Program and Control System
WSPB: Western Society of Business Publications
WS Pen: Washington State Penitentiary
WSPG: White Sands Proving Ground
WSPL: Winston-Salem Public Library
WSPO: Weapon System Project Officer
WSPOP: Weapon System Phase-Out Procedure
WSPU: Women's Social and Political Union
wsr (WSR): weapon system reliability
w/sr: watt(s) per steradian
Wsr: Wesermünde
W & S R: Warren & Saline River (railroad)
WS & RB: Washington Surveying and Rating Bureau
WSRI: World Safety Research Institute
w/srm²: watt(s) per steradian square meter
WSS: Warfare Systems School; Winston-Salem Southbound (railroad); World Ship Society
WSSA: Weapon System Support Activities; World Secret Service Association
WSSC: Weapon System Support Center
WSSCA: White Sands Signal Corps Agency
WSSO: Winston-Salem Symphony Orchestra
WSSS: Weapon System Storage Site
WSS & YP: White Sulphur Springs & Yellowstone Park (railroad)
WST: Whitworth Standard Thread
WSTA: White Slave Traffic Act
WSTC: Winston-Salem Teachers College
WSTF: White Sands Test Facility (NASA)
WSTI: Waterbury State Technical Institute; Welded Steel Tube Institute
WSTNRA: Whiskeytown-Shasta-Trinity National Recreation Area (California)
WSU: Washington State University; Wayne State University; Western State University
w sup: water supply
W Sus: West Sussex
WSUSM: Wayne State University School of Medicine
WSV: Wiener Stadwerke Verkehrsbetriebe (Vienna transportation system)
wsw: white sidewall (tires)
WSW: west southwest
WSWL: Warheads and Special Weapons Laboratory
WSWMA: Western States Weights and Measures Association
WSWS: Wexford Slobs Wildfowl Sanctuary (Ireland)
wt: watch time; watertight; weight; withholding tax (WT)
w/t: wireless telegraph(y)
w/t (W /T): walkie/talkie
WT: war time; withholding tax; winterization test
w & t: wear and tear
W & T: Wrightsville & Tennille (railroad)
WTA: Washington Technological Associates; World Transport Agency
WTAA: World Trade Alliance Association
WTAU: Women's Total Abstinence Union
w/tax: withholding tax
Wtb: Whitby
Wtb: *Wörterbuch* (German—dictionary)
WTBA: Washington Toll Bridge Authority; Water-Tube Boilermakers' Association
WTB & TS: Watchtower Bible and Tract Society (Jehovah's Witnesses)
WTC: World Tanker Corporation (Niarchos); World Trade Center
wtchmn: watchman
wtd: watertight door
WTD: ***World Trade Directory***
WTE: World Tapes for Education
wtf: will to fire
Wft: Waterford
WTFDA: Worldwide TV-FM-DX Association
WTFP: Wolf Trap Farm Park (Vienna, Virginia)
WTG: *Welt-Tierärztegesellschaft* (German—World Veterinary Association)
wthr: weather
WTIS: World Trade Information Service
WTL: Wyle Test Laboratories
wtmh: watertight manhole
WTNR: Wadi Tabor Nature Reserve (Israel)
WTO: Warsaw Treaty Organization
WTP: Weapons Testing Program
wtqad: watertight quick-acting door
wtr: waiter; winter; writer
Wtr: Water (postal abbreviation)
WTR: Western Test Range (formerly Pacific Missile Range)
WTRC: Wool Textile Research Council
wtrz: winterize
wtrzn: winterization
WTS: Watchtower Society; Women's Transport Service
WTSC: West Texas State College
WTTA: Wholesale Tobacco Trade Association
WTUC: World Trade Union Conference
wu: work unit
WU: Washington University; Wesleyan University; Western Union; Wilberforce University; Wittenberg University
W/U: Western Union
WUA: Western Underwriters Association
wuaa: wartime unit aircraft activity
WUAA: Wartime Unit Aircraft Activity
wuc: work unit code
WUCM: Work Unit Code Manual
WUCT: World Union of Catholic Teachers
WUCWO: World Union of Catholic Women's Organizations
WUF: World Underwater Federation; World Union of Free Thinkers
WUI: Western Union International
WUIS: Work Unit Information System
WUJS: World Union of Jewish Students
WULTUO: World Union of Liberal Trade Union Organizations
WUM: Women's Universal Movement
WUMP(S): White Urban Middle-class Protestant(s)
WUNS: World Union of National

Socialists
WUPJ: World Union for Progressive Judaism
Wurst City in the World: Sheboygan, Wisconsin, where making sausage is a specialty
WUS: Western United States; World University Service
WUSL: Women's United Service League
WUSM: Washington University School of Medicine
wut: warmup time
WUT: Washburn University of Topeka
wuts: work-unit time standard
WUX: Western Union (teleprinter) Exchange
wv: wall vent; whispered voice; wind velocity; with view (room with view)
w/v: weight in volume
WV: West Virginia Pulp and Paper Company
W Va: West Virginia; West Virginian
WVA: World Veterinary Association; Wyoming Vocational Association
W Va Turn: West Virginia Turnpike
WVAWRD: West Virginia Water Resources Division
WVC: Wenatchee Valley College
wvd: waived
***WVD:** Werelverbond van Diamantbewerker* **(Dutch—World Alliance of Diamond Workers)**
wvdc: working voltage—direct current
WVEA: West Virginia Educational Association
WVF: World Veterans' Federation
WVIT: West Virginia Institute of Technology
WVL: Warfare Vision Laboratory (USA)
WVMA: Women's Veterinary Medical Association
W V N: West Virginia Northern (railroad)
WVPA: World Veterinary Poultry Association
WVRB: West Virginia Rating Bureau
WVS: Women's Voluntary Service
WVSC: West Virginia State College
wvt: water vapor transfer; water vapor transmission
WVT: Watervliet Arsenal
wvtr: water vapor transmission rate
w/vu: with view
WVU: West Virginia University
WVWC: West Virginia Wesleyan College
ww: warehouse warrant; water white; waterworks; wirewound
***ww:** werkwoord* (Dutch—verb)
w/w: wall-to-wall (carpet, floor covering, linoleum, tile); weight for weight
WW: Walworth (trademark); Woodmen of the World; Woodrow Wilson (28th President of the U.S.); world war; world wide
***WW:** Who's Who*
***Ww:** Witwe* (German—widow)
W & W: Waynesburg & Western (railroad); Winchester & Western (railroad)
WW I: World War I (1914–1918)
WW II: World War II (1939–1945)
WWIVM: World War I Victory Medal
WWIIHSLB: World War II Honorable Service Lapel Button (often called the Ruptured Duck)
WWIIVM: World War II Victory Medal
wwa: with the will annexed
WWA: Western Writers of America
WWB: Walt Whitman Bridge
WWBA: Walt Whitman Birthplace Association; Western Wooden Box Association
WWC: Walla Walla College; Warren Wilson College; William Woods College; World Weather Centers (Melbourne; Moscow; Washington, D.C.)
WWCP: Walking Wounded Collecting Post
WWCTU: World's Women's Christian Temperance Union
wwd: weather working days
***WWD:** Women's Wear Daily*
WWDC: World War Debt Commission
W Wdr: Warrant Wardmaster
wwdShex: weather working days Sundays and holidays excluded
***Wwe:** Weduwe* (Dutch—widow); *Witwe* (German—widow)
WWF: Welder Wildlife Foundation; Woodrow Wilson Foundation; World Wildlife Fund
***WWG:** World Wildlife Guide*
WWHS: Wilbur Wright High School; Woodrow Wilson High School
wwi: whirlwind computer
WWI: Weight Watchers International; World Watch Institute
WWICS: Woodrow Wilson International Center for Scholars
wwio: worldwide inventory objective
WWO: Wing Warrant Officer; World Weather Organization
WWJC: Western Wyoming Junior College
WWMB: Woodrow Wilson Memorial Bridge
WWMC: Woodrow Wilson Memorial Commission
WWMCCS: Worldwide Military Command and Control System
w/wn: with winch
W Wnd Drft: West Wind Drift (Antartic)
WWNFF: Woodrow Wilson National Fellowship Foundation
WWNSSS: World-Wide Network of Standard Seismograph Stations
WWNT: West Wales Naturalists Trust
wwp: water wall peripheral; working water pressure; write without program
WWP: Washington Water Power company
WWPA: Western Wood Products Association
***WWR:** Washington Week in Review* (education television)
WWSA: Walt Whitman Society of America
WWSC: Western Washington State College
WWSN: World-wide Seismology Net (NBS)
WWSPIA: Woodrow Wilson School of Public and International Affairs (Princeton University)
wwss: water wall side skegs
WWSSN: World-Wide Standardized Seismograph Network
WWSU: World Water Ski Union
wwt: whitewall tires
WWTP: Waste Water Treating Process
W W V: call letters of United States Bureau of Standards worldwide radio time signal; Walla Walla Valley (railroad)
WWVH: World Wide Time (US Bureau of Standards, Hawaii)
WWW: World Weather Watch
***WWW:** Who Was Who*
WWWF: Worldwide Wrestling Federation
WWWV: Women World War

Veterans
WWWVA: Wild, Wonderful West Virginia
WWWW: Women Who Want to be Women
wwwwwh: who, what, when, where, why, how (many or much)—reporters' mnemonic for encompassing elements of a news story
WWY: Warwickshire and Worcestershire Yoemanry
wx: waxy
Wx: weather; Wilcox (formation)
wxb: wax bite
WXD: meteorological radar station
wxg: warning
wxp: wax pattern
wy: wey (14 pounds of wool)
Wy: Wyatt; Wycliffe
wyaio: will you accept (the position) if offered?
WYC: Washington Yacht Club; Winthrop Yacht Club
Wycl: Wycliffe
wye: Y (as in wye circuit)
Wyo: Wyoming; Wyomingite
Wyoming Suffragette: Esther Hobart Morris
WYR: West Yorkshire regiment
WZ: *Welt Zeit* (German—world time)
WZO: World Zionist Organization
WZOA: Women's Zionist Organization of America
WZW: *west zuidwest* (Dutch—west southwest)

X

x: an abscissa (symbol); an unknown quantity (symbol); any point on a great circle; by (used between dimensional figures as in 3 × 5 file card); cross; cross reactance (symbol); exchange; extra; frost; mole ratio; no-wind distance; parallactic angle
x: universal symbol standing for things as diverse as hoarfrost in meteorological reports, a kiss, a mechanical defect, a motion picture not suitable for viewing by minors, the spot the body was found or the crime was committed (*x* marks the spot), the position of a craft or anything else on a chart or map, the signature of the illiterate (her or his mark)
x: specific acoustic reactance
x or X: Christ; Christian; Christianity; cross; experiment; experimental (symbol); explosive (symbol); extra; extract(ed); Kienbock unit (symbol); magnification power; reactance (symbol); research aircraft (symbol); single strength; $10 bill; times (multiplied by); univalent negative (symbol); unknown quantity; U.S. Steel Corporation (stock exchange symbol); Xavier; X ray; Xray—code for letter X
X: longitudinal axis
X-2: counterintelligence
X-15: rocket-propelled research aircraft
xa: chiasma; transmission adapter
XA: Crucible Steel (stock exchange symbol)
xaam: experimental air-to-air missile
xact: exact(ly); X (in any computer) automatic code translation
XAE: merchant ammunition ship (3-letter naval symbol)
xafh: X-band antenna feed horn
XAK: merchant cargo ship (3-letter naval symbol)
XAKc: merchant coastal cargo ship, small (3-letter naval symbol)
xal: xenon arc lamp
XAM: merchant ship converted to minesweeper (3-ietter naval symbol)
x-a mix.: xylene-alcohol mixture (insect larva killer)
x-a: mixture: xylene-alcohol mixture
xan: xanthic; xanthine; yellow
Xan: Xanthe; Xanthian; Xanthippe; Xanthus
Xana: Xanadu
Xanadu: nickname Orson Welles gave Hearst Castle in San Simeon, California
xanth: xanthoma(tosis)
XAP: merchant transport (3-letter naval symbol)
XAPc: merchant coastal transport, small (3-letter naval symbol)
x arm: cross arm
XAS: X-band Antenna System
xasm: experimental air-to-surface missile (XASM)
xat: X-ray analysis trial
Xav: Xaver; Xavier; Xaviera
XAV: auxiliary seaplane tender (3-letter naval symbol)
Xavier: Joseph Xavier Boniface's nom de plume
X-axis: horizontal axis on a chart, graph, or map
Xaymayca: (Arawak—Land of Woods and Streams)—Jamaica
xb: crossbar; exploding bridgewire
XB: experimental bomber
X-band: 5,200–10,900 mc
xbar: crossbar
X bear: grizzly bear (abbreviation appearing on many American frontier epitaphs: "killed by an X bear")
Xber: December
xbr: experimental breeder reactor
Xbre: *décembre* (French—December)
xbt: expendable bathythermograph
xbts: exhibits
xc: cross country; ex coupon; X-chromosome
X-c: X-chromosome
XC: experimental cargo aircraft (naval symbol); Xaverian College
xcar: from the railroad car
XCG: experimental cargo glider (naval symbol)
xch: exchange
X-chromosome: female-producing gene found in male sperm
xcit: excitation
xcl: excess current liabilities
XCL: armed merchant cruiser

(naval symbol)
xconn: cross connection
xcp: without coupon
xpt: except
xcs: cross-country skiing
xct: X-band communications transponder
xc & uc: exclusive of covering and uncovering
xut: crosscut
xcvr: transceiver
x cy: cross country
xd: ex dividend
x'd: executed
X'd: crossed out
X-day: launching day
xdcr: transducer
xder: transducer
X & DFLOT: Experimental and Development Flotilla
xdh: xanthine dehydrogenase
xdis: ex distribution (without distribution)
xdiv: without dividend
x'd out: crossed out
xdp: X-ray density probe; X-ray diffraction powder
xdpc: X-ray diffraction powder camera
xdps: X-band diode phase shifter
xdr: transducer
Xdr: Crusader
XDS: Xerox Data Systems; X-ray Diffraction System
xdt: xenon discharge tube
Xe: experimental engine; xenon
xeg: X-ray emission gage
XEG: Xerox Education Group
Xen: Xenia; Xenocratic
xeno: xenodiagnosis; xenodiagnostic; xenogenic; xenograft; xenolith; xenolithic; xenophile; xenophilia; xenophobe; xenophobia
Xeno: Xenocrates; Xenophanes; Xenophon
xenodiag: xenodiagnosis
Xenop: Xenophon
xer: Xerox reproduction
Xer: Xerxes
xerocops: xerocopies (books reproduced by xerography)
xerodups: xerographic duplicates
xerog: xerograph(ic)(al)(ly); xerography
xeromamo: xeromamograph (also called xerox mamograph—xerographic process used in diagnosis of breast cancer)
xerorads: xerographic radiographs
xes: X-ray emission spectra
xf: extra fine
XF: experimental fighter (naval symbol)
xfa: crossed-field acceleration; X-ray fluoresence absorption
xfc: X-band frequency converter
xdf: X-band flow detection
xfer: transfer
xfh: X-band feed horn
Xfher: Christopher
xflt: expanded flight-line tester
xfm: X-band ferrite modulator
xfmr: transformer
xformer: transformer
xfqh: xenon-filled quartz helix
xft: xenon flash tube
xg: crossing
xgam: experimental guided air missile (XGAM)
xh: extra hard; extra heavy; extra high
Xh: Xhosa
XH: experimental helicopter (naval symbol)
x heavy: extra heavy
X-height: height of central portion of lowercase letters exclusive of ascenders and descenders
x-high: of a height equal to a lowercase x of the same face and size
xhil: xenon high-intensity light
xhm: X-ray hazard meter
xhmo: extended huckel molecular orbit
xhr: extra-high reliability
Xhs: Xhosa
xhst: exhaust
xhv: extremely high vacuum
x hvy: extra heavy
xi: ex interest
xia: X-band interferometer antenna
xic: transmission interface converter
xil: xilography; xilogravure (woodcuts)
xim: X-ray intensity meter
xin: without interest
Xin: Xingu
Xina: Christina
XING: crossing (highway or railroad)
xio: execute input-output
xiph: xiphoid; xiphoidal
Xipho: Xiphosura
xirs: xenon infrared searchlight
xis: xenon infrared searchlight
xist: xistoma; xistomiasis
xk: X-band klystron
xl: crystal; crystalline; extra large; extra long
Xl: inductive reactance
xla: X-band limiter anntenuator
xlam: cross-laminate(d)
xlc: xenon lamp collimator
xldt: xenon laser discharge tube
xli: extra-low interstitial
xlnt: excellent
XLO: Ex-Cell-O (precision products; trade name)
xlps: xenon lamp power supply
xlr: experimental liquid rocket
xls: xenon light source
XLSS: Xenon Light-Source System
xlt: cross-linked polyethylene; excellent; xenon laser tube
xl & ul: exclusive of loading and unloading
xlwb: extra-long wheelbase
xm: crossmatch; examine
xm (XM): experimental missile
Xm: Christmas
XM: experimental missile
Xmas: Christmas
XMS: Experimental Development Specification
X-matching: —cross matching
xmfr: transformer
xmit: transmit
xmitter: transmitter
x mod: experimental module
xms: X-band microwave source
xmsn: transmission
xmt: transmit; X-band microwave transmitter
xmtg: transmitting
xmtr: transmitter
xmt-rec: transmit-receive
xn: ex new
Xn: Christian
XN: experimental (USN)
X-note: $10 bill
xnt: excellent
Xnty: Christianity
xo: crystal oscillator
XO: Executive Officer; Experimental Office(r); Turner's syndrome wherein one of the sex-determining pair of XX chromosomes is missing
xob: xenon optical beacon
Xochi: Xochimilco
x-off: transmitter off
x-on: transmitter on
xor: exclusive or (data processing)
xos: extra outside clothing; extra outsize (clothing)
X-O: cross-out test
X-out: cross out; delete; strike out
xover: cross over
X-over: cross over
xp: express paid: xerodema pigmentosum
Xp: fire-resistive protected cabinet, safe, or vault
XP: (Greek—chirho)—first two letters fo the Greek word for Christ
xpa: X-band parametric amplifier; X-band passive array; X-

band planar array; X-band power amplifier
xpaa: X-band planar-array antenna
XPARS: External Research Publication and Retrieval System
XPC: inshore patrol cutter (naval symbol)
xpd: expedite
xper: without privileges
Xper: Christopher
XPG: converted merchant ship (naval symbol)
xpl: explosive
xplo: explosion
xplt: exploit
xpn: expansion
Xpo: *Cristo* (Spanish—Christ)
xpond: transponder
xpp: *exprès payé lettre* (French—express-paid letter)
xppa: X-band pseudo-passive array; X-band pulsed-power amplifier
xpr: ex privileges; without privileges
xprs: express
xps: X-band phase shifter
xpt: *exprès payé télégraphe* (French—express-paid telegraph)
Xpto: *Cristóbal* (Spanish—Christopher)
X-punch: punch in X row (11th row) of an 80-column punchcard
xq: cross-question
XQ: Experimental Target Drone
xqh: xenon quartz helix
xr: ex rights; Xerox radiography
Xr: Christopher; examiner
XR: External Relations (UNESCO)
X-rated movie: moving picture not recommended for minors
Xray: code word for letter X
X-ray: photograph or photography made by X-rays; radiograph; radiography; roentgenograph; roentgenography; roentgen ray
X-ray Discoverer: Wilhelm Konrad Roentgen
xrb: X-band radar beacon
XCR: Extraterrestrial Research Center
xrcd: X-ray crystal density
xrd: X-ray diffraction
X rds: crossroads
xref: cross-reference
xrep: auxiliary report
xrf: X-ray fluorescence
xrii: X-ray image intensifier
xrl: extended-range lance (missile)
xrm: X-ray microanalyzer
xro: xeroradiography
X-roads: crossroads
xrpm: X-ray projection microscope
xrpt: X-ray and photofluorography technician
xrspec: X-ray spectograph
xrt: ex-rights; without rights; X-ray technician
Xrx: Xerox (corporation or copying process)
xs: cross-section; excess; extra strength; extra strong
Xs: atmospherics
xsa: X-band satellite antenna
xsal: xenon short arc lamp
XSB: Xavier Society for the Blind
X-scale: scale of a line parallel to the horizon
x sec: extra sec *(très sec)*—dry champagne
xsect: cross-section
xsf: X-ray scattering facility
xsistor: transistor
XSL: Experimental Space Laboratory
xsm: experimental strategic missile; experimental surface missile
X-sonad: experimental sonic azimuth detector
X-spot: $10 bill
xspv: experimental solid-propellant vehicle
xsr: X-band scatterometer radar
XSS: Experimental Space Station
xsta: X-band satellite-tracking antenna
xstd: X-band stripline tunnel diode
xstda: X-band stripline tunnel diode amplifier
xstr: transistor
x str: extra strong
xstrat: cross-stratified
xt: crosstalk; X-ray tube
Xt: Christ
xta: chiasmata; X-band tracking antenna
xtal: crystal
Xtet: (Swedish—the X)—Sven Erixson
Xth: tenth
Xtian: Christian
xtlo: crystal oscillator
xtnd: extend
xto: X-band triode oscillator
xtra: extra
xtran: experimental language
xtrm: extreme
xtry: extraordinary
xtwa: X-band traveling-wave amplifier
xtwm: X-band traveling-wave masser
Xty: Christianity
xu: x-unit
Xu: fire-resistive unprotected cabinet, safe, or vault
XU: Xavier University
xuv: extreme untraviolet
xva: X-ray videcon analysis
xvers: transverse
XVP: Executive Vice President
xvtr: transverter
xw: experimental warhead; ex warrants; without warrants
X-weld: X-shaped weld
XWS: Experimental Weapon System
xx: without securities or warrants
XX: doublecross; double strength
XX: *Dos Equis* (Spanish—Two X)—Mexican beer
XXer: doublecrosser
xxh: double extra hard; double extra heavy
XX: doublecross; double strength; female (see X chromosome)
XX-note (double-X note): $20 bill
xxs: extra-extra strength
xxx: international urgency signal
XXX: triple strength
XXXX: quadruple strength
XXXXX: quintuple strength
XXY: Klinefelter's syndrome wherein the sex-determining chromosomes are XXY instead of the normal XY
xy: xylography
XY: male
xya: x-y axis
xyat: x-y axis table
xyl: ex young lady (former sweetheart); xylene; xylography
xylo: xylophone
xyloc: xylocain (lidocaine)
xylog: xylography
xyp: x-y plotter
xyr: x-y recorder
x yr dev: ten-year device (US Army service badge)
xyt: x-y table
xyv: x-y vector
XYY syndrome: unusually aggressive male having an extra Y-sex chromosome
XYZ: XYZ Affair leading to undeclared naval war between France and the United States from 1798 to 1800
X zone: adrenal cortex inner zone (of some young mammals)

Y

y: altitude (symbol); depth or height (symbol); an ordinate (symbol); an unknown quantity (symbol); yard; year; yellow; yen (Japanese monetary unit)
Y: Convair (symbol); service test (symbol); yacht; Yankee—code for letter Y; yen (Japanese money unit); YMCA; YMHA; YWCA; YWHA
Y: admittance (symbol); lateral axis (symbol); *ylös* (Finnish—up)
Y1C: Yeoman First Class
Y2C: Yeoman Second Class
Y3C: Yeoman Third Class
Y-18: Ilyushin 18 aircraft
Y-40: Yak 40 aircraft
Y62: Ilyushin Il-Y62 jet airplane
ya: yaw axis
YA: Youth Aliyah; Youth Authority
Y/A: York-Antwerp Rules
YAA: Yachtsmen's Association of America
YAAP: Young Americans Against Pollution
YABA: Yacht Architects and Brokers Association
YACH: Yugoslav-American Cooperative Home
yadh: yeast alcohol dehydrogenase (YADH)
YAEC: Yankee Atomic Electric Company
YAF: Young Americans for Freedom
YAF-PAC: Young Americans for Freedom—Political Action Committee
yag: yttrium aluminum garnet
YAG: district auxiliary miscellaneous (3-letter naval symbol)
yagl: yttrium-aluminum garnet laser
YAIC: Young American Indian Council
Yak: Yakolev; Yakov; Yakovlevich
Yak: *Yakarta* (Spanish—Djakarta)
YAK: Yakolev aircraft (named for its designer)
Yakumo Koizumi: Lafacadio Hearn's Japanese name
yal: yttrium-aluminum laser
YAL: Young Australia League
Yale LJ: *Yale Law Journal*
YAM: Yates American Machine (company)
YAN: Yancey (railroad); Young American Nazis
YANCON: Yankee Conference (intercollegiate sports)
Yank: Yankee; Yankel
YANK: Youth of America Needs to Know
Yankee: code for letter Y
Yankee Clipper: Joe Di Maggio
Yanko-Spanko Conflict: Spanish-American War (so named in 1899 by historian Arthur Bird "Ex-Vice-Consul-General of America at Port-au-Prince, Hayti")
yap.: yaw and pitch
Yar: Yarmouth
YAR: Yemen Arab Republic (Sana—capital); York-Antwerp Rules (insurance)
YARA: Young Americans for Responsible Action
'yard: shipyard
Yard: Scotland Yard
YARD: Yarrow-Admiralty Research Department
Yard(s): Montagnard(s)—nickname derived from pronunciation of the last syllable in Montagnard(s)
yarden: yard + garden
yas: yaw-attitude sensor
YA's: Young Adults (young people)
YASD: Young Adult Services Division (ALA)
Yasnaya Polyana: (Russian—Clear Glade)—Tolstoy family home near Tula about 177 kilometers (110 miles) south of Moscow
YASSR: Yakut Autonomous Soviet Socialist Republic
Yat: *Yatyiopia* (Amharic—Ethopia)
yavis: young, attractive, verbal, intelligent, and successful
YAWF: Youth Against War and Facism
Y-axis: vertical axis on a chart, graph or map
Yb: ytterbium
YB: yearbook
YBA: Young Buddhist Association
YBC: Yerba Buena Center
yBr: yellowish brown
YBR: sludge-removal barge (3-letter naval symbol)
YBRA: Yellowstone-Bighorn Research Association
Y-branch: Y-shaped pipe fitting
yc: yaw channel; yaw coupling; yellow chrome
Y-c: Y-chromosome
YC: open lighter (2-letter naval symbol); Yacht Club; Yankton College; York College; Yuba College
YCA: Yachting Club of America; Young Citizens' Army; Youth Camping Association
YCC: Youth Conservation Corps
YCCA: Youth Council on Civic Affairs
YCCC: Yui Chui Chan Club
YCD: feuling barge (naval symbol); Youth Correction Division (US Dept Justice)
YCF: car float (naval symbol); Young Calvinist Federation
Y-chromosome: male-producing gene found in male sperm
YCI: Young Communist International
YCI: *Yacht Club Italia* (Italian Yacht Club)
YCia: Ybarra Compañía (steamship line)
YCK: open cargo lighter (3-letter naval symbol)
YCL: Yarmouth Cruise Lines; York City Library; Young Communist League
YCNM: Yucca House National Monument
ycp: yaw-coupling parameter
YCS: Young Catholic Students; Young Christian Students
yct: yacht
YCTF: Younger Chemists Task Force
YCU: aircraft transportation lighter (naval symbol)
YC & UO: Young Conservative and Unionist Organisation
YCV: aircraft transportation lighter (3-letter naval symbol)
ycw: you can't win

YCW: Young Christian Workers
yd: yard
yd^2: square yard(s)
yd^3: cubic yard(s)
YD: floating derrick (2-letter naval symbol); Yugoslav dinar
Y & D: Yards and Docks (USN)
YDA: Dawson City, Yukon Territory (airport)
yday: yesterday
ydb: yield-diffusion bonding
ydc: yaw-damping computer
YDCA: Youth Democratic Clubs of America
ydg: yarding
YDG: degaussing vessel (naval symbol)
ydi: yard drain inlet
YDI: Youth Development Incorporated
YDL: Young Development Laboratories
ydmn: yardman
ydmstr: yardmaster
yds: yards
Yds: Yards (postal place-name abbreviation)
YDS: Yale Divinity School
YDSD: Yards and Docks Supply Depot (USN)
YDSO: Yards and Docks Supply Office
YDT: diving tender (naval symbol)
Y-duct: Y-shaped duct
ye: yellow-edged; yellow edges; yellow edging
y^e: (Early English—thou)—also written ye
YE: aircraft homing system
yea.: yaw-error amplifier
YEA: Yale Engineering Association
yearb: yearbook
Year 1905: Shostakovich's Symphony No. 11
Year 1917: Shostakovich's Symphony No. 12
YEB: Yorkshire Electricity Board
Yedo: Tokyo's old name
yeg: yeast extract—glucose
YEG: Edmonton, Alberta (International Airport)
yegg: yeggman (burglar specializing in opening safes and vaults)
yel: yellow
Yellow Emperor: Huang Ti
yellow flag: yellow signal flag flown when a vessel requests pratique; letter Q or Quebec in the international code; also called the quarantine flag
Yellowhammer: Alabama state bird; symbolic nickname of an Alabaman
Yellowhammer State: Alabama
yellowjack: quarantine flag; yellow fever; yellow flag
Yellow River: China's Hwang Ho
Yel NP: Yellowstone National Park
yelsh: yellowish
yem: yeast extract—malt
Yem: Yemen; Yemenite
Yeo: Yeoman
YEO: Youth Employment Office(r)
Yeoman F: Yeoman Female (naval rating)
yeomn: yeomanry
yep: your educational plans
yepd: yeast extract—peptone, dextrose
YES: Youth Educational Services; Youth Employment Service
yesty: yesterday
YEWTIC: Yorkshire, East and West Ridings, Technical Information Centre
yf: wife (simplified orthographic contraction proposed by Benjamin Franklin)
yf (YF): yellow fever
YF: covered lighters (naval symbol)
YF-16: air-superiority single-engine lightweight-fighter aircraft (USAF)
YFB: ferryboat or launch (naval symbol)
YFC: car float (3-letter naval symbol); Young Farmers' Club
YFCU: Young Farmers' Clubs of Ulster
YDF: floating drydock (naval symbol)
YFFP: Yarrawonga Flora and Fauna Park (Australian Northern Territory)
YFN: covered lighter, nonself-propelled (naval symbol)
YFNB: large covered lighter (naval symbol)
YFND: drydock companion craft (naval symbol)
YFNX: special-purpose lighter (naval symbol)
YFP: floating power barge (naval symbol)
YFR: self-propelled refrigerated covered lighter (naval symbol)
YFRN: refrigerated covered lighter, nonself-propelled (naval symbol)
YFRT: covered lighter, range tender (naval symbol)
YFT: torpedo transportation lighter (naval symbol)
yfu: yard freight unit
YfU: Youth for Understanding (teenage exchange program)
YFU: harbor utility craft (naval symbol)
y fwd: yard forward (knitting)
yG: yellowish green
YG: garbage lighter (naval symbol); yellow green
ygl: yttrium-garnet laser
YGN: garbage lighter, nonself-propelled (naval symbol)
YGR: Yankari Game Reserve (Nigeria)
YGS: Young Guard Society
Y-gun: Y-shaped gun used aboard ships for firing depth charges
YH: Youth Hostel
YHA: Youth Hostels Association
Yhama: Yokohama
YHANI: Youth Hostel Association of Northern Ireland
YHB: houseboat (naval symbol)
YHLC: salvage lift craft, heavy (naval ship symbol)
YHt: Young-Helmholtz theory
YHT: heating scow (naval symbol)
Yi: Yiddish
YIC: Yardney International Corporation
Yid: Yiddish; Yiddish-speaking person
Yie: Young interference experiment
yig: yttrium iron garnet (ferrite)
yigib: your improved group insurance benefits
YIJS: Young Israel Institute for Jewish Studies
YIKOR: *Yidishe kultur-organizatsye* (Polish—Yiddish Culture Organization)
yil: yellow indicator lamp
Yinglish: Yiddish-English
yip: yippie (politically-active hippie)
YIP: Detroit, Michigan (Willow Run Airport); Youth International Party (members, including narcotic-addicted hippies, called yippies)
YI & S: Yawata Iron and Steel
Yivo Inst: Yivo Institute for Jewish Research
yj: radar homing beacon (map symbol)
YJC: York Junior College
Y-joint: Y-shaped joint
yk: radar beacon (map symbol)
yl: yellow; young lady
Yk: Yakut; York
YK: Yankee Airlines (2-letter

code)
Yka: Yokohama
YKF: Yiddisher Kulture Farband (Yiddish Culture Club)
YKKK: Yamashita Kisen Kabushiki Kaisha (steamship line)
Yks: Yorkshire
Ykt: Yakut
yl: yellow; yield limit; young lady
Y & L: York and Lancaster
Y & LR: York and Lancaster Regiment
YLA: open landing lighter (naval symbol)
YLI: Young Ladies Institute; Yorkshire Light Infantry
YLJ: *Yale Law Journal*
YLLC: salvage lift crane, light (naval ship symbol)
yl's: young ladies
ym: yacht measurement; yellow metal; your message
YM: dredge (naval symbol); Yehudi Menuhin
YMA: Yarn Merchants Association
ymb: yeast malt broth
YMBA: Yacht and Motor Boat Association
YMCA: Young Men's Christian Association
YM Cath A: Young Men's Catholic Association
YMCU: Young Men's Christian Union
ymd: your message date
Yme: Young's modulus of elasticity
YMF: Young Musicians Foundation
YMFS: Young Men's Friendly Society
YMHA: Young Men's Hebrew Association
YMHAL: Young Men's Hebrew Association Library
YMI: Young Men's Institute
YMLC: salvage lift craft, medium (naval ship symbol)
YMP: motor mine planter (naval symbol)
YMPA: Young Master Printers' Alliance
yms: yield measurement system
YMS: motor minesweepers (naval symbol)
YMT: motor tug (naval symbol)
YMV: Yazoo and Mississippi Valley (railroad)
YM & YWHA: Young Men's and Young Women's Hebrew Association
yn: yen
y-n: yes-no
YN: net tender (naval symbol)
yng: young
YNG: gate vessel (naval symbol)
YNHA: Yosemite Natural History Association
Y-NHH: Yale-New Haven Hospital
YNP: Yellowstone National Park (Idaho, Montana, Wyoming); Yoho NP (British Columbia); Yosemite NP (California)
YNT: net tender, tug (naval symbol)
Ynv: *Ynvar* (Russian—January)
YNWR: Yazoo National Wildlife Refuge (Mississippi)
yo: yarn over (knitting); year old
yo': yore; you; your
y/o: years old
YO: fuel-oil barge (naval symbol); Yerkes Observatory
YOAN: Youth Of All Nations
yob: year of birth
YOC: Youth Opportunity Campaign; Youth Opportunity Center(s); Youth Opportunity Corps
YOC-RSPB: Young Ornithologists' Club—Royal Society for the Protection of Birds
yod: year of death
YOG: gasoline barge, self propelled (naval symbol)
Yogi: Lawrence Peter Berra also known as Yogi Berra
YOGN: gasoline barge, nonself-propelled (naval symbol)
Yok: Yokohama
Yoko: Yokohama
yom: year of marriage
Yom: *Yomiuri* (Japanese—News Crier)—Tokyo's popular newspaper serving nearly six million subscribers
YOM: yellow oxide of mercury
Yomiuri: (Japanese—Reading for Sale)—leading newspaper of Japan
yon: yonder
YON: fuel-oil barge, nonself-propelled (naval symbol)
yood: (slang pronunciation—iud)—intrauterine device; intrauterine diaphragm
YOP: Youth Opportunity Program
York: (turn-of-our-century slang—New York; New York State)
York: *Yorkshire Post*
Yorks: Yorkshire
Yorkshire Queen of Song: Susan Sunderland
York State: New York State (especially the upstate section)
YOS: oil storage barge (naval symbol)
Yos NP: Yosemite National Park
YOU: Youth Organizations United
you'd: you had; you would
you'll: you shall; you will
Young Hickory: James K. Polk—eleventh President of the United States
Youngs: Youngstown
you're: you are
Youth Personified: Juventus (Latin—youth)
youthploit: youth exploitation (commercial exploitation of guillible youngsters)
you've: you have
YOW: Ottawa, Ontario (airport)
yp: yield limit; yield point (psi)
YP: patrol craft (2-letter naval symbol); yellow peril; young people; young person(s)
ypa: yaw-precession amplifier
YPA: Young Pioneers of America
ypd: yaw-phase detector
YPD: floating pile driver (naval symbol)
YPEC: Young Printing Executives Club
YPF: *Yacimientos Petroliferos Fiscales* (Spanish—Government Oil Deposits)—Argentina
YPFB: *Yacimientos Petroliferos Fiscales Bolivianos* (Spanish—Bolivian Government Oil Deposits)
YPG: Yuma Proving Ground
yPk: yellowish pink
YPK: pontoon stowage barge (naval symbol)
YPM: Yale Peabody Museum
YPO: Young Presidents' Organization; Youth Programs Office (Bureau of Indian Affairs)
Yps: Ypsilanti
YPSCE: Young People's Society of Christian Endeavor
YPSL: Young People's Socialist League
Y-punch: punch in Y row (12th row) of an 80-column punchcard
YQX: Gander, Newfoundland (airport)
yr: year; younger; your
y-r: yaw roll
YR: district patrol vessel (naval symbol); floating workshop (2-letter naval symbol)
YRA: Yacht Racing Association
Yr B: Year Book
YRB: submarine repair and berthing barge (naval symbol)

YRBM: submarine repair—berthing and messing barge (naval symbol)
YRC: submarine rescue chamber (naval symbol)
YRD: submarine repair and berthing vessel (3-letter naval symbol)
YRDH: floating drydock hull workshop (naval symbol)
YRDM: floating drydock machinery workshop (naval symbol)
YRL: covered repair lighter (naval symbol)
yrly: yearly
YRNF: Young Republican National Federation
YRR: radiological repair barge (3-letter naval symbol)
yrs: years; yours
Yrs: Yours
YRs: Young Republicans
YRST: salvage craft tender (naval ship symbol)
yrs ty: yours truly
ys: yellow spot (on retina); yield strength
Ys: Yugoslavia; Yugoslavian
YS: Yard Superintendent; Young Socialists
Y & S: Youngstown & Southern (railroad)
YSA: Young Socialist Alliance
ysb: yield-stress bonding
YBS: Yacht Safety Bureau
YSC: Yugoslav Seamen's Club; Youth Studies Center (juvenile correctional facility in Philadelphia)
YSD: seaplane wrecking derrick (naval symbol)
ysdb: yield-stress diffusion bonding
yse: yaw-steering error
Yseult: Isolde
ysh: yellowish
Ysl: Ysrael
YSL: Yves Saint Laurent
YSO: Youngstown Symphony Orchestra
ysp: years service for severance pay purposes
YSP: pontoon salvage vessel (naval symbol)
ysr: you're so right
YSR: sludge-removal barge (naval symbol)
YSS: Young Scots Society
yst: youngest
YST: Yukon Standard Time
YS & T: Youngstown Sheet & Tube
YSTO: Yugoslav State Tourist Office
YSU: Youngstown State University
yt: yoke top
Yt: yttrium
YT: harbor tug (naval symbol); Yukon Territory
Y & T: Tale & Towne
YTA: Yiddish Theatrical Alliance
ytb: yarn to back
YTB: large-harbor tug (naval symbol)
ytf: yarn to front
YTL: small-harbor tug (naval symbol)
YTM: medium-harbor tug (naval symbol)
YTP: *Yeni Türkiye Partisi* (New Turkish Party)—socialist oriented
YTPM: Yuma Territorial Prison Museum
YTS: Yuma Test Station
YTT: torpedo-testing barge (naval symbol)
Y-tube: Y-shaped tube
YTV: Yokohama Television
Yu: Yugoslav; Yugoslavian
YU: Yale University; Yeshiva University; York University; Youngstown University; Yugoslavia (auto plaque)
YUAG: Yale University Art Gallery
Yuc: Yucatan
Yucca: New Mexico state flower
Yucca Country: the Southwest (ern United States)
Yud: Yudel
Yugo: Yugoslav; Yugoslavia; Yugoslavian
Yuk: Yukon
YUK: Youth Uncovering Krud (antipollution society)
YUL: Montreal, Quebec (airport); Yale University Library
Yu-Lin: Betty Yü-Lin Ho
YULRC: Yale University Lung Research Center
YUO: Yale University Observatory
yup: you're uncommonly perceptive
YUP: Yale University Press
Yur: Yuri; Yurievich
Yuri Bilstin: Youry Bildstein
Yus: Yussel
YUSM: Yale University School of Medicine
Yv: Yvette; Yvonne
YV: Young's Version
yvc: yellow-varnish cambric
YVC: Yakima Valley College
YVF: Young Volunteer Force
YVHS: Yorkville Vocational High School
YVJC: Yakima Valley Junior College
YVP: Youth Voter Participation
YVR: Vancouver, British Columbia (airport)
YVRL: Yakima Valley Regional Library
YVT: Yakima Valley Transportation (railroad)
y v v: *y viaje vuelta* (Spanish—and return trip)
YW: water barge (naval symbol)
YWCA: Young Women's Christian Association
YWCAUSA: Young Women's Christian Association of the U.S.A.
YWCTU: Young Women's Christian Temperance Union
YWF: Young World Federalists
YWG: Winnipeg, Manitoba (airport)
YWHA: Young Women's Hebrew Association
YWHS: Young Women's Help Society
YWLL: Young Workers Liberation League
YWN: nonself-propelled barge (naval symbol)
YWS: Young Wales Society
YWU: Yiddish Writers Union
y-y: yaw axis
YY: pseudonymous initials of Robert Lynd noted for his *New Statesman* essays
YYC: Calgary, Alberta (airport)
YYZ: Toronto, Ontario (airport)

Z

z: complex variable (symbol); z-bar; zee (American usage); zed (British usage); zero; zinc; zone
z: *zu* (German—closed; shut)
Z: atomic number (symbol); azimuth (symbol); gram equivalent weight (symbol); impedance (symbol); lighter-than-air aircraft (symbol); obsolete (symbol); radius of circle of least confusion (symbol); zenith; zenith distance; zero meridian time; Zionism; Zionist; Zoroaster; Zoroastrian; Zoroastrianism; Zulu—code for letter Z
Z: normal axis (symbol); *Zeit* (German—time); *Zeitschrift* (German—periodical publication); *zuid* (Dutch—south)
Z¹, Z², Z³: first degree of contraction, second degree of contraction, third degree of contraction
Z39: Library Work, Documentation, and Related Publishing Practices (American National Standards Institute Standards Committee)
za: zero absolute; zero and add
zaap: zero antiaircraft potential
zab: zabaglione; zinc-air battery
za: *zirka* German—about; approximately)
Za: *Zéro absolu* (French—absolute zero)
ZA: *Zuid Afrika* (Afrikaans or Dutch—South Africa)
zab: *zabaglione* (Italian—egg-yolk-and-wine dessert)
Zab: Zaboj
Zab: *Zabriskie's Reports*
Zac: Zacatecas
ZAC: Zale Award Committee; zinc ammonium chloride
Zach: Zachary; Zachariah; Zacharias; Zachary; Zachris
Zack: Zachariah; Zacharias; Zachary
Zad: Zadar; Zadock
ZADCA: Zinc Alloy Die Casters' Association
ZAED: *Zentralstelle für Atomkernenergie Dokumentation* (German—Atomic Energy Documentation Center)
Z-Afrika: *Zuid-Afrika* (Dutch—South Africa)
zag: *zaguán* (Spanish—passageway from street door to central patio of homes in Mexico and American Southwest)
Zag: Zagreb
ZAG: Zagreb, Yugoslavia (airport)
Zahal: *Zva Hagana Leyisrael* (Hebrew—Israel Defense Forces)
Zahlentaf: *Zahlentafeln* (German—table of illustrations)
zai: zero address instruction
zai: *zaibatsu* (Japanese—money clique)—plutocratic oligarchy of wealthy families such as the Mitsubishi, Mitsui, Sumitomo, etc.
Zai: Zaire
Zaire: formerly Congo (Leopoldville), Republic of the Congo, the Belgian Congo
zak: *zaklyuchenny* (Russian—prisoner)—pronounced *zek*
zal: *zaliv* (Russian—bay)
Zal: *Zalmen* (Yiddish—Solomon)
ZALIS: Zinc and Lead International Service
zam: Z-axis modulation
Zam: Zambia; Zamboanga; Zamora
Zamb: Zambia
Zambia: formerly Northern Rhodesia
Zambo: Zamboanga
ZAMPA: Zanzibar and Madagascar Peoples Airway
zam(s): examination(s)
Zan: Zanzibar
ZANU: Zimbabwe African National Union
Zanzi: Zanzibar
zap: zero and add packed; zero antiaircraft potential
zap: *zapad* (Russian—west)
Zap: Zapotec; Zapotecan
zapb: zinc-air primary battery
ZAPU: Zimbabwe Africa People's Union
zar: zeus acquisition radar
Zar: Zaragoza
Zara: Zarathustra (Zoroaster)
ZARPS: *Zuid-Afrikaansche Republiek Polisie* (Afrikaans—South African Republic Police)
zas: zero-access storage
ZASM: *Zuid Afrikaansche Spoorweg Maatschappij* (South African Railway serving the Transvaal at the turn of the century)
zasts: zastrugas
zat: zinc atomspheric tracer
ZAT: *Zaterdag* (Dutch—Saturday)
Z-A test: Zondek-Ascheim test (for pregnancy)
ZAW: *Zuid-Afrikaansche Weehuis* (Afrikaans—South African Orphan Asylum)
Zazen: Zen meditation
zb: zero beat
z B: *zum Beispiel* (German—for instance)
ZB: Zen Buddhist
Z-bar: Z-shaped bar
zbe: zinc battery electrode
zbl: zero-based linearity
Zbl: *Zentralblatt* (German—central publication)
zbr: zero-beat reception; zero-bend radius
ZBS: Zambia Broadcasting Services
ZC: Zale Corporation; Zionist Congress; Zonta Club; Zouave Corps; Zuñian Club
z of c: zones of communication
ZC: Zionist Congress
ZCA: Zirconium Corporation of America
ZCBC: Zambian Consumer Buying Corporation
ZCL: *Zona di Commercio Libero* (Italian—Free Trade Zone)
Z-clip: Z-shaped clip
zcm: zero cerebral muscle
ZCMI: Zion's Cooperative Mercantile Institution
zcn: zinc-coated nut
zcs: zinc-coated screw
ZCSU: Zim Container Service Unit
zcw: zinc-coated washer
zd: zener diode; zero defects
Zd: zenith distance
ZD: zenith description; zero defects (quality-control goal); zond description
ZDA: Zero Defects Association;

Zinc Development Association
zdc: zinc die casting
ZDC: Zero Defects Council
zdg: zinc-doped germanium
Zdm: Zaandam
ZDP: Zero Defects Program; Zero Defects Proposal
zdpa: zero defects program audit
zdpg: zero defects program guideline
zdpo: zero defects program objective
zdpr: zero defects program responsibility
zdr: zeus discrimination radar
ZDR: *Zentraldeutsche Rundfunk* (Central German Radio)
ZDS: Zinc Detection System
zdt: zero-ductility transition
ze: zero effusion; zone effect
Ze: José
Z-E: Zollinger-Ellison (syndrome)
zE: *zum Exempel* (German—for example)
zea: zero-energy assembly
Zeb: Zebedee; Zebulon
zebra.: zero-energy breeder reactor assembly
zebrass: zebra + ass—hybrid of zebra and jenny ass or zebress and jackass
Zebrule: zebra + horse—hybrid of male zebra and domestic mare
zec: zero-energy coefficient
zecc: zinc electrochemical cell
Zech.: Zechariah (book of the Bible)
zed: (obsolete phonetic word—z; zero)
Zed: Zedekiah
Zedland: English shires of Devon, Dorset, and Somerset where *s* is often pronounced so it sounds like *z* or *zed*
Zee: Zellerbach
zeep: zero energy experimental pile
zeg: zero economic growth
zei: zero environmental impact
Zeichn: *Zeichnung(en)* [German—drawing(s)]
Zeke: Ezekiel
zel (ZEL): zero-length launcher
Zel: Zelia; Zelide
Zelda: Griselda
zell: zero-length launching
zen: zenith (highest point)
Zen: Zen Buddhism; Zen Buddhist; Zengo; Zenith; Zenobe; Zenobia; Zenobio; Zenón; Zenophon; Zentippe; Zenus
Zenga: *Zengakuren* (Japanese leftwing students)
zenith: zero-energy nitrogen-heated thermal reactor
Zenith City of the Unsalted Sea: Duluth, Minnesota on Lake Superior leading to the other Great Lakes
ZENRO: *Zen Nihon Rodo Kumiai Kaigi* (Japanese—All-Japan Trade Union Congress)
Zentr: *Zentralblatt* (German—journal)
zeony: zebra + pony (hybrid)
Zep: Giuseppe
Zeph.: Zephaniah (book of the Bible)
zephyr: warm westerly breeze
zepp: zeppelin
Zeppo Marx: Herbert Marx
zep(s): zeppelin(s)
zer: zero-energy reflection
zerc: zero-energy reflection coefficient
zero-g: zero gravity (weightlessness)
Zero Mostel: Sam Mostel
zert: zero-reaction tool
ZES: Zero Energy System
zet: zetetic(s)
zeta.: zero energy thermonuclear assembly
zetr: zero-energy thermal reactor
zeug: zeugma; zeugmatic; zeugmatically
ZEUS: Zero-Energy Uranium System
Zeus: (Greek—Jupiter)—god of the heavens also called Jove
zf: zero frequency
z/f: zone of fire
ZF: *Zagrebacka Filharmonija* (Croatian—Zagreb Philharmonic)
ZFGBI: Zionist Federation of Great Britain and Ireland
ZFMA: Zip Fastener Manufacturers' Association
Z f N: *Zeitschrift für Namenforschung* (German—Journal for the Study of Place-names)
zfp: zyglo-fluorescent penetrant
zfpt: zyglo-flurescent penetrant testing
zfs: zero field splitting
ZFV: *Zentrale für Fremdenverkehr* (German—Central Tourist Association)
z/g: zoster-immune globulin
Zg: Zug
ZG: Zoological Gardens
Z-gas: Zyklon-B gas (deadly)
zge: zero-gravity effect; zero-gravity environment; zero-gravity expulsion
zget: zero-gravity expulsion technique
ZGF: Zero Gravity Facility
zgg: zero gravity generator
zgh: zero-gravity harmonic
ZGM: Zeitner Geological Museum
Z-grams: Admiral Zumwalt's policy statements
zgs: zero-gravity simulator
zgs (ZGS): zero gradient synchrotron
Z-gun: anti-aircraft rocket gun
zh: zinc heads (freight)
zH: *zu Händen* (German—care of; deliver to)
ZH: lighter-than-air search and rescue aircraft (2-letter naval symbol)
ZH: *Zone d'Habitation* (French—residential area)
Zhg: *Zhongguo* (Chinese—China)
zhr: zirconium hydride reactor
Z hr: zero hour
ZHRC: Zinsmaster Hol-Ry Company
zhs: zero hoop stress
ZHS: Zion Historical Society
Zi: Zollner illusion
ZI: Zim Israel (steamship line); Zone of the Inferior; Zonta International
ZI: *Zone Industrielle* (French—industrial zone); *Zone Interdite* (French—prohibited zone)
ZIA: Zone of the Interior Armies
ZID: Zionist Immigration Depot
Zier: Ziervogel process
zig: zero immune globulin
Zig: Ziegfield; Zigfield; Zigfrid; Zigfrids
zig (ZIG): zoster-immune globulin
zig(s): *zigaboo(s)* [(British West Indian—Black(s)]
zigzag line: symbol of water
zil: zillion (a number beyond belief)
ZIL: (Russian—*Zavod Imieni Likhatov*)—Likhatov Auto Factory producing a Packard-like luxury car formerly named for Stalin—the ZIS *(Zavod Imieni Stalin)*
Zilli: Cecilia
zim: zonal interdiction missile
Zim: Zimmerman(n)
Zim: *Zi Mischari* (Hebrew—merchant fleet) as in Zim Israel Line
Zimb: Zimbabwe (African name for Rhodesia)
Zimbabwe: Rhodesia; Southern Rhodesia
Zimco: Zambia Industrial and Mining Company
ZINC: Zim Israel Navigation

Company (Zim Israel Line)
zinco: zincograph
ZINCO: Zim Israel Navigation Company
zincog: zincography)
zinc white: zinc oxide (ZnO)
zineb: zinc ethylenebis (fungicide)
zine(s): magazine(s)
Zinj: Zinjanthropus
Zinoviev, Grigori Evseevich: Hirsch Apfelbaum
zip: zero (slang); zinc impurity photodetector; zipper (slide fastener or similar device)
ZIP: Zone Improvement Plan (US Post Office Zip Code)
zir: zero internal resistance
ZIR: Zug Island Road (Delray Connecting Railroad)
ziram: zinc dimethyldithiocarbamate (fungicide)
ZIRCOA: Zirconium Corporation of America
zircon: zirconium silicate ($ZrSiO_4$)
Zirk Hagen: *Zirkus Hagenbeck* (German—Hagenbeck Circus)
zirox: zirconium oxide (ZrO_2)
ZISS: Zebulon Israel Seafaring Society
zith: zither
zix: zinc isopropyl xanthate
zj: zipper(ed) jacket
zj: *zonder jaartel* (Dutch—without date of publication)
zkrat: *zkratka(y)* [Czech—abbreviation(s)]
zl: freezing drizzle (meteorological symbol)
Zl: zloty (Polish ruble)
ZL: freezing drizzle (symbol)
ZLA: Zambia Library Association
zld: zero level drift; zero lift drag; zodiacal light device
zlg: zero line gap
zll: zero length launch
zm: zoom; zoomar (variable focus lens)
ZM: Zubin Mehta
ZM: *Zeevaart Maatschappij* (Dutch—navigation company); *Zona Militare* (Italian—Military Zone)—restricted area
Z-M: Zuckerman-Moloff (sewage treatment)
Z-man: U.S. Army reserve
zmar: zeus malfunction array radar
Zmbbw: Zimbabwe (Rhodesia; Southern Rhodesia)
ZMC: Zion Mule Corps
Zmd: Zung measurement of depression
zmkr: zone marker
ZMMD: Zurich, Mainz, Munich, Darmstadt (algol processor joint effort of universities in those cities)
ZMRI: Zinc Metals Research Institute
ZMT: Zip (Zone Improvement Plan) Mail Translator (post office sorting device)
Z m Z: *Z mého Zivota* (Czechoslovakian—From my Life)—Smetana's String Quartet No. 1 revealing the happiest and the saddest moments of his life
zn: zenith
zn: *zelfstandig naamwoord:* (Dutch—substantive noun)—any group of words or a pronoun serving as a noun
Zn: true azimuth (symbol); zinc
ZN: *Zuid-Nederlands* (Dutch—South Netherlands)—Belgium
Znak: (Polish—Sign)—Roman Catholic pro-government party
ZnO: zinc oxide
Znpgc: azimuth per gyro compass
ZNP: Zimbabwe National Park (Rhodesia); Zion National Park (Utah)
ZNPM: Zion National Park Museum
ZNPP: Zanzibar and Pemba People's Party
znr: zinc resistor
ZNZ: Zanatska Nabarnoproajna Zadruga (Yugoslavian—Procurement Sales Cooperative)
zo: zero output
ZO: Zionist Organization
ZO: *Zone Occupée* (French—Occupied Zone); *zuidoost* (Dutch—southeast)
ZOA: Zionist Organization of America
ZOB: *Zentral Omnibus Bahnhof* (German—Central Bus Depot)
zoba: bull + yak—hybrid offspring of common bull and yak cow
zobo: cow + yak—hybrid of yak bull and common cow
zoc: *zócalo* (Mexican Spanish—public square)
zod.: *zodiacus* (Latin—circle of animals)—the zodiac
zoe: zero energy; zinc-oxide eugenol
zof: zone of fire
Zog: Ahmed Zogu
Zoh: *Zohar* (The Book of Splendor)
Zola of America: Sir Arthur Conan Doyle's apt nickname for Upton Sinclair who declared: *mankind will not consent to be lied to indefinitely*
Zon: *Zondag* (Dutch—Sunday)
Zondervan: Zondervan Publishing House
Zone: Panama Canal Zone
Zonian(s): American(s) of the Panama Canal Zone
zoo: zoological (garden); zoology
zoochem: zoochemistry
zoogeog: zoogeography
zool: zoologic: zoological; zoologist; zoology
zoomorph: zoomorphic initial letter
zoopal: zoopaleontology
zoopar: zooparasitology
zoopath: zoopathology
zooph: zoophytology
zoopharm: zoopharmacology
zop: zinc-oxide pigment
zor: zone of reconnaissance
Zor: Zoroastrian
zos: zoster; zosteriform; zosteriformal
ZOS: Zapata Corporation (stock exchange symbol)
zot: (slang—zero)
zounds: (euphemistic contraction—god's wounds)
zox: zirconium oxide
zoz: *zie ommezijde* (Dutch—the other side)—please turn over (to the other side of the page)
ZP: lighter-than-air patrol and escort aircraft (naval symbol); Zellerbach Paper
ZP: *Zagrebian Philharmony* (Yugoslavian—Zagreb Philharmonic Orchestra)
Z & P: Zanzibar and Pemba
zpa: zeus program analysis
ZPA: Zeus Program Analysis; Zoological Parks and Aquariums
zpar: zeus-phased array (radar)
zpb: zinc primary battery
ZPC: Zellerbach Paper Company
ZPDA: Zinc Pigment Development Association
zpe: zero-point energy
ZPEN: Zeus Project Engineer Network
zpg: zero population growth
ZPG: Zero Population Growth
zp & j: *zonder plaats en jaar* (Dutch—without place of publication or date)
zpl: *zonder plaats* (Dutch—without place of publication)
Z Plz: Zellerbach Plaza
zpo: zinc peroxide

ZPO: Zeus Project Office
Zpp: Zeiss projection planetarium
zppr: zero-power plutonium reactor
zpr: zero-power reactor
zprf: zero-power reactor facility
ZPRSN: Zurich Provisional Relative Sunspot Number
ZPT: Zero Power Test
zr: freezing rain (meteorological symbol)
Zr: zirconium
Zr^{95}: radioactive zirconium
ZR: freezing rain (symbol); Zenith Radio
Z/R: Zone of Responsibility
zrc: zircorium carbide
ZRC: Zenith Radio Corporation
ZRCL: Zlac Rowing Club Limited
ZRH: Zurich, Switzerland (airport)
znr: zirconium nitride
zrp: zero radial play
zrt: zero-reaction tool
ZRU: *Zone de Rénovation Urbaine* (French—Urban Redevelopment Zone)
zs: zero shift; zero and subtract; zero surpress; zero suppression (of non-significant zeros in computer-printed numerals)
z S: *zur See* (German—of th navy)
Zs: *Zeitschrift* (German—periodical)
ZS: Zoological Society
zsb: zinc storage battery
zsc: zero subcarrier; chromaticity; zinc silicate coat(ing)
ZSC: Zoological Society of Cincinnati
Z-scale: height determination scale
zsd: zebra-stripe display; zinc sulfide detector
ZSDS: Zinc Sulfide Detection System
ZSE: Zagreb Soloists Ensemble *(Solisti di Zagreb)*
zsf: zero skip frequency
zsg: zero-speed generator
zsi: zero-size image
Zsig: Zsigmond
ZSI: Zoological Society of Ireland
ZSL: Zoological Society of London
ZSL: *Zjednoczone Stronnictwo Ludowe* (Polish—United Peasant Party)
ZSM: Zoar State Memorial
ZSN: Zoological Station of Naples
ZSP: Zoological Society of Philadelphia
zspg: zero-speed pulse generator
ZSS: Zinc Sulfide System
ZSSD: Zoological Society of San Diego
Zssg(n): *Zusammensetzung(en)* [German—compound word(S)]
zst: zero strength time (measurement)
ZST: Zone Standard Time
z T: *zum Teil* (German—partly)
Zt: *Zeit* (German—time)
ZT: lighter-than-air training aircraft (naval symbol); Zachary Taylor (12th President U.S.); zero time; zone time
ZT: *Zone Torride* (French—torrid zone)
Z de T: *Zulano de Tal* (Spanish—so and so)
ZTA: Zulu Territorial Authority
Z-test: Zulliger test
Ztg: *Zeitung* (German—newspaper)
Z-time: zebra time or zulu time (jargon for Greenwich Mean Time)
ZTO: Zone Transportation Office(r); Aürich Tonhalle Orchester (Zurich Concert Hall Orchestra)
ztp: zero temperature plasma
Ztr: *Zentner* (German—hundredweight)
Ztschr: *Zeitschrift* (German—periodical)
Z-TWIST: Z-shaped open-band twist
Zu: Zulu
ZU: lighter-than-air utility aircraft (2-letter naval symbol)
Zuck: *Zuckung* (German—contraction)—sometimes abbreviated *Z*
zuid: (Dutch—south)
Zuinglius: Latinization of Ulrich Zwingli's name
Zulu: code word for Greenwich mean time (Zulu time); code word for letter Z
Zur: Zürich
zus: *zusammen* (German—together)
Zus: *Zusammenfassung* (German—summary)
Zuschr: *Zuschrift(en)* [German—communication(s)]
Zut: Zutphen
zuverl: *zuverlassig* (German—authentic)
zv: *zu verfugung* (German—at disposal)
zv: zika virus
Zv: *Zolverein* (German—customs union)
ZVEI: *Zentralverband der Elektrotechnischen Industrie* (Central union of the Electrotechnical Industry)
zvrd: zener voltage regulator diode
zw: zero wear
zw: *zwart* (Dutch—black); *zwischen* (German—between; within)
ZW: *zuidwest* (Dutch—southwest)
zwc: zone wind computer
zwitt: zwitterion (diplole ion)
zwl: zero wave length
ZWO: *Zuiver Wetenschappelijk Onderzoek* (Netherlands Organization for the Advancement of Pure Research)
Zwol: Zwolle
zwp: zone wind plotter
zwv: zero wave velocity
ZYA: Zionist Youth Association
zyg: zygote
Zyg: Zygmunt
zygo: zygomatic; zygomaticus
zym: zymurgy
zymol: zymology
Zyr: Zyrian (Finno—Ugric language spoken by Zyrians in Komi SSR)
zyth: zythum (nancient beer beverage)
zythep: zythepsary (obsolete term for brewery)
zyz: zyzzyva
zz: increasing degrees of contraction (symbol); zigzag
zz.: *zingiber* (Latin—ginger)
z-z: longitudinal axis/roll axis
z-z fold: zig-zag fold (concertina fold)
z Z: *zur Zeit* (German—at present; for the time being)
ZZ: Ariana Afghan Airlines; zz-approach; zed-zed
ZZ: longitudinal or roll axis (symbol)
zza: zamack zinc alloy
ZZB: Zanzibar (tracking station)
zzc: zero-zero condition
zzd: zig-zag diagram
ZZO: *zuidzuidoost* (Dutch—south southeast)
zzr: zig-zag rectifier
z Zt: *zur Zeit* (German—at present; for the time being)
zzv: zero-zero visibility
ZZV: Zanesville, Ohio (airport)
ZZW: *zuidzuidwest* (Dutch—south southwest)
zzz-zzz-zzz: sawing or snoring (cartoonist symbol)

Airlines of the World

AA: American Airlines
AB: Keystone Commuter
AC: Air Canada
AD: Antilles Air Boats
AE: Air Ceylon
Aeronaves: Aeronaves de México (Mexico's largest air system)
AF: Air France
AG: AAT Airlines
AH: Air Algerie
AI: Air India
Air Canada: Canadian international airline
Air France: "the world's largest airline"
Air India: international Indian airline service
Air NZ: Air New Zealand
Air West: "serving 100 cities in the Western United States, Canada and Mexico"
AK: Altair Airlines
AL: Allegheny Airlines
Alaska: Alaska Airlines
Alitalia: international Italian airline
AM: Aeronaves de México
American: American Airlines
AN: Ansett Airlines of Australia
AO: Aviaco
AP: Apache Airlines
AQ: Air Paris
AR: Aerolineas Argentinas
AS: Alaska Airlines
AT: Royal Air Maroc
AU: Austral
AV: Avianca
AVENSA: *Aerovias Venezolanas* (Spanish—Venezuelan Airlines)
AVIANCA: Aerovias Nacionales de Colombia (Spanish—National Airlines of Colombia)
AW: Air Niger
AX: Air Togo
AY: Finnair
AZ: Alitalia
BA: BOAC (British Overseas Airways Corporation)
BD: British Midland Airways
BE: BEA (British European Airways)
BG: Guyana Airways
BH: Bahamas Airways
BI: Braniff International
BJ: Bakhtar Afghan Airlines
BK: BKS Air Transport
BL: Brothers Air Services
BM: Aero Transporti Italiana
BN: Braniff International Airways
BOAC: British Overseas Airways Corporation
BP: Botswana Airways
BR: British United Airways
Braniff: Braniff International
British European: British European Airways
BU: Braathens Air Transport
BV: BEA Helicopters
BW: BWIA (British West Indian Airways)
CB: Caribair
CC: Aerocosta
CD: Cardinal Airlines
CF: Faucett
CH: Chicago Helicopter Airways
CI: China Airlines
CK: Connair
CM: COPA (Compañía Panameña de Aviación—Panamanian Aviation Company)
CN: Craft Airlines
CO: Continental Airlines (Air Micronesia)
Continental: Continental Airlines
CP: CP Air (Canadian Pacific Airlines)
CP Air: Canadian Pacific Airlines
CQ: Aero-Chaco
CR: Commuter Airlnes
CS: Cambrian Airways
CT: Air Commuter Airlines
CU: Cubana Airlines
CW: Channel Airways
CX: Cathay Pacific Airways
CY: Cyprus Airways
CZ: Air Champagne Ardennes
DA: Dan-Air Services
DD: Command Airways
Delta: Delta Air Lines
DJ: Air Djibouti
DL: Delta Air Lines
DM: Maersk Air
DQ: Colony Airlines
DS: Air Senegal
DT: DTA (Divisão de Exploracão dos Transportes Aereos—Exploration Division of Air Transport)
DU: Del Air—Air Cargo
DW: Cross Sound Commuter Airlines
DX: Aerotaxi de Colombia
DY: Florence Airlines
EA: Eastern Airlines
Eastern: Eastern Airlines
EB: Metro-Aire Commuter Airlines
EC: East African Airways
EG: GCS Air Service
EI: Aer Lingus (Irish)
EK: Masling Airlines
El Al: El Al Israel Airlines
EO: Davey Air Services
EP: Aerolineas Peruanas
ER: Caribbean Executive Airlines
ES: Seagreen Air Transport—Air Cargo
ET: Ethiopian Airlines
EU: Compañia Ecuatoriana de Aviación (Ecuadorean Aviation Company)
EV: Elivie
EW: East-West Airlines
EX: Executive Airlines
EY: Europe Aero Service
FA: Florida Airlines
FC: Manufacturers Air Transport Service
FG: Ariana Afghan Airlines
FI: Flugfelag—Icelandair
Finnair: Finnish Airlines
FJ: Fiji Airways
FL: Frontier Airlines
FO: Fjellfly
FS: Key Airlines
FT: Flying Tiger Line—Air Cargo
FW: Wright Airlines
GA: Garuda Indonesian Airways
GB: Air Gabon
GC: Linacongo
GD: Air Antilles
GF: Gulf Aviation
GG: Golden Pacific Airlines
GH: Ghana Airways
GI: Air Guinee
GJ: Airlines of South Australia
GL: Greenlandair
GM: Great Northern Airways
GGN: Transgabon
GQ: Golden West Airlines
GR: General Air
GS: Air Vosges
GT: Gibraltar Airways
GU: Aviateca
GV: Territory Airlines
GX: Great Lakes Air Services
GY: Aurigny Air Services
HA: Hawaiian Air Lines
HB: Air Melanesiae
HD: Aero Servicios
HH: Somali Airlines
HJ: Toa Airways
HK: Cogeair
HL: Holiday Airlines
HN: NLM-Dutch Airlines
HP: Apollo Airways
HQ: Valley Airlines
HR: Pennsylvania Commuter
HS: Scenic Airlines
HT: Air Chad
HU: Cascade Airways
Hughes: Hughes Air West
HX: Virginia Air Cargo
HY: Houston Metro Airlines
IA: Iraqi Airways
IB: Iberia
Iberia: Iberia Air Lines of Spain
IC: Indian Airlines
IE: Solomon Islands Airways
IF: Interflug
IG: Alisarda

IH: Itavia
II: Imperial Airlines
IL: LANSA (Lineas Aereas Nacionales, SA—National Air Lines Corporation)
IM: Massachusetts Air Industries
Imperial: Imperial Airlines
IN: Aerlinte (Irish)
IO: Out Island Airways
IR: Iran National Airlines
Irish: Irish International Airlines
IT: Air Inter
IT: Air Inter
IU: Midstate Air Commuter
IV: Lineas Aereas Guinea Ecuatorial (Equatorial Guinea Airlines)
IW: International Air Bahama
IX: INAIR (Internacional de Aviación)
IY: Swift Airlines
IZ: Arkia-Israel Inland Airlines
JAL: Japan Air Lines
Japan: Japan Air Lines
JB: Aeronaves del Norte
JC: Rocky Mountain Airways
JD: Japan Domestic Airlines
jetliner: jet airliner
JH: Smyer Aircraft
JI: Aeronaves del Este
JL: Japan Air Lines
JM: Air Jamaica
JN: Sun Valley Air
JO: Aeronaves del Oeste
JQ: TAA (Trans-Australia Airlines)
JR: ACSA Airlines
JS: Air Champagne Ardennes
JT: Jamaica Air Service
JU: Jugoslavian Air Transport
JY: Air Caicos
JZ: Aeronaves del Centro
KAL: Korean Air Lines
KB: Kitsap Aviation
KE: Korean Air Lines
KF: Catskill Airways
KH: Time Airways
KK: Shawnee Air
KL: KLM (Koninklijke Luchtvaart Maatschappij—Royal Dutch Airlines)
KLM: Royal Dutch Airlines
KO: Kodiak Airways
Korean Air Lines: KAL
KP: Air Cape
KQ: King Airlines
KR: Dar-Air
KW: Dorado Wings
KX: Cayman Airways
KU: Kuwait Airways
KX: Cayman Airways
KX: Century Airlines
LA: LAN (Linea Aerea Nacional de Chile—National Air Line of Chile)
LB: Lloyd Aereo Boliviano
LC: Loganair Limited
LD: LADE (Lineas Aereas del Estade—State Air Lines)
LE: Lake Geneva Airways
LF: Linjeflyg
LG: Luxair—Luxembourg Airlines
LH: Lufthansa German Airlines
LI: Leeward Islands Air Transport
LJ: Sierra Leone Airways
LK: Alag-Alpine Lift-Trans
LL: Icelandic Airlines
LM: ALM—Dutch Antillean Airlines
LN: Libyan Arab Airlines
LO: Polish Airlines
LP: Air Alpes
LR: LACSA (Lineas Aereas Costarricenses—Costa Rican Airlines)
Lufthansa: Lufthansa German Airlines
LV: LAV (Lineas Aeropostal Venezolana—Venezuelan Aeropostal Lines
LY: El Al Israel Airlines
LZ: Bulgarian Airlines—Balkan
MA: Malev (Hungarian Air Transport)
MD: Air Madagascar
ME: Middle East Airlines
MG: Malta Airlines
MH: Air Manila
MI: Mackey International Air Commuter
MJ: SMB State Lines
MK: Air Mauritius
ML: Malaysia-Singapore Airlines
MM: Sociedad Aeronautica Medellín
MN: Commercial Airways
MO: Mohawk Airlines
MR: Air Mauritanie
MS: United Arab Airlines
MU: Misair
MV: Macrobertson Miller Airlines
MW: Maya Airways
MY: Air Mali
MZ: Merpati Nusantara Airlines
NA: National Airlines
NAC: National Airways Corporation (New Zealand)
National: National Airlines
NB: Newport Air Park
NC: North Central Airlines
ND: Nordair
NE: Northeast Airlines
NH: All Nippon Airways
NI: LANICA (Lineas Aereas de Nicaragua—Air Lines of Nicaragua)
NJ: Air South
NK: Namakwaland Lugdiens
NL: Liberian National Airlines
NM: Mt Cook Airlines
Northwest: Northwest Orient Airlines
NR: Northward Aviation Limited
NS: Northeast Airlines
NU: Southwest Airlines
NV: Combs Airways
NW: Northwest Orient Airlines
NY: New York Airways
NZ: New Zealand National Airways
OA: Olympic Airways
OB: Opal Air Services
OD: Aerocondor
OE: North-Air
OG: Chalk's Flying Service
OH: San Francisco and Oakland —Helicopter
OJ: Stol Commuters
OK: Czechoslovak Airlines
OM: Air Mongol
ON: North American Airlines
ONA: Overseas National Airlines
OO: Borrego Springs Airlines
OP: Air Panama International
OQ: Royale Airlines
OR: Air Comores
OS: Austrian Airlines
OT: Transportes Aereos de São Tome
OX: American Courier
OY: Air North
OZ: Ozark Air Lines
PA: Pan American World Airways
Pan Am: Pan American World Airways
PC: Pacair
PD: Pem Air Limited
PE: Papuan Airlines
PH: Polynesian Airlines
Philippine: Philippine Airlines
PI: Piedmont Aviation
PK: Pakistan International
PM: Pilgrim Airlines
PN: Ansett Airlines of Papua, New Guinea
PP: Phillips Michigan City Flying Service
PQ: Puerto Rico International Airlines
PR: Philipine Airlines
PS: Pacific Southwest Airlines
PSA: Pacific Southwest Airlines
PT: Provincetown-Boston Airline and Naples Airline Division
PU: PLUNA (Primeras Lineas Uruguayas de Navegación Aerea (First Uruguayan Air Navigation Lines)
PV: Eastern Provincial Airways
PW: Pacific Western Airlines
PX: Aspen Airlines
PY: Surinam Airways

PZ: LAP (Lineas Aereas Paraguayas—Paraguayan Air Lines)
QA: Dixie Airlines
QB: Quebecair
QC: Air Congo (Kinshasa)
QD: Sadia
QE: Air Indies
QF: Quantas Airways
QH: St Thomas Tax-Air
QI: Comber Air
QJ: Mel Air Limited
QK: Aroostook Airways
QL: Lesotho Airways
QM: Air Malawi
QN: Bush Pilots Airway
QO: Bar Harbor Airlines
QP: Caspair
QQ: Aerovias Quisqueyana
QS: Air Michigan
QU: Mississippi Valley Airways
Quantas: Quantas Airways (Australian)—originally Queensland and Northern Territory Airways
QV: Monarch Airline
QZ: Zambia Airways
RA: Royal Nepal Airlines
RB: Syrian Arab Airlines
RC: Air Cambodge
RD: Airlift International (Air Cargo)
RG: Varig
RH: Air Rhodesia
RI: Tricon International Airlines
RH: Royal Jordanian Airlines
RK: Air Afrique
RO: TAROM (Transporturile Aeriene Romine—Roumanian Air Transport)
Route of the Red Baron: Lufthansa German Airlines
RU: Rousseau Aviation
RV: Reeve Aleutian Airways
RW:A Hughes Air West
RX: Capitol Air Services
RY: Royal Air Lao
RZ: Aero Mech
SA: South African Airways
***SABENA:** Societe Anonyme Belge d'Exploitation de la Navigation Aerienne* (French—Belgian Corporation for the Exploitation of Aerial Navigation)—Sabena Belgian Airlines
SAS: Scandinavian Airlines System
SB: Seaboard World Airways
SC: Cruzeiro
SD: Sudan Airways
Seaboard: Seaboard World Airways
SG: Aerotransportes Litoral Argentino (Argentine Coastal Air Transport)
SH: Sahsa
SK: SAS (Scandinavian Airlines System)
SL: Southeast Airlines
SN: Sabena (Belgian Airlines)
SO: Southern Airways
SP: SATA (Sociedade Açoriana de Transportes Aeros—Azores Air Transport)
SQ: Norcanair
SR: Swissair
SU: Aeroflot (Soviet Airlines)
SV: Saudi Arabian Airlines
SW: Suidwes Lugdiens
Swissair: Swiss Airlines
SX: Skyways Coach
TA: Taca International
***TAP:** Transportes Aereos Portugueses* (Portuguese—Portuguese Air Transport—Portuguese Airways
TC: Trans Caribbean Airways
TD: Transcarga
TE: Air New Zealand
TG: Thai Airways International
TH: Thai Airways
TJ: Transportes Aereos Buenos Aires
TK: Turk Hava Yollari
TL: Trans-Mediterranean Airways
TM: Direccao de Exploracao dos Transportes Aereos (Mozambique Air Transport)
TN: Trans-Australia Airlines
TP: TAP (Transportes Aereos Portugueses—Portuguese Air Transport)
TQ: Trans Central Airlines
TS: Aloha Airlines
TT: Texas International Airlines
TU: Tunis Air
TV: Trans International Airlines
TW: TWA (Trans World Airlines)
TWA: Trans World Airlines
TX: Transportes Aereos Nacionales (National Air Transport)
TY: Air Caledonie
TZ: Transair Limited
UA: United Air Lines
UB: Union of Burma Airways
UC: LADECO (Linea Aerea del Cobre)
UD: Brower Flight Service
UE: Trans Magic Airlines
UI: Star Airlines
UJ: Air Ulster
UK: British Island Airways
UL: Lansa Airlines of Honduras
UM: Morris Air Transport
United: United Air Lines
UQ: Suburban Airlines
UT: UTA (Union de Transports Aerien)
UU: Touraine Air Transport
UW: Midwest Airlines
UX: Air Illinois
UY: Buckeye Air Service
VA: Viasa
VB: Air Bangui
VD: Port Augusta Air Services
VE: AVENSA (Aerovias Venezolanas—Venezuelan Airlines)
VF: British Air Ferries
VG: Air Siam
VH: Air Volta
VI: STA (Société de Travail Aerien)
VJ: Allen Aviation
VK: Trans Michigan Airlines
VM: Monmouth Airlines
VN: Air Vietnam
VO: BC Airliens
VP: VASP (Viacão Sao Paulo)
VQ: International Dky Cab (Volusia Aviation Services)
VT: RAI (Reseau Aerien Interinsulaire—Tahiti)
VU: Air Ivoire
VV: Viking International Airfreight
VW: Civil Flying Services
VY: Air Cameroun
W: Western Airlines
WA: WAL (Western Air Lines)
WB: Shawnee Airlines
WC: Sien Consolidated Airlines
Western: Western Airlines
WF: Wideroes Flyveselskap
WG: ALAG (Alpine Luft Transport AG)
WJ: Jet Air
WK: Western Alaska
WL: Lao Airlines
WM: Windward Islands Airways
WQ: Georgia Air
WR: Altus Airlines
WS: Northern Wings Limited
WT: Waac-Nigeria-Limited
WU: Avna
WV: West Pacific Airlines
WX: Airlines of New South Wales
WY: Azgec Airways
WZ: Swazi Air Limited
XC: Compañia Chiterena de Aviación
XE: Hub Airlines
XF: Murchison Air Services
XK: Air California
XO: Rio Airways
XQ: Air New England
XT: Southern Airlines
XU: Trans Mo Airlines
XV: Ambassador Airlines
XX: Chicago and Southern Airlines
XY: Downeast Airlines
YE: Yemen Airlines
YH: Amistad Airlines
ZB: Midwest Commuter Airways

ZD: Aztec Airways
ZF: Village Airways
ZH: Royal Hawaiian Airways
ZJ: Aeronaves del Sureste
ZK: Davis Airlines
ZM: Winnipesaukee Aviation
ZN: Cherokee Airways
ZS: Sizer Airways
ZT: SATENA (Servicio Aeronavegacion a Territorios Nacionales —Bogota
ZV: Air Midwest
ZW: Air Wisconsin
ZX: Aeronaves del Mayab
ZY: Skyway Aviation

American Eponyms, Nicknames, and Sobriquets

American: Dvorák's Quartet in F (opus 96) for two violins, viola, and cello
American Apostle of Nonviolent Disobedience: Martin Luther King, Jr
American Beauty Rose: official flower of Washington, D.C.; symbolic nickname sometimes given its girls—American Beauty Roses
American Century: the 20th century marked by invention and industrial activity, highest standard of living for the most people, discovery of the North Pole, landing of men on the moon, victory in two world wars, devotion to the democratic ideal—the 1900s
American Conservationist: title shared by John Muir, William T. Hornaday, Williard G. Van Name, and a very few others who loved nature more than profit or professional approval
American Crusader for Religious Liberty: Roger Williams
American Demosthenes: Robert Ingersoll
American Documentary Film Pioneer: Robert Flaherty
American Eagle: avian symbol of the United States
American Etcher: Joseph Pennell and James Abbott McNeill Whistler share this title with many others
American Expatriate Painter: Benjamin West and James Abbott McNeill Whistler share this descriptive title
American Film Pioneer: David Wark Griffith
America's Forgotten Photographer: Timothy O'Sullivan
American Founder of Women's Suffrage: Elizabeth Cady Stanton (founder and first president of the National Woman Suffrage Association)
American Frontier Romanticist: James Fenimore Cooper
American Gateway to Alaska and the Orient: Seattle
American Historical Painter: Emmanuel Leutzé
American Illustrator: Anton Otto Fischer, Howard Pyle, Norman Rockwell, and others are known by this title
American Impressionist: Childe Hassam
American Industrial Painter: Charles Sheeler
American Infidel: Colonel Robert G. Ingersoll, agnostic attorney and foremost public speaker of his time who was also known as the American Demosthenes
American Karl Marx: Curaçao-born Daniel DeLeon—founder in New York City (where he taught at Columbia University) of the Socialist Labor Party (SLP) and the International Workers of the World (IWW); made some of the first English translations of Karl Marx
American Landscape Painters: Albert Bierstad, George Caleb Bingham, James Britton, Frederic Church, Thomas Cole, Asher Brown Durand, Edward Hopper, Henry Inman, George Inness, J. Francis Murphy, Grant Wood, and Alexander Helwig Wyant share this title
American Libertarian: sobriquet shared by such outstanding freethinkers as Thomas Jefferson, Thomas Paine, Robert Ingersoll, Clarence Darrow, and your favorite American Libertarian
American Lighthouse Painter: Edward Hopper
American Lithographers: Currier & Ives (Nathaniel Currier and James Merritt Ives)
American Medical Historian: William Henry Welch
American Modern: Jackson Pollock
American National Composer: John Philip Sousa
American Neurologist Extraordinary: Silas Weir Mitchell
American Operetta Composers: Irving Berlin, George M. Cohan, Victor Herbert, Jerome Kern, Frederick Loewe, Cole Porter, Richard Rodgers, Vincent Youmans, and your unnamed favorite, must share this title
American Orator Extraordinary: sobriquet shared by Robert G. Ingersoll and Franklin D. Roosevelt
American Portrait Painters: James Britton, John Singleton Copley, Henry Inman, Eastman Johnson, John Singer Sargent, and Eugene Edward Speicher have been among the outstanding holders of this title along with the Peale family, Gilbert Stuart, Thomas Sully, and James Abbott McNeill Whistler
American Pragmatist Trinity: John Dewey, William James, Charles Sanders Peirce
American Primitive Painters: Edward Hicks, Grandma Moses, and others, including the compiler, have been given this title
American Propagandist Novelist: Upton Sinclair
American Railroad Barons: Jay Gould; Edward H. Harriman; James J. Hill; Collis P. Huntington; William H. Vanderbilt
American Sappho: Sarah Wentworth Apthorp Morton of Braintree and Quincy, Mass
American Sculptors: Daniel

Chester French, perhaps the most popular among such as Borglum, Brancusi, Epstein, Lachaise, Manship, Moore, St Gaudens, Ward, and Zorach
American Virgins: U.S. Virgin Islands
American Woodsman: John James Audubon
Americans United: Americans United for Separation of Church and State (AUSCS)
America's Dairyland: Wisconsin's sobriquet
Americanist: Americanist Press
American's Finest City: San Diego, California—in the opinion of its citizens, its mayor, and many seasoned travellers
America's First Financier: Robert Morris
America's First Resort: Newport, Rhode Island
America's First Suffragist: Abigail Smith Adams (*see* Portia)
America's Last Frontier: Alaska
America's Most Useful Citizen: Jane Addams—author of *Twenty Years at Hull-House*
America's Newest Big City: Miami, Florida
America's Nonsense Poet: Ogden Nash
America's Practical Navigator: Nathaniel Bowditch—compiler of *The American Practical Navigator*
America's Premier Air Woman: Amelia Earhart Putnam—first aviatrix to fly across the Atlantic
America's Proudest Musical Possession: Carnegie Hall
America's Safest City: Lakewood, Ohio (suburb of Cleveland)
America's Wintergarden: southern California's Imperial Valley

Astronomical Constellations, Stars and Symbols

And: Andromeda (Princess Enchained), also called Mirach
Ant: Antlia (Bilge Pump)
Aps: Apus (Bird of Paradise)
Aql: Aquila (Eagle); contains Altair
Aqr: Aquarius (Water Carrier)
Ara (Altar)
Arg: Argo or Argo Navis (Ship *Argo* or Ship of the Argonauts); contains Carina (Keel), Malus (Mast), Puppis (Stern), Pyxis (Mariner's Compass), Vela (Sails)
Ari: Aries (Ram); contains Hamal
Aur: Auriga (Charioteer); contains Capella
Boö: Boötes (Herdsman); contains Arcturus
Cae: Caelum (Chisel)
Cam: Camelopardalis (Giraffe)
Cap: Capricornus (Horned Goat)
Car: Carina (Keel), in Argo; contains Canopus
Cas: Cassiopeia (Queen Enthroned); contains supernova 1572
Cen: Centaurus (Centaur); contains Alpha Centauri, Proxima Centauri
Cep: Cepheus (Monarch)
Cet: Cetus (Whale); contains Mira
Cha: Chamaeleon (Chameleon)
Cir: Circinus (Compasses)
CMa: Canis Major (Great Dog); contains Sirius
CMi: Canis Minor (Little Dog); contains Procyon
Cnc: Cancer (Crab); contains Praesepe
Col: Columba (Dove)
Com: Coma Berenices (Berenice's Hair)
CrA: Corona Australis (Southern Crown)
CrB: Corona Borealis (Northern Crown), also called Gemma
Crt: Crater (Cup)
Cru: Crux (Southern Cross); Black Magellanic Cloud nearby
Crv: Corvus (Crow)
CVn: Canes Venatici (Hunting Dogs); contains Cor Caroli
Cyg: Cygnus (Swan); contains Deneb, Northern Cross
Del: Delphinus (Dolphin)
Dor: Dorado, also called Xiphies (Swordfish); Large Magellanic Cloud
Dra: Draco (Dragon)
Equ: Equuleus (Colt)
Eri: Eridanus (Great River); contains Achernar
For: Fornax (Furnace)
Gem: Gemini (The Twins); contains Castor, Pollux
Gru: Grus (Crane)
Her: Hercules; contains Ras Algethi
Hor: Horologium (Clock)
Hya: Hydra (Marine Monster); contains Alphard
Hyd: Hydrus (Water Snake)
Ind: Indus (Indian)
Kif Aus: Kiffa Australis (Southern Breadbasket); contains Zuben el Genubi
Kif Bor: Kiffa Borealis (Northern Breadbasket); contains Zubeneschamali
Lac: Lacerta (Lizard)
Leo (Lion): contains Regulus, Denebola
Lep: Lepus (Hare)
Lib: Libra (Balance or Scales)
LMi: Leo Minor (Little Lion)
Lup: Lupus (Wolf)
Lyn: Lynx
Lyr: Lyra (Lyre); contains Vega
Mal: Malus (Mast), in Argo
Men: Mensa (Table), also called Mons Mensae (Table Mountain)
Mic: Microscopium (Microscope)
Mon: Monoceros (Unicorn)
Mus: Musca (Fly)
Nor: Norma (Rule)
Oct: Octans (Octant)
Oph: Ophiuchus (Serpent Bearer); contains supernova 1604
Ori: Orion (Hunter); contains Betelgeuse, Rigel
Pav: Pavo (Peacock)
Peg: Pegasus (Winged Horse)
Per: Perseus (Rescuer or Champion); contains Algol
Phe: Phoenix
Pic: Pictor (Painter's Easel)
PsA: Piscis Australis or Austrinus

(Southern Fish); contains Formalhaut
Psc: Pisces (Fishes)
Pup: Puppis (Stern), in Argo
Pyx: Pyxis (Mariner's Compass Chest or Binnacle), in Argo
Ret: Reticulum (Net)
Scl: Sculptor (Sculptor's Workshop)
Sco: Scorpio (Scorpion); contains Antares
Sct: Scutum (Shield)
Ser: Serpens (Serpent)
Sex: Sextant
Sge: Sagitta (Arrow)
Sgr: Sagittarius (Archer), Center of Galaxy
Tau: Taurus (Bull); contains Hyades–Aldebaran; Pleiades
Tel: Telescopium (Telescope)
TrA: Triangulum Australe (Southern Triangle)
Tri: Triangulum (Triangle)
Tuc: Tucana (Toucan); Small Magellanic Cloud
UMa: Ursa Major (Great Bear); contains Dubhe, Mizar
UMi: Ursa Minor (Little Bear); contains Polaris (Pole Star)
Vel: Vela (Sails), in Argo
Vir: Virgo (Virgin)
Vol: Volans (Flying Fish)
Vul: Vulpecula (Little Fox), also called Vulpecula cum Ansere (Little Fox with Goose)

ASTRONOMICAL SYMBOLS

⊖☾ : center
☄ : comet
◖ : crescent moon (first quarter)
◗ : crescent moon (last quarter)
⊕ : Earth (symbol shows globe bisected by meridian lines into four quarters)
○ : full moon
◯ : gibbous moon (first quarter)
◯ : gibbous moon (last quarter)
◐ : half moon (first quarter)
◑ : half moon (last quarter)
♃ : Jupiter (symbol said to represent a hieroglyph of the eagle, Jove's bird, or to be the initial letter of Zeus with a line drawn through it to indicate its abbreviation)
⊙̲☾̲ : lower limb
♂ : Mars (symbol represents shield and spear of the god of war, Mars; it is also the male or masculine symbol)
☿ : Mercury (symbol represents head and winged cap of Mercury, god of commerce and communication, surmounting his caduceus)
♆ : Neptune (symbolized by the trident of Neptune, god of the sea)
● : new moon
☽ : moon (symbol depicts crescent moon in last quarter)
♇ : Pluto (symbol is monogram made up of P and L in Pluto, also initials of the astronomer Percival Lowell, who predicted its discovery)
♄ : Saturn (symbol thought to represent an ancient scythe or sickle, as Saturn was the god of seed sowing and hence also of time)
☆ : star
☆-P : star-planet altitude correction
⊙ : sun (symbolized by a shield with its boss; some believe this boss represents a central sunspot)
⊙̄☾̄ : upper limb
♅ : Uranus (symbolized by combined devices indicating the sun plus the spear of Mars, as Uranus was the personification of heaven in the Greek mythology, dominated by the light of the sun and the power of Mars)
♀ : Venus (designated by the female symbol, thought to be the stylized representation of the hand mirror of this goddess of love)

Automatic Data-Processing Abbreviations for Zip-Coded Mail

AK: Alaska
AL: Alabama
AR: Arkansas
AZ: Arizona
CA: California
CO: Colorado
CT: Connecticut
CZ: Canal Zone
DC: District of Columbia
DE: Delaware
FL: Florida
GA: Georgia
GU: Guam
HI: Hawaii
IA: Iowa
ID: Idaho
IL: Illinois
IN: Indiana
KS: Kansas
KY: Kentucky
LA: Louisiana
MA: Massachusetts
MD: Maryland
ME: Maine
MI: Michigan
MN: Minnesota
MO: Missouri

MS: Mississippi	NY: New York	TN: Tennessee
MT: Montana	OH: Ohio	TX: Texas
NB: Nebraska	OK: Oklahoma	UT: Utah
NC: North Carolina	OR: Oregon	VA: Virginia
ND: North Dakota	PA: Pennsylvania	VI: Virgin Islands
NH: New Hampshire	PR: Puerto Rico	VT: Vermont
NJ: New Jersey	RI: Rhode Island	WA: Washington
NM: New Mexico	SC: South Carolina	WI: Wisconsin
NV: Nevada	SD: South Dakota	WV: West Virginia
		WY: Wyoming

Birthstones—Ancient and Modern

	ancient	modern
January	garnet	garnet
February	amethyst	amethyst
March	jasper	aquamarine or bloodstone
April	sapphire	diamond
May	agate	emerald
June	emerald	alexandrite, moonstone, or pearl
July	onyx	ruby
August	carnelian	peridot or sardonyx
September	chrysolite	sapphire
October	aquamarine	opal or tourmaline
November	topaz	topaz
December	ruby	turquoise or zircon

Relative values: diamonds, emeralds, rubies, and sapphires are termed precious stones; all the rest are semiprecious; precious gems are minerals inhanced by the lapidary's art; the pearl, although not a stone, is classed with the gems and depending on its beauty and size may be as valuable as any of the precious stones

Capital Cities of the World

Afghanistan Kabul
Albania Tirana
Algeria Algiers
Andorra Andorra la Vella
Angola Luanda
Argentina Buenos Aires
Australia Canberra
Austria Vienna
Bahamas Nassau
Bahrain Manama
Bangladesh Dacca
Barbados Bridgetown
Belgium Brussels
Benin (Dahomey) Porto-Novo
Bhutan Thimphu
Bolivia Sucre
Botswana Gaborone
Brazil Brasilia
Bulgaria Sofia
Burma Rangoon
Burundi Bujumbura
Cambodia Phnom Penh
Cameroon Yaounde
Canada Ottawa, Ontario
Cape Verde Praia
Central African Republic Bangui
Chad N'Djamena
Chile Santiago
China Peking
China (Taiwan) Taipei
Colombia Bogota
Comoro Islands Moroni
Congo, People's Rep. Brazzaville
Costa Rica San Jose
Cuba Havana
Cyprus Nicosia
Czechoslovakia Prague
Denmark Copenhagen
Dominican Republic Santo Domingo
Ecuador Quito
Egypt (UAR) Cairo
El Salvador San Salvador
Equatorial Guinea Malabo
Estonia Tallinn

Ethiopia	Addis Ababal
Fiji	Suva
Finland	Helsinki
France	Paris
Gabon	Libreville
Gambia	Banjul
German Democratic Rep. (E)	Berlin
Federal Republic of Germany (W)	Bonn
Ghana	Accra
Greece	Athens
Grenada	St. George's
Guatemala	Guatemala City
Guinea	Conakry
Guinea-Bissau	Madina do Boé
Guyana	Georgetown
Haiti	Port-au-Prince
Honduras	Tegucigalpa
Hungary	Budapest
Iceland	Reykjavik
India	New Delhi
Indonesia	Jakarta
Iran	Teheran
Iraq	Baghdad
Ireland	Dublin
Israel	Jerusalem
Italy	Rome
Ivory Coast	Abidjan
Jamaica	Kingston
Japan	Tokyo
Jordan	Amman
Kenya	Nairobi
Korea, Dem. People's Rep. (N)	Pyong Yang
Korea, Republic of (S)	Seoul
Kuwait	Kuwait
Laos, People's Dem. Rep.	Vientiane
Latvia	Riga
Lebanon	Beirut
Lesotho	Maseru
Liberia	Monrovia
Libya	Tripoli
Liechtenstein	Vaduz
Lithuania	Vilnius
Luxembourg	Luxembourg
Madagascar	Tananarive
Malawi	Lilongwe
Malaysia	Kuala Lumpur
Maldives, Rep.	Malé
Mali	Bamako
Malta	Valetta
Mauritania	Nouakchott
Mauritius	Port Louis
Mexico	Mexico City
Mongolian People's Rep.	Ulan Bator
Morocco	Rabat-Salé
Namibia	Windhoek
Nauru	Yaren
Nepal	Katmandu
Netherlands	Amsterdam
New Zealand	Wellington
Nicaragua	Managua
Niger	Niamey
Nigeria	Lagos
Norway	Oslo
Oman	Muscat
Pakistan	Islamabad
Panama	Panama City
Papua New Guinea	Port Moresby
Paraguay	Asuncion
Peru	Lima
Philippines	Quezon City
Poland	Warsaw
Portugal	Lisbon
Qatar	Doha
Rhodesia	Salisbury
Romania	Bucharest
Rwanda	Kigali
San Marino	San Marino
São Tomé and Principe	São Tomé
Saudi Arabia	Riyadh
Senegal	Dakar
Seychelles	Victoria
Sierra Leona	Freetown
Singapore	Singapore
Somalia	Mogadishu
South Africa	Cape Town
Spain	Madrid
Sri Lanka (Ceylon)	Colombo
Sudan	Khartoum
Surinam	Paramaribo
Swaziland	Mbabane
Sweden	Stockholm
Switzerland	Bern
Syrian Arab Republic	Damascus
Tanzania	Dar es Salaam
Thailand	Bangkok
Togo, Rep. of	Lomé
Tonga	Nuku'Alofa
Transkei	Umtata
Trinidad and Tobago	Port-of-Spain
Tunisia	Tunis
Turkey	Ankara
Uganda	Kampala
USSR	Moscow
United Arab Emirates	Abu Dhabi
United Kingdom:	
England	London
Scotland	Edinburgh
Wales	Cardiff
Northern Ireland	Belfast
United States of America	Washington, D.C.
Upper Volta	Ouagadougou
Uruguay	Montevideo
Venezuela	Caracas
Vietnam, Soc. Rep.	Hanoi
Western Somoa	Apia
Yemen	Sana
Yemen, People's Dem. Rep. (S)	Medina al-Eshaab
Yugoslavia	Belgrade
Zaire	Kinshasa
Zambia	Lusaka

Chemical Element Symbols, Atomic Numbers, and Discovery Data

Symbol	*Element*	*Atomic Number*	*Discovered*
Ac	actinium	89	1899 by Debierne
Ag	silver (*argentum*)	47	Before the Christian Era
Al	aluminum	13	1825 by Oersted
Am	americium	95	1944 by Seborg and others
Ar or A	argon	18	1894 by Raleigh and Ramsay
As	arsenic	33	13th century by Magnus
As	astatine	85	1940 by Corson and others
Au	gold (*aurum*)	79	Before the Christian Era
B	boron	5	1808 by Davy
Ba	barium	56	1808 by Davy
Be	beryllium	4	1798 by Vauquelin
Bi	bismuth	83	15th century by Valentine
Bk	berkelium	97	1949 by Thompson, Ghiorso, and Seborg
Br	bromine	35	1826 by Balard
C	carbon	6	Before the Christian Era
Ca	calcium	20	1808 by Davy
Cd	cadmium	48	1817 by Stromeyer
Ce	cerium	58	1803 by Klaproth
Cf	californium	98	1950 by Thompson and others
Cl	chlorine	17	1774 by Scheele
Cm	curium	96	1944 by Seborg and others
Co	cobalt	27	1735 by Brandt
Cr	chromium	24	1797 by Vauquelin
Cs	cesium	55	1861 by Bunsen and Kirchoff
Cu	copper (*cuprum*)	29	Before the Christian Era
Dy	dysprosium	66	1886 by Boisbaudran
Er	erbium	68	1843 by Mosander
Es	einsteinium	99	1952 by Ghiorso and others
Eu	europium	63	1901 by Demarcay
F	fluorine	9	1771 by Scheele
Fe	iron (*ferrum*)	26	Before the Christian Era
Fm	fermium	100	1953 by Ghiorso and others
Fr	francium	87	1939 by Perey
Ga	gallium	31	1875 by Boisbaudran
Gd	gadolinium	64	1886 by Marignac
Ge	germanium	32	1886 by Winkler
H	hydrogen	1	1766 by Cavendish
Ha	hahnium	105	1970 by Ghiorso and others
He	helium	2	1895 by Ramsay
Hf	hafnium	72	1923 by Coster and Hevesy
Hg	mercury (*hydrargyrum*)	80	Before the Christian Era

Symbol	*Element*	*Atomic Number*	*Discovered*
Ho	holmium	67	1879 by Cleve
I	iodine	53	1811 by Courtois
In	indium	49	1863 by Reich and Richter
Ir	iridium	77	1804 by Tennant
K	potassium (*kalium*)	19	1807 by Davy
Kr	krypton	36	1898 by Ramsay and Travers
La	lanthanum	57	1839 by Mosander
Li	lithium	3	1817 by Arfvedson
Lu	lutetium	71	1907 by Welsbach and Urbain
Lw	lawrencium	103	1961 by Ghiorso and others
Md	mendelevium	101	1955 by Ghiorso and others
Mg	magnesium	12	1830 by Bussy and Liebig
Mn	manganese	25	1774 by Gahn
Mo	molybdenum	42	1782 by Hjelm
N	nitrogen	7	1772 by Rutherford
Na	sodium	11	1807 by Davy
Nb	niobium (formerly columbium)	41	1801 by Hatchett
Nd	neodymium	60	1885 by Welsbach
Ne	neon	10	1898 by Ramsay and Travers
Ni	nickel	28	1751 by Cronstedt
No	nobelium	102	1958 by Ghiorso and others
Np	neptunium	93	1940 by Abelson and McMillan
O	oxygen	8	1774 by Priestley and Scheele
Os	osmium	76	1804 by Tennant
P	phosphorus	15	1669 by Brandt
Pa	protactinium	91	1917 by Hahn and Meitner
Pb	lead (*plumbum*)	82	Before the Christian Era
Pd	palladium	46	1803 by Wollaston
Pm	promethium	61	1945 by Glendenin and Marinsky
Po	polonium	84	1898 by P. and M. Curie
Pr	praseodymium	59	1885 by Welsbach
Pt	platinum	78	1735 by Ulloa
Pu	plutonium	94	1940 by Seborg and others
Ra	radium	88	1898 by P. and M. Curie
Rb	rubidium	37	1861 by Bunsen and Kirchoff
Re	rhenium	75	1925 by Noddack and Tacke
Rf	rutherfordium	104	1969 by Ghiorso and others
Rh	rhodium	45	1803 by Wollaston
Rn	radon	86	1900 by Dorn
Ru	ruthenium	44	1845 by Claus
S	sulfur	16	Before the Christian Era
Sb	antimony (*stibium*)	51	1450 by Valentine
Sc	scandium	21	1879 by Nilson
Se	selenium	34	1817 by Berzelius

Symbol	Element	Atomic Number	Discovered
Si	silicon	14	1823 by Berzelius
Sm	samarium	62	1879 by Boisbaudran
Sn	tin (*stannum*)	50	Before the Christian Era
Sr	strontium	38	1790 by Crawford
Ta	tantalum	73	1802 by Eckeberg
Tb	terbium	65	1843 by Mosander
Tc	technetium	43	1937 by Perrier and Segre
Te	tellurium	52	1782 by von Reichenstein
Th	thorium	90	1828 by Berzelius
Ti	titanium	22	1789 by Gregor
Tl	thallium	81	1861 by Crookes
Tm	thulium	69	1879 by Cleve
U	uranium	92	1789 by Klaproth
V	vanadium	23	1830 by Sefström
W	tungsten (wolfram)	74	1783 by d'Elhuyar brothers
Xe	xenon	54	1898 by Ramsay and Travers
Y	yttrium	39	1794 by Gadolin
Yb	ytterbium	70	1878 by Marignac
Zn	zinc	30	Before the Christian Era
Zr	zirconium	40	1789 by Klaproth

Civil and Military Time Systems Compared

Civil	Military	Civil	Military
12.01 A.M. =	0001	12.01 P.M. =	1201
12.02 A.M. =	0002	12.02 P.M. =	1202
12.03 A.M. =	0003	12.03 P.M. =	1203
12.04 A.M. =	0004	12.04 P.M. =	1204
12.05 A.M. =	0005	12.05 P.M. =	1205
12.15 A.M. =	0015	12.15 P.M. =	1215
12.30 A.M. =	0030	12.30 P.M. =	1230
12.45 A.M. =	0045	12.45 P.M. =	1245
1.00 A.M. =	0100	1.00 P.M. =	1300
1.15 A.M. =	0115	1.15 P.M. =	1315
1.30 A.M. =	0130	1.30 P.M. =	1330
1.45 A.M. =	0145	1.45 P.M. =	1345
2.00 A.M. =	0200	2.00 P.M. =	1400
3.00 A.M. =	0300	3.00 P.M. =	1500
4.00 A.M. =	0400	4.00 P.M. =	1600
5.00 A.M. =	0500	5.00 P.M. =	1700
6.00 A.M. =	0600	6.00 P.M. =	1800
7.00 A.M. =	0700	7.00 P.M. =	1900

Civil	*Military*	*Civil*	*Military*
8.00 A.M. =	0800	8.00 P.M. =	2000
9.00 A.M. =	0900	9.00 P.M. =	2100
10.00 A.M. =	1000	10.00 P.M. =	2200
11.00 A.M. =	1100	11.00 P.M. =	2300
12.00 noon =	1200	12.00 midnight =	2400

Climatic Region Symbols

Typical Climatological Regional Divisions Worldwide

Climatic Symbols	Climatic Regions	
Af Am	*Tropical Rainforest*	Tropical rainforests of the Amazon and Middle America from southern Mexico to Colombia and the West Indies; Congo and the Guinea Coast of Africa; jungles of Ceylon, India, Indonesia, Madagascar, Malaya, the Philippines, Southeast Asia
Aw	*Tropical Dry and Wet*	Grassy savannas of Middle America; llanos of eastern Colombia and southern Venezuela; campos of south-central Brazil; damp lowland savannas of Africa and its dry uplands; plains of northern Australia, Burma, India, Pakistan, Southeast Asia
Bsk Bwk	*Midlatitude Dry*	Great plains and prairies of Canada and the United States; arid plains of Patagonia; pampas of Argentina, Bolivia, Paraguay, and Uruguay; Gobi and Takla Makan desert dunes of Asia; Kirghizian steppe of Turkestan; Ukrainian steppe
Bwh	*Tropical Dry*	Afghan, Arabian, Atacaman, Australian, Kalihari, Sahara, Somali, Sonoran, and other subtropical and tropical desertlands of the world
Caf	*Humid Subtropical*	Southeastern United States; northern Argentina; southern Brazil, Paraguay, Uruguay; southeast Africa; southeastern China; southern Japan; eastern Australia
Cfb	*West Coast Marine*	Pacific Northwest of Canada and the United States; southern Chile; west coast of Norway and south coast of Sweden; British Isles and northwestern Europe including northern Spain; south coast of South Africa; southeast coast of Australia; New Zealand
Csa	*Mediterranean Subtropical*	Southern California; central Chile; Mediterranean region including Portugal and most of Spain, southern France, Italy, Yugoslavia, Albania, Greece, Turkey, parts of Morocco and Algeria, much of Israel; Cape of Good Hope area around Cape Town, South Africa
Daf	*Humid Continental*	Southern Canada and the northeastern United States plus much of the Midwest; much of the Soviet Union and the eastern section of China
Dcf	*Continental Subarctic*	Alaska and northern Canada; Siberia and the northern USSR from the Arctic Ocean to the North Pacific Ocean
E	*Tundra*	Arctic coasts of Alaska, Canada, Greenland, northernmost Europe and Asia from northern Norway to easternmost Siberia
Ef	*Polar Icecap*	Interior of Greenland; Antarctica's northernmost tip
H	*Highland*	High valleys and mountains areas of the world where climatic conditions are so variable they almost defy classification

Climatic Symbols Explained

A	Hot and moist equatorial or tropical climate
B	Dry climate with evaporation greater than precipitation
C	Moist and warm with well-defined summer and winter seasons
D	Cold and snowy subarctic with northern boundary the northern limit of forest growth—the taiga
E	Ice climates of the icecaps where ice and snow are perpetual or of the tundra where the growing season above the permafrost is very short
H	Highland climates in mountainous regions where weather conditions are extremely variable and difficult to classify
a	Long and hot summers
b	Short and wet winters
c	Cool or short and moderate summers
d	Very cold and dry winters
f	Moist the year around
h	Hot and moist most of the year
k	Cold and dry most of the year
m	Monsoon conditions
s	Dry summers and wet winters
w	Wet summers and dry winters

Diacritical and Punctuation Marks

´	acute accent (as in Bogotá)
’	apostrophe; single quotation mark
[ ]	brackets
˘	breve
¸	cedilla (as in Curaçao)
^	circumflex (as in *rôle*)
:	colon
)	close parenthesis
,	comma
¨	diaeresis (as in München)
. . . or	ellipsis; leaders
!	exclamation point
`	grave accent (as in *funèbre*)
-	hyphen
?	interrogation or question mark
¯	macron (dictionary pronunciation symbol indicating long vowel, as in dāme)
(	open parenthesis
( )	parentheses
.	period

“ ” quotation marks; quotes
‘ ’ quotation marks, single
; semicolon
˜ tilde (as in São Paulo)
‾ vinculum (mathematics: placed above letters)

Earthquake Table (Richter Scale)

The Richter Scale, devised in 1935 by Dr Charles Francis Richter, seismologist of the California Institute of Technology, is a standardized scale for defining the destructive energy of earthquakes whose force is measured by seismographs. The magnitude of such earthquakes is the logarithm of the largest deflection measured and registered during an earthquake when a seismograph is 100 kilometers (62 miles) from the center of maximum shock, the epicenter of the earthquake, whose exact location is pinpointed by several scattered seismographs.

Numbers of the Richter Scale advance logarithmically and not arithmetically, so earthquakes measuring 8, for example, are ten times greater than those measuring 7, and this relationship is constant throughout the scale.

Earthquakes occurring before 1935, or before the invention of the seismograph in 1841, are approximated in terms of the Richter Scale.

Earthquake Damage and Intensity Devastation Effects Encountered Historically

0 No detectable or measurable earthquake effect although about 100,000 quakes a year can be felt and at least 1000 cause some damage

1 Very slight earthquake effects felt by sensitive persons who may experience dizziness or nausea; other creatures may appear disturbed; gentle swaying may affect bodies of water as well as buildings and trees

2 Slight earthquake effects sensed by sensitive persons as well as other creatures who display uneasiness; hanging lamps and pictures swing slightly; buildings and trees sway slightly

3 Very moderate earthquake effects sensed by a few persons as well as by the most nervous and the most sensitive; dishes on shelves may rattle as may many windows; canned goods stored on shelves may rattle and may fall off; parked vehicles may rock and this is true of shrubs and trees

4 Moderate earthquake sensed by many and sufficient to awaken light sleepers; house frames creak and houses sway slightly; shrubs and trees tremble; parked vehicles may rock and sway

5 Near medium-strength earthquake felt by everyone and frightening most persons who tend to leave buildings and run out of doors to avoid cracking ceilings and crumbling walls; in older buildings plaster falls, ceilings crack, and windows break; pictures may fall off their hangings; dishes and glasses tumble off shelves; heavy desks and tables move and many may topple; old and weak chimneys may crack off at the roofline; ornamental cornices fall from buildings; church bells toll by themselves

6 Full-strength earthquake causing general fright approaching panic; stone walls crack; steep slopes and riverbanks crack; chimneys and towers may crack apart and fall; trees shake violently and often fall as do limbs; the Los Angeles Earthquake of 1971 measured 6.6, caused considerable damage, and took the lives of some 60 persons

7 More devastating and more severe type of earthquake such as occurred in Nicaragua and Guatemala where thousands were killed in 1972 and 1976, respectively; or in the Chile Quake of 1906, preceding the San Francisco Earthquake and Fire by only two days, and causing the loss of 1550 lives in Valparaiso and 452 in San Francisco; both seismic disturbances were calculated in later years as representing 7.8 on the Richter Scale

8 Still more devastating and more severe earthquake causing general panic and marked by widespread land and water disturbances; many dams and dikes break, discharging vast volumes of flooding water; underground cables and pipelines crack and tear apart; railway rails bend and twist; brick, glass, and masonry façades peel off buildings and endanger people as they fall to the ground; loss of life quite severe as in the Peruvian Quake of 1970, accounting for the loss of some 50,000 persons, or the Alaska Quake of 1964, reported as 8.4 on the scale, and marked by heavy damage in downtown Anchorage where 131 lost their lives; earthquakes of even greater magnitude occurred in Lisbon, Portugal in 1755 when 60,000 were lost and lakes in far off Norway were disturbed violently; the Shensi Province Quake, occurring in China in 1566, cost some 830,000 lives, calculated to have been 8.9 on the Richter Scale as was Japan's great quake of 1923, destroying all of Yokohama and half of Tokyo, as well as 143,000 people; the sea bottom in Sagami Bay sank 397 meters or 1300 feet; earthquakes of this magnitude afflicated New Madrid, Missouri in 1811, Charleston, South Carolina in 1886, and are predicted as long overdue along the San Andreas Fault Zone of California extending from below the Mexican Border to San Francisco and northward; overall damage might well equal or exceed the Shinsai or Great Quake felt around Tokyo in 1923; Chinese earthquake of July 26, 1976 registered 8.2 with a 7.9 aftershock the following day; shocks affected an area in and around Peking and Tientsin and some 15 million people.

9 Most devastating and most intense earthquakes, as yet unrecorded on any scale, top of the Richter Scale, extending from 0 to 9, and may never occur due to the good effects of minor earthquakes and tremors, providing stress-relief cracking of and easing the great tectonic energy tension beneath us

Greek Alphabet

ALPHA	A	α	IOTA	I	ι	RHO	P	ρ
BETA	B	β	KAPPA	K	κ	SIGMA	Σ	$\sigma\varsigma$
GAMMA	Γ	γ	LAMBDA	Λ	λ	TAU	T	τ
DELTA	Δ	δ	MU	M	μ	UPSILON	Y	υ
EPSILON	E	ϵ	NU	N	ν	PHI	Φ	ϕ
ZETA	Z	ζ	XI	Ξ	ξ	CHI	X	χ
ETA	H	η	OMICRON	O	o	PSI	Ψ	ψ
THETA	Θ	θ	PI	Π	π	OMEGA	Ω	ω

Fishing Port Registration Symbols (Distinguishing Letters)

England

Aberystwith	AB	Bristol	BL	Dartmouth	DH
Barnstaple	BE	Brixham	BM	Dover	DR
Barrow	BW	Cardiff	CF	Exeter	E
Beaumaris	BS	Cardigan	CA	Falmouth	FH
Berwick-on-Tweed	BK	Carlisle	CL	Fleetwood	FD
Bideford	BD	Carnarvon	CO	Folkstone	FE
Blyth	BH	Chester	CH	Fowey	FY
Boston	BN	Colchester	CK	Gloucester	GR
Briggwater	BR	Cowes	CS	Goole	GE

Grimsby	GY	Newhaven	NN	Shields, North	SN
Hartlepool, West	HL	Newport, Mon.	NT	Shields, South	SSS
Harwich	HH	Padstow	PW	Shoreham	SM
Ipswich	IH	Penzance	PZ	Southhampton	SU
Lancaster	LR	Plymouth	PH	Stockton	ST
Littlehampton	LI	Poole	PE	Sunderland	SD
Liverpool	LL	Portsmouth	P	Swansea	SA
Llanelly	LA	Port Talbot	PT	Teignmouth	TH
London	LO	Preston	PN	Truro	TO
Lowestoft	LT	Ramsgate	R	Weymouth	WH
Lynn	LN	Rochester	RR	Whitby	WY
Maldon	MN	Runcorn	RN	Whitehaven	WA
Manchester	MR	Rye	RX	Wisbech	WI
Maryport	MT	Salcombe	SE	Workington	WO
Middlesbrough	MH	St. Ives	SS	Yarmouth (Norfolk)	YH
Milford	M	Scarborough	SH		
Newcastle	NE	Scilly	SC		

Northern Ireland

Belfast	B	Londonderry	LY
Coleraine	CE	Newry	N

Republic of Ireland

Cork	C	Galway	G	Tralee	T
Drogheda	DA	Limerick	L	Waterford	W
Dublin	D	Skibbereen	S	Westport	WT
Dundalk	DK	Sligo	SO	Wexford	WD

International Civil Aircraft Markings

AN: Nicaragua
AP: Pakistan
B: Formosa
CB: Bolivia
CC: Chile
CCCP: Soviet Union (USSR)
CF: Canada
CR and CS: Portugal and colonies
CU: Cuba
CX: Uruguay
CZ: Principality of Monaco
D: Western Germany
EC: Spain
EI and EJ: Ireland
EL: Liberia
EP: Iran
ET: Ethiopia
F: France and French Union
G: United Kingdom
HA: Hungary
HB: Switzerland
HC: Ecuador
HH: Haiti
HI: Dominican Republic
HK: Colombia
HL: Korea
HS: Thailand
HZ: Saudi Arabia
I: Italy
JA: Japan
JY: Jordan
LN: Norway
LV: Argentine Republic
LX: Luxembourg
LZ: Bulgaria
MC: Monte Carlo
N: United States of America
OB: Peru
OD: Lebanon
OE: Austria
OH: Finland
OK: Czechoslovakia
OO: Belgium
OY: Denmark
PH: Netherlands
PI: Philippine Republic
PJ: Curaçao (Netherlands Antilles)
PK: Indonesia
PP and PT: Brazil
PZ: Surinam (Netherlands Guiana)
RX: Republic of Panama
SE: Sweden
SN: Sudan
SP: Poland
SU: Egypt
SX: Greece
TC: Turkey
TF: Iceland
TG: Guatemala
TI: Costa Rica
VH: Australia
VP; VQ; VR: British Colonies and Protectorates
VT: India
XA; XB; XC: Mexico
XH: Honduras
XT: China (Nationalist)
XY; XZ: Burma
YA: Afghanistan

YE: Yemen
YI: Iraq
YK: Syria
YR: Rumania
YS: El Salvador
YU: Yugoslavia
YV: Venezuela
ZA: Albania
ZK; ZL; ZM: New Zealand
ZP: Paraguay
ZS; ZT; ZU: Union of South Africa
4R: Ceylon
4X: Israel
5A: Libya
9G: Ghana

International Conversions Simplified

area

a (acres)	x	0.4	= ha (hectares)
cm^2 (square centimeters)	x	0.16	= $in.^2$ (square inches)
ft^2 (square feet)	x	0.09	= m^2 (square meters)
ha (hectares)	x	2.5	= a (acres)
$in.^2$ (square inches)	x	6.5	= cm^2 (square centimeters)
km^2 (square kilometers)	x	0.4	= mi^2 (square miles)
m^2 (square meters)	x	1.2	= yd^2 (square yards)
mi^2 (square miles)	x	2.6	= km^2 (square kilometers)
yd^2 (square yards)	x	0.8	= m^2 (square meters)

length

cm (centimeters)	x	0.4	= in. (inches)	
ft (feet)	x	30.0	= cm (centimeters)	
in. (inches)	x	2.54*	= cm (centimeters)	*exactly
km (kilometers)	x	0.6	= mi (miles)	
m (meters)	x	3.3	= ft (feet)	
m (meters)	x	1.1	= yd (yards)	
mi (miles)	x	1.6	= km (kilometers)	
mm (millimeters)	x	0.04	= in. (inches)	
yd (yards)	x	0.9	= m (meters)	

temperature (exact)

C (degrees Celsius or centigrade)	x	9/5	+ 32 = F (degrees Fahrenheit)
F (degrees Fahrenheit)	–	32	x 5/9 = C (degrees Celsius or centigrade)

volume

cups	x	0.24	= l (liters)
fl oz (fluid ounces)	x	30.00	= ml (milliliters)
ft^3 (cubic feet)	x	0.03	= m^3 (cubic meters)
gal (British Imperial gallons)	x	4.6	= l (liters)
gal (U.S. gallons)	x	3.8	= l (liters)
l (liters)	x	2.1	= pt (pints)
l (liters)	x	1.06	= qt (quarts)
l (liters)	x	0.22	= gal (British Imperial gallons)
l (liters)	x	0.26	= gal (gallons)
m^3 (cubic meters)	x	35.00	= ft^3 (cubic feet)
m^3 (cubic meters)	x	1.3	= yd^3 (cubic yards)
ml (milliliters)	x	0.03	= fl oz (fluid ounces)
pt (pints)	x	0.47	= l (liters)
qt (quarts)	x	0.95	= l (liters)
tbsp (tablespoons)	x	15.00	= ml (milliliters)
tsp (teaspoons)	x	5.00	= ml (milliliters)
yd^3 (cubic yards)	x	0.76	= m^3(cubic meters)

weight

g (grams)	x	0.035	= oz (ounces)

kg (kilograms)	x	2.2	=	lb (pounds)
lb (pounds)	x	0.45	=	kg (kilograms)
oz (ounces)	x	28.00	=	g (grams)
st (short tons—2000 pounds)	x	0.9	=	t (tonnes)
t (tonnes—1000 kilograms)	x	1.1	=	st (short tons)

International Radio Alphabet and Code

A: Alpha ·—
B: Bravo —···
C: Charlie —·—·
D: Delta —··
E: Echo ·
F: Foxtrot ··—·
G: Golf ——·
H: Hotel ····
I: India ··
J: Juliet ·———
K: Kilo —·—
L: Lima (leema) ·—··
M: Mike ——
N: November —·
O: Oscar ———
P: Papa ·——·
Q: Quebec (kaybeck) ——·—
R: Romeo ·—·
S: Sierra ···
T: Tango —
U: Uniform ··—
V: Victor ···—
W: Whiskey ·——
X: Xray —··—
Y: Yankee —·——
Z: Zulu ——··

RADIO NUMERALS

0: (zee-ro) —————
1: (wun) ·————
2: (too) ··———
3: (thuh-ree) ···——
4: (fo-wer) ····—
5: (fi-yiv) ·····
6: (siks) —····
7: (sev-ven) ——···
8: (ate) ———··
9: (ni-yen) ————·

International Yacht Racing Union Nationality Codes

Every yacht of an international class recognized by the International Yacht Racing Union must carry on her mainsail, when *racing* in foreign waters, a letter or letters showing her nationality.

A	Argentina
AR	United Arab Republic
B	Belgium
BA	Bahamas
BL	Brazil
BU	Bulgaria
CA	Cambodia
CY	Ceylon
CZ	Czechoslovakia
D	Denmark
E	Spain
EC	Ecuador
F	France
G	West Germany
GO	East Germany
GR	Greece
H	Holland
HA	Netherlands Antilles
I	Italy
IR	Republic of Ireland
K	United Kingdom
KA	Australia
KB	Bermuda
KC	Canada
KG	British Guiana
KGB	Gibraltar
KH	Hong Kong
KI	India
KJ	Jamaica
KK	Kenya
KR	South Rhodesia, Zambia, Malawi
KS	Singapore
KT	West Indies
KZ	New Zealand
L	Finland
LE	Lebanon
LX	Luxembourg
M	Hungary
MA	Morocco
MO	Monaco
MX	Mexico
N	Norway
NK	Democratic People's Republic of Korea
OE	Austria
P	Portugal
PH	Philippines
PR	Puerto Rico
PU	Peru
PZ	Poland
RC	Cuba
RI	Indonesia
RM	Romania
S	Sweden
SA	South Africa
SE	Senegal
SR	Union of Soviet Socialist Republics
T	Tunisia
TH	Thailand
TK	Turkey
U	Uruguay
US	United States of America
V	Venezuela
X	Chile
Y	Yugoslavia
Z	Switzerland

Numbered Abbreviations

o deg lat: zero degrees latitude—the Equator, encircling widest part of the earth
O²: both eyes
¼d: farthing (fourth of an English penny); a fourthling
¼ h: quarter-hard
¼ ly: quarterly
¼ ph: quarter-phase
¼ rd: quarter-round
½ can: narcotics equal to a half can of pipe tobacco
½d: halfpenny (half of an English penny); ha'penny
½ gr: half-gross
½ h: half-hard
½ rd: half-round
½ sovereign: 10 shillings
1b: first base(man)
1/: shilling; also called a *bob*
1/c: single-conductor
1d: an English penny
1s: shilling, also called a *bob*
***1º:** primero(a)* (Spanish—first)
1: Year 1; in the beginning (slang)
1A: available for military service
1-BCE: first century before the Christian era (Caesar's Century)—Julius Caesar conquered Britain and Egypt before he was assassinated in the Roman senate in the year 44
1-C: first century (the Vesuvian Century)—destruction of Pompeii, Herculaneum, and nearby Neapolitan places by the volcano Vesuvius in the year 79 of the Christian era
1C: member or former member of US armed forces with honorable discharge
1 cent: 1 penny (10 mills)
1 Chron: The First Book of the Chronicles
1 Cor: The First Epistle of Paul the Apostle to the Corinthians
1 crown: 5 shillings
1 dime: 10 cents
1 double eagle: S20 (gold)
1 eagle: S10 (gold)
***1er(e):** premier(e)* (French—first)
1 Esd: The First (Apocryphal) Book of Esdras
1 florin: 2 shillings
1 frogskin: S1 bill
1 guinea: 21 shillings
1G, 2G, 3G, etc.: slang for one, two, or three thousand dollars, etc.
1 half crown: 2 shillings, 6 pence
1 half dime: 5 cents
1 half dollar: 50 cents
1 half eagle: S5 (gold)
1 halfpenny: 2 farthings
1 Hen IV: First part of *King Henry IV*
1 Hen VI: First part of *King Henry VI*
1 John: The First Epistle General of John
1 Kings: The First Book of the Kings
1 Macc: The First (Apocryphal) Book of Maccabees
***1mo:** primo* (Italian—first)
1-p: single pole
1 penny: 4 farthings
1 Pet: The First Epistle General of Peter
1 ph: single-phase
1 pound: 20 shillings
1Q: first quarter
1Q66: first quarter 1966
1 quarter dollar: 25 cents
1 quarter eagle: S2.50 (gold)
1 Sam: The First Book of Samuel
1 shilling: 12 pence
1 sixpence: 6 pence
1 sovereign: 1 pound sterling; 20 shillings
1-spot: S1 bill
1st: first
1st cl hon: first-class honors (in academic degrees)
1st Lieut: First Lieutenant
1st Naval District: Boston, Massachusetts
1-striper: ensign (USN); third assistant engineer or third mate (merchant marine); private first class (US Army)
1st Sgt: First Sergeant
1 threepence: 3 pence
1 Thess: The First Epistle of Paul the Apostle to the Thessalonians
1 Tim: The First Epistle of Paul the Apostle to Timothy
1½ striper: naval lieutenant, junior grade
1s & 2s: mixed first and second quality lumber
1-wd: one-wheel drive
1-A: available for military service
I-A-O: conscientious objector available only for noncombatant military service
I-C: member of the armed forces, Coast and Geodetic Survey, or Public Health Service
I-D: member of reserve component or student taking military training
I-O: conscientious objector available only for civilian work contributing to national health, safety, or interest
I-S: student deferred by statute until end of current school year
1st State: Delaware
I-W: conscientious objector performing civilian work contributing to national health, safety, or interest, or who has completed such work
I-Y: registrant does not meet present standards; available for military service only in event of war or national emergency
2/: two shillings; also the coin called a florin
***2º:** segundo(a)* (Spanish—second)
II-A: registrant deferred because of civilian occupation (except agriculture and activity in study) or an apprentice deferred by statute
II-B: registrant deferred because necessary to war production
II-BCE: second century before the Christian era (Roman Century)—Punic wars result in destruction of Carthage by the Roman Legions—the 100s
2b: second base(man)
2 bits: 25 cents
2/c: two-conductor
II-C: registrant deferred because of agricultural occupation
II-C: second century (the Aurelian Century)—reign of the Roman emperior-philosopher Marcus Aurelius—the 100s
II Chron: The Second Book of the Chronicles
2d: second
***2do:** secondo* (Italian—second)
***IIe:** deuxième, second, seconde* (French—second)
II Esd: The Second (Apocryphal) Book of Esdras
2-F: two-seater fighter aircraft (naval symbol)
2g, 3g, 4g, etc.: multiples of acceleration of gravity which at the surface of the earth is 32.2 feet per second
2 Hen IV: Second part of *King Henry IV*
2 Hen VI: Second part of *King Henry VI*
2 i/c: second in command
II John: The Second Epistle of John
II Kings: The Second Book of Kings
II Macc: The Second (Apocryphal) Book of Maccabees
2n: diploid number
2nd: second
2nd Lieut: Second Lieutenant

2-p: double pole
II Pet: The Second Epistle General of Peter
2 ph: two-phase
2Q: second quarter
2Q66: 2nd quarter 1966
2s: two shillings; also the coin called a florin
II-S: registrant deferred because of activity in study
II Sam: The Second Book of Samuel
2-spot: $2 bill
2-striper: corporal (US Army); lieutenant (USN); second assistant engineer or second mate (merchant marine)
2/10–30: 2% discount if paid in 10 days, net in 30 days
2T: double throw
II Thess: The Second Epistle of Paul the Apostle to the Thessalonians
II Tim: Second Epistle of Paul the Apostle to Timothy
2-way: two-way
2-wd: 2-wheel drive
2½-striper: naval lieutenant commander
2-4-D: dichlorophenoxy-acetic acid (weed killer)
2/6: two-and-six (two shillings and sixpence); also called half a crown
2-13: drug addict
2244s: prisoners' petitions for judicial reviews of their cases
2-4-5-T: trichlorophenoxy-acetic acid (antiplant agent and defoliant)
2WW: Second Weather Wing (Air Force—New York)
III-A: registrant with child or children or registrant deferred by reason of extreme hardship to dependents
3b: third base(man)
III-BCE: third century before the Christian era (the Carthaginian Century)—Hannibal crossed the Alps to defeat the Romans—the 200s
3-Bs: Bach, Beethoven, Berlioz; Bach, Beethoven, Bernstein; Bach, Beethoven, Brahms; Bach, Beethoven, Bruckner; etc. (depending on one's favorite composers)
3/c: three-conductor
3C: Computer Control Company
III-C: third century (the Chinese Century)—Chin dynasty rules a reunited China—the 200s
3d: English threepenny; thruppence; third
3-d: dizzy, dopey, and dumb; three dimensional
3d 10h 40m: 3 days 10 hours 40 minutes (Atlantic crossing of SS *United States* in July 1952)
3-Ds: discouragement, disillusionment, disappointment (including frustration and loss)—often leads to suicide, experts insist
IIIe: *troisième* (French—third)
3 Hen VI: Third part of *King Henry VI*
3-I voters: Irish, Israeli, Italian
III John: The Third Epistle of John
3 K's: *Kinder, Küche, Kirche* (German—children, kitchen, church)
3M: Minnesota Mining and Manufacturing Company
3-M: Maintenance and Material Management (USN)
3º: *tercero(a)* (Spanish—third)
3-p: triple pole
3ph: three-phase
3Q: third quarter
3Q66: third quarter 1966
3rd: third
3rd degree: prolonged interrogation designed to produce a confession of guilt
3rd Naval District: New York, New York
3-R's: reading, writing, arithmetic (colloquially, readin', 'ritin', 'rithmetic)
3-star: admiral or general of three-star rank
3-striper: commander (USN); first assistant engineer or first mate (merchant marine); sergeant (US Army)
3T: triple throw
3-way: three-way
3WW: Third Weather Wing (Air Force—Nebraska)
4a: man 38 years or over and deferred from military service by reason of age
IV-A: registrant who has completed service or a sole surviving son
IV-B: government official deferred by statute
IV-BCE: fourth century before the Christian era (the Alexandrian Century)—Alexander the Great of Macedonia defeated the Egyptians, the Persians, and the Indians; encouraged the Greek philosophers and poets—the 300s
4 bits: 50 cents
4/c: four-conductor
4C: Community-Coordinated Child Care Program
IV-C: alien
IV-C: fourth century (the Constantinian Century)—Roman emperor Constantine builds the city of Constantinople on the site of ancient Byzantium and proclaims it capital of the Eastern Empire—the 300s
4-d meat: meat of dead, disabled, diseased, or dying animals
IV-D: minister of religion or divinity student
IVe: *quatrième* (French—fourth)
IV-E: conscientious objector available for, assigned to, or released for work of national importance
4-F: find, feel, fornicate, and forget—code of conduct of certain men in search of casual sexual relationships
IV-F: registrant not qualified for any military service
4-H: 4-H Clubs
4º: quarto (a book about 9 × 12 inches)
4º: *cuarto(a)* (Spanish—fourth)
4-p: quadruple pole
4Q: fourth quarter
4Q66: fourth quarter 1966
4R: Ceylon aircraft
4-star: admiral or general of four-star rank
4-striper: captain (merchant marine or USN); chief engineer (merchant marine)
4th: fourth
4th Naval District: Philadelphia, Pennsylvania
4-way: four-way
4-wd: four-wheel drive
4WW: Fourth Weather Wing (Air Force—Colorado)
4X: Israeli aircraft
5A: Libyan aircraft
V-A: registrant over the age liability for military service
5-and-10: variety store selling articles formerly costing not more than five or ten cents
V-BCE: fifth century before the Christian era (Athenian Century)—Athenians destroy Persian fleet at Salamis; complete the Parthenon in Athens—the 400s
5b: bald man with baywindow, bifocals, bridgework, and bunions (humorous Selective Service rating)
5-B's: Boston baked beans and

brownbread

5BX: five basic exercises (Royal Canadian Air Force physical fitness program)

V^e: *cinquième* (French—fifth)

V-C: fifth century (the Christian Century)—Christianity affirmed as the official faith by two Roman emperors—the 400s

5'er: $5 bill; 5-pound note

5°: *quinto(a)* (Spanish—fifth)

5-percenter: person who for 5 percent arranges introductions leading to valuable orders

5-Ps: (nickname of William Oxberry—British player, poet, publican, publisher, and printer)

5-spot: $5 bill

5th: fifth

5th Naval District: Norfolk, Virginia

5 w's: the *who, what, when, where,* and *why* reporters attempt to include in writing summary paragraphs

6 bits: 75 cents

VI-BCE: sixth century before the Christian era (Babylonian Century)—Babylonians defeat Israelites and make them captive after destroying the temple of Solomon in Jerusalem—the 500s

6/c: six-conductor

VI-C: sixth century (the Persian Century)—Khosru Nushirwan makes peace with the Byzantine Empire and extends Persian rule throughout the Middle East—the 500s

6d: English sixpenny; sixpence

6-dW: Six-day War between Arab countries of Egypt, Jordan, Lebanon, and Syria versus Israel; June 5 to 10, 1967

VIe: *sixième* (French—sixth)

6'er: leader of a pack of six scouts

6°: *sesto(a); sexto(a)* Spanish —sixth)

6-pack: carton containing six of a kind (6 containers of beer, soda, etc.)

6-R's: remedial readin', remedial 'ritin', remedial 'rithmetic

6-shooter: revolver holding six cartridges

6th: sixth

6th Naval District: Charleston, South Carolina

6WW: Sixth Weather Wing (Air Force—Washington, D.C.)

7A: Seven Arts Society

VII-BCE: seventh century before the Christian era (Assyrian Century) when Assyria rules Middle East and conquers Egypt—the 600s

7ber: September

7bre: *Septembre* (French—September); *septiembre* (Spanish—September

7/c: seven-conductor

VII-C: seventh century (the Islamic Century)—marked by Mohammed's flight from Mecca to Medina and his death in 632; Islam began expanding throughout the Middle East and North Africa as well as moving toward France and Spain—the 600s

7 Dec: Pearl Harbor Day (1941)

7ds: seven deadly sins—anger, covetousness, envy, gluttony, lechery, pride, sloth

7^c: *septiembre* (Spanish—September)

7°: *septimo(a)* (Spanish—seventh)

VIIe: *septième* (French—seventh)

7th: seventh

7-Up: a carbonated beverage

7WW: Seventh Weather Wing (Air Force—Illinois)

8: numerical symbol for heroin as H is the eighth of the alphabet

VIII-BCE: eighth century before the Christian era (Chou Century)—eastern Chou dynasty begins ruling China for the next five centuries—the 700s

8 bits: one dollar

8bre: *octobre* (French—October); *octubre* (Spanish—October)

VIII-C: eighth century (the Carolingian Century)—Charlemagne or Charles the Great reigns as King of the Franks and Emperor of the West as well as being chief patron of learning—the 700s

8e: *octubre* (Spanish—October)

VIIIe: *huitième* (French—eighth)

8N: American National 8-thread series

8°: octavo (a book about 9¾ inches high)

8°: *octavo(a)* (Spanish—eighth)

8th: eighth

8th Naval District: New Orleans, Louisiana

8UN: Unified 8-thread series

8va bass.: *ottava bassa* (Italian—octave lower)

IX-BCE: ninth century before the Christian era (Phoenician Century)—Carthage founded by the Phoenicians who trade in all areas of the Mediterranean—the 800s

9ber: November

9bre: *novembre* (French—November); *noviembre* (Spanish—November)

IX-C: ninth century (the Century of Confusion)—Carolingian Empire of Charlemagne disintegrates; European unity dismembered and divided—the 800s

9e: *noviembre* (Spanish—November)

IXe: *neuvième* (French—ninth)

9th: ninth

9th Naval District: Great Lakes, Illinois

9°: *nono(a); noveno(a)* (Spanish—ninth)

9 to 5: everyday job

'10: 1810 (Bolvarian-type Spanish-American Revolutions and wars of liberation, 1810–1826)

10^{-1}: deci (d)

10^{-2}: centi (c)

10^{-3} milli (m)

10^{-6}: micro (μ)

10^{-9}: nano (n)

10^{-12}: pico (p)

10^{-15}: femto (f)

10^{-18}: atto (a)

10: deka (da)

10°: *decimo(a)* (Spanish—tenth)

10^2: hecto (h)

10^3: kilo (k)

10^6: mega (M)

10^9: giga (G)

10^{12}: tera (T)

10 Aug: Ecuadorian Independence Day

X-BCE: tenth century before the Christian era (Israelian Century)—King Solomon reigns and Israelites defeat all enemies and build the great temple of Jerusalem—the 900s

10bre: *décembre* (French—December); *diciembre* (Spanish—December)

Xber: December

X-C: tenth century (the Mayan Century)—great American civilization leaving monumental ruins strewn from Honduras to Yucatan—the 900s

10 Dec: Human Rights Day (Liberia)

10e: *diciembre* (Spanish—December)

X^e: *dixième* (French—tenth)

10 Downing Street: British prime minister's home in west central London

10-gallon hat: cowboy hat

10-spot: $10 bill

10th: tenth
10th Naval District: San Juan, Puerto Rico
10-V: the lowest; the opposite of A-1; the worst
XI-BCE: eleventh century before the Christian era (Century of Saul and David)—King Saul followed by King David as ruler of Israel—the 1000s
XI-C: eleventh century (the Aztecan and Incan Century)—vast monuments in the highlands of Mexico and Peru stand as mute witnesses to these great American civilizations—the 1000s
11th: eleventh
11th Naval District: San Diego, California
11-11-11: eleventh hour, eleventh day, eleventh month of 1918 when Armistice ended World War I
XII-BCE: twelfth century before the Christian era (Trojan Century)—Troy falls to the Greeks after a ten-year siege celebrated in Homer's epic poem the *Iliad*—the 1100s
XII-C: twelfth century (the Portuguese Century when Alfonso I Henriques reigns as king of Portugal soon to emerge as a great maritime power—the 1100s
12N: American National 12-thread series
12°: twelvemo (a book about 7¾ inches high)
12th: twelfth
12th Naval District: San Francisco, California
12UN: Unified 12-thread series
13: numerical symbol for marijuana as M is the thirteenth letter of the alphabet; police radio signal call 13 indicates an officer needs help—this is the highest priority radio call and all units respond
XIII-BCE: thirteenth century before the Christian era (Century of the Exodus)—Moses leads the Israelites out of Egypt—the 1200s
XIII-C: thirteenth century (the Mongol Century) dominated by the reign of the Mongol emperor Genghiz Khan whose hordes conquer China and Russia—the 1200s
13th: thirteenth
13th Naval District: Seattle, Washington
14: numerical symbol for narcotics as N is the fourteenth letter of the alphabet
XIV-BCE: fourteenth century before the Christian era (Century of the Pharoah Tutankhamen)
XIV-C: fourteenth century (Tamerlane's Century)—Mongol emperor Timur (Tamer the Lame) dominates Middle East and western India—the 1300s
14th: fourteenth
14th Naval District: Pearl Harbor, Oahu, Hawaii
15th: fifteenth
15th Naval District: Balboa, Canal Zone
XV-BCE: fifteenth century before the Christian era (Egyptian Century)—Egyptian kingdom extended from the Sahara to beyond the Euphrates—the 1400s
XV-C: fifteenth century (the Italian Century)—powerful families such as the Borgias and the de Medicis bring about the renewal of art and architecture in Italy—the Italian Renaissance—the 1400s
XVI to XXXII BCE: *(see* XXXII-BCE
XXXII-BCE: thirty-second century before the Christian era (Dynastic Century) when the first and second of many Egyptian dynasties began a rule lasting for at least seventeen centuries before the power of the pharoahs began to wane—the 3100s
XVI-C: sixteenth century (the Spanish Century) marked by discoveries and colonizations of much of the New World, circumnavigation of the globe, flowering of art and literature—the Golden Age or *Siglo de Oro*, as well as the defeat of the Spanish Armada by the British—the 1500s
16N: American National 16-thread series
16°: sixteenmo (a book about 6¾ inches high)
16's: 16 rpm phonograph records
16th: sixteenth
16UN: Unified 16-thread series
XVII-C: seventeenth century (the Dutch Century) sees the discovery and settlement of what is now New York as well as South Africa and the East Indies by the Dutch who after a war at sea arrange a mutual defense pact with their British rivals—the 1600s (*see* the Elizabethan Age, *Le Grand Siecle, El Siglo de Oro)*
17-D: modified yellow-fever virus
17th: seventeenth
17th Naval District: Kodiak, Alaska
XVIII-C: eighteenth century (the French Century) of courtesans and kings, poets and playrights, of great territories acquired and lost, of Louis XVI and Marie Antoinette beheaded by the guillotine only to be replaced by Napoleon—the turbulent 1700s (*see* The Enlightenment)
18th: eighteenth
18–19 Sept: Chilean Independence Days
XIX-C: nineteenth century (the British Century) from Napoleon's defeat by Wellington at Waterloo to the defeat of the Boers in South Africa this century is marked by British advances in invention, in the success of its industrial revolution, in its colonization in all parts of the world, and its maritime supremacy on all the oceans—the 1800s
19th: nineteenth
XX-C: twentieth century (The American Century) characterized by industrial advances, victory in two world wars, as well as the development of inventions, the discovery of the North Pole, the placing of men on the moon, the elevation of living standards, the devotion to democratic ideals—the 1900s
20-spot: $20 bill
20th: twentieth; Twentieth Century Limited (New York Central Railroad)
XXI-C: twenty-first century (the Japanese Century)—providing productivity, standard of living, and other growth factors are not disturbed by large-scale earthquakes and world wars—the 2000s
21st: twenty-first
.22: .22-caliber ammunition, pistol, or rifle
22d: twenty-second
22nd: twenty-second
23½ deg N lat: Tropic of Cancer
23½ deg S lat: Tropic of Capricorn
23rd: twenty-third
24°: twenty-fourmo (a book about 5¾ inches high)

24th: twenty-fourth
25: LSD as 25 is part of the chemical name—d-lysergic acid diethylamide tartrate 25
25th: twenty-fifth
26th: twenty-sixth
27th: twenty-seventh
28th: twenty-eighth
29th: twenty-ninth
30: finis symbol used by newspapermen at end of article or story
30 days, etc.: (calendar mnemonic—30 days hath September, April, June, and November; all the rest have 31 save February; 28 are all its score, but in leap year one day more)
30th: thirtieth
.30-'06: 30-caliber American cartridge introduced in 1906; used by US Armed Forces in World Wars I and II for rifles and machine guns
32°: thirty-twomo (a book about 5 inches high)
33's: 33⅓ rpm phonograph records
.38: .38-caliber ammunition or pistol
40: 40 acres
40th: fortieth
40 winks: a nap or short sleep
42nd cousin: a distant relative
.44: .44-caliber ammunition or pistol
.45: .45-caliber ammunition, pistol, or submachine gun
45's: 45 rpm phonograph records
47th State: New Mexico
48: 48-hour weekend liberty pass
48°: forty-eightmo (a book about 4 inches high)
48er: emigrant who came to America in 1848; participant in German revolution of 1848
48th State: Arizona
49er: gold-rush settler who came to California in 1849
49th State: Alaska
.50: .50-caliber ammunition or machine gun
50-spot: $50 bill
50th: fiftieth
50th State: Hawaii
60th: sixtieth
64°: sixty-fourmo (a book about 3 inches high)
66: Phillips Petroleum Company
66 deg 17 min N lat: Arctic Circle
66 deg 17 min S lat: Antarctic Circle
69: pictorial numerical symbol for oral-genital copulation
70th: seventieth
73: best regards (amateur radio)
75's: 75mm cannon
76: Union Oil
'76: 1776
78's: 78 rpm phonograph records
80th: eightieth
88: love and kisses (amateur radio)
89d: 89 days (New York to San Francisco run of American clipper ship *Flying Cloud* in 1854)
89er: Oklahoman who settled in 1889 when the territory was opened
90-day wonder: officer commissioned after only 90 days of training
90 deg N lat: North Pole (zero degrees longitude)
90 deg S lat: South Pole (zero degrees longitude)
90th: ninetieth
93-score: best grade of butter (USDA grade AA)
'96: 1796 (Napoleonic Wars, 1796–1815)
100th: one-hundredth
111: One-Eleven (British Aircraft Corporation short-take-off-and-landing fan-jet aircraft)
240: Convair two-engine transport airplane; trotting horse speed—1 mile in 2 minutes and 40 seconds; synonym for high speed
280: copper alloy (Muntz metal); yellow metal
400: the four hundred; the socially elite (originally designated by Ward McAllister, who drew up a list containing the top 400 in New York society)
415 PC: Section 415 Penal code—disturbing the peace
502: drunken driving (police code)
606: arsphenamine compound sold as Salvarsan; 606th compound developed and tested by Paul Ehrlich for treatment of relapsing fevers and syphilis
707: Boeing Stratoliner jet-transport airplane
720: Boeing medium-range jet-transport airplane
727: Boeing jet-transport with three empennage-mounted engines
737: Boeing short-range twin-jet airplane
747: Boeing jumbo jet-liner (built to transport from 490 to 1000 passengers, depending on the model)
880: Convair 880 jet airplane
911: (police telephone number in many U.S. cities)
990: Convair 990 fan-engine jet airplane
1600 Pennsylvania Avenue: (Washington, D.C., address of the White House)
"*1919*": *Nineteen nineteen* (novel by John Dos Passos depicting World War I era of American life in series of camera-eye closeups)—1919 often used to symbolize this period
"*1984*": *Nineteen eighty-four* (novel of George Orwell describing totalitarian terror in the year 1984)—1984 has become a symbol for anti-libertarian trends
23102a V(ehicle) C(ode): driving under the influence of any intoxicating liquor or drug
2707: Boeing supersonic transport

Numeration

	power	prefix	abbreviation	name
1,000,000,000,000	10^{12}	tera	t	one trillion*
100,000,000,000	10^{11}			one-hundred billion
10,000,000,000	10^{10}			ten billion
1,000,000,000	10^{9}	giga	g	one billion
100,000,000	10^{8}			one-hundred million
10,000,000	10^{7}			ten million
1,000,000	10^{6}	mega	m	one million
100,000	10^{5}			one-hundred thousand
10,000	10^{4}			ten thousand
1000	10^{3}	kilo	k	one thousand
100	10^{2}			one hundred
10	10^{1}			ten
1	10^{0}			one
0.1	10^{-1}	deci	d	one-tenth
0.01	10^{-2}	centi	c	one-hundredth
0.001	10^{-3}	milli	m	one-thousandth
0.0001	10^{-4}			one ten-thousandth
0.00001	10^{-5}			one hundred-thousandth
0.000001	10^{-6}	micro	(*u* - mu)	one millionth
0.0000001	10^{-7}			one ten-millionth
0.00000001	10^{-8}			one hundred-millionth
0.000000001	10^{-9}	nano	n	one billionth
0.0000000001	10^{-10}			one ten-billionth
0.00000000001	10^{-11}			one hundred-billionth
0.000000000001	10^{-12}	pico	p	one trillionth
0.0000000000001	10^{-13}			one ten-trillionth
0.00000000000001	10^{-14}			one hundred-trillionth
0.000000000000001	10^{-15}	femto	f	one quadrillionth
0.0000000000000001	10^{-16}			one ten-quadrillionth
0.00000000000000001	10^{-17}			one hundred-quadrillionth
0.000000000000000001	10^{-18}	atto	a	one quintillionth

* - trillions are followed by quadrillions, quintillions, sextillions, septillions, octillions, nonillions, decillions, undecillions, duodecillions, tredecillions, quattuordecillions, quinquedecillions, sexdecillions, septendecillions, octodecillions, novemdecillions, vigintillions (a thousand novemdecillions)

Proofreader's Marks

- || align; straighten ends of lines
- ⌄' apostrophe or single quotation mark
- bf black face or bold face type (run waved line under text matter)
- ⊗ broken type; damaged type; imperfect type
- cap capital letter
- ≡ capital letters (run triple line under material to be capitalized: George Washington)
- ∧ caret; insertion mark
- ⁀ close up
- :/ colon
- ∧, comma
- ♂ delete or dele; expunge; take out
- ⊔ depress or sink a letter or word
- ⊓ elevate or raise a letter or word
- =/ hyphen
- ital set in *italics* (material to be italicized is underlined)
- lc lower case (run / through letter or letters to be set in /Lower /Case)
- lead insert lead spacing between lines
- ⊏ move to the left
- ⊐ move to the right
- ¶ paragraph
- ⊙ period
- ⊥ push down space which prints as a mark

" " quotation marks

rom set in roman type

;/ semicolon

sc small caps (run double line under material: a.d.)

space; ## double space; etc.

sp spell out (material to be spelled out is encircled: U.S.)

stet let stand that which has been deleted; restore crossed out material (indicate by running dots under the letters of the words to be restored)

tr transpose (indicate in text by ~ or ∽)

@ turn letter right side up

wf wrong font

Railroads of the World

—abbreviations and nicknames
—reporting marks

AA: Ann Arbor Railroad
AAR: Association of American Railroads
A & B: Antofagasta and Bolivia
A y B: *Antofagasta y Bolivia* (Spanish—Antofagasta and Bolivia)—Chilean Railway linking Pacific port with highlands of landlocked Bolivia
ABB: Akron and Barberton Belt Railroad
ABL: Alameda Belt Line
AC: Algoma Central Railway
ACL: Atlantic Coast Line (Seaboard Coast Line Raliroad)
ACY: Akron, Canton and Youngstown Railroad
AD: Atlantic and Danville Railway
ADN: Ashley, Drew and Northern Railway (also AD & N)
AEC: Atlantic and East Carolina
AFE: *Administracion de los Ferrocarriles del Estado* (Spanish—State Railway Administration)—Uruguay
AFL: *Administracion de los Ferrocarriles del Estado* (Spanish—State Railways Administration)—Venezuela
AGS: Alabama Great Southern (Southern Railway)
AF: Alma and Jonquieres Railway
AL: Almanor Railroad
ALM: Arkansas and Louisiana Missouri Railway (also A & LM)
ALN: Albany and Northern Railroad
ALQS: Aliquippa and Southern
ALS: Alton and Southern Railroad
AL & S: Alton and Southern Railroad
Alton Route: Gulf, Mobile and Ohio Railroad
AMC: Amador Central Railroad
AMR: Arcata and Mad River
Amtrac: American (railroad) tracks —(government-sponsored program for reviving city-to-city passenger service)
AN: Apalachicola Northern Railroad
Ann Arbor: Detroit, Toledo and Ironton Railroad
Annie & Mary: (nickname—Arcata and Mad River Railroad) —originally the Union Wharf and Plank Walk Company
ANR: Angelina and Neches River Railroad
APA: Apache Railway Company
APD: Albany Port District
AR: Aberdeen and Rockfish
ARA: Arcade and Attica Railroad
ARC: Alexander Railroad (Southern)
ARR: Alaska Railroad
ART: American Refrigerator Transit
ARW: Arkansas Western Railway (Kansas City Southern)
A & S: Abilene and Southern
ASAB: Atlanta and Saint Andrews Bay Railway
ASDA: Asbestos and Danville
ASLRA: American Short Line Railroad Association
ASR: Association of Southeastern Railroads
ATC: Arnold Transit Company
ATN: Alabama, Tennessee and Northern Railroad
ATSF: Atchison, Topeka and Santa Fe Railway (also AT & SF)
ATW: Atlantic and Western
AUG: Augusta Railroad
AUS: Augusta and Summerville
AVL: Aroostook Valley Railroad
AW: Ahnapee and Western Railway
AWP: Atlanta and West Point Rail Road (includes Western Railway of Alabama and Georgia Railroad)—also A & WP
AWW: Algers, Winslow and Western Railway
AYSS: Allegheny and South Side
B & A: Boston and Albany (Penn Central)
BAP: Butte, Anaconda and Pacific Railway (also BA & P)
BAR: Bangor and Aroostook Railroad
BARC: Baltimore and Annapolis Railroad Company
B & ARR: Boston and Albany Railroad
BART: Bay Area Rapid Transit (San Francisco Bay Area mass transportation system)
Bay Line: Atlanta and Saint Andrews Bay Railway
BB: Birmingham Belt Railroad
BCE Route: British Columbia Electric Route
BCH: British Columbia Hydro and Power Authority
BCK: Buffalo Creek Railroad
BCK: *Bas-Congo au Katanga* (French—Lower Congo—Katanga)—railway of Zaire
BCRR: Boyne City Railroad
BCYR: British Columbia Yukon Railway
BDZ: (Cyrillic transliteration—Bulgarian State Railways)
BE: Baltimore and Eastern Railroad (Penn Central)
BEDT: Brooklyn Eastern District Terminal Railroad
BEEM: Beech Mountain Railroad
BEM: Beaufort and Morehead Railroad

Bessemer: Bessemer and Lake Erie
BFC: Bellefonte Central Railroad
BH: Bath and Hammondsport Railroad
BHS: Bonhomie and Hattiesburg Southern Railroad
Big Four: Cleveland, Cincinnati, Chicago and St Louis Railway (Penn Central)
Birmingham Southern: Birmingham Southern Railraod
BLA: Baltimore and Annapolis
B & LE: Bessemer and Lake Erie Railroad
BM: Boston and Maine Corporation
BME: Beaver, Meade and Englewood Railroad
BML: Belfast and Moosehead Lake
BMT: Brooklyn-Manhattan Transit (subway system)
BMRR: Beech Mountain Railroad
B & MRR: Beaufort and Morehead Railroad
BN: Burlington Northern (combining former Great Northern; Northern Pacific; Chicago, Burlington and Quincy; Spokane, Portland and Seattle; and Pacific Coast railroads)
B & N: Bauxite and Northern Railway
BNT: Buffalo Niagara Transit
B & O: Baltimore and Ohio Railroad (Chessie System)
BOCT: Baltimore and Ohio Chicago Terminal Railroad
BOYC: Boyne City Railroad
BR: British Railways; Burma Railways
BRC: Belt Railway Company of Chicago
BR & W: Black River and Western
BS: Birmingham Southern Railroad
B & S: Bevier and Southern
BTA: Boston Transportation Authority
BTC: Baltimore Transit Company
BTN: Belton Railroad
BU: Budapest Underground (subway system
Burlington Northern: combining Great Northern; Northern Pacific; Chicago, Burlington and Quincy; Spokane, Portland and Seattle; and Pacific Coast railroads)
Burlington Route: Chicago, Burlington and Quincy Railroad
BUSH: Bush Terminal Railroad
BVG: *Berliner Verkehrs Betriebe* (German—Berlin Traffic Management)—Berlin's subway system
BV & S: Bevier and Southern
BWC: Pennsylvania New York Central Transportation Company
BYR: British Yukon Railway
CAD: Cadiz Railroad
CAR: Central Australia Railway
CARR: Carrollton Railroad
CARW: Carolina Western Railroad
CASO: Canada Southern Railway (Penn Central)
CBC: Carbon County Railway
CBL: Conemaugh and Black Lick
CB & Q: Chicago, Burlington and Quincy Railroad
CCCSL: Cleveland, Cincinnati, Chicago and St Louis Railway (Penn Central)
CCFPCS: *Cie des Chemins de Fer de la Plaine du Cul-de-Sac* (French—*Cul-de-Sac Plaine Railroad Company*)—Tahiti
CC & O: Carolina, Clinchfield and Ohio Railway
CC & ORSC: Carolina, Clinchfield and Ohio Railroad of South Carolina
CCR: Corinth and Counce Railroad
CCT: Central California Traction
C & EI: Chicago and Eastern Illinois Railroad
Central: (nickname—New York Central Railroad)—now part of the Penn Central
Central of Ga: Central of Georgia
CF: Cape Fear Railways
CF C-O: *Chemin de Fer Congo-Ocean* (French—Congo-Ocean Railroad)—Congo People's Republic (Brazzaville)
C de F D-N: *Chemins de Fer Dakar-Niger* (French—Dakar-Niger Railways)—Mali
CFF/SFF/FFS: *Chemins de fer Federaux Suisses/Schweizerische Bundesbahnen/Ferrovie Dederali Svizzere/* (French, German, Italian—Swiss Federal Railways)
CFL: *Societe Nationale des Chemins de fer Luxembourgeois* (French—Luxembourg National Railways)
CFM: *Caminho de Ferro de Moçambique*(Portuguese—Mozambique Railroad); *Chemin de Fer Madagascar* (French—Madagascar Railroad)
CFR: *Caile Ferate Ramane* (Romanian—General Direction of the Romanian Railroads)
CFRC: *Chemins de Fer Royaux du Cambodge* (French—Royal Cambodian Railways)
CG: Central of Georgia Railway
C & G: Columbus and Greenville
C of G: Central of Georgia Railway
CGR: Ceylon Government Railway; Cyrenaica Government Railway (Libya)
C & GTR: Canada and Gulf Terminal Railway
CGW: Chicago Great Western
C & H: Cheswick and Harmer Railroad
Chessie System: Chesapeake & Ohio/Baltimore & Ohio
Chicago Outer Belt: Elgin, Joliet and Eastern Railway
Chihuahua-Pacific Railway: *Ferrocarril del Chihuahua al Pacific*—from the border of Texas at Presidio to the Pacific coast at Los Mochis via Chihuahua over route of the Kansas City, Mexico, and Orient
CH-P: Ferrocarril Chihuahua al Pacific. (Chihuahua-Pacific Railway formerly Mexico Northwestern Railway and Kansas City, Mexico and Orient Railway)
CHR: Chestnut Ridge Railway
CHTT: Chicago Heights Terminal Transfer Railroad
CHV: Chattahoochee Valley
CHW: Chesapeake Western
C & I : Cambria and Indiana Railroad
CIC: Cedar Rapids and Iowa City Railway
CIE: *Coras Iompair Eireann* (Gaelic—Irish State Railways)
CI & L: Chicago, Indianapolis, and Louisville Railway (Monon Railroad)
CIM: Chicago and Illinois Midland Railway (also C & IM)
CIND: Central Indiana Railway
CIRR: Chattahoochee Industrial Railroad
C & IRR: Cambria and Indiana Railroad
CIW: Chicago and Illinois Western Railroad
CIWL: *Compangie Internationale des Wagon-Lits* (French—International Sleeping Car Company)
CKSO: Condon, Kinzua and Southern Railroad
CLC: Columbia and Cowlitz
CLCO: Claremont and Concord
Clinchfield: Clinchfield Railroad (Carolina, Clinchfield and Ohio Railway)
CLK: Cadillac and Lake City Railway

CLP: Clarendon and Pittsford Railroad

CLRR: Camp Lejeune Railroad

CMO: Chicago, St Paul, Minneapolis and Omaha (Chicago North Western)

C M StP & P: Chicago, Milwaukee, St Paul and Pacific

CN: Canadian National (includes Canadian National Railways; Central Vermont Railway; Duluth, Winnipeg and Pacific Railway; Grand Trunk Lines in U.S.A.)

C & N: Carolina and Northwestern Railway

CNJ: Central Railroad of New Jersey

CN & L: Columbia, Newberry and Laurens Railroad

CNTP: Cincinnati, New Orleans and Texas Pacific

CNO & TPR: Cincinnati, New Orleans and Texas Pacific Railway

CNR: Chiriqui National Railroad (Panama)

CNW: Chicago and North Western Railway (includes Chicago, St Paul, Minneapolis and Omaha; Litchfield and Madison Railway; Minneapolis and St Louis)

C & NW: Chicago and North Western Railway

C & O: Chesapeake and Ohio (Chessie System)

Coahuila-Zacatecas Railway: Ferrocarril Coahuila-Zacatecas—Mexico

Cog Wheel Route: Manitou and Pike's Peak Railway

COP: City of Prineville Railway

COPR: Copper Range Railroad

Corn Belt Route: St Louis Southwestern Railway

Cotton Belt: Cotton Belt Route (St Louis Southwestern Railway—SSW)

CP: Canadian Pacific Railway (Dominion Atlantic Railway, Esquimalt and Nanaimo Railway, Grand River Railway, Lake Erie and Northern Railway, Quebec Central Railway, Vancouver and Lulu Island Branch)

CP: *Companhia des Caminhos de ferro Portuguese* (Portuguese—Portuguese Railways)

CPA: Coudersport and Port Allegany Railroad

CPF: Cotton Plant—Fargo Railway

CP & LT: Camino, Placerville and Lake Tahoe Railroad

CPR: Canadian Racific Railroad

CP Rail: Canadian Pacific Railroad

CPT: Chicago Produce Terminal

CR: Commonwealth Railways (Australia and Tasmania); Copper Range Railroad (Michigan, Wisconsin, Illinois)

CRANDIC Route: Cedar Rapids and Iowa City Railway

CRC: Cameroon Railways Corporation (West Africa); Cumberland Railway Company (Nova Scotia)

CRI: Chicago River and Indiana

CR & IC: Cedar Rapids and Iowa City Railway

CR & IR: Chicago River and Indiana Railroad

CRN: Carolina and Northwestern (Southern Railway)

CRP: Central Railway of Peru

CRR: Clinchfield Railroad

CRRNJ: Central Railroad of New Jersey

C & S: Colorado and Southern Railway

CSAR: Central South African Railways

CSD: *Ceskoslovenske Statni Drahy* (Czechoslovakian—Czechoslova State Railways)

CSL: Chicago Short Line Railway

CSP: Camas Prairie Railroad

CSS: Chicago South Shore and South Bend Railroad

CSS & SBR: Chicago South Shore and South Bend Railroad

C St P M & O: Chicago, St Paul, Minneapolis and Omaha (Chicago North Western)

CTA: Chicago Transit Authority (elevated and subway railroads)

CTC: Canadian Transport Commission; Cincinnati Transit Company

CTN: Canton Railroad

CTS: Cleveland Transit System

CUTC: Cincinnati Union Terminal Company

CUVA: Cuyahoga Valley Railroad

CV: Central Vermont Railway

CVRy: Cuyahoga Valley Railway

C & W: Colorado and Wyoming Railway

C & WC: Charleston and Western Carolina Railway (Seaboard Coast Line Railroad)

CWI: Chicago and Western Indiana

CWP: Chicago, West Pullman and Southern Railroad (also CWP & S)

CWR: California Western Railroad

DA: Dominion Atlantic Railway (Canadian Pacific)

DB: *Deutsche Bundesbahn* (German—German Railways)

DC: Delray Connecting Railroad

DCI: Des Moines and Central Iowa

DCR: Delray Connecting Railroad (Zug Island Road)

DCT: Washington, D.C. Transit

D & E: De Queen and Eastern

Delay Long and Wait: nickname for the Delaware, Lackawanna and Western Railroad (derived from the initials DL & W)

D & H: Delaware and Hudson

DHR: Darjeeling Himalayan Railway

diner: dining car

DKS: Doniphan, Kensett and Searcy Railway

DL & W: Delaware, Lackawanna and Western Railroad (Erie Lackawanna)

D & M: Detroit and Mackinac

DM & IRR: Duluth, Missabe and Iron Range Railway

DMM: Dansville and Mount Morris

DMU: Des Moines Union Railway

DMWR: Des Moines Western Railway

DNE: Duluth and Northeastern Railroad

DO: Direct Orient (Orient Express)

DORR: Delaware Otsego Railroad

DQ & ERR: De Queen and Eastern Railroad

D & R: Dardanelle and Russellville

D & RGW: Denver and Rio Grande Western Railroad

DRI: Davenport, Rock Island and North Western Railway

DRy: Devco Railway

DS: Durham and Southern Railway

D & S: Durham and Southern Railway

DSB: *Danske Statsbaner* (Danish—Danish State Railways)

DSR: Detroit Street Railways

DT: Detroit Terminal Railroad

D of T: Department of Transportation

DTC: Dallas Transit Company

DTI: Detroit, Toledo and Ironton Railroad (also DT & I)

D & TS: Detroit and Toledo Shore Line Railroad

DVS: Delta Valley and Southern Railway

DWP: Duluth, Winnipeg and Pacific Railway

E: Erie Lackawanna

EAR: East African Railways

EARC: East African Railways Corporation

EAR & H: East African Railways and Harbours
EBR: Emu Bay Railway (Tasmania)
EBRy: Eastern Bengal Railway (East Pakistan)
EDLR: Egyptian Delta Light Railways
EDW: El Dorado and Wesson
EEC: East Erie Commercial Railroad
EFA: *Empresa Ferrocarriles Argentinos* (Spanish—Argentine Railways Enterprise)
EFE: *Empresa de los Ferrocarriles del Estado* (Spanish—State Railways Enterprise)—Chile
EFEE: *Empresa de los Ferrocarriles del Estado Ecuatoriano* (Spanish—Ecuadorian State Railways Enterprise)
EJ & ERy: Elgin, Joliet and Eastern Railway
EJR: East Jersey Railroad
El: Elevated Railroad
EL: Erie Lackawanna Railway (merger of Erie with Delaware, Lackawanna and Western)
ELS: Escanaba and Lake Superior Railroad (also E & LSRR)
E & M: Edgmoor and Manetta
EN: Esquimalt and Nanaimo Railway (Canadian Pacific)
ENF: *Empresa Nacional de Ferrocarriles* (Spanish—National Railways Enterprise)—Bolivia
ER: Egyptian Railways
ERBR: Eastern Region of British Railways
Erie: Erie Railroad (Erie Lackawanna)
ESLJ: East St Louis Junction Railroad
ETL: Essex Terminal Railway
ET & WNC: East Tennessee and Western North Carolina Railroad
Eurailpass: European railroad pass (ticket system valid on almost all European railroads)
EW: East Washington Railway
EYB: *Europa Year Book*
F & C: Frankfort and Cincinnati Railroad
F de C: *Ferrocarriles de Cuba* (Spanish—Cuban Railroads)—Unidad Habana (western Cuba) and Unidad Camaguey (eastern Cuba)
FCAB: *Ferrocarril Antofagasta-Bolivia* (Spanish—Antofagasta and Bolivia Railway)
FCDN: *Ferrocarril del Nacozari* (Spanish—Nacozari Railroad)—Mexico
FCG: Fernwood, Columbia and Gulf Railroad
FCIN: Frankfort and Cincinnati
FCM: *Ferrocarriles Nacionales de México* (Spanish—Mexican National Railways)—includes Nacional de México and Nacional de Tehuantepec
FCP: *Ferrocarril del Pacifico* (Spanish—Pacific Railroad)—links Arizona border with Mazatlan on west coast of Mexico
FC del P: *Ferrocarril Central del Perú* (Spanish—Central Railway of Peru)
FCZ: *Ferrocarril Coahuila-Zacatecas* (Spanish—Coahuila-Zacatecas Railway)—Mexico
FDDM: Fort Dodge, Des Moines and Southern Railway
Feather River Route: Western Pacific Railroad
FEC: Florida East Coast Railway
FEGUA: *Ferrocarriles de Guatemala* (Spanish—Railroads of Guatemala)
FEP: *Ferrocarril Electrico al Pacifico* (Spanish—Pacific Electric Railway)—Costa Rican line linking Pacific port of Puntarenas with mountain capital of San José
FER: Franco-Ethiopian Railway
FES: *Ferrocarril de El Salvador* (Spanish—El Salvador Railway)
F de G a LP: *Ferrocarril de Guayaquil-La Paz* (Spanish—Guayaquil-La Paz Railway)—Peru
FICA: *Ferrocarriles Internacionales de Centro America* (Spanish—International Railways of Central America)
FIPC: *Ferrocarril Industrial del Potosí y Chihuahua (Spanish—Industrial Railroad of Potosi and Chihuahua)—Mexico*
FJG: Fonda, Johnstown and Gloversville Railroad
FLR: Fayum Light Railways (Egypt)
FMS: Fort Myers Southern Railroad
FN: *Ferrocarriles Nacionales* (Spanish—National Railways—Argentina, Chile, Colombia, Cuba, Ecuador, Honduras, Mexico, Panama, Venezuela, etc.)
F del N: *Ferrocarriles del Norte* (Spanish—Northern Railways)—Paraguay
FNC: *Ferrocarriles Nacionales de Cuba* (National Railroads of Cuba nationalized by Castro government and consisting of Consolidated Railroads of Cuba—The Cuba Railroad—Cuba Northern Railways—Guantanamo and Western Railroad—Guantanamo Railroad—Hershey Cuban Railway—et cetera)
FN de H: *Ferrocarriles Nacionales de Honduras* (Spanish—National Railways of Honduras)
FNM: *Ferrocarriles Nacionales de México* (Spanish—National Railways of Mexico)
FOM: *Ferrocarril Occidental de México* (Spanish—Western Railway of Mexico
FOR: Fore River Railroad
F del P: *Ferrocarril del Pacifico* (Spanish—Pacific Railroad)—Mexico
FPCAL: *Ferrocarriles President Carlos Antonio López* (Spanish—President Carlos Antonio Lopez Railways)—Paraguay
FPE: Fairport, Painesville and Eastern Railroad
FP & ER: Fairport, Painesville and Eastern Railway
FPN: *Ferrocarril del Pacifico de Nicaragua* (Spanish—Pacific Railway of Nicaragua)
FR: Feather River Railway
FRDN: Ferdinand Railroad
Frisco: St Louis-San Francisco Railway
FS: *Ferrovie dello Stato* (Italian—State Railway)
FSBC: Ferrocarril Sonora-Baja California (Sonora-Baja California Railroad)
FS del P: *Ferrocarril del Sur del Perú* (Spanish—Southern Railway of Peru)
FSVB: Fort Smith and Van Buren Railway (Kansas City Southern)
FtD DM & S: Fort Dodge, Des Moines and Southern Railway
FUD: *Ferrocarriles Unidos Dominicanos* (Spanish—United Dominican Railways)—Dominican Republic
FUS: Ferrocarriles Unidos del Sureste (United Railways of the Southeast)
FUY: *Ferrocarriles Unidos de Yucatan* (Spanish—United Railways of Yucatan)—Mexico
FWB: Fort Worth Belt Railway
FW & D: Fort Worth and Denver
GA: Georgia Railroad

GANO: Georgia Northern Railway
GASC: Georgia, Ashburn, Sylvester and Camilla Railway
GB & W: Green Bay and Western Lines (includes Kewaunee, Green Bay and Western Railroad)
GC: Graham County Railroad
GCW: Garden City Western Railway
George Washington's Railroad: Chesapeake and Ohio
Georgia: Georgia Railroad
G & F: Georgia and Florida Railway
GFS: Grand Falls Central Railway
GH & H: Galveston, Houston and Henderson Railroad
GJ: Greenwich and Johnsonville Railway
G & J: Greenwich and Johnsonville Railway
GM: Gainesville Midland Railroad
GM & O: Gulf, Mobile and Ohio Railroad
GMRC: Green Mountain Railroad Corporation
GN: Great Northern Railway
GNA: Graysonia, Nashville and Ashdown Railroad
GNW: Genessee and Wyoming Railroad
GNWR: Genesee and Wyoming Railroad
GO Transit: Government of Ontario Transit
G & Q: Guayaquil and Quito
Grand Trunk: Grand Trunk Railway System (Canadian National) and Grand Trunk Western Railroad
Green Bay Route: Green Bay and Western Railroad
GRN: Greenville and Northern Railway
GRNR: Grand River Railway (Canadian Pacific)
GR & PA: Ghana Railway and Port Authority
GRR: Georgetown Railroad
GRSS: Guyana Railways and Shipping Services
GSF: Georgia Southern and Florida (Southern)
GSW: Great Southwest Railroad
GTW: Grand Trunk Western Railroad (Canadian National)
G&U: Grafton and Upton Railroad
GWF: Galveston Wharves
GWR: Great Western Railway
GWWDR: Great Winnipeg Water District Railway
HB: Hampton and Branchville
HBLRR: Harbor Belt Line Railroad
HBS: Hoboken Shore Railroad
HBT: Houston Belt and Terminal
HE: Hollis and Eastern Railroad
HER: Hellenic Electric Railway (Athens-Piraeus subway system linking capital with its seaport)
HH: *Hamburger Hochbahn* (German—Hamburg Elevated Railway)—includes subway system
HI: Holton Inter-Urban Railway
HJR: Hedjaz Jordan Railway
HLNE: Hillsboro and Northeastern
HN: Hutchinson and Northern Railway
HNE: Harriman and Northeastern (Southern)
hovertrain: railroad train supported by an air cushion instead of wheels
HPTD: High Point, Thomasville and Denton Railroad
HRT: Hartwell Railway
HS: Hartford and Slocomb Railroad
HSW: Helena Southwestern Railroad
HTW: Hoosac Tunnel and Wilmington Railroad
i: Illinois Central Gulf Railroad
IAT: Iowa Terminal Railroad
IB&TC: International Bridge and Terminal Company
IC: Illinois Central Gulf (includes Mississippi Central)
ICC: Interstate Commerce Commission
IGA: Indian Government Administration (Railway Board of India)
IHB: Indiana Harbor Belt Railroad
IN: Illinois Northern Railway
IND: Independent (New York subway system)
Indiana Harbor Belt: "connects with all Chicago railroads"
Industrial Railway of Potosí and Chihuahua: (Ferrocarril Industrial del Potosí y Chihuahua)—Mexico
INT: Interstate Railroad
Interstate: Interstate Railroad
IPE: Indian-Pacific Express [Perth to Sydney—2461 miles (3960 kilometers) in 65 hours]
IR: Israel Railways
IRCA: International Railways of Central America (El Salvador, Guatemala, and Honduras)
IRN: Ironton Railroad
IRRys: Iraqi Republic Railways
IRT: Interborough Rapid Transit (New York City subway system)
IRS: Iranian State Railway
ITC: Illinois Terminal Company
ITRC: Iowa Transfer Railway Company
IU: Indiana Union Railway
JE: Jerseyville and Eastern
Jersey Central Lines: Central Railroad of New Jersey and Lehigh and New England
JHSC: Johnstown and Stony Creek Railroad
JNR: Japanese National Railways (world's fastest)
JRC: Jamaica Railway Corporation
JTC: Jacksonville Terminal Company
JWR: *Jane's World Railways*
Katy: Missouri-Kansas-Texas Railroad (MKT)
KBR: Kankakee Belt Route
KCC: Kansas City Connecting Railroad
KCMO: Kansas City, Mexico and Orient Railway (Ferrocarril Chihuahua al Pacifico)
KCNW: Kelley's Creek and Northwestern Railroad
KCPSFO: Kansas City Public Service Freight Operation
KCR: Kanawha Central Railway
K-C Ry: Kowloon-Canton Railway (Hong Kong)
KCS: Kansas City Southern Railway (includes Arkansas Western, Fort Smith and Van Buren, Louisiana and Arkansas railways)
KCT: Kansas City Terminal Railway
KGB: Kewaunee, Green Bay and Western Railroad (Green Bay and Western Lines)—also KGB&W
KIT: Kentucky and Indiana Terminal Railroad
K&M: Kansas and Missouri Railway and Terminal Company
KMRT: Kansas and Missouri Railway and Terminal Company
KNR: Klamath Northern Railway; Korean National Railways
KO&G: Kansas, Oklahoma and Gulf Railway
K&T: Kentucky and Tennessee
L&A: Louisiana and Arkansas Railway (Kansas City Southern) —also LA
LAJ: Los Angeles Junction Railway
LA&LR: Livonia, Avon and Lakeville Railroad
LAMCO: Liberian America Swedish Minerals Company (Liberian Railways)
Land of Evangeline Route: Dominion Atlantic Railway
LART: Los Angeles Rapid Transit
LAWV: Lorain and West Virginia

Railway (Norfolk and Western)
LBR: Lowville and Beaver River Railroad
L&C: Lancaster and Chester Railway
LEE: Lake Erie and Eastern Railroad
LEF: Lake Erie, Franklin and Clarion Railroad
LE&FW: Lake Erie and Fort Wayne
LEN: Lake Erie and Northern Railway (Canadian Pacific)
LHR: Lehigh and Hudson River
LI: Long Island Railroad (Metropolitan Transportation Authority)—M
Lickenpurr: (Hawaiian nickname—Lahaina-Kaanapal and Pacific Rail Road)—nickname derived from abbreviation—LK&PRR
LK&PRR: Lahaina-Kaanapal and Pacific Rail Road (Maui, Hawii)
LM: Litchfield and Madison Railway (Chicago North Western) —also L&M
LM: *Leningrad Metro* (Russian —Leningrad subway)
LMC: Liberia Mining Company
LMRBR: London Midland Region of British Railways
L&N: Louisville and Nashville Railroad
LNAC: Louisville, New Albany and Corydon Railroad
LNE: Lehigh and New England Railway (Central Railroad of New Jersey)
L&NR: Ludington and Northern Railway
L&NRY: Laona and Northern Railway
L&NW: Louisiana and North West Rail Road
LOPG: Live Oak, Perry and Gulf (Southern)
LPB: Louisiana and Pine Bluff Railway
LPN: Longview, Portland and Northern Railway
lrc (LRC): light, rapid, comfortable (high-speed railroad trans)
LRI: Lawndale Transportation Company
LRS: Laurinburg and Southern
L&S: Laurinburg and Southern
LS&BC: La Salle and Bureau County Railroad
LS&I: Lake Superior and Ishpeming Railroad
LSO: Louisiana Southern Railway (Southern)
LSR: Lebanese State Railroads
LST&TRC: Lake Superior Terminal and Transfer Railway Company
LT: Lake Terminal Railroad (also LTRR)
LRB: London Transport Board
LV: Lehigh Valley Railroad
LW: Louisville and Wadley Railway
L&W: Louisville and Wadley Railway
LWV: Lackawanna and Wyoming Valley Railway
M: Metropolitan Transit Authority (New York City's rapid-transit system); Metropolitan Transportation Authority (Long Island Railroad); Monon Railroad
MA: Magyan Allamvasutak (Hungarian—Hungarian State Railways)
MACR: Minneapolis, Anoka and Guyana Range Railroad
Main Line of Mid-America: Illinois Central Railroad
MARR: Magma Arizona Railroad
M-A Ry: Massawa-Agordad Railway (Ethiopia)
M&B: Meridan and Bigbee Railroad
MBI: Marianna and Bloustown Railroad
MBT: Marianna and Blountstown
MBTA: Massachusetts Bay Transportation Authority (Boston's Subway system)
MC: Michigan Central Railroad (Penn Central)
McR: McCloud River Railroad
MCRR: Maine Central Road; Monongahela Connecting Railroad
MCSA: Moscow, Camden and San Augustine Railroad
MD: Municipal Docks Railway of the Jacksonville Port Authority
MD&W: Minnesota, Dakota and Western Railway
M&E: Morristown and Erie Railroad
MEC: Maine Central Railroad
METC: Medesto and Empire Traction Company
Metro: (French short form—*Chemin de fer Metropolitain)* —Paris subway system
Metropolitano: Rome's subway system
Mexican Pacific Railroad: Ferrocarril Mexicano del Pacifico —Los Mochis to Camp
MF: Middle Fork Railroad
MGA: Monongahela Railway
MGU: Mobile and Gulf Railroad
MHM: Mount Hope Mineral Railroad
M&HMRR: Marquette and Huron Mountain Railroad
MI: Missouri-Illinois Railroad
MICO: Midland Continental Railroad
MID: Midway Railroad
MILW: Chicago, Milwaukee, St Paul and Pacific Railroad (Milwaukee Road)
Milwaukee Road: Chicago, Milwaukee, St Paul and Pacific Railroad
MINE: Minneapolis Eastern Railway
MIR: Minneapolis Industrial Railway
Mitropa: *Mitteleuropaische Schlaf und Speiswagen* (German—Middle-European Sleeping Car and Dining Car)
MJ: Manufacturers' Junction Railway
MKC: McKeesport Connecting Railroad
MKT: Missouri-Kansas-Texas Railroad (Katy)
MLD: Midland Railway of Manitoba
MLS: Manistique and Lake Superior Railroad
MMR: Moscow Metro Railway (Moscow's radiating subway system famed for its beautiful stations)
MNF: Morehead North Fork Railroad
MNJ: Middletown and New Jersey Railway
MNS: Minneapolis, Northfield and Southern Railway
MOB: Montreux-Oberland-Bernois (railway)
MON: Monon Railroad
Monon: Monon Railroad (formerly Chicago, Indianapolis and Louisville Railway)
Mon Rys: Mongolian Railways
Montour: Montour Railroad (Youngstown and Southern Railway)
MOP: Missouri-Pacific Lines
Mo-Pac: Missouri-Pacific Lines
MOV: Moshassuck Valley Railroad
MOW: Montana Western Railway
MP: Missouri Pacific Railroad
M del P: Méxicano del Pacifico (Mexican Pacific Railroad formerly Southern Pacific of Mexico)
MPA: Maryland and Pennsylvania
MPB: Montpelier and Barre Railroad
MPPR: Manitou and Pike's Peak Railway

MR: McCloud River Railroad (also McRRR)
M of R: Ministry of Railways (mainland China)
MRA: Malayan Railway Administration
MRL: Malawi Railways Limited
MRR: Mattagami Railroad (Ontario); Mossi Railroad (Upper Volta)
MRS: Manufacturers Railway
MRy: Malayan Railway
MSC: Mississippi Central (Illinois Central)
MSE: Mississippi Export Railroad
M St L: Minneapolis and St. Louis (Chicago North Western)
M&StL: Minneapolis-St Louis (Chicago North Western)
MSTL: Minneapolis-St Louis (Chicago North Western)
MSTR: Massena Terminal Railroad
MSV: Mississippi and Skuna Valley Railroad
MT: Ministry of Transport (USSRs administration of twenty-six railway lines including the de-luxe Leningrad-Moscow and the transcontinental Trans-Siberian linking Moscow with Vladivostok)
MTC: Milwaukee Transport Company; Montreal Transportation Commission (subway and surface railways); Mystic Terminal Company (Boston and Maine)
MTFR: Minnesota Transfer Railroad
MTH: Mount Hood Railway
MTR: Montour Railroad
MTW: Marinette, Tomahawk and Western Railroad
MTWCR: Mt Washington Cog Railway
MWR: Muncie and Western Railroad
NAJ: Napierville Junction Railway
NAP: Narragansett Pier Railroad
NAR: Northern Alberta Railways; Northern Australia Railway
National Railroads of Cuba: Ferrocarriles Nacionales de Cuba (includes nationalized lines of the Cuba Railroad, Cuba Northern Railways, Guantanamo Railroad, Guantanamo Western, Hershey Cuban Railway, etc.)
National Railways of Mexico: Ferrocarriles de México
NB: Northampton and Bath Railroad
NC & StL: Nashville, Chattanooga and St Louis Railway (L&N)
New Haven: New York, New Haven and Hartford Railroad
NEZP: Nezperce Railroad
NFD: Norfolk, Franklin and Danville Railway
NGR: Nepalese Government Railway
NH: New York, New Haven and Hartford Railroad (Penn Central)
NHIR: New Hope and Ivyland Railroad
Nickel Plate: New York, Chicago and St Louis Railroad (merged with Norfolk and Western)
NJ: Niagara Junction Railway
NJI&I: New Jersey, Indiana and Illinois Railroad
NKP: Nickel Plate (New York, Chicago and St Louis Railroad) —merged with Norfolk and Western
NLC: New Orleans and Lower Coast Railroad
NLG: North Louisiana and Gulf Railroad
NM: Nagoya Municipality (subway system)
N de M: Nacional de México (National of Mexico)
NN: Nevada Northern Railway
NNC: Northern Navigation Company
NODM: Ferrocarril Noroeste de México (Northwest Railway of Mexico—Ferrocarril Chihuahua al Pacifico)
NO de M: Noroeste de México (Northwestern of Mexico)
NONE: New Orleans and Northeastern Railroad (Southern)
NOPB: New Orleans Public Belt Railroad
NOPS: New Orleans Public Service
NP: Northern Pacific Railway
N&PB: Norfolk and Portsmouth Belt Line Railroad
NR: Newfoundland Railway (Canadian National); Northern Railway of Costa Rica (from mountain capital of San José to Caribbean seaport of Limón)
NRC: Nigerian Railway Corporation
NRPC: National Railroad Passenger Corporation (Amtrak)
NRRC: National Railroad Company (of Haiti)
NS: Norfolk Southern Railway
NS: *Nederlandsche Spoorwagen* (Dutch—Netherlands Railway Carriage)—Netherlands Railways
NSB: *Norges Statsbaner* (Norwegian—Norwegian State Railways)
NSL: Norwood and St Lawrence Railroad
NSS: Newburgh and South Shore Railway
NSWGR: New South Wales Government Railways
N de T: Nacional de Tehuantepec (Tehuantepec National)
NUR: Natchez, Urania and Ruston Railway
NW: Norfolk and Western
N&W: Norfolk and Western Railway
NWP: Northwestern Pacific Railroad
NWRy: North Western Railway (West Pakistan)
NYC: New York Central Railroad (Penn Central)
NYCTA: New York City Transit Authority (subway systems include BMT, IRT, INDependent)
NYD: New York Dock Railway
NYLB: New York and Long Branch Railroad
NYNH&H: New York, New Haven and Hartford Railroad
NYS: *Nepal Yatayat Samsthan* (Nepali—Transport Corporation of Nepal)
NYSW: New York, Susquehanna and Western Railroad (NYS&W)
NZGR: New Zealand Government Railways
NZR: New Zealand Railways
ÖOB: *Österreichischen Bundesbahnen* (German—Austrian State Railways)
OE: Oregon Electric Railway (Spokane, Portland, and Seattle Railway)
OCE: Oregon, California and Eastern Railway
OGR: *Official Guide of the Railways*
OKT: Oakland Terminal Railway
OL&BR: Omaha, Lincoln and Beatrice Railway
OMTB: Osaka Metropolitan Transportation Bureau (subway system)
ONCF: *Office National des Chemins de Fer* (French—National Railways Office)—Morocco
ONRY: Ogdensburg and Norwood Railway
O&NW: Oregon and Northwestern
ONT: Ontario Northland Railway
ONW: Oregon and Northwestern
OPE: Oregon, Pacific and Eastern
ORER: *Official Railway Equipment Register*
OT: Oregon Trunk Railway (Spokane, Portland, and Seattle Railway)

OUR&D: Ogden Union Railway and Depot
Overland Route: Union Pacific Railroad
PA: Pittsburgh Authority (rapid transit)
PAA: Pennsylvania and Atlantic Railroad
PACC: Pacific Coast Railroad
Pacific Railroad: Ferrocarril del Pacifico (linking American border at Nogales with Mazatlan on Pacific coast of Mexico)
Pacific Railway of Costa Rica: from Pacific port of Puntarenas to San José)
Pacific Railways of Nicaragua: Ferrocarril del Pacifico de Nicaragua—from Corinto on the Pacific to Granada on Lake Nicaragua
PA&M: Pittsburgh, Allegheny and McKees Rocks Railroad
Panama Railroad: Division of the Panama Canal linking Cristóbal and Colón on the Atlantic with Balboa and Panama City on the Pacific and running parallel to the Panama Canal
P&AR: Pacific and Arctic Railway
PATCO: (transportation system linking Camden, New Jersey and Philadelphia, Pennsylvania)
PATH: Port Authority Trans-Hudson Corporation (operates Hudson Tubes between New Jersey and New York)
PBNE: Philadelphia, Bethlehem and New England Railroad
PBR: Patapsco and Back Rivers
PC: Penn Central (Pennsylvania New York Central Transportation Company: Pennsylvania Railroad; New York Central Railroad; New York, New Haven, and Hartford Railroad; Baltimore and Eastern Railroad; Canada Southern Railway; Cleveland, Cincinnati, Chicago and St Louis Railway; Michigan Central Railroad; Peoria and Eastern Railway; Waynesburg and Washington Railroad)
PCL: Peruvian Corporation Limited
PCN: Point Comfort and Northern
PCR: Paraguayan Central Railway
PCY: Pittsburgh, Chartiers and Youghiogheny Railway
PE: Pacific Electric (interurban railway system serving entire Los Angeles area before replacement by smog-producing buses); Pacific Electric Railway of Costa Rica (links Pacific seaport of Puntarenas with mountain capital of San José)—also called *FEP*
P&E: Peoria and Eastern Railway (Penn Central)
Pennsy: (nickname—Pennsylvania Railroad)—now part of the Penn Central
Peoria: Peoria and Pekin Union Railway
P&F: Pioneer and Fayette Railroad
PGE: Pacific Great Eastern Railway
PH&D: Port Huron and Detroit Railroad
P&I: Paducah and Illinois Railroad
PIC: Pickens Railroad
Pick: Pickens Railroad
Pickens: Pickens Railroad
PKP: *Polskie Koleje Panstwowe* (Polish—Polish State Railways)
P&LE: Pittsburgh and Lake Erie Railroad
PLM: Paris-Lyon-Mediterranée
P&N: Piedmont and Northern Railway
PNKA: *Perusahaan Negara Kereta Api* (Indonesian—Indonesian State Railways)
PNR: Philippine National Railways
PNW: Prescott and Northwestern Railroad
Port St Joe Route: Apalachicola Northern Railroad
'Possum Trot Line: Reader Railroad
P&OV: Pittsburgh and Ohio Valley
P&PU: Peoria and Pekin Union
PR: Panama Railroad
P-R: Pennsylvania-Reading Seashore Lines
PRC: Philippine Railway Company
PRCR: Pacific Railway Costa Rica
PRR: Pennsylvania Railroad (Penn Central)
PRS: Pennsylvania-Reading Seashore Lines
PRTD: Portland Railroad and Terminal Division of the Portland Traction Company
PRV: Pearl River Valley Railroad
P y RV: *Potosí y Rio Verde* (Spanish—Potosi and Green River Railroad of Chihuahua)
PS: Pittsburg and Shawmut Railroad
P&SR: Petaluma and Santa Rosa
PTC: Peoria Terminal Company; Philadelphia Transportation Company (also called PATCO includes elevated and subway lines of Philadelphia area)
PTM: Portland Terminal Company
PTR: Parr Terminal Railroad
PTS: Port Townsend Railroad
Pullman: de-luxe railroad cars providing lounging, observation, and sleeping facilities aboard first-class express trains
PVS: Pecos Valley Southern
P&WV: Pittsburgh and West Virginia Railway (Norfolk and Western)
QAP: Quanah, Acme and Pacific
QC: Quebec Central Railway (Canadian Pacific)
QNS&LRC: Quebec North Shore and Labrador Railway Company
QR: Queensland Railways
Quanah Route: Quanah, Acme and Pacific Railway
QUI: Quincy Railroad
RC: Railway Corporation (Nigeria)
RCFA-N: *Regie du Chemin de Fer Abidjan-Niger* (French—Abidjan-Niger Railway Administration)—Ivory Coast
RD: Railway Directorate (Albania)
RDG: Reading Company (formerly Philadelphia and Reading Railroad)
REA: Railway Express Agency; Reader Railroad
Reading Lines: Reading Railway System (formerly Philadelphia and Reading Railroad)
Rebel Route: Gulf, Mobile and Ohio Railroad
RENFE: *Red Nacional de los Ferrocarriles Españoles* (Spanish—Spanish National Railway System)
RFFSA: *Rede Ferroviária Federal SA* (Portuguese—Federal Railway System Corporation— Brazil
RFP: Richmond, Fredericksburg and Potomac Railroad (RF&P)
RF&PRR: Richmond, Fredericksburg and Potomac Railroad
RI: Chicago, Rock Island and Pacific Railroad
Rio Grande: Denver and Rio Grande Western
RKG: Rockingham Railroad
RM: *Rotterdam Metro* (Dutch—Rotterdam Subway)
RNCF: *Reseau National des Chemins de Fer* (French—National Railway System)—Madagascar
Rock Island: Chicago, Rock Island and Pacific Railroad
RR: (abbreviation—Railroad or Rail Road); (reporting mark —Raritan River Rail Road); Rhodesian Railways
RRRR: Raritan River Railroad
RRys: Rhodesian Railways
RS: Roberval and Seguenay Railway

RSP: Roscoe, Snyder and Pacific
R-S Pacific Route: Roscoe, Snyder and Pacific Railway
RSS: Rockdale, Sandow and Southern Railroad
RT: River Terminal Railway
RTM: Railway Transfer Company of Minneapolis
RV: Rahway Valley Railway
Ry: Railway
S&A: Savannah and Atlanta Railway
SAL: Seaboard Airline Railroad (Seaboard Coast Line Railroad is official name adopted to avoid confusion with an airline)
SAN: Sandersville Railroad
Santa Fe: Atchison, Topeka and Santa Fe Railway
SAR: South African Railways; South Australian Railways
SAR&H: South African Railways and Harbours
SATS: San Antonio Transit System
SAVE: Swiss-Alberg-Vienna Express
SB: South Buffalo Railway
SBA: *Subterraneos de Buenos Aires* (Spanish—Buenos Aires Subways)
SBC: Ferrocarril Sonora Baja California (Sonora—Baja California Railway)
SBK: South Brooklyn Railway
SC: Sumter and Choctaw Railway
SCE: Shanghai-Canton Express
SCL: Seaboard Coast Line Railroad (Atlantic Coast Line Railroad, Charleston and Western Carolina Railway, Seaboard Air Line Railroad—former name of the Seaboard Coast Line Railroad)
SC&MR: Strouds Creek and Muddlety Railroad
SCT: Sioux City Terminal Railway
SDAE: San Diego and Arizona Eastern Railway
SD&AE: San Diego and Arizona Eastern Railway
SDTS: San Diego Transit System
SE: Ferrocarril del Sureste (Southeast Railroad)
Seashore Lines: Pennsylvania-Reading Seashore Lines
SERA: Sierra Railroad
SFBRR: San Francisco Belt Railroad
SFMR: San Francisco Municipal Railway (operates the cable cars)
SG: South Georgia Railway (Southern Railway)
SGR: Sa'udi Government Railroad (Saudi Arabia); Surinam Government Railway (Netherlands Guiana)
SH: Steelton and Highspire Railroad
Shawmut: The Pittsburg and Shawmut Railroad
SHK: *Sidirodromi Hellinikou Kratous* (Greek—Hellenic State Railways)—Greece
SI: Spokane International Railroad
SIR: Staten Island Rapid Transit Railway
SIRRI: Southern Industrial Railroad Incorporated
SJ: *Statens Jarnvargar* (Swedish—State Railways)
SJB: St Joseph Belt Railway
SJL: St Johnsbury and Lamoille County Railroad
SJ&LC: St Johnsbury and Lamoille County Railroad
SJTR: St Joseph Terminal Railroad
SKSL: Skaneateles Short Line Railroad
SLC: San Luis Central Railroad
SLGW: Salt Lake, Garfield and Western Railway
SLR: Sierra Leone Railway
SLSF: St Louis-San Francisco Railway
SM: St Marys Railroad
SMA: San Manuel Arizona Railroad
SMR: South Manchurian Railway
SMV: Santa Maria Valley Railroad
SN: Sacramento Northern Railway (also SNRy)
SNCB: *Societe Nationale des Chemins de fer Belges* (French—Belgian National Railways)
SNCF: *Societe Nationale des Chemins de fer Français* (French—French National Railways)
SNCFA: *Societe Nationale des Chemins de Fer Algeriens* (French—Algerian National Railways)
SNY: Southern New York Railway
SOE: Simplon-Orient Express
SOI: Southern Indiana Railway
Sonora—Baja California Railway: Ferrocarril Sonora—Baja California—Mexicali to Benjamin Hill
SOO: Soo Line Railroad
$oo Line: Soo Line Railroad
SOT: South Omaha Terminal Railway
Southern: Southern Railway System (Alabama Great Southern Railroad; Carolina and Northwestern Railway; Cincinnati, New Orleans and Texas Pacific Railway; Georgia Southern and Florida Railway; Harriman and Northeastern Railroad; Live Oak, Perry and Gulf Railroad; Louisiana Southern Railway; New Orleans and Northeastern Railroad; South Georgia Railway)
Southern Pacific: SP
South Shore Line: Chicago South Shore and South Bend Railroad
SP: Southern Pacific (includes Southern Pacific Lines, Sunset Railway, Texas and Louisiana Lines, Texas and New Orleans, etc.)—in fact many school children once said the United States was bounded on the north by Canada and the Great Lakes, on the east by the Atlantic Ocean, and on the south and southwest by the Southern Pacific
SPGT: Springfield Terminal Railway
SPS: Spokane, Portland and Seattle Railway (includes Oregon Electric and Oregon Trunk railways)
SR: Southern Railway
SRBR: Southern Region of British Railways
SRC: Salvador Railway Company (El Salvador)
SRN: Sabine River and Northern
SRRC: Sierra Railroad Company; Strasburg Rail Road Company
SRRCO: Sandersville Railroad Company
SRT: State Railways of Thailand (Siam)
SSDK: Savannah State Docks Railroad
SSLVRR: Southern San Luis Valley Railroad
SSRy: Sand Springs Railway
SSW: St Louis Southwestern Railway (Cotton Belt Route)
STE: Stockton Terminal and Eastern Railroad
STRT: Stewartstown Railroad
STS: Seattle Transit System
SU: Stockholm Underground (subway system)
Sub: Suburban; Subway
Sud Rys: Sudan Railways
SUR: Soviet Union Railways (managed by Ministry of Communications and comprising some twenty-six lines including the Trans-Mongolian and the Trans-Siberian as well as the plush Leningrad-Moscow express)
Susquehanna: New York, Susquehanna and Western Railroad

Syr Rys: Syrian Railways
TAAA: Travelers Aid Association of America
TA&G: Tennessee, Alabama and Georgia Railway
TAG Route: Tennessee, Alabama and Georgia Railway
Tan-Zam: Tanzania-Zambia Railroad
TAR: Trans-Australian Railways
TAS: Tampa Southern Railroad
TASD: Terminal Railway Alabama State Docks
TA&W: Toledo, Angola and Western Railway
TB: Twin Branch Railroad
TBTMG: Transportation Bureau of the Tokyo Metropolitan Government (subway)
TC: Tennessee Central Railway
TCDD: *Turkiye Cumhuriyeti Deviet Demiryollari Isletmesi* (Turkish—Turkish State Railways)
TCG: Tucson, Cornelia and Gila Bend Railroad
TCT: Texas City Terminal Railway
TEBRCL: The Emu Bay Railway Company Limited
TEE: Trans-Europe Express
TENN: Tennessee Railroad
TEXC: Texas Central Railroad
THB: Toronto, Hamilton and Buffalo Railway
The Q: CB&Q (Chicago, Burlington and Quincy)
TM: Texas Mexican Railway; Transport Ministry (USSRs administration of twenty-six railway lines)—TM sometimes used on engines
TMR: Trans-Mongolian Railway
TN: Texas and Northern Railway
T-NM: Texas-New Mexico Rail way
T&NO: Texas and New Orleans (Southern Pacific)—also TNO
TOC: Pennsylvania New York Central Transportation Company (Penn Central)
TOE: Texas, Oklahoma and Eastern Railroad
TOV: Tooele Valley Railway
T&P: Texas and Pacific Railway (also TP)
TPMP: Texas-Pacific-Missouri Pacific Terminal Railroad of New Orleans
TPT: Trenton-Princeton Traction Company
TP&W: Toledo, Peoria and Western Railroad
TR: Tasmanian Railways
TRA: Taiwan Railway Administration
Trans-Sib: Trans-Siberian Railway
TRC: Tela Railway Company (Honduras); Trona Railway Company (California)
TRRA: Terminal Railroad Association of St Louis
TS: Tidewater Southern Railway
TS-E: Texas South-Eastern
TSR: Trans-Siberian Railway
TSU: Tulsa-Sapulpa Union Railway
TT: Toledo Terminal Railroad
T&T: Tijuana and Tecate Railway (freight cars marked TITE)
TTC: Toronto Transit Commission (subway and surface railway systems)
TVG: Tavares and Gulf Railroad
TVRy: Tooele Valley Railway
Tweetsie: (nickname—East Tennessee and Western North Carolina Railroad)—believed to be derived from high-pitched whistles of its engines
T-Z RA: Tanzania-Zambia Railway Authority
U: Underground (London's subway system)
UBR: Ulan Bator Railway
UCR: Utah Coal Route
UFC: United Fruit Company (railroads in Costa Rica and Panama)
UMP: Upper Merion and Plymouth Railroad
UNF: Union Freight Railroad
UNI: Unity Railways
UO: Union Railroad—Oregon
UP: Union Pacific Railroad (includes Oregon Short Line and Oregon-Washington Railroad and Navigation Company)
URR: Union Railroad—Pittsburgh
USSR: (Ministry of Railways administers operation of twenty-six railway boards throughout the USSR)
UT: Union Terminal Railway
UTA: Ulster Transport Authority (railways of six counties in Northern Ireland)
UTAH: Utah Railway
Utah Coal Route: Utah Railway
UTR: Union Transportation Company
U de Y: *Unidos de Yucatan* (Spanish—United Railways of Yucatan, Mexico)
V: *Valtionrautatiet* (Finnish—State Railways)
VBR: Virginia Blue Ridge Railway
VC: Virginia Central Railway
VCS: Virginia and Carolina Southern Railroad
VCY: Ventura County Railway
VE: Visalia Electric Railroad
VGN: Virginian Railway (Norfolk and Western)
Virginian: Virginian Railway (Norfolk and Western)
V&LI: Vancouver and Lulu Island (branch of Canadian Pacific)
V-MNR: Viet-Minh National Railways (North Vietnam)
V-NR: Viet-Nam Railways (South Vietnam)
VR: Victorian Railways (Australia)
V Ry: Verapaz Railway (Guatemala)
VSL: Valley and Siletz Railroad
VSO: Valdosta Southern Railroad
VTR: Vermont Railway
W of A: Western Railway of Alabama
WAB: Wabash Railroad (Norfolk and Western)
Wabash: Wabash Railroad (Norfolk and Western)
WAG: Wellsville, Addison and Galeton Railroad
WAGR: Western Australian Government Railways
WATC: Washington Terminal Company
WAW: Waynesburg and Washington Railroad (Penn Central)
WBCRR: Wilkes-Barre Connecting Railroad
WBT&SRC: Waco, Beaumont, Trinity and Sabine Railway Company
Western Railway of Mexico: Ferrocarril Occidental de México—Culiacan to Limoncito
West Point Route: Atlanta and West Point Rail Road
WHBR: Western Region of British Railways
White Pass: British Columbia Yukon Railway, British Yukon Railway, Pacific and Arctic Railway
White Pass and Yukon Route: British Columbia Yukon Railway, British Yukon Navigation, British Yukon Railway, Pacific and Arctic Railway and Navigation Company
WIM: Washington, Idaho and Montana Railway
WL: *Wagon Lits* (French—sleeping cars)
WLO: Waterloo Railroad
WM: Western Maryland Railway
WMTA: Washington Metropolitan Transit Authority (subway system)
WMWN: Weatherford, Mineral

Wells and Northwestern Railway
WMR: Wasatch Mountain Railway
WNF: Winfield Railroad
W&NO: Wharton and Northern Railroad
WOD: Washington and Old Dominion Railroad
W&OV: Warren and Ouachita Valley Railway
WP: Western Pacific Railroad
WPER: West Pittston-Exeter Railroad
WP&Y: White Pass and Yukon Railway
WRA: Western Railroad Association
WRNT: Warrenton Railroad
WRWK: Warwick Railway
WS: Ware Shoals Railroad
WSR: Warren and Saline River
WSS: Winston-Salem Southbound Railway
WSYP: White Sulphur Springs and Yellowstone Park Railway
WTR: Wrightsville and Tennille Railroad
WVN: West Virginia Northern Railroad
WW: Winchester and Western Railroad
WWV: Walla Walla Valley Railway
WYS: Wyandotte Southern Railroad
WYT: Wyandotte Terminal Railroad
X: express; transport; transportation (as in many private bulk carriers' names such as GATX—General American Transportation)
Xing: crossing (highway or railroad)—also XING
Y&N: Youngstown and Northern Railroad
YAN: Yancey Railroad
YR: Yucatan Railways (*Ferrocarriles Unidos del Sureste*—United Railways of the Southeast)—along the Gulf of Mexico from Coatzacoalcos to Merida
YS: Youngstown and Southern Railway (Montour)
Y&S: Yakutat and Southern Railway
YVT: Yakima Valley Transportation Company
YW: Yreka Western Railroad
ZJZ: *Zajednica Jugoslovenskih Zalesnicca* (Yugoslavian—Community of Yugoslav Railways)
ZR: Zambia Railways
Zug Island Road: Delray Connecting Railroad (DC)

Roman Numerals

I: 1
II: 2
III: 3
IV: 4
V: 5
VI: 6
VII: 7
VIII: 8
IX: 9
X: 10
XV: 15
XIX: 19
XX: 20
XXV: 25
XXIX: 29
XXX: 30
XXV: 35
XXXIX: 39
XL: 40
XLV: 45
XLIX: 49
L: 50
LV: 55
LIX: 59
LX: 60
LXV: 65
LXIX: 69
LXX: 70
LXXV: 75
LXXIX: 79
LXXX: 80
LXXXV: 85
LXXXIX: 89
XC: 90
XCV: 95
XCIX: 99
C: 100
CL: 150
CC: 200
CCC: 300
CD: 400
D: 500
DC: 600
DCC: 700
DCCC: 800
CM: 900
M: 1000
MD: 1500
MDC: 1600
MDCC: 1700
MDCCC: 1800
MCM or MDCCCC: 1900
MCMX: 1910
MCMXX: 1920
MCMXXX: 1930
MCMXL: 1940
MCML: 1950
MCMLX: 1960
MCMLXX: 1970
MCMLXXX: 1980
MCMXC: 1990
MM: 2000
MMM: 3000
MMMM or M$\overline{\text{V}}$: 4000
$\overline{\text{V}}$: 5000
$\overline{\text{M}}$: 1,000,000

Russian Alphabet (transliterated)

Russian Capital Letters	English Capital Letters	Russian Small Letters	English Small Letters	Russian Alphabet Letter Names	Nearest English Equivalent Sounds
А	A	а	a	*ah*	*a* as in *a*rch
Б	B	б	b	*beh*	*b* as in *b*it
В	V	в	v	*veh*	*v* as in *v*est
Г	G	г	g	*geh*	*g* as in *g*et
Д	D	д	d	*deh*	*d* as in *d*ay
Е	Ye	е	ye	*yeh*	*y* as in *y*es
Ж	Zh	ж	zh	*zheh*	*zh* sound as in measure
З	Z	з	z	*zeh*	*z* as in *z*ero
И	I	и	i	*ee*	*i* as in p*ee*l
Й	Y	й	y	*ee s krátkoi*	(short *i* after vowels
К	K	к	k	*kah*	*k* as in *k*ite
Л	L	л	l	*el*	*l* as in woo*l*
М	M	м	m	*em*	*m* as in *m*an
Н	N	н	n	*en*	*n* as in *n*ow
О	O	о	o	*oh*	*o* as in h*o*ax
П	P	п	p	*peh*	*p* as in *p*encil
Р	R	р	r	*err*	*r* as in *r*ye
С	S	с	s	*ess*	*s* as in *s*ay
Т	T	т	t	*teh*	*t* as in *t*ent
У	Oo	у	oo	*ooh*	*oo* as in l*oo*se
Ф	F	ф	f	*eff*	*f* as in *f*ancy
Х	Kh	х	kh	*khan*	*kh* as in lo*ch*
Ц	Ts	ц	ts	*tseh*	*ts* as in ha*ts*
Ч	Ch	ч	ch	*cheh*	*ch* as in *ch*air
Ш	Sh	ш	sh	*shah*	*sh* as in *sh*ave
Щ	Shch	щ	shch	*shchah*	*shch* as in Iri*sh ch*uck
Ъ		ъ		*tvyórdy znak*	(silent-hard sound)
Ы	Y	ы	y	*yery*	*y* as *i* in h*i*t
Ь		ь		*myakhki znak*	(silent)
Э	Eh	э	eh	*eh oborótnoye*	*eh* sound as in d*e*bt
Ю	Yu	ю	yu	*yoo*	*yu* as in *you*
Я	Ya	я	ya	*yah*	*ya* as in *ya*m

Ship's Bell Time Signals

1 bell —12:30 or 4:30 or 8:30 a.m. or p.m.

2 bells—	1:00	5:00	9:00
3 bells—	1:30	5:30	9:30
4 bells—	2:00	6:00	10:00
5 bells—	2:30	6:30	10:30
6 bells—	3:00	7:00	11:00
7 bells—	3:30	7:30	11:30
8 bells—	4:00	8:00	12:00

On many vessels the ship's whistle is blown at noon. On some ships a lightly struck 1 bell announces 15 minutes before the change of watch, usually at 4, 8, and 12 o'clock.

The ship's day starts at noon. The *afternoon watch* is from noon to 4 p.m. The 4 to 8 work period is called the *dogwatch*. From 8 p.m. to midnight is the *first watch*. From midnight to 4 a.m. is the *middle watch*. From 8 a.m. to noon is the *forenoon watch*.

Signs and Symbols Frequently Used

+ add; addition sign; north; plus

& and (ampersand)

&c et cetera (and so forth)

* asterisk

@ at

∵ because

¢ centavo; centime; cent(s)

© copyright

° degree(s)

÷ divide; divided by; division sign

$ dollar sign—used universally for monetary units as diverse as Nicaraguan cordobas; Brazilian cruzeiros; Australian, Bahamian, Barbadian, British Honduran, Canadian, Ethiopian, Guyanian, Hong Kongese, Levantine, Liberian, Malaysian, New Zealand, Taiwan, trade, Trinidadian-Tobagonian, U.S., Viet Namese, West Indian, yuan dollars; Portuguese escudos; Honduran lempiras; Brazilian milreis; Chilean, Colombian, Cuban, Dominican, Mexican, Philippine, Uruguayan pesos; Peruvian soles (often with a lower-case dollar sign, $); Chinese yuans

$A Australian dollar(s)

$b Bolivian peso(s)

$B Bahamian, Barbadian, British dollar(s)

$BH British Honduran dollar(s)

$C Brazilian cruzeiro(s); Canadian dollar(s)

$Col Colombian peso(s)

$E Ethiopian dollar(s)

$Eth Ethiopian dollar(s)

$G Guyanian dollar(s)

$HK Hong Kong dollar(s)

$K $1000 (e.g. $13K = $13,000)

$L Levant(ine) dollar(s)—Maria Theresa thaler(s); Liberian dollar(s)

$M Malay(sian) dollar(s)

$Mal Malay(sian) dollar(s)

$Mex Mexican peso(s)

$NT New Taiwan dollar(s)

$NZ New Zealand dollar(s)

$RD Republica Dominicana peso(s)—Dominican Republic monetary unit(s)

$S Singapore dollar(s)

$T Taiwan dollar(s); trade dollar(s); Trinidad(ian) and Tobago(nian) dollar(s)

$TT Trinidad(ian) and Tobago(nian) dollar(s)

$Ur Uruguayan peso(s)

$US United States dollar(s) [also shown as US$, as are other monetary units where national designations often precede dollar sign: C$—Canadian dollar(s), HK$—Hong Kong dollar(s)]

$VN Viet Namese dollar(s)

$WI West Indian dollar(s); West Indies dollar(s)

$Y yuan dollar(s)

= equality; equals; equal to

G Paraguayan guarani(s)

K certified kosher

LC Cyrian pound(s)

LR Rhodesian pound(s)

− minus; south; subtract; subtraction sign

× multiplication sign; multiplied by; multiply

≥ equal to or greater than

≤ equal to or less than

> greater than

< less than

>> much greater than

<< much less than

fracture(s) (medical); number(s) or pound(s) (commercial); sharp(s) (musical); space(s) (typographical); tic-tac-toe (game symbol); zinc (alchemical)

p Philippine peso(s)

% percent

+ plus; north

± plus or minus

£ pound (*libra*) sign—used universally for monetary units such as the Australian, British, Egyptian, Gambian, Ghanian, Irish, Israeli, Jamaican, Lebanese, Libyan, Malawi, New Zealand, Nigerian, South African, Sudanese, Syrian, Turkish, Western Samoan, Zambian pound

£A pound Australian

£E pound Egyptian (United Arab Republic)

£G pound Gambian; pound Ghanian

£I pound Irish; pound Israeli (also shown as I£)

£J pound Jamaican

£L pound Lebanese; pound Libyan

£M pound Malawi

£N pound Nigerian

£NZ pound New Zealand (also shown as NZ£)

£S pound sterling; pound Sudanese; pound Syrian

£SAf pound South African (also shown as SAf)

£/s/d pounds, shillings, and pence

£T pound Turkish

£WS pound Western Samoan

£Z pound Zambian

R registered

℞ prescription; receipt; recipe; response; reverse

shilling mark; slash; solidus; virgule

∴ therefore

U Union of Orthodox Jewish Congregations of America (symbol for kosher product approved for detergent or dietary use)

XMA$ (symbol—commercialized Christmas)

Y Japanese yen

Steamship Lines

A: Ahearn Shipping Ltd; Alaska Steamship Company; Alcoa Steamship Company; American Export Isbrandtsen Lines; American Mail Line; American Oil Company; American Steamships; Tidewater Oil (capital A between red wings); et cetera

ABRT: A/B Rederi Transatlantic (Pacific Australia Direct Line)

AC: African Coasters

ACL: Atlantic Container Line

ACS: American Coal Shipping

ACSC: Australian Coastal Shipping Commission

AD: Armement Dieppe

AE: African Enterprises

AH: Afred Holt (Blue Funnel Line)

AHB: Great Eastern Line

AHL: Associated Humber Lines

Alcoa: Alcoa Steamship Company

ALL: Anchor Line Limited

All America Cables: All America Cables and Radio

AML: American Mail Line

AMOCO: American Oil Company

ANCAP: *Administracion Nacional de Combustibles Alcohol y Portland* (Spanish—National Administration of Flammable Alcohol and Portland Cement) —Uruguay

ANL: Australian National Line

AP: American Pioneer Lines

AP: *Atlantska Plovidba* (Yugoslavian—Atlantic Line)

APL: American President Lines

ASFS: Alaska State Ferry System

ASN: Atlantic Steam Navigation

ASOK: *Angfartigas Svenska Östasiatiske Kompaniet* (Swedish—Swedish East Asiatic Steamship Company)

ATLANTIC: Atlantic Refining Company

Atlantic Container Line: ACL

AUT: American Union Transport

B: Barber Lines; Booth Line; Branch Lines; Bull Steamship Lines; etc.

BAF: Belgian African Line

BCF: British Columbia Ferries

BCL: Bristol City Line

BCSC: British and Continental Steamship Company

BDS: *Bergenske Dampskibsselskab* (Norwegian—Bergen Steamship Line)—connecting Norway and United Kingdom ports

BFL: Belgian Fruit Lines

BHP: Broken Hill Proprietary

BISNC: British India Steam Navigation Company

B&I SPC: British and Irish Steam Packet Company

BL: Bergen Line; Bibby Line; Booth Line; etc.

B&L: Burns and Laird Lines

BLS: Ben Line Steamers

Blue Star: Blue Star Line

BM: British Methane Limited

BMM: Belfast, Mersey and Manchester Steamship Company

BOC: Burmah Oil Company

BOS: British Oil Shipping

BP: British Petroleum

BPC: British Phosphate Commissioners

BP&Co: Burns, Philp and Company

BR: British Railways (operates many ferry steamers linking England and Scotland with Belgium, France, Ireland, and Holland)

BSC: Baltic Steamship Company

BSL: Black Star Line; Blue Sea Line; Blue Star Line; Etc.

BSNC: Bristol Steam Navigation Company

BTC: Bethlehem Transportation Corporation

B&W: Brocklebank and Well Lines

C: Calmar Line (Bethlehem Steel); Caribbean Steamships Company; Clarke Line; Clyde Line; Etc.

"C": Costa Line

CA: *Carregadores Açoreanos* (Portuguese—Azorean Cargo Carriers)

CAVN: *Compañía Anonima Venezolana de Navegación* (Spanish —Venezuelan Navigation Company)—Venezuela Line

CCAL: Christensen Canadian African Line

CC Co: Commercial Cable Company

CCN: *Companhia Colonial de Navegacão* (Portuguese—Colonial Navigation Company)

CEA: Central Electricity Authority

CF: Compagnie de Navigation Fraissinet

CFPO: *Compagnie Française des Phosphates de l'Oceanie* (French —French Phosphate Company of Oceania)

CGL: Canadian Gulf Line

CGS: Central Gulf Steamships

CGT: *Compagnie Générale Transatlantique* (French—General Transatlantic Company—*$C^{ie}G^{le}T^{rans}$—the French Line*

Chilean Line: (see *CSAV*)

China Merchants Steam Navigation Company: CMSNC

CI: Catalina Island Steamship Line; Christmas Island Phosphate Commission

Cie G^{le} T^{rans}: *Compagnie Générale Transatlantique* (French—General Transatlantic Company)—the French Line

Cities Service: Cities Service Oil Company

CL: Ceylon Lines; Coast Lines

Clipper Line: Wisconsin and Michigan Steamship Company

CM: *Compañía Maritima* (Spanish —Maritime Company)

CMB: *Compagnie Maritime Belge* (French—Belgian Maritime Company)—Royal Belgian Lloyd

CMSNC: China Merchants Steam Navigation Company

CMZ: Compagnie Maritime du Zaire

CNC: China Navigation Company

CNP: *Compagnie Navigation Paquet* (French—Paquet Navigation Company)—Paquet Line

CNS: Canadian National Steamships

COLDEMAR: *Compañía Colombiana de Navegación Maritima* (Spanish—Colombian Maritime Navigation Company)

Columbus Line: HSDG

CP Ships: Canadian Pacific Steamships (*Empress* vessels)

CPV: *Corporación Peruana de Vapores* (Spanish—Peruvian Steamship Corporation)

Crusader: Crusader Line

CSAV: *Compañía Sud-Americana de Vapores* (Spanish—South American Steamship Company)—Chile

CSC: Clyde Shipping Company

CSL: Canada Steamship Lines

CSO: Cities Service Oil

CSSCo: Cunard Steamship Company

CT: Cleveland Tankers

CT: *Compania Transmediterranea* (Spanish—Transmediterranean Company)

CTE: *Compañía Transatlantica Española* (Spanish—Spanish Transatlantic Line)—The Spanish Line
CTL: Coastal Transport Limited
Cunard: Cunard Steam-Ship Company, Limited (includes White Star Line)
D: Delta Line; Donaldson Line; Red 'D' Line; etc.
'D': Red 'D' Line (merged with Grace Line)
DAL: *Deutsche-Afrika Linien* (German—German Affica Line)
d'Amico: d'Amico Line
Day Line: Hudson River Day Line
DBK: Daiichi Bussan Kaisha
D-F: *Dansk-Franske* (Danish-French Line)
Djakarta Line: DL
DL: Djakarta Line
DPLC: Dundee, Perth and London Shipping Company
DS: Dominion Shipping
D-S: Ditlev-Simonsen, Halfdan and Company
E: American Export Isbrandtsen Lines; Eastern Steamship Line; Exxon Tankers; Hellenic Lines and many Greek lines where the letter E stands for Ellas or Hellas—Greece, or for the last name of an owner as in other lands
EAC: East Asiatic Company
E&B: Ellerman and Bucknall Steamship Company
E&F: Elders and Fyffes Ltd
ELMA: *Empresa Lineas Maritimas Argentinas* (Spanish—Argentine Maritime Lines)—formerly *FANU* and uses *FANU* house flag
Empress liners: Canadian Pacific ships
Esso: Esso Petroleum Company
F: Fabre Line; Falcon Tankers; Falkland Islands Trading Company; Farrell Lines; Finnlines; etc.
FAA: *Finska Angfartygs Aktiebolaget* (Finnish—Finnish Steamship Company)—Finland Line
Falline: Federal Atlantic-Lakes Line
FANF: *Flota Argentina de Navegación Fluvial* (Spanish—Argentine River Navigation Fleet)
FANU: *Flota Argentina de Navegación de Ultramar* (Spanish—Argentine High-Sea Navigation Fleet)
Far East Steamship Company: FESCO
FCNCo: Federal Commerce and Navigation Company
Fedpac: Federal Pacific Lakes Line
Fedsea: Federal South East Asia Line
FESCO: Far East Steamship Company
Finald Line: (see *FAA*)
FL: Fesco Pacific Line
FMC: Federal Maritime Commission
FMD: *Flota Mercante Dominicana* (Spanish—Dominican Merchant Fleet)
FMG: *Flota Mercante Grancolombiana* (Spanish—Great Colombian Merchant Fleet)
French Line: (see *CGT*)
FW: Furness, Withy and Company
FWL: Furness Warren Line
G: Glynafon Shipping; Graig Shipping; Arthur Guiness (the brewer); etc.
GAL: German Atlantic Line
GG: Guinea Gulf Line
GL: Greek Line
GO: Gulf Oil
GPRL: Gulf Puerto Rico Lines
GRACE: Grace Line (Prudential-Grace Lines)
Gran Flota Blanca: (Spanish —Great White Fleet)—United Fruit Company (fleet of white steamships)—United Brands
GSA: Gulf and South American Steamship Company
GULF: Gulf Oil Corporation
GYSCo: Great Yarmouth Shipping Company
H: Hansa Line; Heering Line; Horn Line; etc.
HAL: Holland Amerika Lijn (NASM—Nederlandsch-Amerikaasche Stoomvaart Maatschappij)—NASM appears on house flag
HANSA: Hansa Line
Hanseatic-Vaasa Line: VL
HAPAG: *Hamburg-Amerika Paket Aktiengesselschaft* (German—Hamburg-America Packet Company)—Hamburg-America Line
Hapag-Lloyd: Hamburg-Amerika—North German Lloyd Lines
HB C: Hudson's Bay Company
HCL: Hamburg-Chicago Line
HFL: Hawaii Freight Lines
HH: H. Hogarth and Sons
HHA: H.H. Andersen Line
HL: Home Lines
HMS: Her (His) Majesty's Ship (as in HMS *Dreadnought*)
hovercraft: marine craft supported by an air cushion instead of a conventional hull
HSAL: Hamburg South American Line
HSDG: Hamburg-Sudamerikanische Dampfs Gesell (Columbus Line)
H&W: Holm and Wonsild
HWAL: Holland West-Afrika Line
I: Incres Line; Interocean Steamship Lines; Isthmian Lines (U.S. Steel); Ivaran Lines; etc.
ICI: Imperial Chemical Industries
ICSN: Indo-China Steam Navigation Company
IFI: Inter-Freight International
INSCO: Intercontinental Shipping Corporation
Inter-Freight International: IFI
IO Ltd: Imperial Oil Ltd
IOM SPC: Isle of Man Steam Packet Company
IOT: Iron Ore Transport
IPL: Ital Pacific Line
Italia: Italian Line
ITI: Inagua Transports Incorporated
J: Japan Line; John I. Jacobs and Company; Johnson Line; etc.
JBPS: Jamaica Banana Producers' Steamship Co
K: Kavolines; Kawasaki Kisen Kaisha; Kerr Lines; Keystone Shipping (Chas Kurz); Kingsport Shipping; Kirkconnel; Klaveness Line; Knutsen Line; etc.
KG: Koctug Line
KK: Karlander Kangaroo Line
K Line: Kawasaki Kisen Kaisha
KNC: Kingcome Navigation Company
KNSM: *Koninklijke Nederlandsche Stoomboot Maatschappij* (Dutch —Royal Netherlands Steamship Company)
Koctug Line: KL
KSN: Karachi Steam Navigation Line
L: Lauritzen Line; Luckenbach Line; Lykes Line; etc.
LASH: Lighter Aboard Ship Handling
LB: Lloyd Brasileiro
L + H: Lamport and Holt Line
LL: Lauro Line; Link Line
Lloyd's: *Lloyd's Register of Shipping (LRS)*
LRS: *Lloyd's Register of Shipping*
LT: *Lloyd Triestino* (Italian—Trieste Line)
M: Maersk Line; Marine Transport

Lines; Matson Line; Meyer Line; Montship Lines; Moore-McCormack Lines; Munson Line; etc.

Maersk: Maersk Line

MAMENIC: *Marina Mercante Nicaraguense* (Spanish—Nicaraguan Merchant Marine)

Maritime Fruit Carriers: MFC

MCP: Maritime Company of the Philippines

MFC: Maritime Fruit Carriers

MILI: Micronesia Interocean Line Incorporated

Milwaukee Clipper: Wisconsin and Michigan Steamship Company

Mitsui: Mitsui OSK Lines

ML: Manchester Liners

M. M: *Messageries Maritimes* (French—Maritime Mail, Parcel, and Passenger Service)

M/S: Motorship

MS Co: Melbourne Steamship Company

MSTS: Military Sea Transportation Service

MTL: Marine Transport Lines

MV: Motor Vessel

N: Naess Shipping Company; Niarchos Tankers; Nigerian National Line; etc.

NA&G: North Atlantic and Gulf Steamship Company

N-A-L: Norwegian America Line

NASM: (*see* HAL)

NB: Navibel (Belgian Maritime Navigation Company)

NB&C: Norfolk, Baltimore and Carolina Line

NCP : *Naviera Chilena del Pacifico* (Spanish—Chilean Shipping of the Pacific)

Nedlloyd: Nedlloyd and Hoegh Lines

NEE: New England Express

New England Express: NEE

NMB: Navigation Maritime Bulgare (Bulgarian Maritime Navigation)

NNC: Northern Navigation Company

NOL: Norse Oriental Lines

NPCL: North Pacific Coast Line

NTGB: North Thames Gas Board

NYK Line: Nippon Yusen Kaisha

NZSCo: New Zealand Shipping Company

O: Ocean Carriers; Olsen Line; M.J. Osorio; etc.

Official Steamship Guide International: *OSGI*

OG: O. Gross and Sons Ltd.

ØK: *Østasiatiske Kompagni* (Danish—East Asiatic Company) —EAL

Olympic: Olympic Steamship Company

OO: Orient Overseas Line

OSGI: *Official Steamship Guide International*

OSK: Osaka Syosen Kaisha (Osaka Mercantile Steamship Company)—Mitsui Lines

OW: Olof Wallenius Line

P: Panama Line (Panama Canal Company); Pocahontas Steamships; Prudential-Grace Lines; Pure Oil; etc.

P-A: Pan-Atlantic Steamship Corporation

PACE: Pacific America Container Express

Pacific America Container Express: PACE

Pacific Australia Direct Line: (*see* ABRT)

Petrobras: *Petroleo Brasileiro* (Portuguese—Brazilian Petroleum)

PFEL: Pacific Far East Line

P-G: Prudential Grace Lines

PITL: Pacific Islands Transport Line (Thor Dahls Hvalfangerselskap)

PL: Polynesia Line; Port Line; Poseidon Lines; Prince Line

PLA: Port of London Authority

PLL: Prince Line Limited

PLO: *Polskie Linie Oceaniczne* (Polish—Polish Line)

PM: *Petroleos Mexicanos* (Spanish —Mexican Petroleum)

PNL: Philippine National Lines

P&O: Penisular and Occidental Steamship Company; Peninsular and Oriental Line

POE: Pacific Orient Express Line

PPL: Philippine President Lines

Princess Line: Gothenburg-Frederikshavn Line

PSC: Point Shipping Company

PSFL: Puget Sound Freight Lines

PSNC: Pacific Steam Navigation Company

PT: Pope and Talbot

PURE: Pure Oil Company

Q: Qatar Petroleum; Quaker Line; Queensland; Quintessence Navigation; etc.

Q&O: Quebec and Ontario Transportation

R: Rasmussen; Richfield Oil; Ringdal; Robbert; etc.

RIL: Royal Interocean Lines [(*Koninklijke Java-China-Paketvaart Lijnen*—(Dutch—Royal Java-China-Packet Line)]

RL: Regent's Line (Grand Union Shipping)

RLR: Royal Rotterdam Lloyd

RML: Royal Mail Lines

Royal Netherlands Steamship Line: (see *KNSM*)

S: Saguenay Terminals Ltd; Salen; Seatrain Lines; Sinclair Refining; Socony Mobil Oil; Standard Oil of California; States Marine Lines; States Line (seahorse-shaped red-letter S); Sun Oil; Svea Line; etc.

SA&CL: South Atlantic and Caribbean Line

Safmarine: South African Marine Corporation

SAL: *Svenska Amerika Linien* (Swedish-America Line)

Santa ships: Prudential-Grace Line vessels

SC: Submarine Cables Ltd

S&C: Star and Crescent

SCC: Shipping and Coal Company

SCI: Sea Containers Incorporated; Shipping Corporation of India

Scindia: Scindia Steam Navigation

SEGB: South Eastern Gas Board

Shell: Shell Tankers

Shipping Corporation of India: SCI

SL: Southern Lines

SLS: Sea-Land Service

SML: States Marine Lines

SOPONATA: *Sociedade Portuguesa de Navios Tanques Limitada* (Portuguese—Portuguese Tankships Limited)

Sovtorgflot: Soviet Merchant Marine Fleet

Spanish Line: Compañía Transatlantica Española

SS: Steamship (as in SS *Santa Clara)*

STANVAC: Standard-Vacuum Oil Company

STL: Seatrain Lines

SUNOCO: Sun Oil Company

T: Tankers Limited; Texaco (The Texas Company); Thai Mercantile Marine; Thompson Shipping; Thoren Line; Tirrenia; Transatlantic Line; etc.

TCL: Transatlantic Carriers Limited

TCR: Texas City Refining

Texaco: The Texas Company

TH: Thorvald Hansen

Thor Dahls Havalfangerselskap: Pacific Islands Transport Line

TMM: Transportación Maritima Méxicana
Transamerica Trailer Transport: TTT
TS: Tasmanian Steamers
TTT: Transamerica Trailer Transport
U: Union Oil; United Oriental Steamship Company; Universe Tankships; etc.
UA: United Africa Company, Ltd
UBC: United Baltic Corporation
UBL: Union Barge Line
UCMS: Union-Castle Mail Steamship
UFC: United Fruit Company
UIL: Ulster Imperial Line
U.O. Co.: Union Oil Company of California
UPL: United Philippine Lines
USC: Union Steamship Company
USL: United States Lines
USMSTS: U.S. Military Sea Transport Service
USS: United States Ship (as in USS *Constitution*)
USSCo: Ulster Steam Ship Company; Union Steam Ship Company
UT: United Transports
UYL: United Yugoslav Lines
V: Vaccaro Line (Standard Fruit); Valentine Chemical Carriers; Vinke Tankers; Von Sydow; Vulcan Shipping; etc.
VA: *Compañía de Navegación Vasco-Asturiana* (Spanish—Basque-Asturian Navigation Company)
VC: Victory Carriers
VL: Vaasa Line (Hanseatic-Vaasa Line)
VLC: Valley Line Company
VNGC: Van Niervelt, Goudriaan and Company (Rotterdam—South American Line)
VW: Volkswagen (auto-carrier ships)
W: Waterman Steamship Lines; West Line; Westriver Ore Transports; Weyerhaeuser Line; etc.
W&A: Wiel and Amundsen
Wallenius Line: OW (Olof Wallenius)
WHMV & NSSA: Woods Hole, Martha s vineyard and Natucket Steamship Authority
WIL: West India Lines
WIT: West India Tankers
WL: Westfal-Larsen Line
W&L: Westcott and Laurance Line (Ellerman's)
WL&Co: Westfal-Larsen and Company
W&M SS Co: Wisonsin and Michigan Steamship Company (The Clipper Line)
WSFS: Washington State Ferry System
WTC: Western Transportation Company
X: (funnel marking—Chandris America Lines; Southern Cross Steamship Line); Xenophon Navigation Company; etc.
X: (funnel marking—Chandris America Lines; Southern Cross Steamship Line); etc.
Y: Yamashita-Shinnihon Kisen Line; Ybarra Lines; Yukiteru Kaiun; Yung Yang Shipping; etc.
YPF: *Yacimientos Petroliferos Fiscales* (Spanish—Fiscal Petroleum Deposits)—Argentine tanker fleet
Y-S Line: Yamashita-Shinnihon Line
Z: Zacharissen; Zante Navegación; Zillah Shipping; Zim Israel Navigation; Zurga Shipping Company; Etc.
Zim: Zim Israel Line
ZPL: Zim Passenger Line
ZSC: Zeeland Steamship Company

U.S. Naval Ship Symbols

AD: Destroyer Tender
ADG: Degaussing Ship
AE: Ammunition Ship
AF: Store Ship
AFDB: Large Auxiliary Floating Dry Dock (non-self-propelled)
AFDL: Small Auxiliary Floating Dry Dock (non-self-propelled)
AFDM: Medium Auxiliary Floating Dry Dock (non-self-propelled)
AFS: Combat Store Ship
AG: Miscellaneous
AGDE: Escort Research Ship
AGEH: Hydrofoil Research Ship
AGER: Environmental Research Ship
AGF: Miscellaneous Command Ship
AGM: Missile Range Instrumentation Ship
AGMR: Major Communications Relay Ship
AGOR: Oceanographic Research Ship
AGP: Patrol Craft Tender
AGR: Radar Picket Ship
AGS: Surveying Ship
AGSS: Auxiliary Submarine
AGTR: Technical Research Ship
AH: Hospital Ship
AK: Cargo Ship
AKD: Cargo Ship, Dock
AKL: Light Cargo Ship
AKR: Vehicle Cargo Ship
AKS: Stores Issue Ship
AKV: Cargo Ship and Aircraft Ferry
ANL: Net Laying Ship
AO: Oiler
AOE: Fast Combat Support Ship
AOG: Gasoline Tanker
AOR: Replenishment Oiler
AP: Transport
APB: Self-propelled Barracks Ship
APL: Barracks Craft (non-self-propelled)
AR: Repair Ship
ARB: Battle Damage Repair Ship
ARC: Cable Repairing Ship
ARD: Auxiliary Repair Dry Dock (non-self-propelled)
ARDM: Medium Auxiliary Repair Dry Dock (non-self-propelled)
ARG: Internal Combustion Engine Repair Ship
ARL: Landing Craft Repair Ship
ARS: Salvage Ship
ARSD: Salvage Lifting Ship
ARST: Salvage Craft Tender
ARVA: Aircraft Repair Ship (aircraft)
ARVE: Aircraft Repair Ship (engine)
ARVH: Aircraft Repair Ship (helicopter)
AS: Submarine Tender
ASPB: Assault Support Patrol Boat
ASR: Submarine Rescue Ship
ATA: Auxiliary Ocean Tug
ATC: Armored Troop Carrier
ATF: Fleet Ocean Tug
ATS: Salvage Tug
ATSS: Auxiliary Training Submarine
AV: Seaplane Tender
AVM: Guided Missile Ship
AVS: Aviation Supply Ship
AVT: Auxiliary Aircraft Transport
AW: Distilling Ship
BB: Battleship
CA: Heavy Cruiser
CC: Command Ship
CCB: Command and Control Boat
CG: Guided Missile Cruiser

CGN: Guided Missile Cruiser (nuclear propulsion)
CL: Light Cruiser
CLG: Guided Missile Light Cruiser
CVA: Attack Aircraft Carrier
CVAN: Attack Aircraft Carrier (nuclear propulsion)
CVS: ASW Support Aircraft Carrier
CVT: Training Aircraft Carrier
DD: Destroyer
DDG: Guided Missile Destroyer
DE: Escort Ship
DEG: Guided Missile Escort Ship
DER: Radar Picket Escort Ship
DL: Frigate
DLG: Guided Missile Frigate
DLGN: Guided Missile Frigate (nuclear propulsion)
DSRV: Deep Submergence Rescue Vessel
DSV: Deep Submergence Vehicle
E: (Prefix) Experimental Ship
F: (Prefix) Ship being built by U.S. for a foreign nation
FDL: Fast Deployment Logistics Ship
IX: Unclassified Miscellaneous
LCA: Landing Craft, Assault
LCC: Amphibious Command Ship
LCM: Landing Craft, Mechanized
LCPL: Landing Craft, Personnel, Large
LCPR: Landing Craft, Personnel. Ramped
LCSR: Landing Craft Swimmer Reconnaissance
LCU: Landing Craft, Utility
LCVP: Landing Craft, Vehicle, Personnel
LFR: Inshore Fire Support Ship
LFS: Amphibious Fire Support Ship
LHA: Amphibious Assault Ship (general purpose)
LKA: Amphibious Cargo Ship
LPA: Amphibious Transport
LPD: Amphibious Transport Dock
LPH: Amphibious Assault Ship
LPR: Amphibious Transport (small)
LPSS: Amphibious Transport Submarine
LSD: Dock Landing Ship
LSSC: Light SEAL Support Craft
LST: Tank Landing Ship
LWT: Amphibious Warping Tug
MAC: MIUW Attack Craft
MCS: Mine Countermeasures Ship
MON: Monitor
MSB: Minesweeping Boat
MSC: Minesweeper, Coastal (nonmagnetic)
MSD: Minesweeper, Drone
MSF: Minesweeper, Fleet (steel hull)
MSI: Minesweeper, Inshore
MSL: Minesweeping Launch
MSM: Minesweeper, River (Converted LCM-6)
MSO: Minesweeper, Ocean (nonmagnetic)
MSR: Minesweeper, Patrol
MSS: Minesweeper, Special (device)
MSSC: Medium SEAL Support Craft
NR: Submersible Research Vehicle (nuclear propulsion)
PBR: River Patrol Boat
PCE: Patrol Escort
PCER: Patrol Rescue Escort
PCF: Patrol Craft, Inshore
PCH: Patrol Craft (hydrofoil)
PG: Patrol Gunboat
PGH: Patrol Gunboat (hydrofoil)
PTF: Fast Patrol Craft
QFB: Ouiet Fast Boat
RUC: Riverine Utility Craft
SDV: Swimmer Delivery Vehicle
SES: Surface-Effect Ship
SS: Submarine
SSBN: Fleet Ballistic Missile Submarine (nuclear propulsion)
SSG: Guided Missile Submarine
SSN: Submarine (nuclear propulsion)
SST: Target and Training Submarine (self-propelled)
STAB: Strike Assault Boat
T: (Prefix) Military Sealift Command Ship
W: (Prefix) U.S. Coast Guard Ship
X: Submersible Craft (self-propelled)
YAG: Miscellaneous Auxiliary (self-propelled)
YC: Open Lighter (non-self-propelled)
YCF: Car Float (non-self-propelled)
YCV: Aircraft Transportation Lighter (non-self-propelled)
YD: Floating Crane (non-self-propelled)
YDT: Diving Tender (non-self-propelled)
YF: Covered Lighter (self-propelled)
YFB: Ferryboat or Launch (self-propelled)
YFD: Yard Floating Dry Dock (non-self-propelled)
YFN: Covered Lighter (non-self-propelled)
YFNB: Large Covered Lighter (non-self-propelled)
YFND: Dry Dock Companion Craft (non-self-propelled)
YFNX: Lighter (special purpose) (non-self-propelled)
YFP: Floating Power Barge (non-self-propelled)
YFR: Refrigerated Covered Lighter (self-propelled)
YFRN: Refrigerated Covered Lighter (non-self-propelled)
YFRT: Covered Lighter (range-tender) (self-propelled)
YFU: Harbor Utility Craft (self-propelled)
YG: Garbage Lighter (self-propelled)
YGN: Garbage Lighter (non-self-propelled)
YHLC: Salvage Lift Craft, Heavy (non-self-propelled)
YLLC: Salvage Lift Craft, Light (self-propelled)
YM: Dredge (self-propelled)
YMLC: Salvage Lift Craft, Medium (non-self-propelled)
YNG: Gate Craft (non-self-propelled)
YO: Fuel Oil Barge (self-propelled)
YOG: Gasoline Barge (self-propelled)
YOGN: Gasoline Barge (non-self-propelled)
YON: Fuel Oil Barge (non-self-propelled)
YOS: Oil Storage Barge (non-self-propelled)
YP: Patrol Craft (self-propelled)
YPD: Floating Pile Driver (non-self-propelled)
YR: Floating Workshop (non-self-propelled)
YRB: Repair and Berthing Barge (non-self-propelled)
YRBM: Repair, Berthing and Messing Barge (non-self-propelled)
YRDH: Floating Dry Dock Workshop (hull) (non-self-propelled)
YRDM: Floating Dry Dock Workshop (machine) (non-self-propelled)
YRR: Radiological Repair Barge (non-self-propelled)
YRST: Salvage Craft Tender (non-self-propelled)
YSD: Seaplane Wrecking Derrick (self-propelled)
YSR: Sludge Removal Barge (non-self-propelled)
YTB: Large Harbor Tug (self-propelled)
YTL: Small Harbor Tug (self-propelled)
YTM: Medium Harbor Tug (self-propelled)
YW: Water Barge (self-propelled)
YWDN: Water Distilling Barge (non-self-propelled)
YWN: Water Barge (non-self-propelled)

Vehicle Registration Symbols (Index Markers)

British Isles

This Listing includes registration marks for the Republic of Ireland. These marks were introduced before the creation of the Republic of Ireland, which has continued with the same system.

A	London
AA	Hampshire
AB	Worcestershire
AC	Warwickshire
AD	Gloucestershire
AE	Bristol
AF	Cornwall
AG	Ayrshire
AH	Norfolk
AI	Meath
AJ	Yorkshire (NR)
AK	Bradford
AL	Nottinghamshire
AM	Wiltshire
AN	London
AO	Cumberland
AP	Sussex (East)
AR	Hertfordshire
AS	Nairnshire
AT	Kingston-upon-Hull
AU	Nottingham
AV	Aberdeenshire
AW	Salop
AX	Monmouthshire
AY	Leicestershire
AZ	Belfast
B	Lancashire
BA	Salford
BB	Newcastle upon Tyne
BC	Leicester
BD	Northamptonshire
BE	Lincolnshire (Lindsey)
BF	Staffordshire
BG	Birkenhead
BH	Buckinghamshire
BI	Monaghan
BJ	Suffolk (East)
BK	Portsmouth
BL	Berkshire
BM	Bedfordshire
BN	Bolton
BO	Cardiff
BP	Sussex (West)
BR	Sunderland
BS	Orkney
BT	Yorkshire (ER)
BU	Oldham
BV	Blackburn
BW	Oxfordshire
BX	Carmarthenshire
BY	London
BZ	Down
C	Yorkshire (WR)
CA	Denbighshire
CB	Blackburn
CC	Caernarvonshire
CD	Brighton
CE	Cambridgeshire
CF	Suffolk (West)
CG	Hampshire
CH	Derby
CI	Laoighis
CJ	Herefordshire
CK	Preston
CL	Norwich
CM	Birkenhead
CN	Gateshead
CO	Plymouth
CP	Halifax
CR	Southampton
CS	Ayrshire
CT	Lincolnshire (Kesteven)
CU	South Shields
CV	Cornwall
CW	Burnley
CX	Huddersfield
CY	Swansea
CZ	Belfast
D	Kent
DA	Wolverhampton
DB	Stockport
DC	Teesside
DD	Gloucestershire
DE	Pembrokeshire
DF	Gloucestershire
DG	Gloucestershire
DH	Walsall
DI	Roscommon
DJ	St Helens
DK	Rochdale
DL	Isle of Wight
DM	Flintshire
DN	York
DO	Lincolnshire (Holland)
DP	Reading
DR	Plymouth
DS	Peeblesshire
DT	Doncaster
DU	Coventry
DV	Devon
DW	Newport (Mon)
DX	Ipswich
DY	Hastings
DZ	Antrim
E	Staffordshire
EA	West Bromwich
EB	Cambridge
EC	Westmorland
ED	Warrington
EE	Grimsby
EF	West Hartlepool
EG	Huntingdon
EH	Stoke-on-Trent
EI	Sligo
EJ	Cardiganshire
EK	Wigan
EL	Bournemouth
EM	Bootle
EN	Bury
EO	Berrow-in-Furness
EP	Montgomeryshire
ER	Cambridgeshire
ES	Perthshire
ET	Rotherham
EU	Breconshire
EV	Essex
EW	Huntingdonshire
EX	Great Yarmouth
EY	Anglesey
EZ	Belfast
F	Essex
FA	Burton-on-Trent
FB	Bath
FC	Oxford
FD	Dudley
FE	Lincoln
FF	Merionethshire
FG	Fife
FH	Gloucester
FI	Tipperary (NR)
FJ	Exeter
FK	Worcester
FL	Huntingdon
FM	Chester
FN	Canterbury
FO	Radnorshire
FP	Rutland
FR	Blackpool
FS	Edinburgh
FT	Tynemouth

FU	Lincolnshire (Lindsey)
FV	Blackpool
FW	Lincolnshire (Lindsey)
FX	Dorset
FY	Southport
FZ	Belfast
G	Glasgow
GA	Glasgow
GB	Glasgow
GC	London
GD	Glasgow
GE	Glasgow
GF	London
GG	Glasgow
GH	London
GI	London
GK	London
GL	Bath
GM	Motherwell and Wishaw
GN	London
GO	London
GP	London
GR	Sunderland
GS	Perthshire
GT	London
GU	London
GV	Suffolk (West)
GW	London
GX	London
GY	London
GZ	Belfast
H	London
HA	Warley
HB	Merthyr Tydfil
HC	Eastbourne
HD	Dewsbury
HE	Barnsley
HF	Wallasey
HG	Burnley
HH	Carlisle
HI	Tipperary
HJ	Southend
HK	Essex
HL	Wakefield
HM	London
HN	Darlington
HO	Hampshire
HP	Coventry
HR	Wiltshire
HS	Renfrewshire
HT	Bristol
HU	Bristol
HV	London
HW	Bristol
HX	London
HY	Bristol
HZ	Tyrone
IA	Antrim
IB	Armagh
IC	Carlow
ID	Cavan
IE	Clare
IF	Cork (County)
IH	Donegal
IJ	Down
IK	City and County of Dublin
IL	Fermanagh
IM	Galway
IN	Kerry
IO	Kildare
IP	Kilkenny
IR	Offaly
IT	Leitrim
IU	Limerick
IW	Londonderry
IX	Longford
IY	Louth
IZ	Mayo
J	Durham (County)
JA	Stockport
JB	Berkshire
JC	Caernarvonshire
JD	London
JE	Cambridge
JF	Leicester
JG	Canterbury
JH	Hertfordshire
JI	Tyrone
JJ	London
JK	Eastbourne
JL	Lincolnshire (Holland)
JM	Westmorland
JN	Southend
JO	Oxford
JP	Wigan
JR	Northumberland
JS	Ross & Cromarty
JT	Dorset
JU	Leicestershire
JV	Grimsby
JW	Wolverhampton
JX	Halifax
JY	Plymouth
JZ	Down
K	Liverpool
KA	Liverpool
KB	Liverpool
KC	Liverpool
KD	Liverpool
KE	Kent
KF	Liverpool
KG	Cardiff
KH	Kingston-upon-Hull
KI	Waterford
KJ	Kent
KK	Kent
KL	Kent
KM	Kent
KN	Kent
KO	Kent
KP	Kent
KR	Kent
KS	Roxburghshire
KT	Kent
KU	Bradford
KV	Coventry
KW	Bradford
KX	Buckinghamshire
KY	Bradford
KZ	Antrim
L	Glamorgan
LA	London
LB	London
LC	London
LD	London
LE	London
LF	London
LG	Cheshire
LH	London
LI	Westmeath
LJ	Bournemouth
LK	London
LL	London
LM	London
LN	London
LO	London
LP	London
LR	London
LS	Selkirkshire
LT	London
LU	London
LV	Liverpool
LW	London
LX	London
LY	London
LZ	Armagh
M	Cheshire
MA	Cheshire
MB	Cheshire
MC	London
MD	London
ME	London
MF	London
MG	London
MH	London
MI	Wexford
MJ	Bedfordshire
MK	London
ML	London
MM	London
MN	Isle of Man
MO	Berkshire
MP	London
MR	Wiltshire
MS	Stirlingshire
MT	London
MU	London
MV	London
MW	Wiltshire
MX	London
MY	London
MZ	Belfast
N	Manchester
NA	Manchester
NB	Manchester
NC	Manchester
ND	Manchester
NE	Manchester
NF	Manchester
NG	Norfolk

NH	Northampton
NI	Wicklow
NJ	Sussex (East)
NK	Hertfordshire
NL	Northumberland
NM	Bedfordshire
NN	Nottinghamshire
NO	Essex
NP	Worcestershire
NR	Leicestershire
NS	Sutherland
NT	Salop
NU	Derbyshire
NV	Northamptonshire
NW	Leeds (B)
NX	Warwickshire
NY	Glamorgan
NZ	Londonderry
O	Birmingham
OA	Birmingham
OB	Birmingham
OC	Birmingham
OD	Devon
OE	Birmingham
OF	Birmingham
OG	Birmingham
OH	Birmingham
OI	Belfast
OJ	Birmingham
OK	Birmingham
OL	Birmingham
OM	Birmingham
ON	Birmingham
OO	Essex
OP	Birmingham
OR	Hampshire
OS	Wigtownshire
OT	Hampshire
OU	Hampshire
OV	Birmingham
OW	Southampton
OX	Birmingham
OY	London
OZ	Belfast
P	Surrey
PA	Surrey
PB	Surrey
PC	Surrey
PD	Surrey
PE	Surrey
PF	Surrey
PG	Surrey
PH	Surrey
PI	Cork
PJ	Surrey
PK	Surrey
PL	Surrey
PM	Sussex (East)
PN	Sussex (East)
PO	Sussex (West)
PP	Buckinghamshire
PR	Dorset
PS	Zetland
PT	Durham (County)
PU	Essex
PV	Ipswich
PW	Norfolk
PX	Sussex (West)
PY	Yorkshire (NR)
PZ	Belfast
	QA QE QJ QN QB QF QK QP QC QG QL QO QD QH QM QS London: for vehicles temporarily imported from abroad
R	Derbyshire
RA	Derbyshire
RB	Derbyshire
RC	Derby
RD	Reading
RE	Staffordshire
RF	Staffordshire
RG	Aberdeen
RH	Kingston-upon-Hull
RI	City and County of Dublin
RJ	Salford
RK	London
RL	Cornwall
RM	Cumberland
RN	Preston
RO	Hertfordshire
RP	Northamptonshire
RR	Nottinghamshire
RS	Aberdeen
RT	Suffolk (East)
RU	Bournemouth
RV	Portsmouth
RW	Coventry
RX	Berkshire
RY	Leicester
RZ	Antrim
S	Edinburgh
SA	Aberdeenshire
SB	Argyll
SC	Edinburgh
SD	Ayrshire
SE	Banffshire
SF	Edinburgh
SG	Edinburgh
SH	Berwickshire
SJ	Bute
SK	Caithness
SL	Clackmannanshire
SM	Dumfriesshire
SN	Dunbartonshire
SO	Moray
SP	Fife
SR	Angus
SS	East Lothian
ST	Inverness-shire
SU	Kincardineshire
SV	Kinross-shire
SW	Kircudbrightshire
SX	West Lothian
SY	Midlothian
SZ	Down
T	Devon
TA	Devon
TB	Lancashire
TC	Lancashire
TD	Lancashire
TE	Lancashire
TF	Lancashire
TG	Glamorgan
TH	Carmarthenshire
TI	Limerick
TJ	Lancashire
TK	Dorset
TL	Lincolnshire (Kesteven)
TM	Bedfordshire
TN	Newcastle upon Tyne
TO	Nottingham
TP	Portsmouth
TR	Southampton
TS	Dundee
TT	Devon
TU	Cheshire
TV	Nottingham
TW	Essex
TX	Glamorgan
TY	Northumberland
TZ	Belfast
U	Leeds
UA	Leeds
UB	Leeds
UC	London
JD	Oxfordshire
UE	Warwickshire
UF	Brighton
UG	Leeds
UH	Cardiff
UI	Londonderry
UJ	Salop
UK	Wolverhampton
UL	London
UM	Leeds
UN	Denbighshire
UO	Devon
UP	Durham (County)
UR	Hertfordshire
US	Glasgow
UT	Leicestershire
UU	London
UV	London
UW	London
UX	Salop
UY	Worcestershire
UZ	Belfast
V	Lanarkshire
VA	Lanarkshire
VB	London
VC	Coventry
VD	Lanarkshire
VE	Cambridgeshire
VF	Norfolk
VG	Norwich

VH	Huddersfield	XA	London/Kirkcaldy	YS	Glasgow
VJ	Herefordshire	XB	London/Coatbridge	YT	London
VK	Newcastle upon Tyne	XC	London/Solihull	YU	London
VL	Lincoln	XD	London/Luton	YV	London
VM	Manchester	XE	London/Luton	YW	London
VN	Yorkshire (NR)	XF	London/Torbay	YX	London
VO	Nottinghamshire	XG	Teesside	YY	London
VP	Birmingham	XH	London	YZ	Londonderry
VR	Manchester	XI	Belfast	Z	City and County
VS	Greenock	XJ	Manchester		of Dublin
VT	Stoke-on-Trent	XK	London	ZA	City and County
VU	Manchester	XL	London		of Dublin
VV	Northampton	XM	London	ZB	Cork (County)
VW	Essex	XN	London	ZC	City and County
VX	Essex	XO	London		of Dublin
VY	York	XP	London	ZD	City and County
VZ	Tyrone	XR	London		of Dublin
W	Sheffield	XS	Paisley	ZE	City and County
WA	Sheffield	XT	London		of Dublin
WB	Sheffield	XU	London	ZF	Cork
WC	Essex	XV	London	ZH	City and County
WD	Warwickshire	XW	London		of Dublin
WE	Sheffield	XX	London	ZI	City and County
WF	Yorkshire (ER)	XY	London		of Dublin
WG	Stirlingshire	XZ	Armagh	ZJ	City and County
WH	Bolton	Y	Somerset		of Dublin
WI	Waterford	YA	Somerset	ZK	Cork (County)
WJ	Sheffield	YB	Somerset	ZL	City and County
WK	Coventry	YC	Somerset		of Dublin
WL	Oxford	YD	Somerset	ZM	Galway
WM	Southport	YE	London	ZN	Meath
WN	Swansea	YF	London	ZO	City and County
WO	Monmouthshire	YG	Yorkshire (WR)		of Dublin
WP	Worcestershire	YH	London	ZP	Donegal
WR	Yorkshire (WR)	YI	City and County	ZR	Wexford
WS	Edinburgh		of Dublin	ZT	Cork (County)
WT	Yorkshire (WR)	YJ	Dundee	ZU	City and County
WU	Yorkshire (WR)	YK	London		
WV	Wiltshire	YL	London	ZW	Kildare
WW	Yorkshire (WR)	YM	London	ZX	Kerry
WX	Yorkshire (WR)	YN	London	ZY	Louth
WY	Yorkshire (WR)	YO	London	ZZ	Dublin: for vehicles
WZ	Belfast	YP	London		temporarily imported
X	Northumberland	YR	London		from abroad

International

Albania	BSA	Egypt, Arab Reb. of	EOS
Algeria	INAPI	Ethiopia	ESI
Australia	SAA	Finland	SFS
Austria	ON	France	AFNOR
Bangladesh	BDSI	Germany	DIN
Belgium	IBN	Ghana	GSB
Brazil	ABNT	Greece	NHS
Bulgaria	DKC	Hungary	MSZH
Canada	SCC	India	ISI
Chile	INN	Indonesia	YDNI
Colombia	ICONTEC	Iran	ISIRI
Cuba	NC	Iraq	IOS
Czechoslovakia	CSN	Ireland	IIRS
Denmark	DS	Israel	SII

Italy	UNI	Romania	IRS
Jamaica	JBS	Saudi Arabia	SASO
Japan	JISC	Singapore	SISIR
Kenya	KEBS	South Africa, Rep. of	SABS
Korea, Dem. P. Rep. of	CSK	Spain	IRANOR
Korea, Rep. of	KBS	Sri Lanka	BCS
Lebanon	LIBNOR	Sudan	SSD
Malaysia	SIRIM	Sweden	SIS
Mexico	DGN	Switzerland	SNV
Morocco	SNIMA	Thailand	TISI
Netherlands	NNI	Turkey	TSE
New Zealand	SANZ	United Kingdom	BSI
Nigeria	NSO	United States of America	ANSI
Norway	NSF	Union of Soviet Socialist Republics	GOST
Pakistan	PSI	Venezuela	COVENIN
Peru	ITINTEC	Yugoslavia	JZS
Phillippines	PS	Zambia	ZSI
Poland	PKNiM		
Portugal	IGPAI		

Weather Symbols (Beaufort Scale)

WITH CORRESPONDING SEA STATE CODES

Beaufort number	Wind speed				Seaman's term	U. S. Weather Bureau term	Estimating wind speed		Hydrographic Office		International	
	knots	mph	meters per second	km per hour			Effects observed at sea	Effects observed on land	Term and height of waves, in feet	Code	Term and height of waves, in feet	Code
0	under 1	under 1	0.0–0.2	under 1	Calm	Light	Sea like mirror.	Calm; smoke rises vertically.	Calm, 0	0	Calm, glassy, 0	0
1	1–3	1–3	0.3–1.5	1–5	Light air		Ripples with appearance of scales; no foam crests.	Smoke drift indicates wind direction; vanes do not move.	Smooth, less than 1	1		
2	4–6	4–7	1.6–3.3	6–11	Light breeze		Small wavelets; crests of glassy appearance, not breaking.	Wind felt on face; leaves rustle; vanes begin to move.	Slight, 1–3	2	Rippled, 0–1	1
3	7–10	8–12	3.4–5.4	12–19	Gentle breeze	Gentle	Large wavelets; crests begin to break; scattered whitecaps.	Leaves, small twigs in constant motion; light flags extended.	Moderate, 3–5	3	Smooth, 1–2	2
4	11–16	13–18	5.5–7.9	20–28	Moderate breeze	Moderate	Small waves, becoming longer; numerous whitecaps.	Dust, leaves, and loose paper raised up; small branches move.	Rough, 5–8	4	Slight, 2–4	3
5	17–21	19–24	8.0–10.7	29–38	Fresh breeze	Fresh	Moderate waves, taking longer form; many whitecaps; some spray.	Small trees in leaf begin to sway.			Moderate, 4–8	4
6	22–27	25–31	10.8–13.8	39–49	Strong breeze	Strong	Larger waves forming; whitecaps everywhere; more spray	Larger branches of trees in motion; whistling heard in wires.			Rough, 8–13	5
7	28–33	32–38	13.9–17.1	50–61	Moderate gale		Sea heaps up; white foam from breaking waves begins to be blown in streaks.	Whole trees in motion; resistance felt in walking against wind.	Very rough, 8–12	5	Very rough, 13–20	6
8	34–40	39–46	17.2–20.7	62–74	Fresh gale	Gale	Moderately high waves of greater length; edges of crests begin to break into spindrift; foam is blown in well-marked streaks.	Twigs and small branches broken off trees; progress generally impeded.				
9	41–47	47–54	20.8–24.4	75–88	Strong gale		High waves; sea begins to roll; dense streaks of foam; spray may reduce visibility.	Slight structural damage occurs; slate blown from roofs.	High, 12–20	6		
10	48–55	55–63	24.5–28.4	89–102	Whole gale	Whole gale	Very high waves with overhanging crests; sea takes white appearance as foam is blown in very dense streaks; rolling is heavy and visibility reduced.	Seldom experienced on land; trees broken or uprooted; considerable structural damage occurs.	Very high, 20–40	7	High, 20–30	7
11	56–63	64–72	28.5–32.6	103–117	Storm		Exceptionally high waves; sea covered with white foam patches; visibility still more reduced.		Mountainous, 40 and higher	8	Very high, 30–45	8
12 13 14 15 16 17	64–71 72–80 81–89 90–99 100–108 109–118	73–82 83–92 93–103 104–114 115–125 126–136	32.7–36.9 37.[illegible]–41.4 41.[illegible]–46.1 46.2–50.9 51.0–56.0 56.1–61.2	118–133 134–149 150–166 167–183 184–201 202–220	Hurricane	Hurricane	Air filled with foam; sea completely white with driving spray; visibility greatly reduced.	Very rarely experienced on land; usually accompanied by widespread damage.	Confused	9	Phenomenal, over 45	9

Note: Since January 1, 1955, weather map symbols have been based upon wind speed in knots, at five-knot intervals, rather than upon Beaufort number.

Wedding Anniversary Symbols

1st - *Paper* (negotiable paper such as bonds, currency, trust certificates, as well as books, napkins, stationery, and towels)

2nd - *Cotton* (bedspreads, curtains, draperies, pillows, sheets, shirts, socks, underwear, etc.)

3rd - *Leather* (belts, handbags, leatherbound books, luggage, shoes, etc.)

4th - *Linen* (bedsheets, napkins, samplers, scarfs, shirts, tablecloths)

5th - *Wood* (furniture as well as boats and bungalows)

6th - *Iron* (hardware, wrought-iron furniture, ornamental ironwork)

7th - *Wool* (blankets, robes, rugs, socks, suits, sweaters, underwear)

8th - *Bronze* (bells, brassware, bronze objects, gongs, statuary)

9th - *Pottery* (kitchenware, planter's pots, pottery ornaments)

10th - *Aluminum* or *tin* (kitchenware and ornaments)

11th - *Steel* (automobiles, hardware, recreation vehicles, tools)

12th - *Silk* (casual clothes, scarfs, wraps)

13th - *Lace* (bedspreads, curtains, doilies, tablecloths)

14th - *Ivory* (carvings, desk sets, scrimshaw)

15th - *Crystal* (crystal sculpture and glassware)

20th - *China* (chinaware and procelain figurines and tableware)

25th - *Silver* (silver coins and silverware)

30th - *Pearl* (jewelry and mother-of-pearl objects)

35th - *Coral* (jewelry and rare collector's items)

40th - *Ruby* (jewelry)

45th - *Sapphire* (jewelry)

50th - *Golden* (gold coins, gold-plated objects, solid-gold ornaments)

55th - *Emerald* (jewelry)

60th - *Diamond* (jewelry)

65th - *Diamond-and-gold anniversary* (jewelry)

70th - *Diamond-and-emerald anniversary* (jewelry)

75th - *Diamond-emerald-sapphire anniversary* (solid gold dipped in diamonds, emerald, and sapphire chips or stones)

80th - (consult your nearest jeweler; contact the media and the police if you have accumulated all the foregoing wedding anniversary gifts; treat yourself to whatever you want) - this is the *time-flies anniversary* and may earn you a place in the *Guiness Book of World Records*

Zodiacal Signs

♒ : Aquarius (The Water Carrier), eleventh sign of the zodiac, symbolized by two parallel water waves; sun enters this period on January 20

♈ : Aries (The Ram), first sign of the zodiac, symbolized by the ram's horns; the sun enters this period on March 21, marking the spring or vernal equinox

♋ : Cancer (The Crab), fourth sign of the zodiac, symbolized by overlapping crab claws; sun enters this period June 22, marking the summer solstice, the longest day in the year

♑ : Capricornus (The Goat), tenth sign of the zodiac; symbol taken from *tr* of *tragos*, Greek for goat; sun enters Capricorn on December 22, marking the winter solstice, the shortest day in the year

♊ : Gemini (The Twins), third sign of the zodiac, symbolized by wooden statues of Castor and Pollux coupled by horizontal lintels; sun enters this period May 21

♌ : Leo (The Lion), fifth sign of the zodiac, symbolized by stylized figure representing the lion's tufted tail; sun enters this period on July 23

♎ : Libra (The Balance), seventh sign of the zodiac, symbolized by a stylized balance; sun enters this period on September 23, marking the autumnal equinox

♓ : Pisces (The Fishes), twelfth sign of the zodiac; symbolized by two fishes tied by a thong; sun enters this period on February 19

♐ : Sagittarius (The Archer), ninth sign of the zodiac; symbolized by archer's bow and arrow; sun enters this period on November 22

♏ : Scorpio (The Scorpion), eighth sign of the zodiac, symbolized by stylized representation of legs and stinger tail of the scorpion; sun enters this period on October 24

♉ : Taurus (The Bull), second sign of the zodiac, symbolized by the bull's head and horns; sun enters this period April 20

♍ : Virgo (The Virgin), sixth sign of the zodiac; symbol taken from *par* in *parthenos*, Greek for virgin; sun enters Virgo on August 23